ROUTLEDGE HANDBOOK OF ENERGY LAW

The *Routledge Handbook of Energy Law* provides a definitive global survey of the discipline of Energy Law, capturing the essential and relevant issues in Energy today. Each chapter is written by a leading expert, and provides a contemporary overview of a significant area within the field.

The book is divided into six geographical regions based on continents, with a separate section on Russia, an energy powerhouse that straddles both Europe and Asia. Each section contains highly topical chapters from authors who address a number of core themes in Energy Law and Regulation:

- Energy security and the role of markets
- Regulating the growth of renewable energy
- Regulating shifts in traditional forms of energy
- Instruments in regulating disputes in energy
- Impact of energy on the environment
- Key issues in the future of energy and regulation.

Offering an analysis of the full spectrum of current issues in Energy Law, the *Routledge Handbook of Energy Law* is an essential resource for advanced students, researchers, academics, legal practitioners and industry experts.

Tina Soliman Hunter is a Professor of Petroleum and Resources Law at the University of Aberdeen, UK, and Director of the Centre for Energy and Resources Law.

Ignacio Herrera Anchustegui is an Associate Professor at the University of Bergen, Faculty of Law, Norway.

Penelope Crossley is an Associate Professor at The University of Sydney Law School, The University of Sydney, Australia.

Gloria M. Alvarez is a Lecturer at the University of Aberdeen, UK.

ROUTLEDGE HANDBOOK OF ENERGY LAW

Edited by
Tina Soliman Hunter,
Ignacio Herrera Anchustegui,
Penelope Crossley and
Gloria M. Alvarez

Routledge
Taylor & Francis Group
LONDON AND NEW YORK

First published 2020
by Routledge
2 Park Square, Milton Park, Abingdon, Oxon OX14 4RN

and by Routledge
605 Third Avenue, New York, NY 10017

First issued in paperback 2021

Routledge is an imprint of the Taylor & Francis Group, an informa business

Publisher's Note
The publisher has gone to great lengths to ensure the quality of this reprint but points out that some imperfections in the original copies may be apparent.

British Library Cataloguing-in-Publication Data
A catalogue record for this book is available from the British Library

Library of Congress Cataloging-in-Publication Data
A catalog record has been requested for this book

ISBN 13: 978-1-138-32445-9 (hbk)
ISBN 13: 978-1-03-223630-8 (pbk)

DOI: 10.4324/9780429450891

Typeset in Bembo
by codeMantra

CONTENTS

CONTRIBUTORS

Pami Aalto is the Jean Monnet Professor in International Relations at the Faculty of Management and Business, Tampere University, Finland pami.aalto@tuni.fi. He works at the interface of energy policy, international political economy and international environmental governance, and specializes in Europe, the Nordic Countries, Russia and East Asia. Since 2015, he has led the EL-TRAN consortium of some 50 researchers working on energy transitions from various disciplinary backgrounds including engineering, social scientific disciplines, law and future studies.

Gloria M. Alvarez is an international academic on dispute resolution with extensive expertise in the energy and natural resources sectors. She is interested in international economic law, climate and social justice. Gloria has held prestigious fellowships at the Shanghai University of Finance and Economics, Queen Mary University of London, Max Planck Institute and Lauterpacht Centre for International Law, University of Cambridge. Gloria acts as arbitrator and expert in international arbitration proceedings in Africa, Europe and Latin America with experience in ICSID (International Centre for Settlement of Investment Disputes) and LCIA (London Court of International Arbitration). She is the author of *International Investment Arbitration and EU Law: The Present and the Future of the Energy Charter Treaty* (Hart 2020) and co-editor of *The ICSID Convention, Regulations and Rules* (Elgar 2019). Gloria is a Lecturer at the University of Aberdeen and is a Visiting Lecturer at the University of Eastern Finland and Osgood Hall Law School in Canada. She is on the Editorial Board of *ICSID Review*, *Journal of International Arbitration* and *European Investment Law and Arbitration Review*.

Isabella Bellera Landa is an Associate in White & Case's International Arbitration group. Isabella represents and advises private companies, foreign sovereigns and state entities on the resolution of international disputes. She has represented clients in arbitrations before the International Centre for Settlement of Investment Disputes (ICSID), the International Chamber of Commerce (ICC), as well as in litigation in federal district and appellate courts in the United States. Isabella has experience in disputes in a wide range of industries, including infrastructure, power, sovereign debt and textiles. She obtained her Law degree from Universidad de Carabobo (Venezuela) and Juris Doctor Degree from Duke University.

Christian Bergqvist holds a PhD and is currently an Associate Professor in Competition Law at the University of Copenhagen. Bergqvist's interest and work area covers national and EU competition law, with particular interest in its application to the deregulated and network tied sector (telecom, energy, post and transport) and abuse of dominance in general and within these sectors. Moreover, Bergqvist has extensive experience in competition law as academician and practitioner. Before becoming a full-time academician serving five years as lawyer at Tier 1 law firms, representing clients before the judicial and administrative bodies, on competition law matters.

Naomi Briercliffe is a Senior Associate in Allen & Overy's London office specializing in public international law, investment-treaty and international commercial arbitration. Naomi has experience of arbitrations under most major arbitral rules, as well as cases before the International Court of Justice and Iran-U.S. Claims Tribunal. She acts for clients from around the world and operating in different sectors, although she has particular knowledge of the energy, infrastructure and telecoms sectors. Naomi provides training for states on investment treaty policy and has lectured at Sciences Po (Paris) and LSE (London) on investment treaty law and arbitration.

Mikael Collan is a Professor and Academic Director of the Master's Programme in Strategic Finance and Analytics at the LUT School of Business and Management. His research concentrates on real option analysis, applications of fuzzy logic in business and business analytics. He is an ordinary member of the Finnish Society of Sciences and Letters and the past president of the Finnish Operations Research Society.

Penelope Crossley is an Associate Professor in the fields of energy and resources law at the University of Sydney Law School. In particular, her research focuses on the fields of international and comparative renewable energy and energy storage law, electricity market governance, the reform of Australia's National Electricity Law and implementing international best practice in terms of market design, law and governance within the energy and resources sectors. Penelope has also practised in this area in London and Beijing at a leading international law firm, and as In-house Counsel for a global energy company advising on issues related to renewable energy, emerging consumer markets and the integration of new technologies. She holds a PhD in international and comparative renewable energy law from the University of Sydney.

Ruven Fleming is an Assistant Professor at the University of Groningen/Netherlands, working at the Groningen Centre of Energy Law and Sustainability. His research focuses on the regulation of electricity storage and the implementation of 'Hydrogen Economies' in the energy transition, on the implementation of energy democracy in energy projects and the regulation of unconventional hydrocarbons. He is the author of *Shale Gas, the Environment and Energy Security* (Edward Elgar Publishing Ltd 2017) and one of the editors of the standard reference work *Encyclopedia of Energy Law and the Environment* (Edward Elgar Publishing Ltd 2015). He is running a weblog on current energy and climate law affairs www.energyand climatelaw.blogspot.com

Irina Fodchenko is an Associate at Advokatfirmaet Schjødt AS and PhD candidate at the Faculty of Law, University of Oslo (Scandinavian Institute of Maritime Law). She is a dual-qualified lawyer in Norway and Russia with specialisation in petroleum and international law, experienced in both legal systems, cultures and industries.

Andreas Formosa is a Senior Associate in Clifford Chance's energy and infrastructure group and advises energy companies and lenders on energy project development and the relevant regulatory frameworks in the power and gas sectors. Previously, he worked at Ofgem, the GB energy regulator where he advised on networks and wholesale markets. He is particularly interested in how regulation can foster more innovation, competition and decarbonization in power markets. Since 2016 Andreas has been recognized as a Future Energy Leader by the World Energy Council and since 2018 he has been on the board of the FEL-100 community. He is a graduate of the LSE and UCL in London.

María Alejandra Garzón Albornoz is a Lawyer and an LLM candidate on Mining, Petroleum and Energy Regulation. Researcher at the Mining and Energy Law Institute, Externado University, Colombia. She is an Associate attorney at the law firm Estudio Jurídico Montoya & Asociados.

Nate Graham is an assistant for the Energy, Climate Change & Extractive Industries Program at the Inter-American Dialogue. He graduated Phi Beta Kappa from Washington University in St Louis with a BA in Political Science and Economics and a minor in Environmental Studies. He has written about energy and climate policy in Mexico, Venezuela, Brazil and other countries in various publications including *The New York Times, Foreign Policy, World Politics Review* and *Americas Quarterly*.

Scott Hempling is an Adjunct Professor at Georgetown University Law Center, and advises and testifies before utility regulatory agencies and legislative bodies throughout the United States. He has addressed audiences in Canada, Central America, Germany, India, Italy, Jamaica, Mexico, New Zealand, Nigeria, Norway and Peru. He is the author of *Regulating Public Utility Performance: The Law of Market Structure, Pricing and Jurisdiction* (American Bar Association 2013) and *Preside or Lead? The Attributes and Actions of Effective Regulators* (2013). A former Executive Director of the U.S. National Regulatory Research Institute, Hempling received a BA *cum laude* from Yale University in (1) Economics and Political Science and (2) Music; and a JD *magna cum laude* from Georgetown University Law Center.

Ignacio Herrera Anchustegui is an Associate Professor at the Faculty of Law of the University of Bergen and member of the Bergen Offshore Wind Centre (BOW) and the Bergen Center for Competition Law and Economics (BECCLE). Herrera Anchustegui's research focus is the regulation of energy markets, at the intersection between energy, competition and public procurement law, areas in which he has published extensively. He obtained his PhD at the University of Bergen for which he received the Concurrences 2017 Award as best PhD of the year in Competition Law and Economics for his work *Buyer Power in EU Competition Law* (Concurrences 2017) and was recipient of the Meltzer Award for Young Researchers in 2018.

Jie Huan received her bachelor's degree, master's degree and doctorate at the Law School of Wuhan University (China) between 1999 and 2009. Currently, she is an Associate Professor at the School of Public Administration of the China University of Geosciences (Wuhan) and Research Fellow of the Key Laboratory of Natural Resources Law Evaluation of the Ministry of Natural Resources of China. In 2014–2015 and 2017–2018, Dr Huan was a visiting professor at Renmin University of China and the Center for Energy Law at Aberdeen University respectively. Her research focuses are the intersection of Constitution and Natural Resources Law.

David Ingle is a Senior Associate in Allen & Overy's Madrid office specialising in commercial and investment treaty arbitration. David is qualified to practise in England and Wales and is admitted to the Texas bar. He has acted as counsel for a range of clients in numerous international commercial and investment treaty arbitrations and has regularly appeared as advocate in disputes arising under the Energy Charter Treaty. David also lectures on English law and common law at the Universidad Carlos III de Madrid. Before relocating to Madrid, David practised in the Allen & Overy London arbitration team and also spent six months on secondment to the Prague office.

Cameron Kelly is a practising lawyer in the energy and project finance sectors. He has worked in both private practice and in-house counsel roles globally, with the most recent role being legal counsel to a renewable energy project developer/sponsor in Dubai, United Arab Emirates. Dr Kelly completed his PhD in Comparative International Law at the University of East Finland, and is currently the General Counsel at the Australian Renewable Energy Agency (ARENA).

Anna Khalfaoui is the Litigation Fellow at the Open Society Justice Initiative in London. She holds an LL.M. from Harvard Law School and previously studied at the University of Cambridge, King's College London and Sciences Po Paris.

Mariia Kozlova is a post-doctoral researcher at LUT University School of Business and Management, Lappeenranta Finland. Her mainstream research is devoted to renewable energy policy analyses, with a particular focus on Russia. Her publications include "Investment timing and capacity choice under rate-of-return regulation for renewable energy support" (*Energy* 2019), "Real option valuation in renewable energy literature: Research focus, trends and design" (*Renewable and Sustainable Energy Reviews* 2017) and "Modeling the effects of the new Russian capacity mechanism on renewable energy investments" (*Energy Policy* 2016).

Silvia Marchili is a Partner in White & Case's International Arbitration group. Silvia focuses on complex international arbitration and litigation matters involving Latin America and Africa, and a variety of sectors, including oil and gas, power, mining and infrastructure. She regularly appears before tribunals constituted under the Rules of the International Centre for the Settlement of Investment Disputes Convention (ICSID). An expert in investment arbitration, Silvia co-authored, with R. Doak Bishop, the treatise *Annulment Under the ICSID Convention* (Oxford University Press 2012). She obtained her Law Degree from the University of Buenos Aires and Master's Degree from Queen Mary College, University of London.

Miguel Marmolejo-Cervantes, PhD, has been working as commercial Notary Public since 2007. In 2017 he was appointed Research Professor at the Universidad Panamericana and admitted as a member of the National System of Researchers (SNI). He has focused his research and practice on justice and economics affairs brought by the Mexican Energy Reform. He has been a Visiting Academic at the University of Aberdeen, UK and at the Universidad Autónoma de Nuevo León, México. He acts as an OECD advisor in Mexico, is a member of the Academy of Environmental Law and a social witness by the Ministry of Energy.

Milton Fernando Montoya Pardo is the Research Director at the Mining and Energy Law Institute, Externado de Colombia University and Founding Partner at the Estudio

Jurídico Montoya & Asociados, Attorneys at Law. Montoya Pardo holds a PhD from the Universidad Complutense de Madrid, and a Master's Degree in Energy Law, Instituto Superior de la Energía (Spain). He is currently engaged in post-doctoral studies at Dundee University where he is Honorary Lecturer in the Centre for Energy, Petroleum and Mineral Law and Policy. Also, he is a member of the Academic Advisory Group (AAG), the Section on Energy, Environment, Natural Resources and Infrastructure Law (SEERIL), the International Bar Association (IBA and a board member of the Colombian Mining and Petroleum Bar Association.

Alessandro Negri della Torre is a PhD student at the University of Aberdeen and founder of a law firm specializing in emergent technologies. His PhD research is focused on advanced nuclear technology with a particular emphasis on nuclear fusion and the related regulatory challenges. Alessandro holds an LLM from the University of Aberdeen and an LLM from Washington University in St Louis School of Law. He is qualified to practise law in Italy and in the State of New York.

Ernst Nordtveit is a Professor at the Faculty of Law, University of Bergen, Norway. He has been Vice Dean for Research (1996–1998) and Dean of the Faculty (1999–2009). His research interests are on Natural Resource Law, with a particular focus on Energy and Climate Law, and Environmental Law with a special focus on the creation of new legal instruments aimed at creating a sustainable development based on insights from Law and Economics and Behavioural Economics. He has been a member of several public committees preparing legislation and of inter alia the Norwegian Petroleum Price Board (1996–2006). He is head of the Norwegian Conflict Resolution Body for Upstream Gas Pipelines. He also has experience from arbitration cases. He holds a Dr juris Degree from the University of Bergen (1990).

Zuzanna Nowak is an independent energy security and policy expert with a focus on post-Soviet Eurasia. She has held management and international cooperation positions at the Polish Oil and Gas Company (PGNiG) and the Polish National Centre for Nuclear Research. Zuzanna sits on the Polish Committee of the World Energy Council and has previously served as the Head of the Energy Project at the Polish Institute of International Affairs (PISM). She is a graduate of the Paris School of International Affairs, Sciences Po and the College of Europe, Bruges.

Nana Asare Obeng-Darko is a Researcher at the Law School of the University of Eastern Finland. His general research area is International Energy Law and policy. More specifically, he focuses on the regulation of the development of the renewable energy sector across Africa from both legal and policy perspectives. His academic background includes Law, Economics, International Business and Finance.

David M. Ong is the Professor of International and Environmental Law and Director of the Marine Ecological Resilience and Geological Resources (MERGeR) Centre at Nottingham Trent University, UK. He is the principal Rapporteur on the Environment for the International Law Association's Study Group on Asian State Practice in the Implementation of International Law. His research interests range across the Law of the Sea, International Environmental Law, International Investment Law and International Development Finance Law, as well as their interaction.

Indra Overland is a Research Professor and Head of the Centre for Energy Research at the Norwegian Institute of International Affairs (NUPI). His publications include "The geopolitics of renewable energy: Debunking four emerging myths" (*Energy Research and Social Science* 2019), "Financial sanctions impact Russian oil" (*Oil and Gas Journal* 2015) and *Russian Renewable Energy: The Potential for International Cooperation* (Ashgate 2009). He holds a PhD from the University of Cambridge.

Tade Oyewunmi is an Assistant Professor and Senior Energy Research Fellow at the Institute for Energy and the Environment, Vermont Law School, Vermont, USA. He teaches and researches Energy Law, Regulation and Policy. Previously, he was a Visiting Research Fellow at Tulane University Law School, USA, and a Senior Researcher in International Energy Law and Policy at the University of Eastern Finland (UEF) Law School. Dr Oyewunmi also practised in the field of energy and project finance, especially relating to Nigerian oil and gas law and energy policy. He holds an LLB from the University of Ibadan, Nigeria, an LLM from the University of Aberdeen, UK and an LLD from the University of Eastern Finland Law School.

John Paterson is a Professor of Law at the University of Aberdeen and the co-founder of its Centre for Energy Law. He has worked on a range of international research, teaching, training and consultancy projects in energy law and has published widely on a range of topics in the field. He is co-editor of *UK Oil and Gas Law: Current Practice and Emerging Trends*, published in two volumes by Edinburgh University Press and now in its third edition. He has recently held visiting professorships at the National University of Singapore and at the Chinese University of Hong Kong teaching International Oil and Gas Law. He coordinates Aberdeen's involvement in the North Sea Energy Law Programme (with the Universities of Copenhagen, Groningen and Oslo). Recent publications include "Production Sharing Agreements in Africa: Sovereignty and Relationality" in the *Ethiopian Yearbook of International Law* 2019.

Sirja-Leena Penttinen is the Assistant Director and an Adjunct Professor at the Center for Energy Law, Tulane University Law School, as well as Senior Lecturer at the University of Eastern Finland Law School, from where she obtained her PhD. She has published widely on different aspects of international and European energy law; her recent research and consultancy activities have focused on the implications of the sustainable energy transition for markets and investments. Besides her academic activities, she also regularly carries out assignments mainly for the public sector.

Slawomir Raszewski is a Senior Lecturer in the School of Business and Law, University of East London and Visiting Professor in Energy Security and Environmental Protection at the Institute of Political Science and International Relations, Jagiellonian University. His research interests lie at the intersection of international political economy and business strategy. Slawomir's advisory and consulting experience includes political risk, resource governance and regulation. Slawomir holds a PhD from the University of Leeds.

Tina Soliman Hunter is the Professor in Energy and Resources Law at the University of Aberdeen, researching in the area of petroleum law (offshore), Arctic resources law and shale gas law. She has received academic qualifications in marine sediments and geology, political science, applied science and law, completing her PhD at the University of Bergen. She has undertaken teaching, research and consultancies in numerous countries. Soliman Hunter is currently the Leader of the multidisciplinary Consortium of Researchers and Experts in North and Arctic Marine Ecosystems Oil Contamination (CRENAME), and a visiting Professor at Tomsk State University (Russian Federation), Murdoch University (Australia) and the University of Eastern Finland. She has published five books and over one hundred academic contributions. She is currently completing a book on Russian Petroleum Law, the first of its kind in English.

Kim Talus is the holder the James McCulloch Chair in Energy Law at Tulane University and the founding Director of the Tulane Center for Energy Law. He is also a part-time Professor of European Energy Law at University of Eastern Finland Law School and part-time Professor of Energy Law at the University of Helsinki. He also acts as the Editor-in-Chief for Oil, Gas and Energy Law (OGEL). His extensive experience in research and consultancy has centred around international, comparative and European energy law and has authored and co-authored more than 160 publications.

Madeline E. Taylor is an Academic Fellow at the University of Sydney Law School. Her research focuses on natural resources and energy law, and specifically examines comparative energy policies and regulation; unconventional gas and petroleum regulation; and natural resource governance and conflicts within the food–energy nexus. In particular, her research to date performs socio-legal analyses on the fragmented legal relationship and natural resource and energy ownership rights between the State, companies and private landholders – as regulated by numerous and overlapping regulatory regimes. Her publications also examine the legal challenges for regulators in allocating and managing energy and natural resources in the public interest.

Kristen van de Biezenbos is an Assistant Professor with the University of Calgary Faculty of Law. She received her JD, *magna cum laude,* from Tulane University Law School while also serving as an intern at the US District Court for the Eastern District of Louisiana. Van de Biezenbos had practice focused on commercial litigation, oil and gas, maritime law, international law and arbitration. She teaches and writes on energy law and policy, offshore resources and international commercial law. She is a member of the Board of Advisory Editors for the *Tulane Law Review* and the *Loyola Maritime Law Journal.* She has published in the *Michigan Journal of Law Reform,* the *Tulane Law Review*, the *Fordham Law Review* and others.

Lisa Viscidi is the Director of the Energy, Climate Change & Extractive Industries Program at the Inter-American Dialogue. A specialist in Latin American energy issues, Viscidi has written numerous reports and articles on energy policy and regulations, oil and gas markets, climate change, sustainable transport, the social and environmental impacts of natural resources development and the geopolitics of energy in the region. Viscidi conducted her undergraduate work in history at the George Washington University and the University of Barcelona and earned a Master's Degree in Latin American studies with a focus on economic development and public policy from New York University.

Hannah J. Wiseman is Attorneys' Title Professor of Law and Associate Dean for Environmental Programs, Florida State University College of Law. Hannah's research focuses on regulatory and policy design for the intersecting challenges of the environmental and land use-based impacts of fossil fuel and renewable energy development. She received her

JD from Yale Law School and received the award for the best student publication in the *Yale Law Journal*.

Constantinos Yiallourides is a Lecturer in International Law at the University of Aberdeen, and Research Fellow in Law of the Sea and Territorial Disputes at the British Institute of International and Comparative Law, London. Previously he was the JSPS Scholar in International Law at the University of Tokyo, where he conducted research on Japan's legal framework for deep-sea mining. Dr Yiallourides' research expertise spans a number of international law fields with a particular focus on the law of territory, the law of the sea, environmental and natural resources law and the peaceful settlement of international disputes more broadly.

PART I

Introduction

1

INTRODUCTION TO THE *ROUTLEDGE HANDBOOK OF ENERGY LAW*

Tina Soliman Hunter and Ignacio Herrera Anchustegui

1 Introduction

The importance of energy is beyond question. Indeed, few things are as indispensable as energy. As an energy source, no single fuel is more indispensable than petroleum. As noted by prominent political economist Edward Morse, petroleum has proven to be the most versatile fuel source ever discovered, situated at the core of the modern industrial economy.[1] With such versatility has come inevitable growth – increasing growth in the consumption of oil, economic growth fuelled by the consumption of oil (and now gas) and population growth on the back of the 'Green Revolution'.[2] Our reliance on petroleum has come at great costs – political, economic and, most of all, environmental. There is little doubt that the unbridled consumption of hydrocarbons over the last century, from coal to oil to gas, has brought about changes in the climate of the Earth. These climatic shifts, combined with concerns over nuclear energy after the 2009 Fukushima nuclear accident, and technological developments in the field of competitive renewable generation of energy have prompted a shift from the consumption of hydrocarbons to low-carbon energy as society becomes more electrified.

While there are numerous monographs studying different forms of energy, technologies, legal challenges, problems or comparative solutions, this *Handbook* is different. Rather than examining legal aspects related to energy from a source perspective, we have decided to approach the analysis of energy regulation from a geographical perspective. This approach has been undertaken since many issues are confined to regions, rather than sectors. For example, as noted by the *BP Statistical Review of Energy*, the Asia-Pacific region has the highest consumption of hydrocarbons (oil, gas and coal) of any region in the world.[3] By considering existing and emerging energy issues on a regional basis, we are able to highlight regional perspectives and unique issues, as well as place them within a global context.

1 Edward Morse, 'A new political economy of oil' (1999) 53(1) *Journal of International Affairs,* 1–29, 2.

2 The 'Green Revolution' denotes the large increase in the production of crops, especially cereal crops, as a result of the application of artificial fertilisers derived from petroleum products. This revolution commenced in the 1950s, with the global impact occurring during the 1960s..

3 BP, *BP Statistical Review of World Energy* (2019), 10, https://www.bp.com/content/dam/bp/business-sites/en/global/corporate/pdfs/energy-economics/statistical-review/bp-stats-review-2019-full-report.pdf

This unique approach enables us to present a truly worldwide contribution to energy law, illustrating that different regions experience different issues when it comes to the regulation of energy. While some continents, such as Europe, North America and Australia, are more focused on challenges posed by new technologies and energy forms – such as demand side management solutions in electricity markets, disputes over the most efficient regulation of energy markets and competition in them or the impetus given to low-carbon energy forms or non-conventional hydrocarbon sources – other areas, such as Latin America, Russia and the Middle East, remain focused on issues relating to petroleum extraction, state intervention and resource ownership. This however, is not to say that new technologies and low-carbon energy forms are not of importance in these jurisdictions. Although, as demonstrated in this book, these issues are important, the regulatory focus on new technologies in these regions tends to differ, conditioned by the traditional hydrocarbon-based sources. This tension between hydrocarbon-based forms of energy based on the extraction of oil and gas with new low-carbon energy sources is prompted mainly by the political and economic will of many countries to limit climate change and implement less polluting energy forms pursuant to international obligations, such as the Paris Agreement.[4] As the Age of Hydrocarbon Man gives way to the Age of Electricity Man, new regulatory and socio-legal challenges arise. This volume seeks to capture such challenges in this, the era of energy transition.

This chapter introduces the global energy regime today, and the challenges arising now, in the present, but also in the future. Therefore, it will first provide an outline of the current energy landscape. It will consider the origins of Hydrocarbon Man, and the Age of Hydrocarbons, before demonstrating how the Age of Electricity Man is imminent. It will conclude with a consideration of the contents of the book, outlining what each of the regional sections will be considering.

2 The energy landscape

Today's energy landscape is complex. In the last decade, the use of gas as a source for heating and electricity generation has grown markedly.[5] Certainly in the post-war era there was a focus on the use of oil, as outlined in section 3 below. However, this new millennium has been characterised by the use of gas, a most versatile fuel. And in the decades to come the trend seems to shift from gas to society electrification, as we discuss in section 4. Gas can be used directly for heating, the generation of electricity or, in combination with other energy sources, such as coal or renewable energy to 'boost' the energy.

Such a shift from oil to gas has seen a shift in geopolitical power. From the 1960s, the rise of the Organization of the Petroleum Exporting Countries (OPEC), both as an entity and market participant, has delineated a shift in the 'power' of control. Whereas oil production in foreign lands was once the domain of large international oil companies (the 'Seven Sisters'),[6] nationalism in the 1950s and 1960s saw many states take control over production of their oil resources. Most notable of these was Saudi Arabia, with the total nationalisation of its oil operations by

4 Paris Agreement of 12 December 2015.

5 For instance, global demand for gas increased 4.6 per cent in 2018 alone, with the US leading this growth as it switches from coal to gas for the generation of electricity. See the International Energy Agency (IEA), 'Growing demand for gas' (2019), https://www.iea.org/gas2019.

6 The current 'Seven Sisters' (of which there are now four due to mergers) are: BP (former Anglo-Iranian Oil Company); Chevron (comprised of Gulf Oil, Texaco and Standard Oil Company of California); Royal Dutch Shell; and Exxon-Mobil (former Standard Oil company of New Jersey, then Exxon, and Standard Oil company of New York, later Mobil).

the 1980s. Many other nations, such as Mexico, Venezuela and Bolivia, have followed suit, with varying degrees of success. This meant that OPEC grew to dominate the control of oil, particularly during the last three decades of the twentieth century.

A seemingly simple combination of existing technologies (horizontal drilling, hydraulic fracturing and three-dimensional seismic modelling) by non-conventional pioneer George Mitchell in the early 2000s created a tectonic shift in petroleum production resulting in a shift in the energy landscape. As a consequence of this technological coupling, the shale petroleum (both oil and gas) industry was born.[7] With it came two epochal changes. First, was the availability of abundant, cheap gas in the US. This enabled changes in many sectors, fuelled a new wave of US manufacturing and was the basis upon which Donald Trump was able to push for his policy of 'America First'. Secondly, and most importantly, the development and growth of shale oil and shale gas has meant that the US has shifted from being a net energy importer to not only being self-sufficient, but also a net energy exporter. This has shifted the energy geopolitical landscape to one where the US is top dog, and the former dominant force, Saudi Arabia, is no longer the largest energy producer or exporter.

This rise in the power and importance of the US as an energy giant has caused a realignment in approaches to oil in the Middle East. As this chapter is being written, oil facilities in Saudi Arabia are being bombed, forcing the planned Initial Public Offering (IPO) of 5 per cent of Saudi Aramco to be changed to just about 1.5 per cent and which has been received by investors with less enthusiasm than expected. What is of major interest here is not so much the bombing of the oil facilities and the attribution of blame, but the fact that Saudi Arabia is seeking to sell part of the world's largest company, Saudi Aramco. The idea that there will be a partial privatisation of Saudi Aramco is incredible, given decades of public focus on Saudi self-determination. However, as oil resources decline, and global energy sources shift to include low-carbon energy, it is clear that Saudi Arabia needs to effect change. Such change is outlined in the new *Saudi Vision 2030*, which envisages growth in the economy through industrial diversification and support in the renewable energy sector,[8] and the privatisation of government services, including Saudi Aramco.[9]

At a time when oil-associated power is shifting, climate change is contributing to another shift –from hydrocarbon-based energy to low-carbon energy. Recognition of the existence and impact of climate change has been slow. Some movement towards low-carbon energy sources has been significantly developed in the wake of the 2009 Fukushima nuclear accident in Japan. In response to the accident, several countries, particularly Germany, sought to divest themselves of nuclear energy as a source, looking to low-carbon energy sources to fill the energy gap. This move towards low-carbon energy was supported by the European Union's (EU's) third energy package, which sought to increase the percentage of renewable energy in the energy mix, as well as improve energy efficiently, which continues with the 2018–2019 EU 'Clean Energy Package'.

Recently, Greta Thunberg, and her Extinction Rebellion movement, has significantly raised global awareness of the risks associated with climate change. In espousing four interwoven themes (humanity is facing an existential crisis, perpetuated by the current adult

7 Tina Hunter, 'Redefining energy security: the new prize in a time of arctic petroleum resources and technological development' in Slawomir Raszewski, *The International Political Economy of Oil and Gas* (Palgrave Macmillan, 2018), 12–15.

8 Kingdom of Saudi Arabia, *Saudi Vision 2030* (2018) 44, 49, https://www.vision2030.gov.sa/sites/default/files/report/Saudi_Vision2030_EN_2017.pdf

9 Kingdom of Saudi Arabia, *Saudi Vision 2030* (2018), 45, 82–83.

generation, requiring change to solve it, by paying attention to scientists), Thunberg has captured the attention of global youth – and the not so young as well. Through climate strikes aimed at school-age participants, Thunberg seeks to effect changes in energy use and types through today's youth, who will be tomorrow's leaders. It is likely that this movement will provide a significant contribution to the shift from hydrocarbons to low-carbon energy in the years to come.

3 The Age of the Hydrocarbon Man

Is it possible to pinpoint when the Age of the Hydrocarbon Man dawned? Was it when oil was discovered by Colonel Drake in 1859? Was it the mass use of oil as a cheap fuel for electricity and propulsion in the boom period after World War II? Indeed, it was neither. Rather, the Age of Hydrocarbon Man commenced on 20 March 1912, when Lord Admiral Churchill announced in the House of Commons that there was a need to convert the British Navy's fuel source from coal to oil. As noted by Yergin, 'Many thought that was pure folly, for it meant that the navy could no longer rely on safe, secure Welsh coal, but would rather have to depend on distant secure oil supplies'.[10] The reasons for the conversion were strategic – greater speed and more efficient use of manpower.[11] One critical outcome of the conversion was a seismic shift in global geopolitics, one that continues today. In seeking to use oil as the fuel of choice for warships, there was a need to secure foreign oil interests. Indeed, as noted by Lord Churchill,

> the Admiralty must have the power to control an oil field somewhere… what we want now is a proved proposition, a going concern, an immediate supply, and a definite prospect with potentialities of development over which we ourselves can preside. This we find in Persia.[12]

The impact of the need for oil resources on geopolitics has continued throughout the epoch of Hydrocarbon Man. Indeed, a bald illustration of the geopolitical influence of the need for hydrocarbons came in 1980 when in the State of the Union Speech President Carter announced that

> an attempt by any outside force to gain control of the Persian Gulf region will be regarded as an assault on the vital interests of the United States of America, and such an assault will be repelled by any means necessary, including military force.[13]

Today, the Hydrocarbon Man is alive and well.[14] Global oil demand increased by 1.3 per cent in 2018, led by the US and China, and driven by the need for oil in petrochemicals and for jet fuel.[15] In addition, as noted above, consumption of the partner hydrocarbon, gas, has increased. The rise in gas and oil production from shale beds has ensured wide availability of

10 Daniel Yergin, *The Prize: The Epic Quest for Oil, Money & Power* (Free Press, 2008), xiv.

11 Daniel Yergin, *The Prize* (2008), xiv.

12 *Parliamentary Debates,* House of Commons, 20 March 1912, Vol 50 (Winston Churchill, First Lord).

13 President J Carter, *State of the Union Address* (Speech Delivered at the State of the Union, Washington, 23 January 1980).

14 Bright Okugu, *The Middle East and North Africa in a Changing Oil Market* (2003), International Monetary Fund. https://www.imf.org/external/pubs/ft/med/2003/eng/okogu/okogu.html.

15 IEA, *Global Energy and CO_2 Status Report: Oil* (2019), https://www.iea.org/geco/oil

these hydrocarbons have been secured for the US, enabling economic growth to resume on the back of the reliable supply of cheap gas. However, on a global scale, Hydrocarbon Man has also refocused his attention to the most remote of areas – the Arctic.

Containing up to 22 per cent of the world's oil and gas reserves,[16] of which a significant proportion is gas, the Arctic has caused another geopolitical shift. The Arctic is of exceptional geopolitical interest as it is of equal importance to two old foes – the US and Russia. The relevance of the US Arctic as an energy resource was reiterated in 2015 with the re-instatement of drilling rights in the Arctic, and a report from the US National Petroleum Council which recognised that the US Arctic contains petroleum reserves of such size that the position of the US as a global energy producer would be enhanced for at least the next 35 years.[17] Similarly, Russia has iterated the strategic importance of Russian Arctic petroleum through the Russian Marine and Arctic policies. It is the Russian Arctic that has already seen production commence in the Arctic, with oil in small quantities from the Prirazlomnoye Field, and large amounts of gas from the Yamal Peninsula. Combined with the opening of the Northern Sea Route in the Eastern Arctic, enabling rapid transport of Russian gas to Asian markets, global changes in climatic patterns have contributed to continued interest and geopolitical shifts in the Age of Hydrocarbon Man.

In an economic sense, the Age of Hydrocarbon Man has fuelled unrivalled economic growth, particularly in the post-war boom period of the 1950s and 1960s. In the period 1949–72, US oil consumption has rapidly expanded from 5.4 million barrels a day in 1949,[18] to 16.4 million barrels per day in 1972. By contrast, the following 25 years saw growth from 16.4 million barrels per day to 17.7 in 1995,[19] and in the following 25 years to an average of 20.4 million barrels per day in 2018.[20] This rapid growth in oil consumption in the post-war era was not confined to the US, it was also experienced in other countries. In Western Europe in the period 1949–72, oil consumption increased fifteenfold, from 970,000 barrels per day in 1949 to 14.1 million barrels per day in 1972. Similarly, in Japan's great economic growth during the period 1949–72, Japanese oil consumption increased 137 times over, from 32,000 barrels per day to 4.4 million barrels per day by 1972.

Whereas economic growth in the post-war era, fuelled by oil consumption, tended to centre around Western economies (and Japan which was rebuilt after World War II by Western nations), economic growth in the Asian and Middle Eastern region came later, albeit still fuelled by hydrocarbons. The rapid economic growth of China, India and the United Arab Emirates (UAE) has been fuelled largely by access to cheap hydrocarbons. Indeed, without hydrocarbons, China's economic development would have been stymied. This then raises an obvious question – if the Age of Hydrocarbon Man does not continue, albeit with a focus on gas, will economic development be able to continue? In giving way to Electricity Man, has the economic development of hitherto underdeveloped economies been limited or could this be an opportunity to be grabbed towards economic growth?

16 Peter Stauffer, *US Geological Survey (USGS) Circum-Arctic Resource Appraisal: Estimates of Undiscovered Oil and Gas North of the Arctic Circle* (2009), https://pubs.usgs.gov/fs/2008/3049/fs2008-3049.pdf.

17 National Petroleum Council (NPC), *Arctic Potential: Realizing the Promise of U.S. Arctic Oil and Gas Reserves* (2015), http://www.npcarcticpotentialreport.org

18 Yergin, 523.

19 US Energy Information Administration (EIA), *Petroleum and Other Liquids* (2019), https://www.eia.gov/dnav/pet/hist/LeafHandler.ashx?n=PET&s=MTTUPUS2&f=A

20 US EIA, *Petroleum and Other Liquids* (2019), https://www.eia.gov/dnav/pet/hist/LeafHandler.ashx?n=PET&s=MTTUPUS2&f=A

4 The shift to low-carbon energy sources: the Age of the Electricity Man

Even if the Age of the Hydrocarbon Man continues, we are still facing the dawn of a new energy era. This is the shift to modern societies fuelled by low-carbon energy sources and the rise of the Electricity Man. New technologies, coupled with political support, are making renewable energy sources not only a real alternative to fossil fuels but an efficient and economically viable one as output capacity increases and costs quickly decline.[21] No other low-carbon energy source has taken off as electricity produced from renewable sources.[22] Electricity is no longer an energy source used for home appliances or to generate light. It has become a potentially universal source of energy and, therefore, challenges oil's supremacy. More and more, electricity deepens its energy influence and usage in other areas as crucial as transportation and heating, with electricity surplus now used to create a gas fuel that may be stored for future use.

The latest data by the International Energy Agency indicates that in 2017, 23.9 per cent of all the world's electricity was produced thanks to renewable energy sources – with hydropower, solar and wind at the forefront.[23] This trend will continue and generation of electricity from renewable sources in particular – in contrast to nuclear power – is expected to grow to about 30 per cent of the world's total electricity demand by 2022, growing faster than any other source. And unsurprisingly so, as it is expected that by 2020 some solar panel technologies will be able to match the production costs of the most recent coal-fired power plants.[24]

This society electrification and the dawn of the Electricity Man is an increasingly dominant topic in the (energy) political arena, as is shown through the content of this *Handbook of Energy Law*. World debates are centred on reforms to electricity markets, the fast development of new technologies making generation more efficient and readily available, the development of larger storage possibilities, sector coupling, conflicts related to the use of land for energy and agriculture, the need for the development of larger and smarter grids, public financing of projects and tension concerning international investments.

Two key factors merge in this birth of the Age of Electricity Man, having at its core the transition to a low-carbon-based energy society. On the one hand, efforts to shift to these sources are directly related to States' obligations and pledges under Public International Law to mitigate and combat the negative effects of climate change. For example, with the goal to prevent a global temperature rise of more than 2 degrees Celsius this century, as required by the Paris Agreement, but also as part of pledges made concerning the United Nation's Sustainable Development Goals, such as Goal 7 regarding Affordable and Clean Energy, or Goal 13 on Climate Action.[25] Or more regional efforts, for instance the EU's 2030 Energy Strategy with new and more ambitious targets concerning decarbonisation, a cut in greenhouse gas emissions, an increase in energy efficiency and the development of new cross-border transmission lines for electricity and gas.[26]

Additionally, a rise in interest in low-carbon energies must be analysed from a geopolitical perspective. Traditionally 'energy hungry' but rather energy poor countries (in terms

21 https://www.irena.org/publications/2019/May/Renewable-power-generation-costs-in-2018.

22 https://www.iea.org/renewables2018.

23 https://www.iea.org/topics/renewables.

24 https://www.irena.org/publications/2019/May/Renewable-power-generation-costs-in-2018.

25 General Assembly of the United Nations, *Transforming Our World: The 2030 Agenda for Sustainable Development*, 25 September 2015, 70/71.

26 European Commission, *2030 Climate & Energy Framework*, https://ec.europa.eu/clima/policies/strategies/2030_en

of natural resource availability) have been dependent on sources of energy being brought to them from the energy rich. Europe is a clear example of this, with the exception of Norway. For these countries the rise and dawn of the Electricity Man is an opportunity to mitigate their dependence on hydrocarbon rich countries such the US, Russia and the Middle East and improve their energy sufficiency, potentially being able to transform themselves into an energy exporter if produced through renewable technology, for example, thanks to the production of power from offshore wind installations – as happens in the North Sea – or photovoltaic panels. Thus, the rise of the Electricity Man is a business opportunity for new energy rich countries that base this wealth on technology rather than consumable natural resources.

However, the rise of the Electricity Man does not signify the end of the Hydrocarbon Man's age nor does it come without challenges and risks. Geopolitically, if anything, it is a challenge to the former's supremacy and a geopolitical and economic reordering of the energy landscape. Technically, the renewable generation of electricity brings about new and well-known challenges discussed in this *Handbook*, such as variability of supply and therefore system instability and issues of security of supply. The introduction of new forms of electricity supply may also generate stranded costs and investment issues related to the phasing out of non-renewably fuelled power plants or rendering them redundant, thus requiring large infrastructure investments to be integrated into the system to supply other energy sources that now substitute. These issues are complex for both the law and the industry to address. And yet, despite and the efforts to foster low-carbon and renewable energy sources, it is estimated that these will provide less than 15per cent of the world's energy needs by 2023 as heating and transport remain largely dominated by traditional hydrocarbon sources. Thus, while this new era pushes for a low-carbon-based society, the present and near future remain largely dominated by the Hydrocarbon Man. How quickly the transition from Hydrocarbon Man to Electricity Man will occur remains to be seen, however it is likely that the 2020s and 2030s will be critical for both the development of new policy approaches to energy generation, as well as its implementation in both developed and developing states.

Perhaps the greatest change that Electricity Man will bring is the 'nationalisation' of energy. Whereas once upon a time states were dependent upon producer nations for hydrocarbons to use for energy generation, in the era of Electricity Man energy can be produced within national borders. Every state has the capacity to generate electricity from wind, water or the sun. Suddenly, nature's bounty for energy production is shared (somewhat) evenly amongst all nations, rather than a select few. If nothing else, the Age of Electricity Man will become the great equaliser, in a world where all states have the capacity to generate their electricity needs, even if there is neither the political will nor financial capacity to do so at present.

5 The *Routledge Handbook of Energy Law* in a nutshell

Given the shift from hydrocarbons to low-carbon energy, this *Handbook* considers the legal issues arising in this confluence between the Age of the Hydrocarbon Man and the Age of the Electricity Man. Energy and its regulation are the foundation of society, and as a shift occurs from hydrocarbons to low-carbon sources, legal issues and challenges arise. This book and its contents reflect such issues and challenges. To address topical issues of energy regulation we have structured this book in eight sections, six of them being geographical and two, the introduction and the conclusion, focusing on international and security aspects of energy law and the future challenges for energy regulation, respectively. In this book we have aimed to combine expertise in energy law with diversity in legal backgrounds, ethnicities, ages and gender, including contributions from well-known energy law professors and early career researchers alike. Some chapters have been commissioned to provide a broad focus over a little-known topic (such as the regulation of oil and gas in Russia), while others have a narrower and analytical approach, trying to find a good balance between a holistic view of energy and topical and timely topics.

The introductory section of this book, including this contribution, consider the international law aspects of energy, including the issue of energy security. Unlike other parts of this *Handbook of Energy Law*, these chapters are not organised based on their geographical relevance. Instead, in this section we present a general overview of energy law in a worldwide context and a broad content, looking at the role of stakeholders, international law and energy security in light of technological developments and climate change. In Chapter 2, 'From stakeholders to actors? The progressive integration of environmental, social and cultural considerations within international energy law', David M. Ong embarks on an analysis of the role of states and private investors in energy law, showcasing how private investors influence the way in which energy law takes shape as well as its content and how energy regulation is no longer an area for the states. In Chapter 3, Ernst Nordtveit discusses the interplay between international and national law in the regulation of energy matters in 'International energy law in perspective: the relationship between national and international energy law'. This first section concludes with Chapter 4, 'Reconceptualising energy security from a legal perspective in the context of climate change', by John Paterson in which the author stresses how traditional policies on energy security are changing due to the coming of Electricity Man, new sources of energy and technology and efforts to mitigate climate change and how this will require creative and unorthodox legal approaches to the topic.

The European section of this *Handbook* includes five contributions showing two clear and quite local trends: on the one hand, the importance of EU economic law in the regulation and liberalisation of the energy sector, on the other hand, the changes in electricity and renewable energy sources brought about by the Clean Energy Package. In Chapter 5, in 'Energy market liberalisation: from monopolistic to traded markets in the European Union', Sirja-Leena Penttinen discusses the liberalisation process of electricity and gas markets from vertically integrated national champions to wholesale and retail competition in the EU from a historical perspective. This chapter is followed by a further analysis of downstream energy (electricity) markets in Europe and the legal changes brought to them by technological development, the surge of prosumers and the new rules of the Clean Energy Package in Chapter 6 by Ignacio Herrera Anchustegui and Andreas Formosa in 'Regulation of electricity markets in Europe in light of the Clean Energy Package: prosumers and demand response'. Chapters 7 and 8 of this section form a joint read. In these, Christian Bergqvist and Ignacio Herrera Anchustegui discuss the role and importance of two pillars of EU economic regulation. First, in Chapter 7 in 'Uses and abuses of EU competition law in energy' the authors discuss the complementary and even supplementary role of antitrust rules in the energy sector not only to control the abuse of market power or anti-competitive agreements but also to promote sectoral change through structural and merger decisions. Then, in Chapter 8, 'The role of State aid law in energy', the importance of this sub-set of economic rules native to the EU is discussed as a limit but also a means of public intervention in energy markets in case of market failure. In particular, the role of state aid law concerning security of energy supply and capacity remuneration mechanisms is studied as a new and very important development in this field. Chapter 9, by Ruven

Fleming, embarks on an analysis regarding 'Shale gas in Europe: a case study on EU energy and environmental law' as an energy source possibility that is facing a considerable amount of political and social resistance and is conditioned by environmental standards and regulations. This section finishes with Chapter 10 by Naomi Briercliffe and David Ingle with a study on the alternative resolution mechanism landscape and cases in 'Dispute resolution in the European energy sector', in which arbitration has been used concerning renewable energy sources and dealing with investors' expectations and the principle of fair and equitable treatment. It also stresses the importance of international investment treaties to bring about energy security in the region.

Part III of this *Handbook*, 'Russia', follows the section on Europe. Unlike the other parts of the book the whole of it is dedicated to an energy giant and highly influential geopolitical player, sitting between Europe and Asia and conditioning oil and gas markets worldwide. In Chapter 11, 'The regulation of petroleum exploration and production in Russia', Tina Soliman Hunter and Irina Fodchenko provide an overview of the complex regulatory framework that governs access to and production of Russian oil and gas. This contribution is followed by the work of Mariia Kozlova, Mikael Collan and Indra Overland discussing a different and rather unexplored side of 'Russian renewable energy: regulations and outcomes', analysing the legislative framework for these types of energy sources, their very high investment potential and strategic importance to Russia for the future in Chapter 12. The Russia section finishes with Chapter 13, 'Shifting Russian energy geopolitics' by Slawomir Raszewski and Zuzanna Nowak who analyse how Russian petroleum abundance and geopolitical aspirations have moulded its 'new' energy strategy in the twenty-first century.

North America is the subject of Part IV, as an area of vast energy resources that is captured between the boom of shale oil and gas, and the country's electrification and environmental protection. Opening Part IV, in Chapter 14 Hannah J. Wiseman evaluates the boom of shale gas by analysing the economic implications and environmental challenges posed by this nascent industry and the regulatory answers by state and federal agencies in "Shale gas development, economic impacts and regulation". Continuing the theme of regulation, in Chapter 15 Kim Talus discusses the 'Regulation of natural gas pipeline construction and operation in the United States' and how, despite its importance and a state of the art infrastructure, the transmission capacity of gas networks is hampered and rendered inefficient. Of particular relevance is the study of the regulatory permits and competences of different actors. In Chapter 16 Kristen van de Biezenbos presents in "Regulation of low carbon energy sources in the U.S. & Canada" an overview of the US and Canadian regulatory frameworks for low carbon emission energy sources, showcasing the complex dynamics of the law posed by the Federal system which, despite the immense resources of the region, serve to partly explain the timid development of these forms of energy. Scott Hempling concludes Part IV in Chapter 17 with a discussion concerning the rating of electricity utilities by regulatory agencies and whether these tariffs and practices benefit end consumers in 'Formula rate plans and multi-year rate plans: can they serve the public interest, and how?'

The discussion moves south geographically as the *Handbook* now enters Latin America. The chapters in Part V show how this region, rich in energy sources, battles with technological change, political instability and environmental risks posed by energy activity. In Chapter 18 Tina Soliman Hunter and Ignacio Herrera Anchustegui discuss the present and future of shale gas exploitation in the region by analysing Mexico and Colombia as two different examples of countries that have pursued, with varying degrees of enthusiasm, shale gas and unconventional hydrocarbon exploitation amidst plenty of controversy in 'Shale gas regulation in Mexico and Colombia: an uncertain future'. In Chapter 19 Miguel Marmolejo-Cervantes brings the discussion to the realm of the social aspects of energy law through his consideration of energy justice in Mexico as a tool to ensure the reform of the energy industry in 'Energy justice as a key driver to unlock the transition from energy reform to energy counter-reform: the rise of the immutability theory'. Lisa Viscidi and Nate Graham take a comparative perspective in Chapter 20 on 'Low-carbon energy in Latin America: post-Paris advances in renewable and energy efficiency policies', in which they analyse legislative trends and governmental policies in five Latin American countries concerning renewable energy post-Paris Agreement, showcasing that despite important investments these countries have not fully adapted their regulatory framework to embrace and promote these technologies. Chapter 21 by Silvia Marchili and Isabella Bellera Landa, 'Protecting energy investments in Latin America', combines international arbitration, political instability and the changing international investment landscape in the region, by looking at arbitration examples in Venezuela, Ecuador, Argentina and Guatemala, and highlighting key aspects to keep in mind in investment operations and international investment treaties. In Chapter 22 Milton Fernando Montoya Pardo and María Alejandra Garzón Albornoz discuss the regulatory framework in relation to key regional players, Colombia and Brazil. The authors show how, although the regulatory framework in these countries has evolved and expanded, for instance, to include rules concerning low-carbon energy sources and foster electrification, oil and gas activity and its regulation remains at the forefront and is likely to remain so because of these countries' natural reserves and their importance to the economy.

Part VI of this *Handbook* analyses the energy law in Asia and Australia, two different geographical locations, not only because of their energy sources and policies but also their interests and preferred technologies. In Chapter 23, 'Asian energy markets: the impact of shifting global politics', Slawomir Raszewski discusses the influence of liquefied natural gas in shaping energy markets and trading in the Asia-Pacific region and the development opportunities brought by this revolution to the region. Penelope Crossley shows the tension between the Age of the Hydrocarbon Man, the Age of the Electricity Man and climate change in India in Chapter 24 where she explains how India has adapted its legislative framework to promote the energy production shift in 'From coal to clean energy: how the energy transition is being managed in Indian energy law and policy'. China's world character as a superpower is related to the transformation of its economic system and supported by its energy sector and regulation. In Chapter 25 Jie Huan discusses 'Energy law and regulation in China', showing that coal remains a primary source of energy in the country but that is changing, due to technological improvements, international pressure and environmental risks, to low-carbon energy solutions. The final two chapters of this part focus on Australia, covering the past and the future of energy, and the shift from hydrocarbon to renewable energy sources. In Chapter 26 Penelope Crossley discusses how Australia has started to increase its renewable energy production but continues to export hydrocarbons, and how these investment trends are transforming the markets and legislation in 'Renewable energy law in the context of a transforming Australian energy market'. In Chapter 27, 'Is gas security in the "national interest"? An Australian Eastern Gas Market perspective', Madeline E. Taylor examines the relationship between security of energy supply, gas availability and market efficiency for the domestic consumers and discusses how, although they generate revenue, international exports take resources away from the national market.

A handbook of energy law would not be complete without discussing different aspects of energy and its transformation in Africa and the Middle East, two areas in which the importance of hydrocarbon is still fundamental and will remain so in the foreseeable future, but in which renewable sources are starting to penetrate. In Chapter 28 Tade Oyewunmi discusses how the abundance of liquefied natural gas has led to the construction of pipelines for transportation and, therefore, the development of a legal framework in West Africa, showing also how energy policies and politics play a pivotal role in 'Gas commercialisation projects in West Africa: pipelines, LNG and gas-to-power'. Despite the strong presence of hydrocarbons in the region, the coming of the Electricity Man has also had an impact on the African energy landscape. In Chapter 29 Nana Asare Obeng-Darko analyses the legal framework for renewable electricity in sub-Saharan Africa as a way of providing consumers with electricity for their daily activities in 'Legal, policy and regulatory aspects of integrating electricity from renewable energy in sub-Sahara Africa. The case of Ghana, The Gambia and Nigeria'. In the same vein, in Chapter 30, Cameron Kelly shows how 'Developing renewable energy projects in the Middle East and North Africa region' is a reality promoted by different policies and legislative frameworks to push for the development of renewable energy in the region as a way of both reducing dependence on hydrocarbon sources and increasing the export of energy. Finally, the role of geopolitics and borders and maritime conflicts and boundaries in Africa is explored in Chapter 31 by Anna Khalfaoui and Constantinos Yiallourides in 'Maritime disputes and disputed seabed resources in the African Continent', explaining that these territorial disputes, arising as a result of the existence of energy resources in these areas, have accelerated efforts to solve these disputes and delimit borders through the African Union Border Programme and Joint Development Agreements.

The last part of this *Handbook* includes four chapters that look at the future of energy regulation around the globe. These contributions discuss the concept of energy transition, the need for some intermediate solutions to reach a carbon neutral energy society, if that actually is a realistic possibility, as well as the future of dispute settlements in relation to energy. In Chapter 32, 'Energy transitions and the law', Kim Talus and Pami Aalto discuss the role of energy law and policy in promoting the change to sustainable energy sources and the use of liquefied natural gas in this market transition. Although the law pushes for renewable energy sources, increasing the chances of regulatory failure, liquefied natural gas development seems more conditioned by the industry's interest and influence. In Chapter 33 Alessandro Negri della Torre undertakes a study of the future of nuclear energy and its relation to nuclear weapons and how the promotion of one indirectly also promotes the other, while also stressing in 'The future of nuclear energy' that developments in the technology, such as nuclear fusion and safety improvements, would lead to a rethinking of the current legal regime. In Chapter 34, Gloria M. Alvarez studies how legal disputes arising from energy transactions are currently being resolved. In 'The future of dispute resolution in the energy and natural resources sector: setting the scene and looking ahead', Alvarez uses empirical evidence to argue that in a similar fashion to energy law, international dispute resolution has evolved quickly in order to offer an efficient avenue to resolve energy disputes. Unlike national courts, alternative methods of dispute resolution have provided the energy industry with independence, impartiality, neutrality and decision-making know-how. The reordering of our energy systems have also permeated the architecture of international 'energy' arbitration, where there are institutional and policy initiatives to re-model the dispute resolution mechanism so that it is able to adjudicate climate change and environmental and social justice disputes. We end this *Handbook* in Chapter 35 by Penelope Crossley and Gloria M. Alvarez with our 'Concluding thoughts on the global energy transition'.

2

FROM STAKEHOLDERS TO ACTORS?

The progressive integration of environmental, social and cultural considerations within international energy law

David M. Ong

1 Introduction

International energy law as a distinct and specific area or sub-discipline of international law is arguably at a turning point in its evolution. Within international energy law itself, the basic set of relationships revolve around the legal framework for promoting and regulating investment in the energy industry. Previously the *primary actors* within the legal relationships underpinning this field consisted of two States – first, the *home State*, where the investment originates from – and second, the *host State*, the State in which it is invested, as well as the *investors* themselves, whether these be corporate or natural individuals. The basic thrust of this original set of legal relationships has moved over time from its origins within the international legal recognition of the host State's permanent sovereignty over its natural resources, to one in which the (foreign) investor's rights prevail even over that of their host States. Moreover, these investor rights are often confirmed by international trade and/or investment treaties adopted by the host and home States of these investors.

Aside from these *primary actors*, a number of associated entities and groups were also accepted as being part of the overall set of international energy investment relationships. These entities and groups include, *inter alia*, trade unions, local communities, as well as environmental, social and culturally oriented civil society/non-governmental organisations (NGOs). However, the *legal status* of these entities and groups within these existing international energy investment relationships has always been questionable. While they are regarded as important *stakeholders* in the overall set of relationships,[1] their status as *legal actors*

1 In the official 'Frequently Asked Questions' (FAQs) document accompanying the UN-prescribed Ruggie *Principles on Business & Human Rights*, the term 'stakeholder/affected stakeholder' is described as follows: 'A stakeholder refers to any individual who may affect or be affected by an organization's activities. An affected stakeholder refers here specifically to an individual whose human rights have been affected by an enterprise's

within these relationships has remained uncertain. This difference in legal status between a stakeholder and an actor is defined here in *substantive* and *procedural* legal terms. Thus, legal *actors* are provided with *substantive* rights that they may exercise against other actors within a specific legal relationship. Legal *actors* are also accorded the *procedural* legal capacity as designated actors to make legal claims against other actors, often before designated institutional accountability mechanisms and/or third-party dispute settlement bodies. *Stakeholders,* on the other hand, are often introduced as interest-holders, rather than rights-holders. While they may eventually be granted both *substantive* rights and the *procedural* legal capacity to exercise these rights against other actors, their elevation to the status of legal actors within the overall international energy investment relationship is by no means assured.

More recently, however, these stakeholding entities and groups have begun to make inroads within this set of legal relationships underlying international energy law. Thus, it is now at least an arguable case that their interests are beginning to be incorporated as *actors*, rather than merely being addressed as *stakeholders* within these legal relationships. In particular, through various legal and institutional means, these previously disenfranchised *stakeholders* are being provided with certain substantive rights and limited procedural capacity to challenge the unmitigated activities of the established *actors* in the original set of legal relationships underpinning international energy law. The remainder of this chapter will be devoted to interrogating the veracity of the above proposition, as well as examining the emergence of this new, convergent paradigm for the roles of *stakeholders* and *actors* in the international energy investment law relationship(s).

These recent developments in international energy law have taken place in the rule-making and rule-adoption, as well as dispute settlement, aspects of this international legal field/sub-discipline. First, within the international rule-making aspect of international energy law, recent multilateral and bilateral investment treaties (BITs) have shown a greater propensity to include explicit provisions for domestic regulation of higher worker health, safety and environmental protection standards, as well as cultural/religious concerns. In most cases, these new investment treaties incorporate internationally well-accepted environmental, social and cultural protection rules, principles and standards. International 'soft' law instruments such as the Organisation for Economic Co-operation and Development (OECD) Guidelines for Multinational Enterprises (MNEs) have also adopted and/or adapted existing international rules that address health, safety, environmental, social and cultural concerns.[2] Further rule-adoptive regulation of this kind is also manifesting itself within the deliberative processes of public international finance institutions (IFIs) when they make funding decisions for international energy projects. Examples of these international rule-adoption exercises within public IFIs include the World Bank Performance Standards and Environment, Health and Safety (EHS) Guidelines, as well as the International Finance Corporation (IFC)'s Performance Standards. These public IFI Principles, Standards and Guidelines are the product of rule-adoption exercises, drawing their regulations from well-known and well-accepted international environmental instruments, such as the 1992 Rio Declaration on Environment and Development.

Second, in the investor-State dispute settlement aspect of international energy law, there is a growing trend within the international investment case law for arbitral tribunals to accord primacy to host State domestic regulation, even when these are deployed against

operations, products or services.' Accessible at: https://www.ohchr.org/Documents/Publications/FAQ_PrinciplesBussinessHR.pdf.

2 Organisation for Economic Co-operation and Development (OECD), 'Guidelines for multinational enterprises' (2011), accessible at www.oecd.org/corporate/mne.

investor protection interests. Moreover, within the broad meaning of international dispute settlement, there are now an increasing number of public IFI accountability mechanisms that explicitly allow the representation of the worker, community and civil society/NGO interests within these institutional accountability mechanisms. Examples of such accountability mechanisms include the World Bank Inspection Panel and the IFC Compliance Advisor/Ombudsman (Food and Agriculture Organisation of the United Nations (FAO)).

The net result of these normative developments within the rule-making, rule-adoption and dispute settlement aspects of international energy investment law is arguably to provide legally actionable *actor* status to previously non-legally represented *stakeholder* entities and groups that are deemed to be negatively affected by international energy projects. The above propositions will be fleshed-out in the following sections of this chapter with references to the necessary legal authorities and examples. Once these have been elaborated, the discussion will return to the (hypo)thesis proposed at the outset of this chapter, namely, that international energy law has now evolved to include groups and interests that were previously *stakeholders,* but are now *actors* within this legal field/sub-discipline. Thus, where the interests of such *stakeholders* – whether individual or in groups – were hitherto acknowledged, but not afforded the legal capacity to challenge, let alone hold accountable, any industrial or State *actors* responsible for health and safety, environmental, social and cultural risks within international energy investment projects, these *stakeholders* have now been allocated the procedural means to ensure the *institutional accountability* of these actors, even if these mechanisms do not quite ensure the *legal* responsibility of these industry, State or public IFI actors.

2 International rule-making within BITs

A seminal article by Footer outlined at least three ways in which social and environmental issues have been raised and arguably progressively integrated within international investment law.[3] The first trend is in the form of the reassertion by host States of their right to regulate on domestic matters of importance such as worker health and safety, environmental protection, as well as social and cultural values. Where previously the exercise of State regulatory powers in these fields was inhibited due to fear of being challenged by investors as amounting to indirect expropriation, international investment tribunals are arguably showing a greater willingness to accept the legitimacy of State regulatory powers in these fields. A related development that both feeds into and augments this nascent re-assertion of the pre-eminence of State regulatory power is the recent trend within international investment law for States to (re-)negotiate trade promotion and investment protection treaties that explicitly incorporate relevant environmental and social principles, as well as acknowledge cultural values as having similar, if not equal, normative density within these trade and investment regimes.

The second trend is manifested through the increasing role(s) played by civil society groups and NGOs in lobbying on behalf of environmental, social and cultural concerns, especially against oil, gas and mining (OGM) multinationals, in international energy investment litigation by means of *amicus briefs*.[4] When viewed cumulatively, both these trends are evidence of greater consideration given to these environmental, social and cultural concerns within this body of law. They will both be considered in more detail within Section 2 of this chapter of this chapter, on international investment arbitration trends and public IFI accountability mechanisms.

3 Mary E Footer, 'Bits and Pieces: Social and Environmental Protection in the Regulation of Foreign Investment', *Michigan State Journal of International Law* Vol.18, No.1 (2009) 33, at 33–34.

4 Ibid., at 34.

Finally, according to Footer, the third development is the introduction of a more tenable link between business and human rights into investment treaty instruments.[5] Thus, while international investment agreements are traditionally geared towards the protection of investors and their investments, many of them now contain a *quid pro quo*, introducing principles and standards of corporate social responsibility for investors in their operations abroad. The so-called Ruggie Principles on Business and Human Rights represent the culmination of efforts by the United Nations (UN) to consolidate the relevant State responsibility for human rights violations, as well as establish the duty to respect and provide remedies for human rights abuses for businesses operating within these States. As such, these Principles are particularly resonant for multinational energy companies active in developing economies for at least two reasons: First, the proportionately greater environmental and social impacts that these extractively-oriented industries inflict on the domestic polities in which they operate; and second, the relatively longer time periods in which these energy investments are made within these developing economies.

The rise in the significance of human rights and environmental protection within the UN and other related international institutional initiatives has arguably led to their appearance within a new generation of 'model' BITs spearheaded by the governments of the United States (US) and Canada, and emulated by the European Union (EU) as well in its own recent BITs with Canada and Japan. These model BITs seek to balance the competing interests of investor protection, on the one hand, and social and environmental protection, on the other, through the provision of specific clauses on each of these concerns in their treaty-making practice.[6] A significant factor in this regard is that some model BITs aim to incorporate these social and environmental norms by direct reference within the proposed treaty text, alongside the investment protection clauses.[7]

While these three trends within international investment law are undoubtedly continuing, this first section of the chapter will initially focus on how they are in fact converging to shape both present and, especially, future international energy law, through their formal incorporation within new international investment agreements (IIAs) – in the form of both BITs and multilateral trade and investment agreements (MTIAs). Recent examples of the latter type of agreements that will be examined here include the following two MTIAs, namely: 1) the Central American & Dominican Republic-USA Free Trade Agreement (CAFTA-DR),[8] in force since 2007; and 2) the USA-Mexico-Canada Agreement,[9] adopted on 30 November 2018, which has replaced the 1993 North American Free Trade Agreement (NAFTA).[10] Among the BITs highlighted here are: 1) the Comprehensive Economic and Trade Agreement between Canada and the EU (CETA) which entered into force provisionally in September 2017;[11] and 2) the EU-Japan Economic Partnership Agreement which was concluded on 1 February 2019.[12]

5 Ibid., at 34.
6 Ibid., at 34.
7 Ibid., at 35.
8 Initially, the CAFTA-DR Agreement included the US and the Central American countries of Costa Rica, El Salvador, Guatemala, Honduras and Nicaragua, and was called CAFTA. In 2004, the Dominican Republic joined the negotiations, and the agreement was renamed. CAFTA-DR.
9 Full title: Agreement between the United States of America, the United Mexican States, and Canada, adopted on 30 November 2018, but not yet in force. More information and text accessible at: https://ustr.gov/usmca.
10 Adopted in 17 December 1992, and entered into force: 1 January 1994.
11 Adopted on 30 October 2016. The CETA text is accessible at: http://trade.ec.europa.eu/doclib/docs/2014/september/tradoc_152806.pdf.
12 Full title: Agreement between the European Union and Japan for an economic partnership, entered into force on 1 February 2019. Available at: http://ec.europa.eu/trade/policy/in-focus/eu-japan-economic-partnership-agreement.

2.1 *Multilateral trade and investment agreements and bilateral investment treaties*

The inculcation of social and environmental concerns within international investment law instruments, which have particular resonance for the international energy industry, has evolved in at least two ways. First, these agreements have sought to confirm the wide domestic regulatory powers and discretion of host States on environmental, social and cultural (including religious) matters. As we will see below (in Section 2), when we examine the case law on these broadly described powers they have been instrumental in enabling host States to circumscribe legal challenges to their regulatory discretion in favour of investor protection, especially within the context of indirect expropriation claims. Second, not content with the confirmation of host State national sovereignty on these municipal regulation issues, these newer, international trade and investment promotion agreements also explicitly re-iterate both current and (any) forthcoming international obligations accepted by States on environmental, social and cultural concerns, as well as link these obligations directly to the domestic regulatory autonomy already confirmed within the treaty text (above). Within the context of climate change, for example, Gehring et al., have noted that these refinements to 'trade and investment laws, particularly in regional treaties which advance beyond the globally agreed disciplines, do not unduly constrain domestic regulatory flexibility to address climate change, and might even promote more sustainable development'.[13]

Specific environmental provisions are now being expressly included within the substantive chapters of the texts of these major international trade and investment instruments. Viñuales concurs, noting that '[t]he majority of newly-concluded International Investment Agreements (IIAs) contain clauses that relate to environmental concerns'.[14] Empirical evidence for this trend is forthcoming from an OECD report examining the prevalence of environmental concerns within a sample of 1,623 IIAs, involving 49 States and the European Commission, amounting to roughly half of the global investment treaty population.[15] This survey provides a statistical portrait of the extent, kind and frequency of treaty language referring to environmental concerns and the evolution of the use of such language over time. The survey summarises its findings as follows:

> i) over time, more treaties contain such language; ii) only about 8% of the sample treaties include references to environmental concerns; and iii) there are wide variations in the content of such language, both across countries and across time.[16]

The net result of these two converging trends in recent multilateral and bilateral trade and investment agreements is to reinforce the normative equivalence of this set of issues (environmental, social and cultural) over that of the traditional objectives of these agreements, namely, trade promotion and investor protection. Examples of both these trends – first, broader domestic regulatory powers to host States that cannot be challenged as amounting to indirect expropriation, and, second, explicit inclusion of relevant environmental and social goals and principles – within recent MTIAs as well as bilateral investment treaties BITs – will be highlighted in the sub-section below.

13 Markus Gehring, Marie-Clair Cordonier-Segger and Jarrod Hepburn, 'Climate Change and International Trade and Investment Law', in Rosemary Rayfuse and Shirley V. Scott (eds) *International Law in the Era of Climate Change*, Edward Elgar (2012) 84–117, at 108.

14 See remarks attributed to Viñuales in Diepeveen, Levashova and Lambooy (2014) at 147.

15 Gordon and Pohl (2011).

16 Ibid., at 3.

2.1.1 Central American and Dominican Republic-USA (CADR/USA FTA) Free Trade Agreement

Despite being of an earlier vintage than the other Agreements discussed in this section, a close examination of Investment-related provisions of the CADR/USA FTA Agreement arguably contain the seeds of the broad domestic regulatory discretion afforded to States 'hosting' foreign-sourced investment within their individual national jurisdictions. The text under 'Section A: Investment', of Chapter Ten on 'Investment' of this Agreement provide for investor protection against both direct and indirect expropriation. These provisions establish a fairly standard investment treaty approach. However, a specific provision under Article 10.11 on 'Investment and Environment' details as follows:

> Nothing in this Chapter shall be construed to prevent a Party from adopting, maintaining, or enforcing any measure otherwise consistent with this Chapter that it considers appropriate to ensure that investment activity in its territory is undertaken in a manner sensitive to environmental concerns.

Under Chapter Seventeen on the 'Environment', Article 17.1 on 'Levels of Protection' buttresses the domestic regulatory autonomy and discretion for States hosting foreign investors provided by Article 10.11:

> Recognizing the right of each Party to establish its own levels of domestic environmental protection and environmental development policies and priorities, and to adopt or modify accordingly its environmental laws and policies, each Party shall ensure that its laws and policies provide for and encourage high levels of environmental protection, and shall strive to continue to improve those laws and policies.

Article 17.2.1 entitled: 'Enforcement of Environmental Laws', then provides as follows:

> (a) A Party shall not fail to effectively enforce its environmental laws, through a sustained or recurring course of action or inaction, in a manner affecting trade between the Parties, after the date of entry into force of this Agreement.
>
> (b) The Parties recognize that each Party retains the right to exercise discretion with respect to investigatory, prosecutorial, regulatory, and compliance matters and to make decisions regarding the allocation of resources to enforcement with respect to other environmental matters determined to have higher priorities.
>
> Accordingly, the Parties understand that a Party is in compliance with subparagraph (a) where a course of action or inaction reflects a reasonable exercise of such discretion, or results from a bona fide decision regarding the allocation of resources.

Article 17.2.2 then specifically discourages these States from lowering their regulatory standards in the hope of stimulating inward investment – an approach known as the 'race to the bottom', by providing that:

> The Parties recognize that it is inappropriate to encourage trade or investment by weakening or reducing the protections afforded in domestic environmental laws. Accordingly, each Party shall strive to ensure that it does not waive or otherwise derogate from, or offer to waive or otherwise derogate from, such laws in a manner that weakens

> or reduces the protections afforded in those laws as an encouragement for trade with another Party, or as an encouragement for the establishment, acquisition, expansion, or retention of an investment in its territory.

Finally, the CAFTA-DR/USA Agreement also provides for harmonisation in the implementation and enforcement of their domestic environmental regulations Article 17.3.

2.1.2 US-Mexico-Canada Agreement

The US-Mexico-Canada Agreement, replaced the NAFTA and, for the purposes of this chapter, the relevant focus here is on the treaty text relating to the consequences of the expropriation of an 'investment' protected by this Agreement, which is covered by Article 14. While the rest of the provisions under Article 14.8 establish a fairly standard regime for protection of investors against direct and indirect expropriation by their host States, Article 14.8.5 specifies that: 'For greater certainty, whether an action or series of actions by a Party constitutes an expropriation shall be determined in accordance with paragraph 1 of this Article and Annex 14-B (Expropriation)'. Within Annex 14-B on 'Expropriation', the Parties first confirm their shared understanding that: 'An action or a series of actions by a Party cannot constitute an expropriation unless it interferes with a tangible or intangible property right or property interest in an investment'.

Article 14.8.1 (Expropriation and Compensation) then addresses two situations. The first is *direct* expropriation, in which an investment is nationalised or otherwise directly expropriated through formal transfer of title or outright seizure. The second situation addressed by Article 14.8.1 (Expropriation and Compensation) is *indirect* expropriation, in which an action or series of actions by a Party has an effect equivalent to direct expropriation without formal transfer of title or outright seizure. In this context, Article 14.8.1(a) initially provides that:

> a) The determination of whether an action or series of actions by a Party, in a specific fact situation, constitutes an indirect expropriation, requires a case-by-case, fact based inquiry that considers, among other factors:
>
> (i) the economic impact of the government action, although the fact that an action or series of actions by a Party has an adverse effect on the economic value of an investment, standing alone, does not establish that an indirect expropriation has occurred,
> (ii) the extent to which the government action interferes with distinct, reasonable investment-backed expectations, and
> (iii) the character of the government action, including its object, context, and intent.

However, much more significantly, Article 14.8.1(b) further specifies that:

> Non-discriminatory regulatory actions by a Party that are designed and applied to protect legitimate public welfare objectives, such as health, safety and the environment, do not constitute indirect expropriations, except in rare circumstances.

This explicitly worded exclusion of 'regulatory actions' (on such broadly described themes) from the definition of *indirect* expropriation, albeit subject to the non-discrimination principle, clearly expands the regulatory scope of the 'host' State concerned.

This is buttressed by Article 14.16 on 'Investment and Environmental, Health, Safety, and other Regulatory Objectives', which provides that:

> Nothing in this Chapter shall be construed to prevent a Party from adopting, maintaining, or enforcing any measure otherwise consistent with this Chapter that it considers appropriate to ensure that investment activity in its territory is undertaken in a manner sensitive to environmental, health, safety, or other regulatory objectives.

Article 14.17 on 'Corporate Social Responsibility' further provides that:

> The Parties reaffirm the importance of each Party encouraging enterprises operating within its territory or subject to its jurisdiction to voluntarily incorporate into their internal policies those internationally recognized standards, guidelines, and principles of corporate social responsibility that have been endorsed or are supported by that Party, which may include the OECD Guidelines for Multinational Enterprises. These standards, guidelines, and principles may address areas such as labor, environment, gender equality, human rights, indigenous and aboriginal peoples' rights, and corruption.

Moving on from the reiteration and arguably expansion of the regulatory ambit of the 'host' State to any investment made within its jurisdiction, as well as taking on board clear references to both treaty obligations and international standards on a variety of environmental and social considerations, the present US-Mexico-Canada Agreement also includes specific definitions of environmental terms within a whole Chapter (24) of this treaty devoted to the 'Environment'.

Thus, Article 24.1 on 'Definitions', provides that:

> For the purposes of this Chapter: environmental law means a statute or regulation of a Party, or provision thereof, including any that implements the Party's obligations under a multilateral environmental agreement, the primary purpose of which is the protection of the environment, or the prevention of a danger to human life or health, through:
>
> (a) the prevention, abatement, or control of the release, discharge, or emission of pollutants or environmental contaminants;
> (b) the control of environmentally hazardous or toxic chemicals, substances, materials, or wastes, and the dissemination of information related thereto; or
> (c) the protection or conservation of wild flora or fauna, including the protection or conservation of biological diversity, endangered species, their habitat, and specially protected natural areas (as defined by the Party in its law.)

Article 24.2 then elaborates on the 'Scope and Objectives' of such 'environmental law' and its link to, *inter alia*, 'sustainable development' (Art.24.2.1); 'sustainable use and management of their natural resources' (Art.24.2.3); and 'the economic, social, and cultural well-being of indigenous peoples and local communities' (Art.24.2.4). Article 24.3 then returns to the regulatory extent of such 'host' State's domestic environmental regulation, specifying the 'Levels of Protection' for such regulation as follows:

> 1. The Parties recognize the sovereign right of each Party to establish its own levels of domestic environmental protection and its own environmental priorities, and to establish, adopt, or modify its environmental laws and policies accordingly.

2. Each Party shall strive to ensure that its environmental laws and policies provide for, and encourage, high levels of environmental protection, and shall strive to continue to improve its respective levels of environmental protection.

2.1.3 Canada-European Union Comprehensive Economic and Trade Agreement (CETA)

Another recent example of both trends noted here, namely: 1) treaty provision of greater domestic regulatory autonomy, especially over environmental, social and cultural issues; as well as 2) specific inclusion of international environmental principles and standards for application within the domestic jurisdictions of State parties to trade and investment treaties, is to be found within the CETA. Initially, under Chapter 8 on 'Investment', within Section D on 'Investment Protection', Article 8.9 on 'Investment and Regulatory Measures' provides as follows:

1. For the purpose of this Chapter, the Parties reaffirm their right to regulate within their territories to achieve legitimate policy objectives, such as the protection of public health, safety, the environment or public morals, social or consumer protection or the promotion and protection of cultural diversity.
2. For greater certainty, the mere fact that a Party regulates, including through a modification to its laws, in a manner which negatively affects an investment or interferes with an investor's expectations, including its expectations of profits, does not amount to a breach of an obligation under this Section.
   Moreover, under Annex 8-A, entitled: 'Expropriation', the Parties confirm their shared understanding that:
3. For greater certainty, except in the rare circumstance when the impact of a measure or series of measures is so severe in light of its purpose that it appears manifestly excessive, non-discriminatory measures of a Party that are designed and applied to protect legitimate public welfare objectives, such as health, safety and the environment, do not constitute indirect expropriations.

Specifically, on domestic environmental regulation, under Chapter 24 on 'Trade and Environment' of this treaty, Article 24.3 entitled: 'Right to Regulate and Levels of Protection' then provides as follows:

> The Parties recognise the right of each Party to set its environmental priorities, to establish its levels of environmental protection, and to adopt or modify its laws and policies accordingly and in a manner consistent with the multilateral environmental agreements to which it is party and with this Agreement. Each Party shall seek to ensure that those laws and policies provide for and encourage high levels of environmental protection, and shall strive to continue to improve such laws and policies and their underlying levels of protection.

Moreover, Article 24.5 entitled: 'Upholding Levels of Protection', provides as follows:

1. The Parties recognise that it is inappropriate to encourage trade or investment by weakening or reducing the levels of protection afforded in their environmental law.
2. A Party shall not waive or otherwise derogate from, or offer to waive or otherwise derogate from, its environmental law, to encourage trade or the establishment, acquisition, expansion or retention of an investment in its territory.

3. A Party shall not, through a sustained or recurring course of action or inaction, fail to effectively enforce its environmental law to encourage trade or investment.

More substantively, Chapter 23 of this Agreement covers 'trade and sustainable development', while Chapter 24 covers 'trade and environment'. Chapter 24 commits the EU and Canada to putting into practice international environmental agreements and, *inter alia*, protects each side's right to regulate on environmental matters, requires each side to enforce its domestic environmental laws and prevents either side from relaxing their laws to boost trade. This chapter also encourages conservation and sustainable management of forests and fisheries, as well as the involvement of civil society groups/NGOs in ensuring the implementation of the contents of the chapter.

2.1.4 EU-Japan Economic Partnership Agreement

A more recent example is the Agreement between the EU and Japan on an Economic Partnership, which entered into force on 1 February 2019. The use of the word 'economic', rather than just 'trade', in itself arguably signifies an acknowledgement as well as acceptance and, indeed, promotion of the broadening and deepening inter-dependency between these two major economies, namely, the EU and Japan. Despite this acknowledgement and the usual thrust of such Agreements towards harmonisation and even convergence of trade and investment promotion/protection principles and standards, this Agreement is notable for its provisions that emphasise the possibility of opposite outcomes, namely, the entrenchment of domestic environmental, social and culturally based regulation governing these two markets.

Within Chapter 18, entitled: 'Good Regulatory Practices and Regulatory Cooperation', under Article 18.1 on 'Objectives and General Principles', sub-section 2 provides that:

> Nothing in this Section shall affect the right of a Party to define or regulate its own levels of protection in pursuit or furtherance of its public policy objectives in areas such as: (a) public health; (b) human, animal and plant life and health; (c) occupational health and safety; (d) labour conditions; (e) the environment including climate change; (f) consumers; (g) social protection and social security; (h) personal data and cybersecurity; (i) cultural diversity; (j) financial stability; and (k) energy security.

This provision enshrining the regulatory autonomy of each of these two Parties to this Agreement in all of the above areas, is buttressed by Article 18(3), which provides as follows:

> Nothing in this Section shall be construed to prevent a Party from:
>
> (a) adopting, maintaining and applying regulatory measures in accordance with its legal framework, principles[17] and deadlines, in order to achieve its public policy objectives at the level of protection it deems appropriate; and
> (b) providing and supporting services of general interest, including those related to water, health, education or social services.

17 For the EU, such principles include those established in the Treaty on the Functioning of the European Union (TFEU) as well as in regulations and directives adopted pursuant to Article 289 of the TFEU.

Moreover, Article 18(5) enhances this domestic regulatory autonomy by providing that: 'Nothing in this Section shall be construed as obliging the Parties to achieve any particular regulatory outcome'.

By any measure, this is a most unusual set of provisions to be located within an international trade promotion and investment protection agreement. These provisions arguably allow the continuation, if not enshrinement, of domestic regulatory autonomy within each of these two large economies – Japan and the EU, despite their clear potential to disrupt the very trade and investment this agreement was intended to advance. Almost the only type of provision within this agreement that acts as a bulwark against the trade/investment disruptive potential of the rest of these provisions is Article 18(4), which states that: 'Regulatory measures shall not constitute a disguised barrier to trade', with similarly worded provisions in Article 16.2.3, which provides that:

> The Parties shall not use their respective environmental or labour laws and regulations in a manner which would constitute a means of arbitrary or unjustifiable discrimination against the other Party, or a disguised restriction on international trade', and Article 16.4.5, which states that: 'Nothing in this Agreement prevents a Party from adopting or maintaining measures to implement the multilateral environmental agreements to which it is party, provided that such measures are not applied in a manner that would constitute a means of arbitrary or unjustifiable discrimination against the other Party or a disguised restriction on trade.'

As if to emphasise this highly irregular 'anti-harmonisation' approach, in Chapter 16 of this Agreement, entitled: Trade and Sustainable Development', Article 16.1.2 further provides that:

> The Parties recognise the contribution of this Agreement to the promotion of sustainable development, of which economic development, social development and environmental protection are mutually reinforcing components. The Parties further recognise that the purpose of this Chapter is to strengthen the trade relations and cooperation between the Parties in ways that promote sustainable development, and is *not to harmonise the environment or labour standards of the Parties.* (emphasis added)

Article 16.2.1 on the 'Right to Regulate and Levels of Protection', then provides that

> Recognising the right of each Party to determine its sustainable development policies and priorities, to establish its own levels of domestic environmental and labour protection, and to adopt or modify accordingly its relevant laws and regulations, consistently with its commitments to the internationally recognised standards and international agreements to which the Party is party, each Party shall strive to ensure that its laws, regulations and related policies provide high levels of environmental and labour protection and shall strive to continue to improve those laws and regulations and their underlying levels of protection.

Similar to the provision in the CAFTA-DR/USA Agreement (examined in Section 2.1.1 above), Article 16.2.2 then specifically enjoins against any 'race to the bottom' scenarios, whereby States compete against each other to attract inward investment by lowering their regulatory standards, by providing as follows:

> The Parties shall not encourage trade or investment by relaxing or lowering the level of protection provided by their respective environmental or labour laws and regulations. To that effect, the Parties shall not waive or otherwise derogate from those laws and regulations or fail to effectively enforce them through a sustained or recurring course of action or inaction in a manner affecting trade or investment between the Parties.

Not content with the provision (above) of the broad regulatory ambits for each of these two jurisdictions, the Trade and Sustainable Development chapter of this new Agreement then makes explicit references to 'international labour standards and conventions' (Article 16.3); 'multilateral environmental agreements' (Article 16.4); 'trade and investment favouring sustainable development' (Article 16.5); 'biological diversity' (Article 16.6); 'sustainable management of forests and trade in timber and timber products' (Article 16.7); and 'trade and sustainable use of fisheries resources and sustainable aquaculture' (Article 16.8). In each case, similarly worded provisions ensure that each Party reaffirms its commitment to effectively implement in its laws, regulations and practices, the multilateral environmental agreements on sustainable development/biological diversity/sustainable forest management and timber trade/sustainable fisheries resources and aquaculture, etc., to which it is party. Moreover and albeit within the context of an 'economic partnership agreement', the parties nevertheless provide for mutual reporting requirements as to their implementation of these multilateral environmental agreements, with Article 16.4.3 stating that:

> Each Party shall exchange information with the other Party on its respective situation and advancements regarding ratification, acceptance or approval of, or accession to, multilateral environmental agreements, including their amendments, which each Party considers appropriate to be bound by, as well as implementation of such agreements.

2.2 A new asymmetry within international (energy) investment law?

It has been argued by many commentators that the previous asymmetry (or discrepancy) within international investment law was between investor protection and the use of regulatory 'police' powers by the 'host' State, in favour of the former.[18] Summing up the above discussion on the latest multilateral and bilateral investment promotion/protection treaties, it is submitted here that this asymmetry/discrepancy is now being addressed by the introduction of two types of provisions in newly negotiated (multilateral and bilateral) IIAs. First, through the re-casting of the indirect/regulatory expropriation clauses within these IIAs to reflect a much higher threshold and wider interpretation for non-compensable host State regulation; and secondly, through the inclusion of substantive and procedural environmental principles within dedicated environmental chapters of these new IIAs.

Concluding this brief survey of recent multilateral and bilateral trade and investment promotion agreements, it is possible to argue that a new asymmetry is arising within international (energy) investment law. The traditional asymmetrical relationship *within* such treaties

18 See, for example, Munir Maniruzzaman, 'The Pursuit of Stability in International Energy Investment Contracts: A Critical Appraisal of the Emerging Trends', *Journal of World Energy Law & Business*, Vol.1, No.2 (2008) 121–57.

was balanced in favour of investor protection against the regulatory discretion of their 'host' States. These recent multilateral and bilateral international investment agreements, adopted mainly between developed economies such as the US, Canada, the EU and Japan, reflect the new equilibrium which tends to favour 'host' State regulation over that of investor protection. However, older BITs, especially those that continue to apply between developed and developing/emerging economies, have not incorporated these latest 're-balancing' provisions in favour of 'host' States. Therefore, a new asymmetry has now emerged between these older BITs that still apply between developed and developing/emerging economies in favour of investor protection, as against newer MITs/BITs adopted mainly between developed economies that embody this new equilibrium favouring 'host' State regulation over investor protection. Given that the older BITs between developed and developing/emerging economies usually facilitate investment from the developed economy to the developing one, this will continue to have detrimental effects for host developing/emerging States.

3 International rule-adoption within public international finance institutions

As humankind's search for natural resources both widens and deepens across the globe, the international finance packages for funding these projects in remote developing economies, often situated far away from the final market destinations of these resources, have become ever more intricate. International investment risk management is a significant aspect of all these usually mixed – public and privately sourced – international financing arrangements, with the diversity and extent of different types of risk being important factors to be considered in any international/multinational project finance package. Among these different types of investment risks, environmental protection, social resilience and cultural heritage are rapidly becoming imperative considerations.

3.1 World Bank Environmental and Social Framework and the International Finance Corporation Performance Standards

As an example of how these environmental, social and cultural considerations are now intrinsic to the institutional decision-making process of public and private international/multinational financiers of such projects, we will examine the institutional practice of one of the main public international organisations on this point, namely, the International Bank for Reconstruction and Development (IBRD), more commonly known as the World Bank.[19] In this regard, the World Bank Environmental and Social Framework sets out the World Bank's commitment to sustainable development, through the adoption and implementation of a World Bank Environmental and Social Policy, as well as a set of Environmental and Social Standards (ESS) that are designed to support Borrowers' projects, with the aim of ending extreme poverty and promoting shared prosperity.[20] What is notable here is that through this overarching Environmental and Social Framework, the World Bank is adopting principles, rules and standards for both its own behaviour and that of its borrowers.

19 For more information on the World Bank's activities in the international development field, see: https://www.worldbank.org.

20 See: 'Overview of the World Bank's Environmental and Social Framework', at para.1. Accessible at: http://pubdocs.worldbank.org/en/837721522762050108/Environmental-and-Social-Framework.pdf#page=29&zoom=80.

3.1.1 World Bank Environmental and Social Framework

This Environmental and Social Framework comprises the following items:

a) A Vision for Sustainable Development, which sets out the Bank's aspirations regarding environmental and social sustainability.
b) The World Bank Environmental and Social Policy for Investment Project Financing establishes the mandatory requirements that the Bank must follow regarding projects it supports through Investment Project Financing.
c) The World Bank Environmental and Social Standards (ESS), together with their Annexes, establish the mandatory requirements for Borrowers relating to the identification and assessment of environmental and social risks and impacts associated with projects supported by the Bank through Investment Project Financing.[21]

The Bank believes that the application of these standards will encourage Borrowers to focus on the identification and management of environmental and social risks, thereby assisting in the achievement of their goals of reducing poverty and increasing prosperity in a sustainable manner for the benefit of the environment and their citizens. The ESS will:

(a) Support Borrowers in achieving good international practice relating to environmental and social sustainability;
(b) Assist Borrowers in fulfilling their national and international environmental and social obligations;
(c) Enhance non-discrimination, transparency, participation, accountability and governance; and
(d) Enhance the sustainable development outcomes of projects through ongoing stakeholder engagement.[22]

The ten ESS establish the standards that the Borrower and the project will meet through the project life cycle:

Environmental and Social Standard 1: Assessment and Management of Environmental and Social Risks and Impacts;
Environmental and Social Standard 2: Labor and Working Conditions;
Environmental and Social Standard 3: Resource Efficiency and Pollution Prevention and Management;
Environmental and Social Standard 4: Community Health and Safety;
Environmental and Social Standard 5: Land Acquisition, Restrictions on Land Use and Involuntary Resettlement;
Environmental and Social Standard 6: Biodiversity Conservation and Sustainable Management of Living Natural Resources;
Environmental and Social Standard 7: Indigenous Peoples/Sub-Saharan African Historically Underserved Traditional Local Communities;
Environmental and Social Standard 8: Cultural Heritage;
Environmental and Social Standard 9: Financial Intermediaries; and

21 Ibid., at paras 2, 3 and 4.
22 Ibid., at para. 4.

Environmental and Social Standard 10: Stakeholder Engagement and Information Disclosure.[23]

Specifically, ESS 1 applies to all projects for which bank investment project financing is sought. ESS 1 establishes the importance of:

(a) the Borrower's existing environmental and social framework in addressing the risks and impacts of the project;
(b) an integrated environmental and social assessment to identify the risks and impacts of a project;
(c) effective community engagement through disclosure of project-related information, consultation and effective feedback; and
(d) management of environmental and social risks and impacts by the Borrower throughout the project life cycle.[24]

Thus, the Bank requires that all environmental and social risks and impacts of the project be addressed as part of the environmental and social assessment conducted in accordance with ESS 1. ESS 2–10 set out the obligations of the Borrower in identifying and addressing environmental and social risks and impacts that may require particular attention. These Standards establish objectives and requirements to avoid, minimise, reduce and mitigate risks and impacts, and where significant residual impacts remain, to compensate for or offset such impacts.[25] Borrowers and projects are also required to apply the relevant requirements of the World Bank Group Environmental, Health and Safety Guidelines (EHSGs). These are technical reference documents, with general and industry specific examples of Good International Industry Practice (GIIP).[26]

Furthermore, the Framework includes provisions for grievance redress and accountability (discussed in Section 3.4, below). A Bank-supported project will include a number of mechanisms to address concerns and grievances arising in connection with a project. Project-affected parties will have access, as appropriate, to project grievance mechanisms, local grievance mechanisms, the Bank's corporate Grievance Redress Service,[27] and the World Bank Inspection Panel. After bringing their concerns directly to the World Bank's attention and giving Bank Management a reasonable opportunity to respond, project-affected parties may submit their complaint to the World Bank's independent Inspection Panel to request an inspection to determine whether harm has occurred as a direct result of World Bank non-compliance with its policies and procedures.[28]

3.1.2 International Finance Corporation (IFC)

Not to be outdone, the IFC, as the World Bank's private finance support arm, has also adopted its own version of the above environmental and social sustainability principles and standards. This takes the form of the IFC's Sustainability Framework, which articulates the Corporation's

23 Ibid., at para.5.
24 Ibid., at para.6.
25 Ibid., at para.6.
26 Ibid., at para.11.
27 Accessible at: www.worldbank.org/GRS; email: grievances@worldbank.org.
28 Ibid., at para.12.

strategic commitment to sustainable development, and is an integral part of IFC's approach to risk management. The Sustainability Framework comprises IFC's Policy and Performance Standards on Environmental and Social Sustainability, and IFC's Access to Information Policy. The IFC Policy and Performance Standards on Environmental and Social Sustainability (hereinafter, IFC Performance Standards) describes IFC's commitments, roles and responsibilities related to environmental and social sustainability. The IFC's Access to Information Policy in turn reflects IFC's commitment to transparency and good governance on its operations and outlines the IFC's institutional disclosure obligations regarding its investment and advisory services.

As the main private sector-oriented agency of the World Bank, the IFC also performs a significant supporting role providing either finance and/or advisory services for natural resource development and public infrastructure projects in developing countries around the world.[29] In similar fashion to the co-option of international norms by the World Bank through its Environmental and Social Framework, the IFC has initiated an internal standard-setting institutional process in the form of the IFC Sustainability Framework. This Framework articulates the IFC's strategic commitment to sustainable development, and is an integral part of IFC's approach to risk management. The Sustainability Framework comprises IFC's Policy and Performance Standards on Environmental and Social Sustainability, and IFC's Access to Information Policy.[30] For IFC-sponsored projects, updated Performance Standards which apply similar international environmental and social protection standards to those of the World Bank's Environmental and Social Framework were approved by the IFC Board and came into effect on 1 January 2012.[31]

The IFC Performance Standards are directed towards clients, which for these purposes should be regarded as in the same position as 'Borrowers' in the World Bank context. These Performance Standards provide guidance on how to identify risks and impacts, and are designed to help avoid, mitigate and manage risks and impacts as a way of doing business in a sustainable way, including stakeholder engagement and disclosure obligations of the client in relation to project-level activities. In the case of its direct investments including project and corporate finance provided through financial intermediaries, the IFC requires its clients to apply the Performance Standards to manage environmental and social risks and impacts so that development opportunities are enhanced. IFC uses the Sustainability Framework along with other strategies, policies and initiatives to direct the business activities of the Corporation in order to achieve its overall development objectives. These Performance Standards may also be applied by other financial institutions.[32]

Together, the eight Performance Standards establish standards that the client is to meet throughout the life of an investment by IFC:

Performance Standard 1: Assessment and Management of Environmental and Social Risks and Impacts;
Performance Standard 2: Labor and Working Conditions;
Performance Standard 3: Resource Efficiency and Pollution Prevention;

29 More information on the IFC role is accessible from: www.ifc.org/wps/wcm/connect/CORP_EXT_Content/IFC_External_Corporate_Site/What+We+Do

30 More information on the IFC's Sustainability Framework is accessible from: www.ifc.org/wps/wcm/connect/b9dacb004a73e7a8a273fff998895a12/IFC_Sustainability_%2BFramework.pdf?MOD=AJPERES.

31 IFC Performance Standards on Environmental and Social Sustainability, accessible from: www.ifc.org/wps/wcm/connect/c8f524004a73daeca09afdf998895a12/IFC_Performance_Standards.pdf?MOD=AJPERES.

32 'Overview', para.1.

Performance Standard 4: Community Health, Safety, and Security;
Performance Standard 5: Land Acquisition and Involuntary Resettlement;
Performance Standard 6: Biodiversity Conservation and Sustainable Management of Living Natural Resources;
Performance Standard 7: Indigenous Peoples;
Performance Standard 8: Cultural Heritage.[33]

It is no coincidence that these IFC Performance Standards bear an uncanny resemblance to those introduced by the World Bank, specifically – the International Bank of Reconstruction and Development's ESS. Performance Standard 1 establishes the importance of: (i) integrated assessment to identify the environmental and social impacts, risks and opportunities of projects; (ii) effective community engagement through disclosure of project-related information and consultation with local communities on matters that directly affect them; and (iii) the client's management of environmental and social performance throughout the life of the project.[34] The inclusion of Performance Standard 2 on 'Labor and Working Conditions' reflects the acceptance that local worker safety, health and associated rights needed to be integrated into the environmental and social framework for the IFC,[35] as well as the World Bank.

Performance Standards 3–8 establish objectives and requirements to avoid, minimise and, where residual impacts remain, compensate/offset workers, affected communities and the environment for risks and impacts. While all relevant environmental and social risks and potential impacts should be considered as part of the assessment, Performance Standards 2–8 describe potential environmental and social risks and impacts that require particular attention. Where such environmental or social risks and impacts are identified, the client is required to manage them through its Environmental and Social Management System (ESMS) consistent with Performance Standard 1.[36]

Performance Standard 1 applies to all projects that have environmental and social risks and impacts. Depending on project circumstances, other Performance Standards may apply as well. The Performance Standards should be read together and cross-referenced as needed. The requirements section of each Performance Standard applies to all activities financed under the project, unless otherwise noted in the specific limitations described in each paragraph. Clients are encouraged to apply the ESMS developed under Performance Standard 1 to all their project activities, regardless of financing source. A number of cross-cutting topics such as climate change, gender, human rights and water are addressed across multiple Performance Standards.[37]

3.2 International investment arbitration trends and public international finance institutional accountability mechanisms

Moving on from the environmental, social and cultural rule-*making* exercises initially undertaken by States within their bilateral and multilateral trade and investment agreements,

33 Ibid., at para.2
34 Ibid., para.3.
35 See, for example, Franz Christian Ebert, 'The Integration of Labour Standards Concerns into the Environmental and Social Policy of the International Finance Corporation', *Law and Politics in Africa, Asia and Latin America, Thematic Issue: New Actors and Instruments in the Law of Development Cooperation*, Vol. 47, No. 2 (2014) 229–249.
36 Ibid., at para.3.
37 Ibid., para.4.

followed by the rule-*adoption* of these environmental, social and cultural concerns within public IFIs such as the World Bank (WB) group, including the IFC, the next section of this chapter (3.3) will initially focus on the way(s) in which these environmental, social and cultural concerns are increasingly being complemented by similar recognition and acceptance of the legitimacy of these concerns within the jurisprudence of international investment arbitral tribunals – many of these adjudicating on disputes arising between investing multinational oil companies and their 'host' States.

Section 3.4 then builds on the fact that, as these environmental, social and cultural risks become a central plank of the international finance planning process for these types of projects, the inability of domestic governments to adequately address these types of risks within these projects in themselves becomes a significant political risk factor within any international finance decision-making process. The actual (or perceived) inadequacies of *domestic* judicial and administrative review mechanisms have also resulted in the prescription of *international* accountability mechanisms to complement recourse to national modes of accountability. Thus, a striking feature of *public* international financing of natural resources development projects in developing economies is the introduction of institutional accountability mechanisms to ensure that these projects comply with the environmental and social principles and standards adopted by these public IFIs, namely, the WB EHS Guidelines and IFC Operational Standards discussed above. For example, natural resource development projects funded through the WB are subject to the Inspection Panel mechanism for projects of the IBRD, and the Compliance Advisor Ombudsman (CAO) for IFC-supported projects, in relation to complaints about the negative environmental and social impacts of such projects. Both these public *international* financial institution accountability mechanisms will be examined in Section 3.4, with a view to assessing their contributions to the progressive expansion of remedies available to stakeholders negatively affected by such projects, who would otherwise face intractable barriers to their *domestic* resolution.

3.3 Increased consideration of environmental, social and cultural concerns within investor-state arbitration jurisprudence

As mentioned in the Introduction, the first trend observed by Footer in the increasing consideration of environmental and social issues in international investment law is through the expanding body of case law arising from arbitral tribunals. As she notes, within international investment arbitration law, claims arising out of the breach of property rights or investor protection standards are increasingly being challenged by the right of host States to regulate in the fields of social and cultural policy, as well as environmental protection.[38] In relation to the last of these values – environmental protection, for example, Viñuales has pointed out that the importance of environmental concerns can increasingly be observed in investment arbitration: 'In the last ten years, more than 40 investment claims were brought before arbitral tribunals with an environmental component and in comparison, before 1990, only 9 investment claims had an environmental component'.[39]

Footer also noted a second related development in this regard, in the form of the advocacy of broader social and environmental justice issues by civil society groups and/or NGOs before international arbitral tribunals by means of *amicus curiae* briefs.[40] While it is still at the

38 Ibid., at 33.

39 See remarks attributed to Jorge Viñuales on the interaction between investment law and the environment, in Diepeveen, Levashova and Lambooy (2014) at 147.

40 Ibid., at 34.

discretion of an arbitral tribunal to determine whether it will entertain such briefs, there is evidence of their increased permission for use in practice. This trend is set to expand in relation to international investment arbitration tribunals on a range of social and environmental issues. These new rules on greater transparency and participation by non-Parties to an investment dispute are finding their way into several model BITs, and other governments may in the future feel compelled to include similar clauses in their investment treaties.[41] More recently, Mikadze has also explored this nexus between the international investment regime and civil society/NGOs through the medium of *amicus* briefs specifically on environmental protection issues, arguing that NGOs have a crucial role in bringing about or even compelling, as well as shaping, 'collisions' between the investment regime and environmental protection in ways that lead to greater environmental sensitivity within this regime.[42] However, she ultimately concludes that this role has not been fully realised to date.[43] Referring to the case of *Pac Rim Cayman LLC v Republic of Salvador*,[44] for example, Mikadze notes that the decision-making process of the investor-State dispute settlement (ISDS) at the heart of the international investment regime remains 'unresponsive to environmental concerns when confronted with them'.[45] Specifically, securing access to arbitration documentation and oral hearing transcripts is still problematic.[46]

On the other hand, there are clear indications within certain regional trade and investment regimes, notably the (now replaced) NAFTA that allows host State measures to protect health, safety and the environment, as well as for arbitral tribunals in State-investor disputes to accept such State measures as permissible, even at the expense of investor protection rights.[47] For example, in NAFTA-based arbitration awards such as *Methanex v USA* (2005),[48] *Glamis Gold v. USA* (2009)[49] and *Chemtura v. Canada* (2010)[50] private investor protection has been pitted against host State regulations and the relevant investment tribunals have gener-

41 Ibid., at 34.

42 Mikadze K, 'Uninvited Guests: NGOs, Amicus Curiae Briefs, and the Environment in Investor-State Dispute Settlement', *Journal of International Law & International Relations*, Vol.12, No.1 (2016) 35, at 38.

43 Ibid, at 75.

44 ICSID Case No. ARB/09/12 (2008). Accessible at: https://www.italaw.com/cases/783.

45 Mikadze (2016) at 75.

46 Ibid., at 76.

47 Examples of both State practice and investment tribunal jurisprudence confirming these trends are examined in David M. Ong, 'Transnational Investment Law and Environmental Protection: Russian State Intervention in the Sakhalin II Project – The Empire Strikes Back?', *Netherlands International Law Review*, Vol.LVIII, Issue1 (2011) 1–42; and David M. Ong, 'The Contribution of State-MNC "Transnational" Investment Agreements to International Environmental Law', *Yearbook of International Environmental Law*, Vol.17, 2006, Oxford University Press, 168–212.

48 *Methanex Corporation v United States of America,* NAFTA, Award of 3 August 2005. Available at: www.state.gov/documents/organization/51052.pdf.

49 *Glamis Gold Ltd.* v. *USA*, argued before an Arbitral Tribunal constituted under Chapter 11 of the North American Free Trade Agreement and in accordance with UN Conference on International Trade (UNCITRAL) Rules, at the International Center for the Settlement of Investment Disputes (ICSID), Award, 8 June 2009. Accessible from the US Department of State website at: www.state.gov/documents/organization/125798.pdf.
For case notes see S.W. Schill and D.J. Bederman, 'Glamis Gold Ltd. v USA', 104 *American Journal of International Law* (2010) 253–259; and J. Harrison, 'Investment Protection and the Environment: *Glamis Gold Ltd. v USA*', *Journal of Environmental Law,* Vol. 22 (2010) 505–507.

50 *Chemtura Corporation (formerly Crompton Corporation)* v. *Canada,* argued before an Ad Hoc NAFTA Arbitration under UNCITRAL Rules, Award, 2 August 2010. Accessible from the Permanent Court of Arbitration website at: www.pca-cpa.org/showpage.asp?pag_id=1278.

ally concluded that such measures will not easily be deemed adverse to investment. Specifically, the arbitral tribunal in *Methanex Corp v United States* stressed that:

> as a matter of general international law, a non-discriminatory regulation for a public purpose, which is enacted in accordance with due process and which affects, *inter alios*, a foreign investor or investment is not deemed expropriatory and compensable unless specific commitments had been given by the regulating government to the then putative foreign investor contemplating investment that the government would refrain from such regulation.[51]

In *Glamis Gold*, a new Californian state provision to restore culturally sensitive Native American landscapes following proposed gold mining activities was alleged, *inter alia*, to amount to expropriation but the NAFTA-constituted tribunal held that these measures did not cause sufficient economic impact to be regarded as an expropriation of *Glamis*'s investment. It should be noted that this decision does seem to leave open the possibility that if a significant diminution of the investment had in fact occurred, then expropriation requiring compensation would have been found, even if the domestic measure was justifiable from a cultural/ environmental perspective. In *Chemtura* too, the tribunal was of the view that should a 'substantial deprivation' of investment occur as a result of the domestic environmental measure adopted, then this could be held to amount to expropriation, although this was not held to be proven in that case. On the other hand, the Tribunal concluded that irrespective of the existence of a contractual deprivation (whether substantial or not), the measures challenged by *Chemtura* were in any event a valid exercise of Canadian police powers.

Even more indicative of the increasing acceptance of stringent domestic environmental standards by international investment arbitral tribunals is the recent acceptance and adjudication on 'host' State *counterclaims* on environmental damage. In *Burlington Resources v Ecuador* (2018) an investment arbitral tribunal case adjudicated under the International Center for the Settlement of Investment Disputes (ICSID) rules, *Burlington* had initiated a successful claim for, *inter alia*, breach of the expropriation clause of the relevant 1993 BIT between Ecuador and the US.[52] However, Ecuador has successfully counter-claimed for environmental damage caused by Burlington's operational oil activities on a strict liability basis under the applicable Production Sharing Contract (PSC) citing violations of several PSC clauses, *inter alia*, to 'preserve the existing ecological equilibrium in the Contract Area' in accordance with all pertinent standards and the environmental impact studies; and to employ 'qualified personnel, equipment, machinery, materials, operational procedures and, in general, technology which complies with environmental protection standards and practices used in the international petroleum industry, subject to compliance with existing standards in Ecuador'.[53] Moreover, Clause 5.1.20.10 of Block 7 PSC reads as follows:

> The Contractor will take responsibility for cleanup and reforestation of the area with species similar to those originally found at the site, in order to, with time, allow the site to return to its original potential, with environmental conditions similar to those found at the beginning of the operations.[54]

51 *Methanex v USA* (2005) *op. cit.*

52 See: *Burlington Resources Inc. v Republic of Ecuador,* ICSID Case No. ARB/08/5, Decision on Liability, 14 December 2012. Accessible at: https://www.italaw.com/cases/181.

53 *Burlington v Ecuador,* Decision on Counterclaims, 7 February, 2017, at para.219, citing Clause 5.1.20 of Block 7 PSC.

54 Ibid., at paras 219 and 221.

The Tribunal's initial examination of Burlington's legal responsibility for these alleged violations of these PSC provisions then led it to analyse the relevant Ecuadorian environmental liability laws in tort, as opposed to contractual liability under the PSCs.[55] This in turn necessitated an examination of the tort liability regime for environmental harm both pre- and post the 2008 Ecuador Constitution.[56] Here, the Tribunal began by noting that the Parties agreed that the 2008 Constitution establishes strict liability for environmental harm, and that the Constitution also sets the following rules of the strict liability regime:

(i) the burden of proof of the inexistence of harm falls on the operator;
(ii) the operator is only responsible for the harm caused by him; and environmental claims are imprescriptible.[57]

Moreover, the Tribunal noted that:

> The constitutional regime has been clarified in case law. Specifically, the burden of proof of environmental harm was addressed in *Los Vencedores*, a decision dealing with a claim against Perenco for soil contamination in Block 7 that occurred after the entry into force of the 2008 Constitution. The Court held that the burden of proving harm had been reversed by Article 397(1) of the 2008 Constitution, which provides that '[t]he burden of proof regarding the inexistence of potential or real harm shall lie with the manager of the activity or the defendant'.[58]

While observing this reversal of the burden of proof introduced by the 2008 Constitution, the Tribunal nevertheless noted its understanding 'that the plaintiff still has the burden to make a showing of harm plausibly connected to the defendant's activities and the defendant then has the burden of proving its absence'.[59]

According to the Tribunal, when

> [a]pplied to the present case, the rule contained in Article 397(1) (of the 2008 Constitution) means that once Ecuador has made a showing of the existence of environmental harm reasonably related to the Consortium's risky activities, for example by way of the IEMS sampling exercise, Burlington then carries the burden of demonstrating that there is no harm or, if there is harm, what its limits are.[60]

Moreover, the Tribunal noted that:

> Ecuadorian courts have also held that fault is not a requirement of strict liability. The National Court of Justice explained that strict civil liability is the equivalent of 'risk liability' or 'fault-less liability' that is triggered 'regardless of whether there was wilful misconduct or negligence from the person."

55 Ibid., at para.224.
56 Ibid.
57 Ibid., at para.225.
58 Ibid., at para.226.
59 Ibid.
60 Ibid., at para.227.

The Court added that the duty to repair environmental harm is based on the fact that the harm caused "may be materially attributed to a certain activity, not on the existence of fault".'[61] The Tribunal thus concluded that when '(a)pplied to this case, the absence of a requirement of fault implies that Burlington may not avoid liability by raising that it acted diligently'.[62] The Tribunal then went on to observe that 'Another element of strict liability addressed by the courts is the requirement of causation. Under the strict liability regime, causation is presumed.'[63] As the Tribunal goes on to note:

> For present purposes, this holding means that Burlington can be exempted from liability if it proves that the harm was caused by *force majeure*, by a third party, or by Ecuador and in particular by Petroamazonas after the takeover of the Blocks.[64]

However, the Tribunal disagreed with Burlington's position that Ecuador must prove that the harm was caused during the time of the Consortium's operations, stating that:

> Indeed, proof of causation is not required. Causation is presumed, with the result that liability ensues from the mere exercise of a risky activity and the occurrence of harm that is plausibly connected to such activity as far as the type and location of the harm is concerned.[65]

Accordingly, the Tribunal ultimately concluded that the following elements are characteristic of the strict liability regime for environmental harm under Ecuadorian law: (i) the plaintiff must prove harm connected to the defendant's activities; (ii) fault is not required; and (iii) causation is presumed, the defendant being exonerated if he or she proves that the harm was caused by force majeure, the victim or a third party.[66]

It could be argued that the Tribunal in this case was only concerned to apply the applicable domestic environmental strict liability standard on a non-discriminatory and non-retroactive basis to *all* operators within the Ecuadorian hydrocarbon industry, thereby not affording *Burlington* any special status as a foreign investor within this jurisdiction. However, the willingness of this international *investment* Tribunal to actively consider *environmental* counterclaims of this nature, especially when combined with the Tribunal's detailed, even forensic, examination of the negative environmental impact of such operations in order to substantiate Ecuador's counterclaim augurs well for future 'host' State responses of this sort. At the very least, it will act to lift the paralysis inflicted on such 'host' States, caused by the combination of so-called 'freezing clauses' on domestic environmental regulation and the so-called 'chilling effects' of the stabilisation clause within State-investor contracts.[67] These clauses are then buttressed by the ability of investors to resort to international arbitration, rather than domestic courts, for the resolution of any investor-State disputes arising between them. The *Burlington v Ecuador* environmental counterclaims decision suggests that 'host'

61 Ibid., at para.228.
62 Ibid., at para.229.
63 Ibid., at para.230.
64 Ibid., at para.232.
65 Ibid., at para.232.
66 Ibid., at para.238.
67 See, for example, Lorenzo Cotula, 'Reconciling Regulatory Stability and Evolution of Environmental Standards in Investment Contracts: Towards a Rethink of Stabilization Clauses', *Journal of World Energy Law & Business*, Vol.1, No.2 (2008) 158–179.

States can bring their domestic environmental damage claims to the international dispute settlement system to offset the traditional advantage of foreign investors in this regard. In doing so, this decision transforms the host State's traditional status from that of a passive respondent, to that of an active claimant on behalf of a traditionally unheard/unseen 'stakeholder' within such investor-State proceedings, namely, the 'environment'.

3.4 The World Bank Inspection Panel and the Compliance Advisory Ombudsman of the International Finance Corporation

The general acceptance by public international finance institutions of their legal obligation to inculcate sustainable development within their overall mandates is now both well-documented,[68] and a continuing feature of their operational policies. An important aspect of the assumption of this mandate is the co-option of international environmental and social standards by the WB through its Environmental and Social Framework, as well as through the IFC's Performance Standards.

A further aspect of this new policy agenda is focused on ensuring better institutional accountability for the achievement of these goals within the WB group operations. In this regard, the establishment of the WB's Inspection Panel offers lessons for advocates of greater institutional accountability for decision-making within both public and, increasingly also, private IFIs. One of these lessons is arguably to focus advocacy policy and campaigning practice not just on the institution itself, but also on its own sources of finance. In the case of the WB, human rights and environmental NGOs targeted both the Bank itself but perhaps more significantly, its main donor – the US government and specifically, US congressional leaders who controlled funding to WB agencies. Indeed, so successful was this NGO lobbying exercise that the corresponding pressure placed by the US Congress on WB accountability for its operational policies and funding strategies has recently been held up as an example of how to ensure the democratic legitimacy of international organisations generally.[69]

According to Szablowski, it was this pressure that ultimately resulted in the establishment of the Inspection Panel in 1993.[70] He observes however that '[w]hile the Panel operates autonomously of Bank management and with significant public transparency, it lacks independence of a judicial institution'.[71] Moreover, as Fox notes, 'the panel's very existence challenges key assumptions of national sovereignty',[72] by allowing the citizens of borrowing countries that are hosting the projects funded by these international finance institutions to present their claims directly before an international complaints mechanism.[73] This last point resonates with the aims of the present exercise in examining the means to exert accountability against public

68 Gunther Handl, 'The Legal Mandate of Multilateral Development Banks as Agents for Change Toward Sustainable Development', *American Journal of International Law*, Vol.92 (October, 1998) 642.

69 See: Kristina Daugirdas, 'Congress Underestimated: The Case of the World Bank', *American Journal of International Law*, Vol.107, Issue 3 (2013) 517–62.

70 David Szablowski, *Transnational Law and Local Struggles: Mining, Communities and the World Bank*, Hart (2007) at 90–91, citing, *inter alia*, J A Fox and I D Brown (eds), *The Struggle for Accountability: The World Bank, NGOs and Grassroots Movements*, MIT Press (1998) at 8; S Schlemmer-Schulte, 'The World Bank Inspection Panel: A Record of the First International Accountability Mechanism and Its Role for Human Rights', *Human Rights Brief*, Vol.6, No.2 (1998) 279.

71 Ibid., at 91.

72 Jonathan A Fox, 'The World Bank Inspection Panel: Lessons from the First Five Years', *Global Governance*, Vol.6, No.3 (July–Sept. 2000), 279–318, at 288.

73 Szablowski (2007) *op. cit.*, at 91.

international finance institutions, for compliance with social and environmental protection norms. However, it also exposes the potential pitfalls of such an approach. If the success of these mechanisms results in the withdrawal of public international financing for natural resource development projects, this may be perceived as going against the legitimate sovereign decisions of democratically representative developing countries that nevertheless choose to prioritise socio-economic development over social and environmental protection.

On the other hand, Darrow has observed that the establishment of the Inspection Panel helps ensure that the compliance of both the in-country Task Manager, and therefore indirectly also the borrowing country, with the WB's Operational Standards, including those on human rights and environmental protection.[74] The normative significance of such an institutional compliance and accountability mechanism, along with the jurisprudence it has since generated is notable.[75] This is especially the case when it is observed that, in the performance of its latter (accountability) function, the Panel is the first forum in which individuals can hold an international organisation directly accountable for the consequences of its failure to follow its own rules and procedures.[76]

3.4.1 The World Bank Inspection Panel

The foregoing discussion sets the stage for a snapshot assessment of the role, function and effectiveness of the WB's Inspection Panel. As described by the WB itself, '(t)he Inspection Panel is an independent complaints mechanism for people and communities who believe that they have been, or are likely to be, adversely affected by a World Bank-funded project'.[77] The Board of Executive Directors of the WB created the Inspection Panel in 1993 to ensure that people have access to an independent body to address their concerns and seek recourse for any grievances arising from the role of the WB in relation to the project they are affected by. The Panel is an impartial fact-finding body, independent from the WB management and staff, reporting directly to the Board. The Inspection Panel process aims to promote accountability at the WB, give affected people a greater voice in activities supported by the WB that affect their rights and interests and foster redress when warranted.[78] In response to complaints from project-affected people, the Panel has a mandate to review projects funded by the WB, specifically through the IBRD and International Development Association (IDA). Complaints related to the projects supported by other agencies of the World Bank Group, namely, the IFC and Multilateral Investment Guarantee Agency (MIGA), are dealt with by the Office of the CAO.

The Panel assesses allegations of harm to people or the environment and reviews whether the Bank followed its own operational policies and procedures. These allegations often include issues such as:

- Adverse effects on people and livelihoods as a consequence of displacement and resettlement related to infrastructure projects, such as dams, roads, pipelines, mines and landfills;

74 Mac Darrow, *Between Light and Shadow: The World Bank, The International Monetary Fund and International Human Rights Law*, Hart (2003) at 143.

75 Benedict Kingsbury, 'Operational Policies of International Institutions as Part of the Law-Making Process: The World Bank and Indigenous Peoples', in G Goodwin-Gill and S Talmon (eds) *The Reality of International Law: Essays in Honour of Ian Brownlie*, Oxford University Press (1999) 323–342, at 332.

76 D Bradlow, 'International Organizations and Private Complaints: The Case of the World Bank Inspection Panel', *Virginia Journal of International Law*, Vol.34, No.3 (1994) 553–613, at 554.

77 World Bank, https://www.inspectionpanel.org/about-us/about-inspection-panel.

78 World Bank, ibid.

- Risks to people and the environment related to dam safety, use of pesticides and other indirect effects of investments;
- Risks to indigenous peoples, their culture, traditions, land tenure and development rights;
- Adverse effects on physical cultural heritage, including sacred places; and/or
- Adverse effects on natural habitats, including protected areas, such as wetlands, forests and water bodies.

The Inspection Panel consists of three members appointed by the Board of Executive Directors for a five-year non-renewable term. Members are selected on the basis of their ability to deal thoroughly and fairly with the complaints brought to them, their integrity and independence from Bank management and their exposure to developmental issues and living conditions in developing countries. The Panel has a permanent Secretariat that provides operational and administrative support. For its fact-finding and investigations, the Panel also hires independent, internationally recognised experts to ensure objective and professional assessment of the issues under review.

3.4.2 The Compliance Advisory Ombudsman of the International Finance Corporation

Again, like the WB itself, the IFC followed up the promulgation of its Performance Standards with the establishment of a grievance mechanism to ensure IFC institutional accountability for these co-opted international norms, in the form of the CAO.[79] The IFC Sustainability Framework explains the rationale for the CAO as catering for situations where grievances and complaints from those affected by IFC-supported business activities are not fully resolved at the business activity level or through other established mechanisms.[80] Both the IFC and MIGA, as the private sector components of the WB, are accountable to the CAO. The Office of the CAO is the independent accountability mechanism for projects supported by the IFC and MIGA – the private sector arms of the World Bank Group. The CAO was established in 1999 and reports directly to the President of the World Bank Group. The CAO Office is based in Washington, DC. The CAO addresses the concerns of communities who believe they are affected by IFC and MIGA projects. CAO's mandate is articulated in its Terms of Reference, which were endorsed by the President of the World Bank Group in 1999. The mandate of the CAO is to:

1) Address the concerns of individuals or communities affected by IFC/MIGA projects;
2) Enhance the social and environmental outcomes of IFC/MIGA projects; and
3) Foster greater public accountability of IFC and MIGA.[81]

Under this mandate, the IFC has summarised the three complementary roles of the CAO as follows: First, a *dispute resolution* role, whereby when responding to complaints, CAO attempts to resolve the issues raised using a flexible, collaborative, problem-solving approach. The goal of a dispute resolution process is to address specific issues that have contributed to a

79 More information on the IFC CAO is accessible at: www.cao-ombudsman.org/about/whoweare/index.html.
80 IFC Environmental and Social Sustainability Policy, 1 January 2012, Chapter/Section on the CAO, at para. 54.
81 See: IFC CAO website page at: www.cao-ombudsman.org/about/whoweare/index.html.

conflict and help people identify solutions that meet the interests of all the parties. The focus of CAO's dispute resolution role is on communicating directly with those individuals and/or communities affected by the project and assisting them, the (usually corporate) clients of the IFC and any other relevant stakeholders to resolve complaints, ideally by improving environmental and social outcomes on the ground. Second, a *compliance* role, whereby CAO oversees compliance investigations of the environmental and social performance of IFC, to ensure compliance with policies, standards, guidelines, procedures and conditions for IFC involvement, with the goal of improving IFC performance. Third, an *advisory* role, whereby the CAO is a source of independent advice to the IFC President. Advice is based on insights gathered from CAO's dispute resolution and compliance interventions and is focused on broader environmental and social policies, strategic issues and trends, based on the experiences gained through its case work, with the goal of fostering systemic improvements in IFC.[82]

Complaints are eligible for assessment if they meet three criteria: (i) the complaint relates to an IFC or MIGA project; (ii) the complaint raises social and environmental issues; or (iii) the complaint is filed by an individual and/or community directly affected by the project, or filed by their representative(s).[83]

CAO will inform complainants of the eligibility of their case within 15 working days. The CAO does not assess complaints involving fraud or corruption, nor those relating to procurement decisions.[84] The CAO's Operational Guidelines then explain how CAO carries out its work in response to such complaints, as well as requests for audit related to IFC/MIGA supported projects. Specifically, these Operational Guidelines aim to provide a predictable process to guide complainants and other stakeholders through CAO's complaint-handling process. The Guidelines are available in the seven official languages of the World Bank Group.[85]

Although re-titled: 'Dispute Resolution' from the previous 'Ombudsman' role, the CAO's response to complaints from project-affected communities about the social and environmental impacts of IFC/MIGA-supported projects in this regard still retains its ombudsman-type function. For example, when a complaint is accepted for further assessment, CAO has approximately 120 working days to conduct an assessment of the dispute and the stakeholders' alternatives for resolving the issue(s). The purpose of this assessment is to clarify issues raised by the complainant, to gather information on how other stakeholders view the situation and to help the parties determine whether and how they may be able to resolve the complaint. Through this ombudsman-style process, the CAO helps parties identify alternatives for resolving the issues of concern, utilising dispute resolution specialists trained in assisted negotiation methods – including conflict assessment, mediation and dispute resolution, consensus building, multi-stakeholder problem solving and interest-based facilitation and negotiation. When performing this function, the CAO often partners with neutral third-party facilitators who are independent of CAO and IFC/MIGA, and who possess the appropriate cultural and linguistic skills to work effectively with local stakeholders. Based on the results of the initial assessment, CAO specialists will either work with the stakeholders to develop a jointly agreed process of assisted negotiation, mediation or other collaborative strategy for

82 www.cao-ombudsman.org/howwework/ombudsman.
83 Ibid.
84 Ibid.
85 More information on the CAO Operational Guidelines is accessible from: www.cao-ombudsman.org/howwework/documents/CAOOperationalGuidelines2013_ENGLISH.pdf.

addressing issues raised in the complaint, or determine that a collaborative solution is not possible and transfer the case to CAO Compliance for appraisal of IFC's/MIGA's environmental and social performance.

The ombudsman-type function performed by the CAO in this so-called *dispute resolution* role is epitomised by the fact that the CAO neither comes to a judgement on the merits of a complaint, nor does it impose solutions or find fault. Instead, its stated objective is to assist the parties to the dispute in playing leading roles in identifying and implementing their own solutions. When helping the parties craft solutions, the CAO in its *dispute resolution* role will also not support agreements that may be coercive to one or more parties, contrary to IFC/MIGA policies or violate relevant domestic or international laws. In this 'Dispute Resolution' role, the CAO will also respect any requests for confidentiality of stakeholders' identities or information communicated to the CAO. Parties will be advised by the CAO if confidentiality may constrain efforts to seek a satisfactory resolution.

In its *compliance* role, the CAO initiates audits in response to concerns regarding the social and environmental impacts of specific IFC or MIGA projects, or as requested by the World Bank Group President or senior management.[86] The CAO Compliance role assesses how IFC and MIGA assure themselves of environmental and social performance at the project-level. Investigations focus on IFC or MIGA – not the project sponsor – and examine compliance with relevant policies, standards, guidelines, procedures and conditions. CAO compliance investigations are independent of, but complementary to, IFC/MIGA's internal assurance efforts. Compliance investigations are triggered by any of the following situations:

1) At the request of the President of the World Bank Group or senior management of IFC/MIGA;
2) At the discretion of the CAO Vice-President; or
3) When a complaint is transferred from CAO Dispute Resolution where resolution of the issues is not possible.

First, the CAO initiates an appraisal to determine whether a compliance investigation is merited. The appraisal assesses whether there are substantive concerns regarding a project's environmental or social performance. In the event that the issues raised do not merit an investigation, the CAO will close the case. If an investigation is merited, the CAO typically employs one or more independent experts to conduct the investigation. The investigation is based on a review of documents, interviews and observation of project activities and outcomes. Verification of evidence is an important part of the process. In cases where the IFC, MIGA and/or project sponsors are held to be in compliance with relevant environmental and social standards, the CAO will close the investigation with no further action. In cases where the IFC or MIGA is found to be not in compliance, the CAO keeps the investigation open in monitoring until actions taken by IFC or MIGA assure the CAO that the project is in compliance and the case can be closed.

Finally, in its *advisory* role, the CAO provides overarching advice to the President of the World Bank Group, as well as IFC and MIGA management, on broader social and environmental issues related to IFC/MIGA policies, standards, procedures, guidelines, resources and systems. Deriving lessons learned from its caseload, the CAO's advice through this role aims to improve performance in a systemic way and provide guidance to IFC and MIGA on emerging trends and strategic issues.

86 For more information on the CAO's compliance role, see: www.cao-ombudsman.org/howwework/compliance.

4 Conclusions

This chapter asserts that a paradigm shift is taking place within the international energy investment law (sub-)discipline. In doing so, it outlines significant legal changes afoot whereby previous 'stakeholder' *interests*, encompassing worker health and safety concerns, as well as environmental, social and cultural protection, are now being given 'actor' *rights* to uphold via different international institutional mechanisms such as investment arbitral tribunals, the WB's Inspection Panel and the IFC's CAO. These institutional mechanisms are arguably acting to substantiate both the broader domestic regulatory autonomy afforded to 'host' States on environmental, social and cultural concerns, as well as implement international standards on these concerns that have been adopted by States (in their MIAs and BITs) and IFIs) in their WB Environmental and Social Standards as well as IFC Performance Standards. Future research in these areas will hopefully build on this hypothesis and confirm whether the trends discerned here are continuing, as well as chart their onward twists and turns accordingly.

3

INTERNATIONAL ENERGY LAW IN PERSPECTIVE

The relationship between national and international energy law

Ernst Nordtveit

1 Introduction

1.1 Scope and problems

This chapter focuses on the relationship between international law and national energy law, and on how international and national law interacts in defining the total legal regime for energy activity, on the international and the national level.

Energy law is a relatively new legal discipline which is defined from a functional approach, as the rules and regulations that are relevant for energy activity or energy services throughout the whole life span of energy activity, from the division of energy resources, to production, transport, distribution and finally marketing of energy.[1] International and national or domestic energy law has emerged as an important legal discipline over the last 50 years[2] and has undergone a remarkable expansion and transition which is still ongoing.

International energy law encompass public international law that regulates issues of relevance for energy production and distribution. Public international law refers to rules and principles that regulate the relationship between states and between international organizations. Public international energy law includes law based on international legal sources, such as treaties or international customary law regulating issues arising from division of the right to energy resources, for example, the United Nations Convention of the Law of the Sea (UNCLOS) to foreign investment, hereunder energy projects and trans-border transportation of energy.

1 A Bradbrook, "Energy Law as an Academic Discipline" *Journal of Energy & Natural Resources* 14 (1996) p. 193–217 defines energy law as "the allocation of rights and duties concerning the exploitation of all energy resources between individuals and the government, between governments and between states". This definition is now seen as too narrow as it is concentrated on the exploitation of energy resources. Raphael J. Heffron and Kim Talus, "The Evolution of Energy Law and Energy Jurisprudence: Insights for Energy Analysts and Researchers", *Energy Research & Social Science* 19 (2016), 1–10, p. 4, define energy law as "the regulation of energy-related rights and duties of various stakeholders over the energy resources over the energy life-cycle".

2 As pointed out by T W Wälde, "International Energy Law: An Introduction to Modern Concepts, Context, Policy and Players" in J P Schneider and C Theobald, *Handbuch zum Recht der Energiewirtschaft* (2003) p. 1129, one would not have talked about international energy law in 1970.

International energy law also encompasses a large body of legal principles and models developed by nation-states, such as licensing contracts and production sharing contracts in the petroleum industry, systems for the trading of natural gas or electricity, access to transport facilities, etc. that are developed in the international and national energy industry. The multinational companies operating in energy activities is also creating models and standardized practices that lead to the international standardization of private energy law, for example joint venture agreements.[3] Some have argued that one can speak of a *lex mercatoria* of transnational commercial energy transactions, where principles developed in international energy activity will be applied, not the law of any individual state.[4]

All forms of international energy law will be included in this chapter, but the main focus will be on the role of public international law.

The relationship or interface between international and national energy law is part of the more widely discussed question about the relationship between international law and national law in general. The emergence of international energy law and other new international legal disciplines such as international environmental law,[5] trade law, law of the sea, human rights law, etc. have however extended and changed international law in a manner that challenges the traditional theories on the relationship between international and national law.

The common conception of public international law is a legal system that regulates the relationship between states, while national law regulates internal relationships in a state such as the organization of the state, the relationship between the state and the citizens and between individuals within the state. There is no institution above the states to create international law or to enforce it. International law is created by the states themselves by treaty or custom, and it is the states that decide to follow the law or not.[6]

It is an internal legal question if national law shall have priority over international law in a case of conflicting rules. There are traditionally two main theories about the relationship between international law and national law. Monism is the theory that international and national law form one unified system and that cases have to be solved based on both systems. Dualism sees international and national law as two different systems and international law has to be implemented in national law by a national legal act.[7] These theories were developed at a time when there were far fewer political, economic and social interactions between states than today and the existing international law was mainly aimed at solving conflicts between states. The extensive expansion of international law into areas of law which are also regulated by national law such as energy law has led to what Malcolm N. Shaw calls "an increasing interpenetration of international law and domestic law across a number of fields".[8]

International environmental law, law of the sea, human rights law, international investment law, international trade law, and international energy law are examples of new

3 This is something different from 'private international law', which is the rules on selection of the governing law in an individual case where there is a conflict of laws, based on the connection the case has to the countries involved, This question might also occur in energy cases, but the different rules on private international law will not be discussed here. It might, however, be that the devlopment of international rules and principles in private law leads to a situation where traditional private international law will play a less important role in such conflicts.

4 See Wälde, Introduction p. 1131.

5 See P Birnie, A Boyle and C Redgwell, *International Law and the Environment,* Third edition (2009) p. 1–2 on the development of international environmental law.

6 Malcolm N. Shaw, *International Law*, Sixth edition (2008) p. 6.

7 Shaw, *International Law* p. 29–30.

8 Shaw, *International Law*, p. 129–130.

comprehensive regulatory systems aimed at coordinating regulation of important fields in different jurisdictions and to facilitate trans-border cooperation. This creates a new form of interaction or division of functions between national and international law where common policy objectives like protection of the environment, developing of an effective international trading system or securing access to stable energy supply through an international market, are pursued by coordination of national policy and regulation and by facilitating transboundary cooperation by international treaties. International and national law work together in establishing a system for governance of for example the energy sector to establish a transnational and, in some areas, a global system of energy supply. This also includes the establishment of institutions and organizations for developing international law and for dispute resolution.

The traditional divide between monism and dualism appears as unfit or at least inadequate to deal with the relationship between international and national law in this context of dynamic interaction between international and national law. As pointed out by, inter alia, Stephan W. Schill, the theories of dualism and monism are ill-suited to handle the complex relationship and interplay between international and national energy law in the increasingly international and globalized energy market.[9]

The aim of this chapter is not to give a complete or even comprehensive presentation of the complex and extensive international regulation of the energy sector but to analyse the more general character of the relationship between international law and national law in regulating energy activity. A presentation of the development of international energy law will be given in section 1.2 below and some important areas of international energy law in section 2 below, as a background for the discussion of the relationship or the interface between international and national energy law.[10]

1.2 Background for development of international energy law

The development of international as well as national energy law is partly a result of the growing need for access to secure and affordable energy as a basis for international or global economic growth and social development and the general globalization of trade and commercial activity. Another driving force for developing international regulation relevant to energy activity and energy services is the impact of energy production, transport and consumption on the natural environment and especially on the climate, due to the emission of CO_2 from the burning of fossil fuels.[11] The interdependence of states, due to technological and economic development and the trans-border effect of industrial and other activity, makes it necessary to coordinate the activity in different states and put obligations on all or most states to behave in certain manner in a number of fields, in order to prevent freeriders

9 See S W Schill, "The Interface between National and International Energy Law" in K Taulus, *Research Handbook on International Energy Law* (2014) p. 46–47 and more generally J Nijmann and A Nollkaemper (eds.), *New Perspectives on the Divide between National and International Law* (2007).

10 For more comprehensive presentation and discussion of international energy law see T W Wälde, "International Energy Law: An Introduction to Modern Concepts, Context, Policy and Players" in J P Schneider and C Theobald, *Handbuch zum Recht der Energiewirtschaft* (2003), K Talus (ed.), *Research Handbook on International Energy Law* (2014) and C Redgwell, "International Regulation of Energy Activities" in M Roggenkamp, A Rønne, C Redgwell and I del Guayo, *Energy Law in Europe – National, EU and International Law and Institutions*, Third edition (2016) p. 13–136. See also T Meyer "The Architecture of International Energy Governance", *Proceedings of the ASIL Annual Meeting, 106* (2012) 389–394. doi:10.5305/procannmeetasil.106.0389, R Leal-Arcas, A Filis and E S Abu Gosh, *International Energy Governance: Selected Legal Issues* (2014).

11 See more on the background for the development of international energy law under section 1.2. below.

not participating in joint efforts aimed, for example, at stopping ecological degradation, mitigating climate change or increasing energy production. International agreements on joint efforts to minimalize climate change[12] and to reach the sustainable goals of 2030 are now the main drivers of energy transition that is being implemented in most countries including the European Union (EU).

Energy resources are unevenly distributed around the world, making some countries energy exporters and others importers. The growing dependency on a stable energy supply as a basis for economic growth and a comfortable life has made this a high priority for all countries. Countries are interested in obtaining sovereignty over or at least access to energy resources. The development in international law of the sea, culminating in UNCLOS, led to a strong extension of the coastal state's sovereignty over the offshore area and thereby their exclusive rights to energy resources in the exclusive economic zone (EEZ), and the continental shelf. As a result of this development, many states went from being importers to becoming exporters of energy, and also changed their geopolitical position.[13] The outer borders of continental shelves are in some cases not yet settled and some areas are disputed.

For countries that are reliant on importing energy, a stable and well-functioning international market for energy and energy products and services are of crucial importance for their economic development and geopolitical position. To achieve this a legal regime for a secure investment in energy production and energy infrastructure is also important. This is the reason for the existence of the Energy Charter Treaty (ECT), the International Energy Agency (IEA) and other multilateral and bilateral treaties aimed at strengthening international cooperation to increase the production of energy and transport and trade with energy.

The internationalization of the energy sector began as a result of the shortage of oil that became visible around 1970, especially after the oil crisis of 1973–1974 following the Israel-Arab War in 1973 and the Arab Oil Embargo and the closing of the Suez Canal[14] and the Iran-Iraq War in the 1980s. Until the early 1970s most oil was traded within vertically integrated oil companies who controlled the whole value-chain from production fields to refineries and petrol stations. After the nationalization of oil companies in many countries and the emergence of state owned companies in even more countries, the international oil companies no longer owned all the oil fields, and gradually an international market for crude oil developed during the 1980s and early 1990s.[15] The IEA was established in 1974 to work for the security of energy supply through cooperation on long-term energy policy, information, research and development, etc.[16]

Since the late 1990s transboundary pipeline networks for the transport and distribution of natural gas and oil, and cable networks for the transport of electricity have created large international markets for this type of energy. The development of LNG-technology has also made it possible to establish a global market for natural gas.

To increase international investment in energy projects, transport and trade of energy across borders and even globally, a legal regime that facilitates and defines rights and obligations between states and individuals for these purposes has been developed. Internationalization of law through export and import of legal instruments and patterns to achieve effective

12 The Paris Agreement, 2015.

13 See section 2.1.2 below.

14 L. Maugeri, *The Age of Oil. The Mythology, History and Future of the World's Most Controversial Resource* (2006), p 103–119.

15 D Yergin, *The Quest. Energy, Security, and the Remaking of the Modern World* (2011) p. 165–166.

16 On the early historical development of energy law, see Wälde, "International Energy Law", p. 1137–1141.

regulation of the energy sector also lead to a stronger harmonization and internationalization of energy law. States that want to attract international investment in energy projects need to offer a national legal regime that is recognizable and trustworthy for foreign or international companies and investors. They will often use international experts as advisers in drafting national legislation and try to benefit from the experiences of other countries. This has led to a strong harmonization of national legislation in many countries, particularly in the petroleum sector, but also in other areas of energy law. The development of international standards for environmental protection, protection of indigenous people, management of international watercourses, etc. also influence the regulation of energy activity.

The internationalization of the energy sector has developed differently, at different times for different energy sources. Coal, and especially oil and oil products have been traded on an international market for a long time. Energy sources that need infrastructures like pipelines for natural gas or electricity grids for the transport and utilization of energy produced from energy sources like nuclear, hydro, thermal, wind and solar energy have only recently been traded over longer distances and across borders. Because of the energy transition that is now taking place and is expected to continue, the internationalization of electricity production and distribution will also increase.

Another important reason for the development of the relevant international regulation of energy production and distribution is the need to manage the possible negative effects on the environment and climate from energy production, transport and consumption. International regulation of the environment, such as protection of ecosystems and biodiversity, protection against pollution, regulation of emission of greenhouse gases, demands for pollution preparedness, etc. will influence energy projects. The international community is facing a great challenge to provide a sufficient supply of affordable energy to a growing world population in a sustainable manner while keeping global warming within manageable levels, avoiding great ecological damage and not causing a severe negative impact on the climate, ecosystems and biodiversity and not depleting natural resources. These challenges are now expressed in the Sustainable Development Goals (SDGs) adopted by the United Nations General Assembly (UNGA) in September 2015, making "clean and affordable energy" one of the goals.[17] Other SDGs are also particular relevance to the development of the energy sector.

The energy transition that is underway as a result of this will change the energy-mix and lead to an increase in the production of electricity based on renewable energy sources such as solar or wind energy. An increase in the energy produced by the consumers themselves from solar cells or windmills, and the development of new technology for the storage of electricity or the use of hydrogen might in the near future lead to further changes in energy production and transportation. Trans-border network for transport of energy in the form of pipelines and cables for the transport of natural gas, oil or electricity is necessary to establish international markets for energy. This raises questions of sovereignty over the infrastructure and also private international law problems. Sovereignty questions over oil and gas pipelines have been solved by international agreements.

International cooperation in energy activity, as well as transboundary activity in the form of petroleum products from petroleum fields which are crossing international borders, pipelines or cables across other countries' continental shelf will, of course, be governed by international law. Also, activity on the EEZ or the continental shelf has to be in line with international law, even if the activity itself is under coast state jurisdiction. International law

17 SDG 7.

may also in many cases set standards for the content of national law, for example in the area of protection of ecosystems and biodiversity or for emission of climate gases, etc., and thereby create a framework for the activity carried out by or within a state and for the state's internal regulation of activity.

1.3 International energy law; definition and development

In contrast to, for example, the law of the sea,[18] international trade law and international environmental law, energy law is not regulated by one single treaty or some major treaties with global participation. On the international level as on the national level, energy law is defined based on a functional approach. Energy law includes the rules and regulations that are relevant to energy activity or energy services.[19] The international regulation of energy issues is therefore fragmented and based on the general regulation of different issues. There is no single treaty on energy law containing a holistic energy regulation and no central institution harmonizing international energy law as a whole.

International energy law will include the regulation of access to or division of the sovereignty over and rights to energy resources such as hydrocarbons, coal, watercourses, etc., and the production, transport, distribution and marketing of energy. On some issues, there might not be a full consensus on whether or not some rules should be considered as energy law.[20] The regulation of ship transport of crude oil is not usually considered to be part of energy law, but of international maritime law, even if some aspects of maritime law will also apply to energy law. Rules aimed at saving energy, for example, and standards for the insulation of houses or electric equipment are not usually defined as energy law, even if these are increasingly included in the energy strategy of the EU and many other countries.

Both international law and international energy law are derived from legal sources accepted as the basis for international law. The Statute of the International Court of Justice (ICJ Statute), Article 38 lists the sources that the ICJ shall consider when deciding cases and this has widely been seen as a list of sources of international law and is generally seen as a starting point for determining which legal sources international law should be built on. However, this is not an exhaustive list.[21] International conventions and international customs and general principles of law recognized by civilized nations are the core legal sources listed. Judicial decisions and doctrinal teachings are mentioned as subsidiary sources.

Conventions or treaties are only binding on states that are parties to them, while customary international law applies to all states. Some conventions are wholly or partly regarded as an expression of customary international law, and thus binding also on states that are not a party to the convention.

A rather new development is that resolutions from the UNGA have become a source for international law in some cases. UNGA does not have any power to adopt binding decisions, but there seems to be a development where decisions by UNGA will have an impact on the development of international law.[22]

18 The law of the sea is extensively regulated in UNCLOS from 1982, in force from 1995, see section 2.1.2 below.
19 See section 1.1 above.
20 See R J Heffron, A Ronne, J P Tomain, A Bradbrook and K Talus, "A Treatise for Energy Law" in *Journal of World Energy Law and Business* 11 (2018) p. 34–48.
21 See Redgwell (2016) p. 15.
22 Shaw (2008) p. 114–115.

Of great importance concerning energy law is that UNGA in September 2015 unanimously adopted 17 SDGs for the planet,[23] to end poverty, protect the planet and ensure peace and prosperity everywhere. The SDGs came into force 11 January 2016, after having been accepted by all 193 member-countries of the United Nations (UN). Goal 7 is "Affordable and Clean Energy" or more precisely to "Ensure access to affordable, reliable, sustainable, and modern energy for all". Energy or energy services were not included in the "Millennium Development Goals" declared by the UNGA in the year 2000. This shows that the awareness of the need for energy services and the need to make access to energy services an international priority has increased in the last two decades. Other SDGs might also be relevant to energy projects or activity.

The legal status of the SDGs is not quite clear. It is possible to argue that all states that have voted for the principles in the UNGA are bound by them as if they were an international convention.[24] Although the content of the different SDGs is vague and it will be difficult to extract very clear norms for action from them, they might influence the interpretation of other rules and define the direction of international law.[25] The states are expected to report to the UN how the SDGs are implemented.

It is more generally difficult to draw a strict line as to which norms are considered as international "law". The difficulties that exist in developing new international rules by custom or by treaties have been particularly bad within environmental law and led to the widespread use of instruments that are not seen as legally binding, but which still establish standards or norms in the form of guidelines, code of conduct, declaration of principles, etc. Even if these kinds of instruments do not fit the criteria for being considered as sources of law in the meaning of the ICJ Statute Article 38, many of them have had a great impact on the actions of states.[26]

The EU is a special source of international cooperation with its own political and legal institutions that can adopt and enforce legislation that is binding for the Member States and also to a large extent directly binding within the Member States. In 1963 the European Court of Justice (ECJ) stated that the EU is a new legal order of international law.[27] Even if the EU-legislation is not considered to be a part of public international law in the traditional sense, the EU-legislation on energy issues is still of great importance in a study of international energy law. Before 1985 energy activity was not seen as a part of the common policy, but after 1985 the EU has gradually developed extensive energy legislation that has been renewed and extended step by step.[28] The EU has become an international forerunner in developing new energy policy and legislation to create an effective internal market for energy and to promote development towards renewable energy and EU law now serves as a models for similar efforts

23 Declared by the UNGA in "Transforming Our World: The 2030 Agenda for Sustainable Development".

24 See the general discussion above on the legal status of decisions of the UNGA.

25 Redgwell (2009) p. 32–33. See also below on the development related to state sovereignty over natural resources.

26 See generally on the development of "soft-law"-instruments, Redgwell (2009) p. 34–37, concluding that soft law "can make an important contribution to establishing a new legal order in a fast-growing and unsettled field" (p. 37).

27 *Van Gend en Loos v Nederlandse Administratie der Belastingen* (1963) Case 26/62.

28 The first energy package was enacted in 1996/1998, the second package in 2003 and the third in 2009, which consists of directive 2009/72/EC (electricity market), directive 2009/73/EC (natural gas market), regulation (EC) No 714/2009 (condition for access to the networks for cross-border exchanges in electricity), regulation (EC) No 715/2009 (conditions for access to the natural gas transmission networks) and regulation 713/2009 (establishing an Agency for the Cooperation of Energy Regulators (ACER)).

in other parts of the world.[29] In 2016 the Commission launched a new initiative, the "Winter Energy Package" which was completed in June 2019. The Winter package should deliver 'clean energy for all Europeans'. The legislation on the "package" touches on all energy-related sectors, including electricity generation, heating, cooling and transport, but also agriculture and land use, and is intended to clear the way for a cleaner, more competitive and modern energy system. The background for the new package was that the Commission considered that even if the three former legislative packages had mainly fulfilled their objectives, they were not sufficient in a changing electricity market and a new approach was necessary to realize the 'clean energy transition' to a low carbon economy by 2050.[30]

The establishment of the EU Emission Trading Scheme for greenhouse gases (EU-ETS) also has a strong impact on energy development.[31]

Other regional trade organizations like the North American Free Trade Agreement (NAFTA)[32] are also relevant to energy activity in the member countries, mainly through free trade and provisions for investor protection and dispute settlement.

2 Overview of international energy law

2.1 Access to energy resources

2.1.1 The principle of national sovereignty over natural resources

The right of a state to exercise jurisdiction over its natural resources is regarded as a fundamental principle of international law.[33] A state has the right to exploit the natural resources and to natural resource governance within its territory, which means the right to manage its natural resources and set the rules for exploration and exploitation of energy resources, and to receive the benefit from the resources.[34] This also implies the right to decide if the resources shall be exploited and how and when in such a case this shall take place.

The principle of national sovereignty over natural resources follows from general principles of state sovereignty under the Westphalian system but has in modern times been reiterated

29 See an overview of the development up to 2006, Wälde, "International Energy Law" (2006) p. 1135. He states that the EU "constitutes at present the most developed laboratory for international regulation of energy".

30 The Winter Energy Package consists of the following legal acts: Regulation (EU) 2019/941 of the European Parliament and of the Council of 5 June 2019 on risk-preparedness in the electricity sector, Regulation (EU) 2019/942 of the European Parliament and of the Council of 5 June 2019 establishing a European Union Agency for the Cooperation of Energy Regulators, Regulation (EU) 2019/943 of the European Parliament and of the Council of 5 June 2019 on the internal market for electricity and Directive (EU) 2019/944 of the European Parliament and of the Council of 5 June 2019 on common rules for the internal market for electricity and amending Directive 2012/27/EU.

31 See on the EU-ETS, S E Weishaar, *Emission Trading Design. A Critical Overview* (2014) and E Nordtveit and S E Schütz, *Agreement on the European Economic Area – A Commentary* (2018) p. 731–733.

32 NAFTA came into force in 1994. In September 2018, the United States, Mexico and Canada reached an agreement to replace NAFTA with the United States–Mexico–Canada Agreement (USMCA). NAFTA will remain in force, pending the ratification of the USMCA.

33 See Sanita van Wyk, *The Impact of Climate Change Law on the Principle of State Sovereignty over Natural Resources* (2017) p. 33–38, with further references.

34 S R Chowdhury "Permanent Sovereignty over Natural Resources: Substratum of the Seoul Declaration" in P De Waart, P Peters and E Denters (eds) *International Law and Development* (1988) p. 59–80; K Hossain "Introduction" in K Hossain and S R Chowdhury (eds) *Permanent Sovereignty over Natural Resources in International Law, Principle and Practice* (1984) p. ix.

and developed in a series of resolutions by the UNGA in the 1950s and 1960s.[35] This was a reaction to the fact that international companies controlled the exploration for and production of natural resources, especially oil, in colonial and post-colonial states. The resolutions were adopted to strengthen the position of the new states that emerged as a result of decolonization and to remedy the unequal arrangements between developing and developed states regarding natural resource management.[36] The principle is not only of importance to states with energy resources and energy-producing states, it is also considered to apply to energy importing states making energy supply a part of national sovereignty.[37] The principle of national sovereignty over energy resources and the general structure of the energy supply is also upheld in the EU.[38]

The Westphalian principle has been the basis of the international system based on independent states interacting with each other within the international political system. Today, however, this system is challenged by developments in several areas. The increased focus on human rights has raised the question of whether humanitarian intervention is justifiable under international law and how far the principle of non-intervention can be upheld. The question of governance of cyberspace also challenges a territorial sovereignty-based approach, due to the fact that an act committed in one country can have effect in another, and also that the communication might involve other countries. In the management of international watercourses, there has been a shift from strict territorial based sovereignty to cooperation and a "community of interest approach".[39] The climate crisis is also challenging the principle of unlimited state sovereignty.[40]

The principle of sovereignty over natural resources is only a starting point. International treaties, etc. as described above limit the scope of states for action or regulation on the national level. The question of what the state can decide or do in the energy sector is to a large extent dependent on the interpretation of treaties on a wide range of issues, which might be in conflict with the principle of state sovereignty over energy resources and how energy supply is organized.

2.1.2 Sovereignty over offshore energy resources and activity in the offshore area

One important development in international law which has a great impact on energy production is the extension of coast state sovereignty and rights to natural resources in the sea areas outside the sea territory of a states. This took place after the Second World War and led to the adoption of UNCLOS.[41]

UNCLOS establishes two forms of contingency zones outside the territorial waters of a coastal state. Article 56 gives the coastal state jurisdiction over and the right to the living and non-living natural resources in the water column and the seabed of the EEZ. Under Article 77 the coastal state also has jurisdiction over and the right to natural resources in

35 See especially UN Resolution 1803 (sovereignty over natural resources) and UN Resolution 3281 XXIX 1974 (Economic right to dispose of resources as see fit). The principle is also part of the Stockholm Declaration (Declaration of the UN Conference on the Human Environment 1972) and the Rio Declaration (Declaration of the UN Conference on the Human Environment 1992) Principle 21.

36 Van Wyk (2017) p. 34–35 and Heffron et al. (2018) p. 39–41.

37 See Heffron et al. (2018) p. 40.

38 Treaty on the Functioning of the EU (TFEU) Article 194, 2.

39 See Julie Howden, "The Community of Interest Approach in International Water Law. A Legal Framework for Common Management of International Watercourses", PhD-thesis, University of Bergen, 2018.

40 Van Wyk (2018) p. 24–28 and 340–342.

41 See on the history of the law of the sea, D R Rothwell and T Stephens, *The International Law of the Sea* (2010) p. 1–20.

and on the seabed of the continental shelf "throughout the natural prolongation of its land territory to the outer edge of the continental margin" even if that extends further than 200 nautical miles from the baseline.

The sovereignty over the EEZ and the continental shelf is still not as total as overland territory and the territorial waters. The jurisdiction over the EEZ and continental shelf is limited to what is needed for exploration of the natural resources under coast state jurisdiction, see UNCLOS Article 56(1)(a) which states that the coastal state has:

> sovereign rights for the purpose of exploring and exploiting, conserving and managing the natural resources, whether living or non-living, of the waters superjacent to the seabed and of the seabed and its subsoil, and with regard to other activities for the economic exploitation and exploration of the zone, such as the production of energy from the water, currents and winds.

Regarding the continental shelf, UNCLOS Article 77(1) says that the coastal state: "exercises over the continental shelf sovereign rights to explore it and exploit its natural resources".

In addition to this "positive" limitation, Article 56 (2) and Article 78 (2) emphasize that in exercising the rights and duties under the convention in the EEZ and on the continental shelf, the coastal state shall have due regard to the rights and duties of other states, to navigation and other rights and the freedom of other states under the convention.

Within the limits of the sovereignty over the EEZ and the continental shelf, the coastal state will have the same sovereignty and right to resource governance as over natural resources on the land.[42]

The development of coastal state sovereignty over the offshore areas has facilitated a big development of offshore production of petroleum. More than a quarter of the oil produced comes from offshore sources and offshore production of natural gas has risen sharply. Also, offshore production of renewable energy, up till now mainly from wind, has increased rapidly, and new projects for offshore wind are being constructed or planned. Offshore energy production is expected to be an important part of the transition to renewable energy, which is necessary to reduce greenhouse gas emissions from fossil fuels.

The international regulation of the activity in the EEZ and on the continental shelf is not adequate as a basis for carrying out the activity. International law tends to express general principles and goal-based regulations, which have to be completed and clarified by detailed national regulation. Detailed national regulation based on the framework of the international regulatory system will, for example, be needed to regulate complex and extensive offshore energy activity in a demanding weather environment involving risk of accidents and environmental damage. States with offshore petroleum activity have adopted comprehensive petroleum legislation involving acts, regulations, guidelines and manuals governing the activity. Legislation on the production of renewable energy in the offshore area is now also being enacted in many states as the development of offshore energy is growing.

2.1.3 Cooperation in exploiting trans-border or disputed resources

Special legal problems occur concerning energy resources that straddle borders between states, either onshore or offshore, or are situated in an area claimed by two or more states.

42 This follows directly from UNCLOS Article 56(1)(a) and Article 77(1) as cited above.

The most common situation is that hydrocarbon deposits or watercourses straddle the borderlines between states or that hydrocarbon or coal deposits are situated completely or partly within disputed areas, over which two or more states claim sovereignty.

In the case of resources that straddle an international border, each state will have sovereignty over the part of the resource situated in the state's territory, EEZ or continental shelf. The exploitation of the resource by one state will, however, influence the possibility of exploiting the resource from the area under the other state's sovereignty and might have other effects on the ecosystem and environment more generally. The extraction of oil and gas will influence the pressure in the structure where the deposit is situated and make oil and gas flow from the other state's area into the area of the producing state. The building of hydropower plants in a watercourse might influence the water level and often the possibility of exploiting the water resources for energy production or other purposes in the area of the other riparian state(s). It might also have environmental effects.

The question is whether this will limit the freedom of one state to exploit the resource as it sees fit and if there is an obligation to cooperate on the management and exploitation of the resource. Natural resources situated in two or more states' territory, EEZ or continental shelf are considered to be "shared resources". The question of whether there is an obligation to cooperate in the management of shared resources is discussed in international law literature. For natural resources in areas with overlapping claims for EEZ or continental shelf, UNCLOS Articles 74(3) and 83(3) respectively give the party an obligation to "make every effort to enter into provisional arrangements of a practical nature and, during this transitional period, not to jeopardize or hamper the reaching of the final agreement". This shall be done "in a spirit of understanding and cooperation". Also for transboundary resources, the principle of cooperation in the UN Charter Articles 1 and 2 and several UNGA resolutions gives support to the obligation to cooperate and settle disputes peacefully. The principles of good faith and good neighbourliness also support this.[43]

Since 2002 the International Law Commission (ILC) has worked on the topic "Shared Natural Resources of States", considering resources such as oil, gas and groundwater and a draft was submitted to the UNGA in 2008.[44] The work on aquifers carrying oil and gas was discontinued in 2008, because there was a division between the interested governments as to whether the work should lead to a binding convention or a non-binding set of guidelines.

The principle for the management of international watercourses has developed significantly over the last hundred years from a principle of unlimited sovereignty to an obligation to cooperate to "*attain optimal utilization and adequate protection of an international watercourse*".[45] Developing a balance between the interests of the upper riparian states and those of the lower riparian states is however difficult. The principle of shared natural resources involving equitable utilization and cooperation between riparian states has support but has also met

43 See further the extensive discussions of these questions in Natalia E. Ermolina, *The Law of Shared Hydrocarbon Resources and the Question of Shared State Responsibility for Environmental Harm Arising from Their Cooperative Management.* PhD thesis), UiT–The Arctic University of Tromsø, 2019, Chapter 2, 3 and 4.

44 See more on the process *American Society of International Law* 12(18).

45 Convention on the Law of the Non-navigational Uses of International Watercourses, adopted by the UNGA on 21 May 1997, Article 8, cf. Article 5 on "Equitable and Reasonable Utilization and Participation". The convention is, however, an optional framework code or guideline which may be departed from ad hoc by any of the parties, see Article 3(3) and UNGA, 51th Session, Report of the 60th Committee Working Group, GAOR A/51/869 (1997) para 8, in ILM 36 (1997) p. 719 and P. Birnie, A Boyle and C. Redgwell, *International Law & the Environment*, Third edition (2008) p. 546.

with some opposition as the legal implications of the principle is uncertain.[46] Even if the legal situation is currently unclear regarding the duty to cooperate in developing international watercourses, it seems clear that the old "Harmon doctrine" based on full sovereignty for the riparian states has been abandoned. Most new agreements on the utilization of international watercourses are based on some notion of shared resources involving equity and common management to achieve effective utilization of the watercourse from a social, environmental and economic point of view.

2.2 Trans-border infrastructure for transport of energy

The internationalization of the energy market for electricity and natural gas makes it necessary to establish a transboundary infrastructure in the form of networks of pipelines or electrical grids. The development of the offshore production of natural gas or electricity increases the need for transportation capacity to bring energy from the production site to the market. The development of non-adjustable solar or wind energy also makes diversification of energy supply mandatory in order to be able to supply the market in situations when there is low production of solar and wind energy. This also demands transport capacity from alternative energy sources.

UNCLOS Articles 58(1) and 79(1) give any state the right to lay pipelines and cables over the EEZ or continental shelf respectively of another state. The coastal state has the right to protect other activities such as petroleum exploration, fisheries, etc., but might not "impede" the right to lay cables and pipelines across its EEZ or continental shelf.

These rules seem to give other states a positive right, cf. the formulation "all states are entitled to the laying of cables or pipelines". A national regulation allowing such a right or permission from the coastal state does not seem to be necessary, but, in reality, the decision of where to place the pipeline or cable will have to be made in consultation with the environmental authorities in the coastal state, and in line with international and national environmental regulations. The pipeline or cable must not conflict with the coastal state's utilization of the EEZ or continental shelf, but one must assume that the coastal state must accept some nuisance from the cable or pipeline if that is necessary to build them. The coast state must also be entitled to demand that the infrastructure is in line with acceptable safety standards and does not violate environmental regulations in the coastal state. The Russian pipeline Nord Stream and Nordstream 2, for example, needed permission from Finland, Sweden, Denmark and Germany to construct the pipeline. An Environmental Impact Assessment (EIA) was necessary as a basis for the decisions made by the national authorities in these countries and had to be submitted to all countries, including Russia. The same is, of course, the case for other pipelines or cables. The pipelines or cables also have to avoid crossing natural protection areas.

The infrastructure for transport of energy will also include interconnectors in order to make it possible to transport electricity or natural gas in different directions. This will raise new questions of jurisdiction over the cable and pipeline network, which then might be connected to several countries. Infrastructure with connections to two or more states might also

46 P Birnie, A Boyle and C Redgwell p. 541–546. Julie Howden, "The Community of Interest Approach in International Water Law. A Legal Framework for Common Management of International Watercourses". PhD thesis, University of Bergen, 2018 gives a broad analysis of the problems related to international watercourses and argues that the "Community of Interest Approach" can be derived from principles of solidarity, common management through a joint institution, equity, holism and environmental protection.

lead to private international law issues related to ownership, liability for damages and contracts for transport of petroleum or electricity in the network. There are examples of cables between two countries where the ownership of half of the cable belongs to the semi-public company from State A and the other half to the semi-public company from State B. The cable is crossing the EEZ of two other states. The management of the cable is regulated in an agreement with the two semi-public companies owning the cable. This is a structure that obviously might lead to difficult private international questions in case of a conflict. Also, the question of access to pipelines or cables for the transport of petroleum or electricity may occur. These questions are now mainly regulated in treaties between the countries involved and in EU/EEA(European Economic Area)-law.[47]

2.3 *Environmental protection, climate and energy*

Both international and national environmental law have developed over more or less the same timespan as energy law, from around 1970, with a large body of global and regional treaties protecting ecosystems and biodiversity[48] in general and watercourses, ocean areas, etc. against pollution or other forms of interference. Basic principles like the principle of sustainable development, the precautionary principle, the principle of best possible technology, etc. have been developed and permeate all relevant areas of law. Treaties that deal with natural resource management like UNCLOS also contain provisions on the duty to protect the environment.[49]

Energy production involves exploitation of natural resources and infrastructure development that interferes with the natural environment. Environmental regulation will therefore often have a direct impact on energy production projects and energy consumption. Oil production might lead to a discharge of oil into the soil or water, sometimes by accidents like the Macondo accident in the Mexican Gulf in 2010.[50] Hydroelectric plants lead to interference with the water flow in watercourses, change in groundwater level, etc., and windmills kill birds. Energy production also might lead to pollution from petroleum fields or nuclear plants. Environmental considerations are also included in energy legislation, especially petroleum legislation, and in international treaties regulating, for example, the dumping of petroleum installations in the North East Atlantic.[51] With their direct relevance to energy activity a large part of the international environmental law must also be considered as international energy law.

The most pressing environmental problem of our time is climate change, which, to a large extent, is caused by energy produced by burning fossil fuels (coal, oil and gas) which leads to the outlet of CO_2 which changes the composition of the atmosphere. An extensive

47 An example is "Framework Agreement" concerning "Cross-Boundary Petroleum Cooperation" between the UK and Norway from 2006. Article 1(3)(1) states: "Nothing in this Agreement shall be interpreted as affecting the sovereign rights and the jurisdiction which each State has under international law over the continental shelf which appertains to it". All installations belonging to each state shall be under the respective state's jurisdiction. Both states agree to "use their best effort to facilitate Cross-Boundary Projects" and not to "prevent or impede such projects by withholding Authorizations", see Article 1(4)(1). The contract regulates HMS issues, metering systems and inspection, construction of pipelines and access to infrastructure, joint exploitation of trans-boundary reservoirs, dispute settlement, etc.

48 Convention on Biodiversity, United Nations 1992. In the tenth meeting of the Conference of the Parties in Nagoya 2010, a revised and updated Strategic Plan for Biodiversity was adopted for the 2011–2020 period. In the meeting in 2020 the Parties are expected to update the Convention's strategic plan and adopt a global biodiversity framework for the next decade.

49 UNCLOS 192.

50 Also called the Deep Water Horizon accident.

51 OSPAR decision 98/3.

change in energy policy and the energy strategy of most countries is already taking place in order to meet this challenge.[52]

Fulfilment of the Paris Agreement and the goals for reduction of climate gases that the states have committed themselves to under the Paris Agreement and together with the fulfilment of the SDGs will demand a fundamental change in energy production and consumption in the future. The legal instruments to achieve this are only partly in place.

International environmental law will play an important role in future energy development. As a common global effort is needed to meet the ecological and climate crisis, international law is necessary in order to avoid freeriders and to secure the participations of all states in this effort.

2.4 Investment protection

Energy production and transport are capital-intensive operations and are often associated with great financial risk. Energy resources are often located in countries with poorly developed institutions and legal systems that can also be politically unstable. If the host state changes the conditions for concessions or licenses in a way that is detrimental to the investor or expropriated the property of the investor, the investor's only possible remedy is often to call on its home state to try to put pressure on the host state. The national courts are often not expected to be independent and objective in such cases. Since 1965 when the "Convention on the Settlement of Investment Disputes between States and Nationals of other States" was adopted, there has been a movement towards a system with international arbitration as the main form of settlement of disputes between investors and the host state. Through a large number of bilateral and multilateral investment agreements, the protection of foreign investors is regulated and a system of international arbitration is established. The Energy Charter Part V regulates settlements of disputes between an investor and a party to the agreement ("contracting party").[53] These agreements are for several reasons more important for international energy investments than for most other investments.[54]

Through the investment agreements a dispute settlement system for foreign investors is established that does not presuppose an agreement between the investor and the host state, or any arbitration clause agreed between the parties. The basis for the decision will be standards established by international law, not the national law of the host state.[55] The first known bilateral investment treaty to be entered into was in 1959, the number now has risen to 3 300, and around 700 cases are tried or are still pending, creating a large body of jurisprudence on investment protection. This has created a new international system of dispute resolution in cases on foreign investment in energy projects, leaving little room for the national courts.

2.5 Energy justice, human rights protection of minorities and indigenous people

Energy policy and energy law have traditionally been focused on the need to secure energy supply by securing access to energy resources and to promote effective and economic utilization of energy resources. More recently the social and human aspects of energy activity and

52 See section 1.3 above on the development in EU-regulation.

53 ECT Article 26.

54 Wälde, "International Energy Law", p. 1134.

55 C McLachlan, L Shore and M Weiniger, *International Investment Arbitration – Substantive Principles*, Second edition (2017) p. 4–5.

how costs or burdens and benefits of energy activity are distributed between different groups of people has been focused on.[56] Energy projects might have an impact on people's livelihood by occupying land or fishing fields, flooding homes or by polluting rivers or sea areas. This also raises questions about recognition, information and participation in the process leading to decisions on permits and licensing, and about the distribution of benefits from the activity.

Development of human rights in international law might constitute a legal basis for protection from at least some severe interventions in the environment that are affecting people's living conditions. The Charter of the United Nations, the Universal Declaration of Human Rights, or regional treaties on human rights like the European Convention on Human Rights and international human rights law can give some protection. More than 100 states have also adopted provisions in their constitutions that recognize the human right to a sound and healthy environment and protect the citizen's right to a clean and healthy environment. These provisions have been used to oppose energy projects.[57]

There are special treaties on the protection of the rights of minorities and indigenous people's access to natural resources which are needed to uphold their livelihood, culture and language, and will probably provide stronger protection than that which is found in general treaties of human rights.

The UN Covenant on Civil and Political Rights (ICCPR) from 1966, Article 27 protects the right of "ethnic, religious or linguistic minorities" to "enjoy their own culture, to profess and practise their religion, or to use their language". This has also been interpreted as a right to the natural resources the groups in question needs as a basis for upholding their culture.

Another important treaty is the ILO Convention 169 (C169 – Indigenous and Tribal Peoples Convention, 1989), which contains a far more detailed regulation of the rights of groups of people who fall under this convention. The General Assembly adopted the United Nations Declaration on the Rights of Indigenous Peoples (UNDRIP) on 13 September 2007, by a majority of 144 states. This is currently the most comprehensive international instrument on the rights of indigenous peoples.

There are cases in Norway where hydropower projects have been limited by an administrative decision because they would interfere too much with the reindeer herding or other activities of the Samii people, who are accepted as an indigenous people. There is, however, no case where the courts have found interference in Samii interests to be a violation of any of the mentioned treaties.

3 Conclusions

For a number of reasons international energy law has developed from being almost non-existent before 1970, to an important legal discipline, and this development is still ongoing. International energy law is, however, fragmented and based on many legal sources from different legal disciplines and concerned with different problems.

56 A philosophical approach to energy justice is found in B K Sovacool and M H Dworkin, *Global Energy Justice: Principles, Problems, and Practices* (2014). See also K. Jenkins, D McCauley, R Heffron, H Stephan and R Rehner, "Energy Justice: A Conceptual Review", in *Energy Research & Social Science* 11 (2016) p. 174–182.

57 As an example, the litigation raised by several environmental organisations against the Norwegian State, in which it was claimed that the 23rd licensing round for the Norwegian continental shelf, where several licenses were granted in the Barents Sea, was a violation of the Norwegian Constitution Section 112. They lost the case in Oslo City Court 4 January 2018. The case was argued in Borgarting Appeal Court in November 2019 but the Court has not yet made its decision as the book goes into print.

This diversified nature of international energy law makes it difficult to say something definite on the relationship between international and national law as this will vary depending on which field one is speaking about. The methodological challenges will be rather different when applying international regulation to indigenous people's rights to an energy project, from what is the case when applying regulation to the international distribution of electricity. The relationship between international law and national law in a certain field will not only depend on the international regulation, but also on the national regulation.

Many of the relevant legal sources are not solely or even mainly aimed at energy regulation. International law is often vague and confined to determining some main principles, leaving the detailed regulation which is often needed to national law. The international regulation will often leave a certain leeway for the national regulation. If this room has been used to give a comprehensive and detailed national regulation, the national regulation will apply provided it is not in conflict with the international law. The room that international law leaves for national regulation creates a possibility for division of labour between international and national law, where principles and direction are decided in international law, but the more detailed implementation is left to national law. In an increasingly integrated international market for energy, especially electricity, it is, however, necessary to establish increasingly detailed international regulation in order to coordinate the operation of networks.

International energy law influences and limits the content of national law by laying down rules that must be reflected in national law, and also by establishing legal instruments and models for regulation that it is difficult for states to deviate from in a globalized world. The traditional monism-dualism dichotomy is not adequate to capture the relationship between international and national law in the field of energy, as in many other fields.

4

RECONCEPTUALISING ENERGY SECURITY FROM A LEGAL PERSPECTIVE IN THE CONTEXT OF CLIMATE CHANGE

John Paterson

1 Introduction

Not so long ago, writing a chapter on energy security from a legal perspective would have been, if not exactly straightforward, then at least relatively narrowly focused; in all probability the emphasis would have been upon oil, with the key concern being the operation of the international agreements underpinning, on the one hand, the Organisation of Oil Exporting Countries (OPEC) and, on the other, the International Energy Programme (IEP). Those instruments retain undoubted significance, but it is also the case that the world has become a much more complex place, not least for reasons associated very directly with the extent to which oil dominated the energy sector for so long. Now it is impossible to speak of energy security without at the same time having equal regard to the impact of energy production and consumption on climate change. As such, it becomes imperative to understand how the already challenging problem of ensuring energy security can be solved in ways that do not simultaneously risk the viability of human life on the planet. In the context of such manifestly 'wicked problems', which will undoubtedly require human technological prowess to be matched by considerable political sophistication, the concerns of lawyers may appear to be matters of lesser importance. It is the case, however, that whatever political and technological solutions emerge in the years ahead, much will depend upon legal arrangements, first, to promote and facilitate the necessary deliberations and innovations and, secondly, to implement the decisions.

In the same way that political and technological innovations are anticipated, it is likely that legal innovations will also be required. The scale of the challenge is such that a business-as-usual approach in any facet of the response is unlikely to be adequate. This brief chapter does not attempt to provide anything like a definitive view of what those legal innovations might look like; the dynamic nature of energy security and climate change challenges make prediction increasingly complex and high-risk. Rather, it sets out to look at the ways in which we currently conceptualise energy security from a legal perspective and considers the extent to which these might either restrict or facilitate innovation in the face of these dynamic and interconnected challenges. With these thoughts in mind, it then proceeds to ask whether new orientations of law are required and, if so, what these might look like. Inevitably speculative, the aim is not to offer a definitive model; rather it is to encourage lawyers to think outside of current categories, recognising that what has been familiar and comfortable for decades, whether in terms of international collaborative agreements or of business organisational forms, may prove wholly inadequate in the context of challenges to the economy and society unlike anything encountered before, even in war.

2 Traditional conceptualisations of energy security from a legal perspective

Energy security can be defined "as the continuity of energy supplies relative to demand".[1] Insofar as it has traditionally been the case that energy security concerns have tended to focus on oil, it is useful to look at the ways in which these concerns have been conceptualised from a legal perspective in that specific energy sector. This can be done most efficiently by considering, first, the OPEC Statute[2] and, secondly, the Agreement on an International Energy Programme.[3]

2.1 The OPEC Statute

Even as the fortunes of OPEC ebb and flow, it remains a significant force in the oil market, albeit a controversial one (as evidenced by current efforts in the US Congress to curtail its influence).[4] Given the evident geopolitical importance of this discussion, it is surprising that the foundational legal document upon which OPEC operates is rarely if ever referenced in the frequent media discussions of its activities. Instead there tends to be a relatively unquestioned acceptance of the view that the organisation is in some sense the antithesis of the functioning of a free market for oil. Nor, of course, as we shall see, is it difficult to understand the view that this is a body formed with the explicit aim of raising oil prices and with the capacity to use supply disruptions as a political tool. The full facts, however, are somewhat different.

Article 2 of the OPEC Statute is particularly important. This indicates that OPEC's key aim is "the coordination and unification of the petroleum policies" of its members, as well as establishing the best way to protect their individual and collective interests.[5] If one read no further, one could certainly be forgiven for accepting the popular image of the self-serving cartel, but the following words suggest that a more nuanced view is necessary. Article 2 continues that OPEC "shall devise ways and means of ensuring the stabilisation of prices in international oil markets with a view to eliminating harmful and unnecessary fluctuations".[6] This can, of course, be read as code for price fixing in favour of the producer, or perhaps at best as an indication of an unwillingness to allow market forces to operate, but it must surely be conceded that it can also be read as respectful of consumers who have an interest in

1 Christian Winzer, 'Conceptualising Energy Security', EPRG Working Paper 1123, *Cambridge Working Paper in Economics* 1151, July 2011.

2 Organisation of Petroleum Exporting Countries (OPEC), Statute (updated to 2012), https://www.opec.org/opec_web/static_files_project/media/downloads/publications/OPEC_Statute.pdf (visited 27 August 2019), (hereafter referred to as the OPEC Statute).

3 Agreement on an International Energy Program (as amended to 9 May 2014), https://www.oecd-ilibrary.org/the-i-e-p-agreement-of-1974_5lmqcr2jdqlv.pdf?itemId=%2Fcontent%2Fcomponent%2F9789264014947-3-en&mimeType=pdf (visited 27 August 2019), (hereafter referred to as the IEP Agreement).

4 The so-called NOPEC Initiative: 116th Congress, 1st Session, HR 948, a bill to amend the Sherman Act to make oil-producing and exporting cartels illegal, 4 February 2019.

5 OPEC Statute, Article 2(A).

6 OPEC Statute, Article 2(B).

stable prices to facilitate budgetary planning. Article 2 concludes with a further modulated paragraph which states that

> [d]ue regard shall be given at all times to the interests of the producing nations and to the necessity of securing a steady income to the producing countries; an efficient, economic and regular supply of petroleum to consuming nations; and a fair return on their capital to those investing in the petroleum industry.[7]

The first part of this final element of Article 2 is certainly preoccupied with members' interests, but in its entirety, this could just as well be read as a relatively uncontroversial description of what should be expected from a well-functioning free market. In short, it looks as if, far from being a self-serving cartel, OPEC is concerned to balance the interests of all the parties in the crude oil value chain, from investors in exploration and production through to the end consumer, whilst ensuring an appropriate return to the producer state.

Be that as it may, there is no denying that OPEC at times appeared less interested in an orderly market than in asserting the power that comes with the possession of a commodity that others desperately need. The organisation's *1968 Declaratory Statement of Petroleum Policy in Member Countries* "emphasised the inalienable right of all countries to exercise permanent sovereignty over their natural resources in the interest of their national development",[8] which could be translated as a clear warning to international oil companies operating in member countries that the latter reserved the right to nationalise their oil industries. Such an approach was, of course, at odds with the notion of a free market, but it reflected a broader movement among newly independent developing countries at that time who were keen to re-exert control that had been lost during the colonial era. In the case of oil in particular, consumer nations that had enjoyed the advantages of the domination of the market by the so-called Seven Sisters (the five main US oil companies together with BP and Shell)[9] were hardly in a strong position to object. OPEC thus perhaps felt emboldened to deal with this matter by a bald declaration; the United Nations, on the other hand, deliberated for considerably longer, establishing a Commission on Permanent Sovereignty over Natural Resources in 1958,[10] but not producing a tangible outcome until 1974 in the shape of the Declaration[11] and Programme of Action on the Establishment of a New International Economic Order[12] and the Charter of Economic Rights and Duties of States.[13]

Much of the delay had been due to concerns among developing countries that the progress of the discussions indicated an undue concern with the rights of international investors. The 1974 Charter, however, settled the issue of sovereignty fairly unequivocally to the extent that it provided, inter alia, that "[e]very state has and shall freely exercise full permanent sovereignty … over all its wealth, natural resources and economic activities".[14] It equally

7 OPEC Statute, Article 2(C).

8 OPEC, 'Brief History', www.opec.org/opec_web/en/about_us/24.htm (visited 27 August 2019).

9 See Anthony Sampson, *The Seven Sisters: The Great Oil Companies and the World They Shaped*, New York: Viking, 1975.

10 United Nations General Assembly Resolution 1314 (XIII), 12 December 1958, Recommendations Concerning International Respect for the Rights of Peoples and Nations to Self-Determination.

11 United Nations General Assembly Resolution 3201 (S-VI), 14 May 1974.

12 United Nations General Assembly Resolution 3202 (S-VI), 14 May 1974.

13 United Nations General Assembly Resolution 3281 (XXIX), 12 December 1974.

14 Resolution 3281, Article 2(a).

established that when dealing with transnational corporations, a state had the right to regulate them in accordance with "its economic and social policies".[15] Furthermore, a state was also explicitly able to "nationalise, expropriate or transfer ownership of foreign property"—albeit on payment of compensation—and in the event of a dispute to have that settled in its own courts according to domestic law unless the parties had agreed otherwise.[16] OPEC's 1968 declaration may have blown a chill wind through the boardrooms of transnational corporations—and indeed across cabinet tables—but by 1974 it was clear that the organisation had simply been ahead of a now more broadly accepted movement.

By 1974, of course, OPEC had also given consumer nations more tangible cause for concern insofar as in the previous year it (or, more accurately, the Organisation of Arab Petroleum Exporting Countries (OAPEC) or the Arab members of OPEC) had imposed an oil embargo on the United States and certain other countries in response to their support for Israel in the Arab-Israeli War of 1973. It is surely this action which colours the popular perception of the organisation more than any other to the present day. There was, of course, more to this event than the embargo; the 5 per cent production cut imposed by the same countries, to say nothing of the substantial purchases of oil on global markets by the United States and other consumer governments, did nothing to alleviate a sense of panic. This is well exemplified by the 400 per cent increase in crude oil prices at the time. Whatever OAPEC/OPEC thought the result of their action would be, it is unlikely that they would have taken it had they foreseen the reaction of the consumer nations. And here we have perhaps an early indication of the limitations on law's ability to constrain behaviours which are driven by geopolitical considerations.

It is, for example, hard to squarely place a politically motivated embargo and production cut with the objectives of the organisation set out in Article 2 of the OPEC Statute without adopting a very loose interpretation of key terms. It is hard to see how precipitating what became known as the 'First Oil Shock' advances any of the organisation's objectives in terms of market stability or security of supply to consumers. It would require some fairly casuistical reasoning to refute the conclusion that the 1973 action was, in fact and in law, a complete rejection of the organisation's stated aims. It is, therefore, evident that, given the firmly held (and by then increasingly internationally supported) views with respect to permanent sovereignty over natural resources, not only contracts with international oil companies might be disregarded (or at best renegotiated) in the pursuit of national interest, but also international agreements. That is, the unequivocal language of Article 2—and thus the legal obligations which the member countries had taken on—exercised no influence where it was felt that foreign policy considerations supervened. It is instructive that no sanctions from within OPEC were imposed on those members who had been involved in the embargo and production cuts; there are simply no provisions within the Statute that would allow member countries to be disciplined. Furthermore, that the action was led by Saudi Arabia—by some margin the organisation's strongest member—also helps explain the quiescent response; an international agreement such as the Statute may on its face record a series of promises binding all signatories equally, but it says nothing about any lack of equality of power among those same parties. And we have yet further indications of the limits of law in such settings.

It might be difficult to imagine what sort of penalty could have been imposed in the context of a breach by one or more members of OPEC, but this case serves to highlight the serious consequences that can follow where there are simply no sanctions for failure to comply

15 Resolution 3281, Article 2(b).
16 Resolution 3281, Article 2(c).

with commitments. Whereas by one measure the embargo and production cut can be seen to have produced a desired effect in essentially punishing target nations, this turned out to be a blunt instrument insofar as all consumer nations suffered—and that for a prolonged period. Indeed, so blunt was the instrument that by another—more broadly accepted—measure, the action was an abject failure. OPEC's standing was substantially damaged insofar as the linkage between supply and foreign policy undermined the organisation's reliability as a counterparty in oil trade. Article 2 might indicate a nuanced and sophisticated understanding of the multiply-connected oil market, but in the years after 1973 it looked increasingly like a dead letter. There is little evidence to contradict the assertion that the rapid expansion of non-OPEC (and especially non-Middle Eastern) supply during that period as well as energy technology and market innovations are a direct result of this shift in perception.[17] And among the unintended consequences one of the most important, in the context of current concerns, was the reaction of the consumer nations under the auspices of the Organisation for Economic Cooperation and Development (OECD).

2.2 The International Energy Programme

Established in 1961 (a year before the signing of the OPEC Statute), the OECD's main objective was to advance economic development with a view to preserving individual liberty and improving well-being.[18] This was to be achieved by way of cooperation and consultation among the member countries, recognising the extent to which their economies were intertwined. The key means of implementing this cooperation and of achieving those objectives was to be "the further expansion of world trade" on the basis that it "is one of the most important factors favouring the economic development of countries and the improvement of international economic relations".[19] Among the obligations to which the member countries agreed was to "pursue their efforts to reduce or abolish obstacles to the exchange of goods and services and current payments and maintain and extend the liberalisation of capital movements".[20] The organisation was and is accordingly focused on free trade and the liberalisation of global markets. The action of OPEC's Arab members in 1973, therefore, in imposing an embargo and cutting oil production, was completely contrary to the ethos of the OECD. It also revealed how vulnerable consumer nations were to supply cuts from what now appeared to be an unreliable source. This was the context in which the OECD members came together to form the Agreement on the International Energy Program (IEP) which also established the International Energy Agency.[21]

Given what could, therefore, appear to be an emerging clash between two different ways of doing business internationally exemplified by two distinct blocs, it is perhaps surprising that the preamble to the IEP Agreement makes no explicit reference to the OECD's core concern with free trade. It refers instead to the need "to take common effective measures to meet oil supply emergencies by developing emergency self-sufficiency in oil supplies,

17 For a convenient review of these arguments, see Robert Copaken, 'The Arab Oil Weapon of 1973–74 as a Double-edged Sword: Its Implications for Future Energy Security', Working Paper, University of Durham, Centre for Middle Eastern and Islamic Studies, Sir William Luce Fellowship Paper, no. 4, 2003.

18 Convention on the Organisation for Economic Co-operation and Development (OECD), Paris, 14 December 1960.

19 OECD Convention, Preamble.

20 OECD Convention, Article 2(d).

21 See also Richard Scott, *The History of the International Energy Agency 1974–1994, Volume 1: Origins and Structure*, Paris: OECD/IEA, 1994, pp. 27–58.

restraining demand and allocating available oil among [participating countries] on an equitable basis" and "to reduce … dependence on imported oil". What is evident here is a recognition that, even in the context of an organisation with a special mission to promote and develop free markets, governments have a "special responsibility … for energy supply". The overarching concern with the operation of the market is, nevertheless, still implicit insofar as the preamble also indicates that outside of emergency situations the participating countries are keen to foster cooperation between producer and consumer nations and to establish "a comprehensive international information system".[22]

The IEP's methods of achieving these objectives are the following. First, in order to achieve self-sufficiency in the event of an emergency, each participating country is required to hold stock equivalent to 90 days' of net oil imports.[23] Secondly, as part of the response to an emergency, each participating country must be ready to implement a programme of demand restraint "enabling it to reduce its rate of final consumption" by an agreed amount.[24] Thirdly, measures are put in place for the allocation of oil as between participating countries in the event of an emergency[25] with allocation calculations taking account of any non-compliance by a participating country.[26] The mechanisms which would see the emergency provisions activated and deactivated are contained in Chapter IV of the Agreement.

These proposed interventions clearly contradict any idea that the market is best placed to balance supply and demand, but can be justified insofar as they would only come into play in the case of market failure. It is nevertheless significant that the cooperation required from commercial actors under the IEP led to fears of antitrust violations or anti-competitive behaviour sufficient to require specific exemptions under US and EU law.[27] Also noteworthy is the extent to which the IEP seeks to ensure that its operation does not unnecessarily delay the resumption of normal market operations; for example, oil is to be allocated at a price based on the "price conditions prevailing for comparable commercial transactions".[28] Furthermore, it is expressly stated that "[i]t is not an objective of the [IEP] to seek to increase, in an emergency, the share of world oil supply" that the participating countries received "under normal market conditions" and that "[h]istorical oil trade patterns should be preserved as far as is reasonable".[29] Equally, whilst the provisions of the Agreement relating to an information system on the international oil market are "designed to ensure the efficient operation" of the emergency measures, they also provide reliable information to participants at other times, thus assisting in the achievement of stable markets, which is an objective shared by the OECD and OPEC.[30] Finally, and expressing a sentiment familiar to a reader of Article 2 of the OPEC Statute, the IEP Agreement includes provisions reminding participating countries of the need to promote good relations between consumer and producer nations and in

22 IEP Agreement, Preamble.
23 IEP Agreement, Article 2.
24 IEP Agreement, Article 3 and Chapter IV.
25 IEP Agreement, Chapter III.
26 See Catherine Redgwell, 'International Energy Security', in Barton, B., Redgwell, C., Rønne, A. and Zillman, D. (eds), *Energy Security: Managing Risk in a Dynamic Legal and Regulatory Environment*, Oxford: Oxford University Press, 2004, pp. 17–46, 30.
27 For a discussion, see Richard Scott, *The History of the International Energy Agency 1974–1994, Volume 2: Major Policies and Actions*, Paris: OECD/IEA, 1994, pp. 107–109.
28 IEP Agreement, Article 10.
29 IEP Agreement, Article 11.
30 IEP Agreement, Chapter V.

particular of the need to seek "opportunities and means of encouraging stable international trade in oil and promoting secure oil supplies on reasonable and equitable terms".[31]

Despite the turmoil that has beset global oil markets at times in the succeeding years, the full emergency provisions of the IEP have never been activated. The Second Oil Shock of 1979–1980 (associated with supply cuts caused by the Iranian Revolution followed by the commencement of the Iran-Iraq War) required the close attention of the IEA, and countries such as Sweden and Turkey came close to the threshold that would have required specific action, but the group as a whole did not face cuts at the appropriate level. The political action of the participating countries in encouraging a collective reduction in demand (though weak compared to a legally binding action) in tandem with their willingness to allow the individual drawdown of stock, permitted the crisis to be managed without the emergency procedures being activated.[32]

This experience nevertheless offered valuable lessons to participating countries who recognised that binding coordinated action could also be appropriate in circumstances short of a supply cut at the level required under the IEP. Accordingly, in 1984, the Governing Board of the IEA adopted the Decision on Stocks and Supply Disruptions, which established a lighter-touch response mechanism, designated the Co-ordinated Emergency Response Measures system or CERM.[33] Though it reiterates the importance of demand restraint, the CERM emphasises rapid stock drawdown as the key means of calming markets in the event of supply shocks. This "lighter touch" approach has been activated on a number of occasions, including at the start of the first Gulf War in 1991 and in the aftermath of the hurricanes which disrupted production in the Gulf of Mexico in 2005.[34] One could conclude that the IEA has not been eager to activate even the lighter-touch mechanism, preferring where possible (and certainly in circumstances short of war or unprecedented natural disaster) to allow the market to function. It is also important to recognise that the market now operates in full knowledge of the presence of the backstop constituted by the very significant strategic reserves built up under the IEP and CERM.

2.3 The energy security spectrum

Having obtained an insight into the operation of two key international agreements focused on energy security in the oil market, the question is what this indicates in terms of how the concept has been understood from a legal perspective. It is immediately clear that two views dominate thinking in this context. On the one hand, there is a broad recognition of the desirability of having a well-functioning oil market as the most efficient mechanism for balancing supply and demand; on the other, there is a similarly broad recognition that, at times, state interest will trump the default enthusiasm for the market. A superficial reading of the situation under the OPEC Statute and the IEP Agreement could see the IEA countries as essentially forced to take actions (stockpiling; cooperation from oil companies requiring anti-trust exemptions), which in any other setting would be seen as potentially destructive of the market, because of the ability of the OPEC countries to prioritise political objectives over legal obligations in relation to oil supply. If that reading was ever accurate, there are good reasons for suggesting that it is not the case now.

31 IEP Agreement, Article 47.

32 See Scott, note 27 above, pp. 114–120.

33 Decision IEA/GB(84)27, 11 July 1984.

34 See IEA, *IEA Response System for Oil Supply Emergencies*, Paris: OECD/IEA, 2011, p. 11.

First of all, interference in the oil market in the pursuit of individual state interests has a history that predates OPEC and has indeed even been carried out by enthusiasts for free markets such as the United States.[35] Secondly, it is wrong to assume that IEA members have never engaged in actions similar to those of the Arab members of OPEC in 1973; whilst not acting under the auspices of the IEA, some members imposed an embargo on the supply of oil to Yugoslavia during the crisis there in 2000, a situation the IEA has described as "unprecedented".[36] Thirdly, during one of the more recent supply shocks risking market turmoil (the crisis in Libya in 2011) not only did the IEA signal the release of oil to compensate,[37] but OPEC did the same thing (even if the efficient coordination by the IEA was in stark contrast to the difficulties faced by OPEC at the time in reaching an agreed position).[38] Finally, in a world where OPEC's key member, Saudi Arabia, is actively seeking to list its National Oil Company, Saudi Aramco, on global stock exchanges, it is hard to imagine a situation where the oil weapon could be deployed with the same alacrity as it was in 1973.[39]

What may be said, however, is that it is reasonable to look at legal approaches to energy security as lying on a continuum running from strong state control (or the exercise of sovereignty over natural resources), at one end, to pure free markets, at the other, but it is really impossible to find any practical examples that fully embody either extreme on the spectrum. Whether one looks at the agreement among the countries of a producer bloc or that among the countries of an essentially consumer bloc, there is a more nuanced understanding that whereas the default is to allow the market to run as it may, there will be times when the fundamental importance of energy security to the state means that non-market (even anti-market) interventions will be justified. The question is whether the latter can always be confined to responses to market failures as opposed to geopolitical gestures designed to pursue other non-energy agendas. In many respects the next significant international agreement focused on energy security may be understood as an attempt to respond to that question.

2.4 The Energy Charter Treaty

Emerging from the recognition of opportunities for unprecedented international collaboration in the immediate aftermath of the Cold War, the Energy Charter Treaty (ECT)[40] is the most ambitious international legal instrument in the realm of energy security insofar as

35 For an account of US actions in this regard in the aftermath of the Second World War, see James N. Maynard, 'Oil Import Controls: A Critical Appraisal', *Texas International Law Forum*, 1969, 5, 150–163; V. L. Kohn, 'The Oil Import Question: Research, Report, Reaction', *Case Western Reserve Journal of International Law*, 1970, 88(3), 88; and Jeffrey P. Bialos, 'Oil Imports and National Security: The Legal and Policy Framework for Ensuring United States Access to Strategic Resources', (1989) 11(2) *University of Pennsylvania Journal of International Business Law* 235–300.

36 IEA, *Energy Supply Security: Emergency Response of IEA Countries 2014*, Paris: OECD/IEA, 2014, 593.

37 Ibid., 594.

38 Escribano, Gonzalo (2011) 'The International Energy Agency Responds to the Libyan Crisis', Elcano Royal Institute, Energy Programme/International Economy & Trade, ARI 117/2011; www.realinstitutoelcano.org/wps/wcm/connect/bb34e68047aa9fc08137d9076e8e26e4/ARI117-2011_Escribano_IEA_Libyan_Crisis pdf?MOD=AJPERES&CACHEID=bb34e68047aa9fc08137d9076e8e2 6e4 (visited 27 August 2019).

39 See Kingdom of Saudi Arabia, *Vision 2030*, p. 43; https://vision2030.gov.sa/sites/default/files/report/Saudi_Vision2030_EN_2017.pdf (visited 27 August 2019).

40 The Energy Charter Treaty (Annex 1 to the Final Act of the European Energy Charter Conference) 17 December 1994. For details and background see Energy Charter Secretariat, *The Energy Charter Treaty and Related Documents: A Legal Framework for International Energy Cooperation*, Brussels: Energy Charter Secretariat, 2004.

it attempts to establish market conditions across much of Eurasia in relation to investment, transport and trade, especially in oil and gas. In essence, the ECT may be said to seek to apply WTO rules to the energy sector in the contracting parties. The extent to which the Treaty was signed up to with equal enthusiasm in Europe and in the former Soviet republics may be readily understood by the win-win situation it appeared to offer. By providing investment protection to Western companies otherwise nervous of committing capital to countries only recently emerging from the command economy of the USSR, barriers to the flow of funds to former Soviet nations hungry for capital to develop their hydrocarbon industries seemed to have been removed at a stroke.[41] Similarly, by clarifying the terms of trade, those same former Soviet states could find ready and reliable buyers among the consumer nations of Western Europe who were keen to reduce further their dependence on oil imports from the Middle East.[42] Add in the opportunities offered to transit states between producers and consumers to earn income from tariffs on the flow of oil and gas through their territories, and the compelling proposition offered by the ECT looks even harder to turn down.[43] That the Treaty is not well known to those outside of the energy sector is perhaps the readiest indication that, whatever the potential it offered to states at every point on the hydrocarbon value chain, things have not turned out as well in practice as was anticipated at the outset. The reason for this may be found in the question raised at the end of the last section, namely whether non-market energy security interventions can always be confined to responses to market failures as opposed to geopolitical gestures designed to pursue other non-energy agendas, and in the negative answer that experience with the ECT reveals.

For all the apparent broad attractions of the ECT, the project nevertheless experienced tensions from the outset—especially between Russia and the EU. This was primarily in the context of negotiations over the terms of a draft Transit Protocol designed to bolster the provisions relating to this matter in the Treaty.[44] These tensions were manifest especially in the failure of Russia to ratify the Treaty and then its decision to terminate its provisional application of the Treaty in 2009.[45] Examination of the points of contention between the EU and Russia reveal, in essence, very different ideas about the role that the market should play in achieving the objective of energy security, with Russia apparently unwilling to accept the notion of competition and thus the threat to the dominant position of its quasi-state companies.[46] In the end, it appears that the constraints on its ability to exercise sovereignty in relation to its energy resources persuaded Russia that it should no longer subject itself to those restrictions.

41 Energy Charter Treaty, Part III.

42 Energy Charter Treaty, Part II.

43 Energy Charter Treaty, Article 7.

44 Draft Final Act of the Energy Charter Conference with respect to the Energy Charter Protocol on Transit, 31 October 2003.

45 Russia informed the Depository (Portugal) on 20 August 2009 of its intention not to become a Contracting Party to the ECT. As a consequence of the terms of Article 45(3) (a) of the ECT, its provisional application of the Treaty terminated on the expiration of 60 days from that notification, i.e. 18 October 2009. For details see www.encharter.org/index.php?id=414 (visited 27 August 2019). See further P. Szlagowski, 'Review of the "New Legal Framework for Energy Cooperation" and Dispute Resolution Mechanisms in Energy Transit', *International Energy Law Review*, 2010, 5, 147–154.

46 For a discussion, see D. Doeh, S. Nappert and A. Popov (2006) 'Russia and the Energy Charter Treaty: Common Interests or Irreconcilable Differences?', *International Energy Law & Taxation Review*, 2006, 7, 189–191; and K. Hober, and S. Nappert (2007) 'Provisional Application and the Energy Charter Treaty: The Russian Doll Provision', *International Arbitration Law Review*, 2007, 10(3), 53–57.

The decision, which was a major blow to the credibility of the ECT, was perhaps easier to take in the context of a case which revealed to Russia the full potential the ECT's challenge to traditional notions of sovereignty in the context of energy security. Foreign shareholders in the Yukos company whose assets were seized by Russia to cover alleged tax avoidance took the matter to the Permanent Court of Arbitration in The Hague, making use of the investor protection provisions offered by the ECT. That tribunal first of all confirmed, against Russia's objections, that it had jurisdiction and that Russia's obligations in relation to then existing investments persist for 20 years beyond the termination of provisional application.[47] The tribunal's findings on the merits of the case arrived in due course in the form of the most valuable arbitration award ever handed down, finding that Russia had essentially expropriated Yukos' assets and ordering the payment of $50 billion to the shareholders.[48] But whilst the shareholders celebrated and began enforcement of the award in a number of jurisdictions under the New York Convention on the Recognition and Enforcement of Foreign Arbitral Awards of 1958, courts in those jurisdictions have not been keen to find that the commercial interests targeted can be found liable for Russia's actions. More fundamentally, Russia appealed successfully to The Hague District Court, which set aside the award on the basis that the tribunal had erred in relation to the question of provisional application. In contrast to the tribunal's reading of the Treaty, the District Court concluded, inter alia, that the issue was a matter of public law which was not within the competence of the tribunal and that an appropriate reading of the Treaty revealed that Russia was not subject to its arbitration provisions.[49] Whether any further appeal will change this position remains unclear.

3 The supremacy of sovereignty

What is striking, then, in the examination of these three different legal instruments established to assist in the achievement of energy security is, first, the fact that each to a greater or lesser extent is premised on the idea that a market-based approach is not only desirable but optimal and, secondly, that notwithstanding the extent to which the market is prioritised in any such instrument it appears impossible to prevent or even discourage the exercise of sovereignty even in circumstances where stepping back from the market is not about energy per se but rather about the pursuit of other objectives. At best, it appears, we can hope for surrounding circumstances to be propitious and not to increase the temptation for states to engage in activities that undermine the market; a look around the world today, however, suggests that even that limited hope is forlorn. Nor perhaps should we be so surprised at the inability of international agreements to constrain behaviour, even when it is arguably more damaging to the interests of all for the benefit of some. The fact that the very legal act by which a state purports to bind itself in its relations with other states is

47 In the matter of arbitration before a tribunal constituted in accordance with Article 26 of the Energy Charter Treaty and the UNCITRAL Arbitration Rules 1976 between Hulley Enterprises Limited (Cyprus) and the Russian Federation, Interim Award on jurisdiction and admissibility, 30 November 2009, PCA Case No. AA 226.

48 In the matter of arbitration before a tribunal constituted in accordance with Article 26 of the Energy Charter Treaty and the UNCITRAL Arbitration Rules 1976 between Hulley Enterprises Limited (Cyprus) and the Russian Federation, Final Award, 18 July 2014, PCA Case No. AA 226. See also Lena U. Serhan, 'Arbitration Unbound: How the Yukos Oil Decision Yields Uncertainty for International-Investment Arbitration', *Texas Law Review*, 2016, 95(1), 101–121.

49 See http://arbitrationblog.kluwerarbitration.com/2016/04/27/yukos-awards-set-aside-by-the-hague-district-court (visited 27 August 2019).

itself an expression of sovereignty indicates the difficulty in persuading a state that a further legal act negating or at least qualifying the first is thereby ruled out: there is indeed a powerful argument that the very idea is a logical impossibility. In other words, are there any circumstances in which the apparently binding legal obligations entered into by a state can really be regarded unequivocally as such, insofar as any obligation if genuinely binding would constitute a constraint on a state to exercise sovereignty in future—something which the very notion of sovereignty appears to rule out? In such circumstances, the fact that states continue to have recourse to treaties appears to suggest the triumph of hope over experience. And yet, it is precisely because the stakes are so high when it comes to sovereignty over oil and gas resources that law is both indispensable and yet on occasion apparently powerless.

Where does this leave the whole question of energy security which, as the foregoing discussion has demonstrated, remains a key priority for producer and consumer nations alike? Does the analysis in this chapter reveal that there is an inescapable tension between sovereignty and security which not even law in the form of binding obligations is able to resolve? It seems clear that despite the idea (even the ideology) of the market which underpins so much of international discourse about energy security, what ultimately matters is the way in which states as market participants actually behave.

Most significant, perhaps, is the recognition that state actors remain not just important but key to the operation of markets. It is easy to characterise states as being in thrall to markets, but the extent to which markets depend upon states should not be underestimated. Thus, as the various instruments considered above reveal, when it comes to the functioning of global energy markets the divergence between theory and practice, between the ideal and the actual, has produced a succession of legal efforts at the international level aimed at either modifying the behaviour of state actors in particular or compensating for it. And despite the desire in each case to make things better, it could certainly be concluded on the evidence that in many instances these legal efforts actually went some way towards making them worse.

Such an assessment would, however, fail to recognise the magnitude of the task that is set for law in the context of the tension between energy security and sovereignty in the domain of energy. On the one hand, there is perhaps a naivety on the part of states when it comes to their ability to intervene in markets in ways that will produce predictable effects. On the other, there is perhaps a failure on the part of commercial actors to understand the extent to which markets are complex social phenomena as opposed to purely economic mechanisms and thus to understand the limits to what state actors are willing to tolerate in terms of the working out of pure competitive operations.

If we were able to terminate our discussion here, then we would undoubtedly be concerned about the apparent limitations on the ability of legal instruments to achieve desirable energy security objectives despite the compelling offer that is made by proponents of markets to states at every point on the energy value chain. We might, nevertheless, at least feel that with clearer identification of the chokepoints there could be opportunities for progress in the longer term as the downside of self-interested interventions became apparent even to those who made them in the first place. The fracturing of global compacts that is apparent at the time of writing (in the summer of 2019) would of course give considerable pause for thought, but we might optimistically expect that these would play out exactly as suggested in the foregoing sentence: whether one speaks of trade wars and the imposition of tariffs as key indicators of sovereign authority or an increasing unwillingness to engage in regional or global integrated markets to the extent that they threaten sovereignty, one does not need any particularly sophisticated insight to understand that these are measurably self-defeating. So, is it simply the case that we simply have to wait long enough, and things will come back into a better balance where markets are able to help solve energy security problems by efficiently modulating demand and supply? All else equal, that would not be an unreasonable suggestion. All else, of course, is not equal and time is not a luxury we currently enjoy. For, as was mentioned at the outset of this chapter, it is now impossible to speak of energy security without simultaneously speaking of climate change. Given the urgency of the messages from the Intergovernmental Panel on Climate Change (IPCC), it is now surely unthinkable that we could allow individual short-term self-serving interventions in the domain of energy security to compromise necessary actions in the pursuit of climate change mitigation. But if the foregoing discussion of the legal instruments aimed at achieving energy security reveals anything, it is surely that we will find it very difficult to do anything about such actions. In short, therefore, it is apparent that the legal arrangements necessary for the more complex energy security challenges facing the world in the coming decades will need to be qualitatively different from those that have characterised the second half of the twentieth century and which have in essence stumbled on into the early part of the twenty-first.

4 The tragedy of the horizon

In looking for ways to break out of the impasse, it is useful to seek to understand better the obstacles that stand in the way of fuller acceptance of collaborative solutions. In this regard, the analysis offered by a leading central banker in recent years is instructive. Speaking in 2015, Mark Carney, Governor of the Bank of England, analogising from the tragedy of the commons,[50] described the challenge of responding appropriately to climate change as the tragedy of the horizon, in other words, the problem caused by the fact that "the catastrophic impacts of climate change will be felt beyond the traditional horizons of most actors – imposing a cost on future generations that the current generation has no direct incentive to fix".[51] The horizons Carney alluded to were those of the business cycle (perhaps 5–6 years), technocratic authorities (perhaps 10 years) and politics (perhaps 5 years in democracies, longer in autocracies). The fact that these temporal horizons are so short means that the absence of clearly catastrophic problems makes it difficult to take decisions that would avert those very problems: "[i]n other words, once climate change becomes a defining issue … it may already be too late".[52] Paradoxically, then, whereas earlier action would be cheaper, the absence of the emergence of catastrophe makes those cheaper interventions look expensive compared to doing nothing.

With that insight, the question then becomes one of how to lift the eyes of those in each of those settings (economic, technocratic and political) beyond their relatively hard-wired temporal horizons. Taking the privileged view of the second-order observer (the observer who observes *how* others observe), it is easy to see the constraints, but it is less easy to see the keys that might remove them. In the case of economic actors, unless they have the cash (or

50 See Garrett Hardin, 'The Tragedy of the Commons', *Science*, New Series, 13 Dec. 1968,162(3859, 1243–1248.

51 Mark Carney, 'Breaking their Tragedy of the Horizon – Climate Change and Financial Stability', Speech given at Lloyd's of London, 25 September 2015, p. 4; available online at: https://www.bankofengland.co.uk/-/media/boe/files/speech/2015/breaking-the-tragedy-of-the-horizon-climate-change-and-financial-stability.pdf?la=en&hash=7C67E785651862457D99511147C7424FF5EA0C1A (visited 9 August 2015).

52 Ibid.

the leverage) to take a long-term hedging position on catastrophe, it is much more likely that they will be driven by the short-term expectations of shareholders, customers, creditors and the like. And, of course, even the long-term bet might be worthless if the climate catastrophe makes the pay-off something of a Pyrrhic victory. In the case of technocratic actors, their temporal horizons are established by their mandates which in turn are handed down by their political masters. A pessimistic view might, therefore, hold that the likelihood of positive change here is unlikely to the extent that the temporal horizons of those political masters are usually even shorter. More optimistically, however, one might suggest that whereas a shift in the political temporal horizon might be costly (doing the right thing for a period 20 years in the future may impose costs on electorates today who will therefore vote for your opponent), a change in the mandate of a central bank, for example, might be seen by political actors as a way of contracting out the painful decisions and ensuring that they will affect all governing incumbents equally. Previously, the establishment of such independent agencies has been understood as a way of insulating them from politics precisely to avoid short-term self-serving interference in issues regarded as too important to allow them to be the playthings of politicians.[53] In the context of climate change, the optimistic argument here would suggest, politicians might actually welcome the insulation—simultaneously allowing the right decisions to be made for the long term, but avoiding the political cost because the decisions have been taken by independent experts on the basis of the evidence and beyond the scope of government to interfere.

The limitations on the optimistic reading are not hard to find. There are plenty of examples of political leaders either bullying technocrats[54] or even stacking supposedly independent agencies and branches of government with likeminded followers as a means of ensuring that nothing stands in the way of short-term political programmes aimed purely at the maintenance of power.[55] Nor should this surprise us, given that it was precisely the inability to curb the exercise of sovereignty in the pursuit of self-interest that appeared to represent the greatest weakness of the traditional international agreements in the domain of energy security. So, if that remains the case in these observations about the added challenge of climate change, are there alternative legal tools that could be envisaged either to make it more difficult for sovereigns to renege or, if we accept that that might be unduly difficult, to lengthen the temporal horizons of economic actors such that the very context within which sovereigns operate is so fundamentally changed that their ability to intervene in ways that are damaging is progressively limited?

5 New approaches to energy security in the context of climate change

In this penultimate section of the chapter, we will first of all consider some suggestions to refocus international efforts to change the behaviours of states in the domain of energy security where that concept is complexified by the appreciation of climate change, and then look at alternatives which focus on changing the behaviours of economic actors.

53 For a discussion, see Giandomenico Majone, *Evidence, Argument and Persuasion in the Policy Process*, New Haven, CT and London: Yale University Press, 1989.

54 President Trump's onslaught against the Chairman of the Federal Reserve, Jerome H. Powell, during 2019 is a classic example. See, for example, James Politi and Colby Smith, "Trump Unsettles Markets by Taking Aim at Fed and China", *Financial Times*, 30 July 2019.

55 Prime Minister Victor Orbán in Hungary is just one that springs readily to mind from amongst current examples. See James Kirchick, *The End of Europe: Dictators, Demagogues and the Coming Dark Age*, New Haven, CT and London: Yale University Press, 2018, pp. 40ff.

5.1 New approaches aimed at state actors

What stands out in the earlier consideration of international legal efforts to achieve energy security objectives is, first of all, the willingness of state actors to breach obligations aimed at ensuring the functioning of energy markets and, secondly, the relative weakness (and sometimes the absence) of enforcement mechanisms. As such, it might be suggested that refocused efforts to accommodate climate change as well as energy security might usefully channel this observation by insisting on market-based solutions which are backed up by substantive and painful consequences for defection. A recent example of such an approach has been suggested by Todd N. Tucker[56] who begins by developing a plan for the internationalisation of the Green New Deal that has been proposed by Democratic politicians in the United States.[57] In practice, this would involve "establishing a tariff-free zone among countries that institute a Green New Deal and embargoing those that do not".[58] This is nothing if not ambitious, comprising, as it would, a number of steps including: (1) a ten-year suspension of existing international trade treaties during which period countries instituting a Green New Deal would enjoy tariff-free trade, whilst countries that did not would see tariffs imposed equivalent to those applying to non-normal trading relations; (2) existing dispute resolution arrangements would be replaced during the same period by "ad hoc arbitration [for] any investor or civil society group that alleges a government is not upholding its obligations under the Global Green New Deal" with naming and shaming followed by multilateral sanctions in the event of non-compliance; and (3) a range of supportive policies including a financial transaction tax and the free transfer of publicly funded green technology to developing countries.[59]

An immediate question, of course, is why any state would willingly sign up to a treaty which involved such severe consequences for non-compliance (including for the pursuit of a non-green energy agenda). Doubts in this regard could easily persuade us that we are no further forward than we were in the face of the apparent impotence of the international energy security treaties examined earlier. To the contrary, however, it can plausibly be argued that there is very likely to be much less public sympathy for defections from climate change objectives in the coming years as compared to defections from relatively obscure energy security obligations in earlier years—and very likely to be considerable public support for the imposition of sanctions in similar circumstances. Nor is Tucker alone in calling for this form of action in the context of state actors. Edoardo Saravalle has recently argued for a similar approach and has usefully pointed out that in practice "Green sanctions would reach beyond their immediate targets. Risk-averse financial institutions would pause before getting involved in any new coal projects—sanctioned or not."[60] In other words, the internationalised Green New Deal would have the benefit over the traditional more limited energy security arrangements considered above that economic actors would have a rational self-interest in avoiding support for defectors and in channelling funds to those manifesting strong compliance. The recent—and radical—shift signalled by the Business Roundtable

56 Todd N. Tucker, 'The Green New Deal: A Ten-Year Window to Reshape International Economic Law', Roosevelt Institute Working Paper, July 2019, available online at: https://rooseveltinstitute.org/wp-content/uploads/2019/07/RI_GND_Working-Paper-201907.pdf (visited 9 August 2019)

57 See Resolution Recognising the Duty of the Federal Government to Create a Green New Deal, 116th Congress, 1st Session, 7 February 2019, H. Res. 106, available online at: https://www.congress.gov/116/bills/hres109/BILLS-116hres109ih.pdf (visited 26 August 2019).

58 Tucker, note 56 above, p. 2.

59 Ibid., pp. 7–8.

60 Edoardo Saravalle, "Why World Leaders Should Impose Green Sanctions", *Financial Times*, 8 August 2019.

in the United States in its new "Statement on the Purpose of a Corporation" looks at first sight to be a clear indication of the extent to which economic actors increasingly display this preference.[61]

5.2 New approaches aimed at economic actors

It remains the case, however, that we lack a clear indication of what legal means could be deployed to ensure that economic actors do indeed behave in the way implied by the Business Roundtable's new Statement. Most obviously, company law could be modified to restate directors' fiduciary duties—although the complications involved in shifting from a position where such duties are owed solely to shareholders (or, in the case of the UK, to the company for the benefit of shareholders) should not be underestimated. That said, growing public concern about climate change could well persuade policy makers previously nervous of diluting directors' duties that they need to set aside their hesitations. Beyond such formal legal modifications, it is once again the case that market mechanisms might actually prompt change. In this regard, the observation that insurers are increasingly aware of the multidimensional risks associated with climate change suggests that targeted increases in premiums—and even withdrawal of cover—is more likely to influence the choices made by corporations. The UK's Prudential Regulation Authority, for example, has pointed out that in addition to the physical risks from weather-related events, insurers need to factor in transition risks ("the potential re-pricing of carbon-intensive financial assets, and the speed at which any such re-pricing might occur") and liability risks (where "parties who have suffered loss and damage from climate change … seek to recover losses from others who they believe may have been responsible").[62] Of course, this is a chicken-and-egg situation insofar as the transition risks will most likely arise when policy makers, legislators and regulators take decisions which adversely impact the value of carbon producing assets, whilst liability risks will depend upon courts being willing to find against companies who have contributed to global warming. In short, there will need to be legislative or judicial action which changes the economic value of assets and processes which today remain profitable even as they wreak long-term climate damage. In the case of judicial action, this will depend upon it being found to be reasonable in all the circumstances to impose an unprecedented global-scale duty of care on, for example, fossil fuel companies—a move which courts will find easier to make in circumstances where those companies have taken clear steps to lobby disingenuously against clear scientific evidence whilst paradoxically retrofitting their infrastructure to be proof against the effects of climate change, such as rising sea levels. In the case of legislative action, this will depend upon the politicians being able to break free from their short-term temporal horizons, which in turn is likely to depend upon the extent to which the temporal horizons of the governed themselves lengthen and thus change the calculus for the maintenance of political power.

61 Business Roundtable, 'Statement on the Purpose of a Corporation', August 2019, https://opportunity.businessroundtable.org/wp-content/uploads/2019/08/Business-Roundtable-Statement-on-the-Purpose-of-a-Corporation-with-Signatures.pdf (visited 26 August 2019).

62 Bank of England Prudential Regulation Authority, "The Impact of Climate Change on the UK Insurance Sector: A Climate Change Adaptation Report by the Prudential Regulation Authority", September 2015, para. 1.6; https://www.bankofengland.co.uk/-/media/boe/files/prudential-regulation/publication/impact-of-climate-change-on-the-uk-insurance-sector.pdf?la=en&hash=EF9FE0FF9AEC940A2BA722324902FFBA49A5A29A (visited 9 August 2019).

6 Conclusions

This chapter set out to consider the extent to which existing legal conceptualisations of energy would need to change in order to meet the challenges raised by climate change. The limitations of traditional international legal instruments were clearly exposed in the context of their inability to rein in sovereign defection where a non-energy agenda supervened. Extending the analysis to encompass emergent climate change problems revealed both the potential limits imposed by the different temporal horizons of key political, economic and technocratic actors, but also allowed us to speculate about the ways in which legal concepts might develop in tandem with political and economic imperatives so as to overcome those limits. What is intriguing is that, although the co-evolution of political, economic and legal concepts (all responding, of course, to the scientific definition of the problem) produces sometimes radical changes (for example, the restatement of fiduciary duties in company law, the reformation of international trade law), none seems to involve the need for wholly new legal tools. Rather, we see the need for modifications to or the redeployment of familiar legal instruments. Whilst this should offer some reassurance to lawyers preparing themselves for the uncertainties of the climate emergency, it should not be allowed to induce any complacency. What lies ahead is not going to be straightforward and it is going to require lawyers to be ready to innovate and to embrace that which, at times, will be strange and unfamiliar. But the role lawyers play will be vital in supporting necessary political and technological innovation.

PART II

Europe

5

ENERGY MARKET LIBERALISATION

From monopolistic to traded markets in the European Union

*Sirja-Leena Penttinen**

1 Introduction

The European Union (EU) energy markets can be described as downstream energy markets.[1] The separation of upstream, midstream and downstream markets is more familiar to the oil and gas sectors, where the concepts refer to an oil or gas company's location in the supply chain; the closer the operating firm or function is to the end user, the further downstream the operations are.[2] This strict separation of different operations and activities has become somewhat blurred given the changing energy landscape, in particular because of the transition towards a low-carbon energy system with an increasing share of renewables and new roles and actors.[3] Nevertheless, the concept of downstream still provides an overview on how the energy markets in the EU have been organised and what type of regulation has been used in order to break the national vertically integrated monopoly companies in particular in the electricity and gas sectors.

Due to the importance of the energy sector, the EU Member States have been unwilling to embrace the idea of extending their energy markets beyond national borders. The energy sector is considered to fall strictly under the umbrella of state sovereignty and this has been the main reason why Member States have been rather unwilling to allow the EU to exercise any competence in the sector.[4] This is so, even if from the outset, in the Treaty establishing

* The chapter is part of the EL-TRAN-project funded by the Academy of Finland (project No. 293437).

1 See also L. S. Reins, 'Developments in Downstream Energy Regulation in the EU: Accommodating the Changing Role of Energy Consumers', 16 (3) *Oil, Gas and Energy Law (Special Issue on International Energy Law)* (2018).

2 See, e.g., Investopedia, 'Downstream', available at: https://www.investopedia.com/terms/d/downstream.asp (accessed December 2018).

3 Similarly, see, e.g., L. S. Reins, 'Developments in Downstream Energy Regulation in the EU: Accommodating the Changing Role of Energy Consumers', 16 (3) *Oil, Gas and Energy Law (Special Issue on International Energy Law)* (2018), pp. 2–3.

4 See, e.g., L. Hancher, 'A Single European Energy Market Rhetoric or Reality?', 11 (2) *Energy Law Journal* (1990), p. 221. Article 194 Treaty of the Functioning of the European Union (TFEU), introduced in the Lisbon Treaty, provides the EU with a legal basis to adopt secondary legislation in order to achieve objectives related to the functioning of the energy market as listed in Article 194(1) TFEU, as energy falls under shared competences between Member States and the EU. Nevertheless, Article 194(2) TFEU includes a caveat, according to which EU measures 'shall not affect a Member State's rights to determine the conditions for exploiting its

the European Coal and Steel Community (the ECSC Treaty) and the Treaty establishing the European Atomic Energy Community (Euratom), the impression was conveyed that energy was indeed a common European concern.[5]

Member States' national energy sectors were structured in such a way as to ensure that the state exercised control at every stage of the process of energy supply. National energy companies were vertically integrated, often state-owned companies, which were in charge of generation, transportation and energy sales to the final consumer. These companies enjoyed a monopoly over electricity and gas extending through the whole energy value chain and thus dominated Member States' national markets, which were largely isolated from one another.[6] However, it should be emphasised that despite characterising the national incumbents as state-owned utilities, it is the operation, and not the ownership itself, of the utility that is the determining factor that limits the possibilities for cross-border trade in energy.[7]

Companies did not face competition from other suppliers, whether internal or external, nor did they wish to do so. Almost all Member States' energy companies could have been characterised as 'inward-looking monopolies' and they had no interest in breaking out of their boundaries and entering the territories of neighbouring companies.[8]

The existing trade in electricity between Member States was largely conducted as a balancing activity between Member States' national monopoly companies. Whilst some interconnections between national systems existed, they did not provide capacity for substantial net trade. As was the case for electricity, gas trade only took place between national utilities in the Member States concerned and did not enhance competition at the level of the final consumer. Above all, most Member States were reluctant to rely to any significant extent on electricity supplies from outside their own borders. For both gas and electricity, a larger degree of interconnection was envisaged by making it possible to share supplies in emergency situations, thereby enhancing security of supply.[9] Consequently, the creation of an EU-wide energy market area was frequently hindered by the specific features of Member States' domestic energy markets and their historical development.

---

energy resources, its choice between different energy sources and the general structure of its energy supply'. This caveat has been much discussed with reference to renewable energy, and in particular to the national targets set for Member States by the Renewable Energy Directive (Directive 2009/28/EC of the European Parliament and of the Council of 23 April 2009 on the promotion of the use of energy from renewable sources and amending and subsequently repealing Directives 2001/77/EC and 2003/30/EC, OJ L 140, 5.6.2009, pp. 16–62). For an analysis of Article 194(2) TFEU, see, e.g., A. Johnston and E. van der Marel, '*Ad Lucem*? Interpreting the New EU Energy Provisions, and in particular the Meaning of Article 194(2) TFEU' 22 (5) *European Energy and Environmental Law Review* (2013), pp. 181–199. Nevertheless, the General Court recently provided the first interpretation concerning Article 194(2) TFEU and confirmed Member States' energy rights under 194(2) TFEU, see T-356/15 Austria v Commission, EU:T:2018:439, para. 105.

5 At EU level, the initial treaty framework focused specifically on energy; two of the three founding treaties evolved around energy products. The ECSC Treaty sought to establish a common market in coal and steel – coal being the main energy product at the time – and thereby ensure peace and further the reconstruction of post-war Europe. The Euratom, on the other hand, was initially created to coordinate the Member States' research programmes to facilitate the peaceful use of nuclear energy.

6 K. Talus, *Vertical Natural Gas Transportation Capacity, Upstream Commodity Contracts and EU Competition Law* (Kluwer Law International 2011), p. 197.

7 A. Lakatos, 'Overview of the Regulatory Environment for Trade in Electricity', in J. Bielecki & M. Geboye Desta (eds.) *Electricity Trade in Europe: Review of the Economic and Regulatory Challenges* (Kluwer Law International 2004), p. 131.

8 K. Talus, *EU Energy Law and Policy: A Critical Approach* (Oxford University Press 2013), p. 17.

9 The Commission of the European Communities, Communication from the Commission to the Council, New Community Energy Objectives, COM(85) 254 final, paras. 31–35.

The main barriers to the establishment of an EU-wide internal energy market has been the spectrum of different national approaches to energy, and the inability to find common ground and a solution that suits every party.[10] Member States were reluctant to accept the limits that an integrated market would impose on their policy options given the strategic nature of the sector in question. This had already been highlighted as one of the reasons why the ECSC failed: the situation for which it was created never materialised and in its absence Member States preferred market segmentation to market integration – and the High Authority had no supranational powers at its disposal to trump national self-interest.[11]

Similarly, players involved in the electricity and gas industries were of the view that nothing needed changing and that Brussels' involvement was neither necessary nor welcome. The reasons behind this approach reflected both the (monopolistic) industries' need to protect their substantial profits as well as simple fear of change. Both governments and industries alike expressed their differing concerns by relying on the language of security of supply and the need to protect public service obligations.[12]

Therefore, it is of the utmost importance to understand that when it comes to energy market liberalisation the sector in question differs fundamentally from other economic sectors, such as telecommunications, for example. An entire transformation has taken place from a state-driven and planned system to a market-based system. This has not been purely a question of eliminating barriers to a free trade area but has instead entailed a fundamental transformation, at an ideological level, of the approach taken to the organisation of energy markets.[13]

This chapter traces the historical development of energy market liberalisation and energy trading in the EU from a regulatory perspective. It portrays the political climate and legislative developments adopted at the EU level in order to integrate national energy markets into EU-wide energy markets. The emphasis is on electricity and gas, as the EU energy *acquis* focuses to a large extent on the regulation of these sectors. By contrast, EU energy regulation has not similarly touched upon oil markets because of their very different character from electricity and gas: oil markets are international in nature and they are not as dependent on infrastructure as electricity and gas.[14] The remainder of the chapter follows the developments of the EU energy market's liberalisation from the 1980s onwards, and the conclusion addresses some of the future challenges that have an impact on the (regulation of the) energy sector.

2 Security of supply as the first driver for harmonisation measures at the EU level

Despite the fact that energy has been at the very heart of European integration since its early days, the process of integrating national energy markets into an EU-wide energy market in

10 On the early days of the EU's energy policy, see T. Daintith and L. Hancher, 'The Management of Diversity: Community Law as an Instrument of Energy and Other Sectoral Policies', 4 (1) *Yearbook of European Law* (1984), pp. 127–136.

11 K. J. Alter, *The European Court's Political Power: Selected Essays* (Oxford University Press 2009), p. 48; and M. Chick, *Electricity and Energy Policy in Britain, France and the United States Since 1945* (Edward Elgar 2007), p. 46.

12 J. P. Stern, *Competition and Liberalization in European Gas Markets: A Diversity of Models* (The Royal Institute of International Affairs, Energy and Environmental Programme 1998), p. 90.

13 K. Talus, *EU Energy Law and Policy: A Critical Account* (Oxford University Press 2013), p. 99.

14 K. Talus, *Vertical Natural Gas Transportation Capacity, Upstream Commodity Contracts and EU Competition Law* (Wolters Kluwer 2011), p. 4; P. J. Slot, 'Energy and Competition', 31 (3) *Common Market Law Review* (1994), p. 516.

which energy can flow freely has moved forward extremely slowly.[15] Although the Treaty of Rome establishing the European Economic Community (EEC) included provisions on free movement and competition, which, in principle, also applied to the energy sector,[16] energy markets were nationally segmented and dominated by national and heavily regulated energy monopoly companies, which were either publicly owned or publicly supported.[17] These national monopoly companies were often granted either *de jure* or *de facto* the exclusive right to sell, import and export energy, and to construct infrastructure in their particular area.[18]

Energy was considered to fall under the category of a 'public service',[19] which meant that it had to be provided universally to all citizens. Given the strategic nature of energy, self-sufficiency was held by national governments to be the main objective of energy policy.[20]

Some of the first regulatory tools that explicitly concerned the energy sector were adopted to ensure the security of the energy supply. While the ECSC Treaty provided the Commission with broad powers in relation to monitoring the market, including emergency powers to deal with issues such as scarcity in the supply of oil and steel, within this particular framework these powers did not bring about any substantial progress in respect of such issues.[21]

However, the EU began to make modest steps in this area a few decades later. The political volatility in the Middle East during the 1970s resulted in shortages of petroleum exports in addition to elevated prices. This also had repercussions in Europe.[22] While oil supplies were vulnerable, the Commission decided to focus on the pressing issues of the time, such as security of supply, the management of scarcity, reducing energy import dependency and increasing energy savings.[23] Some of the initiatives that addressed these pressing issues ultimately led to the adoption of secondary legislation.[24] The main aim of this was to set up

15 For an overview, see e.g., S-L. Penttinen, 'Free Movement and the Energy Sector in the European Union: The Role of the European Court of Justice' (Routledge 2020).

16 Despite the fact that electricity lacks some of the fundamental qualities of a good, in the early case of 6/64 Costa v ENEL, EU:C:1964:66, the Court held – though without specifically confirming that it is to be considered as a good – that an electricity monopoly falls within the scope of Article 37 TFEU. Decades later, in C-393/92 Almelo, EU:C:1994:171, the Court explicitly confirmed the status of electricity as a good. See 'also S.-L. Penttinen, 'The Treaty Freedoms in the Energy Sector – Overview and State of Play' in S-L. Penttinen & I. Mersinia (eds), *Energy Transitions: Regulatory and Policy Trends* (Intersentia 2017), pp. 75–107.

17 K. Talus, *EU Energy Law and Policy: A Critical Account* (Oxford University Press 2013), p. 15.

18 C. Jones, 'Introduction', in C. Jones (ed.), *EU Energy Law: Volume I, The Internal Energy Market* (Claeys & Casteels Publishing 2016), p. 1.

19 C-157/94 Commission v Netherlands, EU:C:1997:499: C-158/94 Commission v Italy, EU:C:1997:500, and C-159/94 Commission v France, EU:C:1997:501. See also L. Hancher and W. Sauter, 'Public Services and EU Law', in C. Barnard and S. Peers (eds.), *European Union Law* (Oxford University Press 2014), pp. 539–566.

20 See, e.g., J. Bielecki, 'Electricity Trade: Overview of Current Flows and Infrastructure', in J. Bielecki & M. Geboye Desta (eds.), *Electricity Trade in Europe: Review of the Economic and Regulatory Challenges* (Kluwer Law International 2004), pp. 8–9.

21 T. Daintith & L. Hancher, 'The Management of Diversity: Community Law as an Instrument of Energy and Other Sectoral Policies', 4 (1) *Yearbook of European Law* (1984), p. 126.

22 See also Commission of the European Communities, 'Problems, Resources and Necessary Progress in Community Energy Policy 1975–1985', available at: http://aei.pitt.edu/36270/1/A2480.pdf (accessed December 2018).

23 Today, the two concepts of energy savings and energy efficiency are closely intertwined by both environmental and security of supply objectives, see S-L. Penttinen and L. Reins, 'System Boundaries of Nearly Zero-Energy Buildings in the European Union—Rethinking the Legal Framework for Active Consumer Participation' 37 (4) *Journal of Energy and Natural Resources Law* (2019), pp. 389–404.

24 See, e.g., Council Directive 68/414/EEC of 20 December 1968 imposing an obligation on Member States of the EEC to maintain minimum stocks of crude oil and/or petroleum products, OJ L 308, 23 Dec. 1968,

an emergency system within the EU,[25] since – as the Commission itself emphasised – '[e]nergy supply problems are today so largely world problems that attempts to solve them at the national level appear doomed in advance'.[26] These measures, however, remained rather modest in their scope, as they merely served as a tool of coordination and information-sharing rather than a regulatory tool imposing stringent obligations on Member States. In practice, almost all Member States relied primarily on the International Energy Agency's emergency oil-sharing mechanisms once the oil crisis hit Europe. Furthermore, although the EU adopted ambitious long-term goals in respect of energy production, consumption and imports after the first oil shock, no common ground on the concrete measures to be taken to achieve these goals was found.[27] Instead, by holding tightly onto their energy sector sovereignty, each Member State did what they thought was best for them. For example, France decided to invest in nuclear energy in order to make the country less vulnerable to import shortages.

Despite the Commission's acknowledgement of the universal nature of energy supply issues, its approach to energy policy within the EU – and, more precisely to the development and enforcement of EU law in relation to the energy sector – in that period has been characterised as the 'management of diversity'.[28] This essentially denotes an appreciation that Member States chose their own different paths towards the energy policy objectives of both the EU and Member States based on their individual situations.[29] This approach guided the Commission's approach to the energy sector after it became clear that there was no scope to develop and implement a genuinely coordinated energy at EU level at the time, despite the fact that the first energy policy objectives at EU level had been stated as early as 1968. At the time the energy sector fell strictly under the sovereignty of Member States, and their characteristics were regarded as being too different for a common energy policy to be a viable proposition.[30] Instead of seeking full uniformity of energy sector policies among Member States, the Commission aimed to bring about equivalent effort and collective discipline on the part of Member States in the establishment and pursuit of their own national energy policies.[31]

3 The first steps towards restructuring the market at the EU level: the first and second energy packages

Developments in respect of the integration of the EU energy markets can be roughly divided into two main time periods, where different priorities in the underlying policy aspects can clearly be seen to pave the way for legal developments. The first period comprises early

p. 14–16; Council Directive 72/425/EEC of 19 December 1972 amending the Council Directive of 20 December 1968 imposing an obligation on Member States of the EEC to maintain minimum stocks of crude oil and/or petroleum products, OJ L 291, 28 Dec. 1972, p. 154.

25 K. Talus, *EU Energy Law and Policy: A Critical Account* (Oxford University Press 2013), p. 16.

26 Communication from the Commission to the Council, Necessary Progress in Community Energy Policy, COM(72) 1200 final, 4 October 1972, para. 3.

27 J. S. Duffield & V. L. Birchfield, 'Introduction', in V. L. Birchfield & J. S. Duffield, *Toward a Common European Union Energy Policy: Problems, Progress, and Prospects* (Palgrave Macmillan 2011), p. 4.

28 T. Daintith & L. Hancher, 'The Management of Diversity: Community Law as an Instrument of Energy and Other Sectoral Policies', 4 (1) *Yearbook of European Law* (1984), pp. 123–167.

29 T. Daintith & L. Hancher, 'The Management of Diversity: Community Law as an Instrument of Energy and Other Sectoral Policies', 4 (1) *Yearbook of European Law* (1984), p. 123.

30 K. Talus, *EU Energy Law and Policy: A Critical Account* (Oxford University Press 2013), p. 17.

31 T. Daintith & L. Hancher, 'The Management of Diversity: Community Law as an Instrument of Energy and Other Sectoral Policies', 4 (1) *Yearbook of European Law* (1984), pp. 123–167.

developments from the 1980s to the adoption of the first and second energy packages in the mid-1990s and early 2000s. The second period covers the adoption of the third energy package and the climate change legislation.[32]

The EU's focus on energy gradually increased following the example provided by the evolution of 'general' single market integration.[33] In particular, examples from certain US states provided the necessary push for the ideological change that was needed. Similarly, in Europe, the UK in particular offered an example of a successful change in the organisation of energy markets.[34] The ideological movement from heavily regulated monopolies that ensured self-sufficiency in energy towards new policies promoting competition and liberalisation of energy markets slowly began to get underway, and this approach started to resonate from the UK first, and then the rest of Europe.[35]

While the previous approach was based on the assumption that the energy industry was a natural monopoly, the new approach rejected this premise. Instead, it was felt that at least the segments of generation, marketing and distribution could be subjected to competition and that this would lead ultimately to improved economic efficiency.[36] Once the system of energy monopolies was challenged by examples of alternative approaches from the other side of the Atlantic, the sole purpose of the existence of monopoly structures started slowly to be questioned. In particular, consumers realised that the high tariffs they were charged did not reflect the costs involved in securing the functioning of the system and that, after these costs had been met, the surplus income was going into the pockets of the employees and managers of the utilities and the politicians that provided the political and legal support to maintain the monopolistic structures. The wave of changes that occurred ultimately culminated in a wide-ranging corruption investigation in several Member States, which has been considered to have amounted to the reading of the last rites in respect of the legal and moral legitimacy of monopolistic structures within the energy sector, particularly in the eyes of consumers.[37]

This change in the political climate also represented the turning point in terms of the Commission's purpose in relation to the sector, i.e., the aim of achieving a common market in energy through coordinated action at EU level instead of 'just' managing Member States' divergent approaches. This political change indicated a movement towards deregulation and privatisation throughout the economy, and the energy sector was no exception to this.[38] The new ideological approach involved fair and free competition between energy

32 A similar grouping is outlined, e.g., in P. Thaler, 'The European Commission and the European Council: Coordinated Agenda Setting in European Energy Policy', 5 (38) *Journal of European Integration* (2016), p. 571.

33 For a more comprehensive overview on the Single Market Programme of the late 1980s and early 1990s, please refer to P. Craig & G. de Búrca, *EU Law: Text, Cases and Materials*, 6th edition (Oxford University Press 2015), pp. 609–619.

34 See, e.g., M. Chick, *Electricity and Energy Policy in Britain, France and the United States since 1945* (Edward Elgar 2007).

35 J. Bielecki, 'Electricity Trade: Overview of Current Flows and Infrastructure', in J. Bielecki & M. Geboye Desta (eds.), *Electricity Trade in Europe: Review of the Economic and Regulatory Challenges* (Kluwer Law International 2004), p. 9.

36 Ibid.

37 K. Talus, *EU Energy Law and Policy: A Critical Account* (Oxford University Press 2013), p. 18. See also T. Wälde & A. Gunst, 'International Energy Trade and Access to Networks: The Case of Electricity', in J. Bielecki & M. Geboye Desta (eds.), *Electricity Trade in Europe: Review of the Economic and Regulatory Challenges* (Kluwer Law International 2004), pp. 182–183.

38 P. J. Slot, 'Energy and Competition', 31 (3) *Common Market Law Review* (1994), p. 511. However, in the context of EU energy markets, that idea of 'deregulation' is to a certain extent misleading. The concept of deregulation

companies across the EU. This was expected to lead to large efficiency gains, lower and less divergent prices for consumers across the EU, increased competitiveness for energy-intensive industries and, finally, economic growth that would go hand in hand with increased welfare.[39]

In the aftermath of the launch of the general Single Market Programme the Commission decided it was time to focus more explicitly on the internal energy market. This led to the Working Document on the Internal Energy Market in May 1988,[40] which contained the first comprehensive discussion of the European energy sector.

The Commission's Working Document dealt with the general issues involved in the realisation of a single energy market. It specifically identified potential obstacles to achieving free energy flow in Europe and endorsed a competition-oriented approach. This latter provided impetus for further measures in a new political climate that was open to ideological – and further substantive – change. Since then, development has been rapid and the legislation targeting different aspects of liberalisation of energy, in particular the electricity and gas markets, has evolved quickly. To date, three sets of enactments aimed at liberalising the EU's internal energy market have been adopted.[41] These are referred to as the 'energy packages' and comprise different means of addressing, among other things, market access, the need to support the increase of and improvement in interconnection capacity and infrastructure, transparency, security of supply, consumer protection and various issues relating to sustainability and environmental protection.

The Commission presented its first proposals for regulations and directives concerning the energy market following the adoption of the Single European Act in 1986. However, it took several years of negotiation for these to develop into the first energy package, and during the course of the negotiations it became clear that a number of Member States and industry players viewed many of the Commission's proposals as being too ambitious. Despite the differences between electricity and gas, it should be noted that the broad aims of the directives concerning each sector were largely the same.[42] However, it became clear during the early stages of the market opening development that the electricity industry was far more prepared to concede that liberalisation could bring efficiencies and advantages to the industry than were representatives of the European gas industries, who regarded the introduction of

is often used in the context of privatisation and has therefore also been utilised in respect of discussions on energy market liberalisation in the EU. However, deregulation, in general, refers to the process of decreasing state regulation in a given field. No clear role has been played in the energy sector by regulatory authorities in the implementation and policing of competition and liberalisation. Instead, a major part of the EU energy market liberalisation efforts rely on the creation of EU and national level regulatory institutions and regimes, and therefore the concept of deregulation is, within the EU context, quite misleading as these developments should instead be referred to by reference to the concept of 'reregulation'. See, e.g., J. P. Stern, *Competition and Liberalization in European Gas Markets: A Diversity of Models* (The Royal Institute of International Affairs, Energy and Environmental Programme 1998), pp. xxii–xxiii.

39 See, e.g., P. O. Eikeland, 'EU Internal Energy Market Policy: Achievements and Hurdles', in V. L. Birchfield & J. S. Duffield, *Toward a Common European Union Energy Policy: Problems, Progress, and Prospects* (Palgrave Macmillan 2011), p. 13.

40 Commission Working Document on the Internal Energy Market, COM(88) 238 final.

41 The first electricity directive was adopted in 1996, whereas the first gas directive followed in 1998. The second energy package, comprising electricity and gas directives was adopted in 2003, and the third energy package in 2009. See Chapter 6 in this book by Formosa Herrera-Anchustegui and Formosa.

42 H. Vedder, A. Rønne, M. Roggenkamp & I. del Guayo, 'EU Energy Law', in M. Roggenkamp, C. Redgwell, A. Rønne & I. del Guayo (eds.), *Energy Law in Europe: National, EU and International Regulation,* 3rd edition (Oxford University Press 2016), p. 256.

liberalisation 'as the equivalent of the end of civilization'.[43] This is one of the reasons why the electricity sector was able to proceed faster on the details concerning how and when electricity market liberalisation could be introduced.[44]

The original electricity and gas market liberalisation proposals included, among other things, rules on unbundling (the separation of the management and accounting of production, transmission and distribution operations in vertically integrated undertakings), the creation of a transparent and non-discriminatory system for granting licences for the production of electricity and the building of networks and the introduction of a system of third-party access.[45] While in principle Member States affirmed the importance of aiming towards more open, transparent, efficient and competitive electricity and gas markets, they also expressed reservations about the Commission's proposals. Furthermore, the legal basis for the very first proposals was what used to be Article 90(3) of the EEC Treaty,[46] which was criticised by both Member States and industry players alike for being undemocratic.[47]

In response to this opposition, the Commission amended its proposals into something characterised as 'heavily watered-down versions',[48] reflecting the intense negotiation that the proposals required. First of all, the Commission relied on Article 100(a) of the EEC Treaty, which provided for a consensus-based approach, as the legal basis. Unbundling was no longer required; instead the accounts of the utilities were to be drawn up to ensure transparency. Third party access – an important tool in the opening up of national monopolies – was to be realised either through a negotiated third-party access technique (in which conditions of access to the network are subject to negotiations between the transmission system operator and suppliers and customers), regulated access (an obligation to provide access to the network under non-discriminatory and transparent conditions) or by relying on a single buyer procedure (a system in which only a single entity buys and sells electricity).[49] The last option was considered particularly problematic vis-à-vis the establishment of cross-border trade, as the procedure enables a single national company to retain full control over imports.[50] The single buyer option, however, applied only to electricity. While the electricity and gas markets directives followed the same logic, the main difference between them is that in relation

43 J. P. Stern, *Competition and Liberalization in European Gas Markets: A Diversity of Models* (The Royal Institute of International Affairs, Energy and Environmental Programme 1998), pp. 90–91.

44 J. P. Stern, *Competition and Liberalization in European Gas Markets: A Diversity of Models* (The Royal Institute of International Affairs, Energy and Environmental Programme 1998), p. 91.

45 P. J. Slot, 'Energy and Competition', 31 (3) *Common Market Law Review* (1994), p. 544.

46 This article provides the competence for the Commission to take unilateral action.

47 P. J. Slot, 'Energy and Competition', 31 (3) *Common Market Law Review* (1994), p. 543.

48 P. O. Eikeland, 'EU Internal Energy Market Policy: Achievements and Hurdles', in V. L. Birchfield & J. S. Duffield, *Toward a Common European Union Energy Policy: Problems, Progress, and Prospects* (Palgrave Macmillan 2011), p. 19. See also P. J. Slot, 'Cases C-157/94, Commission v. Netherlands; C-158/94, Commission v. Italy; C-159/94, Commission v. France; C-160/94, Commission v. Spain; C-189/95, Harry Franzén; judgments of 23 October 1997, Full Court, [1997] ECR I-5699, I-5789, I-5815, I-5851, I-5909', 35 (5) *Common Market Law Review* (1998), p. 1185.

49 Articles 17 and 18 of Directive 96/92/EC of the European Parliament and of the Council of 19 December 1996 concerning common rules for the internal market in electricity, OJ L 27, 30 Jan. 1997, pp. 20–29; and Articles 15 and 16 of Directive 98/30/EC of the European Parliament and of the Council of 22 June 1998 concerning common rules for the internal market in natural gas, OJ L 204, 21 July 1998, pp. 1–12.

50 P. O. Eikeland, 'EU Internal Energy Market Policy: Achievements and Hurdles', in V. L. Birchfield & J. S. Duffield, *Toward a Common European Union Energy Policy: Problems, Progress, and Prospects* (Palgrave Macmillan 2011), p. 19.

to gas Member States had to make a choice between a system of negotiated access and one involving regulated access.[51]

Despite the adoption of the first energy package, the legislative development was regarded as having been fairly modest in scope and the directives were considered to be relatively weak documents in comparison with the aspirations voiced in the late 1980s.[52] In particular, as the Commission had to agree to certain options in respect of third-party access regimes[53] that are not considered sufficiently effective, the vertically integrated companies were still left with opportunities to obstruct access on the part of competing power supply businesses.[54] While there was an obligation for tariffs to be non-discriminatory and transparent, the directives did not provide any guidance on the methodology to be used to calculate them.[55] Furthermore, they only allowed for partial market opening: only industrial consumers were given the right to choose their electricity supplier.

In addition to the electricity and gas market directives adopted to open up the national electricity and gas markets, some progress was made in relation to the environment as the rise of environmental policy at EU level also impacted upon the energy sector.[56]

These first package directives obliged the Commission to regularly report on possible additional measures that might be needed to harmonise national regulations to remove the remaining barriers to trade and the physical flow of electricity and gas across national borders.[57] Over the years, the Commission produced several reports in which it indicated the remaining shortcomings in the markets.[58] Furthermore, several Member States lagged behind in terms of transposing the obligations imposed by the directives into their national laws and regulations. While some Member States went beyond the obligations stemming from the directives, others maintained systems that were not in line with the directives, and were therefore hampering liberalisation efforts.[59] In this sense, Hancher has described the first electricity directive as:

> a framework in the loosest sense of the word: its objectives are laid down in very general terminology and moreover, Member States are given a substantial degree of choice

51 J. P. Stern, *Competition and Liberalization in European Gas Markets: A Diversity of Models* (The Royal Institute of International Affairs, Energy and Environmental Programme 1998), p. 95.

52 J. P. Stern, *Competition and Liberalization in European Gas Markets: A Diversity of Models* (The Royal Institute of International Affairs, Energy and Environmental Programme 1998), p. 100.

53 On different third-party access regimes, see K. Talus, *Introduction to EU Energy Law* (Oxford University Press 2016) pp. 19–24.

54 P. O. Eikeland, 'EU Internal Energy Market Policy: Achievements and Hurdles', in V. L. Birchfield & J. S. Duffield, *Toward a Common European Union Energy Policy: Problems, Progress, and Prospects* (Palgrave Macmillan 2011), p. 19.

55 J. P. Stern, *Competition and Liberalization in European Gas Markets: A Diversity of Models* (The Royal Institute of International Affairs, Energy and Environmental Programme 1998), pp. 93, 99.

56 J. S. Duffield & V. L. Birchfield, 'Introduction', in V. L. Birchfield & J. S. Duffield, *Toward a Common European Union Energy Policy: Problems, Progress, and Prospects* (Palgrave Macmillan 2011), pp. 4–5.

57 Article 25(1) of Directive 96/92/EC of the European Parliament and of the Council of 19 December 1996 concerning common rules for the internal market in electricity, OJ L 27, 30 Jan. 1997, pp. 20–29; and Article 27 of Directive 98/30/EC of the European Parliament and of the Council of 22 June 1998 concerning common rules for the internal market in natural gas, OJ L 204, 21 July 1998, pp. 1–12.

58 See, for example, Commission Staff Working Paper, 'First Report on the Implementation of the Internal Electricity and Gas Market' SEC(2001) 1957.

59 P. O. Eikeland, 'EU Internal Energy Market Policy: Achievements and Hurdles', in V. L. Birchfield & J. S. Duffield, *Toward a Common European Union Energy Policy: Problems, Progress, and Prospects* (Palgrave Macmillan 2011), p. 20.

> in how they are about introducing more competition into their electricity markets. Indeed, the margin is so substantial that it would seem possible for the determined anti-market countries to avoid introducing any meaningful degree of competition at all.[60]

Against this background, the Commission was asked to prepare a second energy package.

This second package – the so-called acceleration energy package of 2003 – imposed an obligation on the Member States to fully open their electricity and gas markets by improving the existing third-party access regime, which provided for regulated third-party access. It also laid down rules on the legal, operational and information-related unbundling of historically incumbent energy utilities.[61] As distinct from the rules brought in under the first energy package, all consumers were now given the right to choose their supplier. Whereas the first energy package introduced measures aimed at opening up the market and shifted the focus from a state-oriented to a liberalised market, the second energy package focused more on the competition side as the new liberalised markets needed regulation. In addition, environmental policy was on the rise during this time, and a number of directives were adopted in order to promote electricity generation from renewable sources, encourage the use of biofuels and improve energy efficiency.[62]

In 2005 – even though the process of implementing the earlier measures was still unfinished – the Commission launched a sector inquiry into the functioning of the European electricity and gas markets. The inquiry was prompted by the dissatisfaction voiced by energy consumers, who claimed that they were experiencing higher tariff levels than before as well as discrimination in access to grids on the part of vertically integrated companies.[63] The sector inquiry revealed several shortcomings in the EU energy markets. In particular, the Commission was concerned about the continuing market power exercised by national incumbents in many Member States, the inadequate separation of network and supply companies, which had led to new entrants being shut out of the market and had hindered investment, and the lack of cross-border integration of networks and cross-border regulatory supervision. The final report produced by this inquiry revealed several enduring deficiencies in the energy markets, including the following:

- too much market concentration in most national markets
- a lack of liquidity, preventing successful new entry

60 L. Hancher, 'Delimitation of Energy Law Jurisdiction: The EU and Its Member States: From Organisational to Regulatory Conflicts', 16 (1) *Journal of Energy and Natural Resources Law* (1998), p. 42.

61 Directive 2003/54/EC of the European Parliament and of the Council of 26 June 2003 concerning common rules for the internal market in electricity and repealing Directive 96/92/EC, OJ L 176, 15.7.2003, p. 37–56; Directive 2003/55/EC of the European Parliament and of the Council of 26 June 2003 concerning common rules for the internal market in natural gas and repealing Directive 98/30/EC, OJ L 176, 15 July 2003, p. 57–78; Regulation (EC) No. 1228/2003 of the European Parliament and of the Council of 26 June 2003 on conditions for access to the network for cross-border exchanges in electricity, OJ L 176, 15 July 2003, pp. 1–10; Regulation (EC) No. 1775/2005 of the European Parliament and of the Council of 28 September 2005 on conditions for access to the natural gas transmission networks, OJ L 289, 3 Nov. 2005, pp. 1–13.

62 See, e.g., Directive 2001/77/EC of the European Parliament and of the Council of 27 September 2001 on the promotion of electricity produced from renewable energy sources in the internal electricity market, OJ L 283, 27 Oct. 2001, pp. 33–40 and Directive 2003/30/EC of the European Parliament and of the Council of 8 May 2003 on the promotion of the use of biofuels or other renewable fuels for transport, OJ L 123, 17 May 2003, pp. 42–46.

63 P. O. Eikeland, 'EU Internal Energy Market Policy: Achievements and Hurdles', in V. L. Birchfield & J. S. Duffield, *Toward a Common European Union Energy Policy: Problems, Progress, and Prospects* (Palgrave Macmillan 2011), p. 21; C. Jones, 'Introduction', in C. Jones (ed.), *EU Energy Law: Volume I, The Internal Energy Market* (Claeys & Casteels Publishing 2016), p. 4.

- too little integration between Member States' markets
- an absence of transparently available market information, leading to distrust in pricing mechanisms
- an inadequate level of unbundling between network and supply interests, which had negative repercussions for market functioning and investment incentives
- customers being tied to suppliers through long-term downstream contracts
- current balancing markets and small balancing zones that favour incumbents.[64]

The findings identified in the sector inquiry spurred the Commission into taking further action in the form of proposing further regulatory and structural measures. The Commission identified four key areas that called for urgent action: (1) achieving effective unbundling of network and supply activities; (2) removing the regulatory gaps, particularly in relation to cross-border issues; (3) addressing market concentration and barriers to entry; and (4) increasing transparency in market operations.[65]

In addition to the sector inquiry, the Commission published in 2006 a Green Paper on developing a common, coherent European energy policy.[66] This development was initiated by the European Council and ultimately led to the adoption of the third energy package.

4 Towards competitive EU-wide markets: deepening integration through the third energy package

To tackle the shortcomings identified in the inquiry, the Commission started to pursue individual cases under the competition rules.[67] It also started to push for improvements in the regulatory framework. The objective of the third energy package was to liberalise the national energy markets to a greater extent, and to bring about further unbundling of transmission system operations from different interests, i.e. production, supply and trading.

The process of creating a competitive internal energy market within the EU accelerated rapidly with the adoption of the third energy package in July 2009.[68] This imposed significant requirements on transmission companies with regard to ownership unbundling (requiring real and effective separation of transmission companies from those involved in generation and supply),[69] better coordination of the operation and development of networks across borders within Europe, and the introduction of a new actor in the energy sector: the Agency for the Cooperation of the Energy Regulators (ACER).[70] While the ACER was established by

64 Communication from the Commission, Inquiry pursuant to Article 17 of Regulation (EC) No. 1/2003 into the European gas and electricity sectors (Final Report) COM(2006) 851 final.

65 Communication from the Commission – Inquiry pursuant to Article 17 of Regulation (EC) No. 1/2003 into the European gas and electricity sectors (Final Report), COM(2006) 851 final, p. 3.

66 Commission of the European Communities, Green Paper: A European Strategy for Sustainable, Competitive and Secure Energy, COM(2006) 105 final, Brussels 8.3.2006.

67 See Chapter 7 in this volume by Bergqvist and Herrera Anchustegui.

68 C. Jones, 'Introduction', in C. Jones (ed.), *EU Energy Law: Volume I, The Internal Energy Market* (Claeys & Casteels Publishing 2016), p. 1.

69 See also I. Herrera-Anchustegui, 'Transmission Networks in Electricity Competition: Third-Party Access and Unbundling – a Transatlantic Perspective', in J. I. Ruiz Peris, and C. Cerdá Martínez-Pujalte, C (eds), *Competencia en mercados con recursos esenciales compartidos: telecomunicaciones y energía* (Aranzadi 2019), pp. 91–128.

70 Directive 2009/72/EC of the European Parliament and of the Council of 13 July 2009 concerning common rules for the internal market in electricity and repealing Directive 2003/54/EC, OJ L 211, 14 Aug. 2009, pp. 55–93; Directive 2009/73/EC of the European Parliament and of the Council of 13 July 2009 concerning common rules for the internal market in natural gas and repealing Directive 2003/55/EC, OJ L 211, 14 Aug.

a regulation included in the third energy package,[71] it later had new powers conferred upon it under Regulation (EU) No 1227/2011 of the European Parliament and of the Council.[72] The Commission's proposals were accepted with some modifications by the Council and the European Parliament during the negotiations.[73]

In addition to these regulatory developments, the European Court of Justice had to deal, within a short time period, with numerous preliminary references focusing on various aspects of the newly liberalised sector. The judgments handed down by the Court concerned both the interpretation of the existing secondary legislation on energy and the application of general EU law to the energy sector, and the interpretation of that law.[74]

Furthermore, the package introduced parallel measures aimed at responding to environmental concerns, particularly the need for climate change mitigation. These environmental measures covered various matters that fell under the umbrella concept of 'sustainability', including the promotion of renewable energy, energy efficiency, carbon capture and storage and the EU's emissions trading system.[75] This 'environmentally friendly' approach was either embodied in specific measures intended to address environmental concerns or formed part of more general considerations, proposals and policy documents.[76] However, the increase in environmental measures aside, the competition-oriented energy packages concern not only environmental issues but also security of supply. This issue has of course always been on the EU's agenda, although the degree of emphasis placed on it has varied depending on the context.

This development reflects how the relatively single-minded approach adopted towards establishing an EU-wide energy market has gradually developed to involve the pursuit of a wider range of goals.[77] While the liberalisation of national energy markets has been the objective of regulatory reform at EU level, the electricity and gas directives also provide for derogations from the principal competition-oriented rules that they lay down. Consequently, the simultaneous pursuit of other objectives – for instance, general objectives such as environmental protection or more specific objectives such as ensuring security of supply in emergency situations – have been acknowledged in the directives contained in the third energy package.[78]

2009, pp. 94–136; Regulation (EC) No 713/2009 of the European Parliament and of the Council of 13 July 2009 establishing an Agency for the Cooperation of Energy Regulators, OJ L 211, 14 Aug. 2009, pp. 1–14; Regulation (EC) No 714/2009 of the European Parliament and of the Council of 13 July 2009 on conditions for access to the network for cross-border exchanges in electricity and repealing Regulation (EC) No 1228/2003, OJ L 211, 14 Aug. 2009, pp. 15–35; Regulation (EC) No 715/2009 of the European Parliament and of the Council of 13 July 2009 on conditions for access to the natural gas transmission networks and repealing Regulation (EC) No1775/2005, OJ L 211, 14 Aug. 2009, pp. 36–54.

71 Regulation (EC) No 713/2009 of the European Parliament and of the Council of 13 July 2009 establishing an Agency for the Cooperation of Energy Regulators, OJ L 211, 14 Aug. 2009, pp. 1–14.

72 Regulation (EU) No 1227/2011 of the European Parliament and of the Council of 25 October 2011 on wholesale energy market integrity and transparency, OJ L 326, 2 Dec. 2011, pp. 1–16.

73 C. Jones, 'Introduction', in C. Jones (ed.), *EU Energy Law: Volume I, The Internal Energy Market* (Claeys & Casteels Publishing 2016), p. 8.

74 For an overview of the Court's case-law over the course of the process of energy market liberalisation, see S.-L. Penttinen, 'The Role of the Court of Justice of the European Union in the Energy Market Liberalisation', in K. Talus (ed.), *Research Handbook on International Energy Law* (Edward Elgar 2014), pp. 241–271.

75 See also S.-L. Penttinen, 'Sustainability in the Energy Sector: Policy Directions and Implementing Measures', 3 (16) *Oil, Gas and Energy Law (Special Issue on International Energy Law)* (2018), pp. 1–4.

76 A. Johnston & G. Block, *EU Energy Law* (Oxford University Press 2012), p. 26.

77 A. Johnston & G. Block, *EU Energy Law* (Oxford University Press 2012), p. 25.

78 Ibid.

5 Conclusion

The regulatory approach taken in respect of the energy sector has resulted from the changing political climate and encouraging experiences both from within and outside Europe. Due to the ideological changes that have taken place and the regulatory approach that has been adopted, the European energy markets have undergone a gradual and progressive change. The privatisation of national energy companies has, at least to a certain extent, gradually removed the governmental protection those companies traditionally received. This has pushed those companies independently to look for new markets beyond their national borders in order to compensate at least to a degree for the market share lost to new market entrants.[79] Furthermore, cross-border trade has grown due to increased interconnection capacity – technical trade barriers have partially been overcome over the past few decades.

However, while some of the old problems have been overcome, the energy sector is in a state of constant change and new challenges have appeared, of which the growing concern over climate change mitigation is one of the most prominent. In recent years, both environmental concerns and security of supply issues have reappeared on the EU's energy agenda, though in a slightly different light than before. This particularly relates to the challenge posed by 'energy transition'. The key focus of this transition is that of lowering the environmental impacts that arise from energy production and consumption, in particular by increasing the share of renewable energy in the energy mix and improving energy efficiency.[80] Depending on whether the focus is global, EU-wide or local, the energy transition is also anticipated to further several other objectives, ranging from improvement of the security of the energy supply to stimulating different technology innovations. The boost given to the use of clean technology by supporting a sustainable business approach includes, apart from energy efficiency and carbon mitigation, resource reduction and management, pollution control, end of life strategy and waste reduction. Because energy markets within the EU have traditionally evolved around the supply side where (national) monopoly energy companies produce energy from conventional energy sources (fossil fuels), energy transitions require a major shift in the whole ideology underpinning energy production and energy markets.[81]

Although the challenge of energy transition is global, it is being addressed at EU level under the Energy Union framework.[82] The so-called Clean Energy Package has finally been adopted. The rules under the Clean Energy Package reflect the technological, societal and political developments that must be taken into consideration in the changing energy landscape.

79 J. P. Stern, *Competition and Liberalization in European Gas Markets: A Diversity of Models* (The Royal Institute of International Affairs, Energy and Environmental Programme 1998), pp. 174–175.

80 For an overview, see S.-L. Penttinen, 'Sustainability in the Energy Sector: Policy Directions and Implementing Measures', 3 (16) *Oil, Gas and Energy Law, Special Issue in International Energy Law* (2018), pp. 1–22.

81 I. Mersinia and S.-L. Penttinen, 'Introduction: Examining Different Aspects of the Energy Transition', in S. L. Penttinen and I. Mersinia, *Energy Transitions: Regulatory and Policy Trends* (Intersentia 2017), p. 1.

82 Communication from the Commission to the European Parliament, the Council, the European Economic and Social Committee, the Committee of the Regions and the European Investment Bank, 'A Framework Strategy for a Resilient Energy Union with a Forward-Looking Climate Change Policy' COM (2015) 80 final.

6

REGULATION OF ELECTRICITY MARKETS IN EUROPE IN LIGHT OF THE CLEAN ENERGY PACKAGE

Prosumers and demand response

Ignacio Herrera Anchustegui and Andreas Formosa*

1 Introduction

In this chapter we aim to present an introduction to the regulation of energy markets in Europe with a focus on the upcoming legislative acts being adopted through the Clean Energy Package (CEP) – a series of Directives and Regulations that were adopted in 2018 and 2019 to modernize European electricity markets, with a particular focus on decarbonisation and enabling the participation of active consumers.

Traditionally, European energy market regulation has dealt with electricity and gas from a market-oriented perspective in an effort to create a common internal energy market to foster economic efficiency, security of supply and competitiveness.[1] To a lesser extent, European Union (EU) law also deals with oil, shale gas and other unconventional hydrocarbons – industries outside of this chapter's scope.[2] The content of EU energy market regulation initially focused on the transition from public monopolies of vertically integrated energy companies to a competitive market. This topic is discussed in detail by Pentinnen in Chapter 6, which focuses on the grant of access to essential infrastructure.[3] The new set of rules contained in the CEP go

* This contribution has been written as part of the research project "Regulating Energy Markets, a Perspective from EEA/EU Competition and Public Procurement Law", thanks to the financial support of the AkademiaAvtalen programme between the University of Bergen and Equinor ASA. Also, I would like to thank the E.ON Stipendienfonds for their financial support which made possible my visit to the Max Planck Institute for Research on Collective Goods, where part of this research was done.

1 Explanatory memorandum of the European Commission to the proposed rules of the Clean Energy Package, Proposal for a Regulation of the European Parliament and of the Council on the Internal Market for Electricity (Recast) 2016/0379 (COD), p. 1–3.

2 See concerning these: Directive 94/22/EC on the conditions for granting and using authorizations for the prospection, exploration and production of hydrocarbons [1994] OJ L 164/30; Directive 2013/30/EU on safety of offshore oil and gas operations [2013] OJ L 178/66.

3 See also: Ignacio Herrera Anchustegui, 'Transmission Networks in Electricity Competition: Third-Party Access and Unbundling – a Transatlantic Perspective', in J.I. Ruiz Peris and Carmen María Cerdá Martínez-Pujalte (eds), *Competencia en mercados con recursos esenciales compartidos: telecomunicaciones y energía* (Aranzadi 2019).

a step further in the strengthening of the Energy Union,[4] and they seek to adapt the rules dealing with electricity, renewable energy sources, energy efficiency and regulatory energy agencies to speed up the technological changes we have witnessed over the past decade in Europe.

Two factors are key in understanding the reasons behind the regulatory changes and the content of the CEP, which we discuss in this chapter. Energy markets in Europe have been and currently are being transformed as a result of the integration of renewables into the grid. This brings about technical and legal challenges for the transition to "smart markets" in energy as already seen in 2011 by the German Bundesnetzagentur.[5] These changes in generation and consumption require that the market sends the right signals to guide both the generation, consumption and transmission patterns for the future grid. The second guiding element of the CEP is also connected to those technological changes as they now have made possible the active participation of the end-consumer as a responsive and responsible 'prosumer'.

2 EU energy law in a nutshell – before and after the Lisbon Treaty

2.1 Introduction

The core of EU energy regulation deals with the creation of an internal market as a shared competence of the EU and the Member States.[6] Despite energy being at the centre of European integration history with the creation of the European Coal and Steel Community and the Atomic Energy Treaty, it was not until the 1990s that energy matters began to be regulated at a European level as we discuss in section 2.2.[7] For the first time in the Treaty of Lisbon, EU primary law includes an explicit provision granting specific powers to the EU to develop an energy policy for the establishment and functioning of the internal market and improvement of the environmental conditions in its Article 194. Article 194 of the Treaty on the Functioning of the European Union (TFEU) serves as a complement to the general provision that allowed energy regulation to take place through the EU's powers to regulate the internal market in what it is now Article 114 TFEU.

Traditionally EU energy law has focused on the transformation of energy markets, aiming at the creation of competitive markets replacing monopolistic provision of utilities services, often done by a publicly owned national company. This opening up to effective competition started in the late 1980s and continues today with several 'packages' of energy liberalisation focusing on electricity and natural gas, primarily, but also applying to rules on energy efficiency, emission trading schemes and even regulatory agencies. This liberalisation and faith in markets to bring about the benefits of better provision of energy services to consumers does not imply a reduction of the regulation of EU energy markets, in fact, the reality is the opposite. The move to authorising competition in energy markets and regulating this competition at the community and the national level, in a balance between uniformity and room for the fulfilment of national objectives and suiting national conditions,[8] has led to an extensive, detailed and complex amount of regulation, not the absence of it.[9]

4 Communication from the European Commission, *A Framework Strategy for a Resilient Energy Union with a Forward-Looking Climate Change Policy* [* COM/2015/080 final *], (25 February 2015).

5 Bundesnetzagentur, Smart Grid and Smart Market: Summary of the BNetzA Position Paper (Discussion Paper, December 2011).

6 Article 4(2)(i) Treaty of the Functioning of the European Union.

7 K. Talus, *Introduction to EU Energy Law* (Oxford University Press 2016), p. 4.

8 Jacopo Torriti, Mohamed G. Hassan and Matthew Leach, 'Demand Response Experience in Europe: Policies, Programmes and Implementation' 35 *Energy* (2010), p. 1576.

9 Talus (n. 7), p. 4.

In more recent years, with the notable exception of the no longer in force Directive 2001/77/EC on Renewable Energy Sources from 2001, EU energy regulation has extended its scope of action not only to 'energy markets' but also to the fostering of renewable energies, environmental aspects of energy policy and energy efficiency. This is a trend that continues with the rules brought by the CEP (Section 3) and which influences energy market regulation, with the examples of prosumers and demand response we discuss in Section 4.

2.2 EU internal energy market: from national monopolies to a (green and renewable-oriented) Energy Union

2.2.1 First Energy Package

The first legislative move towards an integrated and European-regulated energy market took place with the adoption of the First Energy Package of 1996 and 1998 in electricity[10] and natural gas,[11] respectively. This first attempt was not ambitious in its scope but revolutionary in trying to shift national markets dominated by state-controlled energy vertically integrated undertakings which had exclusive rights to operate in the designated territory. These first European rules focused on access rules to transmission and distribution infrastructure (negotiated or regulated), rules on construction of generation capacity, and basic unbundling demands for energy undertakings. The attempt was to force Member States to open up their internal energy markets to competition and to allow for an internal energy market. These basic rules were insufficient but a gradual step towards authorizing and making energy competition a reality in Europe.

2.2.2 Second Energy Package

In 2003, the Second Energy Package, including rules on electricity,[12] natural gas[13] and access to cross-border network infrastructure, was adopted.[14] These rules built upon their predecessors and contained more detailed and mandatory provisions for Member States concerning unbundling and access to infrastructure. Also, for the first time, they included rules concerning national energy market regulators, and a regulatory framework for cross-border interconnectors.

2.2.3 Third Energy Package

Yet, the rules concerning the creation of a workable and open energy market in Europe were insufficient. Several aspects were still under-developed and an attempt was made to remedy them in the comprehensive and ambitious Third Energy Package of 2009. This package, with most of its rules still in force, went beyond its predecessors by imposing stricter rules to foster well-functioning wholesale energy markets and also to regulate with special interest energy competition in the retail market. It also expanded the scope of EU energy regulation,

10 Directive 96/92/EC concerning common rules for the internal market in electricity [1997] OJ L27/20.
11 Directive 98/30/EC concerning common rules for the internal market in natural gas [1998] OJ L204/1.
12 Directive 2003/55/EC concerning common rules for the internal market in natural gas [2003] OJ L176/57.
13 Directive 2003/54/EC concerning common rules for the internal market in electricity [2003] OJ L176/37.
14 Regulation 1228/2003/EC on conditions for access to the network for cross-border exchanges in electricity [2003] OJ L 176/1.

covering, in addition to the electricity and natural gas internal markets, other aspects related to energy markets in order to move towards a more integrated regulation, integration and promotion of renewable energy sources and environmental aspects, aspects which continue and are developed further by the CEP.

The electricity[15] and gas[16] directives included stricter (yet not mandatory) ownership unbundling rules on transmission networks as well as provisions regarding national regulators. They also included two regulations dealing with revised rules on access to natural gas networks,[17] and cross-border exchanges in electricity[18] were adopted to further the integration of energy markets in Europe.

Moreover, the regulatory aspect of EU energy law was strengthened with the creation of the Agency for the Cooperation of Energy Regulators (ACER), a European entity that helps national regulators in the adoption of issues with cross-border interest, has powers to decide cross-border matters, draft guidelines for the operation of cross-border infrastructure and ensure the well-functioning of energy markets.[19] The powers of ACER were complemented in 2011 with the duty to ensure market integrity and transparency in wholesale markets – sharing competition competences with the EU Commission – through the REMIT Regulation.[20]

In connection with the Third Energy Package, EU legislation has adopted other legislative instruments that regulate more specific energy aspects connected to environmental issues. These documents support the creation of a true Energy Union, a comprehensive project launched in 2015 in which energy market regulation is one of the elements of a medium to long-term plan based on security, sustainability, competitive and affordable energy.[21] Some of these instruments deal with the setting up of the European Emission Trading System, setting an emission cap that diminishes over time and creating a market for the purchase of emission allowances.[22] Also, rules concerning energy efficiency, renewable energy and national energy and climate were adopted, which now have been revised under the CEP, having entered into force in 2018. These rules are contained in the revised Renewable Energy Directive that seeks to achieve a binding target of 32 per cent EU-wide renewable energy generation;[23] the Energy Efficiency Directive, setting an energy efficiency target in goods, the energy system, buildings, billing and tariffs and energy-saving schemes of 32.5 per cent;[24] and the Governance Regulation with requirements for Member States to draw up and implement national energy and climate plans on how to achieve the efficiency and renewable targets.[25]

15 Directive 2009/72/EC concerning common rules for the internal market in electricity [2009] OJ L211/55.

16 Directive 2009/73/EC concerning common rules for the internal market in natural gas [2009] OJ L211/94.

17 Regulation 715/2009/EC on conditions for access to the natural gas transmission networks [2009] OJ L211/36.

18 Regulation 714/2009/EC on conditions for access to the network for cross-border exchanges in electricity [2009] OJ L211/15.

19 Regulation 713/2009/EC establishing an agency for the cooperation of energy regulators [2009] OJ L211/1.

20 Regulation 1227/2011/EU on wholesale energy market integrity and transparency [2011] OJ L326/1.

21 European Commission, Energy Union: secure, sustainable, competitive, affordable energy for every European, 25 February 2015. See also the latest Report on the State of the Energy Union from November 2017, COM(2017) 688 final.

22 Directive 2003/87/EC establishing a system for greenhouse gas emission allowance trading within the Union [2003] OJ L/275/32 last amended by Directive 2018/410 [2018] OJ L76/3.

23 Directive 2018/2001 on the promotion of the use of energy from renewable sources [2018] OJ L328/82.

24 Directive 2018/2002 on energy efficiency [2018] OJ L328/210.

25 Regulation 2018/1999/EU on the governance of the Energy Union and Climate Action [2018] OJ L328/1.

3 CEP revamps the EU energy markets' rulebook

3.1 Why reform?

Section 2 described the EU energy market landscape, which has been liberalised progressively since the 1990s through three energy packages. These packages focused on the harmonisation and liberalisation of energy markets with a particular accent on wholesale markets and the unbundling rules. Yet, the focus of policy-makers has been steadily shifting towards retail competition and the active participation of consumers in energy markets, largely prompted by technological development such as digitalisation.

Despite the Third Energy Package bringing in sweeping reforms, as mentioned above, it was considered (even at the time) that future legislation would be needed. The 2009 package was drafted just before the digital "revolution", the boom in solar and wind energy, and the rise of the "prosumer" model. The CEP therefore follows in a long line of liberalisation and harmonisation packages. The CEP does, however, differ from previous packages in two key ways. First, the CEP does not focus as much on headline grabbing binding targets for renewable energy and energy efficiency.[26] The CEP adopts more market-based arrangements, focuses more on the empowerment of the end-consumer and introduces legislation to strengthen the role of ACER. Secondly, the CEP is much broader than previous packages, and does not only cover market liberalisation and harmonisation, it also includes policies on renewables, energy efficiency and heating. Where the CEP deals with electricity and gas markets, the policies are more focused on market design with a much wider remit than the Third Energy Package. The substantial new rules on capacity mechanisms and procurement of ancillary services are a case in point. It is probably for this reason, i.e. the wider remit, that the CEP was not named the "Fourth Energy Package".

3.2 Legal basis

EU institutions are only empowered to adopt laws which they have the legal competence to enact. The First, Second and Third Energy Packages were all adopted before the Lisbon Treaty, which created a chapter dedicated to the energy competence of the EU, and thus relied on the internal market legal basis.

The legal basis for the CEP is Article 194 of the TFEU, which consolidated and clarified the competences of the EU in the field of energy, establishing an area of shared competences between the Union and the Member States. Article 194 TFEU states the main aims of the EU's energy policy, which are to: ensure the functioning of the energy market; ensure security of energy supply in the EU; promote energy efficiency and energy saving and the development of new and renewable forms of energy; and promote the interconnection of energy networks.

3.3 Brief overview of changes

The CEP is a package of legislation dealing with energy and climate policies. As the European Commission ("the Commission") has stated,[27] the CEP has three main goals: putting

26 The 2007 climate and energy package introduced the "famous" 2020 targets of a 20 per cent reduction in greenhouse gases, 20 per cent of EU energy to come from renewables and a 20 per cent improvement in energy efficiency.

27 See https://ec.europa.eu/energy/en/topics/energy-strategy-and-energy-union/clean-energy-all-europeans.

energy efficiency first; achieving global leadership in renewable energies; and providing a fair deal for consumers. To achieve its three goals, the Commission proposed revising the following eight pieces of legislation, which were adopted during the course of 2018 and 2019:

1. Energy Performance in Buildings Directive;
2. Renewable Energy Directive;
3. Energy Efficiency Directive;
4. Governance of the Energy Union Regulation;
5. Electricity Regulation;
6. Electricity Directive;
7. Risk-Preparedness Regulation; and
8. ACER Regulation.

Much of the CEP builds on the policies of previous energy packages, which had already laid the foundations for a liberalised, integrated European electricity and gas market. Therefore, what the CEP aims to do is primarily twofold. It is responding to dramatic changes in energy technology and its associated cost reductions; and secondly it is trying to integrate the "demand side" of the equation[28] into the market. The Commission, as a proponent of market-based measures, attempts to rely as much as possible on market-based solutions rather than on large subsidy regimes which have underpinned many of EU Member States' renewable energy policies since 2010.

There are, however, elements of the CEP that are new to EU energy market legislation. The draft Governance Regulation[29] is the first time that governance of the EU's single energy market is consolidated into one legislative text, which includes the obligations and targets of all Member States. The Governance Regulation arguably creates more clarity and certainty in the direction of travel of EU policy in the energy field.[30] The Recast ACER Regulation, while building on the 2012 Regulation, goes a step further by creating a more powerful pan-European regulatory agency.[31] It also for the first time creates "Regional Operation Centres", which some argue may eventually lead to regional or a "pan-European ISO (independent system operator)".[32]

28 See Section 6 for more detail on demand response.

29 Regulation on the Governance of the Energy Union, amending Directive 94/22/EC, Directive 98/70/EC, Directive 2009/31/EC, Regulation 663/2009/EC, Regulation 715/2009/EC, Directive 2009/73/EC, Council Directive 2009/119/EC, Directive 2010/31/EU, Directive 2012/27/EU, Directive 2013/30/EU and Council Directive 2015/652/EU and repealing Regulation 525/2013/EU.

30 Some commentators have argued that the proposed Governance Regulation does not go far enough by focusing purely on administrative reporting, monitoring and verification, rather than creating a robust framework acting as a tangible driver to achieve the energy transition. See: https://institutdelors.eu/wp-content/uploads/2018/01/ch1-makingtheenergytransitionaeuropeansuccess-study-pellerincarlinfernandesrubio-june2017.pdf.

31 Under the existing ACER Regulation, ACER, the pan-EU regulatory agency, lacks any robust enforcement powers of its own and largely relies on Member State agencies and the European Commission to introduce policies and enforce against non-compliance.

32 Regional Operational Centres are intended to complement the role of transmission system operators (TSOs) by performing functions of regional relevance and coordinating activities of TSOs in defined regions in the EU.

4 Transforming retail markets through renewable energy integration and consumer participation

4.1 *Introduction*

EU energy market regulation has traditionally focused on the opening up and effective competition in wholesale energy markets for electricity and natural gas. However, EU regulation of retail markets has kept growing since the Third Energy Package, covering aspects such as the opening up of retail competition, setting minimum consumer rights and protection, rules on energy poverty and rules on consumer participation in the market as 'prosumers' or 'active customers'.[33] This new bottom-up energy market focus (and regulation) has two main drivers: technological changes that allow for active consumer participation, and the insertion of renewable energy generation.[34]

On the one hand, new technologies have made possible the economically viable and efficient generation of renewable energy sources on a large scale, with the EU seeking to have up to 32 per cent of its energy production based on renewable energy. The integration of these green but variable energy sources plays an important role in the generation mix and affects short-term energy markets (balancing and intraday) due to their variability and difficulty in forecasting. On the other hand, consumers are no longer passive recipients of energy supply but can and have become producers of their own (and other's) energy by being a 'prosumer', for example by using a rooftop solar panel on top of a residential home, storing energy in household or electric car batteries and/ or selling the energy produced on their own premises.

4.2 *A glimpse into the electricity retail market in light of the CEP*

The CEP contains new and updated provisions with an important impact on the functioning of retail markets. As with its predecessor legislation, European electricity retail markets remain open to competition in all Member States, with prices being primarily based on demand and supply and free choice of electricity supplier across the whole internal market.[35] This is not the case in all international markets, with the US being an example where retail competition is the exception and not the rule.[36] This does not mean, however, that dynamic pricing is the only option available for end consumers in the EU. Despite attempts by the Commission to get rid of fixed tariffs, Member States are free to allow for rate-based tariffs as well as special rules and prices concerning energy poor users.[37]

33 The latter is the term employed in the proposal for an Electricity Directive, Article 2(6). See also its Article 15.

34 Explanatory memorandum of the European Commission to the proposed rules of the Clean Energy Package, Proposal for a Regulation on the Internal Market for Electricity (Recast) 2016/0379 (COD), p. 2–3.

35 Article 3, Regulation (EU) 2019/943 on the internal market for electricity (OJ [2019] L 158/54) ("Recast Electricity Regulation"), and Articles 3 and 4, Directive 2019/944 of the European Parliament and of the Council of 5 June 2019 on common rules for the internal market for electricity and amending Directive 2012/27/EU (OJ [2019] L 158/125) ("Recast Electricity Directive").

36 See, inter alia: Scott Hempling, *Regulating Public Utility Performance: The Law of Market Structure, Pricing and Jurisdiction* (American Bar Association 2015); Severin Borenstein and James Bushnell, 'The US Electricity Industry After 20 Years of Restructuring" (2015) 7 *Annual Review of Economics* 437; Kenneth Rose, 'The State of Retail Electricity Markets in the U.S', 17 *The Electricity Journal* (2004), p. 26.

37 Article 5, Recast Electricity Directive.

Furthermore, the provisions concerning consumer empowerment and protection have been revised with several substantive changes and new provisions included in Chapter III of the Recast Electricity Directive. As stated by the Directive itself, these changes aim at "putting consumers at the heart of the energy market" in a complex balance of rights, alternatives and even responsibilities as system users.[38] Thus, the aim of the new regulation is to transform energy retailing through the empowerment of consumers to also facilitate the incorporation of renewable and intermittent energy. Among the new rules included in the Recast Electricity Directive, Article 10 sets some minimum contractual rights and provider obligations. Related to this and derived from the need to foster demand-side management solutions like demand response, the Directive creates a right for consumers to have a "dynamic electricity price contract" (Article 11) and the ability of customers to switch suppliers without surcharge fees (Article 12). Also, minimum requirements are set concerning billing of end consumers to facilitate their comprehension of charges (Article 18). The new electricity retail rules also allow consumers to enter into contracts with aggregators (Article 13) and form local energy communities (Article 16), topics which we discuss below in more detail. The new provisions also deal extensively with demand response possibilities and metering, including smart meters (Articles 17, 19, 20 and 22, and discussed in *extenso* below).

In the remainder of this chapter, we focus on the evolution of passive consumers to prosumers and demand response programmes and regulation using the CEP and the on-going European experiences as examples of this transformation of retail markets across the Member States.

5 Evolution from consumer to prosumer

5.1 Consumers at the heart of the energy market

One of the defining characteristics of the CEP, and in particular, the communications documents published with the legislative proposals, is to emphasise the critical role of putting consumers at the "heart of the energy market". To understand the role of the prosumer in the CEP, it is first necessary to understand what a prosumer is. As described by Kotilainen and Saari, the concept of the prosumer has its roots in the work of Toffler, who despite not having energy markets in mind was referring to the consumption and production of technology products and services.[39] The European Parliamentary Research Service (EPRS) has broadly defined "electricity prosumers" as "consumers who both produce and consume electricity".[40] It goes go on to describe in further detail that prosumers "self-consume" some of the electricity they produce but sell the excess production to the market. As prosumers are still connected to the public network, when their own production is low, they will import electricity from the grid, thus being consumers at certain times, and producers at other times.

The EPRS[41] divides prosumers into four categories:

1. Residential prosumers: consumers who produce their own electricity, for example with rooftop PV panels

38 Explanatory memorandum of the European Commission to the proposed rules of the Clean Energy Package, Proposal for a Regulation on the Internal Market for Electricity (Recast) 2016/0379 (COD), 4–5.

39 Kirsi Kotilainen and Ulla A Saari, 'Policy Influence on Consumers' Evolution into Prosumers—Empirical Findings from an Exploratory Survey in Europe', 10 *Sustainability* (2018), p. 186.

40 Briefing produced by Nikolina Šajn for the members of the European Parliamentary Research Service, November 2016.

41 Ibid, p. 2.

2. Community/cooperative energy: consumer led cooperatives with community owned generators, such as solar photovoltaic panels, wind turbines or combined heat and power
3. Commercial prosumers: businesses whose main business is not electricity production; however, they reduce their energy bills by installing generators such as rooftop PV, combined heat and power (CHP) and diesel generators, and may participate in demand response
4. Public prosumers: public sector buildings that invest in similar technology to commercial prosumers.

The rise in the prosumer model has arguably come about for three main reasons. The first is economic. The fall in the costs of installing and maintaining solar PV systems, for example, has dropped dramatically since large-scale subsidies were introduced approximately a decade ago. The fall in costs has largely been due to the generous subsidies on offer in various EU Member States, such as Germany and Spain,[42] as well as the low rate of exchange of the Chinese RMB. Consumers could not only take advantage of schemes such as feed-in-tariffs, under which they were paid an above market rate for their power, but the increase in demand lowered the overall cost of PV systems for all consumers as a result of economies of scale in factories in Europe and Asia, which made such systems even more affordable. More recently, due to the drop in costs of battery storage (and other storage systems such as heat pumps), storage systems are also being taken up by energy savvy prosumers, particularly in countries where electricity prices are quite high.[43] Secondly, individual consumers' awareness of the benefits of renewable energy, vis-à-vis the threat of climate change has created a genuine interest among consumers to produce and consume energy from renewables. This trend is demonstrated by a recent survey and report from price comparison website, "Money Supermarket", which found that 13 per cent of all British consumers were on green energy tariffs.[44] Even consumers who are not prosumers are voting with their wallet by signing up to renewable only tariffs with their energy suppliers. Finally, trust in incumbent utilities in some EU Member States[45] is very low, and many individuals feel empowered by producing their own energy, even if it is costlier than importing from the public grid.

Some Member States, including Denmark and the UK, have responded to the growing demand for distributed generation (DG) by businesses and consumers, and have facilitated consumers and businesses transitioning to a prosumer model. The Danish experience serves as a good case-study for the growth in DG. As part of the Danish Government's plan to completely decarbonize the energy system by 2050, the Government introduced policies to support and incentivise the growth in onshore wind (which in Denmark is typically connected to the distribution grid), and electricity and heat generation from combined heat and power (CHP) plants. These two sources now supply approximately 100 per cent of Danish peak demand.[46]

42 For example, at their peak in Spain in 2008, domestic consumers with PV panels could earn €340/MWh compared to wholesale market prices of around €65/MWh.

43 Of note is the fact that the uptake of storage systems has not been driven by subsidies in most countries.

44 https://www.moneysupermarket.com/gas-and-electricity/renewable-energy-home.

45 Second consumer market study on the functioning of the retail electricity markets for consumers in the EU, European Commission, September 2016.

46 S. Ropenus & H. Jacobsen Klinge 'A Snapshot of the Danish Energy Transition. Objectives, Markets, Grid, Support Schemes and Acceptance. Study' (Agora Energiewende 2015). The other major sources of electricity generation in Denmark are thermal power plants and offshore wind energy. Denmark's total installed power capacity exceeds its total demand and therefore it regularly exports the excess power to neighbouring countries through numerous interconnectors.

The Commission, inspired by the rise of prosumers, and perhaps by prosumer-friendly regulations in countries such as Denmark, the UK,[47] and Germany, put the consumer, and by extension the prosumer at the heart of much of the CEP. One of the Commission's primary considerations in introducing the CEP was to integrate all types of consumers into energy markets, as they recognised that integrating the demand side is the only way of truly creating a smart grid and reaping the benefits of a renewables-focused energy mix. As the Commission described in its publication on the CEP proposal, "(a)ctivating consumer participation is therefore a prerequisite for managing the energy transition successfully and in a cost-effective way".[48] For example, the Recast Renewable Energy Directive (RED II) has introduced for the first time a definition of "renewable energy communities"[49] as well as a definition of "renewable self-consumption".[50] The RED has also introduced additional rights for energy cooperatives within national renewables support schemes. Perhaps one of the most impactful additions of the Recast RED is Article 21 which ensures that households who self-consume from renewable electricity sources without feeding that electricity into the public grid are exempt from disproportionate procedures or grid charges that are not cost-reflective. Significant grid charges for the export of excess on-site generation has perhaps been one of the primary reasons the uptake of DG by consumers has been slower than it could have been. By prohibiting this charge, one would expect the proliferation of DG ownership among consumers, and hence a rise in prosumers.

5.2 *Ancillary services and distributed generation aggregation*

Electricity, unlike other forms of energy, cannot be stored easily or cheaply. This means the electricity grid has to remain balanced in real time so that demand for electricity perfectly matches the supply of electricity.[51] The role of balancing the grid has largely been carried out by Transmission System Operators (also known as TSOs) or similar organisations. Historically this function of the TSO was a straightforward task as it was relatively easy to predict supply and demand on any given day.[52] Generation was largely centralised (and therefore "dispatchable"),[53] thermal, nuclear or large hydro, while supply was inelastic. With the exponential rise of variable renewable energy coupled with advances in digital technology that allow consumers to actively participate in energy markets, the role of balancing the grid has changed and become more challenging for traditional TSOs.

47 The British experience with the embedded generation is also very interesting. Strong network charging incentives grew the sector exponentially until the energy regulator, Ofgem, decided that these incentives were not cost-reflective and significantly scaled them back. See also: https://www.ofgem.gov.uk/publications-and-updates/embedded-benefits-impact-assessment-and-decision-industry-proposals-cmp264-and-cmp265-change-electricity-transmission-charging-arrangements-embedded-generators.

48 Proposal for a Regulation on the Internal Market for Electricity (Recast) COM/2016/0861 final – 2016/0379 (COD).

49 Article 2(16) and Article 22, Directive 2018/2001 on the promotion of the use of energy from renewable sources.

50 "Renewable self-consumption" means the generation and consumption, and, where applicable, storage of renewable electricity by renewable self consumers.

51 Andreas Formosa, 'The Regulation of Demand Side Resources to Support the Energy Transition', in Vicente López Ibor Mayor (ed), *Clean Energy Law and Regulation* (Wildy, Simmonds & Hill 2017), p. 137.

52 For example, see: https://www.entsoe.eu/fileadmin/user_upload/_library/position_papers/111104_RESBalancing_final.pdf.

53 A "dispatchable" source of power generation means that it can be turned on or off, and, importantly, it can be dispatched at the request of power system operations.

Ancillary services[54] are the services[55] procured by TSOs from power generators under a market framework (at least in the EU) to be able to balance the electricity grid. As mentioned above, as grids become increasingly dominated by variable renewable energy, the importance and value of ancillary services rises. For example, the cost in the UK of balancing charges[56] has risen from £746m in 2010[57] to £1.19bb in 2018 and are expected to keep rising. The growth in importance of ancillary services also coincides with the closure of thermal power stations that have traditionally provided these services. These market dynamics have created an enormous opportunity for new innovative technologies such as battery storage and demand response to participate in ancillary services markets. As these technologies are predominantly located on the distribution rather than the transmission network, and are often even in "behind the meter"[58] settings, this has created a unique opportunity for prosumers.

The EU began liberalising and harmonising the regulation of ancillary services following the introduction of the Electricity Regulation, which provided for the development of implementing network regulations ("European Network Codes"),[59] aimed at detailing the complex rules of cross-border electricity and gas trading, including at the balancing services level. For example, the Regulation establishing a guideline for electricity balancing[60] imposes market-based rules on TSOs when procuring ancillary services and creates voluntary pan-EU balancing markets that are co-administered by participating national TSOs. As with most aspects of EU electricity legislation, the CEP builds upon the Third Energy Package and European Network Codes that emerged from the Electricity Regulation.

The CEP has done this by clarifying the status of such services, through definitions of previously undefined terms;[61] by requiring that such services be market driven (rather than at the discretion of the TSO) and open to all forms of flexibility (including demand response); and by creating new obligations on distribution system operators (DSOs) to procure equivalent ancillary services on their distribution networks. The combination of these legislative proposals is extremely significant. The CEP has recognised the value of flexibility in non-traditional resources, but it has also recognised the critical role that the DSO will play in balancing the system (alongside the TSO) as more flexible generation and demand is located on the distribution network. This is yet another route to market for prosumers.

The CEP introduces provisions to ensure there is a level playing field in ancillary services, a market that has been historically dominated by a small group of traditional thermal energy generators. For example, Article 17 of the Recast Electricity Directive creates an obligation on Member States to ensure that both TSOs and DSOs treat demand response providers in a non-discriminatory manner when creating the technical rules for the participation in

54 Directive 2009/72/EC defines ancillary service as "a service necessary for the operation of a transmission or distribution system".

55 These services are also known by other names such as "balancing services" or "grid services".

56 These charges recover the cost of system operation and balancing.

57 Michael Joos and Iain Staffell, 'Short-Term Integration Costs of Variable Renewable Energy: Wind Curtailment and Balancing in Britain and Germany', 86 *Renewable and Sustainable Energy Reviews* (2018), pp. 45–65.

58 This refers to flexible load being located on a customer's premises, i.e. behind the meter interfacing the grid, rather than standalone power generation or electricity storage.

59 European Network Codes are legally binding European Commission Implementing Regulations, which govern all cross-border electricity market transactions and system operations.

60 Commission Regulation 2017/2195/EU of 23 November 2017 establishing a guideline on electricity balancing.

61 The Recast Electricity Directive in Article 2 introduces the definition of "ancillary service", which is "a service necessary for the operation of a transmission or distribution system including balancing and non-frequency ancillary services but not congestion management".

ancillary service procurement, as we discuss further in Section 6. In many Member States, explicit discrimination (i.e. a ban on certain technologies participating) is rare, however, the technical specifications used by TSOs have in many cases prohibited demand response and DG from participating, without objective reasons. In most cases this phenomenon is due to antiquated rules not keeping up with technological advances.[62] The Commission has therefore clearly acknowledged this market barrier when drafting the CEP package of legislation.

6 Demand response

6.1 Introduction

While demand response (DR) regulation – a demand side management mechanism that seeks to alter electricity consumption with respect to price variations – is not novel to EU electricity regulation, the downstream and consumer centric approach of the CEP has placed an important emphasis on the regulation of it. This includes new and more detailed rules than before as well as "codifying these" mostly in the Recast Electricity Directive and the Regulation on the Internal Market for Electricity, and no longer in the Energy Efficiency Directive, as it was in the Third Energy Package.[63] The 2012 Energy Efficiency Directive included some basic demands for Member States not to hamper DR participation by setting unnecessary requirements, promoting the use of dynamic tariffs, ensuring that DR was able to participate along with supply on an equal footing in wholesale and retail markets, and included the possibility of DR aggregation. However, the Directive was very succinct and insufficient.[64]

At a national level, the rules have been very varied and few programmes have been implemented,[65] meaning the adoption of DR by electricity users has been low in Europe.[66] This is explained by a myriad factors, including a traditional preference of the EU to resort to measures dealing with energy efficiency and electricity generation rather than demand side management tools, maintaining tariff caps, non-variable electricity prices, lack of technology to facilitate consumer response and a focus on market liberalisation as a priority.[67] This trend and the role given by the EU to DR has changed. In the CEP, demand response has a more relevant role as a demand side management mechanism built around the notion of prosumers, dynamic tariffs and of mart metering to bring flexibility into the system and also prevent price spikes.[68] A change for good reasons. DR can bring about huge economic benefits representing an energy saving of between a 10 and 15 per cent, optimising the use of resources and bringing flexibility to the system.[69] Moreover, from a policy perspective,

62 For a more detailed discussion on the non-explicit barriers to demand side resources participating in electricity markets see Formosa (n 51).

63 Directive 2009/125/EC, amended by Directive 2012/27/EU on energy efficiency (OJ [2012] L 315/1).

64 See, for example, Recitals (44), (45), Article 15.4. and 15.8 of the Directive 2012/27/EU on energy efficiency OJ [2012] L315/1.

65 Nikolaos G. Paterakis, Ozan Erdinç and João P. S. Catalão, 'An overview of Demand Response: Key-elements and International Experience', 69 *Renewable and Sustainable Energy Reviews* (2017), pp. 883–884.

66 Torriti, Hassan and Leach (n 8), p. 1578; Paterakis, Erdinç and Catalão (n 65).

67 Torriti, Hassan and Leach (n 8), p. 1582; International Energy Agency/Organisation for Economic Cooperation and Development, *The Power to Choose – Demand Response in Liberalised Electricity Markets* (OECD/IEA 2003), 1.

68 Article 3.1, Recast Electricity Directive.

69 Recitals (37), (42), (52), Recast Electricity Directive; Recitals (12), (30), Recast Electricity Regulation. See also: European Commission, 'Demand Response – Empowering the European Consumer', Smart Grids, *SETIS Magazine*, March 2014, available at: https://setis.ec.europa.eu/setis-reports/setis-magazine/smart-grids/demand-response-empowering-european-consumer, last visited 19 June 2019.

DR works well with two key aspects of the new regulatory framework: a push for further introduction of renewable sources of electricity generation – as it serves as an instrument to address issues of supply variability – and prosumers, as it allows them to have a dynamic, responsive and price-aware role.

6.2 *Defining benefits brought by, and regulating, demand response*

When customers are exposed to real-time prices, they may respond by either shifting the time of day at which they demand power to an off-peak period, and/or reducing their total or peak demand through energy efficiency measures or self-generation.[70] Price decreases as a consequence of the reduction in purchases because the electricity supply curve is upward sloping (the more it is supplied, the more expensive the unit will be due to capacity constraints). Therefore, a small reduction in demand of power can imply a large price decrease,[71] creating a monopsony like effect. This 'flattens' the load, limiting instances of peak times and market price volatility or shifting consumption when there is excess supply (and even negative electricity prices). Further benefits can be brought to the system as shifts of demand during peak times can reduce the need for higher marginal cost generation, offer lower cost system balancing, decrease grid reinforcement investment and bolster system reliability.[72] In addition, price reduction benefits users as a whole as it decreases electricity prices in general.[73] DR can also play a role in preventing market power exertion by pivotal electricity suppliers.[74] Thus, it is not surprising that DR is said to be "a win-win solution for all".[75] Additionally, DR facilitates renewable energy penetration as it helps to alleviate issues of over and under generation of these sources, balancing power fluctuation and decreasing the need for peak capacity generation.[76] For instance, if offshore wind electricity production is low in the North Sea, participants of a DR programme may shift their demand to another time of the day or reduce their demand altogether, instead of increasing production of non-renewable power plants.[77] DR now acts as a facilitator for more efficient use of renewable electricity and a sponsor of climate change mitigation at the EU level, but this role still needs to be pushed at the national level in order to be effective.[78]

6.2.1 *Legal definition and schemes*

The Recast Electricity Directive defines DR in similar terms as discussed above and largely follows established literature and other governmental definitions. It conceptualises DR as:

> the change of electricity load by final customers from their normal or current consumption patterns in response to market signals, including in response to time-variable

70 International Energy Agency/Organisation for Economic Cooperation and Development (n 67), 17.

71 Paterakis, Erdinç and Catalão (n 65), p. 877.

72 Torriti, Hassan and Leach (n 8), 1575; Anne Hoskins and Paul Roberti, 'The Essential Role of State Engagement in Demand Response' 40 *Harvard Environmental Law Review Forum* (2016), p. 14.

73 Niamh O'Connell, Pierre Pinson, Henrik Madsen & Mark O'Malley, 'Benefits and Challenges of Electrical Demand Response: A Critical Review' 39 *Renewable and Sustainable Energy Reviews* (2014), p. 690.

74 Paterakis, Erdinç and Catalão (n 65), p. 878.

75 European Commission, 'Incorporating Demand Side Flexibility, in Particular Demand Response, in Electricity Markets', accompanying the document 'Delivering the Internal Electricity Market and Making the Most of Public Intervention' SWD (2013) 442 final.

76 O'Connell and others (n 73), p. 687.

77 See also: Paterakis, Erdinç and Catalão (n 65), p. 876.

78 Torriti, Hassan and Leach (n 8), p. 1578.

> electricity prices or incentive payments, or in response to the acceptance of the final customer's bid to sell demand reduction or increase at a price in an organised market as defined in point (4) of Article 2 of Commission Implementing Regulation (EU) No 1348/20141, whether alone or through aggregation.[79]

The Directive includes three different options for using DR modalities.[80] First, a "price-based" or "indirect" DR in which variation in demand takes place due to price fluctuation (of power and/or transportation tariffs). For this to work, dynamic tariffs and active customers (i.e. customers willing to actively respond to price signals) are needed, although this may or may not require customers to adhere to commitments made to reduce consumption. Second, "incentive-based" DR can be implemented when the end user is remunerated for participating in a programme of load reduction usually organized by its electricity supplier, the TSO/DSO or an aggregator. This could take place in direct load control programmes (the utility sends more or less power to an appliance, typically done with heat tanks), or through curtailable load in which the consumers/participants receive a payment to alter their consumption pattern upon previous notification by the load controller. Third, a "direct" or "explicit" DR in which end consumers, individually or through aggregators, offer their availability (consume less or more) to the supplier or the TSO in exchange for a payment.

6.2.2 Demand response aggregation

An aggregator is a third party that pools the flexibility of electricity users and offers this availability to the market (a day ahead, intra-day, balancing or ancillary) in the form of load and offers it for sale, purchase or auction.[81] The aggregator might be a retailer of electricity or an independent party, and could aggregate load, generation or even storage, for which a preference for technology neutral definition is preferred.[82]

One of the most salient aspects of the regulation of DR in the CEP is the importance given to its aggregation to maximize effective consumer participation, as regulated by Article 17 of the Recast Electricity Directive. While not new, aggregation played a minor role in the Third Energy Package, and in some circumstances it was not practically feasible nor legal in some Member States.[83] According to Article 17, Member States should allow and promote DR activities through aggregators and allow final consumers (aggregated or not) to participate in all electricity markets. This requirement also extends to TSOs and DSOs when acquiring ancillary services as they are required to treat demand aggregated users on an equal footing with other forms of electricity supply.

The Recast Electricity Directive creates a set of minimum criteria the national regulation must comply with respect to DR aggregation.[84] Market participants have the right to engage in aggregation without the consent of others, Member States must enact non-discriminatory and clear rules concerning the roles and duties of the aggregators and customers, as well as

79 Article 2(20), Recast Electricity Directive.

80 Article 2(20), Recast Electricity Directive. For some literature discussing demand response modalities see, inter alia: P. Bertoldi, P. Zancanella, B. Boza-Kiss *Demand Response Status in EU Member States*; EUR 27998 EN; doi:10.2790/962868; Paterakis, Erdinç and Catalão (n 65), p. 873

81 Article 2(18) and (19), Recast Electricity Directive.

82 European Commission Workshop, 'The Potential of Electricity Demand Response', Brussels, 30 May 2017, p. 11.

83 Paterakis, Erdinç and Catalão (n 65), p. 884.

84 Article 17.3, Recast Electricity Directive.

non-discriminatory and transparent rules concerning the exchange of data. Further, they must ensure that aggregated market participants are financially responsible for the imbalances caused to the system by either being directly responsible for balancing or delegating it to a balance responsible party of their choice, according to the principle of balance responsibility of Article 5 of the Electricity Regulation. It is also forbidden for electricity suppliers to impose penalties or undue contractual restrictions on customers using independent aggregators, and Member States must create a dispute resolution mechanism between participants involved in aggregation and other market players.

6.2.3 Other regulatory aspects

The CEP governs other more general aspects of DR. For instance, the Energy Efficiency Directive requires the Commission – and Member States – to ensure that DR is able to compete on equal terms with generation, as a substitute and competitor for capacity.[85] Also, the Recast Electricity Directive requires electricity products on all markets, including short-term but also ancillary and capacity markets, to be defined in such a way as to encourage DR participation.[86] Further, DR also plays a role in the process of authorisation for new generation capacity. Member States must take it into account as an award criterion as it constitutes an alternative to new capacity.[87] DR must now be factored in when carrying out the European and national resource adequacy assessments required by the Electricity Regulation,[88] a role it also plays in the Commission's assessment of Capacity Remuneration mechanisms.[89] Furthermore, the CEP requires TSOs and DSOs to take into account DR availability and its full potential when developing their network plans.[90]

While in the majority of cases it is beneficial for system users, DR activation may cause balancing issues and generate costs for other players, such as generators or system operators. The Recast Electricity Directive recognises this and requires the payment of financial compensation by DR users with respect to the "costs incurred by the suppliers of participating customers or the suppliers' balance responsible parties during the activation of demand response".[91] Aggregators and consumers may be required to compensate other markets' participants if these "are affected by demand response activation". This payment mechanism is a reasonable requirement as other participants may have incurred purchases and/or costs as forecasted but that was not consumed due to DR.[92] The compensation calculation should take into account the benefits brought by the aggregators to the other participants, and it should not imply a market barrier for participants in aggregation or flexibility.

Another regulated aspect is the DR interaction with the General Data Protection Regulation (GDPR),[93] as remarked explicitly in Recital (91) of the Recast Electricity Directive. Personal data from end consumers engaged in DR will be under the scope of the

85 Recital (2) of the Directive (EU) 2018/2002 on Energy Efficiency [2018] OJ L328/210.
86 Recital (39), Recast Electricity Directive.
87 Article 9.2(l), Recast Electricity Directive.
88 Articles 23.5(d) and 24, Recast Electricity Regulation.
89 For a discussion of this issue see in this book Chapter 7 by Herrera Anchustegui and Bergqvist.
90 Articles 32 and 51.3, Recast Electricity Directive.
91 Article 17.4, Recast Electricity Directive.
92 European Commission Workshop (n 82) 5.
93 Regulation (EU) 2016/679 on the protection of natural persons with regard to the processing of personal data and on the free movement of such data [2016] OJ L119/1.

GDPR – just as smart meters that process personal data that allows parties to be identifiable will be.[94] The Recast Electricity Directive addresses these relationships through its Article 23 on data management rules, including data derived from DR. It is still unclear how cumbersome the management of personal data for aggregators and electricity undertakings result will be, to some degree, which may also impact the success of DR programs.

6.3 *Regulatory obstacles for DR*

Despite the clear advances made in the CEP concerning DR regulation, some legal hurdles remain for this demand-side management tool to be efficient and entice prosumers to engage in it. These remarks are not aimed so much at the existing EU regulation as at the national implementation of DR which will follow in the next few years.[95]

The most obvious obstacle to the integration of DR resources in the electricity markets structures is the absence of rules that relate to their participation in the electricity markets.[96] This is an issue that the CEP should solve, and even in the absence of national regulation, EU provisions would have a direct effect. Less obvious but perhaps more important is the need for dynamic tariffs and avoidance of price caps to incentivise consumers (especially large ones) to offer their flexibility to the system and avoid wrong market signals.[97] Therefore, governments and regulators should review their price and capping regulations and adjust (or eliminate) them so as not to impede DR programmes.[98]

Technical requirements are another important issue for DR implementation. Traditionally, regulators and system operators have developed requirements to be met by large users and generators, an issue that created problems for DR penetration.[99] Now that DR is to compete with other forms of supply and provide flexibility, the technical and administrative requirements should account for the characteristics of DR, without these being excessive.[100] Among the technical aspects to be considered by a regulator are: technical prequalification requirements, minimum bid size for individual and aggregated customers, bid direction, response times and frequency, duration of response, trading charges, fees, compensation mechanisms in light of Article 17.4 of the Recast Electricity Directive and which and how many DR programmes are available to parties.[101]

Another important barrier for DR is how to ensure its participation in all relevant markets. While the Third Energy Package was in place, DR was primarily active in "emergency contingency support and ancillary services, with limited participation in the day-ahead

94 See discussing more in general the interaction between the GDPR and active customers and smart metering: Alessandra Fratini and Giulia Pizza, 'Data protection and smart meters: the GDPR and the 'winter package' of EU clean energy law' (*EU Law Analysis*, 22 March 2018) http://eulawanalysis.blogspot.com/2018/03/data-protection-and-smart-meters-gdpr.html last visited on 12 June 2019; Dalhammar C and Hjärne A, 'The Use of Consumer Data to Optimize Smart Grids for Electricity and District Heating' [2018].

95 The Recast Electricity Directive and, therefore, its rules concerning demand respond should be duly implemented by 31 December 2020.

96 Paterakis, Erdinç and Catalão (n 65), p. 883

97 European Commission Workshop (n 82), p. 13.

98 International Energy Agency/Organization for Economic Cooperation and Development (n 67) 14.

99 Paterakis, Erdinç and Catalão (n 65), p. 884.

100 See, for example: Recital (61), Article 3.1, Article 17.2, and specially Article 17.5, Recast Electricity Directive. See also Article 6.1, Recast Electricity Regulation.

101 Paterakis, Erdinç and Catalão (n 65) 884; Paolo Bertoldi, Paolo Zancanella and Benigna Boza-Kiss 'Demand Response Status in EU Member States; JRC Science for Policy Report – European Commission' (2016), EUR 27998 EN; doi:10.2790/962868, p. 6.

market".[102] Therefore, not only should DR be active and allowed to participate in balancing markets,[103] but also in other short-term markets such as the day-ahead, intraday or ancillary markets without discrimination.[104]

7 Conclusion

EU energy law to date can be placed in two categories or two distinct "periods" which fall into: (1) the historic European Coal and Steel Community and the Atomic Energy Treaty created at the very beginning of the European Community; and (2) the three gas and electricity market liberalisation "packages" which were born out of a wider liberalisation agenda of the key utilities such as telecoms and postal services. The CEP arguably attempts to create a third and new category of EU energy law. As set out in section 3 of this chapter, the CEP, while building on the liberalisation and harmonisation goals of the three energy packages, has gone a step further. The CEP unlike its predecessors incorporates the EU's climate goals within the legislative package and puts it at its core, hence the name "Clean Energy Package for all Europeans" rather than the "Fourth Energy Package". For example, the CEP includes legislation on energy efficiency and renewable energy, which previously were under separate climate and energy legislative packages. The CEP is also being introduced during a period of rapid technological change, including digitisation, which has had the effect of blurring the lines between traditional generation and consumption of electricity and upstream and downstream electricity markets. Examples include flexibility solutions such as demand response and energy storage, the rise of prosumers and cost-competitive unsubsidised renewable energy generators. As described in section 4 of this chapter, these developments are probably most evident in retail markets where one can see these technologies and new business models converge, for example, retailers offering customers battery storage, power purchase agreements (PPAs) for their excess energy generation and flexible electric vehicle (EV) charging solutions. In our view, there will be two interesting things to look out for as the CEP is implemented. The first will be the approach Member States will take in transposing the Directives within the CEP, as much has been left to the discretion of national governments and regulators. Secondly, and perhaps more importantly, it will be interesting to see whether the CEP will signal a new category of EU energy law that is more holistic by including both market rules and climate action.

102 O'Connell and others (n 73), p. 690.

103 Article 6, Recast Electricity Regulation.

104 Article 7, Recast Electricity Regulation.

7

USES AND ABUSES OF EU COMPETITION LAW IN ENERGY

Christian Bergqvist and Ignacio Herrera Anchustegui

Providers of electricity and natural gas to the European markets are subject to European Union (EU) competition law and the obligations are directed to both public and private undertakings so that Member States do not thwart the adequate and efficient functioning of energy markets. This chapter outlines how the EU competition law provisions dealing with: (1) anticompetitive agreements (Article 101 TFEU (Treaty on the Functioning of the European Union)); (2) abuse of dominant position (Article 102 TFEU); (3) concentrations among undertakings; and iv) the derogations to these undertakings providing services of general economic interest (Article 106 TFEU) have been applied to electricity and gas and used to reshaped European energy markets.

While the EU took an interest in the energy sector early in its life, the introduction of competition only came about much later, representing a fundamental paradigm shift. Until the mid-nineties, energy activities were in most countries reserved for designated utility companies[1] often coupled with regulatory tasks such as system overview and dispatching.[2] Subsequently, liberalization came about through three successive 'energy packages',[3] where the actual market opening in the first (1996/1998) remained somewhat limited and a large number of issues equally dormant, e.g. on third party access to the infrastructure and isolation of regulatory tasks. Not until the second energy package (2003) was this remedied without addressing other issues, e.g. the infrastructure remaining vertically integrated, an issue that came within the scope of the third energy package (2009) along with enhanced cross-border participation and furtherance of regulatory functions.

Creating a single energy market has been a story of slow movements, the sector regulation representing what politically was attainable rather than optimal, and therefore often suffering from regulatory lacunas. The story of competition law applied to electricity and gas has therefore also been a story of incomplete markets where competition law has been used to bridge some of the regulatory deficits and it is even doubtful if any single energy market ever

1 For further information, see e.g. Eugene D. Cross, *Electric Utility Regulation in the European Union – A Country by Country Guide*, Wiley, 1996.

2 Dispatching covers the sequences in which power plants are called to supply to the market.

3 For an outline of the liberalization of electricity and gas see the Chapter 6 by Herrera Anchustegui and Formosa in this volume.

would have come about void of competition law giving teeth to the Commission's bite and bidding for amendments across the three packages.

Rather than structuring the presentation in accordance with the different competition law provisions used, we have divided this chapter according to a time element, distinguishing between the application of competition law before the full energy market opening and post full energy market opening.

1 Competition law before full market opening

1.1 First attempts at applying competition law

Despite early community interest, there was no questioning of the granting of exclusive and special rights to energy companies, if not precluding competition at least reducing it, until the late eighties. This might be attributed to a reading of Article 106(1) of them TFEU with respect to the use of special and reserved rights if serving a legitimate purpose,[4] which is undoubtedly the case of the provision of energy to a modern society. Moreover, it was not until after the *Second Electricity Directive*[5] and *Second Gas Directive*[6] in 2003 that EU law mandated a clear opening to competition in all energy markets from 2007, save for the infrastructure.

More fundamental, perhaps, was the fact that no appropriate case[7] presented itself before the nineties, and even then the Commission application can best be described as lenient. In 1992 in *SHG*,[8] intervention was made against an agreement between the French and Italian system operators (TSOs) paying an independent French electricity generator (SHG), linked exclusively to the Italian grid, under the lower French tariffs. With the help of the Commission, a compromise was brokered, securing payment under the higher Italian tariffs. However, confining itself to reviewing the agreement under Article 101 and rushing for a settlement, an opportunity to appraise the exclusive rights facilitating the involved abuse was missed.[9]

1.2 A limited and later lenient application of competition law

While *SHG* might have represented a missed opportunity to offer clarity on the application of competition law to the energy sector, Article 102 TFEU was made use of in *Small Mines*[10] from 1991, where purchasers of coal were held jointly dominant and their offered terms discriminatory. In the same manner as *SHG*, an understanding was secured and the case closed without further issues. Only in 1994 with *Almelo*[11] did the European Court of Justice (ECJ)

4 See e.g. Christian Bergqvist, *Between Regulation and Deregulation*, DJOEF, 2016, pp. 68–73.

5 Directive 2003/54/EC concerning common rules for the internal market in electricity.

6 Directive 2003/55/EC concerning common rules for the internal market in natural gas.

7 In 13th Report on Competition Policy (1983) recital 291, and 12th Report on Competition Policy (1982) recital 221, a case against Belgium for the retention of an exclusive right on the import of gas is noted. Following commitment, involving reduction of the scope of the exclusive right, the case was closed. An identical case against France is noted in 12th Report on Competition Policy (1982) recital 221, but it is unclear how the case ended.

8 See XXII Report on Competition Policy (1992) recital 97.

9 The same pattern can be seen in *Vertical Agreements between Electricity Generators and Coal Producers*, 19th Report on Competition Policy (1989) recital 32, and *Coramine*, XXII Report on Competition Policy (1992) recital 51.

10 See XX Report on Competition Policy (1990) recital 145, and XXI Report on Competition Policy (1991), recital 107.

11 Case C-393/92 – *Almelo*.

confirm that competition law applied to electricity but Article 106(2) could be invoked in defence as electricity was a service of general interest. While both questions had been prejudiced by *Ijsselcentrale*[12] from 1990 involving an agreement preventing Dutch distributors and end users from importing electricity directly, the late delivery of *Almelo* underlines the respect shown by the Commission. Nevertheless, competition law cases started to surface in the early nineties along with the availability of Article 106(3) of the TFEU to adopt Commission Directives,[13] should progress on a normal council directive stall. Thus, the initial application of competition law to the energy sector can best be described as limited, and later as lenient with a regulatory flavour.

1.2.1 A lenient application with a regulatory flavour

Labelling the application of competition law to the energy sector as lenient follows also from the approach to cases preparing the electricity sector for market opening. In three UK cases from 1991, *Privatization of the electricity industry in England and Wales,*[14] *Privatization of the electricity industry in Scotland*[15] and *Scottish Nuclear,*[16] long-term electricity supply agreements were considered either permissible under Article 101(1) of the TFEU or exemptible under Article 101(3) of the TFEU, conditioned only upon a reduction in duration from 30 to 15 years. Regardless of the potential foreclosure they served to reorganize the UK electricity wholesale market inducing competition in a longer perspective. Exemption under Article 101(3), conditioned upon reductions, was also available in *Jahrhundertvertrag*[17] from 1992, compelling German generators to use domestic (German) coal despite its inferior quality. However, the Commission confined itself to shortening the scope of the agreement to what was reasonably required for the purpose of security of supply, defined as less than 20 per cent of the national consumption by the end of 1995 to be reduced to 15 per cent by 2000. Despite the security of supply argument, it is difficult to see the consumer benefits, meriting the use of Article 101(3) of the TFEU, when German coal was inferior and had to be shielded from competition.

Lenient application also can be seen in *Pego*[18] from 1993 and *Verbändevereinbarung* from 1998.[19] In the former it was held permissible under Article 101(1) to conclude an exclusive supply agreement tying a newly constructed power plant to the Portuguese energy incumbent for 15 years followed by a first right of refusal. As the incumbent was also in a dominant position, the appraisal differed from what normally would have been expected, but did, on the other hand, increase generation capacity for the Portuguese market. In *Verbändevereinbarung* the Commission decided not to act against a national horizontal agreement fixing

12 Case IV/32.732 – *Ijsselcentrale*, O.J. 1991 L 28/32.

13 For further information, see Susanne K. Schmidt, 'Sterile Debates and Dubious Generalisations: European Integration Theory Tested by Telecommunications and Electricity' *Journal of Public Policy*, volume 16, 1997, p. 261. See also Peter D. Cameron, *Competition in Energy Markets, Law and Regulation in the European Union*, Oxford University Press, 2001 p. 123 referring to a circulated draft.

14 See XX Report on Competition Policy (1990) recital 65.

15 See XX Report on Competition Policy (1990) recital 65.

16 Case IV/33.473 – *Scottish Nuclear*, O.J. 1991L 178/31.

17 Case IV/33.151 – *Jahrhundertvertrag*, O.J. 1990C 159/7, O.J. 1991C 116/6.

18 XXIII Report on Competition Policy (1993) recital 222. See also XXVI Report on Competition Policy (1996), p. 133 for an additional example.

19 See XXVIII Report on Competition Policy (1998), pp. 160–163. The tariffs also favoured local (and domestic) producers when calculated against the "travelled" distance, as trading does not require movement. However, this element remained unchallenged until later.

terms and prices for transmission of electricity in Germany.[20] Ignoring what can hardly be considered anything short of a cartel is somewhat unexpected, but should be seen in connection with the lack of mandatory provisions on access matters to transmission infrastructure in the *First Electricity Directive*,[21] the issue was referred to negotiation between the electricity undertakings. Deciding a horizontal agreement on the matter was better than individual discussions with the many German transmission operators, the Commission decided to turn a blind eye to the agreement and have no opinion. A prudent, but unusual move.

The lenient application in *Pego* was recycled in *Electrabel*[22] from 1997, with the court finding compatible with Article 102 that the dominant Belgian supplier had concluded an exclusive arrangement with a local distributor provided that the exclusive element lapse in 2011 and from 2006 had been reduced to 75 per cent. Despite the gradual reduction, the application must be considered lenient as Article 102 of the TFEU normally is considered to, if not preclude, at least limit exclusivity. However, the Commission's practice is not fully consistent. In *REN/Turbogàs*[23] from 1996, also involving a projected power plant and the permissibility under Article 101(1) of the TFEU of 15 years of exclusivity, the Commission was, in contrast to *Pego,* unwilling to accept any obligations following the lapse of the 15 years, even where the contracting party had contributed to the financing of the power plant by paying a surplus for the electricity in exchange for a reduction once the construction costs had been written off. Only a compensation model reflecting the surcharge was acceptable, securing the power plant options to contract with a third party after 15 years.[24]

1.3 The liberal reading involved an active use of competition law

The lenient application of EU competition law outlined above was largely directed at the regulatory lacunas in the access regime to networks as first illustrated by *Verbändevereinbarung*. Despite being of pivotal importance for cross-border trading and transit, transmission capacity remained limited on cross-border connections, and often subject to long-term reservation arrangements predating market opening, referred to as *Grandfather Right*.[25] Here, competition law provided a useful instrument as demonstrated in *Skagerrak Cable*[26] from 2000 and *UK/France Interconnector*[27] from 2001. In these two cases the Commission acted against long-term reservations under Article 101 of the TFEU, closing the investigation subject to relinquishing

20 See Peter D. Cameron, *Competition in Energy Markets,* 2nd Edition, Oxford University Press, 2007 pp. 334–339 for further information, including a parallel gas agreement never reviewed by the Commission.

21 Directive 96/92/EC concerning common rules for the internal market in electricity, Article 17 allowed the Member States to refer the matter to negotiations. Pursuant to SEC 2001 1957 – *Commission staff working paper – First benchmarking report on the implementation of the internal electricity and gas market* p. 9 Germany further refrained from remedying this nationally.

22 XXV Report on Competition Policy (1995) recital 94.

23 See XXVI Report on Competition Policy (1996), p. 134.

24 See also case 37.542 – *PO/Gas Natural + Endesa*, XXX Report on Competition Policy (2000), p. 154 for an example of a gas case closed subject to reductions in time and scope.

25 Further, pursuant to Directive 96/92/EC concerning common rules for the internal market in electricity, Article 24 derogations were available for such rights and initially it was understood that this was granted automatically. However, case C-17/03 – *VEMW and others,* overturned this as detailed by Christopher Jones (Ed.), *EU Energy Law,* Claeys & Casteels, Volume 1, 3rd Edition, 2010, pp. 68–75.

26 Case COMP/E/37.125 – *Statkraft/Elsam – Interconnector capacity.* See XXX Report on Competition Policy (2000), p. 155.

27 See IP/01/341 – *UK-French electricity interconnector opens up, increasing scope for competition.* See also MEMO/01/76 – *Role of interconnectors in the electricity market. A competition perspective* outlining additional cases.

capacity on the cross-border electricity connections. The special interests allotted to the infrastructure were neither isolated to electricity nor the relinquishing of capacity. In *Thyssengas*[28] from 2001 third party access was secured to a gas pipeline controlled by continental European gas companies, not only in terms of granting access but also by rendering this more effective, through improvement in the balancing and congestions regime. Moreover, in *Irish Interconnector*[29] from 1999 the Commission expressed a preference for allocating gas capacity under an auction model, and in *Electricity transmission tariffs in the Netherlands*[30] from 1999 that charges for transmitting electricity had to be cost based. An important comment as trading of electricity and gas does not per se require actual movement creating a risk of excessive pricing, referred to as *pancaking*, if linked to distance or number of systems crossed. Finally, while the Commission expressed frustration about the vertical and horizontal demarcation in the energy sector, with well-established vertical supply chains and a limited appetite for competition,[31] it would fall to the enforcement of the merger regulation to remedy these issues.

1.4 The establishing of early priorities

Both the *First Electricity Directive*[32] (1996) and the *First Gas Directive*[33] (1998) identifies priorities for competition law. The preamble of them refer to the need for avoiding "... *any abuse of a dominant position or any predatory behaviour...*" followed by references to Article 106 of the TFEU. The meaning of this reference is obvious by indicating how the Member States must respect Article 106(1) of the TFEU only reserving activities if required to secure the general supply and permissible under Article 106(2) of the TFEU. Additional principles were provided in 1998,[34] 2001[35] and 2002[36] explaining how effective competition would require freedom from artificial restrictions followed by singling out as priority five principles: i) the securing of effective third party access to the infrastructure, ii) addressing the preference for corporation rather than competition, the preventing of iii) excessive pricing (pancaking), iv) vertical foreclosure and v) cross-subsidization.[37] In practice only the first has guided the actual enforcement as it also was indicated that[38] competition law should serve in an overall role, giving priority to ex ante sector regulation if available, or obtainable, by amendments.

1.5 An active application with a regulatory twist

While competition law from 2000 would start to serve in a more traditional capacity, policing against abuse of market power and collusion, the quasi-regulatory role would not be

28 See IP/01/1641 – *Commission settles Marathon case with Thyssengas*. As detailed later some of the cases would continue until 2004.
29 See *Irish Interconnector*, XXIX Report on Competition Policy (1999), p. 168.
30 Case IV/E3/37.770 – *Electricity transmission tariffs in the Netherlands*, XXIX Report on Competition Policy (1999), p. 168.
31 See XXXI Report on Competition Policy (2001) recitals 98–100 which also indicate potential cases on the matter.
32 See *First Electricity Directive* recitals 37, 16 and Article 3.
33 Directive 98/30/EC concerning common rules for the internal market in natural gas, recitals 14–16.
34 XXVIII Report on Competition Policy (1998) recitals 121 and 126–128.
35 See XXXI Report on Competition Policy (2001) recitals 96–100.
36 See XXXI Report on Competition Policy (2002) recital 84.
37 See XXVIII Report on Competition Policy (1998) recital 121 referring indirectly to this.
38 XXVIII Report on Competition Policy (1998) recitals 126–128.

given up.[39] An example of this can be seen in *Viking Cable*[40] from 2001, where 25 years of exclusive use of a projected interconnector between Norway and Germany was compliant with Articles 101 and 102 TFEU. A somewhat unexpected approach to exclusive arrangements, having indicated access to the interconnectors was a priority. More importantly a derogation from the adopted third party access regime had been amended into the *First Cross Border Transmission Regulation*[41] to incentivize the establishment of new cross-border connectors. *Viking Cable* provided alignment between the enforcements of *ex ante* sector regulation and ex post competition law. A significant move as competition law had found use to secure third party access to the interconnectors, potentially casting doubt on the value of derogations.

1.5.1 The mergers presented the Commission with opportunities

The emerging consolidation in the energy sector also allowed the Commission to move on some of the identified shortcomings. In *EDF/Louise Dreyfus*[42] from 1999 it was stressed that France had failed to implement the *First Electricity Directive*, opening the market as obligated, warranting remedies addressing this for clearance. In *Grupo Villar Mir/EnBW/Hidroelectrica del Cantabrico*[43] from 2001 the Commission identified a risk of strategic underinvestment in transmission capacity between France and Spain following a French company's (EDF) acquisition of local Spanish production capacity. However, clearance was available subject to quadrupling capacity on the interconnector linking the two countries. Even more notable are two mergers involving the German market, as both touched upon the limited appetite for competition in the energy sector and the Commission's frustration[44] about vertical and horizontal demarcation. In *EDF/EnBW*[45] from 2000 an acquisition in the German market could have entrenched EDF's firm grip on the French market by providing instruments to drop prices in the former, and discourage German producers from entering the latter. Regardless, clearance became available following commitment to inject the French wholesale market with capacity. This not only unlocked the otherwise hermetically closed French market but also addressed the alleged preference for collusion by creating a wholesale market. An anti-competitive duopoly was also identified in *VEBA/VIAG*[46] from 2000, between the merged entity and its closest competitor in the German electricity market. Among the elements entrenching the duopoly was a revised horizontal agreement stipulating terms for access to the infrastructure, *Verbändevereinbarung II,* with elements favouring the incumbents. Clearance was, however, available subject to relinquishing control of the interconnector to Denmark and removal of certain elements in the *Verbändevereinbarung II*, improving access to

39 Moreover, the Commission reserved the right to use Article 106(3) to adopt Commission directives, should the Member States refuse to contemplate amendments to instruments already adopted. See e.g. XXXI Report on Competition Policy (2001) recital 94.

40 Case COMP/E-3/37-921 – *Viking Cable*, O.J. 2001C 247/11.

41 Council Regulation 1228/2003 on conditions for access to the network for cross-border exchanges in electricity, Article 7.

42 Case COMP/M.1557 – *EDF/Louise Dreyfus*. The adopted commitment packages prohibited transfer of know-how or assistance to EDF until France had implemented the directive and provided an indirect incentive to provide for this.

43 Case COMP/M.2434 – *Grupo Villar Mir/EnBW/Hidroelectrica del Cantabrico*. The French grid was controlled by a subsidiary securing direct control of any enlargements.

44 See e.g. XXXI Report on Competition Policy (2001) recitals 98–100.

45 Case COMP/M.1853 – *EDF/EnBW*.

46 Case COMP/M. 1673 – *VEBA/VIAG*. See recitals 108–110 and recitals 120–125 for details on *Verbändevereinbarung II*.

the wholesale electricity market. In particular, the latter is notable as the Commission once again ignored a horizontal price agreement, requesting only the removal of discriminatory elements.

1.6 A pattern can be drawn on the application prior to 2003

From the pre-2003 cases, a pattern emerges where competition is applied (or not) for the purpose of supporting the single market by focusing on specific market lacunas and regulatory deficits. This also explains the lenient approach to exclusive agreements in the early years. The task of securing sufficient and adequate electricity (referred to as Public Service Obligation (PSO)) was under the adopted electricity directives allotted to the local distribution companies, explaining the outcome of *Electrabel,* while cases such as *Pego* and *REN/Turbogàs*[47] can be explained by their contribution of new generation capacity outside the direct control of the incumbent. Moreover, the differences between the first and the last on the first right of refusal clause might indicate some post-event rationalization with the Commission now unwilling to accept any restriction beyond 15 years. Furthermore, the outcome of *Jahrhundertvertrag,* giving priority to the indigenous energy source amounting to 15 per cent of the total energy consumption, was later incorporated into the *First Electricity Directive*[48] as part of the PSO system. Finally, the approach to *Grandfather Right* and *Verbändevereinbarung* must be read in conjunction with the deficits in the adopted directives with few provisions securing third party access to the infrastructure, while *Viking Cable* must be read in conjunction with the need for investments in infrastructure. While Article 106 of the TFEU played no official role, it most likely tacitly compelled the Commission to offer concessions in the adopted sector regulation, initially not moving liberalization beyond what would be required under it. While this pattern can explain the outcome of cases pre-2003, including the remarkable level of leniency, it also means that lasting principles can only be extracted with some caution. Most of the cases must be read in close conjunction with the adopted sector regulation and the indicated preference for referring questions to be resolved under this regulation if available or attainable through amendments and reforms.

2 Competition law post full-market opening

Following the adoption of the second energy package in 2003, all segments except for the infrastructure, were to be opened to competition from 2007, and regulatory tasks isolated. The Commission used the opportunity to announce its intention to move to formal decisions,[49] with less clemency for infringements,[50] and later that (unannounced) inspections had been undertaken.[51] While this signalled a more traditional role for competition law enforcement, reality is as always more complex. The Commission retained an appetite for settlements to improve the functioning of the markets, and the use of competition law to facilitate this.

47 This also emerges when comparing *Pego* with *Scottish Nuclear,* both accepting 15 years of exclusivity. However, the latter, involving an existing power plant, required exemption pursuant to Article 101(3).

48 Article 8(4). The provision was in the original draft COM 91 548, p. 15 and Article 13(5) and available in 1992.

49 See e.g. XXXIII Report on Competition Policy (2003) recital 97.

50 IP/04/1310 – *Commission confirms that territorial restriction clauses in the gas sector restrict competition.*

51 See MEMO 06/220 – *Competition: Commission confirms inspections in the energy sector* and MEMO/06/205 – *Competition: Commission has carried out inspections in the EU gas sector in five Member States.*

Moreover, accepting that competition still lagged behind, a sector inquiry under competition law was launched for the purpose of updating the enforcement priorities and preparing for the third energy package.

2.1 The sector inquiries and priorities for competition law enforcement

The *Energy Sector Inquiry*[52] of 2007 was launched to identify obstacles to the creation of a single energy market, in the form of competition law infringement. However, the final report offered a broader insight identifying a number of deficiencies, including: (1) concentrated wholesales markets; (2) insufficient unbundling between network and supply/generation; (3) insufficient cross-border capacities and networks, often controlled by the incumbents; (4) insufficient market information, creating advantages for the vertically integrated incumbents; (5) long-term supply agreements foreclosing the retail markets, and in respect to gas restriction on the use; (6) design of the balancing markets that favours the incumbents; and finally (7) an emerging trend of retail price regulation, potentially inducing margin squeeze of newcomers.[53]

In the *Sector Inquiry* the Commission tables as priorities for competition law the addressing of the high concentration at wholesale level, persistent vertical foreclosure risk from long-term supply agreements and lack of (effective) access to the infrastructure. In contrast, reforms of the sector regulation should pursue structural unbundling of the infrastructure. While the latter ambition was directed at the sector regulation, it would be secured partly through competition law. Furthermore, the adoption of the *Third Electricity*[54] and *Third Gas Directives*,[55] in 2009 highlighted the need to prevent long-term exclusive agreement, abuse of dominance and predatory behaviour, and that national regulation and review did not preclude ex post application of other provisions; being these clear references to competition law and the Commission's power to oversee the correct and full implementation of sectoral regulation.

2.2 Competition law in a quasi-regulatory role

While the opening of formal cases indicated a more traditional role and application for competition law, the quasi regulatory use would resurface. The *Energy Sector Inquiry*, although formally a competition law instrument, was used to set out objectives to be attained under ex ante sector regulation is a prime example of this. *Swedish Interconnectors*[56] being closed against commitments in 2010 is another. Here, the Swedish system operator, supervising the electricity system, had in response to internal Swedish congestion closed the interconnector to Denmark, reserving cheap electricity for the Swedish users. Normally, electricity would

52 SEC 2006 1724 – *DG Competition report on energy sector inquiry*, 10 January 2007. See Executive Summary pp. 7–11 for the findings.

53 There is no direct reference to margin squeeze. However, the concerns appear embedded in the references to the use of a regulated retail price. See e.g. recital 313.

54 Directive 2009/72 concerning common rules for the internal market in electricity, Article 37(1)(k) (long-term exclusive agreement), Article 37(13) (abuse of dominance and predatory behaviour) and Article 37(2) (full application of competition law).

55 Directive 2009/73 concerning common rules for the internal market in natural gas, Article 41(1)(k) (long-term exclusive agreement), Article 41(13) (abuse of dominance and predatory behaviour) and Article 41(2) (full application of competition law).

56 Case COMP/39.351 – *Swedish Interconnectors*.

flow freely from northern Sweden, where cheap access to electricity was available to southern Sweden, and then further on to Denmark. However, in case of congestion between northern and southern Sweden the market price in southern Sweden was suppressed by subsidies and the link to Denmark closed to reduce the costs. Following discussions with the Commission on the compatibility with Article 102 of the TFEU, a settlement was reached, providing for the fragmentation of Sweden into two different bidding (price) zones with congestion management where it occurred and not at the border. A case in 2018 with similar characteristics to *Swedish Interconnectors* has been under scrutiny by the Commission concerning alleged transmission capacity curtailment in the *DK/DE Interconnector* case.[57] The Commission opened an investigation against TenneT (the German TSO) due to possible infringements of Article 102 TFEU as it was allegedly "systematically limiting southward capacity at the electricity interconnector between Western Denmark and Germany", negatively affecting imports to Germany and increasing power prices in Denmark. This curtailment of transmission capacity was done to address congestion issues in Germany due to insufficient North-South transmission capacity and the order of electricity dispatch from other plants, just as in the *Swedish Interconnectors* case. The Commission resorted to competition law application to address a classical regulatory problem: preventing curtailment of transmission capacity and control electricity wholesale prices by requiring TenneT to increase capacity substantially. Unlike *Swedish Interconnectors,* however, no re-arrangement of bidding zones was imposed, even though the split of Germany into at least two different areas would have alleviated the issues of internal congestion and reduced re-dispatching costs. While these cases were addressed through competition law enforcement, they also would have been contrary to the ex-ante regulation in *Cross Border Transmission,*[58] mandating the use of market-based instruments against congestion. Thus, rather than pursuing a normal non-implementation case, competition law served to secure correct national implementation, arguably because it was faster but hard to reconcile with the Commission's intention to pursue formal decisions and give priority to sector regulation.

2.2.1 Ownership unbundling through the backdoor

While *Swedish Interconnectors* and *DK/DE Interconnector* gave teeth to already adopted provisions, other cases closed regulatory gaps and lacunas as illustrated by the double case *German electricity wholesale market*[59] and *German Electricity Balancing Market*[60] from 2008.[61] In the first, had the German energy incumbent E.ON strategically withheld available production capacity driving upwards wholesale prices in a manner potentially infringing Article 102 of the TFEU? No decision was made on the matter, however, as the company offered to

57 40461 – *DK/DE Interconnector* (no public version available at the time of writing).

58 Council Regulation 714/2009 on conditions for access to the network for cross-border exchanges in electricity. *Swedish Interconnectors* was advanced under the former transmission regulation (1228/2003) as the new Regulation had not entered into force. However, following a new Annex in 2006, no differences existed between the two on congestion management.

59 COMP/39.388 – *German electricity wholesale market* recitals 13–20 (dominance) and 28–40 (abuse). A potential identical French case was opened as COMP/39.442 – *French electricity wholesale market.* It is unclear what has happened with this.

60 COMP/39.389 – *German Electricity Balancing Market* recitals 48 (dominance) and 50–54 (abuse).

61 Originally, the cases appear to have involved a third abuse directed at preventing new constructions of production capacity as detailed in SEC 2009 1004 – *Staff Working Document accompanying the Report on Competition Policy 2008,* recital 146.

divest production capacity. Yet, the case appears to be based on a loose reading of Article 102 of the TFEU as E.ON was either single dominant, with a market share below 30 per cent, or a member of a loose trio of collectively dominant undertakings, while the abuse involved retaining electricity when the market price exceeded marginal costs. Normally, excessive pricing is benchmarked against higher standards,[62] indicating either a redefinition of the notions of dominance and abuse or a case that could not have been finalized. The other case involved the same undertaking, E.ON, and its conduct as system operator when procuring balancing power. Often, it had preferred more expensive electricity sourced from group-affiliated providers, passing on the higher costs to the competitors in imbalance and ultimately to the end users.[63] In contrast to the former E.ON case, the potential abuse stands out much more clearly.[64] Labelling the case as quasi regulatory is nevertheless merited as the adopted commitment required the divestment of transmission network,[65] and structural unbundling, which was so strongly desired by the Commission. Obligations later incorporated as a non-mandatory, but preferred solution for transmission networks in the *Third Electricity* and *Gas Directives*. While never officially linked, it appears plausible to see both a connection and how the securing of structural unbundling in a politically significant Member State might have changed the votes in the council. Further, while the *Third Electricity Directive* did not mandate structural unbundling, it did prevent negating already adopted unbundling and, further, specifically allowed voluntary unbundling. While the first prevented Member States from undoing commitments (already) secured under competition law, the latter cemented the instrument as Member States could not prohibit it nationally.

2.2.2 Concentrations are advanced against a loose concept of market power

The principles of *German electricity wholesale market,* where loose forms of oligopoly were identified as problematic, were recycled in the two mergers, *EDF/BRITISH ENERGY*[66] and *EDF/SEGEBEL*[67] from 2008 and 2009. Both involved the French EDF acquisitions on geographical adjacent markets. In the first, where EDF acquired the British BE, the combined market share did not exceed 30 per cent but was nevertheless held problematic for two reasons. First, the concentration would combine BE's mainly baseload and predominantly nuclear capacity with EDF's flexible coal and gas capacity, vesting EDF with an ability to increase market prices by withholding production capacity. The short-term loss would thereby be offset by higher wholesale prices and increased profitability of the electricity supplied. Secondly, the liquidity of the wholesale market would be reduced when EDF's substantial retail business could internalize its procurement. Both elements were somewhat unexpected in the light of the moderate combined market share brought about by the concentration. Clearance was, however, available against divesture of production capacity and a commitment to procure electricity through the wholesale market, rather than the group internal market,

62 See Robert O'Donoghue and Jorge Padilla, *The Law and Economics of Article 102*, 2nd Edition, Hart Publishing, 2013, p. 749.

63 Moreover, the company had prevented the importing of balancing power. See recital 52.

64 The abuse might also have infringed Directive 2003/54/EC concerning common rules for the internal market in electricity, Article 11, dictating that balancing power must be sourced on non-discriminatory terms, which should preclude group favouring.

65 See also COMP/39.402 – *RWE gas foreclosure,* involving the divestment of a German gas transmission network.

66 COMP/M.5224 – *EDF/BRITISH ENERG* recitals 24–37 (retaining of capacity) and 38–82 (reduction of liquidity).

67 COMP/M.5549 – *EDF/SEGEBEL* recitals 60–83 and 128.

thereby improving the liquidity of the former. *EDF/SEGEBEL* follows some of the same elements. Here, EDF acquired a Belgian competitor. In spite of no significant horizontal overlaps and a combined market share below 20 per cent, the merger was nevertheless said to raise issues.[68] According to the Commission, EDF could, as an alternative to acquiring an (existing) domestic producer, have entered the Belgium market by constructing new power plants, of which two were already projected. However, following the acquisition, the incentive to finalize these plants, increasing overall available capacity, was reduced, mandating commitments to sell and/or develop them. Once again, the power to review concentrations was used to improve the functioning of the energy market through commitments. Moreover, this happened in situations that challenged the traditional concept of market power under Article 102 as detailed later in the chapter.

2.3 Using competition law to unlock wholesale and retail markets

In accordance with the enforcement priorities set out as early as 1998 the Commission would act against agreements and behaviour impeding the wholesale and retail markets unlocking these through commitments parallel to improving effective access to the infrastructure. While the latter in principle was secured in the adopted sector regulation, the actual access was hampered by congestion, long-term reservation agreements and sub-optimal balancing regimes as outlined by the (later) *Energy Sector Inquiry*.

2.3.1 Unlocking the wholesale markets and fighting destination clauses

While the Commission had reviewed, often leniently, joint sales agreements,[69] cases like *DUC/DONG*[70] from 2003 and *Synergen*[71] from 2002 allowed the Commission to take a more restrictive approach. In *DUC/DONG* a Danish gas incumbent, *DONG*, and a consortium, *DUC*, accounting for 90 per cent of all Danish gas production, agreed to market gas jointly, reducing the number of resellers. However, the Commission also took issue with vertical provisions reducing the parties' incentive to resell gas and partitioning downstream markets. No formal decision was required as commitments were tendered remedying the identified impediments, and increasing the free flow of gas, topped up with obligations to improve third party access to the DONG offshore gas pipeline, and the Danish wholesale gas market. In *Synergen* a joint venture had been established between the Irish electricity incumbent *ESB* and the Norwegian gas supplier *Statoil*, for the purpose of constructing and operating a new 400 MW power plant. As part of this, a 15 years' exclusive gas supply agreement had been concluded, which could have entrenched ESB's dominant position. Clearance, under Article 101(3) TFEU was available subject to injecting 600 MW, corresponding to half of the total Irish consumption, into the wholesale market. Compared to e.g. *Pego*, a decade before, this was a much more restrictive approach.

Although *DUC/DONG* signalled a more restrictive approach to vertical restrictions preventing or hampering resale this would be developed further. In *NLNG*[72] from 2002 a

68 See also COMP/M.5978 – *GDF SUEZ/International Power* recitals 72–73 for an example of a merger warranting substantial remedies regardless of limited overlaps.

69 See Peter D Cameron, *Competition in Energy Markets, Law and Regulation in the European Union*, 2nd Edition, Oxford University Press, 2007 pp. 301–308 for examples.

70 IP/03/566 – *Commission and Danish competition authorities jointly open up Danish gas market.*

71 Case COMP/E-4/37.732 – *Synergen.*

72 IP/02/1869 – *Commission settles investigation into territorial sales restrictions with Nigerian gas company NLNG.*

Nigerian gas supplier accepted to forego any provisions restricting how the gas was used, including being resold in contracts. These principles were recycled and amended in *Gazprom/ENI,*[73] from 2003, and *OMV*[74] and *Ruhrgas*[75] from 2005, all involving the supply of Russian gas to the European market. Further, the two first also warranted commitments to increase the amount of gas resold, the capacity in the TAG pipeline crossing Austria and third-party access to this. While still closed against commitments, and still short of fines and (official) condemnation, the cases had gradually taken a more formal shape indicating infringements of Article 101 of the TFEU. This was reinforced with the double case *GDF/ENI/ENEL*[76] from 2004, involving the supply of gas to the Italian market. While it was closed to commitments to fold on the provisions, the Commission insisted on adopting formal decisions and issuing a statement of less clemency for such restrictions henceforth. Nevertheless, *BEH Electricity*[77] from 2015 and *Gazprom*[78] from 2018, also involving restriction of the resale of electricity and gas respectively, were closed against commitments lifting the reselling restriction and in *BEH Electricity* supplemented with commitments to establishing an electricity pool. In *Gazprom,* after six years of investigations, the Commission closed the case based on four commitments directed at providing for Russian-on-Russian gas competition, securing availability of alternative gas suppliers and Gazprom's control over the gas infrastructure.[79] The commitments involved the adoption of a gas swapping programme, allowing customers to request deliveries at alternative destinations and providing for cross-border reselling of gas, creating competition across markets void of actual connectors. Also, Gazprom agreed to facilitate flow to and from isolated markets and to contain its ability to leverage its dominance on the gas supply markets to the market of access or control of gas infrastructure.

2.3.2 Preventing foreclosure of the downstream retail markets

Further, Article 102 of the TFEU has been used against attempts to drive up wholesale prices, group favouring and margin squeeze and efforts to foreclose the retailing market. *Deutsche Bahn I/II*[80] from 2013 involved a potential margin squeeze by the German railroad incumbent, (ab)using its control over the German rail network and supply of tractions current. Current, hence electricity, was supplied to group-affiliated subsidiaries at better terms thereby squeezing the equally efficient competitors. No final decision was made following the submission of commitments. A potential margin squeeze was identified in *RWE gas foreclosure*[81] from 2009 where the company involved had allegedly abused its control of the gas transmission system to set transmission and balancing tariffs at artificially high levels in order to squeeze the competitors' margins. However, following the offer of commitments to divest the network the case was closed. Attempts to foreclose the retail

73 IP/03/1345 – *Commission reaches breakthrough with Gazprom and ENI on territorial restriction clauses.*

74 IP/05/195 – *Competition: commission secures improvements to gas supply contracts between OMV and Gazprom.*

75 IP/05/710 – *Competition: commission secures changes to gas supply contracts between E.on Ruhrgas and Gazprom.*

76 COMP/38.662 – *GDF.*

77 Case 39.767 – *BEH Electricity.*

78 Case AT.39.816 – *Upstream gas supplies in Central and Eastern Europe.* See also IP/07/1074 – *Commission and Algeria reach agreement on territorial restrictions and alternative clauses in gas supply contracts* involving a variation of the destination clauses.

79 Case AT.39.816 – *Upstream gas supplies in Central and Eastern Europe.*, recitals 159–183.

80 Case COMP AT.39.678/AT.39.731 – *Deutsche Bahn I/II.* See recitals 42–47.

81 COMP/39.402 – *RWE gas foreclosure,* recital 29–36.

market were also addressed in *Distrigas*[82] from 2007 and in *Long-term contracts France*[83] from 2013. In the first, the Commission voiced concerns over a potential foreclosing of the downstream gas markets in Belgium via long-term supply contracts, while the concern in the latter was directed at the electricity market in France. Both were reviewed under Article 102 and closed against commitments to reduce the span and scope of the agreements, freeing up the retail market. While taking a restrictive stand on the use of an exclusive long-term supply agreement, pragmatism was also demonstrated on the need for long-term planning requiring only a reduction in span and scope rather than full termination. Normally this would have been expected as case law is perceived to preclude exclusive supply agreements under Article 102 of the TFEU.

2.3.3 Retaining interest in securing effective access to the infrastructure

Despite provisions securing third party access in the *Second Energy Package* competition law would remain in a supportive role when it came to securing effective access. While one of the *Marathon* related cases,[84] where a group of European gas incumbents had colluded to prevent access to their gas pipeline, had been settled in 2001, other cases would continue until 2003[85] and 2004.[86] However, eventually the companies entered into commitments to improve: (1) the balancing regime, reducing the risk of enduring imbalances and associated fees; (2) transparencies on available capacity; (3) handling of access requests; and (4) congestion management. Some of the cases even involved additional commitments on (5) gas release and conversion programmes injecting gas into the wholesale markets, and (6) a new transmission tariffs system linked to costs and avoiding pancaking.

Variations of the access issues emerged in *GDF foreclosure*[87] from 2009, *E-on Gas*[88] from 2010, *ENI*[89] from 2010 and *CEZ*[90] from 2013, all involving hoaxing of capacities on existing gas and electricity facilities. In *GDF Suez* and *ENI* this was coupled with strategic under-investments. Regrettably, none of the cases were finalized, thus depriving us of an interesting ruling on the concept of access denial. Rather, they were closed against commitments to reduce reservations and in *ENI* and *CEZ* divestments of the network and production capacity respectively. While strategic hoaxing of capacity, as part of an overall foreclosure plan, might be accommodated under Article 102 of the TFEU, under-investment, regardless of the motive, would likely require an expansive reading of Article 102 of the TFEU. Void of commitments it remains open whether the cases could have been finalized unless additional grievances were uncovered, making the Commission's move for commitments prudent.[91]

82 Case COMP/37.966 *Distrigaz*.

83 COMP/39.386 – *Long-term contracts France*. In contrast, no problems were found in COMP/39.387 *Long-term contracts in Belgium* relating to the Belgium market.

84 See IP/01/1641 *Commission settles Marathon case with Thyssengas*.

85 See IP/03/547 – *Commission's competition services settle Marathon case with Gasunie* and IP/03/1129 – *Commission Settles Marathon Case with German Gas Company BEB*.

86 See IP/04/573 – *Commission settles Marathon case with Gaz de France and Ruhrgas*.

87 Case COMP/39.316 – *GDF foreclosure*.

88 Case COMP/39.317 – *E.On gas foreclosure*

89 Case 39.315 – *ENI*.

90 Case AT.39.727 – *CEZ*.

91 Even the hoaxing of capacity as an abuse is debatable as analysis by Ulrich Scolz and Stephan Purps shows, 'The Application of EU Competition Law in the Energy Sector', *Journal of European Competition Law & Practice*, 2011, Vol. 2 No. 1, pp. 73–77.

2.4 Combatting abusive behaviour and restrictive agreements

Competition law has also served against more traditional forms of infringements, e.g. margin squeeze as seen in *Deutsche Bahn I/II* and *RWE gas foreclosure,* and excessive pricing in *German electricity wholesale market* and *Gazprom.* In the latter because the gas price had been linked to the oil price, and was thus void of actual cost.[92] However, as none of the cases were finalized, it remains debatable whether the behaviour amounted to an abuse. In addition, *German electricity wholesale market* was, as already noted, advanced against a somewhat loose concept of dominance with market share below 30 per cent[93] and an expansive reading of the concept of excessive pricing. Consequently, it is unclear if the case could have been finalized under Article 102 of the TFEU unless there was significant redrafting of the notion of it.

Regardless of the dubious manner in which *German electricity wholesale market* was advanced, the underlying impediment to competition in the form of strategic withholding of capacity for the purpose of driving up wholesale prices is real.[94] Moreover, the ability to exercise market power is aggravated when it comes to electricity. First, demand is inelastic and market prices are dictated by the marginal (pivotal) supplier. Secondly, as demonstrated by the merger *EDF/BRITISH ENERGY,* the different technologies utilized to generate electricity display different characteristics and cost profiles.[95] The number of alternative providers and competitors therefore depends on the market prices vesting generators with small market shares and the occasional ability to exercise market power. The system operator must therefore carefully dispatch the order generators are called to supply electricity to the market. This also provides for market power confined to certain price intervals or congestion in the transmission system, creating a concept of temporary dominance,[96] potentially short of Article 102.

In light of these uncertainties the Commission's interest in settling *German electricity wholesale market* is obvious, but the commitment decision deprives us of what could have been a landmark case on abuse of dominance and the energy sector. In contrast, the abuse in *German Electricity Balancing Market* and *Gazprom* was much clearer, indicating how Article 102 of the TFEU can be used against group favouring, excessive pricing, tying and abuse of regulatory powers. The issue of discrimination was developed further in *Romanian Power Exchange/OP-COM*[97] from 2014 where the Commission doled out a fine of EURO 1,031,000 in response to requirements of Romanian VAT numbers as a trading condition. A finding supported by large, but not further specified, associated costs of securing such number, making it unfounded and discriminatory under Article 102 of the TFEU.[98]

92 The case also involved a bundling element, as supplies on occasion had been conditioned upon contribution to new pipelines.

93 The case could most likely have been advanced against a notion of joint dominance due to structural links between the companies. However, the Commission specifically reserved the right to pursue the case under a single dominance theory despite low market shares.

94 For further on the matter see Panagiotis Tsangaris, *Capacity Withdrawals in the Electricity Wholesale Market,* Springer 2017.

95 For further see e.g. SEC 2006 1724 - *DG Competition report on energy sector inquiry,* recital 370, figure 40.

96 The ability to accommodate this under Article 102 is explored by Christian Bergqvist, *Between Regulation and Deregulation* DJOEF 2016, pp. 62–64.

97 CASE AT 39.984 – *Romanian Power Exchange/OPCOM.* See recitals 163 and 167.

98 Case AT 39.958 – *SU/CEZ* also involved a discriminatory policy but was closed due to a national case on the same matter.

2.4.1 Acting against restrictive agreements under Article 101 of the TFEU

Restrictive agreements and more traditional market sharing arrangements under Article 101 TFEU were reviewed and condemned in *E.ON/GdF*[99] from 2009 and *POWER EXCHANGES*[100] from 2014. In the first, two gas importers had colluded, when importing Russian gas over a shared gas pipeline, not to sell gas into each other's home market. While officially having folded on the agreement in 2004, the Commission found a tacit understanding to continue and levied fines. In the latter case two electricity pools had adopted a non-compete clause as part of an agreement coupling wholesale markets and facilitating cross-border trade. While promoting competition through market coupling the agreement had been given a twist warranting intervention under Article 101 TFEU and fines.

2.4.2 National attempts to negate the market opening

Competition law, in the form of Article 106(1) of the TFEU, has also been used to prevent national attempts to negate the market opening. In *Greek Lignite*[101] from 2008, the Commission used it against an attempt to reserve the Greek lignite (brown coal) market for the national electricity incumbent. While initially overturned by the General Court void of – at least a potential underlying – infringement of Article 102 of the TFEU, the Court of Justice ultimately sided with the Commission condemning the behaviour under Article 106 of the TFEU regardless of any other infringements. The Court confirmed the availability of Article 102 against Member States' actions if distorting energy market competition unless legitimized by e.g. the adopted sector regulation or Article 106(2) of the TFEU. However, following the incorporation of an advanced PSO system into the former, the actual scope for invoking the latter is presumably limited.

2.5 The merging pattern on competition law post 2003

From the application post 2003 a pattern emerges where competition is applied, in a more traditional role, without depriving it of the supportive role with respect to promoting the single energy market project by focusing on improving the functioning of the markets and fighting abusive behaviour. Some of the latter in a novel manner and in ways that challenge and expand the traditional reading of Article 102 of the TFEU. However, parallel to this, which to some extent was to be expected in light of the many particularities of the energy sector, competition law continues to have a quasi-regulatory role. In *Swedish Interconnectors* competition law was used to secure full national implementation of existing obligations, while *German Electricity Balancing Market* paved the way for including infrastructure unbundling in the third energy package, perhaps the very adoption of the package.

3 Summarizing competition law as applied to energy

Articles 101, 102 and 106 of the TFEU establish, in principle, a coherent enforcement system checking impediments to the single market and free competition regardless of its origin.

99 Case COMP/39.401 – *E.On – GdF collusion*. Part of the decision was overturned by the General Court as case T-370/09 – *GDF Suez*.

100 Case AT.39.952 – *POWER EXCHANGES*.

101 Case 38.700 – *Greek lignite and electricity markets*. Overturned with case T-169/08 – *DEI v. Commission* but ultimately upheld with case C-553/12P – *Commission v. DEI*.

While the provisions have remained unchanged across almost 30 years of liberalization neither the governing theories of harms nor the underlying markets have, evolving and supporting (and at times replacing) regulation towards the creation of the internal energy market. Nevertheless, a pattern for the application of competition law to electricity and gas emerges that can be summarized as follows:

1) The Commission has often resorted to competition law to serve in a quasi-regulator role, initially bending competition law to accommodate deficits in the adopted sector regulation and later (ab)using competition law to secure the adoption of amendments. *Verbändevereinbarung* closing a deficit in the *First Electricity Directive* is an example of the former and *German Electricity Balancing Market,* paving the way for the adoption of *Third Electricity Directive,* of the latter. *Swedish Interconnectors* securing national implementation of adopted provisions could also have been cited.
2) Competition law through Article 106 of the TFEU has formed the adopted sector regulation by tacitly compelling the Commission to offer concessions in this, initially not moving liberalization beyond what would be required under Article 106(1) of the TFEU for fear of national attempts to negate on the process and invoke Article 106(2) of the TFEU in defence. Moreover, cases such as *Jahrhundertvertrag* cannot be read separately from the PSO-system later incorporated into the sector regulation, and thus as an attempt to pre-empt the later developments. However, that also means that the scope for invoking Article 106(2) of the TFEU now is very narrow as the PSO system has enshrined most legitimate concerns.
3) The single energy market remains hampered by insufficient cross-border and even generation capacity at peak times. Competition law and commitments have been used to free transmission capacity and improve the access regime, e.g. with respect to balancing and congestion management and pricing. Initially the Commission was confined to behavioural commitments, but has later moved in favour of structural unbundling.
4) While in principle combatting long-term exclusivity agreements, respect for planning and projecting purposes has been demonstrated requesting reduction in scope and duration rather than full termination of long-term supply agreements. However, the assessment has tightened over time and now commitments are requested to improve the wholesale markets.
5) Some of the access cases are advanced against a concept of abuse that might fall short of Article 102 of the TFEU. The alleged abuses in *GDF Suez* and *ENI,* while never finalized, entailed strategic underinvestment in infrastructure beneficial to competitors. The alleged abuse rests upon an expansive reading of Article 102 of the TFEU, compelling the dominant undertaking to promote competition and, in principle, its own demise. However, from cases such as *German electricity wholesale market* and *EDF/BRITISH ENERGY* it follows that the ability to exercise market power might elude detection if only viewed against market shares providing cover for some rethinking.

These patterns are supplemented with an indication of the enforcement priorities. Priority was initially directed at access to the infrastructure and the freeing of capacity and also, partly, in response to regulatory lacunas in the adopted regulation failing to address either. Later, the focus shifted to balancing and the congestion regime and a non-discriminatory application of this, coupled with an interest in checking long-term exclusive agreements, abuse of dominance and that obligations are implemented nationally in full. Embedded in the priority also appears to be a preference for referring issues to be resolved to sector regulation if available and effective. However, the latter ultimately rests with the Commission to appraise.

8

THE ROLE OF STATE AID LAW IN ENERGY

Ignacio Herrera Anchustegui and Christian Bergqvist*

1 Introduction

1.1 An overview of energy and State aid

State aid rules are an integral component of energy regulation in the European Union (EU). They establish negative and positive limits for the provision of State aid (support) to undertakings involved in the generation, transmission and/or distribution of energy in the internal market. These rules, Articles 107 and 108 of the TFEU, preclude Member States from benefiting from an undertaking by granting some advantage, unless the benefit is compatible with the internal market and the measure has been both notified to and approved by the Commission, in order to ensure competition in the market is not distorted.

The importance of State aid rules for the energy sector is pivotal. According to the Commission, 53 per cent of all approved State aid spending was attributed to measures related to environmental and energy services, including renewable energy in 2017.[1] Between 2009 and 2016, around 216 billion euros of approved or block-exempted aid measures were registered showing a trend of increasing aid to the energy sector.[2]

There are several reasons why State aid rules have such an active role in the energy sector.[3] Energy markets tend to be characterized by market failures that market forces alone do not fully address, i.e. natural monopolies, public service obligations, need for investment

* This chapter has been written as part of the research project "Regulating energy markets, a perspective from EEA/EU Competition and Public Procurement Law", thanks to the financial support of the AkademiaAvtalen Programme between the University of Bergen and Equinor ASA. The authors would like to thank Dr Sune Troels Poulsen for his comments on an earlier draft. All errors and omissions are our own.

1 European Commission, 'State Aid Scoreboard 2018: Results, trends and observations regarding EU28 State aid expenditure reports for 2017' (January 2019) 7.

2 Ibid, p. 70.

3 See also: Falk Schöning and Clemens Ziegler, 'What is State Aid?' in Leigh Hancher, Adrien de Hauteclocque and Francesco Maria Salerno (eds), *State Aid and the Energy Sector* (Hart 2018) 4; Hans Vedder and others, 'EU Energy Law' in Martha Margrethe Roggenkamp and others (eds), *Energy Law in Europe: National, EU and International Regulation* (3rd edn, Oxford University Press 2016) para. 4.169.

in renewable markets at a high rate, etc.[4] Additionally, the presence of State aid in energy markets over the last decade is explained by three circumstances. The energy sector requires large financial investment for infrastructural projects, particularly those with very high sunk costs; Member States have a political interest and legal duty to help meet their energy security and environmental law targets, in accordance with the EU rules on renewable energy and national policies; and State support – and not necessarily aid depending on the measure's design – has become necessary frequently to address the problem of adequate generation capacity and security of supply of electricity through capacity remuneration mechanisms.[5]

2 Notion of State aid

State aid is a *sui generis* set of rules part of EU competition regime. These rules are designed to prevent or limit the capacity of Member States to distort the competitive process and intra-community trade in the EU by granting an undertaking with some economic advantage. While granting public aid to one specific energy generator may bring benefits to said entity and end consumers, for instance in the form of lower prices, this advantage brings externalities that negatively impact the market's competitiveness. In such a way, aid creates an uneven playing field between actors across jurisdictions. This distorts competition and it is likely to affect economic welfare. State aid rules share similarities with those setting limits to State subsidies under World Trade Organization (WTO) law, but are broader as the concept of aid embraces the positive benefits and mitigation of costs of an undertaking.[6] State aid rules apply to all economic sectors, including energy.

State aid is an objective and legal EU concept defined in the Treaty of the Functioning of the European Union (TFEU) and subject to interpretation by the EU Courts, but not subject to national courts' interpretation.[7] Article 107(1) of the TFEU defines it as

> any aid granted by a Member State or through State resources in any form whatsoever which distorts or threatens to distort competition by favouring certain undertakings or the production of certain goods shall, in so far as it affects trade between Member States, be incompatible with the internal market.

Whether a State intervention amounts to aid or not must be assessed *in concreto* by the Commission. The Commission has a limited margin of appreciation and its decision is subject to review by the European Courts. The Commission may find that the measure does not constitute aid, or that it does. In the latter case, it may also find that the aid is either illegal or compatible with the internal market.

For a measure to qualify as 'State aid', four cumulative conditions must be met. First, there must be an intervention by the State or through State resources; second, this intervention must be liable to affect trade between Member States; third, a selective advantage must

4 Kim Talus, *Introduction to EU Energy Law* (Oxford University Press 2016) 106.

5 Note the increase in the number of cases concerning CRM structured programmes either as aid schemes or compensation for the provision of a service of general economic interest (SGEI) from one case up to 2014 to six cases between then and August 2018.

6 Judgment of 20 September 2017, *Commission v Frucona Košice*, C-300/16 P, EU:C:2017:706, para. 20. For more on this distinction see: Claire Micheau, *State Aid, Subsidy and Tax Incentives under EU and WTO Law* (Wolters Kluwer 2014); Luca Rubini, *The Definition of Subsidy and State Aid: WTO and EC Law in Comparative Perspective* (Oxford University Press 2009).

7 Judgment of 15 September 2016, *PGE*, C-574/14, EU:C:2016:686, para. 32.

be conferred upon an undertaking; and fourth, the measure must distort or threaten to distort competition.[8] These constituent elements imply that there will be aid whenever: (1) the aid has a State origin; (2) it is granted to an undertaking; (3) said undertaking receives an advantage; (4) the measure is selective; and (5) the aid distorts competition and affects trade between Member States. These elements are discussed below.

2.1 State origin

For a measure to qualify as aid the benefit granted must have a State origin. This implies that the activity must be *imputable* to the State and *State resources must be granted*. These requirements are cumulative and not alternatives as clarified in *PreussenElektra*.[9]

Imputability is fulfilled whenever the aid is granted by a public authority – which could be the State or one of its organs regardless of its internal organization and its autonomy vis-à-vis other entities – or when it is granted by a public or private body that has been entrusted with such task by a public authority.[10] Advantages conferred by private entities, regardless of their effects, do not have a State origin and are not State aid. A public undertaking may also confer aid which may be State imputable depending on whether or not a series of indicators are present. These are its autonomy, the degree of State supervision and its legal status.[11] However, a measure would not be imputable to the State when it is required by EU law without any discretion.

The criterion of State origin has been discussed at length in energy cases. In *PreussenElektra* the European Court of Justice (ECJ) was confronted with the question of whether advantages granted by private parties, but which were required by the state, had State origin. This case dealt with a feed-in tariff scheme which required private electricity undertakings to purchase renewable energy sources at minimum guaranteed prices not subject to the market vagaries. The scheme meant that energy consumers had to partially pay the difference between the market electricity prices and the guaranteed price and granted suppliers of renewable energy with an advantage vis-à-vis generators using fossil fuels. The ECJ found that while the measure was imputable to the State as it had imposed a purchasing obligation through a statute, no State resources were involved. This was due to the lack of State control over the resources and a mechanism to compensate the private operator since the funds originated from private regional electricity companies. Therefore, as the requirement of State funding imputability was not met, no aid was given.[12] This interpretation of State origin and 'State resources' is formalistic and very narrow. Such a view allows measures resembling pseudo fiscal State aid policies to be implemented,[13] as well as granting a (very) broad opportunity for Member States to grant an advantage to certain entities by imposing such a burden on private entities that would ultimately pass on these higher costs to end consumers.

8 *Frucona Košice* (n 6).

9 Judgment of 12 March 2001, *PreussenElektra*, C-379/98, EU:C:2001:160. See, more recently: Opinion of A.G. Sharpston of 22 June 2017 in *Farrell*, C-413/15, EU:C:2017:745.

10 Commission Notice on the notion of State aid as referred to in Article 107(1) TFEU (OJ [2016] C 262/1), paras. 39–43.

11 Judgment of 18 May 2017, *Fondul Proprietatea*, C-150/16, EU:C:2017:388.

12 *PreussenElektra* (n 9) paras. 58–61.

13 See also the opinion of Sánchez Graells in his entry: www.howtocrackanut.com/blog/2013/06/cjeu-incorrectly-analyses-state.html (last accessed on 1 March 2018).

A different but related trend of cases in which State aid was found to exist and also dealing with surcharges has been discussed before the courts, as in *Essent Netwerk Noord*[14] and *Vent De Colère and Others*.[15] In these cases, the EU Courts have declared mandatory surcharges for electricity, levied on undertakings and/or consumers, as funds attributable to the state. This is the case as long as private undertakings had been appointed by the Member State to manage a State resource, holding the presence of aid. In the assessments, it was crucial that the funds were financed through charges imposed by the legislation of the Member State, managed and apportioned in accordance with the provisions of that legislation, even if not managed by the State.[16] That these entities were appointed by the State to manage the State resource and "not merely bound by an obligation to purchase by means of their own financial resources" constituted the decisive factor.[17]

More recently, the concept of State origin was reviewed by the Commission in the *German EEG Surcharge* decision declaring as 'aid' a German scheme imposing an obligation on network operators (distributors and transmission entities) to acquire renewable electricity at prices exceeding the market levels.[18] This renewable electricity was sold on the spot market and if the transmission entities that purchased it were unable to cover their purchasing price, they were entitled to require the payment of the difference from the final consumers through an Erneuerbare Energien Gesetz (renewable energy surcharge) (EEG) surcharge. Additionally, 'electricity-intensive undertakings in the manufacturing service' and 'railways' benefited from a special compensation scheme capping the surcharge to maintain their competitiveness. Despite finding the scheme as constituting aid, moving away from the *PreussenElektra* interpretation of State origin, the scheme was found compatible with the internal market and only a limited portion of the EEG reductions were to be restituted. The Commission's Decision was appealed before the General Court which confirmed it and held that the reduction of EEG on energy intensive users constituted an advantage.[19] The General Court argued that because the funds generated by the EEG surcharge were under the dominant influence of the State through the administration of the transmission entities, and the scheme included a mechanism for private entities to recover the losses imposed by the purchase obligation, the aid had a State origin. The case was decided on 28 March 2019 by the ECJ, overturning the judgment by the General Court and annulling the Commission's Decision as it was incorrect to determine that these EEG surcharges constitute State resources. This was so because the surcharge was not a levy, as it does not require suppliers to pass on the amounts charged to them to end consumers, and the 'in practice' passing them indirectly through higher practices is not sufficient. Also, and more importantly, it was not shown that the State had power to dispose of the funds generated by the surcharge or control the distributors and transmission entities by exercising public control.[20]

2.2 *Undertaking as a recipient*

Only aid granted to an undertaking triggers State aid rules. An undertaking is an entity engaged in an economic activity, regardless of its legal status and the way in which is financed.

14 Judgment of 17 July 2008, *Essent Netwerk Noord and Others*, C-206/06, EU:C:2008:413, para. 74

15 Judgment of 19 December 2013, *Vent De Colère and Others*, C-262/12, EU:C:2013:851, paras. 14–37.

16 Judgment of 28 March 2019, *Germany v Commission*, C-405/16 P, EU: C:2019:268, para. 58.

17 Ibid, para. 59.

18 Commission Decision SA.33995 [2014], C(2014) 8786 final.

19 Judgment of 10 May 2016, *Germany v Commission*, T-47/15, EU:T:2016:281. This case has been appealed before the Court of Justice as C-405/16 P.

20 Judgment of 28 March 2019, *Germany v Commission*, C-405/16 P, EU: C:2019:268, paras. 48–87.

It is the same concept that defines the applicability of EU competition law to an entity. Economic activity is defined as offering goods and services on a given market, regardless of whether the activity is for profit.[21] Non-profit entities that do not offer goods and services on a market are outside State aid's scope.

The classification of an entity as an undertaking is relative to a specific activity, which implies that an entity can be an undertaking concerning some of its functions but not in respect to others. Whether a market exists for certain services or goods depends on the way in which they are organized nationally, and its classification may change over time. Also, the fact that a public authority precludes the provision of an activity for third parties and reserves that activity to the State does not mean the activity would not be economic, as long as there are undertakings that would be willing to provide the service. An entity that exercises public powers (*jus imperium*) or acts in its capacity of an authority does not constitute an undertaking.[22] However, if an entity is entrusted with some tasks in the public

Interest but carries out other economic activities, such as a transmission system operator entrusted with security functions or other infrastructures (such as airports), this does not exempt it from the application of State aid rules as the activities are severable.[23] Also, schemes in the area of social security are unlikely to qualify as undertakings if they are based on the principle of solidarity.[24] Public healthcare and education and research systems are typically not economic activities, as clarified by the Courts. Also, certain cultural, heritage and nature conservation activities are not economic.

In the case of energy, the concept of undertaking as a potential aid recipient carries little controversy as most energy players would be an undertaking due to the nature of their activities. This includes traditional entities that extract or generate energy, transmission entrusted entities or energy retailers. But also applies to private entities created by the State to mitigate climate change,[25] or companies that carry out energy research.

2.3 Advantage

The advantage criterion is pivotal in State aid law. For a measure to qualify as aid some advantage having a State origin must be granted to an undertaking which it otherwise would not have received under normal market conditions.[26] An advantage is a functional concept; the defining characteristic is its effects and not the cause or intention,[27] and the advantage could be direct or indirect. If the benefit reduces the normal financial burden of an undertaking it is an advantage,[28] for instance by relieving or mitigating the costs of carrying out the economic activity. Furthermore, the case law has defined advantage broadly, not only

21 Judgment of 11 July 2006, *Fenin v Commission*, C-205/03 P, EU:C:2006:453, paras. 25–27.

22 Judgment of 12 July 2016, *Compass-Datenbank*, C-138/11 EU:C:2012:449, para. 40.

23 Judgment of 12 December 2000, *Aéroports de Paris v Commission*, T-128/98, EU:T:2000:290; Judgment of 19 December 2012, *Mitteldeutsche Flughafen and Flughafen Leipzig-Halle v Commission*, C-288/11 P, EU:C:2012:821.

24 Judgment of 17 February 1993, *Poucet and Pistre v AGF and Cancava*, C-159/91, EU:C:1993:63; Judgment of 16 March 2004, *AOK-Bundesverband and Others*, C-355/01, EU:C:2004:150.

25 SA.24895 (2011/NN) – United Kingdom.

26 Judgment of 24 July 2003, *Altmark Trans and Regierungspräsidium Magdeburg*, C-280/00, EU:C:2003:415, para. 84.

27 Commission Notice on the notion of State aid as referred to in Article 107(1) TFEU (OJ [2016] C 262/1), para. 67.

28 Judgment of 16 March 2004, *Danske Busvognmænd v Commission*, T-157/01, EU:T:2004:76, para. 57.

covering net payments, subsidies, loans or direct investment, but also negative benefits, such as the relief from the payment of taxes or fiscal charges.[29]

The case law has recognized two exceptions to the scope of Article 107(1) where the granting of a benefit to an undertaking does not constitute an advantage. The benefit was compensation for the provision of services of general economic interest (SGEIs) or the State has acted as a private investor would. Both avenues are of importance for the energy sector as they have allowed financing a provision of some socially sensitive services – like security of energy supply, or the construction of new infrastructure for the transport or generation of energy. Also, if the advantage granted is considered minutiae, because it is too small to create a market distortion, then it will be exempted pursuant the rules on *de minimis* aid.[30] Any aid of less than 200 000 euros granted to an undertaking involved in any economic activity over a period of three years does not need to be notified to the Commission for it to be considered compatible aid.[31]

2.3.1 Advantages granted to finance a SGEI

Compensation granted to undertakings that provide a public service obligation qualifying as a SGEI would not constitute an advantage, and therefore would not be State aid. This is because EU law allows for public intervention in cases in which an activity is not provided to the public under satisfactory conditions, such as related to price, quality, continuity and access to the service in a manner consistent with the public interest by the market operators,[32] revealing the existence of a market failure.[33]

Public service obligations are requirements imposed by public authorities on the provider of a service to ensure that certain public interests are met, such as, for instance, electricity availability for all consumers. In energy law, the Electricity and Gas Directives authorize the Member States to impose "public service obligations which may relate to security, including security of supply, regularity, quality and price of supplies and environmental protection, including energy efficiency, energy from renewable sources and climate protection".[34] These public service obligations must be clearly defined, transparent, non-discriminatory and verifiable and must guarantee access equality for energy undertakings to national consumers.

For the compensation granted to the discharge of a public service obligation not to qualify as an advantage four cumulative conditions must be met in accordance with the *Altmark* test.[35] First, the undertaking must have a duty to discharge a public service obligation which must be clearly defined. Second, the parameters for the calculation of the remuneration must be established in a transparent and objective manner. Third, the compensation cannot

29 Judgment of 20 November 2003, *GEMO SA*, C-126/01, EU:C:2003:622, para. 28.

30 The De Minimis Regulation does not apply to aid granted regarding the sectors of primary production of agricultural products, fishery and aquaculture.

31 Article 3, Commission Regulation (EU) No 1407/2013 on the application of Articles 107 and 108 of the Treaty on the Functioning of the European Union to De Minimis aid (OJ [2013] L 352/1).

32 Communication from the Commission on the application of the European Union State aid rules to compensation granted for the provision of services of general economic interest (OJ [2012] C 8/4), para. 48.

33 Judgment of 16 September 2013, *Colt Télécommunications France v Commission*, T-79/10, para. 154.

34 Article 3(2) of the Directive 2009/72/EC concerning common rules for the internal market in electricity (OJ [2009] L 211/55); and Article 3(2) of Directive 2009/73/EC concerning common rules for the internal market in natural gas (OJ [2009] L 211/94).

35 *Altmark* (n 26) paras 87–95.

exceed what is necessary to cover all or part of the costs incurred in the provision of the public service, taking into account some reasonable profit. Lastly, the undertaking that carries out the public service is either to be chosen following a public procurement procedure, or, in case it is not, the level of compensation must be determined on the basis of an analysis of the costs which a typical undertaking, adequately provided with means to meet the public service requirements, would have incurred to discharge these obligations, including a reasonable profit.

2.3.2 The Market Economy Investor Principle (MEIP)

Article 345 of the TFEU allows public authorities to act as market operators and own undertakings. As an extension of this right, the State is also allowed to invest or offer loans or guarantees to a private or public entity. When the State invests in conditions which would be acceptable for a hypothetical private investor or operator, such market intervention does not amount to State aid. Thus, the investment by the State is done to obtain a rate of return that would satisfy a private investor, not to pursue a public policy objective.[36] In this way, the Treaty allows for the State to intervene in the economy to generate profit but on an equal footing as when compared to a private person.

Under the Market Economy Investor Principle (MEIP) there is no requirement to pursue the most profitable investment or maximize the rate of return, only of performing like a prudent and profit seeking investor.[37] What is demanded is that the return on the investment is on a par with the average in the particular sector of the economy, in the short and/or the long run. It is on the State to demonstrate the soundness of the investment and not on the Commission to prove the contrary. Also, it is irrelevant whether the investment was profitable or not as the measure is not to be evaluated in hindsight.

Due to its nature, the test is complex and varies from case to case. However, a sound principle to determine the appropriateness of the investment and, thus, the inexistence of aid, is not only that a hypothetical market participant would carry out the operation but that indeed there are investors carrying out similar activities.[38] In the energy sector, the MEIP has played an important role in several cases dealing with long-term power purchasing agreements, and concerning the waiver of corporate tax in the re-structuring of an energy company in *Commission v EDF,* in which the test was not originally applied but should have been.[39]

2.4 Selectivity

A State measure only falls into the State aid rules' scope if it favours certain undertakings or the production of certain goods. Therefore, measures that are of a selective nature are captured, while generic measures that benefit all undertakings or goods are not. The selectivity criterion has been interpreted narrowly by the Courts as measures that at a glance appear as

36 Phedon Nicolaides and Sarah Schoenmaekers, 'The Concept of "Advantage" in State Aid and Public Procurement and the Application of Public Procurement Rules to Minimise Advantage in the New GBER' (2015) *European State Aid Law Quarterly* 144.

37 Judgment of 2 March 2012, *Netherlands and ING Groep v Commission*, T-29/10, EU:T:2012:98, para. 97.

38 Ben Slocock, 'The Market Economy Investor Principle' *June Competition Policy Newsletter – European Commission* (2002) 23, p. 24.

39 Judgment of 5 June 2012, *Commission v EDF*, C-124/10 P, EU:C:2012:318.

of a general characteristic that may be selective when implemented.[40] For a measure to be selective, it must distinguish between undertakings in a comparable situation, by favouring one undertaking above others. Such a situation was, for instance, the case regarding the supply of energy on preferential terms to undertakings manufacturing goods in *Adria-Wien Pipeline and Wietersdorfer & Peggauer Zementwerke*.[41] Therefore, the key to this test is finding the adequate comparative benchmark to be applied in the case.[42] This is called the "reference system".[43] The reference system constitutes the set of rules that apply to all undertakings falling in its scope based on objective criteria, and also the way in which the rules are applied, the rights and obligations of the chosen undertakings and its functioning. Once the reference system has been framed, then an analysis of whether the measure differentiates between undertakings in the system – such as by favouring certain undertakings or goods when compared to other undertakings in "a similar factual and legal situation, in the light of the intrinsic objective of the system of reference" – must be undertaken.[44]

The Commission distinguishes between material and regional selectivity. Material selectivity implies that the measure applies to a certain kind of undertakings or economic sectors in a state. Regional selectivity, on the other hand, means that the measure applies to a specific part of a Member State. Regional measures may not be selective under particular circumstances which so far have been only evaluated under tax measures.

Concerning material selectivity, the Commission distinguishes between de jure and de facto selectivity, depending on how the advantage's recipient is chosen. De jure selectivity implies that the result of the award of the benefit is based on legal criteria previously established applicable to a certain type of undertaking. De facto selectivity, on the other hand, implies that despite the existence of a general and objective criteria to award a benefit, the structure of the measure or its interpretation makes it be significantly in favour of a particular group of undertakings.[45] Furthermore, whenever there is a wide margin of appreciation for the public authority to choose the beneficiary of a measure that was designed in a general scheme, there might be selectivity.[46]

Lastly, some measures that might appear as selective may not qualify as State aid because the derogation from the reference system is justified by the nature or general scheme of the system, based on either its guiding principles or because the distinction is necessary for its functioning.[47] This type of exemption from selectivity is often justified in the case of tax schemes which have been connected to energy. For instance, in a German tax scheme distinguishing between the use of energy for heating and motor (taxed) and non-fuel energy uses (non-taxed) allowed for the 'dual use of energy' in certain energy intensive sectors (steel production and mineralogical process) to be exempted due to the nature of the objective pursued by the tax system.[48] Also, tax exemptions in the Netherlands for green electricity

40 Judgment of 29 June 1999, *DM Transport*, C-256/97, EU:C:1999:332, para. 27; Judgment of 6 March 2002, *Diputación Foral de Álava and Others v Commission*, T-127/99, para. 149.

41 Judgment of 8 November 2001, *Adria-Wien Pipeline and Wietersdorfer & Peggauer Zementwerke*, paras. 40–41.

42 Schöning and Ziegler (n 3) 24.

43 Commission Notice on the notion of State aid as referred to in Article 107(1) TFEU (OJ [2016] C 262/1), paras. 128–141.

44 Ibid, para. 135.

45 Ibid, para. 121.

46 Judgment of 29 June 1999, *DM Transport*, C-256/97, EU:C:1999:332, para. 27.

47 Commission Notice on the notion of State aid as referred to in Article 107(1) TFEU (OJ [2016] C 262/1), para 138.

48 N820/2006 Tax exemptions for certain energy intensive processes.

('zero rate') were considered not to be selective measures based on the system's nature – as they did not contribute to the generation of CO_2.[49] However, in *Austria v Commission* the General Court dismissed a claim that the measure was not selective based on the system's nature. It was concluded that

> the Commission was correct to consider that the measure at issue was selective, in that it differentiated between undertakings which, in the light of the objective pursued, were in a comparable factual and legal situation [... and not as the result of the nature and structure of the system ...].[50]

This measure only benefited energy-intensive businesses by limiting their charges for green energy, while other Austrian energy consumers did not benefit from the advantage from the sales.

2.5 *Effect on trade and competition*

Only State interventions that affect trade between Member States and, therefore, competition constitute aid. These two requirements, despite being distinct, are interrelated. However, a measure that affects competition but remains purely internal would not in principle affect trade between Member States.

A measure granted by a Member State that is capable of improving the competitive position of its recipient in comparison to its competitors affects competition. Furthermore, whenever a Member State grants an advantage to an undertaking in a liberalized sector, such as electricity and gas, it distorts competition, even if competition is not actual but possible.[51] The provision 'in-house' of a service would not distort competition if four conditions were met.[52] The service is subject to a legal monopoly which does not exclude competition in the market or for the market, the services is not in competition with others and the provider is active on another market subject to competition and where cross-subsidization is excluded.

In addition to a distortion on competition, the advantage granted must affect trade between Member States to constitute aid, in particular by favouring an undertaking that competes with others in the internal market. This effect does not need to be factual but it is sufficient "only to examine whether that aid is liable to affect such trade and distort competition".[53] Yet, this does not mean that the effect can be merely hypothetical or presumed – there must be an establishment of reasons why the measure is able to affect trade.[54] Furthermore, the Court has clarified that public support can distort trade between Member States even if the recipient in itself is not involved in cross-border trade, because, for instance, the benefit would make entry or the sale of foreign goods more difficult.[55] If the measure has a purely local impact it has no effect on inter-state trade.

49 NN30b/2000 Zero tariff for green electricity.

50 Judgment of 11 December 2014, *Republic of Austria v European Commission*, T-251/11, EU:T:2014:1060.

51 Judgment of 15 June 2000, *Alzetta and Others v Commission*, T-298/97, EU:T:2000:151, paras. 141–147.

52 Commission Notice on the notion of State aid as referred to in Article 107(1) TFEU (OJ [2016] C 262/1), para. 188.

53 Judgment of 14 January 2015, *Eventech*, C-518/13, EU:C:2015:9, para 65.

54 Commission Notice on the notion of State aid as referred to in Article 107(1) TFEU (OJ [2016] C 262/1), para. 195.

55 Judgment of 14 January 2015, *Eventech*, C-518/13, EU:C:2015:9, para. 65.

3 Consequences of granting State aid

In principle, any

> aid granted by a Member State or through State resources in any form whatsoever which distorts or threatens to distort competition by favouring certain undertakings or the production of certain goods shall, in so far as it affects trade between Member States, be incompatible with the internal market.[56]

Illegally granted aid must be stopped and recovered by the Member State and, if this is not done, the Commission and/or another Member State may refer the matter to the ECJ for a Treaty breach. In such a way, State aid rules impose a limit on Member States from 'picking winners and losers' in a given market and, therefore, distorting the competitive playing field.

However, not all economic advantage granted by a Member State to an undertaking is incompatible with the internal market. The Treaty allows Member States to grant an economic advantage to an undertaking(s) in certain circumstances, if such intervention is necessary for a well-functioning economy and to remedy a market failure. In the case of energy, this could be, for instance, to promote certain policy goals, such as the promotion of renewable energy, the general provision of minimum energy services to end consumers or to foster the economic development of less-developed regions by promoting investment in energy infrastructure or renewable sources.

A State measure that qualifies as aid may be declared compatible with the internal market on the basis of either the second or third paragraph of Article 107 TFEU. In the case of Article 107 (2) this provision contains automatic exceptions in which the Commission has no discretion and must declare these types of aid as compatible with the internal market.[57] The provision sets a *numerus clausus* of excluded aids which are: aid of a social character to individual consumers; aid to address natural disasters; and aid for the fostering of former Eastern Germany.

In the case of Article 107(3), certain types of aid may be declared compatible with the internal market pursuant an individual decision. These are discretionary exceptions in which the Commission enjoys a wide margin of appreciation and the Courts have a limited power to review such appreciation. In general, aid in the areas listed under this provision would be compatible with the internal market if it is necessary to obtain the objective it pursues, proportionate regarding its intensity, duration and scope and it shall not distort competition to an extent contrary to the common interest. Aid that can be declared compatible under this provision includes aid: to promote the economic development of particularly underdeveloped geographical areas; aid to promote projects of common European interest or to address a serious disturbance of the economy of a Member State, to facilitate the development of certain economic activities if such aid does not affect trade to an extent contrary to the common interest, for culture and heritage conservation; and other categories of aid specified by a Council decision. To assist Member States and potential recipients of aid, the Commission has issued different State Aid Guidelines clarifying in which circumstances aid to certain activities under specific conditions are to be considered compatible with the internal market. These Guidelines are binding on the Commission and are, therefore, an important source of *soft* law.[58]

56 Article 107(1) of the TFEU.

57 Christopher W. Jones and Leigh Hancher, *EU Energy Law: Vol. 2: EU Competition Law and Energy Markets* (4th edn, Claeys & Casteels 2016) para. 5.320.

58 Judgment of 19 July 2016, *Kotnik and Others*, C-526/14, EU:C:2016:570, para. 40.

4 The General Block Exemption Regulation and energy

Additionally, certain types of State aid benefit from an ex-ante declaration of compatibility with the internal market through 'block exemption regulations' adopted under Article 108(3) and (4) TFEU. These exemptions grant the Council the power to determine categories of aid that do not require to be notified for their approval and the Commission the authority to adopt Regulations indicating certain categories of aid that are ex-ante declared to be compatible with the internal market, respectively. In the following we briefly discuss the current Commission Regulation 651/2014 (the General Block Exemption Regulation (GBER)) in general and in connection with energy.[59]

The GBER allows the granting of State aid without prior notification, alleviating the administrative burden of Member States and the Commission for measures that are likely to benefit from the exception of Article 107(3) of the TFEU. The GBER sets the conditions under which certain measures will be automatically considered as compatible with the internal market. In general, a measure would not be considered illegal State aid if it concerns one of the categories set out in the regulation, serves a purpose in the common interest, has a clear incentive effect, is appropriate and proportionate, granted in full transparency and subject to regular control and does not affect trade to an extent contrary to the common interest.[60] According to the Commission aid amounting to about 41.7 billion euros was exempted under the GBER, representing 38 per cent of all the aid expenditure in the EU, and 96 per cent of all new State aid measures.[61]

The GBER rules have been designed to foster the 'Europe 2020' strategy aims concerning energy, in particular those related to the reduction of gas emissions by 20 per cent when compared to 1990 levels, with at least 20 per cent of energy production coming from renewable sources and an increase of 20 per cent energy efficiency in the EU.[62] The energy-focused rules of the GBER are inspired by the Commission's practice and the Guidelines on Energy and Environmental Protection – a soft law instrument – to determine which type of aid is considered unproblematic and consistent with the Treaty rules and, therefore, not requiring prior notification and approval.[63]

Section 7 of the GBER deals with aids granted for environmental protection. While the category is not directly dealing with aids granted to the energy sector it does so as many of these advantages are designed to "lead to a more efficient use of natural resources, including energy-saving measures and the use of renewable sources of energy".[64] In particular, the GBER includes rules granting a State aid exemption to projects connected to environmental protection, including energy-saving measures (energy efficiency),[65] the use and promo-

59 Commission Regulation (EU) No 651/2014 of 17 June 2014 declaring certain categories of aid compatible with the internal market in application of Articles 107 and 108 (OJ [2014] L 187), amended by Commission Regulation (EU) 2017/1084 of 14 June 2017 (OJ [2017] L 156/1).

60 Ibid, Recital (5).

61 European Commission (n 1) 7, cf. with European Commission, State Aid Scoreboard 2017.

62 European Commission, EUROPE 2020 A strategy for smart, sustainable and inclusive growth, /* COM/2010/2020 final.

63 Communication from the Commission, Guidelines on State aid for environmental protection and energy 2014–2020 (OJ [2014] C 200/1).

64 Commission Regulation (EU) No 651/2014 of 17 June 2014 declaring certain categories of aid compatible with the internal market in application of Articles 107 and 108 (OJ [2014] L 187), amended by Commission Regulation (EU) 2017/1084 of 14 June 2017 (OJ [2017] L 156/1).

65 Ibid, Articles 38, 39 and 40.

tion concerning investment and operation of renewable sources of energy,[66] regional aid related to energy infrastructure and generation,[67] and general aid for investment in energy infrastructure.[68]

The GBER does not apply to aid facilitating the closure of uncompetitive coal mines.[69] Furthermore, the GBER's provisions concerning regional aid – policies which benefit from a more lenient regime whenever pursuing the economic development of a disadvantage region – are not applicable to measures concerning energy generation, distribution and infrastructure and which are regulated by sectoral EU regulation and evaluated under non-Regional aid rules.[70] However, regional policy rules may apply concomitantly with rules relating to aid for environmental protection as discussed above.[71]

5 Capacity remuneration mechanisms

5.1 Understanding Capacity Remuneration Mechanisms (CRMs)

Perhaps the most important and timely development taking place concerning State intervention into energy markets since 2014 is the set-up by Member States and the assessment by the Commission of Capacity Remuneration Mechanisms (CRMs). In this final section we briefly discuss some relevant aspects concerning the assessment of CRMs, in particular the development of their assessment by the Commission and very recently by the EU Courts, as an example of recent developments of State aid application in the energy field.

Security of supply concerning electricity – in particular the need for systems to be reliable and be able to respond quickly and effectively to fluctuations in demand and supply – has been a source of concern among Member States and energy providers.[72] The introduction of renewable energy, its substantial growth, the variability of supply, a reduction in electricity demand and a decrease in fossil fuels have "curbed the profitability of conventional generators and reduced incentives to maintain existing power plants or invest in new ones".[73] This lack of incentives to maintain existing power plants or invest – due to wholesale electricity caps in peak times that hinder recoupment of capacity investment – creates a risk of insufficient available capacity to meet electricity demand and, therefore, puts the reliability of the system at risk.

To tackle these issues of electricity availability, Member States have set up policy tools to ensure adequate additional capacity to ensure an adequate level of security of supply,[74] which should be of a temporary and not indefinite nature.[75] This is usually done through the granting of

66 Ibid, Articles 41, 42 and 43.

67 Ibid, Article 13.

68 Ibid, Article 48.

69 Ibid, Article 13(a).

70 Ibid, Article 13(a).

71 Recital (34) of the Commission Regulation (EU) No 651/2014 of 17 June 2014 declaring certain categories of aid compatible with the internal market in application of Articles 107 and 108 (OJ [2014] L 187), amended by Commission Regulation (EU) 2017/1084 of 14 June 2017 (OJ [2017] L 156/1).

72 Graeme Hawker, Keith Bell and Simon Gill, 'Electricity Security in the European Union—The Conflict between National Capacity Mechanisms and the Single Market' (2017) 24 *Energy Research & Social Science* 51.

73 European Commission, Interim Report of the Sector Inquiry on Capacity Mechanisms {SWD(2016) 119 final}, 13 April 2016, p. 3.

74 Ibid.

75 See the definition of CRM in Article 2 (22) of the Regulation (EU) 2019/943 on the internal market for electricity (OJ [2019] L 158/54).

financial support to generators "for the mere availability of generation capacity",[76] in addition to the revenue obtained from their sale of power, but should also include other providers of capacity, such as demand response or capacity storage suppliers. These mechanisms are significant, complex and novel, as stressed by the General Court,[77] and should be used as a last resort solution.[78]

The literature and practice distinguish a variety of modalities of capacity remuneration mechanisms that vary according to the problem they try to address.[79] They can be designed to address capacity problems in the short term, for instance through a strategic reserve CRM[80] (which is the preferred choice by the newly adopted rules of the Electricity Regulation),[81] or in the long term, by supporting the construction of new capacity through a tender,[82] which applies to the whole market, being either volume or price based;[83] or targeted, as are the majority of the current CRMs in place in Europe.[84]

These financial incentives and support of a public nature tend to qualify as State aid and, therefore, its compatibility with the internal market is to be assessed, as we discuss below.

5.2 Assessment of aid in CRMs: three waves?

In Europe there are more than 35 CRMs in place in at least 13 different Member States.[85] However, only a proportion of these have been subject to scrutiny by the Commission concerning their compatibility with the Treaty rules on State aid. We have observed that through time the design, scrutiny and review of CRM has changed, becoming stricter, due to what we perceive is an increased scrutiny and concern regarding the distorting market effects of these types of aid.[86] This change is palpable in three 'waves' of design, implementation and review of CRM as we discuss below.[87]

76 Communication from the Commission, Guidelines on State aid for environmental protection and energy 2014–2020 (OJ [2014] C 200/1) para. 218.

77 Judgment of 15 November 2018, *Tempus Energy Ltd and Tempus Energy Technology Ltd v Commission*, T-793/14, EU:T:2018:790.

78 Article 21(1) of Regulation (EU) 2019/943 on the internal market for electricity (OJ [2019] L 158/54).

79 For example, the Commission has recently classified CRMs in six different groups in European Commission (n 75) 10; see also: Hawker, Bell and Gill (n 72) 53; Elisabetta Righini and Juan Carlos González Fernández, 'Capacity Mechanisms and State Aid: Between PSOs, Market Liberalisation, and Security of Supply' (2016) 7 *Journal of European Competition Law & Practice* 661.

80 Examples are the Belgian or German mechanisms recently declared compatible with the State aid rules by the Commission. See: SA.48648 *Belgian Strategic Reserve* (OJ [2018] C/121); SA.45852 *German Capacity Reserve* (OJ [2018] L 302).

81 Article 21(3) of the Regulation (EU) 2019/943 on the internal market for electricity (OJ [2019] L 158/54).

82 SA.40454 *Tender for Additional Capacity in Brittany* (OJ [2017] L 235).

83 For instance, through central buyer mechanisms as in Italy in SA.42011 *Italian Capacity Mechanism* (OJ [2018] C 158), or Ireland in SA.44464 *Irish Capacity Mechanism: Reliability Option Scheme* (OJ [2018] C 121).

84 These are the cases of several targeted CRM in place in both Portugal and Spain. See Commission Staff Working Document Accompanying the document: 'Final Report of the Sector Inquiry on Capacity Mechanisms' (2016).

85 Hawker, Bell and Gill (n 72) 53.

86 Even the notion of having CRM as a solution to pure energy-only markets has been put to question and scrutiny in the literature. See for more on this, inter alia, Leigh Hancher, Adrien de Hauteclocque and Malgorzata Sadowska, *Capacity Mechanisms in the EU Energy Market: Law, Policy, and Economics* (Oxford University Press 2015); Arthur Henriot and Jean-Michel Glachant, Capacity remuneration mechanisms in the European market: now but how?, EUI Working Paper RSCAS 2014/84, (2014); Nicolas Hary, Vincent Rious and Marcelo Saguan, 'The Electricity Generation Adequacy Problem: Assessing Dynamic Effects of Capacity Remuneration Mechanisms' (2016) 91 *Energy Policy* 113; Guido Cervigni, *Generation Capacity Adequacy in Europe: What Economic Rationale for Capacity Remuneration Mechanisms?,* Centre of Regulation in Europe (CERRE) (2013).

87 Also identifying 'waves' of scrutiny regarding CRM see: Righini and González Fernández (n 79) 661.

5.2.1 Public service obligation and Article 106(2) of the TFEU

The first set of CRMs that were implemented in Europe were designed as remuneration granted to undertakings entrusted with the operation of a service of general economic interest that was designated as a public service obligation (PSO).[88] By doing so, Member States were able to circumvent the application of EU State aid rules because no aid was granted and only a compensation was given. Thus, no traditional State aid notification and assessment of the CRM had to be made by the Commission as this did not constitute aid pursuant to the derogation of Article 106(2) of the TFEU.[89]

As long as Member States constructed the CRM within the limits imposed by the rules concerning the designation of a public service obligation in line with the *Altmark* criteria, there was no granting of aid and no obligation to report to the Commission, due to the exception of Article 106(2) of the TFEU. In practice, this translated into the Commission carrying out an assessment concerning whether the service constituted a PSO and if the remuneration was in line with the criteria and not concerning the remuneration scheme itself. Two concrete examples of this approach are the cases of Ireland[90] and Slovenia[91] in which this assessment took place.

In the Irish case, the Commission assessed a CRM in the whole of Ireland based on the entry of new capacity supported by a Capacity and Differences Agreement. This system implied that generators would receive payments based on available capacity for up to ten years based on a pool price, ultimately financed by end consumers. Following the *Altmark* criteria, the Commission evaluated the four cumulative requirements and concluded, as all requirements were present, that "the scheme involves no State aid within the meaning of Article [107](1) TFEU of the [TFEU] Treaty to generators".[92] In the Slovenian case, the situation dealt with two power plants that received a support scheme as part of a large investigation concerning stranded costs for electricity generators. The remuneration for the power plant in Trbovlje was built around the support of renewable sources to secure supply of electricity. The Decision reviewed the remuneration paid by the Slovenian State as connected to a PSO and therefore benefiting from an exception to the prohibition of aid, following a succinct analysis of the *Altmark* criteria and it was decided it does not constitute aid.[93]

5.2.2 The Commission's guidelines and follow-up cases

As part of the State aid modernization in 2014 the Commission issued its Guidelines on State Aid for Environmental Protection and Energy 2014–2020 which, for the first time, contain rules for the assessment of CRP in its Section 3.9.[94] These provisions are quite detailed and appear as a mechanism to order and standardize as much as possible the granting of aid to secure adequate electricity generation by Member States to secure sufficient electricity supply.

88 Ibid, 668–669.

89 See Judgment of 24 July 2003, *Altmark Trans and Regierungspräsidium Magdeburg*, C-280/00, EU:C:2003:415; and discussing the imposition of a compensation connected to the discharge of public service obligations and the derogation of Article [106](2) TFEU Judgment of 11 June 2009, *Italy v Commission*, T-222/04, EU:T:2009:194, paras. 107–116. See also: Talus (n 4) 105.

90 N475/2003 *Public Service Obligation (PSO) Notification*.

91 SA.16726 *Slovenian Electricity Tariffs*, Case C7/2005.

92 *Public Service Obligation* (n 90) para. 65.

93 *Slovenian Electricity Tariffs* (n 91) paras. 98–123.

94 Communication from the Commission, Guidelines on State aid for environmental protection and energy 2014–2020 (OJ [2014] C 200/1).

The Guidelines shed light concerning the characteristics CRM should comply with in general to be considered compatible with State aid rules and, therefore, be compatible aid. The objective of the measure, for example being long or short-term security of supply, "should be clearly defined, including when and where the generation adequacy problem is expected to arise".[95] Member States are required to define the nature and causes for the introduction of the CRM, with a detailed and sufficient analysis of technical information, and the reasons why the market is unable to address the failure.[96] Among the relevant information to be assessed is the impact of the CRM on variable generation, on demand-side participation, on the existing or potential interconnection capacity or other elements that may affect generation adequacy and, in particular, on regulated tariffs and price caps. Further, the compensation granted to the undertaking must be appropriate and shall only "remunerate solely the service of pure availability provided by the generator, that is to say, the commitment of being available to deliver electricity and the corresponding compensation for it", excluding any remuneration for the sale of power.[97] Most important, perhaps, is the remark that the CRM must be open to both existing and future generators and be treated in the same manner as other energy efficiency solutions, such as demand-side response or storage.[98] Regarding the amount of aid, the Guidelines state that this should allow for a remuneration which can be considered reasonable and that, whenever possible, this should be determined through a competitive bidding process in order to select the undertaking(s) providing the capacity, ensuring the avoidance of windfall profits.[99] Also, the CRM should be designed to ensure that the compensation paid for capacity automatically tends to zero when there is sufficient available capacity in the system, only being remunerated in cases of strict necessity.[100] Lastly, the Guidelines seek to limit the undue negative side-effects on competition and trade of the CRM. In this sense, the mechanism should be generation-technology neutral, and treat other efficiency solutions in the same way as generation, such as demand-side management, storage or interconnection capacity. Cross-border participation from generators should be encouraged if physically possible and energy-market negative effects should be avoided as much as possible.[101]

The Guidelines kickstarted the review of CRM by the Commission. Since its adoption, 15 mechanisms have been assessed, all of them approved. Only a handful of these have been fully assessed before or after the CRM has been put in place, ensuring its compatibility with the Guidelines after initial doubts,[102] and in most of cases no objections or comments have been raised.[103]

5.2.3 Stricter review by the EU Courts?

In November 2018 the General Court reviewed and annulled the Commission's assessment of a CRM in the UK in *Tempus Energy*.[104] This is the first approved case in accordance with

95 Ibid., para. 221.

96 Ibid, paras. 222 and 223.

97 Ibid, para. 225.

98 Ibid, para. 225.

99 Ibid, paras. 228–230.

100 Ibid, para. 231. This is also explicitly addressed by Article 22 of the Regulation (EU) 2019/943 on the internal market for electricity (OJ [2019] L 158/54).

101 Communication from the Commission, Guidelines on State aid for environmental protection and energy 2014–2020 (OJ [2014] C 200/1), paras. 232 and 233.

102 See the examples of France country-wide capacity mechanism – SA.39621; *France – Tender for additional capacity in Brittany* – SA.40454; and *Germany - German capacity reserve* – SA.45852.

103 http://ec.europa.eu/competition/sectors/energy/state_aid_to_secure_electricity_supply_en.html. Last accessed 27 May 2019.

104 *Tempus Energy* (n 77).

the Guidelines on State Aid for Environmental Protection and Energy 2014–2020,[105] and also the first annulled case of a decision dealing with CRM in Europe. In its assessment, the General Court found that the Commission should have opened a full investigation to assess the compatibility of the measure as there were sufficient doubts concerning its compliance with the Commission's Guidelines, even if the Court did not challenge the need to set up a CRM in the UK to alleviate the capacity shortage.[106] The main grounds for the Court to annul the decision and order a new assessment were the doubts that were raised by Tempus concerning the discriminatory and disproportionate manner in which, allegedly, the CRM installed in the UK privileged capacity offered by generators vis-à-vis demand side response solutions, as required by the Guidelines. Due to the size and role that demand response could have been played to address the issue of capacity in the first place, the Commission must have had doubts as to whether the CRM was even necessary and, therefore, should have opened a formal investigation procedure to allow parties to submit observations and assess in full the need and compatibility of the capacity market.

This case is now being followed up by another action[107] pending decision launched on February 2018 by Grange Backup Power against the decisions by the Commission concerning the compatibility of the CRM in Ireland,[108] and in Northern Ireland.[109]

In our view, these two cases, and the new rules in the Proposed Electricity Regulation, are the start of a series of actions to be brought before the EU Courts by energy undertakings that feel the CRM has been set up by the Member States without a proper detailed assessment by the Commission and that it has distorting effects in competition. As a side-effect of these cases, we also estimate the future Commission Decisions on CRMs to be (even) more detailed than they are currently and focused on the possible discriminatory effects of the remuneration vis-à-vis non-generating electricity undertakings.

6 Conclusion

State aid rules constitute an essential part of EU regulation concerning energy. They set positive and negative boundaries for Member States to intervene in the energy market's structure and performance, by allowing the granting (or prohibiting) of some State benefit to a particular undertaking to address a market failure and advance energy market policies and objectives within the rules imposed by the Treaty. In practical terms, the amount of State aid designated to energy is the second largest of the approved aid in the EU and these funds are being used to transform, modernize and pursue the 'greenification' of energy markets in Europe, with renewable electricity infrastructure and energy efficiency measures at the forefront.

This trend of intense public intervention in energy markets is likely to continue through the granting of aid. This is both to ensure functioning and modern energy markets and to promote the European energy regulation goals, more especially pursuant to the "Clean Energy Package's" rules, and further public intervention in the fostering of renewable energy

105 European Commission, State aid: Commission authorises UK Capacity Market electricity generation scheme, Press Release (23 July 2014).

106 *Tempus Energy* (n 77) para. 267.

107 Case T-110/18, *Grange Backup Power v Commission* (pending).

108 Commission Decision C(2017) 7789 final of 24 November 2017 on the *Irish Capacity Mechanism* (SA.44464 (2017/N).

109 *United Kingdom – Northern Irish Capacity Mechanism: Reliability Option Scheme* – SA.4446.

sources and cross-border infrastructural projects. While we expect that most energy related aid will continue being approved and/or designed to benefit from the GBER,[110] which is the case with more than 95 per cent of general State aid measures being exempted, we also anticipate a stricter scrutiny from the Commission concerning energy aid measures. This is both to promote competition between sources

Furthermore, we expect the importance and scrutiny of CRM and State aid evaluations to keep increasing and becoming more complex, the more so with new rules applicable to them for both long and short-term issues in the Electricity Regulation and the new (but old as they reflect the Commission's Guidelines) principles listed in its Article 21,[111] and the proposed Risk-Preparedness Regulation,[112] respectively.

110 In 2017, more than 95 per cent of the State aid measures fell under the GBER (n 1) 7.

111 Regulation (EU) 2019/943 on the internal market for electricity (OJ [2019] L 158/54). See also: Kaisa Huhta, *Capacity Mechanisms in EU Law: A Comment on the Free Movement of Goods* (Oxford Energy Comment 2018) 7.

112 Regulation (EU) 2019/941 of the European Parliament and of the Council of 5 June 2019 on risk-preparedness in the electricity sector and repealing Directive 2005/89/EC (OJ [2019] L 158/1).

9

SHALE GAS IN EUROPE

A case study on EU energy and environmental law

Ruven Fleming

I Introduction

By the beginning of the 2010s, the debate about new and so-called 'unconventional' forms of energy had reached fever-pitch level in societies around the globe. The reason was shale gas, a hitherto untapped resource of natural gas. The resource was dispersed around the globe and it fuelled imagination and controversy. At the height of the controversy movies were made on the subject.[1] A documentary called *Gasland*, which investigated the early days of the shale gas rush in the (United States (US), even became a nominee for an Oscar.[2] That film entailed a sequence, which captured the public imagination and turned into a symbol for potential issues of shale gas extraction: American house owners were filmed setting their water taps on fire.[3]

The regulatory reaction to these documentaries in Europe was swift and forceful:[4] a number of European Union (EU) Member States put into place moratoria or outright bans on the activity.[5] These quick actions were underpinned by the opinion of some legal scholars, who claimed that it is very easy to prohibit shale gas extraction, whereas it is more complicated to create permissive shale gas regulation.[6]

1 Focus Features, Promised Land Movie (2012) www.focusfeatures.com/promised_land, accessed 22 December 2018.

2 *Gasland* (2010), www.gaslandthemovie.com, accessed 22 December 2018. In 2013, the director launched another movie called *Gasland 2*. For the Oscar nomination see: Mike Soraghan *New York Times* (24 February 2011), 'Groundtruthing Academy Award Nominee "Gasland,"' www.nytimes.com/gwire/2011/02/24/24greenwire-groundtruthing-academy-award-nominee-gasland-33228.html?pagewanted=all, accessed 22 December 2018.

3 It was claimed that their water supplies had been poisoned by shale gas extraction Those claims were later thrown into question by another documentary that defended shale gas extraction called *Frack Nation*. Phelim McAleer, Frack Nation, http://fracknation.com, accessed 22 December 2018.

4 Occasionally, it has, indeed, been a direct reaction to the movies, see the debate on a shale gas moratorium for Northern Ireland in the Northern Ireland Assembly: Northern Ireland Assembly, Debates, 6 December 2011, Vol 69 No 6, cols 305 and 311.

5 Ruven Fleming, 'Shale Gas, the Environment and Energy Security,' (Edward Elgar, Cheltenham 2017), 108–178.

6 Tina Hunter, Emre Usenmez and John Paterson, 'Future Trends in Shale Gas Law and Policy in the United Kingdom,' in Tina Hunter (ed.), *Handbook of Shale Gas Law and Policy*, (Intersentia, Cambridge 2016) 389, fm 40.

But there is also a different view in Europe. In particular, the EU Commission appears to be open to permissive shale gas regulation. Shale gas extraction is viewed as a potential 'game-changer' for the security of energy supplies in Europe.[7] Shale gas has already allowed the US to switch its gas-importer status to that of a gas-exporter.[8] Moreover, shale gas extraction could have the potential to lower gas prices.[9] It is not even necessary for shale gas extraction to actually commence in the EU to achieve that goal.[10] The mere prospect of domestic shale gas extraction in Europe might make current suppliers think twice about further increases in the price of their commodity.[11]

This chapter scrutinizes EU legislation and its applicability to shale gas extraction. Shale gas extraction, being a hitherto unknown way to produce gas in Europe, is a perfect case study on how EU law works when it comes to new energy developments and the dichotomy involved between the pre-existing legal framework and new rules that might have to be drawn up. This regulatory process involves three steps. First the EU requires primary law competence to regulate shale gas extraction in the first place rather than it be left to the Member States. After having established the competence to regulate, a second step, the so-called secondary EU law, needs to be assessed (Regulations, Directives, etc.) to see which components the existing legal framework of the EU has on shale gas extraction. The third step is then dedicated to the EU's recent endeavours to develop shale gas specific regulation in order to close identified gaps in the existing framework, before coming to some conclusions. The remainder of this chapter follows this structure.

2 Primary EU Law and shale gas extraction

2.1 Consideration of a possible legal basis

Due to the division of powers between the EU and its Member States,[12] it is necessary for the EU to have competence, whenever it wishes to act on a certain issue.[13] A competence that will provide the EU with regulatory powers in a particular area[14] must have been conferred upon it[15] by the European Treaties.[16]

7 Maximilian Kuhn and Frank Umbach *Strategic Perspectives of Unconventional Gas: A Game Changer with Implications for the EU* (2011) European Centre for Energy and Resource Security (EUCERS) Strategy Paper No 1 available at: www.eucers.eu/2011/05/06/eucers-strategy-paper-no1_, accessed 24 April 2018.

8 Slawomir Raszewski 'Shale Gas and Energy Security' in Tina Hunter (ed.) *Handbook of Shale Gas Law and Policy* (Intersentia, Cambridge 2016) 124.

9 Affordability of energy is part of the security of supplies, see Leigh Hancher and Sally Janssen, 'Shared Competences and Multi-Faceted Concepts – European Legal Framework for Security of Supply' in Barton B et al. (eds.) *Energy Security: Managing Risk in a Dynamic Legal and Regulatory Environment* (Oxford University Press, Oxford 2004) 93.

10 Commission 'Communication on the Exploration and Production of Hydrocarbons (such as Shale Gas) Using High Volume Hydraulic Fracturing in the EU' (Communication) COM (2014) 23 final/2 at 3 (hereinafter: Commission Shale Gas Communication); Ivan L G Pearson et al. 'Unconventional Gas: Potential Energy Market Impacts in the European Union' (Joint Research Centre of the European Commission, 2012) 59, https://ec.europa.eu/jrc/en/publication/eur-scientific-and-technical-research-reports/unconventional-gas-europe-potential-energy-market-impacts [accessed 9 Dec. 2019], Kuhn and Umbach, n.7, 42.

11 Ibid.

12 Paul Craig and Grainne de Burca *EU Law Texts Cases and Materials* 5th edition (Oxford University Press, Oxford 2011) 75–78.

13 Ibid. 74; Jan H Jans and Hans H B Vedder *European Environmental Law* 3rd edition (Europa Law Publishing, Groningen 2008) 10 (hereinafter: Jans/Vedder).

14 Craig/De Burca 75.

15 Article 5 (2) Treaty on European Union (hereinafter: TEU); Jans/Vedder 10.

16 Craig/De Burca 75–76.

Shale gas extraction strikes at the core of (at least) two vital interests, environmental protection and energy security. Both are laid out as potential areas of EU competence, Article 194 of the Treaty on the Functioning of the European Union (TFEU) for energy and Article 192 of the TFEU for the environment. Due to their link with shale gas extraction these two competences lend themselves naturally for consideration of a legal basis of shale gas regulation at EU level.[17]

Prior to the enactment of the TFEU a third legal basis had been used to justify EU action in both the environmental and the energy spheres, namely what is now Article 114 of the TFEU.[18] Article 114 of the TFEU allows the EU to adopt measures that have the establishment and functioning of an internal market in Europe as their objective.[19] Before the coming into force of the TFEU environmental and energy measures that support the free movement of goods, persons, services and capital had to be adopted under this article and its predecessors.[20] However, the literature commonly agrees that, as opposed to past practice, which relied upon Article 114 of the TFEU, now Article 194 of the TFEU provides the central EU competence in energy matters.[21]

Shale gas, after all, is a form of energy that may be produced in individual Member States. Being a domestic source of energy, other Member States might exceptionally be involved when it comes to shale gas reservoirs that straddle national boundaries. But other than that, the process of shale gas extraction[22] is more directly linked to the specific energy Article 194 of the TFEU than to Article 114 of the TFEU.[23]

In any case, energy regulation has been traditionally singled out by the legal literature as an area of minimum harmonization, where Member States might establish their own legislation within the framework provided by the EU.[24] Several decisions of the European Court of Justice (ECJ) assert that Member States indeed have the right to legislate in the field of energy if the EU has not, not yet or not comprehensively exercised its right to do so.[25]

2.2 The centre of gravity: Article 192 or Article 194 TFEU as legal basis?

It is settled case law of the ECJ that the legal basis of an EU measure must be selected by the legislator based on objective factors that are assessable to judicial review.[26] The legislator shall

17 Elen Stokes 'New EU Policy on Shale Gas' (2014) Volume 16 Issue 1 *Environmental Law Review* 43–44 (hereinafter: Stokes).

18 Angus Johnston and Guy Block *EU Energy Law* (Oxford University Press, Oxford 2012) paragraphs 1.04 and 2.51 (hereinafter: Johnston/Block); Nicolas de Sadeleer *Environmental Law and the Internal Market* 350 (Oxford University Press, Oxford 2014) (hereinafter: De Sadeleer *Internal Market*); Jans/Vedder 94.

19 Article 114 (1) TFEU in conjunction with Article 26 (1) and (2) TFEU.

20 For a concise description of the history of that particular article see: Jans/Vedder 94.

21 De Sadeleer *Internal Market* 350; Johnston/Block paragraph 1.05/1.08.

22 It has to be emphasized that this picture might or might not change when it comes to the question of what happens with the gas after extraction, further downstream. This question, however, lies outside the scope of the current chapter.

23 For a similar assessment see: Stokes 43–44.

24 Johnston/Block paragraph 15.03.

25 Such as Case 6/64 *Flaminio Costa v E.N.E.L.* [1964] ECR I-00585 at 593; for a discussion of this and further cases see Christian Calliess and Matthias Ruffert *EUV/AEUV Kommentar* 4th edition (Beck, München 2011) Article 194 AEUV paragraph 23 (hereinafter: Calliess/Ruffert).

26 Case C-45/86 Commission of the European Communities v Council of the European Communities [1987] ECR I-1493 paragraph 11; Case C-300/89 Commission of the European Communities v Council of the European Communities [1991] ECR I-2867 paragraph 10; Case C-155/91 Commission of the European Communities v Council of the

look for the 'centre of gravity' of a measure, which determines its legal basis.[27] If the 'centre of gravity' is protection of the environment, measures should be brought under Article 192 TFEU.[28] If the measure is mainly concerned with energy Article 194 TFEU is the applicable legal basis.[29]

Concentrating on the 'centre of gravity'-doctrine it seems that in a case like the regulation of shale gas extraction both competences, the energy as well as the environmental competence, should be heavily involved. After all, shale gas extraction might have severe repercussions in both areas. If an act of secondary EU law pursues more than one objective and the pursued objectives have an equal bearing on the regulated issue, the ECJ exceptionally accepts that a measure can be founded on a dual legal basis,[30] as long as practicalities of the legislative procedure can be reconciled.[31] Since shale gas extraction has an intense bearing on both the environmental and the energy sphere, it would be most appropriate to use Articles 192 and 194 of the TFEU as dual legal basis.[32]

3 Secondary EU law and shale gas extraction

Having established a primary EU law basis, it is now necessary to assess how shale gas extraction fits into the existing secondary law framework on energy and the environment. The extent to which European secondary law covers shale gas extraction is subject to an ongoing debate in the scientific literature. Studies on the topic yielded a huge variety of results, ranging from eight different applicable pieces of EU legislation,[33] to over 19[34] and up to approximately 40.[35] This discrepancy is mainly caused by the fact that some studies focus on the most relevant pieces of legislation, while others comprehensively address every legislative bit that might have a potential bearing on shale gas extraction.

European Communities [1993] ECR I-939 paragraphs 10–15 and Case C-187/93 European Parliament v Council of the European Union [1994] ECR I-2857 paragraphs 22–23; Case C-268/94 Portuguese Republic v Council of the European Union [1996] ECR I-6177 paragraph 22; C-176/03 Commission of the European Communities v Council of the European Union [2005] ECR I-7879 paragraph 45.

27 Jans/Vedder 68; Mathew L Schemmel and Bas de Regt 'The European Court of Justice and the Environmental Protection Policy of the European Community' (1994) Vol 17 Issue 1 *Boston College International and Comparative Law Review* 53; Ronald van Ooik 'Cross-Pillar Litigation Before the ECJ: Demarcation of Community and Union Competences' (2008) Volume 4 Issue 3 *European Constitutional Law Review* 399.

28 Ibid.

29 Johnston/Block paragraph 1.05.

30 Case C-300/98 and C-392/98 *Parfums Christian Dior SA v TUK Consultancy BV und Assco Gerüste GmbH and Rob van Dijk v Wilhelm Layher GmbH & Co. KG and Layher BV* [2000] ECR I-11307 paragraph 13; Case C-336/00 *Republik Österreich v Martin Huber* [2002] ECR I-07699 paragraph 31; Jans/Vedder 69.

31 For more on that problem see Ruven Fleming 'Shale Gas, the Environment and Energy Security' (Edward Elgar, Cheltenham 2017) 57–59 (hereinafter: Fleming).

32 Fleming 58–59.

33 Available at: http://ec.europa.eu/environment/integration/energy/pdf/legal_assessment.pdf_[accessed 24 April 2014] (hereinafter: Potocnik Transmission).

34 Mark Broomfield 'Support to the Identification of Potential Risks for the Environment and Human Health Arising from Hydrocarbons Operations Involving Hydraulic Fracturing in Europe' (AEA Technology, Didcot 2012) xi and 77 available at: http://ec.europa.eu/environment/integration/energy/uff_studies_en.htm [accessed 4 Sept 2018] (hereinafter: Broomfield).

35 Didier Bonijoly et al. 'Impacts of Shale Gas and Shale Oil Extraction on the Environment and on Human Health' (European Parliament, 2011) 48 and 54 available at: https://www.europarl.europa.eu/document/activities/cont/201312/20131205ATT75545/20131205ATT75545EN.pdf [accessed 9 Dec. 2019] (hereinafter: Bonijoly et al.).

Due to spatial limitations, this chapter provides a very brief overview of the five most relevant Directives and Regulations on shale gas extraction, and the most prominent legal discussions surrounding them.[36] The assessment focuses on regulations in the Directive on Strategic Environmental Assessment and the Environmental Impact Assessment Directive (Monitoring), the Water Framework and Groundwater Directives (Water Pollution), the REACH Regulation (Chemicals), the Environmental Liability Directive (responsibility and burden of proof) and the Hydrocarbons Licensing Directive (Licensing of hydrocarbon extraction in the EU).[37]

Although these norms were not developed with shale gas extraction in mind, nonetheless they apply to certain aspects of the process.

3.1 Strategic Environmental Assessment and Environmental Impact Assessment

According to the Directive on Strategic Environmental Assessment (SEA Directive) Member States shall undertake environmental assessments in certain cases for large strategic plans or programmes at policy level.[38] This applies to plans and programmes that are likely to have significant environmental impacts.[39] A strategic environmental assessment (or SEA) shall describe and appraise these likely and significant impacts on the environment. This has to be viewed together with the Environmental Impact Assessment Directive (EIA Directive), which covers impact assessments for individual projects.[40]

Article 3 of the SEA Directive determines which plans and programmes in particular have to be subjected to a strategic environmental assessment. According to Article 3(2)(a) of the SEA Directive this is, *inter alia*, the case for town and country planning programmes, which are listed in Annexes I and II of the EIA Directive and set the framework for future

36 Fleming 59–104.

37 Potočnik Annex II page 6 identified seven EU Directives and one EU Regulation. For the four main risks see Sachverständigenrat für Umweltfragen (SRU) Martin Faulstich et al. 'Fracking zur Schiefergasgewinnung Ein Beitrag zur energie- und umweltpolitischen Bewertung Stellungnahme' available at: www.umweltrat.de/SharedDocs/Downloads/DE/04_Stellungnahmen/2012_2016/2013_05_AS_18_Fracking.pdf?__blob=publicationFile (accessed 2 July 2019] 44–45 (hereinafter: SRU Faulstich); Philippe & Partners Law Firm 'Final Report on Unconventional Gas in Europe' (2011) 101–102 available at: http://ec.europa.eu/energy/studies/doc/2012_unconventional_gas_in_europe.pdf [accessed 12 March 2018] (hereinafter: Philippe & Partners); Stokes 43–44.

38 Articles 1 and 2 and 5(1) of Council Directive (EC) 2001/42 of 27 June 2001 on the assessment of the effects of certain plans and programmes on the environment [2001] OJ L 197/30 (hereinafter: SEA Directive).

39 Article 1 SEA Directive. Article 3 SEA Directive determines which plans and programmes in particular have to be subjected to a SEA.

40 Article 1(1) Council Directive (EU) 2011/92 of 13 December 2011 on the assessment of the effects of certain public and private projects on the environment [2012] OJ L 26/1, as amended by Council Directive (EU) 2014/52 of 16 April 2014 amending Directive 2011/92/EU on the assessment of the effects of certain public and private projects on the environment [2014] OJ L 124/1 (hereinafter: EIA Directive). According to Article 14 of Directive 2011/92/EU, this Directive repealed the pre-existing, older version of an EIA Directive, namely Council Directive (EC) 85/337/EEC of 27 June 1985 on the assessment of the effects of certain public and private projects on the environment [1985] OJ L 175/40, which had already been amended several times by Council Directive (EC) 97/11 of 3 March 1997 amending Directive 85/337/EEC on the assessment of the effects of certain public and private projects on the environment [1997] OJ L 73/5 and Council Directive (EC) 2003/35 of 26 May 2003 providing for public participation in respect of the drawing up of certain plans and programmes relating to the environment and amending with regard to public participation and access to justice Council Directives 85/337/EEC and 96/61/EC [2003] OJ L 156/17.

development consents for projects. This provision may apply to shale gas projects in the following way:[41] Annex II to the EIA Directive, in its section on the extractive industry, mentions 'd) deep drillings' and 'e) surface industrial installations for the extraction of coal, petroleum, natural gas and ores, as well as bituminous shale'. It has been argued that, because shale gas is natural gas and deep drillings would be required to access it, a SEA would be required for plans and programmes that are concerned with the town and country planning aspects of shale gas activities.[42]

According to Article 1(2)(a) of the EIA Directive, a project is something that requires the execution of construction works or other interventions in the natural surroundings or landscape, including activities like the extraction of mineral resources. Article 2 (1) of the EIA Directive contains its central provision.[43] It requires Member States to ensure that an environmental impact assessment is carried out before consent is granted to projects that are likely to have significant effects on the environment.

Article 4 of the EIA Directive distinguishes between two different categories of projects. Projects falling under Annex I must be accompanied by an obligatory environmental impact assessment.[44] In case of projects falling under Annex II, the Member States are asked to determine on a case-by-case basis whether or not the project in question should be subjected to an environmental impact assessment.[45]

Shale gas is not explicitly listed in either of these two annexes. However, section 14 of Annex I makes the carrying out of an environmental impact assessment compulsory for 'Extraction of petroleum and natural gas for commercial purposes where the amount extracted exceeds 500 tonnes/day in the case of petroleum and 500 000 cubic metres/day in the case of gas'.[46]

Since shale gas is natural gas produced for commercial purposes, this paragraph could be applicable. However, shale gas wells in Europe,[47] even in its largest Member State,[48] cannot reasonably be expected to have a daily output of gas anywhere near 500 000 cubic metres per day.[49] Even if a project could be defined as consisting of several wells that are drilled from the same plot of land, the output would not reach 500 000 cubic metres per day.[50] Thus, an environmental impact assessment is not compulsory for individual shale gas projects.[51]

However, Article 4(2) in conjunction with Annex II of the EIA Directive establishes that Member States can voluntarily decide whether or not they wish to subject a certain project to an environmental impact assessment, either through case-by-case examination or by setting thresholds or criteria (or both). Annex III of the EIA Directive establishes a list of selection criteria with the help of which Member States shall make that choice.[52]

41 Broomfield 8 and 79.
42 Broomfield 79.
43 Jans/Vedder 312.
44 According to Article 4(1) EIA Directive.
45 Article 4(2) EIA Directive.
46 Section 14 of Annex I Council Directive (EU) 2011/92 of 13 December 2011 on the assessment of the effects of certain public and private projects on the environment [2012] OJ L 26/1.
47 Lechtenböhmer et al. 61.
48 For the example of Germany see: Philippe & Partners 49 paragraph 145.
49 Broomfield 80.
50 Ibid.
51 Ibid.
52 Jans/Vedder 314.

A 2011 guidance note of the European Commission on the application of the EIA Directive to unconventional hydrocarbons stressed that 'unconventional hydrocarbon projects, even exploratory ones, which use deep drillings, are covered by Annex II.2.d'.[53] In addition, paragraph 2(e) of Annex II of the 2011 EIA Directive is applicable to shale gas extraction.[54] Thus, shale gas extraction falls into the scope of the EIA Directive, but only under Annex II and it is up to the Member States to decide on a case-by-case basis if an environmental impact assessment is required.[55]

3.2 Water Framework Directive and Groundwater Directive

The potential contamination of water resources has been a focal point of the political debate on shale gas.[56] Potential threats could, on the one hand, result from the contamination of groundwater by chemicals or hydrocarbons during shale gas extraction. On the other hand, aquifers and groundwater reservoirs could become polluted after the actual extraction process has ceased, namely during the disposal of 'flow back' (water that re-surfaces during the fracturing treatment) in deep ground injection wells.[57]

The Water Framework Directive and the Groundwater Directive both deal with the quality of groundwater and try to achieve a good quality of this resource from two different angles. The Groundwater Directive recommends specific measures to prevent and control groundwater pollution. Its aim is to monitor groundwater quality, which will also have to be done in the context of shale gas extraction.

The Water Framework Directive, however, is the more comprehensive tool and may become a 'sharp sword'. Article 11(3)(j) of the Water Framework Directive prohibits the direct discharge of pollutants into groundwater, subject to specific provisions.[58] But there is an exception: according to its Article 11(3)(j) Member States may allow

> injection of water containing substances resulting from the operations for exploration and extraction of hydrocarbons or mining activities, and injection of water for technical reasons, into geological formations from which hydrocarbons or other substances have been extracted .... Such injections shall not contain substances other than those resulting from the above operations.[59]

The then European Commissioner for the environment, Janez Potočnik, concluded that this exemption does not apply to the deep ground disposal of 'flow back' from shale gas operations.[60] His report provides two arguments for this: first, one of the objectives of the Water Framework Directive is to reach a good status of water resources, which would be endangered by shale gas operations.[61] Second, the exception of Article 11(3)(j) of the Water Frame-

53 European Commission 'Guidance Note on the Application of Directive 85/337/EEC to Projects Related to the Exploration and Exploitation of Unconventional Hydrocarbon' of 12 December 2011 at 3 available at: http://ec.europa.eu/environment/integration/energy/pdf/guidance_note.pdf [accessed 28 April 2019].

54 Broomfield 81 and 85.

55 Philippe & Partners 49 paragraph 145; Lechtenböhmer et al. 61.

56 Fleming 21–40.

57 Potocnik Transmission 7.

58 Broomfield 110.

59 Article 11(3)(j) Water Framework Directive.

60 Potocnik Transmission 7.

61 Ibid.

work Directive has been specifically designed for conventional hydrocarbon operations, as the negotiation history of the Directive highlights.[62]

This argument has been endorsed by a later study on shale gas extraction, prepared for the European Commission.[63] This later study added a third argument that builds upon the wording of Article 11(3)(j) of the Water Framework Directive. According to this argument, only the injection of water containing substances *resulting* from the operations for exploration and extraction of hydrocarbons is subject to the exemption.[64] The last sentence of Article 11(3)(j) of the Water Framework Directive ('*Such injections shall not contain substances other than those resulting from the above operations*') would, thus, preclude the deep ground injection of 'flow back'; 'flow back' does not only contain substances resulting from hydrocarbons extraction, but also the artificially prepared, fracturing fluid plus substances coming from the geological formations.[65] The fracturing fluid, the argument goes, serves a special purpose (maximizing the flow of hydrocarbons) and its existence is not a *consequence* of the operations.[66]

All three arguments have to be dismissed as invalid. In cases where shale gas extraction is not achieved by the use of chemical substances but by other means, like pneumatic fracturing or gel-based fracturing fluids, the existence of a potential threat might be excluded.[67] These methods do not use water-endangering chemicals.[68] Moreover, where chemicals are being used, fracturing fluids are mixed for each well individually and therefore no general assumptions about their risk-potential can be made.

The second argument, that the exemption of Article 11(3)(j) of the Water Framework Directive was originally elaborated with conventional hydrocarbon extraction in mind and does not apply to unconventionals, is also not convincing. Legal interpretation requires, first and foremost, consideration of the plain meaning of the provision in question. The wording of the Directive does not mention any restriction to conventional hydrocarbons.

Furthermore, law evolves in the sense that it may eventually be applied to facts and circumstances that were not foreseen when the regulation was originally promulgated.[69] After all, this whole chapter is concerned with the question of how to apply European environmental legislation to a technological development that was not thought of at the time when EU environmental laws were adopted.

The third argument could be summed up in the following terms: the exemption of Article 11(3)(j) of the Water Framework Directive does not apply to 'flow back', because the latter is not only composed of substances that were originally present in the shale play.

Closer examination of the Article, however, reveals that this definition is incorrect. The wording of Article 11(3)(j) of the Water Framework Directive has the purpose of precluding the disposal of substances which are not in any way associated with the extraction process.[70]

62 Ibid.
63 Broomfield 111.
64 Ibid.
65 Ibid.
66 Ibid.
67 Lucca Gandossi 'An Overview of Hydraulic Fracturing and Other Formation Stimulation Technologies for Shale Gas Production' (Publications Office of the European Union, Luxembourg 2013) 10–50 (hereinafter: Gandossi).
68 Gandossi 49–53.
69 Christine Parker and John Braithwaite 'Regulation' in Peter Cane and Mark Tushnet (eds) *The Oxford Handbook of Legal Studies* (Oxford University Press, Oxford 2003) 122 et sqq.
70 Marleen Van Rijswick 'The Water Framework Directive' in Marleen Van Rijswick (ed.) *The Water Framework Directive: Implementation into German and Dutch Law* (Centrum voor Omgevingsrecht en Beleid, Utrecht 2003) 18–19 and 25–26 (hereinafter: Van Rijswick).

This might be wastewater from other industries or general waste that has nothing to do with the extraction of hydrocarbons.[71] It is, however, not the aim of the Article to exclude the disposal of any substance that does, indeed, result from the extraction process. The natural meaning of the word 'resulting' in Article 11(3)(j) of the Water Framework Directive is 'as a result' and it therefore applies to the entire end-product of the process. 'Flow back' is a natural result of hydraulic fracturing.

To sum up, the deep ground disposal of 'flow back' can be viewed as explicitly endorsed by Article 11(3)(j) of the Water Framework Directive. Although three arguments have been advanced as to why this Article does not cover shale gas extraction, none of them is convincing or coherent.

3.3 *REACH*

Chemical products that are being used in shale gas operations must be regularly disclosed by companies and certified as safe for the specific use by the European Chemicals and Health Agency under Regulations (1907/2006) (REACH).[72] REACH could help to counter the risk of groundwater contamination by holding two different groups of persons accountable for ensuring the safe use of chemicals: first, the producer or importer of a substance[73] and second, the downstream user of the substance,[74] the operator of a shale gas facility.

Manufacturers or importers must register substances under the scope of REACH, which they produce in quantities of one tonne or more per year, with the European Chemicals and Health Agency.[75] There must be an intention to release the substance into the environment under normal or reasonably foreseeable conditions of use.[76]

Although downstream users of chemicals do not have to register directly under REACH, they must make sure that the chemicals are fully registered by manufacturers and importers for their intended use (exposure scenarios). Otherwise, downstream users are simply not allowed to utilize them.[77] Hence, REACH obliges the operator of a shale gas extraction facility (being the downstream user in this case) to assist the supplier in preparing a registration and to check compliance with exposure scenarios.[78] Their primary source of information for making this assessment is an extended safety data sheet that includes exposure scenarios, which has to be provided by the suppliers of the substance.[79] A downstream user shall prepare a chemical safety report on his own for any use outside of the exposure scenarios or for any use his supplier advises against, if the use of the substance would exceed one tonne per

71 Ibid.

72 Regulation (EC) 1907/2006 of 18 December 2006 concerning the registration, evaluation, authorization and restriction of chemicals (REACH) [2006] OJ L 396/1; Potocnik Transmission 8.

73 Articles 3 (32) and 7 REACH.

74 Article 3 (34) and Title V REACH.

75 Articles 6 (1) and 7 (1) REACH.

76 Articles 10 and 14 REACH.

77 Dieter Drohmann and Matthew Townsend *REACH Best Practice Guide to Regulation No 1907/2006* (Beck, Muenchen 2013) 366 (hereinafter: Drohmann/Townsend).

78 Drohmann/Townsend 366–367.

79 Articles 31 (1) and 37 (4) and (5) REACH; Nicolas Herbatschek, Lucas Bergkamp and Meglena Mihova 'The REACH Programmes and Procedures' in Lucas Bergkamp (ed.) *The European Union REACH Regulation for Chemicals Law and Practice* (Oxford University Press, Oxford 2013) paragraph 4.97 (hereinafter: Herbatschek/Bergkamp/Mihova).

year.[80] The downstream user has to communicate this chemical safety report to the European Chemicals and Health Agency.[81]

Alternatively, the downstream user may notify his supplier of the intended use outside of the exposure scenarios and the supplier must then include this use in his exposure scenarios.[82] In any case, the substances may not be used in shale gas operations until these conditions are met.[83] The enforcement of these obligations is up to the Member States.[84] This means that a Member State can and must act if chemical substances are used outside of the scope of intended use or without registration,[85] for instance for unregistered shale gas extraction purposes.

Finally, Article 118 of REACH provides a stipulation for the disclosure of information. Information may not be made publicly available if this would undermine the protection of the commercial interests of the person concerned.[86] However, this non-disclosure only pertains to certain information, like the full composition of a preparation or the precise tonnage of substances.[87] It is also important to note that this merely applies to disclosures to the public. The European Chemicals and Health Agency must be informed in any case.[88] In urgent situations, where the environment or human health is at risk, the Agency itself may disclose sensitive, but relevant information to the public.[89]

To sum up, the provisions of REACH provide a comprehensive net of norms, which could help in countering the potential threat of groundwater contamination brought about by shale gas extraction. The Regulations provide an adequate control mechanism for the use of chemicals and biocides that are associated with shale gas extraction.[90] However, an in-depth study about the applicability of REACH on shale gas extraction concluded that slight amendments to the current reporting praxis of REACH could be made, mainly by clarification of technical terms.[91]

3.4 Environmental Liability Directive

Adopted in 2004, the main aim of Directive 2004/35/EC (Environmental Liability Directive)[92] is to make Member States responsible for ensuring that damage to water, land and

80 Article 37 (4) REACH; Herbatschek/Bergkamp/Mihova paragraph 4.116.

81 Article 38 (1) REACH.

82 Drohmann/Townsend 367–368.

83 Herbatschek/Bergkamp/Mihova paragraph 4.117.

84 Articles 117 and 127 REACH.

85 Herbatschek/Bergkamp/Mihova paragraph 4.117–4.118.

86 Article 118 (2) REACH.

87 Ibid.

88 See Article 118 (1) in conjunction with Article 118 (2) REACH.

89 Article 118 (2) REACH.

90 Stefania Gottardo et al. 'Assessment of the Use of Substances in Hydraulic Fracturing of Shale Gas Reservoirs under REACH' (Publications Office of the European Union, Luxembourg 2013) 8 (hereinafter: Gottardo et al.)

91 Gottardo et al. 8; Fleming 81–85 and 99.

92 Council Directive (EC) 2004/35 of 21 April 2004 on environmental liability with regard to the prevention and remedying of environmental damage [2004] OJ L 143/56 (hereinafter: Environmental Liability Directive). The Directive has been amended three times since by Council Directive (EC) 2006/21 of 15 March 2006 on the management of waste from extractive industries and amending Directive 2004/35/EC [2006] OJ L 102/15, Council Directive (EC) 2009/31 of 23 April 2009 on the geological storage of carbon dioxide and amending Council Directive 85/337/EEC, European Parliament and Council Directives 2000/60/EC, 2001/80/EC, 2004/35/EC, 2006/12/EC, 2008/1/EC and Regulation (EC) No 1013/2006 [2009] OJ L

biodiversity is either prevented and/or remedied.[93] The Environmental Liability Directive, thus, has a dual function. *Prior* to a possible incident, preventive measures against an imminent threat of environmental damage have to be implemented. *After* an incident where environmental damage occurred it demands the taking of necessary restorative measures.[94]

Strict liability applies to environmental damage caused by the operation of any of the activities listed in Annex III of the Directive.[95] Annex III refers to activities covered under other Directives, when assessing a certain activity. The aspects of shale gas extraction that fall under certain other Directives would, thus, be covered by the strict liability regime of the Environmental Liability Directive.[96] This is most likely the case for groundwater issues and issues with the 'flow back', falling into the scope of the Water Framework Directive (paragraph 5, Annex III) and the Mining Waste Directive.[97]

Fault liability occurs when damages to protected species and natural habitats are caused by the operation of any occupational activity, other than those listed in Annex III and/or any imminent threat of such damage, whenever the operator was at fault or negligent.[98] This is of particular importance for shale gas extraction. The Environmental Liability Directive only covers environmental damage of diffuse character, if a causal link between the damage and the activities of individual operators may be established.[99] This will, most likely, be an issue in shale gas cases, given that air emissions and overbearing land use might have several sources and may, hence, be classified as diffuse environmental damage.[100]

To sum up, the Environmental Liability Directive only orders a strict liability regime for groundwater issues and the deep-ground injection of 'flow back', as these issues are covered by the Mining Waste and the Water Framework Directive. Other potential threats, like greenhouse gas emissions and overbearing use of land, are also covered by the Directive, but are not subject to a strict liability regime. This might be perceived as a gap in the legislation.

3.5 Hydrocarbons Licensing Directive

Directive 94/22/EC (Hydrocarbons Licensing Directive)[101] is a key measure for the regulation of gas extraction,[102] which has to be discussed in the shale gas context. However, in contrast to the pieces of legislation considered so far, the Hydrocarbons Licensing Directive does not have environmental protection as its main aim.[103] The Directive is very much of a framework nature, setting broad principles rather than concrete rules concerning access to

---

140/63 and Council Directive (EU) 2013/30 of 12 June 2013 on safety of offshore oil and gas operations and amending Directive 2004/35/EC [2013] OJ L 178/66.

93 Article 1 Environmental Liability Directive; Barbara J. Goldsmith and Lucas Bergkamp *The EU Environmental Liability Directive A Commentary* (Oxford University Press, Oxford 2013) paragraph 00.03 (hereinafter: Goldsmith/Bergkamp).

94 Goldsmith/Bergkamp paragraph 00.04.

95 Article 3 (1) (a) Environmental Liability Directive; Goldsmith/Bergkamp paragraph 03.02.

96 Broomfield 94.

97 See the new paragraph 13 Annex III Environmental Liability Directive that has been inserted by Article 15 Mining Waste Directive.

98 Article 3 (1) (b) Environmental Liability Directive; Goldsmith/Bergkamp paragraph 03.03.

99 Article 4 (5) Environmental Liability Directive.

100 Broomfield 94.

101 Council Directive (EC) 94/22 of 30 May 1994 on the conditions for granting and using authorizations for the prospection, exploration and production of hydrocarbons OJ L 164/3.

102 Johnston/Block paragraph 15.02/03.

103 Ibid.

hydrocarbons[104] and its main task is to ensure fair competition and equitable access in the internal market.[105]

However, Article 6(2) of the Hydrocarbons Licensing Directive allows Member States to attach conditions upon the exercise of authorizations if this is justified, *inter alia*, by environmental protection needs. This provision makes it possible for Member States to draft authorization conditions that are aimed at preventing or mitigating environmental impacts.[106] Environmental considerations are, hence, not absent from the Hydrocarbons Licensing Directive, but may only come into play indirectly as additional criteria.

Thus, in summary the Hydrocarbons Licensing Directive is not an apt legal tool to regulate any of the potential environmental threats of shale gas extraction, because it focuses on ensuring fair competition in the internal market. This is not a shortcoming of the EU's regulatory framework, but rather a logical consequence of the way in which it is built.

4 Critical reflection on shale gas specific legislation in the EU

In 2014 the Commission put into place a new framework, specifically designed to regulate unconventional hydrocarbon extraction. The framework consists of two components, a Communication and a Recommendation. The main act is the Recommendation on exploration and production of shale gas (2014 Shale Gas Recommendation),[107] supplemented by the Communication on the exploration and production of hydrocarbons (such as shale gas) using 'high-volume hydraulic fracturing' (HVHF) in the EU (2014 Shale Gas Communication).[108] The Recommendation targets not only shale gas extraction, but every kind of unconventional gas extraction that uses HVHF.[109] The term means the injection of 1 000 m^3 or more of water per fracturing stage or 10 000 m^3 or more of water during the entire fracturing process into a well.[110] It is unclear why the Commission is making exactly this differentiation and the assessment of the framework shows that it confuses Member States, as described below.

The framework does not impose a particular approach to shale gas regulation on Member States. Instead, it aims to create a level playing field for states that decide to take a permissive approach to shale gas extraction.[111] These states shall apply a set of protective measures as a common baseline in addition to existing EU legislation.[112]

These protective measures address a number of the gaps in EU legislation. The measures will now be scrutinized with a view to their effectiveness in closing such gaps.

The Recommendation urges Member States to always carry out a SEA prior to issuing a licence that *may* lead to the use of HVHF.[113] The Recommendation also calls upon Member States to take the necessary measures to ensure that an environmental impact assessment is

104 Johnston/Block paragraph 15.03.
105 Broomfield 85.
106 Broomfield 85.
107 Commission Recommendation 2014/70/EU of 22 January 2014 on minimum principles for the exploration and production of hydrocarbons (such as shale gas) using high-volume hydraulic fracturing [2014] OJ L 39/72.
108 Commission Shale Gas Communication.
109 See title of both documents.
110 Article 2 (a) Commission Shale Gas Recommendation.
111 Preamble 9 Commission Shale Gas Recommendation; 2014 Commission Shale Gas Communication page 4.
112 Article 1 and Preamble 5 and 9 Commission Shale Gas Recommendation.
113 Article 3.1 Commission Shale Gas Recommendation.

carried out for each project.[114] However, by simply passing the ball to Member States, the EU did not adequately address the main gap in EU environmental impact assessment legislation, that environmental impact assessments are not *obligatory* for shale gas projects under the EIA Directive. If the Commission, as is apparent from the Recommendation, takes the view that an environmental impact assessment should be carried out for every shale gas project, it should have inserted shale gas extraction in Annex I of the EIA Directive.

With a view to groundwater, the Recommendation reinforces the view that direct discharges of pollutants into the groundwater are prohibited,[115] and calls upon Member States to urge operators to use as little water as possible in shale gas extraction processes.[116] Furthermore, Member States have to establish regulations concerning minimum distances between a shale gas site and a water protection area and minimum depth limitations between the fracturing area and groundwater, to avoid pollution and contamination.[117] Crucially, 'baseline studies' of shale gas sites with regard, *inter alia*, to water, soil and air quality should be carried out[118] and these factors should be consistently monitored.[119]

The use of chemicals during shale gas extraction is of considerable concern to the Commission. The framework asks Member States to ensure that as few chemicals as possible are being used in shale gas operations.[120] If chemicals are used, information about their nature must be disseminated amongst the public.[121] The framework mainly reiterates what is already in REACH, but also recommends some clarifications concerning terminology and reporting practices.[122]

Furthermore, the framework dedicates one article to environmental liability issues.[123] It calls upon Member States to apply the provisions on environmental liability to all activities that are taking place at a shale gas extraction site.[124] This request explicitly includes those activities that do not currently fall into the scope of the Environmental Liability Directive.[125]

Finally, the framework features a number of stipulations that relate to the issuing of licences and the Hydrocarbons Licensing Directive. The Recommendation urges Member States to ensure that their national regulatory bodies are efficiently co-ordinated[126] and have adequate resources at their disposal[127] to carry out their task of appraising applications for shale gas licences.

The crucial aspect of the Commission's 2014 framework on shale gas extraction is not its content, but its legal guise: it is soft law not hard law.[128] While Regulations, Directives and Decisions are legally binding to varying degrees, Article 288 of the TFEU states explicitly that Recommendations and Opinions shall have no binding force. A Recommendation,

114 Article 3.3 Commission Shale Gas Recommendation.
115 Article 5.4 Commission Shale Gas Recommendation.
116 Articles 10.2, 9.2 and 9.3 Commission Shale Gas Recommendation.
117 Article 3.2 Commission Shale Gas Recommendation.
118 Article 6 Commission Shale Gas Recommendation.
119 Articles 11.2 and 11.3 Commission Shale Gas Recommendation.
120 Articles 10.1 (b) and 10.2 Commission Shale Gas Recommendation.
121 Article 15 Commission Shale Gas Recommendation.
122 Article 10.1 (a) Commission Shale Gas Recommendation.
123 Article 12 Commission Shale Gas Recommendation.
124 Article 12.1 Commission Shale Gas Recommendation.
125 Ibid.
126 Articles 4 and 5 Commission Shale Gas Recommendation.
127 Article 13 Commission Shale Gas Recommendation.
128 Stokes 47–48.

thus, has no immediate binding effect upon Member States.[129] It constitutes a form of soft law[130] and the EU may not enforce Recommendations directly.[131]

This EU approach to choose a legally non-binding tool for shale gas regulation attracted intense criticism from environmental pressure groups.[132] The European Commission itself had initially put forward four different policy options for EU shale gas regulation, ranging from the now adopted Recommendation to a firm, legally binding Directive.[133] The Commission prepared an impact assessment to outline repercussions of all four options, which concluded that, a Recommendation 'with its non-binding character, is the least effective of the policy options analysed. Clarification of the legal requirements for shale gas operations would provide a more secure environment for investment and therefore enable shale gas developments'.[134]

The fear is that individual states could simply ignore the recommended measures if they do not fit in with their respective agenda on shale gas extraction.[135] After all, no sanctions for non-compliance with these measures have been outlined in the Recommendation or Communication. The adoption of a legally non-binding Recommendation will hardly lead to stringent shale gas regulations among European countries. Instead of creating a level playing field for all Member States, as claimed by the 2014 Shale Gas Recommendation[136] and Communication,[137] these documents could facilitate piecemeal regulation on shale gas in Europe.

Member States only have 6 months to implement the recommended measures[138] and, thereafter, shall submit crucial data on the implementation of measures every 12 months.[139] The Commission had to review the submitted data within 18 months of its publication[140]

So far the individual country reports and overall overviews for 2014, 2015 and 2016 have been made available to the public by the Directorate General on the Environment of the European Commission.[141] Moreover, two reports by external consulting firms on the implementation of the 2014 framework have been issued. The first one deals with the year 2014 and the second with the period 2015–2017.

The first study issued in December 2015 and concerning the year 2014[142] found divergence in the application across Member States (particularly in relation to EIA related principles)

129 Craig/De Burca 107.

130 Ibid.

131 Calliess/Ruffert Article 288 AEUV paragraph 95.

132 See for instance Friends of the Earth 'Europe Opens Doors to Dangerous Fracking' available at: www.foeeurope.org/shale_gas_framework_220114 [accessed: 18 Dec 2018].

133 European Commission 'Executive Summary of the Impact Assessment on Communication COM (2014) 23 final of 22nd January 2014' available at: http://eur-lex.europa.eu/legal-content/EN/TXT/PDF/?uri=CELEX:52014SC0022&from=EN [accessed 2 April 2018] (hereinafter: Commission Impact Assessment).

134 Commission Impact Assessment 4.

135 Stokes 17–48.

136 2014 Shale Gas Recommendation Preamble 9.

137 2014 Shale Gas Communication 4.

138 2014 Shale Gas Recommendation preamble 11.

139 2014 Shale Gas Recommendation Article 16.1.

140 2014 Shale Gas Recommendation Article 16.3.

141 Available at: http://ec.europa.eu/environment/integration/energy/unconventional_en.htm [accessed 3 July 2019].

142 Milieu Ltd. for the European Commission 'Study on the Application in Relevant Member States of the Commission Recommendation on Minimum Principles for the Exploration and Production of Hydrocarbons (such as Shale Gas) Using High-Volume Hydraulic Fracturing' (Publications Office of the European Union, Luxembourg 2015) available at: https://publications.europa.eu/en/publication-detail/-/publication/f840d592-0b70-11e6-b713-01aa75ed71a1 [accessed 3 July 2019] (hereinafter: 2015 Report).

and/or incomplete application of the Recommendation and the Communication (mainly related to the requirement to put into place SEAs prior to starting activities, requirements concerning baseline studies for effective monitoring and shortcomings in requirements related to the dissemination of information).[143]

In July 2018, four years (!) after coming into force, the Commission issued its second and final report on the implementation of the 2014 Recommendation and Communication in the Member States.[144] However, this study focused particularly on the years 2015–2017.[145]

This study also paints a rather mixed picture of what happened in Europe in terms of implementation. Eleven Member States responded that they granted or possibly would like to grant authorization for the use of HVHF, as defined in the 2014 Recommendation (see above).[146] However, many Member States do not differentiate between hydraulic fracturing and HVHF, as mentioned earlier.[147]

On the positive side the majority of Member States stated that principles of the Recommendation are implemented fully or partially[148] and of those states almost all used 'legally binding instruments' for the implementation.[149] On the negative side, however, there are three key principles where approximately half of the Member States (who stated that they have or may grant authorization for the use of HVHF) have not implemented the Recommendation.[150] These three key principles concern, first, the requirement to carry out an SEA prior to granting licenses that pertain to HVHF operations, second the minimum distance between the zone to be fractured and groundwater and, third, the obligation on clear use of the term 'hydraulic fracturing' in chemicals legislation and use sheets.[151]

In practice, of the 11 Member States intending to use HVHF, only a few had actually done so.[152] Only the United Kingdom and Poland were found to have active licences targeting shale gas, whereas in the other nine Member States either licences have expired, or there is a moratorium on the use of hydraulic fracturing.[153] The report claims that as a result the implementation of the 2014 Recommendation and Communication was not very advanced, because there was no actual need to implement the Recommendation.

5 Conclusion

Recent technological advancements mean that shale gas extraction is starting to become a real possibility in Europe. Although it might seem to have stalled at the moment, it might come back in the near future. If this development is not to go unregulated, the extent to

143 2015 Report pages 8–10.

144 DNVGL for the European Commission 'Application in Relevant Member States of the Commission Recommendations on Minimum Principles for the Exploration and Production of Hydrocarbons (such as Shale Gas) Using High-Volume Hydraulic Fracturing and Related Developments Relevant for Hydrocarbon Activities' (Publications Office of the European Union, Luxembourg 2018) available at: https://publications.europa.eu/en/publication-detail/-/publication/821b0b31-78ee-11e8-ac6a-01aa75ed71a1/language-en/format-PDF/source-73186205 [accessed 3 July 2019] (hereinafter: 2018 Final Report).

145 2018 Final Report Part A pages 1 and 2.

146 2018 Final Report Part A page 4.

147 Ibid.

148 2018 Final Report Part A page 15.

149 2018 Final Report Part B page 8.

150 2018 Final Report Part A page 15.

151 Ibid.

152 2018 Final Report Part A page 8.

153 2018 Final Report Part A page 14.

which current EU law applies to shale gas extraction has to be assessed. Such an assessment provides a crucial starting point for discussions on the regulation of shale gas extraction in Member States, since the main pillars of national environmental and energy regulation emanate from EU law.

For the EU to be able to act on shale gas, a competence in primary EU law is required. Shale gas regulation could be based on both Article 192 and Article 194 of the TFEU, although adopting shale gas regulation on the single basis of Article 192 of the TFEU would also be legitimate. Articles 192 and 194 of the TFEU differ slightly in the procedures that need to be followed to adopt secondary law, but the differences are not insurmountable and both procedures may be reconciled.

Having established that the EU has a primary law competence to regulate shale gas extraction, the second step is to investigate to what extent the existing secondary law framework covers the potential issues of shale gas extraction. I found that this framework has a bearing on shale gas extraction but its legally binding part is not shale gas specific. Several gaps or possible inadequacies in the EU environmental legislative framework need to be addressed by shale gas specific supplements to the respective laws.

In 2014 the Commission took action and recommended to Member States a set of measures and operating standards in order to create a level playing field among European states. The measures, indeed, go some way in potentially closing the pre-existing gaps. The sting in the tail is the fact that they are not legally binding. The framework has been moulded into a Recommendation and a Communication, secondary EU law measures with no direct binding force.

Consequently, the national regulatory frameworks take centre stage for shale gas regulation. Member States have the right to take different approaches to shale gas extraction and they have done so. Research, however, has shown that those 11 Member States that are (potentially) interested in shale gas development display variation when it comes to the implementation of the 2014 Recommendation. If the EU wishes to avoid a situation like 2010–2011 where it was caught off-guard by sudden requests for shale gas licences, it is important to urge interested Member States, in one way or the other, to come together and discuss a more strategic approach towards shale gas regulation and learn from each other's best practice.

10

DISPUTE RESOLUTION IN THE EUROPEAN ENERGY SECTOR

Naomi Briercliffe and David Ingle[1]

1 Introduction

In recent years, news relating to dispute resolution in the European energy sector has been dominated by a series of investor-State cases concerning investments in the renewable energy industry. More than 50 cases of this nature have been brought against European States, including Spain, Italy, the Czech Republic, Hungary and Romania, among others. Most of the claims have been brought under the Energy Charter Treaty (ECT). All of them have resulted from States' amendments to incentive regimes that were introduced to meet renewable energy targets established under the 1997 Kyoto Protocol and European Union (EU) directives. The reason for the claims is straightforward. The construction of renewable energy plants typically requires significant, upfront investment, funded on the basis of anticipated long-term returns from the generation of power. The market price of electricity is generally insufficient to induce such investment. To correct this market failure, countries implement incentive schemes, such as feed-in tariffs (FITs) or so-called "green bonuses", in order to encourage investment in renewable energy projects. Investors rely on the stability of those schemes when investing, in particular over the period in which they expect to recover their investments. If the schemes are then changed – as has happened in a number of States across Europe – the impact on the financial viability of renewable energy projects may be vast. In this context, the ECT offers investors important protections. In particular, it requires Contracting States (which, until recently included all EU Member States,[2] as well as the EU itself) to "*encourage and create stable, equitable, favourable and transparent conditions for Investors*" and, in particular, to grant investments "*fair and equitable treatment*" (FET). As this chapter will demonstrate, the FET standard has been interpreted as requiring Contracting States, in certain circumstances, to ensure the stability of their renewable energy incentive schemes.

1 Naomi Briercliffe and David Ingle are Senior Associates at Allen & Overy LLP. The views and opinions expressed in this chapter are those of the authors and do not necessarily reflect the views of Allen & Overy, or those of its clients. Allen & Overy represents a number of investors in various of the ECT claims against the Kingdom of Spain. The observations made in this chapter are based solely on publicly available information.

2 Italy gave notice of its withdrawal from the ECT on 31 December 2014. That notice was effective from 1 January 2016. It is obliged to comply with the terms of the ECT until 1 January 2036, pursuant to Article 47(3) of the ECT (the so-called "sunset clause").

The following sections contain summaries of the awards so far rendered in the European renewable energy cases under the ECT.[3] The chapter concludes with the lessons that may be drawn from those cases as to the scope of the protection offered under the FET standard in the context of regulatory change. Those lessons are not only relevant for renewable energy investors; they also apply to investors in any type of energy project which is premised on significant upfront investment and is dependent on the stability of a particular legal regime. They are also important for States to appreciate as they consider how best to regulate their energy sectors.

2 Claims against Spain

2.1 Overview

The claims against Spain have all arisen as a result of amendments made by Spain to its incentive scheme for renewable energy investments, starting in 2010. The incentive scheme (known as the "Special Regime") was established in the 1990s and was based on a FIT mechanism. Spain introduced a number of versions of the scheme, including, most notably, under Royal Decree 661/2007, which was passed in May 2007 (RD 661/2007). The RD 661/2007 regime had multiple elements, but key among those was that qualifying investments would be guaranteed certain tariffs for their lifetime provided they were registered within a particular window.

Spain's Ministry of Industry, Energy and Tourism promoted the scheme widely, with great success. Subsequently, however, concerns arose about the contribution of the scheme to Spain's large and growing "tariff deficit" (the financial gap between the costs of subsidies paid to renewable energy producers and revenues derived from energy sales to consumers). Those concerns, coupled with the effect of the global financial crisis on the Spanish economy, led Spain to enact legislation between 2010 and 2014 to overhaul the Special Regime.[4]

The new incentive scheme implemented to replace the Special Regime (the New Regime) was introduced by royal decree law in July 2013. The New Regime announced the immediate withdrawal of the Special Regime and the repeal of, *inter alia*, RD 661/2007. The New Regime was then implemented in June 2014, when a new Electricity Law and accompanying regulation were published, setting out the new remuneration scheme applicable to renewable energy installations. The New Regime was applied not only to future renewable energy

3 In addition to the awards addressed in this chapter, a number of further awards and decisions were rendered in European renewable energy cases under the ECT shortly before publication. These include the following. *SolEs Badajoz GmbH v. Kingdom of Spain*, ICSID Case No. ARB/15/38, *OperaFund Eco-Invest SICAV PLC and Schwab Holding AG v. Kingdom of Spain*, ICSID Case No. ARB/15/36, *Stadtwerke München GmbH, RWE Innogy GmbH, and others v. Kingdom of Spain*, ICSID Case No. ARB/15/1, *Cube Infrastructure Fund SICAV, et al. v. Kingdom of Spain*, ICSID Case No. ARB/15/20, *InfraRed Environmental Infrastructure GP Limited, et al. v. Kingdom of Spain*, ICSID Case No. ARB/14/12, *RWE Innogy GmbH and RWE Innogy Aersa S.A.U. v. Kingdom of Spain*, ICSID Case No. ARB/14/34, *Belenergia S.A. v. Italian Republic*, ICSID Case No. ARB/15/40, *WA Investments Europa Nova Ltd. v. Czech Republic*, PCA Case No. 2014–19, *I.C.W. Europe Investments Limited v. Czech Republic*, PCA Case No. 2014–22, *Photovoltaic Knopf Betriebs GMBH v. Czech Republic*, PCA Case No. 2014–21, and *Voltaic Network GmbH v. Czech Republic*, PCA Case No. 2014–20.

4 In the cases against Spain, the claimants also made claims in respect of a law passed by Spain in 2012 (Law 15/2012) which imposed a 7 per cent levy on all revenues obtained from the sale of electricity (the 7% Levy). These claims have been dismissed in every award issued so far on the basis that the 7% Levy constitutes a tax and the ECT states that "Taxation Measures" cannot breach Article 10 of the ECT (see, Article 21(1) of the ECT).

investments, but also to investments that had already been made and were benefitting from the Special Regime.

The changes made by Spain to its renewable energy incentive scheme have precipitated a minimum of 44 investment-treaty claims. All of these claims have been made under the ECT.[5]

Investors have alleged that Spain's actions give rise to a number of breaches of the ECT. In particular, however, the claims focus on Spain's alleged breach of its duty under Article 10(1) of the ECT to accord investments FET. The summaries below compare different tribunals' treatment of that claim specifically.

2.2 Cases

2.2.1 Charanne B.V. and Construction Investments S.à.r.l. v. the Kingdom of Spain, SCC Case No. V 062/2012

The *Charanne* award, rendered on 21 January 2016, was the first award on the merits to be delivered in the series of renewable energy cases against Spain (the Spain Cases). The claimants, Charanne B.V. and Construction Investments S.à.r.l., were Dutch and Luxembourgish companies respectively, and shareholders of Grupo T-Solar Global S.A. (T-Solar), a company involved in the generation and sale of electricity produced from 34 photovoltaic (PV) plants in Spain.[6]

The claimants had acquired their stakes in T-Solar in 2009 relying on the Special Regime of RD 661/2007 and another royal decree, RD 1578/2008.[7] They argued that those rules, being directed at a specific and limited group of investors, constituted specific commitments.[8] As such, the claimants argued they were capable of giving rise, on their part, to a legitimate expectation as to the FITs that would be received by their PV plants.[9]

The claimants alleged that Spain had frustrated their legitimate expectations by introducing measures in 2010 which had broken the stability of the regulatory framework in which they invested.[10] That, they claimed, constituted a breach of Spain's FET obligation under the ECT.

The tribunal (acting by majority[11]) dismissed the claimants' claims. While it agreed that the frustration of legitimate expectations could give rise to a breach of an FET obligation,[12] it disagreed that the claimants could have held a legitimate expectation that the regulatory regime for their investment would remain unchanged.[13] In particular, it disagreed that regulations such as RD 661/2007 and RD 1578/2008,[14] could constitute specific commitments

5 UNCTAD Investment Policy Hub official website, *Investment Dispute Settlement Navigator: Spain*, at https://investmentpolicy.unctad.org/investment-dispute-settlement/country/197/spain/respondent, accessed 24 June 2019.

6 *Charanne B.V. and Construction Investments S.à.r.l. v the Kingdom of Spain* (*Charanne*), SCC Case No. V 062/2012, Award, 21 January 2016, paras 1–5.

7 Ibid, para 297.

8 Ibid, para 297.

9 Ibid, para 297.

10 Ibid, para 294.

11 Dr Guideo Santiago Tawil issued a dissenting opinion, holding that RD 661/2007 and RD 1578/2008 were capable of giving rise to the legitimate expectation on the part of the claimants that their plants would receive the FITs under those regulations for their lifetime (para 12).

12 *Charanne*, para 486.

13 Ibid, para 503.

14 Ibid, para 493.

by Spain generating legitimate expectations.[15] It accepted that Spain had intended to induce investment through implementing the Special Regime.[16] However, it did not agree that the claimants could have – based on that regime – an expectation as to the absolute stability of FITs for the lifetime of their plants.[17]

The tribunal considered that an investor could have a legitimate expectation that, when modifying regulations relied on by investors a state would not act unreasonably, disproportionately or contrary to the public interest.[18] However, it did not consider that the 2010 measures constituted such type of action.[19] As such, the tribunal found no breach by Spain of its FET obligation in the circumstances of the *Charanne* case. Importantly, however, the tribunal stressed that it did not "prejudge the conclusions…[of] another arbitral tribunal based on the analysis of all the norms adopted [by Spain], including the 2013 norms" which fell outside the scope of its enquiry.[20]

2.2.2 Isolux Infrastructure Netherlands B.V. v. the Kingdom of Spain, SCC Case V2013/153

The *Isolux* award was rendered on 17 July 2016, although it was not made public until 2017. Isolux Infrastructure Netherlands B.V. was a Dutch company sitting in the corporate chain between the *Charanne* claimants and T-Solar.[21] It had become an investor in T-Solar and other Spanish companies holding PV assets following its incorporation in 2012.[22]

As with the *Charanne* claimants, Isolux's FET claim centred on an alleged breach of its legitimate expectations. Unlike the *Charanne* claimants, however, Isolux did not argue that RD 661/2007 and RD 1578/2008 contained specific commitments by Spain that the regulatory regime would remain unchanged. Instead, Isolux's position was that the nature of the general regulatory framework for renewables (including RD 661/2007 and RD 1578/2008) was such that it had given rise to a legitimate expectation as to legal stability.[23] That expectation – Isolux alleged – was undermined by the measures introduced by Spain from 2012, although the most flagrant violation was the abolition of the Special Regime in 2013.[24]

The Isolux tribunal (again acting by majority) dismissed the claimant's claims. While it accepted that general regulations could give rise to legitimate expectations of the nature alleged,[25] it held that such expectations could not have arisen in the circumstances in which the claimant invested.[26] Specifically, it noted that as of the date of the claimant's investment, the regulatory framework for renewable energy had already been modified, and such modification was the subject of various studies which would make its further modification inevitable.[27] In addition, the Spanish Supreme Court had confirmed that changes to the Special

15 Ibid, para 492.
16 Ibid, para 497.
17 Ibid, para 503.
18 Ibid, para 514.
19 Ibid, para 539.
20 Ibid, para 542.
21 Ibid, para 8.
22 *Isolux Infrastructure Netherlands B.V. v the Kingdom of Spain (Isolux)*, SCC Case V2013/153, Final Award, 17 July 2016, para 1.
23 *Isolux*, para 421.
24 Ibid, para 411.
25 Ibid, para 775.
26 Ibid, para 785.
27 Ibid, para 787.

Regime were permissible. As a result, the tribunal considered no reasonable investor could have had the expectation that no changes would be made in future.[28] Even the abolition of the Special Regime was, in its view, predictable.[29]

2.2.3 *Eiser Infrastructure Limited and Energia Solar Luxembourg S.à.r.l. v. Kingdom of Spain, ICSID Case No. ARB/13/36*

The *Eiser* award was rendered on 4 May 2017. The claimants were Eiser Infrastructure Limited (EIL), a private limited company incorporated under the laws of the United Kingdom, and Energia Solar Luxembourg S.à.r.l. (ESL), a private limited company incorporated under the laws of Luxembourg.[30] They were indirect investors in three concentrated solar power (CSP) plants acquired in 2007 and 2009.[31]

As with the previous claims, the claimants' FET claim appears to have focused on legitimate expectations. The claimants argued that the regulatory changes adopted by Spain over period 2012–2014 had defeated the claimants' legitimate expectations of stability of the RD 661/2007 regime and of its promised characteristics and advantages.[32] The claimants' expectations were, they argued, legitimate for a number of reasons. Legitimate expectations could be predicated upon a State's legal framework, and changing that framework could lead to liability.[33] The investor's expectations based on RD 661/2007 were confirmed to be legitimate by: (1) Spain's road shows promoting solar investments in Spain; (2) another regulation, RD 1614/2010, which had implemented an agreement in 2010 between producers and the government; (3) other efforts to promote renewables by Spain; (4) resolutions issued by the government in 2011 to the claimants' CSP plants and (5) other official actions which confirmed that the plants would receive the favourable regime established by RD 661/2007.[34]

Departing from the *Charanne* and *Isolux* tribunals, the *Eiser* tribunal found in favour of the claimants. While the tribunal did not accept that RD 661/2007 had given them immutable economic rights that could not be altered by changes in the regulatory regime, it held that the ECT did protect the claimants against the "total and unreasonable change" they had experienced.[35] The tribunal noted that the claimants were "experienced and sophisticated investors".[36] They recognized that regulatory regimes are sometimes adjusted, but within foreseeable limits.[37] However, the evidence showed that:

> Spain eliminated a favourable regulatory regime previously extended to the claimants and other investors in CSP. It was then replaced with an unprecedented and wholly different regulatory approach, based on wholly different premises. This new system was profoundly unfair and inequitable as applied to Claimants' existing investment, stripping Claimants of virtually all of the value of their investment.[38]

28 Ibid, para 787.
29 Ibid, para 804.
30 *Eiser Infrastructure Limited and Energia Solar Luxembourg S.à.r.l. v. Kingdom of Spain (Eiser)*, ICSID Case No. ARB/13/36, Final Award, 4 May 2017, para 2.
31 Ibid, paras 120 and 122.
32 Ibid, para 358.
33 Ibid, para 358.
34 Ibid, para 358.
35 Ibid, para 363.
36 Ibid, para 364.
37 Ibid, para 364.
38 Ibid, para 365.

In other words, Spain's responsibility under the ECT had been engaged as a result of the way in which it had exercised its "acknowledged right to regulate".[39]

The tribunal distinguished the position of the *Eiser* claimants from that of the claimants in *Charanne*. It explained that the "measures complained of in *Charanne* had far less dramatic effects than those at issue" in the *Eiser* case.[40] The 2010 measures at issue in *Charanne* had, the *Charanne* claimants alleged, "reduced the profitability of the plants under RD 1578 by 10% and plants under RD 661/2007 by 8.5%".[41] The new regulatory system implemented by Spain through the measures complained of by the *Eiser* claimants "deprived the Claimants of substantially the total value of their investments".[42]

The tribunal accepted that Spain "faced a legitimate public policy problem with its tariff deficit" and indicated that it did not "question the appropriateness of Spanish authorities adopting reasonable measures to address the situation". However, in doing so, "Spain had to act in a way that respected the obligations it assumed under the ECT, including the obligation to accord fair and equitable treatment to investors".[43]

It was not a sufficient response to the claimants' claims that Spain's Supreme Court had upheld the constitutionality of the measure (RDL 9/2013) that had repealed RD 661/2007 and established the new legal and economic framework for renewables.[44] The "question of conformity with Spain's Constitution and with the requirements of the ECT [were] quite separate".[45]

The tribunal held that the "new system was based on quite different assumptions, and utilized a new and untested regulatory approach, all intended to significantly reduce subsidies to existing plants".[46] That had a "devastating effect on Claimants' investments because of two key characteristics that were or should have been known to Respondent's regulators".[47] Those two key characteristics were that the projects involved "heavy front-end capital investments and [were] highly leveraged".[48] The "sharp fall in revenues from the levels anticipated under the RD 661/2007 regime forced the operating companies into debt rescheduling negotiations"[49] and "deprived the Claimants of essentially all of the value of their investment".[50] Doing so, the tribunal held, "violated the Respondent's obligation to accord fair and equitable treatment".[51]

2.2.4 Novenergia II – Energy & Environment (SCA) (Grand Duchy of Luxembourg), SICAR v. Kingdom of Spain, SCC Arbitration (2015/063)

The *Novenergia* award was rendered on 15 February 2018. The claimant was a Luxembourgish company[52] and the claim was brought in respect of its investment in eight PV plants,

39 Ibid, para 362.
40 Ibid, para 368.
41 Ibid, para 368, citing *Charanne*, para 284
42 Ibid, para 413.
43 Ibid, para 371.
44 Ibid, para 373.
45 Ibid, para 373.
46 Ibid, para 391.
47 Ibid, para 409.
48 Ibid, para 409.
49 Ibid, para 417.
50 Ibid, para 418.
51 Ibid, para 418. The tribunal assessed the damages due to the claimants at €128 million, Ibid, para 474.
52 *Novenergia II – Energy & Environment (SCA) (Grand Duchy of Luxembourg), SICAR v. Kingdom of Spain* (*Novenergia*), SCC Arbitration, Final Award, 15 February 2018, para 1.

structured through a Spanish entity, Novenergia II Energy & Environment España, S.L.[53] The claimant acquired its investment on 3 July 2007.[54]

Novenergia argued, *inter alia*, that its legitimate expectations at the time of investing in Spain had been undermined by Spain's repeal of the Special Regime.[55] The claimant had invested under RD 661/2007 and expected to receive a fixed FIT for the lifespan of its PV plants.[56] Those expectations were legitimate and reasonable, as they arose out of a stable legal framework that was tailored to attract PV investments in the renewable sector by offering income visibility through a guaranteed FIT for the lifetime of such investments.[57]

The tribunal agreed with the claimant's position. It held that the regulatory regime under which the claimant had invested (Law 54/1997 and RD 661/2007) had plainly been enacted with the objective of inducing investment and, in that regard, contained a number of assurances regarding the conditions that investments would benefit from under the regime.[58] Moreover, investors were encouraged to invest by statements in Spain's investment promotion material and its renewable energy plan for 2005–2010.[59]

Spain argued that there were a number of warning signs that should have alerted the claimant to the fact the Special Regime would not remain intact over the course of the PV plants' lifetime, including references in the regulatory regime and Spanish court judgments to the fact that all investors were guaranteed was a reasonable rate of return.[60] However, the tribunal found Spain's arguments unconvincing.[61] It noted that most of the authorities relied on by Spain post-dated the claimant's investments.[62] In those that did not, concepts such as a "reasonable rate of return" were "still generally vague and insufficiently defined" and so could not have had any effect on the claimant's expectations.[63] None of them could have given the claimant the expectation that a "reasonable rate of return" was limited to 7 per cent, that stability and predictability could not be expected, or that the Special Regime could be abolished, which was what Spain argued.[64]

The tribunal also rejected Spain's claim that the claimant did not perform an adequate due diligence prior to making its investment.[65] There was evidence that the claimant had carried out a reasonable analysis of the Spanish regulatory framework and "RD 661/2007 was so adamantly clear that its understanding by common readers did not require a particularly sophisticated analysis".[66]

The tribunal distinguished the circumstances of the *Charanne* and *Isolux* cases on the basis that the former had only addressed legislation enacted by Spain in 2010,[67] while the latter con-

53 Ibid, para 2.
54 Ibid, para 2.
55 Ibid, para 551 *et seq*.
56 Ibid, para 553.
57 Ibid, para 554.
58 Ibid, paras 665–667.
59 Ibid, para 668.
60 Ibid, paras 671–673.
61 Ibid, para 674.
62 Ibid, para 671.
63 Ibid, para 673.
64 Ibid, para 674.
65 Ibid, para 679.
66 Ibid, para 679.
67 Ibid, para 685.

cerned an investment made in October 2012, at a "stage when it must have been clear to the investor that changes were being made to the Special Regime".[68] It held that the factual circumstances and legal issues in *Eiser* were, however, very similar to the ones in the *Novenergia* case.[69]

The *Novenergia* tribunal did not consider it necessary that an investor's investment be obliterated entirely in order for a breach of the FET standard to exist.[70] In the tribunal's view:

> the assessment of whether the FET standard [had] been breached is a balancing exercise, where the state's regulatory interests are weighed against the investor's legitimate expectations and reliance. It is not simply sufficient to look at the economic effect that the challenged measures have had.[71]

It acknowledged, however, that the "economic effect on a claimant's investment is an important factor in the balancing exercise".[72]

Taking into account Spain's statements and assurances prior to and in connection with the implementation of RD 661/2007, the legitimate expectations of the claimant and the changes introduced through RDL 9/2013, the tribunal considered the challenged measures to be "radical and unexpected". Moreover, the measures adopted in 2013 and 2014 had a "significant damaging economic effect on the claimant's investments". Accordingly, the tribunal held that Spain had breached its obligation to provide FET to investors.[73]

2.2.5 *Masdar Solar & Wind Cooperatief U.A. v. Kingdom of Spain, ICSID Case No. ARB/14/1*

The *Masdar* award was rendered on 16 May 2018. The claimant, which was a Dutch company[74] ultimately owned by the Government of Abu Dhabi,[75] invested in three CSP plants with a Spanish joint venture partner, and, through the project company, Torresol Energy Investments S.A.[76] The claimant's investments in the plants appear to have been made over the period 2008–2010.[77]

As regards its FET claim, *Masdar* argued that by the time its CSP plants were operational and had been registered to receive tariffs under RD 661/2007, it "had done all that it was required to do in order to ensure that the RD 661/2007 regime would apply to [those installations]".[78] However, its expectations were dashed by the enactment, in rapid succession, of measures in 2013 and 2014, which provided investors such as Masdar with significantly lower returns and removed the stability that was promised to them "and on the basis of which they entered into these investments in the first place".[79]

68 Ibid, para 686.
69 Ibid, para 687.
70 Ibid, para 694.
71 *Novenergia*, para 694.
72 Ibid, para 694.
73 Ibid, para 695.
74 *Masdar Solar & Wind Cooperatief U.A. v. Kingdom of Spain* (*Masdar*), ICSID Case No. ARB/14/1, Award, 16 May 2018, para 2.
75 Ibid, para 83.
76 Ibid, para 89.
77 Ibid, paras 90–96 and 355.
78 Ibid, para 464.
79 Ibid, paras 464–467.

The tribunal agreed that Spain had failed to comply with its FET obligation. It was:

> in no doubt that the FET constitutes a standard the purpose of which is to ensure that an investor may be confident that (i) the legal framework in which the investment has been made will not be subject to unreasonable or unjustified modification; and (ii) the legal framework will not be subject to modification in a manner contrary to specific commitments made to the investor.[80]

By reason of the loss of the RD 661/2007 regime and the rights accrued to the claimant thereunder pursuant to the disputed measures, that standard had been breached.[81]

Interestingly, the tribunal appears to have been divided over what type of specific commitment could give rise to protected legitimate expectations. It explained that there were two schools of thought on the issue: one which considers that such commitments can result from general statements in general laws or regulations, and one which considers that such commitments must be specific and could not arise from general regulations.[82] The latter position, it noted, was adopted by the majority in the *Charanne* case.[83] It did not, however, need to detain itself over which approach was correct, since the facts of the *Masdar* case supported both.

If legitimate expectations could arise from general regulation then, in light of all the circumstances, including the due diligence undertaken by the claimant, its expectations were reasonable.[84] If specific commitments were required, they were given by Spain in various guises.[85] In particular, the tribunal noted that RD 661/2007 required investors to comply with certain conditions, including registration in the RAIPRE (an administrative register) within a particular window of time.[86] The *Charanne* tribunal had considered that to be a mere administrative requirement with no specific consequences.[87] In the circumstances of the *Masdar* case, however, it was held that the offer to provide stability of benefits upon RAIPRE registration constituted a specific commitment.[88]

2.2.6 *Antin Infrastructure Services Luxembourg S.à.r.l. and Antin Energia Termosolar B.V. v. Kingdom of Spain, ICSID Case No. ARB/13/31*

The award in *Antin* was issued on 15 June 2018. The claimants were Luxembourgish and Dutch companies in the same corporate chain,[89] used by a French professional private equity investment fund to carry out investments in the Spanish renewables sector.[90] Their investments in two CSP plants were made in 2011.[91]

80 Ibid, para 485.
81 *Masdar*, para 522.
82 Ibid, paras 490, 504 and 507.
83 Ibid, para 508.
84 Ibid, paras 496–503.
85 Ibid, paras 512–521.
86 Ibid, para 512.
87 Ibid, para 514, referring to *Charanne*, paras 509–510.
88 Ibid, paras 512–515.
89 *Antin Infrastructure Services Luxembourg S.à.r.l. and Antin Energia Termosolar B.V. v. Kingdom of Spain (Antin)*, ICSID Case No. ARB/13/31, Award, 15 June 2018, para 2.
90 Ibid, para 2.
91 Ibid, para 70.

Once again, the claimants' FET claim was based on the alleged frustration of legitimate expectations. The claimants' claim was not, however, only based on RD 661/2007.[92] They alleged the commitments made in that regulation had been reinforced by another regulation, RD 1614/2010, which was passed in 2010 and had repeated those commitments for CSP technology, specifically.[93]

Spain's main defence, as in other cases, was that the claimants could not expect RD 661/2007 to remain unmodified. In addition, it claimed that when the claimants invested in Spain they were fully aware of the future possibility of regulatory changes to their investments.[94] The claimants could not derive expectations from reports received from a law firm at the time, or from what it claimed to be unverifiable representations allegedly made by public officials.[95]

The tribunal found in favour of the claimants. It analysed the ordinary meaning of Article 10(1) of the ECT in light of the treaty's context, object and purpose[96] and noted that the stated purpose of the ECT suggests it was conceived as enhancing the stability required for long-term cooperation.[97] The tribunal agreed with Spain in that "the ECT limits the regulatory power of States, but does not cancel or 'extremely limit' the State's regulatory power".[98] However, it did not agree that "the ECT sets no more limits on the regulatory power of States than the minimum standard of international law".[99]

In its view, Article 10(1) of the ECT, which sets out to provide FET to investments, "comprises an obligation to afford fundamental stability in the essential characteristics of the legal regime relied upon by the investors in making long-term investments".[100] That did not mean that States were precluded from adapting their regulatory regimes to the changing circumstances of public interest. However, it meant that "a regulatory regime specifically created to induce investments in the energy sector cannot be radically altered – i.e., stripped of its key features – as applied to existing investors in ways that affect investors who invested in reliance on those regimes".[101]

Analysing the text of RD 661/2007 and RD 1614/2010, as well as other documents issued by Spain at the time in connection with them, the tribunal stated that "it had no difficulty in concluding that this falls squarely into the type of conduct that was intended to, and did, give rise to legitimate expectations of the Claimants".[102] Even if Spain had not made a commitment that the regulatory regime applicable to the claimants' plants would remain completely unchanged, it had committed to the stability and predictability of the existing economic regime.[103] The New Regime had eliminated key features of RD 661/2007 and replaced it with a new regime not based on any identifiable criteria.[104] As such, Spain had breached its obligation to accord the claimants' investments FET.

92 Ibid, para 510.
93 Ibid, para 510.
94 Ibid, para 514.
95 *Antin*, para 514.
96 Ibid, para 518. The tribunal awarded the claimant damages assessed at €64.5 million, Ibid, para 520.
97 Ibid, para 520.
98 Ibid, para 530.
99 Ibid, para 530.
100 Ibid, para 532.
101 Ibid, para 532.
102 Ibid, para 552.
103 Ibid, para 553.
104 Ibid, para 572.

2.2.7 Foresight Luxembourg Solar 1 S.à.r.l., Foresight Luxembourg Solar 2 S.à.r.l., Greentech Energy Systems A/S, GWM Renewable Energy I S.P.A. and GWM Renewable Energy II S.p.A. v. Kingdom of Spain, SCC Case No. V 2015–150

The *Greentech* award was rendered on 14 November 2018 and concerned claims brought by Foresight Luxembourg Solar 1 S.à.r.l. and Foresight Luxembourg Solar 2 S.à.r.l., incorporated in Luxembourg,[105] GWM Renewable Energy I S.p.A. and GWM Renewable Energy II S.à.r.l., incorporated in Italy,[106] and Greentech Energy Systems A/S, incorporated in Denmark.[107]

The claimants' investments comprised three PV plants acquired in 2009 and 2010. In bringing their FET claim, the claimants contended that one particular provision of RD 661/2007 – namely Article 44.3 – constituted "a specific assurance giving rise to a legitimate expectation that the Claimants would receive fixed FiTs for the lifetime of their PV plants".[108] Article 44.3 in essence provided that existing installations would be exempted from future revisions to the FIT.[109]

The *Greentech* tribunal agreed with the *Eiser* and *Novenergia* tribunals that the FET standard in the ECT "protects investors from a radical or fundamental change in the legal or regulatory framework under which the investments are made".[110] The tribunal further held that "a State's duty under the FET standard to ensure a stable legal and regulatory framework 'arises when the State has generated "legitimate expectations" of such stability on the part of investors'".[111] To be protected under the ECT, such expectations of legal stability have to be reasonable and objective.

Applying these standards, the tribunal decided that the claimants "did not have legitimate expectations that they would receive the precise [feed-in tariff] standard specified in RD 661/2007 for the entire lifetime of their PV plants", but that they did have the legitimate expectation that "the legal and regulatory framework would not be fundamentally and abruptly altered" such as to deprive them of a substantial part of their revenues.[112]

The tribunal followed *Eiser* in finding that RD 661/2007 did not give investors immutable economic rights,[113] and distinguished *Masdar* on the basis that, in that case, the claimant had received specific clarification from Spain that their facilities would receive the RD 661/2007 FITs for their operating lives.[114] In the absence of such specific commitments, it was held to be unreasonable for an investor not to expect any changes to the RD 661/2007 regime. This was partly because the FIT regime had been amended prior to RD 661/2007 and partly because Spanish Supreme Court jurisprudence prior to RD 661/2007 being enacted had indicated that such changes were permissible.[115]

105 *Foresight Luxembourg Solar 1 S.à r.l., Foresight Luxembourg Solar 2 S.à.r.l., Greentech Energy Systems A/S, GWM Renewable Energy I S.P.A. and GWM Renewable Energy II S.P.A. v. Kingdom of Spain* (*Greentech v Spain*), SCC Case No. V 2015-150, Final Award, 14 November 2018, para 2(a).

106 *Greentech v Spain*, para 2(b).

107 Ibid, para 2(c).

108 Ibid, para 366.

109 The final paragraph of Article 44.3 of RD 661/2007 stated as follows: "The revisions to the regulated tariff and the upper and lower limits indicated in this paragraph shall not affect facilities for which the deed of commissioning shall have been granted prior to January 1 of the second year following the year in which the revision shall have been performed".

110 *Greentech v Spain*, para 359.

111 Ibid, para 352.

112 Ibid, para 365.

113 Ibid, para 366.

114 Ibid, para 367.

115 Ibid, paras 368–371.

The *Greentech* tribunal found that the claimants did, however, have the legitimate expectation that the regulatory framework would not be fundamentally and abruptly changed (as opposed to being merely modified, on which point the tribunal agreed with *Charanne*).[116] The tribunal also agreed with the finding in *Novenergia* that the claimants could not have expected that the reasonable rate of return would be limited to 7 per cent, or that the Special Regime would be abolished.[117]

Like the tribunals in *Charanne Isolux*, *Eiser*, and *Novenergia*, the *Greentech* tribunal held that the changes enacted by RD 1565/2010, RDL 14/2010 or RD 2/2013 did not breach the FET standard,[118] but Spain nonetheless "abrogated RD 661/2007 and replaced it with a new support scheme under RD 413/2014 and MO 1045/2014 pursuant to an entirely new legal and regulatory framework under Law 24/2013".[119]

The majority found that, although sophisticated investors such as the claimants should have expected that RD 661/2007 could be modified within limits, this was not the case with the New Regime.[120] The tribunal followed the *Eiser* tribunal in finding that the New Regime constituted an "unprecedented and wholly different regulatory approach", and followed the *Novenergia* tribunal in finding that the measures enacting the New Regime were "radical and unexpected".[121]

In response to Spain's defence that the claimants had not carried out sufficient due diligence regarding changes under Spanish law, the tribunal found that although the claimants' due diligence was in some respects vague, "it is reasonable for an investor to assume that its legal advisors would have raised a red flag had they detected any risk of fundamental change to the regulatory regime".[122] Thus, Spain's due diligence defence was rejected.

2.2.8 RREEF Infrastructure (G.P.) Limited and RREEF Pan-European Infrastructure Two Lux S.à.r.l. v. Kingdom of Spain, ICSID Case No. ARB/13/30

The tribunal in *RREEF* issued a Decision on Responsibility and on the Principles of Quantum on 30 November 2018. This addressed the merits of the claims brought by RREEF Infrastructure (G.P.) Limited, a company incorporated in Jersey, and RREEF Pan-European Infrastructure Two Lux S.à.r.l., a company incorporated in Luxembourg. The RREEF claimants were part of the Deutsche Bank group and specialized in infrastructure investments.[123]

The *RREEF* claimants first invested in Spain in February 2011 by indirectly acquiring an equity interest in three project companies, which held five wind power parks.[124] In June 2011, they invested in two other CSP plants known as the "Andasol Plants".[125] In July 2011,

116 Ibid, para 377.
117 *Greentech v Spain*, para 378.
118 Ibid, para 388.
119 Ibid, para 390.
120 Co-arbitrator Raúl E. Vinuesa issued a Partial Dissenting Opinion in which he, *inter alia*, dissented from the majority's finding on liability.
121 Ibid, para 397.
122 Ibid, para 380.
123 *RREEF Infrastructure (G.P.) Limited and RREEF Pan-European Infrastructure Two Lux S.à r.l. v. Kingdom of* Spain (*RREEF*), ICSID Case No. ARB/13/30, Decision on Liability and Principles of Quantum, 30 November 2018, para 4.
124 Ibid, para 159 and footnote 128.
125 Ibid, paras 172–174.

the claimants then indirectly invested in a third CSP plant that was in development and is referred to as the "Arenales Plant".[126] Notably, the Andasol plants were the same plants that were the subject of the *Antin* award addressed above.

The claimants alleged that, through the various measures enacted by it between 2012 and 2014, Spain had fundamentally altered the applicable legal and regulatory regime encompassed in RD 661/2007, upon which the claimants had relied when investing in Spain's renewable energy sector.[127]

The tribunal agreed.[128] It found that Spain implemented a favourable legal framework to attract investment.[129] This conduct gave rise to the legitimate expectation that the legal framework would not be significantly modified.[130] In implementing the disputed measures, Spain had radically altered the regulatory framework under which the claimants invested and breached their legitimate expectations.[131]

The tribunal concurred with the tribunal in *Eiser* in that the ECT's "obligation to accord fair and equitable treatment necessarily embraces an obligation to provide fundamental stability in the essential characteristics of the legal regime relied upon by investors in making long-term investments".[132] The tribunal also agreed with the *Eiser* tribunal that the ECT prevented Spain from "radically alte[ring] [the regulatory regimes] as applied to existing investments in ways that deprive investors who invested in reliance on those regimes of their investment's value".[133]

The tribunal accepted that Spain's regulatory regime was sufficient to create legitimate expectations.[134] Unlike other tribunals, however, it considered that "the guarantee of 'reasonable return' or 'reasonable profitability' was the main specific commitment of Spain vis-à-vis the investors in the Special Regime".[135] Therefore, in the tribunal's view, the disputed measures ought to be assessed by analysing their impact on returns on the claimant's investments.[136]

Ultimately, the tribunal found that the disputed measures lowered the return on the claimants' CSP investments below the threshold of a "reasonable return". On this basis, it concluded that Spain had radically altered the regulatory regime in reliance on which the claimants had invested.[137] It therefore found that Spain's implementation of the disputed measures was a breach of Article 10(1) of the ECT and set forth the principle for the quantification of damages, which was to take place in a subsequent phase.

2.2.9 9REN Holding S.à.r.l. v. The Kingdom of Spain, ICSID Case No. ARB/15/15

The final award in *9REN* was rendered on 31 May 2019. The claimant was 9REN Holding S.à.r.l., a Luxembourgish subsidiary of the U.S.-based partnership First Reserve, which

126 Ibid, para 162.
127 *RREEF*, para 250.
128 Ibid, para 600(2).
129 Ibid, paras 386 and 587.
130 Ibid, para 390.
131 Ibid, paras 328 and 600(2).
132 Ibid, para 314 citing *Eiser* Award, para 382.
133 Ibid, para 316 citing *Eiser* Award, para 382.
134 Ibid, para 381.
135 Ibid, para 384.
136 Ibid, para 472: "the Tribunal will be in the position to determine whether the measures taken by the Respondent have adversely affected the Claimants' legitimate expectation for a reasonable return only when it has evaluated the loss sustained by them, taking into account all the relevant element."
137 Ibid, para 328.

invested in eight PV projects in Spain in April 2008.[138] Seven of these were entitled to receive the RD 661/2007 FIT. The eighth and final PV plant was completed in March 2011 and was therefore not entitled to receive the RD 661/2007 FIT but was instead registered to receive the subsequent FIT established under RD 1578/2008.

The claimants' claim centred on the "guarantee of 'stability'" contained at Article 44(3) of RD 661/2007.[139] That provision (it was alleged) "contemplated a 'grandfathering' of benefits" for installations registered under RD 661/2007.[140] This had given rise to the legitimate expectation that the claimants' PV installations would not be subject to future tariff changes.

In determining the claimant's FET claim, the *9REN* tribunal endorsed an observation of the United Nations Conference on Trade and Development (UNCTAD) in a report issued by it in 2012 that "legitimate expectations may arise from 'rules not specifically addressed to a particular investor but which are put in place with a specific aim to induce foreign investments and on which the foreign investor relied on making his investment'".[141] The tribunal thus found there to be:

> no reason in principle why such a commitment of the requisite clarity and specificity cannot be made in the regulation itself where (as here) such a commitment is made for the purpose of inducing investment, which succeeded in attracting the Claimant's investment, and, once made, resulted in losses to the Claimant.[142]

The *9REN* tribunal agreed with the claimants' submission that RD 661/2007 contained a "specific undertaking" at Article 44.3 that future tariff revisions would not affect PV installations already operating.[143] This undertaking created legitimate expectations of stability that had subsequently been frustrated by Spain's changes to the FIT implemented from 2010 onwards.[144]

In reaching this finding, the *9REN* tribunal rejected Spain's defence that the domestic jurisprudence of the Spanish Supreme Court had confirmed that changes to the FIT scheme were permissible under Spanish law. Indeed, the *9REN* tribunal observed that "the *Charanne* tribunal placed too much emphasis" on this domestic jurisprudence:[145]

> This Tribunal does not doubt the constitutional authority of Spain to evolve its regulatory system to keep abreast of changing circumstances. The question is whether under the ECT the cost of such changes should fall on the investors who were attracted to Spain's renewable energy by specific promises of stability rather than fall on Spanish consumers or Spanish taxpayers generally.[146]

Contrary to the position under Spain's domestic law, assessing the claims under the FET standard resulted in a breach of the ECT.

138 *9REN Holding S.à r.l. v. The Kingdom of Spain* (*9REN*), ICSID Case No. ARB/15/15, Award, 31 May 2019, paras 85 and 287.
139 *9REN*, para 87.
140 Ibid, para 88.
141 Ibid, para 294.
142 Ibid, para 295.
143 Ibid, para 257.
144 Ibid, para 259.
145 Ibid, para 253.
146 Ibid, para 253.

2.2.10 NextEra Energy Global Holdings B.V. and NextEra Energy Spain Holdings B.V. v The Kingdom of Spain, ICSID Case No. ARB/14/11

The tribunal in *NextEra* issued a Decision on Jurisdiction, Liability and Quantum Principles on 12 March 2019, which was shortly followed by a final award on 31 May 2019. The claim was brought by the Dutch and Spanish subsidiaries of the US corporation, NextEra Energy Inc. Those subsidiaries invested in two CSP plants.[147] The claimants were engaged in development activities in respect of the plants between 2008 and 2009.[148] The plants were built using project financing in 2011–2012.[149]

The *NextEra* claimants argued that Spain had failed to protect their legitimate expectations in violation of the FET standard.[150] Those legitimate expectations were founded on the regulatory framework as established in RD 661/2007, the registration of its plants in the RAIPRE (which had confirmed the right of their plants to receive the RD 661/2007 FIT), ministerial resolutions issued to the plants confirming the FIT applicable to them and specific statements they alleged had been made to NextEra by Spanish officials.[151] In its analysis of the *NextEra* FET claim, the tribunal noted that:

> it was not convinced that in the circumstances of the present case the mere fact of the Regulatory Framework I [i.e. the Special Regime] was a sufficient basis for the expectation that Claimants would be guaranteed the terms of Regulatory Framework I. The Framework was based on legislation and legislation can be changed.[152]

Likewise, it did not consider that registration in the RAIPRE "did of itself grant any right to the economic regime set out in RD 661/2007".[153] In that regard, the *NextEra* tribunal agreed with the *Charanne* tribunal that registration in the RAIPRE was a "mere administrative requirement".[154] The *NextEra* tribunal was also not persuaded that the Ministerial Resolutions of December 2010, which were issued to the claimant's plants and confirmed the terms of the regulatory regime applicable to them, gave the claimant a legitimate expectation as to the continuation of that regime.[155] It held that all the resolutions did was reiterate the applicable terms of the regulatory regime and the "Ministerial Resolutions could not do what the legislation to which they applied had not done".[156]

The tribunal found, however, that the "primary basis" for the *NextEra* claimant's claim was not the legislation itself, RAIPRE registration or the Ministerial Resolutions, but that "statements and assurances made directly to NextEra by Spanish authorities ... created expectations about the economic regime that would apply to Claimants in respect of their investment".[157] In particular, in making its investments, the *NextEra* claimants had relied on letters from the

147 *NextEra Energy Global Holdings B.V. and NextEra Energy Spain Holdings B.V. v The Kingdom of Spain* (*NextEra*), ICSID Case No. ARB/14/11, Final Award, 31 May 2019, para 168 *et seq.*

148 Ibid, para 168.

149 Ibid, paras 176–177.

150 Ibid, para 582.

151 Ibid, para 583.

152 Ibid, para 584.

153 Ibid, para 585.

154 Ibid, para 585.

155 Ibid, para 565. This can be contrasted with the position that the *Masdar* tribunal took regarding the Ministerial Resolutions issued in that case.

156 Ibid, para 586.

157 Ibid, para 587.

Secretary of State for Energy to NextEra personnel which had confirmed that "the absolute vocation of said legislation is to preserve the legal security of all investments currently underway, thereby guaranteeing the forecasts under which said investments are to be made".[158] In the view of the *NextEra* tribunal, although these letters were not "formal commitments" they could nevertheless give rise to legitimate expectations in the broader context of the regulatory framework.[159]

According to the tribunal, the specific legitimate expectation was not that the RD 661/2007 regime would remain frozen but that "it would not be changed in a way that would undermine the security and viability of [the Claimants'] investment".[160] That expectation had been repudiated by the New Regime, which "fundamentally and radically changed" the regulatory framework.[161] These changes "went beyond anything that might have been reasonably expected by Claimants when they undertook their investment".[162] There was therefore a breach of FET.[163]

3 Claims against the Czech Republic

3.1 *Overview*

As with the claims against Spain, the claims against the Czech Republic concern amendments to renewable energy incentives. The Czech Support Scheme for renewable energy came into effect in March 2005. It broadly consisted of two parts: (1) the continuation of existing tax incentives; and (2) the enactment of Act 180, which is described below.

The tax element derived from a piece of legislation named Act 586/1992 (the "Income Tax Act"), which had been in force since 1993. The Income Tax Act provided that renewable energy producers were to be exempt from income tax in the year a plant first become operational, and for the following five years. It also created an accelerated depreciation period for particular intangible assets of renewable energy producers.

Act 180 established a number of other renewable incentives, including FITs and so-called green-bonuses. Renewable energy producers were entitled to choose between FITs and green bonuses when their plants first went into operation. Each year the Czech regulator, the ERO, determined the rates of FITs and green bonuses for plants connecting to the grid the following year. Under s 6 of the Act, FITs were to be such that investors should receive an adequate return on their capital invested within 15 years (later amended to 20 years), with the proviso that the new tariff set could not be reduced by more than 5 per cent as compared to the preceding year's tariff. That, in effect, imposed a brake on how much FITs could fall year on year (the 5% brake).

The formula and assumptions for the calculation of the FIT rates were published by the ERO in 2005, and were subsequently revised in 2009 through ERO Regulation 140, which stated a targeted annual increase of 2–4 per cent in the FIT rates. Published technical regulations indicated that an adequate return on investment was considered to be 7 per cent per annum.

158 Ibid, para 592.
159 *NextEra*, paras 592–596.
160 Ibid, para 596.
161 Ibid, para 599.
162 Ibid, para 599.
163 Ibid, para 37(2).

From 2010, however, the Czech Republic began to change the favourable investment climate created by the Support Scheme, owing to a dramatic fall in the price of solar panels. The Czech Republic claimed that, as a result, producers stood to earn windfall profits at the expense of consumers. Act 180's provisions were heavily amended; first, in May 2010, by the removal of the 5% brake for plants (per Act 173/2010) and, subsequently, in November 2010, by the restriction of the FITs for PV plants commissioned after March 2011 to only those PV plants with a capacity of up to 30kWh (through Act 330/2010). These changes, however, only applied to plants connected to the grid from January 2011 onwards.

The next change to be made was the removal of the Income Tax Act's exemptions and favourable depreciation programme (per Act 346/2010). That measure had effect from 2011, but applied to all PV plants. Finally, the Czech Republic introduced a new 26 per cent levy applicable to the electricity generated by PV plants benefitting from FITs and put into operation between January 2009 and December 2010 (the Solar Levy) (Act 402/2010). The Solar Levy was withheld at source by the operator of the transmission system and was to apply for a period of three years.

In 2012, Act 180 was entirely repealed and replaced by Act 165/2012, which incorporated the amended FIT and the Solar Levy. The Solar Levy was later extended, at a rate of 10 per cent of the FIT, for plants commissioned in 2010 for the period in which they would receive FITs.

3.2 *Cases*

Two cases have so far been brought as a result of these changes: *Jürgen Wirtgen, Stefan Wirtgen, Gisela Wirtgen and JSW Solar (zwei) GmbH & Co. KG v. Czech Republic* and *Antaris GmbH & Dr Michael Göde v. Czech Republic.* The *JSW* case was brought under the bilateral investment treaty between Germany and the Czech Republic (the BIT) alone and therefore falls outside the scope of this chapter. The *Antaris* case was brought under the ECT and the BIT together. The tribunal's treatment of the claimant's claim relating to a breach of the FET standard under Article 10(1) is addressed below.

3.2.1 Antaris GmbH & Dr Michael Göde v. Czech Republic, PCA Case No. 2014-01

The *Antaris* award was rendered on 2 May 2018. The claimants were Antaris GmbH (Antaris), a German company,[164] and its ultimate shareholder,[165] Dr Michael Göde, a German individual, who together had interests in five PV plants.[166]

As noted above, the claimants brought their claims under the ECT and the BIT together.

The claimants argued that the Czech Government breached the FET clauses of those treaties through the "progressive dismantling"[167] of the incentive regime for PV installations, which undermined their legitimate expectations that: (1) the FIT level would remain stable over the lifetime of their PV plants; and (2) the Income Tax Exemption would last for six years.[168] The claimants argued that the "inherent nature of the Incentive Regime created

164 *Antaris GmbH & Dr Michael Göde v. Czech Republic* (*Antaris*), PCA Case No. 2014-01, Award, 2 May 2018, para 3.
165 Ibid, para 6.
166 Ibid, paras 402–409.
167 Ibid, para 74.
168 Ibid, para 271.

basic expectations and a promise that the Czech Republic would not modify the Incentive Regime".[169] The claimants alleged that their expectations arose from the legislation itself along with the "purpose and context" of the incentive regime, and that they would not have invested without "the guarantee that the Incentive regime should be granted and maintained".[170] They specified that the purpose of the incentive regime was to "attract the investments that the Czech Republic needed to comply with its EU law obligations".[171]

The claimants also argued that "a promise of stability may arise in the absence of a stabilization clause",[172] and that the Czech Republic had an "obligation to provide a stable and predictable legal framework" under both the BIT and the ECT.[173]

The *Antaris* tribunal (acting by majority)[174] rejected the claimants' claims.[175] First, it held that the claimants' complaints with regard to the amendment of Czech tax incentives could not be considered under the ECT as a result of the tax carve-out contained in that treaty.[176] Secondly, the tribunal did not agree that the claimants had held the legitimate expectations they claimed. It accepted that "to establish a legitimate expectation, there is no requirement that there be an express stabilisation provision".[177] However, all of the other arguments made by the claimants failed. The tribunal noted that it was particularly important to take into account the date when the claimants' PV plants were commissioned. The Holýšov plant was commissioned on 18 December 2008. It was not affected by the disputed measures, but the claimants maintained a FET claim in respect of it, on the basis that the Czech Republic's actions had increased uncertainty in the solar energy investment environment, which had a negative impact on the business's enterprise value.[178]

The specific dates of construction and commissioning of the other four plants (Úsliné, Mozolov, Stříbro and Holýšov) have been redacted in the public version of the award.[179] However, elsewhere in the award, it is noted that the plants were constructed and commissioned after Act 173/2010 came into force (i.e. after May 2010), but before 2011 from when Act 173/2010 had effect.[180] Dr Göde explained in his witness evidence that the fact that Act 173/2010 did not affect PV plants already commissioned, or plants that would come online before 2011, gave him comfort that the Czech Republic would not amend the incentive regime for existing plants.[181] The tribunal disagreed, holding that "Dr Göde was essentially an opportunistic investor who saw a window of opportunity and who was aware, or should have been aware, that dealing with the solar boom was a fast-moving and controversial political issue".[182] Notwithstanding his witness testimony, the tribunal considered that there was "no evidence of any real due diligence by Dr Göde".[183]

169 Ibid, para 265.
170 Ibid, paras 274–281.
171 Ibid, para 281.
172 Ibid, para 268.
173 Ibid, para 267.
174 Co-arbitrator Mr Gary Born issued a dissenting opinion.
175 Ibid, para 465.
176 Ibid, para 217. That was, in any event, conceded by the claimants in their Reply. The Solar Levy was not excluded since, on analysis, it was not considered to be a tax (see, paras 218–253).
177 Ibid, para 399.
178 Ibid, para 401
179 Ibid, paras 401–409.
180 Ibid, para 393.
181 Ibid, paras 391–392.
182 Ibid, para 431.
183 *Antaris*, paras 432, 381–398.

The tribunal noted that "[i]nvestors know that the legislative framework may change and evolve in the light of circumstances and political developments".[184] It held that, at the time they invested, the claimants "should have been aware that other legislative changes, especially with regard to tax, were in the air".[185] As such, all the claimants had was "a speculative hope [as to the support scheme they would benefit from] – as opposed to an internationally-protected expectation".[186] The tribunal considered that "an informed investor who had undertaken proper due diligence would have been aware of the use by the ERO of the 7% benchmark" to calculate the FITs to which investors were entitled.[187] It noted that "[a]ll that the measures did was to reduce the rate of return to a level which the State had originally intended".[188] The measures had a legitimate aim of reducing excessive profits and sheltering consumers from excessive energy prices.[189] Accordingly, it considered that the measures were "rational and proportionate".[190]

4 Claims against Italy

4.1 Overview

The claims against Italy also arise from a series of changes made to a regulatory framework that had been implemented to induce investment in Italy's solar energy sector. At the time of writing, these claims have resulted in three final awards: *Greentech*, *CEF Energia* and *Blusun*.

The Italian incentive scheme was established through Legislative Decree No. 387 dated 29 December 2003. This created the framework for the subsequent enactment of a succession of ministerial decrees issued from 2005 onwards (the Conto Energia Decrees). Each Conto Energia Decree implemented a FIT to be paid for a 20-year period commencing from the date of the qualifying installation's entry into operation.

Under the Italian FIT scheme, an individual PV installation's entitlement to the FIT was confirmed by a letter issued by a state-owned company, *Gestore dei Servizi Energetici* (GSE). The GSE letter was then followed by an agreement between GSE and the owner of the PV installation, which specified the FIT to which the installation was entitled. In addition to the FIT scheme, Legislative Decree No. 387 also established a minimum pricing scheme whereby the GSE would directly purchase electricity from smaller renewable energy producers at minimum guaranteed prices.

Italy modified the Conto Energia FIT regime through a sequence of measures primarily aimed at reducing the electricity bill of consumers. Legislative Decree 28 (the Romani Decree), passed on 3 March 2011, retrospectively changed the eligibility criteria for plants to qualify for the Conto Energia Decree FITs in two respects. First, it restricted the eligibility for the FIT established by the third Conto Energia Decree to plants that had entered into operation before 31 May 2011 and not, as originally established, to those in operation by 31 December 2013.[191] Secondly, it provided that any plants entering into operation after

184 Ibid, paras 435 and 437.

185 Ibid, para 433.

186 Ibid, para 435.

187 Ibid, para 440. The same finding was reached by the *JSW* tribunal, which rejected the *JSW* claimants' FET claim under the BIT.

188 Ibid, para 445.

189 Ibid, para 444.

190 Ibid, para 445.

191 *Blusun S.A., Jean-Pierre Lecorcier and Michael Stein v. Italian Republic, ICSID Case No. ARB/14/3* (*Blusun*), Final Award, 27 December 2016, para 103.

29 March 2012 would only be eligible to receive a FIT if they occupied less than 10 per cent of the land in which they were erected.[192]

Subsequently, on 24 June 2014, Law Decree 91 was issued (the *Spalma-incentivi* Decree). The *Spalma-incentivi* Decree offered PV installations already registered a choice as to whether or not to receive the FIT. They could elect to receive: (1) a 17–25 per cent cut to the FIT with the FIT being payable over 24 years instead of the original 20 years; (2) a tariff reduction from –2019 with a promise to increase tariffs in later years; or (3) the default option of a 6–8 per cent cut of the FIT over the 20-year period of the FIT.

Italy also revoked the application of the inflation adjustment under the first Conto Energia Decree;[193] imposed new administrative fees and imbalance costs;[194] altered the prices that had applied under the minimum guaranteed prices scheme;[195] applied a so-called "Robin Hood" tax (which had originally been targeted at companies with an annual gross income of over €25 million) to companies with an annual gross income of €3 million or taxable income over €300,000, thus encompassing certain PV projects operating under the FIT scheme; and classified PV installations as immovable property, resulting in the application of additional charges.

4.2 Cases

The *Greentech*, *CEF Energia* and *Blusun* cases were all brought under the ECT. The summaries below focus on the tribunals' treatment of the claimants' FET claims under Article 10(1) of the ECT.

4.2.1 Greentech Energy Systems A/S, NovEnergia II Energy & Environment (SCA) SICAR, and NovEnergia II Italian Portfolio SA v. The Italian Republic, SCC Case No. V 2015/095

The *Greentech* award was rendered on 23 December 2018 and concerned the claims of Greentech Energy Systems A/S and NovEnergia II Energy & Environment (SCA) SICAR ("NovEnergia") and its subsidiary, NovEnergia II Italian Portfolio SA ("NIP").[196] Greentech is a Danish company, which held interests in a total of 81 PV plants, acquired between 2011 and 2013.[197] NovEnergia and NIP are Luxembourgish companies, which had interests in 52 PV plants, acquired between 2008 and 2013. All of these plants benefitted from the Conto Energia FIT and some were also entitled to the minimum guaranteed pricing scheme

The "main pillar" of the claimants' claims was that the reduction in tariff levels under the *Spalma-incentivi* Decree violated their legitimate expectations and thus breached the FET clause of the ECT. The claimants also contended that the modifications of the minimum guaranteed price scheme, the cancellation of the inflation adjustment, the imposition of the

192 *Blusun*, para 104.

193 *Greentech Energy Systems A/S, NovEnergia II Energy & Environment (SCA) SICAR, and NovEnergia II Italian Portfolio SA v. The Italian Republic*, SCC Case No. V 2015/095 ("*Greentech v Italy*"), Final Award, 23 December 2018, paras 152–155.

194 Ibid, paras 157–159.

195 Ibid, para 140.

196 Ibid, para 1.A.1.

197 Ibid, paras 404–405.

administrative charges and imbalance costs, the Robin Hood Tax and the classification of PV plants as immovable property had frustrated their legitimate expectations.[198]

The *Greentech* tribunal found that it did not have jurisdiction with respect to the dispute concerning the Robin Hood tax and the classification of PV installations as immovable property since these were taxation measures excluded by the "taxation carve-out" at Article 21 of the ECT.[199] Notably, however, the tribunal held that it did have jurisdiction to hear the claims concerning the newly imposed administration fees and imbalance charges.[200] According to the tribunal, since these charges were either established to cover GSE's costs or were specifically related to electricity dispatching services, they were not allocated to the state's general revenue and were not taxes.[201]

As regards the *Spalma-incentivi* Decree, the tribunal, acting by majority,[202] held that the claimants had been led to believe, reasonably, that the FIT would remain the same as specified in the Conto Energia Decrees, the GSE letter and the GSE agreements.[203] These assurances constituted "non-waivable guarantees" that the FITs would remain fixed for 20 years.[204]

The tribunal acknowledged that although "the investor might need to live with some minor adjustments", there was "nothing [that] alerted the Claimants that they would need to accept changes of the magnitude imposed by the Spalma-incentivi Decree".[205] The majority therefore rejected Italy's defence, which relied on its right to regulate and the economic difficulties it faced at the time of enacting the disputed measures. It noted that none of the economic difficulties reached the level of *force majeure* and that the specificity of the assurances made by Italy with respect to the FITs "crossed a threshold such that the reduction of the incentive tariffs by the Spalma-incentivi Decree defeated Claimants' legitimate expectations".[206] This was therefore a breach of the FET standard.

The tribunal rejected the remainder of the claimants' claims concerning the modification of the minimum guaranteed price scheme, the cancellation of the ISTAT inflation adjustment and the imposition of the administrative charges, observing that the scaling back of the minimum guaranteed price scheme, the revocation of the inflation indexation of the FITs and the imposition of imbalance charges and administrative fees were either foreseeable or were not inconsistent with any prior assurance made by the Italian state.[207]

4.2.2 CEF Energia BV v. Italian Republic, SCC Case No. 158/2015

CEF Energia BV is a Dutch entity that acquired equity interests in three PV plants. In its award dated 16 January 2019, the *CEF Energia* tribunal carried out a careful analysis of the date of each individual investment in each of the PV plants, which ultimately had a pivotal impact on the outcome of the award.

198 See paras 478 *et* seq, 507 *et seq* and 521 *et seq.*

199 Ibid, para 227.

200 Ibid, paras 243 and 251.

201 Ibid, paras 244 and 252.

202 Co-arbitrator Professor Giorgio Sacerdoti issued a dissenting opinion (see, *Greentech v Italy*, Dissenting Opinion of Arbitrator Giorgio Sacerdoti, dated 5 December 2018.

203 Ibid, para 447.

204 Ibid, paras 450–451.

205 Ibid, para 448.

206 Ibid, paras 451–453.

207 Ibid, paras 501–502, 518, and 536.

The first investment was the January 2010 acquisition of Sunholding S.r.l., a company that held the rights to the "Megasol" PV project. The Megasol project subsequently obtained its GSE agreement on 2 November 2011.[208] The second investment was the acquisition of an interest in Phenix S.r.l., which held the rights to the "Sugarella" PV project. It subsequently obtained its GSE agreement on 23 November 2011.[209] Finally, on 30 March 2012, the claimant acquired Enersol S.r.l, which held the "Enersol" PV project. The Enersol project was divided into seven subprojects, the last of which obtained their GSE agreements on 2 March 2012.[210] The Enersol acquisition thus occurred *after* the project had already secured its right to the Conto Energia FIT.

As with *Greentech*, the claimants alleged that the *Spalma-incentivi* Decree, the administrative fees and imbalance costs, the Robin Hood tax and the classification of PV installations as immovable property had violated their legitimate expectations as to the stability of the legal and economic regime applicable to the Italian PV sector.[211] The tribunal found that it only had jurisdiction to hear the *Spalma-incentivi* claim since the remaining measures were taxation measures. The *CEF Energia* tribunal thus reached a different conclusion to the *Greentech* tribunal with respect to the administrative fees and imbalance costs. As noted above, the *Greentech* tribunal held that these measures were not taxation measures.

In its assessment of the alleged breach of the FET standard, the *CEF Energia* tribunal endorsed the summary of the FET standard set out in the *Antaris* award, in particular that: "there will be a breach of the FET standard where legal and business stability or the legal framework has been altered in such a way as to frustrate legitimate and reasonable expectations or guarantees of stability".[212] In addition, the *CEF Energia* tribunal emphasized that the only expectations that may be protected as legitimate under the FET standard are those that existed at the time when the investor made the investment.[213] The tribunal stressed that this was "*an important temporal point*".[214]

Applying those principles, the tribunal found that the claimant could only have had legitimate expectations with respect to the Enersol plant, since only that acquisition was made once the entitlement to the FIT had been confirmed in the GSE agreement. In contrast, the Megasol and Sugarella projects had been acquired at a point when the right to the FIT, although ultimately secured, was still uncertain. Thus, at the time of the investment, there was merely an intention to complete Megasol and Sugarella plants and connect them to the grid.[215]

The tribunal held that a number of elements informed the claimants' legitimate expectation that the Enersol plant would receive the FITs for 20 years. Among other things, the GSE letters constituted "an express and unmistakeable invitation on the part of an emanation of the Respondent to sign the relevant GSE agreements as an essential prerequisite to the obtaining of the incentives".[216] Further, the GSE agreements themselves contained "the express language that the only way change could be brought about to contractual terms was by way of a mutual

208 *CEF Energia BV v. Italian Republic*, SCC Case No. 158/2015 (*CEF*), Final Award, 23 December 2018, para 151.

209 Ibid, para 156.

210 Ibid, para 161.

211 Ibid, para 163 *et seq.*

212 Ibid, para 185.

213 Ibid, para 186.

214 Ibid, para 185.

215 Ibid, para 187.

216 Ibid, para 212.

agreement in writing".[217] Amid these representations, in the appreciation of the tribunal, "[n]o reading, no matter how indulgent, could lead anyone to consider anything other than a clear promise of twenty years of constant currency incentives pursuant to a private law contract".[218]

Having found the claimant had a protected legitimate expectation, the tribunal then considered whether that legitimate expectation had been undermined. The tribunal found that the 6–8 per cent tariff cut implemented by the *Spalma-incentivi* Decree was a violation of the commitments recorded in the FIT incentive regime and GSE agreements. In reaching this finding, the *CEF Energia* tribunal clarified that a rigorous scrutiny of Italy's conduct was appropriate given the clear and specific commitments Italy had made under the contracts.[219] The nature of those commitments meant there was a reduced scope for Italy to implement measures that were inconsistent with the expectations created by those commitments.[220] Thus, a measure that was inconsistent with that prior commitment could breach the FET standard even if the measure was in itself reasonable.[221] Since the *Spalma-incentivi* Decree meant that the claimant was not receiving the originally promised FIT, there was a breach of the FET standard.[222]

Given the commitment Italy had made, the reason provided for this measure (i.e. the reduction of electricity bills for consumers) could not prevail over the claimant's entitlement to the FIT.[223] As a consequence, the tribunal held that Italy had breached its FET obligation under the ECT.[224]

4.2.3 Blusun S.A., Jean-Pierre Lecorcier and Michael Stein v. Italian Republic, ICSID Case No. ARB/14/3

The *Blusun* award was rendered before the *CEF Energia* and *Greentech* awards, on 27 December 2016 and, unlike those subsequent cases, concerned a planned PV project that ultimately was never constructed and failed to secure any entitlement to the FIT scheme.

The claim was brought by Blusun S.A. (Blusun), a Belgian company, and its two owners, Jean–Pierre Lecorcier, a French national, and Michael Stein, a German national.[225] Blusun in turn was a shareholder in two Italian companies, Eskosol S.p.A (Eskosol) and Società Interconnessioni Brindisi S.R.L. (SIB).[226] Eskosol owned the SPVs that were to operate 120 separate PV installations[227] and SIB was to build and manage two substations.[228] These PV installations and substations would together comprise the 120MW Puglia project, which would, at the time, have been the largest PV project in Europe.[229]

Between 2008 and 2009 the project obtained the necessary rights and permits for the development of the plants.[230] On 29 December 2010 Eskosol signed a contract for the

217 Ibid, para 214.
218 Ibid, para 217.
219 Ibid, para 243.
220 Ibid, para 243.
221 Ibid, para 243.
222 Ibid, para 238.
223 *CEF*, para 241.
224 Ibid, para 284.
225 *Blusun*, paras 1–4.
226 Ibid, para 2.
227 Ibid, para 62.
228 Ibid, para 61.
229 Ibid, para 376(a).
230 Ibid, para 54.

construction of the plants.[231] In early 2011 Eskosol then received letters from investors interested in financing the project.[232]

Relevant to Blusun's claim was Italy's consolidated system for applying for construction permits.[233] This included a declaratory procedure, Denuncia di Inizio Attivita (DIA), under which smaller PV installations (with capacity below 20KW) could be built without receiving explicit authorization, provided that no formal objection by the competent authority was received within 30 days of relevant paperwork being submitted.[234] The region of Puglia adopted its own laws which allowed the use of the DIA procedure for plants with a much larger capacity (up to 1MW).[235] Authorisation to build many of the claimants' PV plants was applied for (and received) under the Puglia DIA process.[236] On 26 March 2010, however, the Italian Constitutional Court found Puglia's expansion of the DIA to be unconstitutional.[237] A year later, the Romani Decree was issued.[238] Pursuant to the Romani Decree, the GSE published lists indicating which PV installations would be entitled to benefit from the FITs provided they were built by a particular deadline. These lists included numerous errors, which, the *Blusun* claimants argued, created considerable confusion as to whether or not their project would be entitled to the FIT when it was finally built.[239]

Finally, on 11 January 2012 the municipal authorities of Brindisi issued a stop-work order preventing any further work on the *Blusun* claimants' PV project due to, *inter alia,* alleged violations of zoning regulations.[240] Although that order was subsequently annulled by the regional Administrative Court on 7 March 2012, the *Blusun* claimants alleged that that was of no benefit to them since it left insufficient time for them to comply with the 29 March 2012 deadline imposed by the Romani Decree for their plants to enter into operation.[241]

The Blusun claimants argued that the legal instability created by (*inter alia*): (1) the Constitutional Court decision; (2) the Romani Decree; (3) the erroneous lists published by the GSE; and (4) the Brindisi stop-work order prevented them from obtaining the necessary construction financing and, consequently, caused their project to fail. On the claimants' case, such legal insecurity amounted to a violation of the FET standard and the specific requirement to "encourage and create stable, equitable, favourable and transparent conditions for Investors" specified in Article 10(1) of the ECT.[242]

The tribunal made the following observation with respect to FIT schemes and the FET standard:

> In the absence of a specific commitment, the state has no obligation to grant subsidies such as feed in tariffs, or to maintain them unchanged once granted. But if they are lawfully granted, and if it becomes necessary to modify them, this should be done in

231 Ibid, para 96.
232 Ibid, para 100.
233 Ibid, para 66.
234 Ibid, para 67.
235 Ibid, para 68.
236 Ibid, paras 89–90.
237 Ibid, para 92.
238 Ibid, paras 102–105.
239 Ibid, paras 110–112.
240 *Blusun*, para 119.
241 Ibid, para 119.
242 Ibid, para 321.

> a manner which is not disproportionate to the aim of the legislative amendment, and should have due regard to the reasonable reliance interests of recipients who may have committed substantial resources on the basis of the earlier regime.[243]

The tribunal further observed that a legitimate expectations claim does not involve the incorporation of a margin of appreciation type analysis: "if there were 'legitimate expectations that the Third Energy Account would remain in place for its entire duration according to its terms', issues of reasonableness, proportionality and foreseeableness of changes to that Account would not arise".[244] The tribunal found on the case before it that none of the disputed measures amounted to a breach of the ECT. Among other things, the Constitutional Court challenge to the DIA procedure was known to the investors at the time they invested;[245] the Romani Decree maintained "[t]he principle of guaranteed tariffs for a 20-year period" and provided a reasonable 12-month grace period for projects planning on connecting to the grid;[246] Italy acted in good faith in carrying out the difficult task of compiling an extensive list of eligible projects amid a rapidly changing construction scene;[247] and the stop-work order was temporary, issued in accordance with rule of law standards, and immediately withdrawn upon successful challenge by the claimants.[248]

Having found that these measures individually did not violate Article 10(1) the tribunal considered whether their cumulative effect could amount to a breach. The tribunal held that, for this to occur, an investor would need to establish that the cumulative effect of the measures amounted to the "subversion of the legal regime".[249] The claimants had failed to establish that such a threshold had been reached.

The tribunal then carried out a separate analysis of whether the disputed measures were the operative cause of the failure of the project. In the tribunal's determination, the claimants had failed to show this since,

> [[o]f far greater weight [to the Project's failure] was the continued dependence on project financing, and the failure to obtain it was due both to the size of the Project and to justified concerns about the scope of DIA authorisation, on which the legality of the Project depended.[250]

The claim therefore failed as a matter of causation, even if it had been shown that the disputed measures were breaches of the FET standard.

5 Conclusion

A number of useful lessons may be drawn from the awards so far rendered in the European renewable energy sector cases regarding the operation of the FET standard under Article 10(1) of the ECT in the context of regulatory change.

243 Ibid, para 319(5).
244 Ibid, para 366.
245 Ibid, para 329(b).
246 Ibid, para 342(c).
247 *Blusun*, para 350.
248 Ibid, paras 360 and 364.
249 Ibid, paras 363–364.
250 Ibid, para 394.

- First, it appears universally accepted that where a State undermines an investor's legitimate expectations, that will give rise to a breach of the FET standard.
- Second, most awards confirm that it is possible for *erga omnes* regulations – that is to say regulations directed to the world at large, as opposed to specifically addressed measures – to give rise to legitimate expectations. Tribunals are, however, more likely to find that a particular law or regulation gives rise to a legitimate expectation where it has been implemented specifically in order to induce foreign investment.
- Third, the significance of the changes made to a regulatory regime is likely to be considered relevant to an assessment of whether an investor's legitimate expectations based on that regime have been undermined.
- Fourth, some tribunals have considered that significant changes to a regulatory regime may also give rise to a breach of the FET standard irrespective of whether legitimate expectations as regards the nature of a regulatory regime have been established. Those tribunals have held that, under the FET standard, States have a general obligation not to modify existing regulations in an unreasonable manner.
- Fifth, even in cases where tribunals have considered an investor's legitimate expectations as to the effect of a particular regulatory regime to arise from a specific commitment, the tribunals have still gone on to examine the significance of the disputed regulatory change in determining whether or not the investor's expectations were undermined.
- Sixth, the timing of an investment is likely to be important. Investments are unlikely to be protected from later regulatory change where they are made after it was (or should have been) readily apparent that regulatory stability could not be expected. That will be the case even if that later change is fundamental.
- Seventh where it is objectively reasonable for an investor to have held expectations regarding the stability of a particular regulatory regime based on that regime itself, a lack of detailed due diligence on the part of the investor is unlikely to impact its claim. Where, however, a tribunal is unconvinced that a particular regime gave rise, in and of itself, to the expectations alleged by an investor, a lack of due diligence may well be seen to support a finding that the investor could not have legitimately held the relevant expectations.
- Lastly, questions of conformity of State conduct with national laws and with the requirements of the ECT are separate. Accordingly, judgments from a national court confirming the legitimacy of regulatory changes under national law are unlikely to influence a tribunal that considers that those changes have breached an investor's legitimate expectations.

As noted above, these lessons are valuable not only for renewable energy investors, but also investors in other types of energy project which are premised on significant upfront investment and dependent on the stability of a particular legal regime. They are also important for States to consider both in establishing regulatory incentives and implementing regulatory change.

More generally, it is clear that investment treaties – including, in particular, the ECT – have a significant role to play in supporting the stability of the energy sector in Europe. A stable energy investment framework benefits not only energy investors, but also States and energy consumers. Increased investment in regulated energy sectors lowers the cost of capital associated with investing and can decrease energy costs.

Of course, as the cases summarized above demonstrate, investment treaties also give rise to risks for States. Regulatory change that does not conform to stability requirements may result in multiple claims against a State from investors for compensation. For some States, that risk appears to be too great. For example, on 31 December 2014, Italy became the first EU Member State to give notice of its withdrawal from the ECT. That withdrawal became effective on 1 January 2016, although Italy is obliged to comply with the terms of the ECT for a further 20 years pursuant to the treaty's so-called "sunset clause" in Article 47(3).[251]

251 ECT, Article 47(3) states as follows: "[t]he provisions of this Treaty shall continue to apply to Investments made in the Area of a Contracting Party by Investors of other Contracting Parties or in the Area of other Contracting Parties by Investors of that Contracting Party as of the date when that Contracting Party's withdrawal from the Treaty takes effect for a period of 20 years from such date".

PART III

Russia

11

THE REGULATION OF PETROLEUM EXPLORATION AND PRODUCTION IN RUSSIA

Tina Soliman Hunter and Irina Fodchenko

1 Introduction

Russia is handsomely endowed with petroleum reserves. As of 2018, Russia holds proved oil reserves of 14.6 billion barrels (b/bbl) or 6.1 per cent of global reserves, ranking it among the top six proved reserves in the world.[1] In addition, holding 1,375 trillion cubic feet (tcf) of proved gas reserves, Russia has the largest global gas reserves.[2] There has been a long history of petroleum production in Russia, commencing during the late Tsarist period with oil production from the Baku region.[3] During this period, Russia was one of the top global exporters, with the Russian state exercising direct control over production through ownership of all the resources.[4] This altered in 1872 with the auctioning off of state-owned land, placing petroleum-producing land in the hands of private landholders, and led to a rapid increase in production.[5] During the Soviet era, all petroleum ownership and operations were nationalised,[6] which led to a 60-fold growth in oil production from 10 million tons in 1917 to over 600 million tons in the 1980s. In the period 1928–1939, rapid industrialisation occurred under Stalin's five-year plans, laying the foundations for strong growth in petroleum production in the post-war era.[7] After 1945, exploration and production (E&P) gradually shifted from the Caucus/Baku region to the Volga-Ural region, and from 1965 to Western Siberia.[8]

The Soviet industrial management structure crumbled during the 1980s. Under Gorbachev, traditional Soviet administrative structures were undermined as the power of

1 The top proved oil reserves are Venezuela (17.5 per cent global reserves), Saudi Arabia (17.3 per cent global reserves), Canada (9.7 per cent global reserves), Iran (9 per cent global reserves) and Iraq (8.5 per cent global reserves). BP, *BP Statistical Review of World Energy* (BP, 2019), 14.

2 Ibid, 32.

3 A.A. Igolkin, *Russkaja neft, o kotoroj my tak malo znaem* (Olimp-Biznes, 2003).

4 Nat Moser, *Oil and the Economy of Russia, from the Late-Tsarist to the Post Soviet Period* (Routledge, 2018), 13–14

5 Nat Moser, *Oil and the Economy of Russia, from the Late-Tsarist to the Post Soviet Period* (Routledge, 2018), 14.

6 Such nationalisation occurred through a series of decrees in 1918–1920. Nat Moser, *Oil and the Economy of Russia, from the Late-Tsarist to the Post Soviet Period* (Routledge, 2018), 55.

7 Ibid, 51.

8 Ibid, 55.

enterprise directors was strengthened.[9] This had a major effect on the West Siberian oil region, which required colossal infrastructure,[10] leading to a decline in production from the mid-1980s. By the time of the collapse of the Soviet Union in 1991 and the establishment of the Russian Federation, petroleum production had decreased sharply as a result of structural reforms, Soviet enterprise management and practices,[11] inefficient resource use,[12] and barriers to technological advancement, attributable to the Soviet command economy.[13] In the decade after the break-up of the former Soviet Union, many state-owned assets, including oil and gas assets, were distributed into the hands of an elite few (the 'oligarchs'), particularly as a result of the 'loans for shares scheme'.[14] As a result, for the first time since 1872, the Russo-Soviet state lost control over most aspects of the 'commanding heights' of the economy in the 1990s,[15] including oil and gas production.

By the end of the twentieth century, Gazprom[16] and Rosneft[17] had been increasingly privatised through both the voucher scheme and the loans for shares scheme, with the Russian state owning less than 38 per cent of the Gazprom. However, during Putin's first Presidency (2000–2008), many assets were returned to state ownership or control through a programme of 'national champions',[18] with Gazprom ownership growing to its current position of being just over 50 per cent state-owned. Assets of the former oil giant Yukos[19] were acquired by the Russian Government as a result of unpaid income taxes totalling

9 Ibid, 56.

10 Ibid.

11 Ibid, 60–66

12 Ibid, 66–70.

13 Ibid, 71.

14 The 'loans for shares scheme' occurred under Boris Yeltsin who, facing a severe fiscal deficit and shortage of funds for his presidential re-election campaign in 1995, sought to raise cash. Under Presidential Edict No. 478, of 11 May 1995, stocks in 43 major state-owned enterprises were transferred to a consortium of private banks that had been established under Gorbachev's Law on Cooperative Societies in the 1980s, to be held in trust for the government for five years in exchange for a low interest loan to the state. Under this scheme, the rights to the management of the auctions of state companies, particularly mineral, petroleum, telecommunications and food industry companies, were parcelled out among the major banks who contrived to win the auctions they managed at astonishingly low prices. See Tina Soliman Hunter, 'Real Property Privatization in Pre- and Post-Soviet Russia: Different or the Same?' In Alla Pozdnakova, *Russian Revolutions of 1917: Scandinavian Perspectives* (Wildy, 2019), pp. 46–71.

15 This phrase can be traced to Marx's ideas on socialism, and was analysed in the book by Daniel Yergin and Joseph Stanislaw, *The Commanding Heights: The Battle for the World Economy* (Simon & Schuster, 2002).

16 Originally established in 1989 when the Ministry of Gas Industry was converted to a state-owned corporate enterprise, and gas assets in Russia were retained upon the break-up of the Soviet Union, securing a monopoly in the gas sector. See Marshall Goldman, *Petrostate: Putin, Power and the New Russia* (Oxford University Press, 2003).

17 Originally established in 1993 as a unitary enterprise with assets previously held by Rosneftgaz, which was the successor to the Soviet Ministry of Oil and Gas.

18 Under this policy, corporations were to not only be profitable, but also to act in the interest of the state. This policy has been championed by Putin, originally in his PhD thesis 'Mineral Natural Resources in the Strategy for the Development of the Russian Economy', during his presidencies, particularly this first presidency. V.V. Putin, 'Vladimir Putin's Academic Writings and Russian Natural Resource Policy: Mineral Natural Resources in the Strategy for Development of the Russian Economy' (2006) 53(1) *Problems of Post-Communism* 48–54. Note that the writings were from a Putin article from the 1999 annual edition of the *Mining Institute Journal* and published in English in 2006 in the above journal. See pp. 48–49 for an explanation. https://doi.org/10.2753/PPC1075-8216530105 accessed 12 October 2019.

19 Which produced 20 per cent of Russia's oil in the period 1996–2003. See Peter Baker and Susan B. Glasser, 'Moscow Raid Begins to Seize Assets of Yukos Oil', *Washington Post* 8 July 2004, p. A11, www.washingtonpost.com/wp-dyn/articles/A33869-2004Jul7.html accessed 19 October 2019.

over $7 billion,[20] with Rosneft acquiring many of Yukos' assets at state-run auctions. Since 2010, the acquisition of assets, notably TNK-BP and Bashneft shares,[21] has increased state ownership of oil and gas production assets. Currently, Rosneft and Gazprom, both majority owned by the Russian Government,[22] dominate petroleum exploration and production, with Gazprom owning the Unified Gas Supply System (UGSS), which is the exclusive exporter of piped natural gas, controlling the export of gas since the passing of the *Law on Natural Gas Exports* by the Russian Duma in 2006.[23] A third state oil company, Gazprom Neft (owned directly and indirectly 95.68 per cent by Gazprom) also dominates, setting an ambitious goal of producing 100 million tonnes of oil (730 million barrels of oil equivalent) per annum by 2020.[24] Together, these companies control over half of the production in Russia. In addition, they operate in 20 countries internationally.

Today, Russia is a major petroleum country. In 2018, Russia was the third largest global oil producer,[25] producing around 11.4 million barrels of oil per day (m bbl/d). In addition, Russia produced 669 billion cubic metres of gas (bcm), making it the second largest producer behind the US.[26] As such, oil and gas continue to play a significant role in the Russian economy. According to the Ministry of Finance of the Russian Federation, in 2018 oil and gas revenue was 9,017.8 billion roubles ($140 billion), accounting for 46 per cent of Russia's federal revenue, up from just 36 per cent two years earlier.[27] This growth in revenue can be attributed to the increase in gas production in Russia over the last decade, and in particular the 12 per cent increase in production from the decade-low level of 584 billion cubic feet (bcf) in 2015, attributable to the coming on line of the Yamal in 2017.[28] Given the importance of oil and gas in the Russian energy sector, and the efforts by Putin to re-establish state

20 Peter Baker and Susan B. Glasser, 'Moscow Raid Begins to Seize Assets of Yukos Oil'. *Washington Post* 8 July 2004, p. A11 www.washingtonpost.com/wp-dyn/articles/A33869-2004Jul7.html accessed 19 October 2019.

21 Bashneft was a privately owned oil company originally established through transfer of oil-related assets of the Bashkortostan oil ministry. It was privatised by Murtaza Rakhimov, the president of Bashkortostan, in 2002–2003 when the controlling interest was transferred to Rakhimov's son. Controlling interest in Bashneft was acquired in 2009 by Yevtushenkov, who was placed under house arrest in 2014, and 72 per cent of the Bashneft interests were seized by the Russian Government, and ultimately acquired by Rosneft in 2016.

22 The Russian state owns 50 per cent of Gazprom via the Federal Agency for State Property Management and Rosneftgaz. The remaining shares are publicly owned, and listed on the stock markets of Moscow, London and Frankfurt. As of 1 October 2019, Rosneft is owned 50.00000001 per cent- by Rosneftgaz, which is 100 per cent owned by the Russian state. Other major shareholders include BP (19.75 per cent), Qatar Investment Authority (through its subsidiary QH Oil Investments LLC) 18.93 per cent and the National Settlement Repository (Russian non-bank financial institution and professional securities market participant) 10.97 per cent. See https://www.rosneft.com/Investors/Equity/Shareholder_structure accessed 10 October 2019.

23 This monopoly ended in 2013 with the proclamation of the federal statute *On Amending Articles 13 and 24 of the Federal Statute 'On the Foundations of the State Regulation of Foreign Commerce' and Articles 1 and 3 of the Federal Statute 'On Exports of Natural Gas'*. See Roman Sidortsov, 'The Myth of Liberalisation: The 2013 Changes in the Russian LNG Export Regime' (2014) 35(323) *Energy Law Journal* 323–343.

24 Gazprom Neft, *Petroleum and Gas Exploration and Production* (2016) https://www.gazprom-neft.com/company/exploration-and-production accessed 17 October 2019.

25 Behind the US and Saudi Arabia. BP, *BP Statistical Review of World Energy* (BP, 2019), 16.

26 BP, *BP Statistical Review of World Energy* (BP, 2019), 32.

27 Ministry of Finance of the Russian Federation, Report on Execution of the Federal Budget (published 2 September 2019) https://www.minfin.ru/en/statistics/fedbud accessed 29 September 2019.

28 Russian gas production has increased from 611 bcm in 2009 to 669 bcm in 2018. However, 2014–2016 were characterised by production below 600 bcm, with only 584 bcm in 2015 See BP, *BP Statistical Review of World Energy* (BP, 2019), 32. The Yamal Peninsula produced 82 bcm in 2017.

ownership over production, it is not surprising that Russian petroleum and energy policy is strongly state controlled.

This chapter seeks to provide an overview of the complex legal framework for oil and gas E&P in Russia. Section 2 considers policies related to the development of Russian petroleum resources. Section 3 provides a brief overview of the legal framework, considering both the onshore laws and those pertaining to the Russian Continental Shelf (RCS). Section 4 then examines the complex legal framework for Russian petroleum exploration and production. This complexity is in part due to the restrictions in place for deposits of federal significance, as well as the use of both production sharing contracts and licences granting access to Russian petroleum resources. This chapter seeks to simplify and systematise the complex interaction of laws currently applying to petroleum activities in Russia.

2 Russian petroleum resource policy

After the privatisation of Russian petroleum resource assets in the 1990s, the first decades of the twenty-first century have seen the Russian state regain control over the country's natural resources, both in terms of ownership of those resources, and also through an increase in state-owned petroleum companies. Putin articulated the value of natural resources to the Russian economy in his 1997 PhD thesis:

> Sustainable development of Russia's economy in the near term must be based on systematic growth in her developed sectors, and, most of all, on her mineral resource potential. In this regard, sustainable development based on natural resources means guaranteeing the economic security of the country through creating a reliable natural resource base to meet the current and future needs of the Russian economy …[29]

Furthermore, Putin articulated in the strongest terms that the state should be at the forefront of determining the development of Russia mineral resources through the establishment of both law and policy:

> Regardless of whose property the natural resources and in particular the mineral resources might be, the state has the right to regulate the process of their development and use, acting in the interests of society as a whole … . A contemporary strategy for rational use of resources cannot be based exclusively on the possibilities of the market alone.[30]

Since his assent to the Russian presidency, Putin has implemented a programme of 'russification' of Russia's petroleum resources. Aside from the state acquisition of greater stakes

29 V.V. Putin, 'Vladimir Putin's Academic Writings and Russian Natural Resource Policy: Mineral Natural Resources in the Strategy for Development of the Russian Economy' (2006) 53(1) *Problems of Post-Communism* 48–54. Note that the writings were from a Putin article from the 1999 annual edition of the *Mining Institute Journal* and published in English in 2006 in the above journal. DOI: https://doi.org/10.2753/PPC1075-8216530105 accessed 12 October 2019, p. 49.

30 V.V. Putin, 'Vladimir Putin's Academic Writings and Russian Natural Resource Policy: Mineral Natural Resources in the Strategy for Development of the Russian Economy' (2006) 53(1) *Problems of Post-Communism* 48–54. Note that the writings were from a Putin article from the 1999 annual edition of the *Mining Institute Journal* published in English in 2006 in the above journal. doi: https://doi.org/10.2753/PPC1075-8216530105 accessed 12 October 2019, p. 52.

in Rosneft and Gazprom, Putin has also sought to control the participation of non-Russian companies. Since 2003, foreign oil companies have been allowed to participate in large oil and gas projects only as a minority stakeholder, with Russian state-owned enterprises (SOE) holding a controlling interest. In addition, foreign companies are not permitted to acquire fields of 'strategic size', namely those fields in excess of 500 million bbl of oil or 50 bcm of gas.[31] This control of foreign interest is illustrated by BP's participation in TNK-BP. Difficulties in the relationship culminated in BP selling its 50 per cent share of the partnership in 2012, which was acquired by the Russian SOE Rosneft. Similarly, the original production sharing agreement PSA for the development of Sakhalin II comprised a joint venture between Shell, Mitsui, Mitsubishi and the Russian Government. After legal and political pressure was exerted on the consortium, it sold a majority stake to Gazprom in December 2006. Today Shell retains a 27.5 per cent (minus one share) interest in the project.

In addition to the reacquisition of former state-owned oil and gas assets and minimising the role of foreign companies, Putin has set about reforming the policy framework for the exploitation of Russian petroleum resources. This reform has come through three main policy instruments: the Russian Energy Strategy to 2030, the Arctic Strategy and the Russian Maritime Doctrine.

2.1 Energy Strategy 2030

In 2003 the *Energy Strategy 2020* was established, approved and implemented. This was soon revised, and in 2009 the current energy policy, the *Energy Strategy of Russia for the Period up to 2030* (the '2030 Strategy'), was established and implemented. *Energy Strategy 2030* gives high priority to socio-economic[32] and national security objectives. Regarding the development of petroleum resources, it primarily focuses on areas in Eastern Siberia and the RCS. Thus, the 2030 Strategy applies equally to onshore and offshore petroleum resources. The 2030 Strategy suggests that investment in technically complex and risky projects are desirable where the benefits to the parties are mutually advantageous. Whilst this does not expressly discourage foreign investment in the Russian petroleum sector, the 2030 Strategy expressly establishes that the provisions of the Strategy will be used when 'adjusting programs and major projects of energy companies'.[33]

One of the main goals of the 2030 Strategy is to ensure energy security. To meet the state energy policy goals, the 2030 Strategy aims to: develop a system of prospective regulations standards and norms; improve licensing policy by removing unjustified administrative barriers; increase state participation in the development of new areas, including the Arctic continental shelf; and establish a separate tax regime for petroleum activities on the RCS.[34] In May 2019 a new Energy Security Doctrine (ESR) was approved by Putin, replacing the previous one. According to the Kremlin, the new ESR is 'a strategic planning document in the field of national security reflecting the official view on ensuring Russia's energy security'.

Although the 2030 Strategy remains the official version of the government's energy policy, the *Energy Policy 2035* has been drafted, with the Ministry of Energy planning to submit the

31 Herbert Smith Freehills, *Legal Guide for Foreign Investors in Russia* (Herbert Smith Freehills, 2019).

32 Section III of the *Energy Strategy of Russia for the Period up to 2030* (pp. 17–19).

33 President of Russia, *The President Signed Executive Order Approving the Energy Security Doctrine of the Russian Federation* 13 May 2019, http://en.kremlin.ru/acts/news/60516 accessed 13 October 2019.

34 Section V of the *Energy Strategy of Russia for the Period up to 2030*.

draft strategy to the Russian Government in November 2019.[35] Importantly, the draft considers widening access to the RCS to other Russian companies with the necessary competence and financial resources. In the offshore Arctic, at present only the Russian owned companies Rosneft, Gazprom and Zarubezhneft hold the right to obtain licences and operate on the Russian Continental shelf. However, in September 2019 the Natural Resources Minister Dmitry Kobylkin indicated that private oil companies may be granted the right to operate offshore.[36] This would enable other, privately owned Russian giants such as Lukoil, as well as international oil companies, access to the fields.[37] Private sector interest and participation is likely to be heavily influenced by the price of oil, given that Arctic petroleum exploitation is expensive.

2.2 Russia's Arctic Strategy and the Maritime Doctrine

Russian Arctic policies are driven by national interests of competition for natural resources and control of the Northern Sea Route, rather than ideological or geopolitical factors which were the feature of Soviet policy.[38] These national interests are iterated in two strategies, which promote the development of Russian petroleum resources. The *2013 Strategy of the Development of the Arctic Zone of the Russian Federation and the National Security up to 2020* (2013 Arctic Strategy)[39] establishes development of the resources base of the Russian Arctic Zone. Article 11 of the 2013 Arctic Strategy outlines development of the Arctic resources, including the need to identify and implement reserve fund deposits, implement large infrastructure projects on the continental shelf of the Barents, Pechora and Kara Seas and the Yamal and Gydan Peninsulas.[40] In addition, it seeks to ensure the protection of the public interest in the development of hydrocarbon deposits on the Russian Arctic Continental Shelf.

The importance of Arctic offshore petroleum resources was also identified in the 2015 *Maritime Doctrine of the Russian Federation* (Marine Doctrine). Deputy Prime Minister Rogozin emphasised that 'there are the riches of continental shelf, the development of which calls for an attentive approach'.[41] The main goal of the Marine Doctrine is to exercise jurisdiction and sovereign rights over the natural resources on the RCS, and ensure the reasonable use of the natural resources.[42] As such, the Marine Doctrine sees the development of sea vessels as fundamental for the development of a seagoing fleet and support infrastructure to support the development and operations of Russian petroleum activities.[43]

35 'Russian Energy Ministry Submits Draft Energy Strategy for 2035' 20 October 2019, *Russia Business Today* https://russiabusinesstoday.com/energy/russian-energy-ministry-submits-draft-energy-strategy-for-2035 accessed 20 October 2019.

36 Reuters, 'Minister: Russia Open to Private Companies Developing Energy-Rich Arctic Shelf', 4 September 2019, *VOA News* https://www.voanews.com/economy-business/minister-russia-open-private-companies-developing-energy-rich-arctic-shelf accessed 20 October 2019.

37 Tsvetana Paraskova, 'Russia Could Allow Private Oil Firms to Explore Arctic Shelf' (2019) Oil Price.com https://oilprice.com/Latest-Energy-News/World-News/Russia-Could-Allow-Private-Oil-Firms-To-Explore-Arctic-Shelf.html accessed 20 October 2019.

38 Alexander Sergunin and Valery Konyshev, *Russia's Arctic Strategy: Hard or Soft Power* (2018) https://www.researchgate.net/publication/322158448_Russia's_Arctic_Strategy, p 15.

39 Russian Strategy of the Development of the Arctic Zone and the Provision of National Security until 2020 (adopted by the President of the Russian Federation on February 8 2013), N°. Pr-232.

40 Russian Strategy of the Development of the Arctic Zone and the Provision of National Security until 2020 (adopted by the President of the Russian Federation on February 8 2013), N°. Pr-232, Article 11(d) and (e)

41 Russian Federation, *Maritime Doctrine of the Russian Federation* 2015 (2015).

42 Russian Federation, *Maritime Doctrine of the Russian Federation* 2015 (2015), Article 7.

43 Russian Federation, *Maritime Doctrine of the Russian Federation* 2015 (2015), Section 1: General Provisions.

3 Overview of the Russian legal framework pertaining to petroleum exploration and production

The Russian legal system is based on the civil law tradition, utilising a federalist structure. The Russian Constitution of 1993 asserts Russian sovereignty,[44] and establishes the fundamentals of the Russian legal system, the rights of its citizens, aspects pertaining to government and the federalist structure, and delineates the scope and function of judicial power.

Russia's Constitution is based on a separation of competence between federal and regional level (Federal Subjects), establishing a tripartite system pursuant to Chapter 3 of the Russian Constitution. Article 71 of the Russian Constitution enumerates the areas of federal competence. Article 72 articulates areas of joint competence between the Federal Government and the governments of Federal Subjects. Finally, in accordance with Article 73, Federal Subjects have full competence in all areas not articulated in either Article 71 or 72.

As a federalist state, there are two levels of legislation at both a federal level and a regional level.[45] Federal laws are enacted by Russia's Federal Assembly and are classified as either Federal Constitutional Laws or Federal Laws.[46] In the event of conflict, Federal Constitutional Laws take priority over other laws. In several key areas of Russian law, the basic rules are collated into highly compressed and easy-to follow lawbooks or codes, to avoid repeating the same principles in a long series of laws. The value of a regulation will depend on whether it has been updated to reflect any amendments to the primary legislation. For example, the Licensing Regulation may be limited in validity as a legal source if it is not updated and conflicts with its parent law.[47]

The Russian Constitution clearly articulates the role of natural resources in the development of Russia. Article 9(1) of the Constitution establishes that 'land and other resources shall be utilized and protected in the Russian Federation as the basis of life and activity of the people living in corresponding territories'.[48] Furthermore, it recognises that 'land and other natural resources may be in private, state, municipal and other forms of ownership'.[49] Regardless of the form of ownership, Article 8(2) of the Russian Constitution establishes that 'recognition and equal protection shall be given to the private, state, municipal and other forms of ownership'. The recognition and protection of such forms of ownership contrasts starkly with ownership under the former Soviet Union, where the state held and asserted ownership rights over its natural resources.[50] Article 72(c) of the Russian Constitution bestows on the Federal Government and Federal Subjects (regional authorities) joint ownership and management of natural resources on land but does not extend to the natural resources on the RCS. Rather,

44 Article 4 of the Russian Constitution, 1993.

45 This regional level (Federal Subjects) includes cities of federal importance, Autonomous Okrugs, Autonomous Oblasts, Oblasts, Krais and Republics. All of these regional bodies are equal subjects under Article 5(1) of the Russian Constitution. This chapter will only be concerned with Russia's federal laws relating to petroleum activities.

46 Russia's Federal Assembly consists of two chambers: the Federation Council and the State Duma, comprising 450 representatives. The representatives are elected on party lists, with the threshold to win seats being set at 7 per cent of the total vote. The Federation Council consists of two representatives from each of the constituent entities of the Russian Federation.

47 The *Federal Law on Subsoil 1992* (the Subsoil Law), and the *Federal Law on the Continental Shelf 1994* (the Continental Shelf Law).

48 Article 9(1), Russian Constitution. www.constitution.ru/en/10003000-02.htm accessed 15 October 2019.

49 Article 9(2), Russian Constitution. www.constitution.ru/en/10003000-02.htm accessed 15 October 2019.

50 As set out in Lenin's *Decree on Land*, which was passed on 8 November 1917, and implemented in an amended form in the *1922 Land Code of the Russian Soviet Federative Socialist Republic*.

Article 6 of the Continental Shelf Law and Article 3 of the Subsoil Law place resource exploitation on the RCS within the exclusive competence of the Federal Government.

Pursuant to Article 67, clause 2 of the Russian Constitution,[51] Russia exercises sovereignty over the Russian continental shelf. The sovereign rights of Russia as a coastal state, including the sovereign rights of the Russian Federation with regard to exploration for, and the exploitation of, natural resources on the Russian Continental Shelf, are asserted in Article 5 of the Russian Continental Shelf Law which duplicates, with some minor alterations, the provisions of Article 77 of the United Nations Convention on the Law of the Sea (UNCLOS). Accordingly, Russia asserts state ownership over the resources on the RCS.[52] In addition, according to Article 67 of the Russian Constitution, coastal Federal Subjects' jurisdiction does not include adjacent internal maritime waters or territorial sea. Therefore, offshore petroleum operations and infrastructure fall exclusively within the regulatory ambit of the Federal Government.

The Russian Continental Shelf (RCF) is estimated to be the one of world's largest, with over half of the area considered to hold petroleum.[53] Of Russia's petroleum resources, 25 per cent are found on the Continental Shelf, with the remainder found onshore. Of the onshore reserves, an estimated 75 per cent have been developed, although Eastern Siberia remains largely underdeveloped and under explored. In 2001, under Article 76(8) of UNCLOS, Russia made a submission to the Commission on the Limits of the Continental Shelf (CLCS) regarding its claim in the Arctic Ocean, a partially revised submission with regard to its claim over the Lomonosov Ridge was submitted in August 2015[54] and Russia awaits the final decision by the CLCS.

Although Russia has a long history as an oil-producing state, it has not developed specialised laws for oil and gas. Rather, the regulation of oil and gas E&P is regulated as part of natural resources law and mining law, with no distinction made between oil and gas and other mineral resources. This approach is reflected in the primary legislation for oil and gas E&P, the *Federal Law on Subsoil* (the Subsoil Law),[55] the *Federal Law on the Continental Shelf* (the Continental Shelf Law)[56] and the *Federal Law on Production-sharing Agreements* (the PSA Law),[57] which apply to not only petroleum, but all other mineral resources. Given that petroleum is classed with other mineral resources at law, legal issues related to petroleum are part of a general class of issues pertaining to natural resources law.

Several other related laws play a critical role in petroleum resource E&P. In particular, the *Federal Law on Foreign Investments in the Russian Federation*[58] (the 'Foreign Investment Law') and the *Federal Law on the Procedure of Making Foreign Investments in Companies of*

51 Which provides that offshore jurisdiction shall be exercised in a manner that complies with federal and international law.

52 This is asserted under Article 5 of the Continental Shelf Law.

53 According to a study undertaken by the US Geological Survey in 2009. Donald Gautier et al., 'Assessment of Undiscovered Oil and Gas in the Arctic' (2009) 324 *Science* 1175–1179, 1175. This may be regarded as somewhat speculative, given that only 9–12 per cent of the RCF has been explored with seismic survey.

54 United Nations Division for Ocean Affairs and the Law of the Sea, *Submissions, through the Secretary-General of the United Nations, to the Commission on the Limits of the Continental Shelf, pursuant to article 76, paragraph 8, of the Convention on the Law of the Sea of 10 December, 1982,* 'Russian Federation'.

55 Federal Law on the Subsoil of 21 February 1992 no. 2395-1 [last amended 3 June 2016].

56 Federal law on the Continental Shelf of the Russian Federation of 30 November 1995 no. 187 [last amended 3 July 2016].

57 Federal Law on Production Sharing Agreements of 30 December 1995 no. 225 [last amended 5 April 2016].

58 Federal law on Foreign Investments in the Russian Federation of 09 July 1999 no. 160 [last amended 1 May 2017].

Strategic Importance for National Defence and State Security[59] (the 'Strategic Investment Law') play an important role. Adopted in 2008, the Strategic Investment Law has resulted in extensive amendments to both the Continental Shelf Law and the Subsoil Law. In addition, other written sources of law pertaining to petroleum E&P may include presidential decrees and directives, government regulations, regulations by federal ministries and decisions made by other relevant public bodies.[60]

Theoretically, the application of Russian petroleum law is confined to the legislative provisions only. De jure, the Russian legal system does not recognise judicial precedent (wherein a judge is empowered to show discretion) as a source of law, meaning that judges should base their decisions solely on law. However, in interpreting the law relating to petroleum E&P, there have been few judicial proceedings to date.

4 Regulating oil and gas exploration and production in Russia

4.1 Government control in regulation

The power to grant a licence is held by the executive branch of the Russian Federation (RF), which is obliged to ensure the implementation of relevant policies, including onshore energy, offshore energy, Maritime policy and Arctic policy. The Executive branch, comprising the prime minister, the deputy minister and all government ministers, is responsible for granting licenses for petroleum activities on the Russian Continental Shelf. The president has ultimate power to freeze or abolish government regulations if they conflict with Russia's Constitution, federal constitutional laws, federal laws or presidential decrees.

During the Soviet era, ministries were structured according to the industrial sectors, with the petroleum sector treating oil and gas separately. Under the Ministry of Petroleum there were two sub-ministries. The first was the Ministry of Gas Industry, and the second was the Ministry of Oil Industry. Frustratingly, communication between the two sub-ministries was limited in this period and coordinated development of the resources was rare. Since the break-up of the USSR there has been a restructuring of the ministries, although some features of the Soviet system still survive.

At present there is no specific Ministry of Petroleum. Instead there are two relevant ministries first is *Minprirody* (the Ministry of Natural Resources and Environment of the Russian Federation), and *Minergo* (the Ministry of Energy of the Russian Federation). *Minergo* is responsible for the implementation of government policy, the development of the Russian Federation's petroleum sector, petroleum production and production sharing agreements (PSAs). *Minprirody* has responsibility for the management of all of Russia's natural resources, including petroleum on the shelf. It is also responsible for the development and implementation of Russia's natural resources policy, and the development of relevant laws and regulations. To implement such policies, there are five sub-entities of *Minprody:* the Federal Agency for the Use of Subsoil Resources (*Rosnedra*), the Federal Agency for Water Resources (*Rosvodresursy*), the Federal Agency for Forestry (*Rosleskhoz*), the Federal Service for Hydrometeorology and Environmental Monitoring (*Rosidromet*) and the Federal Service for Monitoring the Exploitation of Natural Resources (*Rospirodnadzor*).

59 Federal Law on the Procedure of Making Foreign Investments in Companies of Strategic Importance for National Defence and State Security of 29 April 2008 no. 57 [last amended 4 November 2014].

60 Decrees (Russian: *Ukas*) are often of a normative character, while directives (Russian: *Rasporjashenie*) are more individualised. Government legal acts are issued in the form of decisions (Russian: *Postanovlenie*, hereinafter referred to as 'directives') or orders (Russian: *Rasporjashenie*).

Several of these agencies have particular roles in the regulation of the exploitation of petroleum resources. *Rosnedra* was established pursuant to the Presidential Decree 314 of 9 March 2004[61] and was responsible for the granting of licenses on the RCS (including tenders and auctions) until 2009, when this role was taken over by the Government of the Russian Federation. *Roshidromet* monitors the environment and environmental pollution from petroleum activities, whilst *Rospirodnadzor* oversees compliance with all federal laws concerning the use of federal natural resources and the management of the offshore resources. This includes issuing all the permits necessary for patrolling activities across the upstream cycle. *Rostekhnadzor* is an autonomous Federal Service responsible for environmental protection and industrial safety. Its role is to supervise all of the technical and operational issues concerning all stages of the petroleum cycle and incorporates emergency preparedness. It reports directly to the Russian Government.

Strategic issues pertaining to petroleum activities, particularly in the Barents Sea, are under the control of the Ministry of Defence and the Russian Federal Security Service, known as the FSB.[62] Both agencies report directly to the president,[63] and such a reporting structure enables the president to exert control over the petroleum sector. The FSB also controls border services including the Russian Coast Guard, meaning that the FSB plays a powerful role in offshore petroleum activities, particularly in the Arctic. Interestingly, the FSB also plays a role in international investments. Under the Strategic Investment Law, FSB consent is required for investments where the investment will result in foreign control of a Russian corporation.

Unlike most other petroleum jurisdictions, where access to petroleum for E&P activities is released in rounds, certain onshore fields and the entire Russian Continental Shelf is open for E&P, subject to the provisions of Article 22 of the Subsoil Law, which designates certain areas as 'National Reserves', and places the area in a 'Reserve Fund'. This Fund is for resource fields (including petroleum) that are not yet in production but are deemed critical for the future resource needs of Russia. Such reservation reiterates Russia's constitutional aim of protecting and utilising Russian natural resources for the benefit of life and activity in the Federation.[64]

4.2 Regulating access to Russia's petroleum resources

There are two primary sources of law in Russia pertaining to access to petroleum resources: the Continental Shelf Law and the Subsoil Law. There appears to be overlapping responsibility of these two laws, and the boundaries between the two are unclear. This is complicated

61 Presidential Decree no. 314 of 9 March 2004 concerning systems and structures of federal bodies exercising executive powers.

62 Although the KGB was renamed the FSB, all of the functions of the KGB do not fall to the FSB. During the restructuring of the KGB, international aspects of KGB operations were removed, and are now part of the Foreign Intelligence Service (SVR). The FSB gained control of the Border Guard Service in 2003. Now the FSB essentially controls domestic security, while the SVR undertakes international intelligence and espionage activities outside Russia in conjunction with the Main Intelligence Directorate of the General Staff of the Armed Forces of the Russian Federation (GRU).

63 Article 32 of the *Federal Constitutional Law no 2 of December 17 1997 on the Government of the Russian Federation* states that the president of the Russian Federation 'shall direct the federal bodies of the executive power in charge on matters of defence, security, internal affairs, foreign affairs, the prevention of emergencies and the elimination of the consequences of natural disasters …'.

64 Article 9(1) of the Russian Constitution.

by the fact that both laws contain provisions relating to better licensing regimes and PSAs. Essentially the Russian Continental Shelf Law sets out the law relating to aspects of petroleum activities on the RCS, with the exception of the territorial waters and the internal waters. Where the Continental Shelf Law does not specifically address issues the Subsoil Law will apply.

Geographically, the scope of the Continental Shelf Law, as defined in Article 1, is confined only to the RCS, and does not include the internal waters, territorial sea or the contiguous zone.[65] This demarcation is relevant since Russia has petroleum activities in areas close to the coast. In these areas, licensing arrangements differ to the RCS, and are akin to the regime for land areas of federal importance. However, to date the fields discovered in these areas are small and are of little interest to both the government and oil companies. The geographical scope for the Subsoil Law encompasses the RCS and all Russian land territory, including maritime and territorial waters. Hence, there is an overlap between the Subsoil Law and the Continental Shelf Law.

The Continental Shelf Law applies to all types of natural resources, including some living organisms. Chapter Two of the law governs the exploration and production of all mineral resources which, according to Article 4, covers minerals and other non-living resources, including petroleum. Similarly, the Subsoil Law applies to a broad range of natural resources, making no distinction between different types of mineral or different types of natural resources. Therefore, the application of the Continental Shelf Law and the Subsoil Law is not limited to petroleum but a wide range of natural resources.

Russia is one of the few petroleum producing countries that does not have a specific law addressing the regulation of petroleum exploration and production. An attempt to draft such a law pertaining to oil and gas was made during the 1990s. Industry and other affected parties, including environmental interest groups, were included in the preparation of the petroleum specific legislation, and a comprehensive law was drafted and approved by both chambers of the Russian Federal Assembly. However, the draft law was terminated when President Yeltsin exercised his right of veto in 1998. The reason for this veto was that certain provisions of the draft law contravened the Russia Constitution and Civil Code, hence the capacity for the president to exert his right of veto. Instead, sectoral reform occurred with the amendment of existing legislation, with both the Continental Shelf Law and the Subsoil Law undergoing several key reforms.

4.2.1 Overview of key regulatory instruments

It is difficult to provide a comprehensive overview of the licensing and approval processes required to conduct petroleum activities on the RCF, because many decisions have been taken that have developed over time depending upon general trends in the Russian state's regulation of petroleum activities at that time. Similarly, onshore experience demonstrates that there may be a significant variation between the approval processes required by different authorities. Therefore, it is almost impossible to provide a standardised overview of the process that is used for every petroleum project both onshore and offshore. This analysis will instead focus on key regulatory instruments for licensing: the Continental Shelf Law and the Subsoil Law.

65 Federal Act on the internal maritime waters, territorial sea and contiguous zone of the Russian Federation of 31 July 1998 no. 155.

Regarding the Continental Shelf Law, Article 7 establishes the allocation of blocks on the RCF for regional geological exploration, geological exploration and geological exploration drilling and production of mineral resources, as well as other types that are envisioned in the Subsoil Law. The exercise of these rights is conditional upon the granting of a license under Article 11 of the Subsoil Law. This means that there are several types of licenses operating on the RCF. The first is the license for regional geological exploration on the RCF. The second is a licence granting the right to conduct geological exploration (exploration license). The third grants the right to conduct exploration drilling and production of petroleum (production license). Article 1 paragraph 3 of the licensing regulation establishes that regional geological exploration does not require a license, and this is reflected in practice. The Continental Shelf Law does not define the term 'regional geological exploration', however Article 6 of the Subsoil Law defines it to include regional geophysical work, geological surveys, scientific research and other activities directed towards general investigation of the subsoil without the implementation of materially invasive activities.[66] The period of a Russian license is not regulated by the Continental Shelf Law, but rather is addressed by Article 10 of the Subsoil Law. Under Article 10 of the Subsoil Law areas for geological exploration conducted in internal maritime waters, territorial waters and the Continental Shelf are allocated for periods up to ten years. This period was extended five years in 2007 in response to pressure from Russian oil companies due to the limitations placed on drilling in Artic areas which is often limited to two or three months. A term of ten years applies to Russian exploration licenses and the first phase of a Russian production license, during which time the licensee is expected to undertake work obligations specified in the license. In some circumstances a project will automatically shift to the next phase where the licensee has conducted the geological exploration in accordance with the production licence. The Subsoil Law also allows the licensee to conduct exploration drilling and production on the Continental Shelf in parallel with geological exploration, it is important to note that this is only permitted for companies that are neither foreign investors nor controlled by foreign investors as defined in Article 6(2) of the Subsoil Law. For foreign companies the requirement to obtain approvals in order to progress from exploration to production still remains. In reality this means that in addition to the usual assessment of resources approvals and the coordination of technical projects, these licensees must apply to the Federal Government for approval to continue the project. The limitations and the restrictions that may be placed by the Federal Government are not defined in either law, giving the Russian Government broad scope to impose any conditions it wishes. In addition, the there are no precedents regarding official practice in this area that clarify what conditions may be set. An important provision of the Subsoil Law to note is Article 2.1(5), enacted in 2008, which allows the Russian Government to refuse a licensee that is a foreign investor the right to conduct exploration drilling and production if, during geological exploration, the company establishes the existence of structures that may be a part of a 'field of federal importance', and a situation arises that poses 'danger for the country's defence and national security'.[67] This law can be interpreted very broadly, but it is important to note that any such expenses accrued to date will be refunded to the licensee.[68]

66 This means that it does not permit drilling.

67 Regulation of 16 September 2008 no. 697.

68 Ibid.

4.2.2 Selection of the licensee

Article 7(1) of the Continental Shelf Law establishes that areas of the RCS may be allocated to legal entities satisfying criteria set forth in Article 9(3) of the Subsoil Law:

> Licensees of areas of federal importance on the Russian continental shelf of the Russian Federation, as well as areas of federal importance located within the territory of the Russian Federation and extending over the Russian continental shelf may be juridical persons, which are established in compliance with the legislation of the Russian Federation, have at least five years' experience of developing areas of the Russian continental shelf, and in which the proportion of the share capital owned by the Russian state comprises over 50 per cent and/or in which the Russian state has at its disposal either directly or indirectly over 50 per cent of the total number of votes represented by the share capital of such juridical persons.

Under this provision, the licensee is required to be a juridical person, which is a broad term for a non-natural person. A more precise definition of juridical person occurs in Article 48 of the Russian Civil Code. What is important to note is that under Russian law the juridical person is broader than a concept of a company.

Article 9 of the Subsoil Law requires that the applicant must have at least five years' experience on the RCS. This means that experience on other continental shelves fall outside the scope of this Article. Although Gazprom and Rosneft both satisfy this requirement, Zarubezhneft was not qualified as a licensee in 2008. Zarubezneft did not hold five years' experience in Russian territory, although it had five years' experience on other continental shelves. In 2012, Zarubezhneft bought 100 per cent minus 1 of the shares in Arktikmorneftegasrasvedka, which had the necessary experience of offshore operations on the Russian continental shelf. As a result, Arktikmorneftegasrasvedka formally satisfied the requirements set forth in Article 9 of the Subsoil Law. In August 2013, Minprirody approved Arktikmorneftegasrasvedka to conduct operations on the Russian Continental Shelf, but no offshore production licences have been granted to the company so far.[69] Finally, in order to obtain an offshore license, the applicant must be a company in which the Russian state has 50 per cent or more ownership. This is an important control mechanism in respect of companies pursuant to Article 9 of the Subsoil Law as it allows the Russian state to prohibit a company from receiving any new production licenses or to remove a licensee's right through the reduction of state ownership of that company.

These requirements listed in the Subsoil Law are cumulative, meaning that an applicant must satisfy all three conditions. The sum of such requirements is that privately owned Russian oil companies such as Sintezneftegaz have the experience required to obtain an offshore license but do not satisfy the state ownership requirement. This is also the case for LUKOIL. In practical terms this means that Gazprom, Rosneft and Zarubezneft are the only three companies to satisfy all of the requirements of Article 7(1) of the Continental Shelf Law and Article 9(3) of the Subsoil Law. These companies therefore are currently the only candidates that meet the criteria for the granting of production licenses on the RCS.

In order for a license to be awarded, there is a requirement for a public announcement of the relevant round under Article 13(1) of the Subsoil Law. This applies to rounds involving

69 Based on www.amngr.ru, accessed 9 July 2019.

tender and auctions but does not apply to licenses for the Russian Continental Shelf. This is because Article 7(4) of the Continental Shelf Law establishes that areas on the RCS shall be allocated without tender or auction.[70] Where tendering rounds are held, the price of the license is not the most critical factor. Rather, applicants are competing with each other to demonstrate that their bid maximises economic, environmental and social benefits in exploiting the petroleum. In addition, greater weight is attached to a company's experience, proposed infrastructure obligations and other qualifications. Until 2004, the auction system held by *Rosnedra* emphasised revenue rather than other characteristics, due to the need for money in the Russian budget. Although the law was amended ten years ago, it is still largely unclear as to what conditions will be used for the award of a license. Rules relating to the award of production licenses and of the award process itself were expected to be adopted and classified in the regulations, although this is yet to come to pass.

Article 12 of the Gas Supply Law allows the direct allocation of gas fields to the owner of the United Gas Supply System of Russia, namely Gazprom. Indeed Gazprom has also previously been awarded licenses to develop a number of northern gas reservoirs under the Gas Supply Law. This included two reservoirs in the Kara Sea and the Sea of Okhotsk which is part of the offshore Sakhalin Project. It is highly likely that Gazprom will continue to be allocated gas fields, with oil fields being allocated to Rosneft. Such allocation corresponds to the origins of each company from their respective ministries after the collapse of the former Soviet Union.

4.2.3 Production sharing agreements

The Presidential Decree of 4 December 1993 (the PSA Decree),[71] established a contract-based regime for the allocation of access to Russia's natural resources. Following the dismantlement of the Soviet industrial administrative system an important objective of the Russian Government was to attract investment to the petroleum sector. In order to increase Russian Government revenue in the early 1990s, there was a need to develop a legal regime that would provide greater protection for investors than that under the licensing regime. In particular, the use of stabilisation clauses in PSAs established contractual protection for the investor. On the basis of the PSA Decree, three PSAs were concluded. The first was the agreement for Sakhalin-1 in 2003. Operated by Exxon Neftgas Ltd, the project encompassed three offshore fields around the Sakhalin Island. The second was for the Sakhalin-2 project, which originally was majority-held by Shell, Mitsui and Mitsubishi in a joint venture called the Sakhalin Energy Investment Company Ltd. However, souring of relations between the Russian Federal Government and Shell, particularly over conditions related to local content provisions, cost oil/profit oil splits and royalties meant that Shell was 'encouraged' to divest its interest. The third was the contract for the Kharyaga project,[72] which was signed in December 1999. In this contract the operator was Total (50 per cent) and Statoil Hydro as a participant (40 per cent). In 2009 each participant was required to return 10 per cent to a Russian company, which they divested to Zarubezhneft. Since that time, the operator Total has transferred its operatorship and half of its shares to Zarubezhneft.

70 This was abolished by the amendment of the Continental Shelf Law by Federal Law number 120 of 18 July 2008.

71 Presidential Decree no. 2285 of 24 December 1993 on Issues Concerning Agreements on Production Sharing in the Mineral Resources Sector.

72 This is an onshore field located in the Nenets autonomous *okrug* on the shores of the Kara Sea region.

It is important to note that the PSA Decree provides guidance on the procedure to enter into a PSA, and includes the obligation and rights of the parties, an essential feature of a PSA, but which is difficult to determine given that PSAs are highly confidential and not publicly available.

Shortly after the PSA Decree came into force and these first PSAs were concluded, there was a question as to whether the PSA Decree conflicts with Article 75(3) of the Russian Constitution.[73] This is because Article 75(3) of the Russian Constitution stipulates that the general principles of taxation and the system of taxes in the Russian federation shall be fixed by Federal Law. The imposition of taxation/royalty arrangements within a PSA may thus breach this constitutional article. In response, the Federal Law on PSAs was implemented in December 1995 to replace the PSA Decree. The PSA Law, similar to the Continental Shelf Law and the Subsoil Law, applies to a broader range of natural resources, and is applicable to the exploitation and production of mineral raw materials.[74] Hence, apart from oil and gas, the PSA Law also covers other mineral resource such as gold, diamonds and coal. Furthermore, according to the preamble of the PSA Law it applies to both onshore and offshore projects.

Article 1 of the PSA Law establishes that where activities do not fall under the scope of the PSA Law, other relevant laws will apply. This means that the Continental Shelf Law and the Subsoil Law will be particularly relevant. Where there is a conflict between the various laws, in accordance with the *lex specialis* principle, the provisions of the PSA Law will prevail. The Russian Civil Code is also relevant in relation to the rights and obligations between the parties in the agreement. Upon the enactment of the PSA Law, further regulations and presidential decrees have supplemented the law in order to clarify the legal aspects of this law.[75] In spite of the supplementary regulation, many legal aspects concerning the conclusion and operation of PSAs remain unresolved. The failure of the PSA Law to clarify such obligations and rights is demonstrated by the failure of the only PSA to be enacted under this legislation to be realised in practice.

When both the PSA Decree and the PSA Law are considered, it is clear that Russia has had two PSA regimes. The failure of the PSA Law to clarify the conditions of these contracts means that it is likely that the three PSAs concluded under the PSA Decree are to be the only PSAs in practice in Russia. Thus, with the exception of the three contracts approved under the PSA Decree, the PSA regime is effectively dormant in Russia, and access to petroleum is granted through licenses.

5 Conclusion

Since Soviet times, there have been several structural changes to Russian oil and gas law. Most notable has been the initial privatisation of Russian oil and gas assets under the Yeltsin Government, particularly as a result of the 'loans for shares' scheme. Private owners of oil and gas assets, many of whom also had political aspirations, were brought to heel by Putin during the 2000s, with several companies reacquired by the state as a result of tax evasion and other illegalities. In particular, the Russian state-owned company Rosneft reacquired many of Yukos' assets, effectively bringing it under state ownership.

73 Article 75(3).

74 PSA Law Article 2(1).

75 V.G. Nesterenko (ed.). *Inostrannye investicii i soglashenija o razdele produkcii. Zakonodatel'stvo, kommentarii, sudebnaja praktika* (Nestor Academic Publishers), 2002.

In the Putin era, there has been a major refocus on both petroleum resources and the Arctic as such, three core policy documents of the Russian federation, the Energy Strategy, the Arctic Strategy, and the Maritime Doctrine shaped petroleum development during the 2000s and 2010s. These three complementary strategies will continue to shape Russian petroleum development, and the laws pertaining to this development, at least until 2024, when the fifth Russian president will be elected. Barring a change to the Russian Constitution, the president will not be Putin, and it remains to be seen whether the new president will continue to focus on offshore Arctic development.

Soon after the break-up of the former Soviet Union, new laws were established for the extraction of mineral resources. The Subsoil Law (1992) established the general framework for extraction on land, as well as in territorial and internal waters. In recent years there have been a number of amendments to this law under Putin, although its basic architecture remains unchanged. Similarly, the Continental Shelf Law was established in 1995, and has undergone three major amendments, including that relating to the use of PSAs. The scope of the Continental Shelf Law is confined to the Russian Continental Shelf beyond 12 nautical miles, the seaward boundary of the Territorial Sea. Both laws pertain to all mineral resources, and do not delineate petroleum exploration and production from other forms of mineral resources. In addition, the two laws interact with one another, creating a regulatory framework where the jurisdiction of the Subsoil Law extends to some aspects of petroleum activities offshore.

12
RUSSIAN RENEWABLE ENERGY
Regulations and outcomes

Mariia Kozlova, Mikael Collan and Indra Overland

1 Introduction

This chapter reviews the development of the legal framework for renewable energy in Russia and discusses the current state of renewable energy in the country. The Russian support scheme for renewable energy is elaborated in detail for both the wholesale and retail energy markets, and the outcomes of the policy are assessed based on the current state of renewable energy in Russia.

Russia has introduced an unusual scheme to promote renewable energy: compensating investments in capacity installed and guaranteeing investors a certain return on their investments. This instrument is known in the literature as a 'capacity-based mechanism' or simply a 'capacity mechanism'. The capacity mechanism also imposes some restrictions and incentives to motivate renewable-energy production and attempts to minimise the cost burden of the subsidies on the taxpayer. Renewable-energy investments in other countries are commonly supported by paying projects for the electricity produced, rather than the installed capacity. The Russian approach has practical relevance from the policymakers' perspective because, in contrast to conventional power plants that can be operated non-stop to produce electricity, many forms of renewable energy are not able to guarantee production on command. Paying for actual electricity production encourages investors to select appropriate sites for renewable energy generation. However, the Russian case demonstrates that renewables can also be supported through installed capacity.

In this chapter, we review the academic literature on Russian renewable energy policy, present a short overview of the various changes in policy and analyse the outcomes of the policy in terms of the current state of renewable energy in Russia, paying particular attention to the effect of the capacity mechanism.

2 Existing research on renewable energy in Russia

In this section, we provide an overview of studies focusing on both the regulatory aspects of renewables and on the investment climate for renewable energy in Russia. We cover mainly the period 2008–2019, as the legal framework for renewables in Russia changed significantly during that period, and the older literature is not so relevant any more. However, we also touch on some of the older works that are of particular interest.

The significant potential for renewable energy in Russia has been highlighted repeatedly in the literature. Among the early studies, Martinot[1] analysed market barriers for broad renewable-energy deployment in Russia and emphasised the importance of institutional incentives and market intermediation. Later, Martinot outlined and discussed business models for renewable energy that are also competitive without financial support, such as hybrid wind-diesel and biomass power plants for small settlements.[2] Joint ventures with foreign corporations are presented as tools to overcome some existing barriers and facilitate knowledge and technology transfer.[3]

In their book, Overland and Kjaernet[4] explore the potential for international cooperation in Russia's renewable-energy sector, focusing mostly on EU-Russian and Nordic-Russian partnerships. Based on extensive data gathered through interviews and field trips, the book presents a thorough analysis of both Russian strengths in the renewable-energy sector and barriers to the sector's development in Russia.

The first in-depth analysis of the Russian capacity mechanism is based on the pre-enactment legislative draft and was carried out by Boute,[5] who at the time of writing acted as a legal adviser to the Russia Renewable Energy Program of the International Finance Corporation/World Bank. His article highlights the uniqueness of the choice to support renewable energy through *capacity* remuneration rather than by supporting electricity *output*, as is common in other support schemes around the world. Boute shows that the capacity-based approach possesses stand-alone benefits, including more predictable cash flows for the investors and a reduced incentive to supply electricity to the grid during periods of low demand.

Boute warns of the potential problems of a capacity-based mechanism with regard to properly accounting for the typically variable electricity output from renewable energy projects. Conventional energy power plants can produce electricity throughout the year, whereas wind and solar power are dependent on the weather. Capacity-based support should be adjusted so that it does not favour the construction of renewable energy projects in locations with low resource availability or the building of plants that are left idle, leading to the waste of taxpayers' money. In this vein, Boute reviews the international experiences of how the variable electricity output of renewable energy has been handled in different capacity markets.

After the introduction of the law governing the Russian renewable-energy support mechanism for the wholesale market in 2013, the scholars showed a growing interest in Russian renewable-energy policy, and the volume of research surged (Figure 12.1).

1 'Energy efficiency and renewable energy in Russia: Transaction barriers, market intermediation, and capacity building' (1998) 26(11) *Energy Policy* 905

2 E. Martinot. 'Renewable energy in Russia: Markets, development and technology transfer' (1999) 3(1) *Renewable and Sustainable Energy Reviews* 49; Indra Overland. 'The Siberian Curse: A blessing in disguise for renewable energy?' (2010) 9(2) *Sibirica* 1

3 E. Martinot, 'Renewable energy in Russia: Markets, development and technology transfer' (1999) 3(1) *Renewable and Sustainable Energy Reviews* 49

4 *Russian Renewable Energy: The Potential for International Cooperation* (Routledge, 2009)

5 'Promoting renewable energy through capacity markets: An analysis of the Russian support scheme' (2012) 46(0) *Energy Policy* 68

In his book,[6] Boute presents a comprehensive overview and analysis of Russian electricity and energy-investment law. Vasilieva et al.[7] analyse the effect of the renewable-energy support mechanism on the prices of electricity and capacity in Russia and show that the effect is modest.

A description of the Russian capacity mechanism is provided by Kozlova and Collan,[8] who provide the first comprehensive presentation of the renewable-energy capacity price calculation procedure published in English. The paper presents the results of a numerical analysis of the effect of the Russian capacity mechanism for renewable energy investments on investment profitability. The results of this analysis indicate that the mechanism can reduce market risks for investors. The paper also discusses the requirements of the mechanism that steer investments towards capital costs control and the limits that the mechanism has on paying out subsidies. The capacity mechanism is crucial to enable renewable-energy investments at the wholesale market level as, without support, these investments would be unprofitable.[9]

Smeets[10] analyses the first two-year period of factual implementation of the capacity mechanism. The evidence suggests that investors were reluctant to offer wind-power projects in the first capacity auctions, whereas solar PV projects were offered actively. The reasons proposed by Smeets for the reluctance to offer wind power investments include: (i) lack of local wind-turbine manufacturing facilities, which makes it impossible to meet the local

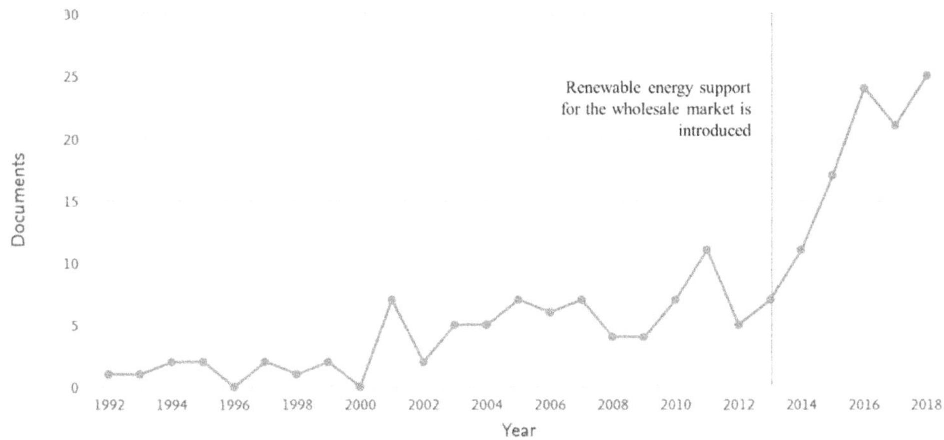

Figure 12.1 Documents per year in Scopus, TITLE-ABS-KEY ("renewable energy" AND Russia AND (policy OR law OR investment))[a]

Source: Scopus bibliography statistics, modified by authors.

a SCOPUS bibliography statistics, modified by authors

6 *Russian Electricity and Energy Investment Law*, Volume 65 (Brill, 2015)

7 Evgeniia Vasileva et al., 'RES support in Russia: Impact on capacity and electricity market prices' (2015) 76(0) *Renewable Energy* 82

8 'Modeling the effects of the new Russian capacity mechanism on renewable energy investments' (2016) 95 *Energy Policy* 350

9 Mariia Kozlova, Mikael Collan and Pasi Luukka, 'Russian mechanism to support renewable energy investments: before and after analysis' in P. Diez et al. *Computational Methods and Models for Transport. Computational Methods in Applied Sciences, Vol. 45* (Springer, 2017) 243

10 'Similar goals, divergent motives. The enabling and constraining factors of Russia's capacity-based renewable energy support scheme' (2017) 101 *Energy Policy* 138

content requirement of the capacity mechanism; (ii) depreciation of the rouble, which made the foreign share of capital costs too expensive; (iii) the possible bias of the design of the support mechanism in favour of solar power (the latter was shown not to be the case by the results of the four subsequent capacity auctions discussed in this chapter). Smeets[11] also shows that both the wind and solar projects selected through the auctions were later delayed.

The monograph by Boute[12] also covers the first two-year period of the implementation of the capacity mechanism. The limited success of the first auction is explained by the short timespan between the activation of the support mechanism and the auction, which left insufficient time for investors to prepare the required documentation. This study suggests that another reason for the partial failure of the two first auctions was simply the lack of investor confidence in the new scheme.

Lanshina et al.[13] emphasise the continuing gap between regulation and implementation of renewable-energy support in Russia, arguing that this is because fossil fuels constitute the main revenue of the Russian government and, thus, have priority for the Russian authorities. However, Smeets[14] argues that Russia's intention to remain an important energy exporter was a driving force for the development of the renewable-energy sector. Here there is an interesting parallel to the Arab Gulf states, though the Arabs went much further in the development of renewable energy than the Russians.[15] The United Arab Emirates, in particular, launched some of the world's largest solar-power projects, helping drive down the price of solar panels globally.[16]

Unlike the capacity mechanism, the electricity tariff scheme for retail markets introduced in Russia in 2015 has not received much academic attention. Boute[17] discusses the role of the regional authorities in developing renewable energy and analyses the barriers in the regulatory framework, one of them being the centralisation of political power. Boute[18] briefly reviews the legal prerequisites for the implementation of the scheme. Kozlova et al.[19] concisely present the newly introduced scheme and highlight the differences and similarities it has with the capacity mechanism. No detailed qualitative or quantitative studies have been carried out that focus on the retail-market support mechanism.

Finally, Russia has been found to have substantial renewable-energy potential, especially in remote areas where renewables are profitable without any support, mostly because they can function as substitutes for fossil fuels that must be transported great distances in small

11 ibid
12 *Russian Electricity and Energy Investment Law* (Volume 65 Brill, 2015)
13 'The slow expansion of renewable energy in Russia: Competitiveness and regulation issues' (2018) 120 *Energy Policy* 600
14 'The Green Menace: Unraveling Russia's elite discourse on enabling and constraining factors of renewable energy policies' (2018) 40 *Energy Research & Social Science* 244
15 A. H. Almasoud and Hatim M. Gandayh, 'Future of solar energy in Saudi Arabia' (2015) 27 *Journal of King Saud University – Engineering Sciences* 153
16 M. Jamil, Farzana Ahmad and Y. J. Jeon. 'Renewable energy technologies adopted by the UAE: Prospects and challenges – A comprehensive overview' (2016) 55 *Renewable and Sustainable Energy Reviews* 1181; Sgouris Sgouridis et al. 'RE-mapping the UAE's energy transition: An economy-wide assessment of renewable energy options and their policy implications' (2016) 55 *Renewable and Sustainable Energy Reviews* 1166
17 'Renewable energy federalism in Russia: Regions as new actors for the promotion of clean energy' (2013) 25(2) *Journal of Environmental Law* 261–291
18 *Russian Electricity and Energy Investment Law* (Volume 65 Brill, 2015)
19 'Renewable energy in emerging economies: Shortly analyzing the Russian incentive mechanisms for renewable energy investments' (International Research Conference 'GSOM Emerging Markets Conference – 2015: Business and government perspectives' Saint Petersburg, Russia 2015)

volumes at a high cost.[20] Boute[21] reviews the legal framework for supporting renewables in remote areas and focuses on hybrid wind and solar-diesel power in the Russian Arctic. Based on his review of the international experience and compatibility with Russian law, he suggests several alternative support mechanisms. Centralised policy coordination is noted to be an important requirement for such support.

3 Russian renewable-energy law and support mechanisms overview

Russia introduced a renewable-energy development strategy in 2009 (Energy Strategy of Russia to 2030).[22] The strategy sets a target of producing 4.5 per cent of electricity from renewable energy sources by 2020. The first real steps towards this target were taken four years later, with the introduction of the renewables support mechanism for the wholesale market.[23] Prior to this, the strategy was considered a failure.[24] However, two years later, amendments to the support scheme were introduced, triggering new investments in renewable energy.[25]

The Russian government also introduced a renewable-energy support scheme for retail markets.[26] This scheme provides a central tariff calculation methodology and delegates the responsibility for supportive measures to the regional energy authorities. The first two years after it was introduced, there were no projects under the scheme.[27] One reason given was the reluctance of the regional energy authorities to work out the regulatory framework for the support-mechanism procedures and formulate the actual contracts that would guarantee investors the promised tariff payments. However, by the end of 2018 there have been a couple of dozen small projects implemented under this scheme, however, their contribution to the overall Russian energy system is negligible.[28]

For all practical purposes, there has been no centralised support mechanism for renewable energy projects in remote areas and isolated energy systems.[29] This makes some sense insofar as renewable energy should be commercially viable without special support mechanisms in many areas. Conversely, a support mechanism could still be useful to help get the ball rolling on renewable-energy developments across Russia's vast northern and eastern

20 P. Lombardi et al., 'Isolated power system in Russia: A chance for renewable energies?' (2016) 90 *Renewable Energy* 532; Z. B. Namsaraev, A. M. Konovalov and G. V. Baturova. 'Study of feasibility of local renewable resources for substitution of fossil fuels in the Far North of Russia' (IOP Conference Series: Earth and Environmental Science, IOP Publishing, 2018) 012022; Indra Overland. 'The Siberian Curse: A blessing in disguise for renewable energy?' (2010) 9(2) *Sibirica* 1

21 'Off-grid renewable energy in remote Arctic areas: An analysis of the Russian Far East' (2016) 59 *Renewable and Sustainable Energy Reviews* 1029

22 8 January 2009 Resolution #1-r on the main directions for the state policy to improve the energy efficiency of the electricity sector on the basis of renewable energy sources for the period up to 2020

23 28 May 2013 Decree #449 on the mechanism of promoting the use of renewable energy in the wholesale market of electric energy and power 2013

24 Anatole Boute, *Russian Electricity and Energy Investment Law* (Volume 65 Brill, Boston 2015)

25 10 November 2015 Decree #1210 on the introduction of amendments to the certain legislative acts regarding the use of renewable energy sources in the wholesale electricity and capacity market 2015

26 23 January 2015 Decree #47 on amendments to some legislative acts of the Russian Federation on promotion of use of renewable energy sources in retail electricity markets 2015

27 A. Zhiharev, 'Renewable energy support on retail markets: Wake-up call' (in Russian). (2017) report by VYGON Consulting 36

28 Tatiana A. Lanshina et al. 'The slow expansion of renewable energy in Russia: Competitiveness and regulation issues' (2018) 120 *Energy Policy* 600

29 Anatole Boute. 'Off-grid renewable energy in remote Arctic areas: An analysis of the Russian Far East' (2016) 59 *Renewable and Sustainable Energy Reviews* 1029

territories. Such developments could, in turn, provide the basis for embryonic markets for renewable-energy equipment and services, which could later be built on as renewable energy spreads to the rest of the country.[30] Nevertheless, some regions have taken the matter into their own hands, developing local renewables by either supporting them with regional funds released from diesel purchasing[31] or by implementing over-sophisticated financing mechanisms for energy performance contracting.[32]

3.1 Wholesale market support

The support mechanism for the wholesale market introduced in 2013[33] differs from renewable energy support schemes in the rest of the world. The Russian scheme originates in the capacity trading system of the Russian energy market. Unlike the electricity-only markets that most countries have, Russia has two commodities in one market, electricity and capacity. By selling capacity, electricity producers pledge that their plants will be available to produce electricity in the future. All wholesale market electricity buyers are obliged to buy a certain amount of capacity corresponding to their peak consumption. This way of organising the market allows for stability in electricity prices, and provides more reliability to the short and long-term electricity supply by providing less risky revenues for investors. Some other countries organise their markets in a similar way,[34] and some of these markets have adopted rules for allowing renewables to participate in the capacity trade.[35] However, the Russian case is the first one in which the capacity trade principle has been used as the foundation for creating a renewable-energy support scheme, rather than supporting renewables with other schemes and simultaneously trying to integrate them into capacity trade as in other jurisdictions.

In the Russian system, planned investment projects are submitted as bids to capacity auctions. The mechanism was set up to conduct annual capacity auctions during the seven-year period 2013–2019. Each auction is used as a mechanism to select the renewable-energy capacity to be installed for the coming four-year period. A total of over 7GW of renewable-energy capacity was planned for construction in Russia by 2024, including 4.4GW of wind power, 1.8GW of solar power and 0.9GW of small hydro power. Selected projects were to benefit

30 Indra Overland. 'The Siberian Curse: A Blessing in Disguise for Renewable Energy?' (2010) 9(2) *Sibirica* 1

31 Margarita Nifontova. 'Vozobnovlyaemaya energetika Yakutii, uravnenie so vsemi izvestnymi [Renewables of Yakutia, equation with all known]' (2019) www.1sn.ru/225334.html

32 N. Zhabin. 'Kamchatka planiruet sozdat' energouzel iz malyh GES na vostoke poluostrova [Kamchatka is planning to create a hydropower generation center in the East of the peninsula]' *neftegaz.ru* (2019) https://neftegaz.ru/news/energy/194234-kamchatka-planiruet-sozdat-energouzel-iz-malykh-ges-na-vostoke-poluostrova

33 28 May 2013 Decree #449 on the mechanism of promoting the use of renewable energy in the wholesale market of electric energy and power 2013

34 Christian Held and Jan Ole Voss. 'Legal limits for electricity capacity markets in the EU and Germany' (2013) 4 *Renewable Energy Law and Policy Review* 245; Benjamin F. Hobbs et al. 'A dynamic analysis of a demand curve-based capacity market proposal: The PJM reliability pricing model' (2007) 22(1) *IEEE Transactions on Power Systems* 3–14; B. Tennbakk et al. 'Capacity mechanisms in individual markets within the IEM' (2013) https://ec.europa.eu/energy/sites/ener/files/documents/20130207_generation_adequacy_study.pdf

35 Sergio Botero, Felipe Isaza and Adriana Valencia. 'Evaluation of methodologies for remunerating wind power's reliability in Colombia' (2010) 14(7) *Renewable and Sustainable Energy Reviews* 2049; Cynthia Bothwell and Benjamin F. Hobbs. 'Crediting wind and solar renewables in electricity capacity markets: The effects of alternative definitions upon market efficiency' (2017) 38 (*KAPSARC Special Issue*) *The Energy Journal*; Seyed Hossein Madaeni, Ramteen Sioshansi and Paul Denholm. 'Comparing capacity value estimation techniques for photovoltaic solar power' (2013) 3(1) *IEEE Journal of Photovoltaics* 407

from capacity payments for 15 years. The selection criterion in the auction is based on investment cost, and only the lowest investment cost projects are selected for subsidisation. Investment cost limits are set for each technology separately. The projects are obliged to use a prespecified share of locally produced equipment; this is called a localisation requirement. In the case of a project failing to fulfil the localisation requirement, the subsidy is to be substantially reduced, possibly making the investment unprofitable.[36]

However, if a project shows compliance with the rules and high performance, its profitability is secured even in the presence of a changing market. The remuneration in terms of capacity price is aimed at a 12 per cent return on investment. The compliance is checked for each project individually, project-specific factors include the project investment costs, localisation of equipment and an annually checked electricity-production performance (the capacity factor). If the average achieved capacity factor is lower than the pre-set target, the remuneration amount for that year is lowered. The critical capacity factor levels are 20 per cent for wind, 10 per cent for solar and 28 per cent for small hydro. This way, the capacity mechanism incorporates the variability of electricity production into the capacity-based support instrument. The capacity price is also annually adjusted based on electricity price variation, inflation and interest rates. This trait of the capacity mechanism reduces market risk for investors, but also ensures the cost-efficiency of the policy by avoiding over-subisidisation during favourable times.

In the first version of the mechanism, the requirements for small hydro and wind power appeared to be too strict. Few projects were offered in the first auctions. To solve this problem, the government introduced amendments with relaxed investment-cost limits and localisation requirements for small hydro and wind power projects.[37]

The next section studies the outcome of the implementation of the Russian support scheme for renewable energy investments and, in particular, the effects of the aforementioned amendments.

3.1.1 Retail markets support

The capacity trade is limited to the wholesale market; therefore, another support mechanism had to be developed for the retail level. The tariff scheme that was introduced is a combination of a feed-in tariff scheme (in which projects are remunerated per unit of electricity produced), a tendering scheme (in which projects compete for funds) and a capacity mechanism (which is embedded in the tariff calculation and guarantees a certain return on investment).[38]

Demand for electricity generated from renewable sources is supported by obliging the electricity-distribution companies to compensate losses in the grid, primarily by using renewable-energy sources. Another principle of the scheme is that the tariff applied varies by region, as it is calculated based on competing investment costs and electricity-production performance. The rate of return on investment, and thus tariff in monetary terms, is calculated by taking the minimum of the pre-set limit and the project-specific planned investment costs. A similar principle is applied to the capacity factor; the maximums of the

36 Mariia Kozlova and Mikael Collan. 'Modeling the effects of the new Russian capacity mechanism on renewable energy investments' (2016) 95 *Energy Policy* 350

37 10 November 2015 Decree #1210 on the introduction of amendments to the certain legislative acts regarding the use of renewable energy sources in the wholesale electricity and capacity market 2015

38 23 January 2015 Decree #47 on amendments to some legislative acts of the Russian Federation on promotion of the use of renewable energy sources in retail electricity markets 2015

pre-set capacity factor and a planned project-specific capacity factor are used. This feature potentially accounts for differences in investment profitability due to differing access to equipment-manufacturing facilities and the availability of renewable resources in different locations.

An important feature of this scheme is that it supports only wind, solar PV and small hydro investments. The regional tariffs are designed for a wider variety of renewable energy sources, also including geothermal, biomass and some other forms of renewable energy.

Although the overall principles and the tariff-calculation methodology are established by central laws, the implementation of the scheme is delegated to the regional authorities. This is both an enabling[39] and a constraining factor.[40] The regional authorities can potentially develop renewable-energy more effectively than the central authorities because they have a more direct interest in local economic and technological development.[41] However, the lack of a more detailed regulatory framework and support procedures at the regional level is one reason for the slow implementation of the scheme[42]

4 Current situation of renewable energy in Russia

In this section, we present the outcome of Russian renewable-energy regulation in terms of existing and planned renewable energy projects. First, we discuss the results of the capacity auctions, followed by some data on all the operational renewable energy projects in Russia.

4.1 Renewable energy projects on the wholesale market

The capacity mechanism discussed above enabled renewables to enter the Russian electricity wholesale market. The results of the capacity auctions reflect the growing role of renewables in the wholesale market and the success of the scheme. However, the specific annual targets for renewable-energy capacity to be built have not been reached as originally planned (see Table 12.1).

Approximately 90 per cent of the targeted renewable energy capacity has been selected in the auctions, with an 80 per cent shortfall for small hydro, a 10 per cent shortfall for wind and a 20 per cent overshoot of the target for solar power. Underperformance was concentrated in the first auctions (2013–2014) and was due to the short time available to prepare for the first auction after the announcement of the support mechanism in 2013 and, as mentioned above, overly strict cost limits and localisation requirements for wind and small hydro power, which were relaxed just before the 2015 auction.

Solar projects have benefited from the existence of domestic manufacturers, making it easier to meet local content requirements[43] and, therefore, reach the targets in 2015. The situation for wind power and small hydro is different. It appears that the capital cost limits

39 Anatole Boute. 'Renewable energy federalism in Russia: Regions as new actors for the promotion of clean energy' (2013) 25(2) *Journal of Environmental Law* 261–291

40 A. Zhiharev, 'Renewable energy support on retail markets: wake-up call' (in Russian). VYGON Consulting (2017)

41 Anatole Boute. 'Renewable energy federalism in Russia: Regions as new actors for the promotion of clean energy' (2013) *Journal of Environmental Law*

42 A. Zhiharev, 'Renewable energy support on retail markets: wake-up call' (in Russian). VYGON Consulting (2017)

43 Niels Smeets. 'Similar goals, divergent motives. The enabling and constraining factors of Russia's capacity-based renewable energy support scheme' (2017) 101 *Energy Policy* 138

Table 12.1 Renewable-energy capacity targeted and auctioned by the planned years of commercialisation

Type	*Capacity*	*2014*	*2015*	*2016*	*2017*	*2018*	*2019*	*2020*	*2021*	*2022*	*2023*	*2024*	*Total*
Wind	target, MW	100	250	250	500	750	500	500	500	500	500	76	***3600****
	auctioned, MW	0	0	50	90	200	509	640	738	530	498	71	**3326**
	auctioned, %	0	0	20	18	27	102	128	148	106	100	94	**92**
Solar	target, MW	120	140	200	250	270	270	270	163	163	0	0	***1520***
	auctioned, MW	35	140	199	255	285	309	295	178	163	-	-	**1858**
	auctioned, %	29	100	100	102	106	114	109	109	100	-	-	**122**
Hydro	target, MW	18	26	124	124	141	159	159	36	36	36	0	***751***
	auctioned, MW	0	0	0	21	0	50	16	25	33	24	-	**168**
	auctioned, %	0	0	0	17	0	31	10	70	93	67	-	**22**
Total	target, MW	238	416	574	874	1161	929	929	698	698	536	76	***5871***
	auctioned, MW	35	140	249	366	485	867	951	941	726	521	71	**5352**
	auctioned, %	15	34	43	42	42	93	102	135	104	97	94	**91**

Source: Computed by the authors based on publicly available results of the renewable energy auctions)[a]

a Total target installed capacity is less than the sum of annual target volumes, it is the initially set objective of the policy according to the *Government of Russian Federation 28 May 2013 Resolution #861-r on amendments being made to Resolution #1-r 8.01.2009 on the main directions for the state policy to improve the energy efficiency of the electricity sector on the basis of renewable energy sources for the period up to 2020* (2013). The annual target volumes for later auctions were pushed higher to compensate for under-selection of earlier auctions.

and localisation requirements were too strict for these technologies initially.[44] Only after the aforementioned amendments in 2015[45] were more projects offered in auctions. This resulted in reaching the targets for installed wind capacity as from 2019 and an increase in installed small hydro as from 2021. The reason for the later fulfilment of the small hydro targets is the longer lead times for their design and construction.

It is also important to understand what happens at the auctions. How many, how big and by whom were the bids? We start the discussion by looking at the average size of the projects submitted in different years; see Figure 12.2.

The first auction saw relatively small projects. From the investor perspective, it made sense to first test the new and unfamiliar system with smaller projects and tie up less capital. As they gained confidence, investors proposed increasingly large-scale projects. The average capacity has had a steady upward trend over the years, except for the last auctions in 2018 and 2019. A number of factors, including the chosen site and land limitations, electricity demand, grid conditions, and so on, affect project size. The decreased average size of the projects proposed in 2018 and 2019 could be a sign that the various factors are reaching an equilibrium. With respect to wind-power investments, there were 19 relatively large projects of 38–39 MW each, but also six projects of 20 MW and one smaller 10 MW wind farm selected in 2018 and one huge 71 MW project in 2019. The size of solar power projects in the same year varies from 5–24 MW. The comparatively small size of hydro power projects

44 ibid

45 10 November 2015 Decree #1210 on the introduction of amendments to the certain legislative acts regarding the use of renewable energy sources in the wholesale electricity and capacity market 2015

Figure 12.2 Average capacity of projects per auction year

Source: Computed by the authors based on the publicly available results of the renewable energy auctions, available at: Trading System Administrator, 'Renewable energy auction results' (available only in Russian) www.atsenergo.ru/vie/proresults/index.htm

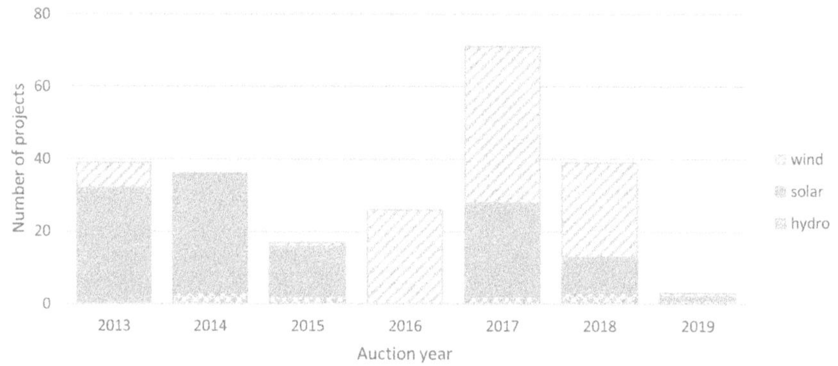

Figure 12.3 Number of projects per auction year

Source: Computed by the authors based on the publicly available results of the renewable energy auctions, available at Trading System Administrator, 'Renewable energy auction results' (available only in Russian) www.atsenergo.ru/vie/proresults/index.htm

could be explained by the fact that they are proffered by companies that are new to the capacity auctions and are testing the waters. Often, a company will offer several projects in an auction, representing the consecutive construction stages of one larger, renewable-energy power plant.

The breakdown of the auction results by the number of selected bids indicates that there is great year-to-year variability in the volumes and types of projects; see Figure 12.3.

There are years with zero projects of a certain kind. For hydro and wind power, this can indicate that the requirements for capital costs and localisation are too strict. For solar, the opposite is the case; an overly successful auction the preceding year causes the administrator to restrict participation because the (longer-term) target capacity has already been reached. Only one project with each technology type was selected in the last 2019 auction, as the target capacities for the later years of the scheme had already been fulfilled.

Figure 12.4 shows the number of companies that participated in the capacity auctions. In total, about 20 different companies have participated in the scheme with the majority of them being involved in the solar-power sector. The entire list of companies and their shares in terms of total selected capacity are presented in Table 12.2.

The Russian wind-power sector is made up of a mix of Russian state-owned companies, foreign investors and Russian–foreign partnerships. The market leader is the Finnish company Fortum, followed by the Russian company VetroOGK (which along with VetroOGK-2 is part of the ROSATOM Group, which is mainly engaged in nuclear power). Vetroparki FRV is a joint company created by Fortum and RUSNANO, and it won capacity agreements for 24 wind farm projects with a combined capacity of 823 MW in the 2018 auction. The secret of their success is the achievement of the local content requirement and lower capital costs. This was made possible by a new Russian wind-turbine manufacturer founded by a partnership of RUSNANO and the Danish company Vestas,[46] the world's leading wind turbine manufacturer.[47] The wind farms are to be commissioned during the period 2019–2023. Both ROSATOM and RUSNANO are government-owned companies. Another entrant in the Russian wind-tech manufacturing market is German–Spanish Siemens Gamesa

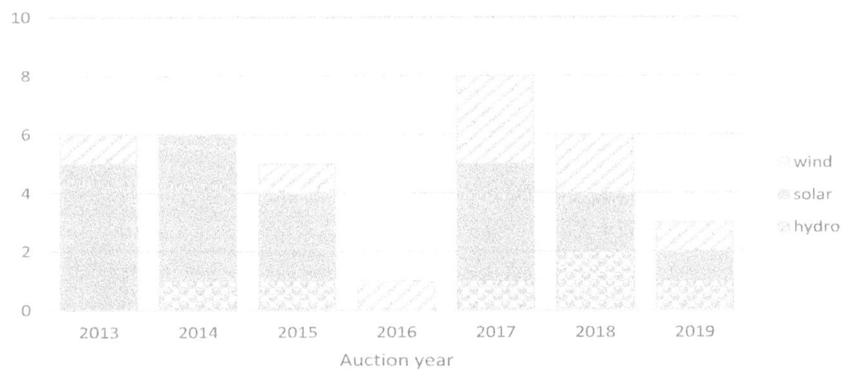

Figure 12.4 Number of companies per auction year

Source: Computed by the authors based on the publicly available results of the renewable energy auctions[a]

Table 12.2 List of companies that have participated in the auctions

Technology type	*Companies*	*Origin*	*Share of the auctioned capacity of that technology type, %*
Wind	Fortum energy	Finland	30
	VetroOGK	Russia	29
	Vetroparki FRV	Russia & Finland	25
	Enel Rossia	Italy	11
	KomplexIndustriya	Russia	3
	VetroOGK-2	Russia	1
	Fortum	Finland	1

(*Continued*)

46 RUSNANO. 'Fond ROSNANO i Fortum poluchil pravo stroitelstva 823 MW vetrogeneracii [Fund of RUSNANO and Fortum received the right to construct 823 MW of windpower]' Press release (2018)

47 REN21, 'Renewables 2018 Global Status Report' (2019) www.ren21.net/wp-content/uploads/2018/06/17-8652_GSR2018_FullReport_web_-1.pdf

Technology type	*Companies*	*Origin*	*Share of the auctioned capacity of that technology type, %*
Solar	Avelar Solar Technology	Russia	25
	Green Energy Rus	Kazakhstan	16
	MRC Energoholding	Russia	13
	Solar Systems	China	12
	T Plus	Russia	11
	KomplexIndustriya	Russia	11
	Fortum	Finland	6
	Kremnievye tehnologii	Russia	4
	Orenburgskaya generirujushaya kompaniya	Russia	1
	MEK-Engineering	Russia	0.6
	Krasnoyarskaya GES	Russia	0.3
Hydro	RusHydro	Russia	42
	NGBP	Russia	30
	Juzhenergostroy	Ukraine	14
	EnergoMIN	Russia	10
	EvroSibEnergo-Gidrogeneracia	Russia	5

Source: Computed by the authors based on the publicly available results of the renewable energy auctions[a]

a Trading System Administrator. 'Renewable energy auction results (Available only in Russian)' atsenergo.ru/vie/proresults/index.htm

(the world's second-largest wind turbine manufacturer),[48] which won its first Russian contract to supply wind turbines for the Russian projects of Italian company Enel in 2017.[49]

In terms of the timeline, the first mover was KomplexIndustriya with a total 105 MW of wind-power projects offered in the 2013 auction. The second mover was Finnish Fortum, which seemingly tested the support scheme with 35 MW in 2015 and then offered a whopping 1,000 MW in 2017. The rest of the wind projects were submitted in the period 2016–2018.

A quarter of the solar power market is in the hands of Avelar Solar Technology, a subsidiary of the largest Russian solar panel manufacturer, Hevel Solar, founded by politician Anatoly Chubais and businessman Viktor Vekselberg, both Russian. Foreign investors involved in the Russian solar sector include Solar Systems founded by the Chinese Amur Sirius Power Equipment, Kazakh Green Energy and Finnish Fortum. A large Russian manufacturer of transformer stations and other electrical equipment, ElectronMash, which has been supplying electrical equipment to the solar projects of Avelar and the wind projects of Vetroparki FRV, is now constructing a solar-panel manufacturing plant.[50]

48 ibid

49 Siemens Gameza. 'Press release: Siemens Gamesa enters Russia with its first order for 90-MW Enel wind farm' (2018) https://www.siemensgamesa.com/newsroom/2018/10/20181005-enters-russia-with-its-first-order-for-90-mw-enel-wind-farm

50 Aleksey Dmitriev. 'Solnechnaya ekonomika. Peterburgskiy Electronmash zapuskaet proizvodstvo ustanovok solnechnyh elektrostanciy [Solar economy. Saint Petersburg's Electronmash starts manufacturing solar panels]' dp.ru (2018) https://www.kommersant.ru/doc/3306333

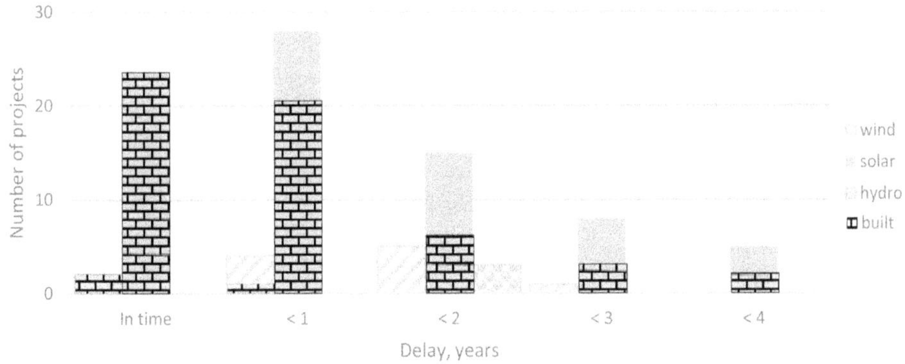

Figure 12.5 Delays in commissioning renewable energy projects

Source: Computed by the authors based on the publicly available results of the renewable energy auctions[a] and the registry of constructed projects[b]

a Trading System Administrator. 'Renewable energy auction results (available only in Russian)' <www.atsenergo.ru/vie/proresults/index.htm>

b NP Market Council. 'Vozobnovlyaemye istochniki energii. Perechen' kvalificirovannyh ob'ektov (Renewable energy sources. The list of the qualified objects)' <https://www.np-sr.ru/ru/market/vie/index.htm>

The bids for solar power projects are more evenly distributed among different companies than the bids for wind and hydropower projects, with the first two auctions receiving bids from five companies each (Figure 12.4).

Small hydro is the smallest renewable energy type in terms of installed capacity (see Table 12.1) and is represented by three Russian companies and one Ukrainian company. RusHydro and NGBP started to participate in the auctions early, in 2014 and 2015. Yuzhenergostroy and EnergoMIN entered the arena in 2018.

These results concern the auctioned renewable-energy projects. Many of them were to start delivering electricity to the grid by 2020. The list of renewable energy projects qualified by the Russian energy authorities[51] reveals substantial delays in the building of the power plants. Only 60 per cent of projects that were supposed to have been built were completed as of January 2020. Figure 12.5 shows the breakdown of the projects in terms of length of delay. The brick pattern indicates already-built projects, whereas the others are still not constructed as of January 2020.

Only 25 per cent of all planned projects were built on time and in accordance with the initial submission dates. The projects that have been constructed on time are the 19 solar projects of Avelar Solar Technology, 3 of T Plus and 1 belonging to Orenburgskaya generiruyushaya kompaniya. Even if the capacity auctions were quite successful for solar power generation, some companies have struggled to realise their plans. Komplexindustriya has not even started the construction of its solar-power projects in the Belgorod and Lipetsk regions, which were originally scheduled for completion in 2015–2016. Possible reasons behind these delays are poor planning of projects and unachievable, overly ambitious low capital costs.[52] In total, 31 solar projects have been built with delays, and 25 have not been built. Three

51 NP Market Council. 'Vozobnovlyaemye istochniki energii. Perechen' kvalificirovannyh ob'ektov [Renewable energy sources. The list of the qualified objects]' https://www.np-sr.ru/ru/market/vie/index.htm

52 Alexander Chizhenok. 'KomplexIndustriya pogasla v Lipecke i Belgorode [KomplexIndustriya faded out in Lipeck and Belgorod]' Komersant (2017) https://www.kommersant.ru/doc/3306333

small hydro power stations by RusHydro were planned to start operating in 2017 and were yet to be built as of January 2020. This was surprising given that RusHydro is a large and well-established actor, and the technology is well-known and simple. Two 25 MW wind projects by Fortum have been built on schedule and one 35 MW project with a minor delay, whereas 7 Komplexindustriya projects planned to start in 2016–2017 still had not been launched as of January 2020. The local media reported that the company was planning to sell the rights to build these windfarms. From 2019, the owner of these rights had to start paying monthly delay fees.[53]

The messy documentation of project implementation makes it difficult to get an overview.[54] In some cases, the owner of a power plant changes during the construction period and so a new one is specified in the list of built projects, but such changes reflect reality. However, errors in some project specifications, e.g., titles and in some cases even identification numbers, make it unnecessarily difficult to get an overview of the situation. Surprisingly, the list of completed renewable energy power plants includes 18 solar projects with a combined capacity of 235 MW that were never selected through the capacity auctions for the specified regions, though they have been assigned ID numbers under the capacity mechanism. It is possible that those projects were built to substitute for other projects that were abandoned somewhere else, but the publicly available documentation does not make it possible to confirm or deny this.

Even if the capacity mechanism for renewable energy was not been as successful as originally intended, it has boosted the development of the renewable-energy sector in Russia and also attracted foreign investors. However, the capacity mechanism ended with its last auction in 2019 and the last renewables to be built under the mechanism should be completed by 2025. Its prolongation is a subject of current political debate.[55] Anatoly Chubais argues that renewable energy investment in Russia will dry up if the support is discontinued. We think this is probably correct, unless a major Russian oil, gas or nuclear company decides to launch renewable projects of its own accord to keep up with international developments and emulate international peers. For broader development of the Russian renewable-energy sector, it is critical that the capacity mechanism is prolonged beyond 2025.

It is informative to contrast the role of foreign investors in the Russian renewables sector with their role in the Russian petroleum sector. In the latter, the law on strategic assets passed in 2008 bars foreign oil companies from taking on a dominant role in the development of oil and gas fields that are deemed to be strategic because of their size and/or location. However, the Russian authorities have also been keen to develop these fields in the hope of securing future income for Russia and have, therefore, warmly invited foreign companies to partner with their Russian counterparts in the development of such fields, as long as the Russian partner remains in control. This has especially been the case in the difficult offshore Arctic projects, where foreign companies are expected to contribute important technologies and experience from other parts of the Arctic.[56] Thus, in the petroleum sector, there is both a

53 Tatyana Dyatel and Sergey Titov. 'Vetryaki menyayut napravlenie [Wind turbines change direction]' (2018) https://www.kommersant.ru/doc/3527423

54 NP Market Council. 'Vozobnovlyaemye istochniki energii. Perechen' kvalificirovannyh ob'ektov [Renewable energy sources. The list of the qualified objects]' https://www.np-sr.ru/ru/market/vie/index.htm

55 Alina Gubaidulina. 'Anatoly Chubais: "Esli ne prinyat" reshenie po DPM-2, vozobnovlyaemaya energetika v Rossii zachahnet' ['Anatoly Chubais: "Without implementing DPM-2, renewable energy in Russia will wither away"']. *Realnoe vremya* (2018)

56 Indra Overland et al., 'Rosneft's offshore partnerships: The re-opening of the Russian petroleum frontier?' (2013) 49(249) *Polar Record* 140–153, https://www.researchgate.net/publication/259431566

push and a pull for foreign companies. By contrast, in the renewables sector, there is neither this push nor this pull. Because renewable energy resources are not seen as strategically valuable, foreign companies are more welcome to take on whatever roles they would like in their development; however, conversely, there is no enthusiasm for the involvement of foreign companies in this sector either. As a result, the involvement of foreign companies is much more natural and both unhindered and unaided in the renewable energy sector than in the petroleum sector in Russia.

4.2 Other renewable energy projects

The total of installed renewable-energy generation capacity in Russia is almost 3 GW, with the projects supported by the capacity mechanism already contributing 40 per cent of this figure. Only 2 per cent of the installed renewable-energy capacity is operating as autonomous power stations. However, they make up over half of the over 600 renewable-energy power plants in the country. Table 12.3 provides an overview of the currently operating renewable-energy power plants in Russia.

Table 12.3 Operating renewable energy projects in Russia

	Wholesale market (capacity mechanism)*			*Other grid connected***			*Autonomous*		
Technology type	*#*	*Average capacity, MW*	*Total capacity, MW*	*#*	*Average capacity, MW*	*Total capacity, MW*	*#*	*Average capacity, MW*	*Total capacity, MW*
Solar PV	72	15.19	1072.70	52	12.65	530.94	156	0.02	2.08
Lighthouses***							86	0.00	0.03
Solar PV-diesel				5	0.03	0.13	6	0.10	0.62
Solar PV-wind-diesel				4	0.17	0.68	5	0.03	0.13
Solar PV-wind				4	0.00	0.01	26	0.04	0.41
Wind	3	28.33	85.00	33	6.81	159.83	12	0.17	1.49
Wind-diesel							16	0.02	0.33
Small hydro				148	5.57	784.98			
Geothermal				24	18.84	294.87	7	8.29	58.02
Tidal				6	0.53	3.20			
TOTAL	75	15.72	1158	247	8.76	1774.65	314	0.21	63.12

* *The data on wholesale market projects are collected from*[a] *the rest of the data are from*[b]
** *Grid-connected, parallel to the grid, reserve, or no data*
*** *Solar PV panels on lighthouses*

a NP Market Council. 'Vozobnovlyaemye istochniki energii. Perechen' kvalificirovannyh ob'ektov [Renewable energy sources. The list of the qualified objects]' https://www.np-sr.ru/ru/market/vie/index.htm

b Research and Educational Center. 'Renewable Energy', Geographical Department of Moscow State University and Joint Institute for High Temperatures of the Russian Academy of Sciences, 'GIS renewable energy sources of Russia'. http://gisre.ru

On the wholesale market level, the participation of renewables is enabled by the capacity mechanism. Thus, the vast majority of these projects are recent, relatively large, with an average installed capacity of 15 MW per project, and so far quite scarce because the support mechanism was introduced so recently. Only wind, solar PV and small hydro power are supported by the capacity mechanism; therefore, no other types have entered the wholesale market.

Other grid-connected renewable power plants are more diverse in terms of technology used. In this group, small hydro, solar PV, geothermal and wind-power plants are present. All small hydro power plants in this group were built before the introduction of the capacity mechanism in 2013. The rest of the grid-connected plants include more exotic types of power, such as tidal power, and various combinations of solar PV, wind and diesel power plants, but their share is small.

Autonomous renewable power plants include a large proportion of geothermal plants with an average size of approximately 8 MW, mostly in the Russian Far East, and a mix of small solar PV, wind and various hybrid plants. Such small hybrid power stations are the single source of electricity for many remote villages in Russia. Combining solar panels and wind turbines with diesel generators can help ensure an uninterrupted power supply.[57] Although autonomous projects constitute a minor share of the total renewable energy installed capacity in Russia, their number exceeds all other renewable energy power plants. Despite the fact that there is no functioning support mechanism for autonomous projects or small distributed capacity, this niche seemingly develops without special incentives. However, more active support from the state could still accelerate the development of them. This would save the local authorities money for diesel and its transport, and improve the market base for renewable-energy actors in Russia.

5 Conclusions

In the global renewable energy landscape, the Russian case has a special place because of the unique instrument for supporting renewables. Originating in the capacity trade, this instrument is meant to secure return on investment for renewable-energy investors. The promise of profitable investments theoretically creates a strong incentive for investors to enter the market; however, in practice, the implementation of this support is more like a steeplechase. Some traits of the mechanism required finetuning and led to the introduction of amendments to the initial legislative document. During the seven-year period that the entire first phase of the capacity mechanism has been in operation (2013–2019), 90 per cent of the targeted capacity (5.9 GW) was auctioned, and to date only 60 per cent of the capacity due has actually been built which constitutes 1.2 GW of wind and solar power as a net current result of the capacity mechanism. However, the industry is gaining momentum, more local manufacturing facilities are being built, and more national and foreign investors are showing interest in the scheme.

The regional-level renewable-energy support has not been very successful, although the framework for it has been created at the national level. However, renewables are penetrating regional markets where they are commercially competitive (e.g., geothermal energy in parts of the Russian Far East or the numerous small autonomous solar or hybrid stations substituting expensive diesel-fired power in isolated or remote areas).

57 Indra Overland. 'The Siberian Curse: A blessing in disguise for renewable energy?' (2010) 9(2) *Sibirica* 1

The scale of renewables in Russia is still, however, negligible. The total 2.6 GW of renewable energy generation capacity built is just 1 per cent of the total Russian power capacity, and, for example, is comparable to the size of a single (though the largest) solar PV project in India. The slow development of renewable energy in Russia creates several risks for the country. First, Russian companies will fall behind in this sector just as it is growing exponentially internationally. Historically, the Russian photovoltaic sector was very strong due to, among other things, the Soviet space programmes, but now they lack a strong home market to buoy their development. The contrast to China is stark, with the Chinese acting highly strategically to secure as big a piece as possible of the rapidly growing global renewables markets. One of the main tools the Chinese are using for this purpose is strong support for domestic deployment of renewable energy. Secondly, the limited development of renewables in Russia means that less-traditional fuels are available for export. Thirdly, it creates a risk that Russian actors are not fully aware and up-to-date on renewable energy developments at the global level. This is because they lack the domestic interface where they can gain experience and exposure. For Russia, as the world's biggest energy exporter, this is a potentially serious concern.

Acknowledgements

We would like to acknowledge financial support from Fortum Foundation (Grant no 201700063); support of the project GIS "Renewable Energy Sources of Russia" (www.gisre.ru), managed by the Faculty of Geography, Moscow State University, Russia and the Joint Institute of High Temperatures of the Russian Academy of Science; funding received from the Finnish Strategic Research Council (Grant no. 313396/MFG40 – Manufacturing 4.0); as well as the support of the Norruss program of the Research Council of Norway for the project "Is this Russia's Kodak Moment?".

13

SHIFTING RUSSIAN ENERGY GEOPOLITICS

Slawomir Raszewski and Zuzanna Nowak

1 Energy security in Russia's energy geopolitics

The Russian Federation has long been playing the role of reliable energy exporter, offering abundant resources and tailor-made deals for its customers, as well as encouraging close relationships with Russian companies through long-term supply contracts. Over the years, Russia has become a vital supplier of energy commodities for the world's numerous economies through its major energy companies. As the companies exporting crude oil or natural gas ultimately generate the lion's share of revenue for the Government, security of demand—understood as insurance against supply risks to ensure sustained revenue flows from the trade of energy resources—has become crucially important for Russia's geopolitics. Geopolitics focuses on the study of ways in which 'politics or ideologies can be explained by means of geographic variables, such as location, size, population, resource or technological development'.[1] The changing dynamics of energy supply and demand across the world is one of the defining features of contemporary geopolitics and energy security. Among many definitions and theoretical perspectives, geopolitics can be defined as 'the study of the changing world political map and an understanding of the "geo" dimension of global, regional and state politics', or simply, 'the political geography of international relations'.[2] The geological dimension of geopolitics—reserves of fossil fuels and the convertibility of such reserves into tradable, commodified resources—makes inroads into the concept of energy security—which is, in itself, understood quite differently by the buyers and sellers of energy. In a nutshell, energy security can be defined as 'reliable supplies of energy at reasonable prices to support the economy and industry'.[3]

1 Michael Leigh, 'Energy: A geopolitical game changer?' [2014] *The International Spectator: Italian Journal of International Affairs* [e-journal], Vol. 49, Issue 2, pp. 1–10, as quoted by Ana Campos and Carla Patricio Fernandes 'The geopolitics of energy', in Carla Patricio Fernandes and Teresa Ferreira Rodrigues (eds) *Geopolitics of Energy and Energy Security* (Instituto da Defesa Nacional, IDN Cadernos no 24, Lisbon 2018), p. 24.

2 David Newman, 'Geopolitics renaissant: Territory, sovereignty and the world political map', [1998] *Geopolitics*, Vol. 1, Issue 1, p. 1.

3 James P. Dorian, Herman T. Franssen, and Dale R. Simbeck, 'Global challenges in energy', [2006] *Energy Policy*, Vol. 34, Issue 15, pp. 1984–1991, quoted by Vlado Vivoda in, 'Evaluating energy security in the Asia-Pacific region: A novel methodological approach', [2010], *Energy Policy*, Vol. 38, Issue 9, pp. 5258–5263, p. 5258.

The legacy of the energy trade between Russia and its consumers means that security of demand remains in place, with Russia's resources treated not as commodities but strategic resources, and control over the energy industry is held by the government through majority stakes in Russia's leading energy companies.

Russia's oil sub-sector examples the case in hand whereby the Government holds 50 per cent (through Rosneftegaz) plus one direct ownership share in the Public Joint Stock Company (PJSC) Rosneft Company. In 2018, Rosneft's total production of liquid hydrocarbons reached 285.5 million tonnes of oil equivalent (mtoe), with the proved reserves totalling 41.4 billion barrels of oil equivalent (bboe) and the proven reserve replacement ratio standing at 173 per cent.[4] Monopoly over the transportation of oil in Russia is held by the Joint Stock Company (JSC) Transneft, which is the largest pipeline company in the world. The natural gas sub-sector has been led by PJSC Gazprom which is both the largest producer—accounting for 498.7 billion cubic metres (bcm) of gas in 2018—and holder of vast proved reserves estimated at about 3.5 trillion cubic metres (tcm) at the end of 2018 (Gazprom 2019). Gazprom retains a monopoly over piped gas exports, while other companies, such as Rosneft and Novatek are allowed to export only liquified natural gas (LNG). Russia's energy status features in nuclear energy led by Rosatom State Nuclear Energy Corporation (Rosatom), which is the largest electricity producer in Russia having accounted for over 204 TWh (gross) production in 2018.[5] Together with its subsidiaries—Rosatom for technology exports and Open Joint Stock Company TVEL Fuel Company for nuclear fuel—Russia is one of the world leaders in the nuclear sub-sector.[6]

The clout Russia carries in the energy sector translates into geopolitics which, in effect, may determine the country's behaviour as far as energy security is concerned. Russia's geopolitical influence is at its greatest since the end of the Cold War: the partitioning of Georgia in 2008, the annexation of Crimea in 2014, exercising influence over the Euro-Atlantic ambitions of Ukraine, giving support to Syria's Assad regime, and the US presidential election meddling have all been credited as the key factors that increased Russia's geopolitical momentum.[7]

In the energy domain, two main ideas—Russia's reassertion of the state's control over strategic resources, and gaining 'primacy over the main pipelines and market channels through which it ships its hydrocarbons to international markets'[8]—have been the main objectives of Russia's energy security.

In the past two decades, the Russian internal energy market has been slowly undergoing reform, its market players have seen only limited growth of domestic competition, and export patterns revived only recently. At the same time, global energy geopolitics has rapidly evolved, undermining Russia's energy security. According to the World Economic Forum's Strategic Intelligence (2019) the key underpinnings of energy geopolitics today are related

4 Rosneft (2019) *Annual Report 2018*, p. 6, available at https://www.rosneft.com/upload/site2/document_file/a_report_2018_eng.pdf

5 The Information and Public Relations Department of Rosenergoatom [2019] 'Rosenergoatom: In 2018 Russian nuclear power plants set a new electricity production record of over 204 bln kWh', available at https://rosatom.ru/en/press-centre/news/rosenergoatom-in-2018-russian-nuclear-power-plants-set-a-new-electricity-production-record-of-over-2

6 Rosatom (2017) 'Performance of State Atomic Energy Corporation Rosatom in 2017: Public Annual Report', available at https://rosatom.ru/upload/iblock/29c/29c061878dad37c189db341648c964b3.pdf

7 National Bank of Canada (2018) 'Can Russia live up to its geopolitical ambitions?', *Geopolitical Briefing, Economics and Strategy*, 27 August.

8 Daniel Yergin, 'Ensuring energy security', [2006] *Foreign Affairs*, Vol. 85, No. 2, pp. 69–82, p. 70.

to the European Union (EU), climate change, China, issues of global governance, the Middle East and North Africa, international security, the Russian Federation, the United States and geo-economics (with the penultimate being at the centre of unconventional production from shale reserves, which has transformed the global picture of energy geopolitics). In addition to this, a number of regional and international undertakings coupled with technological and environmental dynamics make Russia's energy trade more complex than it was previously.

Bearing all the above in mind, this chapter seeks to address the question of to what extent geopolitics is still a relevant lens to analyse Russia and its energy security and how the country's energy resources endowment is used to achieve Russia's objectives elsewhere in the world.

Current as well as anticipated global shifts have a degree of influence on and can determine Russia's behaviour. Its reaction is twofold. Russia must ensure permanent and reliable access to energy consumers in order to maintain budget revenues. This competition for markets will be discussed in the example of Russia's relations with the EU (2.1) and Asia (2.2). Simultaneously, Russia must ensure that it maintains and acquires new zones of energy influence, thus acting effectively on global energy fora and opening windows of opportunity for its own further energy expansion. This quest for influence will be demonstrated with the example of Russian involvement in international energy organisations (3.1) and Russian plans related to the Northern Sea Route (3.2).

2 Energy security—competition for markets

Until recently, energy markets (such as those in the EU, China, or the US) have been largely fragmented, constituting separate areas with distinct pricing of commodities and limited availability of alternative suppliers and consumers. Fragmentation of energy markets—and, thus, structural imbalances between energy supply and demand—in the key consuming regions may incentivise energy suppliers to abuse their dominant position, prioritising energy demand security. Russia has often turned such instances of fragmented markets in its favor by means of a rather realistic 'divide and rule' approach to international energy. Examples of the realistic approach is pipeline diplomacy both within Russia's traditional space of influence, the post-Soviet Eurasia, and the EU.[9] Yet, globalisation and development of new technologies have made for an improved interconnectedness and greater flexibility of international energy markets. Greater interconnectedness, coupled with the shifting geography of energy producers and consumers, has increasingly disabled Russian security of demand imperatives. Russia now takes appropriate measures in order not to lose its existing export markets (such as the EU discussed below) while focusing on identifying new outlets (such as those in Asia as discussed in section 2.2 below).

2.1 EU—reshaping traditional cooperation

Russia-EU energy relations have transformed over the last two decades, driven by concerns over diversification and transit. The EU is Russia's traditional energy resources export market and its largest buyer of natural gas. Also, currently, Russia satisfies the largest share of

9 Dominique Finon and Catherine Locatelli, 'Russian and European gas interdependence: Could contractual trade channel geopolitics?', [2008] *Energy Policy*, Vol. 36, Issue 1, pp. 423–442.

the EU gas market, as 42 per cent of this commodity was imported by the EU from Russia in 2018.[10]

The mutual energy relationship between the EU and Russia can be characterised as a turbulent one, which can be largely ascribed to essential differences in the manner energy as perceived by Brussels and Moscow: for the former it is a commodity which ought to be subject to market exchange whereas for the latter it is a strategic resource that has to be governed by the state.[11] Energy supply from Russia—and prior to 1991 the Soviet Union—is often described as energy secure in terms of lack of supply interruptions. Uninterrupted supply has become an issue in the 2000s, coinciding with EU enlargement into the east of Europe. The eastwards EU enlargement, if seen outside of the EU-led liberal institutional integration process and considered as a geopolitical development, significantly impacted the EU-Russian energy relationship. Accession into the politico-trading bloc of Central and Eastern European (CEE) nations, historically dependent on Russia for their energy supply, produced a new dynamic impacting energy security, and more broadly energy relations between the EU and Russia, including: accelerated liberalisation of energy (natural gas and electricity) markets as a result of the creation of a single energy market within the EU, and reinforced energy security at the EU level with a steady prioritisation of sustainable development objectives and environmental sustainability.[12] While the EU's energy market policy started to take shape in late 2000s following the enactment of the third gas directive (the so-called Third Energy Package (TEP)), for Russia energy policy vis-à vis Europe has been more than just about energy and is often seen as rooted in a strategic relationship whereby—following the commodity strategic resource logic—the former positioned itself as a provider of energy security on the continent rather than just a supplier of a resource.[13] The acceleration of EU energy and climate law witnessed in 2000s profoundly changed the EU-Russia energy relationship. Implementation of the TEP, a body of laws and regulations concerning the workings of the EU's internal energy market, including the provision for 'unbundling', requiring energy companies (in Russia's case, Gazprom) to give up control over business activities in more than one segment of the value chain, produced concerns over the future energy relationship between the two partners. By doing so, 'the EU now intends to redefine the way in which it manages its relations with its main suppliers, such as Russia, by attempting to impose a model based on competition, unbundling of network industries and privatization'.[14]

The politicisation and securitisation of energy relations that followed was intrinsically linked with the EU energy law reforms as well as the drive of CEE nations to shield

10 European Commission (2019) 'European Commission – Press release. Energy Union: Commission welcomes tonight's provisional political agreement to ensure that pipelines with third countries comply with EU gas rules', IP/19/1069. Brussels, 12 February 2019. Available at: https://europa.eu/rapid/press-release_IP-19-1069_en.htm'

11 Richard Youngs 'Europe's external energy policy: Between geopolitics and the market', 20 November [2007], CEPS Working Documents No. 278. Available at: https://ssrn.com/abstract=1337975 or http://dx.doi.org/10.2139/ssrn.1337975; Richard Youngs, *Energy Security: Europe's New Foreign Policy Challenge* (Routledge 2009).

12 Andrei Belyi, 'New dimensions of energy security of the enlarging EU and their impact on relations with Russia', [2003] *Journal of European Integration*, Vol. 25, Issue 4, pp. 351–369, p. 351.

13 Jack D. Sharples, 'Russian approaches to energy security and climate change: Russian gas exports to the EU', [2013] *Environmental Politics*, Vol. 22, Issue 4 (*Energy Security and Climate Change: Conflicts and Synergies*), pp. 683–700.

14 Catherine Locatelli, 'EU-Russia trading relations: The challenges of a new gas architecture', [2015] *European Journal of Law and Economics*, Vol. 39, Issue 2, pp. 313–329.

themselves from the negative consequences of energy geopolitics at the time.[15] The deterioration of EU-Russia energy relations had been seen as a result of EU energy legalism and the expansion of the EU, all of which predated the first Russia-Ukraine gas pricing dispute in the winter of 2005/2006. The politicisation of Russia's energy exports into the EU expedited the Community's supply diversification policies as well as internal market trading, all aimed at curbing the market power of monopolistic entities such as Gazprom by means of a liberalised internal energy market.[16]

The transit of Russia's energy exports to the EU is the second key issue which has been on the agenda since the collapse of the USSR. Due to the existing Soviet-legacy infrastructure and new supply pipelines such as Nord Stream, the Baltic Sea undersea gas pipeline connecting Russia and Germany and Blue Stream, and a gas pipeline under the Black Sea connecting Russia with Turkey, Russia continues to play the leading role in European energy security. The EU-Russian energy relationship demands new policy approaches which the EU has sought to implement by addressing what it sees as two-tier dependence on Russia in terms of sources of supply and routes of supplies of Russian gas.[17]

From the Russian perspective as the producer, the transit has been seen as a challenge both in terms of the cost as well as geopolitical uncertainties. Russia's transit avoidance,[18] a policy dating back to mid-2000s aimed at circumventing traditional transit countries to provide direct supplies to Russia's largest consumers in Germany and, most recently, Turkey has sought to address the geopolitical issue of the transit of natural gas through previously Soviet republics/former Eastern Bloc countries. The former Soviet republics, which after the collapse of the Soviet Union became Newly Independent States (NIS), had been seen as potentially uncertain partners due to their new foreign policies, not least by changing political orientation manifested through membership of Euro-Atlantic organisations such as NATO and the EU. Substituting an onland transit of pipelines and commissioning offshore pipelines such as Nord Stream, which circumvented CEE countries including Poland and Belarus, addressed the new geopolitics of the region. Avoiding transit altogether enabled Russia to engage in pipeline politics as 'control over transport routes and export outlets has been a key instrument for the Russian state to maintain its grip on the oil and gas sectors',[19] while, if not pre-empting, then significantly affecting the physical implementation of the EU internal market.[20]

Following the Ukraine conflict in 2014 and the subsequent annexation of Crimea, Russia sped up the process of transit avoidance with calls to fully bypass Ukraine by using alternative pipelines including the Turkish Stream gas pipeline to Turkey and the Nord Stream 2 pipeline to Germany. Ukraine has traditionally played a key role in natural gas transit to the EU due to the extensive grid of Soviet-era pipelines and storage capacity in the country. While it is unclear whether the transit avoidance will materialise in the next few years

15 Slawomir Raszewski, 'Security and economics of energy in north-east Europe', in Caroline Kuzemko et al. (eds) *Dynamics of Energy Governance in Europe and Russia* (Palgrave Macmillan 2012).

16 Sharples (n 13).

17 Slawomir Raszewski (2015) 'Europe's dependency on Russian gas is not likely to change any time soon', *The Conversation*, 1 March. Available at: https://theconversation.com/europes-dependency-on-russian-gas-is-not-likely-to-change-any-time-soon-38192.

18 James Henderson and Tatiana Mitrova, 'The political and commercial dynamics of Russia's gas export strategy', [2105] *Oxford Institute for Energy Studies Paper*, NG 102.

19 Adnan Vatansever (2017). 'Is Russia building too many pipelines? Explaining Russia's oil and gas export strategy', *Energy Policy*, Vol. 108, pp. 1–11. Available at: 10.1016/j.enpol.2017.05.038.

20 Locatelli (n 14).

as the new capacity is still under construction, it is anticipated that the significance of the Ukraine transit is likely to be diminished in 2020–2025 should the demand not increase.[21] At the same time, Russia's approach has been aimed at operationalising alternative hubs for its gas supply to the EU. At the time of writing, the two pipeline projects—Nord Stream 2 and Turkish Stream—are aiming at just that and, when constructed, will provide greater capacity while, at the same time, effectively avoiding transit via the CEE countries.

2.2 Asia—setting new partnerships

Key demand centres in Asia—led by China and South Korea—have increased demand for energy resources exponentially, a shift attributed to the climate and the economy. The domestic policies of the Asian countries have aimed at a reduction of emissions and the substitution of coal with less CO_2 emitting fuels. Economy wise, energy demand in those Asian economies has increased as a result of economic development. Against this backdrop, Asia has become a promising energy export destination with growing interconnectedness of international energy markets and competitiveness moving from procurement to market-based trade dynamics. A large number of energy supplies have been diverted between Europe and Asia taking into account seasonal supply and demand dynamics and, as a result, the price differentials between the regions.

Globalisation of LNG trade has arguably become the most notable energy shift in recent times. LNG supply has allowed for movement of gas between the key global demand centres—while challenging the traditional piped gas supply—with its flexibility, clearly defined ports of loading and discharge and, possibly, more attractive contractual bases. Several important aspects should be highlighted: the increase in the number of LNG exporters—US LNG exports commenced in 2016[22] and the Russian LNG exports started in 2009[23]—coupled with a shifting in indexation of prices away from oil to hub-based or spot pricing and the narrowing price premium of Asian to European markets. Countries in Asia—led by Japan, China and South Korea—have retained the biggest LNG appetite and were responsible for over 75 per cent of global LNG imports in 2018, while European countries accounted for only 16 per cent of LNG trade.[24] Contrary to a common assumption, rather than an alternative, for Russia the Asian energy market is a parallel one vis-à-vis the EU market despite the two markets being entirely different.

First, the Asian market is developing, particularly for those resources exported by Russia. While the EU market is expected to reduce consumption of fossil fuels, the Asian market is experiencing a boom in consumption.

Secondly, the Asian and European markets have very distinct resource needs in particular with regard to pipeline gas which is particularly sensitive in terms of geopolitics. Russian

21 Simon Pirani, 'Russian gas transit through Ukraine after 2019: The options', [2018] *Oxford Energy Insight*, 41, November.

22 US Energy (2019) 'Interactive Map: U.S. liquefied natural gas exports breaking records', US Energy Department, 15 May, available at https://www.energy.gov/articles/interactive-map-us-liquefied-natural-gas-exports-breaking-records; Tatiana Mitrova, and Tim Boersma, 'The impact of US LNG on Russian natural gas export policy', [2018] *Center on Global Energy Policy*.

23 Tatiana Mitrova 'Russian LNG: the long road to export', [2013] IFRI, Russia/NIS Centre, Russie Nei ReportsNo.16.Availableat:https://www.ifri.org/sites/default/files/atoms/files/defifrimitrovalngengdecember2013.pdf

24 GIIGNL (2019) 'International Group of Liquefied Natural Gas Importers. The LNG Industry GIIGNL Annual Report'.

natural gas (pipeline) resources earmarked for the EU originate in Yamal and those destined for export to Asia are produced in eastern Siberia, meaning that there is a lack of physical price arbitrage between the two. LNG—as opposed to pipeline gas—is different in this respect and exports of the fuel are dependent on seasonal variations and, hence, more dependent on market prices. With the advance of trade and shipping following the construction of Yamal LNG, Russia can now export directly to Asia, although this export route is still subject to weather conditions.

Thirdly, Asian markets are not homogenous in terms of trade rules and are dependent on a number of bilateral agreements between Russia and countries in the region, underpinned by historical and geopolitical legacies of bilateral trade relations. For instance, Japan's geopolitical relations with Russia stall over the Kuril Islands, a contagious foreign affairs challenge which is yet to be resolved. In the absence of an agreement over the Russia-held Japan-disputed territories bloc, a peace treaty between the two countries and, moving forward, provide a degree of uncertainty in the current geopolitical climate in the Asia-Pacific region. Despite this fundamental issue, on the economic front Russia and Japan have collaborated closely as evidenced by the trade between the two countries. Prior to the Ukraine Crisis, the Russia-Japan trade partnership reached $37 billion in 2013, six times the amount recorded a decade earlier, with Russian energy exports to Japan increasing substantially following the nuclear disaster at the Fukushima Daiichi power plant.[25]

Post-Ukraine sanctions meant that Asian countries—in particular China—were indispensable to help secure the necessary funding for Russian energy projects and, as a result, there was a greater degree of concessions from Russia in order to fund its capital-intensive frontier projects such as Yamal LNG.

Asian markets are important to Russia in the longer term and, despite the rhetoric, Russia's Asia 'pivot' does not mean and should not mean Moscow compromises with Europe. With its extensive reserves there is a degree of optimism for continued trade relations between Russia and the EU and, equally, Russia and the key Asian economies. The fact that the US is present in the Asia-Pacific region only heightens the region on Russia's agenda, not least because of energy demand security championed by Russia. On the economic front, Russia has been a late arrival to shale gas development—advanced by the US—and has been historically slow in embracing LNG trade which is key to globalising energy. The shifting geopolitics of European gas supplies as well as a relatively stagnant demand in Europe has led to a refocusing on Asian markets, which Russia is actively pursuing through its strategic oil and gas companies.

New rules on third country pipeline supplies into the EU as well as a degree of coercion in the EU's market legislation, in particular through the Third Energy Package,[26] which have been put in place to ensure more of a supply and demand dynamic on the internal energy market within the EU,[27] led arguably to a desire to create a greater price arbitrage for Russia between Europe and Asia through the expansion of its existing transport capacity. Planned pipelines to connect Russia's production in the east of the country with demand centres in China via planned large-scale transport infrastructure projects evidence the case.

25 Wrenn Yennie-Lindgren, 'New dynamics in Japan–Russia energy relations 2011–2017', [2018] *Journal of Eurasian Studies*, Vol. 9, Issue 2 (July), pp. 152–162.

26 European Commission, 'Third Energy Package'. Last updated 20 August 2019. Available at https://ec.europa.eu/energy/en/topics/markets-and-consumers/market-legislation/third-energy-package.

27 Tatiana Romanova, 'Is Russian energy policy towards the EU only about geopolitics? The case of the Third Liberalisation Package', [2016] *Geopolitics*, Vol. 21, Issue 4, pp. 857–879.

Plans to build two gas pipelines—the Power of Siberia and the Altai Pipeline[28]—to supply the Chinese market have been announced by Gazprom, the former project being underway and the latter's route yet to be finalised.[29]

3 Energy security—quest for influence

Russia aims at increasing its importance as an energy supplier, not only in countable values (volumes or revenues) as discussed in the previous section, but also in terms of strategic decision-making and global geopolitical ambitions.[30] This objective would not be realistic without the robust support of Russia's diplomatic services, close links between business and government, a strong expert community as well as a developed technological and research base. This combined technological and research effort to determine strategic objectives and defend Russia's interests, magnified by the geopolitical weight and territorial size of the country, contributes a great deal towards maintaining Russia's energy security. This chapter describes two key aspects of Russia's quest for influence, one being its involvement in international energy fora and groups through the lens of energy transition (A), the second being the implementation of ambitious and visionary projects having a potential impact on energy geopolitics, such as the Northern Sea Route (B).

3.1 International governmental organisations—advancing foreign policy objectives

Proliferation of international governmental organisations (IGOs) in the energy field is an expression of the need for global governance of the intensifying energy resources trade. States join energy IGOs in order to consolidate or improve their market position (as producers or consumers), coordinate with other states their energy policies and be part of the same international group as their market competitors or infrastructural partners.[31]

Being one of the world's leading oil and gas producers, Russia has been prioritising bilateral relationships over exchanges within or with a multilateral setting. Free of the organisational and bureaucratic burdens characteristic of international organisations, bilateral frameworks allow direct expression of Russia's foreign energy policy, grounded in a willingness to ensure security of demand and to maintain or enlarge spheres of influence and stronger political leverage. Yet, for Russia, as is also the case for other countries whose budgets rely on exports of energy resources, current global trends such as an abundant supply of fossil fuels in markets, volatility of energy prices and energy transition can have a destabilising effect. As a result, Russia has started operationalising multilateral fora as a collateral channel to promote its interests (often other than those that are genuinely energy related, such as military or political interests) and emphasise its desire to continue playing the role of a global actor, taking an assertive, or even offensive posture.[32] Affiliation with an energy

28 Alex Forbes, 'Russia's hunger for second eastern gas outlet grows', [2019] *Petroleum Economist*. Available at https://www.petroleum-economist.com/articles/politics-economics/europe-eurasia/2019/russia-s-hunger-for-second-eastern-gas-outlet-grows.

29 Vatansever (n 19).

30 Nikos Tsafos, 'Who's afraid of Russian gas? Bridging the transatlantic divide', [2018] *CSIS Brief*, 3 May.

31 Leonardo Baccini, Veronica Lenz and Paul Thurner, 'Global energy governance: Trade, infrastructure, and the diffusion of international organizations', [2013] *International Interactions*, Vol. 39, Issue 2, pp. 192–216.

32 Ian Bond, 'Russia in international organizations: The shift from defence to offence', in David Cadier and Margot Light (eds) *Russia's Foreign Policy* (Palgrave Macmillan, 2015), pp. 189–203.

organisation (or an organisation with a distinct energy clout) is a result of long-lasting foreign policy considerations on costs and benefits. Russia's adherence to IGOs and the impact such an adherence would have on energy security and Russia's broader economy and politics does not necessarily mean Russia's full commitment to an IGO's organisational objectives. For example, due among other things to Russia's energy trade-related preoccupations, talks on its admission to the World Trade Organisation lasted 18 years, only gaining accession in 2012. Russia had also been a member of the Energy Charter Conference (and signed the European Energy Charter in 1991, pulling out of the treaty in 2012). The scope of Russian activities in energy IGOs is wide and heterogenous, yet one example of an IGO (of which Russia is not formally a member) deserves more attention, as it shows the impact of global shifts on Russia's energy geopolitics.

The Organisation of the Petroleum Exporting Countries (OPEC) founded in 1960, as stated in its Statute, coordinates and unifies its member states' policies in order to stabilise oil prices on international markets, ensure the security of supplies and receive steady income from their activities. Any country with significant crude exports can join OPEC if it shares similar interests and is accepted by a three-quarters majority of its members. The USSR had a rather 'strained relationship' with OPEC, not only because of their competition on foreign markets, but also due to the 'clash of values' between a Communist regime and an organisation dominated by Islamic states.[33] Later, when Russian oil production revived after the collapse of the USSR, this relationship was mainly characterised by rivalry. However, the 2010s shale revolution coupled with the subsequent drop in oil prices put a new light on OPEC-Russia relations. Against the backdrop of global oil market shifts, Russia and OPEC (with strong Saudi Arabian leadership) realised that their position in terms of market share and pricing would be stronger and activities more effective if they acted together. Hence, still without being an OPEC member, in 2016 Russia joined the so-called OPEC 'plus' initiative, signing the Declaration on cooperation with the cartel. Production adjustments pushing up oil prices effectively helped to balance Russia's budget and softened the sanctions' impact on its economy. The implications of Russia's alliance with OPEC, however, go beyond market considerations and have geopolitical significance for the turbulent Middle East region, the scope of which is yet to be seen.

In addition to energy IGOs, numerous climate protection initiatives aimed at the implementation of energy efficiency measures, promotion of renewable energy sources as well as limiting consumption of fossil fuel have emerged in recent years. Since 'international organizations constrain the predilection of individual and organized interests to diverge from a common or shared perspective of the good',[34] the UN, the world's largest IOG, has therefore become the watchman of the environment and climate. In 2011, Ban Ki-Moon, the then UN Secretary General, observed that 'climate change does not respect border' and therefore has to be treated as a 'global challenge'. This attitude had already been sealed with the United Nations Framework Convention on Climate Change in 1992, its Kyoto Protocol from 1997, and was later confirmed with the Paris Agreement from 2015, outlining a global path towards mitigation of global warming processes. Russia, a member of the UN and one of the biggest world polluters, is particularly concerned about developing climate protection measures which could undermine the foundations of its economy based on fossil fuels and

33 Joseph Mann, 'Russia's policy towards OPEC'. [2009] *Middle Eastern Studies*, Vol. 45, No. 6, pp. 985–1005.

34 James P. Muldoon Jr, *The Architecture of Global Governance: An Introduction to the Study of International Organization*, (Westview Press, 2004).

threaten its energy security. Its perception of the 'good' diverges from that of energy importing countries. For this reason, Russia has been rather reluctant to bind itself with obligations and limitations stemming from an emerging global climate policy and took into account other considerations while committing to climate protection activities. For instance, after years of strong opposition and long deliberations, Russia decided to ratify the Kyoto Protocol in 2004 only when the EU put on the negotiation table an offer to drop objections to Russia's WTO membership. Also, legislation to ratify the Paris Agreement has only recently been submitted to Parliament, the Duma, by the Russian Government. This move can be seen as a means of maintaining an influence on global climate negotiations and an opportunity to protect Russia's interests, especially in view of the US withdrawal from the Agreement, rather than Russia's contribution to climate protection.

3.2 Northern Sea Route—ambitious pioneering

Climate change in the Arctic is provoking an unprecedented increase in temperature, followed by significant melting and retreating of ice. For the Russian Government, however, ice disappearing from the Arctic constitutes an unparalleled opportunity for new developments in the region including economic, political and military installations. Furthermore, development of the Russian Arctic is perceived as a long-term endeavour, 'essential for the future of the Russian Federation'.[35]

First, Russia is interested in developing petroleum and mineral resources locked beneath the Arctic Circle. The Arctic Circle covers around 6 per cent of the Earth's surface and may contain '30% of the world's undiscovered gas and 13% of the world's undiscovered oil' located mainly offshore,[36] and these estimates do not even cover additional unconventional resources such as tight oil and gas. Melting ice facilitates access to oil and gas deposits lying under the seabed, a big share of which can be claimed by Russia. In a similar manner to other Arctic countries, Russia presented a claim to the United Nations to extend its continental shelf beyond the Exclusive Economic Zone (EEC). If the claim is accepted, which might take years of negotiation, Russia will potentially get access to enormous hydrocarbon reserves under the North Pole.

Currently only the state-controlled Russian companies, Gazprom and Rosneft, are allowed to operate in the Russian Arctic, but their activities are limited due to the geological, technological and financial challenges the Arctic waters pose. In addition to the recent challenge of low oil prices, business licences and drillings, the 2014 American sanctions have put Russia's Arctic activities in question, adding more political flavour to the issue and pushing Russia to develop new relations. As a result, the Chinese-Russian strategic partnership can be used not only as a tool to continue efforts towards extraction of the Arctic resources, but also as means of balancing geopolitical interests in the region by outweighing Western influence.

Second, rapidly melting Arctic ice gives Russia an even more valuable geopolitical asset in the short term. Unfrozen waters not only allow an increased military presence in the Arctic region, but, from a commercial perspective, open up an opportunity for Russia to strengthen

35 Tina Soliman Hunter, 'Russian Arctic Policy, petroleum resources – development and the EU: Cooperation or coming confrontation?' in Nengye Liu, Elizabeth A. Kirk and Tore Henriksen (eds) *The European Union and the Arctic'* (Brill Nijhoff, 2017).

36 Donald Gautier et al., 'Assessment of undiscovered oil and gas in the Arctic' [2009] *Science,* Vol. 324, Issue 5931,pp. 1175–1179.

its presence in Arctic shipping lanes and develop one of President Putin's May 2018 Decree flagship economic projects of strategic importance: the Northern Sea Route. Defined by 'Law on the Northern Sea Route Area' (Federal Law N 132-FZ from 28/07/2012) it is the sector of the Russian EEZ located between Novaya Zemlya in the West and the Bering Strait in the East, encompassing Russian strategic ports such as the largest one, Murmansk, and the busiest one, Sabetta (where the Yamal LNG plant is located). Since the transfer of responsibilities from the Ministry of Transport in 2018, the Route has been and is under the administration of Rosatom.

This seaway is expected to grow significantly in importance due to its gradually increasing availability. First, retreating ice will allow an extension of the peak season for transport beyond the current August to October period. Second, Russia will strengthen Rosatom's icebreaker escort fleet and develop new nuclear-powered vessels to keep this path navigable all year-round. The resulting security and reliability of shipments will ensure the competitiveness of the Arctic route with traditional routes connecting European and Asian markets. The Northern Sea Route is two to three weeks faster than the traditional Suez route. In a world where a few weeks can make a difference between the success or failure of an enterprise, an ice-free Arctic shortcut could become a global energy game-changer. All the more so because the majority of goods shipped along the Northern Sea Route will be natural gas and oil destined for Asian markets, characterised by rapidly increasing energy consumption.

Even though the economic viability of the Northern Sea Route choice is questionable for international shipments (especially taking into account high insurance costs, the need for icebreaker escorts and some legal uncertainties) and it has not yet attracted crowds of ships, this navigating path has the potential to become an important part of the broader 'Polar Silk Road' concept launched by China.

4 In lieu of conclusion: Russian energy geopolitics—future challenges

Russian energy geopolitics results from a clash of two forces: internal politics and global conditions. Internal politics, motivated by the imperial aspirations of energy decision-makers,[37] translates into foreign energy relations, both in business and diplomacy. Global conditions—economic, technological and political—shape the world balance of energy resources supply and demand as well as directions of trade. The former—the Russian endogenous force—seeks to exert maximum influence and power on the latter, be it in a reactive or proactive way, to ensure Russia's energy security, understood as guaranteeing demand for Russian energy resources. However, due to the still evolving energy market conditions outlined in this chapter (growing competition, restructuring of trade patterns, climate priority, technological advancements, etc.) it could transpire that the huge resource base and its political use may not be enough for Russia to further extend an important degree of influence.

A number of challenges—economics vs geopolitics—loom high: inconsistency between Russia's geopolitical ambitions and the country's long-term structural economic weaknesses stemming from its relatively small economy.[38] Russia has a relatively small GDP as compared to the US. Based on a purchasing power parity basis the size of Russia's economy is about 20 per cent the size of the US economy while population wise it is 44 per cent that of

37 Stefan Bouzarovski and Mark Bassin, 'Energy and identity: Imagining Russia as a hydrocarbon superpower', [2011] *Annals of the Association of American Geographers*, Vol. 101, Issue 4 (Geographies of Energy), pp. 783–794.

38 National Bank of Canada (n 7).

the US.[39] Russia spends over 5 per cent of its GDP on defence as compared with just over 3 per cent in the US.[40] Finally, Russia's military budget is set at about $70 billion compared to the US $700 billion budget.

First of all, as energy markets undergo continued development, their vulnerability to geopolitical influence decreases. The multitude of actors (importers and exporters), the forces of trade liberalisation and globalisation, contract flexibility, technological progress and, at the other end of the market, the boom in renewable energy sources (RES), the development of distributed energy resources, the growing importance of prosumers—all these challenge the Russian diplomats involved in traditional energy-related geopolitical manoeuvres. However, energy geopolitics is not yet dead. It is being redefined and adapted to current challenges. As energy mixes, based until recently mainly on fossil fuels, are expected to undergo a radical change towards the predominance of renewable energy, new challenges can shape geopolitics, such as access to the critical materials needed for RES installations, rivalry for technology financing, a new wave of resource shortage in RES-intense countries, an increased cross-border electricity trade to name a few.[41] Also, more broadly, mitigation of climate change and a reduction in greenhouse gas emissions is not just a question of environment, but of 'earth governance', hence it is a question which has an increasing potential to shape geopolitics.[42] From this perspective, Russia's energy industry seems outdated and requires substantial modernisation targeted on an increase in energy efficiency as well as decarbonisation. Such a scenario would be relevant if Russia recognised the disastrous impact of climate change on the environment and humanity and was ready to undertake immediate action. However, Russia prefers a hands-off approach, with no meaningful internal climate change mitigation initiatives (despite the formulation of national climate change policies). Moreover, Russia perceives climate change as a domestic asset that will provide savings (e.g., lower expenses for heating), access to new resources (e.g., easier access for oil and gas drilling) or control over transport routes (e.g., Northern Sea Route). Ironically, the global climate change narrative (neglected domestically) is used by Russia in order to increase its presence on global markets. Russia's nuclear technology is sold as a green solution to climate change while natural gas has received a 'clean' label, since it is the cleanest of fossil fuels and constitutes, at least in Russia's main market—the EU—a transition fuel before this economy is able to switch to greener solutions (e.g., the use of hydrogen, which could also come from Russia). After all, Russia is a skilful geopolitical player, constantly striving to secure demand for its energy products.

Second, both in terms of maintaining current and reaching new market outlets (shaping high commodity prices while maintaining significant volumes of export) and gaining spheres of influence (through concluding energy-related agreements with new allies as well as territorial pioneering), Russia is yet to demonstrate an innovative and progressive approach to its energy industry. It has to be underpinned by a coherent energy policy and broader foreign policy strategies, followed by implemented and precisely executed policy guidelines and backed by substantial financing as is the case presently. Construction of Russia's current energy geopolitics is a result of the strong leadership of its president, Vladimir

39 Ibid.

40 Ibid.

41 Megan O'Sullivan, Indra Overland and David Sandalow, 'The geopolitics of renewable energy'. [2017] *HKS Working Paper* No. RWP17-027.

42 Shannon O'Lear and Simon Dalby, 'Towards ecological geopolitics: Climate change reframed' in Shannon O'Lear and Simon Dalby (eds) '*Reframing Climate Change. Constructing Ecological Geopolitics*' (Routledge, 2015).

Putin, who sets national priorities and imposes their implementation on relevant ministries and representatives of industry, over whom he exerts personal control. Hence, not without nuances and slight aberrations resulting from unexpected (or ignored, as in the case of shale boom) events, Russia's regime is perceived as one of the most predictable in the world. However, some trends, such as ageing Russian elites defining Russia's energy policy, with the president himself at the forefront, coupled with rising internal political opposition, highlight the question of the inevitability of political shifts within the country. While it is hard to predict their outcome and the future of Russia, there is no doubt that energy resources will remain one of the most precious of all Russia's assets. Extracted or remaining in deposits, withdrawn from the markets or used to flood them, due to their abundance Russian energy resources can be a global geopolitical tool of influence, capable of creating important short and mid-term shocks. Uncertainty over the future of Russia's internal politics and the use of its energy assets to adapt to or counter global changes together make the geopolitical lens the most appropriate tool to analyse Russia and its energy security.

PART IV

North America

14

SHALE GAS DEVELOPMENT, ECONOMIC IMPACTS AND REGULATION

Hannah J. Wiseman

1 Introduction

Shales, densely packed, are geologic formations with tiny pores and very limited connections between those pores—have long been known to contain natural gas and oil. But techniques for extracting the natural gas and oil from these low porosity, low permeability formations were slow to emerge. The U.S. government, in partnership with a private non-profit institute, funded applied research on unconventional gas extraction methods from the mid-1970s through 1992, and with some success; shale gas production approximately "quintupled" by the late 1990s.[1] But as Professor John Golden and I have noted, this was only the beginning of another significant development—one that built substantially from previous research and technological advances but was indeed a breakthrough of sorts.[2] George Mitchell and his firm Mitchell Energy directly partnered with the U.S. public-private research project in 1991, and by the late 1990s the firm found success in Texas's Barnett shale.[3] Mitchell Energy combined two techniques—horizontal drilling and a new form of hydraulic fracturing called "slickwater" fracturing—and achieved substantial production of gas from the shale.[4] Slickwater fracturing involved larger volumes of water and some different chemicals from those used in previous types of fracturing; horizontal drilling, in turn, exposed more of the shale, and fracturing in stages from different portions of a horizontal wellbore proved to be lucrative. Barnett shale production steadily increased as a result of this combined horizontal drilling-slickwater fracturing technique,[5] and by the mid-2000s, gas prices were sufficiently high, and other companies were sufficiently persuaded of the effectiveness of the technique,

1 John M. Golden & Hannah J. Wiseman, The fracking revolution: Shale Gas as a Case Study in Innovation Policy, vol 64 (*Emory L.J.*, 2015) 955, 983–989.

2 *Id.* at 960–962.

3 *Id.* at 962, n.20.

4 *Id.* at 960.

5 Railroad Comm'n of Tex., 'Texas Barnett Shale, Total Natural Gas Production 2000 through February 2018,' <www.rrc.state.tx.us/media/41507/barnettshale_totalnaturalgas_day.pdf> accessed 24 May 2019. Note that gas production began to fall after 2012. *Id.*

to venture out and apply it to other shales.[6] A nationwide boom in shale gas and oil production ensued. The United States became the world's leading producer of natural gas in 2009 and of petroleum hydrocarbons in 2013.[7]

This chapter focuses on the extraction of gas from shales, in part due to the major economic and environmental impacts of the shale gas boom on the electric power sector. But the massive expansion in production applies to oil, too, with producers in the United States now extracting large quantities of oil from formations such as North Dakota's Bakken shale and Texas's Wolfcamp shale.[8] Much of the attention has focused on shale gas rather than oil because shale gas was the leader of the "boom".

The chapter begins by introducing the market impacts of U.S. shale gas and continues with a discussion of the U.S. regulatory response to the natural gas boom, from the national to the local level. U.S. shale gas production has, in general, generated a domestic decline in both gas prices[9] and price volatility.[10] This has caused natural gas use to rise in the domestic utility sector.[11] The expansion in production has also generated rising U.S. exports of natural gas, both in gaseous form through pipelines to Mexico and Canada and in liquefied form (liquefied natural gas, or LNG) to other countries.[12] Exports to Asia, in particular, will be important because natural gas prices are relatively high there,[13] and countries like China have announced ambitious plans to transition from coal to natural gas.[14] The United States became a net exporter of natural gas in 2017.[15]

6 *See, e.g.*, Jennifer Cruz, Peter W. Smith, and Sara Stanley, U.S. Bureau of Labor Statistics, The Marcellus Shale gas boom in Pennsylvania: employment and wage trends, *Monthly Labor Review* (Feb. 2014), <https://www.bls.gov/opub/mlr/2014/article/the-marcellus-shale-gas-boom-in-pennsylvania.htm> accessed 24 May 2019 (noting growing employment in the U.S. oil and gas industry between 2007 and 2012, including in places such as Pennsylvania and North Dakota, where shale gas and oil development substantially increased during this period).

7 U.S. Energy Info. Admin., United States remains the world's top producer of petroleum and natural gas hydrocarbons (7 June 2017), <www.eia.gov/todayinenergy/detail.php?id=31532> accessed 24 May 2019.

8 Mohammed Izadi, Wolfcamp shale, vol 14 *Oil & Gas Financial Journal* (12 Jan. 2018), <www.ogfj.com/articles/print/volume-14/issue-12/features/wolfcamp-shale.html> accessed 14 Jan. 2019; U.S. Energy Info. Admin., Bakken Region Drilling Productivity Report (May 2018), <https://www.eia.gov/petroleum/drilling/pdf/bakken.pdf> accessed 24 May 2019.

9 U.S. Energy Info. Admin., Natural gas-fired capacity likely to increase over next two years (30 Jan. 2017), <www.eia.gov/todayinenergy/detail.php?id=29732> accessed 24 May 2019. ("Expanded production from shale formations is one of the main reasons that natural gas prices have remained low in recent years.")

10 Douglas J. Gotham et al., State Utility Forecasting Group, Natural Gas Market Study 1 (Nov. 2013), <www.in.gov/iurc/files/Natural_Gas_Market_Study.pdf> accessed 24 May 2019; State Utility Forecasting Group, Natural Gas Price Report Update 1 (Mar. 2017), <www.purdue.edu/discoverypark/sufg/docs/publications/Natural%20gas%20price%20update.pdf> accessed 24 May 2019.

11 U.S. Energy Info. Admin., Competition between coal and natural gas affects power markets (16 June 2017), <www.eia.gov/todayinenergy/detail.php?id=31672> accessed 24 May 2019.

12 U.S. Energy Info. Admin., 'Annual Energy Outlook 2018 with Projections to 2050' (Feb. 2018) 72–73, <https://www.eia.gov/outlooks/archive/aeo18/pdf/AEO2018.pdf> accessed 24 May 2019.

13 Price differentials are declining, however. In November 2019, landed prices at Cove Point in the United States were $4.31 per 1,000 cubic feet, as compared to $5.52 in Korea and China. The differential between the Lake Charles price ($2.55) and Asian markets was greater, however. Fed. Energy Reg. Comm'n, World LNG Estimated Landed Prices (Nov. 19) <https://www.ferc.gov/market-assessments/mkt-gas/overview/ngas-ovr-lng-wld-pr-est.pdf> accessed 12 Dec. 2019.

14 *See, e.g.*, Ma Xinghua, Natural gas and energy revolution: A case study of Sichuan-Chongqing gas province, *Natural Gas Industry* B 4 91, 92–94 (2017) (describing China's "Energy Revolution" and other policies such as "Instruction on Promoting Gas Utilization").

15 U.S. Energy Info. Admin., The U.S. exported more natural gas than it imported in 2017 (19 Mar. 2018), <www.eia.gov/todayinenergy/detail.php?id=35392> accessed 24 May 2019.

Projections of future natural gas production, consumption, prices, and associated market changes are in part dependent on regulation, and in the early years of the boom there were questions about the extent to which regulations might affect the cost and pace of production. In general, there has not been a widespread U.S. effort to stringently regulate shale gas production, although responses at the local and state level have varied, and a few states—most notably New York—have banned or placed moratoria on production,[16] as have many local governments (although many local bans have been preempted by states).[17] At the federal level, the most significant regulations pertain to the capture of methane from hydraulically fractured wells on private and public lands;[18] the Trump Administration has proposed to modify or withdraw several of those regulations.[19]

In summary, U.S. shale gas production has largely forged ahead since the initial boom, causing substantial changes in the domestic economy and having some international economic impacts as well. The international impacts are likely to expand as LNG exports grow, with two terminals currently operating and four LNG export terminals projected to be completed by 2021.[20] While regulations have changed, and in some cases grown alongside rising production, they have not appeared to dramatically impede growth. Indeed, there have been continued calls for more stringent environmental regulation from many members of the environmental community and from residents who live near the areas of highest production, among other stakeholders, while industry has argued that this regulation would stifle an important domestic industry.[21] Debate over the appropriate level of regulation is likely to continue.

16 N.Y. Dept. of Envtl. Conservation, Final Supplemental Generic Environmental Impact Statement on the Oil, Gas and Solution Mining Regulatory Program (29 June 2015), <www.dec.ny.gov/docs/materials_minerals_pdf/findingstatehvhf62015.pdf> accessed 24 May 2019.

17 *See infra* notes 90–96 and accompanying text.

18 Environmental Protection Agency, Oil and Natural Gas Sector: New Source Performance Standards and National Emission Standards for Hazardous Air Pollutants Reviews, 77 *Fed. Reg.* 49490 (16 Aug. 2012) (Final Rule), <www.gpo.gov/fdsys/pkg/FR-2012-08-16/pdf/2012-16806.pdf> accessed 24 May 2019; Oil and Natural Gas Sector: Emission Standards for New, Reconstructed, and Modified Sources, 81 *Fed. Reg.* 35824 (3 June 2016) (Final Rule), <www.gpo.gov/fdsys/pkg/FR-2016-06-03/pdf/2016-11971.pdf> accessed 24 May 2019; Bureau of Land Management, Interior, *Waste Prevention, Production Subject to Royalties, and Resource Conservation*, 81 *Fed. Reg.* 83008 (18 Nov. 2016) https://www.govinfo.gov/content/pkg/FR-2016-11-18/pdf/2016-27637.pdf accessed 20 December 2019.

19 Bureau of Land Management, Interior, Waste Prevention, Production Subject to Royalties, and Resource Conservation; Rescission or Revision of Certain Requirements, 83 *Fed. Reg.* 49184 (28 Sept. 2018) (Final Rule), <www.blm.gov/sites/blm.gov/files/Proposed%20Waste%20Prevention%20Rule%202.12.18.pdf> accessed 24 May 2019; Environmental Protection Agency, Oil and Natural Gas Sector: Emission Standards for New, Reconstructed, and Modified Sources: Stay of Certain Requirements, 82 *Fed. Reg.* 27645 (16 June 2017), <www.gpo.gov/fdsys/pkg/FR 2017-06-16/pdf/2017-12698.pdf> accessed 24 May 2019; Environmental Protection Agency, Oil and Natural Gas Sector: Emission Standards for New, Reconstructed, and Modified Sources Review,, 83 *Fed. Reg.* 50244 (24 Sept. 2019) (proposed rule) <https://www.govinfo.gov/content/pkg/FR-2019-09-24/pdf/2019-19876.pdf>accessed 12 Dec. 2019.

20 U.S. Energy Info. Admin., *supra* note 11, at 73; U.S. liquefied gas exports quadrupled in 2017 (27 Mar. 2018), <www.eia.gov/todayinenergy/detail.php?id=35512> accessed 24 May 2019.

21 For discussion of demands for more regulation, *see, e.g.*, 79 *Fed. Reg.* 28664, 28664, Hydraulic Fracturing Chemicals and Mixtures, Advanced Notice of Proposed Rulemaking, 19 May 2014 (noting "a petition from Earthjustice and 114 other groups . . . requesting that EPA issue . . . [Toxic Substances Control Act] . . . rules requiring toxicity testing of chemicals and mixtures used in oil and gas exploration and production" and proposing a limited rulemaking in response); Earthjustice, Petition to the United States Environmental Protection Agency, Petition for Listing and Rulemaking Under Section 112 of the Clean Air Act to Establish an Area Source Category for Oil and Gas Production Wells and Associated Equipment and to Set National Emission Standards for Hazardous Air Pollutant Emissions (13 May 2014), <https://earthjustice.org/sites/default/files/files/OilGasToxicWellsPetition51314.pdf> accessed 25 May 2019; Joseph De Avila, "Fracking"

2 Shale gas markets

Shale gas has worked profound changes in energy markets because natural gas prices have been notoriously volatile in recent decades. Domestically, it has caused gas prices to decline and has led to rising consumption of natural gas in the industrial and electricity sectors; consumption growth in these sectors is projected to continue through 2050.[22] Growing consumption of natural gas in the U.S. electricity sector, in particular, has generated attention due to its short-term environmental impacts (notably a decline in reliance on coal, and thus a short-term decline in carbon emissions)[23] and its economic impacts on the coal industry; several coal mining and coal utility companies have recently declared bankruptcy.[24]

Electric utility managers, who are responsible for continuously providing an adequate supply of electricity no matter the demand or seasonal conditions, must make long-term infrastructure and fuel commitments, and investing in natural gas plants was historically a risky proposition, at times. Although utilities can fuel switch (meaning they increase electricity production from a plant fueled by an alternative source if one source of fuel becomes more expensive or scarcer), certain plant retirements and other factors limit fuel switching abilities. Utilities were therefore sometimes hesitant to invest too heavily in natural gas. This has changed with the advent of shale gas development. Although natural gas prices are projected to rise, natural gas price volatility has declined since the production boom of 2009.[25] The low price of natural gas, combined with somewhat weaker concerns surrounding price volatility, has led to a surge in new gas plant construction as gas has outcompeted coal and nuclear options in many parts of the country. The Energy Information Administration reported in January 2017 that in the United States there had been a net reduction in "coal-fired generating capacity" for the preceding five year

goes local, *Wall St. J.* (28 Aug. 2012), <www.wsj.com/articles/SB10000872396390444327204577617793552508470> accessed 25 May 2019 (noting that as of 29 Aug. 2012, approximately 35 New York municipalities had banned hydraulic fracturing, and approximately 100 had issued moratoria on the practice, although other local governments, through citizen referenda and other initiatives, supported hydraulic fracturing). For industry objections to and reservations about expanded regulation, *see, e.g.*, 81 *Fed. Reg.* 35824, 35855, Oil and Natural Gas Sector: Emission Standards for New, Reconstructed, and Modified Sources (3 June 2016) (noting industry concerns about the lack of availability of reduced emissions completion (REC) equipment required by a federal rule mandating limits on methane emissions from hydraulically fractured oil and gas wells); Mark Green, American Petroleum Institute, Reducing Methane Emissions: Industry is on It (5 Apr. 2016), <www.api.org/news-policy-and-issues/blog/2016/04/05/reducing-methane-emissions-industry-is-o> accessed 25 May 2019 (noting industry arguments that the methane rule was "an unnecessary regulatory push that could lead to serious negative impacts").

22 U.S. Energy Info. Admin., U.S. natural gas production and consumption increase in nearly all AEO 2018 cases (16 Apr. 2018), <www.eia.gov/todayinenergy/detail.php?id=35792> accessed 24 May 2019.

23 U.S. Energy Info. Admin., U.S. energy-related CO2 emissions expected to rise slightly in 2018, remain flat in 2019 (8 Feb. 2018), <www.eia.gov/todayinenergy/detail.php?id=34872> accessed 24 May 2019 (reporting that "U.S. energy-related carbon dioxide (CO2) emissions declined by 861 million metric tons (14%) from 2005 to 2017" and that much of this decline was due to the fact that "more electricity has been generated from natural gas than from other fossil fuels").

24 Arathy S. Nair, Peabody Chapter 11 tops string of U.S. coal bankruptcies, Reuters, 15 Apr. 2016, <https://www.reuters.com/article/us-usa-coal-bankruptcy/peabody-chapter-11-tops-string-of-u-s-coal-bankruptcies-idUSKCN0XC2KQ>accessed 16 Dec. 2019; David Henry, FirstEnergy nuclear, coal plant units file for bankruptcy protection, Reuters, 1 Apr. 2018), <www.reuters.com/article/us-firstenergy-bankruptcy/firstenergy-nuclear-coal-plant-units-file-for-bankruptcy-protection-idUSKCN1H81GX> accessed 24 May 2019.

25 U.S. Energy Info. Admin., *supra* note 9.

period, accompanied by rising construction of new gas plants and conversion of coal plants to gas.[26] This was due to low gas prices—driven largely by shale gas production—and changes in environmental regulation.[27] In April 2015 natural gas "first exceeded coal as the most common electricity fuel,"[28] and, although losing to coal again in May 2015,[29] annually surpassed coal use in the power sector in 2015 and 2016.[30]

Internationally, U.S. shale gas production has had at least two important impacts. First, the application of horizontal drilling and slickwater fracturing to shales around the country has shown producers that these technologies might be relevant on an even broader geographic scale,[31] albeit with modifications. U.S. success cannot be transferred overnight, of course. In many cases producers in other countries must independently develop technologies, in part due to differences in physical conditions but also because they do not consistently have access to detailed information about U.S. technologies.[32] But production of shale gas in commercial quantities has already been achieved in China, Canada, and Argentina, and the U.S. Energy Information Administration projects that shale gas will comprise "30% of world natural gas production" by 2040.[33]

U.S. gas exports will also likely impact international markets as more LNG terminals become operational. According to some accounts, the current relatively small quantity of U.S. LNG exported is already changing gas contracts in Asia—making them shorter and allowing for more flexibility because importers know that they now have more options for purchasing gas.[34] And as U.S. exports grow—indeed, they quadrupled between 2016 and 2017,[35] and the United States was a net exporter of gas in 2017[36]—there will likely be an impact on global gas prices.

26 U.S. Energy Info. Admin., *supra* note 8.
27 *Id.*
28 U.S. Energy Info. Admin., *supra* note 11.
29 U.S. Energy Info. Admin., Electricity from natural gas surpasses coal for the first time, but just for one month (31 July 2015), <www.eia.gov/todayinenergy/detail.php?id=22312> accessed 24 May 2019.
30 U.S. Energy Info. Admin., *supra* note 11.
31 *See, e.g.*, Xinghua, *supra* note 14, at 92 ("The success of the United States has inspired the enthusiasm of other countries to explore and develop shale gas.").
32 Patent protections may play a role here, too. Although the slickwater fracturing technique itself is not patented, other patents of hydraulic fracturing technologies have increased. *See* John M. Golden & Hannah J. Wiseman, The fracking revolution: Shale gas as a case study in innovation policy, vol 64 (*Emory L.J.*, 2015) 955 (discussing the lack of patent protection for slickwater fracturing); Patent picks: Fracking technology vol 93 issue 4 *Chemical & Engineering News* (26 Jan. 2015) 37, <https://cen.acs.org/content/cen/articles/93/i4/Patent-Picks-Fracking-Technology.html> accessed 24 May 2019 (discussing the growth of other patents). Although Chinese companies invested billions of dollars in U.S. shale plays, they have not generally "negotiated for technology and license rights or the right to jointly operate fields." David Sandalow et al., Columbia Center on Global Energy Policy, 'Meeting China's Shale Gas Goals: Working Draft for Public Release, (Sept. 2014) 32, <https://energypolicy.columbia.edu/sites/default/files/China%20Shale%20Gas_WORKING%20DRAFT_Sept%2011_0.pdf> accessed 24 May 2019.
33 U.S. Energy Info. Admin., Shale gas production drives world natural gas production growth (15 Aug. 2016), <www.eia.gov/todayinenergy/detail.php?id=27512> accessed 24 May 2019.
34 Gaurav Sharma, U.S. LNG exporters reshaping global natural gas markets (7 Mar. 2018), <www.forbes.com/sites/gauravsharma/2018/03/07/u-s-shale-exporters-reshaping-global-natural-gas-markets/#7d3071e01089> accessed 24 May 2019.
35 U.S. Energy Info. Admin., *supra* note 15.
36 U.S. Energy Info. Admin., The U.S. exported more natural gas than it imported in 2017 (19 Mar. 2018), <www.eia.gov/todayinenergy/detail.php?id=35392> accessed 24 May 2019.

Furthermore, although oil prices have long been set largely by global forces due to the relative ease of transporting oil as compared to gas, gas prices have tended to be regional.[37] As LNG exports from the United States and other countries increase, experts predict that gas pricing "hubs" will develop in parts of Asia and elsewhere—physical or virtual locations where enough gas is traded and data is recorded such that prices can be carefully recorded and tracked—thus allowing for more reliance on competitive prices and spot markets and less on long-term contracts tied to the price of oil.[38]

The pace of U.S. shale gas exports is impacted by federal law, which applies to both the siting and construction of LNG export terminals and the actual export of gas. The Federal Energy Regulatory Commission (in consultation with states, which address state and local safety considerations) approves the siting and construction of onshore and near-short LNG export terminals,[39] and the Maritime Administration approves offshore deepwater port LNG export facilities.[40] The Department of Energy approves the export of LNG.[41] Exports to countries with which the United States has a free trade agreement (FTA)—specifically an agreement that requires national treatment for natural gas trade—receive quick approval because they are automatically deemed to be in the public interest.[42] The United States has these types of FTAs with approximately 18 countries, including, for example, Australia, Canada, Mexico, several Central and South American countries, and Korea and Singapore.[43] Exports to non-FTA countries receive more scrutiny and must be deemed by the Department of Energy (DOE) to be in the "public interest" before being approved; the DOE considers economic impacts (particularly on the domestic price of gas), international impacts, security of the natural gas supply, and environmental impacts.[44] As of April 2018 the DOE had approved nearly 30 applications for LNG export from the United States

37 U.S. Energy Info. Admin., Effect of increased natural gas exports on domestic energy markets (Jan. 2012), <www.eia.gov/analysis/requests/fe/pdf/fe_lng.pdf> accessed 24 May 2019 ("Global natural gas markets are not integrated and their nature could change substantially in response to significant changes in natural gas trading patterns.").

38 Mamdouh G. Salameh, U.S. LNG exports could prove a game changer in the global gas market (IAEE Energy Forum, 2016); U.S. Energy Info. Admin., Growing global liquefied natural gas trade could support market hub development in Asia (27 Mar. 2017), <www.eia.gov/todayinenergy/detail.php?id=30512> accessed 24 May 2019.

39 15 U.S.C. § 717b(e).

40 33 U.S.C. § 1503 (providing that the Secretary of Transportation shall be responsible for authorizing the construction of deepwater ports); 33 C.F.R. § 148.3 (noting that "[u]nder delegations from the Secretary of Homeland Security and the Secretary of Transportation, the Coast Guard and MARAD coordinate with each other in processing applications for the issuance, transfer, or amendment of a license for the construction and operation of a deepwater port").

41 15 U.S.C. § 717b (originally vesting the predecessor to the Federal Energy Regulatory Commission with the responsibility to approve exports); 42 U.S.C. § 7151 (transferring certain authority to the Department of Energy).

42 15 U.S.C. § 717b(b).

43 Office of Fossil Energy, How to obtain authorization to import and/or export natural gas and LNG, <www.energy.gov/fe/services/natural-gas-regulation/how-obtain-authorization-import-andor-export-natural-gas-and-lng> accessed 24 May 2019.

44 *See, e.g.*, Order Extending Authorization to Export Liquefied Natural Gas from Alaska, Phillips Alaska Natural Gas Corporation and Marathon Oil Company, DOE/FE Opinion and Order No. 1473 (2 Apr. 1999), <www.ferc.gov/industries/gas/indus-act/angtp/doe1473.pdf> accessed 24 May 2019; New Policy Guidelines and Delegation Orders from Secretary of Energy to Economic Regulatory Administration and Federal Energy Regulatory Commission Relating to the Regulation of Imported Natural Gas, 49 *Fed. Reg.* 6684 (1984).

(excluding Hawaii and Alaska) to non-FTA countries.[45] As noted above, two natural gas export terminals were operating in the United States as of May 2018—Sabine Pass in Louisiana and Cove Point in Maryland[46]—and four others are under construction in Texas, Georgia, and Louisiana.[47]

One of the central concerns surrounding the expansion of gas exports is the possibility that domestic gas prices will rise. The DOE has commissioned four studies to address this concern and other uncertainties associated with the impacts of various levels of LNG exports. Two reports prepared by the U.S. Energy Information Administration concluded that higher levels of gas export would indeed lead to higher domestic gas prices while driving "higher levels of economic output."[48] The third report noted that the economic benefits of expanding gas exports would outweigh the costs of higher domestic gas prices.[49] The fourth study, completed in 2018 and commissioned as part of the DOE's consideration of granting broader-scale approval of gas exports to non-FTA countries, examined the impacts of exporting LNG if the market were the sole determinant of whether or not exports could occur ("unconstrained LNG exports").[50] The report notes that of the gas exports to non-FTA countries that the DOE had approved as of October 2017, there is a 63 per cent chance that this level of exports will be reached by 2040; it will take strong domestic production and favorable markets for this level to be reached. Of the exports for which producers have *applied*, as opposed to have received approval for, there is only a 2 per cent chance that this volume of export could be achieved by 2040.[51] It therefore appears that the current "public interest" export restraint—the approval that exporters must receive before moving forward with an export project—is not substantially limiting export opportunities. The report notes that the direct effects of any level of U.S. LNG exports include "increases in natural gas production, LNG export revenues, wealth transfers in the form of tolling charges on LNG exports, and domestic natural gas price," and that higher LNG demand puts "upward pressure" on domestic natural gas prices.[52] But the report concludes that higher levels of export "lead to larger improvements in welfare."[53]

45 U.S. Dept. of Energy, Long term applications received by DOE/FE to export domestically produced LNG from the Lower 48 States (as of 9 Apr. 2018), <www.energy.gov/sites/prod/files/2018/04/f50/Summary%20of%20LNG%20Export%20Applications_0.pdf> accessed 24 May 2019.

46 Fed. Energy Reg. Comm'n, North American LNG Import/Export Terminals *Existing* (as of October 23, 2018), <www.ferc.gov/industries/gas/indus-act/lng/lng-existing.pdf> accessed 24 May 2019. Kenai, Alaska is also an export terminal but is not usually included within the statistics that describe operating terminals.

47 Fed. Energy Reg. Comm'n, North American LNG Import/Export Terminals *Approved* (23 Apr. 2018) <www.ferc.gov/industries/gas/indus-act/lng/lng-approved.pdf> accessed 24 May 2019.

48 U.S. Energy Info. Admin., Effect of Increased Natural Gas Exports on Domestic Energy Markets (Jan. 2012), <http://energy.gov/sites/prod/files/2013/04/f0/fe_eia_lng.pdf> accessed 24 May 2019; U.S. Energy Info. Admin., Effect of Increased Levels of Liquefied Natural Gas Exports on U.S. Energy Markets 12 (Oct. 2014), <https://www.eia.gov/analysis/requests/fe/pdf/lng.pdf> accessed 24 May 2019, 12.

49 NERA Economic Consulting, Macroeconomic Impacts of LNG Exports from the United States 1 (December 2012), <http://energy.gov/sites/prod/files/2013/04/f0/nera_lng_report.pdf> accessed 24 May 2019.

50 NERA Economic Consulting, Macroeconomic Outcomes of Market Determined Levels of U.S. LNG Exports 12 (7 June 2018), <www.energy.gov/sites/prod/files/2018/06/f52/Macroeconomic%20LNG%20Export%20Study%202018.pdf> accessed 24 May 2019.

51 *Id.* at 49.

52 *Id.* at 64.

53 *Id.* at 66.

To summarize, the effect of U.S. gas on international markets will ultimately depend on a wide range of factors, with a central uncertainty being the extent to which high production levels remain steady and improved extraction technologies continue to emerge.[54]

3 Regulation of shale gas development

Just as the regulation of gas export has affected the pace at which U.S. shale gas has become available globally—and thus the pace at which international economic impacts will occur—domestic regulation affects overall levels of production. As noted above, for the most part the relevant governmental authorities did not respond to the shale gas boom with dramatic regulatory changes, although some, particularly local (municipal and other local governments), did. This section introduces the relevant U.S. regulatory actors, their role in regulating the environmental and social impacts of shale gas development, and the some of the specific regulatory changes implemented by these governments after the shale boom.

The division of governance authority over U.S. shale gas development is complex. The 50 U.S. states have the most important and extensive authority, but local governments (including incorporated municipalities as well as towns, counties, and other local governments), regional governments (groups of states who are permitted by the federal Congress to regulate certain regional resources, such as rivers), and the federal government also play an important role.

3.1 Federal regulation

At the federal level, the Endangered Species Act,[55] Bald and Golden Eagle Protection Act,[56] and Migratory Bird Treaty Act[57] impact the location of gas well sites in addition to well operations. All of these acts prohibit the "taking" of protected species,[58] and "take" has in some cases (particularly under the Endangered Species Act) been broadly defined to include acts that are not targeted at the species but still harm it, such as habitat modification.[59] So when oil and gas companies are siting a potential shale gas well they typically have to avoid the habitat of endangered or threatened species altogether or, more commonly, work with the federal Fish and Wildlife Service to obtain an "incidental take permit" under the Endangered Species Act. This permit allows for limited impacts on threatened or endangered species but specifies the steps that the oil and gas operator must follow to avoid undue harm to those species. Further, well operators must be aware of the potential impacts on threatened and endangered species off-site, such as erosion from well sites that can negatively impact the habitat of fish in nearby streams. For example, soon after the shale gas boom hit the Mid-Atlantic United States (particularly Pennsylvania and, to a somewhat lesser extent, West Virginia), the U.S. Fish and Wildlife Service listed the diamond darter of West Virginia as endangered and later designated critical habitat for the fish.[60] This critically endangered

54 *Id.* at 25.
55 16 U.S.C. ch. 35.
56 16 U.S.C. §§ 668–668d.
57 16 U.S.C. §§ 703–712.
58 16 U.S.C. § 1538 (a); 16 U.S.C. § 668a; 16 U.S.C. § 703.
59 *Babbitt v. Sweet Home Chapter of Communities for a Great Oregon*, 515 U.S. 687 (1995).
60 Department of the Interior, Endangered and Threatened Wildlife and Plants; Designation of Critical Habitat for the Diamond Darter (*Crystallaria cincotta*), 78 *Fed. Reg.* 52364, 2013 (22 Aug. 2013) (Final Rule), <www.govinfo.gov/content/pkg/FR-2013-08-22/pdf/2013-20449.pdf> accessed 25 May 2019.

fish—of which only "19 individuals have been collected in the last 30 years"—lives in "clean sand, gravel, and cobble runs of small to medium rivers" and can be negatively impacted by soil and other runoff from oil and gas operations.[61]

Operators also sometimes must modify the location or timing of operations in order to avoid disturbing active eagle nests so that they comply with the Bald and Golden Eagle Protection Act (BGEPA).[62] Another concern that applies specifically to migratory birds is the maintenance of surface impoundments or "pits" at oil and gas sites. Operators commonly store large quantities of wastewater, including the natural saline "produced" water that comes out of wells along with oil and gas and the flowback that comes out of the well after fracturing, in lined pits on the surface of the site. Migratory birds often mistake these pits for welcoming water bodies and are injured or die in the pits when they land in them.[63] The Migratory Bird Treaty Act (MBTA) is a strict liability statute, meaning that oil and gas operators or other entities need not intend to harm a bird in order to be criminally liable for harm that occurs. Thus, U.S. Fish and Wildlife Service officers deemed oil and gas companies to be criminally liable under the MBTA when dead ducks and other birds were found in pits at well sites—for example, sites in Bakken shale of North Dakota, which is along a major migratory route for birds.[64] However, a federal district court in North Dakota interpreted the MBTA differently, finding that an oil and gas operator's activities had to be directed at birds in order for the operator to be liable.[65] A federal circuit court reached a similar finding with respect to birds that flew into open tanks at oil refineries.[66] The issue of whether the MBTA is truly a strict liability statute has not yet been taken up by the U.S. Supreme Court.

Another prominent statute that impacts U.S. gas drilling and fracturing is the Clean Air Act. Administrative agencies acting under President Obama issued three regulations under the Act that limited the amount of volatile organic compounds and methane that could be released from hydraulically fractured wells on both public and private lands.[67] After fracturing, when fracturing fluid flows back out of the well as flowback, gas and other volatile organic compounds also flow out of the well and were, traditionally, either flared (burned) or vented (released into the air). The crux of these regulations was to require the separation of gas and other substances that volatilized from the flowback and to require that operators

61 *Crystallaria cincotta*, IUCN Red List of Threatened Species, <www.iucnredlist.org/details/202435/0> accessed 25 May 2019.

62 *See, e.g.*, U.S. Fish & Wildlife Serv., National Bald Eagle Management Guidelines 12 (May 2007) (for BGEPA compliance purposes, recommending that oil and gas activities be conducted at least 660 feet from a nest if the "activity will be visible from the nest"), <www.fws.gov/southdakotafieldoffice/NationalBaldEagleManagementGuidelines.pdf> accessed 25 May 2019.

63 *See, e.g.*, *United States v. Brigham Oil and Gas, K.P.*, 840 F. Supp. 2d 1202, 1204–1207 (United States District Court, North Dakota 2012) (noting bird deaths in pits).

64 *Id.* at 1204–1207

65 *Id.* at 1213–1214.

66 *United States v. Citgo Petroleum Corp.*, 801 F.3d 488, 492–494 (United States Court of Appeals, Fifth Circuit 2015).

67 Waste Prevention, Production Subject to Royalties, and Resource Conservation, 81 *Fed. Reg.* 83008 (18 Nov. 2016) (Final Rule) (codified at 43 C.F.R. pts. 3100, 3160, 3170) (applies to wells drilled and fractured on federal lands); Oil and Natural Gas Sector: Emission Standards for New, Reconstructed, and Modified Sources, 81 *Fed. Reg.* 35824 (3 June 2016) (Final Rule) (covers emissions of methane and volatile organic compounds and applies to all newly-fractured and refractured wells as of a specific date on private lands); Oil and Natural Gas Sector: Reconsideration of Additional Provisions for New Source Performance Standards, 79 *Fed. Reg.* 79018 (31 Dec. 2014) (Final Rule) (covers emissions of volatile organic compounds and applies to all newly-fractured wells as of a specific date on private lands).

send the gas through gathering lines or use it onsite, such as in a natural gas generator. The Department of the Interior has proposed to eliminate these gas capture requirements for wells drilled and fractured on public lands.[68]

The Environmental Protection Agency (EPA) under the Obama administration also finalized a rule under the federal Clean Water Act that prohibited well operators from sending wastewater from hydraulically fractured wells to publicly owned treatment works (POTWs)—facilities that accept sewage and other waste from homes, businesses, and industry; treat the waste; and then release it, sometimes directly into a freshwater source.[69] Wastewater from these wells includes produced water and flowback. The EPA proposed and finalized this rule after concluding that POTWs in states such as Pennsylvania were potentially inadequately treating the waste and emitting waste with radiation levels that exceeded regulatory limits, as well as other wastes such as "organic chemicals, metals and total dissolved solids."[70] Wastewater from shale gas wells and conventional wells contains natural radiation and salts picked up from the rocks in which it sits underground.

In most states, operators of shale gas wells were already sending produced water and flowback to an alternative disposal site—the "underground injection control" (UIC) well—before the EPA prohibited disposal through publicly owned treatment works. UIC wells are wells drilled underground to accept and permanently store liquid wastes. Under the federal Safe Drinking Water Act, the EPA regulates these wells to prevent their endangerment of underground sources of drinking water, primarily through requirements for cementing adequate casing (steel lining) into the wells, among other regulations.[71] In most states, the EPA has delegated its regulatory and permitting authority over UIC wells, including "Class II" UIC wells, which accept oil and gas wastes, to state environmental agencies.[72] The operators of Class II UIC wells that accept the bulk of liquid wastes from fractured gas wells must therefore comply with federal requirements to minimize the likelihood of waste leakage from these wells into underground water sources, and the federal requirements are administered through state regulations and permits.

However, one aspect of UIC wells is not federally regulated: the fact that UIC wells drilled and operated in certain locations cause earthquakes, also called "induced seismicity."[73] The pressure from large volumes of water injected underground can cause natural faults to "slip," thus triggering an earthquake. These earthquakes are typically minor, but some—particularly in states such as Oklahoma—have been substantial.[74] Congress has not

68 Waste Prevention, Production Subject to Royalties, and Resources Conservation; Rescission or Revisions of Certain Requirements, 83 *Fed. Reg.* 7924, 7929–7930 (22 Feb. 2018) (Proposed Rule).

69 Effluent Limitations Guidelines and Standards for the Oil and Gas Extraction Point Source Category, 81 *Fed. Reg.* 41845, 41853 (28 June 2016) (Final Rule); Effluent Limitations Guidelines and Standards for the Oil and Gas Extraction Point Source Category—Implementation Date Extension, 81 *Fed. Reg.* 88126, 88126 (7 Dec. 2016) (Final Rule) (proposing to extend the compliance date to 2019 for existing wastewater sources that were already discharging to treatment works between 2015 and 2016).

70 Letter from Shawn M. Garvin (Regional Administrator, U.S. Envtl. Protection Agency, Region III) to Michael Krancer (Acting Secretary, Penn. Dept. of Envtl. Protection) (7 Mar. 2011), <www.epa.gov/sites/production/files/2015-06/documents/pdep_march_7.pdf> accessed 25 May 2019.

71 42 U.S.C. §§ 300h–300h-5.

72 U.S. Envtl. Protection Agency, Primary Enforcement Authority for the Underground Injection Control Program, <www.epa.gov/uic/primary-enforcement-authority-underground-injection-control-program> accessed 25 May 2019.

73 *See, e.g.*, Katie M. Keranen et al., Potentially induced earthquakes in Oklahoma, USA: Links between wastewater injection and the 2011 Mw 5.7 earthquake sequence, 45 *Geology* 699 (26 Mar. 2013).

74 *Id.*

modified the Safe Drinking Water Act to address the risk of earthquakes; nor has the EPA changed its regulation under the Act to address earthquakes. However, some states that administer federal UIC programs have elected to regulate induced seismicity from UIC wells that accept oil and gas wastes. These regulations typically require entities applying to drill a UIC well to map the faults around the well or otherwise demonstrate the extent to which there is a risk that earthquakes could occur due to naturally-occurring faults or earthquake histories in the area.[75] Some state regulations also require continuous monitoring of pressures in the UIC well and well shut-down if certain pressures are exceeded.[76]

One might think that because the injection of liquid wastes underground is regulated under the Safe Drinking Water Act (with the exception of earthquakes caused by this injection), the injection of fracturing fluids to hydraulically fracture a well would be similarly regulated. Indeed, one federal court found this to be the case. For the Alabama UIC well program, a federal court determined that the state was wrong to treat hydraulically fractured wells as falling under an alternative part of the UIC regulations. Instead, the court determined, hydraulic fracturing should be covered by the Class II program that applies to oil and gas waste disposal.[77] Congress responded in 2005, directly exempting hydraulic fracturing, with the exception of fracturing that uses diesel fuel, from the definition of "injection" in the Safe Drinking Water Act.[78] Therefore, before hydraulically fracturing a well, operators need not first obtain a Safe Drinking Water Act permit that ensures that the well will avoid endangering underground sources of drinking water. States, however, regulate the casing of fractured wells to varying degrees, thus helping to prevent this type of endangerment. Rare cases of underground water contamination from fractured wells have still occurred.[79]

Another large exemption from federal law that is important for hydraulically fractured wells is the exemption of many oil and gas "exploration and production" (E&P) wastes from the hazardous waste portion of the Resource Conservation and Recovery Act (RCRA). RCRA applies to on-land generation, storage, transportation, and disposal of wastes. Most E&P wastes from fractured gas wells—even wastes that have hazardous or toxic characteristics—are exempt from the hazardous waste portion of the act, meaning that well operators do not have to follow heightened restrictions when storing the wastes on site, use a special trucking system to transport these wastes, or send the wastes to a specialized, more heavily-regulated disposal facility.[80] This is in part why operators may store substances like produced water and flowback in open pits on oil and gas sites.

Despite these exemptions, a final federal law applies to retroactively address some pollution of soil, surface water, and groundwater from hydraulic fracturing, waste storage and handling, or other practices at shale gas sites. The Comprehensive Environmental Response, Compensation, and Liability Act holds operators liable for contamination of a site with hazardous substances like fracturing fluids; they must clean up the contamination or pay for the

75 Ohio Admin. Code § 1501: 9-3-06; Okla. Admin. Code § 165: 10-5-7; 16 Tex. Admin. Code § 3.9.

76 Ohio Admin. Code § 1501: 9-3-07

77 *Legal Envtl. Assistance Found. v. U.S. Envtl. Protection Agency*, 275 F.2d 1253, 1264 (United States Court of Appeals, Eleventh Circuit 2001).

78 Energy Policy Act of 2005, Public Law 109-58, § 322 (8 Aug. 2005).

79 U.S. Envtl. Protection Agency, Hydraulic Fracturing for Oil and Gas: Impacts from the Hydraulic Fracturing Water Cycle on Drinking Water Resources in the United States 6–21 (Dec. 2016).

80 Exemption of Oil and Gas Exploration and Production Wastes from Federal Hazardous Waste Regulations 9–11 (2002), <https://archive.epa.gov/epawaste/nonhaz/industrial/special/web/pdf/oil-gas.pdf> accessed 25 May 2019 (showing that the exemption applies to "[w]ell completion, treatment, and stimulation fluids" as well as "produced water" and other wastes).

clean-up. The Act exempts pollution of sites from oil or gas[81] but does not exempt substances such as flowback or produced water.

As shown by the variety of federal statutes that apply to shale gas development (not all of which are discussed here), federal regulation applies to some aspects of this development. However, the bulk of regulation of shale gas development occurs at the state level, as discussed in the following section.

3.2 State regulation

The 50 U.S. states have historically been primarily responsible for regulating oil and gas development. States originally focused on ensuring that when oil and gas wells were drilled, the maximum amount of oil and gas would be produced from the ground. These anti-"waste" regulations were not environmental in nature but were rather aimed at preventing the waste of oil and gas—in other words, preventing the drilling of a well that failed to fully extract all of the available oil and gas underground. However, State regulations began to be more environmentally-focused. Today, some states have detailed environmental regulations that address the impacts of oil and gas development, including shale gas development. A comprehensive survey of state regulations would require a full book, or more, but this section describes the types of environmental impacts from shale gas development that state laws focus on.

One way of controlling a variety of impacts from shale gas development is to require that well sites, or the well itself, be located a minimum distance from important natural or human resources, such as water wells. Therefore, many states have setback requirements for wells or well sites, and some have updated these requirements for shale gas and oil wells, specifically. For example, Pennsylvania prohibits unconventional wells from being drilled within 500 feet of a building or private water well, 1,000 feet of a public water supply, and 300 feet of wetlands or streams, and the "edge of the disturbed area associated with any unconventional well site must maintain a 100-foot setback" from streams.[82]

Another important substantive regulation that states place on oil and gas wells to prevent underground water contamination is the casing regulation. This comprises of a suite of rules that require the lining of wells to be of a minimum strength, be cemented into the ground using certain techniques, and, typically, to be placed below, through, and above underground sources of drinking water, thus helping to ensure that oil, gas, and wastes flowing through the well do not enter groundwater. States such as Texas updated casing regulations when more shale gas and oil wells began to be fractured, acknowledging that fracturing can place additional pressure on the casing and can cause it to fail. Among other provisions, the state requires that casing be able to withstand "1.10 times the maximum pressure to which the casing string will be subjected", that well operators pressure test the casing before fracturing occurs, and that operators monitor the spaces between different layers of casing during fracturing to determine whether pressure is building up in this space.[83] A pressure build-up outside of the casing suggests that the casing might be at risk of being compromised.

81 42 U.S.C. § 101(14).

82 58 Penn. Statutes and Consolidated States § 3215.

83 Railroad Commn. of Tex., Summary of Amendments to Statewide Rule 13, <www.rrc.state.tx.us/oil-gas/compliance-enforcement/rule-13-geologic-formation-info/summary-of-amendments-to-swr-13> accessed 25 May 2019; 16 Tex. Admin. Code § 3.13(a)(7).

As a complement to casing regulations, many states also have requirements for operator use of blowout prevention technologies. A well blowout, which can occur onshore or offshore, is when a well "explodes," either underground or aboveground, as a result of uncontrolled pressure build-up. The Deepwater Horizon oil spill in 2010 off the U.S. Gulf Coast was caused by a well blowout.[84] Many states require operators to install specific types of blowout preventers and to periodically test them to ensure that they are working.[85]

Another means by which states address concerns about groundwater is to require that well operators test the quality of groundwater before they begin drilling or fracturing a well. This allows state regulators, litigants, and other parties to better determine whether drilling or fracturing might have caused contamination of water or whether the contamination predated drilling and fracturing. For example, Michigan requires well operators to complete a "hydrogeological investigation" before drilling, including water quality sampling, "a determination of the direction of groundwater flow and depth to the groundwater in the uppermost aquifer," and a specific chemical analyses for benzene, ethylbenzene, toluene, and xylene, among other factors.[86] Operators must also install and maintain at least one groundwater monitoring well below all storage areas for produced water and hydrocarbons.[87] Many of the states with the largest volumes of oil and gas produced from unconventional wells also require well operators to disclose the chemicals and water volumes used in hydraulic fracturing, although in most of these states operators may avoid disclosing specific chemicals by asserting that they are a trade secret.[88]

Some states have done more than others to update their regulations in the midst of booming shale gas and oil development, and regulations among the states still vary considerably. For example, Pennsylvania substantially revised requirements relating to well casing, setbacks of well sites, presumptions of liability for groundwater contamination and other rules specific to hydraulically fractured wells.[89] Texas, on the other hand, primarily focused on changing only its casing requirements for these wells.[90] However, as shown by this brief discussion, several states have taken meaningful steps to adjust requirements based on changing technologies and practices.

3.3 *Local regulation*

Some of the most important but overlooked regulation of shale gas development occurs at the local government level, where both municipalities (towns, townships, cities, and the like)

84 The Bureau of Ocean Energy Management, Regulation and Enforcement, Report Regarding the Causes of the April 20, 2010 Macondo Well Blowout (14 Sept. 2011), <www.bsee.gov/sites/bsee.gov/files/reports/blowout-prevention/dwhfinaldoi-volumeii.pdf> accessed 25 May 2019.

85 *See, e.g.*, 2 Colo. Code Regs. § 404-1:317; La. Admin. Code tit. 43:XIX, § 111; Okla. Admin. Code §§ 78.72, 78.84.

86 Mich. Admin. Code R. § 324.1002 (3)(a).

87 *Id.*

88 Keith B. Hall, Hydraulic fracturing, Trade secrets and the mandatory disclosure of fracturing water composition, 49 *Idaho L. Rev.* 399 (2013).

89 *See, e.g.*, Hannah J. Wiseman, Risk and response in fracturing policy, 84 *U. Colo. L. Rev.* 729, 779 notes 299, 326–327 (2013) (describing changes in Pennsylvania). For an assessment of states' regulations and their stringency, see Nathan Richardson et al., Resources for the Future, The State of State Shale Gas Regulation (2013), <www.rff.org/documents/524/RFF-Rpt-StateofStateRegs_Report.pdf> accessed 25 May 2019.

90 *See supra* note 83 and accompanying text.

and counties have surprisingly detailed requirements for drilling and hydraulic fracturing. Local governments control these practices using a variety of tools.

One of the most common controls is the zoning regulation, in which local governments divide up their territory into different zoning districts, such as residential, industrial, commercial, and agricultural districts and specify the districts in which certain types of land uses are or are not allowed. Oil and gas drilling is often listed as a "conditional use" only in specific districts, meaning that the local government anticipates that the use will be allowed within certain parts of the districts but must approve it on a case-by-case, property-by-property basis. In some cases, oil and gas development is a conditional use within an overlay district, which means that an oil and gas operator must first obtain legislative approval from the local government to place a new oil and gas zoning district on top of an underlying district (such as an agricultural district) and obtain approval for drilling an oil and gas well on a particular property within that district.[91]

Other common local rules beyond zoning regulations include local permitting of oil and gas drilling, requirements that oil and gas operators have environmental liability and other forms of insurance that will cover a specific amount of damage, requirements for the posting of bonds in the event that drilling and fracturing cause damages that are not addressed by the oil and gas operator, restrictions on the level of noise permitted near a well site, requirements for landscaping around sites or fencing them in, requirements for 24-hour security or night watchmen to remain at the site, and general prohibitions on pollution, among other provisions.[92]

Although cities like Fort Worth, Texas, which host numerous fractured gas wells, have detailed regulations that address drilling and fracturing,[93] many states have preempted local control. This has occurred through two main avenues. First, in states such as Ohio,[94] Louisiana,[95] New Mexico,[96] and West Virginia,[97] courts have found that existing preemptive statutory language prohibits some or all local control over oil and gas operations. Second, in states such as Oklahoma,[98] Pennsylvania,[99] and Texas,[100] state legislatures have enacted new legislation that preempts most local control. In Pennsylvania, the state supreme court deemed this preemptive language to violate the state constitution,[101] but relatively broad preemption in Oklahoma and Texas, enacted in 2015, remains in place. One issue that remains unresolved in some state courts is whether local governments may use their land use powers, as opposed to other types of regulatory powers, to regulate or even ban hydraulic fracturing. In New York, the highest court has determined that a local ban on fracturing pursuant to a government's land use authority is not preempted by state law.[102] Another remaining question is

91 *See, e.g.*, Cecil Twp., Pa., Ordinance No. 09-2011 § 3 (2011).

92 *See* Hannah J. Wiseman, Governing fracking from the ground up, 93 *Tex. L. Rev. See* also 29, 39–40 (2015).

93 Fort Worth, Tex., Ordinance No. 18449-02-2009 (3 Feb. 2009), <https://perma.cc/4HKN-X7YK> accessed 25 May 2019.

94 *State ex rel. Morrison v. Beck Energy Corp.*, 143 Ohio St.3d 271, 280 (2015).

95 *Energy Mgmt. Corp. v. City of Shreveport*, 397 F.3d 297, 306 (5th Cir. 2005).

96 *Swepi v. Mora Cty.*, 81 F. Supp. 3d 1075, 1203 (D.N.M. 2015).

97 *Ne. Nat. Energy, LLC v. The City of Morgantown*, No. 11-C-411, 2011 WL 3584376 (W. Va. Cir. Ct. Aug. 12, 2011).

98 Okla. Stat. tit. 52, § 52137.1 (2015).

99 58 Pa. Cons. Stat. § 3304.

100 Tex. H.B. No. 40, 2015 Tex. Gen. Laws c. 30.

101 *Robinson Twp. v. Commonwealth*, 623 Pa. 564, 701 (Pa. 2013).

102 *Wallach v. Town of Dryden*, 16 N.E.3d 1188, 1203 (N.Y. 2014).

the extent to which local governments may regulate, ban, or place long-term moratoria, on hydraulic fracturing. The Colorado Supreme Court has determined that bans and long-term moratoria are preempted but has not yet ruled on the regulatory issue.[103]

One additional yet important type of government that regulates U.S. shale gas development exists at the regional (multi-state) scale. For example, the Susquehanna River Basin Regulation regulates withdrawals of water for fracturing, mandating that these withdrawals not cause streams to drop below a minimum flow level and placing other limits on withdrawals.[104]

4 Conclusions

In summary, the U.S. landscape of shale gas regulation involves a complex layering of governmental authority and, due to the primary reliance on state regulation, varies geographically. Under the Obama Administration, the federal government updated some water and air quality regulations to address the boom in development. The Trump Administration has proposed to delay compliance dates for some of these rules or to withdraw them entirely, although these efforts have not been consistently successful.[105] States have focused on a range of regulatory issues, with some changing almost none of their oil and gas regulations and others completing a relatively comprehensive revision of rules. Local governments have also shown a spectrum of responses. Some have banned hydraulic fracturing, others have allowed it but regulated it relatively comprehensively, and still others have welcomed oil and gas development and placed few restrictions on it.

103 *City of Longmont v. Colo. Oil & Gas Assn.*, 369 P.3d 573, 585 (Colo. 2016); *City of Fort Collins v. Colorado Oil and Gas Association*, 369 P.3d 586, 594 (Colo. 2016).

104 James L. Richenderfer et al., Water Use Associated with Natural Gas Shale Development: An Assessment of Activities Managed by the Susquehanna River Basin Commission July 2008 through December 2013 (Apr. 2016), <www.srbc.net/our-work/reports-library/technical-reports/299-natural-gas-water-use-susquehanna/docs/water-use-natural-gas-report.pdf> accessed 25 May 2019.

105 *See, e.g., Clean Air Council v. Pruitt*, 8620 F.3d 1, 14 (D.C. Cir. 2017) (rejecting a Trump Administration proposal to stay a rule that limits emissions from hydraulically fractured oil and gas wells).

15

REGULATION OF NATURAL GAS PIPELINE CONSTRUCTION AND OPERATION IN THE UNITED STATES

Kim Talus

1 Introduction

Between a natural gas field and the consumer of the natural gas there is an important and often less discussed link: the pipeline. These pipelines connect upstream with downstream markets, the seller and the buyer of natural gas, and the producer and the consumer. Without this transportation link between the two, trade cannot be concluded, and natural gas has little value. In fact, and as discussed below, without this link, natural gas can become a problem.

In the early days of the oil and gas industry in the United States (US), gas was mainly consumed locally, only with the progress in the steel industry that made the construction of long-distance, high-pressure steel pipeline structures possible, could the markets start to expand.[1] Today, the natural gas pipeline network in the US is dense and natural gas is transported via a highly sophisticated pipeline system involving around 500 000 km of interstate and intrastate transmission pipelines and over 11 000 delivery points.[2]

Even with this extensive pipeline network, the problem of missing pipelines is very apparent in the US. Rapidly changing markets have created shortages in the transmission capacities: in 2017 alone, natural gas production from the Permian Basin of West Texas rose 26.4 percent, averaging almost 5 billion cubic feet per day (Bcfd).[3] The existing pipeline capacities have not been able to accommodate this surge in shale-based production. As a result, the Texas Railroad Commission, the agency competent to regulate the oil and natural gas industry and pipeline transporters in Texas, has been forced to allow flaring of significant volumes of natural gas.[4] The Permian Basin is not alone in this problem. Many other shale-based production areas in the US are facing similar issues. Nor is this a local state-level question, interstate pipelines need to be put in place to serve both existing consumption centers in the US as well as new LNG export facilities.

1 D Yergin, *The Prize: The Epic Quest for Oil, Money, and Power* (Free Press 2008) p. 64 and 72–73, for example.

2 For an overview of US natural gas markets and infrastructure, see <https://www.eia.gov/energyexplained/index.php?page=natural_gas_pipelines> accessed April 2, 2019.

3 <https://www.ferc.gov/market-oversight/reports-analyses/st-mkt-ovr/2017-som-A-3-full.pdf?csrt=7101744648658170122>.

4 See for example, 'In America's Hottest Drilling Spot, Gas Is Going Up in Smoke: With Consent from Texas Regulators, Producers Flare Freely in Permian Basin', *The Wall Street Journal,* August 29, 2018.

In this situation, the construction of new pipeline capacities as well as optimal utilization of existing capacities is imperative. Approximately 1 250 km of new natural gas pipeline capacity under the Federal Energy Regulatory Commission (FERC) jurisdiction went into service in 2017. Approximately 4 400 km of new pipelines where certified over the same year, with new pipelines connecting shale areas like Marcellus and Utica – shale-based fields to markets in the Northeast and Midwest. Similarly, new pipelines move natural gas towards the Gulf Coast and its existing and planned LNG export facilities.[5]

Pipelines can also be controversial. The Keystone XL pipeline is a good example of this. The rationale for this pipeline is to transport crude oil from Alberta to the US. In addition to being a commercial project, it is a project that has become highly political. The pipeline construction was blocked for climate impact reasons (the oil would originate from Alberta oil sands) by the Obama administration. The new Trump administration overturned this decision within days of taking office and opened up the licensing and permitting for the pipeline.[6] Months later, the US State Department issued a permit to start building the pipeline. In issuing the permit, the State Department considered a range of factors, "including but not limited to foreign policy; energy security; environmental, cultural, and economic impacts; and compliance with applicable law and policy."[7] The pipeline is currently seeking the other necessary permits. Similar examples of highly political pipelines can be found both in the US[8] and abroad.[9]

This chapter will focus on US regulation of interstate natural gas pipeline construction and operation. In the EU context, natural gas pipeline regulation has been discussed in numerous commentaries.[10] Similarly, international pipelines are a frequent topic for academic commentators.[11] What is less discussed is the permitting and licensing required for the construction of these pipelines. In comparison, the US approach to pipeline construction and operation is a less discussed topic. This chapter will first provide an overview of the competence to regulate interstate pipelines. Thereafter the chapter's focus will move to first construction and then the operation of these pipelines.

2 Competence to certify and regulate natural gas pipelines

In the earliest days of the natural gas markets in the US, the gas pipeline business was organized through entities that were vertically integrated with either the natural gas

5 <https://www.ferc.gov/market-oversight/reports-analyses/st-mkt-ovr/2017-som-A-3-full.pdf?csrt=7101744618658170122>.

6 The original Presidential Order 13337 of April 30, 2004 was replaced by a new Presidential Order to the same effect on March 29, 2019.

7 <https://www.state.gov/r/pa/prs/ps/2017/03/269074.htm>.

8 For example, Bayou Bridge Pipeline is a controversial pipeline project that would transport oil from Texas to Louisiana crossing the vulnerable wetlands of Louisiana coast.

9 For an example from Europe, see the developments surrounding the Nord Stream 2 pipeline construction. Kim Talus, 'Application of EU Energy and Certain National Laws of Baltic Sea Countries to the Nord Stream 2 Pipeline Project' 10 (2017) 1 *Journal of World Energy Law & Business*, p. 30–42.

10 See for example, Kim Talus, 'Decades of EU Energy Policy: Towards Politically Driven Markets', 10 (2017) 4 *Journal of World Energy Law & Business*, p. 380–388 or Kim Talus, *Introduction to EU Energy Law* (Oxford University Press 2016), Chapter 8.3.

11 For example, K. Yafimava, *The Transit Dimension of EU Energy Security: Russian Gas Transit Across Ukraine, Belarus and Moldova* (Oxford University Press 2011) or various contributions in Martha M. Roggenkamp, Lila Barrera-Hernández, Donald N. Zillman, and Iñigo del Guayo (eds.), *Energy Networks and the Law: Innovative Solutions in Changing Markets* (Oxford University Press 2012).

producers or distributors. Gas markets were largely local, created around the production areas. In these early days, natural gas was largely what is today called "associated gas", i.e. gas found in association with oil deposits.[12] In 1920, the progress in the steel industry made the construction of long-distance, high-pressure steel pipeline structures possible.[13] The first large-scale gas pipelines from Texas to Chicago in 1931 initiated the development of an interstate gas pipeline network.[14] This started the progress towards a US wide natural gas market.

During this period, the federal licensing and rate regulation (setting of transmission tariffs) did not exist.[15] Pipelines were only regulated by state legislation and where a pipeline crossed a border, it also left the jurisdiction of one state and entered another. This resulted in various problems with conflicting orders from various jurisdictions, on the one hand, and complete lack of regulation, on the other. To address these issues, the US Supreme Court issued opinions essentially stating that the regulation of interstate pipelines fell under federal jurisdiction.[16]

The passing of the Natural Gas Act of 1938 started the federal regulation of the interstate gas trade. The Natural Gas Act is still in force today and, while it has been subject to modifications, it continues to regulate interstate pipeline business.

Under the division of competences between the state and federal level created by the Supreme Court opinions and subsequently by the Natural Gas Act, the competence to regulate both pipeline certification and operation in the US is divided into the federal and the state level. The interstate gas markets of the US are regulated by the Federal Energy Regulatory Commission (hereinafter FERC) pursuant to the Natural Gas Act.[17] The FERC does not regulate the state markets, which are subject to state regulation. The FERC's jurisdiction is limited to the transportation in the interstate pipelines and to certain sales as well as to persons engaging in these transactions. In addition to this, the FERC has jurisdiction over specific issues such as the siting of LNG re-gasification terminals.[18]

12 In the case of remote oil fields, associated natural gas was flared. In the 1950s about 20 percent of the natural gas produced was wasted. See M. Raymond and W. Leffler, *Oil and Gas Production in Nontechnical Language* (PennWell 2006), p. 13.

13 R. Pierce, 'The Evolution of Natural Gas Regulatory Policy' 10 (1995) 1 *Natural Resources and Environment*, p. 53. Daniel Yergin describes the establishment of the US natural gas industry and the construction of the first pipelines to bypass the market power of Standard Oil. See D. Yergin, *The Prize: The Epic Quest for Oil, Money, and Power* (Free Press 2008), p. 10.

14 R. O'Neill, 'Natural Gas Pipelines', in D. Moss, *Network Access, Regulation and Antitrust* (Routledge 2005), p. 107–120.

15 More generally on this period, see D. Bryce, 'Pipeline Gathering in an Unbundled World: How FERCs Response to "Spin Down" Threatens Competition in the Natural Gas Industry', 89 (2004–2005) 537 *Minnesota Law Review*, p. 540–542.

16 *Phillips Petroleum Co v Wisconsin*, 347 US 672 (1954).

17 Natural Gas Act, 15 USC x 717 et seq.

18 US Code 15 USC x 717(b) as modified by the Energy Policy Act of 2005. Under the federal law, the FERC has the exclusive authority to approve or deny an application for the siting, construction, expansion, or operation of an LNG terminal, matters which are still subject to state regulation. In particular: states' rights in the authorization of LNG facilities include the ability to effectively "veto" a project by denying permits required under the Clean Water Act, the Coastal Zone Management Act, and the Clean Air Act. During the review of a project under the National Environmental Policy Act by the FERC, a state can also act as a cooperating agency and can therefore contribute to the environmental review. For a brief overview of the relationship between state and federal legislation (including doctrines such as commerce clause), see R. Clingman and A. Cumming, 'The 2005 Energy Policy Act: Analysis of the Jurisdictional Basis for Federal Siting of LNG Facilities' 57 (2006) *Texas Journal of Oil, Gas, and Energy Law*, p. 57–91.

This historical development of the US natural gas markets is very different from that of the EU, where the market creation has primarily been a result of administrative and legislative measures to create EU-wide markets. Today's US markets and regulatory set-up are the result of various developments involving re- and de-regulation, always followed by heavy litigation. In general, it seems as if the emphasis is moving from a state-centered regulatory system towards a federally regulated market.[19] As a result of these historical developments the competences of the FERC within natural gas and natural gas pipeline markets in particular, include:

- Regulation of construction of pipeline, storage, and liquefied natural gas facilities
- Regulation of interstate natural gas transport
- Issuance of certificates of public convenience and necessity to prospective interstate pipeline and natural gas storage companies
- Regulation of abandonment of natural gas facilities
- Regulation of rates for services
- Regulation of the transportation of natural gas under Natural Gas Policy Act and Outer Continental Shelf Lands Act
- Oversight of the construction and operation of import and export pipelines.

3 Permitting and licensing of interstate natural gas pipeline construction

Under the Natural Gas Act a "(n)atural-gas company" means a person engaged in the transportation of natural gas in interstate commerce, or the sale in interstate commerce of such gas for resale.[20]

Under Section 7 of the Natural Gas Act,

> no natural-gas company or person which will be a natural-gas company upon completion of any proposed construction or extension shall engage in the transportation or sale of natural gas, subject to the jurisdiction of the Commission, or undertake the construction or extension of any facilities therefor, or acquire or operate any such facilities or extensions thereof, unless there is in force with respect to such natural-gas company a certificate of public convenience and necessity issued by the Commission authorizing such acts or operations.[21]

In other words, a company seeking to build an interstate gas pipeline must obtain certificates of public convenience and necessity from the FERC. This entails that the FERC examines the "public interest" for a new pipeline construction. "Public interest" in this context has a specific meaning which is closely related to the purposes for which the Natural Gas Act was adopted. The principal purpose of the Natural Gas Act was to "encourage the orderly development of plentiful supplies of electricity and natural gas at reasonable prices."[22] It is from this point of view that the public interest has to be understood.

19 Although states retain the power to regulate state markets, there are certain developments that shift the competence for specific areas, such as LNG terminals, to the federal level.
20 15 U.S. Code § 717f – Construction, extension, or abandonment of facilities.
21 Ibid.
22 *NAACP v. Fed. Power Comm'n*, 425 U.S. 662, 669–670 (1976).

The regulatory process for this pipeline certification can be divided into several stages:[23]

Pre-filing; where the main idea is the engagement with all the stakeholders, including governmental agencies, property owners, and so on in order to solicit input that can be used to improve the project's design. At the end of this stage, the project developer will prepare the final application for the FERC. This stage is already part of the regulatory process and thus requires an application and FERC approval.

Application for the FERC certificate: the project developer formally applies for the certificate of public convenience and necessity with detailed information on the pipeline route, construction schedule, environmental impacts of different routes, overview of all other permits and licenses from various government entities, and so on.[24] The decision from the FERC is based on the project meeting the public interest test. This test incorporates questions like impact on competition, potential environmental impact, impact on existing customers, overbuilding, amongst many others. The key considerations in this test boil down to public need vs. impact on private property and environment. As such, the environmental review is an important part of the process.

Environmental review: the National Environmental Policy Act (NEPA) requires federal agencies to take the environmental impact of their actions into account. The National Energy Policy Act of 2005 places the FERC in the lead for coordination of NEPA compliance and all other applicable federal authorizations relating to pipeline certificate applications. It is noteworthy that the environmental review has a strong public comment component and includes hearings, access to documents, and appeal possibilities.

Where the FERC approves the application and grants the certificate, including the approved pipeline route, the pipeline developer acquires the eminent domain authority allowing them to use private lands for the pipeline. However, in considering the impact of new construction projects on existing pipelines, the Commission's goal is to appropriately consider the enhancement of competitive transportation alternatives, the possibility of overbuilding, the avoidance of unnecessary disruption of the environment, and the unneeded exercise of eminent domain.[25]

Post certificate proceedings consist of possible appeals over the FERC approval. A request for rehearing by the FERC must be lodged within 30 days of the final approval. There are no time limits for the FERC to consider or conclude the rehearing, after which the pipeline construction can begin.

Overall, one of the concerns of the industry is that the granting of this certificate takes too long. There have been proposals to create a mandatory 12-month deadline for the FERC.[26]

The next section will provide an overview of the FERC regulation of interstate pipeline operation and the main developments towards the *status quo*.[27]

23 The process has been described in simple graphs at <https://www.ferc.gov/resources/processes/gas-pipe-stor-perm.asp>.

24 Section 7(c) of the Natural Gas Act [15 U.S.C. 717f]; 18 C.F.R. 157. See also 18 C.F.R. 153.2, 380.5.

25 Federal Energy Regulatory Commission, Certification of New Interstate Natural Gas Pipeline Facilities (Policy Statement), 88 FERC 61, 227, 1999.

26 Paul W. Parfomak, 'Interstate Natural Gas Pipelines: Process and Timing of FERC Permit Application Review' Congressional Research Services (January 16, 2015).

27 The historical overview is based on and updated from Kim Talus, 'Long-term Natural Gas Contracts and Antitrust Law in the European Union and the United States', *AIPN Research Paper* (2011).

4 Regulatory regime for interstate natural gas pipelines

Pipeline companies operate a natural monopoly, which can often not reasonably be duplicated, and access to the pipeline is necessary to compete in the supply market for natural gas. In order to control the abuse of the monopoly power that the pipeline companies possess this activity must be subject to a regulatory framework that sets certain basic rules. Initially, the Natural Gas Act did not adopt an open-access type of "common carrier" model but rather opted for a cost-of-service rate-making model.[28] These pipeline rates would have to be just, reasonable, and non-discriminatory.[29]

The Natural Gas Act did not extend the price regulation to the price of natural gas (the wellhead price), only to the transportation service. While this approach is both logical and in line with free market thinking, it did not last. In 1954, the Supreme Court gave its opinion in *Phillips Petroleum Co. v. Wisconsin*[30] finding that natural gas companies as defined by the Natural Gas Act and their sales in the interstate natural gas business "are subject to the jurisdiction of, and rate regulation by, the Federal Power Commission". The Supreme Court also held that Congress did not intend to regulate only interstate pipeline companies. Rather the legislative history indicates a congressional intent to give the Commission jurisdiction over the rates of all wholesales of natural gas in interstate commerce, whether by a pipeline company or not and whether occurring before, during, or after transmission by an interstate pipeline company.

This meant that the wellhead price, the price that a producer could ask for its gas from the pipeline company for gas to be traded at the interstate level, was to be regulated at federal level. The federal jurisdiction and, consequently, the control of wellhead price did not extend to the state-level trade. This resulted in the creation of distinct interstate and intrastate markets. It is important to note that these two markets had very different price levels, due to the state-level price controls. As the price levels for the interstate trade were much lower than what they were for intrastate trade, it became relatively unattractive for producers to sell into this market, creating the false impression of a shortage of gas. This led to a rush to conclude long-term contracts for the supply of natural gas.[31] When deregulation revealed the true availability of supply, prices fell sharply, and the pipelines found themselves obliged to take volumes of gas which were at prices well above those created by new market conditions. This led to court proceedings (*pacta sunt servanda* v. *force majeure* and other legal doctrines) and the enactment of laws that would circumvent pre-existing contract terms.[32]

By this time, the contractual structure of the gas industry was based on long-term agreements throughout the gas chain: producers and pipeline companies had long-term take-or-pay contracts[33] in place, pipeline companies and local distribution companies had entered into long term minimum bill contracts (similar to take-or-pay agreements), local distribution companies had captive customers, and the price of gas was rising. Industrial players with switching capability opted for other fuels and this obviously worsened the

28 F. Bosselman, J. Rossi, and J. Weaver, *Energy Economics and the Environment* (Foundation Press 2015), p. 546.

29 ABA Section of Antitrust Law, *Energy Antitrust Handbook: A Guide to the Electric and Gas Industries* (American Bar Association 2002), p. 12.

30 *Phillips Petroleum Co. v Wisconsin* [1954] 347 U.S. 672.

31 F. Bosselman, J. Rossi, and J. Weaver, *Energy Economics and the Environment* (Foundation Press 2000), p. 551–554.

32 Ibid.

33 A take-or-pay clause requires that the buyer commit to certain volumes of gas. In the event the buyer cannot take the gas, it is still required to pay for the agreed take-or-pay volume. Typically, this take-or-pay obligation does not cover all the volumes bought under the contract but a certain part of it.

situation.[34] State regulatory authorities, alarmed at the impact on consumers, began to invalidate minimum bill provisions, allowing distribution companies to extricate themselves from their obligations. This left pipeline companies contracted to take or pay for gas at prices far above market levels. In this situation the FERC started working towards a comprehensive restructuring of the natural gas industry in the US.

After a number of attempts to rectify the problems discussed in the previous paragraphs, the FERC and state regulatory commissions gave a series of "open access" orders that enabled industrial users to bypass the pipelines, reducing their role to a transport service for gas that it did not hold title to. Buyer and seller could enter into a contractual relationship and enter into a transport contract with the pipeline.[35] This was the beginning of a new era, that of the modern deregulated gas market.

At first, the FERC approved these transportation transactions on a case-by-case basis but the issuance of Order 436 gave the interstate pipelines a general right to provide transportation services to third parties. Essentially, Order 436 instituted the model of open-access, non-discriminatory transportation to permit local distribution companies, industrial users, and other players in the downstream gas markets to purchase natural gas directly from gas merchants as an alternative to purchasing their requirements from the pipeline companies in a particular distribution area under the pipelines' bundled sales services.

To achieve this, Order 436 adopted three key provisions:

1. The pipelines were required to permit their firm sales customers to convert their firm sales entitlements to a volumetrically equivalent amount of firm transportation service over a five-year period.
2. The pipelines were required to offer their open-access transportation services without discrimination or preference.
3. The pipelines were required to design maximum rates to ration capacity during peak periods and to maximize throughput for firm service during off-peak periods and for interruptible service during all periods.

These open-access transportation services were not mandatory, but if the pipeline company decided to provide these services it had to respect the requirements of the Order. This included separating the pipeline's merchant (sale of gas) and transportation functions. A large number of pipelines opted for this possibility and the number of applications and approvals for the status of an open-access carrier grew rapidly. In three years, virtually all the major pipelines had been converted to open-access pipelines.[36] As some commentators observed:

> (b)y 1989, a mature form of competition had come to natural gas. Enough pipelines had opened their systems to form a pipeline network. Markets had evolved far enough to coordinate gas and transmission trading. The gas market had gained the broad participation of buyers and sellers, giving it the depth and liquidity characteristic of a competitive market. The gas pipeline industry is no longer a natural monopoly.[37]

34 Ibid.

35 A. De Vany and W. D. Walls, 'The Triumph of Markets in Natural Gas' (April 1995) *Public Utilities Fortnightly*, p. 15–21.

36 ABA Section of Antitrust Law, *Energy Antitrust Handbook: A Guide to the Electric and Gas Industries* (American Bar Association 2002), p. 15 and A. De Vany and W. D. Walls, 'The Triumph of Markets in Natural Gas' (April 1995) *Public Utilities Fortnightly*, p. 15–21.

37 A. De Vany and W. D. Walls, 'The Triumph of Markets in Natural Gas' (April 1995) *Public Utilities Fortnightly*, p. 15–21

Another important policy change that was implemented in conjunction with Order 436 was the "shipper-must-have-title" policy. Under this policy the shipper must have the title to the gas (meaning he must be the owner of the gas volumes transported) when it is delivered to the transporter and while the gas is in transit.[38] The rationale behind this policy was to prevent private and unauthorized brokering or withholding of capacity and to promote transparency in the markets.[39]

However, despite the success of Order 436 and the open access rules, important market imperfections remained. For example, pipelines offered a superior service for bundled sales (as opposed to transportation services only).[40] This made transportation services less effective.

These remaining problems were addressed in Order 636, the most significant restructuring measure by the FERC. The objective was to:

> finalise the structural changes in the [FERC's] regulation of the natural gas industry ... [which] will therefore reflect and finally complete the evolution to competition in the natural gas industry (...) so that all natural gas suppliers, including the pipeline as merchant, will compete for gas purchasers on an equal footing ... because ... this promotion of competition among gas suppliers will benefit all gas consumers and the nation by ensuring an adequate and reliable supply of clean and abundant natural gas at the lowest reasonable price.[41]

While Order 436 (and other previous orders) had tried to promote non-discriminatory access to the transportation service without dealing with issues relating to vertical integration, Order 636 required functional unbundling of transportation and sales. Merchant pipelines were forced to separate their sales activities and transportation services into different units. Order 636 did not require any kind of divestiture in the form of ownership unbundling but required that the companies engage in an internal restructuring of their activities.[42] The idea behind this functional unbundling was to ensure non-discriminatory transportation services for third-party gas and the pipeline company's own gas. Functional unbundling had the desired result, increasing competition between various gas sellers and mitigating the market power of pipeline companies.[43]

The key provisions and requirements of Order 636 are:

- Functional unbundling
- Non-discriminatory transportation services
- Encouragement to develop market centers where various pipeline systems interconnect
- Expanded access to interstate storage facilities
- Capacity release program and related electronic bulletin boards
- Common rate design

38 Consolidated Gas Transmission Corp., 38 FERC 61,150, at 61,408 (1987) (citing *Texas Eastern Transmission Corp.*, 37 FERC 61,260, at 61,683–685 (1986)).

39 In re MGTC, Inc., 121 FERC 61,087.

40 ABA Section of Antitrust Law, *Energy Antitrust Handbook: A Guide to the Electric and Gas Industries* (American Bar Association 2002), p. 17.

41 Order 636, Introduction.

42 F. Bosselman, J. Rossi, and J. Weaver, *Energy Economics and the Environment* (Foundation Press 2000), p. 554.

43 <www.eia.doe.gov/oil_gas/natural_gas/analysis_publications/ngmajorleg/ferc636.html>.

Concurrently with the provisions of Order 636, the FERC regulation provides for the release of firm capacity where this capacity exceeds 31 days at a price less than the maximum tariff rate. In such a case, the information about the release has to be posted for competitive bidding on the pipeline's Electronic Bulletin Board.[44] Even discounted releases or releases for less than 31 days have to be notified within 48 hours of the release, even if the transaction is exempted from the competitive bidding requirements.[45] The rationale behind these posting requirements is obviously to promote transparency and hence provide the opportunity for interested parties to bid for available capacity. Similarly, the rationale behind the bidding requirement is to ensure that the capacity is allocated to the player that most values it. Together these requirements promote transparency and efficiency and eliminate undue preference and discrimination in the natural gas transportation market.[46] They form an integral part of the FERC pipeline open-access program.[47]

These changes, Order 636 in particular, altered the US natural gas markets very profoundly, creating the conditions for a competitive market structure to emerge.[48] Order 636 turned many of the pipeline companies into pure transporters of natural gas, instead of purchasers and re-sellers. Many services that these pipeline companies abandoned in changing their business approach were then picked up by newly created hubs (connection between various pipelines including physical transportation from one to another and balancing).[49] As a consequence, the wholesale markets in the US have moved from the wellhead to the hubs. Major hubs are typically operated by one or more of the interstate pipeline companies and are located at the interconnections between several pipelines.[50] As one author put it: "(i)n short, the utility world after Order No. 636 looks entirely different from the utility world of the early 1980s."[51]

Of course, markets continued to develop and the progress in the US natural gas market regulation did not come to a halt with Order 636. Order 637[52] was issued to modify the existing regulatory framework and to improve the efficiency of the market and provide captive customers with the opportunity to reduce their cost of holding long-term pipeline capacity while continuing to protect against the exercise of market power.

44 18 C.F.R. § 284.8 (2007).

45 Ibid.

46 In re BP Energy Co., 121 FERC 61,088 (issued October 25, 2007).

47 Ibid. In this case, the FERC also found that "flipping" (i.e., repeated, short-term releases of discounted rate capacity to two or more affiliated replacement shippers on an alternating monthly basis in order to avoid the competitive bidding requirement for discounted long-term capacity release) violates the FERC capacity release rules. Similarly, the FERC noted that buy/sell transactions were prohibited. (A prohibited buy-sell transaction is a commercial arrangement by which a shipper holding interstate pipeline capacity buys gas at the direction of, on behalf of, or directly from another entity (e.g., an end-user), ships that gas through its interstate pipeline capacity, and then resells an equivalent quantity of gas to the downstream entity at the delivery point.)

48 R. Pierce, 'The State of the Transition to Competitive Markets in Natural Gas and Electricity' 10 (1994) 15 *Energy Law Journal*, p. 323 and 324.

49 J. Tobin, 'Natural Gas Market Centers and Hubs: A 2003 Update'. Available at: <www.eia.doe.gov/pub/oil_gas/natural_gas/feature_articles/2003/market_hubs/mkthubsweb.html>.

50 See <www- wds.worldbank.org/external/default/WDSContentServer/WDSP/IB/1998/04/01/000009265_3980630181135/Rendered/PDF/multi_page.pdf>.

51 J. Petrash, 'Long-Term Natural Gas Contracts: Dead, Dying or Merely Resting?' 27 (2006) 2 *Energy Law Journal*, p. 556.

52 90 FERC ¶ 61,109 (issued February 9, 2000).

In particular, the Order 637 amends the FERC pricing policy to enhance the efficiency of the market by waiving price ceilings for short-term released capacity for a two-year period and permitting pipelines to file for peak/off-peak and term differentiated rate structures.

The Order 637 also effects changes in regulations relating to scheduling procedures, capacity segmentation, and pipeline penalties to improve the competitiveness and efficiency of the interstate pipeline grid. Importantly, it also narrows the right of first refusal to remove economic biases in the current rule, while still protecting captive customers' ability to re-subscribe to long-term capacity. Here, it is noteworthy that in the US natural gas market context, long-term translates to one year, which is much shorter than anywhere else.[53]

Order 720[54] from 2010 extended FERC regulation to certain intra-state pipelines. It requires major intrastate pipelines to post daily scheduled volume information and other data for certain points. These modifications include a requirement that major intrastate pipelines post information for receipt and delivery points at which design capacity is unknown. The underlying idea is that these requirements will facilitate price transparency in markets for the sale or transportation of physical natural gas in interstate commerce to implement section 23 of the Natural Gas Act.[55] This and many other new acts and cases have gradually extended the FERC competence to regulated US natural gas markets beyond its original scope. This is arguably a logical development that is connected with the growth and general developments in US natural gas markets.

5 Conclusion

US natural gas markets are arguably the most competitive gas markets in the world. The gas pricing does not rely on oil price indexation or energy product baskets as it tends to do in many other parts of the world. The prices are set at competitive and liquid hubs, of which the Henry Hub in Louisiana is arguably the best known internationally.

Natural gas in the US markets is moving through a dense pipeline network which connects producers and customers in consuming regions. Pipelines also connect certain producing regions with liquefied natural gas export projects along coastal areas, the Gulf of Mexico in particular. For LNG exports to grow, however, there is a need for additional pipeline capacity to be built, in particular from the Permian basin located in Texas. That region is currently performing less efficiently than it should due to lack of sufficient gas pipeline capacity. This has resulted in an increasing volume of natural gas being flared, something that is both an economic waste and environmentally harmful.

New pipeline projects require permitting and licensing. For interstate pipelines the permitting authority is the FERC. In some areas it is the permitting authority, in other areas it has a coordination function. The centralized system created by the Natural Gas Act of 1938 functions fairly well, especially in an international comparison. While there is some discussion on the duration of the proceedings, the situation is better than in many other countries.

The operational regimes for natural gas pipelines are the key factor for optimal market functioning. Natural gas pipelines can be seen as natural monopolies. As such they need to be regulated. In line with this, the US regulatory scheme is based on non-discriminatory

53 In the EU context or international LNG context, a long-term agreement would be something in the range of 10–15 years.

54 130 FERC ¶ 61,040 (issued January 21, 2010).

55 15 U.S.C. 717t-2 (2000 & Supp. V 2005).

third-party access. However, there are a number of exceptions to this rule. For example, gathering lines from the fields to the main pipelines is outside the scope of third-party access. Again, this is in line with international practise in this area of energy law. For example, EU energy law imposes similar (though not identical) non-discriminatory third-party access obligations for transmission and distribution pipelines.[56] It also includes an exemption for upstream pipelines (similar to the US exemption on gathering lines).

Finally, this chapter has examined the regulatory frameworks for onshore interstate pipelines. Here, the primary authority lays with the FERC. For intra-state pipelines, similar functions are under the competence of State Regulatory Commissions. It must also be noted that while the FERC is the key authority for interstate pipelines, many other agencies have specific roles to play: for example, the Department of Transportation's Pipeline and Hazardous Material Safety Administration (PHMSA), acting through the Office of Pipeline Safety (OPS), regulates, monitors, and enforces safety in pipeline operations. Also, the Environmental Protection Agency (EPA) has a role to play under the Environmental Policy Act, the Clean Water Act, the Coastal Zone Management Act, the Endangered Species Act, and the Clean Air Act.

It may be argued that this chapter has only provided a partial picture of the US natural gas pipeline regulation. However, given the central role of interstate pipelines for a natural gas market and the central role played by the FERC in this area, it is crucial that the non-US readers understand this important part of the puzzle.

56 Chapter VII ('Organisation of Access to the System'), and especially Article 32, of the Directive 2009/73/EC of the European Parliament and of the Council of 13 July 2009 concerning common rules for the internal market in natural gas and repealing Directive 2003/55/EC (OJ L 211, August 14, 2009, p. 94).

16

REGULATION OF LOW CARBON ENERGY SOURCES IN THE U.S. AND CANADA

Kristen van de Biezenbos

1 The U.S.

In the U.S., federal, state, and local governments all play a role in the regulation of low carbon energy sources. Despite the lack of regulatory uniformity, the U.S. is one of the largest producers of hydroelectric, geothermal, nuclear, wind, and solar power in the world,[1] and a major destination for international investment in renewable technologies.[2] Under the U.S. Constitution, the federal government has jurisdiction over activities taking place on federal land or involved in interstate commerce.[3] This includes the licensing of energy projects and electricity transmission lines on federal land, as well as the generation and transmission of electricity. However, with respect to the generation and transmission of electricity, the Federal Energy Regulatory Commission (FERC) does not handle the siting or construction of power plants (including wind and solar facilities) or transmission lines unless they are entirely located in federal lands.[4] If any part of such a project is on state or private lands, the proponent must apply to each state's utility commission for approval, as well as obtain a surface lease or right-of-way easement from each private land owner.[5] There have been some attempts to change this, as under the Energy Policy Act of 2005, but thus far FERC may only exercise siting authority if a state refuses to allow some types of energy infrastructure to be built in a federally-designated energy corridor.[6] If, however, the state

1 International Renewable Energy Agency, 'Capacity and Generation Country Rankings', <http://resourceirena.irena.org/gateway/dashboard/?topic=4&subTopic=18>.

2 United Nations Environment Programme & Bloomberg New Energy Finance, 'Global Trends in Renewable Energy Investment 2018' (2018) 22, <https://drive.google.com/file/d/1Smhal-WAcmEMqR8R9oL5FxnOcZ0kfY8Z/view>.

3 See U.S. Department of Energy, 'Electricity Transmission: A Primer' (2004) 39–48, <https://www.energy.gov/sites/prod/files/oeprod/DocumentsandMedia/primer.pdf>.

4 See FERC, *About FERC – What FERC Does*, <https://www.ferc.gov/about/ferc-does.asp>.

5 See U.S. Constitution art. I, sec. 8, cl. 3; *FPC v. Florida Power & Light*, 404 U.S. 453 (1972). There was an attempt to give FERC backstop siting authority in the Public Utilities Regulatory Policies Act, but that authority was never successfully exercised by FERC and was removed by the Energy Policy Act of 2005.

6 See Debbie Swanstrom & Meredith J. Jolivert, 'DOE Transmission Corridor Designations & (and) FERC Backstop Siting Authority: Has the Energy Policy Act of 2005 Succeeded in Stimulating the Development of New Transmission Facilities?' 30 (2009) *Energy Law Journal* 415.

takes no action on an application (as opposed to rejecting it) in such a corridor, FERC does not have the authority to take action in its stead.[7]

Instead, FERC generally confines its authority to regulating wholesale power rates and transmission tariffs.[8] This means that FERC has regulatory authority over approving open access transmission tariffs for connecting to existing grid infrastructure (through Order 888, which also applies to transmission line interconnections between the US and Canada),[9] and approving whole power generation rates. Both of these issues are of concern to generators of low carbon electricity, especially wind and solar facilities which are often located in rural areas and must be assured access to the grid in order to sell their power.[10] Additionally, wind and solar power purchase agreements are approved by FERC, as are applications by generators to sell on electricity spot markets, if the generator is located in a competitive wholesale power market.[11]

Some incentives for low carbon energy investment are also federal, mostly in the form of tax breaks. Most of the regulation intended to spur low carbon energy development comes from the states, especially in the form of Renewable Portfolio Standards, which often include a renewable energy credit trading system, and Feed-in Tariffs. Renewable Portfolio Standards set targets for adding a certain amount of renewable sources to the jurisdiction's energy mix and use a variety of legal and non-legal tools to reach those goals.[12] Feed-in Tariffs guarantee a long-term set price per kilowatt hour of generated renewable energy that is fed into the jurisdiction's grid.[13] California and Washington both have state-wide carbon caps (though Washington's is more qualified that California's), and ten states in the northeast—Massachusetts, New York, Delaware, Maine, Connecticut, Maryland, New Hampshire, Rhode Island, Vermont, and New Jersey—participate in the Regional Greenhouse Gas Initiative, a cap and trade program that targets power plants. California's cap is state wide and applies to all large emitters. They were previously joined in their carbon trading market by Quebec and Ontario, but in 2018 Ontario left the market.

These state-level initiatives have been extremely successful in bringing more wind and solar into the country's energy mix. For example, the renewable portfolio standard in Texas was such a success that the state is now not only the largest producer of wind power in the U.S., but it is the sixth largest producer of wind power in the world.[14] But, for various reasons, nuclear and hydropower have not benefitted to the same extent. One primary reason is cost, but states also lack regulatory authority over nuclear and hydropower. As will be explored in more depth below, both of those energy sources are federally regulated and involve time-consuming approval processes that have slowed the growth of both hydroelectric and nuclear power in the U.S.

7 See *ibid.*

8 See *supra* note 4.

9 See Ignacio Herrera Anchustegui, 'Transmission Networks in Electricity Competition: Third-Party Access and Unbundling – A Transatlantic Perspective' in Ruiz Peris and Juan Ignacio (eds), *Competencia en mercados con recursos esenciales compartidos: telecomunicaciones y energía* (Valencia: University of Valencia, 2018). https://papers.ssrn.com/sol3/cf_dev/AbsByAuth.cfm?per_id=2335166.

10 See FERC, 'Overview of FERC', <https://www.ferc.gov/about/ferc-does/overview-print.asp>.

11 Ibid.

12 See National Conference of State Legislatures, 'State Renewable Portfolio Standards and Goals', </www.ncsl.org/research/energy/renewable-portfolio-standards.aspx>.

13 See U.S. Energy Information Administration, 'Feed in Tariff: A Policy Tool Encouraging Deployment of Renewable Electricity Technologies', <https://www.eia.gov/todayinenergy/detail.php?id=11471>.

14 See Powering Texas, 'Texas: America's Wind Energy Leader', <https://poweringtexas.com/wp-content/uploads/2019/01/Powering-Texas-Legislative-Guide.pdf>.

1.1 Nuclear

Despite the fact that few reactors have been built since the Three Mile Island incident in 1979,[15] nuclear power still represents about 20 per cent of the electricity generation in the U.S.[16] There are currently 60 nuclear power plants and 98 reactors operating in 30 states, making the U.S. the largest producer of nuclear power in the world.[17] Nuclear power safety is regulated by a federal agency, the Nuclear Regulatory Commission, an independent agency (meaning that it is not part of a larger department, such as the Department of Energy), although many other agencies play a role in the mining and transportation of uranium and the environmental assessment of proposed nuclear power plants.[18] Although the U.S. is a major nuclear power, both in terms of energy and weaponry, many of the nuclear power plants in the country are aging, and all of them require semi-annual maintenance that can be extremely expensive. Further, the costs of new nuclear power plants are astronomical—although there have been three new plants permitted by the NRC since 2017, only two of them have even started construction, while the other has already been cancelled due to high costs.[19] As in Canada, nuclear power in the U.S. is often discussed but rarely deployed.

1.2 Hydropower

The U.S. has a long history of using hydroelectric power plants, from the earliest use of Niagara Falls to generate direct current electricity to power lights to large-scale hydroelectric projects like the Grand Coulee and Hoover Dams.[20] Indeed, FERC was originally formed by the 1920 Federal Power Act to regulate hydropower, and it still oversees the licensing, overseeing ongoing operations, and relicensing of hydropower facilities. In *S. D. Warren Co. v. Maine Board of Environmental Protection*, the U.S. Supreme Court held that states also play a role in the licensing of dams that release water back into navigable waters.[21] Under Clean Water Act Section 401, any activity that results in a discharge of a substance into navigable waters must not violate federal or state water quality laws.[22] As a result, hydroelectric dams are licensed by FERC, but may also need to pass an environmental review by a state agency

15 In 1979, a nuclear reactor in Pennsylvania had a partial meltdown and released radioactive material into the surrounding area. See United States Nuclear Regulatory Commission, 'Backgrounder on the Three Mile Island Accident', <https://www.nrc.gov/reading-rm/doc-collections/fact-sheets/3mile-isle.html>.

16 See World Nuclear Association, 'Nuclear Power in the USA', <http://www.world-nuclear.org/information-library/country-profiles/countries-t-z/usa-nuclear-power.aspx>.

17 See *ibid*; Nuclear Energy Institute, 'Top 15 Nuclear Generating Countries', <https://www.nei.org/resources/statistics/top-15-nuclear-generating-countries>.

18 For example, the mining of uranium is overseen by the Nuclear Regulatory Commission (NRC), although most of the U.S. states where uranium is located are "agreement states", and have been authorized by the NRC to issue mining permits. See World Nuclear Association, 'U.S. Uranium Mining and Exploration', <https://www.world-nuclear.org/information-library/country-profiles/countries-t-z/us-uranium-mining.aspx>. The transportation of uranium is overseen by the U.S. Department of Transportation while it is in transit. See U.S. Department of Energy, 'Packaging, Transportation, and Storage of Radioactive Materials', <https://www.energy.gov/sites/prod/files/2014/04/f14/rmem2_0.pdf>.

19 See Brad Plumer, 'U.S. Nuclear Comeback Stalls as Two Reactors Are Abandoned' *The New York Times* (31 July 2017), <https://www.nytimes.com/2017/07/31/climate/nuclear-power-project-canceled-in-south-carolina.html>.

20 U.S. Bureau of Reclamation, 'Hydropower Program: The History of Hydropower Development in the United States', <https://www.usbr.gov/power/edu/history.html>.

21 *S. D. Warren Co. v. Maine Bd. of Environmental Protection* [2006] 547 U.S. 370.

22 Ibid; see also 33 U.S.C. §1341.

as well. It may, in addition, be necessary to consult with Native American tribes or bands, if a project is planned on reservation land.[23] FERC also requires that proposed hydropower projects be consistent with any existing comprehensive plans for the development of particular waterways, such as navigation, fishing, wildlife habitat, or flood control.[24]

The design and construction of large hydro projects in the eastern part of the U.S. are overseen by the U.S. Army Corps of Engineers, while the U.S. Bureau of Reclamation oversees hydroelectric projects in the western part of the country (which covers over a dozen states, including Texas and California).[25] The Bureau of Reclamation also oversees the operation of completed projects within its regions, and is the second largest producer of hydroelectric power in the U.S.[26] There are also some non-federal projects, most of which are operated by private energy companies or municipal utilities. A federally-owned corporation, the Tennessee Valley Authority, operates hydroelectric (as well as nuclear, wind solar, and coal) facilities in the Southeast, and is the largest public utility in the country.[27] All dams are subject to FERC's regulation, and because of the potentially devastating impacts on the ecosystem that large dams can cause, a host of federal regulations and agencies may also be involved, particularly in ensuring that the project is compliant with federal environmental and wildlife protection laws. Older dams have already caused permanent, irreversible damage to Native American sacred sites and local fish populations.[28]

1.3 Wind and solar

Unlike nuclear and hydropower, wind and solar power in the U.S. is largely subject to state regulation, with the exception of rates (which are overseen by FERC) and environmental review if the wind or solar farm is located on federal land.[29] There have been numerous federal incentive policies and regulations meant to bolster wind and solar capacity, some of which provided tax breaks and others required a certain percentage of the power used by the

23 When a hydropower project is proposed on a Native American reservation, FERC appoints a tribal liaison officer to facilitate consultation with affected tribes. See FERC, <https://www.ferc.gov/industries/hydropower/indus-act/order-2002/tribal-policy.pdf>. Additionally, under the National Environmental Policy Act, National Historic Preservation Act, and Native American Graves Protection and Repatriation Act, tribes must be consulted when proposed projects may negatively impact sacred sites or burial grounds, even if they are not on reservation land. See 42 U.S.C. §§ 4321 et seq. (2006); 6 U.S.C. §§ 470a et seq. (2006); 25 U.S.C. §§ 3001–3013. (2006).

24 FERC, 'Hydropower, General Information, Comprehensive Plans', <https://www.ferc.gov/industries/hydropower/gen-info/comp-plans.asp?csrt=2092015266497394104>.

25 U.S. Department of Energy, 'History of Hydropower', <https://www.energy.gov/eere/water/history-hydropower>.

26 Ibid.

27 Tennessee Valley Authority, 'Our History', <https://www.tva.gov/About-TVA/Our-History>; U.S. Energy Information Administration, 'Tennessee State Energy Profile', <https://www.eia.gov/state/print.php?sid=TN>.

28 For example, Chota and Tanasi, both once important Cherokee cities, were destroyed by the Tennessee Valley's Tellico Dam Project. Wendell Rawls, Jr., 'Forgotten People of the Tellico Dam Fight' *The New York Times* (11 Nov 1979). The Grand Coulee Dam was not properly equipped with salmon ladders, causing salmon to vanish from the Columbia River and depriving Native American groups along the river of their traditional source of food. See Emily Schwing, 'After 70 Years, Salmon Could Return to Columbia River Above Grand Coulee' *NW News Network* (16 Mar 2018).

29 See Interstate Renewable Energy Council, 'Solar Licensing Table', <https://irecusa.org/2010/08/solar-licensing-information>; National Conference of State Legislators, 'State Legislative Approaches to Wind Energy Facility Siting', <http://www.ncsl.org/research/energy/state-wind-energy-siting.aspx>.

federal government to be from wind, but all of those policies and regulations have lapsed or were repealed.[30] An exception is the Renewable Electricity Production Tax Credit, which wind and solar facilities can still qualify for, though the tax incentives were set to be lower going forward in 2018.[31]

Wind and solar facilities that are sited on state or private land are, with the aforementioned exception on rates, subject to state regulation. Many states have policies in place that encourage wind and solar power, such as renewable portfolio standards, feed-in tariffs, or cap and trade.[32] The result of these policies, which often include tax incentives and power purchase agreements (long-term contracts which can guarantee wind and solar power producers a certain price per kilowatt hour), are that the U.S. is the second largest producer of wind power in the world,[33] the fourth largest producer of photovoltaic solar power, and the second largest producer of concentrated solar power.[34] Additionally, while wholesale power rates or the ability to sell electricity in competitive wholesale power markets is regulated by FERC, distribution rates—including rates to residential customers—are determined by state utility regulators.[35] The state regulators do not have the power to overrule FERC rates, however, and must consider them in determining a utility's revenue requirement; that is, the total amount that a utility must be able to recoup via distribution rates in order to stay financially viable.[36] State environmental agencies are also responsible for environmental assessment and ensuring compliance with state laws for wind and solar facilities on state land.

1.4 Geothermal

The U.S. has significant geothermal resources, especially in the western parts of the country, and is the world's largest producer of geothermal electricity.[37] Many of the same federal laws meant to promote renewable energy technologies also apply to geothermal power, with the addition of the Energy Independence and Security Act of 2007's provisions, entitled the Advanced Geothermal Research and Development Act of 2007.[38] Leasing for geothermal projects on federal lands is regulated by the U.S. Department of the Interior and the Minerals Management Service in accordance with the John Rishel Geothermal Leasing Amendments passed in the Energy Policy Act of 2005.[39] Leasing on state lands is regulated by state agencies and may also be subject to local ordinances. As with other low-carbon energy facilities, geothermal wells are subject to federal and state environmental laws, and wholesale electricity prices from geothermal plants are set by FERC.

30 See Timothy Cama, 'White House Jumps Into Fight Over Energy Subsidies' *The Hill* (4 Dec 2018), <https://thehill.com/policy/energy-environment/419736-white-house-jumps-into-fight-over-energy-subsidies>.

31 See Department of Energy, 'Renewable Electricity Production Credit', <https://www.energy.gov/savings/renewable-electricity-production-tax-credit-ptc>.

32 See U.S. Environmental Protection Agency, 'State Renewable Energy Resources', <https://www.epa.gov/statelocalenergy/state-renewable-energy-resources>.

33 World Wind Energy Association, 'Wind Power Capacity Worldwide Reaches 600 GW, 53,9 GW Added in 2018', <https://wwindea.org/blog/2019/02/25/wind-power-capacity-worldwide-reaches-600-gw-539-gw-added-in-2018>.

34 See PowerWeb, 'Renewable Energy', <www.fi-powerweb.com/Renewable-Energy.html>.

35 U.S Energy Information Agency, 'Renewables 2018', <https://www.iea.org/renewables2018/power>.

36 See *supra* note 4.

37 U.S. Energy Information Agency, Geothermal Explained, 'Use of Geothermal Energy', <https://www.eia.gov/energyexplained/index.php?page=geothermal_use>.

38 Geothermal Energy Association, 'Key Geothermal Laws', <http://geo-energy.org/KeyGeothermalLaws.aspx>.

39 Ibid.

2 Canada

Canada's electricity sector is dominated by low carbon energy sources, particularly hydropower.[40] In 2016, 81 per cent of the country's electricity was generated from non-greenhouse gas emitting sources, the highest percentage in the Organisation for Economic Co-operation and Development (OECD).[41] Despite this, the distribution of hydropower resources is not uniform across the country, and some provinces and territories are almost entirely dependent on fossil fuels and biomass—mainly wood—for electricity and heat.[42] Canada also has one of the highest energy intensities in the developed world, because of its reliance on fossil fuels for transportation and heating. Canada is the second largest country in the world by area, but has a relatively small and population spread out over great distances, and has very cold, long winters.[43] Large swaths of Canada's north is inaccessible for part of the year because of extreme cold.[44] Further complicating the move towards low carbon energy is the complex federalism picture. Under the Constitution Act of 1982, jurisdiction over natural resources rests exclusively with the provinces, unless a particular project crosses provincial borders.[45] As a result, most provinces regulate their own low carbon energy sources, both on the electricity and transportation side, while the federal government regulates for the territories.[46]

This does not mean the federal government plays no role in regulating low carbon energy, but its oversight is often limited to the environmental review of projects (unlike the natural resources themselves, the air, soil, water, and flora and fauna are national in nature, and thus are subject to federal jurisdiction).[47] In order to address its energy intensity and to meet its commitments under the Paris Agreement, Canada has embarked upon a strategy to further decarbonize, addressing the coal-fired power plants in the prairie provinces, the use of diesel generators in Newfoundland and the country's northern areas (both provincial and in the territories), and renewable fuels.[48] However, the primary piece of legislation supporting this strategy—the Pan Canadian Framework on Clean Growth and Climate Change—is currently in peril, as political and legal resistance to its initiatives is growing across the country.[49]

It is also important to note the role of indigenous people and their rights in the development of low carbon energy projects, both on the federal and provincial levels. When the rights of indigenous peoples may be affected by a project, there are Constitutional duties of meaningful consultation, the existence of contracts (especially community contracts

40 Natural Resources Canada, 'Electricity Facts', <https://www.nrcan.gc.ca/energy/facts/electricity/20068>.
41 Natural Resources Canada, 'Energy & Greenhouse Gas Emissions (GHGs)', <https://www.nrcan.gc.ca/energy/facts/energy-ghgs/20063>.
42 National Energy Board, 'Energy Use in Canada's North: An Overview of Yukon, Northwest Territories, and Nunavut', <https://www.neb-one.gc.ca/nrg/ntgrtd/mrkt/archive/.../nrgsncndnrthfct-eng.pdf>.
43 The Conference Board of Canada, 'Energy Intensity', <https://www.conferenceboard.ca/hcp/Details/Environment/energy-intensity.aspx?AspxAutoDetectCookieSupport=1>.
44 Statistics Canada, 'Transportation in the North', <https://www150.statcan.gc.ca/n1/pub/16-002-x/2009001/article/10820-eng.htm>.
45 Constitution Act of 1982, section 93.
46 Ibid.
47 Ibid.
48 See Government of Canada, 'Pan-Canadian Framework on Clean Growth and Climate Change', <https://www.canada.ca/en/services/environment/weather/climatechange/pan-canadian-framework.html>.
49 See Paul Wells, 'A Carbon Tax? Just Try Them' *Macleans's* (7 Nov 2018), <https://www.macleans.ca/politics/ottawa/a-carbon-tax-just-try-them>.

called Impact and Benefits Agreements), and other considerations that must be taken into account.[50] However, in recent years, more and more indigenous groups have begun partnering with energy companies and even forming their own energy companies—both low carbon and fossil fuel—in order to play an active role in how, when, and where these projects come to fruition.[51]

The next sections give an overview of the regulation of specific low carbon energy sources as well as regulations meant to encourage the use of low carbon energy.

2.1 Nuclear

Nuclear power is unique among low carbon energy sources, in that it is exclusively regulated by the federal government.[52] Canada's history with nuclear power is significant. In the 1940s, a group of scientists working at the University of Montreal created a new type of nuclear reaction using heavy water, and by the 1960s, the national company Atomic Energy of Canada Limited built its Canada Deuterium Uranium (CANDU) reactors both in Canada and around the world. Currently, however, there are no plans to build any new CANDU or its more modern counterpart, the Advanced CANDU reactor, and Atomic Energy of Canada Limited's nuclear laboratories are now operated by Canadian Nuclear Laboratories Ltd.[53] Despite this, there are still five reactors operational, all in Quebec, Ontario, and New Brunswick.[54] Ownership of these reactors varies; some are private and some are public.[55]

As in the U.S., nuclear power in Canada is federally regulated, and the current regulator is the Canadian Nuclear Safety Commission (CNSC).[56] Under the Nuclear Safety and Control Act, the CNSC has the authority to oversee nuclear power and materials in a way that is safe, environmentally sound, and secure (since the nuclear fuel, particularly plutonium, can be used to make nuclear weapons).[57] More specifically, the CNSC reviews and issues licenses for nuclear power plants, ensures compliance with safety regulations, and oversees the decommissioning and abandonment of facilities.[58] There are also other federal agencies that play a role in related aspects of nuclear power, such as Transport Canada (overseeing the transportation of nuclear material to and from power plants) and Health Canada (taking

50 See Robert Hamilton & Joshua Nichols, 'The Tin Ear of the Court: Ktunaxa Nation and the Foundation of the Duty to Consult', 56 (2019) 3 *Alta L Rev*, 729; Alastair R. Lucas, 'Participatory Rights and Strategic Litigation: Benefits Forcing and Endowment Protection in Canadian Natural Resource Development' in Lilia Barrera-Hernandez et al, (eds), *Sharing the Costs and Benefits of Energy and Resource Activity* (Oxford: Oxford University Press, 2016) 339, 343.

51 See Kyle Bakx & Geneviève Normand, 'More than 100 First Nations Could Purchase the Trans Mountain Expansion Pipeline' *The Globe and Mail* (15 Jan 2019), <https://www.cbc.ca/news/business/tmx-irc-indigenous-1.4975243>; Brent Jang, 'First Nations Group Offers to Buy Stake in Coastal GasLink Pipeline' *The Globe and Mail* (8 Apr 2019), <https://www.theglobeandmail.com/business/article-first-nations-group-offers-to-buy-225-per-cent-stake-in-transcanadas>.

52 See Nuclear Safety and Control Act (S.C. 1997, c. 9).

53 Natural Resources Canada, Nuclear Energy, <https://www.nrcan.gc.ca/energy/uranium-nuclear/7711>.

54 See Canadian Nuclear Laboratories, 'News Release: Launch of Canadian Nuclear Laboratories', <http://www.cnl.ca/en/home/news-and-publications/news-releases/2014/141030.aspx>.

55 World Nuclear Association, 'Nuclear Power in Canada', <www.world-nuclear.org/information-library/country-profiles/countries-a-f/canada-nuclear-power.aspx>.

56 See Canadian Nuclear Safety Commission, <https://www.cnsc-ccsn.gc.ca/eng>.

57 Ibid.

58 Canadian Nuclear Safety Commission, 'Licensing Process for New Nuclear Power Plants in Canada', May 2008, <https://nuclearsafety.gc.ca/pubs_catalogue/uploads/I0756_R1_e.pdf>.

steps to prevent and treat radiation exposure).[59] As with all major energy projects, proposed nuclear power plants may also be required to undergo an environmental impact assessment, which takes into consideration all five stages of the power plant's life cycle: siting, construction, operation, decommissioning, and abandonment.[60]

2.2 Hydropower

About 7 percent of the world's accessible renewable fresh water is in Canada, and thus it is not a surprise that most of the country's electricity—almost 60 percent—is provided by hydropower.[61] Canada is also the second largest producer of hydropower in the world, after China.[62] Hydro resources are not evenly distributed across the country, however. Nearly all large-scale hydro is in just four provinces: British Columbia, Quebec, Ontario, and Newfoundland and Labrador.[63] These provinces regulate their hydroelectric power plants through (mostly) municipal utilities, which are in turn overseen by utility regulators empowered by provincial legislatures. For example, BC Hydro and Power Authority is the municipal electric utility for British Columbia, and provides the majority of electricity in the province.[64] Between 1960 and 1980, BC Hydro built several large dams in accordance with the Columbia River Treaty, an agreement between the United States and Canada allowing British Columbia to alter the flow of bodies of water that also cross the border with the United States.[65] Although the power generated from these hydro facilities is almost entirely free of greenhouse gas (GHG) emissions, more recent projects put forward by BC Hydro have met with stiff resistance from environmental and indigenous groups.[66]

An illustration of the current problems surrounding new hydro facilities is BC Hydro's planned Site C, an earth-fill hydro facility that would both help ease the burden on aging dams and be the fourth largest hydro facility in British Columbia in its own right. Site C is currently under construction on the Peace River in the northeastern part of the province, which is home to several indigenous communities. There is also an existing hydro facility on the Peace River, the Bennet Dam, the construction of which permanently altered the surrounding ecosystem and severely impeded the ability of nearby indigenous groups to continue their traditional way of life and subsistent patterns.[67] Because Site C would exacerbate these existing problems and would flood land also used for agriculture and other industry, it

59 Canadian Nuclear Safety Commission, <https://www.cnsc-ccsn.gc.ca/eng>.

60 Ibid.

61 Ibid.

62 Government of Canada, 'Water: Frequently Asked Questions', <https://www.canada.ca/en/environment-climate-change/services/water-overview/frequently-asked-questions.html>; Natural Resources Canada, Electricity Facts, <https://www.nrcan.gc.ca/energy/facts/electricity/2006>.

63 Natural Resources Canada, 'About Renewable Energy', <https://www.nrcan.gc.ca/energy/renewable-electricity/7295>.

64 See National Energy Board, 'Canada's Energy Transition: Historical and Future Changes to Energy Systems', <https://www.neb-one.gc.ca/nrg/ntgrtd/mrkt/cndsnrgtrnstn/trndsncnd-eng.html?=undefined&wbdisable=true>.

65 See BC Hydro, 'About Us', <https://www.bchydro.com/toolbar/about.html>.

66 See, for example, Sarah Cox, 'The United Nations Instructs Canada to Suspend Site C Dam Construction Over Indigenous Rights Violations', *The Narwhal* (9 Jan 2019), <https://thenarwhal.ca/united-nations-instructs-canada-to-suspend-site-c-dam-construction-over-indigenous-rights-violations>.

67 See Gavin Fisher, 'BC Hydro Acknowledges Dark Past of W.A.C. Bennett Dam in New Exhibit' *CBC News* (15 June 2016), <https://www.cbc.ca/news/canada/british-columbia/bc-hydro-acknowledges-dark-past-of-wac-bennett-dam-1.3637489>.

has been delayed numerous times due to legal challenges from First Nations, Metis groups, and coalitions of farmers and landowners.[68] Though those challenges were unsuccessful, the project still suffers from ballooning costs and construction problems. Even so, Site C is expected to be cheaper than the alternatives in the long-run, given BC Hydro's extensive experience with hydropower and its regulation.[69] This is also true for hydro resources in Quebec, Ontario, and Newfoundland, although there is interest in wind and solar to complement the large capacity hydro dams in all of those provinces.

2.3 *Wind and solar*

Adding wind and solar generation in Canada can be challenging because of the lack of east-west transmission line interties and the extremely cold weather, which can put stress on solar panels and on wind turbine blades (the latter tend to become covered by frost and ice, which diminishes their aerodynamics). The majority of Ontario's electricity is generated by wind, following a feed-in tariff (FIT) program that encouraged wind and solar producers to build in the province.[70] Although this is an encouraging sign of non-hydro renewable power making its way into the country, a rise in electricity rates in Ontario after the implementation of the FIT makes the wind power in that province controversial.[71] Wind power in the Maritimes, Alberta, and Quebec is not as widespread as in Ontario, but it has a foothold in those provinces and the wind sector is expected to grow steadily. In Alberta, wind power has been especially popular due to the province's goal of reaching 30 percent renewable power by 2030.

Licensing for wind power infrastructure, including turbines, is generally overseen by a mosaic of provincial regulators. Additionally, most provinces, with the notable exception of Alberta, have wind energy leasing systems to encourage the siting of turbines on Crown (government) land, where lease payments will benefit the province.[72] Setting up a system like this generally requires provincial legislation to be passed, and the leases are also generally overseen by provincial regulators. In British Columbia, for example, a wind power project proposal would be submitted to the Integrated Land Management Bureau, which would issue the permit to investigate a site for wind potential and, later, to build the turbines.[73] The surface lease would be overseen by the Ministry of Energy, Mines, and Petroleum Resources,

68 Andrew Kurjata, 'Work on Site C Suspended Prior to First Nations Lawsuit' *CBC News* (27 Feb 2018), <https://www.cbc.ca/news/canada/british-columbia/site-c-work-suspended-1.4554007>

69 See Justin McElroy, 'B.C. Government to Go Ahead with Site C Hydroelectric Dam Project' *CBC News* (11 Dec 2017), <https://www.cbc.ca/news/canada/british-columbia/site-c-dam-decision-1.4435939>.

70 See National Energy Board, 'Market Snapshot: Ontario and Quebec Are Among the Leaders in North American Wind Power Capacity' (9 Mar 2018), <https://www.neb-one.gc.ca/nrg/ntgrtd/mrkt/snpsht/2018/05-01ntrqbcldrs-eng.html>.

71 See Stewart Fast et al, 'Lessons Learned from Ontario's Wind Energy Disputes' 1 (2016) *Nature Energy* 15028; Brian Hill, 'Ontario Energy Minister Admits Mistake with Green Energy Program' *Global News* (24 Feb 2017), <https://globalnews.ca/news/3272095/ontario-energy-minister-admits-mistake-with-green-energy-program>. The failure of the FIT program was that it locked municipal utilities into long-term contracts with wind power producers, forcing consumer prices to rise considerably. See *ibid*.

72 See Allan Ingelson, 'Wind Energy Development on Public Lands in Alberta: A Missed Opportunity', ABlawg (14 June 2018), <http://ablawg.ca/wp-content/uploads/2018/06/Blog_AI_Wind_Development_Public_Lands.pdf>.

73 See Government of British Columbia, 'Land Use: Wind Power', <https://www2.gov.bc.ca/gov/content/industry/crown-land-water/crown-land/crown-land-uses/clean-energy/wind-power?keyword=wind>.

which sets the rents for wind facilities on Crown land in British Columbia.[74] Other provinces would have a different set of agencies in charge of issuing permits and setting rents.

There are also wind facilities in the northern part of the country, including Yukon and the Northwest Territories, although these are mainly installed and maintained by mining companies to provide power for their operations.[75] Many parts of Canada's far north are dependent on diesel powered generators for electricity, and most villages and towns do not have the resources that mining companies have to make the switch to wind power (solar would not be a good option, given that there is so little sunlight during the winter).[76] However, there are examples of microgrids running on wind and run-of-the-river hydropower throughout the territories. Since there is no comprehensive grid in this part of Canada, generation tends to be located close to the point of consumption. The distance between these remote parts of Canada and more populated areas many hundreds of miles to the south make interties uneconomic and practically very difficult.

2.4 Geothermal

As of this writing, there are no utility-scale geothermal plants in Canada, although there are sufficient geothermal resources in parts of the country to make this a possibility in the future. There is one planned five-megawatt geothermal plant in Saskatchewan, which would be the first geothermal plant built from the ground up in the country.[77] This facility, once it is operational, will be run by Saskatchewan Power, the province's municipal utility, and regulated by the Saskatchewan Rate Review Panel.[78] There are also proposed small geothermal generation sites, which would be created from repurposed oil and gas wells, in Alberta and Saskatchewan. Because of the technical difficulties in converting the wells, the provincial oil and gas regulators would likely be the de facto regulators of this small-scale geothermal power generation.

2.5 Laws promoting low carbon energy: carbon tax

Canada is set to implement a mandatory minimum carbon price of $20 per tonne in 2019, rising to $50 per tonne by 2022.[79] This minimum, also called the backstop, is part of Canada's federal climate action plan, the Pan Canadian Framework on Clean Growth and Climate Change.[80] The backstop uses output based pricing restrictions instead of a single price that applies to all emitters, meaning that some industries may be able to emit a certain amount of carbon before the tax kicks in. This makes the backstop similar to the provincial carbon

74 Ibid.

75 See Jimmy Thomson, 'How Can Canada's North Get Off Diesel?' *The Narwhal* (11 Feb 2019), <https://thenarwhal.ca/how-canadas-north-get-off-diesel>.

76 Ibid.

77 Arthur White-Crummey, 'Canada's First-ever Geothermal Power Plant in the Works for Torquay Area' *Regina Leader-Post* (18 May 2018), <https://leaderpost.com/news/saskatchewan/canadas-first-ever-geothermal-power-plant-in-the-works-for-torquay-area>.

78 Natural Resources Canada, 'Saskatchewan's Electric Reliability Framework', <https://www.nrcan.gc.ca/energy/electricity-infrastructure/18849>.

79 Government of Canada, 'Technical Paper: Federal Carbon Pricing Backstop', <https://www.canada.ca/en/services/environment/weather/climatechange/technical-paper-federal-carbon-pricing-backstop.html>.

80 See Government of Canada, 'Pan-Canadian Framework on Clean Growth and Climate Change', <https://www.canada.ca/en/services/environment/weather/climatechange/pan-canadian-framework.html>.

tax in Alberta, which is currently $30 per tonne with an output-based pricing scheme that exempts some emissions from industries like oil and gas, and exempts all emissions from other specified sources, like farm fuels.[81] In contrast, British Columbia's carbon price is a flat $50 per tonne for all emitters, including individuals who buy gasoline and diesel (the price is attached to the fuels). Because both Alberta and British Columbia's carbon prices meet or exceed the backstop, at least for 2019 and 2020, the backstop would not be applied to them. This is also true for Quebec, which participates in a carbon cap and trade market with California.[82]

Other provinces that do not have a carbon price, or have a carbon price that is lower than the federal backstop, had to adopt the backstop in 2019.[83] However, the provinces of Ontario and Saskatchewan have mounted a legal challenge to the backstop, arguing that the federal government does not have the authority to impose a nationwide carbon price.[84] Alberta, which has a carbon tax, elected a new government in 2019 that has promised to repeal the tax and it is likely that, upon doing so, the province will also join the legal challenges to the backstop.[85] The future of Canada's national carbon price is therefore in doubt.

Both the United States and Canada have made strides in employing legislation and other tools to encourage the use of low carbon energy sources, but in both countries, progress can be hindered by the politicizing of energy issues more generally. Despite the success of integrating wind and solar power into the grid, both countries are still largely dependent on fossil fuels for transportation, heating, and, in some places, electricity. Real strides to change this may be on the horizon, but currently regulatory efforts are likely not bold enough to accomplish this. For both countries, there are ways to promote and sustain low carbon energy sources, but the will to do so is not always there when there is an actual or perceived economic downside.

81 See Government of Alberta, 'Carbon Levy and Rebates', <https://www.alberta.ca/climate-carbon-pricing.aspx>.

82 This was also true of Ontario until 2018, when the province withdrew from the cap and trade market with California and Quebec. See David V. Wright, 'Enforcement and Withdrawal Under the California-Quebec (and not Ontario) Cap-and-Trade Linkage Agreement' (2018) Canadian Institute of Resources Law, <https://cirl.ca/files/cirl/d-wright-enforcement-and-withdrawal.pdf>.

83 See Environment and Climate Change Canada, 'Estimated Results of the Federal Carbon Pollution Pricing System', <https://www.canada.ca/en/services/environment/weather/climatechange/climate-action/pricing-carbon-pollution/estimated-impacts-federal-system.html>.

84 See Tyler Dawson, 'With Legal Battle over Carbon Tax Set to Start in 2019, Here Are the Major Players' Arguments' *National Post* (2 Jan 2019), <https://nationalpost.com/news/politics/with-legal-battle-over-carbon-tax-set-to-start-in-2019-here-are-the-major-players-arguments>.

85 United Conservative Party, 'Platform: Scrapping the Carbon Tax', <https://www.albertastrongandfree.ca/scrapping-the-carbon-tax>.

17

FORMULA RATE PLANS AND MULTI-YEAR RATE PLANS

Can they serve the public interest, and how?

Scott Hempling

Overview

In most of the United States, electric service is provided by companies known as "public utilities". Most of these entities are investor-owned, for-profit companies that have received exclusive franchises (sometimes called "concessions") from a state-level legislature or regulatory agency (known as a public utility commission). Each utility's rates are set by a regulatory agency and placed in a public file in the form of legal tariffs.[1] This chapter addresses a series of questions about how these regulatory agencies set their utilities' rates.

When setting a utility's rates for a given service, regulators can choose between two very different questions: "What does this service cost?" vs. "What should this service cost?" In competitive markets, the second question dominates, causing sellers to push their costs to the lowest level necessary to achieve customer satisfaction. Customers don't pay for costs; they pay for performance. But retail electricity markets are usually monopoly markets, so the first question dominates. Utilities submit data on what they intend to spend—accounting data. Rarely do regulators require the utility to submit data on what they should spend—competitive market data. Rate cases focus on aligning rates with costs; they should focus instead on aligning compensation with performance.

This inefficient practice, of basing rates on costs rather than performance, is exacerbated and entrenched by the current popularity—among utilities, that is—of formula rate plans (FRP) and multi-year rate plans (MYRP). A utility designs its FRP and MYRP proposals to increase the certainty of recovering its costs, so that its actual return on equity (ROE) will equal or exceed its authorized ROE. Utilities label these proposals "performance-based ratemaking." That phrase offers no value, because all ratemaking is, or should be, performance-based ratemaking. Overusing the term "performance" without accountability causes observers to confuse plans that address only earnings with plans that actually induce performance. This chapter provides readers the analytical alertness necessary to avoid that confusion. *Part One* deals with substance; *Part Two* addresses strategy.

1 For a discussion about the legal underpinning of public utilities in the United States, *see generally* Scott Hempling, *Regulating Public Utility Performance: The Law of Market Structure, Pricing and Jurisdiction* (American Bar Assoc. 2013), especially Chapters 2 and 6.

On substance: *Sections I* and *II* address formula rate plans and multi-year rate plans, respectively. For each type of plan, I offer definitions, purposes, and characteristics. The main sources are statutes, rules, and orders enacted or issued by U.S. state legislatures or regulatory commissions.

On strategy: *Section III* returns to the key public interest purposes and asks, "How might those purposes be undermined by proposals that appear innocuous?" Because undermining public interest purposes can occur through language, *Section IV* presents phrases that utilities feed into regulatory conversation to produce emotions unrelated to facts or logic, hoping to gain approvals that increase their earnings while shifting their risks. *Section V* then presents a set of questions with which policy-makers can evaluate proposed plans. *Section VI* closes the chapter with this recommendation: regulatory commissions should start generic proceedings on FRPs and MYRPs, to establish appropriate expectations for public interest plans. The alternative—a regulatory habit of passively waiting for a utility's proposal—makes the utility's goals central and the consumers' needs marginal.

This chapter originated as a task for, and is funded by, the District of Columbia Office of People's Counsel.

Part One Substance

1 Formula rate plans: definition, purposes, characteristics

1.1 Definition and purposes

A formula rate plan trues up actual ROE to authorized ROE. At the end of each specified period, it adjusts rates for the next period as necessary to correct for any over-earning or under-earning, relative to an authorized ROE, that occurred in the preceding period. The formula rate plan can be designed to true-up the utility's overall ROE, or only the ROE as applied to particular investments. The plan is an insurance policy against over- or under-earnings. Like any insurance policy for a utility, it comes—or should come—at a cost to the utility: a reduction in the authorized ROE to reflect the reduction in shareholder risk.[2]

There is a distinction between a "bare" formula rate plan and a "performance-based" formula rate plan. The bare formula rate plan periodically adjusts rate levels for one reason only: to keep the earned ROE close to the authorized ROE (possibly subject to a "dead-band," sometimes called a "collar," and some means of allocating between shareholders and ratepayers any deviations from that band). The performance-based formula rate plan includes that purpose, but also adjusts the actual earnings based on the utility's performance on specified parameters—like infrastructure investment, job creation, productivity increases, cost decreases, and rate stability.

1.2 Characteristics

1.2.1 As between utility and commission, who has power and discretion over what?

The power to propose is the power to influence. State statutes differ on how they allocate, between utility and commission, the power and discretion to propose or impose a plan, as

2 For a discussion of the relationship between risk-reducing plans and the authorized return on equity, see Scott Hempling, *Riders, Trackers, Surcharges, Pre-Approvals, and Decoupling: How Do They Affect the Cost of Equity?* (March 2012), ElectricityPolicy.com <www.scotthemplinglaw.com/files/pdf/ppr_riders_oge_hempling112711.pdf> accessed 28 May 2019.

well as the power to choose the details. These powers and discretions can differ between two time periods: before the plan's adoption, and while the plan is in effect.

1.2.1.1 BEFORE ADOPTION OF THE PLAN

Does the statute require the commission to accept the utility's proposal, allowing the commission to modify it only to the extent necessary to render it consistent with some statutory standard? Or may the commission go beyond the proposal, making changes not legally necessary but commission-preferred? Alternatively, does the commission have the power to impose an FRP on the utility even if the utility does not propose one or want one? Some statutes require the commission to allow an FRP if the utility wants it.[3] Other statutes allow the commission to adjust the utility's proposal to make it reflect the commission's preferences.[4]

1.2.1.2 AFTER ADOPTION OF THE PLAN

Once the plan goes into effect, what powers does the commission have? Questions arise about monitoring, changes, and termination.

Monitoring: Does the commission have the power to require periodic information on utility costs, profit, and other issues—and then to adjust numbers based on an audit? If the plan provides these opportunities, then what information comes forth and at what intervals? One statute requires the utility to provide information quarterly and allows the commission to adjust numbers after an audit.[5]

Changes to the plan: During the plan's operation, does the commission have the power to investigate its reasonableness, then make changes? Some statutes allow the commission to change the plan prospectively.[6]

Termination: Does the utility have a right to escape the plan if it dislikes the outcomes? Is there a reciprocal right in the customers, or reciprocal power in the commission to terminate the plan if its outputs conflict with the public interest? If there is a right in the utility but not one for the consumer or commission, what prevents the utility from keeping the plan when it raises rates but escaping the plan when it lowers rates? Some statutes require the utility to stay in the plan until the plan terminates.[7] Other statutes allow the utility to escape if a *force majeure* event occurs.[8] Still other statutes allow the utility to escape the plan whenever it wishes.[9]

1.2.2 Proposal design

Of the many design parameters used to shape formula rate plans, there are nine that appear most frequently.

3 Arkansas Code §§ 23-4-1201, et seq.; South Carolina Code §§ 58-5-415, et seq.
4 Arkansas Code §§ 23-4-1201, et seq.
5 South Carolina Code §§ 58-5-415, et seq.
6 220 Illinois Code 5/16-108.5, et seq.
7 South Carolina Code §§ 58-5-415, et seq.
8 *Alabama Metallurgical Corp. v. Alabama Public Service Commission*, 441 So.2d 565, 1983 Ala. LEXIS 4745 (Ala. 1983).
9 220 Illinois Code 5/16-108.5, et seq.

For what period does the FRP last? The frequent choices are: (a) until the utility proposes and the commission establishes new rates;[10] (b) no more than five years, unless the commission expressly extends the plan for another five years;[11] and (c) indefinitely, until the utility decides to terminate its plan.[12]

What is the initial cost level and ROE level? The frequent choices are: (a) the most recently approved cost of service, or a newly filed (and approved) cost of service, whichever the utility prefers;[13] (b) a cost of service based on utility-selected test period;[14] and (c) a newly established cost of service.[15]

Is there a "collar" around the authorized ROE? What type of "sharing" exists outside the band? Frequent options include: (a) 100 basis point[16] collar, with profit above collar "shared"[17] 75/25 (customers/shareholders);[18] (b) 100 basis point collar, with no "sharing" above or below the collar;[19] and (c) 50 basis point collar, with no "sharing" above or below the collar.[20]

Is there a cap on the size of rate adjustments? Some plans limit the size of the rate adjustment, such as at 2.5 percent[21] and 4percent.[22]

What is the cost basis for each adjusted rate? Some plans use the official cost data reported annually to the U.S. Federal Energy Regulatory Commission (FERC), adjusted to reflect projections for the upcoming year and to reflect any reconciliations of over- or under-recovery from the prior year.[23] An alternative cost basis is simply the existing rate, adjusted for any necessary reconciliations.[24]

How does the FRP process relate to the general rate case process? Some statutes allow the request for an FRP to accompany a general rate application;[25] others allow requests for an FRP at any time.[26] And for some, the utility may initiate a general rate case while an FRP is in effect.[27]

During the FRP's period, may the commission examine costs for prudence, outside of a general rate case? Some statutes prohibit the commission from questioning the prudence of a utility's costs, once the state has made those costs the basis for a plan.[28] Other statutes expressly preserve that commission authority.[29]

10 South Carolina Code §§ 58-5-415, et seq.; Arkansas Code §§ 23-4-1201, et seq.
11 Arkansas Code §§ 23-4-1201, et seq.
12 220 Illinois Code 5/16-108.5, et seq.
13 South Carolina Code §§ 58-5-415, et seq.
14 Arkansas Code §§ 23-4-1201, et seq.
15 220 Illinois Code 5/16-108.5, et seq.
16 A basis point is 1/100 of a percentage point.
17 For a discussion of the term "sharing," see Section IV.A.
18 *In the Matter of an Application for a General Change or Modification in Centerpoint Energy Arkla, a Division of Centerpoint Energy Resources Corp.'s, Rates, Charges and Tariffs*, Cause No. PUD 200400187, 2004 Okla. PUC LEXIS 226.
19 South Carolina Code §§ 58-5-415, et seq.; Arkansas Code §§ 23-4-1201, et seq.
20 220 Illinois Code 5/16-108.5, et seq.
21 220 Illinois Code 5/16-108.5, et seq.
22 Arkansas Code §§ 23-4-1201, et seq.
23 220 Illinois Code 5/16-108.5, et seq.
24 Arkansas Code §§ 23-4-1201, et seq.
25 Arkansas Code §§ 23-4-1201, et seq.
26 South Carolina Code §§ 58-5-415, et seq.
27 *In the Matter of an Application for a General Change or Modification in Centerpoint Energy Arkla, a Division of Centerpoint Energy Resources Corp.'s, Rates, Charges and Tariffs*, Cause No. PUD 200400187, 2004 Okla. PUC LEXIS 226.
28 South Carolina Code §§ 58-5-415, et seq.
29 220 Illinois Code 5/16-108.5, et seq.; *In the Matter of an Application for a General Change or Modification in Centerpoint Energy Arkla, a Division of Centerpoint Energy Resources Corp.'s, Rates, Charges and Tariffs*, Cause No. PUD 200400187, 2004 Okla. PUC LEXIS 226.

Does the FRP affect revenue allocation and rate design? Under some statutes, the FRP can adjust the allocation of costs—both among customer classes and between the fixed and variable components of the existing rate structure.[30] Other statutes require the FRP to track the pre-existing allocations, until the commission changes them in the next general rate case.[31]

Does the FRP require specific performance achievements? With what rewards or penalties? Some statutes require FRPs to include specific performance metrics, such as: job creation, investment in distribution upgrades and smart grid projects, reliability achievements, line losses, estimated bills, uncollectible accounts, contracts with minority and female-owned businesses, and low-income program support. There can be financial penalties if the utility fails to achieve these metrics.[32]

2 Multi-year rate plans: definition, purposes, characteristics

2.1 Definitions

A multi-year rate plan determines the rate path for a multi-year period, usually at least three years (although some have lasted for eight years). During that period there is no general rate case. The plan could, but need not, specify the actual rates for each year; more likely it describes how those rates will change during the period.

Accompanying the rate path can be other elements: performance metrics, "sharing" mechanisms for when actual ROE exceeds or falls below a collar, and "trackers" that true-up the costs of (and therefore reduce the shareholder risks associated with) certain types of expenditures. A utility could have an MYRP along with one or more adjustment mechanisms, as well as targeted performance "incentives."

What distinguishes an MYRP from conventional cost-of-service ratemaking? A general rate case sets fixed rates—rates that do not change until re-set in a new general rate case (not counting fuel adjustment clauses and other trackers). In an MYRP, the rates can change during the period according to pre-set conditions. So, the inevitable divergence of actual results from projected results that occurs in a traditional rate case does not necessarily occur in an MYRP—at least not to the same extent. Why? Because the MYRP's rate path can anticipate and address the events that cause divergence, such as inflation and productivity. Reflecting those factors in the rate path reduces the likelihood that actual results will vary from projections.

What distinguishes MYRP from FRP? As explained in Section II, an FRP's main purpose is to true-up actuals to projections. An MYRP does not true-up actuals to projections (although it can reduce divergences); rather, it assigns consequences for the inevitable variations of actuals from projections (although an FRP can do that with a "sharing" mechanism). Also, under an FRP, a new rate case can be initiated at any time (by the utility, the commission, or an intervenor). Under an MYRP, in contrast, no one can start a rate case during the multi-year period—unless the plan provides for one. In that case the plan would not really be an MYRP.

30 *In the Matter of an Application for a General Change or Modification in Centerpoint Energy Arkla, a Division of Centerpoint Energy Resources Corp.'s, Rates, Charges and Tariffs*, Cause No. PUD 200400187, 2004 Okla. PUC LEXIS 226.

31 South Carolina Code §§ 58-5-415, et seq.; 220 Illinois Code 5/16-108.5, et seq.

32 Illinois statute.

Like an FRP, an MYRP does not ignore cost-of-service ratemaking. Its design starts with base rates set in a general rate case. But the MYRP differs from cost-of-service ratemaking and the FRP in a key respect: *It reduces the amount of information available to regulators on actual costs incurred during the MYRP period.* In the FRP, the commission receives the actual cost information so it can reconcile projections to actuals. The MYRP does not ensure that information flow. During the MYRP period, the only information the regulator has is the old information used to set base rates prior to the MYRP period; the utility, in contrast, always has internally (and privately) the most up-to-date cost information. So, an MYRP increases the asymmetry of knowledge, thereby lessening the regulator's ability to assess whether the MYRP is causing the utility to operate more efficiently or is merely enabling the utility to increase its earnings.

2.2 Purposes

MYRP proponents describe several purposes. By increasing the period between rate cases and by eliminating true-up guarantees, an MYPR encourages the utility both to: (a) reduce costs; and (b) invest in projects having multi-year construction periods and multi-year benefits. The latter benefit is more likely to occur if the MYRP includes a tracker for capital expenditures (as will be discussed in Section II.C.2.b). When the rate path is specific, the utility is "clear about the extent to which a successful effort to control costs will result in increased earnings."[33] At the same time, "[l]oosening the link between its own cost and revenue gives a utility an operating environment more like that which competitive markets experience."[34] When the MYRP has factors reflecting new capital projects, the utility can recover its capital expenditures on a schedule closer to their actual incurrence, thus reducing capital costs. Certain variations can encourage utilities to reduce total costs by eliminating bias towards capital expenditures (capex) and against operating expenses (as will be discussed in Section II.C.1.c).

An MYRP can be designed for at least four additional purposes. First, adding performance metrics, accompanied by rewards and penalties can hold utilities accountable on specific performance dimensions. Second, adding a factor for inflation makes rate increases more frequent, smaller, and more predictable, thus reducing "rate shock."[35] Third, adding "efficiency carryover mechanisms"—devices which allow the utility to maintain rates above cost beyond the MYRP period—gives the utility more reason to reduce costs. And fourth, an MYRP can reduce the number of rate cases, thereby freeing management, intervenors, and the commission to focus on other things.

2.3 Characteristics

Discussed next are six main characteristics of MYRP proposals.

2.3.1 The base revenue requirement and adjustments

2.3.1.1 A BASE RATES

The MYRP begins with base rates, such as those established in the most recent, or current, rate case. Some plans start not with the most recently approved cost-of-service, but with the

33 The Brattle Group, *Performance Based Regulation Plans: Goals, Incentives and Alignment* at viii (December 2017).

34 M.N. Lowry et al., *Regulation Using Multiyear Rate Plans for U.S. Electric Utilities* at iii (July 2017).

35 *See* Section V.F, questioning whether "rate shock" is necessarily a bad thing.

costs reported to the Federal Energy Regulatory Commission in the FERC Form 1.[36] But Form 1 cost levels are not necessarily prudent cost levels. Form 1 reports what happened, not what should have happened. The better data source on what should have happened is not data from the applicant utility but data from the best performing utilities.

A note on depreciation: The rate paths provided by MYRPs do not necessarily track the decline in rate base arising from paper depreciation.[37] The original rate base remains at that level for the entire plan period, even as that rate base is being depreciated for accounting purposes. The result, if all other costs match projections, is over-earnings. While that risk of over-earning exists in the normal practice (because depreciation continues in the period between general rate cases), with MYRPs that period is longer.

2.3.1.2 INCREASES TO THE BASE RATES

A typical MYRP adjusts base rates to increase the revenue over time. Some plans specify the precise change in rates for each MYRP year. A series of specified stair-steps makes the rates known in advance.

Instead of specifying annual rate changes, some MYRPs identify indices that raise the rates automatically. Some call these indices "attrition relief mechanisms."[38] An inflation factor could reflect either general inflation in the economy, or inflation in the cost basket specific to the type of utility at issue. By accounting for rising costs while not ensuring recovery of the utility's specific costs, this technique reduces the utility's financial risk while preserving an "incentive" to cut costs (unlike an FRP's true-up approach, which removes that incentive). This revenue-increasing factor can be applied to operating costs, capital expenditures, or both; one in fact could apply a different inflation factor to each of those categories. Some plans address capital expenditures through trackers; doing so removes them from the cost-disciplining purpose of the MYRP—making their treatment more like a true-up FRP.

Caution: An MYRP that is rhetorically emphatic about "efficiency," but places major capital expenditures in a tracker, is closer to a discipline-reducing FRP than an efficiency-increasing

36 The Federal Energy Regulatory Commission describes its Form 1 as "a comprehensive financial and operating report submitted for Electric Rate regulation and financial audits." It contains details on operational indicators, operating costs, and capital expenditures. Each utility subject to FERC's jurisdiction files its Form 1 annually. *See* <www.ferc.gov/docs-filing/forms/form-1/data.asp> accessed 28 May 2019.

37 An excellent explanation of depreciation and its role in the utility ratemaking appears in *Louisiana Public Service Commission v. FCC*, 476 U.S. 355, 364–365 (1986):

> Depreciation is defined as the loss in service value of a capital asset over time. In the context of public utility accounting and regulation, it is a process of charging the cost of depreciable property, adjusted for net salvage, to operating expense accounts over the useful life of the asset . . . [A] regulated carrier is entitled to recover its reasonable expenses and a fair return on its investment through the rates it charges its customers, and . . . depreciation practices contribute importantly to the calculation of both the carrier's investment and its expenses. [citations omitted] The total amount that a carrier is entitled to charge for services, its "revenue requirement," is the sum of its current operating expenses, including taxes and depreciation expenses, and a return on its investment "rate base." The original cost of a given item of equipment enters the rate base when that item enters service. As it depreciates over time—as a function of wear and tear or technological obsolescence—the rate base is reduced according to a depreciation schedule that is based on an estimate of the item's expected useful life. Each year the amount that is removed from the rate base is included as an operating expense.

38 *See, e.g.*, M.N. Lowry et al., *Regulation Using Multiyear Rate Plans for U.S. Electric Utilities* at iii (July 2017) (using the phrase "attrition relief mechanism" to describe a tariff term that "escalates rates or revenue between rate cases to address cost pressures such as inflation and growth in number of customers independently of the utility's own cost").

MYRP. What matters is not the plan's label (e.g., "FRP" or "MYRP"); *what matters is its scope* (*i.e.*, which costs are inside the plan—thus subject to the risk of under-recovery—and which costs are outside the plan—thus recovered, risk-free, through riders and trackers).

2.3.1.3 THE CAPITAL EXPENDITURE BIAS

In traditional cost of service ratemaking, for-profit utilities earn a profit on their capital expenditures (capex), if those expenditures are prudent and used and useful. Operating expenses (opex), in contrast, are recovered from ratepayers without a profit. As a result, a utility with a choice between meeting its customers' need with a capital expenditure (such as a new generating plant) or with operating expenditures (such as a purchase of power from another entity) prefer the capital expenditure. This preference for capex over opex does not disappear with an MYRP. To solve this problem, the United Kingdom focused on totex (total expenditures)—making the utility's total profit indifferent between opex and capex, with the total profit subject to a cap. To equalize incentives between capex and opex, the United Kingdom's regulator, Ofgem,

> fixed the amount of total expenditures that could be capitalized at 85 percent. Newly capitalized costs would be recovered over a 45-year period, while existing rate base costs would be recovered over a 20-year period. The remaining 15 percent would be expensed.[39]

A utility could pursue its capex bias by including in the MYRP a capex amount representing particular projects, but then defer those projects to a year outside the plan. That deferral means the utility would have collected MYRP revenues for a project that had not been carried out. Then, in the next MYRP, the utility would try to include the deferred projects—hoping to get paid twice for the same project.

2.3.1.4 PRODUCTIVITY ADJUSTMENT

The typical MYRP couples the expectation of rising costs with an expectation of rising productivity. Known as the "X factor," the productivity adjustment is a subtraction from the inflation factor, intended to make the utility "stretch" to maintain or increase its earnings.[40] Ontario used X factors based on peer groups, such as samples of Ontario power distributors and U.S. distributors.[41]

2.3.2 *Other possible accompaniments*

2.3.2.1 INCLUSION OF FRP WITHIN THE MYRP?

Some utilities have proposed what they call an MYRP, but what is actually a multi-year series of FRPs. The multi-year period has no rate case, but each year has a true-up of

39 Ibid at text accompanying n.167.

40 Ibid defines "X factor" as "a term in a rate or revenue cap index that reflects the impact of productivity growth on cost growth. It may also incorporate stretch factors and adjustments for other considerations such as the inaccuracy of the inflation measure," x.

41 Ibid at p.6.30.

projected to actual costs, so that the utility bears no risk of under-recovery (or some risk if there is a deadband (a range within which there is no sharing) and "sharing"). While this approach ensures that each year's rates are based on the most recent data, the promise of annual true-ups removes operational discipline. Putting an FRP into an MYRP is like creating a tracker, discussed next—but a tracker for the entirety of costs rather than only for specified costs.

2.3.2.2 TRACKERS

Trackers (also called riders) remove certain costs from the MYRP's efficiency-and-stretch purpose, placing them into an FRP-like true-up purpose. This tracker option allows the plan designer to assign different risks to different costs, like using objective indexing for operations and maintenance, but true-ups for certain capital expenditures. A close cousin to the tracker is deferred accounting: The tracker promises retroactive true-up; deferred accounting preserves the utility's ability to argue for retroactive true-up. Utilities seek these devices for costs they assert are hard to predict and hard to control. The Hawaii Commission used a tracker-surcharge to finance renewable energy infrastructure.[42]

2.3.2.3 PERFORMANCE INCENTIVE METRICS

A bare MYRP—one having no performance metrics—has only one function and result: to reward the utility for reducing costs during the plan period (and to "share" savings with customers). But cutting costs without attention to performance is like cutting taxes while ignoring children's education. To avoid cost-cutting that harms performance, MYRPs typically include a performance feature.

When placed in an MYRP, a performance feature has four dimensions: (a) the subject of the performance (*e.g.*, outages, demand reduction, consumption reduction, renewable energy interconnections); (b) a target or benchmark (*e.g.*, percentage reduction in hours or frequency of outages, mW reduction of demand or mWh reduction of consumption, percentage increase in renewable energy); (c) a range of expected performance within which there is no reward or penalty (the deadband); and (d) specific penalties or rewards for performance below or above that range.

2.3.2.4 EARNINGS SHARING MECHANISMS

The earnings sharing mechanism in an MYRP plays the same role as in an FRP: to allocate between ratepayers and shareholders the over-earnings and under-earnings relative to a deadband. While the notion of "sharing" is not inherently wrong (although the term "sharing" is misleading word-play, because anything above authorized ROE is monopoly rent and therefore "extraction," not "sharing"—see Section IV.A below), its application can harm customers. Calculating rewards as basis-point adjustments to the ROE, for example, encourages the utility to grow its rate base (since the higher ROE is multiplied by the rate base). The California Commission prefers calculating the reward "in reference to basis-point changes and then fixed in dollar amounts."[43]

42 Hawaii Public Utility Commission, Decision and Order No. 32177 (July 1, 2014).

43 M.N. Lowry et al., *Regulation Using Multiyear Rate Plans for U.S. Electric Utilities* at iii (July 2017) at 6.17.

2.3.3 Review of prudence during the plan

During an MYRP period, rates rise without a general rate case. Are those rate increases subject to any regulatory review? An MYRP's very purpose is to insulate the increases from review (just like commissions don't review the prudence of costs incurred between rate cases, because of the prohibition against retroactive ratemaking). An exception is Minnesota, where a Commission order on MYRPs had this passage:

> The Commission will require utilities seeking a multi-year rate plan to acknowledge that imprudent rate increases during the plan will be subject to refund, and to waive any claim that such a decision would be barred as a form of retroactive ratemaking.[44]

This order effectively converted the MYRPs' rate increases into rate caps, subject to review for prudence of the underlying costs.

2.3.4 Off-ramps

Some MYRPs include off-ramps, *i.e.*, plan terminations, for situations where earnings fall dangerously outside of expectations, either below (due to *force majeure* events) or above.

2.3.5 Relation to general rate case

During an MYRP period, the utility cannot seek a general rate case. As the Minnesota Commission explained, a "new rate case would undermine the rate certainty promised by the plan, while consuming more administrative resources."[45] But the Ontario Energy Board once allowed distribution companies, if they needed to make new capital expenditures, to file a rate case before their plans expired.[46]

2.3.6 When the plan ends, what will the rates be?

In a world without MRPs. this question has an obvious answer: The utility would file a general rate application, then the commission would decide rates in the normal way. The MYRP world is not that simple. Utilities have proposed "efficiency carryover mechanisms." After the MYRP period, these devices allow the utility to maintain rates above prudent cost, thus withholding from ratepayers cost reductions created during the plan period. The ostensible goal? To give the utility a profit-oriented reason to achieve long-term efficiencies (long-term meaning beyond the plan period)—efficiencies that the utility would not otherwise achieve.

The problem: Given its government protection from competition, the utility already had a legal obligation to achieve those efficiencies, so it has no reason to expect supranormal returns for achieving them. In fact, the implicit resistance to achieving them without the extra returns is grounds for revoking the utility's franchise, not granting the extra returns.

44 MN PUC Order at 9.
45 Ibid.
46 M.N. Lowry et al., *Regulation Using Multiyear Rate Plans for U.S. Electric Utilities* at 6.31 (July 2017).

Part Two Strategy

3 Public interest purposes: how are they undermined?

The preceding sections have described the common and optional features of FRPs and MYRPs. To win approval for these measures, utilities typically associate them with generic public interest purposes, six of which I discuss here. But a proposal's specifics can undermine those stated purposes. For each of six common purposes, this section explains how this undermining can occur.

3.1 Align rates with costs

When a utility asserts that its purpose is to align rates with costs, it means align rates with the *utility's* costs, whatever they are. That approach replaces objectivity with subjectivity. The outcome conflicts with the utility's legal obligation to charge customers for reasonable costs only.[47] For rates to satisfy the law—to be just and reasonable—they must align not with the utility's costs, but with the right costs.

Commissions that focus on continuously re-aligning the utility's rates with the utility's costs risk being drawn into a series of rate increases. Each increase might seem small. But for major capital projects that series of approvals can bring the commission past the "point of no return"—the point at which it no longer makes economic sense to consider alternatives because the incremental cost of completing and operating the original project becomes less than the total cost (construction and operation) of a not-yet started alternative—one that, had it been the original option, would have cost less. To prevent this result, commissions using FRPs or MYRPs should not approve expenditures for major capital projects unless the projects have emerged from a rigorous integrated resource planning process.

A related problem: If for a capital project a commission's pre-expenditure approvals are based on the utility's cost estimates, the utility has an incentive to underestimate its costs. And then, having gotten the commission committed to the utility's preferred option, the utility can increase the recoverable amount later using the "point-of-no-return" argument just noted. There is also the converse risk of the utility over-estimating its costs, winning approval for the expenditure, then touting project completion "under budget" as evidence of prudence when the prudent cost was actually lower than the final cost. To protect against these tactics, commissions will need independent, expert assistance, equivalent to the utility's expertise, for each major approval request.

The utility should also bear a continuing burden of proving, at the time of each successive cost recovery request, that the capital project still makes economic sense in light of feasible alternatives. New options can emerge, interest rates can change, fuel prices can rise or fall.

47 Beginning with the Interstate Commerce Act of 1887, economic regulatory statutes in the United States have required that a utility's rates be "just and reasonable." The just and reasonable principle has been echoed in numerous court cases, requiring that a public utility must, at all times, "operate with all reasonable economies," *El Paso Natural Gas Co. v. FPC*, 281 F.2d 567, 573 (5th Cir. 1960); incur the "lowest feasible cost *Potomac Elec. Power Co. v. Pub. Serv. Comm'n of the D.C.*, 661 A.2d 131, 137 (D.C. 1995); and use "all available cost savings opportunities," *Midwestern Gas Transmission Co. v. E. Tenn. Natural Gas Co.*, 36 FPC 61, 70 (1966), *aff'd sub nom. Midwestern Gas Transmission Co. v. FPC*, 388 F.2d 444 (7th Cir. 1968). For a detailed discussion of utility ratemaking, *see* Scott Hempling, *Regulating Public Utility Performance: The Law of Market Structure, Pricing and Jurisdiction* (American Bar Assoc. 2013), especially chapter 6.

The integrated resource planning process that initially approved the project should not remove the utility's continuing obligation to act cost-effectively.

Finally, at each cost request, the commission should assign expressly, between ratepayers and shareholders, the prospective risk of results varying from estimated costs. Not all risks must fall on ratepayers. Otherwise the discipline normally imposed by competition is lost.

3.2 Create incentives to cut costs

3.2.1 The "incentive" problem

Utilities that propose FRPs and MYRPs argue that the prospect of a ROE exceeding normal levels is a necessary "incentive" to performance. This argument ignores facts. Performance depends on performers. Shareholders are not performers; they are investors. They invest in a company, not in a particular service, product, or effort by that company. The productivity and efficiency actions under discussion in FRPs and MYRPs are not inanimate behaviors caused by abstract forces; they are efforts undertaken by human beings: workers, not shareholders. While the ROE must be sufficient to attract capital, any "performance" incentives must go to the performers—executives, managers, and line workers.

If employees' base salaries already reflect competitive levels, their obligation to achieve ordinary standards is given. They should get extra compensation—"incentives"—only for excellence. They should also face penalties for shortcomings. With these employee incentives in place, shareholder incentives add nothing.

Paying extra compensation to achieve higher standards must align with a reasonable benefit-cost analysis. Not every higher standard is worth the extra cost; indeed, where a utility can increase its earnings by increasing its investments, "gold-plating" is a risk. If the quality difference between first-quartile and second-quartile performance is barely noticeable, but costly to achieve, ratepayers should not pay for it.

Executive compensation raises a different problem: The potential for conflict with the customers' interest. Compensation based on stock price or earnings encourages executives to seek earnings beyond the authorized level, beyond what customers should have to pay. Some commissions disallow this type of compensation from rates. But doing so removes only a tiny percentage of the utility's multi-billion dollar revenue requirement;[48] it does not remove the adverse incentive.

3.2.2 The cost-cutting problem

An FRP and an MYRP affect cost-cutting differently. Pure FRP merely reconciles rates to costs; it does not reward cost-cutting. Indeed, if applied thoughtlessly, it makes the utility indifferent to costs. MYRP, with its longer-than-normal regulatory lag, does encourage cost-cutting. But cost-cutting is not performance—not if the cost cuts lead to more frequent and longer outages due to poor plant maintenance or require higher expenditures later. For the utility, the larger and sooner the cost cut, the larger and sooner the addition to earnings. Careless cuts now can lead to higher costs later. Reducing vegetation management now can produce costly distribution outages later, reducing employee training can mean less productivity later, deferring maintenance now can cause larger repairs later.

48 For example, the Illinois statute says that charges for incentive compensation "based on net income or an affiliate's earnings per share shall not be recoverable under the performance-based formula rate."

3.2.3 The time horizon problem

Common to traditional cost-of-service ratemaking, FRPs, and MYRPs is the challenge of time horizon. Regulators seek to align in time three things: investment, cost recovery, and customer benefit. But a rate case deals with only a limited future period. That period's length depends on multiple factors: the utility's decision to file rates, the customer representative's decision to file complaints, and/or a commission's decision to start a rate case. The time dimensions for performance are different. Payback periods vary for new meters, for a renewable energy investment, and for pipeline repair. None of these performance time periods bears any connection to rate case time periods. As a result, regulation always faces mismatches among three time slots: when expenditures are incurred, when costs are recovered, and when benefits are produced.

These plans, especially MYRPs, do offer timing flexibility—different time periods for expenditures, cost recovery, and benefit production. But so do normal rate cases—especially when we distinguish operating costs (which are recovered currently) from capital expenditures (which are amortized over a project's useful life). The key is to treat each major expenditure option as a question: When is the money needed, when will the benefits arrive, and how do we set rates to answer both questions appropriately? These questions exist in normal ratemaking, FRPs, and MYRPs. As far as the time horizon problem is concerned, FRPs and MYRPs offer no inherent advantage over normal ratemaking.

3.3 Align rates with performance

A Lexus costs more than a Volkswagen; a car costs more than a bicycle. In competitive markets, people pay for performance. For a utility commission to align rates with performance, it first must determine what performance to require; then determine the prudent cost of achieving that performance.

To produce that performance, the FRP or MYRP must specify performance metrics, with appropriate consequences for failing to achieve those metrics. The typical FRP or MYRP proposal does not follow that analytical path. Instead it states a goal of full cost recovery; then attaches a limited set of performance metrics with associated adjustments that the utility has designed.

Once the commission has established performance standards, the shareholder compensation should be, and needs to be, no more than prudent cost, plus normal profit. An above-normal performance metric might increase the *expenditure* but need not increase the required *return*. Only if the higher quality means a higher probability of failing to meet that quality—and only if that failure would cause a penalty—would there be additional risk to the shareholders, justifying an increase in the return. Absent a showing of unique risk uncompensated by a ROE increment, a supranormal return is monopoly rent. Calling it an "incentive" does not change this economic fact.

3.4 Avoid "rate shock"

Proponents of FRPs and MYRPs say it is better for rates to rise by small increments annually rather than by a large amount suddenly.[49] Gradualism does have a value. Customers should

49 *See, e.g.*, Oklahoma Commission (2004) ("[A]ny rate increases passed on to customers would tend to be in smaller increments under the PBRC than might result from a general rate order."); Ark. Code § 23-4-1202(b)

always face prices that reflect the cost of consumption; so that as costs change, so do prices. But the "rate shock" argument assumes that costs always rise. That is not the case with all products, especially those involving investment in new technologies such as renewable power.

3.5 Encourage utility to make investments when necessary, rather than awaiting the next rate case

Absent a capital expenditure rider or some form of "construction work in progress," conventional ratemaking provides the utility with no compensation for its capital expenditures until the new facility enters commercial operation. Utilities argue that this limitation causes them to defer necessary capital expenditures until they have reason to file a general rate application. An MYRP, in contrast, can schedule ratepayer funding to synchronize with capital expenditures.

This argument for MYRPs has a premise that no commission should accept—and that no utility dares say out loud: that a utility would violate its obligation to serve by intentionally delaying a necessary expenditure (investment withholding) until it receives the rate treatment it wants. If the utility sees a public need for a capital expenditure, it has a legal obligation to make that expenditure.[50] The regulator then has an obligation to set rates appropriately. If the regulator fails to act, the utility has a right to relief in court; it does not have a right to avoid its obligation.

3.6 The problem of asymmetrical knowledge

If an FRP or MYRP otherwise has merit, it will serve the public interest only if the commission has the information and expertise equivalent to the utility's. Here are six examples of how, in the context of an FRP or MYRP, a differential in expertise or information can affect outcomes:

1. The *base cost structure* is the starting point for all rate increases and decreases. It has to be reasonable. The utility will know more than the commission about what it actually costs to run the utility in the base year.
2. Even where *cost escalation factors* are based on external, objective data, the utility will know more than the commission about how its actual costs are likely to compare to that data. That knowledge will help the utility design a reward-penalty structure to its advantage.

(aspiring to "stable rates"); and Section 4 of Arkansas's enacting bill ("[T]here is a need to maintain stable rates and to mitigate the magnitude of future rate changes.")

50 An "obligation to serve" is at the core of every utility's relationship to its government franchising authority. Washington State's provision is typical: "Every telecommunications company shall, upon reasonable notice, furnish to all persons and corporations who may apply therefor and be reasonably entitled thereto suitable and proper facilities and connections for telephonic communication and furnish telephone service as demanded." Wash. Rev. Code § 80.36.090." The obligation is to serve not only current needs but future needs. As the New Jersey Supreme Court explained:

> The burden assumed [by accepting a franchise] . . . was a community service; it was not limited to the establishment of a system suitable only to the then current needs. Included also was the utility's duty to keep in view the probable growth of the township, both in population and in structural development, and to make gradual extensions of its mains to meet the reasonable demands that would inevitably result.
>
> Bd. of Fire Comm'rs of Fire Dist. No. 3, *Township of Piscataway v. Bd. of Pub. Util. Comm'rs*, 142 A.2d 85, 87 (N.J. 1958)

3. For predictions of *capital expenditures*, the utility will know more than will the commission about the types and timing of capital needs, and the alternative means of meeting those needs. That knowledge allows the utility to insert numbers it can beat.
4. Where the plan purports to distinguish *controllable from uncontrollable costs* (placing a cap on the controllable but allowing auto-recovery of the uncontrollable), the utility will know more than the commission about what it can and cannot control. Many external cost influences do fall outside the utility's control: fuel, labor, concrete and steel; legislative and regulatory actions like environmental rules; and storms, floods, and hurricanes. But the uncontrollability of external costs does not mean uncontrollability of utility costs. The utility negotiates with suppliers, schedules purchases, influences the mix of generation and non-generation alternatives (generation being vulnerable to input costs, weather, and environmental rules), and manages plant operations and vegetation (which affects frequency and duration of outages. And a utility's vulnerability to fuel costs depends in part on how it maintains the plant and how it provides for alternatives when outages occur.

Absent full access to this information, a commission cannot credibly predict or assess the utility's performance. The resulting knowledge gap disables the commission both from establishing realistic standards, and from designing compensation schemes that induce the utility to comply with those standards. Distinct from information access is technical mastery. To credibly judge the utility's performance the regulator must be expert in that performance. The greater the information-and-mastery differential, the greater the utility's temptation and opportunity to exploit it. By holding back performance data, by deferring performance improvement in the hopes of higher rewards later, and by timing investments and rate cases to maximize net income rather customer welfare, the utility can exploit its knowledge advantage in ways that undermine the public interest.

4 Utility persuasion through misuse of language

Proponents of FRPs and MYRPs often use phrases whose positivism masks less public-spirited intentions. Below are three examples.

4.1 "Sharing"

Commission orders often use the term "sharing" to describe the allocation, between shareholders and ratepayers, of profit that exceeds the authorized level.[51] "Sharing" implies giving, volunteering, parting with something valuable for a cause larger than oneself. The truth is the opposite. The excess return is monopoly rent. In an effectively competitive market, monopoly rent is competed away. So what the utility is "sharing" is money that both market forces and regulatory principles say belongs to the ratepayers: any earnings above what is authorized—earnings that landed in the utility's hands initially because the formula used to establish rates was imperfect. Only if the extra return is attributable to supra-normal performance—creating a cost efficiency no one ever heard of—would monopoly rent be appropriate (thus paralleling the concept in antitrust law allowing supra-normal profit earned

51 *See, e.g.*, In the Matter of Application for a General Change or Modification in CenterPoint Energy Arkka's Rates, Charges and Tariffs, Cause No. PUD 200400187, 2004 Okla PUC LEXIS 226 (Dec. 28, 2004) (stating that return on equity between 10.75 percent and 11.75 percent "shall be shared" 50/50).

from a monopoly position lawfully obtained—such as through a scientific discovery leading to a patent). Even then, the reward should go to the employees who created the benefit.

4.2 *"Encourage"*

Plan proponents assert that that the prospect of additional profit will "encourage" them to perform better.[52] But encouragement is necessary only for performance beyond the obligatory. Only if the regulator fails to define an obligation, leaving the utility free to act as it wishes, does "encouragement" become necessary to produce the desired performance. But defining obligatory performance is precisely what regulation is meant to do. The utility has an obligation to serve; the regulator has an obligation to define and enforce that obligation to serve—and then to compensate the utility commensurate with its performance. "Encouragement" is irrelevant.

4.3 *"Incentive""*

The term "incentive" suffers from the same flaws as "encourage." Shareholders are volunteers—they don't have to invest in the company. So, the regulator must calculate the authorized return to coax the shareholders to invest. But the utility is not a volunteer. Once it accepts the obligation to serve, it must carry that obligation out.

5 Evaluation criteria to make plans meet public interest purposes

To test whether a plan serves the public interest rather than a utility's private interest, below is a set of questions in six categories.

5.1 *Clarity of purpose*

Does the plan state clear public interest goals?

Does the plan aspire to results consistent with what effective competition would produce?

5.2 *Commission's role*

Does the plan make the commission passive—luring it into a series of pre-approvals and auto-approvals?

Does the plan ensure that the commission has the information, expertise, and time necessary to distinguish (a) reasonable from unreasonable costs, and (b) innovative performance from run-of-the-mill performance?

5.3 *"Incentives"*

Does the plan deal logically with the chain of causation from shareholder profit to board obligations, to CEO salary, to managers' salaries, to line employees' pay?

Does the plan reward the employees who cause improvement?

52 *See, e.g.*, Direct Testimony of Herbert Emmrich on behalf of San Diego Gas & Electric Co., Application 10-12-005 before the California Public Utilities Commission (Dec. 2010) (proposing "earnings and productivity sharing incentive mechanisms to continue to encourage the utility to invest in innovative technology to improve the efficiency of company operations").

Does the plan reward utility resistance to improvement, by promising normal profit for low performance, then awarding extra returns for improved performance?

The plan aside, are there inside-the-company "incentives" for executives and management that conflict with the utility's obligations to ratepayers; thus undermining the plan's asserted purposes?

Does the plan remove the utility's capital expenditure bias?

Does the "sharing" mechanism, when it allows supracompetitive returns (which is what "sharing" does), allow those returns only for supracompetitive performance; or are those supracompetitive returns allowed even when attributable to external factors unrelated to performance?

5.4 Accountability for costs and performance

Does the plan ensure that the utility absorbs all unreasonable costs?

Does the plan induce the utility to favor short-term solutions at the expense of long-term solutions?

Does the plan properly assign to the utility the normal business risks that cause executives and managers to act carefully?

Does the plan assign appropriate consequences for failing to meet expectations?

5.5 Responsiveness to consumers' needs

Does the plan induce customers to take actions to lower their costs—or is the focus solely on ways for executives to increase shareholder return?

Does the plan, implicitly or explicitly, perpetuate the utility's monopoly by inviting, allowing, or requiring the utility to invest in products or infrastructures that alternative providers should have a chance to provide more cost-effectively?

5.6 Overall logic of the plan

Is the plan asymmetrical, *e.g.*, guaranteeing rate increases with inflation but promising no rate decreases due to efficiencies?

Is the plan's purpose undermined by any adjusters that are outside the plan? Does the plan, when combined with all existing adjusters, make sense?

Does the plan properly adjust the authorized return on equity to account for the plan's risk reduction effects?

6 Conclusions and recommendation for regulatory procedure: generic proceeding to shape new plans

Rather than accept utility proposals passively, commissions should hold generic proceedings on the positives and negatives of, and alternative designs for, FRPs and MYRPs. The question must be, "*What performance do consumers need, and what method of compensating and disciplining the utility will produce that performance at minimum cost?*" This recommended proceeding should focus on how to design proposals that address the concerns and criteria discussed in this chapter. It would ask the following questions, among others:

1. *For each utility activity, what performance levels should define the utility's obligation to serve?* Designing a rate plan without first defining performance is utility-centric and

backwards—the opposite of what competition would produce. Furthermore, determining the quality level is not only about setting a standard, such as "average," "above average," "excellent" or "first quartile." Quality also is defined by innovation and creativity. A commission should insist on, and base compensation on, utilities remaining alert to new technologies and new service offerings, especially those that empower customers to make efficient decisions. Without addressing these questions, and without integrating the answers fully into the plan, FRPs and MYRPs risk becoming mere spreadsheets and risk-shifters.

2. *How might we reduce the time horizon conflicts between rate cases and productivity investments?* A rate case deals with a limited future period. Performance has different time dimensions. Payback periods vary for new meters, for employee education, for a long-term purchase of renewable energy, and for creating new staff slots to master technology. These performance time periods bear no connection to rate case time periods. As a result, there are multiple mismatches between the period in which rates are in effect, the period in which capital expenditures must occur, and the periods necessary to realize the benefits from expenditures. There is a legitimate concern that this period mismatch creates a risk-reward mismatch, for shareholders and for consumers.
3. *Do the existing multiple mechanisms for standard-setting and cost recovery work well together?* The general rate case is only one of several places where performance and compensation intersect. There also are power purchase cases, riders and surcharges, energy efficiency obligations, power plant performance incentives, and other measures. A commission needs to ask whether there are already so many cost recovery mechanisms, all having unclear effects on performance and cost recovery, that they need first to understand the interactions and combined effects before adding new mechanisms.
4. *Is the utility, automatically and necessarily, the correct entity to perform every service?* FRPs and MYRPs assume that every service whose cost is covered by the plans is a service that only the utility can perform. (Otherwise government-assured cost recovery would be unnecessary.) Approving a plan thus locks in, for the plan period, an assumption about the incumbent utility's monopoly role. But that premise deserves continuous rethinking, especially now, when distributed resource technology can enable market entry by multiple competing providers of new services. Regulatory passivity risks missing the most important question to be answered by regulation.
5. *For each service at issue, who is the most cost-effective provider?* This question is especially important when a utility seeks a supra-normal return to perform services at a quality level for which competitive markets provide a normal return.
6. *Under what circumstances should the commission terminate a plan?* A conditional plan is a plan that is subject to circumstances—the most important one being that the utility does not engage in behavior that conflicts with the public interest. Conflict will arise if:

    a. the utility fails to provide accurate and timely data requested by the commission or intervenors;
    b. the utility seeks recovery of costs that a reasonable utility would know are imprudent;
    c. the utility's affiliations with other members of the holding company family create conflicts with the utility's obligation to act unconditionally for the benefit of its customers;
    d. the magnitude or nature of other business activities in the corporate family have caused, or created substantial risk of causing, harm to the utility's ability to serve its customers cost-effectively;

e. a rating agency has downgraded, or has indicated the possibility of downgrading, the utility's debt ratings due to its affiliations with other members of the holding company family;
f. an affiliate resists commission requests for information about business activities that could affect the utility's well-being or its ability to carry out its obligation to serve;
g. the utility fails to act neutrally in any situation where there is an opportunity for a non-utility entrant to offer a product or service that will benefit consumers.

PART V

Latin America

18

SHALE GAS REGULATION IN MEXICO AND COLOMBIA

An uncertain future

*Tina Soliman Hunter and Ignacio Herrera Anchustegui**

1 Introduction and background

The Latin American region possesses some of the largest reserves of shale gas[1] in the world, with more than 20 per cent of the total reserves,[2] and accounting for about 1.907 billion cubic feet, more than double the region's conventional gas reserves.[3] Over the last decade, some states and companies have been keen to open up these markets to exploration and production (E&P), creating or modifying the legal rules governing these types of activity with mixed results. In this chapter, we have chosen two countries, Mexico and Colombia, to illustrate this development – or lack thereof – and the avenues other Latin American countries could follow with regard to the development of extraction of shale gas. Both of these countries are typical of the Latin American approach to hydrocarbon extraction, where state control of the exploitation of hydrocarbons remains strong, and the market has little influence.

It is important to note that the idea of developing shale gas resources derives from the success of the US, turning itself from a net oil and gas importer to the largest oil and gas producer in the world.[4] The success of the US in developing its shale gas lies in three key aspects: innovative use of existing technologies, the importance of market forces, and existing infrastructure for efficient and cost effective extraction and transport of the oil and gas. None of these features exist in Mexico and Colombia, both of which are state-centric, dominated by state oil companies (SOC), and lack the necessary land-based infrastructure. Therefore,

* This chapter has been written as part of the research project "Regulating energy markets, a perspective from EEA/EU Competition and Public Procurement Law", thanks to financial support of the AkademiaAvtalen programme between the University of Bergen and Equinor ASA.

All electronic references cited in this chapter were last accessed on 1 August 2019.

1 Note that the term 'shale gas' here refers to both shale gas and shale oil, with shale gas the generic term used to cover both

2 Andrés Arroyo and Andrea Perdriel, *Gobernanza del gas natural no convencional para el desarrollo sostenible de América Latina y el Caribe: Experiencias generales y tendencias en la Argentina, el Brasil, Colombia y México* (United Nations Economic Commission for Latin America and the Caribbean 2015), 7.

3 Ibid, 20.

4 According to the US Energy Information Agency (EIA) as of 20 August 2019, the US is now the largest oil and gas producer in the world. EIA, 'The U.S. leads global petroleum and natural gas production with record growth in 2018' (2019) https://www.eia.gov/todayinenergy/detail.php?id=40973.

aside from the physical challenges associated with geology, there are a number of challenges that these jurisdictions face, all of which typify the likely experience of other Latin American jurisdictions in the development of their shale gas reserves.

Although the Mexican and Colombian approaches to shale gas resource exploitation have occurred against a similar backdrop of SOC involvement, strong state control of the hydrocarbon sector, and a need to increase revenue from petroleum resources, their approaches have differed markedly, with Mexico reluctant to develop its shale gas resources, whilst Colombia actively seeks to develop the resources quickly. Therefore, this chapter will consider the approach each of these states has taken in attempting to develop their shale resources, set against the political backdrop and changing legal landscape. It will consider the constitutional position with regard to shale gas development, the regulatory framework for shale gas development, the role of the respective SOC in development and each state's consideration of the environment. In undertaking this analysis, this chapter seeks to demonstrate that for Latin American countries, there is a choice of options in developing the shale gas reserves – strong state participation as in the case of Mexico, or strong state regulation with diversified participation, as in the case of Colombia. Thus, what follows is an analysis of each country's experience to date and the relationship of each to the larger conventional petroleum industry within an often-shifting political landscape.

2 Shale gas in Mexico

2.1 Introduction

In 2013 at the dawn of the Energy Reform ('the Reform') in Mexico, the stage appeared to be set for a new kind of revolution in Mexico, one involving not only politics, but also petroleum. The Reform comprised critical constitutional changes, as well as the adoption of 21 new and/or modified laws. The effect of these laws transformed the legal landscape in a country in which for almost 80 years the state held an energy monopoly through the state oil company: PEMEX. Part of the Reform focused on shale gas exploitation,[5] since production of conventional hydrocarbons had been falling in Mexico, coupled with a constant need to import natural gas from the US since the 2000s,[6] for electricity generation uses.[7] Although the Mexican economy has traditionally been based on petroleum exploitation, production peak was reached in 2004 with an annual production of 178 323 thousand tonnes, and which has declined steadily since, sitting now at 11 482 thousand tonnes in 2016.[8] Similarly, natural

5 See stressing the role of shale gas to promote the Energy Reform: Pedro Gutiérrez-Yurrita and María Peláez Gálvez, 'La reforma energética y la legislación sobre el fracking en México' in Germán Valencia Martín and Juan Rosa Moreno (eds), *Derecho y Fracking* (Thomson-Reuters Aranzadi 2016), Chapter IX.

6 Angel de la Vega Navarro and Jaime Ramírez Villegas J, 'El gas de lutitas (shale gas) en México: Recursos, explotación, usos, impactos' [2015] 12 *Economía UNAM*, 79, 92. In 2017, about 62 per cent of all natural gas consumed in Mexico was imported from the US, see: 'México "se guarda" su gas shale; prefiere comprarlo a EU in El Economista', https://www.eleconomista.com.mx/empresas/Mexico-se-guarda-su-gas-shale-prefiere-comprarlo-a-EU-20181003-0028.html.

7 In 2015, natural gas was used to generate about 51 per cent of Mexico's total electricity, Arroyo and Perdriel, (n 2), 14. In 2017 Mexico resorted to gas to generate 50.2 per cent of its electricity: Secretaría de Energía (SENER), 'Prospectiva del Sector Eléctrico 2017–2031' (2017), https://www.gob.mx/cms/uploads/attachment/file/284345/Prospectiva_del_Sector_El_ctrico_2017.pdf, 17.

8 https://www.iea.org/statistics/?country=MEXICO&year=2016&category=Energy%20supply&indicator=OilProd&mode=chart&dataTable=OIL.

gas production has declined from 1,883,374 terrajoules (TJ) in 2013 to 1,415,746 TJ in 2016. This decline in production reversed after March 2018, with gas production increasing from approximately 50,000 standard cubic feet per day to 177,000 thousand standard cubic feet per day by April 2019.[9] Furthermore, the Mexican government seeks to continue this increase, peaking at around 10 400 million cubic feet by 2025.

Therefore, the need to explore other energy sources such as the seemingly plentiful shale gas, appeared to be an opportunity for the country, even though under and unexploited reserves of gas remained, and conventional gas production has increased. This desire to exploit shale rested on the notion that Mexico has been said to have the "best near-term opportunities for shale gas development of any country [other than the US] if energy reform there can be successfully implemented".[10] Given the political instability and economic challenges that Mexico has faced in the last 30 years, such an approach is not surprising.

Mexican shale gas reserves are vast, and considered to be the sixth largest reserves in the world. According to the Mexican Ministry in Energy (SENER) there are about 36.8 trillion cubic feet (Tcf) of "humid gas" and 104.7 Tcf of "dry gas".[11] These reserves, located in eight different formations, were estimated in 2015 by the US Energy Information Agency (US EIA) to comprise (technically recoverable) 545 Tcf of shale gas and 13 billion barrels of shale oil.[12] Out of these, it is estimated that 16 billion cubic feet of shale gas are economically recoverable.[13] More recent numbers issued by the National Commission of Hydrocarbons (CNH) were released in 2018, indicating that the total gas reserves, including shale gas, were 10 trillion cubic feet for P1 reserves, 19 trillion MMM cubic feet for P2 reserves and 30trillion MMM cubic feet for P3 reserves.[14] Whichever estimates are to be believed, there is no doubt that Mexico is seemingly awash with shale gas resources with excellent potential.

The desire to develop shale plays in Mexico was not merely an outcome of the Reform. In 2010 PEMEX started exploration of potential shale gas reservoirs with minor pilot projects.[15] Indeed, in 2013 the US EIA noted that PEMEX envisioned commercial shale gas production to commence by 2015, with up to 2 billion cubic feet (Bcf) per day to be produced by 2025, and an investment of US$1billion to drill 750 wells.[16] However, unconventional development started slowly, and has continued rather timidly since the Reform, with a bold venture into shale gas developed and outlined only a few years before the Reform nowhere to be seen. Such reticence, both before and since the Reform, can be ascribed to a number of factors, including controversy surrounding fracking and public opposition to the process.[17]

9 https://www.iea.org/statistics/?country=MEXICO&year=2016&category=Energy%20supply&indicator=NatGasProd&mode=chart&dataTable=GAS.

10 Thomas Tunstall, 'Shale development and Mexico' in Yongsheng Wang and William Hefley (eds), *The Global Impact of Unconventional Shale Gas Development: Economics, Policy, and Interdependence* (Springer International Publishing 2016), 237.

11 www.senado.gob.mx/comisiones/cambio_climatico/reu/docs/presentacion_231017-7.pdf.

12 U.S. Energy Information Administration, *Technically Recoverable Shale Oil and Shale Gas Resources: Mexico September 2015* (2015) https://www.eia.gov/analysis/studies/worldshalegas/pdf/Mexico_2013.pdf.

13 Comisión Nacional de Hidrocarburos, 'Reservas de hidrocarburos en México'. Conceptos fundamentales y análisis 2018, 7.

14 Ibid, 48.

15 de la Vega Navarro and Ramírez Villegas (n 6), 95.

16 U.S. Energy Information Administration (n 12),P II-2.

17 See also highlighting the little encouragement given to unconventional hydrocarbons in Mexico (and Brazil): Arroyo and Perdriel (n 2), 7.

2.2 The Mexican Energy Reform and shale gas

To speak about shale gas (and shale oil) regulation in Mexico without referring to the 2013 Energy Reform is almost impossible.[18] The state monopoly model that governed Mexico's petroleum exploitation for almost 80 years came to an end with the reform of Articles 25, 27 and 28 of the Mexican Constitution,[19] transforming the energy regulatory framework (of both petroleum and electricity). Regarding petroleum, the Reform enabled private participation in upstream petroleum activities for the first time in over 50 years, with certain caveats and forms of participation in both upstream and downstream hydrocarbon activities. In the case of natural gas, the Reform was preceded by several constitutional changes in 1995 that allowed for some private participation in a number of activities related to the transport, storage and distribution but not in relation to E&P.

Under the Reform, the nationalized and monopolistic upstream petroleum sector has been opened up to private and international investors. This was more out of necessity (the need for investment and technology to explore deep-water conventional and land-based unconventional deposits) rather than competitive-market convictions.

At the heart of the Reform was the alteration of the constitutional position regarding the exclusive right of the state to conduct hydrocarbon activities in Mexico. In reforming Article 27 of the Mexican Constitution,

> the State has property over the shale gas resources located in the subsoil, and this property is inalienable and imprescriptible, and no concessions shall be granted to any actors, the exploitation of those reserves can be done by the state and private entities. Exploration and extraction activities (E&P) shall be conducted through assignations or contracts to generate revenue to the nation by both public and private entities.[20]

In addition, the Reform established a Mexican Oil Fund for the Stabilization and Development to administer and distribute the revenue generated by E&P activities carried out by different public and/or private entities.[21] By 2018 this fund controlled ca. US$1 billion and administered financial aspects of 111 contracts that Mexico has entered into concerning E&P activities since the first bidding round.[22]

The Mexican Energy Reform has attracted much controversy. Whilst some, including the political parties that promoted it, saw it as a necessary change to attract much-needed international investment, to modernize the corporate structure and technologies of PEMEX and generate additional revenue for the state,[23] others see it as a neo-liberal US-backed intervention designed to benefit a small circle of power in the nation,[24] and foster greater social and class division. Arguably, the reality is something in between. What is certain is that the Reform sought to bring about change in order to revive a flagging petroleum

18 For a comprehensive overview of the Energy Reform of 2013 see: Miguel Marmolejo-Cervantes and Tina Soliman Hunter 'State control in the aftermath of petroleum policy and governance reform in Mexico: capable of fulfilling constitutional objectives?' [2019] 12 *Journal of World Energy Law and Business* 169–195.

19 For a detailed analysis see Eduardo González-Canales, 'Mexican energy law: industry renaissance or chronicle of a death foretold?: Part 1: Upstream ventures in Mexico' [2015] 8 *The Journal of World Energy Law & Business* 45.

20 Article 27 of the Mexican Constitution.

21 Article 28 para. 6 of the Mexican Constitution.

22 This is further discussed in section 2.3.2 below.

23 Gonzalez-Canales (n 19), 45.

24 Gutiérrez-Yurrita and Peláez Gálvez (n 5).

industry, with shale gas extraction an important component, particularly given the success of shale gas development in the US. Furthermore, clear goals of revenue maximization and long-term social development were imbued within the Mexican Constitution. As noted by Marmolejo-Cervantes and Soliman Hunter, in order to accomplish an increase in revenue, it is necessary to either raise petroleum revenue through taxation and royalties, or to increase the production of oil and gas.[25] Clearly, Mexico sees the increase in production, from both conventional and unconventional sources, as a way of maximizing revenue to meet constitutional goals.

2.3 Shale gas regulation in Mexico

2.3.1 Institutional and regulatory framework post-Reform

As part of the Reform, there were a number of significant institutional changes. The role and sphere of influence of SENER, the central body for the regulation of hydrocarbons in Mexico charged with defining and conducting the energy policy of Mexico and defining the areas available for E&P activities and technical requirements,[26] was curtailed. At the same time, the role of the CNH was expanded to that of an independent body which provides technical knowledge to SENER concerning geological and operative information, organizes the bidding rounds for awarding E&P, assigns contracts and the authorizes different exploitation techniques for the areas and wells. The authority of CNH is supported by constitutional reforms, granting technical autonomy and supported by the Supreme Court of Justice's recent developed doctrine of the 'regulator state'.[27] This enables the CNH to have the flexibility and adaptability required to regulate petroleum extraction activities so long as it implements scientific and technical criteria through resolutions, administrative general provisions, technical standards, guidelines, handbooks and Mexican official norms. In addition, the role of the National Agency for Industrial Safety and Environmental Protection of the Hydrocarbons Sector (ASEA) has expanded, becoming an independent regulator at arm's length from SENER.

The core of the Energy Reform was the establishment of a new upstream petroleum law – the *Hydrocarbons Law 2014* (the Hydrocarbons Law) subsequently reformed in 2016.[28] The Hydrocarbons Law regulates all aspects of petroleum activity and establishes the contractual framework and contractual arrangements for E&P. The Hydrocarbons Law is complemented by the Regulation of the Hydrocarbons Law and the Regulation for the Title III Activities of the Hydrocarbons laws, focusing on exploration and extraction activities and industry activities, respectively. Article 1 of the Hydrocarbons Law 2014 clarifies that all hydrocarbons, irrespective of their physical state (and therefore applying to shale gas) located in the subsoil of the national territory are direct property of the nation, being this property inalienable and imprescriptible, which is an international trend rather than the exception.[29] This public ownership of petroleum resources applies also to those found in the continental shelf and

25 Marmolejo-Cervantes and Soliman Hunter (n 18), 189.

26 Decree which reforms and adds provisions to the Mexican Constitution in Energy of 20 December 2013, Transitory Disposition Ten(a).

27 Marmolejo-Cervantes and Soliman Hunter (n 18), 179.

28 Ley de Hidrocarburos of 11 August 2014 and last reformed on 15 November 2016 and published in the Official Gazette of said day. Available (in Spanish) at: www.diputados.gob.mx/LeyesBiblio/pdf/LHidro_151116.pdf (Hydrocarbons Law).

29 Tunstall (n 10), 233.

the exclusive economic zone. While the law defines different terms, including natural gas, associated gas, non-associated gas and petroleum liquated gas,[30] it does not specifically identify unconventional gas or shale gas. However, since the gas extracted from shale deposits is 'natural gas' (i.e. methane), then essentially the Hydrocarbons Law directly applies to shale gas. Given the broad nature of the Hydrocarbons Law, it does not consider the techniques utilized for the production of petroleum. As such, hydraulic fracturing, a controversial well stimulation technique required to produce shale gas, is not specifically considered in the law, nor are other well stimulation techniques. Instead, the *Regulation of the Hydrocarbons Law* and the *Regulation for the Title III Activities of the Hydrocarbons Laws* considers these activities in greater detail. [31]

While there is no specific law addressing shale gas extraction and the use of hydraulic fracturing techniques, the regulation concerning unconventional gas forms part of the general Hydrocarbons Law 2014 and the myriad of instruments that deal with petroleum and its derivatives in different instruments.

2.3.2 Licensing rounds and contractual forms

Since the Reform, Mexico has undertaken four licencing rounds, including "Round Zero", which was an 'exclusive' round where PEMEX was the sole bidder and entitled to request E&P over areas in which it had been already active before the Reform. In this 'zero' round, 83 per cent of Mexico's proven reserves of hydrocarbons were assigned to PEMEX and 21 per cent of its prospective reserves, including shale gas deposits, as well as 100 per cent of the producing areas in which PEMEX was already active were granted to PEMEX.[32] Regarding unconventional hydrocarbons, PEMEX was less successful, with SENER granting only 44 per cent of the areas requested.[33] Arguably, PEMEX was less fortunate with unconventional hydrocarbon deposits because it lacked experience and the technological and investment capacity required to efficiently and effectively develop shale gas resources. After this first round, PEMEX was required to compete on an equal footing with other bidders for acreage released for E&P activity.

Licencing Rounds One and Two only offered conventional petroleum acreage, with no unconventional deposits available to prospective bidders. Whether related to the unavailability of shale gas or not, these early rounds were less than successful.[34] In Round Three, opened in late 2018, the first shale gas acreages were offered in Burgos, Tamapulipas near the Gulf of Mexico.[35] However, shortly after the tender was opened and at least nine bids had been received, the CNH cancelled this bidding round, on 11 December 2018, amidst political debate in part fuelled by Mexico's new president López Obrador's criticism of hydraulic fracturing.[36]

30 Article 4, XVI, XVII, XVIII and XIX, respectively of the Hydrocarbons Law.

31 Also highlighting that there is no particular shale gas or unconventional hydrocarbon regulation, even in the Hydrocarbons Law 2014, see: Arroyo and Perdriel (n 2), 71.

32 https://www.mayerbrown.com/-/media/files/perspectives-events/publications/2014/08/analysis-of-mexicos-new-hydrocarbons-legal-regime/files/get-the-full-report/fileattachment/updateanalysisofmexicos newhydrocarbonslegalregime.pdf, 1.

33 The assigned areas represented about 6.5% of the total unconventional reserves. See Arroyo and Perdriel (n 2), 54.

34 Tunstall (n 10), 240.

35 https://rondasmexico.gob.mx/esp/rondas/ronda-3/cnh-r03-l032018/áreas-contractuales/información.

36 https://rondasmexico.gob.mx/esp/rondas/ronda-3/cnh-r03-l032018/seguimiento-y-transparencia; https://www.naturalgasintel.com/articles/116752-mexicos-cnh-cancels-upcoming-oil-natural-gas-bid-rounds.

Where a licence is granted to a bidder, be it conventional or unconventional, the bidder and the state enter into a legal arrangement through some form of public contract. Under the Hydrocarbons Law, such a legal arrangement can be one of four different modalities: i) licenses; ii) production-sharing contracts; iii) profit-sharing contracts; and iv) service contracts. These contracts can only be entered into by the Mexican State, through the CNH and the other party, following the bid/tender procedure.[37] In these E&P contracts the state can require the inclusion of the participation of the state, along with the party assigned the contract, if the area coexists at a different depth with an assignation area, to foster transfer of technology to state enterprises (which could well be shale gas operations as PEMEX has relatively little expertise in this), or when the state wishes to promote the project through public financing.[38] Shale gas is expected to be initially developed by foreign companies with expertise in such development. Indeed, Tunstall argues that in the near future it is unlikely that PEMEX will aggressively pursue shale gas exploration and extraction.[39]

One aspect of unconventional hydrocarbons not subject to the licencing and contractual regime set out in the Hydrocarbons Law is the production of natural gas found from coal as part of the coal mining process.[40] There is no additional requirement to bid for a petroleum license where miners already hold a mining concession, as stated in Article 27 of the Hydrocarbons Law. Therefore, the production of coal seam gas, as a by-product from the mining of coal, is covered under a mining concession. However, where natural gas, rather than coal, is the primary product produced from coal measures, it is likely that laws relating to hydrocarbon extraction, rather than mining laws, would apply.

2.3.3 *Environmental sustainability and fracking controversies*

A major criticism of shale gas development in Mexico is the lack of a clear environmental policy and real concern regarding hydrocarbons and shale gas exploitation in Mexico, in particular regarding the use of hydraulic fracturing (often referred to as fracking).[41] The Hydrocarbons Law's provisions regarding environmental protection are scant, indicating that ASEA is competent to enact the applicable administrative rules concerning environmental protection for the promotion and development of hydrocarbon activities in a sustainable way.[42] However, the law does require participants to undertake all practices and comply with all rules to prevent and repair environmental damage, nor does it impose liability for environmental wrongdoing.[43]

Although generally there is a lack of attention to environmental protections, some effort has been made to protect vulnerable areas. While in principle shale gas and hydrocarbon exploitation can take place in any area, some "Zones of Protection" can be established by a Presidential Decree, at the suggestion of SENER, prohibiting any E&P activity in the declared area.[44] In addition, ASEA has issued several detailed instruments dealing with environmental protection and hydrocarbon activity of an administrative nature.[45] The Ministry

37 Articles 15 and 23 of the Hydrocarbons Law.
38 Article 16 of the Hydrocarbons Law.
39 Tunstall (n 10), 231.
40 Article 27 of the Hydrocarbons Law.
41 See, for example: Gutiérrez-Yurrita and Peláez Gálvez (n 5).
42 Article 129 of the Hydrocarbons Law.
43 Article 130 of the Hydrocarbons Law.
44 Articles 41 and 42 of the Hydrocarbons Law.
45 See a list of the relevant regulation in this matter at https://www.gob.mx/asea/acciones-y-programas/leyes-y-normas-del-sector.

of Environment and Natural Resources has also produced documents concerning shale gas operations, including the 2015 "Environmental Criteria Guide for the Exploration and Extraction of Hydrocarbons Contained in Lutites" ("Shale Guide").[46]

The Shale Guide incorporates a series of suggestions to implement that might appear vague or left to be developed by other instruments. Among these, the petroleum companies "*should* incorporate the criteria" of the Shale Guide in an "Environmental Impact Manifestation" required in accordance with the Law on Ecological Equilibrium and Environment Protection. Before any shale gas activity can be carried out, a base study is required, considering aspects such as air quality, aquifers, bodies of superficial water, floral and animal species, soil conditions, contaminated areas, environmental passives, seismicity, fractures and geological faults. Particular relevance is given to the use of water, including its quality, source, retention and recuperation. Also, operators should have financial guarantees to cover environmental impact and process all toxic residues in compliance with the applicable law.[47]

Hydraulic fracturing for shale gas exploitation is the subject of much controversy in Mexico. The use of the technique is implicitly authorized – by not being barred – in different decrees deriving from the Energy Reform.[48] Indeed, it has been used regularly in Mexico both before and after the Energy Reform to stimulate conventional wells, and by 2017 the SENER estimated that this technique had been used in 7,568 wells (for both oil and gas).[49] In 2019 it was estimated to be 8,457 wells, and out of those, only 27 have been drilled for unconventional hydrocarbons.[50] While the technique is not prohibited under any administrative provision, the Shale Guide does warn against its impact on water contamination, excessive use of water, global warming, soil and atmospheric contamination, harm to road and housing infrastructure and loss of biodiversity.[51] Although the Shale Guide seeks to establish both base line studies prior to the activity and environmental protection during the activity, it must remembered that it is only a soft law instrument, and has been criticized for leaving many important issues unresolved.[52]

Hydraulic fracturing was used in February 2019 when CNH approved a PEMEX pilot project to drill eight shale gas exploratory wells in the Tampico-Misantla region, which predicted a production potential of up to 775,000 barrels per day.[53] In June 2019 CNH also approved the use of hydraulic fracturing to extract shale gas from PEMEX's Laxix-1EXP well in the Humapa block.[54] The following day, at an official press conference, President López Obrador argued that an

> authorization in November past year was made and was finished in these months and, effectively, it has been authorized the exploitation of a field, a well with fracking,

46 Secretaría de Medio Ambiente y Recursos Naturales, "Guía de Criterios Ambientales para la Exploración y Extracción de Hidrocarburos Contenidos en Lutitas" (2015), available at: http://biblioteca.semarnat.gob.mx/janium/Documentos/Ciga/Libros2011/CD001945.pdf.

47 Ibid, 11–13.

48 Gutiérrez-Yurrita and Peláez Gálvez (n 5), 415.

49 www.senado.gob.mx/comisiones/cambio_climatico/reu/docs/presentacion_231017-7.pdf.

50 Comisión Nacional de Hidrocarburos, 'El fracturamiento hidráulico es una técnica de producción de uso intensivo en campos de gas', 20 August 2019, available at: https://hidrocarburos.gob.mx/media/2792/pozos-con-fracturamiento_200819.pdf.

51 Secretaría de Medio Ambiente y Recursos Naturales (n 46), 7.

52 Gutiérrez-Yurrita and Peláez Gálvez (n 5), 425.

53 It is important to note that any increase in production will generate greater revenue for the state, as well as decreasing US gas dependence.

54 This block is located between the states of Veracruz and Puebla https://www.plenglish.com/index.php?o=rn&id=43742&SEO=cnh-gives-pemex-fracking-approval-in-mexico; https://www.milenio.com/negocios/pemex-solicito-fracking-cnh-administracion-campo-humapa.

> and this authorization is now suspended. We shall not use fracking for hydrocarbons exploitation.[55]

Such open criticism combined with only soft law instruments governing its use, indicates that shale gas extraction utilizing hydraulic fracturing is unlikely to progress at the expected or necessary pace.

2.3.4 Land use issues

Article 27 of the Mexican Constitution states that "ownership of the lands and waters within the boundaries of the national territory is vested originally in the Nation, which has had, and has, the right to transmit title thereof to private persons", and that "(t)he Nation shall at all times have the right to impose on private property such limitations as the public interest may demand". Most importantly, this constitutional provision also stipulates that "(i)n the Nation is vested the direct ownership of all natural resources of the continental shelf ... all minerals or substances ... deposits of precious stones ... solid mineral fuels; petroleum and all solid, liquid, and gaseous hydrocarbons ...". Thus, all Mexican landholders are entitled to use the surface of the land, but do not own the subsoil resources, and must make way for their development. Furthermore, the Mexican hydrocarbon regime establishes that E&P activities are of public interest and, therefore, prevail over any other that requires the use of the surface or subsoil, including agricultural activities.[56] Where E&P activities affect private land, there is a requirement for the landowner to be compensated, first through negotiations between the parties (which may even lead to purchase of the land), and, if no agreement is reached, ultimately through litigation.[57] These negotiations shall comply with a detailed process, including the legal requirements set out in Chapter IV (Articles 100–117) of the Hydrocarbons Law.

3 Shale gas in Colombia

3.1 Introduction

Whereas Mexico represents a timid or even adversarial position as regards shale gas E&P, Colombia appears to adopt a more positive position, offering a detailed regulatory framework and governmental support for exploitation of unconventional hydrocarbons, including shale gas.[58] Since the early 2010s, Colombia has had the most developed laws relating to unconventional hydrocarbon exploitation within in Latin America.[59] The use of gas for electricity generation is much lower than in Mexico. According to official statistics, as of August 2018, 69 per cent of all electricity was generated through hydropower, with natural gas representing 9.61 per cent of generation, and the rest generated through coal-fired power plants.[60] Gas is also used for other uses such as cooking. Thus, the total energy use of gas is

55 https://www.milenio.com/negocios/pemex-solicito-fracking-cnh-administracion-campo-humapa (author's translations).

56 Articles 25, 27 and 28 of the Mexican Constitution.

57 Articles 100 and ss of the Hydrocarbons Law.

58 Arroyo and Perdriel (n 2), 7.

59 See also in this sense: Ibid, 47.

60 Subdirección de Energía Eléctrica, 'Informe Mensual de Variables de Generación y del Mercado Eléctrico Colombiano' (August 2018), www.siel.gov.co/portals/0/generacion/2018/Informe_de_variables_Ago_2018.pdf.

less than 25 per cent of the energy mix in Colombia.[61] Given the relatively low domestic reliance on gas in Colombia, shale gas exploitation is perceived more as an export possibility to generate revenues rather than substituting or reducing imports, as in the Mexican case. This could explain why shale gas exploitation is of great interest to the Colombian government, and its exploitation has received its endorsement.

Differing markedly from Mexico, Colombia has detailed and specific regulations for unconventional petroleum E&P activities, including regulation concerning hydraulic fracturing. In addition, Colombia has awarded licence areas for unconventional E&P activities, although no production has occurred as of August 2019. Despite this, at the time of writing this chapter (August 2019), the regulation concerning unconventional petroleum extraction, including the use of hydraulic fracturing techniques, is under legal scrutiny before the Colombian Council of the State at the same time as it is defending a legal challenge to the constitutionality of some of the rules for unconventional hydrocarbon exploitation. Similar to the above analysis on Mexico, this section will consider the Colombian stance on the development of unconventional hydrocarbons, examining the regulatory framework that currently exists for such development. This section will also examine the environmental issues and current social attitudes towards shale gas development.

3.2 Hydrocarbons regulatory framework

3.2.1 Constitutional framework

Like Mexico, the fundamental legal basis for petroleum resource development stems from the Colombian Constitution, which establishes that all the non-renewable natural resources located in the subsoil are the property of the nation,[62] and the state shall control and intervene in the exploitation of the natural resources and the use of the soil with the aim of improving citizens' welfare.[63] In order to exploit any hydrocarbons, including shale gas, the interested parties require the grant of a "habilitating title", similar to a licence.

The Colombia Constitution establishes robust environmental protection, which is strongly linked to shale gas activities, and which sets the parameters for further regulation related to environmental impact and environmental harm by the legislator and administration.[64]Article 8 of the Colombian Constitution makes it a duty of the state to protect the natural and cultural riches of the nation, which, when read in conjunction with Article 79 of the Constitution, establishes the right of all citizens to enjoy a healthy environment, and the responsibility of the state to protect the diversity and integrity of the environment. Together, these provisions clearly establish that the Colombian State is responsible for protecting the environment. Furthermore, the exploitation of all natural resources, including shale gas, is required to be managed with the aim of guaranteeing its sustainable development and conservation, as well as the obligation to "prevent and control the environmental deterioration, impose legal sanctions and demand the reparation of caused damages".[65] It is against the

61 Arroyo and Perdriel (n 2), 15.

62 Article 332 of the Colombian Constitution.

63 Article 334 of the Colombian Constitution.

64 See also expressing this strong protection of the environment the Decree 2372 of 2010 issued by the Consejo de Estado. See also: Milton José Pereira Blanco, 'Hacia la construcción de un derecho energético ambiental como disciplina autónoma' [2016] 12 *Jurídicas CUC* 1.

65 Article 80, paragraph 2 of the Colombian Constitution.

background of these strong environmental rules that the validity of unconventional petroleum development is being disputed, as discussed in section 3.4 below.

3.2.2 General hydrocarbons regulatory framework

The hydrocarbon regulatory framework in Colombia builds upon a complex web of legal instruments. Unlike Mexico, where the regulation stems from the Hydrocarbons Law, most regulatory instruments in Colombia are administrative in nature, and include presidential decrees, regulations, administrative provisions and agreements. The framework distinguishes between upstream, midstream and downstream activity, with the first of them being the focus of this chapter. In Colombia, as in Mexico, there is a relatively clear division of regulatory powers concerning the administration and oversight of petroleum exploitation. On the one hand, the Ministry of Mines and Energy is entrusted with the regulation of technical matters, while, on the other hand, the National Agency of Hydrocarbons (ANH) has powers concerning tendering of E&P contracts and areas selected for development.

For upstream E&P activity, Colombian law resorts to public procurement and tender-like procedures to grant access to petroleum areas for exploration and, ultimately, production. Article 76 of Law 80 of 1993 of Public Contracting contains fundamental provisions for the regulation of contracts for E&P of natural resources.[66] In accordance with this norm, the regulation for these types of public contracts is done by special regulation. This special regulation, which is based on administrative acts, 'agreements' and presidential decrees, is the framework for hydrocarbon activity in Colombia; forming a complex regulatory web.

At the core of this regulatory web are two primary legal instruments regulating all hydrocarbon activities, including the development of shale gas. Agreement 2 of 2017 ("Agreement 2") issued by the ANH, establishes the rules concerning the adjudication of E&P contracts.[67] Presidential Decree 1073 of 2015 (Decree 1073) establishes the Single Regulatory Decree of the Administrative Sector of Mines and Energy.[68] Decree 1073 sets a general framework concerning the functioning and structure of the mining energy sector in Colombia, granting powers to the Ministry of Mines and Energy (MME) to formulate, adopt, direct and coordinate energy policies. It also entrusts the ANH with the administration of the hydrocarbon reserves of the nation and the promotion of its optimal and sustainable use.[69] Given that shale gas is a hydrocarbon resource, although Decree 1073 does not specifically identify shale gas regulation, it presumably regulates shale gas given that it defines shale gas as a hydrocarbon.

Agreement 2 replaced a previous administrative regulation by the ANH, Agreement 4 2012, which set rules concerning the adjudication of E&P hydrocarbon contracts (and which was modified by Agreement 3 2014 that deals in particular with unconventional hydrocarbons).[70] Agreement 2 2017 is an extensive and detailed piece of regulation governing the assignation of areas for hydrocarbon E&P, the selection of the contracting parties and it sets out

66 Ley 80 De 1993 (octubre 28) Diario Oficial No. 41.094 de 28 de octubre de 1993 por la cual se expide el Estatuto General de Contratación de la Administración Pública, last modified in January 2018.

67 Acuerdo No. 02 de 2017, Consejo Directivo de la Agencia Nacional de Hidrocarburos (ANH).

68 Article 2.2.1.1.1.1., Decreto 1073 de 2015 (mayo 26) por medio del cual se expide el Decreto Único Reglamentario del Sector Administrativo de Minas y Energía.

69 Articles 1.1.1.1.1 and 1.2.1.1.1.1., Decreto 1073 de 2015 (mayo 26) por medio del cual se expide el Decreto Único Reglamentario del Sector Administrativo de Minas y Energía.

70 Article 110, Acuerdo No. 02 de 2017, Consejo Directivo de la Agencia Nacional de Hidrocarburos (ANH).

the adjudication and governing aspects of the contracts.[71] The rules in Agreement 2 include provisions governing the selection procedure, the form of the public tender, selection and award criteria, contractual and non-contractual responsibilities and obligations, fines and criminal liabilities, social and environmental aspects, economic rights derived from hydrocarbon activities (in a highly detailed section), control and oversight of contract compliance and termination rules. In the following we comment on some of these general rules that are also applicable to shale gas activity. In addition, Agreement 2 contains a detailed series of rules that interested parties must comply with in order to be admitted to the Registry of Interested Parties which in turn allows them to participate in licensing procedures. Furthermore, Agreement 2 sets stringent and detailed rules concerning technical, legal, economic, environmental and social responsibility capacity.[72]

Colombian legislation establishes four contractual modalities for upstream hydrocarbon activities that are applicable also to shale gas. The first is a "convention" entered into by the ANH and the Colombian state-owned oil company, Ecopetrol, for exploration and/or exploitation of areas under its control before 2003. All other contracts entered into by Ecopetrol must follow the rules for the other three type of agreements. The second type are Technical Evaluation Agreements (TEAs), which grant the licensee an exclusive right to carry out an analysis in its designated area to determine its capability and it receives a payment for the use of soil and subsoil and a share of the benefits in case the area is subject to an E&P contract later on.[73] The third type are E&P agreements, which grant the licensee an exclusive right to carry out explorative and productive activities with respect to the hydrocarbons property of the state and to receive a benefit in the form of royalties and economic benefits.[74] Lastly, the law allows for special contracts which differ from E&P and TEA contracts.[75]

Agreement 2 also establishes the tender procedure to select contracting parties and the areas. So far, these have been done in "rounds" (*Rondas*), and among these, some areas have been assigned for unconventional hydrocarbons and shale gas activity. The main criteria in adjudicating public contracts is through three types of competitive tender: an open procedure in which the ANH selects the best tender for the offers made by any entity in the registry;[76] a closed procedure in which the ANH invites a number of potential tenderers (at least two) to submit the tenders and choose the most favourable one;[77] or the ANH may directly award an area to a legal person because they comply with the minimum requirements established and for some particular reason, such as lack of technical information, public interest or public order.[78]

71 Article 1, Acuerdo No. 02 de 2017, Consejo Directivo de la Agencia Nacional de Hidrocarburos (ANH). Agreement 2 sets up three clear phases for E&P contracts: i) precontractual, involving previous analysis and preparation of the award/tender procedure and adjudication of the contract; ii) a contractual phase dealing with the phase between the celebration of the agreement and its termination; and iii) a post-contractual phase concerning obligations that extend beyond the liquidation of the contract, and for which environmental liability is of special importance for shale gas E&P activities.

72 See Articles 21–27, Acuerdo No. 02 de 2017, Consejo Directivo de la Agencia Nacional de Hidrocarburos (ANH).

73 Article 35.2, Acuerdo No. 02 de 2017, Consejo Directivo de la Agencia Nacional de Hidrocarburos (ANH).

74 Article 35.3, Acuerdo No. 02 de 2017, Consejo Directivo de la Agencia Nacional de Hidrocarburos (ANH).

75 Article 35.4, Acuerdo No. 02 de 2017, Consejo Directivo de la Agencia Nacional de Hidrocarburos (ANH).

76 Article 36.1.1, Acuerdo No. 02 de 2017, Consejo Directivo de la Agencia Nacional de Hidrocarburos (ANH).

77 Article 36.1.2, Acuerdo No. 02 de 2017, Consejo Directivo de la Agencia Nacional de Hidrocarburos (ANH).

78 Article 36.2, Acuerdo No. 02 de 2017, Consejo Directivo de la Agencia Nacional de Hidrocarburos (ANH).

Furthermore, Resolution 18 1495 of 2009 implements aspects of the constitutional position regarding natural resources by establishing the main rules requiring hydrocarbon activities to maximize their recovery.[79] Finally, the Law on the General System of Royalties[80] defines the manner in which the Colombian State will be compensated for the exploitation of Colombian petroleum resources. It includes a specific provision to promote E&P of unconventional hydrocarbons.

3.3 *Shale gas specific regulation*

The instruments outlined in section 3.2 above stipulate the legal basis for oil and gas exploration and production in Colombia. In addition, unlike Mexico, Colombia has established a specific regulation for unconventional petroleum, including shale gas since 2012.[81] Colombian law includes several definitions of unconventional petroleum. Probably the most complete (and recent) of them is found in Decree 1073 of 2015, which defines it as a "rocky formation with low primary permeability and to which stimulation must be made to improve the mobility and capture of hydrocarbons".[82] This definition explicitly covers "gas and petroleum of lutites (shale)",[83] which is the same as the definition of it in the Presidential Decree 3004 of 2013 (the Presidential Decree").[84]

The primary regulatory instruments for shale gas are the Administrative Resolution 9 0341 of 27 March 2014 issued by the MME, which establishes the technical and procedural requirements for exploration and exploitation of unconventional hydrocarbons,[85] and ANH Agreement 3 of 26 March 2014 (Agreement 3).[86]

Agreement 3 was established as the result of a 2013 Presidential Decree that required the MME to "enact the technical and procedural norms concerning well integrity, hydraulic stimulation, production water injection, return fluids and other technical matters associated to the exploration and exploitation of unconventional deposits".[87] It incorporates rules and parameters applicable to the Regulation of Contracts for Exploration and Exploitation of Hydrocarbons, originally to Agreement 4 2012,[88] applied specifically to unconventional deposits and work in conjunction with Agreement 2 of 2017 (that replaced Agreement 4 2012) with respect to the specific aspects developed in it, i.e. the detailed regulation of

79 Resolución 18-1495 de 2009 (septiembre 02) por la cual se establecen medidas en materia de Exploración y Explotación de Hidrocarburos.

80 Ley 1530 de 2012 por la cual se Regula la Organización y el Funcionamiento del Sistema General de Regalías.

81 https://www.slideshare.net/AIDA_Americas/regulacin-del-fracking en colombia; https://www.larepublica.co/economia/colombia-tiene-una-regulacion-robusta-para-iniciar-los-primeros-pilotos-de-fracking-2864560.

82 Artículo 2.2.1.1.1.1., Decreto 1073 de 2015 (mayo 26) por medio del cual se expide el Decreto Único Reglamentario del Sector Administrativo de Minas y Energía.

83 Artículo 2.2.1.1.1.1., Decreto 1073 de 2015 (mayo 26) por medio del cual se expide el Decreto Único Reglamentario del Sector Administrativo de Minas y Energía.

84 Article 1, Decreto 3004 de 2013 (diciembre 26) por el cual se establecen los criterios y procedimientos para la exploración y explotación de hidrocarburos en yacimientos no convencionales.

85 Resolución 9 0341 de 27 marzo 2014, Ministerio de Minas y Energía, por el cual se establecen requerimientos técnicos y procedimientos para la exploración y explotación de hidrocarburos en yacimientos no convencionales.

86 Acuerdo 3 de marzo 26 de 2014, Agencia Nacional de Hidrocarburos.

87 Article 2, Decreto 3004 de 2013 (diciembre 26), Ministerio de Energía y Minas, por el cual se establecen los criterios y procedimientos para la exploración y explotación de hidrocarburos en yacimientos no convencionales.

88 Acuerdo 4 de 2012, por el cual se establecen criterios de administración y asignación de áreas para exploración y explotación de los hidrocarburos propiedad de la nación, Agencia Nacional de Hidrocarburos (ANH).

unconventional deposits.[89] Together, these administrative regulations open the door to shale gas development in Colombia, as well as setting the contractual forms for carrying out these activities.[90]

Agreement 3 stipulates that unconventional hydrocarbon activity will be limited in time based on the type of contract and activity undertaken. For exploration contracts, the period of activity is nine years (which may be extended), divided into three phases. This exploration contract requires a detailed Exploratory Program with a minimum investment requirement based on market prices. The Exploration Program may co-exist with the one for conventional deposits or replace it.[91] Production contracts for shale gas and other unconventional deposits in designated areas are for 30 years, also with the possibility of extension.

In undertaking unconventional hydrocarbon operations, Agreement 3 sets minimum thresholds for the capacity of the contract holder. Article 42 stipulates the economic and financial capacity to develop these types of depositions, in principle requiring economic activity that during the three previous years is equal or superior to US$200 million per year, per area to exploit. This requirement essentially excludes the small to medium players, meaning that shale gas exploration becomes the purvey of large international oil companies. Such a view is supported by the caveat where if the party(ies) is included in the index of the last publication of some specialized energy finance journals or have a BBB credit risk classification, no financial assessment is required.

Article 43 of Agreement 3 requires operators to prove experience and expertise in unconventional hydrocarbon exploitation according to international best practices. They are required to prove minimum requirements of company reserves (equivalent to 50 million barrels), and a minimum operational production equivalent to 20,000 barrels per day. Again, if the party(ies) is included in the index of the last publication of some specialized energy finance journals it is not required to prove this capacity. Concerning the award procedure, parties must comply with previous qualification requirements, submitting a proposal to develop unconventional wells alongside the business plan. The ANH must evaluate the proposal, and confirm it complies with the requirements.

Once all of these minimum requirements are verified, the contractor is authorized to carry out operations of "Exploration, Evaluation, Development and Production for this kind of Unconventional Deposits",[92] and special contracting conditions apply. For gas contracts, no methane gas associated with carbon seams may be explored or produced, nor hydrocarbons in bituminous sands.[93] Also, for unconventional deposits, it is not possible to return areas before the expiration of the exploration period, unless the contractor has returned the area when carrying out exploration for conventional deposits.

These two shale gas instruments build upon political decisions by the ANH and the central government to give priority to unconventional hydrocarbon development as part of the Nation's Development Plan 2010–2014.[94] The legal base of these rules is Presidential Decree 3004 of 2013 (Decree 3004), which instructed the Ministry of Mines and Energy and

89 Article 110, Acuerdo No. 02 de 2017, Consejo Directivo de la Agencia Nacional de Hidrocarburos (ANH).

90 Jaramillo Velázquez, David, Reglamento de Contratación para la Exploración y Producción de Hidrocarburos Provenientes de Yacimientos No Convencionales" in Montoya Pardo and Milton Fernando (eds.) *Lecturas en Regulación Energética y de Hidrocarburos*, (Universidad Externado de Colombia 2016), 146.

91 Article 40.2, Acuerdo 3 de marzo 26 de 2014, Agencia Nacional de Hidrocarburos.

92 Article 48, Acuerdo 3 de marzo 26 de 2014, Agencia Nacional de Hidrocarburos (emphasis in original).

93 Article 49.1., Acuerdo 3 de marzo 26 de 2014, Agencia Nacional de Hidrocarburos.

94 https://colaboracion.dnp.gov.co/CDT/PND/PND2010-2014%20Tomo%20I%20CD.pdf, 285. This Nation's Development Plan was later incorporated in the legal framework through the Law N. 1450 of 16 June 2011.

the ANH to regulate unconventional hydrocarbons from a technical and contractual perspective, respectively.[95] This existing unconventional hydrocarbons regulatory framework is currently under scrutiny, with some of the rules (the Resolution 9 0341 of 27 March 2014 and the Decree 3004) being suspended by the Colombian Council of the State due to ongoing litigation concerning the constitutionality of the rules for hydraulic fracturing. This ongoing procedure has not only suspended these administrative rules concerning fracking (and also shale gas and unconventional hydrocarbons) but also all activity in the assigned areas, currently leaving shale gas regulation in limbo in Colombia.

3.3.1 Shale gas technical regulation

Resolution 9 0341 of 2014 is extremely thorough in setting out the technical and procedural requirements for unconventional hydrocarbon activities in order to guarantee "the sustainable development of the industrial activity".[96] This rule governs the activity *ratione specialis* but in case of a lacuna, then Resolution 18 1495 of 2009 aplies,[97] which establishes the main rules concerning hydrocarbon activities to maximize their recovery from a more general perspective.[98]

Additionally, Resolution 9 0341 inserts detailed standards to carry out activities, which vary depending on the stage of the activity. Article 7 regulates the carrying out of a production trial test, which is to be carried out after the perforation, stimulation and termination of the well, and the results are to be reported to the MME for the potential of the well to be evaluated. For a production well, Article 8 requires a pilot project for up to two years (reporting monthly), which can be extended for contractual or technical reasons. To get this pilot project authorized, the operator is required to submit a report concerning the facilities, installations and operations according to national and international rules and standards.

Article 9 of Resolution 9 0341 sets technical requirements for exploratory wells (including vertical sampling), while Article 10 regulates stratigraphic wells. Article 11 sets detailed technical rules for the cementing of unconventional wells, the cementation of exploratory and development wells for unconventional hydrocarbons, including particularities on conductor and superficial coating, intermediate coating and productive coating.

3.3.2 Licensing

Similar to Mexico, several licensing rounds have taken place in Colombia, with the 2012 and 2014 rounds including unconventional hydrocarbons and shale gas. The 2012 *Ronda Colombiana* included the first authorizations to undertake E&P operations of unconventional reservoirs in emerging zones. Out of 12 areas with reservoirs of unconventional hydrocarbons 5 were awarded, while out of the 18 areas with little or no geological information that

95 Article 1, Decreto 3004 de 2013 (diciembre 26), Ministerio de Energía y Minas, por el cual se establecen los criterios y procedimientos para la exploración y explotación de hidrocarburos en yacimientos no convencionales.

96 Article 1, Resolución 9 0341 de 27 marzo 2014, Ministerio de Minas y Energía, por el cual se establecen requerimientos técnicos y procedimientos para la exploración y explotación de hidrocarburos en yacimientos no convencionales.

97 Resolución 18-1495 de 2009 (septiembre 02) por la cual se establecen medidas en materia de Exploración y Explotación de Hidrocarburos.

98 Article 2, Resolución 9 0341 de 27 marzo 2014, Ministerio de Minas y Energía, por el cual se establecen requerimientos técnicos y procedimientos para la exploración y explotación de hidrocarburos en yacimientos no convencionales.

were tendered, none were awarded and none were adjudicated under the figure of contracts of technical evaluation.[99] In the 2014 round, 18 areas for E&P of unconventional hydrocarbons were tendered. However, only 1 of those areas was awarded to Parex Resources Colombia.[100]

According to data from 2017, out of 48 identified unconventional hydrocarbon blocks, 11 contained exploration activities and 1 had commenced production. However, with the ongoing litigation concerning the validity of unconventional hydrocarbon rules all operations have been stopped and no further shale gas areas can be awarded until a decision is made.

The Colombian SOC, Ecopetrol[101] enjoys some privileges regarding acquisition of areas for shale gas exploration. Article 56 of Agreement 3 establishes special rules applicable to agreements between the ANH and Ecopetrol for unconventional hydrocarbons, which exempt it to prove technical, economic, operational or juridical capacity to operate in the designated areas.

3.3.3 Financial promotion of shale gas activities

In addition to an extensive and detailed regulation of shale gas activities, unconventional hydrocarbon exploitation is promoted through a more lenient system of royalties payable to the Colombian State. Article 14.1 of the Law on the General System of Royalties sets the rules applicable to unconventional hydrocarbons which are more lenient than the general system of royalties to incentivize their exploration and exploitation. According to this provision, the royalties that apply are 60 per cent of the participation royalties that apply to the exploitation of conventional crude, which represents a rather attractive economic benefit.

Also, the Colombian legislation aims to promote unconventional and shale gas exploitation by allowing producers and other private companies to carry out thermoelectric generation activity directly as long as they use the gas extracted.[102] Additionally, the MME, the ANH and the Comision de Regulacion de Energia y Gas (CREG) may also adopt additional incentives to promote unconventional E&P activities in a wide and flexible provision.[103]

3.4 Controversy and litigation surrounding the validity of shale gas regulation and fracking

As in Mexico, the use of hydraulic fracturing as a technique to exploit shale gas deposits has been the subject of much controversy, as have Colombian legal procedures established for the activity, with the constitutional validity of these procedures being challenged.

As discussed in section 3.2.1 above, Colombia's Constitution establishes detailed and broad environmental protection, premised on the notion of protection of the environment as a collective good, and the need to repair it in case of damage. Colombian regulation includes a set of comprehensive, modern and complex environmental protection rules to be

99 Arroyo and Perdriel (n 2), 52.

100 Ibid, 52–53.

101 Founded in 1951, Ecopetrol (Empresa Colombiana de Petróleos) is a mainly state owned oil company in which the Colombia State holds 88 per cent of the shares and the rest are in the hands of private investors, JP Morgan Chase being the largest of them with 2.60 per cent of the shares.

102 Artículo 2.2.2.2.27., Decreto 1073 de 2015 (mayo 26) por medio del cual se expide el Decreto Único Reglamentario del Sector Administrativo de Minas y Energía.

103 Artículo 2.2.2.2.27, paragraph 1, Decreto 1073 de 2015 (mayo 26) por medio del cual se expide el Decreto Único Reglamentario del Sector Administrativo de Minas y Energía.

applied to unconventional hydrocarbons, which have been adopted through administrative resolutions.[104] These instruments have been adopted by the Ministry of Environment and the ANH.

On 23 August 2016, a lawsuit was filed before the Council of the State[105] requesting the nullity of the Colombian rules concerning unconventional hydrocarbon exploitation through fracking mechanisms.[106] The lawsuit aims at annulling Presidential Decree 3004 of 2013 and Resolution 9 0341 of 2014 issued by the MME on the grounds that they conflict with Articles 79 and 80 of the Constitution, which deal with environmental and health protection.

The Council of the State admitted the lawsuit and on 8 November 2018 granted an interim injunction, suspending the entirety of the Decree 3004 of 2013 and Administrative Resolution 9 0341 of 2014, but not discussing the validity of Agreement 3 2014 or Agreement 2 of 2017, both issued by the ANH. The Council of the State granted the injunction on the grounds that it was

> necessary, proportional and adequate ..., as the administrative provisions, in principle, do not comply with the precautionary approach and obligation of general due diligence that imposes taking all necessary measures to prevent the potential damage or risks derived from activities associated to *fracking*.[107]

In April 2019, a Commission of 13 experts released a Fracking Report of non-binding nature and independent of the ongoing litigation. The report, which was requested by the Executive Power, concluded that "before determining whether or not to do fracking with commercial purposes in Colombia",[108] the Commission recommends carrying out several pilot projects based on a previous and a post-phase divided into three stages, to take into account the impact concerning social, technical and institutional aspects, the *in situ* fracking operations and a result evaluation and to define whether or not to carry out commercial exploitation in defined areas.[109] These conclusions have been reported in the specialized press as being a "green light" to fracking activity,[110] interpreting them as allowing pilot projects to determine the consequences and benefits of the technique prior to authorizing fully-fledged commercial fracking operations across the country.

104 See for example, Resolution 0421 of 2014 issued by the Ministry of Environment and Sustainable Development setting the requirements for developing an Environmental Impact Study for exploratory perforation of hydrocarbons.

105 Colombia's Consejo de Estado is the Supreme Court for Administrative Law matters, akin to the French Conseil d' État.

106 Consejo de Estado, Case No 57.819, Esteban Antonio Lagos González vs State-Ministry of Energy and Mines (pending), documents of the case available at http://servicios.consejodeestado.gov.co/testmaster/nue_actua.asp?mindice=11001032600020160014000

107 Consejo de Estado, Case No 57.819, *Esteban Antonio Lagos González vs State-Ministry of Energy and Mines* (pending), Decision on Interim Injunction of 8 November 2018, 51 (emphasis in original).

108 Informe sobre Efectos Ambientales (Bióticos, Físicos Y Sociales) y Económicos de la Exploración de Hidrocarburos en Áreas con Posible Despliegue de Técnicas de Fracturamiento Hidráulico de Roca Generadora Mediante Perforación Horizontal (April 2019), 116.

109 Informe sobre Efectos Ambientales (Bióticos, Físicos Y Sociales) y Económicos de la Exploración de Hidrocarburos en Áreas con Posible Despliegue de Técnicas de Fracturamiento Hidráulico de Roca Generadora Mediante Perforación Horizontal (April 2019), 109.

110 https://www.americasquarterly.org/content/fracking-colombia-real-time; https://www.dinero.com/pais/articulo/se-puede-hacer-fracking-en-colombia-segun-comision-de-expertos/267160; https://sostenibilidad.semana.com/actualidad/articulo/decision-de-la-comision-de-expertos-sobre-fracking-genera-polemica/42987;https://www.pulzo.com/economia/si-habra-fracking-colombia-comision-expertos-PP643139.

Following the Fracking Report and continuing with the annulment action, the Council of the State in the Initial Audience of 7 June 2019 ordered the creation of a group of experts appointed by the National University of Colombia. This group is entrusted with submitting a report within three months to determine the environmental impact that fracking may have when carrying out E&P operations of unconventional hydrocarbons.[111] At the time of the writing of this chapter, the report has not been produced and the case is still pending before the Council of the State.

The debate regarding shale gas development is certainly not over, rather it has stepped into the legislative arena. There are currently three law proposals concerning fracking under discussion before the Colombian Congress. Two of them request prohibiting fracking activity, while a third one suggests suspending fracking activities until there are sufficient studies to reveal whether or not it is safe.[112]

4 Conclusion: the future of shale gas in Mexico and Colombia

In this chapter, we analysed current regulation and the status of unconventional hydrocarbons and shale gas in Latin America, focusing on two vastly differing jurisdictions, Mexico and Colombia. This chapter shows two different approaches to shale gas exploitation and regulation, revealing both the advantages and disadvantages of shale gas. On the one hand, these Latin American countries and their governments had initially perceived shale gas exploitation as a possible way of increasing financial revenues for the country, and an opportunity to develop expertise and technology for the national SOC. However, the environmental impact of shale gas exploitation, its clash with environmental law provisions, a critical public perception and, in some cases, reservations or rejection concerning the hydrocarbon policy by a new government, has generated controversy and opposition to it, especially whenever the hydraulic fracturing is undertaken. This controversial aspect of shale gas exploitation has led to Presidential action, in the case of Mexico, and the revoking of already awarded E&P permits. In Colombia, a critical lawsuit against the framework that allows and develops shale gas and unconventional exploitation activities is underway, with the outcome likely to determine the future of shale gas exploitation forevermore.

In Mexico, shale gas activity takes place within the Energy Reform of 2013, which transformed the upstream petroleum industry and allowed private parties' participation in hydrocarbon exploitation alongside PEMEX. During this process of change, shale gas and unconventional hydrocarbons were seen as an opportunity to improve the competitiveness and profitability of the Mexican hydrocarbon industry, and to reduce dependence on US imports, especially of natural gas. Despite the need for increased gas production, the Mexican legal framework has not adopted specific legal or administrative rules to directly regulate exploitation of unconventional hydrocarbon resources or the fracking technique. This, however, has not led to an absence of unconventional hydrocarbon activity, as some areas have been awarded for E&P activities. Authorization for the use of hydraulic fracturing was also granted by the competent authority, only to be overruled by the Mexican president the following day.

111 Consejo de Estado, Case No 57.819, *Esteban Antonio Lagos González vs State-Ministry of Energy and Mines* (pending), Act of Initial Audience of 7 June 2019, 12 and 13.

112 https://sostenibilidad.semana.com/actualidad/articulo/decision-de-la-comision-de-expertos-sobre-fracking-genera-polemica/42987.

Colombia, on the other hand, shows a different trend. Like Mexico, it possesses large shale gas and unconventional hydrocarbon deposits and has a history as a petroleum producer. Yet, its hydrocarbon legal framework contains the most advanced and specific regulation for the exploitation of unconventional hydrocarbons, including shale gas, in Latin America, as well as regulating the hydraulic fracturing which is required to produce shale gas. Also, unlike Mexico, the Colombian government saw exploitation of shale gas not as an opportunity to reduce dependency on gas imports, but to increase its hydrocarbon exports, and to utilize such production as an opportunity to develop new techniques and technologies for the SOC, Ecopetrol.

Colombia's specific shale gas regulation builds upon the general hydrocarbons framework but recognizes the need for specific and detailed regulation developed through administrative resolutions and issued by competent hydrocarbon agencies and presidential decrees. Such a legal framework enables flexibility, perhaps to the detriment of legal certainty. Another aspect to highlight is that while the regulation is specific for shale gas exploitation, there is as yet no practical experience of its application. Furthermore, the legal validity of the specific shale gas legal framework is currently under scrutiny, with accusations of the laws being unconstitutional. Furthermore, it appears also that in Colombia, the challenge in developing shale gas resources lies in the practical implementation of the law, and institutional capacity and independence, rather than the legal framework or the quality of the regulation.

Despite these similitudes and differences displaying a relatively diverse landscape in Latin American shale gas regulation, what the examples of Mexico and Colombia alike demonstrate is a resistance to shale gas activities. We distinguish three aspects from our analysis as the source of this controversy. First, these Latin American countries, like the majority of those in the region, see their natural resources policy dictated by political (presidential) interests, which are at times very varied within the same country in a short period of time. In the case of shale gas, in both Mexico and Colombia there has been a major interest in promoting the industry but in the Mexican case this has now faded and is the industry is strongly opposed by the new government. Second, shale gas development, and the use of hydraulic fracturing to achieve such development, is resisted by the general population, with such resistance primarily attributable to the perceived environmental impacts, previous Latin American experiences in controlling environmental damage and prior experiences in the intervention and impact of large corporations on Latin American society. Thirdly, and most legally relevant, some of the provisions allowing for shale gas exploitation utilizing hydraulic fracturing have been deemed by some in Colombia to breach constitutional provisions guaranteeing high environmental standards and a right to a healthy environment.

All in all, if anything, the future of shale gas in Latin America still seems distant, facing a myriad of obstacles given the Mexican and Colombian experiences. If other countries in the region look upon the experiences of these two countries, it is likely that a path of wariness is likely to be trod.

19

ENERGY JUSTICE AS A KEY DRIVER TO UNLOCK THE TRANSITION FROM ENERGY REFORM TO ENERGY COUNTER-REFORM

The rise of the immutability theory

Miguel Marmolejo-Cervantes

1 Introduction

In Mexico, private parties have been actively participating in petroleum operations (upstream) since 2015 by virtue of the energy reform (ER) enacted in 2013. As of July 2018, 102 petroleum contracts and 3 farm outs have been executed satisfactorily, representing investments of around US$4,072 million.[1]

Despite the outcomes achieved in a relatively short period of time, a radical movement limiting private investment is getting stronger, which is seen as the energy counter-reform (ECR).[2] President Andres Manuel López Obrador has expressed, although inconsistently, his desire to adjust the ER to fiercely point out a higher intervention of the State.[3] However, given the type of incentives for private participants, if any, it is unclear how they are intended to accomplish a constitutional fair balance between acquired ownership rights,[4] legal certainty[5] and

1 Ministry of Energy, 'Five-year Plan on Hydrocarbon Exploration and Extraction Bidding 2015–2019' (Ministry of Energy, 2014) 13 <www.gob.mx/cms/uploads/attachment/file/395318/Prog._Quinquenal_-_septiembre.pdf> accessed 23 October 2018.

2 Self-conception.

3 Keith Johnson, 'Mexico's Populist New President Unlikely to Derail Energy Reform' (Foreign Policy, 3 July 2018) <https://foreignpolicy.com/2018/07/03/mexicos-populist-new-president-unlikely-to-derail-energy-reform-amlo-pemex-oil> accessed 23 October 2018. Ana Isabel Martinez and Marianna Parraga, 'President-elect López Obrador Slams Mexico's Pemex for Crude Import Plan' (*CNBC*, 23 October 2018) www.cnbc.com/2018/10/23/reuters-america-president-elect-lopez-obrador-slams-mexicos-pemex-for-crude-import-plan.html> accessed 25 October 2018.

4 In terms of article 27 of the Mexican Constitution which entitles private participants to get access to petroleum activities.

5 Respect of the rule of law.

the principle of non-retroactivity[6]. Unless the ghost of direct or indirect expropriation is returning, the appetite of investors to maximise the State's revenues might not be accomplished.[7]

Therefore, the key question is: to what extent does the ECR affect the current ER governance structure? Secondly, it should also be asked if such an impact would allow the co-existence of present and future private participants to maximise oil revenues as the Mexican Constitution mandates.

Such questions will be answered based on the assumption that the new (old school) model proposed by President López Obrador excludes direct private participation in petroleum activities, or imposes limits on private participants that might prevent direct access to petroleum extraction operations.

This chapter intends to provide a solution in terms of the concept known as energy justice as a key driver to solve the transition from ER to ECR. In order to achieve this, the immutability theory will be built on the fundamentals of the energy justice concept and subsequently these arguments will be tested on the government's Five-Year Plan.

2 Energy justice and the immutability theory

2.1 Energy justice

The concept of energy justice has recently emerged with the objective of applying justice principles to energy policy, energy production and systems, energy consumption, energy activism, energy security, the energy trilemma, the energy political economy and climate change.[8] Energy justice evaluates: 1) where injustices emerge; 2) which of the affected sections of society are ignored; and 3) which processes exist for their remediation to reveal and reduce such injustices.[9]

Key aspects of the energy justice theory have been discussed since the 1980s.[10] A contemporary interest in energy justice can be identified in different initiatives led by the Resources for the Future group, the work of the Brundtland Commission and the studies of the World Energy Council and United Nations. For instance, the United Nations Development Programme Report entitled 'Energy and the challenge of sustainability'[11] touches on energy justice when addressing subjects related to energy, -social issues and energy security. More recently, the concept of energy justice gained prominence as an explicit theme of the UK Energy Research Council.[12]

Energy justice can be defined through universal and particular concepts.[13] Universal energy justice is understood as a global energy system that fairly disseminates both the benefits

6 Political Constitution of the United Mexican States, article 14: "No law shall be given retroactive effect to the detriment of any person whatsoever". Therefore, when it represents a concrete benefit to any person, it shall not be considered retroactive.

7 The ghost of direct expropriation is understood when former President Lázaro Cárdenas signed an order that expropriated the assets of nearly all of the foreign oil companies operating in Mexico. Mexican Expropriation of Foreign Oil, 1938. <https://history.state.gov/milestones/1937-1945/mexican-oil> accessed 3 June 2019. Additionally, the ghost of indirect expropriation is meant in terms of the international investment law provisions, particularly when the legitimate expectations of investors are made and then broken without legal justification. Indeed, Mexico signed the ICSID Convention on 11 January 2018 to reinforce its commitment to respect investments accordingly. <https://icsid.worldbank.org/en/Pages/about/Database-of-Member-States.aspx> accessed 3 June 2019.

8 Kirsten Jenkins et al., 'Energy Justice: A Conceptual Review' [2016] 11 *ERSS* 174, 175 accessed 31 October 2018.

9 Ibid.

10 Kirsten Jenkins et al., 'Energy Justice: A Policy Approach' [2017] 105 *Energy Policy*, 631 accessed 27 October 2018.

11 Ibid.

12 Ibid.

13 Michael Carnegie LaBelle, 'In Pursuit of Energy Justice' [2017] 107 *Energy Policy* 615, 616 accessed 30 October 2018.

and costs of energy services and has a representative and impartial energy decision-making process. This definition stems from other interpretations of justice: procedural, distributional and cosmopolitan. Procedural, as in the delivery and protection of energy services through administrative or judicial means. Distributional, which facilitates other human rights like education, health and access to energy services. And cosmopolitan, defined as a collective approach to creating meaningful global change specifically in energy behaviours and attitudes.

Additionally, energy justice specifically analyses justice within local experiences as an accounting of local issues and interpretations of social, political and economic actions affecting access to energy resources and services. This is significant because cultural and environmental factors of a domestic character influence the choice of energy technologies and policy preferences for the distribution of energy services. Within this type of justice is recognition justice, which provides representation for groups with features such as social, ethnic and gender differences.[14]

A conceptual framework recognises eight principles surrounding energy justice, suitable to strengthen the immutability theory will be discussed below (Table 19.1).[15]

2.2 *Immutability theory*

The immutability theory that will be developed in this chapter is understood as the fusion of various national and international principles or models, based on constitutional, legal or case law sources. Their content allows the analysis and assessment of the degree of legal certainty and safety that exists in the decision-making process carried out by the government in relation to the energy field in the long term.

At the national level the principles taken into account are: 1) the principle of the non-retroactivity of the law to the detriment of any person; 2) the principle of legality; 3) the principle of acquired rights; and 4) the principle of maximisation of oil revenue under the terms of constitutional article 27. At the international level, the principles are those of sustainable development, which are enacted by the United Nations.

Thus, nationally, the principle of non-retroactivity is understood as the restrictions on the government to modify specific conditions to the detriment of the people governed. The principle of legality refers to the government's respect for the legal decisions made, whether in the form of administrative resolutions or contracts. The principle of acquired rights is understood as respect for the ownership and stability of the applicable law. Finally, the principle of maximisation of oil revenues refers to the constitutional mandate aimed at getting State revenues to contribute to the country's long-term development.

On the other hand, internationally, the United Nations sustainable development goals are: no poverty, affordable and clean energy, decent work and economic growth, climate action and peace, justice and strong institutions.

In this way, the immutability theory establishes that the government's legal decisions must not be altered, especially to the detriment of any person (principle of non-retroactivity), they must be upheld (principle of legality), and they must comply with the constitutional goal of maximising State revenue for long-term development (principle of maximisation). In other words, the content of a government decision is immutable: if it upholds one of the State's main sources of revenue to combat poverty; if affordable and clean energy is achieved; if decent work and economic growth is reachable; and if peace, justice and the strengthening of institutions are well served.

14 Ibid.

15 Benjamin K. Sovacool and Michael H. Dworkin, *Global Energy Justice: Problems, Principles and Practices* (1st edn, Cambridge University Press, 2014) 367–371.

The highest threshold would be a situation whereby an immutable decision is made for an unlawful purpose, and whether these are sufficient grounds to revoke that decision. In particular, one of the bases of the immutability theory is the fulfilment of a constitutional goal—that is, the maximisation of oil revenues—which is valid and lawful. This means that one of the State sources of revenue is constitutionally protected, as is the mechanism to achieve that goal (allowing the private sector to participate in oil bidding rounds as well as the development of unconventional oil fields).

In the case that the State changes or reinterprets the constitutional goal of revenue maximisation, is it valid to determine that all legal acts executed for achieving it are now considered revoked? This chapter argues that the answer is no, because this would violate the principles of non-retroactivity and legality and possible rights acquired by third parties. This may not only be a violation of rights, but fundamentally, this measure expressed in public policies could impoverish current and future generations and might jeopardise the State's financial stability.

But what if the constitutional goal is considered unlawful over time? In this case, the State has the power to establish an orderly non-abrupt transition based on the principles of the immutability theory itself as well as by respecting the rule of law, transparency in the decision-making process and fostering a meaningful dialogue between the stakeholders.

In this sense, if the State proceeds to an orderly non-abrupt transition, then is obliged to get all the evidence available, accounting for best practices and successfully proven international models, which effectively have produced long-term maximisation of revenue, in a sustainable manner. The State is also obliged to seek not only social justice, but also the hope of energy justice that best and equally balances social, economic and environmental issues, within an ecosystem whereby the State and the private sector may coexist equally.

Analogically we can use the case of the United Kingdom and the *Petroleum and Submarine Pipelines 1975 Act*. This Act was possible due to intensive negotiations for several years accompanied by many assurances to the licensees (and their banks) concerning the exercise of the new powers it contained. Two main values can be extracted from this case, transparent dialogue and reciprocal guarantees of good behaviour. In this context, it is still feasible for a government to re-introduce unilateral modifications to legal framework of hydrocarbons and, consequently, be able to exercise new powers over the contracts already signed.[16]

On the other hand, the mere argument that the participation of the private sector weakens the State's direction is inaccurate, given that article 25 of the Mexican Constitution provides for a mixed participation model between public and private capital in order to achieve economic development.

Likewise, it is inaccurate to argue that State revenue is enough to provide sufficient energy to satisfy the estimated demand, in a country with a demographic bonus that is growing exponentially, particularly when the State is facing a serious financial situation. That is why private investment is amply justified.

In any case, energy justice is compromised if the sovereign model proposed by the new administration fails to offer a better and greater State source of revenue that would allow the maximisation of oil revenues, or fails to provide a better model guaranteeing the governability of the oil industry in comparison with the current model established in the constitution.

16 Omon Anenih, 'The UK Petroleum Production Licence – Is it a Contract or Regulation and Does it Matter?' (ResearchGate, 2019) <www.researchgate.net/publication/267772867_The_UK_Petroleum_Production_Licence_-_Is_it_a_Contract_or_Regulation_and_Does_it_Matter> accessed 31 January 2019.

2.3 Correlation between energy justice and the immutability theory

Table 19.1 analyses the eight principles of energy justice (first two columns 'Principles of energy justice' and 'Energy justice')[17] and their relationship with the immutability theory (last two columns 'Immutability theory' and 'Relationship between the two concepts'), seeking to analyse the fairness of this theory.

Table 19.1 Energy justice principles and the immutability theory

Principles of energy justice	*Energy justice*	*Immutability theory*	*Relationship between the two concepts*
Availability	Seeks to ensure that a market, economy or system can guarantee both sufficient and high-quality energy resources to its people.	Administrative decisions already made by the Federal government in the energy sector promoted a greater availability of energy resources and services, at least as a fiscal funding source.	Revoking the structure established by an earlier administration may limit the availability of energy resources and services.
Affordability	People should pay no more than 10 per cent of their income for energy services. Prices must be lowered while energy needs are still met.	The energy reform (ER) sought to increase the production of energy resources, which would in turn reduce costs.	Not continuing with the strategy enforced by the former administration, based on the constitutional principle of revenue maximisation, might create uncertainty regarding the prices to be paid by energy consumers.
Due process	Countries must respect the established procedures and recognised human rights in the production and use of energy. It necessitates judicial and administrative recourses.	Factually revoking the former administration's established energy strategy blatantly violates the immutability theory.	The leaders of the new administration can make decisions regarding energy strategies undertaken by the outgoing administration. By interrupting the Ministry of Energy's five-year plan, the current administration is unjustly breaching the immutability theory.
Information	To minimise corruption and improve accountability, people should have access to information about energy, as well as fair, transparent and accountable forms of energy decision-making.	The new administration has interrupted the energy strategies of its predecessors. This *de facto* decision is not properly substantiated nor has sufficient information been provided to relevant parties.	Revoking these energy-sector decisions, merely seeking to undermine the prior administration without a comprehensive analysis regarding the substantial value of such decisions, is inconsistent with the principle of information and is not based on accountable forms of decision-making.

17 Ibid 16.

Principles of energy justice	*Energy justice*	*Immutability theory*	*Relationship between the two concepts*
Sustainability	Refers to a development that meets the needs of the present without compromising the ability of future generations to meet their own needs. Regarding energy, countries have the responsibility not to deplete resources too rapidly.	The previous administration's energy-sector strategies sought to properly exploit resources so that future generations have the possibility of satisfying their own needs. Revoking these strategies creates uncertainty regarding the sustainability of a new strategy.	An inadequate administration of the energy sector, which includes decision-making by one leadership political group and an unjustified revocation by another, might lead to the misuse of energy resources, which can compromise the possibility of future being able to access them.
Intragenerational equity	People have the right to access energy services fairly, and they are entitled to sufficient energy services, which enables them to enjoy a minimum of well-being.	An earlier administration of the Mexican government promoted higher and more efficient production of energy resources to satisfy the country's energy needs, an essential part of its social and economic development. Withdrawing these strategies jeopardises the possibility of the Mexican population having fair access to energy resources and services.	The reversal of the former administration's decisions plainly obstructs the right to access sufficient and adequate energy resources and thus compromises people's social and economic well-being.
Intergenerational equity	Future generations have the right to enjoy a good life undisturbed by the damage that energy systems inflict on the world today.	A poor administration of energy resources can inflict damage upon future generations' rights to access such resources.	Implementing and within a short period of time revoking energy-related decisions will have consequences on future generations' rights to access energy resources and services.
Responsibility	Nations must protect the natural environment and minimise energy-related environmental threats.	An inadequate energy-sector strategy enables threats both to the environment and to people's right to fairly access its energy resources.	A responsible administration implements well-planned strategies and, ideally, ensures a continuation and improvement of strategies from one administration to another, not the outright halt of such decisions.

Source: First two columns Sovacool and Dworkin,[a] last two columns added by author.

a Ibid 16.

2.3.1 Fairness of the immutability theory in terms of energy justice

The immutability theory is legitimated and strengthened by the above-mentioned principles of energy justice, mainly because it is fair for a government decision to prevail and perpetuate in the long term, thus allowing social peace or even better an energy peacekeeping to be maintained.

Thus, a government decision on energy is immutable if energy justice criteria are met as follows:

Availability: legitimately and objectively proven to result in energy supply sufficiency
Affordability: feasible economic burden

Due process: effective democratisation and adoption of agreements by stakeholders
Information: effective information on the respective energy public policy terms and scope
Sustainability: the guarantee that necessary and sufficient oil resources will be exploited for the long-term development of the country at a prudent and sustainable rhythm, wisely and strategically administering the real threat of stranded assets[18]
Intragenerational equity: the guarantee of a minimum level of welfare and subsistence avoiding energy poverty
Intergenerational equity: the availability of energy resources for future generations together with a permanent public policy for the current generations, aimed at providing education based on responsible energy consumption
Responsibility: the reduction of environmental impact.

If this is the case, then this decision must be immutable given that it is a legally binding legal decision, as it is the decision made through the issuance of the Five-Year Plan in which the immutability theory allows the reinforcement of its validity and execution.

It is the State's responsibility to protect basic goods, such as energy resources, and to guarantee everyone's access to sustainable modern energy. This must be carried out especially through adequate social, legal, economic—and environmental—agreements, with the application of international decisions. In fact, the State is always expected to accompany economic private agents in the adoption of sustainable behaviours for the environment and society. It is done by the establishment of public–private cooperation rules and the defence of adequate public policies to manage licences in the extraction of resources. It is also done by taking social and environmental responsibilities in commercial activities.[19]

Private extractive industries can contribute to sustainable development, provided they respect the environment, their projects are well-implemented, the rights of the people involved are protected and the benefits generated are properly used.[20]

Consequently, the State–private sector binomial relationship is assumed to be a necessary development model, at least by the Pontificio Consejo de 'Justicia y Paz', who believes that the perception of the relationship between energy, justice and peace will always be complex, and, if not satisfactorily resolved, it may be a serious threat to these basic goods. Conversely, if harmoniously resolved, it may contribute to a real, comprehensive and sustainable development.[21]

18 Stranded assets are defined as assets that have suffered from unanticipated or premature write-downs, devaluations or conversion to liabilities (Caldecott, Howarth, and McSharry, Oxford University Press, 2013). Stranded assets resulting from environment-related risk factors, including the effects of physical climate change and societal and regulatory responses to climate change, have become increasingly prominent, driven in large part by changes in the real economy (e.g., the falling cost of renewables), as well as by the attention generated by the Paris Agreement. *Stranded assets could be a systemic risk to financial stability and should therefore be a topic of concern for central banks and financial regulators.* There are also issues related to macro and micro prudential regulation and the conduct and practices of financial institutions that make stranded assets of relevance to supervisory bodies. Much of the work in this area has been led by the Bank of England, with the Financial Stability Board and the European Systemic Risk Board also producing work: Ben Caldecott et al., 'Stranded Assets: A Climate Risk Challenge' (Inter-American Development Bank, 2015) <https://publications.iadb.org/bitstream/handle/11319/7851/Stranded-Assets-A-Climate-Risk-Challenge.pdf?sequence=1&isAllowed=y> accessed 13 November 2018.

19 Pontificio Consejo, *Justice and Peace* (Editrice Vaticana, 2014), Foreword by Peter K. A. Cardenal Turkson and Mario Toso 'Energy, Justice and Peace, a Reflection on Energy in the Current Context of Development and Environmental Protection' 104–105.

20 World Bank, 'Striking a Better Balance – The World Bank Group and Extractive Industries: The Final Report of the Extractive Industries Review' (World Bank, 17 September 2004) Executive summary.

21 Consejo (n 21) 6–7.

The Mexican petroleum legal framework adopted this State-private binomial. It fosters private investment and, at the same time, energy justice and peacekeeping are being served. It contains international best practices as can be appreciated when it is compared *to* the petroleum law essential elements, as stipulated in the *Legislative frameworks used to foster petroleum development*.[22] Analysis which suggests the following:

1. State ownership of hydrocarbons is kept by the Mexican State.
2. The competent authority to implement government policy is clearly identified, as in the case of the National Hydrocarbon Commission (NHC).
3. Petroleum operations are conducted only under a duly issued permit or licence, as in Mexico biddings are conducted by the NHC, ending in an awarding contract in terms of the Hydrocarbon Law provisions and based on further secondary regulations whereby both PEMEX (Petróleos Mexicanos) and any other private petroleum company, regardless of its nationality, is able to participate.
4. Petroleum agreements are available to the public once the bidding call is published,[23] although the Ministry of Energy proposes a contract model. Regulations are subsidiary instruments. The NHC is expressly authorised to produce and to amend its own regulation, from time to time, consistent with public policy and objectives in terms of the petroleum law.
5. Qualifications, duties and rights of rights holders or contractors are validated by the NHC which is entitled to conduct due diligence to evaluate financial participants' sources, technical competence and professional skills and to enforce the Hydrocarbon Law and petroleum agreement duties such as petroleum discovery reporting and a development plan for commercial petroleum discoveries.[24] All petroleum operations are conducted in accordance with good international petroleum industry practice. Indeed, international standards are being incorporated into the upstream regulation to standardise best practice.[25] In return, the rights holder is granted the exclusive right to carry out petroleum operations within the area covered by the petroleum agreement.
6. Taxation of profits, although a complex and grey area in Mexico, in general terms, represents a stable tax forum based on a worldwide network of international agreements regarding double taxation avoidance. However, fiscal duties derived from entitlements or contracts are handled in terms of the Hydrocarbon Revenue Law and tax duties in accordance with the tax legal framework. Both concepts are duly incorporated in the Petroleum Agreement in specific provisions as a tax duties rule. Mexico is an investment-friendly forum due to its extensive free trade advocacy contained in free trade agreements and bilateral investment treaties, no exchange controls are applicable. A fiscal stabilisation is also incorporated in the Petroleum Agreement as an amendments and relinquishments provision.

22 William T. Onorato, 'Legislative Frameworks Used to Foster Petroleum Development' (World Bank, February 1995) <http://documents.worldbank.org/curated/en/761771468765623659/pdf/multi-page.pdf> accessed 26 November 2018.

23 Contract models and contracts awarded are available at the NHC website: <https://www.gob.mx/cnh> (digital warehouse) and <https://rondasmexico.gob.mx> English versions are also available.

24 Government of Mexico, 'Exploration and Extraction Contracts Bidding Administrative Regulations' (*Federal Official Gazette*, 28 November 2014) <www.dof.gob.mx/nota_detalle.php?codigo=5372660&fecha=28/11/2014> accessed 30 November 2018.

25 Well drilling guidelines refer directly to the American Petroleum Standards: National Hydrocarbons Commission, 'Well Drilling Guidelines' (National Hydrocarbons Commission, 2016) <https://cnh.gob.mx/regulacion/docs/Lineamientos%20de%20Perforaci%C3%B3n%20de%20Pozos%20Versi%C3%B3n%20Compilada.pdf> accessed 30 November 2018.

7. Environmental protection and safety is covered in terms of the National Agency for Industrial Safety and Environmental Protection of the Hydrocarbons Sector (ASEA)'s functions and regulations, particularly through its own law which is based on a regulatory function to issue general administrative regulations and Mexican official norms on onshore and offshore petroleum extraction. The content of such regulations adopts international standards generally accepted by the industry around the world to achieve efficient and safe exploration and production of petroleum.

In general terms all the key points outlined in the chapter are met by the Mexican petroleum legal framework, particularly those related to essential elements of a petroleum law model for attracting investments fairly.

3 Immutability Theory applied to the Five-Year Plan

3.1 Background

Energy regulation relies on the participation of private investors, either in oil fields awarded directly to PEMEX as State Productive Enterprise (known as Round 0).[26] Private investment participation can also be awarded via bidding rounds. Bidding rounds are conducted by the regulator (the National Hydrocarbon Commission). Lastly, once the awarding process has been finalised, the National Hydrocarbon Commission will grant exploration and extraction contracts based on the satisfaction of economic criteria (Rounds 1, 2, 3 and so on).[27]

In 2015, the Mexican Ministry of Energy released a Five-Year Plan for Exploration and Production of Oil and Gas Bids. Its latest version was published on October 2018.[28] The Five-Year Plan contains elements such as the prioritisation of oil fields, their classification, mechanisms, qualifications and frequency of biddings.[29] The strategy of the Five-Year Plan is to increase oil and gas production among others.[30]

Special consideration should be taken of the industry nominations, where in terms of the regulations, any state-owned or private company (private investor) may propose an area (oil field) to the Ministry of Energy in which there is an interest in carrying out oil and gas

26 Available at <https://www.gob.mx/sener/articulos/ronda-cero-y-migracion-de-contratos-de-pemex> accessed 11 April 2019.

27 Available at <https://rondasmexico.gob.mx> accessed 11 April 2019.

28 Ministry of Energy, 'Five Year Plan on Hydrocarbon Exploration and Extraction Bid 2015–2019: 2018 Evaluation' (Government of Mexico, 2018) <www.gob.mx/cms/uploads/attachment/file/396006/Plan__Quinquenal_Evaluacion_2018_Final.pdf> accessed 25 October 2018.

29 Priority is given to areas with mature or discovered fields, where the entire geologic column is kept in the same area. The areas are classified as in the previous evaluation: 1) Deep water; 2) Shallow water; 3) Onshore unconventional (Chicontepec and shale); and iv. Onshore conventional. Every year at least one invitation to bid will be carried out for each type of area. The opening of proposals will take place approximately six months after the invitation to bid announcement. Prior to the announcement of an invitation to bid there is a three-month period during which companies can nominate areas they wish to be included in the subsequent invitation to bid. These areas must be accompanied by a technical study considering the information available at the National Center for Hydrocarbon Information (Centro Nacional de Información de Hidrocarburos), derived from an Authorisation for Surface Exploration (Autorización de Reconocimiento y Exploración Superficial) or from an institutional source. Other aspects of the bidding rounds will continue to be simplified, such as the prequalification requirements. Ministry of Energy, 'Executive Summary: Five Year Plan for Exploration and Production of Oil and Gas Bids 2015–2019' (Government of Mexico, 2017) 4–5 <www.gob.mx/cms/uploads/attachment/file/291463/FiveYearPlan_ExecutiveSummary_2017.pdf> accessed 25 October 2018.

30 Ibid 5.

exploration and extraction activities. The Ministry of Energy will evaluate these proposals and, if applicable, include them in the Five-Year Plan. The Ministry of Energy has invited companies to nominate their areas of interest and companies have sent their nominations, with subsurface information, and reasons for supporting their request. In order not to interfere with fair competition conditions, information regarding nominations is not disclosed.[31]

One of the key features of the ER is that the energy policy is deeply embedded in the constitutional provisions with the aim of providing legal certainty[32] along with financial security which is provided by the investment international treaties that foster and protect private investments.[33] Mexico represents a world class investment forum.

This legal framework sets the rights and duties of private participants within a governance structure. This is formed by the interactions between agencies of the Federal Government and regulators, to rule and incentivise them, on a collaborative basis. These interactions aim to achieve the ultimate goal of the State: to obtain revenues derived from petroleum activities in order to contribute to the long-term development of the Nation.

3.2 Legal analysis

Nevertheless, what would happen if ECR takes place and suddenly the new administration cancels the Five-Year Plan for Exploration and Production of Oil and Gas Bids and bans private participation? Would that be legally possible?

First, above all, and in terms of ER, the current legal framework protects investors from any regulatory change. Obviously, the State is entitled to make amendments that are constitutional, such as the principle of non-retroactivity. Moreover, if the exercise of power has been turned into an administrative act then it becomes a concrete administrative resolution on behalf of the investors. This resolution shall be upheld by the new administration unless an extinction cause arises, like cancellation, which is not an available remedy in terms of the hydrocarbons legal framework.[34]

Within the Five-Year Plan for Exploration and Production of Oil and Gas Bids, the Ministry of Energy plays an active role in choosing the oil fields (contractual areas) to be the subject of bidding. The Ministry is also responsible for the issuance of the Plan, which is public and can be amended in terms of the administrative regulation. This Plan can never be cancelled because the Ministry of Energy does not have any legal powers in relation to the Hydrocarbon Law.[35]

Furthermore, article 33 section VII of the Organic Law of the Federal Public Administration states that the Ministry of Energy has the authority to set (not to reset) oil fields to

31 Hydrocarbon Law Administrative Regulation, articles 26–28.

32 As can be appreciated in articles 25 paragraph four, 27 paragraph seven and 28 paragraph four of the General Constitution, as well as its extensive 21 transitory provisions derived from the Energy Reform constitutional amendment. Contents that are reflected subsequently into the Hydrocarbon Law, Hydrocarbon Revenues Law, Law of Coordinated Energy Regulatory Agencies, Environmental and Industrial Safety for the Hydrocarbons Sector Law, PEMEX Law and the Foreign Investment Law. The aforementioned laws are also governed by further secondary regulation.

33 There are 12 Free Trade Agreements and 32 Bilateral Investment Treaties in force exerted by Mexico. Ministry of Economy, 'Foreign Commerce / Countries with Treaties and Agreements signed with Mexico' (Government of Mexico, 2015) <www.gob.mx/se/acciones-y-programas/comercio-exterior-paises-con-tratados-y-acuerdos-firmados-con-mexico> accessed 13 November 2018.

34 Federal Administrative Procedural Law, article 11 section VI.

35 Article 29.

Exploration and Extraction contracts. These same powers are established in article 16 of the Ministry of Energy Internal Regulation. This internal regulation explains that the Deputy Minister is in charge of approving the selection of oil fields for exploration and extraction purposes to be incorporated into the bidding rounds. Additionally, he is in charge of its approval. Finally, he is in charge of issuing and publishing the Five-Year Plan for Exploration and Production of Oil and Gas Bids. Again, there is no power to cancel it.

Article 29 sections I and II of the Hydrocarbon Law states the Ministry of Energy has the power to choose oil fields, it is also in charge of the approval and issuance of the Five-Year Plan for Exploration and Production of Oil and Gas Bids, which is public. Indeed, the Plan can be added to or modified later, even if it has been published in accordance with the secondary administrative regulation of the Hydrocarbon Law.[36]

Interestingly, article 26 clearly states that the Ministry of Energy shall resolve the Five-Year Plan approval within 60 working days of its reception and shall be published electronically.[37] Such a Plan shall contain the planning of the oil fields already selected for bidding over the following five years as well as their main features. In addition, article 27 states that the Five-Year Plan shall be evaluated every year within its first quarter and shall be added to or amended, if applicable, with the technical assistance of the National Hydrocarbon Commission (which acts as the market regulator in the context of the hydrocarbons sector). Finally, article 28 incorporates a democratic mechanism for investors containing a right to nominate (to propose) the most attractive oil fields according to their interests the logic being that they may make a successful bid. The Ministry of Energy shall assess the information received by investors which shall be treated as confidential. Then the Ministry shall place the oil fields proposed into the Five-Year Plan or in its future amendments.

This nomination mechanism has been controversial, even in Congress, where Senator Benjamín Robles Montoya, from the Parliamentary Group of the Revolutionary Democratic Party, urged the suspension of the new strategy of the Five-Year Plan due to its biases and violations of the legal framework, based on the argument that confidentiality on the nomination mechanism could lead to corruption. In the end, the Ministry of Energy may exert discretionary power when choosing oil fields and the Ministry of Finance similarly when the economic terms are set.[38] Controversial or not, it is an investor's right once exerted and subject to be acknowledged by the new Ministry of Energy.

To sum up, the Five-Year Plan is not a simple manifestation of the energy policy at all, but a predictable administrative resolution based on an executed energy policy instructed by the Constitution, whereby investors, if nominated, can have a legitimate expectation that their rights will be protected in terms of receiving fair and equitable treatment in accordance with international investment law, pointing out that investors shall not bear an equivalent expropriation or nationalisation measure upon their investments.

Moreover, the second chamber of the Mexican Supreme Court of Justice[39] has ruled that administrative resolutions cannot be self-cancelled by the authority. Indeed, the Supreme Court has stated under the concept known as legitimate trust that decisions must follow a

36 In terms of articles 26, 27 and 28. A complete section describing the Five-Year Plan is developed within the administrative regulation of the Hydrocarbon Law.

37 The notion of "shall resolve" is meant to be interpreted as an administrative resolution in terms of article 1 of the Federal Administrative Procedural Law.

38 Parliamentary Gazette of the Mexican Chamber of Senators of 23 March 2017 <www.senado.gob.mx/64/gaceta_del_senado/documento/69850> accessed 1 November 2018.

39 Docket number: 2013882. Available at the Supreme Court of Justice website <https://sjf.scjn.gob.mx/SJFHome/Index.html>.

reasonable expectation created on behalf of the citizen in order to get a stable and foreseeable status around the decision. If legitimate trust is broken, then the judge should decide whether or not the cause is considered a superior collective interest, if it is, it should prevail over the private one and, thus, the administrative resolution might be amended accordingly, but, if not, then it must be upheld.

In the case of the Five-Year Plan, the bidding expectation over oil fields is based on a collective interest (maximisation of revenues) merged with a private one (nomination). In other words, it is the consequence of boosting private investment to achieve revenues coming from petroleum activities and that cannot be undone.

Indeed, in terms of the last Five-Year Plan evaluation published in October 2018, there are 528 oil fields for bidding rounds, 112 for deep waters, 113 shallow waters, 117 on shore conventional resources and 186 on shore unconventional resources. Those areas are still available at the time of the writing of this chapter for bidding in 2019 and are to be the subject for bidding processes in 2019.

In addition, the Plan acknowledges nominations exerted by private investors,[40] whereby the Ministry of Energy invited companies to nominate their areas of interest. Then companies sent their nominations, with subsurface information, and the reasons for making their request. Information is treated as confidential to avoid interference with fair competition.[41]

Then, what if the new government decides: 1) to deselect all oil fields incorporated into the Five-Year Plan through future amendments; or 2) to stop the bidding processes? What would happen if the nomination is executed? To what extent is this legally possible? In general, it is not possible to deselect all oil fields without proper justification. There have to be technical or economic reasons behind it, and it always has to be based on the maximisation of revenues standard. For instance, when analysing the Five-Year Plan, it can be observed that some oil fields were being deselected, but in the majority of cases it was for technical reasons.[42] The State exercised its sovereignty through the Ministry of Energy when issuing the Five-Year Plan until 2020, it represents a legal resolution, whereas those oil fields were incorporated on it and, therefore, were available for bidding rounds and awards only. Consequently, it is potentially the only constitutional way to maximise revenues through private investors. In this sense, what the constitution is protecting is the governance system as a whole, whereby investors will be choosing whether or not to place their investment in the petroleum industry.

If the new government decides to stop the bidding process, it will be a violation of the maximisation of revenues standard, a mandate instructed by the Constitution as well as a breach of the resolution contained in the Five-Year Plan.

The main notion here is that once the power is exerted it cannot be re-exerted again, it is a done deal, because the Constitution clearly states a process whereby power can be exerted, beginning with the possibility for the State to maximise revenues through the selection of oil fields for bidding and awarding to private investors.

40 Ibid 42.

41 Ministry of Energy (n 25).

42 For instance, on 22 February 2018, in accordance to the ninth extraordinary session, the Hydrocarbon National Commission Governance Committee approved amendments of the bidding terms and conditions of such a bidding call, to adjust grid references of contractual areas 27 and 31, as a result the reduction of 223 kilometres to avoid overlapping with the establishment of the Natural Protected Area project named "Arrecife los Tuxtlas". Thus, a technical reason supports the reduction of the contractual area. Ministry of Energy (n 25).

Once the power has been exerted, the areas contained in the Five-Year Plan emerge as the only way in which the State has decided it can maximise its revenues. until those oil fields, particularly the 528 already contained in the Five-Year Plan, are duly exhausted at the maximum rate in terms of technical and economic feasibility whether in deep waters, shallow waters, onshore conventional or unconventional resources, which, incidentally, were targets contained in the national energy policy enacted by the earlier administration of the Mexican government.

However, what happens if the constitution is amended and the mandate is not the maximisation of revenues through private investors, but that in future, it will be done by the State exclusively (participatory intervention) by means of its National Oil Company (PEMEX) and respecting the principle of non-retroactivity?[43]

There are three possible different answers to this question:

1. If oil fields are already placed in the Five-Year Plan and currently under a bidding process, then the bidding process has to be completed by the National Hydrocarbon Commission, and oil fields must be awarded in terms of the current bidding rules to private investors if the necessary requirements are fulfilled.
2. If oil fields are already placed in the Five-Year Plan but not currently under a bidding process, then the bidding process has to be scheduled by the National Hydrocarbon Commission, and the oil fields must be awarded in terms of the current bidding rules to private investors if the necessary requirements are fulfilled. The nomination right exerted by private investors over oil fields has to prevail.
3. If oil fields have never been incorporated in the Five-Year Plan, then a new energy policy by the actual government can be implemented constitutionally. New oil fields must be selected mandatorily and shall be distinct from the 528 already selected for bidding and awarding in the Five-Year Plan to private investors. However, the 528 available oil fields cannot be put on hold. That would be unconstitutional.

In any case, the Hydrocarbon Law would also be amended to incorporate a deselection and/or cancellation power for the Ministry of Energy as a discretionary authority. Probably this last option would not be strategic as it does not take into consideration the competition from overseas for private investment, especially in Brazil, Argentina and Colombia.[44]

43 Positively upheld by the Supreme Court of Justice almost 100 years ago on behalf of private companies, when the government tried to retroactively apply article 27, amended by President Venustiano Carranza. Indeed matters relating to petroleum affairs and the recognition of the oil concessions by the Mexican Government were items argued at the Bucareli Conferences, whereby the confirmatory concessions regime was accepted stating the rejection of the argument in which private companies claimed full ownership of the subsoil as well as the right to explore and exploit petroleum. However legal resolutions issued by the Supreme Court recognising the non-retroactivity principle of the new constitutional provisions were taken as the defence of private companies with the support of their governments. Roberto Ortega Lomelín, *The Constitutional Evolution of the Energy since 1917* (National Institution for the Study of Mexican Historical Revolutions, 2016) ch 2, 27 <https://inehrm.gob.mx/recursos/Libros/SENERGIA.pdf> accessed 27 November 2018.

44 Despite the fact that Mexico has the most attractive government take (65– 70 per cent) between countries with high production in the region. Ramón Espinasa, Ramón Medina and Gustavo Tarre, 'Law and Hydrocarbons: A Comparison of Latin American and Caribbean Legal Frameworks' (Inter/-American Development Bank, 2016) 96 <https://publications.iadb.org/bitstream/handle/11319/7948/La-ley-y-los-hidrocarburos-Comparacion-de-marcos-legales-de-America-Latina-y-el-Caribe.pdf?sequence=4&isAllowed=y> accessed 27 November 2018.

4 Conclusion

The immutability theory is based on the stability and predictability of the energy governance system, as well as the principle of non-retroactivity, a constitutional standard upheld traditionally by the Supreme Court of Justice which embodies the rule of law.[45]

The immutability theory was made to gain the trust of private investors in order to get sufficient predictability about this new model in Mexico. Similarly, the State's goal is to increase the chances of a better award system of the oil fields resulting, eventually, in more revenues to contribute to the country's long-term development.

At the end of the day, the immutability theory looks after past fair energy decisions, by enforcing them now, for a better energy justice in the future. If followed, the transition from the ER to the ECR in Mexico should be carried out successfully.

As stated by Thomas W. Wälde, although one can discuss the different views on the principle of 'rule of law', at the core of the principle are the notions that legal rules should be predictable and that acquired rights should be (within parameters set by law) respected, because the notion of the 'rule of law' also underlies modern treaty-based investment protection practice, such as the NorthAmerican Free Trade Agreement (NAFTA) or the Energy Charter Treaty (ECT).[46]

In other words, there is a link between the rule of law, foreign direct investment and economic development in policies based on the incentives that the rule of law creates for investment and trade.[47] The importance of the rule of law is broadly accepted across countries and regions, and the link between the rule of law, growth and development is often echoed in international policy documents.

As stated before, the Mexican petroleum legal framework fosters private investment and takes into consideration energy justice fundamentals in terms of international best practices. Ultimately this is the achievement of peacekeeping.

Lastly, and emulating Steve King[48] but rephrasing his quote, 'That's the key: get the constitution in place. Get rule of law in place, capital will come, oil will flow and energy justice will be served'.

45 It is highly advisable to analyse the following research paper. Tony Payan and Guadalupe Correa-Cabrera 'Security, the Rule of Law, and Energy Reform in Mexico' (Baker Institute, 2016) <www.bakerinstitute.org/research/security-mexicos-energy-reform> accessed 27 November 2018.

46 The immutability theory is based on the stability and predictability of the energy governance system in the principle of non-retroactivity, a constitutional standard upheld by the Supreme Court of Justice traditionally. Thomas W. Wälde, 'Renegotiating Acquired Rights in the Oil and Gas Industries: Industry and Political Cycles Meet the Rule of Law' [2008] 1 *JWELB* 55–97 <https://academic.oup.com/jwelb/article/1/1/55/1005126> accessed 26 November 2018.

47 The Economist Intelligence Unit et al., 'Risk and Return: Foreign Direct Investment and the Rule of Law' (*Roleuk*, 2014) Section 2.2, 20 and 26 <www.roleuk.org.uk/resources/example-resources-2> accessed November 2018.

48 "That's the key: get the constitution in place. Get rule of law in place, capital will come, electricity will follow" Steve King. Brainy Quote, 'Rule of Law Quotes' (Brainy Quote, 2001) <https://www.brainyquote.com/quotes/steve_king_406879?src=t_rule_of_law> accessed 27 November 2018.

20

LOW-CARBON ENERGY IN LATIN AMERICA

Post-Paris advances in renewable and energy efficiency policies

Lisa Viscidi and Nate Graham

1 Introduction

The world has seen transformative technological and commercial developments in low carbon energy in recent years. Innovations in smart grids and energy storage are improving the technical and economic viability of both utility scale and distributed energy systems. Improvements in energy efficiency have allowed many countries to decouple energy demand and carbon emissions from economic growth. These developments are critical as electricity (along with heating) represents the largest source of greenhouse gas emissions globally. The Paris Climate Agreement signed in December 2015 has provided a catalyst for countries around the world to introduce new regulations and policies to take advantage of these developments and accelerate the transition to clean power.

As a region, Latin America boasts extremely low per capita electricity emissions by global standards, thanks to the heavy reliance in a number of countries on hydroelectric generation. Brazil, Chile, and Mexico ranked in the top 10 global markets for renewable energy investment in 2015, while Costa Rica, Uruguay and Paraguay all generate virtually 100 per cent of their electricity through renewables. This largely explains why at the time of the signing of the Paris Climate Agreement, Latin America accounted for only 5 per cent of global carbon emissions despite having 8.6 per cent of the global population. Several countries are also seeing rapid growth in non-hydro renewable energy sources, particularly wind and solar. According to the International Renewable Energy Agency, between 2014 and 2016 non-hydro renewable energy investment in the region grew eleven-fold, compared to a six-fold increase worldwide.

However, policies in most countries do not sufficiently incentivize the use of other technologies to decarbonize the power sector, such as distributed renewable energy and energy efficiency technologies. A World Bank project called Regulatory Indicators for Sustainable Energy (RISE), which in 2016 rated countries on a scale from 0–100 based on 12 energy efficiency metrics, awarded just 1 of 14 Latin America and the Caribbean (LAC) countries

(Mexico) a score above 55.[1] UN Environment has estimated that standards for electric appliances could create annual savings of $20 billion in the region.[2]

This chapter will compare the steps taken to foment renewable energy and improve energy efficiency within the NDC frameworks of Latin America's five largest economies, which are also the region's five largest emitters (excluding Venezuela, which has extremely high fuel subsidies that encourage demand). As the following analysis focuses on the most recent developments in energy policy, in particular those which have taken place since the Paris Agreement in 2015, the impact on energy consumption and emissions is still unclear in some cases. The goal of this chapter will thus be to provide an overview of how policies in renewable generation and energy efficiency have responded to the commitments made under the Paris Agreement by Latin America's five largest economies, and what more needs to be done. The steps being taken in these countries are of great importance: together they account for 72 per cent of the region's emissions.[3]

2 Brazil

Brazil has the highest greenhouse gas emissions in Latin America and was the world's sixth-largest emitter, accounting for 3.5 per cent of global emissions, in 2015.[4] Brazil's nationally determined contribution (NDC) commitment to a 43 per cent reduction by 2030 in emissions relative to 2005 levels only represents a 7 per cent decrease relative to 2012.[5] This is because of drastic decreases in the rate of deforestation between 2005 and 2012. Though Brazil is already largely powered by renewable energy (mostly hydropower), remaining hydropower potential is limited, and the power demand of the country's 207 million inhabitants[6] is expected to bounce back as the country exits a crippling recession.[7] Thus, Brazilian policies must address the need for aggressive growth in wind and solar power and achieve major gains in energy efficiency. Its auction system is producing impressive results for wind and solar investment (it was a top ten[8] global market in 2017) but comprehensive energy efficiency regulations are needed to reverse the rising energy intensity of gross domestic product (GDP).

1 'Rise, Regulatory Indicators for Sustainable Energy'. (World Bank, 2016). <http://rise.worldbank.org/scores> accessed 7 January 2020.

2 Godoy, Emilio. 'Why Latin America and the Caribbean are missing energy efficiency'. (Energytransition.org, 29 December 2017). <https://energytransition.org/2017/12/why-latin-america-and-the-caribbean-are-missing-energy-efficiency> accessed 7 January 2020.

3 'Global Carbon Atlas'. (GCP, 2017). <www.globalcarbonatlas.org/en/CO2-emissions> accessed 5 November 2018.

4 'The road from Paris: Brazil's progress toward its climate pledge'(NRDC, November 2017). <https://www.nrdc.org/sites/default/files/paris-climate-agreement-progress-2017-brazil-ib.pdf> accessed 5 November 2018.

5 'Climate Action Tracker – Brazil' (Climate Action Tracker, 2017). <https://climateactiontracker.org/countries/brazil/pledges-and-targets> accessed 5 November 2018

6 *The World Factbook: South America – Brazil* (CIA, October 2018). <https://www.cia.gov/library/publications/the-world-factbook/geos/br.html> accessed 5 November 2018

7 Dezem, Vanessa and Sergio Lima, Mario. 'Brazil bets on power demand recovery in 2018 as economy improves'. (Bloomberg, 11 August 2017). <https://www.bloomberg.com/news/articles/2017-08-11/brazil-bets-on-power-demand-recovery-in-2018-as-economy-improves> accessed 7 January 2020.

8 'UN Environment Programme – environment for development' (Bloomberg, UN Environment, 2017). <https://europa.eu/capacity4dev/unep/documents/global-trends-renewable-energy-investment-2018> accessed 5 November 2018.

2.1 Renewable power generation

At the time of the Paris Accord in 2015, the share of renewables in Brazil's electric generation was already 75 per cent,[9] almost entirely due to hydroelectric plants.[10] However, the concentration of remaining hydropower potential in environmentally sensitive areas has shifted new hydro investment into run-of-river plants that tend to be much smaller in scale than large hydro. Anticipating a decrease in hydro's share of power generation, Brazil's NDC commits to increasing the share of renewables other than large hydropower (nonconventional renewable energy, or NCRE) to 23 per cent of the power supply by 2030 (up from 19 per cent of the energy matrix in 2017).[11] Furthermore, the Ten-Year Energy Plan approved by the Ministry of Mines and Energy in December 2017 raises this goal to nearly 26 per cent by 2026,[12] with 8 per cent of power coming from biomass. However, because Brazil's electricity demand is rapidly increasing (3.7 per cent annual growth is expected through to 2026)[13] as hydroelectric growth slows, NCRE generation will mostly displace hydro's share of the power matrix rather than that of natural gas and oil. The newly installed capacity over this period is expected to be 75 per cent renewables (of which two-thirds will be NCRE)—roughly the current share of renewables in power generation.[14] Thus, as hydropower drops below 50 per cent of installed capacity, the total share of renewables will increase only nominally, if at all.

Concrete implementation strategies to accomplish the proposed changes to Brazil's energy matrix are scarce. The government has been preoccupied with an economy that contracted for much of 2015 and 2016 and the massive Lava Jato (Car Wash) corruption scandal. Some renewable energy auctions had to be cancelled due to low demand amid the economic recession. Even so, renewable energy has recently enjoyed enormous growth under the programs and regulations already in place.

In 2017 Brazil's installed capacity of wind increased by 24 per cent to 10.6 gigawatt (GW) (doubling since 2015) and the government aims for a wind capacity of 28.4 GW by 2026, which would account for around 12 per cent of the total power supply.[15] Wind auctions for power purchase agreements (PPAs) have been highly successful, with an auction in April 2018 (for capacity to come online in 2022) producing a contract with Electricité de France

9 'Brazil renewable energy matrix reaches 41.2%'. (EBC, 6 June 2016). <http://agenciabrasil.ebc.com.br/en/economia/noticia/2016-06/brazil-share-renewable-energy-matrix-reaches-412> accessed 7 January 2020.

10 Johnson, Slade and Berndt, Kirstin. 'Hydroelectric plants account for more than 70% of Brazil's electric generation' (EIA, 11 August 2016). <https://www.eia.gov/todayinenergy/detail.php?id=27472> accessed 7 January 2020.

11 'Latin America Energy Insights' (EnergyNet World, 2016). <www.energynet.co.uk/webfm_send/2089> accessed 5 November 2018.

12 Morais, Lucas. 'Brazil expects renewables to hit 48% share in 2026 energy' (RenewablesNow, 6 December 2017). <https://renewablesnow.com/news/brazil-expects-renewables-to-hit-48-share-in-2026-energy-593600> accessed 7 January 2020.

13 'Brazilian Government presents 10-year energy plan'. (Medium.com, 6 August 2017). <https://medium.com/the-brazil-opportunity/brazil-ministry-of-energy-10-year-plan-pde-2026-9ae919bd33f7> accessed 7 January 2020

14 'Brazilian Government presents 10-year Energy Plan (PDE 2026)'. (Medium.com, 19 July 2017). <https://medium.com/the-brazil-opportunity/brazil-ministry-of-energy-10-year-plan-pde-2026-9ae919bd33f7> accessed 7 January 2020.

15 'Brazil's wind production is surging again in 2017' (Enerdata, 19 December 2017). <https://www.enerdata.net/publications/executive-briefing/brazil-wind-power-generation-increase-2017.html> accessed 7 January 2020.

SA to sell power for $20.23/MWh (megawatt hour). This number approaches the record low bid set in Mexico by Enel SpA in November 2017.[16]

Solar has also benefited from Brazil's auction scheme and thus not required major feed-in tariffs as in the United States (Concentrated Solar Power in Particles (CSP2)).[17] From June 2016 to June 2017 Brazil's solar capacity saw a 930.5 per cent increase,[18] and solar investment was up 204 per cent in 2017[19] from 2016. The total installed solar power in Brazil was estimated at about 2.2 GW in 2019.[20] Auctions have been adapted to account for variations in renewable energy production, including via a settlement mechanism that allows power to be delivered and settled on an annual basis, and by moving away from reserve energy auctions in which capacity allocations were made by the government rather than by bidders.[21] The government has not included large scale photovoltaic (PV) projects in A-6 auctions (those awarding contracts for generation to be delivered in six years), citing rapidly declining solar costs and the consequent inability to predict prices in the long term. However, an A-4 auction in December 2017 awarded 0.6 GW,[22] and in 2019, the average solar power price in a Brazilian A-6 auction reached $20.52/MWh.[23] Overall, the government hopes to have 9.6 GW of installed solar capacity by 2026, including 4.5 GW from 1.2 million consumers participating in distributed generation (DG) schemes, such as solar rooftop installations.[24] Few new incentives for DG have been introduced since the Paris Agreement, but previous government measures, including improvements on the original net metering regulation that took effect in December 2012, *Normative Resolution No. 482/2012*, have allowed DG to flourish.[25] DG has accounted for nearly half of the recent rise in Brazilian solar capacity.[26] Prosumers (energy consumers that also produce their own energy, especially via small-scale PV) with excess energy production can earn credits to reduce their future bills and contribute to group installa-

16 Dezem, Vanessa. 'Wind power cheaper than ever almost as low as Mexico CSP'. (Bloomberg, 4 April 2018). <https://www.bloomberg.com/news/articles/2018-04-04/wind-power-cheaper-than-ever-in-brazil-almost-as-low-as-mexico> accessed 7 January 2020.

17 Malagueta, Diego et al. 'Assessing incentive policies for integrating centralized solar power generation in the Brazilian electric power system'. (Elsevier, 15 March 2013).

18 Yaneva, Mariyana. 'Distributed solar power set for spectacular growth in Brazil'. (Renewables Now, 18 October 2017). <https://renewablesnow.com/news/report-distributed-solar-power-set-for-spectacular-growth-in-brazil-587534> accessed 7 January 2020.

19 Ibid 8.

20 Sanchez Molina, Pilar and Bellini, Emiliano. 'Average solar power price in Brazilian A-6 auction reaches $20.52/MWH'. <https://www.pv-magazine.com/2019/10/21/average-bids-for-solar-in-brazils-a-6-auction-reaches-20-52-mwh> accessed 8 January 2020.

21 Bellini, Emiliano. 'There is a long positive road ahead for solar in Brazil'. (*PV Magazine*, 2 March, 2018). <https://www.pv-magazine.com/2018/03/02/in-brazil-there-is-still-a-tremendous-road-ahead-for-solar> accessed 7 January 2020

22 Timperley, Jocelyn. 'The Carbon Brief Profile: Brazil' (CarbonBrief, 7 March 2018). <https://www.carbonbrief.org/the-carbon-brief-profile-brazil> accessed 7 January 2020.

23 Sanchez Molina, Pilar and Bellini, Emiliano. 'Average solar power price in Brazilian A-6 auction reaches $20.52/MWH'. <https://www.pv-magazine.com/2019/10/21/average-bids-for-solar-in-brazils-a-6-auction-reaches-20-52-mwh> accessed 8 January 2020.

24 Kenning, Tom. 'Brazil's historic net metering revision comes into force' (PV-Tech, 1 March 2016). <https://www.pv-tech.org/news/brazils-historic-net-metering-revision-comes-into-force> accessed 7 January 2020.

25 Calixton, Carlos Alberto. 'Net Metering Scheme in Brazil: regulation and perspectives' (CIRED 18 June 2015). <http://cired.net/publications/cired2015/papers/CIRED2015_0831_final.pdf> accessed 7 January 2020.

26 Yaneva, Mariyana. 'REPORT – distributed solar power set for spectacular growth in Brazil' (18 October 2017). <https://renewablesnow.com/news/report-distributed-solar-power-set-for-spectacular-growth-in-brazil-587534>

tions, with each member receiving credits proportionate to their *financial input*.[27] Installations with a maximum capacity of 5 MW can participate, up from 1 MW originally. Since 2015, 23 of Brazil's 26 states have adopted *Convenio ICMS 16/2015*, a measure that introduced an exemption such that solar power producers (up to 1 MW) only pay VAT on the quantity of their electricity bill that is not discounted by excess production credits.[28]

2.2 Energy efficiency

Energy efficiency is of major importance in Brazil, which increased its primary energy intensity of GDP every year from 2013 to 2016 while global energy intensity decreased.[29] In 2016, for instance, global energy intensity fell by 1.8 percent while in Brazil it increased by almost 2 percent. In recognition of this problem, Brazil's NDC[30] includes a 10 percent energy efficiency improvement target for 2030. However, this goal is not particularly ambitious relative to regional peers with lower energy intensity, and implementation measures are lacking.

Brazil has two major government programs associated with energy efficiency, the National Program for Energy Conservation (PROCEL) and the Energy Efficiency Program (PEE). Over the last 32 years, PROCEL has produced savings of 128.6 TWh (terawatt hour), including 21.2 in 2017, corresponding to 4.57 percent of national electricity consumption.[31] Its programs include energy efficiency labelling for equipment and buildings. In 2016, PROCEL was strengthened by an amendment of law enacted in 2000 (9.991)[32] that requires electricity distributors to invest a small percentage of their business revenue in energy efficiency activities. Under the new law (13.280) PROCEL is now entitled to 20 percent of that investment (close to 100 million reais, or $27 million, per year).[33] PEE led to a reduction in electricity consumption of 9.48 TWh per year from 2000 to 2017.[34] in June 2016, the sale of incandescent bulbs was banned and consumers were encouraged to replace them with LEDs, improving energy efficiency in lighting.[35]

However, of a list of 23 countries[36] ranked by the American Council for Energy Efficiency Economy (ACEEE) in 2017, Brazil came second to last, partly because of low

27 Kenning, Tom. 'Brazil's historic net metering revision comes into force' (PV-Tech, 1 March 2016). <https://www.pv-tech.org/news/brazils-historic-net-metering-revision-comes-into-force> accessed 7 January 2020.

28 Bellini, Emiliano. 'Another Brazilian state introduces ICMS exemption for solar' (*PV Magazine*, 11 December 2017). <https://www.pv-magazine.com/2017/12/11/another-brazilian-state-introduces-icms-exemption-for-solar>

29 'Energy Efficiency 2017'. (International Energy Agency, 2017). accessed 5 November 2018.

30 'Federative Republic of Brazil intended nationally determined contribution towards achieving the objective of the United Nations framework convention on climate change' (UNFCCC). <www4.unfccc.int/submissions/INDC/Published%20Documents/Brazil/1/BRAZIL%20iNDC%20english%20FINAL.pdf> accessed 5 November 2018.

31 'Resultados Procel 2018 – Ano base 2017' (PROCEL, Electrobras, 2018). <www.procelinfo.com.br/resultadosprocel2018/docs/Procel_rel_2018_web.pdf> accessed 5 November 2018

32 'Presidência da República Casa Civil Subchefia para Assuntos Jurídicos: LEI No 9.991'. (Government of Brazil, 24 July 2000). </www.planalto.gov.br/ccivil_03/Leis/L9991.htm> accessed 7 January 2020.

33 'Nova Lei fortalece ações de eficiência energética' (Governo do Brasil, 4 June 2016). <www.brasil.gov.br/noticias/infraestrutura/2016/05/nova-lei-fortalece-acoes-de-eficiencia-energetica>

34 Diogne de Souza, Silva, Rogério, Cavalcante de Oliveira, Rosana, and Emília de Lima Tostes, Maria. 'Analysis of the Brazilian Energy Efficiency Program for electricity distribution systems' (MDPI, 2017) accessed 5 November 2018.

35 'Lâmpadas incandescentes de 41W a 60W deixam o mercado nacional' (Inmetro.gov, 2016). <www.inmetro.gov.br/imprensa/releases/lampadas-incandescentes.pdf> accessed 5 November 2018.

36 Diogne de Souza Silva, Rogério, Cavalcante de Oliveira, Rosana, and Emília de Lima Tostes, Maria. 'Analysis of the Brazilian Energy Efficiency Program for electricity distribution systems' (MDPI, 2017) accessed 5 November 2018

investment in energy efficiency per capita (one-tenth that of Germany, the first-place country), and partly for having few companies that meet international energy management standards. Brazil has 23, compared with Germany's 3402 certified companies. Besides the additional revenue for PROCEL, there is little recent legislation that suggests progress towards the 10 percent increase in energy efficiency proposed by Brazil's NDC. Brazil's 2026 Energy Expansion Plan[37] projects a 7 percent cut in final energy consumption due to energy efficiency measures but it also projects electricity consumption to grow 1.5 times faster than GDP. The plan does not specify what energy efficiency measures will be taken and acknowledged that Brazil's existing initiatives have thus far failed to create a sustainable market for energy efficiency.

There is ample room for improvement, which is made evident by an April 2018 study released by the energy efficiency branch of Comerc (an electric power distribution company), and based on estimates by the government's Energy Research Company.[38] The report indicates that with energy efficiency measures, Brazilian industry could save 4 billion reais ($1 billion) per year in 2020, and 2.4 billion reais in the commercial sector. Together these savings would correspond to 8.6 $MtCO_2$ (million metric tons of CO_2) emitted. In reaction to the findings, the president of the Brazilian Association of Energy Conservation Service Companies (Abesco) pointed out that this potential will not be realized unless companies are obliged by the government to be efficient. A sweeping energy efficiency law is needed in Brazil to comply with its NDC and achieve major savings in the power sector.

Thus, Brazil is making important progress toward increasing the share of nonconventional renewables in its power matrix, even raising the goal originally proposed in its NDC, but forecasts of rising power demand and decreasing additional hydropower potential mean that it should be even more ambitious. Moreover, Brazil must take bold steps to legislate on and regulate energy efficiency and comply with the 10 percent improvement included in its NDC. This could reap potentially enormous economic and environmental gains.

3 Mexico

Mexico's ratification of the Paris Agreement in September 2016 formalized its intention to unconditionally reduce its greenhouse gas (GHG) emissions to 22 percent below its business as usual (BAU) projection by 2030. This includes a 31 percent decrease in emissions from electricity generation, which accounts for almost 30 percent of the total reduction proposed in the country's NDC. The Secretariat of Environment and Natural Resources (SEMARNAT) and the National Ecology and Climate Change Institute (INECC), which was created to develop, conduct, and evaluate national climate change policy under the 2012 General Climate Change Law, have proposed *30 measures* to reach Mexico's emissions target.[39] These include plans to spur renewable investment and improve efficiency, and further legislation has expanded on the groundwork laid by the NDC. Recent growth in renewable investment has been massive, and energy efficiency gains could be on the horizon.

37 Ibid 13.

38 Santa Rita, Bruno. 'Eficiência energética pode poupar ao Brasil R$ 6,4 bilhões em 2020' (*Coreio Braziliense* 10 April 2018). <https://www.correiobraziliense.com.br/app/noticia/economia/2018/04/10/internas_economia,672555/eficiencia-energetica-pode-poupar-ao-brasil-r-6-4-bilhoes-em-2020.shtml> accessed 7 January 2020.

39 'Costos de las Contribuciones Nacionalmente Determinadas de México' (INECC, May 2018). <https://www.gob.mx/cms/uploads/attachment/file/330857/Costos_de_las_contribuciones_nacionalmente_determinadas_de_M_xico__dobles_p_ginas_.pdf> accessed 5 November 2018.

3.1 Renewable power generation

Mexico's NDC aims to achieve 35 percent renewable electricity generation by 2025 and 43 percent by 2030. The Energy Transition Law of 2015 added intermediate benchmarks of 25 percent renewable generation by 2018 and 30 percent by 2021. Important progress has been made towards these goals since the enactment of the Electricity Industry Law in 2014, under which private companies have been able to participate in wholesale renewable energy auctions since 2016. Indeed, in 2017 new investment in renewable energy in Mexico grew by 810 percent to $6 billion,[40] placing it in the top ten countries for new renewable investment. Continuing this trend could unlock major results: Mexico's wind potential is more than 8 times current installed wind capacity, and its solar resources are 75 times total installed capacity.

The Electricity Industry Law incentivized renewable investment through the introduction of tradeable clean energy certificates that electricity distributors have to acquire to reach quotas, thereby ensuring an increase in the renewable share of power generation. As a result of these changes, the first clean energy auction, held in 2016, drew commitments equalling 173 percent of the solar and wind capacity installed in Mexico over the previous 18 years.[41] In 2017, an auction[42] established record low prices for onshore wind and solar PV. The Electricity Industry Law also encouraged the creation of renewable projects, often in remote locations, by allowing *private contracting* to improve and expand Mexico's decrepit transmission and distribution system.[43] SEMARNAT and INECC have established the goal of 222.7 TWh of clean generation by 2030, which would save 41.74 $MtCO_2e$ (metric tons of carbon dioxide) relative to the BAU scenario.

Mexico also has strong policies to support small-scale renewable generation, particularly distributed rooftop solar power. The Electricity Industry Law provides contracts for small-scale domestic and commercial solar energy producers (below 500 kW) to sell their excess energy back to the grid through net metering, net billing, or total sale. By the end of 2017, 60,000 such contracts had been signed.[44] Installed capacity of such projects is currently around 400 MW, up 63 percent from 2016. It is estimated that by 2030 this figure could reach 19,000 MW, or more than 10 percent of Mexico's installed capacity.[45]

Mexico's expansion of renewable energy has been rapid, at least in terms of investment (much of which is relatively recent and has not yet been realized as installed capacity), but is beginning from a low base relative to the rest of Latin America. Mexico's installed capacity is less than 25 percent renewable compared to around *50 percent* in the region on average (its large hydroelectric resources are much less significant than those of other

40 Ibid 8.

41 Lucas, Hugo. 'Renewable energy tenders and community [em]power[ment]' (REN21, 2017). <www.ren21.net/wp-content/uploads/2017/09/LAC-Report.pdf> accessed 5 November 2018.

42 Ibid 8.

43 Viscidi, Lisa. 'Mexico's renewable energy future: a working paper' (Wilson Center Mexico Institute, May 2018). <https://www.wilsoncenter.org/sites/default/files/mexico_renewable_energy_future_0.pdf> accessed 5 November 2018.

44 García, Karol. 'CFE destraba incentives para detonar techos solares' (*El Economista*, 8 July 2018). <https://www.eleconomista.com.mx/empresas/CFE-destraba-incentivos-para-detonar-techos-solares-20180708-0109.html> accessed 7 January 2020.

45 Chaudhry, Nadim. 'It's only the beginning, Mexico to hit 51% Clean Energy in 2030!' (MIREC, 19 April 2018). <https://www.linkedin.com/pulse/mexico-hit-51-clean-energy-2030-nadim-chaudhry> accessed 7 January 2020.

neighbouring countries).[46] Thus, as Mexico's renewable capacity expands it can also benefit from replacing coal and petroleum with a lower carbon fossil fuel, natural gas. SEMARNAT and INECC's NDC strategy proposes substituting natural gas for other fossil fuels in new thermoelectric plants. This measure could produce annual savings of 0.6 $MtCO_2e$ by 2030.

Finally, renewable generation could be further incentivized by the introduction of a carbon emissions trading system. More than 100 businesses participated in an emissions trading simulation that concluded at the end of June 2018,[47] and Mexico plans to begin the scheme in 2022 after a three-year pilot program which started in 2019.[48] Mexico's emissions registry, RENE, is set to undergo improvements, including the accreditation of new third-party verifiers, which will be a necessary complement for the success of the "carbon market." Further, in 2013 Mexico enacted a tax on carbon from fossil fuel use, though it is low at $3.50 per ton of emissions (and natural gas is zero-rated).[49] It is expected to produce an annual reduction of 1.6 $MtCO_2e$, just 0.33 percent of Mexico's total emissions.[50]

3.2 *Energy efficiency*

The 2015 Energy Transition Law sets explicit goals for final energy consumption intensity, with an average annual decrease of 1.9 percent from 2016 to 2030 and of 3.7 percent from 2031 to 2050. Energy efficiency measures proposed by Mexico in the electricity sector are being applied to both the supply side and the demand side.

On the supply side, Mexico has committed to converting thermoelectric plants that reach the end of their life between 2014 and 2030 to combined cycle or fluidized bed generation rather than rehabilitating them in their current form. By 2030 INECC estimates that 43 TWh will be generated by plants modernized in such a way, saving 14 $MtCO_2e$ relative to the BAU scenario.[51] However, the economic proposals of the 2018 president, Andrés Manuel López Obrador, cast doubt on these plans with a vague mention of an intention to "rehabilitate thermoelectric plants."[52]

Mexico also intends to reduce technical losses in its transmission system, the National Electric System (SEN). Opening the transmission system to private contracting is a promising step to attract the investment necessary to reach Mexico's goal of reducing technical losses from 7.9 percent in 2012 to 5.3 percent in 2030. Through this measure annual savings

46 Viscidi, Lisa. Graham, Nate. 'AMLO puede convertir a México en el líder mundial de la energía limpia' (*New York Times*, 23 June 2018). <https://www.nytimes.com/es/2018/07/23/opinion-viscidi-amlo-energia-limpia-mexico/?smid=tw-espanol&smtyp=cur> accessed 7 January 2020.

47 'Finaliza la primera simulación de Mercado de CO2' (*En Concreto*, 28 June 2018). <https://www.grupoenconcreto.com/finaliza-la-primera-simulacion-de-mercado-de-co2> accessed 7 January 2020.

48 'Mexico announces 2022 start to its emissions trading scheme' (*Carbon Pulse*, 19 September 2018). <http://carbon-pulse.com/58994> accessed 7 January 2020.

49 Altamirano, Juan-Carlos and Martínez, Julia. 'Mexico's 3 big steps towards comprehensive carbon pricing' (World Resources Institute, 14 April 2017). <https://www.wri.org/blog/2017/04/mexicos-3-big-steps-towards-comprehensive-carbon-pricing> accessed 7 January 2020.

50 Belausteguigoitia, Juan Carlos. 'Economic analyses to support the environmental fiscal reform'. (Centro Mario Molina, 29 May 2013).

51 'Costos de las contribuciones nacionalmente determinadas de México' (INECC, May 2018). <https://www.gob.mx/cms/uploads/attachment/file/330857/Costos_de_las_contribuciones_nacionalmente_determinadas_de_M_xico__dobles_p_ginas_.pdf > accessed 5 November 2018.

52 Navarro, María Fernanda. 'Propuestas 2018 | Las dudas sobre el plan económico de AMLO' (16 April 2018). <https://www.forbes.com.mx/propuestas-2018-las-dudas-sobre-el-plan-economico-de-amlo> accessed 7 January 2020.

of 6.6 $MtCO_2e$ are projected by 2030.[53] A report by SEMARNAT and INECC notes that this is the only electricity generation measure in the NDC that does not produce a negative net cost (that is, monetary savings).[54] However, it is necessary to substantially improve the efficiency of Mexico's aging transmission system.

On the demand side, Mexico's NDC strategy proposes two measures to improve residential and commercial energy efficiency: reduce demand for heated water by making 75 percent of installed shower heads efficient by 2030 and replace conventional water heaters with instantaneous and solar water heaters. These two measures are projected to save 5 $MtCO_2e$ in 2030. Additionally, Mexico introduced a measure in 2016 increasing energy efficiency standards for certain air conditioners.[55] Since 2013, small and medium-sized businesses have been eligible for "eco-credits," financial compensation for the replacement of low-efficiency appliances. In September 2017 it was announced that more than one billion pesos ($53 million) in credits had been distributed.[56]

In March 2017 the Secretariat of Energy (in collaboration with the INECC and a number of other organizations) put together a detailed "roadmap" of how Mexico will improve its building efficiency standards in compliance with its 2015 Energy Transition Law and 2016 Climate Change Mid-Century Strategy.[57] The International Energy Agency (IEA) projects that energy efficiency measures could contribute to a 49 percent reduction of CO_2 emissions and a 35 percent reduction in final energy consumption by 2050.[58] The roadmap outlines mechanisms for improving compliance with existing codes and adopting new ones.

In the last decade Mexico has experienced by far the most rapid renewable investment growth in the region, and the continuation of the auctions and policies that have led to this growth will be key to unlocking the country's enormous solar and wind potential and achieving the ambitious renewable power share targets in its NDC.

4 Argentina

Argentina's unconditional goal under the Paris Agreement is a reduction of roughly 18 percent of emissions relative to a BAU scenario by 2030, and a large share of this (71 percent) will come from reductions in emissions from the energy sector. Argentina was another

53 'Costos de las contribuciones nacionalmente determinadas de México' (INECC, May 2018). <https://www.gob.mx/cms/uploads/attachment/file/330857/Costos_de_las_contribuciones_nacionalmente_determinadas_de_M_xico__dobles_p_ginas_.pdf> accessed 5< November 2018.

54 'Costos de las contribuciones nacionalmente determinadas de México' (INECC, May 2018). <https://www.gob.mx/cms/uploads/attachment/file/330857/Costos_de_las_contribuciones_nacionalmente_determinadas_de_M_xico__dobles_p_ginas_.pdf> accessed 5 November 2018.

55 'Mexico: Mexico approved standard NOM-026-ENER-2015 of Energy Efficiency' (TÜV SÜD, September 2016). <https://www.tuv-sud.com/home-com/resource-centre/publications/e-ssentials-newsletter/consumer-products-e-ssentials/e-ssentials-13-2016/mexico-approved-standard-nom-026-ener-2015> accessed 5 November 2018.

56 'Eficiencia energética en PyMEs rebasa la marca de los mil mdp' (Redacción Pymempresario, 11 September 2017). <https://www.pymempresario.com/2017/09/eficiencia-energetica-en-pymes-rebasa-la-marca-de-los-mil-mdp> accessed 7 January 2020.

57 'Roadmap for building energy codes and standards for Mexico' (SENER, March 2017). <https://www.gob.mx/cms/uploads/attachment/file/215224/Hoja_de_Ruta_para_el_C_digo_y_Normas_EE_para_Edificaciones_M_xico_EN_Fin....pdf> accessed 5 November 2018.

58 'Roadmap for building energy codes and standards for Mexico' (SENER March 2017). <https://www.gob.mx/cms/uploads/attachment/file/215224/Hoja_de_Ruta_para_el_C_digo_y_Normas_EE_para_Edificaciones_M_xico_EN_Fin....pdf > accessed 5 November 2018.

strong renewable energy market in 2017 as a result of renewable energy targets made law in 2015 and tenders held to meet these targets. If Argentina does meet these targets, 16 percent of the total emissions reduction will result from an increased share of renewable energy. Further steps to reduce energy related emissions are detailed in the National Energy & Climate Change Action Plan, one of three sectoral plans produced by the National Climate Change Cabinet, a body created by decree in 2016 to oversee planning related to Argentina's NDC compliance. The plan will break Argentina's strategy down into four categories, two of which are renewable energy and energy efficiency.

4.1 Renewable power generation

Expanding the renewable share of Argentina's electricity mix has been a major priority in recent energy legislation. The renewable energy law (Law 27.191), published at the end of 2015 calls for an increase in the share of NCRE to 20 percent of total power generation by 2025. The three renewable energy auctions (RenovAr) that have been carried out to implement it have yielded impressive results. In 2016 these sources accounted for just 2 percent of total power generation,[59] but renewable energy investment increased by $1.8B in 2017 (a 777 percent increase on 2016).[60] The auctions have already awarded 4466.5 MW[61] of NCRE capacity, an amount equal to more than 12 percent of Argentina's installed capacity in 2015.[62] An important caveat is that an extension of the electricity grid is underway to increase the capacity for these projects and future tenders, and the lack of a clear timeline could delay the implementation of both.[63]

Another important step was taken in distributed renewable energy with the passage of Law 27.424 in 2017. This net metering law allows users of the distribution network to inject surplus renewable energy into the electricity grid and prohibits distribution companies from charging for network maintenance and use or installation.[64] In terms of off-grid distributed energy, the second round of Argentina's PERMER (Renewable Energies in Rural Markets Project) accepted tenders in early 2018 for the installation of solar PV kits for 120,000 rural households not connected to the power grid.[65]

In addition to RenovAr's clean energy licensing rounds, in May 2017 through Resolution 287 the Secretary of Electric Energy commissioned a new call for efficient electricity generation bids via combined-cycle and cogeneration plants.[66] The round, completed

59 'Climatescope 2017: Argentina' (Climatescope, 2017). <http://global-climatescope.org/en/country/argentina/#/enabling-framework> accessed 5 November 2018.

60 Ibid 8.

61 Morais, Lucas. 'Argentina signs 210 MW of RenovAr round 2 contracts' (Renewables Now, 13 July 2018). <https://renewablesnow.com/news/argentina-signs-210-mw-of-renovar-round-2-contracts-619910> accessed 7 January 2020.

62 'South America: Argentina, The World Factbook' (CIA, 24 October 2018). <https://www.cia.gov/library/publications/the-world-factbook/fields/2236.html> accessed 7 January 2020.

63 'Argentina: current policy projections' (Climate Action Tracker, 30 April 2018) <https://climateactiontracker.org/countries/argentina/current-policy-projections> accessed 7 January 2020.

64 Bellini, Emiliano. 'Argentina: new distributed generation provisions come into force' (*PV Magazine*, 2 January 2018). <https://www.pv-magazine.com/2018/01/02/argentina-new-distributed-generation-provisions-come-into-force> accessed 7 January 2020.

65 Bellini, Emiliano. 'Argentina launches tender for supply of 120,000 solar kits' (*PV Magazine*, 12 January 2018). <https://www.pv-magazine.com/2018/01/12/argentina-launches-tender-for-supply-of-120000-solar-kits> accessed 7 January 2020.

66 'Resolución SEE 287 - E/ 2017 – Convocatoria Abierta a Interesados – Cierre Ciclos Combinados y Cogeneración' (CAMMESA, 2017). <http://portalweb.cammesa.com/Pages/Res420.aspx> accessed 5 November 2018.

in October 2017, awarded more than 1800 MW of capacity expected to come online in mid-2020. The Ministry of Energy had hoped to increase capacity by 3300 MW, partly in order to decrease power outages during the hottest days of the summer, on which energy demand reaches 25,000 MW.[67] Argentina also hopes to replace fossil fuels with natural gas in electricity generation, though no specific policies have yet been put in place to this end.

Like Mexico, Argentina has a carbon tax, and as in Mexico, there is widespread skepticism about its effectiveness. At 10 US$/ton of CO2e, national NGOs have dismissed it as simply an effort to align Argentine policies with those of the Organisation for Economic Co-operation and Development (OECD) countries to increase the likelihood of admittance to the body.[68] Some studies have found that a tax four or more times higher would be necessary for compliance with the Paris Agreement.[69]

4.2 Energy efficiency

Argentina's climate change planners recognize the importance of energy efficiency, projecting that residential, industrial, and public and private lighting efficiency measures will account for 50 percent of the energy sector's share of emissions reduction. Argentina's energy efficiency efforts are organized under a designated Subsecretariat of Energy Savings & Efficiency, which was created by decree in 2015 under the Ministry of Energy & Mining. The body estimates that by 2030 efficiency measures could produce energy savings of 10 percent, with accumulated savings in 2017–2030 equalling the total electricity demand in 2016. Nearly half of these savings will come from improvements to domestic appliances and residential lighting and insulation. Progress in 2017 included the publication of four new energy efficiency norms (including for electric ovens and ceiling fans), seven norms reaching obligatory status (televisions, microwaves, and others), and the completion of a norm for washing machines that was to be applied in 2018. In 2017 the Subsecretariat's projects included a revision of residential buildings standards, a pilot program carried out in 350 residences in the city of Rosario to develop an index for classifying the energy use of homes, the inauguration of a national home energy use poll, guides for the development and management of public and multi-family housing, and programs to replace public lighting with LED technology,[70] including via public-private partnership.[71] Lighting is also the subject of a major measure currently in the legislature (which has been endorsed by the Chamber of Deputies' Energy and Fuels Commission): a ban on the import and sale of halogen lightbulbs.[72] According to

67 Spaltro, Santiago. 'Adjucian proyectos par aampliar el 10% la capacidad de generacíon elétrica' (*El Cronista*, 4 September 2017). <https://www.cronista.com/economiapolitica/Adjudican-proyectos-para-ampliar-el-10-la-capacidad-de-generacion-electrica-20170904-0032.html> accessed 5 November 2018.

68 'La reforma tributaria y el impuesto al carbono' (Fundación Ambiente y Recursos Naturales, 19 December 2017). < https://farn.org.ar/archives/23151> accessed 7 January 2020.

69 'Argentina: current policy projections'. (Climate Action Tracker, 30 April 2018). <https://climateactiontracker.org/countries/argentina/current-policy-projections> accessed 7 January 2020.

70 'Plan Alumbrado Eficiente (PLAE)' (Argentina.gob.ar., 2017). <https://www.argentina.gob.ar/energia/ahorro-y-eficiencia-energetica/alumbrado-publico-eficiente> accessed 5 November 2018.

71 'Eficiencia Energética en Alumbrado Público. 'Proyecto de Participación Público Privada Etapa 1'. (Argentina.gob.ar, 19 January 2018). <https://www.argentina.gob.ar/energia/ahorro-y-eficiencia-energetica/alumbrado-publico> accessed 7 January 2020.

72 'Tras el mensaje de Macri, avalan un proyecto para fomentar el uso de lámparas LED'. (Parlamentario.com, 29 May 2018). <www.parlamentario.com/noticia-110131.html> accessed 7 January 2020.

the officials backing the plan, replacement of these bulbs with LED technology would eliminate 1700 tCO_2 annually, as LED bulbs are up to 50 percent more efficient.[73]

The elaboration of Argentina's NDC implementation strategies will reveal much more about the next steps in attracting renewable investment and improving energy efficiency. Its renewable auction system has already showed promise, as have individual energy efficiency programs. However, broadening the amount of energy consumption regulated by stringent nationwide efficiency standards will have a much greater impact in fulfilling Argentina's Paris commitments.

5 Chile

Chile's NDC commits to unconditionally reducing the emission intensity of its GDP by 30 percent in 2030 compared to 2007 levels. It is cited as a motivating factor in Chile's official Energía 2050 Plan, the country's national energy policy signed by President Michelle Bachelet in December 2015, the same month as the Paris Agreement.[74] The plan aspires to increase the share of NCRE in electricity generation to 40% percent by 2035, with 60 percent of electricity generation coming from all types of renewables. This is an improvement on the previous goal, established in 2013, that 20 percent of the power matrix should be NCRE by 2025. Though Chile's NDC makes no explicit mention of energy efficiency, this concept is incorporated into the Energía 2050 Plan. The three broad mitigation strategies in electricity generation are to increase renewable participation in the electricity matrix, increase the efficiency of the generation system and use of low-emission fuels, and support the implementation of low-carbon technologies. Together, official estimates place the potential impact of these measures at around an 8 percent reduction of GHG emissions in 2030 relative to a BAU scenario. Because of the nature of Chile's NDC, whether or not this reduction is sufficient is heavily dependent on GDP growth over the period.

5.1 Renewable power generation

Chile has made more advances in developing nonconventional renewable energy, particularly solar power, than the rest of Latin America, due largely to the country's more favourable investment climate and high levels of solar irradiation in the Atacama Desert. In 2017 Chile registered \$1.5 billion of new NCRE investment, one quarter of the amount in Brazil, which has a population and land area more than ten times greater.[75] In 2016 Chile was one of the top 10 countries for added solar capacity,[76] and in June 2018 solar, wind, biomass, and small hydro combined to comprise 19.2 percent of installed capacity, including 9 percent solar PV and just over 6 percent wind.[77]

73 Villalonga, Juan Carlos and Heinz, Andrea. 'Eficiencia energética: adiós a las lámparas halógenas'. (*Clarin*, 24 May 2017). <https://www.clarin.com/opinion/eficiencia-energetica-adios-lamparas-halogenas_0_S1m94QfZ-.html> accessed 7 January 2020.

74 'Energía 2050, Poítica Energética de Chile'. (Minsterio de Energía). <www.energia2050.cl/wp-content/uploads/2016/07/Politica-Energetica-Nacional.pdf> accessed 5 November 2018.

75 Ibid 8.

76 'Renewables 2018 Global Status Report'. (REN21, 2017). <www.ren21.net/wp-content/uploads/2017/06/17-8399_GSR_2017_Full_Report_0621_Opt.pdf> accessed 5 November 2018.

77 'Reporte Mensual Sector Energético'. (Comisión Nacional de Energía). <https://www.cne.cl/wp-content/uploads/2015/06/RMensual_v201807.pdf> accessed 5 November 2018.

In recent years Chile has taken some important legal steps to foment the development of renewable energy sources and discourage further development of plants that burn fossil fuels. In 2013 Law 20.698 mandated that electric utilities with an operational capacity of greater than 200 MW generate 20 percent of their electricity from renewable sources by 2025, an increase from a 2007 law that set this number at 10 percent. The law, cited in Chile's NDC, also establishes a system of transferable certificates that can be acquired in lieu of a generator reaching the 20 percent share. A law passed in early 2015 also modified electrical generation auctions in ways that made them more favourable to renewable energy projects. One important change to the Power Purchase Agreement (PPA) auctions was the replacement of take-or-pay contracts with hourly blocks, a mechanism that catalyzes the integration of intermittent energy sources like wind and solar with conventional sources. The onus is placed on generators to provide an alternative source of energy on days with little sun or wind by using other generation methods at their disposal or purchasing from the spot market.[78] Officials cite this modification as well as accommodations for the seasonality of variable energy sources as drivers of the competition that brought average renewable auction prices down to 32.5 $/MWh in the 2017 auction, 75 percent lower than the average price in 2013.[79] While impressive, the punctual completion of the awarded projects is not a given. A 2017 analysis showed that less than half of the capacity expected to come online in 2016 and 2017 (corresponding to projects awarded between 2013 and 2015) had been connected.[80] According to the report, the contracts awarded have weak penalties for noncompliance and in some cases even allow for delays. As the prices of renewable energy projects continue to fall rapidly, it is in companies' interests to continue delaying construction. More recently, in 2019, successful bidders have secured a 15-year power supply deal and some 5.6 TWh of electricity is expected to be generated annually as a result of the new capacity.[81]

Furthermore, advances have been made in the ability to connect new projects, including the slew of new renewable energy projects and distributed installations, to the transmission system. A 2016 measure, Law 20.936, reformed the Chilean transmission system, designating an independent Coordinator of the Electric System, mandating open access to the grid for new installations (even if new capacity must be created), and simplifying remuneration schemes.[82] The law complements Chile's net billing law (20.571), which came into force in October 2014 and allows prosumers with generation (via renewables or efficient cogeneration) up to 100 kW to sell their excess production to distributors at regulated prices.[83] However, the net billing mechanism, through which distributors buy excess production

78 Valencia, Leonardo. 'Licitación eléctrica: todos miran fijamente a Chile'. (*El Monstrador*, 21 November 2017). <https://www.elmostrador.cl/mercados/2017/11/21/licitacion-electrica-todos-miran-fijamente-a-chile> accessed 7 January 2020.

79 Bellini, Emiliano. 'Subasta eléctrica de Chile termina con precio promedio de 32,5 $/MWh'. (*PV Magazine*, 3 November 2017). <https://www.pv-magazine-latam.com/2017/11/03/subasta-electrica-de-chile-termina-con-precio-promedio-de-325-mwh> accessed 7 January 2020.

80 Bellini, Emiliano. 'Chile: menos de la mitad de los proyectos licitados entre 2013 y 2015 está en operación' (*PV Magazine*, 30 November 2017). <https://www.pv-magazine-latam.com/2017/11/30/chile-menos-de-la-mitad-de-los-proyectos-licitados-entre-2013-y-2015-esta-en-operacion> accessed 7 January 2020.

81 Bellini, Emiliano. 'Chile to hold a new energy action in June'. <https://www.pv-magazine.com/2019/11/19/chile-to-hold-new-energy-auction-in-june> accessed 8 January 2019.

82 Sepúlveda, Juan Manuel Contreras. 'Resumen de la nueva ley de transmisión'. (CTG Energía, 28 October 2016). <https://www.ctgenergia.com/single-post/2016/10/28/Resumen-de-la-Nueva-Ley-de-Transmisi%2525C3%2525B3n> accessed 7 January 2020.

83 'Ley de Generación Distribuida (Ley 20,571)'. (División de Energías Renovables – Minsterio de Energía de Chile, May 2017). <https://www.leychile.cl/Navegar?idNorma=1038211>accessed 5 November 2018.

from prosumers at wholesale prices, is controversial (it has been called "net bullying" and accused of favouring distributors over prosumers).[84] The lack of net metering has stalled widespread distribution generation (DG) uptake. In May 2018 installed capacity was just 18.3 MW, a disproportionately tiny number relative to Chile's globally recognized large-scale PV capacity.[85] The Ruta Energética Plan[86] proposed by current President Sebastián Piñera promises improvements to distributed generation, including development of new financing sources for small-scale generation both by small and medium businesses and residences, and expansion of the benefits of renewable distributed generation to rural areas. It also promises to modernize the energy grid and add flexibility to incorporate renewable energy sources.

To incentivize renewables uptake it will also be important to create disincentives to using fossil fuels, especially coal, which in 2017 accounted for 39 percent of Chile's electricity generation.[87] Chile's NDC cites the implementation of a carbon tax (which came into force in 2017) as one such measure, but at just 5 US$/ton of CO2 emitted, it has been shown to be "wholly ineffective" in reducing emissions.[88] Nonetheless, coal is on the decline in Chile, and in January 2018 the government reached an agreement with operators of coal-fired power plants stating that no new coal plants would be built without carbon capture and sequestration systems, and that a working group would be created to phase out any such existing plants.[89]

5.2 *Energy efficiency*

Energy efficiency constitutes one of three "pillars" of Chile's Energía 2050 Plan, which outlines ambitious goals for improving the energy efficiency of buildings, domestic products, and transportation, but implementation has been limited. As a nation approaching the consumption levels of developed countries, Chile is basing its energy efficiency efforts on a motivation to decouple GDP growth from energy consumption—that is, to reduce the energy intensity of GDP (a reduction of emissions intensity is the target of Chile's NDC). To this end, Chile's energy plan states that by 2050, 100 percent of new buildings will meet OECD construction efficiency standards and that 100 percent of mainstream electronic products will be energy efficient. In the case of these domestic appliances the plan does not elaborate on what the precise standard of energy efficiency will be. If Chile is to elevate and expand its Minimum Energy Performance (MEP) standards to OECD levels, the legislature and regulatory bodies will have significant work to do, as the country currently finds itself well above the OECD average in terms of energy intensity of GDP.[90] One analyst says there have been "no relevant achievements in the matter."[91]

84 Sohr, Raúl. 'Alejandro Guillier. De cara al país: conversaciones con Raúl Sohr'. (Penguin Random House Grupo Editorial Chile, 1 April 2017). <https://tinyurl.com/y9w6wjcd> accessed 7 January 2020.

85 Proaño, Maximiliano. 'Is an energy revolution underway in Chile?'. (Energytransition.org, 9 July 2018). <https://energytransition.org/2018/07/is-an-energy-revolution-underway-in-chile>

86 'Ruta Energética 2018-2022 liderando la modernización con sello ciudadano' (Ministerio de Energía, 2017). <www.energia.gob.cl/rutaenergetica2018-2022.pdf> accessed 5 November 2018.

87 'Will coal soon be history in Latin America?'. (TheDialogue, 11 May 2018). <https://www.thedialogue.org/analysis/will-coal-soon-be-history-in-latin-america>

88 Mardones, Cristian and Flores, Belén. (Latin American Research Review, 2017) 'Evaluation of a CO2 tax in Chile: emissions reduction or design problems?'. accessed 5 November 2018.

89 'Ruta Energética 2018–2022 liderando la modernización con sello ciudadano' (Minsterio de Energía, 2017). <http://www.energia.gob.cl/rutaenergetica2018-2022.pdf> accessed 5 November 2018.

90 'Energía 2050, Poítica Energética de Chile'. (Minsterio de Energía). <www.energia2050.cl/wp-content/uploads/2016/07/Politica-Energetica-Nacional.pdf> accessed 5 November 2018.

91 Proaño, Maximiliano. 'Is an energy revolution underway in Chile?'. (Energytransition.org, 9 July 2018). <https://energytransition.org/2018/07/is-an-energy-revolution-underway-in-chile> accessed 7 January 2020.

Perhaps that will change under the new administration. Piñera's Ruta Energética commits to introducing heating efficiency standards for buildings and incorporating new items, including stoves, washers, vacuums, microwaves, and electric ovens, into the country's energy efficiency standards. The Energy Efficiency Law approved in 2018 has made up for the absence of energy efficiency provisions in Chile's NDC and complement Chile's impressive growth in NCRE, which is expected to continue advancing towards a 40 percent share of generation by 2035.

6 Colombia

Colombia is the most recent Latin American country to ratify the Paris Agreement (July 2018), though its intention to do so was never in doubt.[92] Indeed, the Paris Agreement was the primary planning instrument for the country's 2017 National Climate Change Policy. Colombia's NDC commits to a 20 percent reduction of CO_2 equivalent emissions relative to a BAU scenario by 2030.[93] Through SISCLIMA (the National Climate Change System, created by Decreto 298 in 2016), ministries collaborate to identify appropriate mitigation goals and actions for each sector of the economy, with the objective of reducing emissions by 20 percent in each sector in accordance with Colombia's NDC goal. The sectoral plan for electrical energy includes three policy lines: demand-side energy efficiency, efficiency of national energy system operations, and nonconventional renewable energy sources (PAS_Energia_Electrica).

6.1 Renewable power generation

Colombia's Sectorial Mitigation Action Plan (SMAP) for Electrical Energy includes a policy plan for an increased share of nonconventional renewable energy sources in the national energy system, but it consists of broad strokes (for instance, a directive to "promote and support the implementation of large-scale nonconventional renewable energy sources in the national energy system") and does not set a goal for the share of renewables or for the amount of emissions to be reduced by their increase. More regulatory detail and the creation of specific incentives will be necessary to foster the country's nascent solar and wind industries.

A policy approved in July 2018 (created by CONPES, the National Economic and Social Policy Council) took some important steps in this regard. Essentially a roadmap for Colombia's "green growth" policy, CONPES 3934 indicated that NCRE resources represented just 2 percent of the country's total capacity (hydropower counts for 70 percent), with wind energy accounting for just 18 MW out of an estimated potential of 29,500 MW.[94] To increase this share, the policy stresses the importance of implementing Decree 570, which the Ministry of Mines and Energy (MME) issued in March 2018.[95] The decree charges UPME

92 Monterrosa, Heidy. 'Colombia ratifica Acuerdo de París frente al cambio climático' (*La República*, 16 July 2018). <https://www.larepublica.co/economia/colombia-ratifica-acuerdo-de-paris-frente-al-cambio-climatico-2749718≥ accessed 5 November 2018.

93 'Intended nationally determined contribution: Colombia'. (Gobierno de Colombia, 2015). <www4.unfccc.int/ndcregistry/PublishedDocuments/Colombia%20First/Colombia%20iNDC%20Unofficial%20translation%20Eng.pdf> accessed 5 November 2018.

94 'Documento Conpes – Consejo Nacional de Política Económica y Social'. (República de Colombia – Departamento Nacional de Planeación, 10 July 2018).

95 Monterrosa, Heidy. 'Colombia ratifica Acuerdo de París frente al cambio climático'. (*La República*, 16 July 2018). <https://www.larepublica.co/economia/colombia-ratifica-acuerdo-de-paris-frente-al-cambio-climatico-2749718> accessed 7 January 2020

(the national Mining and Energy Planning Unit) and CREG (the Energy and Gas Regulatory Commission) with developing a long-term contracting mechanism for NCRE projects that promotes competition and reduces energy provision risk from extreme climate events such as el Niño via diversification of the energy matrix. The policy also recommends that by 2020 the MME develop protocols for intra-day energy provision from diverse sources, storage, and connection of new sources to the grid. Finally, it recommends that the Ministry of Environment modify the Unified Environmental Regulation Decree (the legislation comprising the complete body of environmental regulation in Colombia) to exempt NCRE projects from conducting environmental evaluations of possible alternatives to a project, in 2019. UPME's goal is that by 2029 wind energy will comprise 5 percent of the electricity matrix and solar energy 1 percent.[96]

The uptake of nonconventional renewable energy sources into Colombia's energy matrix is primarily regulated and incentivized by Law 1715 (2014).[97] The law includes tax deductions for investments made in related projects, VAT and tariff exemptions for materials associated with NCREs, and accelerated depreciation schedules for the associated assets. However, the executive director of Colombia's renewable energy association reported in 2017 that a lack of personnel had slowed the process of actually accessing these incentives.[98] Within the framework of Law 1715, a 2018 resolution by the Energy and Gas Regulatory Commission (Resolution CREG 030)[99] regulates small-scale distributed renewable generation (up to 1 MW), guaranteeing a buyer for prosumers and a price very close to the value paid by prosumers for their energy consumption under Colombia's net billing program. The resolution was seen as an important step for small-scale self-generation by Colombia's solar energy association.

In 2016 Law 1819 established a carbon tax on natural gas, liquified petroleum gas (LPG), gasoline, kerosene, jet fuel, diesel, and fuel oil, equal to slightly more than 5 US\$/tCO_2e in 2017.[100] This law aims to advance the goals in Colombia's NDC, as the burning of fossil fuels accounts for 27 percent of the country's greenhouse gas emissions. In 2017, Decree 926 created an exemption from paying this tax to companies that neutralize some or all of their emissions from these fuels through renewable energy, reforestation, energy efficiency, sustainable agriculture, and other carbon reduction projects.[101] However, in order to incen-

96 Sarmiento, Sergio Rodríguez. 'Ya está lista la hoja de ruta para el crecimiento verde de Colombia'. (*El Colombiano*, 10 July 2018). <www.elcolombiano.com/negocios/economia/conpes-de-crecimiento-verde-en-colombia-LK8972094> accessed 7 January 2020

97 'Law 1715/2014, regulating the integration and promotion of nonconventional renewable energy (FNCER.)'. (LSE – Grantham Research Institute on Climate Change and the Environment, 2014). <www.lse.ac.uk/GranthamInstitute/law/law-1715-2014-regulating-the-integration-and-promotion-of-non-conventional renewable-energy-fncer≥ accessed 5 November 2018.

98 '¿Por qué no avanzan los proyectos de eficiencia energética en Colombia?'. (Semana-Sostenible, 6 December 2017). <https://sostenibilidad.semana.com/actualidad/articulo/eficiencia-energetica-en-colombia-por-que-no-avanzan-los-proyectos en el pais/39122> accessed 7 January 2020

99 Molina, Pilar Sánchez. 'Colombia issues regulation for distributed solar generation'. (*PV Magazine*, 5 March 2018). <https://www.pv-magazine.com/2018/03/05/colombia-issues-regulation for solar distributed-generation> accessed 7 January 2020

100 'Principales preguntas frente al impuesto nacional al carbono y la solicitud de no causación por carbono neutralidad'. (Minambiente, 2017). <www.minambiente.gov.co/images/abc_carbono_final29ago.pdf> accessed 5 November 2018.

101 'Principales preguntas frente al impuesto nacional al carbono y la solicitud de no causación por carbono neutralidad'. (Minambiente, 2017). <www.minambiente.gov.co/images/abc_carbono_final29ago.pdf> accessed 5 November 2018.

tivize companies to opt for this exemption, or reduce emissions to avoid the tax, the cost of implementing alternative carbon-reduction projects must be lower than the carbon tax itself. Based on research questioning the efficacy of carbon prices of the same level in Chile and Mexico, it is doubtful that the function of this tax will extend well beyond that of a public revenue source.

6.2 Energy efficiency

Colombia's most important document related to energy efficiency is the Energy Efficiency Action Plan 2017–2022 (PAI), which was released in December 2016 by the MME in order to update the Rational and Efficient Energy Use Program (PROURE).[102] In the 2017–2022 Plan the MME adopted goals for energy efficiency in the transport, industry, services, and residential sectors, adding up to a total energy savings of 9.05 percent over the period. The plan is detailed and comprehensive, and includes actions to be taken in each of the four sectors previously mentioned, such as design and implementation of Energy Management Systems (SGE), design and construction of energy efficient buildings, and energy efficiency improvements in public lighting, air conditioning, heating, and refrigeration. To incentivize these actions and ensure their alignment with the goals set forth in the PAI, Decree 1564 (2017) stipulated that the existing VAT exclusion for "equipment, parts, and machinery for projects, products, programs, or activities related to reduction in energy consumption and/or energy efficiency" could not be approved by the National Environmental Licensing Authority unless the item(s) in question corresponded to the goals used by the MME in the PAI, the same goals (9.05 percent energy savings to 2022) set by the Ministry of Environment and Sustainable Development in Resolution 1988 (2017).[103]

CONPES 3934, the "green growth" roadmap, also expands Colombia's energy efficiency goals and recommends measures to meet them. It proposes a 22 percent reduction in energy intensity of GDP by 2030 and states the importance of expanding the amount of energy consumption that is regulated by minimum energy performance standards, charging UPME with this task.[104] The policy also plans for the Ministry of Mining and Energy to create a real-time hourly-rate scheme for energy consumption in 2019.

Colombia's NCRE sector is still in its early days, and pending contract mechanisms should mimic other successful models from the countries discussed previously. An update to Colombia's NDC to reflect its new goals and strategies for enhancing renewable investment and energy efficiency and reducing energy intensity of GDP could provide additional weight and legitimacy to the country's climate commitments.

102 'Plan de acción indicativo de eficiencia energética 2017–2022 una realidad y oportunidad para Colombia'. (UPME, December 2016). <www1.upme.gov.co/DemandaEnergetica/MarcoNormatividad/PAI_PROURE_2017-2022.pdf> accessed 5 November 2018.

103 'Resolución no. 1988' (Ministerio de Ambiente y Desarrollo Sostenible, 29 September 2017).

104 'Conpes de Crecimiento Verde consolida logros del gobierno en materia ambiental con visión a 2030' (Presidencia de la República, 10 July 2018). <http://es.presidencia.gov.co/noticia/180710-Conpes-de-Crecimiento-Verde-consolida-logros-del-gobierno-en-materia-ambiental-con-vision-a-2030> accessed 7 Janaury 2020

7 Conclusion

The legal frameworks and policies encouraging the expansion of renewable energy generation and energy efficiency measures vary widely among Latin America's largest economies. Some countries have already developed very detailed plans to implement their energy-related NDCs while others still have only general strategies. Brazil, Mexico, Argentina, and Chile have attracted considerable investment in large-scale nonconventional renewable generation through successful PPA auctions. The achievements in distributed generation are more limited; several countries have recently developed policies to promote DG but few residences and businesses are taking advantage of them. Carbon pricing schemes to disincentivize fossil fuel use are woefully ineffective throughout the region. Energy efficiency is also a weak point in Latin American energy policy overall, with massive economic and environmental gains yet to be realized throughout the region. Chile and Colombia stand out as countries appearing to make an effort to reduce their energy intensity, while Brazil is in great need of overarching energy efficiency legislation.

The legislative and regulatory steps taken over the next few years in these economies will play an important role in the global fight against climate change, despite the fact that even their *combined* share of global emissions is nowhere near that of the United States or China. The efforts of developing nations, especially ones with important economies like those in Latin America, to comply with the Paris Agreement will increase pressure on prosperous nations to do so as well. With a recent change of government in Chile, new presidents and legislatures taking the helm in Mexico, Brazil, Colombia, and Argentina, many politicians will have the opportunity to take a leadership role in their respective domestic fights against climate change and set an example for the region.

21

PROTECTING ENERGY INVESTMENTS IN LATIN AMERICA

*Silvia Marchili and Isabella Bellera Landa**

1 Latin American energy investments: regional trends and the need for investment protection

Investments in the energy sector face significant challenges. On the one hand, investors in this field commit significant upfront capital and technology investments, required for the development of energy resources, with the hope of obtaining high profits in the long term.[1] On the other hand, States commonly own and extensively regulate these resources, subjecting any investments to regulatory changes and political risk. In many countries, moreover, the development of energy resources is of such macro-economic and political importance that the State often acts as the indirect or direct operator.[2] The stability of the legal and political framework of a host State is therefore fundamental to the attraction of investments of this nature.[3]

In light of these unique features, if a dispute regarding an energy investment arises, both the investor and the host State are under significant economic and political pressure to obtain a favourable outcome.[4] It is thus not surprising that disputes arising out of the energy industry have paved the way for the development of legal and contractual forms of protection of foreign investment.[5] It also is not surprising that, as reported by the 2018 Queen Mary University survey, 85 percent of interviewed arbitration users believe that international arbitration "is likely to increase even more in the future" for the energy sector.[6]

* The authors thank Madeline Gootman for her collaboration with the authors on this publication.

1 Nigel Blackaby and Caroline Richard, 'Regulatory Change in Oil and Gas Arbitration: The Latin American Experience' in James M. Gaitis ed., *The Leading Practitioners' Guide to International Oil & Gas Arbitration* (Juris, 2015) 79.

2 Mark W. Friedman, Dietmar W. Prager and Ina C. Popova, 'Expropriation and Nationalisation' in J. William Rowley QC, Doak Bishop and Gordon Kaiser (eds), *The Guide to Energy Arbitrations* (David Samuels, 2018) 17.

3 Blackaby and Richard (n 2).

4 Friedman et al. (n. 3).

5 Peter D. Cameron, *International Energy Investment Law: The Pursuit of Stability* (Oxford University Press, 2010) 7.

6 Queen Mary University of London and White and Case LLP, 'The 2018 International Arbitration Survey: The Evolution of International Arbitration' (White & Case LLP, 9 May 2018) <https://www.whitecase.com/publications/insight/2018-international-arbitration-survey-evolution-international-arbitration> 29.

Energy investments in Latin America are no exception to these risks and hence the need for investment protections. The region is home to some of the largest oil exporters in the world and holds more than 20 percent of global proven oil reserves, the second largest outside the Middle East.[7] Latin America, moreover, has one of the world's highest shares of renewable energy, building on the historical role of hydropower and bioenergy.[8] In conjunction with exportation opportunities, a recent study estimates that the demand for electricity in the region will double by 2040, and to meet this demand an average of US$ 24 billion in investments will be required each year.[9]

Despite its potential, investors in the energy sector in Latin America need to take into account a complicated history of state involvement in and regulation of energy resources, and, at times, resistance to providing protection for foreign investors.[10]

In many Latin American countries, the subsoils belong to the State, and the participation of foreign investors may be limited or restricted by law, including by the State's constitution.[11] Among many requirements, domestic legal constraints may mandate partnerships or direct participation of the State.[12] A number of States, moreover, have privatized activities beyond exploration and exploitation of traditional raw materials, including the generation and distribution of electricity, maintaining strict regulatory controls.[13] The State is therefore distinctly involved in these investments, increasing the risk of changes in the regulatory framework and politically driven measures, particularly in times of high commodity prices (which may lead to resource nationalism) or macro-economic instability.

More than any other region in the world, Latin American countries have invited foreign investment in periods of resource discovery and low commodity prices, and have occasionally sought to claw back the profits of investors through regulation or direct expropriation when States have deemed them excessive or circumstances have changed.[14] In the twentieth century, moreover, certain Latin American States notably included so-called "Calvo clauses" in their constitutions and contracts, under which foreign investors were not entitled to more favourable treatment than domestic investors, and could only resort to domestic courts for the enforcement of their rights.[15] As a result, in Latin America States provided investors with little to no protection against the unilateral actions with respect to energy resources.

7 International Renewable Energy Agency, 'Renewable Energy Market Analysis, Latin America' (IRENA 2016) 23; Roger Tissot, 'Latin America's Energy Future' (Inter-American Development Bank Discussion Paper No. IDB-DP-252, 2012), 5–7.

8 ibid 49.

9 Rigoberto Ariel Yépez-García, Michelle Hallack, Yi Ji and David López Soto, 'The Energy Path of Latin America and the Caribbean' (Inter-American Development Bank, 2018) 4

10 Francisco Monaldi, 'First Take: Latin America's Oil and Gas, After the Boom, a New Liberalization Cycle?' [2015]. *Harvard Rev. Latin America* <https://revista.drclas.harvard.edu/book/ first-take-latin-america%E2%80%99s-oil-and-gas>.

11 For example, the Constitution of Guatemala provides that the State owns the subsoil, hydrocarbon and mineral deposits, as well as any other organic or inorganic substances from the subsoil. *See* Constitution of Guatemala, Art. 121. Similarly, the Peruvian Constitution states that the subsoil is inalienable. *See* Constitution of Peru, Art. 54.

12 For example, in Brazil, companies organized under Brazilian law through concession agreements or under production sharing regimes can only perform the exploration, development, and production of hydrocarbons. Further, Law 12.276/10 provides that only Petrobras, a State-owned enterprise, is granted the right by the Federal Government to explore and produce hydrocarbons in certain areas without having to go through a bidding procedure.

13 Manuel Dussan, 'Electric Power Sector Reform in Latin America and the Caribbean' (Working Papers Series IFM-104 1996) 6, 12–13.

14 See Blackaby and Richard (n 2) 79, 112–114.

15 Cameron (n 6) 234.

In Latin America, the 1990s and the first decade of this century are the most relevant examples of a wave of investment attraction, all which were followed by episodes of resource nationalism and ex-post regulation. In the 1990s, as part of a regional effort to attract investment, a number of States executed diverse programs and initiatives, including legal stability agreements, having the effect of protecting investors against any changes in the regulatory framework.[16] The vast majority of Latin American States, moreover, abandoned the Calvo Doctrine and instead ratified the New York Convention on the Recognition and Enforcement of International Arbitration Awards, joined the Convention on the Settlement of Investment Disputes between States and Nationals of Other States (ICSID Convention) of 1965, and concluded bilateral investment treaties (BITs) providing substantive protection and access to international arbitration.[17] Such was the case, for example, of Argentina, Bolivia, Colombia, and Venezuela, which signed the ICSID Convention in the early 1990s.[18]

This pro-investment agenda, however, changed at the turn of the century, largely due to a dramatic increase in oil prices. This change in circumstances created tension between States and investors because of the gains that investors could receive in accordance with conditions agreed upon at an earlier period (when prices were significantly lower).[19] Consequently, certain States, particularly Venezuela, Bolivia, Ecuador, and Argentina, engaged in unilateral actions to increase their gains from the oil price boom. These actions included increases in taxes, forced renegotiation of contracts, direct expropriations, or a combination of these measures.[20]

In addition to resource nationalism, unilateral actions that affected investments in the energy field were also found in States' responses to macro-economic conditions and political agendas. One example was Argentina's response to its 2001–2002 economic downturn when it dismantled the regulatory framework that had been specifically established to attract foreign investment.[21] Another source of disputed measures was the privatization of the generation and distribution of electricity and the ensuing review of applicable tariffs, as was the case with Guatemala.[22]

As seen in the twentieth century, foreign investors and States were involved in disputes in light of these unilateral actions derived from resource nationalism and changes in macroeconomic conditions. There was, however, one significant difference from previous disputes: the investment protection offered in international treaties, contracts, and domestic laws in the 1990s provided significant leverage for investors to negotiate settlements or seek recovery before international arbitral tribunals. As a result, arbitral institutions witnessed a dramatic increase in the number of arbitration requests against Latin American States or State-owned entities. Indeed, to date, out of 750 cases, 224 cases have been brought under the Rules of the International Centre for Settlement of Investment Disputes (ICSID Rules)

16 ibid 235.

17 Jonathan Hamilton, Omar Garcia and Hernando Otero, 'Latin American Arbitration and Investment Protections' in *Latin American Investment Protections* (Martinus Nijhoff Publishers, 2012) 1–2. A notable exception to this trend is Brazil, which has never signed the ICSID Convention and only signed the New York Convention in 2002. *See* ICLG.com, Brazil: International Arbitration 2019 available at <https://iclg.com/practice-areas/international-arbitration-laws-and-regulations/brazil> accessed 5 September 2019.

18 Jonathan Hamilton, Omar Garcia and Hernando Otero, 'Latin American Arbitration and Investment Protections' in *Latin American Investment Protections* (Martinus Nijhoff Publishers, 2012) 1–2.

19 Cameron (n 6) and Monaldi (n 11).

20 Cameron (n 6) and Monaldi (n 11).

21 Cameron ibid 235.

22 ibid 236.

against Latin American States or their State-owned enterprises, of which almost 53 percent were filed before 2010, and almost 27 percent involved an investment made in the energy sector.[23]

Despite more investor-friendly policies by certain Latin American States in recent years, these proceedings continue to emerge, and international arbitration remains a preferred choice for investors to settle disputes in the energy field. As the International Centre for Settlement of Investment Disputes (ICSID) reports, Latin American States are respondents to 26 percent of all current ICSID cases, with 69 pending cases, 6 of which are in the energy sector.[24] Similarly, the International Chamber of Commerce (ICC) reports that cases involving Latin American parties have steadily increased since 2009,[25] with Latin American nations representing 14.9 percent of all parties to disputes before the ICC in 2018.[26]

As explained below, these disputes have resulted in a number of international arbitration awards, which provide valuable lessons, including with respect to the limits of State regulation *vis-à-vis* long-term investments and the need to effectively structure foreign investments to gain access to substantive protections and neutral dispute settlement mechanisms.

After years of uncertainty and a period of lower commodity prices, it appears that a new wave of liberalization and attraction of foreign investment is taking place in Latin America. Some of these developments include Mexico's constitutional reform to allow foreign investment in the oil industry and its signature of the ICSID Convention; Argentina's assurances to new investors in the oil and gas sector; as well as regular auctions by Guatemala and Colombia for oil exploration.[27] In light of the experience gained over the last three decades, prospective and current investors in this new wave are uniquely positioned to learn from the past and design effective investment protection and dispute management strategies.

This chapter therefore has the following purposes: Section 2 examines key investment disputes in the last three decades in the energy field. Section 3 describes key lessons from these disputes regarding dispute management. Finally, Section 4 reflects upon current investment trends in the energy sector.

2 Selected energy disputes in Latin America

2.1 Venezuela and its direct expropriations of the Orinoco River oil fields

No other country in the region provides a more clear-cut example of foreign investment – followed by resource nationalism – than Venezuela. In 1975, Venezuela nationalized its oil industry and created Petróleos de Venezuela, S.A. (PDVSA), a State-owned oil company, to carry out activities in the oil industry, and replaced multinational companies then operating in the country.[28] While the law establishing PDVSA stated that PDVSA had to operate by

23 Figures based on the author's own calculation using data derived from the ICSID Case Database. ICSID Secretariat, 'ICSID Case Database Advanced Search,' (2019) <https://icsid.worldbank.org/en/Pages/cases/AdvancedSearch.aspx>.

24 ibid.

25 Claudio D. Salas and Nicolás Costábile, 'Energy Arbitration in Latin America,' in *The Arbitration Review of the Americas* 2019, 20.

26 International Chamber of Commerce, 'ICC Dispute Resolution 2018 Statistics', (2019) 8 <www.iccwbo.org/dr-stat2018> accessed 11 September 2019.

27 Monaldi (n 11).

28 Luis E. Giusti, 'La Apertura: The Opening of Venezuela's Oil Industry' (1999) 53 *Journal of International Affairs* 117–128.

corporate principles, by the early 1990s, the State-owned entity was unable to effectively explore new oil fields because of a lack of technology and financing.[29]

Accordingly, in the 1990s, Venezuela adopted a series of measures known as the *Apertura Petrolera* (Oil Opening), which allowed foreign investors to participate in the oil industry.[30] At the same time, Venezuela ratified the ICSID Convention and concluded several BITs, including one with the Netherlands in 1991.[31] These measures allowed and incentivized private firms, including Mobil (prior to its 1998 Exxon merger) and ConocoPhillips, to form strategic associations (equivalent to joint ventures) and operational agreements with PDVSA.[32] Mobil and ConocoPhillips were among several other companies that invested in oil fields located in the Orinoco region.[33]

This liberalized system of oil production lasted until the early 2000s, shortly after Hugo Chavez became Venezuela's president. In 2001, Venezuela enacted a new hydrocarbons law that reserved production to the State and only allowed private participation through mixed enterprises in which the State held a majority share.[34] Agreements from the Oil Opening era, entered into before 2001, were initially unaffected by the new law, but by 2006, the era's economic incentives had been unilaterally withdrawn and taxes increased.[35] By this time, Exxon Mobil and ConocoPhillips had restructured their investments to gain international protection under the Netherlands-Venezuela BIT.

Shortly thereafter, in February 2007, President Chavez issued Decree No. 5200, which mandated that the 2001 hydrocarbons legislation would apply retroactively, and thus, the previously unaffected companies would have to conform to its requirements and transform into mixed companies in which PDVSA or its subsidiaries would own at least a 60 percent stake.[36] Companies were given four months to negotiate compliance, and if negotiations failed, the State would directly assume their operations.[37] In May 2007, while these negotiations were pending, President Hugo Chavez announced on national television that the government would take over the Orinoco River oil fields.[38]

Whereas some companies such as Chevron and British Petroleum agreed to migrate their investments to the mixed company model, such was not the case with several other investors,

29 ibid 1.

30 ibid 18. *See* 'The Apertura allowed foreign direct investment under attractive financial terms and provided a contractual protection regime that included fiscal stabilization clauses, choice of external law, and the government's consent to international arbitration' in Julian Cardenas Garcia *Rebalancing Oil Contracts in Venezuela* (2018) July 24 *Hous. J. Int'l L.* 239.

31 Agreement on Encouragement and Reciprocal Protection of Investments between the Kingdom of the Netherlands and the Republic of Venezuela, 22 Oct. 1991 (entered into force on 1 Nov. 1993).

32 Giusti (n 29) 18.

33 *Conoco Phillips Petrozuata B.V., ConocoPhillips Hamaca B.V., ConocoPhillips Gulf of Paria B.V., ConocoPhillips Company v. Bolivarian Republic of Venezuela*, ICSID Case No. ARB/07/30, Decision on Jurisdiction and the Merits (3 Sep. 2013), para 106, 141; *Venezuela Holdings, B.V., Mobil Cerro Negro Holding, LTD., Mobil Venezolana de Petróleos Holdings, Inc., Mobil Cerro Negro, LTD., Mobil Venezolana de Petróleos, Inc. v. Bolivarian Republic of Venezuela*, ICSID Case No. ARB/07/27, Award of the Tribunal (9 Oct. 2014), para 45.

34 Decree No. 1510 Hydrocarbons Organic Law (2 Nov. 2001) (Venezuela).

35 Blackaby and Richard (n 2) 88.

36 Alberto F. Ravell, 'A Brief Overview of Venezuela's Oil Policies' Lex Petrolera, 2011 10, <lexology.com/library/detail.aspx?g=01cf61f2-9591-4ac3-9ceb-59ac37090e13> accessed 12 January 2020.

37 Cardenas Garcia (n 31) and Ravell ibid.

38 Natalie Obiko Pearson, 'Chávez Finishes Nationalizing Venezuela Oil', *Seattle Times* (Venezuela, 2 May 2007), <https://www.seattletimes.com/nation-world/chvez-finishes-nationalizing-venezuela-oil> accessed 4 September 2019.

most notably ExxonMobil's various holdings and ConocoPhillips.[39] Instead, ExxonMobil and ConocoPhillips commenced international arbitrations under the Netherlands-Venezuela BIT and their association agreements with PDVSA, which provided for ICC arbitration.[40]

In an award rendered on October 9, 2014, the *Mobil v. Venezuela* ICSID tribunal found that the expropriation of ExxonMobil's assets, a fact undisputed by Venezuela, was a *lawful* expropriation because it complied with the requirements for expropriation set out in the Netherlands-Venezuela BIT.[41] The tribunal also noted that the lack of compensation to an investor did not automatically render an expropriation unlawful; and that, instead, such legality depended on the content of any compensation offer.[42] In light of this finding, the tribunal awarded US$ 1.6 billion to ExxonMobil in compensation, which was calculated on the basis of the fair market value *at the time of expropriation in 2007*, rather than the fair market value at the time of the dispute, when oil prices were significantly higher.[43] Venezuela was subsequently successful in obtaining an annulment of this decision by an ICSID *ad hoc* panel on the grounds that the tribunal had exceeded its powers by inappropriately applying the compensation standard under international law, when the parties had agreed to a "price cap" in their underlying agreements.[44]

In turn, in September 2013, the *ConocoPhillips* ICSID tribunal issued a decision on jurisdiction and merits finding that Venezuela had *unlawfully*[45] expropriated ConocoPhillips' investments in Venezuela, by breaching its "obligation to negotiate in good faith for its taking of the ConocoPhillips assets ... on the basis of market value as required by Article 6(c) of the BIT."[46] Six years later, on 8 March 2019, the tribunal awarded US$ 8.7 billion in

39 BBC, 'Venezuela profile – Timeline' *BBC News* (Venezuela, 25 Feb. 2019) <https://www.bbc.com/news/world-latin-america-19652436> accessed 2 September 2019, and Cardenas Garcia (n 31) 242.

40 While both companies also brought commercial arbitration claims before the ICC, this chapter focuses on the treaty claims brought before ICSID. *See Mobil Cerro Negro, Ltd. v. Petróleos de Venezuela S.A. and PDVSA Cerro Negro, S.A.*, ICC No. 15416/JRF/CA, Award dated 23 Dec. 2011; *Phillips Petroleum Company Venezuela Limited, ConocoPhillips Petrozuata B.V. v. Petróleos de Venezuela, S.A., Corpoguanipa, S.A., PDVSA Petróleo, S.A.*, ICC No. 20549/ASM/JPA Final Award (24 Apr. 2018).

41 *Venezuela Holdings v Venezuela* (n 34) paras 297, 299, 306–307.

42 ibid para 301.

43 ibid para 307. Nina Howell, Sarah Vasani and Greg Lazarev, 'ExxonMobil Decision by ICSID: A Win for ExxonMobil or Venezuela?' (8 December 2014) <https://www.kslaw.com/blog-posts/exxonmobil-decision-icsid-win-exxonmobil-venezuela> accessed 4 September 2019.

44 *Venezuela Holdings, B.V., Mobil Cerro Negro Holding, LTD., Mobil Venezolana de Petróleos Holdings, Inc., Mobil Cerro Negro, LTD., Mobil Venezolana de Petróleos, Inc. v. Bolivarian Republic of Venezuela*, ICSID Case No. ARB/07/27 Decision on Annulment (9 Mar. 2017) para 188; Chuck Stanley, 'ICSID Nixes $1.4B Exxon Award for Venezuelan Oil Assets' (Law 360, 10 Mar. 2017); Caroline Simson, '3 Takeaways from the Mobil Cerro Negro Award Annulment' (Law 360, 20 Mar. 2017).

45 The violation of Article 6(c) rendered the expropriation unlawful because fulfilment of the Article was a necessary condition for the lawfulness of the expropriation. *ConocoPhillips Petrozuata B.V., ConocoPhillips Hamaca B.V., ConocoPhillips Gulf of Paria B.V., ConocoPhillips Company v. Bolivarian Republic of Venezuela*, ICSID Case No. ARB/07/30, Award (8 March 2019) para 46: "The tribunal recalled in its 2017 Interim Decision (para. 147) that the 2013 Decision noted that the requirement of compensation was one of the necessary conditions for an expropriation to be "lawful" (paras. 334, 343, 401). Using the same logic, the finding that one of these conditions has not been met must be understood as having the effect of rendering the expropriation in June 2007 unlawful".

46 *Conoco Phillips Petrozuata B.V., ConocoPhillips Hamaca B.V., ConocoPhillips Gulf of Paria B.V., ConocoPhillips Company v. Bolivarian Republic of Venezuela*, ICSID Case No. ARB/07/30, Decision on Jurisdiction and the Merits (3 Sep. 2013) para 404(d); Greg Coughlin, 'ICSID Tribunal Awards Conocophillips USD 8.7 Billion Plus Interest in Dispute with Venezuela', <https://iisd.org/itn/2019/04/23/icsid-tribunal-awards-conocophillips-usd-8-7-billion-plus-interest-dispute-venezuela-gregg-coughlin> accessed 4 September 2019.

compensation to ConocoPhillips, the largest ICSID award to date against any sovereign.[47] Given its finding that the expropriation was unlawful, the *ConocoPhillips* tribunal calculated the compensation based on the fair market value of the date of the award, as opposed to the date of expropriation, resulting in significantly higher damages.[48] Notably, in contrast to the finding of the *ad hoc* committee in the *Mobil v. Venezuela* case, the *ConocoPhillips* tribunal did not limit ConocoPhillips' recovery to the price cap in its association agreement. This is because the tribunal found that the association agreements and Venezuelan law, while relevant, were not dispositive on compensation because the claim had arisen out of a BIT violation.[49]

2.2 *Ecuador and its change of legal regime applicable to oil contracts*

Similar to Venezuela, in the early 1990s, Ecuador established a favourable investment regime for investors.[50] Prior to 1993, the model for oil contracts was the service contract by which the government owned the oil and was the sole seller.[51] If an investor found oil under the service contract, the investor would be compensated with a fee and reimbursed of any expenses.[52] The low price of oil at that time, however, imposed high costs on Ecuador.[53] Accordingly, in 1993, Ecuador passed a new hydrocarbons law that changed the preferred model of investment from service contracts to production sharing contracts (PSCs).[54] Under the PSCs, investors would carry the entire risk for the oil exploration, but they would receive a share of any oil found.[55] The PSCs also included tax stabilization clauses.[56] This new model for contracting was perceived as beneficial to both the State and investors as the State enjoyed a lower risk profile from other types of contracts, and investors enjoyed new freedom with their operations and potential for higher profits.[57] Among the investors in Ecuador's oil fields was a consortium comprised of Perenco Ecuador Limited and Burlington Resources, Inc., which sought to develop blocks in the Amazonian region.[58] In addition to changing its contracting model, Ecuador followed the regional trend of signing numerous BITs and joining the ICSID Convention.[59]

By 2005, oil had more than doubled in price.[60] Ecuador thus sought, unsuccessfully, to renegotiate the PSCs to get a larger share of the profits from the oil production. In 2006, Ecuador enacted Law 42, which awarded 50 percent of "extraordinary profits," *i.e.*, any amount earned at a market price higher than the price of oil at the time that the PSCs were

47 *Conoco Phillips v Venezuela*, Award (n 47) and Coughlin ibid.
48 *Conoco Phillips v Venezuela* ibid para 40.
49 ibid para 169 and Coughlin (n 47).
50 Cameron (n 6) 244.
51 Blackaby and Richard (n 2).
52 ibid 99.
53 Cameron (n 6) 244.
54 ibid.
55 ibid.
56 ibid.
57 Blackaby and Richard (n 2).
58 *Burlington Resources Inc. v. Republic of Ecuador*, ICSID Case No. ARB/08/5, Decision on Liability (14 Dec. 2012) para 15.
59 Cameron (n 6) 244.
60 In 1993, the price of oil was US$ 14.25 per barrel, and in 2005 the price was US$ 50.28. US Energy Information Administration, 'Petroleum and Other Liquids: Data', <https://www.eia.gov/dnav/pet/hist/LeafHandler.ashx?n=PET&s=F000000__3&f=A> accessed 13 September 2019.

originally negotiated, to Ecuador.[61] Subsequently, following the election of President Rafael Correa in 2007, Ecuador raised the tax under Law 42 to 99 percent through a decree.[62] As a result, several investors that had entered into PSCs with Ecuador commenced arbitration claims under the BITs and the PSCs.[63] The cases described below illustrate the potential liability resulting from regulatory reforms, as well as the issue of potential counterclaims involving environmental claims.

Such was the case of Burlington Resources, Inc., which brought treaty claims against Ecuador over its investments in development blocks in the Amazonian region. In 2008, Burlington Resources brought claims under the U.S.-Ecuador BIT,[64] arguing that Law 42 violated the BIT's protections against expropriation and fair equitable treatment (FET).[65] In a decision rendered on 2 June 2010, the tribunal rejected Burlington's FET claims on the ground that the BIT did not extend to taxation measures.[66] The tribunal also rejected Burlington's expropriation claims on the ground that the value of the investment had not been substantially deprived.[67] In 2011, while the proceedings were still ongoing, Ecuador raised US$ 2.7 billion in counterclaims for harm to the environment.[68] Ecuador claimed that Burlington was strictly liable under Ecuadorian law for damage to the environment in the Amazonian development blocks.[69] In this regard, the tribunal agreed with Ecuador that Burlington was strictly liable and ordered Burlington to pay for restoration and the remedy of infrastructure.[70]

Perenco Ecuador Ltd., Burlington Resources' consortium partner, also brought treaty claims against Ecuador under the France-Ecuador BIT.[71] In this ICSID arbitration, Ecuador raised a similar counterclaim regarding alleged environmental harm.[72] Perenco argued that Law 42 had violated the protections of fair and equitable treatment (FET) and indirect expropriation.[73] In its decision on jurisdiction and liability, the Perenco tribunal found that the 99 percent tax was a breach of the treaty.[74] Specifically, the tribunal found that the PSCs

> were anchored in a legislative framework duly considered and enacted by the Nation's Congress ... [which] set out certain key features of the new contractual regime ... [that] any contractor could reasonably expect that the contract's structure would not be altered .. unilaterally or undone by State action ... except in accordance with their terms and the State's law.[75]

61 Law No 2006–42 Amending the Hydrocarbons Law (Law 42) (Ecuador).
62 Executive Decree 662, 18 Oct. 2007 (Ecuador).
63 Blackaby and Richard (n 2) 101–102.
64 *Burlington v. Ecuador* (n 59) para 67.
65 Burlington also brought an umbrella clause claim, but the tribunal found no jurisdiction over the claim, *ibid* para 546(B)(1).
66 *Burlington Resources Inc. v. Republic of Ecuador,* ICSID Case No. ARB/08/5 Decision on Jurisdiction (2 June 2010) paras 200, 208.
67 *Burlington v Ecuador* (n 59) paras 433, 457.
68 *Burlington Resources Inc. v. Republic of Ecuador,* ICSID Case No. ARB/08/5, Decision on Counterclaims (7 Feb. 2017) paras 6, 52.
69 ibid para 52.
70 ibid para 1099.
71 *Perenco Ecuador Ltd v. Republic of Ecuador and Empresa Estatal Petróleos del Ecuador (PetroEcuador),* ICSID Case No ARB/08/06, Decision on Remaining Issues of Jurisdiction and Liability (12 Sep. 2014) para 4.
72 *Perenco v Ecuador,* Decision on Remaining Issues of Jurisdiction and Liability (n 72) 536, 632.
73 ibid para 713.
74 ibid.
75 ibid para 671, 690.

The tribunal nonetheless did not find that there had been an expropriation.[76] With respect to the environmental counter-claims, the tribunal held that they did not have enough knowledge at the time to make a decision, but indicated that Perenco would likely be liable for some damage.[77] The tribunal nonetheless did not find that there had been an expropriation. Ecuador presented similar counter-claims regarding environmental harm – which raised issues of double recovery by Ecuador in light of the Burlington tribunal's prior order to pay damages for what was, according to Perenco, the same harm. In this respect, the Perenco tribunal found that the tribunal-appointed expert had been in a "better position to capture and delineate the extent of the contamination," resulting in a higher damages quantification. The Perenco tribunal thus treated the damages paid by Burlington as a "down payment towards the total amount of damages" and adjusted the final amount that would be due by Perenco to Ecuador.

2.3 Argentina and its dismantling of the energy legal framework

Starting in 1990, Argentina began a liberalization process for its energy sector.[78] At the time, the Argentine State controlled all forms of energy production, including the oil and gas industry, as well as the provision of energy.[79] Yacimientos Petrolíferos Fiscales (YPF), the State-owned oil company, had a monopoly and private companies could only operate on the basis of service contracts.[80] The transmission and distribution networks for natural gas were also controlled by the State.[81] Furthermore, any oil or gas produced in the country was required to be delivered to State companies for a pricing control regime.[82]

In the early 1990s, in the context of an economic crisis that resulted in severe hyperinflation, the newly-elected government of President Carlos Menem enacted economic measures to liberalize Argentina's economy.[83] This included the privatization of the gas distribution company, Gas del Estado, as well as the establishment of regulatory agencies to oversee the energy industry and, eventually, the privatization of YPF.[84] Argentina also passed the Convertibility Law, which implemented a fixed exchange rate by pegging the Argentinian peso to the U.S. dollar.[85] Furthermore, Argentina ratified the ICSID Convention and entered into more than 50 BITs.[86]

Following an economic downturn in the early 2000s, Argentina began dismantling the above-described legal framework.[87] Argentina enacted a series of emergency laws that undid the financial liberalization commitments previously made, such as the parity between the

76 *Perenco Ecuador Ltd v. Republic of Ecuador and Empresa Estatal Petróleos del Ecuador (PetroEcuador*), ICSID Case No ARB/08/06, Interim Decision on the Environmental Counterclaim (11 Aug. 2015).

77 *Perenco Ecuador Ltd v. Republic of Ecuador and Empresa Estatal Petróleos del Ecuador (PetroEcuador*), ICSID Case No ARB/08/06, Award (27 Sep. 2019), paras. 898–899.

78 ibid.

79 Cameron (n 6) 245.

80 ibid.

81 ibid.

82 ibid.

83 ibid.

84 ibid and Blackaby and Richard (n 2) 106.

85 ibid.

86 Cameron ibid and ICSID, 'Database of ICSID Member States', <https://icsid.worldbank.org/en/Pages/about/Database-of-Member-States.aspx> (indicating that Argentina became of a member of ICSID on 18 November 1994) accessed 2 September 2019.

87 Cameron ibid 246.

Argentinian peso and the U.S. dollar.[88] Most importantly, Argentina disregarded the tariff regime applicable to utilities, which originally provided U.S.-dollar based tariffs, and subjected gas transmission and distribution licenses to renegotiation. In addition, a new State-owned entity, Energía Argentina (Enarsa) was also created for the oil and gas industry.[89] Moreover, in 2012, Argentina expropriated YPF, which at the time was controlled by the Spanish energy company Repsol.

These regulatory changes, revocations, and expropriations negatively affected many foreign investors, including in the energy sector. As a result, investors filed more than 35 ICSID arbitration claims against Argentina through the mechanisms laid out in the BITs between Argentina and the investors' respective home countries. Argentina advanced two main arguments in defense of its emergency actions: the non-precluded measures (NPM) provisions, under the US-Argentina BIT, and the defense of necessity, under international customary law.

Argentina invoked both of these arguments in an effort to avoid liability in multiple ICSID arbitrations but was largely unsuccessful. Indeed, most tribunals rejected Argentina's defenses and found it liable for the damage caused to investors by the restructuring of their investments under the emergency laws.[90] Specifically, tribunals found that Argentina's actions violated the FET standard because Argentina had deviated from the regulatory framework, which had formed the basis of the investors' expectations.[91]

The *CMS Gas Transmission Company* tribunal, for example, found that Argentina had failed to provide FET under the US-Argentina BIT by violating the stability and predictability of the investment[92] because "[t]he measures … did in fact entirely transform and alter the legal and business environment under which the investment was decided and made."[93] The *Enron* and *Sempra* tribunals also found that Argentina had violated the FET standard, holding in similar terms that where there had been business certainty and stability for investors, there was no doubt and ambiguity.[94] In the words of the *Enron* tribunal, "[t]he long-term business outlook enabled by the tariff regime, ha[d] been transformed into a day-to-day discussion about what comes next" and Argentina had "failed to provide a final and definitive framework for the operation of business in the energy sector."[95]

The *Enron* and *Sempra* awards, however, were subsequently annulled by *ad hoc* committees at the request of Argentina, pursuant to the procedure established under the ICSID Rules. In the case of *Sempra*, the *ad hoc* committee found that the tribunal had not applied the

88 ibid.

89 ibid.

90 William W. Burke-White, 'The Argentine Financial Crisis: State Liability Under BITs and the Legitimacy of the ICSID System', (2008) *University of Pennsylvania Faculty Scholarship* 11 (discussing *CMS v. Argentina, Enron v. Argentina, and Sempra v. Argentina*).

91 *See, e.g., BG Group Plc. v. Republic of Argentina,* UNCITRAL, Final Award (24 Dec. 2007) para 307; *CMS Gas Transmission Co. v. Argentine Republic,* ICSID Case No. ARB/01/8, Award (12 May 2005) para 276; *LG&E Energy Corp., LG&E Capital Corp., and LG&E Int'l, Inc. v. Arg. Republic,* ICSID Case No. ARB/02/1, Decision on Liability (3 Oct. 2006) paras 132–139.

92 *CMS v Argentina* (n 93) paras 276, 281.

93 ibid para 275.

94 *Sempra Energy International v. Argentine Republic,* ICSID Case No. ARB/02/16, Award (28 Sep. 2007) paras 303–304; *Enron Corporation Ponderosa Assets, L. P. v. Argentine Republic,* ICSID Case No. ARB/01/3, Award (22 May 2007) paras 266, 268.

95 *Enron Corporation Ponderosa Assets, L. P. v. Argentine Republic,* ICSID Case No. ARB/01/3, Award (22 May 2007) para 266.

applicable law (specifically Article XI of the BIT) and hence, had exceeded its powers.[96] The *Enron ad hoc* committee in turn, agreed to annul the Enron award because the tribunal had failed to consider certain issues in its legal interpretation of Argentina's necessity defense.[97] These decisions, however, continue to be controversial in the international arbitration community as they are part of a group of annulment decisions that showed "an unprecedented level of activism."[98]

2.4 Guatemala and the electricity tariff review process

As noted in Section 1 above, certain Latin American States have privatized activities including the generation and distribution of electricity. Such was the case of Guatemala, which in 1996 passed the General Electricity Law in order to address an electricity crisis. The General Electricity Law provided that it had the purpose of "increas[ing] the production, transmission, and distribution of … energy resources through the liberalization" of the electricity sector.[99] This law further established the National Commission of Electric Energy (CNEE), a regulatory agency required to publish electricity tariffs every five years.[100]

While these tariffs consist of various components, one of the most significant is the formula for "Value Added for Distribution" (VAD), by which the distributors recoup their investments and make a profit. Under the General Electricity Law, the VAD is calculated based on the study of an independent consultant engaged by the distributor and pre-qualified by the CNEE, whose findings may be subject to an *ad hoc* expert commission in the event the distributor and the CNEE have a disagreement regarding the study.

As part of its liberalization strategy, in the late 1990s, the Republic of Guatemala privatized certain assets in the electricity sector, which included the largest distributor in the country: Empresa Eléctrica de Guatemala (EEGSA).[101] As a result, in 1998, 80 percent of EEGSA's equity was purchased by a consortium formed by: Iberdrola Energía, S.A. (Iberdrola), TECO Guatemala Holdings, LCC (TECO), and Electricidad de Portugal S.A. A decade later, however, a dispute arose between Guatemala and EEGSA because of Guatemala's disregard for its regulatory framework and international obligations in the review and establishment of the electricity tariffs applicable to EEGSA for the 2008–2013 period. Subsequently, two of the consortium members, Iberdrola and TECO, commenced separate international arbitration proceedings against Guatemala. As explained below, these proceedings had entirely different outcomes.[102]

96 *Sempra Energy International v. Argentine Republic*, ICSID Case No. ARB/02/16, Decision on the Argentine Republic's Application for Annulment of the Award (29 June 2019) para 208; R. Doak Bishop and Silvia M. Marchili, 'Annulment Under the ICSID Convention' (Oxford University Press, 2012) 29–30.

97 *Enron Creditors Recovery Corp. Ponderosa Assets, L.., v. The Argentine Republic*, ICSID Case No. ARB/01/03, Decision on the Application for Annulment of the Argentine Republic (30 July 2010) paras 377, 392–339 and Bishop and Marchili ibid 31–32.

98 Christoph Schreuer, 'From ICSID Annulment to Appeal' (2011) *The Law and Practice of International Courts and Tribunals* 213 and 215. Argentina systematically challenged adverse awards, one of which was the subject of a decision by the U.S. Supreme Court on the issues of arbitrability of local litigation requirements. *See BG Group plc v. Republic of Arg.*, 572 U.S. 25 (2014).

99 General Law of Electricity published by Decree No. 93–96 dated 21 Nov. 1996 (General Electricity Law), Preamble.

100 General Electricity Law, Art. 4.

101 UN Conference on Trade and Development, 'Guatemala, Investment Policy Review' (2010) 13.

102 *See* generally *TECO Guatemala Holdings LLC v. Republic of Guatemala,* ICSID Case No. ARB/10/17, Award (19 Dec. 2013); *Iberdrola Energía S.A. v. Republic of Guatemala,* ICSID Case No. ARB/09/5, Award (17 Aug. 2012)).

Iberdrola brought its claim under the Spain-Guatemala BIT, but failed to proceed past the jurisdictional stage.[103] In its award, the tribunal held that Iberdrola had failed to demonstrate that Guatemala had breached international law by failing to adhere to the local regulatory framework.[104] Specifically, the tribunal referred to how the parties' pleadings and argument in the hearing "discussed at length ... how certain provisions of Guatemala law should be interpreted" and "focused [up]on the technical and financial differences for calculating the VAD and its components," but that "[e]xcept marginally, there [had been] no debate about the violations of the Treaty or international law, or about which actions of the Republic of Guatemala, in exercise of State authority, had violated certain standards contained in the Treaty."[105]

TECO brought its claim under the Free Trade Agreement between the Dominican Republic, the United States, and Central America (DR-CAFTA) and survived Guatemala's jurisdictional challenges.[106] TECO successfully established that the CNEE's conduct amounted to a breach of the FET standard under DR-CAFTA because such standard "prohibits State officials from exercising the authority in an abusive, arbitrary, and discriminatory manner," and obliges the State to observe due process in administrative proceedings.[107] The *TECO* tribunal, moreover, held that "in disregarding without providing reasons the Expert Commission's report, and in unilaterally imposing a tariff based on its own consultant's VAD calculation," repudiating fundamental principles of the regulatory framework, the CNEE "acted arbitrarily and in violation of fundamental principles of due process in regulatory matters."[108] This liability finding survived a challenge by Guatemala in a subsequent annulment proceeding.[109] TECO, moreover, sought and was successful in annulling the tribunal's findings limiting the quantum of compensation it was entitled to, and the extent of interest it would receive on the compensation TECO was awarded.[110] That, and the related question of allocation of costs based on the relative success of the parties in the arbitration, are questions that became the subject of a resubmitted arbitration, which is presently ongoing.

As evidenced by the events described in this section, Latin America is one of the most volatile areas for investments in the energy sector. In the past few decades, certain States invited investments, but then sought to claw back investors' profits when they were obtaining what the State considered a windfall. In other cases, investments in the energy sector were profoundly affected by the macro-economic policies enacted by States to respond to macro-economic crisis. As we explained above, such was the case of Venezuela, Argentina, and Ecuador at the turn of the century, leading to a significant increase in the number of disputes filed by investors against those States or their State-owned entities. Some States like Ecuador and Venezuela, moreover, not only dismantled the domestic regulatory framework for investments, but also subsequently reneged on the substantive procedural and substantive protections afforded in international treaties to investors by terminating or forcibly renegotiating investment treaties and withdrawing from the ICSID Convention.[111]

103 *See* generally *Iberdrola Award*.

104 *Iberdrola v Guatemala* (n 99) paras 350, 356.

105 ibid paras 351–352.

106 ibid para 18.

107 ibid para 587.

108 ibid para 664.

109 *TECO Guatemala Holdings LLC v. Republic of Guatemala*, ICSID Case No. ARB 10/17, Decision on Annulment (5 Apr. 2016) paras 215–238, 246–259, 274–300, 308–323, 327–331, 337–343, 348–351, 358–362.

110 ibid paras 123–139, 183–198, 358–362.

111 Bolivia denounced ICSID in 2007, followed by Ecuador in 2009 and Venezuela in 2012. *See* Belén Olmos Giupponi, *Latin American States, International Arbitration and Trade in Investment Agreements: Quo Vadis?* (Kluwer

3 Latin America's volatility requires risk mitigation strategies for existing and future investments

After years of uncertainty, it appears that a new investment phase is beginning in Latin American States as a result of the enactment of investor-friendly policies, a renewed confidence in the price of oil, and the thriving renewable energy sector. Over the last few years, there have been significant governmental efforts to attract, or re-attract, foreign investors to the region in the energy sector. As part of these efforts, many Latin American countries have become more open to energy investment and enacted market-friendly policies and regulatory reforms to attract private capital and international expertise. These include, for example, Ecuador's proposal to introduce new investment agreements called "bilateral investment agreements," with the aim of attracting investments and solving any differences with investors in "a friendly and constructive way."[112] Similarly, Brazil removed the requirement that Petrobras be the sole operator in pre-salt fields with a minimum 30 percent stake, as well as local content requirements for its oil industry, which required oil and gas operators to obtain a certain level of supplies from Brazilian sources.[113] In a slightly different fashion, as part of its energy reform, Mexico has agreed to settle disputes arising out of its hydrocarbon exploration and extraction contracts through arbitration under the UNCITRAL Rules.[114]

These efforts have striking similarities to the promises made and frameworks built in the early 1990s.[115] Investors, therefore, need to design and execute a comprehensive strategy in order to protect their long-term investments in the energy sector in Latin America against political actions and adverse changes in the regulatory framework. Drawing from the lessons learned over the past three decades, this section describes risk mitigation strategies and best practices that investors may take into consideration. These recommendations are also intended to serve as a guide for States to consider to reduce litigation risks while enacting measures to attract and promote foreign investments.

As set forth below, these risk-mitigation strategies include: (i) structuring investments to gain protection under international law; (ii) incorporating substantive protection under contractual arrangements; and (iii) implementing best practices to avoid and prepare for potential disputes.

Structuring investments to gain protection under international investment treaties: Prospective investors should take into account the investment protection provided under BITs, free trade agreements, or other forms of multilateral investment protection when structuring their

---

Arbitration Blog, 16 June 2019) <http://arbitrationblog.kluwerarbitration.com/2019/06/16/latin-american-states-international-arbitration-and-trade-in-investment-agreements-quo-vadis/> accessed on 4 September 2019.

112 Ministerio de Relaciones Exteriores y Movilidad Humana, 'Ecuador Proposes New Investment Agreements that Protect the Country and Defend Human Rights' (8 Mar. 8, 2018) <https://www.cancilleria.gob.ec/en/ecuador-proposes-new-investment-agreements-that-protect-the-country-and-defend-human-rights> accessed on 2 September 2019.

113 Lisa Viscidi and Rebecca O'Connor, 'US-Latin America Energy Investment: Proposals for Policy Engagement, Energy Working Paper' (2017) *The Dialogue*, 6; CMS Law, 'Brazil Proposes Relaxation of Local Content Requirements' (CMS Law, 2 Feb. 2017) <https://www.cms-lawnow.com/ealerts/2017/02/brazil-proposes-relaxation-of-local-content-requirements>_accessed on 2 September 2019.

114 See, e.g., Contract for the Exploration and Extraction of Hydrocarbons under the Shared Production Modality between National Commission of Hydrocarbons, Pemex Exploración y Producción and Servicios Multiples de Burgos, S.A. de C.V. dated 2 Mar. 2018, Cl. 27.5 <https://www.gob.mx/cms/uploads/attachment/file/304938/CNH-M3-MISI_N-2018.pdf> accessed on 2 September 2019.

115 Monaldi (n 11).

investments in Latin America. In so doing, investors should take a close look at the substantive protection afforded by each treaty, as well as whether there is availability of access to international arbitration to allow the enforcement of such protection before a neutral forum.[116] Absent the access to international arbitration, the only alternative would be to sue the host State before local courts, which in most jurisdictions would raise concerns of bias and the independence of the judiciary.

When selecting a jurisdiction in which to structure an investment in Latin America, the prospective or existing investor should conduct a comparative analysis of the available treaties and jurisdictions with a particular emphasis on the following factors:

- *Definition of investor*: certain treaties provide broad definitions of investor only requiring, for example, that a legal entity merely have the nationality of the relevant jurisdiction.[117] In contrast, other treaties may require investors to have substantial business activities in the relevant jurisdiction.[118]
- *Definition of investment*: certain treaties provide broad definitions of investment, which encompass all kinds of assets owned by a natural or legal entity.[119] Other treaties may expressly incorporate the so-called *Salini* factors, *i.e.*, commitment of capital or other resources, the expectation of gain or profit, and the assumption of risk.[120]
- *Substantive protections*: most investment treaties provide fair and equitable and most-favoured nation treatment, as well as protection against expropriation or measures with similar effect without prompt and adequate compensation. Careful attention, however, should be paid to any potential limitations to those substantive protections. For example, certain treaties limit the fair and equitable and most-favoured nation treatments or disputes involving certain types of measures.[121]
- *International arbitration*: most investment treaties provide for arbitration under the ICSID and/or UNCITRAL Rules. However, the investor must evaluate whether the treaty provides limitations to the commencement of such proceedings, including the waiver of

116 For example, the Italy-Nicaragua BIT allows for both UNCITRAL and ICSID arbitration. Agreement Between the Government of the Republic of Nicaragua and the Government of the Italian Republic on the Promotion and Protection of Investments, 20 Apr. 2004 (entered into force 22 May 2006). Similarly, the Belgium-Luxembourg Economic Union-Colombia BIT also allows for both UNCITRAL and ICSID arbitration. Agreement Between the Belgium-Luxembourg Economic Union, on the one hand, and the Republic of Colombia, on the other hand, on the Reciprocal Promotion and Protection of Investments, 4 Feb. 2009 (signed but not in force).

117 See, e.g., Agreement between the Kingdom of Spain and the Republic of Colombia for the Promotion and Reciprocal Protection of Investments dated 31 Mar. 2005 (entered into force on 22 Sep. 2017).

118 See, e.g., The Dominican Republic – Central America – United States Free Trade Agreement, 5 Aug. 2004; Bilateral Agreement for the Promotion and Protection of Investments between the Government of the United Kingdom of Great Britain and Northern Ireland and the Republic of Colombia dated 17 Mar. 2010 (entered into force on 10 Oct. 2014).

119 See, e.g., Agreement between the Republic of Chile and the Kingdom of Spain for the Protection and Reciprocal Promotion of Investments dated 2 Oct. 1991 (entered into force on 28 Mar. 1994).

120 See, e.g., United States – Chile Free Trade Agreement, 6 June 2003, Bilateral Agreement for the Promotion and Protection of Investments between the Government of the United Kingdom of Great Britain and Northern Ireland and Republic of Colombia, 17 Mar. 2010 (entered into force 10 Oct. 2014).

121 See, e.g., The Dominican Republic – Central America – United States Free Trade Agreement, 5 Aug. 2004 (including terms requiring "like circumstances"); Bilateral Agreement for the Promotion and Protection of Investments between the Government of the United Kingdom of Great Britain and Northern Ireland and Republic of Colombia, 17 Mar. 2010 (entered into force 10 Oct. 2014) (excluding taxation from the scope of the treaty).

domestic proceedings, fork-in-the-road provisions, the requirement to resort to submitting the dispute to local courts for a certain period of time, or waiting for "cooling-off" periods before resorting to international arbitration.

Absent specific requirements in the relevant treaty, tribunals have commonly accepted the legitimacy of restructuring investments in order to gain the protections of investment treaties. The tribunal in *Alapi v. Turkey* affirmed that restructuring in good faith is permitted so long as there is not an "actual dispute" or "specific future dispute as a high probability" between the parties.[122] In the Latin American context, the tribunal in *ExxonMobil v. Venezuela* similarly found that Mobil's restructuring of their investments in 2005 and 2006 in order to gain access to arbitration under the ICSID Rules under the Netherlands-Venezuela BIT was a "perfectly legitimate goal."[123]

Smart contract drafting: As explained in Section I, most energy concessions or contracts require investors to sign a contract with a State or its State-owned entities. Therefore, in addition to strategic structuring under existing investment treaties, investors can include a variety of clauses in their contracts to protect their investments, including stabilization, indemnification, and force majeure clauses, as well as access to international arbitration. Of course, the ability to achieve these contractual protections will vary enormously depending on the State and the investor's respective bargaining power.

The inclusion of these types of clauses is of fundamental importance, particularly if the host State is not a signatory to the ICSID Convention or otherwise does not have an investment treaty with any viable jurisdiction. Below are some of the main contract clauses that investors should consider with a view to mitigating risks when investing in the Latin American energy sector:

- *Stabilization clauses*: these clauses provide that their investments will be protected against changes in the legal framework of the host State. While these clauses do not restrain a State's ability to change the regulatory framework, they assure that adverse effects from changes in the law will be set off economically by the State. For example, in the Ecuadorian production sharing contracts discussed above, Ecuador had agreed to tax stabilization clauses whereby if Ecuador changed the tax scheme in a way that adversely affected investment under the production sharing contract, then Ecuador had to readjust oil participation shares to "absorb the impact of the tax increase."[124]
- *Indemnification clauses*: typically included in contracts with State-owned entities, these clauses provide compensation to an investor if a specific event occurs, for example, a tax increase or an expropriation.[125] These clauses, therefore, help mitigate the effects of

122 *Alapi Elektrik B.V. v. Republic of Turkey*, ICSID Case No. ARB/08/13, Award (16 July 2012) paras 402–403 (discussing the "dividing line between a good faith (re)structuring to get access to international arbitration and a bad faith restructuring ...").

123 *Venezuela Holdings, B.V., Mobil Cerro Negro Holding, LTD., Mobil Venezolana de Petróleos Holdings, Inc., Mobil Cerro Negro, LTD., Mobil Venezolana de Petróleos, Inc. v. Bolivarian Republic of Venezuela*, ICSID Case No. ARB/07/27, Decision on Jurisdiction (10 June 2010) para 199.

124 See *Burlington Resources Inc. v. Republic of Ecuador*, ICSID Case No. ARB/08/5, Decision on Liability (14 Dec. 2014) para 114; *see also Perenco Ecuador Ltd v. Republic of Ecuador and Empresa Estatal Petróleos del Ecuador (Petro-Ecuador)*, ICSID Case No ARB/08/06, Decision on Remaining Issues of Jurisdiction and Liability (12 Sep. 2014) paras 361–366, 378 (noting that the Tribunal did not consider the tax clause to be a true stabilization clause because it did not freeze regulations at the time of contracting).

125 D. Brian King and Jue (Allie) Bian, 'Back to the Future? Investment Protection at a Time of Uncertainty' (2019) *ITA in Review*, 12.

adverse governmental action in contracts to which the government is not itself a party, by creating a strict liability-like result in the event of a particular action. An example of such a clause can be found in Venezuela's association agreements from the *Apertura Petrolera* era. Pursuant to such clause, ExxonMobil was able to bring an arbitration claim to the ICC against PDVSA based on PDVSA's agreement to indemnify the company if such "discriminatory measures" occurred.[126] The ICC tribunal found in favour of ExxonMobil's claim because Venezuela took discriminatory measures against ExxonMobil that caused a "materially adverse impact."[127]

- *Force majeure clauses*: typically indicate when a party is not liable for breach of contract because of circumstances out of its control.[128] Properly crafted clauses can reduce this risk by indicating when the State-owned entity is responsible for mitigating the effects of the State action or when direct liability lies with the State-owned entity for breach.[129]
- *International arbitration*: investors should strongly consider including an arbitration clause providing for the resolution of any disputes through international arbitration in order to avoid the use of the courts of the host State for such purpose. In this respect, it is advisable for the investor to seek specialized international arbitration counsel when drafting these clauses in order to prevent potential procedural difficulties in the event a dispute arises. At a minimum, the investor should rely on the model clauses provided by relevant international arbitration institutions such as the International Chamber of Commerce and ensure that seat of arbitration is a neutral State with advanced international arbitration laws. Investors and States could also consider incorporating ICSID arbitration clauses in their contracts with the State and State-owned entities in order to benefit from the recognition and enforcement protections afforded by the ICSID Convention. Indeed, as ICSID reports, over 60 percent of its contract-based cases arise from energy-related contracts, with sub-Saharan African countries being the most active respondents.[130]

Monitor State conduct and implement best practices to avoid (but be prepared for) disputes: when investing in the energy sector in Latin America, investors should implement best practices in order to avoid disputes with the States, while maintaining appropriate records in the event of adverse government action. These best practices include the following:

- Investors should maintain records of all formal and informal communication with the State and its State-owned entities. These communications include formal letters, resolutions, records of meetings, as well as any informal communications with government officials or executives of the State-owned entity.
- Investors should also take steps to ensure compliance with domestic and international law when investing, in order to avoid an argument by the host State that the investment has not been made in accordance with domestic law.

126 See *Mobil Cerro Negro v. Petróleos de Venezuela S.A., PDVSA Cerro Negro, S.A.*, ICC Case No. 15415/JRF/CA, Final Award dated 23 Dec. 2011 ¶¶ 2, 236: see also *Venezuela Holdings, B.V., Mobil Cerro Negro Holding, LTD., Mobil Venezolana de Petróleos Holdings, Inc., Mobil Cerro Negro, LTD., Mobil Venezolana de Petróleos, Inc. v. Bolivarian Republic of Venezuela*, ICSID Case No. ARB/07/27, Award dated 9 Oct. 2014 ¶ 216.

127 *Mobil Cerro Negro v. Petróleos de Venezuela S.A., PDVSA Cerro Negro, S.A.*, ICC Case No. 15415/JRF/CA, Final Award (23 Dec. 2011) 3.

128 King and Bian (n 126).

129 ibid.

130 ICSID, 'Spotlight on Contract-Based Disputes at ICSID', <https://icsid.worldbank.org/en/Pages/resources/Spotlight-on-Contract-based-Disputes-at-ICSID.aspx> accessed 2 September 2019.

- Investors should further monitor State action in the industry, even if the action is not directly adverse to the investor, to anticipate future action. As we saw in the Venezuela example, explained above in Section 2, Venezuela initially exempted certain companies from the application of the 2001 Hydrocarbons Law, but then extended those regulations to the originally exempted entities. Therefore, monitoring the regulations or administrative actions against similarly situated entities from an international perspective may allow the investors to be pro-active and design strategies to avoid potential losses and maximize their chances of successfully settling the dispute.

4 Future trends

Despite the forewarned volatility of the Latin American energy market, the sector's potential for great returns is increasing. For instance, the World Energy Outlook of 2018 predicts an increase in total primary energy demand by 250 million tons of oil equivalent (MTOE) in Latin America between 2017 and 2040.[131] Commentators also have recently recognized that "[a]ll the [oil] supply boom in the world is coming from the Americas;" emphasizing that "[t]he center of the universe in oil is moving that way."[132] Compatible with its expansive ownership of oil reserves, Latin America also has the biggest share of renewable energy in the world,[133] which countries in the region are rapidly seeking to exploit. The demand for electricity in the region will double by 2040, requiring an influx of around US$ 24 billion each subsequent year.[134]

The following developments have taken place in energy investment in Latin America recently:

- *Peru*: has significantly developed its oil and gas sector since the 1990s as a result of its liberal legislation, which allowed State-owned companies to enter into exploration and exploitation contracts with private enterprises.[135]
- *Brazil*: under new leadership, Brazil has announced a plan to privatize State-owned companies, including assets belonging to State-owned oil company, Petrobras.[136]
- *Argentina*: fracking prospects in the Vaca Muerta shale fields have attracted foreign investors since recent reforms in the oil and gas industry.[137] Argentina has also enacted legislation providing for commercial arbitration in public-private contracts.[138] The influx of investment in the Vaca Muerta fields and the new legislation for arbitration could increase the number of arbitral disputes arising from Argentina's energy sector, especially

131 International Energy Agency, 'World Energy Outlook 2018' 35 <https://www.iea.org/weo2018> accessed on 13 September 2019.

132 Robbie Whelan, Paulo Trevisani and Bradley Olson, 'Major Oil Companies Embrace Latin America', *Wall Street Journal* (21 May 2018) <https://www.wsj.com/articles/major-oil-companies-embrace-latin-america-1526907600> accessed 2 September 2019.

133 Lisa Viscidi and Ariel Yépez, 'The Energy Solution Latin America Needs', *New York Times* (12 Feb. 2018), <https://nyti.ms/2FzZkdW> accessed 2 September 2019.

134 Yépez-García et al. (n 10).

135 Salas and Costábile (n 26).

136 Steven Tredennicket al., 'Optimism Abounds for LatAm's Oil & Gas Sector After a Quiet 2018', White & Case LLP (7 May 2019), <https://mergers.whitecase.com/highlights/optimism-abounds-for-latams-oil-gas-sector-after-a-quiet-2018> accessed 2 September 2019.

137 Tredennick et al. ibid and Whelan et al. (n 133).

138 Salas and Costábile (n 26).

if the Argentinian Government ultimately fails to observe its commitments to investors in the Vaca Muerta shale fields.[139]

- *Guyana*: has also been blessed with several significant offshore discoveries that have led to significant investments. For instance, ExxonMobil is confident that its wells in the Stabroek Block will produce more than 750,000 barrels of oil per day by 2025.[140] As a result, over the next decade, Guyana could become the second-largest oil producer in Latin America.[141]
- *Mexico*: showing increasing signs of openness in the early 2010s, Mexico signed the ICSID Convention and now allows the arbitration of disputes relating to hydrocarbons.[142] This is notable since Mexico's constitution prohibited foreign investment in most energy sectors until 2013.[143] Following this constitutional change, Mexico awarded more than 100 contracts for energy projects ranging from offshore drilling to solar installations.[144] However, the Lopez-Obrador administration has placed these contracts under review, heightening the uncertainty for international investments in the sector.[145] The administration has also halted all energy auctions for new projects.[146] At the time of writing this chapter, it is not clear what ultimate course of action the Lopez-Obrador administration will take with regard to foreign energy investment, though the administration has focused more heavily on promoting and investing in Pemex, Mexico's State oil company.[147] How the Lopez-Obrador administration continues to treat foreign investment, particularly the investments made during the previous administration, will determine the extent of disputes arising in Mexico's energy sector.[148]
- *Ecuador*: despite having left ICSID, Ecuador is seeking to attract foreign investment by renegotiating previously terminated treaties, as well as proposing a new draft investment law.[149] Early in 2019, Ecuador awarded new oil exploration contracts to Frontera and Geopark; the bids for these contracts indicated that Ecuador would receive 60 percent of the oil production from the new fields.[150] Ecuador needed this new investment in the oil sector to increase crude output because of high fiscal deficits and large foreign debt obligations.[151]

Based on these trends, investors should take advantage of investment opportunities arising in countries that are opening their markets and developing investor-friendly schemes.

139 Tom Sanzillo and Kathy Hipple, 'IEEFA Argentina: Government Cannot Afford Subsidies for Vaca Muerta Oil and Gas Producers', *Institute for Energy Economics and Financial Analysis* (8 Feb. 2019) <https://ieefa.org/ieefa-argentina-government-cannot-afford-subsidies-for-vaca-muerta-oil-and-gas-producers>.
140 Tredennick (n 138).
141 ibid.
142 Salas and Costábile (n 26).
143 Viscidi and O'Connor (n 115).
144 ibid.
145 ibid.
146 ibid.
147 ibid.
148 See Chapter 19 in this volume: 'Energy justice as a key driver to unlock the transition from energy reform to energy counter-reform: the rise of the immutability theory'.
149 Salas and Costábile (n 25).
150 'Gran Tierra, Frontera-GeoPark Consortium Win Ecuador Oil Contracts', *Reuters* (10 Apr. 2019) <https://www.reuters.com/article/ecuador-oil/gran-tierra-frontera-geopark-consortium-win-ecuador-oil-contracts-idUSL1N21S13Y> accessed 2 September 2019.
151 ibid.

However, given the historical trends of negative changes in investment regimes once prices and returns for investors rise, it is recommended that investors utilize the aforementioned strategies to protect their investments, such as structuring an investment to take advantage of treaty protections including arbitration. While no investment is free from the risk of disputes, following the aforementioned recommendations can help lead to a positive investment experience in the ever-growing energy sector in Latin America.

22

REGULATORY FRAMEWORK FOR THE ENERGY SECTOR IN COLOMBIA AND BRAZIL

*Milton Fernando Montoya Pardo and María Alejandra Garzón Albornoz**

1 Introduction

The electricity and hydrocarbon sector are important elements of a national public policy, not only because of their key role in the economy but also because of the necessities they meet. Besides, both sectors are directly related to sustainable development goals where energy poverty is also relevant.[1] In Colombia and Brazil, the electricity and hydrocarbon sectors are of pivotal importance for both their economic impact (as net producers of energy) as well as social impact. This chapter seeks to characterize the electricity and hydrocarbon market in these countries. In doing so, we shall briefly discuss the main regulations, the institutions involved and the general framework.

2 Colombia

2.1 The main features of the energy industry

The energy sector in Colombia is closely related to the development and strengthening of the economy because it entwines aspects such as economic growth, private investment, job creation, satisfaction of needs, technological development and living standards. Thus, the importance of this sector is paramount. During 2017, the gas and electricity sector made up 2.4 per cent and the mining-oil sector made up 6.1 per cent of the gross domestic product (GDP), respectively. The crude reserves will only last until 2024 and the gas reserves until 2029.[2]

Regarding the foreign investment in the sector, the Banco de la República de Colombia valued the flow of investment for the oil sector at $US 2.537 million dollars and 64 million dollars

* All electronic sources used on this chapter were last visited on 20 June 2019 unless otherwise stated.

1 See also Milton Montoya et al., 'Energy Justice and Energy Poverty in Latin America', *Energy Justice* (Oxford University Press 2020, forthcoming).

2 MacMaster, Bruce. 'Una nueva mirada del sector minero energético', 7ª Colombia Genera 2018 La ANDI habla de Petróleo, Energía, Minería y Gas (March, 2018) Cartagena, Colombia, available at: www.andi.com.co/Uploads/Presentaci%C3%B3nBMM.pdf.

for the electricity, water and gas sector.[3] In general terms, Colombia has five main energy challenges to face: i) guarantee energy security, reliability, diversification of the energy matrix and increase the coverage of the service; ii) increase the percentage of non-conventional renewable sources; iii) increase the hydrocarbon reserves; iv) incorporate the new regulatory trends like digitalization and disruptive technologies, among other solutions; v) foster competition and create incentives for private national and foreign investment.

Concerning the exports during 2018, they amounted to about $US 16 billion this being a significant decrease when compared to the exports for 2015 ($US 24 billion); 2016 ($US 19 billion) and 2017 ($US 17 billion). The exports of electricity for the year 2018 reached 16.064 GWh. At the time of writing, the Plan Nacional de Desarrollo 2018–2022 is in force. This is a planning document which lays out the vision and goals of the current government. According to this planning document, the energy sector framework includes the following objectives:[4]

- building a mining-energy sector with social and environmental responsibility
- diversifying the energy matrix to ensure energy security
- making use of solar, wind and biomass energy
- increasing the hydrocarbon reserves
- developing a new model of interrelations between government and the regions
- issuing a technical and environmental regulation to address the development of non-conventional energy sources
- Producing recommendations from the commission of experts about the future of the non-conventional fields of hydrocarbons in Colombia.

Accordingly, the Colombian government has estimated that by 2022 there will be an increase of renewable energy in the country's energy matrix, where the effective net capability will increase from 17.319 MW to 21,329 MW, achieving a wind generation of 5 per cent and a solar generation of 1 per cent. Some aspects that will help to ensure this target is achieved are wind speed in some of the Colombian regions and a higher generation potential based on sun and wind than hydroelectrical power.[5]

2.2 *Constitutional considerations*

The Colombian Constitution mentions some principles that frame the energy sector in Colombia. Among these we can highlight: the ownership of resources because it established that the public goods belong to the State,[6] which means that the State is the also the owner of the non-renewable resources,[7] and is in charge of planning the use of those according to sustainable development considerations.[8]

3 Banco de la República de Colombia. 'Flujos de inversión directa – balanza de pagos', www.banrep.gov.co/es/inversion-directa.

4 Departamento Nacional de Planeación. 'Plan Nacional de Desarrollo 2018–2022. Pacto por Colombia pacto por la equidad' (2019), https://colaboracion.dnp.gov.co/CDT/Prensa/Resumen-PND2018-2022-final.pdf. Ley 1955 de 2019 por el cual se expide el Plan Nacional de Desarrollo 2018–2022. "Pacto por Colombia, pacto por la Equidad".

5 Ministerio de Minas y Energía, 'Iniciativa cluster de energía renovables del Caribe', www.andi.com.co/Uploads/11%20Ministra%20de%20Minas.pdf.

6 Political Constitution of Colombia 1991, Article 102.

7 Ibid, Article 332.

8 Ibid, Article 80.

It is noteworthy that in order to protect the cultural and national wealth of the country and because of the ethnic and cultural diversity of Colombia,[9] local communities must be advised of all projects that may affect them and cause environmental or territorial impacts. Those requirements can be met through mechanisms like agreements or prior consultation.[10] Although this topic is beyond the scope of this chapter, we must mention that many of the energy and mining projects of the industry have been paralyzed due to the challenging relationship with communities and the lack of social licenses or acceptance.[11] Thus, this issue of consultation and agreement with local communities is an important topic for Colombian energy law. In fact, a project in the mining sector cannot proceed in Colombia without the agreement of local authorities and communities.[12] Besides, the generation of electricity and hydrocarbon activities have been categorized as 'of public utility',[13] which in general terms produces the possibility of expropriation and imposing easement because of its importance and general interest of the Nation.

Electricity and some hydrocarbon activities have also been categorized as a public service,[14] and are consequently inherent to the social purpose of the State.[15] Therefore, it the State's duty to ensure the efficient provision of this service throughout the national territory. In Colombia, while the State does not reserve the right to provide these activities, it has exclusive competence over the regulation, control and auditing of these services.

On the other hand, the Colombian Constitution establishes that the law must state the competences and responsibilities related to the provision, coverage, quality, funding, fees, system of providing these public services, bearing in mind the costs, solidarity and redistribution of income criteria.[16] Municipalities are required to be responsible for the provision of public services based on their technical and economic characteristics.

Finally, the Colombian Constitution has determined that the State should be compensated for the exploitation of non-renewable natural resources through royalties.[17] Royalties are the payments made by the companies that exploit the areas of non-renewable resources. For example, oil companies give the State between 8 and 25 per cent of their income in royalties. Such resources are used to address the basic unmet needs of the population, such as to reduce poverty, distribute wealth, promote regional development, encourage small and medium size energy projects, etc., according to the principles of the General System of Royalties.[18]

9 Ibid, Article 7.

10 Ibid, Article 8.

11 Portafolio, '¿Cómo lograr que las comunidades no sigan frenando grandes proyectos en el país?', https://www.portafolio.co/economia/en colombia-grandes-proyectos-se-frenan-por-culpa-de-las-comunidades-498527.

12 Montoya Pardo and Milton Fernando, 'The new reality of participation of local authorities in mining projects in Colombia: Interpretation of constitutional principles, new opportunities and participation mechanisms', (2017) *Journal of Energy & Natural Resources Law*, Vol 35 No 4, p. 391; Milton Fernando Montoya Pardo, 'Participation of territorial authorities in mining activities in Colombia', in Lila Barrera-Hernandez, Barry Barton, Lee Godden, Alastair Lucas and Anita Ronne (eds), *Sharing the Costs and Benefits of Energy and Resource Activity: Legal Change and Impact on Communities* (Oxford University Press, 2016), p. 355.

13 Political Constitution of Colombia 1991, Article 58,

14 Being a public utility renders the possibility of enforcing assessment.

15 Political Constitution of Colombia 1991, Article 365.

16 Political Constitution of Colombia 1991, Article 367.

17 Political Constitution of Colombia 1991, Article 360.

18 Ley 1530 de 2012 por la cual se regula la organización y el funcionamiento del Sistema General de Regalías (mayo 2012). Article 2.

2.3 Legal system

2.3.1 Hydrocarbons

The current regulations relating to hydrocarbons are found mainly in the Decree 1073 of 2015 in the section 'Administrativo de Minas y Energía', where the Colombian State compiled and rationalized the rules that govern the sector. Different topics are regulated such as exploration, exploitation, valuation, accounting of reserves and the description of the properties of natural resources.

From a broad perspective, the regulation of the hydrocarbons sector is made up of international conventions, the Colombian constitution, the Petroleum Code, general and specific laws, as well as technical regulation and policies. Likewise, the fiscal, environmental, transactions, easement, gas procurement, hydrocarbon transport policies should be taken into account along with the Civil, Commercial, Criminal and Administrative Codes.

As background information for the hydrocarbons sector in Colombia, we can start with the creation of ECOPETROL (Colombian Oil Company) in 1951 which is responsible for the management of existing fields. Later, in 1953 the Petroleum Code was issued.[19] In this regulation the public utility of the activity[20] is acknowledged and highlighted, as is the identification of oil as private property, and the regulation of the exploration, exploitation, transportation, refinery and distribution activities of hydrocarbons and derived products. Some years later, Law 20 of 1969, which was later interpreted by Law 97 of 1993, stated that hydrocarbons are private property when they are linked to a field discovered no later than 22 December 1969. And finally, in 1974 ECOPETROL was made responsible for the administration of the hydrocarbon resources of the country through joint venture where activities of exploration and exploitation take place.

In terms of the evolution of the contractual framework, historically there have been four types of contract: concession contracts, joint ventures, agreements for technical assessments contracts and exploration and production (E&P) contracts. Regarding E&P contracts, the exploration period was between 6 and 9 years whereas the exploitation right was between 24 and 30 years. The contractor conducts the activities at its own cost and risk and must obtain the necessary permissions and licenses to explore the land of the subcontracted area to produce hydrocarbons that are State property.

The regulations relating to the transportation of hydrocarbons and the technical conditions are found in Resolution 72145 of 2014. In this resolution, the transportation activity is recognized as a public utility, and Resolution 72146 of 2014 makes a reference to the remuneration for this service. Its legal recognition is found in the Petroleum Code. Since 2001, the access to oil pipelines has been regulated.[21]

The distribution and marketing of fuels is also considered a public utility. The first regulation of these activities was in Decree 285 of 1986 in which the chain of distribution and marketing was established. The current regulation laid out in Decree 1073 of 2015 governs the activities involved in downstream activities.

According to the Colombian regulation, the activities of exploration, exploitation, refinery, transportation and distribution are public utilities.[22] This means that it is possible to

19 Decree 1056 of 1953 (20 April 1953), Oil Legal Code.

20 It is important to highlight that in Law 20 of 1969 private property for hydrocarbons is acknowledged but only for those who meet certain requirements.

21 Ministerio de Minas y Energía, Resolution 181258, 2010.

22 Decree 1056 of 1953. Op. cit. Article 4.

enforce expropriation and easement. The easements must be mentioned when discussing public utility because in relation to hydrocarbons they have the characteristics of being legal, not having a dominant and serviant estate and must have a monetary compensation. The legal recognition can be found in Law 1274 of 2009 where the procedures and formalities for valuation and the mechanisms for the attendance of easements are also stated.

It is important to note that regulations regarding natural gas are separated into the various stages of petroleum production, taking into account that it is largely ruled by the regulations in Law 142 of 1994. The supply of gas is established in Decree 2201 of 2003 which seeks to promote and guarantee the supply of natural gas.

Agreement 02 of 2017, issued by the Agencia Nacional de Hidrocarburos deserves special attention. With this instrument, the main topics related to the exploration and exploitation of hydrocarbons are developed. Topics included are: areas, the registration of interested parties, criteria for the selection of contractors, management, settlement, monitoring, exploratory programmes, area allocation, selection of contractors, assessment and proposal awarding, generating rock fields, environmental and social aspects, tracking, monitoring and follow-up and measures to mitigate the negative effects from a fall in international oil prices.[23] The main purpose of the agreement was to promote and maintain investment in exploration.

As regards the current context of shale oil and gas expansion, in Colombia the Ruling Number 18074 of 2012 was issued whereby the procedures to explore and exploit hydrocarbons and unconventional fields were established. Decree 3004 of 2013 expanded the unconventional hydrocarbons regulation further by setting criteria and procedures for exploration and exploitation activities and, finally, ordered the Ministry to issue the technical rules and procedures that are necessary, which were regulated in Resolution 90341-2014. However, in 2019 the Council of State suspended the technical regulations that were previously mentioned as it was considered that the measures needed to be adjusted to reflect the parameters of environmental care and the precaution principle but to allow the development of pilot projects based on the fracking technique.[24]

Regarding the gas sector, the main regulation is Law 142 of 1994. This law divides the productive gas chain into: (i) production; (ii) transportation; (iii) distribution; and (iv) commercialization areas. As with the electricity sector, there are restrictions on market participation in order to avoid a dominant position in the market.[25] There is also freedom of entry and exit from the market,[26] and open access,[27] and the fees are governed by remuneration principles.[28]

Gas production is done through an E&P) contract and the sales should be done in compliance with the regulation that governs commercialization issues established by the Commission for Energy and Gas Regulation (CREG), while the transport activity is complementary to the public domiciliary service of gas and is constituted as a natural monopoly.

23 Agencia Nacional de Hidrocarburos, 'La Agencia Nacional de Hidrocarburos – ANH socializa Acuerdo 02 de 2017', www.anh.gov.co/Sala-de-Prensa/Lists/Anuncios/Noticias.aspx?ID=266&ContentTypeId=0x01040072853B5EA34F2842806117375623237C.

24 Consejo De Estado, 'Consejo de Estado suspende normas que regulan el fracking', www.consejodeestado.gov.co/news/consejo-de-estado-suspende-normas-que-regulan-el-fracking. See also Chapter 18 in this book: 'Shale gas development in Mexico and Colombia; an uncertain future'.

25 Article 73 of Law 142 of 1994, establishing the regime for domicile public services and other provisions. *Official Gazette* No. 41.433 of 11 July 1994.

26 Ibid, Article 10.

27 Ibid, Article 73.

28 Ibid, Articles 87 and 88.

The wholesale market of natural gas comprises of the primary and secondary market where in the former the producers are the only participants and in the latter there are non-regulated users, which can participate as buyers.

2.4 Electricity sector

In general terms, the regulatory framework in Colombia for electricity is integrated in several legal instruments. Among these are, the Political Constitution, Law 142 of 1994, Law 143 of 1994, Decree number 1073 of 2015, Ministry Resolutions, the Committee for the Regulation of Energy and Gas resolutions, Andean Decision number 536 of 2002 and the recommendations of the OECD's Organización Latinoamericana de Energía (OLADE), without prejudice of the cross-sectional regulation such as environmental regulation. Law 143 of 1994[29] is a special law for the electricity sector and is paramount because it sets the regulatory framework. It mentions the responsibility of the government as head of the sector, the advocacy for free competition, the regulation of the natural monopoly (distribution and transmission), user protection, power coverage for different regions of the country.

The State is not solely responsible for providing electricity; nonetheless it is important to note that the State is the only body responsible for the regulation and auditing of it. The principles that rule and control the electrical energy market in Colombia are:[30] freedom of enterprise,[31] free competition,[32] competition between the wholesale market and the retail market[33] and a price system according to the structure of the mainstream market.[34] However, Law 142 lists two electricity regimes. On the one hand, the regime of freedom of activity where there is competition as in the case of generation and commercialization and, on the other hand, the regime of monopoly where there is no competition, as in the case of the natural monopolies of transmission and distribution.

As far as the electricity service is concerned, the basic legal principles defined by Law 143 of 1994[35] are: efficiency, quality, continuity, adaptability, neutrality, equity, solidarity and redistribution. The composition of the electricity matrix in Colombia is made up as follows: (i) water 69.18 per cent, (ii) bagasse (0.81 per cent), (iii) biogas (0.02 per cent), carbon (9.75 per cent), fuel oil (1.74 per cent), gas (9.61 per cent), jet-A1 (0.25 per cent), gas-jet A1 (1.49 per cent), solar rad (0.06 per cent), wind (0.10 per cent).

2.4.1 Types of systems (SIN-ZNI)

There are two kinds of electricity systems in Colombia. The National Interconnected System (Sistema Interconectado Nacional, SIN) and the Non-Interconnected Zones (ZNI). The Non-Interconnected Zones (ZNI) are characterized by several elements. First, they are made up[36] of the municipalities, localities or hamlets where the public service for electrical

29 Law 143 of 1994 establishing the regime for the generation, interconnection, transmission, distribution and commercialization of electricity in the national territory and granting authorizations in energy.

30 Luis Ferney Moreno Castillo, 'Los modelos de regulación de electricidad en América Latina y en particular el modelo de Colombia', in Luis Ferney Moreno Castillo and Victor Rafael Hernández Mendible (coord.) *Derecho de la Energía en América Latina* (Book I, Universidad Externado de Colombia, Bogotá, 2017) p. 715–742.

31 Article 333 Political Constitution of Colombia.

32 Law 142 1994, Article 2.

33 Law 143 1994, Article 11.

34 Law 142 1994, Articles 86 and 88 42 *Law* 143 1994.

35 Law 143 1994, Article 6.

36 Law 855 of 2003, Article 1.

energy is not provided through the SIN. Second, the generation of the ZNI is done mainly through diesel, solar panels and small hydroelectric plants.[37] Third, the ZNI coverage represents more than 50 per cent of the national territory, where this percentage comprises 12,000 localities of which 1,440 localities have energy services with an installed capacity of approximately 165 MW, which equates to 1.1 per cent of the total national installed capacity. Fourth, the provision of energy service varies according to the conditions of each locality. In some cases, the service is provided with no interruptions, in other cases the service is only available a few hours a day and in other cases there is no provision at all. The number of hours of provision on a daily basis depends on the type of locality, which is defined by the number of users provided with the service.[38]

The main difference between SIN and ZNI is that[39] in the SIN there is competition in both the wholesale market and the retail market whereas in the ZNI there is only one vertical integrated market.[40] The companies which provide this service of public energy to the ZNI can develop their joint activities of generation, distribution and commercialization.[41]

2.5 Renewable energy

The most relevant legal instrument to renewable energy is Law 1715 of 2014 where: (i) non-conventional energy sources are fostered, promoting energy efficiency and demand, (ii) the Ministry of Mines and Energy must develop a policy that encourages the use of non-conventional renewable sources (Fuentes no Convencionales de Energía Renovable (FNCER)); (iii) the Ministry authorizes the sales of surplus electricity for distributed generation; (iv) creates tax and fiscal incentives for non-conventional renewable sources of energy; (v) creates the fund to fostering non-conventional renewable energy source and efficiency Fondos de Energías No Convencionales y Gestión Eficiente de la Energía (FENOGE).

Since the ratification of Law 1715 of 2014, Colombia has developed a normative framework that applies to renewable sources of energy and energy efficiency, through legislation like Decree 0570 of 2018 in which the Ministry of Mines and Energy called for bidding for contracts in order to promote diversification of the energy matrix, reduction of CO_2 emissions and the fostering of renewable sources of energy and Resolution 40009 (4 January 2019) in which the Ministry of Mines and Energy provides annual energy in the long term for generation projects in the wholesale market.

Finally, it is important to mention Law 1931 of 27 July 2018, known as the Climate Change Law, which is the law that establishes the guidelines to deal with climate change in the decisions of any private or public persons, nation, departments, districts, metropolitan areas and environmental authorities. This law also mentions the reduction of greenhouse gases.[42]

37 Commission for the regulation of Energy and Gas 'CREG- *Zonas No Interconectadas*', www.creg.gov.co/index.php/es/sectores/energia/zni-energia.

38 Commission for the Regulation of Energy and Gas (CREG), 'Propuesta para remunerar la generación, distribución y comercialización de Energía Eléctrica en las ZNI' (2014), https://creg.gov.co/sites/default/files/propuesta_para_remunerar_la_generacion_distribucion_y_comercializacion_de_energia_electrica_en_las_zni.pdf (accessed 6 January 2018).

39 Moreno Castillo (n. 30).

40 Law 633 of 2000, Article 81.

41 Law 143 of 1994, Article74.

42 Law 1931 of 2018, establishing a framework for climate change management.

2.5.1 Renewable energy projects

In 2018 the number of potential projects to generate renewable energy reached a total of 400: 11 biomass projects, 20 wind projects, 92 hydraulic projects, 322 solar projects and 4 thermic projects.[43]

Currently there are a number of projects being developed using renewables in new methods to generate electricity. An example of this is in the Guajira department where four projects solar and wind projects are being analyzed by the authorities like the Ministry of Mines and Energy. Referring to projects like these the Colombian President, Ivan Duque said:

> (t)he national strategy for use of large scale non conventional energy sources will make the country pass from 50MW of installed capacity (similar to the consumption of energy in a city like Ibague) to 1.5000MW (equivalent to the consumption of a city like Medellin and Cali combined together during the year) this or the year 2022.[44]

Another project underway is Hidroituango, the biggest hydro project currently being developed in Colombia. Its generation capacity is 2,400 MW which represents 17 per cent of the electrical energy demand in the country.[45]

The importance of renewable energy in Columbia and the commitment of the government to the transition and diversification of the energy matrix is clear:

> Currently, the Colombian electrical system has 16.8 GW of power generation connected to the Colombian power system, from which 66 % are hydraulic, 28 % thermal and approximately 6 % from smaller plants. Nevertheless, it is expected that by 2023 the Colombian electrical system presents important changes in its energy matrix, integrating at least 1.7 GW of solar PV and wind plants that currently have a connection concept from UPME. According to information from UPME, in the future, these numbers are expected to increase significantly, as requests for connection of approximately 10 GW of solar and wind plants have been reported ...[46]

2.6 Authorities of the energy sector

The Ministry of Mines and Energy is in charge of formulating, adopting and implementing the public policy for the management of the mining and energy sector.[47] With regard to energy the Ministry is specifically responsible for the following aspects:

1. the generation, transmission, distribution and commercialization of energy and the issuance of technical regulations
2. the rational use of energy policy, developing alternative sources of energy and ensuring the development of programmes and adopting plans to expand the supply of electricity

43 Unidad de Planeación Minero Energética (UPME).

44 Ministry of Mines and Energy (2018), 'La Guajira, potencia de energías renovables no convencionales en Colombia', https://www.minminas.gov.co/historico-de-noticias?idNoticia=24048509.

45 Hidroeléctrica Ituango (2019), https://www.hidroituango.com.co/proyectos/proyecto-hidroelectrico-ituango/38.

46 XM, Colombia Renewable Integration, https://www.xm.com.co/Renovables/Paginas/Colombia-renewable-integration.aspx.

47 Article 2 of Decree 0381 of 16 February 2012.

3. managing the financial support fund to supply energy to the non-interconnected areas and the rural interconnected areas.

In the case of hydrocarbons the Ministry is responsible for the following aspects

1. the policy for exploration, exploitation, transportation, refinery, processing, benefit, transformation and distribution of hydrocarbons and biofuels and their regulation
2. the regulation of the transport of crude through oil pipelines
3. auditing the exploration and exploitation of the deposits
4. defining the prices and fees of the oil, diesel (ACPM) biofuels
5. checking the plan to expand the polyducts
6. controlling and auditing the activities related with upstream activity.[48]

The Ministry of the Environment and Sustainable Development, the National Authority of Environmental Licensing and the Autonomous Regional Corporations are in charge of the environmental public policy, environmental licensing and the environmental control and monitoring of hydropower and hydrocarbon projects (ANLA–CARS [Autoridad Nacional de Licencias Ambientales—Corporaciones Autónomas Regionales]). The competent authority depends on the characteristics of the project.[49]

The National Agency of Hydrocarbons is in charge of the comprehensive management of the reserves of potential hydrocarbon of the nation. Furthermore, it also has the general functions of: identifying and assessing the hydrocarbon potential in the country, helping the Mining Ministry in the formulation of the public policy; designing, fostering, negotiating, holding and managing the contracts and agreements of exploration and exploitation; and fixing the prices of hydrocarbons for the liquidation of royalties, among other functions.[50]

CREG was created to regulate the technical activities in the electricity supply chain (generation, transmission, distribution and commercialization).[51] It also responsible for developing a regulatory framework that encourages investment in expanding the generation and transmission capacity of the interconnected system.[52] Later it was entrusted with the power to issue the economic regulation for the liquid fuel derived from hydrocarbons chain,[53] as well as the transportation price per product.[54]

CREG also has certain control powers in accordance with Law 142 of 1994: the division of a public services company,[55] the merger of a company[56] and the liquidation of a company with a monopoly.[57]

48 President of Colombia. 'Decree 0381 of 2012 modifies the structure of the ministry of mines and energy', Article 12.
49 Law 99 of 1993, which created the Ministry of the Environment, reorganized the public sector in charge of the management and preservation of the environment and renewable resources, organizing the National System of Environment SINA and established other determinations.
50 Decree Law 4137 of 2011 (3 November 2011) changed the legal nature of the National Agency of Hydrocarbons, ANH.
51 Law 142 of 1994.
52 Ibid, Article 18.
53 Decree 1260 of 2013, which modified the structure of the Commission for Energy and Gas Regulation CREG Article 1.
54 Decree 4130 of 2011, which reassigned some functions.
55 Article 73.13, Law 142-1994.
56 Ibid, Article 73.14.
57 Ibíd, Article 73.15.

Furthermore, CREG is the authority that specializes in gas regulation in its different phases, such as transport and commercialization, in order to ensure an adequate infrastructure, continuity in the service provision and sufficient competitiveness.

3 Brazil

Brazil is the region's main economy and it has particular characteristics that make it different from the other countries such as its vast territorial extension, the agricultural relevance and the size of tits energy infrastructure. Given its qualities, Brazil has a common baseline with developed countries. That said, it must be mentioned that Brazil as a country has suffered from an increase in pollution from gas emissions In 2016 it recorded 2,278 gross tons of carbon dioxide, an 8.9 per cent increase from 2015.[58] In 2012, the energy sector was responsible for 26 per cent of the gas emissions, while forestry al/land utilization absorbed 44 per cent of the emissions. Whereas in 2018 electricity generation was responsible for 12.9 per cent of gas emissions and the transport sector for 46.5 per cent. However, despite the emissions, the country's energy matrix is clean, as its generation source is 79 per cent renewable, 18 per cent conventional and 3 per cent nuclear.[59] The electricity market is highly decentralized,[60] with 778 power producers, 122 transmission companies and 46 distributors. Brazil is one the countries with the greatest hydrocarbon potential, it is the third largest oil producing country (2,734, barrels per day), after the United States (13,057 barrels per day) and Canada (4,831 barrels per day). On the other hand, the proven oil reserves estimated for 2017 in Brazil correspond to 12,999,999,488 barrels, in comparison Colombia has 2,002,000,000 barrrels per.[61] With regard to oil, it is important to highlight the rise in exports with an increase of about free on board (FOB) 6,551,200 thousands of US dollars.[62]

3.1 Constitutional framework

Article 20 of the Brazilian Constitution states that the mineral resources belong to the Union and the research, exploration, refinement, importation, exportation and maritime transport activities are considered to be a State monopoly.[63] With Amendment No. 9 of 1995, the State is allowed to hire third parties (public or private companies) to carry out activities that are considered to be monopolies, and PETROBAS has an exclusive monopoly.[64]

The Constitution regulates several aspects of the electricity industry. For instance, hydropower generation potential is public property belonging to the nation, and the Federation operates the electricity services and energy installations through a concession, permission or authorization.

58 Agencia Efe. 'Emisiones de gases contaminantes de Brasil en 2016 fueron mayores en 9 años' (25 October 2017), https://www.efe.com/efe/america/sociedad/emisiones-de-gases-contaminantes-brasil-en-2016-fueron-mayores-9-anos/20000013-3419226.

59 Latin-American Energy Organization. 'OLADE, Energy Outlook for Latin America and the Caribbean' (2019), http://biblioteca.olade.org/opac-tmpl/Documentos/old0416b.pdf.

60 Mattos Filho, Veiga, Marrey Jr. and Quiroga Advogados. *Brazil,* in Daniel Hagan (ed.), *Electricity Regulation* (Getting the Deal Through, 2015), p. 20–25.

61 Ibid.

62 Ibid.

63 Article 177, Political Constitution 1988.

64 Margarita Teresa Nieves Zarate, 'Aperturas del sector petrolero. Los casos de Noruega, Brasil y Colombia' in María del Pilar Rodriguez Ibáñez et. al. (eds.), *Regulación de servicios públicos y energía, lecturas selectas* (Porrúa, 2016), p. 173–195.

3.2 Legal framework

3.2.1 Hydrocarbons

By constitutional mandate, the ownership of resources that exist in the subsoil belongs to the Federal Union.[65] The supply of fuels is a public utility service.[66] Law 9.478 of 1997 sets the national energy policy and the hiring of third parties is regulated in the same way as the concession regime for the exploitation and production of oil and gas. Moreover, Law 9.478 of 1997 establishes that in the case of hydrocarbons, the Federal Union reserves the monopoly of the following activities: the investigation and exploration of oil, natural gas, hydrocarbon and fluid reserves, the refining of domestic or foreign oil, the importation and exportation of the products derived from the aforementioned activities and marine transport of crude oil of national origin or oil derivatives, including transport via pipelines.[67]

In 2009, Law 11.909 was issued, known as the Gas Law, as it regulates the exploitation, development, production, import, export, processing, treatment, transport, loading, storage, conditioning, liquefaction, regasification, distribution and commercialization of gas, as well as the related to liquified natural gas (LNG). Subsequently, a regulatory framework has been issued related to the pre-salt areas, Law 12.351 concerning the production sharing regime and Law 12.276 that makes reference to the conveyance of consideration.[68] From the aforementioned it can be concluded that Brazil has different legal regimes that apply according to the deposit's location or its strategical character, and they are divided in the following way:[69] in a concession regime the oil company is responsible for the research and evaluation activities of the area at its own risk. In this regime, the production belongs to the concessionaire, but must pay for government participation according to the contract. It precedes bidding in accordance with the legal provisions and is celebrated between the ANP and the winner of the tender, PETROBRAS participates in conditions of equality. Law 9.478/1997 regulates the concession regime for oil and gas production.

In pre-salt areas a production distribution regime applies. Here, the evaluation activities are carried out at the oil company's own expense and risk, but if oil is discovered, the production is divided between the contractor and the Union. Compensation is paid for the initial costs and risks and the profit is divided proportionally between the contractor and the Union.

3.2.2 Electricity

While there is no definitive list of the principles applicable to the energy sector in Brazil's legal system, it is possible to identify the constitutional principles of protection of free

65 In the case of gas, it is argued within the doctrine that the contract concession for this type of resource is on the public good and not on the activity.

66 Gilberto Bervovici, 'Petróleo y soberania energética en Brasil', in Luis Ferney Moreno Castillo and Victor Rafael Hernández Mendible (coord.), *'Derecho de la Energía en América Latina'* (Book I, Universidad Externado de Colombia, Bogotá, 2017), p. 629–659.

67 Vitor Rhein Schirato, 'El régimen de la industria del Gas Natural en Brasil', in Luis Ferney Moreno Castillo and Victor Rafael Hernández Mendible (coord.), *Derecho de la Energía en América Latina* (Book I, Universidad Externado de Colombia, Bogotá, 2017), p. 661–710.

68 Floriano de Azevedo Marques Neto and Marina Fontao Zago, 'El marco regulatorio del petróleo y el gas en Brasil', in Luis Ferney Moreno Castillo and Victor Rafael Hernández Mendible (coord.), *Derecho de la Energía en América Latina* (Book I, Universidad Externado de Colombia, Bogotá, 2017).

69 Ibid.

competition, defence of the consumer, national development and protection of the environment,[70] regularity of public utilities, efficiency, security, timeliness and relevance, general availability, courteous presentation, consumer protection, system security and supply security.[71]

In constitutional and historical terms, from the Charter of 1934 to the Federal Constitution of Brazil of 1988, three main topics are identifiable.[72] The first one is the ownership of goods. The potentials of hydraulic hydroelectric energy are public goods and their owner is the Federal Union, therefore they may not be utilized by any private individual without an enabling title. It is important to warn that according to the specialized doctrine,[73] those goods with potential for hydroelectric generation of energy are not public goods by their very nature but because of their potential to generate electricity. Another important consideration is legislative power which belongs exclusively to the Federal Union. A third aspect jurisdiction, e all the activities of the energy sector are part of the Union's jurisdiction and may be developed directly or via a third party by means of a concession, a permit or an authorization.[74]

In Brazil there is no one general law relating to the electricity market, instead there are different legal provisions that regulate the matter. Federal Law 9.074 of 1995 is the main regulation for the sector. From this law and from the general legal framework it is possible to identify the following activities[75] concerning generation, transmission, distribution and commercialization: this is subject to the legal regime for public utilities. There are two special cases, one of them being generation of hydroelectric power destined for the provision of public utilities and the other being independent generation of electric power. The enabling title for the pursuit of this activity will depend on the source of generation. Another special case is generation of electric power in amounts under 3,000 KW. In this case, the authorization of the Federal Union is not necessary, only a registration with the competent authorities.

Transmission is an activity that belongs to the public utility's regime, meaning that it can only be performed by means of a public utility concession granted by the Federal Union. Under Law 9.648, the operational control of electricity generation and transmission within the SIN will be performed by the National Operator of the Electric System (ONS).[76] In terms of commercialization, the marketeer, by long-term contract or market spot, is the one responsible for the purchase, importation, exportation and sale of electric energy from/to other marketeers or consumers. Marketing is not subject to the public service regime, therefore, authorization is required to carry it out. Finally, distribution belongs to the public utility regime. Authorization must be requested. In the case of thermoelectric power, the bidding process is not necessary only an administrative granting process. Part of the supply of

70 Principles applicable to concessions, Law 8.987 of 1995.

71 Vitor Rhein Schirato, 'A regulação do sector eléctrico brasileiro', in Milton Fernando Montoya Pardo (ed.), *Trends and Challenges in Electricity and Oil Regulation* (12 Colección de Regulación Minera y Energética, Universidad Externado de Colombia, 2017), p. 131–166.

72 Floriano de Azevedo Marques Neto, 'Bens públicos: função social e exploração econômica. O regime jurídico utilidades públicas' (Belo Horizonte Forúm, 2009), p. 157 e ss.

73 Ibid.

74 Article 21 of the Constitution, subparagraph XII, Section B, a material jurisdiction of the Federal Union.

75 Rhein Schirato (n. 71).

76 André Saddy, 'Regulación del sector eléctrico brasileño', in Luis Ferney Moreno Castillo and Victor Rafael Hernández Mendible (coord.), *Derecho de la Energía en América Latina* (Book I, Universidad Externado de Colombia, Bogotá, 2017), p. 575–602.

energy to the final user is completed in this phase. There are different kinds of user according to the purpose and quantity of the usage.[77]

In the Brazilian electricity sector, three different political and legislative frameworks converge: (i) public utility laws; (ii) public goods exploitation laws; and (iii) private economic activity laws. As in most countries, the electricity sector in Brazil comprises two markets. On the one hand, there is the wholesale market comprised of the generators and concession owners of electric power distribution and the independent generators retailers and consumers of electric power. In this market there are different levels of competence (regulated contracting/independent contracting). On the other hand, the retail market mainly comprises distribution and retailing. It is strictly regulated, with prices based on tariffs, and there is no possibility of competition.

3.2.3 Renewable energy

Concerning renewable energy, there is huge potential for renewable energy in Brazil and big projects to exploit it.[78] In the context of the Paris Agreement,[79] Federal Decree No. 9.073 of 2017 was implemented. As a result, the promotion of programmes, funding and credit lines with the objective of implementing renewable energy is expected. In 2002, the government created a program intended to incentivize the use of renewable energy (PROINFA) by means of the implementation of small hydroelectric power stations and eolic and biomass power plants. The marketing of energy projects is secured by long-term purchase agreements of energy. In the same way, in 2015 Law 13.203 established that biomass, eolic and solar power plants will also receive a discount on fees as long as their capacity is below 300 MW.

3.3 Competent authorities for the energy sector

The Ministry of Mines and Energy is the authority in charge of planning and formulating public policies and advises the presidency on the formulation of public policies as well as coordinating with the different authorities.

The National Council for Energy Policies (CNPE) is the authority in charge of proposing national energy policies. It is responsible for fostering the rational use of energy resources, taking into account energy grids. It is also responsible for authorizing the National Agency for Petroleum to offer blocks under the concession and production sharing regime.[80] The National Agency for Petroleum (ANP) is the entity which has the jurisdiction to regulate, hire and inspect the activities that integrate the industry of oil, gas and their derivatives. The Brazilian Institute of the Environment and Natural Resources is the entity in charge of environmental regulation regarding *upstream offshore* activities. For activities on land, other local authorities have the jurisdiction of regulating *upstream* activities.[81]

The National Agency of Electric Power (ANEEL) is in charge of the regulation of the electricity sector. ANEEL is an independent entity created by Law 9.427 of 1996 entrusted

77 Ibid.

78 Private Participation in Renewable Energy Database. Brazil, http://ppi-re.worldbank.org/snapshots/country/brazil.

79 Paris Agreement, 12 December 2015.

80 Giovani Loss, Felipe Rodrigues Caldas Feres Felipe, and Mattos Nilton, 'Brazil', in Christopher B. Strong (ed.), *The Oil and Gas Law Review* (Third Edition, Law Business Research Ltd, 2015), p. 1–12.

81 Ibid.

with the task of regulating the Brazilian energy sector and ensuring it performs well, maintaining equilibrium in all parts of the sector. As such, its jurisdiction includes carrying out duties that deal with user protection and conflict resolution. It has ample regulatory power, arbitration competency and can define the granting of auctions for the generation of electricity.[82] The Chamber of Electric Power Commercialization (CCEE) is a private law entity whose main objective is the control and oversight of power generation, transfer and marketing activities, as well as recording all the agreements for the provision of energy in accordance with the guidelines of the Ministry of Mines and Energy.[83] Additionally, the National System Operator (ONS) is an entity composed of public and private agents in charge of coordinating the purchase and sale of power in the national market, financial settlements, or determining the debt and credit conditions between agents, and the general safety and functionality of the Brazilian energy system. The Committee for Monitoring of the Energy Sector (CMSE) is in charge of evaluating the conditions of energy supply and proposing corrective and preventive measures to guarantee the satisfaction of demand.[84]

4 Conclusion

The ownership of resources is key in several countries in Latin America as is the case for Colombia and Brazil. This means that the system depends on the legal framework for its use and that in accordance with this, the States regulate and establish the requirements for access, operating licenses and developing conditions for energy activity. It is important to mention that the regulation of the energy sector is changing and evolving according to the needs of the time and the vision for the sector. At the beginning of its existence the government had a dominant role in the sector and this has slowly been changing as markets are being opened up to liberalization and competition.

In any given case, even with the participation of private companies in the sector, the States still have the power to regulate, survey and control those parties who are exploiting their resources through different government entities.

Finally, it is important to highlight three topics that are current in the existing agenda. First, energy self-sufficiency; Colombia and Brazil, and other countries in the region, are looking for alternatives to guarantee energy security and avoid dependence. Second, there is a trend towards the diversification of the energy matrix and the incorporation of renewable energy, with a series of regulatory conditions as benefits and legal liabilities to integrate this type of alternative sources within the parameters of climate change. This is part of the global energy transition and de-carbonization. However, there is still concern over the storage, the technologies, the costs and the reliability of the supply of electricity. Lastly, the relationship between communities and the social licensee is a core object, phenomena such as social responsibility, community rejection of the projects, human rights and extractive industry have generated change within the sector.

82 Ibid.

83 Law 10.848 of 2004.

84 Mattos Filho, Veiga, Marrey Jr. and Quiroga Advogados (n. 60).

PART VI

Asia and Australia

23

ASIAN ENERGY MARKETS

The impact of shifting global politics

Slawomir Raszewski

1 Introduction

Energy has been one of the key defining features of the Asia Pacific due to the regional nature of the markets, the environment and the complex interplay of geopolitics and geoeconomics.[1] The Asia Pacific emerged as a region over half a century ago primarily due to the strategic considerations of the United States and its allies. The emergence of the construct allowed Australia to reposition itself in the world of trade and reach out to Asia and, effectively, become part of what later became the world's fastest growing economic region.

Since 2010 the Asia Pacific region has been transformed largely due to China being an economic powerhouse but also other nations' economies, in particular Japan and South Korea. Trade within the region has blossomed, transforming Australia's regional role within the Asia Pacific as largely a raw materials and energy commodity exporter. Coal and natural gas have been two key commodities traded with Asia Pacific enhancing the economic welfare of Australia while, at the same time, ensuring secure supplies to the Asian markets. Australia has benefited both directly and indirectly from the renewed trade in energy, as well as non-energy (primarily finance and education) sectors. Shifting global politics – including the international political economy of energy in and outside of Asia Pacific – are relevant not only for the region itself but the entire world economy due to energy demand and supply the region generates. With the environment and geopolitics playing an ever-greater role, trade in liquified natural gas (LNG) has become an important phenomenon which, simultaneously, strengthens the fuel's global outlook. Energy supply security concerns, uncertainty concerning the organisation of environmental protection in the aftermath of the Paris Agreement and the rise of geoeconomics – led by state capitalist enterprise –have all changed the way markets in Asia operate. It is more relevant than ever for Australia to engage in a carefully crafted energy policy to allow it to continue the extent of its regional trade engagements within the region in the foreseeable future.

1 While there is no single definition, geoeconomics is widely understood as a state-led advancement of geopolitical and strategic objectives by means of economic tools. Geoeconomics as an academic concept was first laid out by Luttwak (1990). For a recent, critical overview of the concept please see Scholvin and Wiggel (2018).

2 Asia Pacific – energy and the environment

'Asia Pacific' emerged as a concept in the 1960s and 1970s 'promoted by countries such as the United States, Japan and Australia as a means of linking East Asia to the wider Pacific region' (McDougall 2016: 6). The Asia Pacific concept expanded geographical domain – beyond what otherwise would normally be known as East Asia – offering the United States legitimisation over its involvement in the political and international affairs of East Asia and its nations. This was despite the former not being an Asian power *per se* but having extensive international trade and security interests in the region. The expanded construct of Asia Pacific allows countries such as Australia as well as Canada and New Zealand to be actively engaged politically and economically in the region without the strategic, security weight ascribed to the United States (McDougall 2016: 6). While not being directly involved in 'hard' politics, in particular international security, Australia does play a significant role in 'soft' politics in the region in areas such as the trade and energy markets.

Energy has been one of the key defining features of the Asia Pacific due to the regional nature of the market, environment concerns, as well as geopolitical and geoeconomic considerations. Energy markets have been fundamentally transformed due to the region's demand for energy. From the market perspective, the China-led Asia Pacific has become a global manufacturing powerhouse (McKay and Song 2010) taking both the world's energy demand and carbon emissions to new, unprecedented levels. Asia Pacific's spectacular economic growth and rapidly growing energy demand driven by the region's developing economies – particularly China and India – have transformed energy markets globally due to their 'sheer size and pace of growth' (Vivoda 2010: 5258).

As shown in Figure 23.1, Asia Pacific is the global heavyweight in energy consumption. In 2018, Asia Pacific's primary energy consumption accounted for 42.5 percent – or

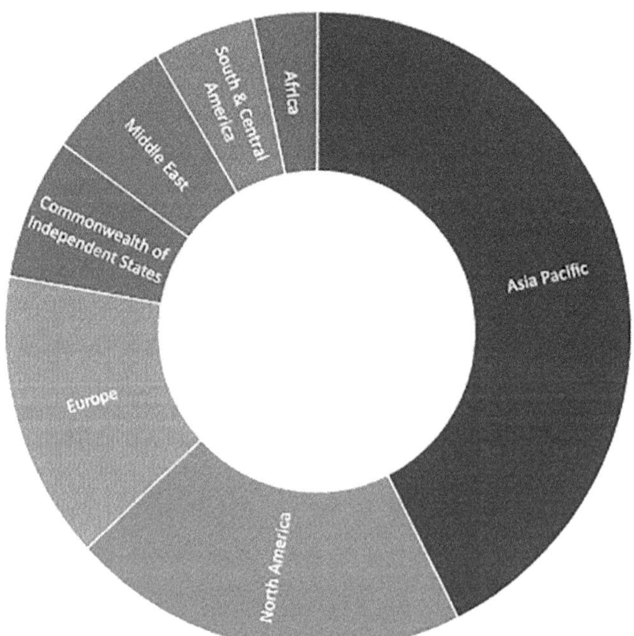

Figure 23.1 World primary energy consumption by region

Source: Author's own compilation using data from BP 2018.

Table 23.1 Asia Pacific primary energy consumption

Asia to Asia Pacific – Primary Energy Consumption						*Growth rate per annum*		*Share of total*
Million tonnes oil equivalent	*2013*	*2014*	*2015*	*2016*	*2017*	*2017*	*2006–2016*	*2017*
Australia	132.9	135.1	138	139.5	139.4	0.2%	1.1%	10%
Bangladesh	25.5	26.8	31.1	31.9	33	3.6%	6.5%	0.2%
China	2907	2973.5	3009.8	3047.2	3132.2	3.1%	4.4%	23.2%
China Hong Kong SAR	28	27.3	28.1	28.8	30.9	7.4%	1.6%	0.2%
India	623.6	666.8	686.9	722.3	753.7	4.6%	5.7%	5.6%
Indonesia	177.6	166	165.4	167.4	175.2	5.0%	2.9%	1.3%
Japan	471.3	456.7	453	451.2	456.4	1.4%	–1.6%	3.4%
Malaysia	93.1	93.9	95.1	97.6	99.6	2.4%	2.9%	0.7%
New Zealand	20.2	21.1	21.3	21.7	22.1	2.2%	1.2%	0.2%
Pakistan	64.8	66.7	70.2	76.5	80.9	6.1%	2.8%	0.6%
Philippines	33.1	34.9	38.3	40.6	43.3	6.9%	4.6%	0.3%
Singapore	73.6	75.8	80.6	83.6	86.5	3.7%	4.9%	0.6%
South Korea	276.7	279.3	284.9	292.2	295.9	1.6%	2.5%	2.2%
Sri Lanka	6.1	6.4	7. 4	7.4	7.7	4.8%	3.3%	0.1%
Taiwan	111.9	114.4	112.9	114	115.1	1.3%	0.6%	0.9%
Thailand	118.7	122.1	124.9	126.9	129.7	2.5%	3.6%	10%
Vietnam	57.2	62.7	68.8	73.6	75.3	2.7%	10.0%	0.6%
Other Asia Pacific	48.6	53.3	55.5	63.1	66.5	5.8%	3.4%	0.5%
Total Asia Pacific	5269.9	5382.9	5472.4	5585.5	5743.6	3.1%	3.5%	42.5%

Source: Author's own compilation using data from BP 2018.

5743.6 million tonnes of oil equivalent (mtoe) – of the world's total consumption. This makes the region the most important demand centre (BP 2018).[2] China, which is not just Asia Pacific's but also the world's single biggest consumer of energy, accounted for over 23 percent of global demand – or 3132.2 mtoe – in 2018. This was following strong year on year and aggregate demand growth since 2013 (Table 23.1). India is the region's second biggest consumer of energy with the country's energy demand still accounting for roughly four times less than that of China. In 2018, India's share of the world's primary energy consumption equalled 5.6 percent. India's primary energy demand growth rate has been consistently high since 2013 as demonstrated in Table 23.1. Japan and South Korea are two demand centres within the Asia Pacific accounting for a combined 5.6 percent share of the world's primary energy consumption. Of the countries listed in Table 23.1, Japan was the only country to witness negative compounded annual growth of primary energy demand since 2013, which can be ascribed to Japan's emphasis on energy conservation and efficiency measures, particularly following the Fukushima plant disaster. Because of its very limited energy resources domestically which since 2012 following the disaster have met only 10 percent of the country's overall demand – Japan has pursued domestic energy efficiency measures aimed at enhancing the country's energy security while, at the same time, addressing reduction of carbon dioxide emissions (U.S. Energy Information Agency 2017).

2 With the United States included Asia Pacific's energy consumption is nearly 60 percent of the world's total.

Asia Pacific's energy mix is comprised of all the major types of energy: coal, oil, natural gas, hydroelectricity, nuclear energy and renewables. Asia Pacific's spectacular economic growth since the millennium has produced large energy demand which has been met by a rapidly growing supply of coal. The 'Renaissance' of coal in Asia Pacific's developing economies has been a growing environmental concern, largely driven by low prices when compared to oil or natural gas (Steckel, Edenhofer and Jakob 2015). Consumption of coal is Asia Pacific's key feature as it accounts for nearly half of the regional energy mix at the time of writing this chapter. By comparison oil is the second most consumed source of energy in the region accounting for almost a third of all fuel types consumed, followed by natural gas which constitutes roughly a tenth of all energy consumption within Asia Pacific. Asian economies have a long-standing coal trade with Australia, which for some of the Asian nations dates back to the early 1970s. Australian coal exports have been an essential source of steady income and demand security over the decades. Between 1970 and 2010, over 80 percent of Australia's coal was exported to Asia, primarily to Japan, South Korea and Taiwan with only a marginal 2 percent of all those historical exports having been exported to China. Large exports of Australia's coal to China only began in 2008, with a spectacular twenty-fold demand growth between 2008 and 2012 (Lucas 2016: 56). In 2018, China accounted for nearly half of the global coal consumption putting pressure on carbon emissions. In a short-term perspective, Australia's coal exports to China constitute an important part of its commodity exports worth US$43.3 billion in 2017 alone (World Bank 2017).

Asia Pacific's second largest energy consumer, India, has increased its coal consumption and its coal imports – as a measure to offset dwindling production of coal domestically – and countries such as Vietnam, Philippines, Malaysia and Pakistan are forecasted, according to International Energy Agency (IEA) data, to increase their use of coal in the coming years (International Energy Agency 2018a). As for the supply side, Australia is set to remain the largest exporter of coal through to 2022 (International Energy Agency 2017: 5).

3 The environment

Affordability and availability have been the main drivers of coal consumption in Asia Pacific. Yet, the lack of balance between the economic and the environmental dimensions has led to a policy shift in the region's largest polluter. In 2013, China initiated a set of policy measures (Feng and Liao 2016) to tackle air pollution in the country including the introduction of bans on new coal-burning capacity (Parker 2018). The success of China's clean air policy may affect future imports of coal (Woodhouse 2019). The changing environmental and climate objectives of the key consumer of coal mean that Australia's coal export dependence on China is one of the areas of the two countries' mutual trade which may change in the near future. The reason for such a change is attributed to China rapidly changing policies, promoting switches from coal to natural gas to tackle air pollution (Matsumoto 2019). Tackling air pollution in China and the coal-to-gas switches as a result of the policy is an unprecedented development which may have a negative effect on coal imports. At the same time the switches are likely to promote imports of natural gas moving forward, a development which China's state-owned enterprises and investments funds have been painstakingly addressing through upstream investments and stakes.[3] It is forecast that demand in Asia for LNG is likely

3 A recent example includes investments in the Russian LNG projects in the Arctic. China's oil and gas companies have consistently invested in upstream developments internationally to ensure energy supply security due to limited energy resources of their own (see: Bambawale and Sovacool 2011).

to double by 2025 due to China's clean air policy. Indeed, China increased imports of LNG by 45 percent in 2017 (Chamorro 2018). Investments in Russia's Arctic LNG 1 and 2 projects to secure imports of gas demonstrate the trend, while opening up new transport routes may serve as evidence of consistency in China's LNG policy (Maritime Executive 2017). Importantly, the LNG and natural gas imports are part of the Chinese environmental strategy. Having started imports of LNG in 2007, six years later in 2013 China imported around 15 percent of its natural gas needs through LNG from more than 11 countries (Vivoda 2017). China has witnessed a dramatic increase of built LNG receiving capacity which is expected to reach around 70 mtpa in 2020 (Miyamoto and Ishiguro 2018: 31). As of 2019 the country's 21 LNG receiving terminals, which have been built by state major companies, China National Offshore Oil Corporation (CNOOC), China National Petroleum Corporation (CNPC) and China Petroleum & Chemical Corporation (SINOPEC) – with the exception of a few terminals run by private companies such as Energy Holding Limited (ENN) – are expected to boost imports of LNG into China (Aizhu and Jaganathan 2019). LNG imports into China have grown year on year and high utilisation of existing LNG capacity – which in 2017 stood at a total of 77.2 percent for all of the country's regions (Miyamoto and Ishiguro 2018: 32) – has driven the demand. The dramatic increase in the existing LNG capacity coupled with strong import demand owing to the Chinese government's supportive policies mean that China is forecast to overtake Japan as the world's largest LNG importer in the early-to-mid-2020s (Yun Fan and Moore 2019). In addition to the large-scale LNG import capacity led by state-owned oil and gas companies, implementation of China's clean air policy also includes investments in new engineering solutions along with energy efficiency measures, increasing renewable energy and the introduction of stricter pollution control mechanisms (World Bank 2018).

Australia's approach to energy has been one of a free market rather than geoeconomics. Conceptually, free market and geoeconomics are ascribed to, respectively, liberal and realist thinking of international relations. Broadly speaking, for free marketers betterment of economic exchange is the mean for market development (economic objective). For geoeconomic state-actors the market is the mean to gain more power (strategic objective). Empirically, free market and geoeconomics may rely on specific set of tools deployed to ensure distinct outcomes with comparably alternate means to an end. Examples may include but are not limited to: (1) excessive state ownership – characterised by absence of (or inadequate) separation between constitutive management aspects of an enterprise resulting in the state's ability to exercise wide powers in determining the objectives of the enterprise – undermining or replacing the free market's supply and demand logic; (2) reliance on geographical factors as a geopolitical leverage in the development of international trade – political considerations rather than economics play a greater role in the allocation of finance and are aimed at serving relative power ('greatness') – rather than the economy *per se* – of the given nation as the strategic objective.

Belief in free markets and private firms being responsible for serving the interests of the country while delivering the 'right' price as a result of a balance between supply and demand have been the dominant feature of Australia's energy policy or, indeed, absence of thereof. In contrast, China has focused on state-ownership and geoeconomics where the economic tools are used to serve the enterprise of strategic importance. Australia, on the other hand, does not have a national oil company despite being endowed with large reserves of strategically important energy and natural resources. Instead, the country's energy is exploited by international oil companies which often exert a lot of power in the political process (Hancock and Vivoda 2014). At the other end of spectrum, the key importer in Asia Pacific, China, relies almost entirely on its national oil companies to guarantee energy supply security with a heavy state role in ensuring control over energy markets. The planned nature of the Chinese economy may appear to be delivering tangible results, however it depends heavily on direct and indirect subsidisation, particularly in the energy sector (Lin and Jiang 2011). Principally, heavily subsidised economic development goes against the free market objectives as it places the state through its constitutive executive branches – including 'strategic' enterprise that the energy/oil and gas sectors are part of – at the forefront of such an (geo)economic development strategy. In essence, geoeconomics is China's response to geopolitical projects where the state through its state-owned enterprises is the ultimate guarantor of supply security, negotiations and finance.

4 Asia Pacific's consumption, production and reserves of natural gas

Consumption of natural gas in Asia Pacific is the second largest in the world after North America. China, Japan and South Korea are the three top consumers of natural gas in Asia Pacific. China has increased its consumption of natural gas over the last decade or so at an impressive 13.7 percent (see Table 23.2). The rate of annual growth of China's natural gas consumption – with a year-on-year increase of 15.1 percent in 2017 alone – is attributed to increased imports and, simultaneously, the importance of natural gas in the country's energy mix. In addition to China, Taiwan, India and Pakistan have all witnessed high rates of annual growth of gas consumption evidencing an upward trend for the region. Asian LNG demand is growing driven by the above-explained China's coal-to-gas switch policy (Wood Mackenzie 2018).

The Asia Pacific region is ranked third after the Middle East and the Commonwealth of Independent States (CIS) regions when it comes to the global share of its natural gas reserves, which in 2018 was estimated at 19.3 trillion cubic metres (tcm) or 10 percent of the world's proved gas reserves (BP 2018). While the reserves do not automatically translate to readily available resources that can be economically produced, the regional production is, indeed, extensive and expanding rapidly. Asia Pacific ranks fourth in terms of natural gas production – after North America, the CIS and the Middle East regions – with a global share of 16.5 percent of total gas production (BP 2018). While being a net importer of energy, China ranks as the largest producer of natural gas within the Asia Pacific region at nearly 150 billion cubic metres (bcm) produced in 2017 accounting for 4.1 percent of the share of global natural gas production. Australia is the fastest growing producer of natural gas in Asia Pacific (Table 23.2). In 2017 Australia produced 113.5 bcm reaching a staggering 18 percent increase year on year. China remains a large producer of natural gas within the region of Asia Pacific as demonstrated by its regional production share standing at 4.1 percent in 2018 (Table 23.2). Yet, China's large production – standing at 149.2 bcm in 2018 – is primarily for domestic consumption due to the country's vast energy needs. Asia Pacific's developing nations – such as Bangladesh, Myanmar, Thailand and Vietnam – have all increased their natural gas production between 2013 and 2017 despite relatively modest reserves and production as compared with the key regional natural gas players (Table 23.3). Some of the region's smaller producers – Myanmar, for instance – has prioritised exports over domestic consumption, a policy which is currently being revised due to the country's energy demand being fuelled by economic growth (Htwe 2018). Australia's production is destined for both domestic consumption and exportation. In 2018 Australia ranked the world's second (after Qatar) LNG exporter at 56.2 million tonnes per annum (mtpa) which equated to 19.2 percent of the global LNG market share (International Gas Union 2018). Malaysia is the third biggest producer of natural gas in the region with 78.4 bcm production followed by Indonesia (fourth biggest producer in the region) accounting for 68 bcm production (BP 2018).

Table 23.2 Asia Pacific primary energy production

Asia-Pacific – Natural gas production (in bcm)						*Growth per annum*		*Share of total*
	2013	*2014*	*2015*	*2016*	*2017*	*2018*	*2006–16*	*2018*
Australia	61.8	66.6	76	96.4	113.5	18.0%	9.0%	3.1%
Bangladesh	22	23	25.9	26.5	26.6	0.8%	6.3%	0.7%
Brunei	11.9	11.6	12.2	11.7	12	2.5%	0.4%	0.3%
China	121.8	131.2	135.7	137.9	149.2	8.5%	8.9%	4.1%
India	31.9	30.2	29.2	27.3	28.5	4.5%	−0.3%	0.8%
Indonesia	77.6	76.4	76.2	70.7	68	3.6%	−0.6%	1.8%
Malaysia	72.9	72	73.9	75.6	78.4	4.1%	1.0%	2.1%
Myanmar	12.9	16.5	19.2	18.3	18	1.4%	4.0%	0.5%
Pakistan	35.6	35	35	34.7	34.7	0.2%	0.4%	0.9%
Thailand	43.3	43.6	41.2	40.4	38.7	4.0%	4.8%	1.1%
Vietnam	9.4	9.9	10.3	10.2	9.5	7.4%	4.2%	0.3%
Other Asia Pacific	18.6	23.5	29.3	30.5	30.6	0.6%	7.7%	0.8%
Total Asia Pacific	519.6	539.4	564	580.3	607.5	5.0%	4.0%	16.5%

Source: Author's own tabulation using data from BP 2018.

Table 23.3 Liquefied natural gas and market share by country (in mtpa) in 2017

Country	*Exports*	*Market share*
Qatar	81.0	27.6%
Australia	**56.2**	**19.2%**
Malaysia	**26.4**	**9.0%**
Nigeria	21.3	7.3%
Indonesia	**16.2**	**5.5%**
US	13.1	4.5%
Algeria	12.4	4.2%
Russia	11.1	3.8%
Trinidad	10.8	3.7%
Oman	8.4	2.9%
PNG	7.7	2.6%
Brunei	**7.0**	**2.4%**
UAE	5.2	1.8%
Peru	4.1	1.4%
Norway	4.1	1.4%
Angola	3.7	1.3%
Eq. Guinea	3.6	1.2%
Egypt	0.8	0.3%

Source: Author's own tabulation using data from International Gas Union 2018.

Due to the nature of exploration and production, trade and transportation, gas production in Asia Pacific has been predominantly exchanged as LNG. It is, however, worth noting that China's new foreign policy strategy – discussed below in details – aims well beyond the confines of the regional constructs. Hence, outside of the Asia Pacific concept China and its state-owned enterprises are pursuing multi-vectoral import diversification policies aimed at additional, non-LNG supplies from Central Asia as well as Russia's Siberia. Despite the added premium as far as cost is concerned, LNG remains the option of choice for China because of its transport flexibility.

5 Liquified natural gas

Natural gas has been one of the key underpinnings of regional energy markets comprised of both producing and consuming nations, net exporters and net importers of natural gas. Yet, it is China that has transformed supply and demand by doubling its LNG import capacity from 30bcm in 2015–2016 to 63 bcm in 2017–2018 (Bethune 2018).

In 2017, the Asia Pacific region exporters were responsible for over 36 percent[4] of global market share worth of exports or nearly 106 mtpa. Australia (56.2 mtpa), Malaysia (26.4 mtpa) and Indonesia (16.2 mtpa) were among the top five LNG exporters in 2017. Japan and China – Asia Pacific's key demand centres and key net importers – have been the key destinations for LNG in Asia Pacific (International Energy Agency 2018: 6) Globally LNG growth has been led by projects in Australia and the United States. Existing LNG capacity at Wheatstone LNG, Prelude FLNG and Ichthys LNG has been increased by additional trains at Australia Pacific LNG and Gorgon LNG, and increased production from existing trains increased Australia's LNG output adding an extra 11.9 million tonnes per annum (mta) in 2017 alone.[5] Indeed, Australia witnessed the single greatest increase in exports of LNG due to new trains at Pacific LNG T2 and Gorgon LNG T3 and new plans at Wheatstone LNG T11 as well as higher utilisation at existing facilities (International Gas Union 2018).

Demand for LNG has grown in Asia Pacific, which as a region has been the key driver of LNG trade growth with an impressive flow of intra-regional LNG trade, amounting to approximately 125 mta in 2017 and being made possible thanks to Australian production and Chinese demand. Chinese LNG imports in 2016 alone increased by 12.7 mta, an unprecedented LNG demand growth for any single country (International Gas Union 2018). The source of demand has been attributed to anti-pollution environmental policies which have favoured switches from coal to gas.

In addition to China, South Korea and Pakistan have increased their LNG imports adding to the liquidity of the LNG market. The Asia Pacific region's second largest LNG exporter, Malaysia, added new capacity through Petronas' floating liquified natural gas (FLNG) or Petronas PFLNG Satu project (Lewis 2018). Australian LNG is supplied to Asian customers primarily under the Japan Custom-Crude (JCC) price largely tracking the price of Brent. The Australian Competition and Consumer Commission, which started reporting LNG netback prices in 2018 expects that the LNG netback price will increase to the level of A$8.35 a gigajoule in January 2020 from the historical LNG netback price of A$5.1 a gigajoule in August 2019 (Australian Competition and Consumer Commission 2019). High production growth, coupled with favourable market conditions, in particular strong gas demand in China, has positioned Australia as a major exporter of LNG, a position it has since sought to strengthen by overtaking Qatar as the world's largest exporter of the fuel (Hunter and Raszewski 2015).

4 All exporters combined, the total market share was reported to be as high as 38.6 percent (International Gas Union (IGU) 2018).

5 The US production increased by 10.2 million tonnes driven by Sabine Pass LNG as a result of two new trains being added in 2017 (IGU 2018).

So far Australia's quest to lead the global LNG export market share has not materialised due to a lower-than-anticipated utilisation of capacity as well as lower recoverability (Yep 2018). Australian LNG export commitments coincide with higher than expected domestic demand for natural gas in the power sector. Internal factors play an important role in the country's ability to expand its LNG export capacity. In the absence of one consistent national energy policy and the pressure of higher domestic demand for gas, the Australian Government was forced to introduce the Australian Domestic Gas Security Mechanism in 2017 with a possible impact on exports (Taylor and Soliman Hunter 2018). Australia's approach to domestic security of supply reverberates beyond its shores and may affect export capacity and the credibility of Australia as a major exporter of LNG. There were reports of a domestic gas shortage leading to a reduction in LNG export capacity in 2018 (Richardson 2018), a trend which may continue if Australia's security of gas supply deteriorates. Plans to build receiving terminal to import LNG into Australia are underway evidencing the challenge faced by producers and exporters of gas (Smyth 2018).

In addition, Australia's Asia Pacific exports may be affected in the near future by external factors. The Australian LNG export price may be affected by arbitrage with new supplies coming from Russia and the United States and the fairly inflexible contractual terms Australian LNG is traded on, in particular the 'take or pay' clause (LNG World News 2018).

6 Energy markets

Australia's role in trade, investment and security within the Asia Pacific has been one of the research themes subject to substantial academic literature (Farrar, Hiscock and Lo 2015). Energy, in particular, has been one of the key drivers of the closer relationship between the Australian and Asian economies, a phenomenon particularly clear since 2010 following enhanced coal trade with China. New developments, such as the growth of Australia's LNG natural gas sales to the Asian markets, have accelerated the exchange of finance, investments, trade and education between the two regions. Since 2013 uncertainty in the energy domain about trade has increased due to the impact of the Asian energy demand on Australia's national energy security. Growth of Australia's LNG natural gas sales to the Asian markets and the impact of Australia's security of LNG demand as opposed to domestic security of gas supply have both been affecting the delicate equilibrium between domestic supply and external demand needs (Hunter and Raszewski 2015). The Asian economies have been the dominant demand generators for Australia's energy exports, driving the latter's export-oriented trade policies. Australia's LNG exports in 2017 were worth nearly US$19.7 billion (World Bank 2017). In its bid to become world's largest LNG exporter the value of Australian international sales is expected to increase in the coming years also driven by rising price of oil (LNG World News 2018).

In 2017, the primary energy demand in Asia Pacific accounted for a staggering 42 percent of the total global demand (BP 2018). Being the world's most populous nation and globally oriented economy, in 2017 China accounted for over 23 percent of the global primary energy demand, the highest demand in the world at present. Within Asia Pacific, China's demand is followed by India's which – despite being the world's second largest nation—still relies on a fairly 'modest' 5.6 percent of global primary energy demand. Both China and India are considered to be developing economies with a high growth rate in their respective primary energy demands (see Table 23.1). Within the Asia Pacific region three more nations deserve our particular attention: Australia, Japan and South Korea. Australia's primary energy demand is the sixth largest within the region on a par with Thailand (BP 2018).

Being a mature, developed economy Japan has already gone down the path of energy efficiency measures – both on environmental and energy supply security grounds – with the result that its consumption of LNG remains stable at present. Japan continues to invest in the Asian LNG infrastructure and Singapore positioned itself as the region's LNG trading hub (Chamorro 2018). Being the region's mature market for LNG, developments involving pricing as well as supply options are still to a large extent led by the Japanese economy. However, with the rapid growth in Chinese LNG imports the existing trading structures are undergoing a profound change. South Korea is a major energy power in the region with important energy market changes that may ultimately redefine the role natural gas is set to play in the country. In 2017 a new presidential administration was sworn in heralding a new approach to the energy sector in the country, focusing on the transition away from coal and enhancing renewable energy and natural gas. It is still unclear, however, which direction of travel the approach is going to take for economic, environmental and political reasons. The South Korean economy depends on stable supplies of energy not least to fuel its shipyard and car manufacturing industries. South Korea's natural gas imports are dominated by Korea Gas Corporation (KOGAS), which operates three out of four LNG import terminals (Paik 2018). Environmental challenges – including high seismicity – inform the country's energy policy. Finally, some of the options such as the 'peace pipeline' – a trans-Korea gas pipeline linking Russia's natural gas network to South Korea via North Korea – is politically sensitive due to current sanctions against Russia and, possibly, the US preference for continued promotion of LNG in the region (Chung 2018).

China has been at the forefront of both regional and global LNG market developments. Supply security concerns, investment opportunities for China's national oil and gas companies and investment funds and strategic considerations have all played an important role in the promotion of LNG. Finally, the environment has been high on the policy agenda in China, an unprecedented development as compared with Beijing's approach in the early 2000s. Attempts to improve air quality in its cities by switching from coal to natural gas has both created more demand and a price increase on regional markets. Rather than being saturated the LNG market has grown, driven by Chinese demand which went up by 18.2 in 2018 on a year-on-year basis reaching 202 bcm while the county's indigenous production of gas went up by a mere 6.3 percent necessitating growth in gas imports which increased by 37.6 percent to a total of 87 bcm (Bethune 2018).

China is currently the biggest importer of gas, which it receives both as LNG and pipeline gas. The latter are deliveries from Central Asia and Myanmar. The future of China's natural gas policy is likely to change due to the expanding trade relationship with Russia. Direct pipeline projects connecting Russia's Far East gas production with China's demand centres via the Power of Siberia natural gas pipeline are adding new volumes to China's natural-gas-hungry energy market (Forbes 2019).

7 Geopolitics and geoeconomics

As outlined above the market and environmental dynamics are at the core of the Asia Pacific region. Energy supply and demand are critical for sustaining the economic development of regional economies, particularly that of China. As demonstrated above, the diversification of China's primary energy consumption and restructuring the country's high-carbon economy to increase energy efficiency are key objectives. To address these key objectives China has opted for a mega foreign policy project, the Belt and Road Initiative (BRI). The BRI is a policy initiative aimed at economic cooperation by means of a new transport infrastructure to connect China with Asia, Africa and Europe. The breadth and scope of China's BRI is underpinned by China's anticipated international leadership, including its international economic cooperation with the rest of the world (Wang 2016). Indeed, boosting regional economic cooperation is the stated objective of BRI (Huang 2016) which is hoped to be achieved by means of connecting China to existing and new trading partners. The BRI economic cooperation is to be achieved by means of policy coordination, connectivity of facilities, facilitation of trade, financial integration and people-to-people contacts (Cullinane et al. 2018). Because of the wide array of policy objectives the initiative seeks to achieve – cutting across markets and security – China's BRI has been essentially viewed as a geopolitical policy project (Fallon 2015). The geopolitical significance of BRI is evident in the planned resource allocation and span of countries to which the strategy seeks to connect infrastructurally: an estimated US$1.3 trillion in loans is expected to be allocated by 2027. This represents around ten times higher financial integration than the post-World War II, US-led Marshall Plan and will include 76 countries around the world (Lipton 2019). Energy supply chains are an essential part of the strategy with overseas energy investments being a central part of BRI (Duan et al. 2018).

China's strategic policy objectives are to be realised by means of large China-financed infrastructural projects such as those linking China with the Central Asian nations. China's 'Silk Road' energy strategy aimed at Central Asia has led to investments in and the development of an energy infrastructure network connecting the region's energy rich countries – Kazakhstan, Turkmenistan and Uzbekistan – creating a degree of energy integration with the region (Smith Stegen 2015). At the same time, this initiative is putting pressure on alternative westward energy export routes that other regional players such as the European Union have long hoped to have implemented. China's success in ensuring eastward energy exports from Central Asia has wider ramifications involving security. The US response to China's regional and global economic and diplomatic outreach has been one of scepticism. Being part of the Asia Pacific the United States has raised its political and security posture in the region with its 'pivot to Asia' seeking to reorient US foreign policy towards Asia Pacific in anticipation of Asia Pacific becoming the key political and economic space in the twenty-first century (Campbell and Andrews 2013).

Against the backdrop of the geoeconomics of energy infrastructure projects there is a degree of institutionalisation which plays an increasingly important role in the region, including in the domain of free trade (Dent 2010). China's power, understood in economic, political and security terms, has increased exponentially since the millennium. An institutional approach to counterbalance the growing power of China in the region (Beeson 2016) has been taken by the Association of Southeast Asian Nations (ASEAN) founded in 1967.[6] ASEAN has sought to promote a unity within the bloc as a counterweight to China's economic policies within the region which are seen by some as aimed at rewriting the current geopolitical landscape (Fallon 2015).

Another inter-governmental forum comprising 21 Pacific Rim economies is the Asia-Pacific Economic Cooperation (APEC). APEC is focused on the promotion of free trade throughout the Asia Pacific region (APEC Website 2018). Bearing in mind the strategic implications of China's politico-economic revival in Asia Pacific, the United

6 ASEAN member states are: Brunei Darussalam, Cambodia, Indonesia, Lao PDR, Malaysia, Myanmar, Philippines, Singapore, Thailand and Vietnam.

States has previously sought to engage with the region by means of the (now defunct) Trans-Pacific Partnership (TPP), a free trade agreement (Aggarwal 2016; Cheong and Tongzon 2013). China has sought to counterbalance the TPP by proposing an alternative mega free trade agreement, the Regional Comprehensive Economic Partnership (RCEP), which has been seen as a 'balancing strategy' against the US influence in Asia Pacific (Wilson 2015).

Asia Pacific is arguably an area with a high propensity for dangerous unrest involving global powers (Christensen 1999). The geopolitical challenge has grown exponentially because of maritime security between China and Southeast Asia. At the heart of the maritime security in the region has been the physical occupation and physical control of the Nansha (or Spratly) Islands by some of the coastal states (Odgaard 2002) and, increasingly, security challenges as a result of the international legal disputes within the South China Sea (Buszynski 2012; Gao and Jia 2013). While

> all the claimants in the South China Sea disputes have engaged in various degrees of island-building on many of the geographic features in the Spratly Islands ... none has been on the scale of Chinese island-building on the features which it occupies.
>
> *(Davenport 2018: 76)*

The construction and militarisation of artificial islands in South China Sea puts pressure on the region, particularly in cases of overflight and maritime activities. There have been reports recently of an exclusion zone being imposed by China restricting flights over the region as well as passage of vessels (Thayer 2015). It remains to be seen what arrangements will be taken to ensure the balance of power in the region, with a variety of proposed solutions, including a regional alignment of states, possibly Australia-India-Japan-United States (Chellaney 2018).

8 Concluding remarks

Asian energy markets are undergoing a profound change in consumption, production and transportation of energy resources. The change has been largely attributed to the growth of China driven by the country's markets, the environment, geopolitics and geoeconomics. The unprecedented growth of developing economies within Asia Pacific is expected to continue, further strengthening Asia Pacific's role in the global economy and energy. Net-exporters are likely to soon become net-importers of energy against a backdrop of population growth, urbanisation and, most importantly, a dwindling domestic resource base. The environmental policy is rapidly changing in the region's biggest polluter, China, driven by state intervention.

Australia has long been part of the Asia Pacific region both economically and politically. However, increasingly, due to the changing nature of economic development, Australia is at a crossroads with its energy and environmental politics. Asia Pacific remains Australia's key geographical space yet the geoeconomic developments led by state-ownership and the greater role of geopolitics require a new approach. Energy and climate change are Australia's two biggest political issues at present. Despite all the effort of exporting a billion dollars' worth of coal and LNG to some of the fastest-growing economies of Asia Pacific, the Australian Government is struggling to ensure energy security at home: shortages of natural gas, infrastructure and investment shortages are responsible for spiralling costs which have had an impact on the country's economy (*Financial Times* 2018).

In order to address the rapidly changing dynamics in the region it wants to be part of, Australia has to prioritise its commitment to sustainable energy markets – balancing demands of exports and domestic consumption. The geoeconomics of energy and climate in China helped the country to manage its key sectors to achieve its policy objectives at an accelerated rate with little resort to markets. For its part, Australia has long relied on markets to manage its energy and mining sector. With the regional dynamics increasingly driven by geoeconomics and geopolitics, Australia needs to reinstate its environmental policy objectives to minimise the impact of changing energy markets in the region.

References

Australian Competition and Consumer Commission (2019) 'Gas inquiry 2017–2020', LNG netback price series, 1 August 2019. https://www.accc.gov.au/regulated-infrastructure/energy/gas-inquiry-2017-2020/lng-netback-price-series

Aggarwal, V.K. (2016) 'Mega-FTAs and the trade-security nexus: the Trans-Pacific Partnership (TPP) and the Regional Comprehensive Economic Partnership (RCEP)', *Asia Pacific Issues*, Analysis from the East-West Center No. 123, March. https://scholarspace.manoa.hawaii.edu/bitstream/10125/40004/1/api123a.pdf

Aizhu, C. and Jaganathan, J. (2019) 'China's CNOOC explores opening up LNG terminals under reform pressure: sources', Reuters, 11 March. https://www.reuters.com/article/us-china-gas-cnooc/chinas-cnooc-explores-opening-up-lng-terminals-under-reform-pressure-sources-idUSKBN1QS13J

APEC Website (2018) History. https://www.apec.org/About-Us/About-APEC/History

Bambawale, M.J. and Sovacool, B.K. (2011) 'China's energy security: the perspective of energy users', *Applied Energy*, Vol. 88, Issue 5, pp. 1949–1956.

Bethune, Greame (2018) 'China's hunger for LNG confounds all forecasts', *Petroleum Economist*, 18 December. https://www.petroleum-economist.com/articles/midstream-downstream/lng/2018/china-s-hunger-for-lng-confounds-all-forecasts

Beeson, M. (2016) 'Can ASEAN cope with China?', *Journal of Current Southeast Asian Affairs*, Vol. 35, Issue 1, pp. 5–28.

BP (2018) 'BP statistical review of world energy', June 2018. https://www.bp.com/content/dam/bp/business-sites/en/global/corporate/pdfs/energy-economics/statistical-review/bp-stats-review-2018-full-report.pdf

Buszynski, L. (2012) 'The South China Sea: oil, maritime claims, and U.S.–China strategic rivalry', *The Washington Quarterly*, Vol. 35, Issue 2, pp. 139–156.

Campbell, K. and Andrews, B. (2013) 'Explaining the US "Pivot" to Asia', Chatham House, August. https://kritisches-netzwerk.de/sites/default/files/explaining_the_us_pivot_to_asia_-_kurt_campbell_and_brian_andrews_-_the_asia_group_-_august_2013_-_9_pages_1.pdf

Chamorro, D. (2018) 'Seizing opportunity in Southeast Asia's energy market', Forbes, 20 August. https://www.forbes.com/sites/riskmap/2018/08/20/seizing-opportunity-in-southeast-asias-energy-market/#366ace236a9c

Chellaney, B. (2018) 'Why the South China Sea is critical to security', *Japan Times*, 26 March. https://www.japantimes.co.jp/opinion/2018/03/26/commentary/world-commentary/south-china-sea-critical-security/#.XJfgA5P7Sb8

Cheong, I. and Tongzon, J. (2013) 'Comparing the economic impact of the Trans-Pacific Partnership and the Regional Comprehensive Economic Partnership', *Asian Economic Papers*, Vol 12, Issue 2, pp. 144–161.

Christensen, T.J. (1999) 'China, the U.S.-Japan alliance, and the security dilemma in East Asia', *International Security*, Vol. 23, Issue 4, pp. 49–80.

Chung, J. (2018) 'Trans-Korea gas pipeline project reappears, but challenges remain', Reuters, 29 June. https://uk.reuters.com/article/uk-northkorea-southkorea-gas-russia/trans-korea-gas-pipeline-project-reappears-but-challenges-remain-idUKKBN1JP0V6

Cullinane, K.P.B., Lee, P.T.W., Yang, Z. and Hu, Z.H. (2018) 'Editorial: China's Belt and Road Initiative', *Transportation Research Part E: Logistics and Transportation Review*, Vol. 117, pp. 1–4.

Davenport, T. (2018) 'Island-building in the South China Sea: legality and limits', *Asian Journal of International Law*, Vol. 8, Issue 1, pp. 76–90.
Dent, C.M. (2010) 'Free trade agreements in the Asia-Pacific a decade on: evaluating the past, looking to the future', *International Relations of the Asia-Pacific*, Vol. 10, Issue 2, pp. 201–245. https://doi.org/10.1093/irap/lcp022
Duan, F., Ji, Q., Liu, B-Y. and Fan, Y. (2018) 'Energy investment risk assessment for nations along China's Belt & Road Initiative', *Journal of Cleaner Production*, Vol. 170, pp. 535–547.
Fallon, T. (2015) 'The new Silk Road: Xi Jinping's grand strategy for Eurasia', *American Foreign Policy Interests: The Journal of the National Committee on American Foreign Policy*, Vol. 37, Issue 3, pp. 140–147.
Farrar, J., Hiscock, M. and Lo, V.I. (eds) *Australia's Trade, Investment and Security in the Asian Century*. Singapore: World Scientific Publishing Co. Pte. Ltd.
Feng, L. and Liao, W. (2016) 'Legislation, plans, and policies for prevention and control of air pollution in China: achievements, challenges, and improvements', *Journal of Cleaner Production*, Vol. 112, pp. 1549–1558.
Financial Times (2018) Energy is at the root of Australia's political crisis. https://www.ft.com/content/2ad3c68c-a6cd-11e8-926a-7342fe5e173f
Forbes, Alex (2019) 'Russia's hunger for second eastern gas outlet grows', *Petroleum Economist*, 15 February. https://www.petroleum-economist.com/articles/politics-economics/europe-eurasia/2019/russia-s-hunger-for-second-eastern-gas-outlet-grows
Gao, Z. and Jia, B.B. (2013) 'The Nine-Dash Line in the South China Sea: history, status, and implications', *American Journal of International Law*, Vol. 107, Issue 1, pp. 98–123.
Hancock, Kathleen J. and Vivoda, Vlado (2014) 'International political economy: a field born of the OPEC crisis returns to its energy roots', *Energy Research & Social Science*, Vol. 1, pp. 206–216. https://doi.org/10.1016/j.erss.2014.03.017
Htwe, C.M. (2018) 'Myanmar's gas production dilemma', *Myanmar Times*, 18 October. https://www.mmtimes.com/news/myanmars-gas-production-dilemma.html
Huang, Y. (2016) 'Understanding China's Belt & Road Initiative: motivation, framework and assessment', *China Economic Review*, Vol. 40, pp. 314–321.
Hunter, Tina and Raszewski, Slawomir (2015) 'Australia's national interest in supplying gas resources to the Asian markets' (Chapter 10), In: J. Farrar, M. Hiscock and V.I. Lo (eds) *Australia's Trade, Investment and Security in the Asian Century*, pp. 155–173. Singapore: World Scientific Publishing Co. Pte. Ltd.
International Energy Agency (2017) 'Coal 2017: analysis and forecast to 2022 (Executive Summary)', IEA Market Report Series. https://www.iea.org/Textbase/npsum/coal2017MRSsum.pdf
International Energy Agency (2018a) 'Global coal demand set to remain stable through 2023, despite headwinds', IEA, 18 December. https://www.iea.org/newsroom/news/2018/december/global-coal-demand-set-to-remain-stable-through-2023-despite-headwinds.html
International Energy Agency (IEA) (2018b) 'Key energy statistics 2018'. IEA. https://webstore.iea.org/download/direct/2291?fileName=Key_World_2018.pdf
International Gas Union (2018) 'World LNG report 2018: 27th World Gas Conference Edition'. https://www.igu.org/sites/default/files/node-document-field_file/IGU_LNG_2018_0.pdf
Lewis, Ian (2018) 'FLNG enters new age', *Petroleum Economist*, 31 August. https://www.petroleum-economist.com/articles/upstream/technology/2018/flng-enters-new-age
Lin, Boqiang and Jiang, Zhujun (2011) 'Estimates of energy subsidies in China and impact of energy subsidy reform', *Energy Economics*, Vol. 33, Issue 2, pp. 273–283.
Lipton, G. (2019) 'Graphic truth: one belt, one road, two worlds?', *GZeroMedia*, 19 March. https://www.gzeromedia.com/graphic-truth-one-belt-one-road-two-worlds
LNG World News (2018) 'Higher volumes, price to bump Australia's LNG export income', 2 July. https://www.lngworldnews.com/higher-volumes-price-to-bump-australias-lng-export-income
Lucas, Adam (2016) 'Stranded assets, externalities and carbon risk in the Australian coal industry: the case for contraction in a carbon-constrained world', *Energy Research & Social Science*, Vol. 11, pp. 53–66.
Luttwak, E.N. (1990) 'From geopolitics to geo-economics: logic of conflict, grammar of commerce', *The National Interest*, No. 20 (Summer), pp. 17–23.
Maritime Executive (2017) 'Novatek signs Chinese deals for Arctic LNG 2', 4 November. https://www.maritime-executive.com/article/novatek-signs-chinese-deals-for-arctic-lng-2

Matsumoto, Fumi (2019) 'Coal expected to be Australia's most valuable export in 2018–19: recovering demand lifts prices, underscoring dependence on China', *Nikkei Asian Review*, 13 January. https://asia.nikkei.com/Business/Markets/Commodities/Coal-expected-to-be-Australia-s-most-valuable-export-in-2018-19

McDougall, Derek (2016) *Asia Pacific in World Politics*. 2nd ed. Boulder, CO: Lynne Rienner Publishers. https://www.rienner.com/uploads/5772df0a12b70.pdf

McKay, Huw and Song, Ligang (2010) 'China as a global manufacturing powerhouse: strategic considerations and structural adjustment', *China & World Economy*, Vol. 18, No. 1, 2010, pp. 1–32.

Miyamoto, A. and Ishiguro, C. (2018) 'The outlook for natural gas and LNG in China in the war against air pollution', Oxford Institute for Energy Studies Paper NG139. https://www.oxfordenergy.org/wpcms/wp-content/uploads/2018/12/The-Outlook-for-Natural-Gas-and-LNG-in-China-in-the-War-against-Air-Pollution-NG139.pdf

Odgaard, L. (2002) *Maritime Security between China and Southeast Asia: Conflict and Cooperation in the Making of Regional Order*. London: Routledge.

Paik, W.K. (2018) 'South Korea's energy policy change and the implications for its LNG imports', Oxford Institute for Energy Studies NG132. June. https://www.oxfordenergy.org/wpcms/wp-content/uploads/2018/06/South-Koreas-Energy-Policy-Change-and-the-Implications-for-its-LNG-Imports-NG132.pdf?v=79cba1185463

Parker, J. (2018) 'How China cut its air pollution', *The Economist*, 25 January. https://www.economist.com/the-economist-explains/2018/01/25/how-china-cut-its-air-pollution

Raszewski, S. and Hunter, T. (2014) 'Gas and energy security policy in Australia: Japan as a secure energy consumer', *Centre for International Minerals and Energy Law Briefing Paper*. https://www.researchgate.net/publication/320508586_Gas_and_Energy_Security_Policy_in_Australia_Japan_as_a_secure_Energy_Consumer

Richardson, Nathan (2018) 'Australia cuts 2018–19 LNG export forecasts again amid domestic gas shortage', S&P Global Platts, 3 July. https://www.spglobal.com/platts/en/market-insights/latest-news/natural-gas/070318-australia-cuts-2018-19-lng-export-forecasts-again-amid-domestic-gas-shortage

Scholvin, S. and Wigge, M. (2018) 'Power politics by economic means: geoeconomics as an analytical approach and foreign policy practice', *Journal of Comparative Strategy*, Vol. 37, Issue 1, pp. 73–84.

Smith Stegen, Karen (2015) 'Understanding China's global energy strategy', *International Journal of Emerging Markets*, Vol. 10, Issue 2, pp. 194–208.

Smyth, Jamie (2018) 'Australia's LNG export surge fuels domestic supply concerns', *Financial Times*, 12 December. https://www.ft.com/content/912a7de8-fdc3-11e8-aebf-99e208d3e521

Steckel, J.C., Edenhofer, O. and Jakob, M. (2015) 'Drivers for the renaissance of coal', *Proceedings of the Natural Academy of Sciences of the United States of America*, Vol. 112, Issue 29, pp. E3775–E3781. https://www.pnas.org/content/pnas/112/29/E3775.full.pdf

Taylor, M. and Soliman Hunter, T. (2018) 'A paradox of plenty: the Australian domestic gas supply regulatory dilemma', *The Journal of World Energy Law & Business*, Vol. 11, Issue 6, pp. 465–486.

Thayer, C. (2015) 'No, China is not reclaiming land in the South China Sea', *The Diplomat*, 7 June. https://thediplomat.com/2015/06/no-china-is-not-reclaiming-land-in-the-south-china-sea

U.S. Energy Information Agency (2017) 'Country analysis brief: Japan'. Last updated: 2 February 2017. https://www.eia.gov/beta/international/analysis_includes/countries_long/Japan/japan.pdf

Vivoda, V. (2010) 'Evaluating energy security in the Asia-Pacific region: a novel methodological approach', *Energy Policy*, Vol. 38, Issue 9, pp. 5258–5263.

Vivoda, V. (2017) 'LNG import diversification and energy security in Asia', *Energy Policy*, Vol. 129, pp. 967–974.

Wang, Y. (2016) 'Offensive for defensive: the Belt and Road Initiative and China's new grand strategy', *The Pacific Review*, Vol. 29, Issue 3, pp. 455–463.

Wilson, J.D. (2015) 'Mega-regional trade deals in the Asia-Pacific: choosing between the TPP and RCEP?', *Journal of Contemporary Asia*, Vol. 45, No. 2, pp. 345–353. http://content.csbs.utah.edu/~mli/Economies%205430-6430/Wilson-Choosing%20between%20TPP%20and%20RCEP.pdf

Woodhouse, A. (2019) 'Australian coal miners stumble in wake of China import restrictions', *Financial Times*, 22 February. https://www.ft.com/content/4fc3f78c-3638-11e9-bd3a-8b2a211d90d5

Wood Mackenzie (2018) 'New wave of growth on the horizon for Asia-Pacific's oil and gas sector', Comment, 15 October. https://www.woodmac.com/press-releases/new-wave-of-growth-on-the-horizon-for-asia-pacifics-oil-and-gas-sector

World Bank (2017) 'Australia trade at a glance: most recent values', *World Integrated Trade Solution*, https://wits.worldbank.org/CountrySnapshot/en/AUS
World Bank (2018) 'Helping China fight air pollution', 11 June. https://www.worldbank.org/en/news/feature/2018/06/11/helping-china-fight-air-pollution
Yep, Eric (2018) 'Australia's bid to be the world's largest LNG exporter may fizzle out', S&P Global Platts Blog, 18 October. https://blogs.platts.com/2018/10/18/australia-bid-world-largest-lng-exporter-may-fizzle-out
Yun Fan, S. and Moore, J. (2019) 'Asian LNG landscape shifts as emerging markets liberalize', S&P Global Platts, 31 July. https://www.spglobal.com/en/research-insights/articles/asian-lng-landscape-shifts-as-emerging-markets-liberalize

24

FROM COAL TO CLEAN ENERGY

How the energy transition is being managed in Indian energy law and policy

Penelope Crossley

Introduction

With India having the second largest population in the world, and a rapidly developing and growing economy,[1] securing an adequate supply of energy to meet the ever-increasing demand has long been a central concern of successive governments. Indeed, India is now the third largest consumer of energy in the world after the USA and China.[2] Further, India's energy consumption is predicted to increase by 156 per cent on its 2017 levels by 2040,[3] accounting for more than 25 per cent of net primary global energy demand growth.[4] This puts India, a country that has long valued self-reliance and energy independence, in the uncomfortable position of being heavily dependent on fuel imports.[5] At the same time, the Indian Government has been trying to ensure that energy remains affordable to assist with its commitment to provide access to energy for all its citizens and also address concerns about air pollution and climate change.[6] Section 1 of this chapter will outline the current Indian energy mix. In Section 2, the complex regulatory framework that governs the energy sector will be critically analysed, while in Section 3 the legal and policy drivers, as well as the central government governance structures for electricity and each of

1 International Energy Agency, 'Understanding Energy Challenges in India: Policies, Players and Issues' (International Energy Agency, 11 December 2015) 11 <https://www.oecd-ilibrary.org/energy/understanding-energy-challenges-in-india_9789264247444-en> accessed 27 August 2019.

2 Directorate General of Hydrocarbons, Ministry of Petroleum and Natural Gas, Government of India, 'India's Hydrocarbon Outlook 2017–18: A Report on Exploration and Production Activities' (Ministry of Petroleum and Natural Gas, New Delhi, 2018) 7 <http://dghindia.gov.in/assets/downloads/ar/2017-18.pdf> accessed 27 August 2019.

3 BP p.l.c., 'BP Energy Outlook 2019 (BP p.l.c., 2019) 2 <https://www.bp.com/content/dam/bp/business-sites/en/global/corporate/pdfs/energy-economics/energy-outlook/bp-energy-outlook-2019-country-insight-india.pdf> accessed 27 August 2019.

4 Ibid 1.

5 International Energy Agency, 'Understanding Energy Challenges in India: Policies, Players and Issues' (International Energy Agency, 11 December 2015) 7 <https://www.oecd-ilibrary.org/energy/understanding-energy-challenges-in-india_9789264247444-en> accessed 27 August 2019.

6 Ibid 10.

the major energy sources (coal, oil and gas, renewable energy and nuclear energy) used in the Indian economy will be discussed. Section 4 will then turn to the greatest challenge currently faced by the Indian energy sector, that of, how to manage its transition from being a coal-fuelled economy to using cleaner energy sources. This will require the delicate balancing of India's four key pillars of energy policy: (i) energy security, (ii) affordability and access, (iii) environmental concerns, such as air pollution and climate change, and (iv) energy efficiency, which in the context of rapidly rising energy demand is no easy task. The chapter will conclude in Section 5.

1 The Indian energy mix

Energy is viewed as a key enabler for the Indian economy. The National Institute for Transforming India (the Indian national planning and policy think-tank) has said that it believes that 'India is set to be at the centre of the world's energy stage',[7] in coming decades. Such a view is also supported by the Indian Prime Minister, Narendra Modi, who recently stated: 'The power and energy sectors are the biggest constituents of the infrastructure sector. If you ignore them, no development will happen.'[8]

The central focus on the Indian energy sector is partly explained by its current heavy reliance on coal-fired generation, its dependence on foreign fuel imports,[9] particularly for crude oil and high-grade coal, and its rapid growth in energy demand.[10] This means that India is likely to experience a far greater and much more rapid shift than many other economies, which have been gradually managing the energy transition over several decades.

The Indian economy currently utilises coal and lignite, petroleum and natural gas, diesel, renewable energy (including hydropower) and nuclear energy.[11] India is the world's second largest importer of coal[12] and the third largest importer of crude oil.[13] It currently accounts for approximately 4 per cent of global electricity generation, and 4.3 per cent of renewable

7 Simi Thambi, 'India's Energy and Emissions Outlook: Results from India Energy Model' (National Institution for Transforming India, Government of India, 2018) 7 <https://www.niti.gov.in/sites/default/files/2019-07/India%E2%80%99s-Energy-and-Emissions-Outlook.pdf> accessed 27 August 2019.

8 Amol Sharma, 'Q&A: Gujarat Chief Minister Narendra Modi' (*The Wall Street Journal,* India, 29 August 2012) <https://blogs.wsj.com/indiarealtime/2012/08/29/qa-gujarat-chief-minister-narendra-modi> accessed 27 August 2019.

9 International Energy Agency, 'India Energy Outlook' (*World Energy Outlook Special Report*, 27 November 2015) ch 1, 30 <https://www.gita.org.in/Attachments/Reports/IndiaEnergyOutlook_WEO2015.pdf> accessed 27 August 2019.

10 Office of the Chief Economist, Department of Industry and Science, Australian Government, 'Coal in India 2015' (Office of the Chief Economist, Department of Industry and Science, Australian Government, June 2015) 12 <https://www.industry.gov.au/sites/g/files/net3906/f/June%202018/document/pdf/coal-in-india.pdf> accessed 27 August 2019.

11 Lari Tiewsoh, Jakub Jirasek and Martin Sivek, 'Electricity Generation in India: Present State, Future Outlook and Policy implications' (2019) 12(7) *Energies*, 3.

12 Office of the Chief Economist, Department of Industry and Science, Australian Government, 'Coal in India 2015' (Office of the Chief Economist, Department of Industry and Science, Australian Government, June 2015) 5 <https://www.industry.gov.au/sites/g/files/net3906/f/June%202018/document/pdf/coal-in-india.pdf> accessed 27 August 2019.

13 International Energy Agency, 'India Energy Outlook' (*World Energy Outlook Special Report*, 27 November 2015) 14 <https://www.gita.org.in/Attachments/Reports/IndiaEnergyOutlook_WEO2015.pdf> accessed 27 August 2019.

energy generation, boasting sizeable quantities of installed capacity from wind power and concentrated solar power.[14] As at 31 July 2019, the Central Electricity Authority reported that of India's total electricity generation:

- 63.2 per cent came from thermal power generation sources, specifically 54.3 per cent coal, 6.9 per cent gas, 1.7 per cent lignite and 0.2 per cent diesel;
- 22 per cent came from renewable energy sources, including wind, solar, biomass, biogas, waste to energy and small scale hydropower projects;
- 12.6 per cent came from large scale hydropower projects;
- 1.9 per cent from nuclear power.[15]

Strikingly, India is anticipated to account for 11 per cent of global electricity generation by 2040,[16] with a large portion of the increase predicted to come from renewable energy sources (40 per cent by 2030 alone).[17] Despite this, India is likely to remain a predominantly coal-fuelled economy,[18] at least for the foreseeable future, in large part due to its central role in the Indian Government's industrial policy, which will be discussed further below.

2 The regulatory framework governing the Indian energy sector

2.1 The Indian constitutional framework

The Indian Constitution establishes India as a federated union of states, consisting of 28 states and seven union territories.[19] As shown in Table 24.1, the Seventh Schedule to the Constitution of India (1949)[20] allocates responsibility over subjects to either the Union, the States or to be managed concurrently by both the Union and the States.[21] As such, the regulatory framework of the energy sector in India is dictated by its complex constitutional underpinnings. The allocation of energy-related subject matter in the Indian Constitution is as follows:

14 India Brand Equity Association, 'Renewable Energy (India Brand Equity Association, June 2018), 8.

15 Government of India Ministry of Power, 'Power Sector at a Glance ALL INDIA' (Government of India, 21 August 2019) <https://powermin.nic.in/en/content/power-sector-glance-all-india> accessed 27 August 2019.

16 World Coal Association, 'The Role of Coal in India's Energy Ambitions' (World Coal Association, 14 February, 2019) <https://www.worldcoal.org/role-coal-india%E2%80%99s-energy-ambitions> accessed 27 August 2019.

17 International Energy Agency, 'India Energy Outlook' (*World Energy Outlook Special Report*, 27 November 2015) 13 <https://www.gita.org.in/Attachments/Reports/IndiaEnergyOutlook_WEO2015.pdf> accessed 27 August 2019.

18 Office of the Chief Economist, Department of Industry and Science, Australian Government, 'Coal in India 2015' (Office of the Chief Economist, Department of Industry and Science, Australian Government, June 2015) 18 <https://www.industry.gov.au/sites/g/files/net3906/f/June%202018/document/pdf/coal-in-india.pdf> accessed 27 August 2019.

19 International Energy Agency, 'Understanding Energy Challenges in India: Policies, Players and Issues' (International Energy Agency, 11 December 2015) 11–12 <https://www.oecd-ilibrary.org/energy/understanding-energy-challenges-in-india_9789264247444-en> accessed 27 August 2019.

20 Constitution of India, 1949 art 246 (as amended).

21 Amit Maheshwari and Neeraj Menon (Trilegal), 'Electricity Regulation in India' (*Lexology*, 26 March 2019) <https://www.lexology.com/library/detail.aspx?g=72d8a27b-af85-4a0e-ab46-dc4928a6d4f9> accessed 27 August 2019.

Table 24.1 Allocation of responsibility for energy in the Indian Constitution (1949, as amended)

List I – Union List	*List II – State List*	*List III – Concurrent List*
6. Atomic energy and mineral resources necessary for its production.[a]	17. Water, that is to say, water supplies, irrigation and canals, drainage and investments, water storage and water power subject to the provisions of entry 56 of List I.[b]	38. Electricity.[c]
53. Regulation and development of oil field and mineral oil resources; petroleum and petroleum products; other liquids and substances declared by Parliament by law to be dangerously inflammable.[d]	23. Regulation of mines and mineral development subject to the provisions of List I with respect to regulation in development under the control of the Union.[e]	
54. Regulation of mines and mineral development to the extent to which such regulation development under the control of the Union is declared by Parliament by law to be expedient in the public interest.[f]	25. Gas and gas-works.[g]	
55. Regulation of labour and safety in mines and oilfields.[h]	50. Taxes on mineral rights subject to any limitations imposed by Parliament by law relating to mineral development.[i]	
56. Regulation and development of inter-State rivers and river valleys to the extent to which such regulation in development under the control of the Union is declared by Parliament by law to be expedient in the public interest.[j]	53. Taxes on the consumption and sale of electricity.[k]	

Source: Compiled by the author.

a Constitution of India, 1949 art 246, List I – Union List, 6.
b Ibid List II – State List, 17.
c Ibid List III – Concurrent List, 38.
d Ibid List I – Union List, 54.
e Ibid List II – State List, 23.
f Ibid List I – Union List, 54.
g Ibid List II – State List, 25.
h Ibid List I – Union List, 55.
i Ibid List II – State List, 50.
j Ibid List I – Union List, 56.
k Ibid List II – State List, 53.

As a result of this allocation of powers, nuclear energy,[22] petroleum and coal are subject to Union legislation from the central Parliament,[23] gas and hydropower are subject to state legislation, and electricity (and thus it follows, renewable energy, with the exception of hydropower) is subject to concurrent legislation.[24] The effect of electricity being listed on the Concurrent List is that both the central Parliament and the state legislatures may legislate in this area.[25] However, should any repugnancy or inconsistency arise between Union and state-based legislation, then to the extent of the repugnancy the state legislation will be void.[26]

2.2 The governance of energy at a Union level

The governance of energy at a Union level is managed by four separate Ministries and one Government Department: the Ministry of Power, the Ministry of Petroleum and Gas, the Ministry of New and Renewable Energy, the Ministry of Coal and the Department of Atomic Energy (see Figure 24.1 below).[27] The national strategy and plans for energy are devised by a separate national think-tank, NITI Aayog, which holds broad responsibility for strategic forward planning for all aspects of the Indian economy and society.[28]

The splitting of responsibility in this way has long been criticised, with it being said that 'all are bent on to protecting their narrow turf',[29] and that this structure makes devising and

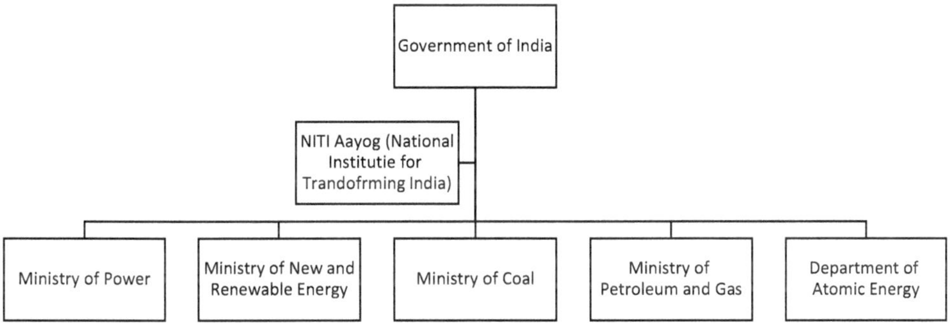

Figure 24.1 Governance structure of the Indian energy sector at the Union level

22 International Energy Agency, 'Understanding Energy Challenges in India: Policies, Players and Issues' (International Energy Agency, 11 December 2015) 9 <https://www.oecd-ilibrary.org/energy/understanding-energy-challenges-in-india_9789264247444-en> accessed 27 August 2019.

23 Ibid 49.

24 Ibid 12.

25 Ibid 12.

26 Constitution of India, 1949 art 254(1). See the discussion of this point in *Bhagwanti Bai v The State of Madhya Pradesh,* W.P. 6563 of 2016, H.C.M. P., 15 May 1997.

27 International Energy Agency, 'Understanding Energy Challenges in India: Policies, Players and Issues' (International Energy Agency, 11 December 2015) 19–20 <https://www.oecd-ilibrary.org/energy/understanding-energy-challenges-in-india_9789264247444-en> accessed 27 August 2019.

28 Press Information Bureau, Government of India, Planning Commission, 'Objectives and Functions' (Press Information Bureau, Government of India, Planning Commission, 1 January 2015) <https://pib.gov.in/newsite/PrintRelease.aspx?relid=114273> accessed 27 August 2019.

29 International Energy Agency, 'Understanding Energy Challenges in India: Policies, Players and Issues' (International Energy Agency, 11 December 2015) 20 <https://www.oecd-ilibrary.org/energy/understanding-energy-challenges-in-india_9789264247444-en> accessed 27 August 2019.

implementing a unified national energy strategy difficult and creates regulatory and policy uncertainty.[30] However, the politics of the central Union Parliament is such that critics such as Madan have stated that despite there being obvious benefits that would flow from the merging of responsibilities into a single Ministry of Energy, this is unlikely to occur.[31]

2.3 The governance of energy at a state level

In addition to the central government governance structures, each Indian state also has its own ministry of power, with its own electricity regulatory commission governing intra-state trade, its own state electricity board, its own ministry of new and renewable energy, as well as its own ministry of mines.[32] While these entities are tasked with different responsibilities to the central government agencies in accordance with the national constitution, the effect of placing electricity on the concurrent list is to increase the risk of regulatory overlap.[33] Moreover, in the absence of efforts to harmonise state energy laws, this adds significant regulatory and policy complexity for market participants seeking to operate across state borders.[34]

3 Legal and policy issues associated with India's energy supply

3.1 Electricity

In 2017–2018, the total Indian electricity generation from utilities and non-utilities was 14,86,493 GWh.[35] This electricity can currently be accessed by 92.6 per cent of the population, with a goal that 100 per cent of the population will have access by 2022.[36] While the Indian states play an important role in regulating their state energy sectors, the central Ministry of Power is 'responsible for General Policy in the electric power sector and issues relating to energy policy and coordination thereof … [including] cutting across sectors, fuels, regions, and intra country and inter country flows'.[37] More recently, the Ministry of

30 Vivek Sen, Kuldeep Sharma and Gireesh Shrimali, 'Reaching India's Renewable Energy Targets: The Role of Institutional Investors' (The Global Commission on the Economy and Climate, November 2016) 14 <https://climatepolicyinitiative.org/wp-content/uploads/2016/11/Reaching-Indias-Renewable-Energy-Targets-The-Role-of-Institutional-Investors_conference-draft.pdf> accessed 27 August 2019.

31 Tanvi Madan, 'The Brookings Foreign Policy Studies Energy Security Series: India' (The Brookings Institution, November 2006) 27–28 <https://www.brookings.edu/wp-content/uploads/2016/06/2006india.pdf> accessed 27 August 2019.

32 Dibyanshu, Anuj Rastogi, Sathyajith Nair and Khaitan & Co, 'Electricity Regulation in India: Overview' (Thomson Reuters, 1 May 2019) <https://uk.practicallaw.thomsonreuters.com/w-012-2860?transitionType=Default&contextData=(sc.Default)&bhcp=1> accessed 27 August 2019.

33 International Energy Agency, 'Understanding Energy Challenges in India: Policies, Players and Issues' (International Energy Agency, 11 December 2015) 12 <https://www.oecd-ilibrary.org/energy/understanding-energy-challenges-in-india_9789264247444-en> accessed 27 August 2019.

34 Ibid 91.

35 Central Statistics Office, Ministry of Statistics and Programme Implementation, Government of India, 'Energy Statistics – 2019, 26th Issue' (Ministry of Statistics and Programme Implementation, Government of India, March 2019) 36 <www.mospi.gov.in/sites/default/files/publication_reports/Energy%20Statistics%202019-finall.pdf> accessed 27 August 2019.

36 Bigsna Gill, Astha Gupta and Debajit Palit, 'Rural Electrification: Impact on Distribution Companies in India' (The Energy and Resources Institute, 2019) 4 <https://www.teriin.org/sites/default/files/2019-02/DUF%20Report.pdf> accessed 27 August 2019.

37 Government of India, Ministry of Power, 'Responsibilities' (Government of India, August 2019) <https://powermin.nic.in/en/content/responsibilities> accessed August 2019.

Power has directed the state government entities and licensed distribution businesses which procure electricity that they are only to procure thermal power through competitive reverse auction bidding processes using standard form long-term power purchase agreements (PPAs) that are issued by the Ministry.[38] The Ministry is also currently in the process of releasing new medium-term PPAs.[39] The Central Electricity Regulatory Commission acts as the regulator for interstate trade in the electricity sector. The Central Electricity Authority acts as the technical and safety adviser to the government.[40]

As will be discussed in 3.2 below, the majority of India's electricity is currently fuelled by coal-fired generation, which is supplied by a majority government owned enterprise at discounted prices to the international coal price. More recently, the Indian Government has committed to substantially increase the volume of renewable electricity generation in its electricity mix.[41]

3.1.1 The Electricity Act *2003*

The *Electricity Act* 2003 is the primary legislation governing the electricity sector throughout India.[42] Prior to 30 October 2019, this legislation did not apply to the special autonomous state of Jammu and Kashmir.[43] However, following the re-election of the nationalist Bharatiya Janata Party in 2019,[44] on 9 August 2019 both houses of the Indian Parliament voted to enable the President to amend Article 370 of the Indian Constitution and extend the application of the Indian Constitution in its entirety to Jammu and Kashmir.[45] The effect of this extension of application is that Jammu and Kashmir will now also be subject to the *Electricity Act* 2003, which will be truly national in its coverage for the first time since India's independence.

This legislation has acted as a source of significant industry and legislative reform, both in its original enactment, and through its amendment in 2007. It has consolidated and replaced a number of older pieces of legislation such as the *Indian Electricity Act* 1910, *The Electricity*

38 Amit Maheshwari and Neeraj Menon (Trilegal), 'Electricity Regulation in India' (*Lexology,* 26 March 2019) <https://www.lexology.com/library/detail.aspx?g=72d8a27b-af85-4a0e-ab46-dc4928a6d4f9> accessed 27 August 2019.

39 Ibid.

40 Ibid.

41 Vivek Sen, Kuldeep Sharma and Gireesh Shrimali, 'Reaching India's Renewable Energy Targets: The Role of Institutional Investors' (The Global Commission on the Economy and Climate, November 2016) I <https://climatepolicyinitiative.org/wp-content/uploads/2016/11/Reaching-Indias-Renewable-Energy-Targets-The-Role-of-Institutional-Investors_conference draft.pdf> accessed 27 August 2019.

42 Dibyanshu, Anuj Rastogi, Sathyajith Nair and Khaitan & Co, 'Electricity Regulation in India: Overview' (Thomson Reuters, 1 May 2019) <https://uk.practicallaw.thomsonreuters.com/w-012-2860?transitionType=Default&contextData=(sc.Default)&firstPage=true&bhcp=1> accessed 27 August 2019.

43 *The Economic Times*, 'Article 370: Why is Kashmir Tense about It & What Can India Do?' (*The Economic Times*, 5 August 2019) <https://economictimes.indiatimes.com/news/politics-and-nation/article-370-why-is-kashmir-tense-about-it-what-can-india-do/articleshow/70508922.cms?from=mdr> accessed 27 August 2019.

44 *India Today*, 'Narendra Modi-led Bharatiya Janata Party Retains Power in India: All You Need to Know about Indian Elections 2019' (*India Today*, 24 May 2019) <https://www.indiatoday.in/elections/lok-sabha-2019/story/all-you-need-to-know-about-indian-election-results-2019-1533352-2019-05-24> accessed 27 August 2019.

45 The *Jammu and Kashmir Reorganisation Act* 2019, Act 34 of 2019, 9 August 2019, *The Gazette of India* <http://egazette.nic.in/WriteReadData/2019/210407.pdf>. See also, Namit Saxena, 'Legal Hurdles Could Derail Modi Govt's Big Kashmir Move' (*Deccan Herald,* 5 August 2019) <https://www.deccanherald.com/opinion/comment/a-chip-on-my-shoulder-756764.html> accessed 27 August 2019.

(Supply) Act 1948 and the *Electricity Regulatory Commission Act* 1998. One of the most significant changes brought about by this legislation was contained in s.7,[46] which de-licensed the generation of electricity (with the exception of nuclear energy and larger hydroelectricity projects)[47]. In addition, generators were given the right in s.10(2)[48] to sell their electricity direct to end-consumers rather than the licensees or state electricity boards, in an effort to facilitate greater competition in the retail supply market.[49] This meant that consumers could avail themselves of PPAs with a generator much more readily and was designed to encourage greater private sector participation and foreign direct investment in the Indian energy sector. Other key developments included: empowering the central government to develop a National Electricity Policy and National Electricity Tariff Policy in consultation with state governments; unbundling the state electricity boards to create a structural separation between their generation, distribution and transmission activities; non-discriminatory access to transmission and distribution lines; and the introduction of a purchase obligation for renewable generation.[50]

3.2 Coal

India's natural resource endowments predominantly take the form of coal and lignite, with India boasting 220 years' worth of coal reserves at its current rate of production (320BT) and 472 years of coal resources.[51] Similar to other energy resources, India's coal and lignite deposits are not spread evenly geographically, with the eastern and south-central states of Jharkhand, Odisha, Chhattisgarh, West Bengal, Madhya Pradesh, Telangana and Maharashtra accounting for 98.26 per cent of the total coal reserves in the country.[52] However, Indian coal is poor quality with a 'very high ash content and a low calorific value',[53] meaning that higher-grade coal needs to be imported to meet the growing demand and help curb air pollution. In 2016, India accounted for 16 per cent of global coal consumption and coal is predicted to remain the dominant energy source in India until at least 2031–2032.[54]

The Ministry of Coal describes its goal as being 'to secure availability of coal to meet the demand of various sectors of the economy in an eco-friendly, sustainable and cost-effective manner'.[55] Coal-fired generation has grown rapidly since 2011, with a 12.7 per cent

46 S.7, *Electricity Act* 2003.

47 S.8, *Electricity Act* 2003.

48 S.10(2), *Electricity Act* 2003.

49 International Energy Agency, 'Understanding Energy Challenges in India: Policies, Players and Issues' (International Energy Agency, 11 December 2015) 30 <https://www.oecd-ilibrary.org/energy/understanding-energy-challenges-in-india_9789264247444-en> accessed 27 August 2019.

50 Ibid 91.

51 Central Statistics Office, Ministry of Statistics and Programme Implementation, Government of India, 'Energy Statistics – 2019, 26th Issue' (Ministry of Statistics and Programme Implementation, Government of India, March 2019) 100 <www.mospi.gov.in/sites/default/files/publication_reports/Energy%20Statistics%202019-finall.pdf> accessed 27 August 2019.

52 Ibid 14.

53 Chaturvedi, AVSM, VSM (Retd) and Maj Ajay Kumar, *Nuclear Energy in India's Energy Security Mix: An Appraisal* (Vij Books India Private Limited, 2014), 17.

54 Ajit Kumar Singh, 'Energy and Sustainable Development – An Indian Perspective' (2018) 1(1) *International Journal of Scientific Current Research and Development* 1.

55 Government of India, Ministry of Coal, 'Vision' (Government of India, 10 September 2014) <https://www.coal.nic.in/content/vision> accessed 27 August 2019.

compound annual growth rate to 2017.[56] This is double the growth in demand for electricity, leaving some states with a surplus of electricity supply.[57] However, given the recent push by Prime Minister Modi to reduce India's coal imports by a third by 2024[58] as a means of redressing the terms of trade, and with an additional 50GW of coal-fired generation currently under construction,[59] coal production will have to grow at a compound annual growth rate of 7.7 per cent until 2024 to meet the predicted shortfall in domestic demand.[60]

In 2019 there were 127 thermal coal-fired power plants in India, which combined provide 53.4 per cent of India's electricity generation.[61] Following the nationalisation of the Indian coal industry in 1971, a single company, Coal India Limited (CIL), which is majority owned by the Indian Government provides almost 85 per cent of India's domestic coal production. Coal India Limited also supplies 126 of the 127 coal-fired power plants.[62] This makes it the world's largest coal mining company,[63] and a sizeable contributor to central revenue in India through dividend payments, royalties on the coal production and other associated taxes. It is also a major employer, directly employing close to 300,000 people,[64] with a further 70,000 contractors employed, across its 369 mines, 16 coal washeries and corporate offices.[65] The importance of CIL to the Indian economy cannot be understated, the coal it supplies to the thermal power plants is at a rate that is discounted to international prices, thus it is designed to 'insulate Indian coal consumers against price volatility in the international market'.[66] Thus, its ultimate purpose is to make India's 'end user industry globally competitive'.[67]

Two other public sector/joint sector undertakings, which also report to the Ministry of Coal, make up much of the remaining coal production in India.[68] The first, NLC India Limited, is a public sector undertaking, which owns three lignite mines and four thermal power stations, as well as numerous wind and solar projects.[69] In total, NLC India Limited provides power-generating capacity of 4834.5MW.[70] This structure of vertical integration within the

56 Rahul Tongia, 'Understanding India, Its Energy Needs and Ambitions, and the Global Implications for Carbon Emissions' Brookings (Blog Post, 18 September 2018) <https://www.brookings.edu/blog/planetpolicy/2018/09/18/understanding-india-its-energy-needs-and-ambitions-and-the-global-implications-for-carbon-emissions>.

57 Ibid.

58 Institute for Energy Economics and Financial Analysis, 'India Looking to Slash Coal Imports by One-Third in the Next Five Years' (IEEFA, 5 August 2019) <http://ieefa.org/india-looking-to-slash-coal-imports-by-one-third-in-the-next-five-years> accessed 27 August 2019.

59 Tim Buckley, 'No New Coal Fired Power Plants for India' (*Renew Economy*, 20 December 2016) <https://reneweconomy.com.au/no-new-coal-fired-power-plants-india-80026> accessed 27 August 2019.

60 Rajesh Singh, 'India, World's No.2 Coal Buyer, Plans to Cut Imports by a Third' (Bloomberg, 1 August 2019) <https://www.bloomberg.com/news/articles/2019-08-01/india-world-s-no-2-coal-buyer-plans-to-cut-imports-by-a-third> accessed 27 August 2019.

61 Ministry of Power, Government of India, 'Annual Report 2017/2018' (Ministry of Power, Government of India, New Delhi 2018) 4 <https://powermin.nic.in/sites/default/files/uploads/MOP_Annual_Report_Eng_2017 18.pdf> accessed 27 August 2019.

62 Ministry of Coal, Government of India 'Annual Report 2018-19' (Ministry of Coal, Government of India, 2019) ch 5, 45 <https://coal.nic.in/sites/upload_files/coal/files/coalupload/AnnualReport1819.pdf> accessed 27 August 2019.

63 Ibid ch 1, 8.

64 Ibid ch 1, 8.

65 Ibid ch 1, 8.

66 Ibid ch 5, 45.

67 Ibid ch 5, 45.

68 Ibid ch 1, 7.

69 Ibid ch 1, 9.

70 Ibid ch 1, 9.

power sector of miner and generator is very unusual compared to other major economies in the unbundled and competitive market era. The second, the Singareni Collieries Limited (SCCL) is a joint sector undertaking.[71] This means it is a joint venture formed between the State Government of Telanganan and the Government of India, with an equity participation ratio of 51:49.[72] SCCL currently holds 10475MMT of proven coal reserves and provides 9 per cent of total Indian coal production.[73] It too is an active participant in electricity generation, operating a 1200MW thermal power station, with various solar power stations also proposed.[74]

In addition to these public sector/joint sector undertakings, a number of smaller privately owned and operated coal mines and coal-fired generators have now entered the market, following the de-licensing of electricity generation under the *Electricity Act* 2003.[75] Both private coal mining companies and coal-fired generators have reported serious difficulties obtaining the necessary land,[76] environmental approval and permits.[77] Further, the coal-fired generators have stated that they have faced acute difficulties since entering the market as they have been placed at a disadvantage when compared to the public sector/joint sector undertakings when it comes to obtaining coal supply (a 'coal linkage agreement') and in signing PPAs to sell their power.[78]

A further interesting development is the recent approval of the large Indian owned Adani Carmichael coal mine in Queensland, Australia. This mine has the potential to supply 2.3 billion tonnes of high-quality coal to India over the next 60 years, though how this development will interact with the Indian Government's commitment to significantly reduce their energy imports and improve their air quality is opaque.[79]

3.3 *Conventional hydrocarbons*

The Ministry of Petroleum and Natural Gas is responsible for the 'exploration and exploitation of petroleum resources, including natural gas', and the 'production, supply, distribution, marketing and pricing of petroleum including natural gas and petroleum products'.[80] With its rapid economic development and growing middle class,[81] India has recently experienced

71 Ibid ch 1, 8.
72 Ibid ch 1, 8.
73 Ibid ch 1, 8.
74 Ibid ch 1, 9.
75 International Energy Agency, 'Understanding Energy Challenges in India: Policies, Players and Issues' (International Energy Agency, 11 December 2015) 47, 56–57 <https://www.oecd-ilibrary.org/energy/understanding-energy-challenges-in-india_9789264247444-en> accessed 27 August 2019.
76 Ibid 38.
77 Ibid 90.
78 Amit Maheshwari and Neeraj Menon, Power Generation in India (*Lexology*, 25 July 2019), <https://www.lexology.com/library/detail.aspx?g=94ea53cd-3fab-4b86-a245-66ba399480ac> accessed 27 August 2019.
79 Stephen Long, Wayne Harley and Mary Fallon, 'Adani Carmichael Coal Mine: Former Indian Minister Sounds Alarm on Adani's Track Record, Mega-Mine's Viability' (Australian Broadcasting Corporation News, 2 October 2017), <https://www.abc.net.au/news/2017-10-02/former-minister-sounds-alarm-on-adanis-track-record-in-india/9005596> accessed 27 August 2019.
80 Ministry of Petroleum and Natural Gas, 'About the Ministry' (Ministry of Petroleum and Natural Gas, 3 August 2017) <http://petroleum.nic.in/about-us/about-ministry> accessed 27 August 2019.
81 International Energy Agency, 'India Energy Outlook' (*World Energy Outlook Special Report*, 27 November 2015) ch 2, 77 <https://www.gita.org.in/Attachments/Reports/IndiaEnergyOutlook_WEO2015.pdf> accessed 27 August 2019.

its largest ever increases in oil consumption.[82] Despite the first commercially successful oil discovery occurring in India in 1889,[83] India possesses limited reserves of crude oil and natural gas, making it one of the world's largest importers of crude oil.[84] It has been estimated that almost 80 per cent of India's petroleum is imported,[85] primarily from the Middle East.[86]

The domestic reserves India does have are spread over 26 sedimentary basins spanning 3.36 million km^2 of land, offshore up to 400m isobaths and in deep water beyond 400m isobath.[87] The total estimated balance recoverable reserves within India of oil and oil equivalent of gas are 1917MMT.[88] Only seven basins are currently in commercial production: Cambay, Assam Shelf, Mumbai offshore, Krishna Godavari, Cauvery, Assam Arakan Fold Belt and Rajasthan.[89]

Domestic crude oil production is currently approximately 35.68MMT per annum.[90] This production is split on an almost 70:30 basis[91] between a nomination regime operated by two Indian Government enterprises, Oil and Natural Gas Corporation Limited and Oil India Limited, and a production sharing contract regime operated by private joint venture companies. Gas production operates on a similar basis, with approximately 32.65BCM[92] being produced on a 75:25 split[93] between the government enterprises operating under the nomination regime and the private joint venture companies operating under the production sharing contract regime.

3.3.1 The Nomination Regime

From 1948 until 1980, the oil sector in India was operated as a state monopoly,[94] with only public sector upstream oil companies able to participate in exploration and production activities. Two national oil companies (NOCs), the Oil and Natural Gas Corporation Limited and

82 Ibid 11.

83 Directorate General of Hydrocarbons, Ministry of Petroleum and Natural Gas, Government of India, 'India's Hydrocarbon Outlook 2017–18: A Report on Exploration and Production Activities' (Ministry of Petroleum and Natural Gas, New Delhi, 2018) <http://dghindia.gov.in/assets/downloads/ar/2017-18.pdf> accessed 27 August 2019.

84 International Energy Agency, 'India Energy Outlook' (*World Energy Outlook Special Report*, 27 November 2015) 14 <https://www.gita.org.in/Attachments/Reports/IndiaEnergyOutlook_WEO2015.pdf> accessed 27 August 2019.

85 Narendra Dalei, Anshuman Gupta and Hiranmoy Roy, 'Crude Oil Import of India from Its Major Oil Trade Partner Countries: An Empirical Evidence Using Panel Data Analysis' (2017) 2(5) *International Journal of Advanced Research and Development*, 726 <https://www.researchgate.net/publication/322069253_Crude_oil_import_of_India_from_its_major_oil_trade_partner_countries_An_empirical_evidence_using_panel_data_analysis> accessed 27 August 2019.

86 International Energy Agency, 'India Energy Outlook' (*World Energy Outlook Special Report*, 27 November 2015) ch 1, 33 <https://www.gita.org.in/Attachments/Reports/IndiaEnergyOutlook_WEO2015.pdf> accessed 27 August 2019.

87 Directorate General of Hydrocarbons, Ministry of Petroleum and Natural Gas, Government of India, 'India's Hydrocarbon Outlook 2017–18: A Report on Exploration and Production Activities' (Ministry of Petroleum and Natural Gas, New Delhi, 2018) 103 <http://dghindia.gov.in/assets/downloads/ar/2017-18.pdf> accessed 27 August 2019.

88 Ibid 103.

89 Ibid 103.

90 Ibid 4.

91 Ibid 9.

92 Ibid 4.

93 Ibid 9.

94 Ibid 23.

Oil India Private Limited, were formed during this period.[95] The first, the Oil and Natural Gas Corporation Limited, was initially established as the Oil and Natural Gas Directorate (ONGC) in 1955[96] and tasked with carrying out geological surveys, before changing its status to a statutory body under an Act of Parliament in October 1959.[97] The role of ONGC was

> to plan, promote, organize and implement programs for the development of Petroleum Resources and the production and sale of petroleum and petroleum products produced by it, and to perform such other functions as the central government may, from time to time, assign to it.[98]

The second NOC, Oil India Private Limited (OIL), was initially established to take over the Burma Oil Company's (BOC's) affairs in Assam.[99] At its incorporation on 18 February 1959, the company was two-thirds owned by the Assam Oil Company/BOC and one-third owned by the Government of India. In 1961, OIL was restructured into a joint venture company, with the venturers becoming equal partners in the new entity.[100]

3.3.1.1 FEATURES OF THE NOMINATION REGIME

The Nomination Regime was a state-based monopoly regime,[101] with the NOCs engaging in exploration and production on blocks assigned to them by the precursor to the Ministry of Petroleum and Gas.[102] These projects had no minimum expenditure requirement.[103] Although these projects did pay a royalty, the hydrocarbons produced were priced at the prevailing rate in accordance with subsidy arrangements.[104]

3.3.2 The Production Sharing Contract Regime

The Production Sharing Contract (PSC) Regime existed in India from 1980 until 2015.[105] Throughout this period, the government sought to de-regulate (1980–1995)[106] and then liberalise (1997–2010)[107] the exploration and production of petroleum. During this period, the government launched the New Exploration Licensing Policy (1997) in an effort to 'attract significant risk capital from Indian and foreign companies, state of the art technologies, new geological concepts and best management practises to explore oil and gas resources in the country and meet rising demands for oil and gas'.[108] This liberalisation of the sector introduced international competitive bidding, and placed domestic and foreign companies on an equal footing.[109] This meant that the NOCs no longer had a carried interest, with the

95 Ibid 24.
96 Ibid 16.
97 Ibid 16.
98 Ibid 16.
99 Ibid 17.
100 Ibid 16.
101 Ibid 22–23.
102 Ibid 23.
103 Ibid 160, 163.
104 Ibid 158.
105 Ibid 23.
106 Ibid 23.
107 Ibid 23.
108 Ibid 20.
109 Ibid 20.

government interest now taking the form of royalties, income taxes and a share of profit oil based on a sliding scale linked to post-tax rates of return.[110]

3.3.3 *The Revenue Sharing Contract Regime*

On 10 March 2016, the government introduced the Hydrocarbon Exploration and Licensing Policy (HELP), in an attempt to stimulate domestic oil and gas production, fast track exploration, enhance transparency and thereby reduce import dependency.[111] The HELP introduced a revenue sharing contract regime.[112] Another significant development linked to the HELP was the introduction of the Open Acreage Licensing Policy (OALP).[113] The OALP enables companies to initiate *suo moto* an Expression of Interest to propose a potential block for release for exploration and production rather than having to wait for it to come up in a licensing round.[114] Once a block has been proposed, the Directorate General of Hydrocarbons will open up the block to competitive bidding[115] subject to specified conditions such as a work programme and environmental, health and safety regulations being met.[116]

The model revenue sharing contract provides a number of benefits, with the operators now having the freedom to market and price any hydrocarbons produced at international market prices under Article 19 and the government no longer having to monitor expenditure on cost oil.[117] Rather the government merely has to monitor the production levels and that the oil is marketed at arm's length international fair market prices.[118] There are also reduced royalty rates and extended exploration and production periods to encourage deep water and ultra-deep water exploration.[119]

3.4 *Unconventional hydrocarbons*

In addition to conventional hydrocarbon resources, India also possesses recoverable reserves of coal bed methane (also known as coal seam gas) of approximately 280.3BCM, and is estimated to possess other sedimentary basins bearing shale gas/oil resources.[120] Until recently, the development of unconventional hydrocarbons was limited because the licences issued and the regulatory framework specified that the hydrocarbon produced would be crude oil or conventional natural gas.[121] In August 2018, a new policy framework was introduced to accelerate the exploration and production of unconventional hydrocarbons. A key feature of

110 Ibid 160–163
111 Ibid 6–8.
112 Ibid ch 2, 34.
113 Ibid ch 2, 34.
114 Ibid ch 2, 34–35.
115 Ibid ch 2, 34.
116 Ibid ch 1, 22.
117 Ibid ch 8, 159.
118 Ibid ch 2, 35, 40.
119 Ibid ch 2, 35.
120 Ministry of Petroleum and Natural Gas, Government of India, 'Annual report 2015–2016' (Ministry of Petroleum and Natural Gas, Government of India, 2016) 22 <http://petroleum.nic.in/sites/default/files/AR15-16.pdf> accessed 27 August 2019.
121 Directorate General of Hydrocarbons, Ministry of Petroleum and Natural Gas, Government of India, 'India's Hydrocarbon Outlook 2017–18: a report on exploration and production activities' (Ministry of Petroleum and Natural Gas, New Delhi, 2018) 23 <http://dghindia.gov.in/assets/downloads/ar/2017-18.pdf> accessed 27 August 2019.

this framework is that it provides a uniform license for the exploitation of oil and gas[122] (i.e., operators that currently work a crude oil or natural gas project that also has reserves of shale oil, shale gas, gas hydrates or coal bed methane are now able to exploit all of the hydrocarbons within their license area).

Other recent developments include the introduction of the National Biofuel Policy in 2018, which was designed to encourage the use of domestic agricultural and industrial waste as feedstock in both the energy and transportation sectors.[123]

3.5 Renewable energy

India is rapidly becoming a world leader in renewable energy, with installed renewable electricity capacity more than doubling between 2014 and 2019.[124] India is currently on track to exceed its Paris commitment under its Intended Nationally Determined Contribution (INDC) of 175GW of renewable capacity installed by 2022.[125] This target is made up of 100GW of solar energy, 60GW wind energy, 10GW of biomass and biogas and 5GW from small hydropower.[126] It is not surprising that India has met this target given the strong commitment and range of renewable energy policies and incentives that are available at both a central and state level.[127] Indeed, as of June 2018, the Indian Government set a revised target of 225GW of renewable energy by 2022.[128] The success in achieving these targets is in large part due to the success of the National Solar Mission, solar power capacity increased over eightfold between 2014 and 2018 from 2630MW to 22,000MW in 2017–2018, while wind power capacity has increased 1.6 times over the same period to 35.62GW.[129] In addition, India also has over 1100 small hydro projects[130] and 500 biomass and cogeneration power projects installed,[131] which

122 Ibid 6.

123 Amit Maheshwari and Neeraj Menon (Trilegal), 'Electricity Regulation in India' (*Lexology,* 26 March 2019) <https://www.lexology.com/library/detail.aspx?g=72d8a27b-af85-4a0e-ab46-dc4928a6d4f9> accessed 27 August 2019.

124 Office of the Chief Economist, Department of Industry, Innovation and Science, Australian Government, 'Coal in India 2019' (Office of the Chief Economist, Department of Industry, Innovation and Science, Australian Government, 2019) 22 <https://www.industry.gov.au/sites/default/files/2019-08/coal-in-india-2019-report.pdf> accessed 27 August 2019.

125 Natural Resources Defense Council, 'The Road From Paris: India's Progress Toward Its Climate Pledge' (Natural Resources Defense Council, December 2018) 3 <https://www.nrdc.org/sites/default/files/indias_progress_towards_its_climate_pledge_2018.pdf> accessed 27 August 2019.

126 Press Information Bureau, Government of India, Ministry of New and Renewable Energy, 'Year End Review 2018 – MNRE' (Ministry of New and Renewable Energy, 10 December 2018) <https://pib.gov.in/Pressreleaseshare.aspx?PRID=1555373> accessed 27 August 2019.

127 International Energy Agency, 'Understanding Energy Challenges in India: Policies, Players and Issues' (International Energy Agency, 11 December 2015) 19–20 <https://www.oecd-ilibrary.org/energy/understanding-energy-challenges-in-india_9789264247444-en> accessed 27 August 2019.

128 Skipper Limited, 'Scaling Diversifying Winning: Annual Report FY2017–18' (Skipper Limited, 2018) 46 <https://repository.skipperlimited.com/investor-relations/pdf/Annual-Report-2017-2018.pdf> accessed 27 August 2019.

129 Ministry of New and Renewable Energy, Government of India, 'Four Year Achievement Booklet' (Ministry of New and Renewable Energy, Government of India), <https://mnre.gov.in/sites/default/files/uploads/MNRE-4-Year-Achievement-Booklet.pdf> accessed 19 August 2019.

130 Ministry of New and Renewable Energy, Government of India, 'Annual Report 2018–19' (Ministry of New and Renewable Energy, Government of India) ch 4, 50 <https://mnre.gov.in/file-manager/annual-report/2018-2019/English/pdf/chapter-4.pdf> accessed 27 August 2019.

131 Ibid ch 4, 48.

provide an additional 4593MW[132] and 9075MW of generation capacity to the Indian electricity sector,[133] respectively. India currently boasts the fourth largest volume of installed wind and renewable electricity capacity globally,[134] and the fifth largest volume of solar energy capacity.[135] One of the greatest achievements of the Indian renewables programme is the tangible difference it makes to poorer households. For example, 2.5 million solar lamps were distributed to Indian students between 2015 and 2019.[136]

India has a revised electricity tariff that mandates quota-based schemes, and a renewables purchasing obligation.[137] The renewables purchase obligation (RPO) mandates that all State Electricity Commissions must supply at least 8 per cent of renewable energy[138] and 10.5 per cent of solar electricity in their generation mix by 2022.[139] The RPO has an effective floor price of US$144 per MW of electricity.[140] The landmark Indian Supreme Court case of *Hindustan Zinc Limited v Rajasthan Electricity Regulatory Commission* (Civil Appeal No. 4417 of 2015)[141] challenged whether the RPO applied to all wholesale purchasers of electricity. The outcome of this case was that because of the need to support the transition to renewable energy, the Supreme Court held that the RPO is to be imposed on all purchasers of electricity including captive generators and open-access consumers. The Court also ruled that RPO empowers electricity regulators to impose penalties on entities that fail to meet their RPO obligations. As a result of the adoption of reverse auction bidding against the benchmark tariffs set up by the Central Electricity Regulatory Commission, prices for solar energy fell throughout India at a much faster rate than had been previously anticipated.[142] Inter-state transmission charges, which are the purview of the Central Government of India, are also waived for both wind and solar energy.[143]

132 Ibid ch 4, 50.

133 Ibid ch 4, 48.

134 Press Information Bureau, Government of India, Ministry of New and Renewable Energy, 'Year End Review 2018 – MNRE' (Ministry of New and Renewable Energy, 10 December 2018) <https://pib.gov.in/Pressreleaseshare.aspx?PRID=1555373> accessed 27 August 2019.

135 Ibid.

136 Ministry of New and Renewable Energy, Government of India, 'Four Year Achievement Booklet' (Ministry of New and Renewable Energy, Government of India), <https://mnre.gov.in/sites/default/files/uploads/MNRE-4-Year-Achievement-Booklet.pdf> accessed 19 August 2019.

137 Ministry of New and Renewable Energy, Government of India, 'Annual Report 2018–19' (Ministry of New and Renewable Energy, Government of India) ch 4, 60 <https://mnre.gov.in/file-manager/annual-report/2018-2019/English/pdf/chapter-4.pdf> accessed 27 August 2019.

138 Ministry of New and Renewable Energy, Government of India, 'Solar RPO Requirements for States' <https://mnre.gov.in/sites/default/files/uploads/solar-RPO-requirement-by-2022_0.pdf> accessed 18 August 2019.

139 Ministry of New and Renewable Energy, Government of India, 'Annual Report 2018–19' (Ministry of New and Renewable Energy, Government of India) chs 1 and 2 <https://mnre.gov.in/file-manager/annual-report/2018-2019/English/pdf/chapter-1.pdf> accessed 27 August 2019.

140 India Brand Equity Foundation, 'Renewable Energy' (India Brand Equity Foundation, February 2018) 17 <https://www.ibef.org/download/Renewable-Energy-February-2018.pdf> accessed 27 August 2019.

141 *Hindustan Zinc Limited v Rajasthan Electricity Regulatory Commission* (2015) 12 S.C.C. 611.

142 LexCounsel Law Offices, 'Low Tariff for Solar PV Projects: The Good and the Not So Good' (International Lawyers Network, 9 February, 2016) <https://www.ilntoday.com/2016/02/low-tariff-for-solar-pv-projects-the-good-and-the-not-so-good> accessed 27 August 2019.

143 Manu Aggarwal and Arjun Dutt, 'State of the Indian Renewable Energy Sector: Drivers, Risks, and Opportunities' (Council on Energy, Environment and Water, September 2018) 20 <https://www.ceew.in/sites/default/files/CEEW_State_of_the_Indian_Renewable_Energy_Sector_report_31Oct18.pdf> accessed 27 August 2019.

Going forward, India has set a national target to increase its share of non-fossil fuelled electric capacity to 40 per cent by 2030.[144] The INDC also commits to reducing India's greenhouse gas (GHG) emissions intensity per unit of GDP by 33–35 per cent below 2005 levels by 2030, and 'to create an additional carbon sink of 2.5 to 3 billion tonnes of carbon dioxide through additional tree cover'.[145] It has also shown international leadership in the area of solar energy deployment, establishing the International Solar Alliance (ISA) in 2015, a treaty-based organisation with 122 member states,[146] which is headquartered in Gurugram, India.[147] ISA members are committed to promote solar energy and facilitate over a US$1 trillion in investments to install 1TW of solar power by 2030.[148]

3.6 Nuclear energy

India's nuclear energy law and policy has long been focused on making India's energy sector more self-reliant. Indeed, this principle has been so prevalent that when India's Atomic Energy Programme commenced in 1948[149] under the supervision of the Indian Atomic Energy Agency, the agency's motto was 'self-reliance'.[150] India currently generates 6780MW of electricity a year from its nuclear power stations, though this is predicted to increase to 20,000MW by 2020.[151] Increasing nuclear generation is a core strategy of the Indian Government, with 25 per cent of its electricity generation by 2050 planned to come from nuclear sources.[152] Private ownership of nuclear energy generation assets is not permitted.[153]

India's Nuclear Power Programme is being implemented in three key stages. In Stage 1 a Public Sector Enterprise, the Nuclear Power Corporation of India Limited (NPCIL) deployed pressurised heavy water reactors (PHWR) to generate electricity.[154] NPCIL currently

144 International Energy Agency, 'Nationally Determined Contribution (NDC) to the Paris Agreement: India' (International Energy Agency, 22 February 2018) <https://www.iea.org/policiesandmeasures/pams/india/name-155210-en.php?s=dHlwZT1jYyZzdGF0dXM9T2s,&return=PG5hdiBpZD0iYnJlYWRjcnVtYiI-PGEgaHJlZj0iLyI-SG9tZTwvYT4gJnJhcXVvOyA8YSBocmVmPSIvcG9saWNpZXNhbmRtZWFzdXJlcy8iPlBvbGljaWVzIGFuZCBNZWFzdXJlczwvYT4gJnJhcXVv> accessed 27 August 2019.

145 Ibid.

146 International Solar Alliance, 'ISA Member Countries' (International Solar Alliance, 19 August 2019), <http://isolaralliance.org/MemberCont.aspx> accessed 19 August 2019.

147 United Nations Framework Convention on Climate Change, 'International Solar Alliance Enters into Force' (United Nations Framework Convention on Climate Change, 7 December 2017) <https://unfccc.int/news/international-solar-alliance-enters-into-force> accessed 27 August 2019.

148 The World Bank, 'Solar Energy to Power India of the Future' (The World Bank, 30 June 2016) <https://www.worldbank.org/en/news/feature/2016/06/30/solar-energy-to-power-india-of-the-future> accessed 27 August 2019.

149 This programme was facilitated by the introduction of the Atomic Energy Agency Act 1948. This legislation was subsequently replaced by the Atomic Energy Act 1962.

150 Chaturvedi, AVSM, VSM (Retd), Maj Ajay Kumar, *Nuclear Energy in India's Energy Security Mix: An Appraisal* (Vij Books India Private Limited, 2014), 99.

151 Prerna Gupta and M. V. Ramana, 'A Decade After the Nuclear Deal' (The India Forum, 3 May 2019) <https://www.theindiaforum.in/article/decade-after-nuclear-deal> accessed 27 August 2019.

152 International Energy Agency, 'India Energy Outlook' (*World Energy Outlook Special Report*, 27 November 2015) ch 3, 135 <https://www.gita.org.in/Attachments/Reports/IndiaEnergyOutlook_WEO2015.pdf> accessed 27 August 2019.

153 International Atomic Energy Agency, 'Country Nuclear Power Profiles, 2018 Edition, India' (International Atomic Energy Agency, 2016) <https://www-pub.iaea.org/MTCD/Publications/PDF/cnpp2018/countryprofiles/India/India.htm> accessed 27 August 2019.

154 Department of Atomic Energy, Government of India 'Annual Report 2017–18' (Department of Atomic Energy, Government of India) ch 1, 3 <http://www.dae.nic.in/writereaddata/areport/ar1718.pdf> accessed 27 August 2019.

operates 22 nuclear power reactors with an installed capacity of 6780MW.[155] However, this process is still ongoing, with a further 6 PHWR currently under construction and a further 14 PWHR projects, with a combined capacity of approximately 15,700MW,[156] sanctioned by the government as part of a fast ramp up strategy for nuclear generation. Stage 2 of the Nuclear Power Programme involves the development of Fast Breeder Reactors (FBR) by the Indira Gandhi Centre for Atomic Research, Bhartiya Nabhikiya Vidyut Nigam Ltd and the Bhabha Atomic Research Centre.[157] FBR offer benefits over other technologies because they use a mixed oxide of uranium and plutonium for fuel and utilise liquid sodium for cooling, therefore producing more fuel than they consume.[158] Stage 3 of the Nuclear Power Programme focuses on developing new advanced nuclear technologies for the development on a commercial scale of power generation such as Thorium-232 based reactors.[159] Thorium-based reactors offer a range of benefits, including advanced safety features, but also, more importantly for the Indian market, they use a fuel stock that has far larger world resources than uranium.[160]

India is not a party to the Nuclear Non-Proliferation Treaty (NPT)[161] and has signed but not ratified the Comprehensive Test Ban Treaty (CTBT).[162] Ordinarily, this would prelude India from being able to purchase foreign supplies of uranium, plutonium and thorium feedstocks.[163] The 48 members of the Nuclear Suppliers Group (NSG), a voluntary association of states who have decided to coordinate their export controls to non-nuclear weapon states, have long held a rule that they will not sell to countries who are not parties to both the NPT and the CTBT.[164] However, on 6 September 2008[165] following the signing of the Indo-US Nuclear Civilian Agreement[166] and intense lobbying by the USA of the other NSG member states, [167] the NSG gave India a 'clean waiver'[168] from its existing rules, including the requirement that recipient countries must have comprehensive International Atomic

155 Nuclear Power Corporation of India Limited, 'About Us' (Nuclear Power Corporation of India Limited, 2017) <https://www.npcil.nic.in/content/328_1_AboutNPCIL.aspx> accessed 27 August 2019.

156 Amit Maheshwari and Neeraj Menon (Trilegal), 'Power Generation in India' (*Lexology*, 25 July 2019) <https://www.lexology.com/library/detail.aspx?g=94ea53cd-3fab-4b86-a245-66ba399480ac> accessed 27 August 2019.

157 Department of Atomic Energy, Government of India 'Annual Report 2017–18' (Department of Atomic Energy, Government of India) ch 2, 53 <http://www.dae.nic.in/writereaddata/areport/ar1718.pdf> accessed 27 August 2019.

158 Ibid ch 2, 53.

159 Ibid ch 3, 75.

160 Ibid ch 3, 75.

161 Nuclear Threat Initiative, 'India' (Nuclear Threat initiative, June 2019) <https://www.nti.org/learn/countries/india> accessed 27 August 2019.

162 Rakesh Sood, 'India and Non-Proliferation Export Control Regimes' (Observer Research Foundation, April 2018) 24 <https://www.orfonline.org/wp-content/uploads/2018/04/ORF_OccasionalPaper_150_NonProliferation_FinalForUpload.pdf> accessed 27 August 2019.

163 International Energy Agency, 'Understanding Energy Challenges in India: Policies, Players and Issues' (International Energy Agency, 11 December 2015) 81 <https://www.oecd-ilibrary.org/energy/understanding-energy-challenges-in-india_9789264247444-en> accessed 27 August 2019.

164 Arms Control Association, 'The Nuclear Suppliers Group (NSG) at a Glance' (Arms Control Association, August 2017) <https://www.armscontrol.org/factsheets/NSG> accessed 27 August 2019.

165 Rakesh Sood, 'India and Non-Proliferation Export Control Regimes' (Observer Research Foundation, April 2018) 28 <https://www.orfonline.org/wp-content/uploads/2018/04/ORF_OccasionalPaper_150_NonProliferation_FinalForUpload.pdf> accessed 27 August 2019.

166 Ibid 4.

167 Ibid 6.

168 Ibid 13.

Energy Agency (IAEA) safeguards covering all nuclear activities.[169] In return, India had to provide a commitment that it would not share its nuclear technology or material with any other country and that it would uphold its voluntary moratorium on the testing of nuclear weapons. Since 2008, India has entered into nuclear supply agreements with a number of NSG member states including Australia, Russia, France, the USA, Mongolia, Namibia and Canada.[170] This has uniquely positioned India in being able to engage in civil nuclear commerce.[171]

One positive feature of the Indian nuclear sector is its strong emphasis on the indigenous development of its nuclear energy industry.[172] More recently, the Indian Government has sought greater levels of foreign participation in the nuclear industry, particularly in the context of the supply of technology and other equipment. One of the key issues for foreign suppliers has been the requirement imposed by both s.4 of the Civil Liability for Nuclear Damage Act 2010 and Article 10 of the Convention on Supplementary Compensation for Nuclear Damages, which India has also ratified, mandating a strict liability civil nuclear liability clause,[173] which was said to be hampering foreign participation.[174] The Indian Government has since released FAQs which have stated that within a contract between the NPCIL, as the operator of nuclear power plants, and a foreign supplier it was not mandatory to include a civil liability clause.[175] However, for this to be effective two things will need to occur, first, NPCIL must be willing to accept having the foreign supplier pass the liability that they would otherwise have borne onto them, and second, the FAQs must be deemed to be legally binding. This latter issue seems particularly unconvincing, especially as the government has publicly stated that it will not be amending the *Civil Liability for Nuclear Damage* (CLND) *Act* 2010 to effect the change.[176] Furthermore, the approach suggested in the FAQs must not be deemed to be in breach of the Convention on Supplementary Compensation.[177] Thus there seems to be a lot of issues for foreign suppliers to get comfortable with prior to entering into a contract with NPCIL on the basis of the FAQs.

169 Arms Control Association, 'The Nuclear Suppliers Group (NSG) at a Glance' (Arms Control Association, August 2017) <https://www.armscontrol.org/factsheets/NSG> accessed 27 August 2019.

170 Nuclear Threat Initiative, 'India – Nuclear' (Nuclear Threat Initiative, August 2016) <https://www.nti.org/learn/countries/india/nuclear> accessed 27 August 2019.

171 Ibid.

172 International Energy Agency, 'India Energy Outlook' (*World Energy Outlook Special Report*, 27 November 2015) ch 3, 135 <https://www.gita.org.in/Attachments/Reports/IndiaEnergyOutlook_WEO2015.pdf> accessed 27 August 2019.

173 Amit Maheshwari and Neeraj Menon (Trilegal), 'Electricity Regulation in India' (*Lexology*, 26 March 2019) <https://www.lexology.com/library/detail.aspx?g=72d8a27b-af85-4a0e-ab46-dc4928a6d4f9> accessed 27 August 2019.

174 International Energy Agency, 'India Energy Outlook' (*World Energy Outlook Special Report*, 27 November 2015) ch 3, 136 <https://www.gita.org.in/Attachments/Reports/IndiaEnergyOutlook_WEO2015.pdf> accessed 27 August 2019.

175 Ministry of External Affairs, Government of India, 'Frequently Asked Questions and Answers on Civil Liability for Nuclear Damage Act 2010 and Related Issues' (Ministry of External Affairs, Government of India, 8 February 2015) <https://www.mea.gov.in/press-releases.htm?dtl/24766/Frequently_Asked_Questions_and_Answers_on_Civil_Liability_for_Nuclear_Damage_Act_2010_and_related_issues> accessed 27 August 2019.

176 First Post, 'Liability Law Regarding Nuclear Reactors will not be Amended, Says Govt' (First Post India, 8 February 2015), <https://www.firstpost.com/india/liability-law-regarding-nuclear-reactors-will-not-amended-says-govt-2086787.html>, accessed 17 August 2019.

177 Ibid.

4 Managing the Indian energy transition

There are four key pillars to India's energy policy:

1. energy security
2. universal access to energy and energy affordability
3. environmental concerns, such as air pollution and climate change
4. improving energy efficiency.[178]

While the first pillar, energy security, has long been interpreted within the Indian context as meaning energy independence or self-reliance, and thus supports the continuing use of domestic coal, the other pillars all act as drivers for the energy transition.

4.1 Energy security

Due to its long history of linking energy security with national security, India's approach to energy security has long been based on the premise of increasing its domestic production,[179] as opposed to the regional approaches used by the European Union[180] or the diversified energy sources and diversified supply approaches adopted by the Chinese Government. These factors, along with a concern about the impact of a heavy import dependence within the energy sector on the Indian terms of trade,[181] led Prime Minister Modi to announce a one-third reduction in coal imports by 2024.[182] This is likely to have a negative impact on both India's air pollution, GHG emissions and energy efficiency, as domestic sources of coal are generally a lower grade than the imported coal and possess a higher ash content, with result that they do not burn as efficiently.[183] The exploitation of other domestic sources such as conventional and unconventional hydrocarbons and renewable energy sources, as well as the development of thorium reactors are all outworkings of this approach to energy security.[184]

178 Narendra Modi, 'Hydrocarbons to Fuel the Future – Choices & Challenges' (Petrotech, New Delhi, 5 December 2016) <http://archive.petrotech.in/documents/PM-address-at-the-Inaugural-Session-of-PETROTECH-on-December-5-2016.pdf> accessed 27 August 2019.

179 Narendra Modi, 'Hydrocarbons to Fuel the Future – Choices & Challenges' (Petrotech, New Delhi, 5 December 2016) <http://archive.petrotech.in/documents/PM-address-at-the-Inaugural-Session-of-PETROTECH-on-December-5-2016.pdf> accessed 27 August 2019.

180 Christian Egenhofer and Jacques de Jong, 'Thinking the Unthinkable: Promoting Regional Approaches to EU Energy Policies for a More United and Effective Europe' (*Istituto Affari Internazionali*, May 2014) 1–3 <https://www.clingendaelenergy.com/files.cfm?event=files.download&ui=B83D7BE0-5254-00CF-FD03F122B6DF5885> accessed 27 August 2019.

181 June Ma and Ivan Roberts, 'Economic Trends in India' (The Reserve Bank of Australia, 21 June 2018) 4 <https://www.rba.gov.au/publications/bulletin/2018/jun/pdf/economic-trends-in-india.pdf> accessed 27 August 2019.

182 Rajesh Singh, 'India, World's No. 2 Coal Buyer, Plans to Cut Imports by a Third' (Bloomberg, 1 August 2019) <https://www.bloomberg.com/news/articles/2019-08-01/india-world-s-no-2-coal-buyer-plans-to-cut-imports-by-a-third> accessed 27 August 2019.

183 Chandra Bhushan, Sanjeev Kanchan, Soundaram Ramanathan, Angeline Suresh, Priyavrat Bhati, N. Sai Siddhartha and Abhisehek Rudra, 'Coal Toll' (DownToEarth, 7 July 2015) <https://www.downtoearth.org.in/coverage/pollution/coal-toll-48581> accessed 27 August 2019.

184 See, e.g., McKinsey & Company, 'India: Towards Energy Independence 2030' (McKinsey & Company, January 2014) 9 <https://www.mckinsey.com/~/media/McKinsey/Industries/Oil%20and%20Gas/Our%20Insights/India%20Towards%20energy%20independence%202030/India-Towards-energy-independence-2030.ashx> accessed 27 August 2019.

4.2 Universal access to energy and energy affordability

India's electrification project has been described by the International Energy Agency (IEA) as 'one of the largest successes in the history of electrification'.[185] In 2000, only 43 per cent of the Indian population had access to energy.[186] By 2017, following concerted efforts by subsequent governments over 92 per cent of the Indian population had access to electricity.[187] The government is committed to achieving universal access, including through the SAUBHAGYA Scheme which was launched by Prime Minister Modi in September 2017.[188] This scheme seeks to ensure the universal electrification of all census villages by December 2018,[189] with the government aiming to provide all households with access to a continuous 24 hour supply of electricity by 2022 under the Deen Dayal Upadhyay Gram Jyoti Yojana Scheme.[190]

Energy affordability goes hand-in-hand with the strategies designed to support the universal access to energy. As a developing country with a sizeable rural and remote population, many consumers are extremely price sensitive.[191]

4.3 Environmental concerns

The air pollution associated with Indian power generation is the most pressing environmental concern for the Indian Government, with over 1 million Indian citizens said to die prematurely each year[192] as a result of large particulate matter in the air from coal-fired generation and the use of traditional biomass for cooking in poorer communities. In addition, and as detailed in section 3.5 above, India has ratified the United Nations Framework Convention on Climate Change, the Kyoto Protocol and the Paris Agreement, and thus has committed to substantially reduce its GHG emissions.[193] Neither of these concerns will be easy to achieve, especially when coupled with the conflicting commitment to increase the use of domestically produced low-grade coal by 2024.

185 International Energy Agency, 'Energy Access Outlook 2017 From Poverty to Prosperity' (International Energy Agency, 2017) 3 <https://www.iea.org/publications/freepublications/publication/WEO2017SpecialReport_EnergyAccessOutlook.pdf> accessed 27 August 2019.

186 Ibid.

187 The World Bank, 'Access to Electricity (% of Population)' (The World Bank, 2019) <https://data.worldbank.org/indicator/eg.elc.accs.zs?end=2017&start=2017&view=map> accessed 27 August 2019.

188 Bigsna Gill, Astha Gupta and Debajit Palit, 'Rural Electrification: Impact on Distribution Companies in India' (The Energy and Resources Institute, 2019) 4 <https://www.teriin.org/sites/default/files/2019-02/DUF%20Report.pdf> accessed 27 August 2019.

189 Ibid 11.

190 Ibid 4, 11.

191 Peter Varghese, 'An India Economic Strategy to 2035: Navigating from Potential to Delivery' (Department of Foreign Affairs and Trade (Australia), 12 July 2018) ch 7, 167 <https://dfat.gov.au/geo/india/ies/pdf/dfat-an-india-economic-strategy-to-2035.pdf> accessed 27 August 2019.

192 Ibid ch 7, 167.

193 *The Economic Times*, 'India ratifies 2nd commitment period of Kyoto Protocol' (*The Economic Times*, 9 August 2017) <https://economictimes.indiatimes.com/news/politics-and-nation/india-ratifies-2nd-commitment-period-of-kyoto-protocol/articleshow/59983651.cms> accessed 27 August 2019.

4.4 Improving energy efficiency

Improving the energy efficiency of the existing coal-fired generation fleet is seen as a key means of reducing air pollution and GHG emissions.[194] Any strategies established to enhance energy efficiency are also likely to positively impact both the terms of trade and allay concerns about an ever-increasing import dependency.

5 Conclusion

Fossil fuels are still expected to remain the primary energy sources within the Indian economy by 2030.

Despite this, renewable energy and nuclear power are expected to play an ever-increasing role in meeting the growing demand for energy and electricity. India is in a difficult position, its historic reliance on its plentiful coal supply means that its electricity transition will need to be more rapid and profound than many other countries. This comes with impacts on its terms of trade, as India will either have to import more foreign energy supply at great cost, thereby giving up its traditional values of energy independence and self-reliance, or markedly increase its use of renewables and nuclear power. Either option is invariably more expensive than the status quo and that risks a decline in energy affordability for low-income households and puts India's significant gains in energy access in jeopardy. That said, such a move also presents several benefits if the renewables and nuclear option is chosen by reducing large particulate matter and air pollution, thereby lessening deaths caused by poor air quality, as well as helping India to meet their Paris commitments on climate change. This means that India's policymakers and legislators have a difficult task ahead trying to balance their competing national objectives for the energy sector when trying to pick the option that best provides India with a stable, clean, reliable, secure, affordable and accessible energy supply.

194 Ian Barnes, 'Upgrading the Efficiency of the World's Coal Fleet to Reduce CO_2 Emissions' (World Coal Association, 8 April 2015) <https://www.worldcoal.org/upgrading-efficiency-worlds-coal-fleet-reduce-co2-emissions> accessed 27 August 2019.

25

ENERGY LAW AND REGULATION IN CHINA

Jie Huan

1 Introduction

China has become the world's largest energy producer and consumer.[1] China is also the world's largest producer of energy-intensive goods.[2] At present, in China, a multi-fuel energy production system of coal, oil gas and renewable energy has been formed.[3] The energy sector is shifting, divesting itself of coal and moving to clean energy sources, with the development momentum accelerated from conventional to unconventional energy.[4] China's energy security guarantees are based on the domestic market while simultaneously strengthening international cooperation in energy. With the "One Belt One Road"[5] energy cooperation and pragmatic advancement, oil and gas import capacity has been steadily improved, and the structure continues to be optimized.[6] The energy consumption per unit of gross domestic

1 China's total energy production, installed capacity and power generation are among the highest in the world. The installed scale of hydropower, wind power and photovoltaic power generation and the scale of nuclear power construction are ranked first in the world. National Development and Reform Commission, National Energy Administration, 'The 13th Five-Year Plan for Energy Development' (December 2016) <www.ndrc.gov.cn/fzgggz/fzgh/ghwb/gjjgh/201705/W020170517396324850569.pdf> accessed 3 March 2019; Kehua Jia, 'Unreasonable Energy Structure Cannot be Attributed Solely to Resource Endowments' *China Energy News* (Beijing, 25 January 2016) 4.

2 IEA, 'International Energy Outlook 2018'.

3 Energy Department of the National Bureau of Statistics, 'Achievements in Energy Development and Achievements in Energy Saving, and Consumption Reduction is Remarkable – 12th Series of Reports on Economic and Social Development Achievements in the 40 Years of Reform and Opening Up' (11 September 2018) <http://www.stats.gov.cn/ztjc/ztfx/ggkf40n/201809/t20180911_1622051.html> accessed 3 March 2019.

4 ibid.

5 The "One Belt One Road", also known as the Silk Road Economic Belt and the 21st-century Maritime Silk Road, is a development strategy adopted by the Chinese Government involving infrastructure development and investment in countries in Europe, Asia and Africa. 'What is the "One Belt One Road"?' <http://www.yidaiyilu.gov.cn/info/iList.jsp?tm_id=540> accessed 4 March 2019.

6 Compared with 2012, Chinas total net energy imports increased by 7.3 per cent annually. Among them, raw coal is down by 1.2 per cent annually, crude oil is growing at an average annual rate of 9.1 per cent and natural gas is growing at an average annual rate of 18.4 per cent. Energy Department of the National Bureau of Statistics (n3).

product (GDP) has shown a downward trend nationally.[7] China participates in international cooperation on climate change and has become an important participant, contributor and a leader of global ecological civilization construction.[8]

However, the problem of structural overcapacity in China's traditional energy production is still prominent. The development of renewable energy faces multiple bottlenecks. The task of clean energy substitution is arduous, and energy conservation and consumption are facing increasing pressure. The contradiction between energy resources allocation across provinces is serious.[9] Furthermore, the market-oriented changes in the energy sector are far from complete. In order to meet these challenges, the 19th National Congress of the Communist Party of China (2017) put forward the new development concept of "innovation, coordination, green, openness, sharing",[10] making "promoting the energy production and consumption revolution and building a clean, low-carbon, safe and efficient energy system"[11] an important component of green development growth. The energy revolution has become an important element in "accelerating the reform of the ecological civilization system and building a beautiful China".[12] The completion of this task requires the support of a sound energy law and policy system.

2 China's current energy structure

China's domestic energy endowment is not high, and the per capita possession of coal, oil and natural gas is low.[13] In 2018, China's total energy production was 3.77 billion tons of standard coal, of which the proportion of raw coal production was 69.3 per cent, crude oil accounting for 7.2 per cent, natural gas accounting for 5.5 per cent, and primary electricity and other energy[14] accounting for 18 per cent.[15] In 2018, China's total energy consumption was 4.64 billion tons of standard coal, of which crude oil accounted for 18.8 per cent, natural gas accounted for 7.0 per cent, and primary electricity and other energy accounted for 13.8 per cent.[16] After the 18th National Congress of the Communist Party of China (2012), the advance of the construction of an ecological civilization and the promotion of continuous structural reforms on the energy supply side in China contributed to the following positive changes. First, China's raw coal accounted for the lion's share in total energy production, basically maintaining between 70 and 80 per cent (1978–2016, but fell to 69.6 per cent in 2017).[17] Second, the proportion of crude oil fell from 23.7 per cent in 1978 to an all-time low

7 Energy Department of the National Bureau of Statistics (n3).

8 Jinping Xi, 'Report at the 19th National Congress of the Communist Party of China' (27 October 2017) <http://www.gov.cn/zhuanti/2017-10/27/content_5234876.htm > accessed 3 March 2019.

9 National Development and Reform Commission, National Energy Administration (n1).

10 Xi (n8).

11 ibid.

12 ibid.

13 Information Office of the State Council, 'China's Energy Policy (2012)' (24 October 2012) <http://www.gov.cn/zwgk/2012-10/24/content_2250617.htm > accessed 3 March 2019.

14 The primary electricity and other energy means the primary electricity generation such as hydropower, nuclear energy and other dynamic energy (wind energy, geothermal energy, etc.). National Bureau of Statistics of the PRC, *China Statistical Yearbook 2017* <http://www.stats.gov.cn/tjsj/ndsj/2017/indexch.htm> accessed 3 March 2019.

15 National Bureau of Statistics of the PRC, *China Statistical Yearbook 2019* <www.stats.gov.cn/tjsj/ndsj/2019/indexch.htm> accessed 12 December 2019.

16 ibid.

17 Energy Department of the National Bureau of Statistics (n3).

of 7.6 per cent in 2017.[18] Third, the proportion of clean energy such as natural gas, primary electricity and other energy sources continued to increase, with natural gas increasing from 2.9 per cent in 1978 to 5.4 per cent in 2017.[19] It is clear that the mainstay of China's energy sector is still coal, and domestic energy production cannot meet the demand for energy consumption. In particular, there is a big disparity between the demand and the domestic supply of crude oil and natural gas necessitating a reliance on imports.

There is also a large deficit in China's existing energy sector regarding requirements for safe, green, low carbon and high efficiency energy sources. In addition to the traditional consumption structure of over-reliance on coal and natural gas shortages, there is still a problem of the mismatch between the supply and demand for new energy. The new energy resources and load demand are reversely distributed, and the trans-regional power transmission and the flexible operation of the power grid are insufficient, which hinders the consumption of renewable energy.[20] The problem of "abandoning wind power and abandoning photovoltaic solar cells" in areas with concentrated wind and solar resources is a major one.[21]

Bearing all this in mind, the "Revolutionary Strategy for Energy Production and Consumption" (2016–2030) developed by the National Development and Reform Commission and the National Energy Administration,[22] proposed a revolution in energy production and consumption. The main points are: first, to achieve green production and clean use of coal; second, to promote low-cost, large-scale development of unconventional natural gas, such as coalbed methane, shale gas and tight gas, and steadily promote the trial production of natural hydrates; third, to vigorously develop renewable energy; fourth, nuclear to develop nuclear power safely and efficiently. The "13th Five-Year Plan for Energy Development" developed by the National Development and Reform Commission and the National Energy Administration (NEA) proposed continuing to strengthen the exploration and development of domestic conventional oil and gas resources, increasing reserves and stabilizing production, both onshore and offshore. It also sought to increase the exploration and development of unconventional oil and gas resources and to establish a foothold within China to ensure the supply security of oil and gas resources.[23]

3 China's energy law and policy framework

China has established an energy law and policy framework based on the constitutional provisions and laws and regulations applying specifically to energy, guided by a holistic energy strategy and various energy plans, with energy policies as the mainstay. International Energy Law also has an impact on the framework with its development of best practice in energy development regulation.

18 ibid.

19 ibid.

20 Research Center of Energy Security and National Development, National Development Research Institute, Peking University, and the Joint Research Group of the Department of Energy Economics, School of Economics, Renmin University of China, 'Subsidy Crisis and Large-Scale Curtailment of Wind and Solar Power in China' (2018) (No.4) *International Economic Review* 67.

21 Jian Han and Fei Sun, 'Reform of "Simple Administration, Decentralization, Integration, and Optimization of Services" in the Energy Field: Progress, Problems and Solutions' (2018) (No.1) *Theoretical Exploration* 98.

22 National Development and Reform Commission, National Energy Administration, 'Revolutionary Strategy for Energy Production and Consumption (2016–2030)' (29 December 2016) <http://www.ndrc.gov.cn/zcfb/zcfbtz/201704/W020170425509386101355.pdf> accessed 5 March 2019.

23 ibid.

3.1 International Energy Law

In international energy cooperation, China has assumed a wide range of international obligations and played a positive and constructive role. In terms of bilateral cooperation, China has established energy dialogue and cooperation mechanisms with countries such as the United States, the European Union, Japan, Russia, Kazakhstan, Turkmenistan, Uzbekistan, Brazil, Argentina and Venezuela, in a range of energy commodities, including oil, gas, coal, electricity and renewable energy.[24]These arrangements seek to strengthen dialogue, exchanges and cooperation in the fields of energy, technology equipment and energy policy. In terms of multilateral cooperation, China joined the International Atomic Energy Agency in 1984, the International Renewable Energy Agency in 2013, became an associate member of the International Energy Agency in 2015 and signed the International Energy Charter Declaration in 2015. China is also an observer state of the Energy Charter Treaty, and maintains close ties with the Organization of Petroleum Exporting Countries. The twenty-first-century Maritime Silk Road, the Bangladesh-China-Myanmar Economic Corridor and the China-Pakistan Economic Corridor all seek to strengthen bilateral and multilateral cooperation in international energy.[25]

3.2 National constitution[26]

The energy or energy-related provisions in the Constitution of the People's Republic of China (PRC) are listed below.

Sovereignty and ownership of energy resources. Article 9, paragraph 1, states that mineral deposits are owned by the State. This provision clarifies the State's ownership of energy resources. Article 9, paragraph 2, clarifies the obligations of the State and the private entities in relation to the protection of natural resources. Article 12 provides for the protection of public property, including the protection of national natural resource property.

Energy mining property rights. Article 13 provides for the protection of private property and its expropriation for the public interest. Article 14 provides for a socialist market economy. These two provisions are important for private entities participating in energy development because these two provisions establish the constitutional protection of private property (including the energy mining rights owned by the private entities) and give the market the legal authority to allocate natural resources. Article 18 stipulates that it "allows foreign enterprises and other economic organizations or individuals to invest in China in accordance with the laws of the PRC and carry out various forms of economic cooperation with Chinese enterprises or other economic organizations", which provides a constitutional foundation for international economic cooperation, including energy development cooperation.

National policy on basic energy. Article 14 sets out the national policy on science and technology and the national policy on thriftiness. It provides a constitutional foundation for energy technology innovation and energy conservation systems in the energy sector. Article 26 stipulates that "the state protects and improves the living environment and ecological

24 Information Office of the State Council (n13).

25 General Office of the State Council, 'Energy Development Strategic Action Plan (2014–2020)' (7 May 2014) <www.nea.gov.cn/2014-12/03/c_133830458.htm> accessed 5 March 2019.

26 Eduardo G. Pereira and Kim Talus, *Upstream Law and Regulation: A Global Guide* (Globe Business Publishing Ltd. 2013) 9.

environment, and prevents pollution and other public hazards", which provides a constitutional basis for the State to carry out environmental regulation in the field of energy development.

It should be noted that China has not established a judicial review mechanism for decisions involving the application of the Constitution, so the above-mentioned provisions of the Constitution are mainly implemented through legislation and statutory tools. A state-owned energy resources regime was established in 1986, and is protected by laws and administrative rules and regulations. Energy mining rights are protected through legislation. Social obligations are imposed on the energy developers through legislation and supporting administrative regulations. These legal systems are then enforced by administrative agencies and become the judicial decision basis for energy-related cases. Thus, the Constitution has an indirect and significant impact on the energy sector.

3.3 *Energy strategy and policy*

China's most recent energy strategy is the National Energy Development and Consumption Revolution Strategy (2016–2030) issued by the National Development and Reform Commission and the NEA in 2016. This document systematically expounds China's energy situation, clarifies the strategic goals and tasks of the energy production and consumption revolution and puts forward the requirements of the energy technology revolution and the energy system revolution. The requirements for international energy cooperation, energy security and key breakthroughs in important areas have been clarified. The key breakthroughs include the following 13 actions: national energy conservation, total energy consumption and intensity control, demonstration of near zero carbon emissions, power demand side management of demand side power, clean coal use, promotion of natural gas utilization, a leap-forward in the development of non-fossil energy, new rural energy, promotion of access to energy on internet, breakthroughs in key energy technology and equipment, structural reform of supply side energy, improvement and upgrading of energy standards and cooperation in "One Belt One Road" energy.[27] In addition, the NEA issued the Energy Development Strategic Action Plan (2014–2020) and the National Energy Security Strategic Action Plan (2013–2020). Although China's energy strategy has only recently emerged, it has set the direction for the PRC's energy law and regulation system.

China has a relatively complete energy planning system. Energy planning is divided into three categories: comprehensive, specific and regional. Energy planning is introduced at both the national and local level. At present, four comprehensive energy plans have been promulgated from the "10th Five-Year Plan" to the "13th Five-Year Plan". A number of specific plans have been enacted for different kinds of energy resources, or for specific issues, including coal, oil, natural gas, coalbed methane, shale gas, electricity, nuclear power, renewable energy, energy regulation, energy conservation, energy infrastructure and the production of clean energy. These plans only exist at the top-level design, and they need to be coordinated, refined and enhanced with the introduction of legislation and rules.[28] The implementation mechanisms of the plan need strengthening. [29]

27 National Development and Reform Commission, National Energy Administration (n22).

28 Wei Sun and Yang Liu, 'Analysis of Japan's Energy Management and Its Enlightenment to China' (2015) 200 (No.2) *Contemporary Economy of Japan* 72. < DOI: 10.16123/j.cnki.issn.1000-355x.2015.02.008>.

29 National Development and Reform Commission, National Energy Administration (n1).

China has also enacted a large number of energy policies. Energy policy is implemented by the government or government departments and covers a wide range of areas such as energy production layout, investment, technical equipment, prices, taxes, credit, trade, etc. There are a large number of technical quantitative norms and standards. The formulation and implementation of energy policy is convenient and flexible, and there is a certain amount of scope for administrative discretion.[30] Recent policies include the Biodiesel Industry Development Policy, Shale Gas Industry Policy, Guiding Opinions of the NEA on Regulating Total Coal Production and Optimizing Industrial Layout and the Guiding Opinions of the National Development and Reform Commission on Accelerating the Construction of Gas Storage Facilities, among others. The main objective of the current approach is to "improve policies related to fiscal, taxation, investment, and finance related to energy development, strengthen policy guidance and support, and promote sustainable development of the energy industry".[31]

3.4 Energy legislation

Energy legislation includes comprehensive or basic energy legislation and energy legislation in specific areas. Legislative sources include laws, administrative regulations and local legislation. In China, "Energy Law", which was highly regarded by scholars as "the keystone of the establishment and arrangement of the energy law development and transformation system"[32] has been delayed,[33] resulting in a lack of basic law in the energy field. The root cause of the delay in energy law legislation is the stagnation of market-oriented reforms in the energy sector.[34] The reason for the delay in reform is the multi-headed energy management team, which makes the department's interests difficult to coordinate.[35] As a result, the country's top-level design of energy policy has not been completed or improved. [36] As for Energy Law, and whether it should be categorized as a basic law or a comprehensive law, scholars have different attitudes. In the former case, the terms "basic law" and "comprehensive law" are considered to have the same meaning and are used indiscriminately.[37] In the latter case, Energy Law should be a comprehensive law. For example, Professor Li Yanfang demonstrated that Energy Law should be categorized as comprehensive legislation in the field of energy as Energy Law mainly regulates comprehensive issues related to energy security, energy efficiency,

30 ibid.
31 ibid.
32 Guoxing Xiao, 'The Transformation of Energy Development and the System Choice of the Energy Law' (2011) (No.12) *Law Science* 3.
33 In 2006, the drafting of Energy Law was initiated, and a drafting group composed of 15 ministries (committees, bureaus and offices) of the State Council was established to form an expert group. In 2007, the National Development and Reform Commission promulgated Energy Law (consultation draft). The "Energy Law" was included in the "2015 Legislative Work Plan of the State Council". The drafting of the Basic Energy Law was restarted, but in the "2016 State Council Legislative Work Plan", the "Energy Law" was reorganized as a "preparatory legislative project".
34 Guoxing Xiao, 'The Energy Revolution and the System Dimension of the Energy Law' (2018) 51 (No.6) *Journal of Zhengzhou University (Philosophy and Social Sciences)* 32.
35 The research group on Promoting the Revolutionary Strategy of Energy Production and Consumption, 'The Proposal to Introduce the "Energy Law" as Soon as Possible' in *China Think Tank Economic Watch (2017)* (China International Economic Exchange Centre 2018).
36 Desheng Hu, 'On the Qualitative Positioning of the Proposed Energy Law' (2015) 36 *Journal of Jiangxi University of Science and Technology* 18. <DOI: 10.13265/j.cnki.jxlgdxxb.2015.06.005>.
37 The research group on Promoting the Revolutionary Strategy of Energy Production and Consumption (n35).

energy management and energy and environmental protection. The function of Energy Law is to macro-manage and coordinate and supplement energy-specific legislation.[38] Professor Xiao Guoxing indicated that the comprehensive Energy Law stipulates both energy strategy and energy policy, as well as major regimes or prominent issues that are important or involve the overall situation in the energy-specific energy laws.[39] A third view is that Energy Law should be the basic law in the energy field. For example, Professor Hu Desheng defined the Energy Law as the basic law in the energy branch of the legal system. He indicated that the content of the Energy Law should be based on policy, principle and framework, and that the name "Basic Law on Energy Policy" is appropriate.[40]

There are six energy laws in specific areas. They are as follows: the Electricity Law (promulgated in 1995, latest revision in 2015), the Coal Law (promulgated in 1996, latest revision in 2013), the Energy Conservation Law (promulgated in 1997, latest revision in 2016), the Renewable Energy Law (promulgated in 2005, the latest revision in 2016), the Oil and Gas Pipeline Protection Act (promulgated in 2010) and the Nuclear Safety Law (promulgated in 2018). There are no major laws such as the Oil and Gas Law or the Atomic Energy Law.[41] Specialized public utility legislation and energy regulation legislation are also absent. In the field of oil and gas, legislation only covers pipeline protection legislation and does not cover all aspects of oil and gas development and utilization. There is no specific legislation or administrative regulation for non-traditional fossil energy such as shale gas and coalbed methane.[42] In terms of the legislative concept, there is an insufficient response to issues such as sustainable development and climate change;[43] insufficient attention is paid to the function of market instruments in the allocation of energy resources.[44] The adjustment scope, promulgation time, legislative causes and objectives of these laws are all quite different. Thus, they are still not systematic.[45] As a result, there is unnecessary duplication and conflict between existing laws, and the importance of macro issues and holistic issues has not been addressed.[46] The above-mentioned laws have the problem that "the clauses are principled, instructive and policy-declarative, and there are no adequate, specific and effective safeguard measures to match them",[47] which greatly restricts the actual effect of the laws.

Administrative regulations in specific areas of energy are mainly concentrated in the areas of international cooperation and development, nuclear energy safety, coal mine safety, oil and gas infrastructure, energy conservation and renewable energy.

38 Yanfang Li, 'On the Formulation of China's "Energy Law" – Comment on "Energy Law of the People's Republic of China" (Draft for Comments)' (2008) 20 (No.2) *The Jurist* 92. <DOI: 10.16094/j.cnki.1005-0221.2008.02.007>.

39 Guoxing Xiao, 'Several Issues that should be Considered in the Drafting of China's Energy Law' (2007) (No.2) *Legal Science* 111.

40 Hu (n36).

41 Zewei Yang, 'The Legal Issues of "Two-type Society" and the Development and Utilization of Nuclear Energy in Hubei' (2009) 27 *Law Review* 56.

42 Jiejun Yang, 'The Problems and Bottlenecks in Contemporary China's Energy Legislation and the Solutions' (2013) (No.12) *Nanjing Social Sciences* 92. <DOI: 10.15937/j.cnki.issn1001-8263.2013.12.012>.

43 Bo Ma, Peiliang Liu, 'An Analysis on Legal Problems Concerning China's Energy Security' (2015) 17 (No.3) *Journal of Southwest Petroleum University (Social Sciences Edition)* 18.

44 Yang (n42).

45 Guoxing Xiao, 'The Puzzle and Way Out for the Design of the Energy Law System' (2012) (No.8) *Law Science* 3.

46 Li (n38).

47 Mingyuan Wang, 'Can the "Visible Hand" Mold a Bright Future for China's Renewable Sources of Energy Industry?—A Study Based on the Renewable Energy Act of the PRC' (2007) 29 (No.6) *Modern Law Science* 155.

China is a vast country with large geographical differences. These differences are reflected in various aspects such as population, geographic conditions, level of economic and social development and historical and cultural traditions. Article 72 of the Legislation Law of the PRC (promulgated in 2000 and newly revised in 2015) authorized the local legislative power to the People's Congresses and their Standing Committees of the Provinces, Autonomous Regions, Municipalities directly under the Central Government and Large Cities with Districts. Article 73 clearly stipulates that the above-mentioned institutions may formulate local regulations for the enforcement of laws and administrative regulations, and for dealing with local issues. The natural resources are buried in the land and cannot be repositioned, which determines that in the field of natural resources, local legislation that focuses on regional affairs is valued and adopted because local legislation can respond to the differentiated needs of natural resource legislation. In practice, in a unitary state like China, local "experimental legislation" can also reduce the trial and error costs of the establishment of formal regimes throughout the country. Thus, the central government often explicitly or implicitly supports or encourages local legislation. This situation is also reflected in the field of energy legislation. For example, the Heilongjiang Province Energy Conservation Regulations (promulgated in 2008, the latest revision in 2018), the Sichuan Rural Energy Regulations (promulgated in 2017) and the Regulations on the Development, Utilization and Protection of Climate Resources in Guizhou Province (promulgated in 2012, latest revision in 2017). Although in practice, local legislation is not ideal for local characteristics,[48] it should still be an integral part of the Energy Law and policy framework, starting with the vision of development of legislative technology and the actual needs of energy management.

3.5 *Energy regulation*

Energy development and utilization involve the country's basic economic system and multiple social relationships. In addition to energy-specific legislation, laws governing areas such as natural resources, environmental protection, competition and industrial policies also regulate energy activities.[49] These laws include the Land Administrative Law, Mineral Resources Law, Environmental Protection Law, Environmental Impact Assessment Law, Circular Economy Promotion Law, Clean Production Promotion Law, Air Pollution Prevention and Control Law, Property Law, Anti-Unfair Competition Law, Enterprise Income Tax Law, Environmental Protection Tax Law and Safe Production Law. The regulation of the energy sector established in the above legislation can be broadly divided into four categories. First, resource regulation: this includes energy mining rights licences and supervision of energy development activities. Second, environmental regulation: the Environmental Protection Law and various specific environmental protection laws have established general ecological environmental protection obligations for energy developers, including environmental impact assessment, environmental taxes, pollution control, resource conservation, information disclosure and so on. Third, health and safety regulations: energy developers have labour protection, safety protection and safe production obligations. Fourth, energy taxes and fiscal

48 Jie Huan, Xirun Tan and Yi Wang, 'Empirical Study on the Featured Local Legislation—The Case of the Natural Resources Local Legislation in Hubei Province' (2017) 17 (No.2) *Journal of China University of Geosciences (Social Sciences Edition)* 49. <DOI: 10.16493/j.cnki.42-1627/c.2017.02.007>.

49 Jing Song, 'On the Endogenous and Exogenous Complementation of Energy Legal System' (2018) 51 (No.3) *Journal of Zhengzhou University (Philosophy and Social Sciences Edition)* 38.

tools: incentives in the form of fiscal and taxation tools[50] promote the development of renewable energy and new energy, ensure environmental security and achieve a more equitable sharing of energy resource development benefits and development social costs.

4 Energy mineral resources

In China, coal, coalbed methane, stone-like coal, oil shale, oil, natural gas, oil sands, natural asphalt, uranium, plutonium, geothermal energy shale gas, and methane hydrate are all legally defined as mineral resources. Thus, the upstream development of energy mineral resources is governed by the Mineral Resources Law of the PRC and its supporting administrative regulations, departmental regulations and a large number of regulatory documents. These include the Deep-Sea Submarine Regional Resources Exploration and Development Resource Law of the PRC, the Regulations on Cooperation and Exploitation of Onshore Petroleum Resources and the Regulations on Foreign Cooperation in Exploitation of Offshore Oil Resources. To a certain extent, the Mineral Resources Law has made up for the lack of a basic energy law. However, as China implements a separate system for the regulation and management of energy minerals and other mineral resources, energy resource management still lacks a legal system, instead mainly "managing to rely on policy".[51]

China's energy mineral resources are owned by the State, and entities seeking to explore and develop energy minerals must obtain an exploration rights licence and an exploitation rights licence. The exploration rights licence and exploitation rights licences are both granted by the Ministry of Natural Resources which keeps a register of the rights held by different entities. The only exceptions are coalbed methane and geothermal heat, which can be registered and granted by the appropriate Department of Mineral Resources of the relevant Provincial People's Government authorized by the State Council. The development of energy mineral resources is based on the principle of paid use. The government has initiated the sale of the mining rights of coal, geothermal energy, coalbed methane and shale gas through tendering processes and auctions, which are open to all social entities. In 2015, the Ministry of Land and Resources, with the approval of the State Council, took the lead in carrying out reform pilots in Xinjiang and successfully sold four blocks through open tendering.[52] However, state-owned enterprises, especially central state-owned enterprises, are still the mainstay of energy upstream development, and private capital or private enterprises are still subject to obstruction. The monopoly of central state-owned enterprises in both the oil and gas and the nuclear energy industry is unlikely to change in the short term.

Entities that are engaged in the exploration and exploitation of energy mineral resources must meet the required qualifications, set out in the legal and administrative regulations and the normative documents of the Natural Resources Management Department. Special access conditions for mining rights that are transferred in a competitive manner through tendering and auctions will be listed in detail in the tender and auction announcements.

50 Xisheng Huang and Zhenyuan Zhang, 'Research on Energy Taxation Legal System Based on Energy Structure Adjustment' (2018) (No.3) *Journal of Fujian Normal University (Philosophy and Social Sciences Edition)* 24. <DOI: 10.12046/j.issn.1000-5285.2018.03.004>.

51 Desheng Hu, *Energy Law* (Peking University Press 2017) 73; Junju Ma, Xiangqian Gong, 'On the Reform of Energy Law' (2007) (No.3) *China Legal Science* 147. <DOI:10.14111/j.cnki.zgfx.2007.03.011>.

52 Department of Geological Exploration of the Ministry of Land and Resources, '2015 National Oil and Gas Resources Exploration and Exploitation Bulletin' (4 July 2016) <http://test.mlr.gov.cn/gk/tzgg/201607/t20160707_1991801.html> accessed 3 March 2019.

The conditions generally include compliance with mineral resources planning, energy planning, adequate funding, appropriate technologies, equipment and personnel, approved mining plans, necessary safety production conditions and environmental protection measures. To obtain the mining rights of energy minerals according to an unsolicited application, the developer needs to go through the following steps: first, the energy project is reviewed by the NEA or approved by the appropriate Development and Reform Commission, and the scope of the mining area is demarcated. It should be noted that the approval regime for the overall development programmes of the international cooperation project for oil and gas (including coalbed methane) by the National Development and Reform Commission has been changed to the record filing system.[53] Second, the developer must submit the application for mining rights to the competent authority, and obtain the necessary approvals. Third, the developer signs the mining rights transfer contract with the competent department. Fourth, the developer pays royalties in exchange for the mining right, as required. Fifth, the developer applies for the registration of mining rights, and the competent authorities review the application approvals and register the mining rights. The developer then finally obtains the mining rights.

The process of obtaining energy mineral rights is competitive. First, the appropriate department issues the mining rights bidding or auction announcement. The conditions and competition methods for market access will be detailed in the announcement. Second, the interested developer participates in the bidding or auction. Third, the winner of the bidding or auction makes the confirmation of the transfer of mining rights and signs the transfer contract with the competent department. Fourth, the developer pays royalties in exchange for the mining right. Fifth, the developer applies for the registration of mining rights, and the competent authorities review the application and register the mining rights. Finally, the enterprise obtains mining rights.

In the process of exercising energy mining rights, the contractual obligations and related legal obligations must be fulfilled. The State sets limits on the mining rights as follows. Regarding the exploration rights, first, the developer has to complete the required investment and exploration work. Second, the developer must report the work to the competent authorities. Third, the developer must comply with the laws and regulations on labour and production safety, land reclamation and environmental protection. Fourth, after the completion of the operation, the developer must fulfil the statutory seal, the formalities and other risk prevention measures. The land that is destroyed by the temporary construction of energy exploration infrastructure construction and other construction activities, the entities of energy development are the land reclamation obligor. Fifth, the developer must send geological data to the competent authorities.

Regarding the exploitation rights, first, the developer has to mine according to the approval period, mining area and mining programme. Second, the developer must extract the product effectively and rationally, and utilize mineral resources comprehensively. Third, the developer has to pay taxes and fees in accordance with the law and the transfer contract. Fourth, the developer must comply with national laws and regulations concerning labour and production safety, soil and water conservation, land reclamation and environmental protection. Fifth, the developer must submit a statistical report on the development and utilization of mineral resources to the competent authorities. Sixth, the developer must apply for

53 State Council of the PRC, 'Decision of the State Council on the Abolition and Decentralization of a Number of Administrative Licensing Matters' (6 March 2019) <http://www.gov.cn/zhengce/content/2019-03/06/content_5371253.htm> accessed 3 March 2019.

the closure of mining. In the process of exploration and exploitation of energy mining rights, the Ministry of Natural Resources, the Ministry of Ecology and Environment, the Ministry of Emergency Management, the Ministry of Industry and Information Technology and their local agencies at all levels supervise development activities. Despite the fact that there is some overlapping of functions in law or practice, these regulators have their respective powers and legal status and coexist without a lead supervisory agency. On the same regulatory matter, the local administrative agency is led by its superior administrative organs. The regulatory authorities strive to use planning, legal obligations and penalties, technical norms, standards and guidance, environmental impact assessment, environmental taxation and various types of subsidies, administrative contracts and other regulatory tools comprehensively. In general, China's current energy mercerization is low, government administrative control measures are excessive, and market supervision mechanisms are weak. In the field of energy upstream development the market's allocation of resources has not yet been realized. Mining rights in the conventional oil and gas sector are monopolized by a small number of large state-owned enterprises. Limited by qualifications, capital and technical conditions, only a few private enterprises have been involved in the development of shale gas and coalbed methane. It is the government, not the market, that plays a decisive role in the allocation of resources. As a result, in the above policies and legal tools, the government mainly relies on rigid administrative licensing and punitive measures. The regulator's ability to use economic tools such as subsidies, taxation, and property rights transactions is insufficient.

4.1 New and renewable energy

The Renewable Energy Law of the PRC states in Article 2:

> renewable energy as used in this Law refers to non-fossil resources such as wind energy, solar energy, hydro energy, biomass energy, geothermal energy, ocean energy, etc. The application of hydropower to this Law, it shall be prescribed by the competent department of energy under the State Council and submitted to the State Council for approval.

At present, the main development and utilization of industrialization in China is wind energy, solar energy and hydropower.[54] Hydropower is not governed by the Renewable Energy Law. So, the following section elaborates on hydropower resources and other renewable energy sources separately.

5 Hydropower

China has an abundancy of hydropower resources, and its technical developable capacity is 542 million kilowatts, ranking first in the world.[55] Hydropower is the mainstay of China's clean energy, accounting for 24 per cent of the country's installed capacity and 19 per cent of power generation.[56] Moreover, the price of hydropower is also the lowest among all types of electricity prices, which plays a significant role in stabilizing electricity prices. In 2017, China's

54 Jian Ke, 'Legal Promotion of Renewable Energy Development in the Background of Global Climate Change: Reflecting and Reshaping Renewable Energy Law of China' (2015) (No.4) *Journal of Political Science and Law* 75.

55 Information Office of the State Council (n13).

56 Guobao Zhang, 'Read Energy Statistics Correctly and Develop a Correct Development Strategy' (11 March 2019) <https://mp.weixin.qq.com/s/aHuA-1QY_11_VYCYwV-9aw> accessed 12 March 2019.

hydropower generation capacity was 341.19 million kilowatts.[57] This means that, in 2017, China had already achieved the target (the total installed capacity of conventional hydropower reached 340 million kilowatts) set out in the "13th Five-Year Plan" for Power Development (2016–2020) ahead of schedule.[58] As Mr. Zhang Guobao, former director of the National Energy Administration, pointed out, with years of high-intensity hydropower development, the potential of hydropower generation in China is getting smaller and smaller, and the potential sites for hydropower are becoming fewer and fewer.[59] Therefore, the focus of China's hydropower legislation and regulation should change from promoting large-scale development of hydropower to the quality, efficiency and safety of existing projects, and coping with the problem of ecological and environmental damage accumulated by hydropower development.

In China, hydropower resources are managed by the Ministry of Water Resources. The Ministry of Water Resources is responsible for the supervision and management of national water rights transactions. The development and utilization of hydropower resources is shifting from the unpaid model of administrative orders to the market-based model of paid use. Article 7 of the Water Law of the PRC (Promulgated in 2002, latest revision in 2016) stipulates that "China implements a water intake permit regime and paid use of water resources regime". Article 2 of the Regulations on Water Licensing and Management of Water Resources Fees includes water intaking for hydropower stations within the scope of water intake permits. The regulations stipulate the management authority, permit conditions and approval procedures for water intaking permits, and the standards for the water resources fees. In 2006, the State Council promulgated the Regulations on the Water Collection Permits and Water Resources Fees Acquisition Management 2006, in which it established the regime of paid use of water resources and water rights. However, the regime still has the following areas that need to be improved. First, the content of water rights and the boundaries of rights are still unclear, and the phenomenon of disorderly development and utilization of water resources and ecological destruction has not been fundamentally reversed. Second, the government controls the allocation and development of water resources by planning. Where and to what extent water resources will be developed is determined by various plans and by setting permits to access the development. The role of the market in water allocation has not been fully realized. Third, it is difficult to collect all the water resources fees. With reference to hydropower, national legislation lacks special provisions for the development and utilization of water resources. The standards, conditions, procedures and relief mechanisms for the development and utilization of water energy resources are not well developed.[60] In order to solve the problem of water resources protection, and to clarify the boundaries of the water resources ownership and utilization rights, the State Council promulgated the Proposal of the State Council on Implementing the Strictest Water Resources Management Regime 2012, the Ministry of Water Resources promulgated the Interim Measures for the Administration of Water Rights Transaction 2016 and the Ministry of Water Resources and the former Ministry of Land and Resources jointly issued the Pilot Program for Water Flow Property Rights Confirmation 2016. These documents allow for differential and transitional

57 National Bureau of Statistics of the PRC (n15).

58 National Development and Reform Commission, National Energy Administration, 'The 13th Five-Year Plan for Power Development (2016–2020)' (5 May 2017) <www.ndrc.gov.cn/fzgggz/fzgh/ghwb/gjjgh/201706/W020170605632835660561.pdf> accessed 12 March 2019.

59 Zhang (n56).

60 Mingyuan Wang, 'Research on the System of Development and Utilization Rights of Water Resources for Energy in China' (2010) (No.2) *Academic Journal of Zhongzhou* 102.

institutional and policy arrangements to promote reform of the water rights regime in an orderly manner. The actual effect of the reforms remains to be observed.

The New Energy and Renewable Division of the NEA regulates hydropower, including draft plans and policies, organizes the implementation of new projects and is also responsible for the day-to-day supervision of hydropower project safety. The safety of small rural hydropower projects and important dangerous reservoirs is supervised by the Ministry of Water Resources. Hydropower production implements a hydropower dam safety inspection and rating regime, an operational safety registration regime, a safety management responsibility regime and a hydropower facility safety operation regime to ensure safe production of hydropower. Since hydropower projects and facilities are highly valued, safety regulation has achieved good results in practice.

Hydropower project construction and hydropower production is also required to comply with the provisions of the Environmental Protection Law, the Wildlife Protection Law and other laws and regulations on ecological environmental protection. In recent years, the ecological and environmental hazards brought about by hydropower development have received increasing attention. The main concern is that hydropower development changes the water environment in the basin and causes secondary environmental disasters; the destruction of biological habitats threatens biodiversity; the hydrological characteristics of the basins risk causing geological disasters; the changes in water and sediment transport processes cause water pollution. The Construction of the Three Gorges Reservoir has produced 1.2 million immigrants and triggered serious reflection on the impact of the project on the ecological environment.[61] The Yunnan Nujiang hydropower development was put on hold due to strong opposition from experts, the Environmental Protection Agency and the public.[62] Sichuan Jinsha River hydropower development caused controversy.[63] In 2015, the Ministry of Environmental Protection stopped the planned Xiaonanhai Hydropower Project in the Jinsha River Basin, which was strongly supported by the Chongqing Municipal Government and had a planned investment of 32 billion yuan. This decision to halt the project received universal praise from public opinion.[64] Hydropower development should coordinate hydropower development and ecological protection, adhere to ecological priorities. This has been officially written into China's 13th Five-Year Plan. Against this background, the national environmental protection agencies have changed from being weak to strong in environmental law enforcement. It is foreseeable that environmental legislation and regulatory tools for hydropower development can really have an effective role.

6 Other renewable energy resources

The Renewable Energy Law does not stipulate the upstream development of renewable energy resources. The law only stipulates that the energy department of the State Council

61 Mingde Cao, 'Ecological Environment and Rule of Law Establishment in the Three Gorges Reservoir Area' (2003) (No.1) *Tribune of Economic Law* 459.

62 'Four Geologists Wrote to the State Council Against the Development of Nujiang Hydropower' (4 March 2011) <http://news.sina.com.cn/green/news/roll/2011-03-04/123522052607.shtml> accessed 12 March 2019.

63 Hong Cheng and Yajie Zhao, 'Environmental Externalities of Hydropower Development and Its Legal Adjustment: Example of Jinsha River Basin' (2015) 33 (No. 3) *Journal of Economics of Water Resources* 56. <DOI: 10.3880/j.issn.1003-9511.2015.03.013>.

64 Deng Jiansheng (ed.), 'The People's Daily Said: To Give Thumbs Up for the Stop of the Xiaonanhai Hydropower Station Project' *The People's Daily* (Beijing, 13 April 2015) 16.

shall undertake unified management of the development and utilization of renewable energy throughout the country, and the department responsible for energy management at the county level or above shall be responsible for management of renewable energy development and utilization within the administrative region. (Article 5) Then the law stipulates that the energy department of the State Council is responsible for organizing and coordinating the investigation of renewable energy resources throughout the country and formulating the medium and long-term total targets for the development and utilization of renewable energy in the country and formulating plans for its development and utilization. (Chapter 2) In addition, the law stipulates that state finance establishes special funds for renewable energy development to stimulate the development and utilization of renewable energy (Chapter 6).

In practice, investors and developers are selected for concession projects through a competitive bidding process and the government is committed to coordinate the power grid connection and purchase all the electricity generated by the concession projects.[65] Solar PV power and wind power concessions were granted by concession bidding. In addition, new and renewable energy development activities are regulated by the laws and regulations on ecological environmental protection and safe production and numerous renewable energy programmes and regulations. At present, China's wind, solar and biomass power generation costs are still relatively high compared to traditional fossil energy, and the dependence on policy support is high.[66] The most critical of the support policies of renewable energy is the subsidy policy. However, China's renewable energy subsidies are problematic because of the lack of substantive and procedural legal rules, and the lack of coordination of other public policies. The gap in subsidy funds is large, and there are systemic shortcomings that interfere with market supply and demand and undermine fair competition.[67]

Based on the current situation of China's lacunae and lag in energy legislation, the 13th Five-Year Plan of Energy Development proposes that "energy development has laws to follow"[68] as the goal of energy legislation. The basic energy law and energy-specific law should cover the entire industrial chain and all kinds of energy resources and cope with all aspects of energy regulation and management activity. They should form a comprehensive and coordinated legal system for energy legislation, covering power, coal, oil and gas, atomic energy, renewable energy, energy conservation, energy science and technology, etc. These laws should also be linked to energy strategy, planning, industrial policy, guidance and industry standards. At the same time, these laws must accelerate the pace of market-oriented reforms in the energy sector and create a favourable market environment for energy legislation. In addition, this legislation must promote energy system reform, break through institutional barriers in energy legislation and reduce departmental constraints in the energy legislation process.[69]

65 Sufang Zhang, Philip Andrews-Speed; Xiaoli Zhao and Yongxiu He, 'Interactions between Renewable Energy Policy and Renewable Energy Industrial Policy: A Critical Analysis of China's Policy Approach to Renewable Energies' (2013) 62 *Energy Policy* 342.

66 National Development and Reform Commission, 'The 13th Five Year Plan for Renewable Energy Development' (10 December 2016) <www.ndrc.gov.cn/zcfb/zcfbtz/201612/W020161216659579206185.pdf> accessed 12 March 2019.

67 Hui Feng, 'Research on the Legal Regulation of Government Subsidies for the New Energy Automobile Industry' (2017) (No. 12) *Political Science and Law* 22. <DOI:10.15984/j.cnki.1005-9512.2017.12.003>.

68 National Development and Reform Commission, National Energy Administration (n 1).

69 'The Energy Revolution Needs the Thinking of Rule of Law—Thoughts on the Work of Energy Law in China in the New Era' *China Mining News* (Beijing, 16 January 2018) 3.

With the advancement of socialist market economy reform, China's energy management system has been going through a transformation process. The focus of the current reform is to give full play to the basic role of market allocation of resources and further transform government functions,[70] establishing an open, fair, scientific and effective regulatory system. Specifically, it includes: attaching importance to the strategic planning and macro-control of energy development and comprehensively applying planning, policies, standards and other means to implement the management of the industry. It seeks to reduce government intervention in micro-issues and simplify the system of administrative approval. The reform also should strengthen the management of forecasting energy statistics and improve energy statistics, monitoring, forecasting and early warning systems about the risks of the imbalance of energy supply and demand, and unexpected events in the energy sector.[71]

7 China's institutional system for energy management

The highest level of deliberation and coordination of energy management in China is the National Energy Commission established in 2008.[72] Its main responsibilities are to research and draft national energy development strategies, review major issues in energy security and energy development and coordinate major issues in domestic energy development and energy international cooperation. It does not have an entity in itself, nor does it decide on specific issues. The main energy management agency of the Chinese central government is the National Development and Reform Commission and the NEA which is subordinate to the Commission. The National Development and Reform Commission[73] is primarily responsible for the macro management of energy. Its principal responsibilities in relation to energy are as follows. First, the Commission promotes the sustainable development strategy. Second, the Commission is responsible for the comprehensive coordination of energy conservation and emissions reduction. Third, the Commission organizes the formulation of comprehensive energy conservation and utilization planning and policy measures. Fourth, the Commission coordinates environmental protection and clean production promotion, and organizes the formulation of major strategies, plans and policies to address climate change. In addition, the National Development and Reform Commission manages the NEA in accordance with the regulations of the State Council. The NEA[74] is a specialized energy management regulatory agency with 12 internal institutions. Its main responsibilities are include as follows. First, the NEA drafts energy laws, regulations and strategies, plans, policies, standards, etc., and participates in the formulation of policies concerning energy-related resources, energy-related subsidy and taxation, environmental protection and climate change. Second, the NEA promotes and guides the innovation of energy technology. Third, the NEA manages energy conservation and the comprehensive utilization of resources in the energy sector,

70 General Office of the State Council (n 25).

71 Information Office of the State Council (n 13).

72 State Council, 'Notice of the State Council on the Establishment of the Coordination Mechanism' (21 March 2008) <http://news.xinhuanet.com/fortune/2010-01/28/content_12888948.htm> accessed 5 March 2019.

73 State Council, 'Notice of the State Council on the Establishment of Institutions' (26 April 2008). <http://www.gov.cn/zhengce/content/2008-04/26/content_7621.htm> accessed 5 March 2019; National Development and Reform Commission, 'The main responsibility of the National Development and Reform Commission' <http://www.ndrc.gov.cn/zwfwzx/jj> accessed 5 March 2019.

74 National Energy Administration, 'Introduction to the National Energy Administration' <http://www.nea.gov.cn/201809nyjjj.htm> accessed 5 March 2019.

including recommendations for controlling total energy consumption. Fourth, the NEA is responsible for energy forecasting and early warning, and participates in energy operation regulation and emergency support. Fifth, the NEA manages national oil and gas emergency reserves. Sixth, the NEA examines, approves and authorizes nuclear energy fixed assets investment projects, and manages nuclear power projects. Seventh, the NEA guides and coordinates rural energy development work. Eighth, the NEA regulates the operation of the electricity market. Ninth, the NEA approves or examines major overseas investment projects of energy (coal, oil, natural gas, electricity, etc.) in accordance with the prescribed authority. In addition, the NEA needs to undertake the specific work of the National Energy Commission, and other matters assigned by the National Development and Reform Commission and the State Council.

There are other national institutions with regulatory authority for energy management. First, according to the 2018 "Organizational Reform Plan of the State Council",[75] the newly established Ministry of Natural Resources is responsible for the management of natural resources including energy resources. Its Mining Rights Management Department manages the approval and registration of important energy mining rights such as oil and gas. Second, the newly established Ministry of Ecology and Environment, in addition to environmental regulation, is also responsible for addressing climate change and emission reduction. Third, the newly established Ministry of Emergency Management and its National Coal Mine Safety Administration is responsible for the supervision of energy production safety. The National Coal Mine Safety Supervision Bureau is responsible for the supervision of coal mine production safety. Fourth, the State Administration of Science, Technology and Industry for National Defence is the Chinese Government's nuclear industry authority, which is managed by the Ministry of Industry and Information Technology of the PRC. It is responsible for the regulation of China's peaceful use of the nuclear energy industry (except nuclear power, which is regulated by the NEA).[76]

China's existing energy regulatory system has been sharply criticized by scholars. First, multiple regulatory agencies in the energy sector have overlapping functions and the coordination between them is poor. Wu Bing and Wang Hongwei pointed out that the functions of the National Energy Commission, which is the highest coordination and advisory body, have not been fully utilized. Although the National Energy Administration is a specialized energy regulatory department, it is only a bureau under the Development and Reform Commission. It has limited authority and cannot coordinate the regulatory functions of the allocation of energy resources and the ecological environment, and health and safety regulation is dispersed among other relevant ministries.[77] Second, the institutional reforms in the energy sector are in serious conflict with existing laws and regulations which were promulgated in the last century. Yang Jiejun pointed out the reform of the energy system is based on policies, not laws. Policies changes quickly, resulting in a lack of stability and

75 The institutional reform of the State Council is to strengthen and improve the government's economic regulation, market supervision, social management, public services and ecological environmental protection functions. The establishment of the new ministries is to make the market play a decisive role in resource allocation, and to promote the coordination and efficiency of the functions of state institutions. 'State Council Institutional Reform Program' (17 March 2018) <http://www.xinhuanet.com/politics/2018lh/2018-03/17/c_1122552185.htm> accessed 5 March 2019.

76 China Atomic Energy Authority, 'Institutional Responsibility and Function' <http://www.caea.gov.cn/n6758879/index.html> accessed 5 March 2019.

77 Bin Wu and Hongwei Wang, 'The Direction and Focus of China's Energy System Reform' (2014) 36 (No.6) *Energy of China* 5. <DOI:10.3969/j.issn.1003-2355.2014.06.001>.

continuity of reform. The predictability of reform is insufficient and it is difficult to continue and deepen.[78] Third, the energy management tools have a strong administrative colour and are overplanned. Zheng Jianing indicated that the energy management is too reliant on the administrative power to control the energy sector and cannot meet the requirements of comprehensive management with good service and adaptability.[79] In practice, the institutional barriers hinder the healthy development of the energy sector, thus, the "Revolutionary Strategy for Energy Production and Consumption (2016–2030)"[80] has proposed that the goal of the energy system revolution is to accelerate the transformation of government functions, continue to promote the decentralization of power, integrate management, optimize service reform, strengthen strategic planning, introduce innovative macro-policy supporting mechanisms and re-establish the energy regulatory system.

8 Conclusion

China has become a major energy producer and consumer in the world, but is far from being a powerful country for energy management. The objective of having overall energy security and improving energy development strategies, policies and legislation in China is still a work in progress. Achieving it requires adhering to the strategy of safety-oriented, energy-efficient, green and low-carbon innovation, giving full play to the decisive role of market mechanisms in resource allocation and increasing the role of government of building a clean, efficient, safe and sustainable modern energy resource system. This is necessary in order to achieve national energy security and social energy equity, cope with climate change and protect the ecological environment.

Acknowledgement

This work was supported by the State Social Science Fund Project (grant number 17BFX087: 2017).

78 Yang (n42).

79 Jianing Zheng, 'From Administrative Management to Comprehensive Management: Energy Management System Reform in China' (2010) (No.3) *Administrative Law Review* 62.

80 National Development and Reform Commission, National Energy Administration (n22).

26

RENEWABLE ENERGY LAW IN THE CONTEXT OF A TRANSFORMING AUSTRALIAN ENERGY MARKET

Penelope Crossley

Introduction

Australia is in an unusual quandary when it comes to energy policy. On the one hand, it is the world's largest exporter of coal, and soon to be the world's largest exporter of liquefied natural gas (LNG), while also being a major supplier of uranium for use in nuclear power facilities. On the other hand, Australia also has some of the world's best solar and wind resources, exceptionally high electricity prices, an internationally islanded grid and, as a result, is being used as a global test market for new energy technologies. This chapter examines the complex legal and governance framework that supports the deployment of renewable energy in Australia. The chapter begins by describing the current energy mix in the National Electricity Market (NEM), and how that mix is transforming as a result of the very high penetration of residential photovoltaic (PV) solar and the development of larger-scale renewable energy projects. In Section 2, the chapter considers the constitutional settlement, which led to the responsibility for energy being shared between the Commonwealth Government and the states prompting a very complex set of cooperative governance arrangements. It is argued in Section 3 that the existing governance arrangements for the NEM lead to the lowest common denominator decision-making, are not transparent and make changes to the status quo, which is largely designed for the incumbent fossil fuel generators, difficult to achieve. Section 4 of the chapter then critically analyses the national Renewable Energy Target (RET) and some of the state and territory laws that operate to support the deployment of renewable energy. Section 5 of the chapter examines the recent ef forts to create an integrated energy and climate policy through the development of the National Energy Guarantee (NEG), critiques the draft design and considers how the outcome of the 2019 Federal election is likely to impact on its adoption. The chapter concludes in Section 6.

1 The Australian energy mix in a time of energy market transformation

The need to prepare for a changing energy mix is particularly acute in Australia, with the Australian electricity sector being one of the most carbon intensive electricity sectors in the world. In 2017–2018, black and brown coal generators accounted for 41 per cent of registered capacity within the NEM but supplied 73 per cent of output.[1] Gas powered generators

1 Australian Energy Regulator, *State of the Energy Market 2018* (Australian Government, 2018), 81.

accounted for 21.3 per cent of registered capacity, but only supplied 9.5 per cent of output.[2] Hydroelectric generators accounted for 14.3 per cent of registered generation, but only supplied 7.4 per cent of output.[3] Wind energy accounted for 9.1 per cent of registered capacity but only supplied 6.3 per cent of output.[4]

However, these statistics are slightly deceptive. Australia is undergoing a profound electricity market transformation, most notably among small-scale renewables, which are exempt from registration within the NEM. Over 2 million homes currently have residential PV solar panels, making it the highest penetration of residential PV solar in the world.[5] Meanwhile, battery storage and other distributed energy resources have already become cost competitive in a number of regions of Australia without the need for subsidies, leading to Australia being used as a test market for new energy technologies. The uptake of these new energy technologies has had a corresponding impact on the demand for electricity from the NEM, with grid consumption steadily declining since 2015.[6] This trend is predicted to continue, with the Australian Energy Market Operator projecting that 'consumption met by grid-supplied electricity is forecast to remain relatively flat for the next 20 years, despite projected 30 per cent growth in population and projected growth in the Australian economy.'[7]

Several factors have supported the rapid growth of renewable energy in Australia. Australia has excellent solar and wind resources, which are geographically widespread throughout the Australian continent.[8] This coupled with high and rapidly rising electricity prices, a steep decline in the costs of the renewable technologies and very favourable state government policies supporting renewable energy, has spurred the deployment of both small and large-scale renewable energy.

2 The history of electricity markets in the Australian federal system

Under the constitutional settlement between the Commonwealth Government and the Australian states at the time of Australia's Federation in 1901, the regulation of electricity was largely the purview of the Australian states.[9] Thus prior to the electricity market reforms of the early to mid-1990s, vertically integrated state government-owned monopolies provided all aspects of electricity supply including generation, transmission, distribution and retail services to customers. During this period, each state had its own agencies responsible for planning, developing, commissioning and operating their own electricity supply system, with only limited interconnection between the states.[10]

2 Ibid, 82.

3 Ibid, 83.

4 Ibid, 84. The disparity between capacity and generation can be attributed to variable weather conditions.

5 Clean Energy Council, 'Number of Australian homes with rooftop solar tops 2 million … and counting' (Media Release, 3 December 2018), <https://www.cleanenergycouncil.org.au/news/2018/December/2-million-solar-households.html>.

6 Australian Energy Regulator, 'National Electricity Market Electricity Consumption 2018,' <https://www.aer.gov.au/wholesale-markets/wholesale-statistics/national-electricity-market-electricity-consumption>.

7 Australian Energy Market Operator, '2018 Electricity Forecasting Insights' (March 2018), <https://www.aemo.com.au/Electricity/National-Electricity-Market-NEM/Planning-and-forecasting/NEM-Electricity-Demand-Forecasts/Electricity-Forecasting-Insights/2018-Electricity-Forecasting-Insights>.

8 George Goddard and Megan A. Farrelly, 'Just transition management: Balancing just outcomes with just processes in Australian renewable energy transitions' (2018) 225 *Applied Energy* 110, 111.

9 Constitution of the Commonwealth of Australia s.107.

10 Australian Government, Senate Select Committee on Electricity Prices, 'Report on reducing energy bills and improving energy efficiency' (Parliamentary Paper, 2012), 2.10.

Several reviews of the electricity sector in the early 1990s found that the existing market structure was inefficient, with low productivity and high barriers to entry.[11] This prompted negotiations between the Commonwealth, states and territories about the future governance of the electricity sector and the need to implement market competition. These negotiations resulted in the National Electricity Market Legislation Agreement (NEMLA),[12] which sought to introduce a uniform single wholesale electricity market across eastern and southern Australia, and harmonise the laws and regulations governing electricity supply in participating jurisdictions.[13] These reforms were designed to facilitate interstate trade, lower barriers to competition, increase regulatory certainty and improve productivity within the electricity sector as it transitioned from being dominated by large unbundled state-owned monopolies to privatised corporations. In 1996, the National Electricity Law[14] (NEL) was enacted, which in its own right was a major achievement, being only the second time co-operative legislation had been agreed to and passed by the jurisdictions.[15] Then in 1998, the NEM commenced operations.

3 The national electricity market

The NEM is a wholesale electricity market through which generators generate, sell, transmit and distribute electricity across six jurisdictions in eastern and southern Australia – namely, Queensland, New South Wales, the Australian Capital Territory (ACT), Victoria, South Australia and Tasmania. Despite its name, the NEM is not a truly national market, with Western Australia and the Northern Territory continuing to operate as separate markets 'because the long transmission distances involved make efficient interconnection difficult.'[16] As it is, the NEM is already one of the longest continuous alternating current (AC) transmission networks in the world. It consists of 40,000kms of transmission lines[17] across the five states and one territory linking 240 large generating units and 13 major distribution networks via six cross-border interconnectors.[18] The NEM currently has an installed capacity of 55,590MW.[19] The NEM supplies electricity to 9.7 million residential and business customers in participating jurisdictions.[20]

11 See, e.g., Frederick Hilmer, 'Independent Committee of Inquiry into Competition Policy in Australia' (1993), <http://ncp.ncc.gov.au/docs/National%Competition%20Policy%20Review%20report,%20The%20Hilmer%20Report,%2020August%201993.pdf>.

12 *Australian Energy Market Agreement*, signed 30 June 2004 [2004], <https://web.archive.org/web/20130505164040/http://www.ret.gov.au/Documents/mce/_documents/IGA_FINAL_(30JUNE2004)2004071310032320041112162849.pdf>. In 2004, the Commonwealth, state and territory governments replaced the NEMLA with the Australian Energy Market Agreement (AEMA). This agreement sets the ongoing agenda for a transition from standalone electricity systems to national energy regulation. The AEMA also aims to 'promote the long term interests of consumers with regard to the price, quality and reliability of electricity and gas services.' Id. at 6.

13 Ibid.

14 *National Electricity (South Australia) Act* 1996, Sch. 1. (as amended).

15 See Australian Energy Market Commission, *National Energy Market. A Case Study in Successful Microeconomic Reform*, 31 (2013), <www.aemc.gov.au/getattachment/8c426f7d-ea5c-4823-9b86- 510dfd4e82dd/The-National-Electricity-Market-A-case-study-in-mi.aspx>.

16 *National Electricity (South Australia) Bill* 1996: Second Reading Speech, South Australian Parliamentary Debates, Legislative Council, 1481 (1996).

17 Australian Energy Market Operator, 'National Electricity Market' (2019), <https://www.aemo.com.au/Electricity/National-Electricity-Market-NEM>.

18 See note 1, 75.

19 Ibid.

20 Ibid.

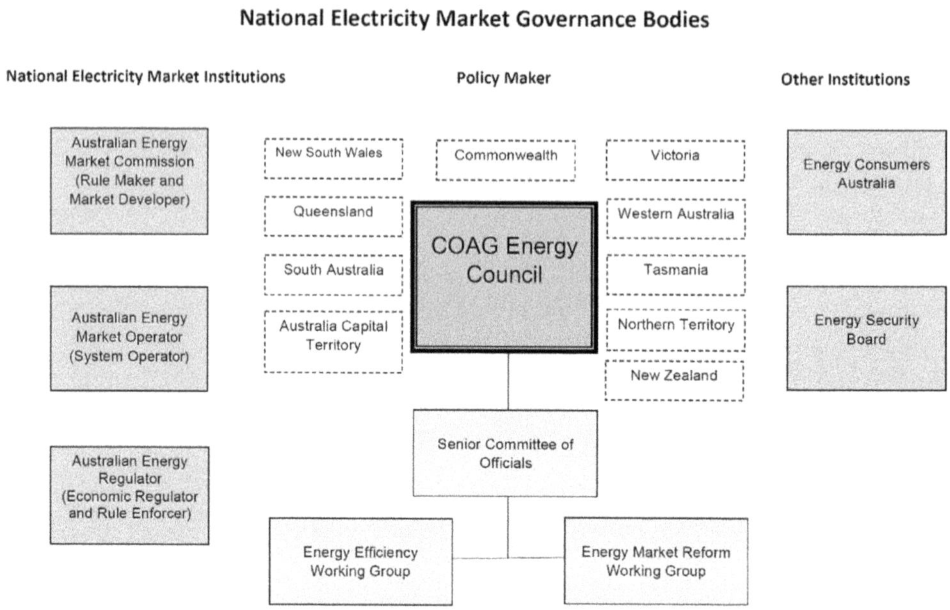

Figure 26.1 The governance structure of the Australian NEM[a]

a Diagram compiled by Author.

3.1 *The institutional and governance structure of the NEM*

As shown in Figure 26.1, the institutional and governance structures of the NEM are highly complex. The key market institutions are:

1. the Council of Australian Governments (COAG) Energy Council,[21] which is made up of the Ministers from the Commonwealth, each state and territory, and New Zealand, with portfolio responsibility for energy and resources, as the entity responsible for national energy policy and strategy;
2. the Australian Energy Market Commission (AEMC) as the entity responsible for rulemaking, in the form of developing changes to the National Electricity Rules, the statutory framework under the National Electricity Law, and market development;[22]

21 The original form of the COAG Energy Council was the Ministerial Council on Energy (MCE), which was established on 8 June 2001. It was designed to be the forum through which the Commonwealth, state and territory Ministers having primary responsibility for energy matters could meet to formulate national energy policy. The role of the MCE is described in cl 4 of the AEMA (as amended on 9 December 2013). Over the past 14 years, three institutions have held these legally enduring roles and powers:

1. the MCE 8 June 2001–16 September 2011;
2. the Standing Council on Energy and Resources (SCER) 17 September 2011–12 December 2013;
3. the COAG Energy Council 13 December 2013–present.

Council of Australian Governments Energy Council, 'Terms of Reference' (2019), <www.coagenergycouncil.gov.au/about-us/council-membership>.

22 While ostensibly this appears to be a mundane regulatory function, the reality of the operations of the AEMC has been as chief policy-maker in relation to electricity in the NEM.

3. the Australian Energy Market Operator (AEMO) as the system operator and the entity responsible for market development;
4. the Australian Energy Regulator (AER) as the economic regulator responsible for implementing the rules, conducting monitoring and ensuring compliance;
5. Energy Consumers Australia (ECA) as the entity charged with promoting the long-term interests of consumers and advocating on their behalf.

The most recent addition to the governance structure of the NEM is the Energy Security Board (ESB), established in 2017 following a series of reliability issues, including blackouts and the retirement of a number of large fossil fuel fired generators on very short notice. Its role is to oversee implementation of the national energy market reform agenda, and to provide whole-of-system oversight for security and reliability.

These institutions must act in accordance with the National Electricity Objective (NEO), contained in Section 7 of the NEL, which states:

> The objective of this Law is to promote efficient investment in, and efficient operation and use of, electricity services for the long term interests of consumers of electricity with respect to-
>
> (a) price, quality, safety, reliability and security of supply of electricity; and
> (b) the reliability, safety and security of the national electricity system.[23]

One of the most striking features about the design of the NEM and the laws and governance structure that support it, is that at the time that they were designed the only renewable generator providing generation to the energy market was the Snowy Hydroelectric Scheme. This has prompted subsequent criticisms that its structural design, which has been largely unchanged since it commenced operation, acts as a barrier to the deployment of renewable energy and innovative energy technologies. In particular, there have been criticism that the NEM was designed to support the incumbent large fossil fuel generators with traditional models of transmission and distribution, with each market participant in the unbundled energy market only being permitted to perform one function.[24] This structure makes innovations such as the widespread implementation of embedded generation, distributed generation, peer-to-peer energy trading or even deploying energy storage technologies challenging. This challenge is heightened when any changes to the laws or governance of the NEM in the COAG Energy Council are largely achieved through consensus (and hence often the lowest common denominator) decision making across the nine jurisdictions and the process is rarely transparent.[25] In addition, the NEO has long been criticised,[26] with questions increasingly being asked about whether it is still fit for purpose. In particular, concerns have been expressed that its narrow focus on the economic interests of consumers limits the ability of the Australian energy market institutions to adequately plan for the long-term future of the electricity sector, especially in relation to growing concerns about the environment and sustainability.[27]

23 *National Electricity (South Australia) Act* 1996, Sch 1 s.7.

24 See, e.g., Penelope Crossley, 'Review of the institutional governance arrangements for the national electricity market' (Report commissioned by the Public Interest Advocacy Centre, 2015).

25 Ibid.

26 Ibid.

27 This may be contrasted with the position of the EU and China, which both include a focus on sustainability within their equivalent provisions.

4 The laws governing renewable energy in Australia[28]

Given the complex governance structure of the NEM, it is no surprise that the mechanisms that support the accelerated deployment of renewable energy in Australia are also a complex, and at times overlapping, combination of Federal and state laws. The most significant of these laws is the national RET.

4.1 The Renewable Energy Target

The Australian RET was enacted under the *Renewable Energy (Electricity) Act* 2000 (Cth), the *Renewable Energy (Electricity) (Small-scale Technology Shortfall Charge) Act* 2010 (Cth), the *Renewable Energy (Electricity) (Large-scale Generation Shortfall Charge) Act* 2000 (Cth) and the *Renewable Energy (Electricity) Regulations* 2001 (Cth). It was one of the first national renewable energy targets introduced, and unlike the renewable energy laws in the vast majority of countries in the world, its legislative objectives have always been solely focused on improving environmental protection and addressing climate change.[29] This focus on the environment has made the law far more vulnerable to political attack than the renewable energy laws in other countries, which tend to be focused on energy security concerns, industrial policy and national development.

Under its original design, the RET was 'projected to reduce emissions by about 200 Mt CO2 e (cumulatively) between 2015 and 2030.'[30] It is essentially a 'technology pull' scheme that requires liable entities to buy renewable energy certificates to meet their RET liability. The RET is divided into two schemes – the Small-scale Renewable Energy Scheme (SRES) and the Large-scale Renewable Energy Target (LRET).

4.1.1 The Small-scale Renewable Energy Scheme

The SRES creates a financial incentive for residential households and small businesses to install eligible small-scale renewable energy systems such as solar water heaters, heat pumps, PV solar systems, small-scale wind systems, or small-scale hydro systems.[31] Eligible small renewable systems may create Small-scale Technology Certificates (STCs) at the time of installation, for the amount of electricity the systems are expected to produce or displace for the expected lifespan of the system.[32] For example, eligible PV solar systems are permitted to create, at the time of installation, one STC for each megawatt hour of eligible renewable electricity either generated or displaced by the system over the 15 years of the expected

28 It is important to note at the outset that while New Zealand is a participating member of the COAG Energy Council, it does not use the same legislative regime to support renewable energy, and in fact does not have a national renewable energy law.

29 Penelope Crossley, *Renewable Energy Law: An International Assessment* (Cambridge University Press, 2019), Chapter 4.

30 Australian Government Climate Change Authority, 'Towards a Climate Policy Toolkit: Special review on Australia's climate goals and policies' (2016), 45, <http://climatechangeauthority.gov.au/sites/prod.climatechangeauthority.gov.au/files/files/Special%20review%20Report%203/Climate%20Change%20Authority%20Special%20Review%20Report%20Three.pdf>.

31 *Renewable Energy (Electricity) Act* 2000 (Cth); see also Clean Energy Regulator, 'How the scheme works,' *Renewable Energy Target* (Web Page, 31 May 2018), <www.cleanenergyregulator.gov.au/RET/About-the-Renewable-Energy-Target/How-the- scheme-works>.

32 *Renewable Energy (Electricity) Act* 2000 (Cth), ss.20B–23E.

system output.[33] The government has legislated demand for STCs, with RET-liable entities with an obligation under the LRET also having a legal requirement under the SRES to buy STCs and surrender them.[34] Individual owners of renewable energy systems rarely create and sell the STCs themselves, rather accredited installers usually create the STCs and then sell them in larger bundles, offering either a discount on the installation price or cash to the owner in return.[35]

4.1.2 The Large-scale Renewable Energy Target

Similar to the SRES, the LRET creates a financial incentive for the establishment or expansion of renewable energy generators, such as wind and solar farms or hydroelectric power stations. It does this by legislating demand for Large-scale Generation Certificates (LGCs), through annual targets, which must be met by liable entities.[36] One LGC can be created for each megawatt hour of eligible renewable electricity produced by an accredited renewable power station.[37] LGCs can be sold to entities (mainly electricity retailers) who surrender them annually to the Clean Energy Regulator to demonstrate their compliance with the RET scheme's annual targets.[38] The revenue earned by the power station for the sale of LGCs is additional to that received for the sale of the electricity generated.[39]

4.1.3 The RET reviews

Since its inception the RET has been formally reviewed by: the Tambling Review in 2003; the Rudd Commonwealth Government in 2009; twice by the Climate Change Authority in 2012 and 2014; the Warburton Renewable Energy Target Expert Review Panel in 2014 and, most recently, was also considered by the Australian Competition and Consumer Commission's (ACCC's) Retail Electricity Pricing Inquiry in 2018. Each of these reviews has arguably introduced uncertainty into the market, making investments more risky until the reviews were concluded.

These reviews have led to the RET undergoing significant re-design twice. In 2009, the *Renewable Energy (Electricity) Amendment Act* 2009, changed the Mandatory Renewable Energy Target of 9,500GWh of renewable generation by 2010 to the RET, which was initially set at 45,000GWh by 2020 (41,000GWh for Large-scale and a target of 4,000GWh for Small-scale). The 2009 Amendment Act also introduced a solar multiplier and allowed for the partial exemption under the RET of emissions-intensive trade-exposed industries.

Following the election of a more conservative Commonwealth Government in late 2013, the newly elected Coalition Government, which had run on a platform of scrapping

33 *Renewable Energy (Electricity) Regulations* 2001 (Cth), Reg 19D(2)(d).

34 *Renewable Energy (Electricity) Act* 2000 (Cth), ss.38AA–38AI.

35 Clean Energy Regulator, 'Claiming small-scale technology certificates' (2019), <www.cleanenergyregulator gov.au/RET/How-to-participate-in-the-Renewable-Energy-Target/Financial-incentives/Claiming-small-scale-technology-certificates>.

36 *Renewable Energy (Electricity) Act* 2000 (Cth), ss.36–38.

37 *Renewable Energy (Electricity) Act* 2000 (Cth), s.18(1).

38 *Renewable Energy (Electricity) Act* 2000 (Cth), ss.20, 44A. The Clean Energy Regulator is an independent statutory body established in 2012 under the *Clean Energy Regulator Act* 2011 (Cth). Its role is to administer the government schemes to reduce greenhouse gas emissions and to increase the use of clean energy in Australia: See *Clean Energy Regulator Act* 2011 (Cth), s.11.

39 *Renewable Energy (Electricity) Act* 2000 (Cth), s.8.

a number of policies supportive of renewable energy and addressing climate change, announced another review of the national renewable energy laws. In 2014, Australia held an expert RET Review chaired by Dick Warburton, the former Chairman of Caltex Oil in Australia.[40] The Review was launched after concerns were raised by the electricity industry that in the context of declining electricity demand and greater energy efficiency, the volumetric requirement of the LRET of 41,000GWh of electricity coming from large-scale renewable energy by 2020 meant that approximately 27 per cent of electricity generation had to come from renewable energy sources.[41] This was significantly higher than the 20 per cent that had originally been intended when the RET scheme was designed and was squeezing out other sources of generation. The Review

> found the RET had led to the abatement of 20 million tonnes of carbon emissions and, if left in place, would abate a further 20 million tonnes of emissions per year from 2015 to 2030—almost 10 per cent of electricity sector emissions.[42]

Further, the Review found that while the cumulative impact on household energy bills over the period of the RET was likely to be small, the RET was 'an expensive emissions abatement tool that subsidises renewable generation at the expense of coal fired electricity generation.'[43] The Review recommended that in order to protect existing generators, instead of the volumetric target, a revised 'true 20 per cent target' for large-scale renewable generation (equivalent to approximately 33,000GWh) should be achieved through a series of yearly targets, set one year in advance, that correspond to 50 per cent of growth in electricity demand.[44] On 23 June 2015, these changes were adopted through legislative amendments to the existing scheme.[45]

In July 2018, the ACCC held an Inquiry into Retail Electricity Pricing. This Inquiry recommended as Recommendation 24 that the SRES should be abolished by 2021 rather than 2030 as scheduled, to reduce electricity prices.[46] This Recommendation has not been adopted as policy by either of the two major national political parties, probably because of the popularity of the SRES with the populace and the short period of time between these Recommendations being made and the 2019 Federal election.

4.2 State and territory government approaches

In addition to the national approach under the *Renewable Energy (Electricity) Act* 2000 (Cth), there are also a number of state and territory initiatives, which operate to support the deployment of renewable energy in Australia. For example, both Victoria and the Australian Capital Territory (ACT) have legislated renewable energy and emissions reduction targets; in Victoria under the *Renewable Energy (Jobs and Investment) Act* 2017 and *Climate Change Act*

40 Dick Warburton et al., 'Renewable Energy Target Scheme: Report of the Expert Panel' (Commonwealth of Australia, 2014), <http://apo.org.au/system/files/41058/apo-nid41058-82456.pdf>. ['Warburton Review'].

41 Ibid, 120.

42 Ibid, 60.

43 Ibid, 18.

44 Ibid, iii–iv.

45 *Renewable Energy (Electricity) Amendment Act* 2015 (Cth).

46 Australian Competition and Consumer Commission, 'Restoring electricity affordability & Australia's competitive advantage – Retail Electricity Pricing Inquiry Final Report,' Chapter 9, Recommendation 24.

2017; and in the ACT under the *Electricity Feed-in (Large-scale Renewable Energy Generation) Act* 2011 and the *Climate Change and Greenhouse Gas Reduction Act* 2010 in the ACT. The other states have not adopted legislated approaches but have had comparatively stable policy positions, with both New South Wales and Queensland aiming to reduce greenhouse gas emissions to net zero by 2050. These state schemes have played an important role in supporting the deployment of renewable energy, particularly in the absence of an integrated energy and climate regime at the Commonwealth level.

While the impact of these initiatives has largely been positive for the Australian renewable energy sector, they have also led to significant differences emerging amongst the states and territories potentially undermining the efforts towards national harmonisation. This has created real issues within the context of the NEM, as some states have elected to encourage very high levels of deployment of intermittent renewable generation and shut down their older coal fired generators. However, due to the lack of a coordinated national approach, this means that some states are at times dependent on their ability to import baseload fossil fuel fired generation from interstate across the interconnectors. This in turn limits the ability of the exporting states to change their own energy mix. These state-based initiatives have also had the effect of making it more difficult for the companies who operate across state borders or on a national scale, as they have to manage regulatory compliance on a state-by-state rather than national basis. This level of complexity and potential regulatory overlap between the Commonwealth and state regimes may act as a market barrier to new entrants considering entering the market.

5 The draft National Energy Guarantee

Recently both major political parties at the Commonwealth level have called for the closer integration of energy and climate policies, and sought to improve the reliability and stability of the network given the increased use of intermittent renewables. This has been visible most recently in the development of the draft NEG, which was developed following the 2016 Independent Review into the Future Security of the National Electricity Market (the Finkel Review).[47] One of their key recommendations was the establishment of the ESB to 'oversee the implementation of the blueprint and coordinate whole-of-system oversight for security and reliability.'[48] In turn, the ESB recommended the development of a NEG as a mechanism to ensure reliability, restore investor confidence and address affordability while lowering emissions in the electricity sector.[49]

On 17 October 2017, then Prime Minister Malcolm Turnbull along with the then Minister for Energy and the Environment, Josh Frydenberg, announced that the Commonwealth Government would introduce a NEG.[50] The NEG was designed by the Energy Security Board as a means of integrating Australia's national energy and emissions policies to ensure

47 Department of the Environment and Energy, 'Independent Review into the Future Security of the National Electricity Market' (2016) <https://www.energy.gov.au/government-priorities/energy-markets/independent-review-future-security-national-electricity-market>.

48 Australian Energy Regulator, *State of the Energy Market 2017* (Commonwealth of Australia, 2017), 6.

49 Kerry Schott, 'Letter from the Board of the Energy Security Board to the Ministers of the COAG Energy Council on the High Level Design of the National Energy Guarantee' (13 April 2018), <www.coagenergycouncil.gov.au/sites/prod.energycouncil/files/publications/documents/ESB%20Letter%20to%20Ministers_High-level%20design%20document.pdf>.

50 Malcolm Turnbull, 'Press Conference with the Minister for the Environment and Energy and Members of the Energy Security Board' (17 October 2017, Parliament House Canberra), Transcript ID 41247.

that 'more affordable, reliable and clean power [could be delivered] to Australian households and businesses.'

It consisted of two key obligations on energy retailers and some large energy users within the National Electricity Market (who opt into the NEG):

1. The Retailer Reliability Obligation;
2. The Emissions Reduction Requirement.

5.1 The Retailer Reliability Obligation

The Retailer Reliability Obligation was outlined in the amendments to the National Electricity Law in the draft *National Electricity (South Australia) (Retailer Reliability Obligation) Amendment Bill* 2018 (Reliability Draft Bill), released for comment in November 2018. The Draft Bill was devised following the widespread blackouts in South Australia in September 2016, which had been erroneously attributed by a number of state and Federal politicians to an inherent failure in renewable energy output.[51]

The Reliability Obligation requires AEMO to assess whether the annual reliability forecast within each NEM region meets the minimum level of the NEM reliability standard of 99.998 per cent[52] and has an appropriate mix of fast and slow starting dispatchable capacity. In the event of a shortfall, these forecasts should send a clear signal to the market that liable market entities should either invest in new capacity in dispatchable energy resources or make additional dispatchable capacity available to the NEM.[53]

If it does not appear that the voluntary market response will be sufficient to address the gap, AEMO may make a written request to the AER to issue statutory reliability instruments. These instruments have the force of law, and effectively compel the liable entities 'to hold forward contracts or invest directly in dispatchable energy resources that cover a predetermined percentage of their forecast peak load.'[54] The liable entities for the reliability requirement are 'registered NEM participants who purchase electricity directly from the NEM spot market (including Market Customers) unless otherwise prescribed,'[55] noting that other 'non-liable customers' may choose to opt into the reliability obligation. This capacity mechanism has been designed to be technology neutral and may include demand response, distributed energy resources such as batteries or additional hydropower, coal or gas fired generation.

Reliability instruments must specify the NEM region in which the gap will occur, the duration of the forecast gap and 'AEMO's one-in-two-year peak demand forecast for the forecast reliability period.'[56] Under the NEG, two different reliability instruments may be

51 Australian Energy Market Operator, *Black System: South Australia 28 September 2016* (Final Report, March 2017).

52 Australian Energy Market Commission, 'Reliability standard and settings Review 2018' (30 April 2018), <https://www.aemc.gov.au/markets-reviews-advice/reliability-standard-and-settings-review-2018>.

53 See also generally, Energy Security Board, 'Consultation on National Energy Guarantee Amendments,' COAG Energy Council Bulletin, August 2018.

54 Energy Security Board, *Overview of the Retailer Reliability and Emissions Guarantee*, COAG Energy Council (Commonwealth of Australia, 2018) 2. <www.coagenergycouncil.gov.au/sites/prod.energycouncil/files/publications/documents/Energy%20Security%20Board%20Overview%20of%20the%20National%20Energy%20Guarantee.pdf>.

55 *National Electricity (South Australia) (National Energy Guarantee) Amendment Bill* 2018 ('*NEG Amendment Bill* 2018'), s.14ZB.

56 *NEG Amendment Bill* 2018, s.14ZG.

issued by the AER, the T-3 reliability instrument (issued three years prior to the forecast reliability gap) and the T-1 reliability instrument (issued one year prior).[57] The key difference between the T-3 and T-1 reliability instruments is whether liable entities '*may*' or '*will*' be required to hold net contract positions sufficient to meet liable entities' share of the one-in-two year forecast peak demand for the forecast reliability gap period.[58]

AEMO will be the procurer of last resort if a T-1 reliability instrument is issued for a particular region and AEMO believes there are insufficient qualifying contracts to secure the dispatchable capacity required to cover the reliability gap period. If AEMO acts as the procurer of last resort, it may recover its costs from the non-compliant entities. The draft bill limits the liability for costs of a defaulting liable entity to $100 million.[59] However, the liable entity may also be subject to a civil penalty under a statutory compliance action, which will not exceed $1 million for the first breach relating to a reliability gap period, and $10 million for a breach relating to a second or subsequent reliability gap period.[60]

5.2 The Emissions Reduction Requirement

The Emissions Reduction Requirement was outlined in the *National Electricity (South Australia) (National Energy Guarantee) Amendment Bill 2018* (Draft NEG Bill) that was released for comment in August 2018. It was predicated on the understanding that a national electricity emissions intensity target would be established under a new Commonwealth Act, the *National Energy Guarantee (Targets) Act* 2018. This target would reflect the contribution that the Australian Government plans the electricity sector will play in meeting its Paris commitments.

Australia's Nationally Determined Contribution under the Paris Agreement is an economy-wide reduction in greenhouse gas emissions by 26 to 28 per cent below 2005 levels by 2030.[61] In order to meet this target, the cumulative emissions reductions between 2021 and 2030 need to range between 868 Mt Co2-e and 934 Mt CO2-e.[62] While Australia is currently on track to overachieve its earlier 2020 target set under the Kyoto Protocol, since the repeal of the Carbon Pollution Reduction Scheme on 17 July 2014, there has been an increase in greenhouse gas emissions every year.[63] The electricity sector is responsible for the largest sectoral contribution to the national greenhouse gas inventory, representing 34 per cent of the total emissions in the year to March 2018.[64] These emissions were predominantly the result of combusting fossil fuels, and in particular coal, for electricity generation.

Once the national emissions intensity target has been set it will then be allocated across the NEM to impose a level of emissions intensity on individual 'liable customers.' For the purposes of the Draft NEG Bill, 'liable customers' are all registered market participants in

57 *NEG Amendment Bill* 2018, s.14ZE.

58 See note 50, and *NEG Amendment Bill* 2018, s.14ZG.

59 *NEG Amendment Bill* 2018, s.14ZR.

60 See note 50, 6.

61 Australian Government, 'Australia's intended nationally determined contribution to a new climate change agreement,' Nationally Determined Contribution Registry, United Nations (August 2015).

62 Department of Environment and Energy (Cth), 'Australia's emissions projections 2017,' Commonwealth of Australia (December 2017), 3.

63 Ibid, 9; Department of Environment and Energy (Cth), 'Review of climate change policies,' Commonwealth of Australia (December 2017), 5.

64 Department of Environment and Energy (Cth), *Quarterly Update of Australia's National Greenhouse Gas Inventory: March 2018*, Australia's National Greenhouse Accounts (Commonwealth of Australia, 2018), 8.

the NEM who buy directly from the wholesale market or other large customers who opt in.[65] The emissions intensity will be based on an assessment of preliminary emissions intensity of the liable customer's liable load (its market load adjusted for exempt loads, scaling, non-market load and GreenPower load) within a compliance year,[66] as well as any carry forwards, deferrals or offsets.[67]

An emissions intensity requirement may be met by entering into contracts with existing generators or by investing in new generation capacity. Each contract purchased will specify both the amount of electricity procured, as well as its emissions level. If the liable entity purchases generation 'from the spot market without a contract, [it] will be assigned the average emissions level of the uncontracted generation capacity available to the market.'[68] The emissions intensity for supply from the spot market is likely to be highly emissions intensive, as it is anticipated that the least cost lower emitting electricity sources will be subject to existing contracts and not available for the spot market. In order to meet the emissions obligation, liable entities will need to show the AER their 'contract and spot market purchases they have used to meet their emissions guarantee'[69] for each annual compliance period. AEMO will establish an emissions registry, in which 'every mega-watt hour of generation that occurs in a compliance year will be recorded in the registry for allocation against every MWh of market customer load in that compliance year'[70] to help facilitate efficient compliance.

If a 'liable customer' overachieves on procuring emissions reductions in a given compliance year, they are permitted to carry forward up to 10 per cent of their first-year emissions intensity target plus a fixed amount of 60,000tCO2-e.[71] Conversely, they may also defer some of their emissions liability, with the deferral limits currently set at 10 per cent over two years.[72] The conditions applicable to carry forward and deferral permitted under the NEG have not yet been released and will be contained in amendments to the National Electricity Rules.

In the event that a 'liable customer' does not have sufficient emissions reductions in the emissions register to meet their obligations and has used up their deferrals, the AER has a suite of options at their disposal and wide discretion to enforce compliance in a least cost manner. In the event of non-compliance, the Australian Energy Regulator can also apply to the courts for the imposition of a civil penalty of up to $100 million for a body corporate.[73]

5.3 Criticisms of the draft NEG design

The ESB famously argued that the 'status quo is not an option,'[74] and that 'an unstable and uncoordinated policy environment exacerbates these issues.'[75] Modelling of the NEG conducted for the ESB estimates that it will lead to a reduction in wholesale electricity prices over the period of 2020 to 2030 of 23 per cent, with the average household expected to save

65 *NEG Amendment Bill* 2018, s.14G.
66 *NEG Amendment Bill* 2018, s.14L.
67 *NEG Amendment Bill* 2018, s.14J.
68 See note 51, 2.
69 Ibid.
70 Energy Security Board, *National Energy Guarantee – Final Detailed Design* (Commonwealth of Australia, 1 August 2018).
71 Ibid, 2.
72 Ibid, 35.
73 *NEG Amendment Bill* 2018, s.14H.
74 See note 67, 9.
75 Ibid.

$150 compared to business as usual.[76] Indeed, the industry consensus appears to be that while the NEG is not the preferred policy option of most organisations some policy certainty in the sector has to be preferable to a complete absence of policy. That said, the current design of the NEG still presents many issues for the sector, four of which will be discussed below.

First, the NEG does not address the issue of reliability and emissions in either the Northern Territory or Western Australia, as they do not form part of the NEM. These jurisdictions are responsible for 22 per cent of the emissions nationally[77] and not to have a truly national emissions reduction target for the electricity sector is a major failure. Secondly, while the NEG is designed to provide clear short–medium term investment signals to the market for dispatchable resources and distributed energy resources, it does not create policy stability post 2030. Most major energy projects are currently financed on loans that have to be fully repaid by 2030 due to the uncertainty in the post 2030 regime. The NEG does not address this issue and thus does not inspire the confidence needed to encourage investment post 2030. Thirdly, it has been argued that the emissions target contained in the NEG is not suitably ambitious. The Clean Energy Council has argued that the emissions target within the NEG is insufficient as it represents 'only a minor reduction from what is expected under business as usual (excluding any impact from state government promises beyond the renewable energy reverse auctions already in train).'[78] They further argue that the lack of ambition in the target is unlikely to attract sufficient new investment in generating capacity to address the concerns around reliability, affordability and emissions, it is inconsistent with the Australian Government's commitments under the Paris Agreement and it fails to address the need for a clear emissions trajectory post 2030.[79] The final issue with the NEG is that it is a very complex legislative scheme that is entering into a policy environment with a number of existing overlapping laws and policies such as the RET and the state-based schemes. It is important that the addition of the NEG does not have unforeseen consequences on existing investments and that the regulatory burden of adhering to multiple schemes in different jurisdictions is minimised.

5.4 The current status of the NEG

On 7 September 2018, the new Prime Minister, Scott Morrison announced that the NEG was 'dead.'[80] Despite this statement, there appeared to be strong support among the Coalition for implementing the NEG's reliability obligation, however they announced they had scrapped the emissions obligation. Between September and December 2018, the Coalition Commonwealth Government continued to pursue the Reliability Obligation, petitioning the other members of the COAG Energy Council for the need to implement it. At the COAG Energy Council meeting in December 2018, the member jurisdictions announced an intention to adopt the Reliability Obligation that had been proposed under the draft

76 Ibid, 52.

77 Clean Energy Regulator, 'State and territory emissions profile 2016 17,' (28 February 2018), <www.cleanenergyregulator.gov.au/NGER/Pages/Published%20information/Data%20highlights/2016%E2%80%9317%20factsheets/State-and-territory-emissions profile 2016%E2%80%9317.aspx>.

78 Clean Energy Council, 'National Energy Guarantee' (2018), <https://www.cleanenergycouncil.org.au/policy-advocacy/national-energy-guarantee.html>.

79 Clean Energy Council, 'National Energy Guarantee – Clean Energy Council Submission to Consultation Paper' (March 2018), 6.

80 Simon Benson, 'National Energy Guarantee 'dead' as Morrison sets new course' *The Australian*, 8 September 2018, <https://www.theaustralian.com.au/national-affairs/climate/national-energy-guarantee-dead-as-morrison-sets-new-course/news-story/1e0db1f87ba30117317cdcc24f537a88>.

NEG. The final version of the Reliability Obligation has now been published with the basic elements remaining the same.

In the meantime, on 21 November 2018, the Labor Shadow Cabinet endorsed the NEG in its entirety in an attempt to encourage a bipartisan and integrated climate and energy policy for the 2019 Federal election.[81] They also announced that they would adopt an emissions reduction target for electricity of 45 per cent by 2030 and be seeking to have an energy mix that is made up of 50 per cent renewable energy by 2030.[82] Thus had Labor won the 2019 Federal election and been able to successfully get the amendments to the National Electricity Law passed in both the House of Representatives and the Senate, the NEG may still have been adopted. However, as the Coalition won the election, only the reliability obligation from the NEG has been adopted, meaning that Australia still does not have an integrated energy and climate policy. This makes Australia one of the few developed countries in the world that has failed to integrate these two key policy areas. However, even if the NEG had been wholly adopted, it would still not have created a national approach to emissions reductions in the energy sector. This is because the NEG would only apply to NEM jurisdictions, meaning that both the Northern Territory and Western Australia, which combined account for over 22 per cent of national emissions,[83] will not be subject to the NEG. Therefore the existing Commonwealth and state support schemes for renewable energy will continue to play an important role in supporting the development of the sector.

6 Conclusion

The national RET has been highly effective for almost 20 years in supporting the transformation of the Australian energy sector by increasing the renewable generation contained within the national energy mix. However, increasing electricity prices, and concerns about the reliability and system stability issues associated with growing volumes of intermittent and non-dispatchable generation have led to calls that the status quo will no longer meet the needs of Australian energy consumers. In particular, consumers are now seeking a reliable energy supply that is affordable and addresses climate concerns. However, energy policy in Australia has long been a political battleground that is ideologically driven. Because of this, there has been a lack of regulatory certainty in how the electricity sector will manage the transition to cleaner renewable energy sources and address climate change. This has increased the risk for those investing and operating within the energy sector and for both commercial and residential customers. There is currently strong popular support for reforming the energy sector to enable energy and climate policies to be integrated, which prompted the development of the draft NEG. Following the election of the Coalition Government in 2019, the NEG was formally scrapped as government policy. The government did, however, subsequently introduce the Retail Reliability Obligation (RRO). The RRO has already been enacted and the first T-3 events reported. The outcome of this is that the Australian energy sector still lacks an integrated approach to energy and climate law. Going forward, it will be important that the design and implementation of any further legislative developments are carefully managed to ensure that they are interoperable with the existing Commonwealth and state support schemes, minimise regulatory overlap and provide the policy and regulatory certainty that the sector has been sorely lacking.

81 ABC Radio, 'Transcript of an interview between Fran Kelly and Mark Butler, Shadow Minister for Climate Change and Energy for Radio National Breakfast' (22 November 2018), <https://www.markbutler.net.au/news/transcripts/rn-breakfast-221118>.

82 Ibid.

83 See note 74.

27

IS GAS SECURITY IN THE 'NATIONAL INTEREST'?

AN AUSTRALIAN EASTERN GAS MARKET PERSPECTIVE

Madeline E. Taylor

1 Introduction

The pattern of natural gas regulation in Australia is increasingly uncertain, inconsistent and *ad hoc*. States and territories continue to create evidentially divergent natural gas policies and pathways in the absence of federal gas policy of a lasting nature, ranging from moratoria on unconventional gas exploitation to the creation of liquid natural gas (LNG) export and import terminals.[1] This is due to the ownership of onshore natural resources being conferred to Australian states and territories, rather than at the federal level.[2] While renewable energy sources continue to be developed in Australia, oil (39.7 per cent), coal (32 per cent) and natural gas (25 per cent) remain the dominant energy sources consumed.[3] Onshore coal seam gas (CSG), a form of unconventional gas, consisting of 1,290 petajoules or 34 billion cubic metres, represents one-third of the natural gas produced in Australia and two-thirds of the gas produced on Australia's East Coast.[4] Asian jurisdictions continue to seek long-term LNG export contracts from energy-export states, such as Australia, in the wake of increasing support for gas as the primary 'transition' fuel to bridge the shift to renewable energy sources.[5] Domestically, the average annual growth for gas consumption is expected to rise 2.9 per cent annually for the next decade within Australia's energy rubric, while the current dominant energy source of coal will decrease by 1.9 per cent annually until 2030.[6] Consequently, the Australian Eastern Gas Market is at a pivotal regulatory moment. Historically it has enjoyed

1 The Port Kembla LNG import terminal is the first in New South Wales and was given approval for construction in April 2019.

2 As the Commonwealth of Australia does not hold specific constitutional powers to legislate for the production and exploration of mineral and petroleum resources, ownership is vested in the Australian states and territories.

3 Australian Government Department of the Environment and Energy, 'Australian Energy Update' (August, 2018) <www.energy.gov.au/sites/default/files/australian_energy_update_2018.pdf> accessed 15 November 2018, 7.

4 Ibid 20.

5 Vaclav Smil, *Natural Gas: Fuel for the 21st Century* (John Wiley and Sons 2015).

6 Australian Government Department of the Environment and Energy (n 3). The importance of coal in Australia's energy export portfolio and energy mix was solidified in the recent final state environmental approval of the Carmichael coalmine in June 2019.

relative security of supply from both conventional and unconventional gas exploitation, however, it is now faced with a gas shortage, increasing gas prices and network outages. In a real sense, the LNG export industry is a victim of its success, as the rush to secure long-term LNG export contracts by consortia in Queensland[7] has resulted in supply constraints for domestic consumers and increased gas prices. This is coupled with the confidential nature of export contract conditions, often bearing penalty clauses for a failure to meet export supply terms, creating regulatory uncertainty and deliverability concerns.[8]

This regulatory dilemma occurs at a time when natural gas is moving beyond being a mere bridging fuel, and becoming a permanent and major source of electricity generation in the global energy mix. The likelihood of natural gas as a permanent fixture in energy policy, regulation and consumption is echoed by Yergin in that; 'by the end of the 2030s, it is likely that natural gas will pull ahead to become the world's No. 1 fuel'.[9] In 2016–2017 alone, natural gas production in Australia increased by 23 per cent spearheaded by three LNG export consortia projects commencing in Queensland in 2014 and 2015.[10] Yet the Eastern Gas Market of Australia is facing a security crisis, coupled with the 'hot' debate of domestic energy pricing and speculation on how to create 'better' regulation of its gas markets.[11] 'Better' regulation scholarship focuses on regulatory strategies that are responsive and risk-based in a legal philosophical shift from deregulation to: (1) clarify regulatory objectives and definitions of problems; (2) ensure regulatory objectives are achieved effectively; and (3) identify alternative options for achieving desired objectives.[12] Inadequate regulation and ill-defined policy causes misallocation of resources and may require regulatory intervention by the State. This raises key questions concerning the long-term viability of the export of LNG in the Eastern Market at a time when managing energy security is a legislative and policy priority.

The Australian Domestic Gas Security Mechanism (ADGSM) represents the latest Australian federal policy attempt to secure reliability and affordability of gas for consumers, while seeking to accelerate the export and use of LNG without binding regulation. The introduction of the ADGSM to curb the security crisis of a gas shortfall is classified as a policy 'trigger' to 'direct LNG projects to limit exports or find new gas sources if their gas consumption causes a domestic supply shortfall'.[13] However, to avoid 'triggering' the ADGSM in 2017 the Federal Government signed, and in 2018 re-signed, a Heads of Agreement with LNG producers to divert LNG to avoid a predicted gas shortfall.[14] The Heads of Agreement

7 The three LNG export terminals for the Eastern Gas Market consist of: Queensland Curtis LNG (online in 2014); Gladstone LNG (online in 2015); and Australia Pacific LNG (online in 2015).

8 Malcolm Abbott and Xiaoying Ma, 'Economic Regulation in Australia: The Case of the New South Wales Gas' (2017) 36(3) *Economic Papers* 250.

9 Daniel Yergin, 'Daniel Yergin on the Future of Energy: Big Gains for Coal and Natural Gas' *The Wall Street Journal* (New York, 7 July 2014).

10 Of this figure, CSG, mostly produced in Queensland, accounted for one-third of Australian gas production and two-thirds of total gas production in the Eastern Market in 2016–2017. Australian Government Department of the Environment and Energy (n 3).

11 Robert Baldwin, 'Better Regulation: Tensions Abroad the Enterprise' in Stephen Weatherill (ed), *Better Regulation* (Bloomsbury Publishing 2007) 34.

12 Ibid 34.

13 Australian Energy Regulator, 'State of the Energy Market 2018' (December, 2018) <https://www.aer.gov.au/publications/state-of-the-energy-market-reports/state-of-the-energy-market-2018> accessed 14 December 2018, 21.

14 The ADGSM has not been triggered since the policy was established in 2017 due to the annual agreements struck with industry in the form of Heads of Agreement to avoid shortages in the Eastern Gas Market.

and the ADGSM policy has clear potential to limit prices within the Eastern Gas Market of Australia. Indeed, the Heads of Agreement have attributed to the lowering of gas prices from a high mark of $22/GJ in March 2017 with the average prices for 2020 currently forecasted at $9.20/GJ.[15]

The wider economic and legal implications of governmental intervention in gas markets is receiving critical scholarly attention in which the question is increasingly posed – which actor should bear the cost of the use and security of consumer pricing and supply? Resolution of a regulatory direction within the Eastern Gas Market is crucial to the long-term effectiveness of any reform to achieve gas security, especially as Australia seeks to retain its position as a leading LNG-exporting nation. A States operating in a public resource proprietary ownership framework must afford its citizens a 'duty of development'[16] in the public interest. As examined throughout this chapter, market-based mechanisms to curb gas pricing do not adequately address strategic and long-term gas security. A regulatory interventionist model is increasingly being accepted and adopted in comparative jurisdictions to ensure long-term energy security and adhere to the principle of public resource ownership.

The purpose of this chapter is to review the current approach to gas security on Australia's East Coast and to consider the role of an expanded and defined 'national interest' test for gas exports as a potential solution to gas insecurity. This chapter poses the broad question of what regulatory direction Australia should take in the increasingly urgent and strident calls for legislative reform and 'better' regulation[17] for the Eastern Gas Market to ensure its reliability and security. By examining the current patchwork of gas policies, rules and governing administrative bodies at the federal level and events of gas insecurity within other Australian markets, such as Western Australia, this chapter provides a critique of the approaches adopted to date in Australia against energy security as a regulatory objective.

There are a number of different economic, policy and regulatory aspects to the analysis of any single gas market. Rather than an overarching analysis of the gas retail market and downstream supply chain, this chapter focuses on two important aspects of gas regulation. First, is the question as to whether the necessary features of energy security have been sufficiently incorporated into Eastern Gas Market regulation and policies to date. Second, are the potential regulatory solutions to a state of long-term gas insecurity. The discussion which follows argues that the underlying rationale and implementation of traditional energy security principles is absent within the scope of the ADGSM and Heads of Agreement instruments in Australia. The chapter first provides an outline of the traditional facets of energy regulation, followed by an examination of the federal administrative structure of the Eastern Gas Market in Australia. The chapter then reviews the ADGSM and the Heads of Agreement representing current market-based policy responses, before examining events of

15 Australian Competition and Consumer Commission, 'Future of Gas Market Regulation' (March, 2019) <https://www.accc.gov.au/speech/future-of-gas-market-regulation> accessed 3 July 2019. As stated by the Australian Energy Market Operator (AEMO), gas shortages within the Eastern Gas Market will be evident: 'From 2029, assuming no further developments beyond existing and committed projects, supply limitations across eastern and south-eastern gas production facilities are also forecast to drive shortfalls in Queensland LNG exports, with 8 PJ of CSG production needed to be diverted to ensure Queensland domestic demand is met in 2029, and 25 PJ in 2030'. Australian Energy Market Operator, 'Gas Statement of Opportunities' (March, 2019) <https://www.aemo.com.au/-/media/Files/Gas/National_Planning_and_Forecasting/GSOO/2019/2019-GSOO-report.pdf> accessed 19 December 2019, 40.

16 Samantha Hepburn, 'Public Resource Ownership and Community Engagement in a Modern Energy Landscape' (2017) 34 *Pace Environmental Law Review* 379, 379.

17 Robert Baldwin (n 11) 27.

gas insecurity in Australia and proposing new regulatory directions to ensure gas security. The difficulties in resolving the tension between the regulatory goal of a commercially viable energy export nation and the need for gas security indicates the necessity for a major regulatory reappraisal of the existing approach to managing gas supplies. As examined within this chapter, this points to a need for consolidation, rather than further fragmentation, of the differing statutory regimes of Australian gas markets.

2 Energy security as a regulatory benchmark

Energy security, as a regulatory concept, is an indispensable aspect of energy regulation in all states. The role of energy law, in part, is to implement the fundamental vision of a state's energy policy. The legal and regulatory frameworks to support such a policy are rapidly changing in Australia. This is evident within the significant gaps and divergences in regulatory approaches amongst the Western, Eastern and Northern Gas Market Regions of Australia and coupled with a broad federal energy policy that is currently in flux, since the partial abolishment of the proposed National Energy Guarantee in September 2018.[18] This has led to continued discrepancies within stated gas policies, legislative intent and regulatory execution in the security of gas supply within the Eastern market.

Once linked exclusively to the amount of oil reserved in a country, and upon the US reaching peak oil production in 1970,[19] energy security was linked to geospatial national security in conjunction with security of other energy sources including gas. The broader contemporary two-tier definition of energy security is now recognised by the International Energy Agency (IEA) as being a definition founded upon both the long and short-term facets including:

> uninterrupted availability of energy sources at an affordable price ... long-term energy security mainly deals with timely investments to supply energy in line with economic developments and environmental needs ... short-term energy security focuses on the ability of the energy system to react promptly to sudden changes in the supply-demand balance.[20]

Gas insecurity can thus be attributed to either a lack of physical supply of the gas itself, or a lack of affordable and accessible pricing due to market failure. In order to address the issue of

18 The Retailer Reliability Obligation has been operational since 1 July 2019 to support the reliability of the National Electricity Market. The Retailer Reliability Obligation is partly based on the National Energy Guarantee and requires retailers to invest in new capacity or offer additional existing capacity to the electricity market if a reliability gap is identified. Once a reliability gap is identified by AEMO, the Reliability Obligation is triggered, and all liable entities 'must assess their likely share of system peak demand and secure sufficient qualifying contracts to cover this by the Contract Position Day (T-1)'. See COAG Energy Council, Energy Security Board Retailer Reliability Obligation Final Rules Package (May, 2019) <www.coagenergycouncil.gov.au/sites/prod.energycouncil/files/publications/documents/Retailer%20Reliability%20Obligation%20-%20Cover%20Paper_1.pdf> accessed 19 December 2019.

19 Although Hubbert's theory of peak oil was reached in the US in 1970, due to the advent of hydraulic fracturing a post-peak decline has not been evident in the US, and some commentators question whether peak oil has indeed been reached. See Duncan Clarke, *The Battle for Barrels: Peak Oil Myths & World Oil Futures* (Profile Books 2007).

20 International Energy Agency, 'Oil Information 2018: Overview' (July, 2018) <https://webstore.iea.org/oil-information-2018-overview> accessed 5 December 2018.

security of supply, it is critical to identify the source of disruption to resolve the shortage of such supply. Demand and growth for gas globally is intrinsically linked to demand volatility and price sensitivity in shaping LNG trade growth. Physical supply shortage, as was evident in the early twentieth century prior to the invention of hydraulic fracturing in creating the ability to access unconventional gas, is no longer the pressing regulatory issue for gas. Rather, ensuring the security of supply for the domestic market and pricing affordability due to insufficient capacity and long-term supply agreements is the new security threat within Australia's Eastern Gas Market. For example, Australia supplied the largest share of LNG imports on the back of China's energy security crises in 2017 in providing 7.35 billion cubic metres (bcm) of gas via long-term contracts.[21] Yet, domestic Eastern gas prices peaked at \$20–22/GJ in March 2017, being significantly above the LNG netback price.[22]

The broader federal energy security policy of Australia is currently defined by the Department of the Environment and Energy as striving to ensure

> adequate, reliable and competitive supply of energy across the electricity, gas and liquid fuel sectors—where: adequacy is the provision of sufficient energy to support economic and social activity; reliability is the provision of energy with minimal disruptions to supply; and competitiveness is the provision of energy at an affordable price.[23]

Elements of long-term energy security strategies coupled with resilience to withstand market fluctuations are evidently missing from the Australian definition of energy security, when compared to the IEA's two-fold definition of energy security. The current Australian energy security policy also falls within the definition of a market-based approach.

Market-based regulation and policies are defined by the encouragement of domestic market efficiency through non-interventionist industry-led guidelines and polices without 'hard' regulatory intervention. Energy is thus viewed as a standard tradable commodity and is exposed to the same conditions and market forces to comparable commodities and industries in relying on private gas distributors to deliver energy at the most competitive price while ensuring adequate and reliable supplies, thus reducing the need for government intervention.[24] The underlying assumption is that market liberalisation will best serve Australia's interests in providing optimal market outcomes in terms of both price and balancing supply and demand. The Productivity Commission of Australia outlines the difficulties with such a market-based approach:

21 Followed by Qatar (3.47 bcm) and Malaysia (2.24 bcm). The US supplied 1.84 bcm more than it did in 2016. International Energy Agency, 'Global Gas Security Review' (October, 2018) <https://webstore.iea.org/global-gas-security-review-2018> accessed 11 December 2018.

22 As per the Explanatory Statement for the enactment of the Customs (Prohibited Exports) Amendment (Liquefied Natural Gas) Regulations 2017 (Cth), 'it is clear that gas prices struck under new contracts have risen sharply, with offerings up to \$20 per gigajoule being quoted in 2017. These prices are significantly above LNG netback prices (allowing for transport and distribution/retail costs), making it theoretically more profitable for an LNG producer to sell gas domestically than to export it.' Explanatory Note to the Customs (Prohibited Exports) Amendment (Liquefied Natural Gas) Regulations 2017 (Cth), 11.

23 Australian Government Department of the Environment and Energy, 'Energy Security' (2019) <https://www.energy.gov.au/government-priorities/energy-security> accessed 1 July 2019.

24 Vlado Vivoda, 'State-Market Interaction in Hydrocarbon Sector: The Cases of Australia and Japan' in Andrei Belyi and Kim Talus (eds), *States and Markets in Hydrocarbon Sectors* (Palgrave Macmillan 2015) 240. See generally Barry Barton et al., *Energy Security: Managing Risk in a Dynamic Legal and Regulatory Environment* (Oxford University Press 2004).

> Markets characterised by the exercise of enduring market power would fail to attain the best outcomes for the community. In such markets, individual companies have some control over prices and can increase their profit by restricting output below optimal levels over time. They are also subject to less pressure (compared to companies in competitive markets) to reduce production costs, and may have less incentive to innovate and to improve the quality of their goods or services.[25]

The clear market-based approach in the reliance on private actors in realising energy security policies is expressly recognised by the Australian Federal Government as being a 'shared responsibility between governments, market institutions and energy businesses'.[26] This is in further contrast to the IEA's recent call for Australia to 'develop competitive, liquid and adequate domestic gas supplies and transportation capacity by swiftly completing the gas market reforms';[27] rather than relying upon industry-based solutions to gas security.

The National Gas Objective as per the *National Gas Law* (NGL), as drafted by the Australian Energy Market Commission (AEMC) under the *National Gas (South Australia) Act 2008* (SA) Div 1 s 23, and adopted into all Australian state and territory legislation, echoes this market-based gas security policy. As evident in the enshrinement of market efficiency and investment in the National Energy Objectives, 'to promote efficient investment in, and efficient operation and use of, natural gas services for the long term interests of consumers of natural gas with respect to price, quality, safety, reliability and security of supply of natural gas'.[28] Albeit with a recognition of the long-term interests of consumers broadly, rather than domestic consumers specifically. It is against this regulatory objective, the ADGSM and Heads of Agreement framework is examined within this chapter.

3 Assessing the Eastern Gas Market framework

High demand for gas, regulatory restrictions on gas exploitation and a lack of interconnection in gas pipelines has led the Australian Competition and Consumer Commission (ACCC) to label the National Energy Market, made up of the Eastern Gas Market states,[29] as 'dysfunctional'.[30] Each gas market in Australia is complex and distinct in nature, due to the separation of the three gas markets on the basis of regulatory jurisdiction and gas basin geography. The basins comprise of: the Eastern Gas Region supplying Australia's eastern and southern states and territories; the Western Gas Region supplying western Australia;

25 Australian Government Productivity Commission, 'Examining Barriers to More Efficient Gas Markets' (March, 2015) <https://www.pc.gov.au/research/completed/gas-markets/gas-markets.pdf> accessed 25 September 2018, 29.

26 Australian Government Department of the Environment and Energy, 'Energy Security' (n 23).

27 International Energy Agency, 'Energy Policies of IEA Countries Australia 2018 Review' (February, 2018) <https://www.iea.org/publications/freepublications/publication/EnergyPoliciesofIEACountriesAustralia 2018Review.pdf> accessed 5 January 2018, 21.

28 Australian Energy Market Commission, 'National Energy Objectives' (2019) <https://www.aemc.gov.au/regulation/national-energy-objectives> accessed 10 June 2019.

29 The Eastern Gas Market consists of Queensland, South Australia, Victoria, Tasmania, the Australian Capital Territory and New South Wales. Thus, the National Electricity Market comprises the transmission of energy to the five physically connected regions on the East Coast of Australia. For further detail see Alexandra Wawryk et al., *Energy Law in Australia* (Kluwer Law International 2018).

30 Australian Competition and Consumer Commission, 'Gas Inquiry 2017–2020 Interim Report July 2018' (July, 2018) <https://www.accc.gov.au/system/files/Gas%20inquiry%20July%202018%20interim%20report.pdf> accessed 14 September 2018, 18.

and the Northern Gas Region supplying the Northern Territory. The issue of gas pricing uncertainty, coupled with opaque supply agreements and a lack of supply reservation is not new. Lockhart J in 1997 highlighted these policy gaps as laying the foundations for gas insecurity:

> Given the lack of physical connection between the gas supply systems serving each mainland Australian state, given past interventions by state governments to protect local interests when the gas supply arrangements were being formulated, and given the need for substantial borrowed funds for the various gas production and transmission projects, with the lender requiring that repayment be secured against project revenues, the Tribunal finds it unsurprising and perhaps inevitable, that the primary supply and gas haulage contracts in Australia have been … long-term contracts with a term of 20 years or more, incorporating some form of "take-or-pay" or similar provision.[31]

Since 1997, the economic and market-based approach of the Eastern Gas Market has indeed seen the proliferation of long-term supply agreements and a lack of new exploitation. For example, since the moratorium on coal bed methane extraction and exploitation in New South Wales (NSW) was enacted in 2012, no new exploration licenses have been granted.[32] The Camden coal bed methane project has remained the state's most significant gas production site and is earmarked to cease production in 2023.[33]

Since 2015, Australia, and Queensland in particular, has exported vast quantities of LNG to Asian markets. This is due to the geographically strategic location of Australia, being in close proximity to Japan, South Korea and Taiwan, and the rapidly growing energy markets of China and India.[34] The result of increasing export pressures is the domestic price of gas on Australia's East Coast being in the range of $$8–11/GJ, reaching parity with export LNG netback prices and creating a lack of accessibility, affordability and security for domestic consumers. This is an improvement from the previous high peak price of $20–22/GJ in March 2017.[35] Yet, as recognised by the ACCC,

31 *Alliance Petroleum Australia Ltd, Re* (1997) ACompT VG 1 of 1996, 24.

32 The proposed Narrabri project by Santos will represent a $3 billion gas operation, representing 850 coal seam gas wells, and will make gas available to the East Coast Market in linking into the existing Moomba to Sydney pipeline. As at December 2019, an Environmental Impact Statement for the project has been lodged for consideration and the Commonwealth Government pursuant to the *Environment Protection and Biodiversity Conservation Act 1999* (Cth) as the project has been referred to the Minister as a 'controlled action' in 2014 and NSW State Government pursuant to Division 4.1 Part 4 of the *Environmental Planning and Assessment Act 1979* (NSW) must approve the project. If approved, the Narrabri project is recognised by the NSW Gas Plan as a Strategic Energy Project with the potential to supply up to 200 terajoules of natural gas per day and meet half of NSW's natural gas demand. The NSW Gas Plan echoes the market-based regulatory approach in securing commitments from distributors and proposed gas projects to 'supply substantive amounts of gas to the NSW market'. New South Wales Government, 'NSW Gas Plan Protecting What's Valuable, Securing Our Future' (2014) <https://www.resourcesandgeoscience.nsw.gov.au/__data/assets/pdf_file/0005/534830/NSW-Gas-Plan.pdf> accessed 4 October 2018, 3. It is likely a decision will be made on the project in early 2020.

33 Ian Cronshaw and Quentin Grafton, 'A Tale of Two States: Development and Regulation of Coal Bed Methane Extraction in Queensland and New South Wales, Australia' (2016) 50 *Resources Policy* 253; Xunpeng Shi and Quentin Grafton, 'Reforming the Eastern Australian Gas Market' (2018) 5 *Asia Pacific Policy Studies* 641.

34 Daniel T. B. Leather et al., 'A Review of Australia's Natural Gas Resources and Their Exploitation' (2013) 10 *Journal of Natural Gas Science and Engineering* 68.

35 Australian Competition and Consumer Commission, 'Gas Inquiry 2017–2020 Interim Report July 2018' (n 30) 12.

> With production costs increasing and gas prices in the Eastern Gas Market being shaped by international LNG prices, domestic prices are unlikely to return to historical levels. International LNG prices are volatile and domestic prices might increase to reflect recent expectations of higher Asian LNG spot prices.[36]

Although gas is legally categorised as a public utility,[37] the pricing of gas and the role of the State in regulating the sector has become an increasingly sensitive policy and regulatory issue. Beyond the role of licensing and concessions granting rights of production and exploration to private firms of the Crown's natural resources, being both offshore and onshore unconventional and conventional gas, the Federal Government has not actively intervened in regulating the Eastern Gas Market to date. In consequence, strategic and operational decisions increasingly lie with private actors who explore for and exploit gas which is then on-sold to wholesale distributors. As Australia does not have a nationally integrated gas pipeline, natural gas produced within a state or territory has encouraged and solidified the fragmentation of the three distinct gas markets. This fragmentation creates the impetus for a market-based regulatory approach currently found at the federal level in Australia evident within overlapping policies, legislation and administrative oversight bodies each regulating three separate areas of the Eastern Gas Market.

State and territory governments have historically preferred to direct their natural gas for distribution domestically, rather than export or ship the gas to another state that may be gas-poor. For example, in a number of recent policy instruments, the Queensland Government has indicated its support for the domestic sales of its gas or export of gas to Asian markets via the Curtis Island facilities, rather than transporting its gas to southern states.[38] Therefore, the physically distinct gas markets of Australia not only operate under widely separate systems of supply of gas sales, regulation surrounding the security of gas supply, and the corresponding gas price, also differs widely. In this vein, rather than providing a single-window approach to energy market regulation, supply contracts between distributors and customers within the National Electricity Market[39] are subject to three overarching categorisations namely: the Electricity Market; the Gas Market; and the Energy Retail Market. Each of these market categories is overseen by four different governance bodies: the COAG Energy Council; the Australian Energy Regulator; the Australian Energy Market Commission and the Australian Energy Market Operator. The National Gas Rules create regulations that uphold the National Gas Objective as per s 23 'to promote efficient investment in, and efficient operation and use of, natural gas services for the long term interests of consumers of natural gas with respect to price, quality, safety, reliability and security of supply of natural gas'.[40] As previously discussed within this chapter, while energy security is not expressly mentioned as a regulatory benchmark, the reliability and security

36 Ibid 13.

37 José Alberto Hernández Ibarzábal, 'Natural Gas Infrastructure Investment, Regulation and Ownership: The Australian Case' (2011) 32(3) *Policy Studies* 231.

38 Queensland Government Department of Energy and Water Supply, 'Powering Queensland Plan' (2018) <https://www.dnrme.qld.gov.au/__data/assets/pdf_file/0008/1253825/powering-queensland-plan.pdf> accessed 3 December 2018; Queensland Government Department of Natural Resources and Mines, 'Queensland Gas Supply and Demand Action Plan' (2016) <https://www.cabinet.qld.gov.au/documents/2016/Oct/GasSupply/Attachments/Paper.pdf> accessed 2 September 2018.

39 Consisting of the Eastern Gas Market states.

40 *National Gas (South Australia) Act 2008* (SA) Div 1, s 23.

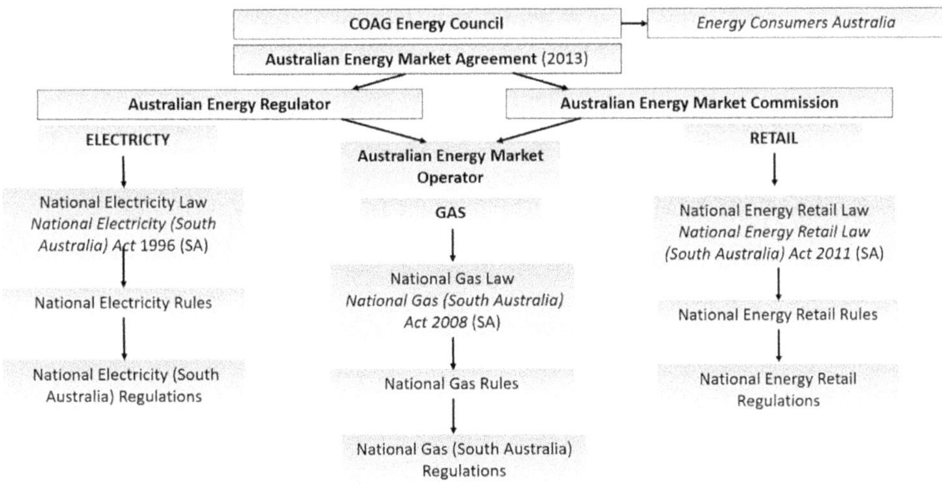

Figure 27.1 Overarching National Electricity Market regulatory framework

Source: Compiled by author. The laws are applied by state and territory application legislation in NSW, Queensland, Victoria, South Australia, Tasmania and the Australian Capital Territory, and to a limited extent in the Northern Territory and Western Australia. Australian Energy Market Commission, 'National Energy Governance' (2018) <https://www.aemc.gov.au/regulation/national-energy-governance> accessed 4 November 2018.

of supply is seen as one of the overarching National Gas Objectives. Figure 27.1 provides an illustration of the overarching governance structure of the National Electricity Market.

As can be seen from Figure 27.1, the National Electricity Market legal framework of Australia is complex, overlapping and rule-based,[41] in line with a market-based approach to policy and regulation. The Eastern Gas Market is the subject of detailed rules, regulation and administrative bodies which may give rise to regulatory inconsistencies, causing rigidity and promulgating 'creative compliance' or 'box ticking'[42] in order to comply with the National Gas Law, National Gas Rules, Australian Energy Market Operator (AEMO), Energy Security Board, Australian Energy Regulator (AER) and AEMC directions.

Further, each state and territory across Australia holds its own environmental protection authority, compliance and enforcement of conditions for onshore gas activities in the relevant state or territory. While enforcement and compliance are an element of regulatory intention to hold applicable actors within the regulatory system to account, compliance is not in and of itself 'good regulation'.[43] The recognition of this has led to the 'better regulation' movement since the millennium, which emphasises the importance of the regulatory philosophical switch from market-based deregulation to 'better regulation'.[44] The movement is founded on

41 Rule-based regulation is traditionally defined as 'command and control' in style and is born out of the need to ensure coercive compliance in the respective regulated sector. See Arie Freiberg, *The Tools of Regulation* (Federation Press 2010).

42 Robert Baldwin, *Rules and Government* (Clarendon Press 1995) 7.

43 Ibid, 145.

44 Stephen Weatherill, *Better Regulation* (Bloomsbury Publishing 2007).

the concept of bad regulation being burdensome and that 'better' regulation should be responsive and risk-based, and recognises the 'evidence and consultation in the regulatory cycle and a more systematic and principled approach to compliance and enforcement'[45] as being highly important. In the nuanced debate surrounding 'better regulation' it is an accepted premise that regulation is 'necessary for the functioning of a market economy, but that regulatory oversight remains essential in the running of public services, especially those involving naturally monopolistic elements, such as networks'.[46] Gas naturally falls within Baldwin's description and example of a public service network requiring 'better' and responsive regulation.

The recognition of the need for regulatory amendment of the National Gas Rules is evident in the AER's *Better Regulation Reform Program* finalised in 2014. The key principles of reform were based on 'incentive-based economic regulation; necessary and efficient investment being encouraged and a stronger consumer engagement framework'.[47] Interestingly, the main outcome of the Better Regulation Program did not result in a regulatory overhaul in merging the three sections of the energy market, creating a single-window operator for the NEM gas market or condensing the regulatory process for gas concerning gas security. Rather, the program created a series of guidelines to better inform consumers of the AER's role. An extension of the Better Regulation Program focusing on condensing federal gas market legislation and governance bodies generally, in the interests of energy security, could be beneficial in achieving a stable regulatory environment and creating a 'national interest' regulatory test, as will be explored in Section 6 of this chapter.

4 Gas security at risk: explosions and disruptions to supply

Numerous studies focus on the differing regulatory and policy approaches of state and territory governments within the gas sector in Australia.[48] Yet, arguably, the most pressing legal issue facing the Eastern Gas Market of regulating energy security through legislative intervention has not been substantially examined to date. As examined throughout this chapter, the rubric of gas legislation, administrative bodies and the National Gas Objective has largely left the policies of security of gas supply unexamined. Perplexingly, the 'world-leading expertise'[49] in the development of conventional and unconventional gas in Australia, coupled with plentiful gas basins, has not curbed the

> significant concerns about the price and the availability of natural gas amid moratoriums on gas production in the eastern market … in such a tight market, any disruption, outage or extreme weather event will require an even more robust emergency preparedness and response[50]

45 Arie Freiberg, *Regulation in Australia* (Federation Press 2017) 157.

46 Robert Baldwin, Martin Cave and Martin Lodge, *Understanding Regulation* (2nd edn, Oxford University Press 2011) 9–10.

47 Australian Energy Regulator, 'Overview of the Better Regulation Reform Package' (April, 2014) <https://www.aer.gov.au/system/files/AER%20Overview%20of%20the%20Better%20Regulation%20reform%20package.pdf> accessed 6 August 2018.

48 Nicola Swayne, 'Regulating Coal Seam Gas in Queensland: Lessons in an Adaptive Environmental Management Approach?' (2012) 29(2) *Environmental and Planning Law Journal* 163; Brian Towler et al., 'An Overview of the Coal Seam Gas Developments in Queensland' (2016) 31 *Journal of Natural Gas Science and Engineering* 249; Chantelle A. Rebello et al., 'Understanding Coal Seam Gas Associated Water, Regulations and Strategies for Treatment' (2016) 13 *Journal of Unconventional Oil and Gas Resources* 32.

49 International Energy Agency, 'Energy Policies of IEA Countries Australia 2018 Review' (n 27) 15.

50 Ibid.

according to the IEA.[51] Indeed, the IEA proposes that a safety net for gas system operation during periods of system adequacy risks could be built upon AEMO's Reliability and Emergency Reserve Trade mechanism to provide gas reserves in the short to medium term, although the Reserve Trader Scheme in this context is yet to be explored.[52]

While the IEA advocates the use of market-based mechanisms to be used prior to introducing export restrictions guaranteeing domestic supply under the ADGSM, it points out distribution to security of supply will probably be most evident in the event of a supply disruption. This is primarily due to the 'radial and long transmission grid and a weak level of interconnections with the National Energy Market' of Australia.[53] Therefore, peak demand, outages or the loss of interconnection capacity will lead to gas supply shortages due to the isolation of the three geographically distinct gas markets. The low physical resilience of energy infrastructure in Australia, which spurred the refinement of Western Australia's Domestic Reservation policy, is evident within the High Court case of *Electricity Generation Corporation (Verve) v Woodside Energy Ltd* [2014] HCA 7.

Woodside Energy concerned the long-term gas supply agreement between Verve Energy Ltd[54] and Woodside Energy Ltd. The supply agreement committed Woodside to make available to Verve a proportionate share of a maximum daily quantity of gas to a common gas supply stream to the best of its 'reasonable endeavours' and taking 'into account all relevant commercial, economic and operational matters'.[55] An explosion occurred on 3 June 2008 at the Apache Energy Ltd gas plant, the principle gas supplier in Western Australia, which caused the cessation of gas production at the plant on Varanus Island. The explosion, in turn, created a reduction in the supply of natural gas to the Western Australian gas market of 30–35 per cent leading to demand exceeding supply. During June–September 2008 Woodside provided Verve gas at the market price pursuant to short-term agreements, which greatly exceeded the price under the long-term supply agreements. This led to Verve commencing proceedings arguing a breach of clause 3.3 and Verve suffering consequential economic duress. The High Court of Australia dismissed the appeal of Verve and construed the terms of the short-term supply agreements according to what a 'reasonable businessperson'[56] would have understood. 'Reasonable endeavours' in the circumstances as per Clause 3.3 was interpreted by the High Court as not requiring the supply of gas to be rerouted to the domestic market, as it was deemed 'uncommercial and objectively unlikely' to reroute gas under long-term supply agreement terms.[57] In applying the observations of Sellers J in *Terrell*,[58] the High Court found an obligation to use reasonable endeavours 'would not oblige the achievement of a contractual object "to the certain ruin of the company or to the utter disregard of the interests of the shareholders"'.[59]

In applying *Woodside* to the Eastern Gas Market in the event of a gas supply distribution due to infrastructure failure, private contractual supply agreements will not require

51 Ibid.

52 Australian Energy Market Operator, 'RERT Guidelines' (July, 2018) <https://www.aemc.gov.au/sites/default/files/2018-07/RERT%20guidelines%202018.pdf> accessed 28 November 2018.

53 International Energy Agency, 'Energy Policies of IEA Countries Australia 2018 Review' (n 27) 15

54 Verve Energy was a state-owned electrical generation company that has now been succeeded by Synergy Ltd.

55 As per clause 3.3 of the Supply Agreement.

56 As per the standard set out in the seminal case *Hospital Products Ltd v United States Surgical Corp* (1984) 156 CLR 41.

57 *Electricity Generation Corporation (Verve) v Woodside Energy Ltd* [2014] HCA 7 [38].

58 Ibid [236].

59 Ibid [42].

producers to supply distributors in the interests of preserving gas security, if it is against their own business interests to supply gas to the domestic market due to unfavourable business conditions. Indeed, this creates a commercial environment whereby commercial contracts will govern the supply price and terms to any given gas market, irrespective of prior contractual terms, in the event of a supply disruption causing gas insecurity. The approach in leaving private actors to act in their own best interests for the benefit of its shareholders, as a central maxim of corporate law, produced the landscape in which the Western Australian State Government reaffirmed and expanded its Domestic Reservation Policy. This is because an obligation to use 'reasonable endeavours' does not apply where the result would be the 'utter disregard of the interests of the shareholders'.[60]

As a direct amendment in response to the reasoning of the *Woodside* case in 2012, the Western Australian Domestic Reservation policy established an Independent Gas Market Monitor,[61] to enforce regulation of all new gas developments to reserve 15 per cent of their LNG to supply the Western Gas Market domestically. Indeed, the Economics and Industry Standing Committee, established after the Varanus Island explosion in 2008, found the 'Domestic gas reservation obligations remain a valuable tool for policy makers to ensure that a proportion of the state's gas reserves are supplied to local consumers in volumes and at prices that are consistent with a well-functioning market'.[62] This produces a policy environment to avoid commercial contracts purely governing pricing and supply terms in the event of a shortfall led by State intervention;[63] as opposed to applying a market-based policy based on an industry agreement to supply gas.

5 The Australian Domestic Gas Security Mechanism and Heads of Agreement: market-based solutions?

An unsustainable rise in gas prices in recent years on Australia's East Coast has led to increasingly strident and threatening calls for regulatory overhaul.[64] Since the signing of long-term

60 *Electricity Generation Corporation (Verve) v Woodside Energy Ltd* [2014] HCA 7 [41–43].

61 As recommended by the Economics and Industry Standing Committee, the purpose of the Gas Market Monitor is to: 'continually monitor the supply/demand balance and requirements in the Western Australian gas market; identify deficiencies or failings across the gas supply chain and facilitate discussion between government and market participants on corrective measures; and provide advice to the Minister on appropriate volumes and processing capacity requirements under future domestic reservation agreement'. Economics and Industry Standing Committee, 'Inquiry into Domestic Gas Prices Report No 6 in the 28th Parliament of Western Australia' (March, 2011) <http://www.parliament.wa.gov.au/publications/tabledpapers.nsf/displaypaper/3813232af0e096cabecf9c8e4825785e0004c326/$file/3232.pdf> accessed 7 January 2018, 24.

62 Ibid 22.

63 A historically similar circumstance took place in September 1998 when a gas explosion caused the Esso natural gas plant at Longford in Victoria to cut the gas supply in the state for two weeks and killed two employees and seriously injured eight persons. After the Longford Royal Commission in 1999 found Esso guilty of breaching workplace safety laws, the Director of Public Prosecutions brought proceedings in 2001. Cummins J in *DPP v Esso Australia Pty Ltd* [2001] VSC 263 surveyed the 11 offences in contravention of ss 21, 22 and 47 of the *Occupational Health and Safety Act 1985* (Vic) due to an unsafe workplace environment and failure to conduct adequate hazard identification and adequately assess risk at the plant on behalf of Esso Australia leading to a payable sum of $2 million. A class action suit representing business users, domestic users and stood-down workers commenced proceedings in which Gillard J granted an application for the settlement of a $32 million compensation package, see *Johnson Tiles Pty Ltd v Esso Australia Pty Ltd (No 4)* [2004] VSC 466.

64 Michele Laidlaw, 'ACCC East Coast Gas Market Report: Is Infrastructure Regulation "Fit for Purpose"?' (2016) 35(2) *Australian Resources and Energy Law Journal* 125; Madeline Taylor and Tina Hunter, 'A Paradox of

LNG export contracts in Queensland,[65] gas exporters have experienced an immense growth of demand from international markets. Indeed, according to the December 2018 *Resources and Energy Quarterly* by the Office of the Chief Economist, 'Australia's LNG exports are forecast to increase from 62 million tonnes in 2017–18 to 78 million tonnes in 2019–20'.[66] This has led to the increasing allocation of natural gas to international markets, leaving insufficient gas supply available for Eastern Australia. The response by the Australian Government is the ADGSM introduced in July 2017 under the Customs (Prohibited Exports) (Operation of the Australian Domestic Gas Security Mechanism) Guidelines 2017 (Cth). The ADGSM represents the first nation-wide gas security policy mechanism. The mechanism, when 'triggered' provides an optional power for the Federal Government to impose export control restrictions, upon the declaration of an energy 'shortfall' year. However, in line with a market-based approach to energy insecurity, the ADGSM is a guideline, not a legislative instrument and is operable at the Ministers discretion only, as acknowledged in s 5 of the policy.[67] However, despite forecast growth as new onshore and offshore gas projects come online, particularly in the Northern Territory, coupled with the introduction of the ADGSM, meeting forecast production rates of 456 petajoules (PJ) in 2020 will require further exploitation of undeveloped gas reserves classified as 2C contingent resources.[68] As recognised by AEMO,

> This shift from 2P reserves[69] to 2C resources is most noticeable in the southern states, where quantities of 2P developed reserves have dropped by 32% – nearly 1,100 PJ in the past year – with only a 270 PJ rise in 2P undeveloped reserves. This pushes forward the time when contingent resources from southern basins, or alternatively gas imports from northern states or LNG imports, will be required to meet domestic demand.[70]

The ADGSM represents the crystallisation and confirmation of a market-based approach as a guideline 'triggered' at the discretion of a minister. The ADGSM is similar to all environmental approvals under the *Environmental Protection and Biodiversity Act 1999* (Cth) (EPBC Act) in requiring ministerial assent. Yet, the ADGSM remains without a mandatory component unlike within the EPBC Act and this discretionary guideline is unlikely to be 'triggered', and indeed was not triggered throughout the 2017–2019 gas security crises. Rather, the second mechanism proposed under the ADGSM regulatory reform package was applied

---

Plenty: The Australian Domestic Gas Supply Regulatory Dilemma' (2018) 11(6) *The Journal of World Energy Law & Business* 465.

65 According to the Office of the Chief Economist, 'Most LNG in Asia is sold on long term contracts, sometimes in excess of 20 years, where the price of LNG is linked to the price of oil. Oil-linked contract prices have been rising steadily since early 2016'. Australian Government Office of the Chief Economist, 'Resources and Energy Quarterly' (December, 2018) <https://publications.industry.gov.au/publications/resourcesandenergyquarterlydecember2018/documents/Resources-and-Energy-Quarterly-December-2018.pdf> accessed 25 January 2019, 43.

66 Ibid 43. The LNG export value increase will represent $50 billion worth of LNG exports in 2018–2019, up from $31 billion worth of exports in 2017–2018.

67 As per s 5 of the Customs (Prohibited Exports) (Operation of the Australian Domestic Gas Security Mechanism) Guidelines 2017 (Cth).

68 Meaning potentially recoverable yet not currently commercially recoverable resources.

69 2P reserves are categorised as proven and probable reserves.

70 Australian Energy Market Operator, 'Gas Statement of Opportunities' (March, 2019) <https://www.aemo.com.au/-/media/Files/Gas/National_Planning_and_Forecasting/GSOO/2019/2019-GSOO-report.pdf> accessed 10 July 2019, 6.

in 2017, 2018 and 2019, being the Heads of Agreement. The Heads of Agreement between major LNG suppliers in 2017 was reaffirmed for the 2019 period. This purely market-based response curtails any need for direct State regulatory interference by market participants agreeing to supply gas 'on reasonable terms'.[71] Such a 'reasonable term' is not defined, and as most LNG exporters are bound by long-term supply contracts for an average term of 20 years. For example, an argument could be made that to re-route export-bound gas to the domestic market is unreasonable. No enforcement provisions are offered within the Heads of Agreement, rather LNG exporter compliance will be based on periodic reporting to the ACCC on offers to sell, bids and sales.

A Head of Agreement is legally categorised as a non-binding agreement, similar to a Memorandum of Understanding, to potentially form a contract at a future date. The traditional common law position of Heads of Agreement is stipulated by *Masters v Cameron*[72] that upon true construction, a Heads of Agreement may only be binding if it is intended to be so, as illustrated in the following scenarios outlined by the High Court:

> The parties have reached finality in arranging all the terms of their bargain and intend to be immediately bound to the performance of those terms, but at the same time propose to have the terms restated in a form which will be fuller or more precise but not different in effect. Or, secondly, it may be a case in which the parties have completely agreed upon all the terms of their bargain and intend no departure from or addition to that which their agreed terms express or imply, but nevertheless have made performance of one or more of the terms conditional upon the execution of a formal document. Or, thirdly, the case may be one in which the intention of the parties is not to make a concluded bargain at all, unless and until they execute a formal contract.[73]

Within the current Heads of Agreement and in applying the *Masters*[74] categorisations, there is no evidently binding intent found between the parties, or the agreement being subject to the condition of a binding contract being executed. Thus, the Heads of Agreement is a private agreement and market-based response, rather than a government intervening regulatory tool that does not carry penalties or remedies for redress.

As previously examined within Section 2 of this chapter, the current gas security policy found within the National Gas Objective of providing 'efficient operation and use of natural gas services in the long-term interest of consumers in relation to reliability and security of supply'[75] is unlikely to be met via a non-binding Heads of Agreement arrangement. Without the weight of regulatory enforcement and intervention, arguably the National Gas Objective cannot be met without State regulation and corresponding gas security cannot be guaranteed. Simshauser critiques the ADGSM in this light as 'not being a credible policy because the fundamental internal supply-demand imbalance of the market has not been altered *per se*, it is merely a contingent policy and limited to assessing the market imbalance one year at

71 Australian Government, 'Heads of Agreement – The Australian East Coast Domestic Gas Supply Commitment' (September, 2018) <https://www.industry.gov.au/sites/default/files/heads-of-agreement-2018-prime-minister-and-east-coast-lng-exporters.pdf> accessed 10 April 2019.

72 *Masters v Cameron* (1954) 91 CLR 353.

73 Ibid [9].

74 Ibid.

75 *National Gas (South Australia) Act 2008* (SA) Div 1, s 23.

a time'.[76] Long-term pricing, supply scarcity and the imbalance between the domestic and international markets will likely remain under the ADGSM model.

Prior to the introduction of the ADGSM, s 95H(1) of the *Competition of Consumer Act 2010* (Cth) and in response to increasing gas prices on the Eastern coast, an ACCC Inquiry was triggered to propose measures in improving 'the transparency of gas supply arrangement in Australia; the supply and demand for natural gas extracted or produced in Australia; and the supply of, an demand for natural gas transportation services in Australia'.[77] In the first of its gas inquiries in 2015, the ACCC reported on the significant changes that had occurred due to the unprecedented amount of private gas supply contracts negotiated spearheaded by the opening of LNG export terminals in Queensland. This resulted in complex and opaque gas markets where the majority of gas is earmarked for export, and domestic commercial and industrial users (C&I) facing the hurdle of negotiating supply contracts against increasing gas prices in the East Gas Market. Each C&I contract is confidential, leading to speculation and an opaque market without a reliable estimate of increasingly changeable gas prices. Consequently, the ACCC introduced a LNG Netback Price, to improve transparency within the East Gas Market. The Netback Price is calculated by 'taking the price that could be received for LNG and subtracting or "netting back" the costs incurred by the supplier to convert the gas to LNG and ship it to the destination port'.[78] Yet, the introduction of the Netback Price has led to higher prices for C&I users and further calls for reform.[79]

The ACCC report outlined a 55 PJ domestic gas demand shortfall and an upper band domestic demand shortfall of 108 PJ for 2018 and prices of $22/GJ in March 2017. However, in July 2018, the ACCC revised this anticipated shortfall and found prices offered for gas supply in 2019 will be within a $8–$11/GJ range. As reported by the ACCC, Queensland LNG producers have anticipated an excess of 98 PJ in excess of their domestic and export supply contracts, and have indicated this gas may be sold either domestically or exported.[80] The Heads of Agreement between gas suppliers to avoid the need to trigger the ADGSM, coupled with the anticipated increase of gas supply from the Northern Gas Pipeline, has largely caused this revision.

Despite price volatility and the constant revision of position by the ACCC, AEMO and the Federal Government over whether a shortfall in domestic supply is imminent on the Eastern Gas Market, the Federal Government is yet to present a holistic regulatory solution to gas insecurity. The domestic Eastern Gas Market price is permanently linked to the Asian LNG spot price, now being far beyond a simple supply and demand equation and resulting in high gas prices on the East Coast, despite Australia being a gas abundant nation.

76 Paul Simshauser, 'Garbage Can Theory and Australia's National Electricity Market: Decarbonisation in a Hostile Policy Environment' (2018) 120 *Energy Policy* 697, 711.

77 Australian Competition and Consumer Commission, 'Inquiry for Improving the Transparency of Gas Supply in Australia' (April, 2017) <https://www.accc.gov.au/system/files/Gas%20market%20transparency%20measures%20Terms%20of%20reference.pdf> accessed 16 November 2018, 2.

78 Australian Competition and Consumer Commission, 'Gas Inquiry 2017–2020 Guide to the LNG Netback Price Series' (October, 2018) <https://www.accc.gov.au/system/files/Guide%20to%20the%20LNG%20netback%20price%20series%20-%20October%202018.pdf > accessed 11 March 2019.

79 Matthew Stevens, 'ACCC Turns Gas Guns on Retailers' *The Australian Financial Review* (18 December 2018) <https://www.afr.com/business/accc-turns-gas-guns-on-retailers-20181218-h1997n>.

80 Australian Competition and Consumer Commission, Gas Inquiry 2017–2020 Guide to the LNG Netback Price Series' (n 78) 14.

Although the Northern Gas Pipeline is touted to ease supply shortages within the Eastern Market in supplying 90 terajoules (TJ) a day of conventional gas,[81] the unconventional gas Beetaloo play has not been proven commercially viable as yet.[82] Further, the IEA recognises the Northern Gas Pipeline is not enough to satiate and avert an energy insecurity crisis in Australia, 'For natural gas to play a role as a transition fuel to a low-carbon economy, resource development, additional pipeline capacity and market integration are critical'.[83] Greater pipeline capacity, and importantly integration, remains crucial to long-term energy affordability and accessibility.

A national pipeline or 'virtual pipeline' via links of supply through import terminals, including the recently approved Port Kembla LNG import terminal, all represent infrastructure solutions to gas insecurity. However, arguably unintended gas disruption through infrastructure failure requires more than a piecemeal approach to policy and regulation, as evident in the *Woodside Energy* case. Calculating the risk of remaining gas insecure lends itself to the conclusion that regulatory inaction will create a failure for the domestic market, and tangentially intermittency and overcapacity followed by a failure to reach emission targets through a lack of reliability of the 'transition' fuel. In order to avoid unintended market-based regulatory outcomes based on uncertain pricing and a lack of secure capacity for domestic consumers, two alternative solutions may provide a safe harbour for the Eastern Gas Market currently in flux. The first proposal is to create a 'national interest' statutory test of review applied on a case by case basis to each new export contract proposed by the LNG consortia in Queensland, the Northern Territory LNG terminal, the North West Shelf LNG terminals and the Floating LNG Terminals. The second proposal is to create a gas reservation policy, currently enacted in Western Australia as a reaction, in part, to the Varanus Island gas explosion.

6 Gas security within the 'national interest'? Options for regulatory reform

As affordability and availability issues continue to reign in the energy policy landscape, the Eastern Gas Market has been forced to increase gas supply by bringing online onshore unconventional gas. Although the moratoria on CSG development in NSW is currently in place, it is arguably highly likely this will be lifted to enable the approval of the proposed Narrabri Gas Project. Narrabri is touted as a strategic state project within the NSW Gas Plan.[84] Recently, Infrastructure NSW has called for new additional sources of CSG to be earmarked for LNG export and connected to the national transmission network to increase security of supply.[85] Interestingly, Infrastructure NSW uses the term 'national' transmission in a regulatory environment with three separate gas markets and supports a similar move by Queensland in approving an LNG export terminal – despite the reoccurring gas insecurity for the domestic Eastern market. This regulatory goal echoes the position of the

81 Jemena Northern Gas Pipeline Pty Ltd, 'Environmental Management Plan' (March, 2017) <https://jemena.com.au/documents/pipeline/negi/399-rp-ev-026-environmental-management-plan.aspx> accessed 26 November 2018.

82 If the Beetaloo gas play proves commercial, an extra capacity of up to 700 TJ a day could be added to the Eastern market via the Northern Gas Pipeline.

83 International Energy Agency, 'Energy Policies of IEA Countries Australia 2018 Review' (n 27) 244.

84 New South Wales Government, 'NSW Gas Plan Protecting What's Valuable, Securing Our Future' (n 32).

85 Infrastructure NSW, 'Energy' (2018) <http://www.infrastructure.nsw.gov.au/media/1141/sis_report_section110_print.pdf> accessed 2 November 2018, 145.

COAG Energy Council of a 'market-focused policy' environment centring on the pillars of 'Competitive Supply; Transparency and Price Discovery; Risk Management; and Removing Unnecessary Regulatory Barriers'.[86] The market-based outcome of new, unconventional gas well-site development is the clear preferential policy approach of federal energy bodies, while market interventions on a national scale including export controls and gas reservation policies are not supported.[87]

Australia is at a gas 'crossroads', as simply increasing gas exploration and production licenses in NSW will not guarantee long-term energy security for the Eastern Gas Market. This has resulted in policy instability and lack of gas security as surmised by Simshauser,

> given the importance and desirable attributes of natural gas as a transitional fuel, any country expanding into LNG production needs to be purposeful from a policy perspective to ensure that exports do not destabilise domestic markets, as has been the case in Australia's National Energy Market.[88]

By continuing to focus on LNG export competitiveness and encouraging investment without regulation prioritising gas security, Australia will continue down the path of policy flux, energy pricing uncertainty for trade and commerce and regulatory relapses. An alternative approach to ensure gas security is the proposal for a 'national interest' test and corresponding statutory regime. While the COAG Energy Council,[89] the Productivity Commission[90] and other scholars[91] have been historically opposed to a 'national interest' test, given the renewed regulatory focus on gas market intervention, the regulatory climate may be ripe to re-examine such a proposal. It must also be noted that the previously proposed 'national interest' policy by the Productivity Commission categorised such a test as being akin to a domestic reservation scheme, 'the underlying mechanism (of a 'national interest' test) – a diversion of some gas supply to domestic users that would have otherwise been destined for export'.[92] This chapter seeks to reformulate a 'national interest' test proposal based on regulatory review of future LNG export projects. A comparative example of a regulatory 'national interest' test is found in Australia's Foreign Acquisitions and Takeovers scheme and serves as a useful illustration of how such a test could be reformulated and applied to gas security regulation.

Australia has had a case-by-case approach to the review of proposed foreign investments and acquisition based on the 'national interest' at the federal level since the enactment of the *Foreign Acquisitions and Takeovers Act 1975* (Cth) (FATA). The FATA empowers the Treasurer,

86 Council of Australian Governments, 'Gas Vision' (December, 2014) <http://www.coagenergycouncil.gov.au/sites/prod.energycouncil/files/publications/documents/COAG-Energy-Council-Australian-Gas-Market-Vision-Dec-2014-FINAL.pdf> accessed 12 January 2018, 2.

87 Ibid 3.

88 Paul Simshauser (n 76) 712.

89 Council of Australian Governments, 'Gas Vision' (n 86).

90 Australian Government, Productivity Commission, 'Examining Barriers to More Efficient Gas Markets' (n 25)

91 Kelly Neill, 'Western Australia's Domestic Gas Reservation Policy The Elemental Economics' (2015) Discussion Paper 15.98 <http://www.business.uwa.edu.au/__data/assets/pdf_file/0010/2712196/15.08-Neill,-K.-WESTERN-AUSTRALIAS-DOMESTIC-GAS-RESERVATION-POLICY-THE-ELEMENTAL-ECONOMICS.pdf>.

92 Australian Government, Productivity Commission, 'Examining Barriers to More Efficient Gas Markets' (n 25) 20.

assisted by the non-statutory advisory body the Foreign Investment Review Board, to approve or reject applications in relation to significant actions by a foreign person.[93] A 'significant action' is broadly outlined by s 39 as 'action to acquire interests in securities, assets or Australian land, or otherwise take action in relation to entities (being corporations and unit trusts) and businesses, that have a connection to Australia'. For an action to be a significant action, the action must result in a 'change in control involving a foreign person or be taken by a foreign person'.[94] Therefore, an action will be a significant action if it meets the applicable threshold test as found in the scenarios outlined within the s 51 FATA table. The threshold test for entities and business is outlined under the Foreign Acquisitions and Takeovers Regulations 2015 (Cth).[95]

A 'national interest' test is not defined within the FATA in order to provide for the subjective case-by-case review mechanism. However, it is clarified by the Australian Foreign Investment Review Board (FIRB) that the default position and presumption is that 'foreign investment is beneficial, given the important role it plays in Australia's economy'.[96] The onus rests on the Treasurer to discharge this presumption and find the investment or acquisition contrary to the 'national interest', rather than the onus of proof resting with the foreign person. The 'national interest' threshold is categorically negative in nature and national security is recognised as a sub-set category within the national interest factors to be considered. National security is defined as 'the extent to which investments affect Australia's ability to protect its strategic and security interests'.[97] The government relies on 'advice from the relevant national security agencies for assessments as to whether an investment raises national security issues'.[98]

While the acquisition or takeover of an Australian gas exploration, production and export company would trigger the FATA mechanism, as evident in the recent consideration of the foreign interest acquisition of APA Ltd,[99] there is no specialised category and indeed recognition of gas production and export as a strategic category to afford protection against foreign acquisition and investment. As one of Australia's most strategic assets, it is arguably in the national interest to enact a new categorisation of conventional and unconventional gas export contracts as a proposed activity that must be approved according to a regime similar to the FATA. This would be in a similar vein to the national interest case-by-case analysis of the FATA legislation, but would apply in requiring new LNG export projects to be approved in the 'national interest'.

In the absence of a domestic reservation policy or construction of a national pipeline, a similar security-based test applied to gas export contracts and trade could provide a mechanism for the effective review of currently privately negotiated gas export contracts. Looking beyond a short-term and purely industry-led market-based approach within the Heads of

93 For a detailed analysis of the Foreign Investment Scheme of Australia see Vivienne Bath, 'Foreign Investment, the National Interest and National Security – Foreign Direct Investment in Australia and China' (2012) 34(1) *Sydney Law Review* 5.

94 *Foreign Acquisitions and Takeovers Act 1975* (Cth), s 3.

95 Foreign Acquisitions and Takeovers Regulations 2015 (Cth) Pt 4.

96 Australian Government, 'Australia's Foreign Investment Policy' (January, 2018) <https://cdn.tspace.gov.au/uploads/sites/82/2017/06/Australias-Foreign-Investment-Policy.pdf> accessed 14 November 2018, 8.

97 Australian Government, 'Australia's Foreign Investment Policy' (January, 2018) <https://cdn.tspace.gov.au/uploads/sites/82/2017/06/Australias-Foreign-Investment-Policy.pdf> accessed 14 November 2018, 8.

98 Ibid.

99 Australian Government, 'Final Decision on the Proposed Acquisition of APA' (November, 2018) <http://jaf.ministers.treasury.gov.au/media-release/055-2018> accessed 14 February 2018.

Agreement, providing the requirement for approval for new gas export contracts on a case-by-case basis, and weighted against a national interest test, could align Australia's commercial export goals with the protection of gas security domestically. Similar treatment of gas exports and trade to the acquisition of agribusiness interests and agricultural land in Australia could provide an effective legislative category and heightened scrutiny of gas contracts. However, in order to implement such a mechanism effectively, a statutory definition of 'national interest' must be defined. Calls for a codified and specified national interest test are not new, indeed such an option was explored by the *Senate Standing Committees on Economic Foreign Investment Review Framework Report* in 2016.[100] The general and unfocused nature has been criticised by the Agricultural Management Company leading to criticism that:

> ultimate judgement to the Treasurer without the requirement for clear justification of reasoning or decisions made. Decision-making that is open to interpretation and unjustified does not portray the message of transparency and accountability that Australia proudly promotes as a point of difference and will deter investment interest in Australia.[101]

A factorial matrix could be outlined within the proposal of any new gas export contracts to uphold Australia's energy security within the national interest and avoid any further gas shortfalls and gas price. For example, whether there will be adequate mechanisms in place to divert exported gas into the domestic market within any long-term export contract could be a factor to ensure the project is within the national interest. Any national interest test arguably must be outlined by a variety of factors, including national security, where gas is afforded special categorisation as a strategic commodity. For example, a definition incorporating, in part, a positively focused 'national security' definition found within the *Security of Critical Infrastructure Act 2018* (Cth) could be another viable option. The *Security of Critical Infrastructure Act 2018* (Cth) establishes a Register of Critical Information Assets as administered by the Critical Infrastructure Centre and requires a 'reporting entity' to report operational information[102] to improve transparency of ownership and operational control

100 Australian Government, Senate Standing Committees on Economics, 'Chapter 2 Australia's Foreign Investment Review Framework' (April, 2016) <https://www.aph.gov.au/Parliamentary_Business/Committees/Senate/Economics/Foreign_Investment_Review/Report/c02> accessed 10 February 2018.

101 Ibid 45.

102 Defined in s 7 of the *Overseas Investment Act 2005* (NZ) as:

> (a) the location of the asset;
> (b) a description of the area the asset services;
> (c) the following information about each entity that is the responsible entity for, or an operator of, the asset:
> (i) the name of the entity;
> (ii) if applicable, the ABN of the entity, or other similar business number (however described) if the entity was incorporated, formed or created (however described) outside Australia;
> (iii) the address of the entity's head office or principal place of business;
> (iv) the country in which the entity was incorporated, formed or created (however described);
> (d) the following information about the chief executive officer (however described) of the responsible entity for the asset:
> (i) the full name of the officer;
> (ii) the country or countries of which the officer is a citizen;
> (e) a description of the arrangements under which each operator operates the asset or a part of the asset;
> (f) a description of the arrangements under which data prescribed by the rules relating to the asset is maintained;
> (g) information prescribed by the rules for the purposes of this paragraph.</ext>

of foreign acquisition of Critical Infrastructure.[103] The purpose of the regime is to understand and mitigate national security risks that risk 'sabotage, espionage and coercion'.[104] The Register of Critical Information Assets is confidential and Critical Infrastructure is defined as including electricity, gas[105] and water assets that are critical to '(i) the social or economic stability of Australia or its people; or (ii) the defence of Australia; or (iii) national security; and (b) there is a risk, in relation to the asset, that may be prejudicial to security'.[106] A Critical Gas Asset is identified by s 12 as a special category of asset and includes a 'gas transmission pipeline that is critical to ensuring the security and reliability of a gas market'. The Critical Infrastructure regime has, for the first time, adopted a statutory definition of national security in relation to energy meaning 'Australia's defence, security or international relations',[107] rather than taking an *ad hoc* subjective case-based approach as in the national interest foreign investment review regime. This could provide an initial basis for a 'national interest' test based on critical gas assets that must only provide LNG to exporting countries in taking into account long-term gas security concerns. Arguably, a broader definition of national interest concerns must also be formulated and adopted in not only considering traditional warfare and defence issues, but other important facets within the national interest, including climate and environmental security.

As energy security concerns both national security and the national interest, a similar framework requiring any future Eastern Gas Market LNG exports to meet a national security threshold test may avoid any future gas shortfalls. This would facilitate a transparent review process to be administered by a statutory board, similar to the Critical Infrastructure Centre, specifically for energy exports. There is some criticism and caution surrounding implementing a 'national interest' as it is unlikely to have an impact on medium-term gas security, as there are no new proposals for LNG export facilities on the East Coast currently.[108] However, as the Northern Territory lifts its moratoria on hydraulic fracturing and the North-West

103 In which non-compliance with obligations may result in civil penalties, ss 3 and 4 defined the outline and purposes of the *Security of Critical Infrastructure Act 2018* (Cth).

104 Mathias Cormann, 'Security of Critical Infrastructure Bill 2017, Security of Critical Infrastructure (Consequential and Transitional Provisions) Bill 2017, Second Reading Speech' (December, 2017) <https://parlinfo.aph.gov.au/parlInfo/search/display/display.w3p;query=Id:%22chamber/hansards/5d592247-329b-4d73-aa23-cc7010d35d45/0091%22> accessed 9 December 2018.

105 Specifically, s 12 of the *Security of Critical Infrastructure Act 2018* (Cth) defines a critical gas assets as:

> (a) a gas processing facility that has a capacity of at least 300 terajoules per day or any other capacity prescribed by the rules;
> (b) a gas storage facility that has a maximum daily quantity of at least 75 terajoules per day or any other quantity prescribed by the rules;
> (c) a network or system for the distribution of gas to ultimately service at least 100,000 customers or any other number of customers prescribed by the rules;
> (d) a gas transmission pipeline that is critical to ensuring the security and reliability of a gas market, in accordance with subsection (2).
>
> Note: The rules may prescribe that a specified critical gas asset is not a Critical Infrastructure asset (see section 9).
> (2) For the purposes of paragraph (1)(d), the rules may prescribe:
> (a) specified gas transmission pipelines that are critical to ensuring the security and reliability of a gas market; or
> (b) requirements for a gas transmission pipeline to be critical to ensuring the security and reliability of a gas market.

106 *Security of Critical Infrastructure Act 2018* (Cth), s 9.

107 Ibid, s 5.

108 Tim Nelson, 'East-coast Australian Gas Markets—Overcoming the Lumpiness of Capital Allocation and Temporal Instability' (2018) 59 *Economic Analysis and Policy* 103.

Pipeline edges closer to completion, it is likely another LNG export facility will be built as Australia shores up its position as the largest LNG exporter in the world, eclipsing Qatar. Another solution is an LNG import port and LNG floating storage and regasification storage units (FSRU). Five such proposals have been proposed to import LNG by 2020.[109] However, the difficulty in finding LNG cheap enough to import remains an issue to be addressed as AEMO recognises, 'from 2025 … the total forecast demand is between 90 PJ and 150 PHJ per annum higher than in … 2016 … LNG exports are expected to increase to maximum production capacity, motivated by increasing international demand for LNG after 2023.[110]

A second option to consider is a strategic reserve. In line with Australia's market-based and reactive, rather than proactive, responses to energy security, Australia is non-compliant with the IEA obligation to hold at least 90 days of oil supply.[111] The Liquid Fuel Security Review[112] due for completion by the end of 2019 is likely to recommend increased oil reserves to increase fuel security and meet the IEA obligation by 2026 and the ability to withstand global oil price spikes and trade distribution. As recognised by Laidlaw,[113] concerns over liquid fuel insecurity have been echoed since the first oil shock of 1973–1974, as recommended by the National Energy Advisory Committee:

> with regard to supply insecurity … Consideration be given as a matter of high priority to the specific form and location of strategic stockpiles[,] the timing of their purchase, the methods of their release and their relationship to those required as a result of Australia's IEA membership. Methods of financing or of providing incentives for such stockholdings should also be examined.[114]

While liquid fuel security is a different energy source, a lack of gas supplies represents a similar challenge to reliability and security of the energy market. The resilience to withstand interruption is clearly low in the Eastern Gas Markets, as evident in the upwards of 23 studies or reviews since 2011,[115] numerous alternative policy proposals and consumer dissatisfaction with increasing prices. The increasing reliance on market triggers calls for a

109 Australian Government Department of Industry, Innovation and Science, 'Asian LNG Trade and Australian LNG Imports: Resources and Energy Quarterly June 2018' (June, 2018) <https://publications.industry.gov.au/publications/resourcesandenergyquarterlyjune2018/documents/Resources-and-Energy-Quarterly-June-2018-Asian-LNG-trade.pdf> accessed 20 December 2019.

110 Australian Energy Market Operator, '2018 Gas Statement of Opportunities' (June, 2018) <https://www.aemo.com.au/-/media/Files/Gas/National_Planning_and_Forecasting/GSOO/2018/2018-Gas-Statement-Of-Opportunities.pdf> accessed 14 January 2019.

111 Parliament of Australia, 'Australia's Transport Energy Resilience and Sustainability' (June, 2015) <https://www.aph.gov.au/Parliamentary_Business/Committees/Senate/Rural_and_Regional_Affairs_and_Transport/Transport_energy_resilience/Report/c03> accessed 14 January 2019.

112 Liquid fuel, such as petrol, diesel and jet fuel, accounts for 37 per cent of Australia's energy use, including 98 per cent of transport needs. Australian Government, Department of the Environment and Energy, 'Liquid Fuel Security Interim Report' (April, 2019) <https://www.environment.gov.au/system/files/consultations/7cf6f8e2-fef0-479e-b2dd-3c1d87efb637/files/liquid-fuel-security-review-interim-report.pdf> accessed 5 June 2019.

113 Hunter Laidlaw, 'Liquid Fuel Security: A Quick Guide' (July, 2018) <https://www.aph.gov.au/About_Parliament/Parliamentary_Departments/Parliamentary_Library/pubs/rp/rp1819/Quick_Guides/LiquidFuelSecurity> accessed 9 December 2018.

114 Ibid.

115 As identified by Alan Finkel, 'Independent Review into the Future Security of the National Electricity Market – Blueprint for the Future' (June, 2017) <https://www.energy.gov.au/sites/default/files/independent-review-future-nem-blueprint-for-the-future-2017.pdf > accessed 23 September 2018.

renewed perspective and solution to the current gas crisis. A number of EU countries including Finland and Sweden have set strategic reserves within their energy systems.[116] This requires a regulator to set an appropriate reserve volume and stipulate how the reserved supply is dispatched in times of shortfall and distribution; or, in the event a pre-defined fixed market price is exceeded, set the 'reserve trigger price'. However, as explored within Section 5 of this chapter, strategic reserve regulation is unlikely to hold favour in the current policy climate of the Eastern market.

In contrast, to Australia, the EU has also recently revised its gas policy in response to political conflicts, representing an example of the traditional definition of an energy security threat. The marked shift in energy security regulation in the EU stems from the Russia-Ukraine gas crisis of 2009 whereby the Ukrainian gas transit pipeline transporting the majority of gas to the EU had a severe reduction in supply due to pricing disagreements.[117] The response to the gas crisis stimulated the enactment of Regulation (EU) 994/2010, recently amended and resulting in the Gas Security of Supply Regulation (EU) 2017/1938.[118] The underpinning policy within the regulation is 'solidarity', a reoccurring theme within EU regulations, and centres on EU Member States aiding neighbouring states suffering an energy security crisis by diverting gas to said Member States requesting solidarity as per article 13.[119]

Such a compensatory regulatory measure may not be a viable tool for a single nation with three distinct gas markets such as Australia. However, the evident shift towards regulatory interventions in 'steering' gas supplies in the context of national security is of note in the latest EU gas security regulatory instalment and could provide a viable regulatory model to adopt in a gas crisis scenario in Australia. Such a legislative basis could simulate the *Liquid Fuels Emergency Act 1984* (Cth) which provides regulation over the management of liquid fuel emergencies in Australia triggered by the relevant Minister largely for purposes related to the defence of Australia and ensuring trade or commerce between states and places outside Australia.[120] Gas security regulation stipulating structured measures to divert gas supply to regions within the Eastern Gas Market suffering severe gas supplies, for example due to severe weather events, could have a positive impact on security of supply within the region.

As examined throughout this chapter, a 'national interest' test, in taking a regulatory direction similar to the Critical Infrastructure and Foreign Acquisitions and Takeovers scheme in Australia, would arguably produce a 'better' regulatory regime to ensure gas security. Such a regime would enforce accountability for the failure of private actors to comply with the National Gas Objective with 'respect to price, quality, safety, reliability and security of supply of natural gas'.[121] This, in turn, would provide a regime that would achieve long-term gas security of an enduring nature coupled with ensuring that regulatory objectives are achieved effectively. While the ADGSM and Heads of Agreement represent policies that partly address short-term gas insecurity, without regulatory intervention, and in the absence

116 Karsten Neuhoff et al., 'A Coordinated Strategic Reserve to Safeguard the European Energy Transition' (2016) 41 *Utilities Policy* 252.

117 Ekaterina Svyatets, *Energy Security and Cooperation in Eurasia Power, Profits and Politics* (Routledge 2015).

118 Regulation (EU) 2017/1938 of the European Parliament and of the Council of 25 October 2017 concerning measures to safeguard the security of gas supply and repealing Regulation (EU) No 994/2010.

119 Ruven Fleming, 'A Legal Perspective on Gas Solidarity' (2019) 124 *Energy Policy* 102.

120 *Liquid Fuels Emergency Act 1984* (Cth), s 6.

121 *National Electricity (South Australia) Act* 1996 (SA), s 7.

of an appropriate regulatory regime to provide clear and binding commitments from the State and legislative action to prevent a supply or infrastructure gas security crisis, Australia will remain at risk of ongoing domestic shortfalls.

7 Conclusion

While several policy and regulatory market-based options have been explored by energy bodies, scholars and the Federal Government in Australia, the response to gas insecurity at a federal level currently consists of the ADGSM and a Heads of Supply Agreement. The rapid rise in wholesale gas prices in the Eastern Gas Market and supply shortfalls has provoked calls for export controls, market transparency, a national pipeline and incentives for load shedding from large electricity users in the National Electricity Market. While a number of solutions are evident, including simply lifting moratoria or increasing exploration and production of unconventional gas, a new regulatory regime centring on the 'national interest' and defined by legislative factors could provide a regulatory tool to increase the security of the Eastern Gas Market.

The experience of Western Australia, including the acknowledgement of its unstable and vulnerable gas market after the Varanus Island explosion, and after facing similar domestic gas shortages in both 2007 and 2009, led to its successful strategic reserve regulation. This has ensured adequate and secure domestic gas supply, including power generation, at competitive and reliable prices. While a domestic reservation regulation is unlikely to find favour at the federal level in Australia, a security mechanism based on yearly review will probably fail to enhance accessibility or ensure affordable pricing. Such market-based tools are unlikely to provide long-term gas security to the Eastern Gas Market. In sum, selecting a regulatory strategy to regulate public resources is an evolving task for the State.

Regulation may require adaptation over time: this may be due to regulatory underperformance, changing policy or the need for amendment based on a new set of risks and risk actors. This requires a regulatory 'responsiveness' from states to assess their own performance and 'institute the orders of change that are required for optimal regulation'.[122] There can be no single silver bullet legislative act to exhaustively address the current Eastern Gas Market crisis. However, the introduction of a defined 'national interest' test as an extension of the ADGSM, modelled on the foreign investment and takeovers regime and the new Critical Infrastructure Assets regime, may create a principled approach to enacting 'better' regulation to safeguard both short and long-term gas security for Australia's East Coast.

122 Robert Baldwin (n 47) 132.

PART VII

Africa and the Middle East

28

GAS COMMERCIALISATION PROJECTS IN WEST AFRICA

Pipelines, LNG and gas-to-power

Tade Oyewunmi

1 Introduction

Over the next couple of decades, energy demand in Africa (especially for electricity) is projected to grow at 3.5 per cent per annum (p.a.), much faster than the global average of 1.3 per cent p.a.[1] The continent holds about 488 trillion cubic feet (Tcf) of proven gas reserves.[2] Gas production is projected to increase by 110 per cent, driven by commercialisation in resource-rich countries as more dynamic and international liquid natural gas (LNG) markets evolve and domestic supply projects are successfully executed to meet growing demand.[3] Within the past decade, about 30 per cent of global oil and gas discoveries have been in sub-Saharan Africa.[4] Countries such as Ghana, which hitherto relied mainly on imports, have recently announced exploration and production licensing rounds. Despite being parties to large-scale cross-border gas pipeline projects such as the West African Gas Pipeline (WAGP), Ghana has made considerable progress in developing its domestic gas reserves from recent discoveries such as in the Sankofa and Gye Nyame fields, Offshore Cape Three Points (OCTP) area, the Tweneboah-Enyennra-Ntomee (TEN), etc.[5] Given the resource

1 BP Plc, *Energy Outlook 2018: Country and Regional Insights – Africa* (BP Publications, 2018) (accessed 21.05.2018); Snam, International Gas Union (IGU) and The Boston Consulting Group, *2018 Global Gas Report* (IGU Publications, 10 November 2018) 1–55 (accessed 20.11.2018).

2 BP Plc, *Statistical Review of World Energy 2018* (67th Edition, June 2018) 1–53 at 26.

3 Tade Oyewunmi, 'The Evolving International Gas Market and Energy Security in Nigeria' in Sola Adesola and Feargal Brennan (eds), *Energy in African Developing Economies: Policy, Management and Sustainability* (Palgrave Macmillan, 2019) 237, 117–145; Rahmat Poudineh and Tade Oyewunmi, 'Natural Gas in Nigeria and Tanzania: Can It Turn On Lights?' *Oxford Energy Forum Issue 115 Electrifying Africa*, (Oxford Institute for Energy Studies, September 2018) 14–20.

4 Yinka Omorogbe and Tade Oyewunmi, 'OGEL Special Issue on "Oil and Gas Law and Policy in West Africa" – Editorial' *The Oil, Gas & Energy Law Intelligence Journal* (*OGEL*) 1 (2017) at <www.ogel.org/article.asp?key=3665#_ftn2> (accessed 05.04.2018).

5 The World Bank, 'Ghana – Sankofa Gas Project' (World Bank Group Report 96554, Washington, DC, 2015) 1–114 available at <http://documents.worldbank.org/curated/en/173561467986250592/Ghana-Sankofa-Gas-Project> (accessed 21.05.2018); Mike Fulwood and Thierry Bros, 'Future Prospects for LNG Demand in Ghana' *Oxford Institute for Energy Studies, Energy Insight* 26 (2018) 1–15. Ghana's first oil and gas licensing round was announced on 15 October 2018. See <https://www.ghanalr2018.com> (accessed 04.01.2019).

potentials and demand projections, operators in the sub-region have also ventured into several gas commercialisation options ranging from traditional large-scale to small-scale LNG projects, Floating Storage and Regasification Units (FSRUs) and Floating Liquefied Natural Gas (FLNG). The main constraints to timely investment decisions and successful project execution have typically bordered on the challenges of (i) whether or not end-users can afford a market-based cost-reflective price for delivered gas; and (ii) downstream power sector liquidity and creditworthiness, which in some cases becomes more complicated due to high technical and commercial losses.[6] As these issues arise and projects are being structured to overcome the various risks, it is important to highlight that the institutional framework of laws, regulations, policies, licensing and contracts relating to the exploration, production and supply of gas plays an instrumental role in meeting any underlying security of supply and competitiveness objectives. By discussing developments in Nigeria and Ghana, this chapter will examine the range of interrelated international petroleum transactions, legal, policy and risk assessment issues that underpin gas utilisation and commercialisation objectives in the West African sub-region.

2 Gas supply and energy in West Africa

Natural gas, whether produced from oil-rich reservoirs (i.e., associated gas) or gas only fields (i.e., non-associated gas) is capital-intensive to process, supply and store, although it is efficient in the generation of electricity and for other energy purposes such as cooking. It is also widely considered to be more environmentally-friendly than other hydrocarbons like coal and diesel oil. Before investments go into building essential networks of processing facilities and pipelines required to supply demand centres, the economic, security and reliability risks must be critically examined and subjected to the necessary due diligence assessments. In most cases, the role of the state as the owner of oil and gas resources *in situ*, and administrator through the licensing and regulatory framework is often made more complicated with the archetypical role granted to national oil and gas corporations in joint ventures or petroleum exploration and production agreements with international and local private operators. Primarily, the host government's objective is to earn export revenues and meet energy security challenges. Such rational expectations come with socio-political undertones and the need to ensure affordability, which may sometimes be at variance with the equally legitimate expectation of private investors and financiers to recover invested capital and earn reasonable returns plus profit. Thus, the legal and regulatory framework for gas projects, which defines applicable rights, interests and obligations regarding exploration and production, transmission and disposal, processing or acquisition, gas utilisation and payments for gas volumes delivered, should be of the highest quality, enhance efficiency and work to meet the objectives of both public and private stakeholders.

6 Ghana, Côte d'Ivoire, etc. have all dabbled in the FSRU option within the past decade, while the Nigerian LNG project remains one of the biggest LNG suppliers globally, other projects such as the Brass LNG and Olokola LNG export projects were mothballed or stalled. See Tade Oyewunmi, *Regulating Gas Supply to Power Markets: Transnational Approaches to Competitiveness and Security of Supply* (Wolters Kluwer Law International, 2018) 323, 40–43; Yinka Omorogbe, 'Law and Investor Protection in the Nigerian Natural Gas Industry' (1996) 14(2) *Journal of Energy & Natural Resources Law* 179–192; Thierry Bros, 'Can Small LNG Meet the Challenge of Empowering Africa?' in *Oxford Energy Forum – Issue 110, Searching for Natural Gas Demand in the Next Decade* (Oxford Institute for Energy Studies, August 2017) 46–47.

For instance, the background facts and issues leading to the case *Process and Industrial Developments Limited vs. Federal Republic of Nigeria and Ministry of Petroleum Resources*[7] underscores the need for due diligence in developing and investing in gas projects. In this case, Process and Industrial Developments Limited (PIDL), a company incorporated by two Irish nationals in 2006 primarily to execute a natural gas processing project in Nigeria, was to receive "wet gas" for free from the Nigerian government and convert it into "lean gas". The Nigerian government could thereafter supply the lean gas to domestic power producers. As compensation, PIDL could freely sell the natural gas liquids (NGLs) produced as by-products of the processing. The company commenced feasibility and engineering studies and plans for the project as well as executing a Gas Supply and Processing Agreement (GSPA) with the Nigerian Ministry of Petroleum (NMP)[8] in 2010. Even though PIDL and NMP agreed to have wet gas delivered by the Nigerian government from oil mining leases (OMLs) 123 and 67 operated by Addax Petroleum and ExxonMobil respectively, both Addax and ExxonMobil were not parties to the GSPA. Later on, the unwillingness of Addax and ExxonMobil to supply the wet gas volumes became a deal-breaker for PIDL and NMP. Thus, PIDL commenced arbitration proceedings against Nigeria under the GSPA, and three arbitrators were appointed accordingly. Among other things, the arbitral tribunal issued an award on liability in 2015, deciding that (i) the Nigerian government was in breach of its obligations under the GSPA to deliver wet gas to the facility which was to be built by PIDL; (ii) although the GSPA identified OMLs 123 and 67 operated by Addax and Exxon as the source gas, the Nigerian government, as the party to the GSPA, was obliged to and could obtain the wet gas from other sources when Addax and Exxon refused to supply PIDL.

Regarding damages, a dissenting arbitrator held that damages should be limited to US$250 million; while two arbitrators awarded PIDL US$6,597,000,000 plus 7 per cent pre- and post-award interest as compensation for a breach of contract.[9] In 2016, the Federal High Court in Nigeria gave an order setting aside the liability award,[10] while two years later PIDL filed a petition in the US seeking to enforce the award among other claims under the Convention on the Recognition and Enforcement of Foreign Arbitral Awards, 10 June 1958. Without going into the merits and demerits of the ongoing claims and counterclaims or appeals, the PIDL case is an instructive example on how agreements and the need to bring all the necessary parties to the table could impact the successful realisation of gas commercialisation projects. It also highlights the need to fully appreciate the local institutional and regulatory regime, how it works and influences broader international petroleum transactions framework as well as the assessment of pre- and post-project completion risks.

7 Case 1:18-cv-00594-CRC at the Washington, DC Circuit, 08/27/18.

8 The NMP, headed by the Minister of Petroleum Resources, is responsible for the administration and governance of the Nigerian petroleum industry, while the Nigerian National Petroleum Corporation (NNPC) is a government owned corporation through which the government participates in the commercial and technical aspects of the industry through Joint Ventures/Joint Operating Agreements (JV/JOAs) or Production Sharing Contracts with international and Nigerian private companies. See the Petroleum Act 1969 CAP P10 Laws of the Federation of Nigeria 2004; NNPC Act CAP N123 Laws of the Federation of Nigeria 2004; Oyewunmi (n6) at 127–146; Tade Oyewunmi, 'Regulatory and Policy Issues for Natural Gas Supply to Power Markets: Examining the Energy Supply Crisis in Nigeria' *Oil, Gas & Energy Law Intelligence (OGEL) Journal* 1 (2017) at <www.ogel.org/article.asp?key=3677> (accessed 23.05.2017).

9 See Sophia Morris, *Nigeria's Immunity Appeal of $9B Award Allowed by Judge* (Law360, 2 November 2018) at <www.law360.com/articles/1098282> (accessed 15.11.2018).

10 *Minister of Petroleum Resources vs Process and Industrial Developments Limited BVI*, No. FHC/L/CS/264/2016 (Federal High Court, 24 May 2016).

2.1 Regulatory and contractual matters

In both international and domestic energy projects, where the host government plays the vital role of both administrator and business partner, it is important to understand the legal and contractual nature of property rights and licenses. Such property rights are in the class of "profit-à-prendre" or "right of taking" which empowers the relevant operator(s) to find, produce, take away, process and sell oil and gas resources.[11] The typical gas supply value chain comprises of the (i) upstream exploration and production (E&P); (ii) the midstream gas (processing, storage and transportation); and (iii) downstream (sales and distribution) segments. The upstream producers hold a license to explore and produce gas, which is thereon gathered through small diameter pipelines (gathering lines) from oil or gas fields; the gas molecules then go through the processing facilities to remove water and impurities or by-products such as NGLs as in PIDL's case above. The dry gas is then compressed to flow into large transmission pipelines (midstream) and then transported to offtakers such as gas-fired power generators, storage or other distribution centres (downstream). Transmission pipelines can be for domestic or cross-border transmission such as the WAGP.

2.1.1 Upstream licensing and contracts

Generally, international upstream arrangements are based on licenses and concessions; Joint Venture/Joint Operating Agreements (JV/JOAs); Production Sharing Contracts (PSCs); and Service Contracts (i.e., Risk Service Contracts (RSCs) and Pure Service Contracts).[12] In recent times, it is more common to find hybrid or model agreements reflecting elements of a typical concession/royalty system and a PSC or JV/JOA adopted in West African and sub-Saharan African countries, as opposed to Service Contracts, which are more common in South America and Middle Eastern countries. For instance, the Ghanaian 2008 OCTP area Petroleum Agreement[13] between ENI Ghana Exploration & Production Limited (ENI) as operator, Vitol Upstream Ghana Limited (Vitol) and Ghana National Petroleum Corporation (GNPC) and the 2006 Deepwater Tano Petroleum Agreement between Tullow Oil as operator, Anadarko Petroleum, Kosmos Energy, PetroSAGhana Limited and GNPC have elements of both a concession/royalty system and production sharing.[14] In commercial terms, the Ghanaian hybrid approach represents a tax and royalty-based system with minority state participation, unlike in Nigeria where concessions granted as licenses and leases in combination with JV/JOAs from the 1960s–1980s now have government-owned NNPC holding majority stakes.[15] In Ghana, the OCTP Area operations led to the discovery of Sankofa & Gye Nyame fields, while the Deepwater Tano operations led to developments such as the TEN projects, which are now considered as crucial in meeting growing domestic demand

11 See Oyewunmi (n6) at 14–28.

12 Mohd Naseem and Saman Naseem, 'World Petroleum Regimes', in Kim Talus (ed) *Research Handbook on International Energy Law* (Edward Elgar, 2014) 149–180.

13 Participating interests in the acreage is allocated between ENI, Vitol and GNPC as 44.44 per cent, 35.56 per cent and 14 per cent respectively. See 'Ghana Petroleum Register – Offshore Cape Three Points' available at <www.ghanapetroleumregister.com/sankofa> (accessed 12.11.2018).

14 Participating interests in the acreage is allocated between Tullow (35.48 per cent), Anadarko (24 per cent), Kosmos Energy (24 per cent), PetroSAGhana (2.52 per cent), GNPC (14 Per cent). See 'Ghanaian Petroleum Register – Deepwater Tano' at <www.ghanapetroleumregister.com/deepwater-tano> (accessed 12.11.2018).

15 Yinka Omorogbe, *Oil and Gas Law in Nigeria* (Malthouse Press, 2003).

in Ghana due to unreliable imports via the WAGP.[16] In Nigeria, JV/JOAs account for about 49 per cent of petroleum operations, while PSCs, Sole Risk Concessions and Marginal Field Licenses constitute about 41 per cent, 6 per cent and 4 per cent respectively.[17]

Licenses and concessions granted by a host government to a private international or local company confers non-possessory interests in a defined area within the State's territorial jurisdiction, to find, produce, take and dispose of oil and gas, subject to the payment of taxes, royalties and rents as required by law. Most host governments manage the award of licenses and industry participation through a ministry (e.g., the NMP) and one or more regulatory agencies such as the Department of Petroleum Resources (DPR) in Nigeria.[18] Host governments also acquire participating interests in commercial and operational activities through their national oil corporations (NOCs) such as the NNPC and the GNPC, thereby entering into JV/JOAs or other variants of E&P agreements. The Nigerian oil prospecting license (OPL) and oil mining lease (OML) granted by the Minister of Petroleum are a type of modern concession, following which a JV/JOA is formed with international and local private E&P companies.[19] In this context, the interests and liabilities are typically "joint and several" to the extent of their respective participating interests. The JV comprises the participation agreement, which defines the relationship and participating interests of the parties, while the JOA defines the legal and operational relationship of the co-venturers by providing for issues such as the operating committees and operator for the concession, work programme and budget, development or disposition of discovered gas, transfer of participating interests, etc.[20] Note that clause 9.3 of the Association of International Petroleum Negotiators (AIPN) Model JOA 2012, which often serves as a benchmark for industry negotiations and arrange-

16 The OCTP is located about 60 km off Ghana's Western Region coast. The fields have about 770 million barrels of oil equivalent (mboe) in place comprising of about 500 million barrels of oil and 270 mboe of non-associated gas (about 40 billion cubic metres). The project entails the production and utilisation of gas entirely for Ghana's domestic market. A 63 km pipeline transports gas to Sanzule's Onshore Receiving Facilities (ORF), where it is processed and transmitted to Ghana's national grid, supplying approximately 180 million standard cubic feet per day (mmscfd). See 'Ghana Petroleum Register – Sankofa & Gye Nyame Fields' at <www.ghanapetroleumregister.com/sankofa-1> (accessed 12.11.2018).

17 Oyewunmi (n6) at 133; DPR Nigeria, *2017 Nigerian Oil and Gas Industry Annual Report* (Department of Petroleum Resources, 2018) 1–111 29. <www.dpr.gov.ng/wp-content/uploads/2018/10/2017-NOGIAR-WEB.pdf> (accessed 12.11.2018).

18 Tade Oyewunmi, 'Examining the Legal and Regulatory Framework for Domestic Gas Utilization and Power Generation in Nigeria' (2014) 7(6) *Journal of World Energy Law & Business*, 538–557.

19 The NNPC-ExxonMobil JV in which ExxonMobil subsidiary – Mobil Producing Nigeria – is operator has NNPC with 60 per cent participating interest and ExxonMobil 40 per cent relates to about four OMLs, while the NNPC-Chevron JV operated by Chevron with NNPC holding 60 per cent and Chevron holding 40 per cent interests relates to about eight OMLs. Other JVs include (i) the NNPC (60 per cent), Agip (20 per cent), Phillips Petroleum (20 per cent); (ii) the NNPC (60 per cent) and Total E&P Nigeria Limited (TEPNG) (40 per cent). The Shell-operated JV accounts for more than 40 per cent of Nigeria's total oil production from about 80 fields. The JV is composed of the NNPC (55 per cent), Shell (30 per cent), Elf (10 per cent) and Agip (5 per cent). Since 2017, the IOCs in the Shell-Elf-Agip/NNPC JV have divested their 45 per cent stake in several concessions to various Nigerian-owned independents such as SEPLAT Petroleum Development Company and NECONDE Energy, see the Energy Mix Report, 'Upstream Assets Divestment in Nigeria: Update, Outlook and Challenges', 1 July 2014, available at <http://energymixreport.com/upstream-assets-divestment-in-nigeria-update-outlook-and-challenges> (accessed 11 November 2014). Such divestments have led to the emergence of JVs between Nigerian-owned independents and NNPC or the subsidiary called Nigerian Petroleum Development Company (NPDC) like NNPC and SEPLAT and NPDC and NECONDE JVs.

20 Tade Oyewunmi, 'Natural Gas Exploration and Production in Nigeria and Mozambique: Legal and Contractual Issues' *OGEL* 1 (2015) 1–25; Ernest E. Smith *et al., International Petroleum Transactions* (3rd Edition, Rocky Mountain Mineral Law Foundation, 2010).

ments amongst other things, includes the following provision regarding the disposition of natural gas:

> The Parties recognise that, in the event of individual disposition of Natural Gas, imbalances may arise with the result being that a Party will temporarily have disposed of more than its Participating Interest share of production of Natural Gas. Accordingly, if Natural Gas is to be produced from an Exploitation Area, the Parties shall, in good faith and no later than the date on which the Development Plan for a Natural Gas project is approved by the Operating Committee, negotiate and conclude the terms of a balancing agreement to cover the disposition of Natural Gas produced under the Contract, regardless of whether all of the Parties have entered into a sales arrangement or sales contract for their respective Entitlement of Natural Gas.

Given that the ownership rights and liabilities of parties is "joint and several" as created by the combination of a license, concession or OML with a JV/JOA; an efficient contractual framework on the disposition of natural gas by co-venturers in a JV/JOA is essential to ensure fair and equitable allocation of entitlements and resources produced from an acreage. Additionally, the physical features of gas, as well as the requirement for huge upfront investments and technical issues for producing, processing or storing and utilising, means that quantifying, metering and balancing are key to creating appropriate economic and commercial value for the co-venturers with "joint and several" interests. Each party has entitlements equal to their respective participating interests and there is usually a delivery point for allocating such volumes. Moreover, unless otherwise agreed, no "agency" or "trust" relationship is *ipso facto* assumed between the parties regarding the disposition of produced gas. The other interesting JOA provisions include the Allocation of Hydrocarbons to Parties and Principles of Natural Gas Agreement(s) with the host government.

Host governments are typically responsible for regulating and managing domestic gas supply networks through a gas transmission and marketing subsidiary of the NOC.[21] Thus, it becomes pertinent to establish clear guiding rules between the private and public stakeholders involved, such as:

a) the right to dispose of all or part of gas entitlements, including the government's share where necessary or as may be agreed, to the highest value outlets in the domestic or export market;
b) considerations for the level of infrastructural and commercial development of the local market;
c) gas reserves to be produced for their full economic life;
d) access to infrastructure and pipeline capacity for gas processing and transportation at a competitive tariff.

PSCs and Service Contracts are essentially agreements in which the host government, through the NOC, holds the concession and appoints a private international and local E&P company or a consortium as the contractor to carry out upstream operations. Under the PSC arrangement, the parties agree to share produced oil and gas from the defined contract area in predetermined percentages, following the allocation and payment of relevant tax, royalties

21 Oyewunmi (n6) 14–28; Oyewunmi (n18) *Domestic Gas Utilization and Power Generation in Nigeria*, ibid.

and fees usually in kind.[22] The contractor bears all the exploration and production risks and is generally in charge of operations and the management of the contract area unless the State party agrees to participate in the venture directly. If no petroleum is found, the contractor typically receives no compensation. Upstream arrangements pertaining to (i) the duration of the E&P period, (ii) the evaluation and announcement of a commercial discovery, (iii) developing a feasible gas utilisation or supply project, and (iv) deciding which party will be primarily responsible for marketing as well as balancing issues in cases of multiple interest holders, are some of the key provisions to be considered for consolidating midstream gas projects. Such requirements will need to synchronise well with supply and delivery arrangements, take-or-pay and sales obligations to be established under a GSPA and Gas Transportation Agreement (GTA).[23]

In Nigeria, an OPL holder may submit a feasibility study programme or proposal for gas utilisation within five years of commencement of crude oil production. Although, the Petroleum Act 1969 empowers the Federal Government to (i) take produced gas free of charge or at a price without payment of royalty, and (ii) approve the price for gas sales by upstream producers to the domestic market; the agreements define the actual dealings between the government's NOC and upstream operators.[24] The Nigerian 2005 Model PSC provides, among other things, that when the contractor discovers enough gas quantities that could justify commercial development, it shall report to the NNPC. The contractor then investigates and submits proposals for development while considering local strategic needs as identified by the NNPC. Both the contractor and the NNPC will also execute further gas development agreement(s) which recognises the former's right to participate in development projects, the right to recover costs and share in profits. The contractor is also obliged to submit a Field Development Programme to the NNPC.

2.1.2 Midstream arrangements and contracts

Negotiating and concluding GSPAs, LNG Sale and Purchase Agreements (SPAs), etc. is essential in securing the upstream gas producers' commitment to sell and the buyers' obligations to take and pay for specified volumes of gas for delivery to offtakers such as a gas-fired power utility or a LNG or processing facility, subject to a predetermined pricing and/or rate-of-return framework. The agreement would typically include conditions for the seller, buyer and transporter as well as determining when such conditions are fulfilled and what happens if they aren't. The terms usually include obtaining all necessary approvals

22 Ibid.

23 See further discussion on the 'Gas Supply Value Chain' in Oyewunmi (n6) 14–20; Tade Oyewunmi, 'Examining the Role of Regulation in Restructuring and Development of Gas Supply Markets in the United States and the European Union' (2017) 40(1) *Houston Journal of International Law* 191–296, 200–210.

24 See Oyewunmi (n6) 132–150. Guidelines and regulations made pursuant to the National Domestic Gas Supply and Pricing Policy 2008 and the National Gas Policy 2017 currently allow for a regulated cost-of-service approach for the pricing of gas supplies to the power sector. For instance, the recent Flare Gas (Prevention of Waste and Pollution) Regulations, 2018 and the DPR guidelines on (i) Grant of Permit to Access Flare Gas Sites, 2018; (ii) Flare Gas Measurement Data Management & Reporting Obligations 2018; (iii) Flare Payments by Upstream Gas Producers 2018; and (iv) Producers Associated Gas Utilisation Projects 2018 provide for the legal and regulatory framework of commercialising associated gas which would ordinarily be flared by producers. See also Oluwaṣeun Ọkẹ, 'Gas Flaring in Nigeria and the Flexed Muscles of the 2018 Regulations: Key Implications and Investment Considerations' *OGEL* 1 (2019) at <www.ogel.org/article.asp?key=3806> (accessed 02.02.2019),

and agreements for (i) development, production and sale of gas by the seller; (ii) purchase, receiving and use of gas acquired by the buyer; and (iii) conveying and delivery of committed volumes by the transporter. Arrangements for siting, construction and financing are also necessary, as well as representations and warranties as to creditworthiness and authority to perform obligations.

A GTA provides the relevant terms governing the transmission of gas, such as transportation tariffs and ancillary service obligations by the pipeline operator.[25] In both domestic and cross-border pipeline supply contexts, these arrangements should be consolidated before upstream producers, suppliers and their financiers commit to investing in the project.[26] In a transnational context, the transportation agreement would also include provisions for transit fees, allocation of risks between suppliers and the pipeline owner/operator in cases where third-party access is allowed and applicable tariffs for such services.[27] The main commercial and transportation risks to be considered by suppliers and the pipeline company are: (i) the availability of gas volumes from upstream associated and non-associated gas fields, as well as whether a functioning, secure or reliable pipeline capacity is available; and (ii) if pipeline capacities are secured, whether gas volumes from upstream sources are already committed to other uses or lack of creditworthiness of the consumers/offtakers to pay for the volumes or services to be rendered by the pipeline company. In a developing West African economy context in which the typical offtakers and consumers are mostly state-owned power utilities with liquidity and affordability constraints as well as state-centred government control, these risks may become more common but surmountable. Creditworthiness and the financial ability to fulfill obligations under supply arrangements are typically established by a guarantee or a standby letter of credit issued by a bank, an on-demand bond issued by a surety corporation, a corporate or government guarantee or such other financial security as is agreed between parties.

The requirement for project financing or support from international financial institutions and corporations in meeting the significant upfront costs and capital from a project's 'pre-completion' to 'post-completion' and through the stages of feasibility studies, front-end engineering, detailed design and construction to operational phases underscores the need for thorough due diligence and risk assessment. Contractual clauses and mechanisms such as take-or-pay (ToP), deliver-or-pay (DoP), ship-or-pay, price adjustment and review and *force majeure* provisions are instrumental in securing the necessary commitments. Although damages arising from claims of a 'breach' or 'non-performance' against a sovereign may prove complicated as seen in the PDIL's case above, and as between sovereigns in a transnational or cross-border context, such as between Nigeria and Ghana in the light of defaults and unreliability issues in the WAGP Project. In reality, parties resort to negotiations, mediation, arbitration and political solutions.

A ToP clause obligates a purchaser to make payment even if it fails to take the negotiated percentage of the quantity of gas that it has committed to pay for under the contract. This type of clause recognises the interest of the producer in seeking to secure guaranteed cash flow to cover *ex ante* costs. These arrangements also protect the purchaser by providing for

25 Oyewunmi (n6) 20–25.

26 Peter Roberts and Ruchdi Maalouf, 'Contractual Issues in the International Gas Trade: LNG – the Key to the Golden Age of Gas' in Kim Talus (ed), *Research Handbook on International Energy Law* (Edward Elgar, 2014) 329–357.

27 Thomas J. Dimitroff, 'Cross-Border Oil and Gas Pipeline Risk and Sustainable Mitigations' (2014) 7(4) *Journal of World Energy Law & Business* 287–339.

make-up-rights, by which a buyer that incurs ToP liabilities in one year can recoup those amounts or part of them by taking more gas than the minimum in subsequent years.[28] On the other hand, DoP clauses are designed to protect the buyer's interests and ensure contracted gas is actually delivered as agreed in the contract. They require a seller that fails to supply negotiated amounts to make compensatory payments. It is usually necessary to allow periodic price adjustments to reflect changes in the value of the product over time, taking into account the traditional long-term duration of supply contracts. Parties also seek to reconcile the interests of buyers and sellers over the long-term period of the contract.

2.1.3 Transnational and cross-border pipeline contracting issues

Most of the arrangements and issues relating to a typical domestic gas supply framework apply to the cross-border pipeline scenario. However, the involvement of two or more governments in a transnational, cross-border context requires bespoke instruments such as Intergovernmental Agreements (IGA), Host Government Agreements (HGAs), multilateral treaties establishing *among other things* a joint, multinational agency as in the WAGP Authority and other project financing and development agreements.[29] An IGA between the host governments across which a cross-border pipeline is constructed and operated would be backed by multilateral and bilateral trade, double taxation and investment agreements. HGAs and project related agreements are also executed between the pipeline company and each of the host governments where appropriate. As in the WAGP Project involving Nigeria, Togo, Benin and Ghana, the respective countries may also be constitutionally required to enact enabling law(s) to domesticate the applicable multilateral treaty within the legal framework of the participating states.[30] Generally, IGAs should cover issues relating to state-to-state dealings with the project company and transported gas volumes such as the freedom to transit, access, protecting the rights and obligations of upstream and downstream states and investors and exemption of pipeline company from double taxation.[31]

2.2 Pipelines or LNG – the WAGP, NLNG and others

At the moment, the Nigerian domestic gas pipeline infrastructure comprises two unintegrated pipeline networks: (i) the Alakiri-Obigbo–Ikot Abasi Pipeline (the Eastern Network); and (ii) the Escravos–Lagos Pipeline System (ELPS) (the Western Network) in addition to the dedicated pipeline infrastructure owned by the NLNG company, the NNPC-Shell JV and the NNPC-Chevron JV.[32] The ELPS is the main trunkline which connects gas reserves in the oil and gas-rich Niger Delta to industrial and power generation users in the south-west

28 Oyewunmi (n6) 20–25.

29 Dimitroff (n27) 318.

30 See the West African Gas Pipeline Treaty, 31 January 2003 ("WAGP Treaty"); Enabling Legislations – (i) Bénin – Régime juridique et fiscal applicable au projet du GAO 2005, (ii) Ghana – West African Gas Pipeline Act, 2004, (iii) Nigeria – West African Gas Pipeline Act, 2005, and (iv) Togo – Régime juridique et fiscal applicable au projet du GAO 2004; WAGP Regulations – (i) Bénin – Règlement du Gazoduc de l'Afrique de l'Ouest, 2005, (ii) Ghana – West African Gas Pipeline Regulations, 2005, (iii) Nigeria – West African Gas Pipeline Regulations 2006, and (iv) Togo – Règlement du Gazoduc de l'Afrique de l'Ouest 2005; and the WAGP Access Code governing access to Transportation Services, 2004 at <www.wagpa.org/project-documentation/> (accessed 15.10.2018).

31 Dimitroff (n27).

32 Oyewunmi (n6) 42.

of the country and also feeds the WAGP system, which goes on to neighbouring Benin, thereafter to Togo and Ghana. From 1990–2000, Nigeria's gas utilisation projects such as the NNPC-Shell JV's NLNG Project, the ExxonMobil JV Oso Condensate Project, the Chevron JV GTL Escravos Gas Project and the WAGP (expected to receive gas from NNPC-Shell JV and NNPC-Chevron JV) were more about boosting government export revenue and less about domestic energy supply, although some NGLs, liquified petroleum gas (LPG) and cooking gas is produced as by-products for domestic use. There has been a growing drive to enhance domestic utilisation and supply for power and energy uses in industrial and commercial centres. Through its gas transmission and marketing subsidiary, the Nigerian Gas Company Ltd (NGC), NNPC has the primary responsibility to develop the domestic gas supply market as well as operate and manage the main transmission pipelines and network.[33]

2.2.1 Nigerian LNG projects

Sponsored by the NNPC-Shell JV, the Nigeria LNG Limited (NLNG) is a special purpose project company incorporated in 1989 to produce LNG and NGLs for export. The company's shareholding and equity distribution comprise the Federal Government, represented by NNPC (49 per cent), Shell (25.6 per cent), Total (15 per cent) and Eni (10.4 per cent).[34] The project is situated on 2.27 square kilometres of largely reclaimed land in Bonny Island, offshore Rivers State, in the Nigerian Niger Delta. It is designed to receive diversified supplies of associated and non-associated gas from the upstream JV sponsors, with six transmission pipeline systems.[35] The project itself had been under consideration since 1976 but only received a Final Investment Decision (FID) in 1995. Consequently, a turnkey Engineering, Procurement and Construction (EPC) contract was executed to construct Trains 1 and 2 of the liquefaction plant, the Gas Transmission System and the Residential Area (RA). LNG production commenced in 1999, followed by FIDs for expansion to Train 3, including NGL and LPG production facilities, which became operational in 2002. Further expansions to Trains 4, 5 and 6 commenced with a FID in 2002 for Trains 4 and 5 and in 2004 for Train 6. Operations and start-up commenced in 2005, 2006 and 2007 respectively, with Train 6 including additional condensate processing, LPG storage and jetty facilities, giving the entire facility a capacity to produce 22 million tonnes per annum (mtpa) of LNG, and 5 mtpa of NGLs from 3.5 billion cubic feet per day (Bcf/d) of natural gas intake.[36]

The original idea was to ship LNG to the US and Europe; thus in 1999, the first shipments went to destinations in Italy, Spain and Portugal.[37] Early interest by companies such as Cove Point Trading of Maryland US, Cabot of Boston, Snam of Italy and Enagas of Spain

33 Oyewunmi (n6) 42. The NGC was recently unbundled into the Nigerian Gas Processing & Transportation Company (NGPTC) and the Nigerian Gas Marketing Company (NGMC). The Escravos Gas project was developed by the NNPC/Chevron JV to process and utilise associated gas. The gas is developed, compressed and piped to a liquid extraction facility where LPG and condensates are removed. The LPG is transported by pipeline to an offshore floating storage and offloading vessel, while the condensate is blended with the Escravos crude oil stream and the remaining dry gas is sold to the NGC/NGPTC.

34 See the NLNG Ltd, *Facts and Figures on NLNG 2018* (5 July 2018) available at <www.nlng.com/Media-Center/Pages/Fasts-and-Figures.aspx> (accessed 12.11.2018).

35 Ibid.

36 Ibid. The Final Investment Decision (FID) for the NLNG project's Train 7 was recently approved, thus boosting the production capacity of NLNG from 22 MTPA to 30 MTPA. See *LNG World News*, 'Nigeria LNG makes Train 7 FID' at <www.lngworldnews.com/nigeria-lng-makes-train-7-fid> (accessed 05.01.2010).

37 Oyewunmi (n3) 'The Evolving International Gas Market'.

led to SPA negotiations. However, the pace of initial negotiations was slow and affected by the political instability and lack of firm government interest. Later on, other companies also expressed interest and joined in negotiations, such as British Gas and Enel. Consequently, it took several years for SPAs to be agreed.[38] The initial set of long-term SPAs were signed with GdF (France), Enel (Italy) and Enagas (Spain) as offtakers, later on by Botas (Turkey) on a delivered ex-ship (DES) basis. The finance negotiations were completed by the end of 2002, and unlike most LNG projects, which are paid for through project finance, the NLNG was financed through the balance sheet of the shareholders sponsoring it.[39] After Trains 1–3, the financing of Trains 4-6 was done by giving lenders security for the loan over the whole liquefaction project without asset segregation, with a financing structure that is understood to have an unusually high equity share (around 50 per cent).[40]

The contractual, financing and equity arrangements meant that a considerable amount of NLNG's volumes was contracted to offtakers not linked to any specific destination including some of the project sponsors themselves. Thus, even though about a quarter of the overall NLNG volumes were sold under contracts intended to serve the US and Spain, there was considerable destination flexibility which permitted easier diversions to other demand centres in the wake of a shale gas production boom in the US which meant demand and supply of Nigerian LNG to the US plummeted. The key issues that underpinned the viability of an eventual FID in this project centred on the stability of the regulatory environment and the provision of contractual "safeguards" in respect of fiscal incentives and guarantees. The ability to conclude investment and supply negotiations efficiently and with government support was also undeniably critical.

2.2.2 Legal tussles and political solutions?

The NLNG Project was established pursuant to the Nigerian LNG (Fiscal Incentives, Guarantees and Assurances) Decree no. 39 of 1990, and amended by Decree no. 113 of 1993 (the "NLNG Act").[41] Among other things the NLNG Act provided for:

1. a 10-year tax relief period to the NLNG;
2. exemptions from all customs duties, levies, charges and imposts of a similar nature; pre-shipment inspection of import waivers;
3. no export duties, taxes or other duties, levies, charges or impost of a similar nature shall be payable or imposed on NLNG;
4. guarantees, assurances and undertakings shall be in effect throughout the lifespan of the venture;
5. the government's commitment:
    a) not to amend the fiscal regime except with the prior written agreement of the shareholders;
    b) to ensure that the guarantees shall not be suspended, modified or revoked during the life of the venture, except with the mutual consent of the government and shareholders

38 The IEA, *Global Gas Security Review 2016* (IEA Publications, France, 2016) 1–117 (accessed 25.12.2016).
39 Ibid.
40 Ibid, 54.
41 Now an Act of the National Assembly referred to as the Nigerian LNG (Fiscal Incentives, Guarantees and Assurances) Act Cap N87 Laws of the Federation of Nigeria 2004.

Some provisions of the NLNG Act prohibiting any future legislation that might affect the assurances and guarantees granted as a means of "investment stability" for the project have been contentious and controversial.[42] In *Niger Delta Development Commission (NDDC) v Nigeria Liquefied Natural Gas Company Ltd* (2005) FHC/PH/CS/313/2005, the NDDC sued the NLNG and others claiming that according to the NDDC Act 2002, the NLNG is a gas processing company operating in the Niger Delta Area, and thus is obliged to pay an annual levy of 3 per cent of the NLNG's total annual budget to the NDDC. While the Federal High Court held, among other things, that the provisions of the NLNG Act hampering the government's legislative powers to make new laws were unconstitutional, the Court of Appeal and Supreme Court upheld the validity of the NLNG Act and refused the NDDC's claim. However, various stakeholders and local groups have called for an amendment of the NLNG Act by the National Assembly (legislature) because it is more than ten years since the project was commissioned in 1999. The role of the Federal Government as a stakeholder in the project has commercial, economic and socio-political ramifications. Arguably, such 'government' role ensure that the project's economics and viability is insulated from various legal and security risks that the company could have faced while operating in Nigeria. With assets worth about US$15.4 billion and a global LNG market share of about 7.2 per cent (as of 2017),[43] the NGLG project is arguably one of the most successful Nigerian commercial ventures with government involvement. The Nigerian Government benefits from its share of payments for feed-gas supplied by upstream JV sponsors, as well as dividends and company income tax via its shareholding through the NNPC.

Other LNG ventures that have been considered in the recent past include Brass LNG and Olokola LNG (OKLNG). These proposed projects have been awaiting a FID for several decades mainly because of questions about the availability of feed-in gas and divestments by the IOCs.[44] For instance, ConocoPhillips withdrew from Brass LNG, while Chevron and British Gas withdrew from OKLNG. Arguably, the risks relating to the uncertainties and over-politicisation of the future investment climate in the Nigerian oil and gas industry following the protracted process of legal and regulatory reform were considered too high, as was the growing desire of the government to channel more resources to the domestic supply of gas to power and industries.

2.2.3 More Nigerian condensates and NGL projects

The Oso Condensate Project involves the commercial development of the condensates from an OML held by the NNPC-Mobil Producing Nigeria (MPN) JV and operated by MPN. Although it was discovered in 1967, it remained undeveloped for over 24 years. The government's push for more gas utilisation and the ban on flaring triggered project plans. The primary financing (both equity and debt) and development arrangements were concluded between 1988 and 1990–1992.[45] Equity financing accounted for about 35 per cent, while debt financing for MPN was provided by the International Finance Corporation (IFC), the

42 See also Bayo Adaralegbe, 'Stabilizing Fiscal Regimes in Long-Term Contracts: Recent Developments from Nigeria', (2008) 1(3) *Journal of World Energy Law & Business* 239–246.

43 See the International Gas Union (IGU), *IGU World LNG Report – 2017 Edition* (IGU Publications 2018) 1–94, 9.

44 Oyewunmi (n6) 43; Hakim Darbouche, *Issues in the Pricing of Domestic and Internationally-Traded Gas in MENA and Sub-Saharan Africa* 1–37 (OIES, NG 64, June 2012).

45 Omorogbe (n6).

US Exim Bank and commercial banks. Loans to the NNPC were from the World Bank, the IFC, international Export-Import banks and financial institutions.[46] The Federal Government also promulgated the Oso Condensate Project Decree No. 15 of 1990, which enabled the NNPC to borrow money in any currency for the project, as well as to pledge any of the money, revenue and assets received by it for the project.[47] The NNPC also had the power to create escrow accounts outside Nigeria from which the capital and interest on money earned for the project shall be paid. Thus, the decree arguably ensured that payments due to the project creditors are not delayed or otherwise hampered because of any inefficiencies in the Nigerian legal and administrative framework.

2.3 The WAGP and energy supply in Ghana

At about the same time as the NLNG project was gaining traction, from the late 1990s to 2000s, the WAGP project was being consolidated with the aim of (i) improving the competitiveness of the energy sectors in Ghana, Benin and Togo through the supply of "cheaper" and more "environmentally-friendly" gas from Nigeria; (ii) diversifying energy sources in the importing countries and replacing solid and liquid fuels used for power generation, industrial and commercial purposes; and (iii) fostering regional economic growth and political integration by supporting the West African electricity market.[48]Article II.1(3) of the WAGP Treaty provides that, as defined in the International Project Agreement (IPA),[49] the WAGP shall be a high-pressure gas pipeline, with associated compression and metering stations, interconnection points and laterals to Cotonou (Benin), Lomé (Togo) and Tema (Ghana), together with such extensions and expansions as the state parties shall from time to time agree, connecting the outlet point of the ELPS in Nigeria to Takoradi in western Ghana and transiting through the territorial waters of the states. Article II.2 makes the WAGP an open access transporter as contemplated under the IPA. The 678 kilometre-long pipeline terminates at Ghana's Takoradi Power Stations, with the possibility of being extended to other West African countries such as the Côte d'Ivoire.

The WAPG Authority was established under Article III of the WAPG Treaty as an international institution having legal personality and financial autonomy recognised in each state party. It is empowered, *inter alia,* to (i) monitor compliance with obligations under the IPA, (ii) facilitate the grant, renewal or extension of project authorisations, (iii) negotiate and conclude pipeline development plans, the terms of amendments to the conditions on which pipeline licenses are granted, as well as agree with the pipeline company on the terms of the access code in accordance with the IPA. The authority does not set tariffs, as these are regulated by contract and the pipeline access code.

The transactional and regulatory aspects of the project comprised:

1. contracts for the design, engineering, construction, ownership, operation and maintenance, oversight, political risk mitigation and guarantees;

46 Ibid; World Bank, 'Nigeria – Oso Condensate Field Development Project' (World Bank, Wahington, DC, 1991) (accessed 23.9.2015).

47 Ibid.

48 The World Bank, 'West African Gas Pipeline Project: Implementation Completion Report Review' (World Bank Group, No. ICRR14706, Washington, DC, 2005) 1–10; WAGP Treaty.

49 An IPA was executed between the pipeline company and operator, West African Gas Pipeline Company Limited (WAPCo) and the state parties.

2. contracts for
   (i) the purchase of gas from the upstream producers in Nigeria, i.e., the NNPC-Shell JV and NNPC-Chevron JV;
   (ii) gas transportation and sales to designated power utilities;
   (iii) environmental assessments and resettlement action plans.[50]

The following corporate entities were entrusted with the implementation of the project:

- West African Gas Pipeline Company Limited (WAPCo), the pipeline project company owned by Chevron (36.9 per cent), NNPC (24.9 per cent), Shell (17.9 per cent), Takoradi Power Company Limited (16.3 per cent), Société Togolaise de Gaz (2 per cent) and Société BenGaz (2 per cent). It was established to build, own, operate and transport gas through the WAGP system.
- N-Gas Limited, comprising of NNPC (62.35 per cent), Chevron (20 per cent) and Shell (17.65 per cent). The company arranges for the purchase of gas from the producers under long-term GSPAs, which will be transported by NGC and WAPCo, and sold to Ghana's Volta River Authority (VRA)[51] and Communauté Electrique du Bénin (CEB)[52] also on a long-term basis, i.e., 20-year term;
- The NGC, which, as NNPC's gas transmission and marketing subsidiary, is contracted by N-Gas to transport gas from the upstream sources via the ELPS to a terminal near Lagos, thereafter taken up by WAPCo into the WAGP system.

The principal project agreements comprise:

1. the IPA between the four states and WAPCo, providing for the development, financing, construction, ownership and operation of the WAGP by WAPCo;
2. the Takoradi GSA between VRA and N-Gas, providing for the sale by N-Gas and purchase by VRA of up to 120 million standard cubic feet per day (MMscf/day) of gas on a ToP and ship-or-pay basis;
3. the Takoradi GTA between WAPCo and N-Gas for the gas being sold by N-Gas under the Takoradi GSA;
4. the VRA Direct Agreement between VRA, WAPCo and N-Gas whereby N-Gas assigns to WAPCo (as security for N-Gas's payment obligations to WAPCo under the Takoradi GTA) the component of the VRA termination payment and arrears owing to N-Gas under the Takoradi GSA corresponding to the same component payable to WAPCo by N-Gas under the Takoradi GTA;
5. the Government Consent and Support Agreement (GCSA) under which Ghana, in compliance with its undertaking under the IPA, irrevocably and unconditionally guarantees to N-Gas and WAPCo the performance obligations of VRA under the Takoradi GSA and the VRA Direct Agreement.

50 The World Bank, *IDA Provides an Innovative Partial Risk Guarantee in Support of the West African Gas Pipeline Project (English). Project Finance and Guarantees Notes* (World Bank Group, No. 35903, Washington, DC, 2005) at <http://documents.worldbank.org/curated/en/746201468203977304/IDA-provides-an-innovative-partial-risk-guarantee-in-support-of-the-West-African-Gas-Pipeline-Project> (accessed 13.12.2018).

51 The VRA is Ghana's state-owned power generation corporation.

52 The CEB is an international corporation co-owned by the governments of Bénin and Togo, responsible for developing electricity infrastructure in both countries which are heavily dependent on energy imports from Ghana.

The reliability of supply from Nigeria on a ship-or-pay basis and the capacity of the foundational buyers to take-and-pay for delivered gas are critical to the project, mainly because the VRA and CEB were expected to underwrite the costs of the pipeline system, backed by government guarantees and international project financing arrangements.[53] The initial US$590 million cost was designed to be financed through direct equity and shareholder loans to WAPCo, whereas subsequent expenditures are expected to be funded by cash flow from transport operations. As in a typical long-term supply project with a long pay-back period, WAPCo is expected to recover its investments through gas transportation charges under its GTA with N-Gas and other future shippers; while the NGC recovers any operational and maintenance expenses through transportation charges under its GTAs with N-Gas. The upstream producers will also recover any project related costs (e.g., upgrading and installing gas gathering systems and treatment facilities upstream of ELPS) through gas sales under GSAs with N-Gas or any other entity that ships gas through WAGP.[54]

Later on, the project design and contractual framework will be rigorously tested to the extent that it would not take due cognisance of exogenous risk factors and supply-side risks from Nigeria. The project sponsors appear to have focused more on guaranteeing and mitigating the demand-side risks from Ghana. The actual total cost of pipeline commissioning became higher than estimated. There were construction delays, pipeline ruptures and sabotage and some operational challenges, thus the deliveries scheduled for 2006 eventually commenced with interruptible gas supplies starting in late 2008. It is noted that not all the receiving stations or the compressor station in Nigeria were operational when the pipeline was completed. The actual start date, when the contractual commitments were triggered, was not achieved until November 2011.[55] Also, connections to power plants in Benin, Togo were only completed at the end of 2013. Unfortunately, the period between 2009 and 2012 was notorious for vandalism and sabotage by miscreants in the Nigerian Niger Delta area, which happens to be the primary source of feed-in gas.[56] A ship's anchor ruptured the pipeline off the coast of Togo in 2012.[57] During the same timeframe, Nigeria was also intensifying efforts to increase gas supply to domestic uses with structural reforms and policies such as the Nigerian Gas Master Plan 2008 which required upstream producers to comply with domestic gas supply obligations.[58] These complex issues meant that supply contracts were implemented under *force majeure* effectively after the start date of 2011. Arguably, the current Nigerian government has been better able to address the insecurity issues in the Niger Delta compared to previous administrations.

Regarding commercial risks, it is noted that between 2014 and 2016, the VRA stopped paying for the gas delivered due to downstream liquidity and financial issues in Ghana's electricity market. Reportedly, the VRA was not receiving payment from the local electricity distributors, who in turn were not being paid by most of their customers, principally the Government of Ghana.[59] According to the World Bank's project Implementation Completion Review (ICR), the Partial Risk Guarantee (PRG) framework did not adequately

53 Ibid.

54 Ibid.

55 Fulwood and Thierry Bros (n5).

56 See the US Energy Information Administration (EIA), *Nigeria Country Analysis* (2016) at <www.eia.gov/beta/international/analysis.php?iso=NGA> accessed (21.09.2018).

57 Ibid.

58 Oyewunmi (n6) 117, 148–149; Oyewunmi (n18).

59 Fulwood and Thierry Bros (n5).

incorporate the implications of parallel developments such as the potentials for domestic gas production in Ghana and ongoing sector reforms and policy initiatives in Nigeria.[60] Also, perhaps due to the socio-political complexities and the limited development of the gas market in the consuming countries, the governing institutions have not been able to make any significant strides in finding a solution to the *force majeure* issue. Such resolutions and conciliation processes would be better managed by or through the WAGP Authority.

Generally, a host government's multifaceted participation in both cross-border and domestic supply arrangements comes with considerable political risks, e.g., because of changes in the governing administration and political dispositions or difficulties in government-owned utilities such as the VRA meeting contractual obligations. Thus, the World Bank system makes available partial political-risk guarantees to cover payments owed by the government, e.g., due to termination of the Takoradi GSA with VRA. The private sector participants take up the construction- and operations-related risks, while the public sector takes up the payment risks under the GSAs, which are on a ToP basis. *Force majeure* events are shared among the parties; however, a default by the upstream producers in delivering gas in Nigeria should result in the payment of liquidated damages to the foundation customers, but only in the case of default due to negligence rather than sabotage or accidents.

2.3.1 Production and supply from Ghana

Recent discoveries of gas offshore from Ghana include the Jubilee and TEN fields with about 490 billion cubic feet (Bcf) and 363 Bcf of associated gas reserves respectively, and the Sankofa field with non-associated gas reserves of approximately 1,107 Bcf. Thus, one could contend that Ghana's energy supply security and reliability challenges can now be reasonably addressed to the extent that the production and commercialisation of the domestic resources are guaranteed. This, however, depends on adequate investment, building new gas infrastructure and the effectiveness of the institutional and regulatory framework for domestic gas-to-power vis-à-vis imports through the WAGP and LNG sources. Upstream operations following petroleum agreements between GNPC and IOCs led to the discovery of oil in 2007 and domestic gas production in 2014 when the pipeline and processing plant necessary to commercialise the associated gas was commissioned to supply power plants in the Takoradi area.[61]

Operators of the TEN concession began production of gas in 2016, and the Sankofa Field project began supplies to the Takoradi area in 2018 with a 63-kilometre submarine pipeline transporting gas to onshore receiving facilities where it is processed and transmitted downstream. The Takoradi offtake point on the WAGP is being reconfigured as an entry point to allow the delivery of domestic offshore gas supplies from Takoradi in the west to augment unreliable supplies in the Tema area in the east, where most of the supplies from Nigeria are delivered. The Sankofa project is expected to deliver 180 mmscfd, split between the Takoradi and Tema power plants with a GSA between Eni/Vitol and GNPC for an estimated

60 The World Bank, 'West African Gas Pipeline Project: Implementation Completion Report Review' (World Bank Group, No. ICRR14706, Washington, DC, posted 13 April 2015).

61 Fulwood and Thierry Bros (n5) supra; Ghana Ministry of Petroleum, *Gas Master Plan* (July 2016) 1–246 at <https://www.thegasconsortium.com/documents/GMP-Final-Jun16.pdf> (accessed 21.09.2018).

19-year period, including a ToP provision which requires GNPC to pay for 90 per cent of the agreed quantity of gas.[62]

The most pressing challenges for the viability of the domestic gas-to-power market include:

(i) the VRA's financial difficulties and under-investment in power generation attributable to unreliability in gas imports leading to the use of more expensive light crude oil for thermal power generation, as well as non-cost-reflective electricity tariffs;
(ii) the state-owned wholesale electricity purchasers, i.e., the Electricity Company of Ghana and the Northern Electricity Distribution Company, are also facing significant liquidity difficulties and poor creditworthiness as power offtakers;
(iii) high technical and non-technical losses and arrears from public sector consumers as with most developing economies in the region.[63]

It is worth noting that the wholesale gas market in Ghana is currently based on bilateral contracts between Nigerian gas suppliers and VRA, although there are steps being taken towards sectorial reforms and a new pricing policy for natural gas to enhance competitiveness.

2.3.1.1 LNG OPTIONS FOR GHANA

On the one hand, the Sankofa project is expected to be in production for almost two decades, whereas it is anticipated that other fields currently in operation in Ghana will decline rapidly after 2020.[64] On the other hand, the emerging legal, political and economic issues may continue to make WAGP supplies less reliable than agreed and performance enforcement could remain equally complicated in reality. As a result, Ghana has been looking into LNG imports to meet its medium- to long-term energy demand as the domestic market grows. Notably, the Government of Ghana signed a Memorandum of Understanding (MoU) with Equatorial Guinea in August 2017 for about 150 mmscfd of natural gas in LNG supplies to Ghana. The MoU also provides for the building and operation of a LNG regasification terminal in Takoradi.

Additionally, in September 2017, Russia's Gazprom signed a GSA with the GNPC due to commence from 2019 for an initial period of 12 years, providing a second potential source of long-term LNG.[65] However, it appears that because of the current market development and institutional issues highlighted earlier, the LNG and FSRU options have not been successful. The notable projects experienced significant delays or were mothballed in this regard. The Tema LNG project, which includes a FSRU facility to receive, store, regasify LNG and

62 Ibid; The World Bank, 'Ghana – Sankofa Gas Project' (World Bank Group Report 96554, Washington, DC, 2015) 1–114.

63 Ghana Ministry of Petroleum (n.61), Thierry Bros, 'Can Small LNG Meet the Challenge of Empowering Africa?' in *Oxford Energy Forum, Issue 110, Searching for Natural Gas Demand in the Next Decade*, (Oxford Institute for Energy Studies, August 2017) 16–17; Poudinch and Oyewunmi (n3).

64 The Sankofa Gas Project – World Bank Group Report (n62).

65 Fulwood and Bros (n5). see also African Center for Energy Policy (ACEP), 'ACEP Urges Gov't to Suspend Tema LNG Project … over Fears of US$820m Liability to GNPC, 9 December 2019 at <https://thebftonline.com/2019/editors-pick/acep-urges-govt-to-suspend-tema-lng-project-over-fears-of-us820m-liability-to-gnpc> (accessed 01.24.2020)..

deliver gas on a build-own-operate-transfer basis, with the assets transferring to the GNPC after the project's 20-year term. The West African Gas Limited (owned by Nigeria's NNPC (60 per cent) and Sahara Energy (40 per cent)), signed a five-year contract with Golar for a FSRU to be moored inside the port of Tema, Ghana. Even though a 10-year GSA with the Ghanaian Government was approved in October 2016, the project was stalled, and the Golar Tundra FSRU has since left Ghana.[66]

3 Conclusion

For the developing economies in West Africa, the issues bordering on energy affordability are not merely a function of pricing, access or availability of gas upstream, but the integrity of pipeline and supply infrastructure, as well as liquidity and creditworthiness of the electricity market and electricity end-users. Intentions to enter into legal relations by relevant parties to the underpinning international and domestic arrangements are often not enough. Property rights and agreements need to remain valid and enforceable, while projects should be practically feasible throughout their life-cycle and typically long-term duration. Although project financing and due diligence by private sector stakeholders are essential factors; provisions of government-backed assurances, guarantees and institutional support are clearly fundamental to securing FIDs and project execution as seen in the case of the NLNG, the WAGP and others highlighted above. Although, such guarantees, promises, agreements and assurances must also be enforceable, valid and not defective *ab initio* to avoid the sort of controversies that arose with the NLNG project or the more recent PIDL case. As seen in the cross-border WAGP project scenario, the handling of both demand-side and supply-side risks through the legal and contractual framework proved crucial to realising the project's objectives. In particular, having reliable supplies from upstream gas sources on a ship-or-pay basis remains equally important as the capacity of the offtakers in the power sector to take-and-pay for delivered gas.

66 Ibid.

29

LEGAL, POLICY AND REGULATORY ASPECTS OF INTEGRATING ELECTRICITY FROM RENEWABLE ENERGY IN SUB-SAHARAN AFRICA

The case of Ghana, The Gambia and Nigeria

Nana Asare Obeng-Darko

1 Introduction

In 2015, the international community agreed on a set of 17 global developmental goals—Sustainable Development Goals (SDGs)—that are to be achieved by 2030.[1] Energy and, particularly, access to modern energy services such as electricity is vital to the sustainable development—economic, social and environmental development—of nations. SDG 7 has the aim to 'ensure access to affordable, reliable, sustainable and modern energy for all'.[2] Quintessential to realising this goal is the appeal to significantly increase the share of renewable energy (RE) in the global energy mix. This relies upon expanding and upgrading the technology and infrastructure used to supply modern and sustainable energy services in developing countries in order that they may develop universal supply in accordance with their respective programmes of support.[3]

The sub-Saharan Africa region[4] has the fastest growing young population in the world.[5] It is both economically and culturally diverse with an enormous potential for rapid economic growth. Economic growth needs an uninterrupted supply of energy to drive it. The unfortunate situation is that sub Saharan Africa currently lacks adequate energy for its economic expansion. Representing 14 per cent of the world's population, the region only accounts

1 UNGA Res 70/1 (21 October 2015) UN Doc A/RES/70/1 2015.

2 ibid.

3 ibid 19.

4 The sub-Saharan Africa region comprises all countries totally or partially geographically located south of the Sahara Desert in Africa. For a list of countries found in this region, see UNDP, 'About Africa' (UNDP in Africa) <www.africa.undp.org/content/rba/en/home/regioninfo.html> accessed 11 March 2019.

5 African Development Bank, Organisation for Economic Co-operation and Development and United Nations Development Programme, *African Economic Outlook 2016 Sustainable Cities and Structural Transformation: Sustainable Cities and Structural Transformation* (OECD Publishing 2016) 5.

for about 4 per cent of energy investment globally.[6] The percentage of people without electricity access in sub-Saharan Africa currently stands at 57 per cent.[7] This is a relatively high percentage compared to 3 per cent both in Latin America and the Middle East and to 11 per cent in Southeast Asia.[8] While sub-Saharan Africa has a substantial rate of lack of electricity access, there is a considerable abundance of renewable energy sources such as solar, hydro and biomass in the region which, if effectively tapped into, would generate adequate power to drive sustainable development in the region. This means that a lot has to been done by way of law, policy and implementable actions if sub-Saharan Africa is to ensure access to affordable, reliable, sustainable and modern energy for all.

Access to electricity is crucial to attaining most of the goals of the 2030 Agenda.[9] Electricity access is also necessary to improve human development and promote social inclusion of everyone in all societies. In its new policy scenario, the International Energy Agency (IEA) in 2017 projected that over 60 per cent of those who will gain access to electricity by 2030 will have done so through generation from renewable energy sources, mainly solar and hydro.[10]

The purpose of this chapter is to examine the legal, policy and regulatory issues affecting the integration of renewable energy sources into the electricity generation mix in sub-Saharan Africa by assessing the cases of Ghana, The Gambia and Nigeria. While not claiming to cover every issue impeding renewable electricity integration in sub-Saharan Africa, key legal, regulatory and policy issues assessed in this chapter seek to serve as bedrock research upon which further future research can be based to fully explore impeding factors to achieving renewable energy targets in sub-Saharan Africa and the ways to overcome those impediments. Following this introduction, this chapter analyses the legal and policy issues on renewable energy integration in selected case study countries. Section 2 begins with the identification of renewable energy policy targets for Ghana and proceeds to examine the policy and legal barriers to achieving the renewable energy targets. Sections 3 and 4 also examine policy and legal issues to achieving set renewable energy integration goals in The Gambia and Nigeria respectively. Conclusions are drawn in Section 5.

6 Subhes C Bhattacharyya, 'Financing Energy Access and Off-Grid Electrification: A Review of Status, Options and Challenges' (2013) 20 *Renewable and Sustainable Energy Reviews* 462, 464; International Energy Agency, 'Energy Access Outlook 2017: From Poverty to Prosperity' (International Energy Agency 2017) World Energy Outlook Special Report 76 <https://www.iea.org/publications/freepublications/publication/WEO2017SpecialReport_EnergyAccessOutlook.pdf> accessed 13 February 2018; Angus McCrone et al., 'Global Trends in Renewable Energy Investment 2017' (Frankfurt School-UNEP Centre/BNEF 2017) Global Trends Reports 23 <http://fs-unep-centre.org/sites/default/files/publications/globaltrendsinrenewableenergyinvestment2016lowres_0.pdf> accessed 3 October 2017.

7 Shonali Pachauri et al., 'Access to Modern Energy: Assessment and Outlook for Developing and Emerging Regions' (International Institute for Applied Systems Analysis (IIASA) 2012) 13 <www.iiasa.ac.at/web/home/research/researchPrograms/Energy/IIASA-GEF-UNIDO_Access-to-Modern-Energy_2013-05-27.pdf> accessed 10 November 2016; IEA (n 6) 75; Dayann Obeng-Darko, 'Renewable Energy and Goal Seven of the Sustainable Development Goals: A Perspective from the Ghanaian Renewable Energy Law and Policy' (2017) 35 *International Energy Law Review* 122, 122.

8 IEA (n 6) 42.

9 International Council for Science, 'A Guide to SDG Interactions: From Science to Implementation' (International Council for Science (ICSU) 2017) 130 <www.icsu.org/publications/a-guide-to-sdg-interactions-from-science-to-implementation> accessed 20 November 2018.

10 IEA (n 6) 39.

2 Ghana

Ghana, like most countries in sub-Saharan Africa is amply endowed with renewable energy resources such as biomass, hydro and solar[11] that could potentially produce enough electricity, yet nearly 16 per cent of the country's population is without access to electricity.[12] Even though Ghana enjoys a relatively high electrification rate (84 per cent) in sub-Saharan Africa, it would be able to improve its electricity supply if it could more effectively tap into its renewable energy potential to generate electricity.[13]

The Government of Ghana aims to boost electricity generation to ensure security of electricity supply in the country by tapping into the nation's renewable energy potentials. In its efforts to develop the nation's renewable energy resources for efficient utilisation and production of electricity through legislation, the Ghanaian Government has enacted a law, called the *Renewable Energy Act 2011* (hereinafter RE Act 2011).[14] The RE Act 2011 primarily sets the legal and regulatory framework within which renewable energy targets are to be achieved. In addition to the RE Act 2011, the Ghanaian Government has also adopted two key energy policy documents that contain the renewable energy policy aims as envisioned by the government. These two key policy documents are the Strategic National Energy Plan (SNEP) 2006–2020[15] and the National Energy Policy (NEP) 2010.[16]

2.1 The Ghanaian Renewable Energy Act

The primary objective of the RE Act 2011 is 'to provide for the development, management and utilisation of renewable energy sources for the production of heat and power in an efficient and environmentally sustainable manner'.[17] Among other provisions, the government aims to achieve this objective by promoting public education on renewable energy production and utilisation, creating an enabling environment to attract investment, improving access to electricity using renewable energy sources and regulating the production and supply of wood-fuel and biofuel.[18] The Ghanaian Government also wishes to diversify energy supplies to ensure energy security and the renewable energy sources supported under these objectives include wind, solar, hydro, biomass, biofuel, landfill gas, sewage gas, geothermal energy, ocean energy and any other energy sources to be designated in writing by the Minister for Energy and Petroleum.[19]

11 International Renewable Energy Agency (IRENA), 'Ghana Renewables Readiness Assessment' (IRENA RRA Ghana, 2015) <www.irena.org/DocumentDownloads/Publications/IRENA_RRA_Ghana_Nov_2015.pdf> accessed 1 October 2016; Antonio Castellano et al., 'Powering Africa | McKinsey & Company' <www.mckinsey.com/industries/electric-power-and-natural-gas/our-insights/powering-africa> accessed 1 October 2016.

12 IEA (n 6) 83.

13 Nana Asare Obeng-Darko, 'Renewable Energy and Power: A Review of the Power Sector Reform and Renewable Energy Law and Policy Nexus in Ghana' (2018) 11 *Africa Review* 17, 28.

14 Renewable Energy Act, 2011 (Act 832) of the Parliament of the Republic of Ghana 2011 (RE Act 832).

15 Energy Commission, 'Strategic National Energy Plan (SNEP) 2006–2020, Main Report' (2006) <www.energycom.gov.gh/files/snep/MAIN%20REPORT%20final%20PD.pdf> accessed 13 June 2016.

16 Ministry of Energy, 'National Energy Policy (NEP) 2010' (2010) <www.ecowrex.org/system/files/repository/2010_national-energy-policy_ministry-of-energy.pdf> accessed 13 June 2016.

17 Renewable Energy Act, 2011 (Act 832) of the Parliament of the Republic of Ghana s 1(1).

18 ibid 1(2).

19 ibid 2.

2.2 Strategic National Energy Plan (SNEP) 2006–2020

The SNEP 2006–2020 was the first policy instrument that included in detail the plans that the Ghanaian Government had regarding the exploitation and the utilisation of renewable energy sources to produce electricity. In the SNEP, the Government of Ghana set a clear target it wants to achieve regarding the utilisation of the country's renewable resources for its energy needs. The target for renewable energy development for electricity production is thus to 'accelerate the development and utilization of renewable energy and energy efficiency technologies so as to achieve 10 percent penetration of national electricity by 2020'.[20] The situation currently is that, as of December 2018, Ghana has only been able to achieve a 0.2 per cent integration rate of electricity from renewable energy sources in its total generation mix.[21]

2.3 National Energy Policy 2010

The NEP is an interim update to the SNEP, which reaffirms the Ghanaian Government's target for renewable energy development in the nation. In this policy instrument, the government aims to increase the share of renewable energy, particularly solar, wind, mini hydro[22] and waste-to-energy, in the total national energy mix and ensure its efficient production and use.[23] Through developing its renewable energy potential for electricity production, the Ghanaian Government further aims to contribute to the mitigation of climate change.[24]

2.4 Legal, regulatory and policy issues

The Ghanaian RE Act 2011,[25] creating the legal environment for achieving renewable energy targets, also prescribes the regulators of the renewable energy sector the specific functions and regulatory measures to be adopted to give effect to the object of the law. There are, however, key issues in the legal, regulatory and policy frameworks, which, if not addressed, will hinder the effective regulation of the Ghanaian renewable sector in achieving sector objectives. These key issues will be discussed below.

2.4.1 Definitional issues

The legal definition for hydro in the RE law concerning renewable energy may pose an impediment to achieving the renewable energy penetration target in Ghana. 'Hydro' as a renewable energy source is defined in the RE Act 2011 as 'a water-based energy system which produces electricity with generation capacity not exceeding one hundred megawatts'.[26] In terms of electricity production, hydro is the biggest single source in Ghana. Ghana gener-

20 Energy Commission, 'SNEP 2006–2020' (n 15) 31.

21 Energy Commission, '2019 Energy (Supply and Demand) Outlook for Ghana' (Energy Commission on Ghana 2019) 1 <www.energycom.gov.gh/planning/data-center/energy-outlook-for-ghana#> accessed 13 November 2019.

22 Mini hydro in the Ghanaian context refers to a hydropower project with generating capacity of less than 1 megawatt (MW).

23 Ministry of Energy (n 16) 6.

24 ibid 17.

25 Renewable Energy Act, 2011 (Act 832) of the Parliament of the Republic of Ghana.

26 ibid 51.

ates 1,580 MW, representing 35.9 per cent of its power generation, from three hydro power plants; with Akosombo generating 1,020 MW, Bui 400 MW and Kpong 160 MW respectively.[27] These hydro power plants do not constitute electricity generators from renewable energy sources as a result of the legal definition in the RE Act 2011. If the definition for hydro in the RE Act 2011 were to include all hydro sources, Ghana would have far exceeded its renewable energy target for electricity production.

The narrow legal definition for hydro as a renewable energy source is not an isolated case limited to the Ghanaian context. Other countries with renewable energy legislation also have limited definitions for what constitutes hydro as a renewable energy source in terms of generational capacity. For example, the Danish Promotion for Renewable Energy Act considers any hydropower station of less than 10 MW production capacity to be a renewable energy source.[28] The Czech Republic's RE law also restricts water (hydro) as a renewable energy source to 10 MW generation capacity.[29] Another example is the Spanish law (Royal Decree 661/2007), where hydroelectric plants with less than 10 MW of capacity are considered sources of renewable energy.[30] However, there are some countries that do not restrict the capacity of the plant in the legal definition for hydro as a renewable energy source. The Gambian Renewable Energy Act of 2013, for example, defines hydropower broadly as including all hydro-based energy systems.[31] While it is not clear why Ghana opted for the restrictive definition for hydropower in its renewable energy law, a reason to justify such an approach could be to reduce the ecological impacts generally associated with large hydro generation plants (dams) such as destruction of fish life and biodiversity in water bodies.[32]

2.4.2 Risk of regulatory failure

The RE Act 2011 identifies certain regulators to perform key functions in the regulation of the Ghanaian renewable energy sector. These regulatory agencies are the Minister (responsible for energy), the Energy Commission and the Public Utilities Regulatory Commission (PURC). The Minister is tasked with the duty of providing policy direction for achieving the integration targets.[33] The Energy Commission is responsible for the technical regulation of the renewable energy sources utilisation and development. To fulfil its role, the Energy Commission is tasked with advising the Minister on renewable energy matters and creating a platform for the collaboration between the government, private sector and civil society for the promotion of renewables.[34] The PURC is responsible for economic regulation in the

27 Energy Commission, '2018 Energy (Supply and Demand) Outlook for Ghana' (April 2018) 1 <www.energycom.gov.gh/planning/data-center/energy-outlook-for-ghana?Download=76:energy-outlook-for-ghana-2018> accessed 20 September 2018.

28 Promotion of Renewable Energy Act, Act No. 1392 of 27 December 2008 s 50(6) (unofficial translation).

29 ACT No. 165 of 31 January 2012 on Promoted Energy Sources and Amendment to Some Laws of the Czech Republic.

30 Real Decreto 661/2007, de 25 de mayo, por el que se regula la actividad de producción de energía eléctrica en régimen especial.

31 Renewable Energy Act 2013 of the Republic of The Gambia, 12 December 2013.

32 See, e.g., David Anderson et al., 'The Impacts of "Run-of-River" Hydropower on the Physical and Ecological Condition of Rivers' (2015) 29 *Water and Environment Journal* 268; Lluís Benejam et al., 'Ecological Impacts of Small Hydropower Plants on Headwater Stream Fish: From Individual to Community Effects' (2016) 25 *Ecology of Freshwater Fish* 295.

33 Renewable Energy Act, 2011 (Act 832) of the Parliament of the Republic of Ghana s 3.

34 ibid 4.

renewable energy sector. For its implementation purposes, the RE Act 2011 requires the PURC to approve the rates chargeable for the purchase of electricity from renewable energy sources by public utilities and approve charges for grid connection.[35] There are, however, regulatory risk factors such as regulation inaction and independence issues, which threaten the effective governance of the Ghanaian renewable sector if not properly addressed.

2.4.2.1 REGULATORY INACTION

In the legal framework for the Ghanaian renewable energy sector, the RE Act 2011 obliges the various regulatory bodies to regulate the sector by means of legislative instruments. None of the regulators have so far issued any legislative instrument on any aspect of regulating the sector as required in the RE Act 2011. Legislative instruments for regulating prescribed fees and charges, conditions of licences, schemes for trading and extinguishing renewable energy certificates and, critically, the legislative instrument for regulating the provision of financial and other incentives necessary for development, production and utilisation of renewable energy sources in Ghana have not yet been instituted. No reason has been given by any of the responsible agencies as to why the required legislative instruments necessary for the effective regulation of the Ghanaian renewable energy sector have not been initiated. The pervasive lack of legislative instruments suggests regulatory weakness in the institutional structure in the renewable energy sector in the country.

Besides the issue of the lack of legislative instruments in the regulatory framework, there is also the problem of determining the required 'specified percentage' of renewable electricity as demanded by the law. It currently appears that regulation of the Ghanaian renewable energy sector is ineffective. Under the 'requirements for electricity generation' title in the RE Act 2011, a renewable energy purchase obligation (REPO) has been established that obliges a distribution system operator (DSO) to purchase a percentage of its total purchase of electricity from renewable energy sources or, as an alternative, pay a premium to the Energy Commission as determined by the Commission.[36] The PURC and the Energy Commission, which are the two agencies responsible for establishing the 'specified percentage', have not yet determined the 'specified percentage' level of electricity to be purchased by the DSOs from renewable electricity producers as required by the law.[37] The result of this situation is that DSOs cannot be held liable for failing to purchase a portion of electricity from renewable energy sources or even be obliged to do so since the REPO requirements under the RE law is currently ineffective due to the non-performance of regulators.

2.4.2.2 ISSUES ABOUT THE INDEPENDENCE OF THE RENEWABLE ENERGY AUTHORITIES

Section 53 of the RE Act 2011 dictates that an independent renewable energy authority shall be established by an Act of the Ghanaian Parliament. This independent agency will be

35 ibid 5.

36 ibid 26(4)(a)–(b).

37 Dayann Obeng-Darko, 'Regulatory Rationale and Theoretical Approaches: Ghana's Renewable Energy Law and Policy Perspective' (2018) 16 *Oil, Gas & Energy Law Journal* (*OGEL*) 15 <https://www.ogel.org/article.asp?key=3725> accessed 8 February 2018; Energy Commission, '2017 Energy (Supply and Demand) Outlook for Ghana' (April 2017) 51 <www.energycom.gov.gh/data-center/energy-outlook-for-ghana?download=31:energy-outlook-for-ghana-2017> accessed 10 November 2017.

known as the Renewable Energy Authority (RE Authority) when it comes into existence. The RE Authority, according to the law, shall be the regulator whose sole purpose will be the implementation of renewable energy policies and regulatory measures in the sector. The RE Authority shall be responsible for governing the implementation of renewable energy activities in the country, implementing renewable energy projects initiated by the State or in which the State has an interest and overseeing the assets in the renewable energy sector on behalf of the State.[38]

The current issue in the institutional framework in the Ghanaian renewable energy sector is that it does not have an independent renewable energy regulator as the law intended on the adoption of the RE Act in 2011. It is not apparent why the Ghanaian Government has not yet established the RE Authority. This is at odds with the government's own vision to show credibility in the institutional structure regulating the nation's renewable energy sector and commitment to policy and regulatory objectives in order to attract investment into the sector.[39] The effect of the absence of the RE Authority is that investors may believe that the government is not committed to developing the nation's renewable energy sector. Investors may have little confidence in the government's renewable energy development plan for the country and subsequently underinvest in the renewable energy sector.

If, therefore, commitment and credibility have become the issues that the Ghanaian Government is seeking to overcome, the establishment of a RE Authority independent from political influences will be a major step in the right direction for the nation. Investors in the renewable energy industry who rely on the stability of regulatory regimes and predictability of regulatory agencies will therefore be able to make investment decisions favourable to the development of the nation's renewable energy sector. Indeed, independent regulatory agencies are seen as offering a buffer against fluctuations in the preferences of current and future governments.[40]

2.4.3 Lack of clarity in policy goals

As an energy policy instrument depicting the policy aims for renewable energy, the NEP, which is an interim update to the SNEP, lacks clarity on the reaffirmation of the renewable energy target as it was clearly stated in the SNEP. The renewable energy target as stipulated in the NEP is to increase the share of renewable energy, particularly solar, wind, mini hydro and waste-to-energy, in the total national energy mix and ensure its efficient production and use.

Whereas the Ghanaian government in the SNEP had set a specific timeframe within which the target for renewable energy is to be achieved—from 2006 to 2020—the authorities failed to define a timeframe within which the reaffirmed renewable energy target should be attained in the NEP. This could be interpreted as meaning that the target for renewable energy in the SNEP is not attainable within the set time (i.e., by the end of 2020), and that is why in its updated energy policy document, the NEP, the government failed to set a new or maintained the original timeframe within which it aims to achieve the target.

38 Renewable Energy Act, 2011 (Act 832) of the Parliament of the Republic of Ghana s 53.

39 Dayann Obeng-Darko, 'Regulation of the Renewable Energy Sector and the Proposed Renewable Energy Authority in Ghana: An Examination' (2017) 8 *Renewable Energy Law & Policy Review* 7, 18.

40 Christopher Decker, *Modern Economic Regulation: An Introduction to Theory and Practice* (Cambridge University Press 2015) 191.

This failure on the part of Ghana's authorities in the NEP may indicate to investors that the Ghanaian Government may have changed its mind concerning the policy goals for the renewable energy sector, particularly in respect of the period within which the target is to be achieved.

The policy aims in the NEP are also contradictory. For instance, on the one hand, the Ghanaian Government intends to reduce dependency on wood-fuel and charcoal use for energy consumption due to deforestation and the negative impact on health, particularly indoor air pollution from cooking with charcoal.[41] Yet, on the other hand, it intends to promote the creation of dedicated woodlots for wood-fuel production.[42]

3 The Gambia

The Gambia is the smallest country on mainland Africa. It is situated in West Africa on the Atlantic coast and surrounded by Senegal. The main source of energy supply in The Gambia is biomass (wood-fuel and charcoal). However, the main energy source for electricity production in the country is heavy fuel oil and diesel oil the majority of which is imported into the country.[43] Due to the importation of these energy products for the production of electricity in the country, The Gambia has one of the highest electricity tariffs within the sub-Saharan Africa.[44] Foreign exchange is a major contributory factor to the high electricity tariff; and the country, due to import dependency, is susceptible to price volatility in global oil prices. The electrification rate in The Gambia is estimated at 35 per cent[45] for a population of 2.1 million.

To improve accessibility to electricity and the security of its supply, The Gambia is turning to renewable energy sources to diversify and bolster its energy supply sources for electricity production. Renewable energy represents a tremendous opportunity for The Gambia and the government intends to utilise the country's potential for electricity generation. In this regard, the nation in 2005 adopted a policy instrument—the Energy Policy (2005)—setting the targets for renewable energy integration into the nation's energy mix for electricity production. In 2018, the Gambian Government adopted its National Development Plan (NDP) 2018–2021,[46] which sets the national agenda and goals—including renewable energy targets—to be achieved by the end of 2021. To provide a legal and regulatory environment within which policy goals for renewable energy will be achieved, The Gambian renewable energy law—*Renewable Energy Act 2013* (RE Act 2013) was adopted in 2013.[47]

41 Ministry of Energy (n 16) 7.

42 ibid 20–21.

43 UNDP, 'Sustainable Energy for All: Rapid Assessment and Gap Analysis – The Gambia' (United Nations Development Programme 2012) 15 <https://www.seforall.org/sites/default/files/Gambia_RAGA_EN_Released.pdf> accessed 30 November 2018.

44 ibid 16; IRENA, 'Gambia Renewables Readiness Assessment' (International Renewable Energy Agency 2013) 13 <https://www.irena.org/-/media/Files/IRENA/Agency/Publication/2013/RRA_Gambia.pdf> accessed 30 November 2018.

45 The Gambian Ministry of Finance and Economic Affairs, 'The Gambia National Development Plan (2018–2021)' (2018) 77 <www.thegambiatimes.com/wp-content/uploads/2018/02/1.-The-Gambia-National-Development-Plan-2018-2021-Full-Version.pdf> accessed 3 December 2018; IEA (n 6) 115.

46 The Gambian Ministry of Finance and Economic Affairs (n 45).

47 Renewable Energy Act 2013 of the Republic of The Gambia, 12 December 2013.

3.1 The Gambian renewable energy law

The Gambian *Renewable Energy Act 2013* (RE Act 2013) was passed by the President and National Assembly in December 2013 to set the 'legal, economic and institutional basis to promote the use of renewable energy resources and for connected matters'[48] in a bid to achieve the nation's renewable energy targets. Crucial to the achievement of renewable energy targets, the RE Act 2013 specifically instructs the Ministry (responsible for energy)[49] to 'recommend middle and long-term national targets for the use of renewable energy resources in electricity generation, which may include targets related to geographic location and diversity'.[50] The Ministry is also to 'report annually to the Cabinet on progress towards these targets, including a review of the performance of the incentives provided under this Act'.[51] In addition to the RE Act 2013, the production of electricity for renewable energy sources is promoted in the Electricity Act (2005) of The Gambia.[52] As part of the objectives of The Gambian Electricity Act, Article 3(l) encourages the production of electricity through the use of renewable energy.

3.2 Energy Policy (2005)

The objectives of the Gambian Government concerning the energy sector and the renewable energy sub-sector are contained in the Energy Policy (2005). The primary objective for re newable energy development is to 'ensure the promotion and utilisation of renewable energy in support of sustainable development in the country'.[53] To achieve this overarching aim, the following specific objectives are to be achieved:

- promote the utilisation of renewable forms of energy such as solar, wind and biomass;
- promote the use and develop, to the extent possible, a domestic production capacity for renewable energy fuels and technologies;
- ensure the sustainable supply of renewable energy fuels/devices/technologies at competitive prices through private sector participation.[54]

3.3 The Gambia National Development Plan (NDP) 2018–2021

The goal set by the Gambian Government regarding renewable energy integration in its NDP is to increase the share of renewable energy in total electricity generation from 2 per cent to 40 per cent between 2018 and 2021.[55] According to the NDP, the government aims to achieve this target by the use of appropriate technology, research and development and other efficient measures. Additionally, the Gambian Government aims to improve electricity access in the country, which is currently estimated at 40 per cent,[56] by combining renewable energy with energy efficiency measures to reduce waste and increase energy conservation in the country.[57]

48 ibid 1.
49 The Minister of the Ministry of Petroleum and Energy is responsible for energy matters in The Gambia.
50 Renewable Energy Act 2013 of the Republic of The Gambia, 12 December 2013 s 4(1).
51 ibid 4(2).
52 Electricity Act, 2005 of the Republic of The Gambia 2005 s 3(I).
53 UNDP (n 43) 37.
54 ibid.
55 The Gambian Ministry of Finance and Economic Affairs (n 45) 73.
56 ibid 76.
57 ibid 261.

3.4 Legal, regulatory and policy issues

3.4.1 Lack of regulatory measures

The regulatory agencies responsible for the regulation and implementation of the Renewable Energy Act 2013 are the Ministry of Energy, the Public Utilities Regulatory Authority (PURA) and the National Water and Energy Company (NAWEC).[58] The Ministry is primarily responsible for overseeing the overall implementation of the RE Act 2013. The PURA, serving as the economic regulator, is responsible for formulating feed-in tariff rules and managing the Renewable Energy Fund which is established under Section 5 of the RE Act 2013.[59] Occupying the role of technical regulator, NAWEC is predominantly responsible for determining the safety and technical capability of the grid to connect electricity generated from renewable energy resources.[60]

The Renewable Energy Act 2013 under Section 19 instructs the Minister to make regulations for the implementation of the law, and in Section 20 they are to work closely with the NAWEC on such aspects as pertain to electricity generation. Essential to the instructions in both Sections 19 and 20 is the adoption of the proposed Biomass Strategy[61] by the Minister following the conduct of an impact assessment a year after the RE Act 2013 came into effect. At the time of writing, such a strategy is yet to be adopted. It may be assumed at this point that the impact assessment of the use of biomass for electricity generation is yet to take place. While this is only an assumption, it helps throw light on the low rate of renewable energy integration in the country's electricity generation mix, which currently stands at 1 megawatt (MW), representing about 0.8 per cent of total electricity production.[62] The RE Act 2013 bars projects generating electricity exceeding 1 MW from biomass energy from benefiting from feed-in tariffs or any other incentives until the impact assessment on biomass has been undertaken by the Ministry.[63] This is a serious deterrent to generating electricity from biomass sources to bolster electricity access in the country since project investors whose electricity production from biomass may exceed 1 MW may feel discriminated against and ultimately decide against investing in the renewable energy sector.

It is important to note at this point that the Ministry is yet to make any regulations to give effect to the various provision of the Renewable Energy Act 2013. Unlike the regulatory mechanism in the Ghanaian renewable energy sector where the law defines specific objectives for which legislative instruments are to be adopted in implementing the provisions of the RE Act 2011, this is not the case in the Gambian renewable energy sector. The Ministry of Petroleum and Energy is to make regulations for the implementation of the Act[64] but no specific aims are identified for which regulations are targeted.

58 The National Water and Energy Company is the 'Responsible Network Utility' in the RE Act 2013. In the RE Act 2013, the 'Responsible Network Utility' means the holder of a distribution or transmission licence (as applicable) granted by the Authority under the Electricity Act at the receiving point at which electric energy is delivered directly from a generating facility. The National Water and Energy Company is the only and elected transmission and distribution company for electricity in The Gambia. See The Gambian National Water and Electricity Co. Ltd, 'About NAWEC – NAWEC' <http://nawec.gm/?page_id=171> accessed 4 December 2018.

59 Renewable Energy Act 2013 of the Republic of The Gambia, 12 December 2013 s 3(2).

60 ibid 3(3).

61 ibid 15.

62 See 'Gambia | ECOWAS SE4ALL NETWORK' <www.se4all.ecreee.org/content/gambia> accessed 4 December 2018.

63 Renewable Energy Act 2013 of the Republic of The Gambia, 12 December 2013 s 15(3).

64 ibid 19.

Similar to the Ghanaian context, the issue of ineffectiveness in regulatory performance is a problem in the Gambian case. For instance, the RE Act 2013 instructs the PURA to formulate, with the approval of the Minister for Energy, feed-in tariff rules that shall conform to the conditions stipulated under Section 11(3) of the RE Act 2013 within six months of the law coming into force. Such feed-in tariff rules are yet to be formulated and made accessible. It appears compliance with the provisions of the law is not a regular practice for regulatory agencies in both The Gambia and Ghana.

3.4.2 Weak licencing regime

The Gambian RE Act 2013 provides for a permitting process for the facilities or projects producing electricity from renewable energy sources. The RE Act 2013 contains a title called 'streamlined permitting', which essentially aims to make the application and process of issuing permits to renewable electricity project operators as smooth as possible.[65] Section 16 of the RE Act 2013, for example, instructs the Ministry (of Petroleum and Energy) to issue clear guidelines for application processing[66] and to collaborate with other ministries in simplifying the permitting process regarding such things as the environmental impact on land use and water use.[67] The streamlined permitting title of the RE Act 2013 does not, however, provide qualification standards for obtaining a licence or permit, the conditions under which a permit may be awarded, the duration of a permit, conditions for renewal and, more importantly, the agency responsible for the issuance of permits.

The law only mandates the Ministry, working with other agencies, to issue clear and simple guidelines on the processing of applications but not the power to issue permits. In fact, the RE Act 2013 does not elect or grant the power to award licences to any of the regulatory agencies in the renewable energy sector of The Gambia. This raises the question of issuance of permits by the competent regulatory authority. The Ministry (of Petroleum and Energy) could easily be mistaken to be the agency responsible for issuing permits under the RE Act 2013 given the Ministry's prominent role in the regulation of the sector even though such authority is not expressly dedicated to it. On the contrary, one may argue that the power to issue permits or licences by default lies with the Secretary of State, usually on the advice of the Public Utilities Regulatory Authority as the Secretary of State generally has the power to issue licences under both The Gambia Public Utilities Regulatory Authority Act 2001 and the Electricity Act 2005.

In comparison to the Ghanaian Renewable Energy Act, The Gambian RE Act 2013 lacks depth when it comes to its licencing regime. The Ghanaian RE Act 2011, for example, has provision for the requirement for licences, specifying in detail the qualification, conditions for granting, conditions for the suspension or cancellation, conditions for renewal, the responsible authority and a mechanism for settling disputes.[68] It also lists the commercial activities that are to be engaged by the project operator in the Ghanaian renewable energy sector. These are missing in The Gambian renewable energy law.

65 ibid 16.
66 ibid 16(3).
67 ibid 16(2).
68 Renewable Energy Act, 2011 (Act 832) of the Parliament of the Republic of Ghana.

3.4.3 Overambitious policy goals

It is the aim of the Gambian Government to increase the integration rate of renewable energy into the total electricity generation mix from less than 2 per cent in 2018 to 40 per cent by the end of 2021.[69] While this is a laudable idea, it appears to be an overambitious aim. Due to present technological and technical impediments to uptaking renewable electricity because of outdated grid systems and lack of the substantial financial investment needed to upgrade them,[70] it is highly improbable that an integration rate of 40 per cent can be achieved in the space of three years. According to the Gambian Government, a quarter of grid electricity transmission was lost in 2017[71] through inefficient transmission systems and aged electricity infrastructure, and is expected to increase to 29 per cent in 2018.[72] It is estimated that the country would need about US$2 billion to upgrade ageing electricity infrastructure.[73] It is certainly not impossible to achieve such a feat, but the chances of it being achieved considering all the factors—inefficient regulation, ageing infrastructure, financial and technical constraints—seems unlikely. A modest, yet realistic and achievable target may prove to be a catalyst for attracting investment into the sector. The reason is that, should the Gambian Government fail to deliver a 40 per cent renewable energy integration by 2021 –moving the goalpost as it were, investors may tend to believe that the government is not committed to its renewable energy developmental target for the nation and may be deterred from investing in the renewable energy sector.

4 Nigeria

Nigeria has huge hydrocarbon resources and is a member of the Organization of the Petroleum Exporting Countries (OPEC). The endowment of the primary energy resources (crude oil and natural gas) in Nigeria is such that over half of the country's economy is dependent on crude oil.[74] It accounts for about 70–80 per cent of Nigeria's federal government's revenue and contributes nearly 30 per cent to the country's gross domestic product (GDP).[75] In terms of electricity generation, petroleum (oil and gas) accounts for about 70 per cent of the total generation mix while large hydropower accounts for about 30 per cent.[76] The Nigerian State nevertheless is unable to meet electricity demand due to inadequate supply,[77] and inaccessi-

69 The Gambian Ministry of Finance and Economic Affairs (n 45) 73.

70 See UNDP (n 43) 16; IRENA (n 44) 14.

71 The Gambian Ministry of Finance and Economic Affairs (n 45) 78.

72 World Bank, 'Projects: Gambia Electricity Support Project' <http://projects.worldbank.org/P152659/?lang=en&tab=documents&subTab=projectDocuments> accessed 5 December 2018.

73 AF-MERCADOS EMI, 'Development of an Electricity Strategy and Renewable Energy Law' (AF-Mercados Energy Markets International 2012) 2 <www.euei-pdf.org/sites/default/files/field_publication_file/1312_Gambia_-_Final_Report_v1-0_2012-12-18.pdf> accessed 30 November 2018.

74 Mohamed Shaaban and J O Petinrin, 'Renewable Energy Potentials in Nigeria: Meeting Rural Energy Needs' (2014) 29 *Renewable and Sustainable Energy Reviews* 72, 73.

75 Embassy of Nigeria, Sweden, 'Nigerian Economy' (4 August 2013) <http://nigerianembassy.nu/economy> accessed 13 March 2019; PwC, 'Nigeria Looking beyond Oil Report' (PricewaterhouseCoopers Inc 2016) 7 <https://www.pwc.com/ng/en/assets/pdf/nigeria-looking-beyond-oil-report.pdf> accessed 13 March 2019; Sunday Olayinka Oyedepo, 'On Energy for Sustainable Development in Nigeria' (2012) 16 *Renewable and Sustainable Energy Reviews* 2583, 2584.

76 Abubakar Sadiq Aliyu, Joseph O Dada and Ibrahim Khalil Adam, 'Current Status and Future Prospects of Renewable Energy in Nigeria' (2015) 48 *Renewable and Sustainable Energy Reviews* 336, 338.

77 Udochukwu B Akuru and others, 'Towards 100% Renewable Energy in Nigeria' (2017) 71 *Renewable and Sustainable Energy Reviews* 943, 943; Aliyu, Dada and Adam (n 76) 338.

bility to electricity by a substantial portion of the population continues to plague not only economic growth but social and environmental development as well. Current data shows that the electrification rate in Nigeria stands at 52 per cent.[78]

To ensure security of electricity supply to satisfy all developmental demands, the Nigerian Government thought it prudent to diversify its electricity generation sources. A number of policy instruments have been issued by the government, which set renewable energy targets in the Nigerian economy. Those key policy instruments under consideration are: the National Energy Policy 2003 (NEP), the Nigeria Vision 20:20202 (NV20:2020), which was commissioned in 2009, the Renewable Energy Master Plan 2011 (REMP) and the National Renewable Energy and Energy Efficiency Policy 2015 (NREEEP).

Unlike Ghana and The Gambia, Nigeria does not have specific legislation on renewable energy establishing the both legal and regulatory environment for achieving renewable energy integration targets for the country. What does the absence of a renewable energy law mean for the Nigerian renewable energy integration target? What legal and/or regulatory issues does it pose to achieving the government's renewable energy developmental aims? Answers to these questions will be attempted in Subsection 4.2.

4.1 Policy targets

The Nigerian NEP has several overall policy objectives, but chief among them is the objective to 'ensure the development of the nation's energy resources, with diversified energy resources option, for the achievement of national energy security and an efficient energy delivery system with an optimal energy resource mix'.[79] Regarding the nation's development of its renewable energy sector, the government hopes, among other things, to significantly increase the integration rate of electricity generation from renewable energy sources in the total energy mix and attract private sector investment in the renewable energy sector.[80] The NV20:2020 is a long-term plan for stimulating a sustained and rapid socio-economic growth in Nigeria. In its NV20:2020, the Nigerian Government envisions utilising the nation's renewable energy resources for power generation in a bid to achieve security of power supply.[81]

The REMP is another policy instrument in which the Nigerian Government sets specific renewable energy integration targets and the timeframe within which they hope to achieve the set target. In the REMP, the government aims to increase the supply of electricity generated from renewable energy sources from 13 per cent of total electricity generation in 2015 to 23 per cent in 2025 and 36 per cent by 2030. Renewable electricity would then account for 10 per cent of Nigerian total energy consumption by 2025.[82] The NREEEP is the policy

78 IEA (n 6) 115.

79 Energy Commission of Nigeria, 'National Energy Policy' (April 2013) 8–9 <http://wacee.net/getattachment/21cca4e4-ef1b-4c59-8501-98b3e8624b88/National_Energy_Policy_Nigeria.pdf.aspx> accessed 10 December 2018.

80 ibid 23–34.

81 Nigeria National Planning Commission, 'Nigeria Vision 20:2020' (2009) <www.nationalplanning.gov.ng/images/docs/NationalPlans/nigeria-vision-20-20-20.pdf> accessed 12 October 2018.

82 IEA, 'Nigeria Renewable Energy Master Plan' (2011) <https://www.iea.org/policiesandmeasures/pams/nigeria/name-24808-en.php?s=dHlwZT1yZSZzdGF0dXM9T2s,&return=PG5hdiBpZD0iYnJlYWRjcnVtYiI-PGEgaHJlZj0iLyI-SG9tZTwvYT4gJnJhcXVvOyA8YSBocmVmPSIvcG9saWNpZXNhbmRtZWFzdXJlcy8iPlBvbGljaWVzIGFuZCBNZWFzdXJlczwvYT4gJnJhcXVvOyA8YSBocmVmPSIvcG9saWNpZXNhbmRtZWFzdXJlcy9yZW5ld2FibGVlbmVyZ3kvIj5SZW5ld2FibGUgRW5lcmd5PC9hPjwvbmF2Pg> accessed 11 December 2018.

document that integrates both the renewable energy and energy efficiency aspirations of the Nigerian Government. The NREEEP sets out 'a framework for action to address Nigerians challenge of inclusive access to modern and clean energy resources, improved energy security and climate objectives'.[83] Regarding renewable energy specific targets in the NREEEP, the government hopes to 'ensure the development of the nation's energy resources, including renewables, to achieve of national energy security'.[84] It also aims to guarantee an adequate, reliable, affordable, equitable and sustainable supply of renewable energy at suitable costs and in an environmentally sustainable manner, to the various sectors of the economy, for national development.[85]

4.2 Legal, regulatory and policy issues

As stated earlier, there is no renewable energy legislation in Nigeria. In fact, the only recognition of renewable energy as a viable energy source for electricity in the nation's laws exists in the country's Electric Power Sector Reform Act (Act No. 6 of 2005) (hereinafter, EPSR Act) where 'renewable energy' is mentioned only once in the entire EPSR Act. Article 88(9) (c) of the EPSR Act provides that the Minister (for Power and Works and Housing) is to provide a quarterly progress report on Rural Electrification Strategy and Plan, which shall include information on renewable energy power generation. The EPSR Act does not provide any mechanisms (financial, technical or otherwise) to support renewable development and its integration into the nation's electricity generation mix.[86] The lack of law on renewable energy raises the question of legal issues with renewable energy integration targets. Another issue that presents itself as a consequence of this lack of an existing renewable energy law or act is that of regulatory concerns.

4.2.1 Lack of legal definitions

Laws concerning renewable energy generally provide the legal and regulatory environment for achieving policy targets.[87] As is presently the case in Nigeria, there are no legally defined concepts such as 'renewable energy', 'support schemes', 'hydropower', 'biomass' and 'power purchase agreement' (PPA), which are commonly found in the renewable energy laws of other jurisdictions.[88] Without these legal definitions, it may be quite difficult to determine,

83 Nigeria Ministry of Power, 'National Renewable Energy and Energy Efficiency Policy (NREEEP)' (20 April 2015) xi <www.power.gov.ng/download/NREEE%20POLICY%202015-%20FEC%20APPROVED%20COPY.pdf> accessed 11 December 2018.

84 ibid 9.

85 ibid.

86 Peter Kayode Oniemola, 'Integrating Renewable Energy into Nigeria's Energy Mix through the Law: Lessons from Germany' (2011) 2011 *Renewable Energy Law and Policy Review* 29, 34.

87 Dayann Obeng-Darko, 'Renewable Energy in Ghana and the Lessons from the EU: An Examination of the Regulatory Support Schemes' (2016) 7 *Renewable Energy Law & Policy Review* 46, 53.

88 See, e.g., Renewable Energy Act, 2011 (Act 832) of the Parliament of the Republic of Ghana; Renewable Energy Act 2013 of the Republic of The Gambia, 12 December 2013; Renewable Energy (Electricity) Act 2000 of Australia, Act No. 174 of 2000 2016; Promotion of Renewable Energy Act, Act No. 1392 of 27 December 2008; Directive 2009/28/EC of the European Parliament and of the Council of 23 April 2009 on the promotion of the use of energy from renewable sources and amending and subsequently repealing Directives 2001/77/EC and 2003/30/EC, OJ 5.6.2009 L 140/16. 2009.

for instance, which renewable electricity production projects or aspects of such projects qualify for financial support under 'support schemes' titles.

While the lack of a renewable energy legislation in Nigeria presents the legal problem of defining and interpreting key concepts, it does not necessarily mean that those (or some) concepts do not actually exist in the Nigerian context. On the contrary, some concepts are delineated in a number of the Nigerian renewable energy policy instruments. The NREEEP, for instance, provides a definition for renewable energy, as:

> energy obtained from energy sources whose utilization does not result in the depletion of the earth's resources. … that have minimal environmental impacts, such as less intrusive hydro and certain biomass combustion. These sources of energy normally will include solar energy, wind, biomass, small and medium hydro, geothermal, tide and wave energy.[89]

While a definition is provided for renewable energy, there are no definitions for the various renewable energy sources mentioned in the description for renewable energy as stated in the NREEEP. For instance, it would be difficult to extrapolate the meaning of 'less intrusive hydro' and 'certain biomass combustion' from the government's definition for renewable energy given that no explanations for those terms were advanced in the policy document.

Another example of a definition existing elsewhere in the absence of a Nigerian renewable energy law is the definition of PPA. There is a regulatory tool known as the 'Regulations on Feed-In Tariff for Renewable Energy Sourced Electricity in Nigeria' (Regulations on Feed-In Tariff) in which a definition of PPA is provided.[90] It is defined as a 'power purchase agreement between the investor and the Off-taker together with any related agreement'.[91] The Regulations on Feed-In Tariff has been promulgated to boost power supply in Nigeria, establish a guaranteed price for renewable electricity for a fixed period (20 years) that provides an adequate return on investment and attract private sector investment to support the creation of a self-sustaining renewable energy market.[92] Additionally, the Feed-In Tariff Regulations provides priority access to the national grid for renewable electricity and establishes an obligation to purchase power produced from renewable energy sources.[93]

4.2.2 *Ineffective regulation*

With the absence of any law(s) promoting renewable energy development in Nigeria, the regulation of the sector is weak. As with most legal documents on renewable energy development, regulators and the specific functions are to a certain extent, defined. In the Nigerian case, regulators of the renewable energy sector and their roles in achieving targets have not been identified in any legal, regulatory or policy instruments except one—the Nigerian Electricity Regulator Commission (NERC). In the exercise of its powers to make regulations conferred to it by Sections 32(1) and 96 of the EPSR Act, the NERC has adopted

89 Ministry of Power (n 83) 1–2.

90 'Regulations on Feed-In Tariff for Renewable Energy Sourced Electricity in Nigeria, 2015'.

91 ibid 2.

92 ibid 3.

93 ibid 3.

the Regulations on Feed-In Tariff and the Regulations for the Procurement of Generation Capacity 2014,[94] which by default makes the NERC the economic regulator when it comes to regulating renewable energy in Nigeria. Even though the NERC is the only recognised regulator in the renewable energy sector, it could generally be assumed that the Minister (for Power and Works and Housing) may direct policy goals for renewable energy development in Nigeria. This stems from the general mandates conferred to them under the EPSR Act. Be that as it may, no other regulations besides the Regulations on Feed-In Tariffs and the Regulations for the Procurement of Generation Capacity 2014 have been adopted to implement legal or regulatory objectives regarding renewable energy development for electricity production in Nigeria.

The licencing regime in the Nigerian energy sector, which also applies to the renewable energy market, also poses a regulatory hurdle in the market. The EPSR Act provides that renewable electricity producers may generate electricity not exceeding 1 MW without a licence[95] with licencing powers granted to the NERC. However, in the NERC rules under its Regulations for the Procurement of Generation Capacity 2014, licence requirements only apply to electricity production projects exceeding 10 MW in capacity.[96] The licence requirement in both the EPSR Act and the Regulations for the Procurement of Generation Capacity 2014 are therefore contradictory. Given the contradictory situation, it appears that the Regulations for the Procurement of Generation Capacity 2014 as adopted does not give effect to the licensing provisions of the EPSR Act. Furthermore, it is not clear whether or not renewable electricity projects with capacities exceeding 1 MW, but less than 10 MW, require a licence to operate.

Due to the high cost involved and the lengthy time period needed, about 18 months minimum, to complete the process of negotiating a PPA with the Nigerian Bulk Electricity Trading Plc (NBET),[97] investors seeking to engage in renewable energy projects may be deterred as they may not wish to engage in such an expensive endeavour prior to obtaining the required permits for investment operations. In fact, it is reported that no PPA has been concluded by NBET for either a small hydropower, a wind power, a solar PV or a concentrated solar power plant as at the time of writing.[98] The lack of an existing PPA between NBET and renewable electricity producers presents another layer of impediment to future investment. This is because prospective investors would not know the sort of financial model they can operate under without an existing PPA template or model.[99]

The absence of a renewable energy legislation in Nigeria has not led the country to perform any worse in terms of achieving renewable targets when compared to The Gambia or Ghana–both countries with renewable energy legislation. Nigeria is not an isolated case when it comes to lack of legislation on RE. Most nations in sub-Saharan Africa do not have

94 'Nigerian Regulations for the Procurement of Generation Capacity 2014'.

95 Electric Power Sector Reform Act, 2005 s 62(2).

96 See GOPA-International Energy Consultants GmbH, 'The Nigerian Energy Sector: An Overview with a Special Emphasis on Renewable Energy, Energy Efficiency and Rural Electrification' (Deutsche Gesellschaft für Internationale Zusammenarbeit (GIZ) GmbH 2015) 99 <https://www.giz.de/en/downloads/giz2015-en-nigerian-energy-sector.pdf> accessed 12 December 2018.

97 Nigerian Bulk Electricity Trading Plc is a state-owned public liability company established in line with the provisions of the EPSR Act with the mandate to engage in the purchase and resale of electricity in the interim until such a time as the Nigerian electricity market is fully privatised.

98 GOPA-International Energy Consultants GmbH (n 96) 98.

99 ibid.

legislation on renewable energy development.[100] In fact, policies establishing renewable energy targets are commonly adopted among nations.

It is evident that while a law on renewable energy does not exist in Nigeria, certain key regulatory instruments have been adopted in an effort by the country's authorities to increase renewable energy integration into the nation's electricity production mix. The NERC has promulgated the country's 'Regulations for the Procurement of Generation Capacity 2014' and the 'Regulations on Feed-In Tariff 2015' as regulatory support mechanisms to not only enhance the attainment of the national targets on renewable electricity but also to attract investment to support the establishment of a self-sustaining renewable market.[101] The rules on licencing are established in the country's EPSR Act. All these are necessary regulatory measures for achieving renewable energy targets.

4.2.3 Incoherent targets

Nigeria, like Ghana and The Gambia, suffers from setting overambitious renewable energy targets that are often inharmonious between different policy instruments and deficient in both aims and implementation measures. For instance, while the government sets out policy objectives in the various policy documents, there appears to be inadequate provisions for financial support to achieve those objectives. The Nigerian feed-in tariff scheme is the only financial support mechanism instituted to help achieve renewable energy integration targets. While this support scheme is important as it aims to attract private investment to the renewable energy market, there is no other financial support in place to fund or support government implementation strategies to achieve its renewable energy policy objectives found both in the REMP and the NREEEP. This is in contrast to Ghana and The Gambia, in which the governments have established Renewable Energy Funds that are earmarked for providing financial resources for the promotion, development and utilisation of renewable energy sources.[102]

Another example of the policy issues is evident in the differences between the targets set by the Nigerian Government in both the 2011 Renewable Energy Master Plan (REMP) and the 2015 National Renewable Energy and Energy Efficiency Policy (NREEEP). The government, in the REMP, aims to increase the supply of renewable electricity from 13 per cent of total electricity generation in 2015 to 23 per cent in 2025 and 36 per cent by 2030. Yet, in the NREEEP, the government set an integration target rate of 18 per cent in 2020 rising to 20 per cent in 2030. Even though projection for 2015 stood at 13 per cent in the REMP, the actual integration rate that was achieved was 10 per cent. Integration stood at 1.3 per cent when large hydropower was excluded.[103] It would appear that the renewable integration target set by the Nigerian Government to be achieved by 2030 in the REMP was too high to achieve and, having realised this, the government reduced the targeted percentage in the NREEEP four years later. Incoherence in projected renewable electricity integration targets does not signify serious commitment to policy objectives on the part of government to in-

100 For list of countries in the world with legislation on renewable energy, see IEA and IRENA, 'Global Renewable Energy' <https://www.iea.org/policiesandmeasures/renewableenergy> accessed 25 March 2019.

101 See 'Regulations on Feed-In Tariff for Renewable Energy Sourced Electricity in Nigeria, 2015' (n 90) 6.

102 See Renewable Energy Act, 2011 (Act 832) of the Parliament of the Republic of Ghana s 32; Renewable Energy Act 2013 of the Republic of The Gambia, 12 December 2013 s 5.

103 Ministry of Power (n 83) 36; GOPA-International Energy Consultants GmbH (n 96) 96. In the Nigerian NREEEP, large hydropower is any water-based power plant with a capacity exceeding 100 MW.

vestors. As indicated in the Ghanaian case, investors positively see adherence to policy targets as an indication of commitment from governments and are more likely to make investments in the market.

5 Conclusion

The trend across sub-Saharan Africa is that governments of the various nations are looking to develop their renewable energy resources and increase their share in electricity production. This trend, which is becoming popular in the region, is driven by the necessity to provide access to electricity to all people in the region. This, in turn, will support economic, social and environmental growth, all key principles underlying the sustainable development goals agenda in sub-Saharan Africa. Achieving renewable electricity integration targets across sub-Saharan Africa will be a monumental feat fraught with legal, policy and regulatory issues, as is evident from the Ghanaian, the Gambian and the Nigerian case studies in this chapter. These issues are all in addition to the technical, financial and technological obstacles to developing and utilising renewable energy resources for electricity production.

From the case studies, legal issues, particularly those dealing with the deficiency of adopted legislation on renewable energy, are pervasive. Regulations are unstructured and ineffective, while policy targets set by the governments appear to lack enough detail and clarity, especially on implementation strategies to achieve these targets. This creates a weak and ill-defined environment in which to achieve both legal and policy goals for renewable energy; a scenario that creates an impediment to attracting investment in the market. In a bid to attract investment in their renewable energy markets, the governments have each set ambitious targets that have either not been achieved (in the case of Nigeria) or are not feasible to achieve (Ghana, The Gambia and Nigeria).

A renewable energy law is not essential to the efficient regulation of the renewable energy market to attain integration targets. What is important is that regulations do exist in some form where regulatory authorities are clearly identified and granted mandates to adopt regulatory or legislative instruments under the nation's laws to implement the measures necessary to achieve national renewable energy development targets. It is imperative that all necessary efforts are taken by governments to convert renewable electricity policy targets into practice. With rising concerns about energy security, the security of electricity supply and climate change and its mitigation factors, further research is needed on the subject in the African context to fully comprehend the importance of utilising renewable energy resources for electricity.

30

DEVELOPING RENEWABLE ENERGY PROJECTS IN THE MIDDLE EAST AND NORTH AFRICAN REGION

Cameron Kelly

1 Introduction

In 2015, the United Arab Emirates (UAE) made global renewable energy headlines by awarding utility-scale solar PV capacity at less than US$0.06 per kilowatt hour (kWh) – some 12 months later, the UAE awarded further capacity at half this price.[1] Many market participants proclaimed that such prices were unrealistic and would never survive construction,[2] yet such prices have remained intact and have afforded the Middle East and North African (MENA) region with unprecedented renewables growth potential.

Contrary to what some market participants may have predicted, the 2014 fall in oil prices did not in and of itself significantly impact MENA clean energy investment. Oil is predominately used for transport (with some heating) while renewables are predominantly used to generate electricity. Regional electricity costs have continued to remain relatively high irrespective of the price of oil. Solar energy is typically priced well below diesel produced electricity, hence the cost of a barrel of oil would have to drop significantly beneath current (2019) prices to have any real impact on solar uptake.[3]

Renewables remain a sound investment proposition to MENA economies irrespective of whether oil prices are high or low. Under high oil prices, renewables facilitate more fossil fuel exports by allowing a greater proportion of domestic generation from cheaply priced renewables; low oil prices also facilitate increased renewables deployment, with financing preferencing forms of generation with the best rates of return.[4] On a levelised cost of energy

1 Eversheds Sutherlands and Price Waterhouse Coopers (PWC) (2016) *Developing Renewable Energy Projects – A Guide to Achieving Success in MENA*, 4th edition, p 4, www.pwc.com/me. Accessed 18 January 2019.

2 Bloomberg New Energy Finance (2016) 'Is Dubai's new record about to set a new normal for solar tariffs?' https://reneweconomy.com.au/is-dubais-new-record-about-to-set-a-new-normal-for-solar-tariffs-42945 (11 May 2016) Accessed: 27 February 2019.

3 Eversheds Sutherlands (2016) 'The journey of renewable energy in the MENA region'. *Electrical Energy Storage International Magazine* January 2016. See: https://www.ibesalliance.org/index.php?id=31&tx_ttnews%5Btt_news%5D=187&cHash=054195527https://www.ibesalliance.org/index.php?id=31&tx_ttnews%5Btt_news%5D=187&cHash=0541955273095ae623acf6ebeb1a8860 (7 March 2016) Accessed: 18 February 2019.

4 Eversheds Sutherlands and PWC (2016) above n.1 p 4.

(LCOE) basis, renewables remain cheaper than most oil or gas-fired power generation, both of which renewables can complement as part of an overall cost effective energy mix.[5]

Beyond cost, renewables – together with energy efficiency, storage, demand response and smart(er) grids – are rapidly becoming new growth sectors in MENA economies.[6] Such sectors can smooth volatile oil and gas prices and assist regional economies' diversification strategies – a clear focus in many 2020 and 2030 strategic plans. Ongoing population growth, industrialisation and economic development all require diversified and sustainable energy sources that can meet increasing demand for energy and water while simultaneously hedging against unpredictable thermal energy prices.[7]

All 22 MENA Member States attended the United Nations Framework Convention on Climate Change's 21st Conference of the Parties in Paris in December 2015, with 15 MENA countries signing the Paris Agreement the following year.[8] Projects such as Dubai's Mohammed Bin Rashid Solar Park, large-scale solar and wind initiatives in Egypt and Jordan and Saudi Arabia's recently announced objective of 9.5 gigawatts (GW) of renewables by 2030 all point to the scale of ambition in the region.[9]

Most Arab countries have significantly scaled up their interest in renewables since 2014, especially in onshore wind and solar power generation, both of which offer the highest technological and market maturity.[10] Support mechanisms like feed-in-tariffs (FITs), net metering and competitive auctions afford long-term certainty and encourage project developers, sponsors and financiers alike to enter the market – such mechanisms are underpinned by short (2020) and long (2030) term renewable energy targets (RETs).

Renewable energy financing in the MENA region is also experiencing major change. 2016 saw the launch of a US$10 billion investment by the National Bank of Abu Dhabi, the Dubai Electricity and Water Authority's Green Energy Fund and Dubai's Green Climate Fund, amongst others.[11] In the same year, US$11 billion was invested in renewables across the Arab region (compared to just US$1.2 billion in 2008), a nine-fold increase in eight years.[12] Between 2016 and 2017, MENA renewable investment increased 11 per cent (to US$10.1 billion); investment increased nearly six-fold in Egypt (to US$2.6 billion), 26 per cent in Jordan (to a record US$1.1 billion) and 29-fold in the UAE (to US$ 2.2 billion).[13]

1.1 Renewable energy targets

Though not legally binding, MENA RETs can be interpreted as relatively ambitious when compared to the region's historically high (and ongoing) reliance on fossil fuels.[14] Morocco leads the region, with a pledge to produce over half (52 per cent) of its electricity through renewables by 2030; Jordan has a RET of 11 per cent to be achieved by 2025, the UAE aims to increase its share of renewables to almost a quarter (24 per cent) of the country's energy

5 Ibid.
6 Ibid.
7 IRENA (2016), *Renewable Energy in the Arab Region. Overview of Developments.* (Abu Dhabi: International Renewable Energy Agency) p 5.
8 Eversheds Sutherlands and PWC (2016) above n.1 p 5.
9 Ibid.
10 IRENA (2016) above n.7 p 5.
11 Eversheds Sutherlands and PWC (2016) above n.1 p 5.
12 IRENA (2017) www.irena.org/mena. Accessed: 12 December 2018.
13 REN21 (2018) *Renewables 2018 Global Status Report* (Paris: REN21 Secretariat) p 143.
14 IRENA (2016) above n.7 p 13.

mix by 2021 (up from just 0.2 per cent in 2014), and Egypt has a 20 per cent target to be achieved by 2022.[15]

Table 30.1 sets out RETs in the MENA region, as at 2016.

1.2 Supporting policies

The preferred policy option for utility-scale projects in the MENA region has tended to involve (public) competitive bidding by independent power producers (IPPs).[16] Successful project developers are appointed based on the most competitive (lowest) bid, and are entitled to execute a power purchase agreement (PPA) with guaranteed government offtakers. FIT schemes as well as direct proposal submissions have also proved to be popular in countries

Table 30.1 Renewable energy targets in the MENA region (as at 2016)

	Renewable energy targets							
	Wind	*PV*	*CSP*	*Biomass*	*Geothermal*	*Total*		
	MW	*MW*	*MW*	*MW*	*MW*	*MW*	*%*	*Target date*
Algeria	1,010	3,000	–	360	5	4,375	15	2020
	5,010	13,575	2,000	1,000	15	21,600	37	2030
Bahrain	–	–	–	–	–	250	5	2030
Djibouti	300	200	–	–	500	1,100	100	2025
Egypt	7,200	2,300	–	–	–	9,500	20	2022
Iraq	–	300	–	–	–	300	1	2020
Jordan	800	800	100	50	–	1,750	10	2020
Kuwait	700	4,600	5,700	–	–	11,000	15	2030
Lebanon	400	150–100		–	–	950–900	12	2020
Libya	600	344	125	–	–	1,069	7	2020
	1,000	844	375	–	–	2,219	10	2025
Mauritania	30	30	–	–	–	60	20	2020
Morocco	2,000	2,000		–	–	6,000	42	2020
	4,200	4,560		–	–	10,090	52	2030
State of Palestine	44	45	20	21	–	130	10	2020
Qatar	–	–	–	–	–	1,800	20	2030
Saudi Arabia	9,000	16,000	25,000	3,000	1,000	54,000	30	2040
Sudan	680	667	50	68	54	1,582	11	2020
	1,000	1,000	100	–	–	2,100	20	2030
Syrian Arab Republic	1,000	2,000	1,300	250	–	4,550	30	2030
Tunisia	1,755	1,510	460	–	–	3,725	30	2030
UAE (Abu Dhabi)	–	–	–	–	–	–	7	2020
UAE (Dubai)	–	5,000		–	–	5,000	25	2030
Yemen	400	8.25	100	6	200	714.25	15	2025

Source: IRENA (2016) above n.7 p 14.

15 IRENA (2016) above n.7 p 20.
16 IRENA (2016) above n.7 p 18.

Table 30.2 Renewable energy support mechanisms in the Arab region

	Competitive bidding	*Direct proposal submission*	*Feed-in-tariff*	*Net metering*
Algeria			X	
Egypt	X	X	X	X
Jordan	X	X	X	X
Kuwait	X			
Lebanon	X			X
Morocco	X			X
Oman	X			
State of Palestine	X		X	X
Syrian Arab Republic	X		X	X
Tunisia				X
United Arab Emirates	X			X
Yemen	X			

Source: IRENA (2016) above n.7 p 19.

like Jordan (see Section 3.3 below) and Egypt. Direct proposal submissions target large, GW-scale investments, competitive bidding schemes target projects of several hundred megawatts (MW) and FITs tend to be preferred for smaller projects (of less than 100 MW).[17]

Auctions have seen spectacular growth in both the Middle East and globally in recent years[18]– the scheduling of successive competitive rounds permits real-time price discovery, incentivises competition and reduces information asymmetry between the public sector and private financiers/developers. Auctions can also be tailored to country-specific objectives (like increasing local content requirements over successive rounds). The factors behind the record low prices achieved by renewable auctions in recent years include a combination of country-specific conditions (such as resource availability together with the relative cost of land, labour and finance), investor confidence and the design of the auction itself.[19]

Table 30.2 sets out the key policies supporting renewable energy in the Arab region.

1.3 Recent trends

In recent years, several key developments have enabled renewable energy generation to out-compete conventional (thermal) generation – this applies equally to the Middle East as it does to other regions around the world. First, ongoing decreases in cost in mature core technologies like solar PV and onshore wind have made these projects significantly more bankable.[20] Secondly, the trend towards storage in the form of electrochemical batteries used to back up (or "firm") renewables is rapidly redefining how renewables can be integrated into grids – it is this opportunity to create a "dispatchable" (as opposed to "baseload")

17 Ibid.

18 More than 70 countries had adopted auctions to procure renewable energy by the end of 2016. See: IRENA (2018), *Renewable Energy Outlook: Egypt* (Abu Dhabi: International Renewable Energy Agency) p 41.

19 IRENA (2018) above n.18 p 41.

20 Eversheds Sutherlands and PWC (2016) above n.1 p 3.

energy system which has the potential to turn energy markets on their head.[21] The final development relates to the unique combination of physical and socio-economic and political circumstances of the MENA region itself – these include some of the best solar and wind resources in the world, together with governments who understand and are prepared to fully embrace the renewables opportunity.

In 2016, the estimated annual cost of energy subsidies in the MENA region was estimated to be greater than the total cost of achieving regional 2020 RETs.[22] Depressed oil prices (with a related decline in Arab government revenues) delivered an urgent need for subsidy and gas price reforms. In 2016, the UAE announced an intention to reduce regional energy subsidies and to allocate US$25 billion to renewable projects by 2020.[23] Egypt, Saudi Arabia, Bahrain and others have also revived plans for a phased reduction in unsustainable energy subsidies.

Project financed renewable energy projects in the Middle East typically involve special purpose vehicle (SPV) non-recourse models in which a project sponsor's assets are insulated from the underlying project's liabilities.[24] Many MENA banks are unable to lend over the lifetime of utility-scale solar and wind projects, so project sponsors must rely on external financing from government banks, private sector finance and multilateral development banks (MDBs).[25] MDBs can lend at concessional rates, offer debt over longer tenures and are generally more familiar with the nuances of lending into utility-scale renewables projects.[26]

2 Egypt

2.1 Context and key drivers

The Arab Republic of Egypt is the most populous country in the MENA region and possesses one of the most rapidly growing populations globally. Fossil fuels are an important part of the country's energy mix – the country is Africa's largest non-OPEC oil producer and second largest natural gas producer.[27] Eygpt's natural gas exploitation is geared towards high domestic demand: more than three-quarters of the country's energy comes from gas-fired plants (power consumption increased by 14 per cent in 2017).[28] A shortage of natural gas has contributed to several electricity blackouts since 2011 – the government is attempting to address this issue by importing liquefied natural gas (LNG) and constructing new power plants.[29] In late 2018, Egypt's Minister of Petroleum Tarek El Molla stated that ENI's Zohr offshore gas

21 Ibid.
22 Eversheds Sutherlands (2016) above n.3.
23 Ibid.
24 Ibid.
25 MDBs active in the MENA region include the World Bank's International Finance Corporation and the European Bank for Reconstruction and Development.
26 The Sukuk market is a relatively new but a growing area of Middle Eastern renewable project finance – these bond-like instruments permit investors to approach capital markets to raise significant sums of capital over long tenures, thereby avoiding the higher costs of typical bank financing. See: Eversheds Sutherlands (2016) above n.22.
27 Eversheds Sutherlands and PWC (2016) above n.1 p 24.
28 McDonald, S (2018) *Here's How Egypt Could Become a Major Gas Exporter.* https://nationalinterest.org/feature/heres-how-egypt-could-become-major-gas-exporter-27056 (29 July 2018) Accessed: 27 February 2019.
29 The West Nile Delta offshore natural gas project will significantly increase gas supply to the country. See: Eversheds Sutherlands and PWC (2016) above n.1 p 24.

field (off the north coast of Egypt) had increased its production six-fold since commencing production in January 2018.[30] This increase has removed the need for LNG imports, with Cairo's first commercial LNG exports occuring in 2019.[31] Gas production in the coming years is expected to increase substantially, not only by already anticipated volumes offshore but also due to production increases and new onshore discoveries in the Western Desert.[32]

Key drivers behind increasing domestic production of renewable energy in Egypt include:

- *Freeing up domestic gas for more profitable uses.* Historically, potential natural gas exports in Egypt have been diverted to the domestic market to meet growing energy demand, resulting in declining export revenues.[33] Developing domestic renewable energy means that more natural gas (in the form of LNG) can be exported.
- *Meeting growing energy demand and enhancing energy security.* Egypt's peak energy demand is expected to grow at a rate of 5 per cent annually – this increase in demand (combined with declining oil and gas production) means that Egypt needs to diversify energy production or potentially face further blackouts.[34]
- *Leveraging abundant natural resources.* Egypt has rich renewable energy resources – direct normal irradiation in Egypt is significantly above the global average and wind full load hours (especially in the Gulf of Suez) are amongst the highest in the MENA region.[35]

2.2 Renewable energy targets

In 2008, Egypt's Supreme Energy Council (SEC) announced a RET of 20 per cent by 2022 (12 per cent wind, 2 per cent solar and 6 per cent hydro).[36] By the following year, the contribution of renewable energy resources to primary energy production in Egypt stood at just 4 per cent (mainly from hydro (3 per cent) and wind (1 per cent)).[37] By 2011, political instability and economic uncertainty meant that the RET had not been implemented. The Ministry of Electricity and Renewable Energy issued a new 20-year strategy titled the Integrated Sustainable Energy Strategy 2015–2035 (ISES 2035). ISES 2035 outlines several scenarios for Egypt's energy mix out to 2035 and is based on a number of key factors, including:

- energy import dependence;
- diversification of primary energy supply;
- CO^2 intensity;
- fuel savings through energy efficiency;
- primary energy intensity;
- total discounted subsidies.[38]

30 Total production at present is said to be around 2 billion standard cubic feet (Bcf) per day, a staggering increase from the 350 million cubic feet (mcf) per day in January 2018. See: Verocy (2018) 'Egypt's gas exports future looks bright, planning however still diffuse'. https://verocy.com/saudi-strategic-upd/egypts-gas-exports-future-looks-bright-planning-however-still-diffuse (14 September 2018) Accessed: 27 February 2019.

31 Verocy (2018) above n.30.

32 Ibid.

33 Eversheds Sutherlands and PWC (2016) above n.1 p 24.

34 Ibid.

35 Ibid.

36 IRENA (2018) above n.18 p 31.

37 IRENA (2018) above n.18 p 22.

38 IRENA (2018) above n.8 p 32.

Taking the above factors into consideration, ISES 2035 identifies a "most likely" scenario for its energy mix, as follows:

1. *Renewable energy:* supply 20 per cent of generated electricity from renewable sources by 2022, with 42 per cent by 2035.[39]
2. *Efficiency:* reduce energy use by over 8 per cent by 2022 (with a base year of 2006/2007).[40]
3. *Climate action:* phase out energy subsidies within 3–5 years with, potentially, a national carbon market which recognises low and zero-carbon sources of energy.[41]
4. *Nuclear:* install 4–5 GW of nuclear generation by 2025/2026 (which should account for 4 per cent of installed power generation capacity by 2030).[42]
5. *Natural gas and oil:* contribute 49 per cent of installed power generation capacity by 2030 (decreasing from 90 per cent in 2014/2015).
6. *Coal:* source 16 per cent of electricity generation from coal by 2030.[43]

The "most likely" scenario modelled a least-cost approach where subsidies are eliminated after 2020, and where coal and nuclear compete directly with renewables. Natural gas and coal in the primary energy supply mix plateau, with renewable energy expected to make up a quarter of total installed capacity in 2019/2020, and coal representing 2.1 per cent.[44] With nuclear introduced in 2025, the scenario contemplates renewables making 42 per cent of total installed capacity (with coal, natural gas and nuclear making up 15.8 per cent, 37.35 per cent and 3.27 per cent respectively) by 2034/2035.[45]

Table 30.3 shows the projected development of installed capacity for renewable technologies between 2009 and 2035.

Table 30.3 Evolution of installed renewable energy power capacity in Egypt (GW)

Source	*2009/10*	*2012/13*	*2029/30*	*2034/35*
Hydro	2.8	2.8	2.9	2.9
Wind	0.5	13.3	20.6	20.6
PV	0	3	22.9	31.75
CSP	0	0.1	4.1	8.1
Total	**3.3**	**19.2**	**50.5**	**62.6**

Source: IRENA (2018) above n.18 p 40.

39 Ibid.
40 Ibid.
41 Egypt ratified the UNFCCC's 21st CoP Paris Agreement on 29 June 2017 it entered into force on 29 July 2017. See: IRENA (2018) above n.18 p 33.
42 IRENA (2018) above n.18 p 33.
43 Ibid.
44 IRENA (2018) above n.18 p 34.
45 ISES 2035 also confirms Egypt's ambition to become an energy hub between Europe, Asia and Africa by expanding grid interconnections across the Arab region and beyond. See: IRENA (2018) above n.18 p 34.

2.3 Legislation

Table 30.4 details the evolution and scope of the principal pieces of legislation relevant to the Egyptian renewable energy sector.

2.4 Contracts, counterparties and governing laws

A developer will need to enter into several contracts to develop a renewable energy project in Egypt. Table 30.5 sets out the relevant counterparty, governing law and function applicable to each key contract.

The choice of governing law in the finance documents is usually agreed by negotiation between the parties. If finance is obtained outside Egypt, English law is the most common system of governing law.

Table 30.4 Evolution of Egyptian renewable energy legislation and regulations[a]

Legislation	*Function*
Law No 102 of the year 1986 establishing the New and Renewable Energy Development and Usage Authority (as amended in 2015)	• Established the NREA (primary responsibility for promoting and developing renewable energy in Egypt)
Renewable Energy Law (Decree Law 203/2014)	• Regulates power generation from renewable projects and details the rules which allocate land for such projects, connecting to the national grid and sale of the power
Cabinet Decree No. 1947 of the year 2014 on Feed-in-Tariff	• Establishes FITs for electricity generated from renewable sources (25 years for solar and 20 years for wind)
Prime Ministerial Decree No. (37/4/15/14) of the year 2015	• Regulations to avail land for renewable energy projects
New Electricity Law No. 87 of 2015 (together with the Law's Executive Regulations)	• The Electricity Law of 2015 established a competitive electricity market that encourages private sector involvement • The Egyptian Electricity Transmission Company (EETC) became an independent company under the Law with responsibility for electricity transmission and network operation • EgyptERA approves tariffs and develops rules and procedures which enhance the efficiency of electricity usage and prevent monopolistic practices
EgyptERA SPV Incorporation Guidelines issued 17 March 2015	• Provides for the incorporation and operation of FIT project companies

Source: IRENA (2018) *Renewable Energy Outlook: Egypt* (Abu Dhabi: International Renewable Energy Agency) p 41.

a IRENA (2018) above n.19 p 36.

Table 30.5 Contracts, counterparties and governing laws for Egyptian renewable energy projects

Contract	*Counter-parties*	*Governing law*	*Function*
Real Estate Contract (freehold/leasehold) for the Special Purpose Vehicle (SPV) premises	Owner/ Landlord	Egyptian	Provision of freehold/leasehold access to relevant plot(s) of land
Usufruct Agreement (for the project's plot of land)	NREA	Egyptian	Establishes the user's rights of usufruct over the site
Usufruct Agreement and Cost Sharing Agreement Direct Agreement	NREA, Lenders	Egyptian	
SPV Bylaws	Shareholders	Egyptian	Rules governing establishment and operation of project companies
Network Connection Agreement	EETC	Egyptian	Provides for how a power producer may connect to the transmission system to supply electricity to the buyer under the Power Purchase Agreement
Cost Sharing Agreement	EETC and NREA	Egyptian	Establishes a framework whereby each Developer pays its share of costs to enable EETC and NREA to construct required energy and road infrastructure
Network Connection Agreement and Cost Sharing Agreement Direct Agreement	EETC, Ministry of Finance, Lenders	Egyptian	
Power Purchase Agreement	EETC	Egyptian	Terms and conditions for the construction, operation and maintenance of the (renewable) power facility and the sale and purchase of electricity
PPA Direct Agreement	EETC, Ministry of Finance, Lenders	Egyptian	Provides for financiers' right to step into the Power Purchase Agreement in case of an SPV default
Guarantee	Ministry of Finance	Egyptian	Government guarantee over the buyer's payments under the Power Purchase Agreement
Engineering, Procurement & Construction (EPC) Contract	EPC Contractor	Negotiable (English)	Design and construction of the facility by the EPC Contractor
Operations & Maintenance (O&M) Agreement	O&M Contractor	Negotiable (English)	Operations and maintenance requirements for the facility by the O&M Contractor

Source: Eversheds Sutherlands and PWC (2016) above n.1 p 31.

2.5 Support mechanisms

Within the regulatory framework described above, the following schemes are applied for implementing Egyptian renewable energy projects.

1. *Build, own & operate schemes and competitive auctions*

   In the early 2000s, Egyptian power projects typically involved build, own and operate (BOO) schemes, wherein prequalified bidders submit technical and commercial proposals for evaluation, and EETC would execute a PPA with the successful bidder. In 2009, EETC launched the first auctions for large-scale private projects under a BOO model.[46] In 2015, an IPP scheme was launched,[47] with electricity sold directly to either (small-scale) end-users or (large-scale) distribution utilities. In 2016, EETC announced competitive bidding processes for wind, solar PV and concentrated solar power (CSP) projects with an overall capacity of more than 1,000 MW under a BOO model in Gulf El Zayt.[48] In addition, 100 MW of CSP and 1,000 MW of solar PV projects under three competitive bidding schemes, as well as a 600 MW solar PV project under direct negotiation, were approved.[49] In 2017, Egypt transitioned to a fully competitive bidding auction mechanism.[50]
2. *FIT schemes: the Nubian Suns FIT Financing Program*

   Prime Ministerial Decree No. (37/4/15/14) of 2015 allocated over 7,500 square kilometres of land in Benban (Aswan province), Zafarana (Gulf of Suez) and West of Nile for renewable energy projects through usufruct rights.[51] Sixty solar and 25 wind developers were selected by the New and Renewable Energy Authority (NREA) to develop over 4 GW of solar and wind projects.[52] The Benban Solar Park hosts over 30 power plants (each between 20 and 50 MW in capacity) across 37 square kilometres with a total capacity of 1.8 GW, and was supported by Egypt's Nubian Suns FIT Financing Program.

   Round one of the Nubian Suns Program involved a PPA which – despite offering an attractive FIT (of almost US$0.15 per kilowatt hour (kWh) – was deemed to be unbankable by international financiers.[53] Local Egyptian banks also had difficulties financing in circumstances where the FIT was paid in Egyptian pounds but project debt raised in US dollars.[54] The second round of the program was implemented in 2016[55] – the FIT was cut by almost 50 per cent, with foreign exchange (FX) risk minimised through a greater

46 In the subsequent years, a number of other tenders were launched by EETC: 200 MW of solar PV in 2013; 250 MW of wind, 200 MW of solar PV and 100 MW of CSP in 2015. See: IRENA (2018) above n.18 p 40.

47 Ibid.

48 Ibid.

49 Ibid.

50 Dooa Farid, 'Electricity Ministry Will Shift to Auctions to Encourage Investment'. www.egypttoday.com/Article/3/28109/Electricity-Ministry-will-shift-to-auctions-to-encourage-investment (17 October 2017) Accessed: 12 November 2018.

51 IRENA (2018) above n.18 p 44.

52 5,700 km² for wind projects (75 per cent share) and 1,900 km² for solar energy projects (25 per cent share). See: IRENA (2018) above n.18 p 28.

53 These included the seat of arbitration located in Cairo, which represented an unacceptable venue for project developers, sponsors and debt financiers alike.

54 Jennifer Runyon, 'Egypt Readies for 2 GW of Solar PV Capacity'. https://www.renewableenergyworld.com/articles/2018/01/egypt-readies-for-2-gw-of-solar-pv-capacity.html (17 January 2018) Accessed: 1 December 2018.

55 Prime Minister's Decree No. 2532, dated 30 September 2016.

proportion of the revised FITs pegged to a (fixed) exchange rate.[56] Under this round, a consortium of nine international banks (led by the World Bank's International Finance Corporation (IFC)) invested for the first time in Egypt's renewable energy sector[57] by providing a US$ 650 million debt package to 13 solar power projects. The financing represented the largest private sector solar PV financing package in the MENA region to date.[58]

3. *Other support mechanisms*

In addition to mechanisms like FITs and competitive auctions, the applied customs on components and spare parts for renewable projects are levied at discounted rates, while VAT is also reduced.[59] Further mechanisms include the provision of sovereign guarantees, concessional government loans and dedicated funds for enhancing transmission and distribution grids.[60]

3 Jordan

3.1 Introduction

Like Egypt, Jordan is blessed with substantial renewable resources – it has one of the highest solar irradiance levels in the world and has a large tract of land with high annual average wind speeds.[61] Unlike some of its neighbours, however, Jordan has very limited fossil fuel resources: the country imports 96 per cent of its energy and relies heavily on fuel imports.[62] Historically, some 40 per cent of the nation's energy requirements has been supplied by the Arab Gas Pipeline from Egypt – this gas supply has been susceptible to disruptions, often requiring diesel and heavy fuel oil back-ups.[63] As in Egypt, such geopolitical circumstances have helped define a clear business case for renewables as a means of energy diversification.

3.2 Key legislation and regulators

Law no. 13/2012 on Renewable Energy and Energy Efficiency (REEEL) as amended in 2014, was adopted to promote investment in renewable energy.[64] The REEEL supports

56 For phase one, only two developers of large-scale PV projects were able to achieve financial closure, while for phase two, 30 companies achieved financial closure for their PV projects with a total capacity of 1,465 MW by October 2017. See: IRENA (2018) above n.18 p 42.

57 The consortium includes the European Bank for Reconstruction and Development, the Africa Development Bank; the Asian Infrastructure Investment Bank; the Arab Bank of Bahrain, CDC Group Plc of the United Kingdom, Europe Arab Bank, Green for Growth Fund, FinnFund, Industrial & Commercial Bank of China and Development Bank of Austria.

58 The Multilateral Investment Guarantee Agency, another member of the World Bank Group, provided US$200 million in political risk insurance. See: 'Egypt Secures Largest Ever Middle East PV Financing; US ITC Calls for 35% Panel Tariffs'. http://newenergyupdate.com/pv-insider/egypt-secures-largest-ever-middle-east-pv-financing-us-itc-calls-35-panel-tariffs (8 November 2017) Accessed: 30 November 2018.

59 IRENA (2018) above n.18 p 44.

60 In 2016 EETC proposed with the NREA and EgyptERA a transmission code for the interconnection of wind projects. The code was approved by EgyptERA, in addition to the rules and regulations for the interconnection of solar PV systems.

61 Eversheds Sutherlands and PWC (2016) above n.1 p 40.

62 Ibid.

63 In 2015, the cost of consumed energy accounted for 10 per cent of GDP. See: Eversheds Sutherlands and PWC (2016) above n.1 p 40.

64 Energy Charter Secretariat (2018) *Energy Investment Risk Assessment (EIRA)* p 81. https://eira.energycharter.org/. Accessed: 21 December 2018.

Jordan's General Electricity Law (2002) which provides the licensing and regulatory regime (generation, transmission and distribution) for developing renewable energy projects. REEEL introduced several significant enabling measures for the development of renewable energy, including:

- empowering the Ministry of Energy and Mineral Resources (MEMR)[65] and the National Electric Power Company (NEPCO) to issue tenders and attract competitive proposals;
- establishing the direct proposal regime to enable private companies to negotiate directly with MEMR (see Section 3.3 below)
- obliging NEPCO to purchase electricity generated by renewable energy projects/IPPs and to pay for grid connections;[66]
- exempting all renewable energy project systems and equipment from customs duties and sales tax.[67]

The Energy and Minerals Regulatory Commission (EMRC) is the regulator of Jordan's energy and minerals sector, and is responsible for:

- issuing generation, distribution and transmission licenses;
- determining electricity tariffs and connection fees;
- issuing and updating Jordan's Transmission Grid Code and Distribution Code;
- metering of sold electricity;
- dealing with disputes between consumers and licensees.

3.3 *Jordan's National Energy Strategy and the Direct Proposal regime*

Jordan's National Energy Strategy Plan 2007–2020 (together with its updated version, the National Energy Strategy 2015–2025) includes a RET of 10 per cent by 2020.[68] From just 1 per cent in 2014, renewable energy increased to 5 per cent of Jordan's total generation in 2016 – halfway to 2020's 10 per cent RET.[69] The National Energy Strategy has already seen over 1,000MW of renewable projects come into operation in Jordan, over half of which were realised in the first half of 2019. Following the completion of a third auction round in October 2018, the government suspended the programme to give NEPCO the opportunity to complete a new power sector plan reviewing the technical feasibility of integrating a larger share of renewables into a still developing grid. Despite this temporary freeze linked to grid capacity constraints and the introduction of a 35 per cent local content requirement in round three, stable policies and transparent incentives have allowed Jordan to become a regional leader in renewable energy.[70]

65 MEMR is responsible for overseeing interconnections with neighbouring countries, attracting international capital for investment in the energy sector and setting policy for the energy, minerals and oil sectors.

66 Electricity is then purchased from NEPCO and distributed by Jordan's (three) retail supplier companies.

67 Bloomberg New Energy Finance (2018) *ClimateScope – Jordan*. http://global-climatescope.org/en/country/jordan/#/enabling-framework. Accessed: 18 November 2018.

68 Ibid.

69 Ibid.

70 Ibid.

Four hundred and thirty MW of solar and wind projects were approved under the first round of the Direct Proposals scheme in 2014 – solar projects received US$100 million in loans from MDBs (including the European Bank for Reconstruction and Development (EBRD) and the French development finance institution Proparco) and were commissioned in 2016.[71] The wind projects experienced grid constraints and connection delays as they will be connected to the "Green Corridor" (an initiative to address Jordan's chronic grid constraints by expanding the grid with an extra 1,000 MW of capacity). As in Egypt, the second round saw bid prices halved.[72] In total, the government hopes to commission some 1,800 MW of solar and wind capacity by 2019.[73]

The Direct Proposal process typically involves the following key project agreements:

- Power Purchase Agreement;
- Transmission Connection Agreement;
- Government Guarantee Agreement;
- Land Lease Agreement or Land Ownership Documents;
- Generation License;
- Engineering, Procurement and Construction Contract;
- Operation and Maintenance Agreement.

The standard form PPA involves a long-term (20-year) offtake, with NEPCO's payment obligations guaranteed by the government. Between signing the PPA and reaching project financial close, the generation license,[74] connection agreement, financing documents (including the PPA Direct Agreement as well as the On and Offshore Security Agreements)[75] and the Engineering, Procurement & Construction EPC and Operations and Maintenance (O&M) Agreements need to be executed. Relevant environmental permits also need to be secured. From financial close until the project's commercial operation date, the facility itself as well as the interconnection facilities and substations need to be commissioned. The PPA is governed under Jordanian law and typically addresses the following matters:

- metering;
- invoicing and payments;
- emission reduction credits;
- insurance (during construction and operations phases);
- *force majeure* (including government and other *force majeure* events) and prolonged *force majeure* events;
- total/partial loss and restoration;
- change in law protection (one time as well as ongoing);
- defaults, termination and consequences of termination;
- interface with lenders (including direct agreements, notices, step-in rights and assignment);
- dispute resolution, expert determination and arbitration;

71 Eversheds Sutherlands and PWC (2016) above n.1 p 44.

72 Bloomberg New Energy Finance (2018) above n.67.

73 Eversheds Sutherlands and PWC (2016) above n.1 p 45.

74 An application for the generation licence is made to the Energy and Minerals Regulatory Commission, which takes approximately two months.

75 The Onshore Security Package of agreements includes:

- restrictions on transfer of shares in the project company;
- decommissioning.

3.4 Support mechanisms

To date, renewable power projects in Jordan have been supported via government tenders or through Direct Proposal FITs. Tenders contemplate EPC and O&M arrangements under BOO models, with the government retaining ownership of the project's assets.[76] Net metering (which permits sale of surplus energy back into the grid) was introduced by the EMRC in 2012. However, it was relatively slow to develop; to facilitate uptake, the EMRC published Wheeling Regulations in 2014 which enable off-site renewable energy production for on-site consumption by corporate offtakers.[77]

4 United Arab Emirates

4.1 Introduction

The UAE consists of a federation of seven independent (separate) emirates.[78] The Emirates of Abu Dhabi and Dubai represent the majority of the population, land mass and developmental ambitions for renewable energy within the UAE. Key incentives for the development of renewable energy include:

- *Alleviate domestic gas shortages and increase oil exports.* The UAE is blessed with substantial fossil fuel resources, possessing the sixth largest oil and seventh largest gas reserves (respectively) in the world.[79] Like Jordan, it also relies on imported gas for production of some of its electricity. In 2008, the UAE became a net gas importer, importing gas via the Dolphin pipeline from Qatar.[80]
- *Address unsustainable fuel subsidies.* The UAE has historically supported generous fuel subsidies. Between 2013 and 2016, Dubai increased its electricity prices three-fold (and linked a portion of the electricity tariff to international prices), while, in 2014, Abu Dhabi implemented a new electricity and water tariff structure under which expatriates experienced a significant increase in utility bills.[81]
- *Meet growing energy demand.* Annual economic growth has been around 5–7 per cent in both Abu Dhabi and Dubai – regional electricity consumption is growing at around the same rate.[82]
- *Facilitate economic diversification.* There is a strategic focus in Abu Dhabi (and Dubai) on diversification such that the economy is less reliant on oil and gas to assist in ensuring the long-term security and sustainability of energy.[83]

76 Eversheds Sutherlands and PWC (2016) above n.1 p 57.
77 Eversheds Sutherlands and PWC (2016) above n.1 p 45.
78 Eversheds Sutherlands and PWC (2016) above n.1 p 94.
79 Eversheds Sutherlands and PWC (2016) above n.1 p 140.
80 Ibid.
81 Eversheds Sutherlands and PWC (2016) above n.1 p 147.
82 Eversheds Sutherlands and PWC (2016) above n.1 p 140.
83 Ibid.

- *Leverage the advantageous geography and climate.* As in both Egypt and Jordan, there is high potential for renewable energy development in the UAE due to high solar irradiation and availability of land.
- *Address carbon emissions.* The UAE has had one of the highest greenhouse gas (carbon dioxide) footprints in the world, mostly due to a high reliance on gas to generate electricity and desalinated water.[84]

4.1.1 Abu Dhabi

Though blessed with the clear majority of the UAE's fossil fuel (oil and gas) reserves, long-term gas contracts with Qatar are unable to meet all of Abu Dhabi's energy requirements, hence the emirate relies heavily on its (more expensive) domestic gas supplies.[85] The Abu Dhabi Future Energy Company (Masdar) is a subsidiary of the Mubadala Development Company, which in turn is a subsidiary of the Abu Dhabi government. Masdar continues to be the main sponsor of renewable projects in Abu Dhabi, and is largely guided by the Abu Dhabi Economic Vision 2030.[86] In 2015, Masdar commissioned the Shams 1 solar power project, a 100 MW CSP project employing a BOO model similar to that used by the emirate in the conventional power sector. The project company sells energy to the local utility (Abu Dhabi Water and Electricity Company (ADWEC)) under a long-term PPA. Masdar has also sponsored several high-profile, utility-scale wind and solar projects in Spain, the UK, Oman, Egypt and Jordan.[87] The main governmental organisations tasked with producing, transmitting and distributing electricity in Abu Dhabi are the utility (the Abu Dhabi Water & Electricity Authority (ADWEA)) and its associated regulator, a single buyer (ADWEC), a transmission company and several distribution companies.[88]

4.1.2 Dubai

Like Jordan, Dubai is relatively fossil fuel poor, possessing less than 5 per cent of the UAE's total fossil fuel reserves – it therefore relies heavily on imports of gas from both Abu Dhabi and Qatar for electricity generation.[89] Although it has entered the renewable market later than neighbouring Abu Dhabi, Dubai's position has become more prominent in recent years, reflecting its rising input fuel prices and the success of its IPP programme.[90] The Dubai Electricity and Water Authority (DEWA) is Dubai's exclusive provider of electricity and water services.

84 Ibid.
85 Eversheds Sutherlands and PWC (2016) above n.1 p 142.
86 Ibid.
87 Ibid.
88 Ibid.
89 Eversheds Sutherlands and PWC (2016) above n.1 p 145.
90 Parkinson, G (2015) 'Dubai set to lead MENA with 25% by 2030 solar goal'. https://reneweconomy.com.au/dubai-set-to-lead-mena-with-25-by-2030-solar-goal-read-more-httpwww-pv-magazine-comnewsdetailsbeitragdubai-set-to-lead-mena-with-25-by-2030-solar-goal_100022178ixzz3t25atktn-54510 (1 December 2015) Accessed: 4 October 2018.

4.2 Key projects: Mohammad Bin Rashid Al Maktoum Solar Park

Dubai's Mohammad Bin Rashid Al Maktoum Solar Park involves both solar PV and CSP technologies and is managed and operated by DEWA. In 2013, US$32.4 million was invested in the park's first, 13 MW solar PV phase.[91] In the park's second phase (in 2015), DEWA issued a request for proposal (RfP) for project developers to submit bids for 200 MW of capacity under a BOO model for a fixed tariff over a 25-year period. Saudi-owned Acwa Power submitted a world record-breaking winning bid of US$0.0584 per kWh.[92] Acwa also proposed to build the entire 1 GW of capacity at a further discounted tariff of US$0.054 per kWh.[93]

Some market participants suggested that the Al Maktoum's second phase winning bid was so low as to be incapable of being built. However, when comparing such prices to that observed for solar PV in Germany, some interesting facts emerge. Solar insolation in Dubai is a little more than twice that in Berlin. On the basis of contemporaneous German prices (around US$0.185 per kWh), the prices in Dubai would be around US$0.054 per kWh – precisely what Acwa proposed if it could construct the entire 1,000 MW solar park.[94]

The Al Maktoum Solar Park's third phase (involving 800 MW of capacity) saw bid prices drop once again to a new world record low. In 2016, the winning bid of 2.99 cents per kilowatt hour (c/kWh) (unsubsidised) from Masdar and FRV was cheaper than all available fossil fuel options in Dubai, and effectively halved the cost of the equivalent bid the previous year.[95] The third phase is due to commence commercial operations in 2020.

In addition to access to cheap debt (at rates of less than 5 per cent), the record-breaking prices for the second and third phases of the Al Maktoum Solar Park were undoubtedly assisted by low labour costs and high capacity factors.[96] Nonetheless, the fact that the price of large-scale solar in a key Middle Eastern jurisdiction halved in just 12 months remains globally significant, and is a dramatic example of just how far and how fast the cost of PV can fall with appropriate support mechanisms.[97]

91 Chadha, M (2015) 'Dubai to invest $3b to boost solar power project capacity to 3GW'. https://reneweconomy.com.au/dubai-to-invest-3b-to-boost-solar-power-project-capacity-to-3gw-43275 (16 April 2015) Accessed: 3 October 2018.

92 The average price of the ten finalists' bids was US$0.0935 per kWh. See: Chadha, M (2015) above n. 91 Accessed: 3 October 2018.

93 Upadhyay, A (2014) +9 (29 November 2014) Accessed: 18 October 2018.

94 In desert environments, panel efficiency would be reduced by both the dust as well as the higher operating temperature. Regular cleaning of the PV modules can only add to the cost. See: Upadhyay, A (2014) above n.93 Accessed: 18 October 2018.

95 In the US, solar tenders are regularly below 3c/kWh, although these include tax incentives and other subsidies. See: Parkinson, G (2016) 'Solar prices plunge to new lows as Dubai auction nets under 3c/kWh'. https://reneweconomy.com.au/solar-prices-plunge-to-new-lows-as-dubai-auction-nets-under-3ckwh-84894 (3 May 2016) Accessed: 15 October 2018.

96 Parkinson, G (2016) above n.95 Accessed: 12 October 2018.

97 In 2015, DEWA awarded the Hassyan coal power station at a much higher tariff of 5.177c/kWh; gas-fired generation in Dubai remains even more expensive. Even at US$10 a barrel, oil cannot match these sorts of prices. See: Parkinson, G (2016) above n.95 Accessed: 15 October 2018.

In 2016, an auction for 200 MW of solar thermal and storage capacity under the Solar Park's fourth phase attracted a new global low for CSP technology of US$94.50/MWh.[98] This phase will host both the world's tallest solar tower and largest thermal energy storage capacity,[99] and has since been increased from 750 to 900 MW in capacity (at a new record low cost of US$24/MWh).[100] Construction is due for completion in 2021.[101]

In 2013, the installed capacity target for the Al Maktoum Solar Park was 1 GW to be completed by 2019 for a cost $3 billion.[102] In 2015, the Park's installed capacity was increased to 3 GW (over a proposed area of some 50 square kilometres) to be completed by 2030, and has since increased again (under Dubai's Clean Energy Strategy 2050 (see Section 4.3 below)) to 5 GW, making the Al Maktoum Solar Park the largest solar park in the world.[103]

4.3 Dubai's Clean Energy Strategy 2050

In 2015, the Dubai Clean Energy Strategy was launched. The Strategy involves a RET of 75 per cent by 2050, aims to make rooftop solar mandatory for all buildings by 2030[104] and seeks to position Dubai as a global centre of clean energy. The Strategy consists of five components, namely infrastructure, legislation, funding, capacity building and a sustainable energy mix. The infrastructure component includes initiatives like the Al Maktoum Solar Park, funding includes the Dubai Green Fund (worth almost US$30 billion)[105] while capacity building involves global training programmes in cooperation with organisations like IRENA. The final component seeks to create a more sustainable energy mix involving solar (25 per cent), nuclear (7 per cent), "clean" coal (7 per cent) and gas (61 per cent) by 2030, with solar increasing to 75 per cent by 2050.[106]

98 Graves, L (2017) 'Dubai set for world's cheapest night-time solar power' https://www.thenational.ae/business/dubai-set-for-world-s-cheapest-night-time-solar-power-1.35494 (5 June 2017) Accessed: 11 September 2018.

99 The tower will be 260 metres in height and involve 15 hours of storage to permit 24/7 dispatchability of electricity.

100 Graves, L (2017) above n.98. Accessed: 7 November 2018.

101 Hill, J (2017) 'Dubai expands mega solar project at "record" low price'. https://reneweconomy.com.au/dubai-expands-mega-solar-project-at-record-low-price-15757 (7 November 2018) Accessed: 13 October 2018.

102 Ibid.

103 Gifford, J (2015) 'Dubai set to lead MENA with 25% by 2030 solar goal'. https://reneweconomy.com.au/dubai-set-to-lead-mena-with-25-by-2030-solar-goal-read-more-httpwww-pv-magazine-comnewsdetailsbeitragdubai-set-to-lead-mena-with-25-by-2030-solar-goal_100022178ixzz3t25atktn-54510 (1 December 2015) Accessed 22 September 2018.

104 Eversheds Sutherlands and PWC (2016) above n.1. p 110.

105 This fund will provide concessional loans for smart grid, storage and other clean energy investors.

106 UAE Government (2018) 'Dubai Clean Energy Strategy'. https://government.ae/en/about-the-uae/strategies-initiatives-and-awards/local-governments-strategies-and-plans/dubai-clean-energy-strategy (12 November 2018) Accessed: 10 October 2019.

Table 30.6 Contracts, counterparties and governing laws for UAE renewable energy projects

Contract	*Counterparties*	*Governing law*
Musataha (Lease)	Landlord (ADWEA/DEWA)	UAE
PPA	ADWEC/DEWA	UAE
Shareholders Agreement	Masdar or another entity in Abu Dhabi/ DEA in Dubai	UAE
EPC Contract	EPC Contractor	Negotiable
O&M Contract	O&M Contractor	Negotiable
Finance documents	Banks/finance provider	Negotiable

Source: Eversheds Sutherlands and PWC (2016) above n.1 p 152.

4.4 Governing laws

Project developers typically need to enter into a suite of contracts when sponsoring or developing a renewable energy project in the UAE. Table 30.6 above sets out the likely counterparties to each of the key contracts under the current regulatory framework:

As in Egypt and Jordan, finance documents are usually governed by English law where finance is obtained from outside the UAE.

4.5 Support mechanisms

Abu Dhabi's independent water and power producer (IWPP) programme involves a "single buyer model", wherein the government offtaker (ADWEA) assumes demand risk under "take or pay" arrangements.[107] ADWEA appoints the winning bidder following an RfP which contains the relevant draft project agreements.

As Dubai's government offtaker, DEWA is a vertically integrated utility, with ownership of generation, transmission and distribution assets. As with Abu Dhabi, a separate regulator is responsible for the development of an independent electricity and water regulatory regime. Dubai commenced its own IWPP programme in 2010.[108]

5 Conclusion

With high electricity demand coupled with an abundant solar resource and high levels of deployable finance, the MENA region (and in particular, the Gulf States) has long been thought ideal for high levels of utility-scale solar PV deployment. Despite this clear potential, as at 2015 a clear majority (nearly 80 per cent) of renewable (non-hydro) energy growth was concentrated in just 4 of the 22 MENA countries, with renewable energy making up just 6 per cent of total installed generation capacity.[109] There are clear signs, however, that such circumstances are changing. The region has begun to appreciate the socio-economic benefits of integrating significant amounts of renewable energy into national grids – this is perceived

107 The successful procurement of the 100 MW solar PV Shams 1 project through the conventional IWPP model is likely to be repeated for other large-scale renewable energy projects in Abu Dhabi. See: Eversheds Sutherlands and PWC (2016) above n.1 p 158.

108 Eversheds Sutherlands and PWC (2016) above n.1 p 165.

109 IRENA (2016) above n.7 p 20.

by a clear majority of MENA governments as a real opportunity for energy diversification, economic growth through increased fossil fuel exports, capacity building and technology transfer. National plans to fulfil each country's short and long-term RETS, as well as policy, regulatory and technical frameworks which facilitate the scaled-up deployment of renewables, will be indispensable.[110]

Political unrest in Egypt – while undoubtedly increasing country risk – has failed to erode the country's long-term commitment to renewables investment. The government's intention to eliminate fuel subsidies, a dedicated governmental authority[111] tasked with supporting renewable energy, attractive FITs and provision of significant tracts of land for project development have all assisted the bankability of Egyptian renewables projects. Jordan's renewable energy market has transitioned from being virtually non-existent in 2013 to a market now worth hundreds of millions of dollars, and in the UAE utility-scale solar auctions conducted between 2015 and 2017 delivered prices that made a significant contribution to the evolution of utility-scale solar PV globally. There is little doubt that the Arab world is actively engaged in leveraging its local advantages by taking bold steps to advance renewables, and in so doing is poised to play a significant role in the global energy transition.[112]

110 Ibid.

111 The New and Renewable Energy Authority.

112 IRENA (2016) above n.7 p 5.

31

MARITIME DISPUTES AND DISPUTED SEABED RESOURCES IN THE AFRICAN CONTINENT

Anna Khalfaoui and Constantinos Yiallourides

1 Introduction

Less than half of the world's maritime boundaries have been settled upon, but the numbers on the African continent are far lower than this average.[1] A few figures illustrate the scale of the issue of overlapping maritime claims and undefined borders in Africa. There are around 27 mainland coastal African States and seven sets of island States whose offshore presence impacts on the maritime delimitation of the coastal States,[2] as it can be seen in Figure 31.1.

The African Union first set 2010 and then 2017 as the deadline for African States to delimit and demarcate their land and maritime borders.[3] To date, however, only 30 per cent of the continent's borders have been delimited or demarcated.[4] A 2014 study identified 100 maritime boundaries in Africa and found that only 32 had been resolved, leaving 68 unresolved or disputed.[5]

Maritime disputes may crystallise in many ways. Neighbouring States can disagree over the boundaries that delimit their maritime zones, as was the case in *Qatar v Bahrain* and *Cameroon v Nigeria* before the International Court of Justice (ICJ), and more generally in the Gulf of Guinea.[6] Neighbouring States may dispute overlapping entitlements to maritime

1 Gbenga Oduntan, *International Law and Boundary Disputes in Africa* (Routledge 2015).

2 Tim Daniels, 'Africa' in David A Colson and Robert W Smith (eds) *International Maritime Boundaries: Volume V* (BRILL 2005) 3429–3437.

3 Fred Oluoch, 'East Africa Yet to Resolve Border Disputes Ahead of Deadline' (*The East African*, 19 January 2017) <https://www.theeastafrican.co.ke/news/East-Africa-yet-to-resolve-border-disputes-ahead-of-deadline/2558-3523420-dw106oz/index.html> 19 January 2017.

4 Strictly speaking 'boundary delimitation' refers to the selection of a boundary site and its definition. Another close concept, 'boundary demarcation', refers to the construction of a boundary line on the ground, Victor Prescott and Gillian Triggs, *International Frontiers and Boundaries* (Martinus Nijhoff 2008) 11–12, 147–148; Theodore Okonkwo, 'Maritime Boundaries Delimitation and Dispute Resolution in Africa' (2017) 8(1) *Beijing Law Review* 55–78.

5 Wendell Roelf, 'Spike Seen in African Offshore Disputes, Oil Companies Watching' (Reuters, 6 November 2014) <https://uk.reuters.com/article/uk-africa-oil-disputes-idUKKBN0IQ1OL20141106>.

6 Oduntan Gbenga, *International Law and Boundary Disputes in Africa* (Routledge 2015).

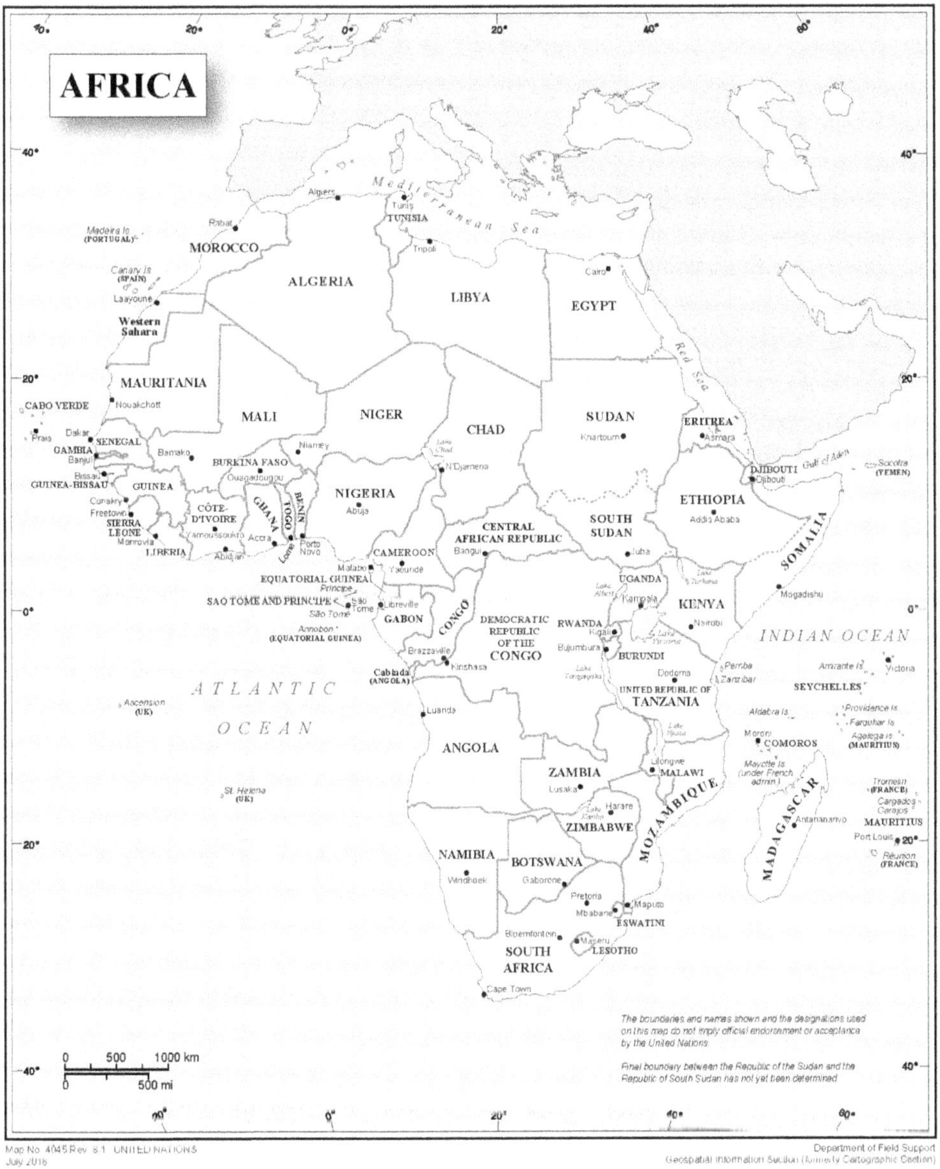

Figure 31.1 Map of Africa

Source: United Nations Cartographic Section – Map No. 4045 Rev. 8.1 (July 2018).

rights and jurisdiction. This includes the right to conduct naval manoeuvres, as in the South China Sea;[7] to exclude fishermen from other States and to exercise powers of arrest, as has

7 Robin R Churchill and Vaughan Lowe, *The Law of the Sea* (3rd edn, Manchester University Press 1999); see also Jing Geng, 'The Legality of Foreign Military Activities in the Exclusive Economic Zone under UNCLOS' (2012) 28(74) *Utrecht Journal of International and European Law* 22–30.

been the case between Namibia and South Africa;[8] to continue fishing in a disputed territory, as in the Western Sahara;[9] or, importantly for our purposes, to exploit highly lucrative seabed resources such as oil or hydrocarbons in a disputed area.[10]

Article 56 of the United Nations Convention on the Law of the Sea (UNCLOS) guarantees that a State, within its exclusive economic zone (EEZ), has "sovereign rights for the purpose of exploring and exploiting, conserving and managing the natural resources".[11] Resolution of a maritime dispute requires delimitation of a maritime boundary according to the provisions laid out in UNCLOS, pursuant to which States may freely decide how to settle their dispute peacefully.[12]

Maritime disputes must be distinguished from territorial disputes which include the contested delimitation of lakes and islands and are also particularly common in Africa, such as around Lake Victoria between Kenya, Uganda and Tanzania; Lake Albert between the Democratic Republic of the Congo (DRC) and Uganda; and Lake Malawi (Nysa) between Tanzania and Malawi.[13]

Undelimited maritime boundaries coupled with abundant disputed seabed resources raise the spectre of conflict in the African Continent. The African Union has laid out the problem clearly:

> Since African countries gained independence, the borders – which were drawn during the colonial period in a context of rivalries between European countries and their scramble for territories in Africa – have been a recurrent source of conflicts and disputes in the continent. Most of the borders are poorly defined. The location of strategic natural resources in cross-border areas poses additional challenges.[14]

Maritime boundary disputes in Africa have typically pre-dated the discovery of seabed resources, in particular oil and gas, but they have been intensified by a recent flurry in exploration activities off its coasts.[15] Since the 2000s, African States have exhibited high growth rates, fuelled by their abundant wealth of natural resources. In 2017, Africa as a whole produced 8,072 thousand barrels of oil daily, totalling 8.7 per cent of world oil production

8 Thara Srinivasan, Reg Watson and Sumaila Rashid, 'Global Fisheries Losses at the Exclusive Economic Zone Level, 1950 to Present' (2012) 36(2) *Marine Policy* 544–549.

9 Oduntan (2015).

10 David Anderson, 'Negotiating Maritime Boundary Agreements: A Personal View' in Rainer Lagoni and Daniel Vignes (eds) *Maritime Delimitation: Volume 53* (BRILL 2006) 129–150.

11 United Nations Convention on the Law of the Sea (adopted 10 December 1982, entered into force 16 November 1994) 1833 United Nations Treaty Series 3.

12 Anne Sheehan, 'Dispute Settlement under UNCLOS: The Exclusion of Maritime Delimitation Disputes' (2005) 24(1) *University of Queensland Law Journal* 165.

13 Oduntan (2015).

14 African Union, 'Conclusions' in *Pan-African Conference on Maritime Boundaries and the Continental Shelf for the Implementation of the African Union Border Programme*, Accra, Ghana (2009), < www.peaceau.org/uploads/conclusions-accra-eng-.pdf >.

15 Wafula Okumu, 'Resources and Border Disputes in Eastern Africa' (2010) 4(2) *Journal of Eastern African Studies* 279–297; Mark Osa Igiehon, 'The ICJ Bakassi Decision: Prospects and Implications for the Exploitation of Petroleum Resources in Contested Waters' in Edwin E Egede and Mark Osa Igiehon (eds) *The Bakassi Dispute and the International Court of Justice: Continuing Challenges* (Routledge 2017) 138–156.

and is estimated to hold 8.5 per cent of the world's proven oil reserves.[16] Hydrocarbons have become a major source of dispute and latent conflicts between African States as neighbouring countries seek to lay claim to the continent's natural resources.[17] In turn, the presence or prospect of oil and gas precipitates the need for maritime delimitation between States.[18] Unequal resources and increased competition over offshore hotspots can magnify disputes.[19] This is concerning given the propensity of sovereignty disputes to escalate into outbreaks of violence and armed conflict.[20] In the Gulf of Guinea in Western Africa alone, it is estimated that the lack of ability to exercise effective control over maritime entitlements and the resulting pervasive insecurity has resulted in more than US$ 2 billion in annual financial losses, constrained investments and crimes such as piracy.[21] Companies in Africa's offshore oil and gas sectors may incur significant costs as a result of maritime disputes, including as a result of legal delays. Operators which were granted licenses to operate in the disputed area are particularly vulnerable.

This chapter provides an overview of some of the most significant maritime boundary disputes in Africa, both past and ongoing, and the interplay between these disputes and the exploration and exploitation of seabed resources. This chapter cannot do justice to the breadth of maritime boundary disputes on the continent, given their sheer numbers, complexities and varieties, fuelled by the ramifications of Africa's colonial past and the presence of externally defined, artificial boundaries. Instead, this chapter concentrates on how the exploration and exploitation of disputed seabed resources have fuelled maritime disputes and how African States have attempted to resolve their differences. Particular focus is paid to cases where the disputing parties were able to sidestep their disagreements over maritime entitlements and boundary delimitation by agreeing to a joint development agreement (JDA) providing for joint exploration and development of seabed resources in the areas of overlap. Joint development involves the creation of a geographic area where joint operations are to be conducted, commonly known as a Joint Development Zone (JDZ). This is often the maritime area in which both States claim sovereign rights, or, as Fox defines it, the area to which "both or either" of the participating States are entitled by international law.[22]

16 'BP Statistical Review of World Energy' (2018) <https://www.bp.com/content/dam/bp/en/corporate/pdf/energy-economics/statistical-review/bp-stats-review-2018-full-report.pdf>.

17 Maurice Kamga, *Délimitation maritime sur la Côte Atlantique africaine* (Bruylant 2006).

18 Gerald Blake and R. F. Swarbrick, 'Hydrocarbons and International Boundaries: A Global Overview' in Gerald Henry Blake, Matt Pratt, Clive Schofield and Janet Allison Brown (eds) *Boundaries and Energy: Problems and Prospects* (Kluwer Law International 1998); Tanga Biang, 'The Joint Development Zone between Nigeria and Sao Tome and Principe: A Case of Provisional Arrangement in the Gulf of Guinea International Law, State Practice and Prospects for Regional Integration' (United Nations – The Nippon Foundation of Japan Fellowship Programme 2010) 187.

19 William Zartman, 'The Foreign and Military Politics of African Boundary Problems' in Carl Gosta Widstrand (ed) *African Boundary Problems* (1st edn, Nordiska Afrikainstitutet 1996) 79–100, Joseph Kum, 'The Central African Subregion' in *Disarmament: Workshop on the Role of Border Problems in African Peace and Security* (United Nations Publications 1993) 49–71.

20 Constantinos Yiallourides, Markus Gehring and Jean-Pierre Gauci, 'The Use of Force in Relation to Sovereignty Disputes over Land Territory' (BIICL 2018) <https://papers.ssrn.com/abstract=3208384>.

21 Junaidu Bello Marshall, 'Joint Development of Offshore Oil and Gas in the Gulf of Guinea: A Case of Energy Security for Nigeria and Cameroon' (2014) 32 *Journal of Law, Policy and Globalization* 2224–3240.

22 Hazel Fox et al. (eds) Joint Development of Offshore Oil and Gas (1st edn, BIICL 1989) 45.

The concept of joint development of resources in disputed maritime areas emerged in the second half of the 1950s.[23] As has been stressed by Anderson:

> The solution of a joint area may be second best to an agreed boundary; but a joint area may well be better than seeing a dispute remain unresolved and possibly grow more serious. The governments may prefer a compromise to a defeat in litigation. An effective treaty providing for joint development may allow the industry to work and produce benefit for many years in an area which would otherwise have remained blighted by dispute over jurisdiction. 'Half a loaf is better than no bread', as the saying goes.[24]

A JDA is an important confidence-building measure which may ultimately lead to a final resolution of the maritime dispute.[25] Articles 74(3) and 83(3) UNCLOS expressly provide for provisional arrangements similar to a JDA where there are overlapping claims within the continental shelf or EEZ.[26] JDAs have also received judicial support, by the ICJ in the *North Sea Continental Shelf* case,[27] by the Arbitral Tribunal in *Guyana v Suriname*[28] and by the International Tribunal for the Law of the Sea (ITLOS) in *Ghana/Côte d'Ivoire.*[29] While there are considerable disagreements between experts as to the definition and essential characteristics of a JDA,[30] this chapter prefers the elastic definition adopted by Fox:

> [A]n agreement between two States to develop so as to share jointly in agreed proportions by interstate cooperation and national measures the offshore oil and gas in a designated zone of seabed and subsoil of the continental shelf to which both or either of the participating States are entitled in international law.[31]

This chapter is structured as follows. First, the chapter discusses the interplay between seabed resources and maritime disputes which were adjudicated or arbitrated or are pending adjudication or arbitration. It then discusses maritime disputes where bilateral or multilateral negotiations achieved maritime delimitation or joint management and exploitation of seabed resources. In the second section, the chapter queries the existence of a presumption of joint and cooperative development of seabed resources in disputed maritime areas in the African Continent.

23 Thomas A Mensah, 'Joint Development Zones as an Alternative Dispute Settlement Approach in Maritime Boundary Delimitation' in Rainer Lagoni, Daniel Vignes and Thomas A Mensah (eds), *Maritime Delimitation: Volume 53* (Brill 2006) 143–152.

24 David Anderson, 'Strategies for Dispute Resolution: Negotiating Joint Agreements' in Gerald Blake, Matt Pratt, Clive Schofield and Janet Allison Brown (eds), *Boundaries and Energy: Problems and Prospects* (Kluwer Law International 1998) 475.

25 Robin R Churchill, 'Joint Development Zones: International Legal Issues' in Hazel Fox et al. (eds) *Joint Development of Offshore Oil and Gas: Volume 2* (1st edn, 1989) 55; Zhiguo Gao, 'The Legal Concept and Aspects of Joint Development in International Law' (1998) 13(1) *Ocean Yearbook* 107–124; Constantinos Yiallourides, 'Joint Development of Seabed Resources in Areas of Overlapping Maritime Claims: An Analysis of Precedents in State Practice' (SSRN Working Paper 2018) <https://ssrn.com/abstract=3258976>.

26 Yiallourides, ibid.

27 *North Sea Continental Shelf Cases (Germany/Denmark; Germany/Netherlands)* (Judgment) [1969] ICJ Rep 3 para 101(c)(2).

28 Arbitration between Guyana and Suriname (Annex VII Tribunal) (2008) 47 *International Legal Materials* 166 paras 459–486.

29 *Delimitation of the Maritime Boundary in the Atlantic Ocean (Ghana/Côte d'Ivoire)* (Judgment of 23 September 2017) para 263 [hereafter, *Ghana/Côte d'Ivoire case*].

30 For a discussion, see Yiallourides (2018) 25.

31 Fox et al. (1989) 45.

2 Resolving maritime disputes through adjudication or arbitration

Many African maritime disputes have been heard before the ICJ, ITLOS and Arbitral Tribunals or are pending adjudication or arbitration. This section details the intersection between such cases and disputed seabed resources.

2.1 Tunisia-Libya – Continental Shelf cases *[1982 and 1985] before the ICJ*

The Libya-Tunisia Agreement of 8 August 1988 is an example of a JDA which was struck following the adjudication of a maritime dispute and the delimitation of the States' maritime boundary before the ICJ in the 1982 *Continental Shelf* case.[32] The ICJ first held that oil and gas concessions were not a relevant consideration in the context of maritime delimitation, except in so far as these oil concessions are based on the States' express or tacit agreement.

Following the proceedings, Libya and Tunisia agreed on a JDZ lying astride the maritime boundary separating their respective continental shelves delimited in the ICJ's judgment.[33] A Libyan-Tunisian Joint Oil Company was established with a special status as an offshore enterprise to exploit the gas in the north-west part of the joint zone.[34] A separate agreement further stipulated that Tunisia would receive 10 per cent of the proceeds from future oil production on the Libyan continental shelf, the south-east section of the zone.[35] Miyoshi notes that the agreement struck by Libya and Tunisia closely mirrored the scheme proposed by Judge *ad hoc* Evenson in his dissenting opinion to the 1982 judgment.[36] There, Judge Evenson proposed a joint development scheme as an alternative solution to the maritime boundary dispute.[37]

2.2 Guinea-Guinea-Bissau – Guinea/Guinea-Bissau *Award [1985]*

Offshore oil was at the centre of the maritime dispute between neighbouring Guinea and Guinea-Bissau. In 1958, Portugal gave US-based Esso (now Exxon) exclusive oil prospecting rights in Guinea-Bissau.[38] In 1979 Guinea granted Union Texas Petroleum an offshore oil concession and exploration began shortly after. The exploratory work conducted by both Esso and Union Texas revealed the likely existence of a transboundary deposit.

Both States turned to arbitration in 1983, less than a year after the signing of UNCLOS.[39] The Tribunal adopted a regional perspective which consisted of joining two coastal points on the continent, from Almadis Point in Senegal to Cape Shilling in Sierra Leone.[40] Aquarone notes that "the driving force of the delimitation process, the prospect of oil in the

32 *Continental Shelf Case (Tunisia/Libya)* (Judgment) [1982] ICJ Rep 18.

33 Biang (2010).

34 Fox et al. (1989).

35 ibid.

36 Masahiro Miyoshi, 'The Basic Concept of Joint Development of Hydrocarbon Resources on the Continental Shelf' (1988) 3(1) *International Journal of Estuarine and Coastal Law* 1–18.

37 "An arrangement for joint exploration, user or even joint jurisdiction over restricted overlapping areas may be a corollary to other equity considerations", *Continental Shelf Case (Tunisia/Libya)* (Judgment) (Diss Op Judge Evensen) [1982] ICJ Rep 18, 306–307.

38 Marie-Christine Aquarone, 'The 1985 Guinea/Guinea-Bissau Maritime Boundary Case and Its Implications' (1995) 26 *Ocean Development & International Law* 413–431.

39 Aquarone (1995), ibid.

40 *Guinea/Guinea-Bissau: Dispute Concerning Delimitation of the Maritime Boundary* (Award of 14 February 1985) (1986) 2 *International Legal Materials* 251–305 para 110.

region, came to nothing; no oil was subsequently found".[41] The award, as it involved two other countries, directly implicated Senegal and Sierra Leone.

2.3 *Senegal-Guinea-Bissau* – Arbitral Award *[1989]* and Guinea-Bissau v Senegal *[1991]*

Less than a month after the *Guinea/Guinea-Bissau* Award, Senegal and Guinea-Bissau challenged the 1960 maritime boundary agreement that was signed by France and Portugal. The arbitral award found that the existing line created by the 1960 agreement concerning the delimitation of the territorial sea, contiguous zone and the continental shelf had force of law between the newly independent States. Guinea-Bissau unsuccessfully challenged the arbitral award before the ICJ. The Court rejected Guinea-Bissau's 1991 request for the Court to delimit all maritime zones between the two countries.[42]

Senegal and Guinea-Bissau were free to choose either the same delimitation line, upheld by the arbitral award, or another line; "[b]ut they agreed instead on a zone straddling the boundary line for the purpose of joint development of EEZ resources".[43] On 14 October 1993, the two States entered into a JDA covering both oil and gas as well as living marine resources. The agreement was later supplemented by a Protocol Relating to the Organization and Operation of the Agency for Management and Cooperation signed on 12 June 1995.[44] Article 2 of the Agreement on the sharing of resources stipulates that access to fishing resources is on equal terms and that revenue from oil and gas is divided 85 per cent for Senegal and 15 per cent for Guinea-Bissau. These proportions apply only to oil already discovered in Senegalese waters. The Agreement also provides, first, for the establishment of an intergovernmental authority to oversee the exploration and exploitation of resources and, second, for joint enforcement and policing powers in the Zone. The Senegal-Guinea-Bissau is a stark example of a peaceful resolution of a boundary dispute and of an agreement which deepened maritime security cooperation by enhancing economic and security ties between the two States.[45]

2.4 *Eritrea-Yemen* – Eritrea/Yemen Award *[1999]*

The likelihood of offshore oil exploitation fuelled the territorial and maritime dispute between Eritrea and Yemen, eventually leading to its arbitration. The dispute concerned a number of uninhabited islands in the southern Red Sea. The Hanish Archipelago is strategically located between the Arabian Peninsula and the Horn of Africa at the entrance of the Bab el-Mandeb Strait which links the Red Sea to the Indian Ocean. The islands were

41 Aquarone (1995) 425.

42 Irini Papanicolopulu, 'Some Thoughts on the Extension of Existing Boundaries for the Delimitation of New Maritime Zones' in Rainer Lagoni and Daniel Vignes (eds) *Maritime Delimitation: Volume 53* (BRILL 2006) 231–244.

43 Masahiro Miyoshi, *The Joint Development of Offshore Oil and Gas in Relation to Maritime Boundary Delimitation* (IBRU 1999) 36.

44 Management and Cooperation Agreement (Senegal/Guinea-Bissau) (adopted 14 October 1993, entered into force 21 December 1995) (1993 Senegal/Guinea-Bissau 1993 Agreement) Management and Cooperation Agreement (Senegal/Guinea-Bissau) (adopted 14 October 1993, entered into force 21 December 1995) (1996) 31 *Law of the Sea Bulletin* 40; Protocol to the Senegal/Guinea-Bissau 1993 Agreement (adopted 12 June 1995, entered into force 21 December 1995).

45 Maurice Kamga, *Délimitation maritime sur la Côte Atlantique africaine* (Bruylant 2006).

occupied by the armed forces of the two States at successive points during the 20th century: the Yemen Arab Republic deployed troops there during the 1973 Arab-Israeli War and during the Ethiopian Civil War.[46] Tensions heightened in 1995 over suspicions that this part of the Red Sea may hold large reserves of offshore oil and natural gas.[47] Eritrea granted US-based Anadarko Petroleum Corporation the rights to explore for gas and oil in the 'Zula Block'. Situated north of the Hanish Islands, the block's south-eastern corner encompassed sections of two Yemeni exploration zones, Yemen's 'Block 23 Antufash' and 'Block 24 Al-Khatib'.[48] The dispute escalated to an armed conflict in the islands during November and December 1995.

The two parties agreed to arbitration in 1996. The Tribunal in Phase I in 1998 awarded most of the archipelago to Yemen and the smaller islands of South West Rocks, the Mohabbakah and Haycock groups to Eritrea. In Phase II, the Arbitration Tribunal delimited the 380 kilometre-long maritime boundary between the two countries. The Tribunal recommended both parties to "give every consideration to the shared or joint or unitized exploitation" of their offshore natural resources.[49]

2.5 *Cameroon-Nigeria* - Cameroon v Nigeria *[2002] before the ICJ*

The Cameroon-Nigeria maritime and boundary dispute led to the ICJ's influential judgment in the *Case Concerning the Land and Maritime Boundary between Cameroon and Nigeria* [2002]. The dispute related to the entire length of their 2,000-kilometre boundary extending from Lake Chad to the waters of the Gulf of Guinea.[50] The dispute crystallised over the oil and natural gas-rich Bakassi Peninsula, which at the time was estimated to hold about 10 per cent of the world's oil and gas reserves.[51] Both States claimed they were entitled to these seabed resources on the basis of their perceived sovereignty over Bakassi. Several scholars have argued that the conflict between the two countries in the Bakassi Peninsula was influenced by the scramble for oil.[52] Indeed, the beginning of border frictions between the two countries in the early 1980s coincided with a period of falling oil prices and repeatedly poor economic performances.[53] Nigeria at the time was heavily dependent on its oil and gas sector. Oil production in Nigeria dramatically increased from approximately 5,100 barrels per day to 2.68 million barrels per day between 1960 and 2012.[54] In 2011 revenues from its oil and gas

46 Daniel Dzurek, Clive Schofield and Shelagh Furness, 'Parting the Red Sea: Boundaries, Offshore Resources and Transit' (IBRU 2001).

47 Jeffrey A Lefebvre, 'Red Sea Security and the Geopolitical-Economy of the Hanish Islands Dispute' (1998) 52(3) *Middle East Journal* 367–385.

48 Lefebvre, ibid.

49 *Award of the Arbitral Tribunal in the Second Stage of the Proceedings between Eritrea and Yemen (Maritime Delimitation)* 17 December 1999, XXII Reports of International Arbitral Awards 335–410 para 86.

50 Daniel-Erasmus Khan, 'Land and Maritime Boundary between Cameroon and Nigeria Case (Cameroon v Nigeria)' *Max Planck Encyclopedia of Public International Law* (Online Version, Updated 2007) <http://opil.ouplaw.com.ezp.lib.cam.ac.uk/view/10.1093/law:epil/9780199231690/law-9780199231690-e156>.

51 Ndumbe Anyu, 'The International Court of Justice and Border-Conflict Resolution in Africa: The Bakassi Peninsula Conflict' (2007) 18(3) *Mediterranean Quarterly* 39–55.

52 Anyu, ibid; Piet Konings, 'The Anglophone Cameroon-Nigeria Boundary: Opportunities and Conflicts' (2005) 104(415) *African Affairs* 275–301.

53 Obasesam Okoi, 'Why Nations Fight: The Causes of the Nigeria–Cameroon Bakassi Peninsula Conflict' (2016) 9(1) *African Security* 42–65.

54 Uwafiokun Idemudia, 'The Resource Curse and the Decentralization of Oil Revenue: The Case of Nigeria'. (2012) 35 *Journal of Cleaner Production* 183–193.

sector continued to account for half of Nigeria's GDP, 90 per cent of its exports and 85 per cent of government revenues.[55]

Cameroon started proceedings against Nigeria before the ICJ in 1994 asking, among other things, for the Court to determine the maritime boundary between the two States. The maritime dispute related to two different sectors. The first ran from the mouth of the Akwayafe River to point G, which Cameroon claimed was delimited by three different treaties, and the second, beyond point G which had not been delimited. Cameroon argued that the maritime delimitation should be drawn by an equidistance line adjusted to account for the concavity of Cameroon's coastline without which Cameroon would be left with practically no EEZ or continental shelf.[56] Nigeria rejected the validity of the three treaties and argued that a strict equidistance line should be preferred regardless of Cameroon's geographic disadvantages.[57] Nigeria asserted that its granting of oil concessions over the disputed Bakassi waters played a very important role in establishing maritime boundaries and that the Court could not redistribute such oil concessions.[58] Cameroon conversely maintained that the existence of oil concessions was not a valid consideration in the delimitation of maritime boundaries.[59]

The ICJ awarded the Bakassi Peninsula to Cameroon on the basis of an unadjusted equidistance.[60] It further found that the granting of oil concessions in and of itself would not be given consideration in the maritime boundary delimitation absent an express or tacit agreement on the part of the disputing State to the other State's grant of license.[61] Otherwise, considering the mere presence or the potential presence of mineral resources as bearing on the delimitation would encourage a right of capture.[62]

A Cameroon-Nigeria Mixed Commission was established to oversee the implementation of the judgment in 2002.[63] The Mixed Commission approved the recommendations of the Working Group on the Maritime Boundary, which include provisions relating to cross-border cooperation on hydrocarbon deposits straddling the maritime boundary.[64] In 2011, the two countries drew up an agreement for joint management and exploitation of oil and other cross-border reserves in the Bakassi Peninsula.[65] The head of the Nigerian

55 Alex Gboyega et al., *Political Economy of the Petroleum Sector in Nigeria* (Policy Research Working Papers, World Bank 2011) <https://doi.org/10.1596/1813-9450-5779>.

56 *Case Concerning the Land and Maritime Boundary between Cameroon and Nigeria (Cameroon v Nigeria, Equatorial Guinea intervening)* [2002] ICJ Rep 303 para 272.

57 ibid para 280.

58 ibid para 282.

59 ibid para 283.

60 ibid para 287.

61 ibid para 304.

62 Barbara Kwiatkowska, 'Resource, Navigational and Environmental Factors in Equitable Maritime Boundary Delimitation' in Jonathan I Charney and Lewis M Alexander (eds), *International Maritime Boundaries* (Martinus Nijhoff 2005) 3223.

63 Eddy Wifa, Mark Amakoromo and Ibiateli Johnson-Ogbo, 'The Role of a Joint Development Agreement (JDA) in Resolving the Conflicts and Uncertainties over Maritime Boundary Delimitation: A Missed Opportunity in the Bakassi Case' in Edwin Egede and Mark Osa Igiehon (eds) *The Bakassi Dispute and the International Court of Justice* (Taylor & Francis 2015) Ch 9.

64 United Nations Office for West Africa and the Sahel (UNOWAS), 'Cameroon-Nigeria Mixed Commission', United Nations Office for West Africa and the Sahel (25 April 2016) <https://unowas.unmissions.org/cameroon-nigeria-mixed-commission>.

65 'Cameroon, Nigeria Plan Joint Oil Work; Addax May Handle' (Reuters, 12 March 2011) <https://www.reuters.com/article/ozabs-cameroon-nigeria-oil-20110312-idAFJOE72B05D20110312>.

delegation, Prince Bola Ajibola, then stressed that it would be "cheaper, better and faster for Cameroon and Nigeria to set up one or several joint ventures to exploit these cross-border hydrocarbon and biotic resources for the mutual benefit of our people".[66] This is in line with the many scholars who have argued that the implementation of a joint development zone would be the best solution for the Nigeria-Cameroon boundary conflict. Progress towards the agreement's implementation has so far, however, remained limited.

2.6 *Ghana-Côte d'Ivoire* – Ghana/Côte d'Ivoire *[2017] before ITLOS*

Ghana discovered major oil resources at the Jubilee Field 32 nautical miles off the Ghanaian coast in 2007 which attracted significant attention from foreign investors.[67] In March 2009, Tweneboa, Enyenra and Ntomme (TEN) Fields were discovered in the area immediately adjacent to Jubilee Field. Côte d'Ivoire continuously objected to Ghana's exploitation activities, claiming that these were in fact conducted in its maritime area. In 2009, Côte d'Ivoire petitioned the United Nations (UN) to complete the delimitation of its maritime boundary with Ghana.[68]

By the time the issue of maritime delimitation was brought into bilateral negotiations between the parties, the TEN and Jubilee Fields were all under development by a consortium of companies led by London-based Tullow Oil. A report in a Ghanaian newspaper claimed that: "[a] major crude oil-induced border dispute could break out between Ghana and neighbouring Côte d'Ivoire if immediate steps are not taken to enter into appropriate negotiations to redefine the international boundary between the two West African nations".[69] The area was reported to contain reserves of 2 billion barrels of oil and 1.2 trillion cubic feet of natural gas.[70]

Côte d'Ivoire continued to object to the ongoing oil activities of Ghana, asserting that those activities were being undertaken in the Ivorian maritime area. It was in response to this assertion that the parties agreed to establish the "Joint Ivoiro-Ghanaian Commission on Maritime Border Demarcation" (Boundary Commission) and maritime delimitation negotiations commenced. On 3 December 2014, in view of the lack of progress in diplomatic negotiations, Ghana and Côte d'Ivoire agreed to submit the maritime boundary dispute to a Special Chamber of ITLOS.

Shortly afterwards, in April 2015, a Special Chamber of ITLOS granted Côte d'Ivoire's request for provisional measures. It recognised that drilling causes a "permanent physical modification" of the disputed area.[71] Ghana was, among others, ordered to refrain from engaging in "new drilling" and was required to "take all necessary steps" to prevent information resulting from past, ongoing or future exploration activities conducted by Ghana

66 ibid.

67 Constantinos Yiallourides, 'Calming the Waters in the West African Region: The Case of Ghana and Côte d'Ivoire' (2018) 26(3) *African Journal of International and Comparative Law* 507, 525–526.

68 Djibril Moudachirou, 'Ocean Resources' Ascendancy over African States Friendship Relations: Can UNCLOS Help Resolve Current or Future Maritime Boundary Delimitation Dispute Issues?' (2016) 5(1) *Journal of Water Resources and Ocean Science* 6–7.

69 'Cote d'Ivoire Lays Claim to Ghana's Oil' (GhanaWeb, 3 April 2010) <www.ghanaweb.com/GhanaHomePage/NewsArchive/Cote-d-Ivoire-lays-claim-to-Ghana-s-oil-177840>.

70 Kingsley Kobo, 'Ivory Coast, Ghana Seek Peaceful Oil Dispute Solution' (AA, 6 October 2014) https://www.aa.com.tr/en/economy/exclusive-ivory-coast-ghana-seek-peaceful-oil-dispute-solution/152473.

71 Dispute concerning Delimitation of the Maritime Boundary between Ghana and Côte d'Ivoire in the Atlantic Ocean (Ghana/Côte d'Ivoire) (Provisional Measures Order of 25 April 2015) paras 89–90.

"from being used in any way whatsoever to the detriment of Côte d'Ivoire".[72] Importantly, the Special Chamber did not order Ghana to suspend all operations as this would entail "considerable financial loss to Ghana and its concessionaries".[73]

In its award on the merits, in September 2017, the Special Chamber held that an unadjusted equidistance line was an equitable solution in this case.[74] It found that no consideration put forward by the parties, such as the location of seabed resources and the conduct of the parties, including in conducting seismic surveys and exploiting existing wells, was a relevant circumstance in maritime delimitation.[75] The Special Chamber held that where one State engages in unilateral petroleum activities on the EEZ or continental shelf of a disputed area which is found to belong to another State, the former State will not necessarily violate the latter State's sovereign rights if it acted with the honest belief that these areas were within its territory.[76] As one of us has argued, "[t]he finding that an initiating state bears no international responsibility for alleged violations of the other claiming state's alleged rights could encourage more unilateralism in areas with seabed resources".[77]

The Ghana-Côte d'Ivoire example illustrates how maritime disputes may adversely affect the profitability of oil and gas discoveries. The intensification of the maritime dispute and its submission to ITLOS cast doubt on the profitability of TEN. On 2 March 2015, Tullow Oil lost US$ 308 million of its market value due to concerns that the project would be severely delayed.[78] By the time of the provisional order of 25 April 2015, Tullow Oil and other concessionaries had already invested over US$ 2 billion in the TEN Fields. Ghanaian concessionaries had already drilled 10 wells and were prevented from drilling the further 14 that were planned for the oil field's full development, significantly decreasing the rate of oil production.

Shortly after the ITLOS judgment, Ghana and Côte d'Ivoire agreed to sign a Strategic Partnership Agreement announcing six areas of strategic cooperation, including maritime cooperation.[79] The joint committee established to implement the ruling agreed to develop a document that will show the plotted maritime boundary for both countries and will, in future meetings, discuss the "draft framework agreement on cooperation in the areas of maritime boundary, hydrocarbons and other natural resources".[80] This could be the first step to the establishment of a JDZ for petroleum fields transcending the established boundary.

72 *Ghana/Côte d'Ivoire (Provisional Measures)* para 108(b).

73 *Ghana/Côte d'Ivoire (Provisional Measures)* paras 99–108(1).

74 *Delimitation of the Maritime Boundary in the Atlantic Ocean (Ghana/Côte d'Ivoire)* (Judgment of 23 September 2017) paras 402–480.

75 For a commentary, see Constantinos Yiallourides, 'Calming the Waters in the West African Region: The Case of Ghana and Côte d'Ivoire' (2018) 26(3) *African Journal of International and Comparative Law* 507–526.

76 *Ghana/Côte d'Ivoire* (Judgment) para 592.

77 Constantinos Yiallourides, 'Calming the Waters in the West African Region: The Case of Ghana and Côte d'Ivoire' (2018) 26(3) *African Journal of International and Comparative Law* 507, 525–526.

78 'Tullow Falls on Worries Legal Dispute Could Delay Ghana Project' (Reuters, 2 March 2015) <https://af.reuters.com/article/investingNews/idAFKBN0LY1K720150302>.

79 'Ghana, Cote d'Ivoire Sign Strategic Partnership Agreement' (GhanaWeb, 17 October 2017) <www.ghanaweb.com/GhanaHomePage/NewsArchive/Ghana-Cote-d-Ivoire-sign-Strategic-Partnership-Agreement-591780>.

80 Maritime Dispute: Ghana, Côte d'Ivoire Agree Guidelines on Boundaries' (GhanaWeb, 8 December 2018) <www.ghanaweb.com/GhanaHomePage/NewsArchive/Maritime-dispute-Ghana-C-te-d-Ivoire-agree-guidelines-on-boundaries-676066>.

2.7 Somalia-Kenya – pending before the ICJ

Oil blocks awarded by Kenya to foreign oil companies are at the heart of the maritime dispute between Somalia and Kenya which is pending adjudication before the ICJ. In 2009, Kenya and Somalia reached a Memorandum of Agreement agreeing to demarcate the maritime boundary between the States by negotiation.[81] This was later rejected by the Somalian Parliament. In 2012, Kenya awarded exploration licenses for eight offshore blocks to foreign oil companies in the Indian Ocean, including Italy-based Eni, France-based Total and Anadarko Petroleum.[82] Somalia protested, contending that Kenya had contravened Somalia Law no. 37 defining Somalia's continental shelf and exclusive economic zone. Abdullahi Haji, then Somalia's minister of foreign affairs, proclaimed that "[t]he issue between Somalia and Kenya is not a dispute; it is a territorial argument that came after oil and gas companies became interested in the region".[83]

Somalia approached the ICJ in 2014 asking the Court to determine the maritime boundary between the two States, including the continental shelf. Kenya favours a maritime boundary based on a straight-line running parallel to the line of latitude. Somalia, conversely, asserts that maritime delimitation should be achieved on the basis of a median line, according to Article 15 UNCLOS. In 2017, the ICJ assumed jurisdiction, rejecting Kenya's preliminary objection that the 2009 Memorandum of Agreement precluded recourse to the jurisdiction of the ICJ. As it stands, the pending dispute casts significant doubt on existing oil and gas investments in the disputed area. The prospective judgment may cause the discharge of Kenya's privately held petroleum contracts in the disputed area, therefore inflicting serious damages on existing oil investments.[84] Cooperation in the form of a JDA is a possible way forward but given the ongoing litigation, is not currently a priority for the disputing States.

2.8 Gabon-Equatorial Guinea – pending referral to the ICJ

The territorial and maritime dispute between Gabon and Equatorial Guinea concerns the ownership of the three small islands Mbane, Cocotiers and Conga in the Corisco Bay.[85] The offshore waters are thought to possess several hundred thousand barrels of oil.[86] The dispute escalated when Ali Bongo Ondimba, then Defence Minister and current President of Gabon, visited the islands in 2003 and asserted Gabon's sovereignty. This was swiftly decried by Equatorial Guinea. Equatorial Guinea began producing oil in 1995 and increased its oil and gas production rapidly, with its production peaking at 425,000 barrels per day in 2005, overtaking its much larger neighbour.[87] Equatorial Guinea has since struggled to halt the decline

81 Mark Osa Igiehon, 'The ICJ Bakassi Decision: Prospects and Implications for the Exploitation of Petroleum Resources in Contested Waters' in Edwin E Egede and Mark Osa Igiehon (eds), *The Bakassi Dispute and the International Court of Justice: Continuing Challenges* (Routledge 2017).

82 Moudachirou (2016).

83 Kelly Gilblom, 'Kenya, Somalia Border Row Threatens Oil Exploration' (Reuters, 20 April 2012) <https://www.reuters.com/article/us-kenya-exploration-idUSBRE83J0M120120420>.

84 Marianthi Pappa, 'The Impact of Judicial Delimitation on Private Rights Existing in Contested Waters: Implications for the Somali-Kenyan Maritime Dispute' (2017) 61(3) *Journal of African Law* 393–418.

85 Oduntan (2015).

86 Moudachirou (2016).

87 Robert Perkins, 'Interview: Equatorial Guinea Warns of African Asset Grab by Oil Majors | S&P Global Platts' (*S&P Global*, 6 September 2018) <https://www.spglobal.com/platts/en/market-insights/latest-news/oil/090618-interview-equatorial-guinea-warns-of-african-asset-grab-by-oil-majors>.

in its oil production as its economy remains largely dependent on hydrocarbons which has fed its claims on the Corisco Bay islands.

In January 2004, Equatorial Guinea and Gabon agreed for their dispute to be settled by a UN mediator. In July 2004, both States concluded an agreement allowing joint oil exploration in disputed territories until a final resolution is worked out under UN mediation. In the absence of progress, including towards the implementation of a framework for joint management, the two countries in February 2016 signed a special agreement referring the dispute to the ICJ.[88]

3 Resolving maritime disputes through bilateral and multilateral negotiations

Several maritime disputes on the African Continent have been mediated directly between States without requiring recourse to adjudication or arbitration. In such instances, as will be seen in this section, joint management and exploitation of seabed resources was frequently achieved by the States through direct negotiations.

3.1 The influence of the African Union Border Programme

The African Union, building on the work of its predecessor, the Organisation of African Unity (OAU), has strongly encouraged maritime delimitation and demarcation in Africa through negotiated settlements between disputing States, together with better management and exploitation of maritime resources. Key delimitation and demarcation principles have been laid down and further specified over time in the OAU Charter (1963); the OAU's Resolution on Peace and Security in Africa through Negotiated Settlement of Border Conflicts (1986); and the Constitutive Act of the African Union (2000). They include the principle of intangibility, which upholds the territorial integrity and existing borders of African States at the time of their independence, and the principle of peaceful settlement of disputes within an African network.[89]

The OAU's Assembly of Heads of State and Government held in Durban, South Africa, in July 2002 stressed the urgent need to delimit and demarcate African boundaries. An important breakthrough came about with the 8th Ordinary Session of the Assembly of Heads of State and Government of the African Union, in January 2007 in Addis Ababa which established the African Union Border Programme (AUBP). The AUBP aims to assist governments in the delimitation, demarcation and reaffirmation of their boundaries; increase regional integration; facilitate cross-border cooperation; and develop institutions for the structural prevention of conflict on a pan-African level. In 2009, the Pan-African Conference on Maritime Boundaries and the Continental Shelf for the Implementation of the African Union Border Programme stressed the continued need for expedited action by African States to delimitate their maritime boundaries.[90] The Conference noted with satisfaction

88 'Secretary-General's Opening Statement at Signing Ceremony on the Border Dispute between the Republic of Equatorial Guinea and the Gabonese Republic [as Delivered] | United Nations Secretary-General' (15 November 2016) <https://www.un.org/sg/en/content/sg/statement/2016-11-15/secretary-generals-opening-statement-signing-ceremony-border-dispute>.

89 African Union Border Programme (AUBP), 'Delimitation and Demarcation of Boundaries in Africa. The User's Guide' (2nd edn, AUBP 2014) <www.peaceau.org/uploads/au2013-en-delim-a-demar-of-bound-gen-iss-a-studies-elec2.pdf>.

90 Okonkwo (2017).

initiatives furthering individual and collective capacities for the management of maritime resources, "including the joint exploitation and management of trans-boundary resources".[91] The African Charter on Maritime Security, Safety and Development was adopted in 2016 "to solidify Africa's commitment to an efficient and effective management of its oceans, seas and waterways, so as to ensure sustainable, equitable and beneficial exploration of these critical resources".[92]

The African Union's (AU's) soft-law, non-binding approach, has led to a number of successful negotiations on complex maritime boundary delimitation.[93] On 5 December 2011, as part of the implementation of the AUBP, the governments of the Comoros, Mozambique and Tanzania signed four agreements on the delimitation of the maritime boundaries between their respective countries as a result of direct negotiations between the parties. On 17 February 2012, similarly, as part of the AUBP's implementation, the Governments of the Comoros, the Seychelles and Tanzania agreed to the delimitation of their maritime borders. These sets of agreements are welcome news for the stability of the area as the waters of the Indian Ocean are rich in natural gas and probably also in oil and mineral nodules which have sparked a flurry of exploration in recent years.[94] The agreements have seemingly fuelled this drilling activity. Comoros awarded its first oil and gas exploration license in 2012 to Kenya-based Bahari Resources and in 2014 for a further three blocks to Bahari Resources and to a unit of UK-based Discover Exploration in a context of substantial gas finds in Mozambique and Tanzania.[95]

3.2 *Negotiations for maritime delimitation and JDAs in the Gulf of Guinea*

The offshore and deep-water areas of the Gulf of Guinea, as has already been indicated in the context of the Cameroon-Nigeria maritime dispute in Part II, hold enormous oil and gas reserves. The Gulf of Guinea, stretching from Senegal to Angola, with an approximately 6,000 kilometre coastline, is now regarded as the world's leading region for oil reserves' renewal.[96] Exploitation in the Gulf of Guinea benefits from several advantages: its oil is light and sweet with lower sulphur content; its long coast allows exploitation in the entire offshore area; and its deep waters and proximity to both Europe and the US enable easy transportation.[97]

91 African Union, 'Conclusions', Pan-African Conference on Maritime Boundaries and the Continental Shelf for the Implementation of the African Union Border Programme. Accra, Ghana (2009), < www.peaceau.org/uploads/conclusions-accra-eng-.pdf>.

92 African Union, African Charter on Maritime Security, Safety and Development (Lomé Charter) (2016), <https://au.int/sites/default/files/treaties/33128-treaty-0060_-_lome_charter_e.pdf>.

93 Gbenga Oduntan, 'The Demarcation of Straddling Villages in Accordance with the International Court of Justice Jurisprudence: The Cameroon–Nigeria Experience' (2016) 5(1) *Chinese Journal of International Law* 79–114.

94 Matthew Richmond 'Oil, Gas and Renewable Energy' (Regional State of Coast Report for the Western Indian Ocean, 2016) 342–359 <https://doi.org/10.18356/d48eeaba-en>.

95 Ahmed Ali Amir, 'Comoros Grants Oil and Gas Exploration Licences for Six Blocks' (Reuters, 19 March 2014) <https://af.reuters.com/article/comorosNews/idAFL6N0MG2EO20140319>.

96 Gbenga Oduntan, 'Modalities for Post Boundary Dispute, Cross Border JPZs/Unitisation Upstream Hydrocarbon Exploitation in the Gulf of Guinea?' (2009) 7(4) *Oil, Gas & Energy Law Journal* (*OGEL*) <https://www.ogel.org/article.asp?key=2943>.

97 Groupe de Recherche et d'Information sur la Paix et la Sécurité (GRIP), 'Géopolitique du pétrole dans la CEEAC' (GRIP, 5 June 2014) https://www.grip.org/sites/grip.org/files/NOTES_ANALYSE/2014/Notes%20DAS%20-<%20Afrique%20EQ/OBS2011-54_GRIP_NOTE-9_G%C3%A9opolitique%20du%20p%C3%A9trole%20dans%20la%20CEEAC.pdf>.

Allen, in particular, has highlighted the importance of the region for meeting the energy needs of oil importing countries given fears of global energy insecurity.[98] Also, according to Daniel, "[t]he necessity for certainty in the Gulf of Guinea, particularly as far as commercial interests are concerned, has been a driving force in the high level of maritime boundary making activity which has taken place there over the past ten years".[99]

As will be shown in this section, the Gulf of Guinea has seen numerous examples of maritime boundary agreements and agreements for joint exploitation and development of resources which have both averted conflicts and strengthened economic relations between States. The "evolving practice of peaceful resolution"[100] in the Gulf of Guinea and West Africa was formalised by the establishment in 2001 of the Gulf of Guinea Commission by Angola, the Republic of the Congo, Gabon, Nigeria and São Tomé and Príncipe to serve as

> [A] framework of consultation among the countries of the Gulf of Guinea for cooperation and development, as well as for the prevention, management and resolution of conflicts that may arise from the delimitation of borders and the economic and commercial exploitation of natural resources within the territorial boundaries, particularly in the overlapping Exclusive Economic Zones (EEZ).[101]

Cameroon and the DRC joined the Commission in 2008.

On the most northern part of the Gulf of Guinea, Senegal early on delimited its maritime boundaries with both the Gambia (1975)[102] and Cape Verde (1993).[103]

Nigeria has sought to delimit the limits of its EEZ in the Gulf of Guinea which contains one of the world's richest offshore hydrocarbon areas. Nigeria signed a maritime boundary agreement with Equatorial Guinea in 2000 which was "very much driven by oil-based considerations".[104] The agreement provides for the possibility of setting up a joint exploitation zone over the pool of oil which straddles the Zafiro oil field of Equatorial Guinea and the Nigerian Ekanga-1 reservoir.[105]

In 2001, Nigeria and São Tomé and Príncipe concluded a Treaty on Joint Development of Petroleum and other Resources. Negotiations towards maritime delimitation had started in 1998 but came to a halt as the two countries disagreed on the delimitation method.[106] São Tomé and Príncipe claimed an equidistance line boundary, while Nigeria argued that its longer coastline warranted a substantial adjustment of that line. In August 2000, in light of their differences, the two heads of State agreed not to seek a final maritime boundary delimitation and instead to strike a provisional arrangement in the form of a JDA.[107] The treaty

98 Fidelis Allen, 'Oil and Security in the Gulf of Guinea: Reflections on the External and Domestic Linkages' (2012) 5(4) *Journal of Sustainable Development* 132.

99 Daniel (2005) 3432.

100 Igiehon (2017) 250.

101 Treaty Establishing the Gulf of Guinea Commission (3 July 2001) <https://cggrps.com/wp-content/uploads/Tratado-EN1.pdf>.

102 Treaty Fixing the Maritime Boundaries between the Republic of the Gambia and the Republic of Senegal (signed and entered into force 4 June 1975).

103 Treaty on the Delimitation of the Maritime Frontier between the Republic of Cape Verde and the Republic of Senegal (signed 17 February 1993, entered into force 25 March 1994).

104 Daniel (2005) 3433.

105 Kamga (2006); Ali (2015).

106 Wifa, Amakoromo and Johnson-Ogbo (2017).

107 Kamga (2006).

establishes a joint development zone of 28,000 square kilometres, in the area where their EEZ claims overlap, for the orderly exploration and exploitation of petroleum and other resources.[108] The parties share all benefits in the proportions of Nigeria 60 per cent and São Tomé and Príncipe 40 per cent. The treaty also lays out a joint development authority with civil and administrative jurisdiction to regulate and manage activities in the joint zone. The JDZ's exploration results have not been promising so far. US-based ChevronTexaco, which drilled the first exploration wells in Block 1 in 2006, announced that the oil was not commercially exploitable, and a number of blocks have since remained abandoned. There have also been reports that the overstaffed JDA has become a financial burden, since 2008 São Tomé and Príncipe has not paid its 40 per cent share of the JDA's operating costs.[109]

Nigeria agreed to a maritime boundary with Benin in 2006 on the basis of equidistance.[110] Nigeria and Ghana in 2017 signed a memorandum of understanding (MOU) on maritime operation to strengthen trade, together with economic and security cooperation.[111] It is to be hoped that this memorandum may lead to further negotiations as to the maritime delimitation between the two countries. Ghana, informed by its dispute with Côte d'Ivoire, has expressed its desire to open negotiations with Nigeria, Togo and Benin as to the delimitation of its maritime boundaries.[112] Reports indicated that Togo and Ghana began boundary negotiations in June 2018 after Togolese authorities prevented Ghana's seismic vessels from carrying out exploration in waters claimed by both countries in December 2017 and May 2018.[113]

In addition to its maritime boundary agreement with Nigeria, São Tomé and Príncipe delimited its maritime borders with Equatorial Guinea in 1999.[114] In 2001, São Tomé and Príncipe also signed a maritime delimitation agreement with Gabon.[115]

In the southern extremities of the Gulf of Guinea, Angola has entered into a JDA with two of its neighbours: the Republic of the Congo and the DRC. Angola and the Republic of the Congo began negotiations towards a maritime boundary agreement in 1998. As talks faltered, the two States instead agreed in September 2001 to a protocol to a joint exploitation zone over the waters off the Congolese Kouilou region and the Angolan enclave of Cabinda.[116] In 2002, the two States finalised the terms of a JDA which provides for the creation

108 Treaty between the Federal Republic of Nigeria and the Democratic Republic of São Tomé and Príncipe on the Joint Development of Petroleum and Other Resources, in respect of Areas of the Exclusive Economic Zone of the Two States (signed 21 February 2001, entered into force 16 January 2003).

109 Gerhard Seibert, 'São Tomé and Príncipe 1975–2015: Politics and Economy in a Former Plantation Colony' (2016) 42(3) *Estudos Ibero-Americanos* 987–1012 <www.redalyc.org/articulo.oa?id=134618568009>.

110 Treaty on the Maritime Boundary and Memorandum of Understanding (Benin/Nigeria) (signed 4 August 2006).

111 Sulaimon Salau, 'Nigeria, Ghana Sign MoU on Maritime Operations' (*The Guardian*, 18 October 2017) <https://guardian.ng/business-services/nigeria-ghana-sign-mou-on-maritime-operations>.

112 'Ghana to Define Maritime Boundaries with Nigeria, Togo and Benin', 24 September 2014. < www.ghanaweb.com/GhanaHomePage/NewsArchive/Ghana-to-define-maritime-boundaries-with-Nigeria-Togo-and-Benin-327272>.

113 Adu Koranteng, 'Ghana Begins Maritime Boundary Talks with Togo | Comprehensive Ghana Oil and Gas News, Information, Updates, Analysis' (Reporting Oil and Gas, 6 January 2018) < www.reportingoilandgas.org/ghana-begins-maritime-boundary-talks-with-togo-2>.

114 Treaty concerning the Delimitation of the Maritime Boundary between the Republic of Equatorial Guinea and the Democratic Republic of Sao Tome and Principe (signed 26 June 1999).

115 Agreement on the Delimitation of the Maritime Border between the Gabonese Republic and the Democratic Republic of Sao Tome and Principe (signed 26 April 200).

116 Kamga (2006).

of an Angolan-Congolese shared zone of 696 square kilometres in the undelimited area.[117] Under the agreement, revenues from Congo's Haute Mer and Angola's Block 14 are shared equally. At the signing, the Angolan Deputy Oil Minister declared that "[t]his accord is a peaceful way to resolve the problems between the two countries", while the Congolese Oil Minister added "[w]e thought the best formula was to exploit it together".[118] In 2004 Chevron Overseas Congo, a subsidiary of US-based ChevronTexaco Corp, reported a significant petroleum discovery in the unitised zone at the Lianzi-1 exploration well; exploitation began in 2015.[119]

The establishment in principle of a JDZ between Angola and the DRC also followed the two States' failure to agree on permanent maritime boundary delimitation. The DRC has an extremely narrow access to the sea of 37 miles which cuts through Angola, separating Angola from its enclave of Cabinda. The dispute is complicated by Cabinda's abundant offshore natural resources to which the DRC has laid claims.[120] A number of Angolan blocks of Cabinda severely restrict DRC's access to the sea and have been contested by Kinshasa.[121] Failing a maritime boundary agreement, in May 2003 the two States signed a MOU to endeavour to resolve the maritime dispute by peaceful means. In 2007, the States agreed in principle to an agreement creating a common interest zone for the exploration and production of hydrocarbons, which to date has not been implemented.[122] Tensions between the two countries have continued to grow with the DRC accusing Angola of stealing its offshore oil and Angolan troops of trespassing onto its territory.[123] In April 2013, Sonangol, the Angolan State oil company, reached a preliminary trade agreement with its counterpart for the DRC, Cohydro, for joint oil production in the common interest zone.[124] This may constitute a first step towards the implementation of the 2007 agreement and the de-escalation of tensions between the two countries through joint exploration and exploitation of the disputed offshore resources.

3.3 Negotiations for maritime agreements and joint development agreements in the Red Sea

The rich waters of the Red Sea on the eastern coast of Africa have enflamed both maritime and territorial boundary disputes between the coastal States of Djibouti, Egypt, Eritrea, Israel, Jordan, Saudi Arabia, Sudan and Yemen. Exploration in the Gulf of Suez basin, north

117 'Angola and Congo-Brazzaville Sign Agreements for Cross Border Oil Exploration' (Macauhub, 19 March 2012) < www.macauhub.com.mo/en/2012/03/19/angola-and-congo-brazzaville-sign-agreements-for-cross-border-oil- exploration>.

118 'Angola and Congo End Maritime Border Dispute' (Rigzone 2002) <https://www.rigzone.com/news/oil_gas/a/2943/angola_and_congo_end_maritime_border_dispute>.

119 'Le Congo assume la présidence du Comité d'exploitation du champ pétrolier Lianzi – Économie – Angola Press – ANGOP' (*Agencia Angola Press*, 8 April 2018) <www.angop.ao/angola/fr_fr/noticias/economia/2018/7/31/Congo-assume-presidence-Comite-exploitation-champ-petrolier-Lianzi,a063076c-5828-4572-b41a-a0689ac3ce0d.html>.

120 Moudachirou (2016).

121 ibid.

122 ibid.

123 'Angola Accuses Congo of Violating Common Border' (Reuters, 17 December 2009) <https://www.reuters.com/article/angola-congo-dispute-idAFLDE5BG0VD20091217>.

124 Michael Kavanagh, 'Sonangol, Cohydro of Congo Reach Agreement on Offshore Oil Block' (Bloomberg, 22 April 2013) <https://www.bloomberg.com/news/articles/2013-04-22/sonangol-cohydro-of-congo-reach-agreement-on-offshore-oil-block>.

of the Red Sea, started as early as the 19th century. By the 2000s, more than 1,900 wells had been drilled in the Gulf of Suez, defining more than 120 fields.[125] Despite its riches, exploration in the Red Sea itself has remained limited owing to the sea's deep waters and complicated topography, resulting in the average deep-water rig cost being estimated at US$ 600 million.[126] This has not prevented the escalation of disputes between the neighbouring States. Besides the Eritrea-Yemen dispute discussed in Section II, a number of States have engaged in bilateral negotiations to delimit their maritime boundaries and, thus, remove barriers to the exploration of the Red Sea's seabed resources.

As early as 1974, Sudan and Saudi Arabia signed a JDA for the joint exploitation of seabed and subsoil resources in a common zone in the Red Sea.[127] The agreement provides for national zones where each country has exclusive sovereign rights from the shore up to 1,000 metres into the sea and a Common Zone between the two national zones where the two States have equal sovereign rights in all the natural resources of the Common Zone (Articles 3– 5). The Saudi-Sudanese Red Sea Joint Commission was established in 1975 to oversee the exploitation of natural resources in the Common Zone. Article 14 provides that where deposits accumulate across the boundary of a national zone into the Common Zone, the Joint Commission shall determine how these resources are to be exploited on the basis of an equitable share of the proceeds of exploitation. Little exploration activity in fact took place in the Common Zone due to a combination of deep waters and falling global ore prices which led the Germany-based Pressaug AG to abandon its mining plan in the early 1980s.[128] In 2010, the Joint Commission granted a 30-year license for the "Atlantis II" area in the Common Zone to Saudi company Manafa International with which Canada-based Diamond Fields has a joint venture.[129] Following studies revealing large reserves of zinc, copper and silver, production in the joint area was initially expected to start in 2014 but operating costs have delayed the start of production.[130]

Efforts to achieve maritime delimitation in the Red Sea have so far remained limited although a number of maritime boundary agreements have been enacted. Israel and Jordan signed a maritime boundary agreement in 1996 defining their boundaries in the Northern Gulf of Aqaba.[131] Saudi Arabia and Yemen settled their land and maritime boundaries in a 2000 agreement.[132] Exploration sites had in the past been affected by the dispute. In the early 1990s, Saudi Arabia had sent warning letters to six oil companies operating in Yemen claiming that the companies were in fact operating on Saudi territory.[133] British Petroleum

125 Dzurek et al. (2001).
126 Ibid.
127 Agreement between Sudan and Saudi Arabia Relating to the Joint Exploitation of the Natural Resources of the Seabed and Subsoil of the Red Sea in the Common Zone (16 May 1974); for a discussion, see Miyoshi (1999).
128 Erich Blissenbach and Zohair Nawab, 'Metalliferous Sediments of the Seabed: The Atlantis-II-Deep Deposits of the Red Sea 1' (1982) 3(1) *Ocean Yearbook Online* 77–104.
129 Paula Park, 'What Might Red Sea Mining Bring to Saudi Arabia and Sudan?' (SciDev.Net, 14 September 2012) <www.scidev.net/index.cfm?originalUrl=/global/biodiversity/feature/what-might-red-sea-mining-bring-to-saudi-arabia-and-sudan-.html&>.
130 'Deep-Sea Mining Remains out of Reach, for Now' (Stratfor, 13 May 2016) <https://worldview.stratfor.com/article/deep-sea-mining-remains-out-reach-now>.
131 Maritime Boundary Agreement between the Government of the State of Israel and the Government of the Hashemite Kingdom of Jordan (signed 18 January 1996, entered into force 17 February 1996).
132 International Border Treaty between the Republic of Yemen and the Kingdom of Saudi Arabia (signed 12 June 2000, entered into force 4 July 2000).
133 John Roberts 'The Saudi-Yemeni Boundary Treaty' (2000) 8(2) *Boundary & Security Bulletin* 70–73.

interrupted its drilling in the Yemeni Antufash offshore block in the Red Sea claiming at the time that it had rethought its priorities.[134]

Similar problems of establishing oil rights in a context of undelimited boundaries have also occurred between Egypt and Sudan. In December 1991, Sudan granted an onshore and offshore exploration block covering 10,300 square kilometres to Canada's International Petroleum Corporation (IPC) in the Halaib triangle disputed by the two States.[135] This was immediately contested by Egypt which in early 1992 responded by issuing a tender for four exploration blocks in the Red Sea with one block, Block D, overlapping with IPC's concession in Halaib. IPC suspended its exploration in the area until the resolution of the dispute. Negotiations started between the two States and a joint legal committee was established to resolve the dispute. In 1998, Sudan and Egypt issued a joint communiqué pledging to resolve the issue of the dispute in the Halaib triangle "in an integrational brotherly context that would form a lead in the process of full integration between the two countries".[136]

In 2014, Saudi Arabia and Egypt concluded a maritime boundary delimitation agreement which ceded the Red Sea islands of Tiran and Sanafir to Saudi Arabia.[137] Following the signature of the agreement, which has been hugely unpopular in the country, Egypt's State-run Ganoub El Wadi Petroleum Holding Company signed a US$ 750 million contract for international extraction companies to conduct seismic and geophysical studies off its coast for the first time.[138]

4 Presumption of joint development of seabed resources

As mentioned above, joint development is linked to the legal obligation provided in Articles 74(3) and 83(3) of UNCLOS, to make every effort to enter into provisional arrangements of a practical nature, pending final boundary delimitation. But are States obliged to enter into such arrangements pending the delimitation of their borders?

A number of scholars have argued that in the absence of agreed boundaries, joint development is "legally necessary" as a matter of customary international law.[139] Article 38(1) of the Statute of the ICJ, which is widely regarded as an authoritative statement of sources of international law, defines international custom as "evidence of a general practice accepted as law".[140] Two important elements must be established in order to find that a particular legal principle enjoys the status of customary international law: a) an objective one, consisting

134 David Pike, 'Cross-Border Hydrocarbon Reserves' in Richard N Schofield (ed) *Territorial Foundations of the Gulf States* (Routledge 2016) 187–199.

135 ibid.

136 Dzurek et al. (2001) 6.

137 Askar H Enazy, 'The Legal Status of Tiran and Sanafir Islands' (Dirasat 2017) <www.kfcris.com/pdf/01b7caee30524d724432198c6819bb035988303421a61.pdf>. See also US Library of Congress 'Egypt/Saudi Arabia: Egyptian Parliament Ratifies Maritime Border Demarcation Agreement' (26 June 2017) <www.loc.gov/law/foreign-news/article/egyptsaudi-arabia-egyptian-parliament-ratifies-maritime-border-demarcation-agreement>.

138 Ahmed Megahid, 'Egypt Prepares for Oil and Gas Exploration in Red Sea' (*The Arab Weekly*, 11 December 2017) <https://thearabweekly.com/egypt-prepares-oil-and-gas-exploration-red-sea>.

139 William T Onorato, 'A Case Study in Joint Development: The Saudi Arabia-Kuwait Partitioned Neutral Zone' (1985) 10(3) *Energy* 539, 541; see also, David M Ong, 'Joint Development of Common Offshore Oil and Gas Deposits: "Mere" State Practice or Customary International Law?' (1999) 93(4) *American Journal of International Law* 771.

140 United Nations, 'Statute of the International Court of Justice' (26 June 1945) 33 United Nations Treaty Series 933.

of State practice which must be constant, uniform and common to a significant number of States, particularly those whose interests are affected; and b) a subjective one, consisting of the subjective conviction that a certain practice is required under customary international law (*opinio juris*).[141]

As has been shown in this chapter, several JDAs have been adopted between African States: in 1974 between Sudan and Saudi Arabia; in 1988 between Libya and Tunisia; in 1993 between Senegal and Guinea-Bissau; in 2001 between Nigeria and São Tomé and Príncipe; in 2002 between Nigeria and Equatorial Guinea and between the Republic of the Congo and Angola; in 2004 between Equatorial Guinea and Gabon; in 2007 between Angola and the DRC: and in 2011 between Cameroon and Nigeria. One could also point to the signature in August 2019 of an agreement between São Tomé and Príncipe and Equatorial Guinea for joint oil exploration and talks of increased cooperation over offshore activities between Ghana and Côte d'Ivoire since the ITLOS ruling.

However, despite the development of a significant body of State practice on interstate cooperation over offshore activities in disputed maritime areas, such practice does not appear to be uniform. There is a great disparity between the different types of arrangements concluded by States involved in boundary disputes and between the particular terms and conditions attached to each arrangement. This is largely because each arrangement, provisional though it may be, is naturally tailored to the specific geographical, economic and political circumstances against which it is negotiated and corresponds to an achievable outcome rather than any previously undertaken legal commitment.[142]

State practice does not provide concrete evidence that the various JDAs concluded to date in the African Continent have been a result of the fact that States considered that they were legally compelled to enter into such agreements. Neither the language used in these agreements nor the States' rhetoric provides any indication that States have concluded these agreements out of a perception of a customary international law obligation. On the contrary, it would appear that the majority of these agreements were the result of the concerned States' genuine desire to access potentially valuable offshore natural resources and improve their international relations at a bilateral or regional level. The willingness of States to cooperate towards the joint exploration and exploitation of overlapping areas has mostly been based on economic and political motives rather than on the perception of a legal obligation. Therefore, although examples of State practice have continued to accumulate, there is no evidence of *opinio juris* on the part of African States on the legal necessity of establishing joint development of disputed seabed resources.[143]

At most, the notion of joint development as an emerging rule of customary law would be an obligation of means to consult and negotiate with neighbouring States for the exploration and exploitation of natural resources in the disputed area, rather than an obligation of result to achieve a JDA. As a matter of international law, the obligation to make every effort to conclude arrangements of a practical nature pending delimitation, does not, in any way, imply an obligation to agree upon any provisional cooperative scheme. States are under an obligation to make every effort to settle their disputes through peaceful means in conformity with Chapter VI of the UN Charter and to act in good faith; however, States are not legally obliged to reach a successful outcome or indeed any outcome.

141 See Michael Wood, 'Second Report on Identification of Customary International Law' (International Law Commission Report, 22 May 2014) 7–70 <http://legal.un.org/docs/?symbol=A/CN.4/672>.

142 Miyoshi (2009).

143 Oduntan (2015).

5 Concluding remarks and resolving ongoing maritime disputes in Africa

JDAs may not constitute a permanent solution to African maritime disputes but are an effective means of dialling down conflicts by promoting economic cooperation and ensuring better management of seabed resources. Efforts at achieving peaceful coexistence through negotiations in view of maritime delimitation through the framework of the AUBP or a JDA should thus be encouraged. This is particularly important for Africa's shores where there are large reserves of natural resources and where so far progress towards the resolution of maritime disputes has been limited.

The southern coasts of Africa have remained largely undelimited, with the notable exception of the two tripartite maritime agreements reached under the auspices of the AUBP between the Comoros, Mozambique and Tanzania, and between Comoros, the Seychelles and Tanzania, previously discussed in Section III. None of the maritime boundaries of South Africa have so far been delimited.[144] The maritime dispute between Namibia and South Africa has been fuelled by the presence of oil and diamonds around the disputed islands in the mouth of the Orange River and the immediate offshore area.[145] South Africa has also so far failed to delimit its maritime boundary with its north-eastern neighbour Mozambique. Here the maritime boundary may be affected by the presence of Madagascar, whose maritime boundaries in turn are complicated by the presence of the French islands of Ile Juan de Nova, Ile Europa and, potentially, the Iles Glorieuses further north, as these islands are claimed by Madagascar. In the case of Mozambique, apart from the agreed maritime boundary with Tanzania in 1988, all other maritime boundaries with neighbouring States (Comoros, Madagascar and South Africa) are still pending.

In the north of the continent, the uncertain status of Western Sahara greatly complicates the delimitation of maritime boundaries on the northwest coast of Africa where significant offshore oil discoveries have been made. Mauritania and Cape Verde settled their maritime boundary in 2003, but efforts at maritime delimitation further north which implicate Morocco and Spain through the Canary Islands have stalled. Morocco, which depends almost exclusively on fossil fuel imports for its energy supply,[146] issued exploration licenses in 2013 to two multinational oil companies, UK-based Cairn Energy and US-based Kosmos Energy, for offshore blocks in the Atlantic waters off Western Sahara.[147] This was swiftly disputed by the government of the partially recognised Sahrawi Arab Democratic Republic (SADR) which itself has purported to grant offshore exploration and exploitation licenses.[148] The complex dispute shows no sign of resolution.

While this chapter has highlighted the progress that has been achieved, notably in recent years, towards delimitation of maritime boundaries and joint development of seabed resources in Africa, a look at the north and south of the continent illustrates that much remains to be done to bring about the certainty necessary for the stability and economic prosperity of many neighbouring African States.

144 For a detailed account, see Patrick Vrancken, *South Africa and the Law of the Sea* (Martinus Nijhoff 2011).

145 Daniel (2005); Moudachirou (2016).

146 International Energy Agency, 'Energy Policies Beyond IEA Countries – Morocco 2014'. <https://webstore.iea.org/energy-policies-beyond-iea-countries-morocco-2014>.

147 'Simmering Saharan Conflict Stirred by Offshore Oil Search' (13 January 2014) <https://www.reuters.com/article/westernsahara-oil-idUSL6N0KN1I120140113>.

148 'Saharawi Government Responds to Oil Development in Western Sahara' (Western Sahara Resource Watch, 20 November 2013) <https://www.wsrw.org/a105x2717>.

PART VIII

Conclusion

32

ENERGY TRANSITIONS AND THE LAW

Kim Talus and Pami Aalto

1 What is an energy transition?

At the most basic level, 'energy transition' can be understood as a fundamental change to the pre-existing state of the energy system. Usually it is expected that these changes concern large trends taking place at the international or global level, and that the changes are long lasting and also shape the societies in question. This relatively simple notion of energy transition is not the only possible option. Theoretically driven transition studies refer to 'transitions' as entailing 'far reaching changes to sectors of economy in which new technologies, institutional structures and organizations emerge and existing ones change or decline. Such transitions are referred to as socio-technical transitions'.[1] Socio-technical systems that are fundamentally transformed can be viewed as a 'network of actors (organizations but also individuals) and institutions, such as societal and technical norms, standards, regulations or user practices as well as material artefacts and knowledge'.[2]

Today, the energy world is going through a number of fundamental transitions. The most commonly discussed and examined of them is the transition towards a more sustainable energy system.[3] For energy transition researchers who focus on this area of transition studies, '(s)ustainability transitions are long-term transformational processes of established industries, socio-technical systems and societies to more sustainable modes of production and consumption'.[4] Sustainability transitions or sustainable development can be defined as 'development that meets the needs of the present without compromising the ability of future generations to meet their own needs'.[5] It has a strong environmental aspect built into it (environmental

1 F. Kern and J. Markard, 'Analysing Energy Transitions: Combining Insights from Transition Studies and International Political Economy'. In: T. Van de Graaf, B. Sovacool, A. Ghosh, F. Kern and M. Klare, *The Palgrave Handbook of the International Political Economy of Energy* (Palgrave 2016), p. 291.

2 Ibid, p. 293.

3 'Energy system' here includes generation, transmission and distribution as well as end-use. Moving to a more sustainable energy system requires changes in all these areas, including the introduction of renewable energy, energy efficiency measures, adaptation of network regulation and so on.

4 Transitions network, https://transitionsnetwork.org/about-strn.

5 'Our Common Future: Report of the World Commission on Environment and Development' (1987), 41 www.un-documents.net/our-common-future.pdf.

sustainability),[6] but it also has an economic and social aspect to it. The 1992 Rio Declaration also includes the following elements: 'States should cooperate to promote a supportive and open international economic system that would lead to economic growth and sustainable development in all countries, to better address the problems of environmental degradation'.[7] In practice, combining these environmental, social and economic aspects of sustainability often presupposes increased resource efficiency, that is, actions extracting more outputs from a smaller amount of resources.[8]

Such transitions affect all stakeholders, from industries with vested interests, to governmental actors and end consumers. The impact is, of course, not symmetric and highly dependent on the actors.[9] The drivers of such transitions also vary, ranging from technological breakthroughs and innovations to specific efforts to change through governmental policies and laws that reflect these policies. Also, in reality, they are often a combination of these and other influencing factors. For example, the United States (US) shale revolution is primarily credited to the innovative and entrepreneurial spirit of the US energy industry, as well as private ownership of the subsoil.[10] It is somewhat underappreciated what a significant role the federal government has played in this 'revolution'. Among other things, the US federal government pursued research and development (R&D) focusing on energy technologies, which subsequently served the profit interests of the industry and eventually the fiscal interests of the federation. The federal government was directly involved in drilling in the 1970s, and introduced tax incentives in the 1980s and research funding in the 1980s and 1990s. This paved the way for two significant technological innovations – horizontal drilling and hydraulic fracturing – forming the bedrock of the shale revolution by enabling the industry to increase productivity and efficiency to control production costs and, ultimately, via a combination of bankruptcies and successes in the industry, make large-scale development profitable.[11] In other words, the success story behind the US shale gas revolution is a combination of industry activities, government funded research and governmental policies.

This chapter will examine the role of law and policy in creating and facilitating energy transitions. It will examine two areas of energy markets that are currently undergoing a significant transition: the sustainable energy transition, and the liquefied natural gas (LNG) market transition. In both cases, law and policy play a role. In the case of the sustainable energy transition, this role is that of creator. It is the driving force in the path towards a more sustainable energy system. For LNG, the role of law and policy is that of a facilitator. Law and policy support the increasingly liquid and global LNG markets. The chapter is organized to first provide some background to energy market transitions. It will discuss and show how the energy industry has always been subject to change and has undergone several significant

6 Term used, for example, at UN Environment programme at https://www.unenvironment.org/about-un-environment/sustainability/why-sustainability-matters.

7 'Rio Declaration on Environment and Development' www.unep.org/documents.multilingual/default.asp?documentid=78&articleid=1163, Principle 12.

8 United Nations Environment Programme, *Towards a Green Economy: Pathways to Sustainable Development and Poverty Eradication* (2011), http://web.unep.org/greeneconomy/resources/green-economy-report.

9 P. Aalto, M. Bilgin and K. Talus, 'How to Manage Energy Transitions? Interests, Frames and the Structuration of Energy Policies in the USA and Germany' (forthcoming), article manuscript under review in an international journal.

10 Some of these elements have been well discussed in M.-K. Pyhäranta, 'State ownership of petroleum resources: an obstacle to shale gas development in the UK?' 10 (2017) 4 *Journal of World Energy Law and Business*, p. 358–366.

11 O. Anderson, 'Shale Revolution or Evolution: Opportunities and Challenges for Europe', 4 (2013) *Global Business Law Review*, pp. 1–26.

transitions. After this background, the chapter will first examine the transition of the LNG market from a local and rigid market to an increasingly liquid and global market. Finally, it will focus on the sustainable energy transition.

2 Transitions and the energy industry

The energy industry has undergone several significant and fundamental transitions. Over the decades, it is an industry that has transitioned from local markets to increasingly international markets. While the increase in the gross consumption of hydrocarbon-based fuels is a trend that has continued since the early days of industrialization, a notable change that has taken place over recent decades relates to the relative importance of different fuel types. In the early days of industrialization, the modern economy was largely fuelled by coal. This came to an end between World War I and II, when oil replaced coal as the primary energy carrier in the world. Similarly, initially the oil industry was primarily for lighting purposes and local in scope. Only with the automotive industry (and electric lighting) did the oil industry transform into a more significant and international industry.[12]

Today's energy mix is a result of such transitions. According to the International Energy Agency (IEA), the current global energy mix is much more balanced than before, with oil comprising 31.9 percent, coal 27.2 percent, natural gas 21.9 percent, renewables 14.0 percent and nuclear power 4.9 percent of the world primary energy demand in 2016.[13] For global electricity generation in 2016, coal still stands for 37 percent of the overall supply, with its share decreasing from 2000 by only two percentage points. The most notable long-term change, however, is the decrease in the share of oil in electricity generation, dropping from 24.8 percent in 1973 to 4 percent in 2016. Its share has largely been replaced by natural gas based production (from 12.1 to 24 percent).[14] The IEA has developed different scenarios for the future development of the world's energy system, and its New Policies scenario suggests that by 2040, the world's energy demand is covered almost equally by oil, gas, coal and low-carbon sources (renewables and nuclear power).[15] BP Energy Outlook for 2040 suggests a similar scenario.[16]

As such, while today's energy transitions can, and should, be viewed as revolutionary, they can also be viewed as continuing the long-term change in the industry. The energy industry has never been a stable industry but rather an industry that has always developed and evolved. Given that this is an industry that plays a vital role in the existence of other sectors of the economy and in the existence of modern societies more generally, it is of paramount importance to understand these transitions and their underlying drivers.

The next section will focus on the LNG market transition.

12 The role of oil for the industrial world has been excellently captured by Daniel Yergin in his now notorious book *The Prize* (Free Press 1991). He illustrates the change from coal to oil in a section discussing how wars were previously fought along the railway lines. This came to an end when the French army deployed the taxi fleet of Paris to move troops to a critical location. The decision to move away from coal to oil in sea transportation and to nationalize what is today BP is also discussed in detail by Yergin.

13 International Energy Agency *World Energy Outlook 2018*, p. 79.

14 Ibid.; IEA, *Key World Energy Statistics 2017*, available at https://www.iea.org/publications/freepublications/publication/KeyWorld2017.pdf.

15 IEA *World Energy Outlook 2018*, p. 79.

16 See BP, 'Energy Outlook 2040', (2018), p. 69, https://www.bp.com/content/dam/bp-country/de_ch/PDF/Energy-Outlook-2018-edition-Booklet.pdf.

3 Liquefied natural gas market transition

LNG markets are going through a rapid and fundamental transition. Where the previous era for LNG deliveries was marked by point-to-point sales from an exporting country to an end-destination importing country, today's LNG world looks very different and is rapidly moving towards a liquid global commodity market. The growth of this market in the 2010s has been rapid, not only within the pivotal Asian LNG markets where the traditional pattern witnessed East Asia's emerging economies importing LNG primarily from South East Asia and the Middle East.

Infrastructure development, alongside technological innovation in areas such as floating LNG liquefaction and regasification facilities, has allowed East Asian states to increase the volumes they produce and new countries to join the LNG trade. Japan alone accounts for a third of global LNG imports, followed by China, South Korea and India with roughly a tenth each.[17] Notably, in the course of the 2010s each one of them has sought additional security of supply from Russian LNG, produced in the Sakhalin Island since 2008 and, since 2017, also in the Yamal Peninsula's Arctic conditions.[18] US and Australian LNG is also entering the Asian markets forcefully. By contrast, in the EU context, for example in Lithuania, interest in introducing competition to pipeline-based deliveries from Russia's Gazprom and responding to the perceived weaknesses in the security of supply underpinned the floating LNG regasification terminal completed in 2014. Similar interest in diversifying supply drove the three LNG agreements with US suppliers signed by Poland's PGNiG in 2018; these may eventually lead to the existing agreement with Gazprom being allowed to expire by 2022.[19] These decisions must be understood in the context of new perceptions of Russian supplies following several conflicts over price and transit fees between Gazprom and its counterparties in Ukraine and Belarus.[20] Finally, some countries have moved to natural gas or LNG for environmental reasons. Malta is an example that combines environmental interests with infrastructure improvements. Its investment in a floating LNG regasification terminal allowed the small Mediterranean island to move its power production from oil to a natural gas based system.

The number of end-destination buyers and sellers has grown significantly: For long-term contract deliveries the markets have moved from six importing countries and three exporting countries in 1971 to 11 importing countries and 12 exporting countries in 2000, and in 2017 markets had reached 40 importing countries and 19 exporting countries.[21] Players in the energy spot market have increased in a similar fashion: from eight importers and six exporting countries in 2000 to 33 end markets and 29 exporting countries in 2017, including

17 International Gas Union, '2017 World LNG Report' https://www.igu.org/sites/default/files/103419-World_IGU_Report_no%20crops.pdf.

18 S. Tabata and X. Liu, 'Russia's Energy Policy in the Far East and East Siberia'. In: P. Aalto (ed.), *Russia's Energy Policies: National, Interregional and Global Levels* (Cheltenham: Edward Elgar 2012), pp. 156–184; P. Aalto and I. Jaakkola, 'Arctic Energy Policy: Global, International, Transnational and Regional Levels'. In: G. Hønneland and L.C. Jensen (eds) *Handbook of the Politics of the Arctic* (Cheltenham: Edward Elgar 2015), pp. 128–143.

19 T. DiChristopher, 'Poland's Goal of Ditching Russian Natural Gas Bolsters American LNG and Trump's Energy Agenda', *CNBC News*, 19 December 2018, https://www.cnbc.com/2018/12/19/polands-goal-of-ditching-russian-gas-yields-opportunity-for-us-lng.html.

20 M. Balmaceda, 'Russia's Central and Eastern European Energy Transit Corridor: Ukraine and Belarus'. In: P. Aalto (ed.) *Russia's Energy Policies: National, Interregional and Global Dimensions* (Cheltenham: Edward Elgar 2012).

21 International Gas Union, '2017 World LNG Report'. Available at https://www.igu.org/sites/default/files/103419-World_IGU_Report_no%20crops.pdf.

re-exports, most of which took place in Europe and East Asia. The market share of non-long-term deliveries (meaning spot and short-term contract deliveries) was 30 percent of all deliveries in 2017.[22] While new long-term contracts are still signed, for new projects in particular, the share of non-long-term deliveries is rising.

New types of players in the markets have also emerged. In addition to the traditional sellers and end-destination buyers, various types of portfolio players have emerged and become increasingly important in the market.[23] Not only do these new players add to the number of buyers and sellers in the market, they also increase liquidity as they can buy large volumes of LNG without necessarily having locked demand for all volumes.[24] Also re-exportation has become more economical with ample available capacities in regasification terminals driving down the price of offloading and reloading. The growth of both trading parties and non-user sellers has contributed to the growing liquidity of the markets.

These changes in the markets have not come without changes in the legal frameworks or their application. Similarly, the changes have put pressure on the traditional contracting methods, such as LNG sale and purchase agreements (SPAs).[25] Some of the changes seen in the markets include: a shortening of contract duration; more frequent price revisions; moves away from oil price indexation of natural gas prices; and increasing flexibility. These changes can be traced back to the development of genuine LNG markets with larger available volumes, more liquidity and an increasing number of players.

Markets and industry are primarily driving these changes, but for some elements of the transition there is also a regulatory push. This includes, among other factors, the move away from destination clauses and other diversion clauses, as well as profit-sharing mechanisms. In this area, the efforts by the European Commission (EC) and the Japanese Fair Trade Commission (JFTC) are particularly important. EU competition law investigations by the EC focusing on various pipeline and LNG contracts and practices in the early and mid-2000s,[26] and the more recent antitrust report by the JFTC in 2017 focusing on international LNG trade, have reached partially similar conclusions.[27] While the concerns of EC were primarily related to the liquidity of EU internal gas markets, the JFTC focused on free trade in LNG and the liquidity of international LNG markets. However, it is possible to see common elements and concerns. Both the EU and Japan are concerned with the impact of cargo diversion restrictions, which are commonly used in LNG SPAs. These clauses prevent the buyer from redirecting the LNG to alternative delivery destinations.

22 Ibid.

23 See, for example, *LNG Journal*, 'Commodities Firms Continue to Increase Their Volumes of LNG for Trading from Key Producers', https://lngjournal.com/index.php/latest-news-mainmenu-47/item/95821-commodities-firms-continue-to-increase-volumes-of-lng-for-trading-from-key-producers.

24 Bloomberg, 'Tankers Going Nowhere Indicate LNG Market Becoming More Like Oil', https://www.bloomberg.com/amp/news/articles/2018-11-27/tankers-going-nowhere-indicate-lng-market-becoming-more-like-oil?__twitter_impression=true.

25 Generally on these agreements, see R. Maalouf, 'International LNG Contracts', *Oil, Gas and Energy Law (OGEL)* 3 (2018), www.ogel.org.

26 An overview of these cases is provided in K. Talus, 'Long term natural gas contracts and antitrust law in the European Union and the United States', *Journal of World Energy Law and Business* 4 (2011) 3, 1–67. For an analysis of destinations clauses in LNG contracts, see: E. Wäktare, 'Territorial Restrictions and Profit Sharing Mechanisms in the Gas Sector: The Algerian Case' (2007) 3 *Competition Policy Newsletter* 19 and H. Nyssen and I. Osborne, 'Profit splitting Mechanism in a Liberalised Gas Market: The Devil Lies in the Detail' (2005) 1 *Competition Policy Newsletter* 25–30.

27 Japan Fair Trade Commission, *Survey on LNG Trades* https://www.jftc.go.jp/en/pressreleases/yearly-2017/June/170628.html.

Historically, many LNG SPAs included destination clauses that prevented the buyer from diverting a cargo to any destination (or terminal) other than the original contractual destination (or terminal). Other similar clauses used in both historical contracts and more recent contracts include other types of diversion clauses, such as consent clauses, requiring the consent of the seller to any diversion, and profit-sharing clauses, enabling the seller to participate in any additional net profit generated by the buyer at the new destination.[28] With increasing LNG trade and the growing liquidity of international LNG markets, such traditional clauses have in many cases been viewed as anticompetitive and have the potential to violate various national or regional antitrust laws. Today's practices relating to LNG cargos are moving towards increasing destination flexibility. This development is particularly visible in US-based LNG, which does not include destination restrictions. As such, the buyer of US LNG is free to divert the cargo as it wishes.

It is obvious that these types of destination restrictions are problematic from the perspective of increasing the liquidity of LNG markets internationally. It is precisely because of this that the antitrust authorities have provided guidance on which types of diversion clauses are to be seen as anticompetitive and thus prohibited and which types of clauses can still be accepted from the antitrust perspective. Furthermore, in order to support the development towards a liquid global LNG trade and to provide clarity and certainty for LNG market participants, a working group supported in the context of an ongoing project initiated by the EC and the Japanese Ministry for Economy, Trade and Industry created a model diversion clause that can be used as part of LNG SPAs.[29]

As noted above, changes in the market, including increasing liquidity, is primarily due to 'real world' changes, as opposed to changes in the 'legal world'. The role of law in LNG market transformation can be described as facilitative. The primary drivers for change have been industry innovation and market economics, while security of supply issues have fuelled new demand for increasing import volumes in Asia and Europe in particular. At the same time, Vivoda, for example, notes how energy security issues are fundamentally complex, as they involve several variables and attributes. In addition to the supply of LNG, demand side management and conservation, policy measures, efficiency of use, links to the vulnerability of critical infrastructure, technology reliability risks, as well as acceptance issues and environmental externalities, issues where, for example, Asian states vary considerably.[30] Variation among the EU Member States regarding the variables of gas supply security is also considerable.[31] In a word, law and policy adjust to these changes in innovation, market developments and energy security needs, and further support the developments in the direction required by the evolving energy system and needs of energy policies.

The next section will focus on the other significant transition: the transition towards a more sustainable energy system.

28 For an overview of past and present contractual models in LNG projects, see R. Maalouf, 'International LNG Contracts', *OGEL* 2018 (www.ogel.org) or, in more detail, P. Roberts, *Gas and LNG Sales and Transportation Agreements, Principles and Structure* (Croyden: Sweet & Maxwell, 5th ed., 2017).

29 The model diversion clause and a guidance note to accompany the model clause are available at: https://www.ogel.org/legal-and-regulatory-detail.asp?key=21040. An academic article explaining the background is available at: https://www.ogel.org/journal-advance-publication-article.asp?key=575.

30 V. Vivoda, 'Evaluating Energy Security in the Asia-Pacific Region: A Novel Methodological Approach', *Energy Policy* (2010) 38(9): 5258–5263.

31 F. Proedrou, *EU Energy Security in the Gas Sector: Evolving Dynamics, Policy Dilemmas and Prospects* (Abingdon: Routledge 2012).

4 Sustainable transition towards low carbon energy systems

The transition to a more sustainable power system is primarily driven by public sector intervention in energy markets. It is not, or at least not primarily, traceable to technological innovation or economic advances, as was the case with the LNG market transition, but rather to governmental decision-making at national and, very importantly, international level. At the same time, the rapidly decreasing deployment cost of renewable energy, in particular wind power and solar PV technology, has significantly facilitated national and international governance. For example, in the US the levelized costs of wind power make it close to being competitive with natural gas in many states, while in some states solar power is cheaper.[32] In Germany, the levelized costs of renewable power (including the Co_2 price and investment costs) in 2015 were already competitive with those of fossil fuels for newly built power plants.[33]

The basic framework created in order to drive energy systems towards a more sustainable direction is international in nature. These frameworks do not always include binding or directly applicable provisions, but rather provide for a general framework for regional or national action. An example is the UN Framework Convention on Climate Change, which establishes a wide framework for policy action to mitigate climate change. It has led to a number of important international mechanisms that directly or indirectly support sustainable energy policies. For example, it supports sustainable energy initiatives through the Technology Mechanism,[34] and funding through the Financial Mechanism.[35] The majority of the technical assistance has been energy related,[36] and many of the intended nationally determined contributions in this context have related to renewable energy deployment (feed-in tariffs and investment in renewable generation and grid infrastructure, for example) and energy efficiency.[37] Similarly to this, the Paris Agreement (COP 21) reinforces international cooperation in this area, including in terms of financial support.[38] Like many other international frameworks, the Paris Agreement is based on recognition of national sovereignty and imposes few binding rules on nation states.

These international frameworks drive national policies. The national policies are in turn implemented in the form of soft and hard law instruments. It is these instruments, hard law in particular, that often drive the transition towards a more sustainable energy law. This section will use as an example the EU measures to transition the energy production system to a more sustainable system. Given that energy transition in this sense is perhaps more central to the energy policy of the EU than for many of its partners and competitors, this choice is logical.

32 T. Covert, M. Greenstone and C. R. Knittel, 'Will We Ever Stop Using Fossil Fuels?', *Journal of Economic Perspectives*, 30(1) (2016), 117–138.

33 Agora Energiewend, 'Insights from Germany's Energiewende: State of Affairs, Trends and Challenges' (2015) https://www.agora-energiewende.de/fileadmin/Projekte/2015/Understanding_the_EW/Key_Insights_Energy_Transition_EN_Stand_7.10.2015_web.pdf.

34 UNFCCC, 'Technology Mechanism' http://unfccc.int/ttclear/templates/render_cms_page?TEM_home.

35 UNFCCC, 'Climate Finance' http://unfccc.int/cooperation_and_support/financial_mechanism/items/2807.php. See also UNFCCC Decision 3/CP.17, 'Launching the Green Climate Fund, Annex: Governing Instrument for the Green Climate Fund' (15 March 2012) UN Doc FCCC/CP/2011/9/Add.1, paras 37–38.

36 CTCN, 'Progress Report: January 2014 – August 2015' (2015) 26, https://www.ctc-n.org/sites/www.ctc-n.org/files/ctnc_progressreport_final.pdf .

37 UNFCCC, 'Synthesis Report on the Aggregate Effect of the Intended Nationally Determined Contributions: Note by the Secretariat (30 October 2015) UN Doc FCCC/CP/2015/7, paras 154–155.

38 Generally, see R. Leal-Arcas and R. Minas (2016) 'Renewable Energy Law'. In: E. Morgera and K. Kulovesi (eds) *Research Handbook in International Law and Natural Resources* (Cheltenham: Edward Elgar).

5 Sustainable transition: the European Union as an example

What we need is 'improvements in the implementation of existing legislation, integrating environmental concerns into other policies, encouraging the market to work for the environment, and empowering citizens and changing behavior'.[39] As this quote from the EC illustrates, the idea is to persuade citizens to do what is expected of them on a voluntary basis, and if this approach does not work, then they must be compelled to act as required by harder instruments of law. In practice, this is what has largely taken place. After using less formal instruments of persuasion, which are still used in some areas, the EC has moved to these harder instruments of law. The EU moved from 'voluntary targets' for renewables and biofuels, as set out in the first Directives in this area, to binding targets under the current Directive 2009/28/EC.[40]

The progress to the *status quo* in the EU has been a result of progressive steps towards the binding targets that exist under Directive 2009/28/EC. As a first step, Directive 2001/77/EC *on the promotion of electricity produced from renewable energy sources in the internal electricity market*[41] set an indicative target of doubling the share of renewables in EU energy consumption from 6 percent to 12 percent in 2010. This meant the renewable share for electricity production should be 22 percent.[42] This overall EU target was then translated into national targets. Both targets were related to the EU's Kyoto commitments. To achieve the targets, Member States *could* provide for rules giving renewable energy sources priority access to transmission and distribution channels on a mandatory basis, though, unlike after the 2009 Renewable Energy Directive,[43] this was not mandatory.[44]

Today, the backbone for the current EU climate and renewable energy policy measures is provided by the '20-20-20 by 2020' climate and energy targets set in 2007.[45] For renewable energy, the objective is a legally binding 20 percent overall share of renewable energy production in the EU by 2020. The '20-20-20 by 2020' objectives also include 20 percent targets for increasing energy efficiency and reducing greenhouse gas emission which are, however, beyond the scope of the present chapter.[46] The overall objective of a 20 percent share for renewable energy in the EU by 2020 has been translated into a national renewable energy target for each of the 28 Member States. Unlike the previous EU legal regime for

39 European Commission, 'European Climate Change Programme, Report' (June 2001), pp. 45–46.

40 Directive 2009/28/EC of the European Parliament and of the Council of 23 April 2009 on the promotion of the use of energy from renewable sources and amending and subsequently repealing Directives 2001/77/EC and 2003/30/EC, *OJ L 140*, 5 June 2009, 16–62.

41 Directive 2001/77/EC of the European Parliament and of the Council of 27 September 2001 on the promotion of electricity produced from renewable energy sources in the internal electricity market, *OJ L* 283, 27.10.2001, 33–40.

42 Directive 2001/77/EC of the European Parliament and of the Council of 27 September 2001 on the promotion of electricity produced from renewable energy sources in the internal electricity market, *OJ L* 283, 27.10.2001.

43 Directive 2009/28/EC of the European Parliament and of the Council of 23 April 2009 on the promotion of the use of energy from renewable sources and amending and subsequently repealing Directives 2001/77/EC and 2003/30/EC (*OJ L* 140, 5.6.2009, 16).

44 Article 7 (1) of Directive 2001/77/EC.

45 'Renewable Energy Road Map. Renewable Energies in the 21st Century: Building a More Sustainable Future' (COM(2006) 848 final), Brussels, 10 January 2007. For analysis, see K. Kulovesi, E. Morgera and M. Muñoz, 'Environmental Integration and Multifaceted International Dimensions of EU Law: Unpacking the EU's 2009 Climate and Energy Package', 48 *Common Market Law Review* (2011), 829–891.

46 These are discussed in S.-L. Penttinen and K. Talus, 'The Development of Sustainability Aspects in EU Energy Law', *Research Handbook in Climate Change Mitigation Law* (Cheltenham: Edward Elgar 2015). See also A. Johnston and G. Block, *EU Energy Law* (Oxford: Oxford University Press 2012).

renewable energy,[47] Directive 2009/28/EC[48] (the 'Renewable Energy Directive') also made the national targets binding. For example, the 2020 target for Finland is 38 percent (from a 2005 level of 28.5 percent) and the French target is 23 percent (from a 2005 level of 10.3 percent). These targets can be achieved by using various measures within the country but also through joint projects[49] or 'statistical transfers' between Member States. They can even be achieved through cooperation with non-EU countries[50] as long as the electricity is consumed within the EU, under certain conditions which eliminate the most obvious problems connected with third country cooperation, such as only new installations and no double support. The binding nature of the national targets has resulted in a considerable increase in investment in renewable energy in the EU.[51] However, this trend is not limited to Europe, as investment in this area has increased globally. In most cases, the development can be traced to the regulatory frameworks that enable investments in this area.[52]

For the EU, the development has been remarkable. The quantity of renewable energy produced within the EU increased overall by 66.6 percent between 2006 and 2016, translating to an average increase of 5.3 percent per year.[53] The EU's climate and energy objectives and targets were first updated through a Council Decision on 24 October 2014,[54] and were included in the Energy Union framework,[55] and the 'summer package' adopted in July 2015.[56] The 2016 Clean Energy Package,[57] continued and suggested a binding renewable energy target of at least 32 percent, with an upwards revision clause by 2023,[58] and an energy efficiency target of at least 32.5 percent by 2030.[59] Today, there is a political agreement over these targets, which has translated into binding legislation.[60]

Without going into the details of the new objectives, the fact that the new rules on renewable energy involve replacing individual targets for Member States with an EU-wide binding target to raise the share of renewables in the energy mix to at least 32 percent by 2030 is worth highlighting. It is possible that this decision will have a negative effect on

47 Directive 2001/77/EC of the European Parliament and of the Council of 27 September 2001 on the promotion of electricity produced from renewable energy sources in the internal electricity market (*OJ L* 283, 27.10.2001, 33).

48 Directive 2009/28/EC of the European Parliament and of the Council of 23 April 2009 on the promotion of the use of energy from renewable sources and amending and subsequently repealing Directives 2001/77/EC and 2003/30/EC (*OJ L* 140, 5.6.2009, 16).

49 Articles 7 and 8 of Directive 2009/28/EC.

50 Article 9 of Directive 2009/28/EC.

51 http://ec.europa.eu/eurostat/statistics-explained/index.php/File:Electricity_generated_from_renewable_energy_sources,_EU-28,_2003%E2%80%9313_YB15.png.

52 www.worldbank.org/en/topic/energy/publication/rise---regulatory-indicators-for-sustainable-energy.

53 https://ec.europa.eu/eurostat/statistics-explained/index.php/Renewable_energy_statistics#Renewable_energy_produced_in_the_EU_increased_by_two_thirds_in_2006-2016.

54 See also communication from the EC to the European Parliament, the Council, the European Economic and Social Committee and the Committee of the Regions, 'A Policy Framework for Climate and Energy in the Period from 2020 to 2030', COM/2014/015 final.

55 See http://ec.europa.eu/priorities/energy-union/index_en.htm

56 European Commission Press Release, 'Transforming Europe's Energy System – Commission's Energy Summer Package Leads the Way' IP 15/5358, Brussels, 15 July 2015.

57 https://ec.europa.eu/energy/en/topics/energy-strategy-and-energy-union/clean-energy-all-europeans.

58 Directive (EU) 2018/2001 of the European Parliament and of the Council of 11 December 2018 on the promotion of the use of energy from renewable sources (*OJ L* 328, 21.12.2019, 82–209).

59 Directive (EU) 2018/844 of the European Parliament and of the Council of 30 May 2018 amending Directive 2010/31/EU on the energy performance of buildings and Directive 2012/27/EU on energy efficiency (*OJ L* 156, 19.6.2018, 75–91.

60 http://europa.eu/rapid/press-release_STATEMENT-18-4155_en.htm.

renewable energy deployment in many EU Member States. However, it is also possible that the trend towards more renewable energy created through binding laws and regulations which have had their intended impact and sparked development in this area far enough to drive down the price of renewable energy.

A similar process has also taken place in relation to energy efficiency.[61] The initial 'soft' instruments included:

- voluntary agreements with industry groups to introduce more energy- or environment-efficient equipment,[62] (mainly voluntary agreements between industry sector competitors, often grouped together in an industry association, facilitated by and then formally notified by the Commission);[63]
- best practice initiatives aimed at identifying and then spreading environment-efficient innovations;
- efforts to build up 'EU energy/environmental labels' into 'environmental brands' able to attract a consumer following;
- setting of 'targets' for energy efficiency intended to focus attention on and galvanize efforts to achieve the target.[64]

As is illustrated using EU renewable energy targets as the example, law and policy have been the primary drivers behind the transition towards sustainable energy systems. Hard law and binding targets subsequently replaced the initial approach, which was based on soft law and voluntary targets. This approach has now shown its effectiveness, and the EU is on its way to the overall objective of a 20 percent share for renewable energy in the EU by 2020. The impact of the EU approach, together with various government initiatives around the world, has been remarkable. The volumes of renewable energies coming on-stream have been significant. Due to the opportunities for private investment and innovation this has provided, the prices of renewable energy technologies and cost of generation has declined rapidly and, as noted, is now becoming market competitive without any government involvement in the form of subsidy. In this sense, the command-control approach taken has been successful.

That law and policy driven energy transition is taking place at an increasing speed can be well illustrated by referring to the case of Finland. It features from the outset a somewhat tricky case for a full-scale energy transition despite already having 39 percent of primary energy consumption from renewable sources in 2015 – mostly consisting of biomass and hydropower.[65] The constraints to the transition include that Finland is highly energy intensive

61 For this, see K. Talus, *EU Energy Law and Policy – A Critical Account* (Oxford: Oxford University Press 2013).

62 For example, agreement with lamp manufacturers to increase the sale of compact fluorescent lights (CFLs) by 2005 and with the car industry on reduction of CO_2 emissions, 'EUC Climate Change Report of June 2001 at p. 46; with the European Automobile manufacturers association, with Japanese and Korean car manufacturers, see: COM (1999) 4446 final; COM (1996) 561; COM (1998) 495 final; EU Green Paper on greenhouse gas emissions trading COM (2000) 87 final, pp. 20–21.

63 'A unilateral commitment of the industry that the Commission takes note of and covers by a corresponding recommendation addressed to industry'. See, for example, para. 32 of the Green Paper on greenhouse gas emissions trading within the EU COM/2000/0087 final.

64 Note in particular the discussion of initiatives in the Commission Report, 'European Climate Change Programme' (June 2001); for an example of EC initiatives to encourage oil companies to undertake voluntary agreements to refrain in the future from chartering tankers older than 15 years, see (COM (2000) 603 final, 27 September 2000.

65 Statistics Finland, 'Energian hankinta ja kulutus 2015', pp. 28–33,https://tilastokeskus.fi/til/ehk/2015/ehk_2015_2016-12-07_fi.pdf, .

with significant heavy industries in the forestry, chemical and metal sectors that together account for some 90 percent of energy consumption in the industry.[66] The country has relatively cold winter temperatures and is sparsely and unevenly populated, while significant industrial clusters are situated far away from the major export ports, therefore requiring the use of road and fossil fuel-based transport. These features, accompanied by a relatively centralized energy system and an energy industry traditionally geared to satisfying the industrial demand and building heating needs during peak demand situations, mean significant inertia for ambitious regulation and policy.[67]

Against this background, a major turnaround has taken place. The country's 2015 Climate Change Act (609/2015) proceeds from many United Nations Framework Convention on Climate Change (UNFCCC) and EU level commitments. In line with the EU's 2011 Energy Roadmap, which seeks to reduce greenhouse gas emissions by 80–95 percent compared to 1990,[68] the Act sets the target of 80 percent less emissions by 2050. It is, however, true that for a long time 'merely' complying with UN and EU level regulation and policy was characteristic of Finnish energy policy targets, and this target, too, adopts the minimum of the 80–95 percent range despite being an ambitious, albeit a very long-term, goal. In fact, a great deal of domestic policy debate for a long time revolved around the commitment to reaching the EU's 20-20-20 target by 2020. Yet, following the 2015 Paris Agreement, and consequent new policy momentum on European and Nordic levels, the Finnish debate decisively turned towards accepting and working on a full-scale energy transition.[69]

To kick-start the transition, the Ministry for Economic Affairs and Employment launched a wide-based working group on smart grids in 2016. In 2018, the group issued several recommendations for new regulation and policies pushing on the agenda of the EU's 2016 winter package by seeking to involve consumers, and enable energy communities and corresponding new business models to maintain competitiveness in the context of energy transition.[70] An independent report on the implementation of the Paris targets also found a compelling need for more ambitious targets in renewable energy, energy efficiency and overall emission reduction, and attracted considerable policy attention.[71] In 2018, the Government of Finland made a political commitment to become carbon-free by 2045, following a parliamentary agreement; Sweden had concluded a similar agreement in 2016 for a 100 percent carbon

66 Työ- ja elinkeinoministeriö [TEM], '100-prosenttisesti uusiutuviin energialähteisiin perustuva energiajärjestelmä: Kansalliseen energia- ja ilmastostrategiaan liittyvä tarkastelu 24.11.2016' (2016). https://tem.fi/documents/1410877/3570111/100+prosenttia+uusiutuvaa+tarkastelu.pdf/8e4ee341-77c5-4447-b6ce-1f2686a3daec/100+prosenttia+uusiutuvaa+tarkastelu.pdf.pdf, accessed 4 February 2019

67 P. Toivanen, P. Lehtonen, P. Aalto, T. Björkqvist, P. Järventausta, S. Kilpeläinen, M. Kojo, F. Mylläri, 'Finland's 2030 Energy System as Envisioned by Expert Stakeholders', *Energy Strategy Reviews* (2017) 18: 150–6 (doi: 10.1016/j.esr.2017.09.007).

68 European Commission, 'Energy Roadmap 2050', Communication from the Commission to the European Parliament, the Council, the European Economic and Social Committee and the Committee of the Regions, Brussels, 15 December 2011 COM(2011) 885 final, https://eur-lex.europa.eu/legal-content/EN/TXT/PDF/?uri=CELEX:52011DC0885&from=EN.

69 S. Kilpeläinen and P. Aalto, 'Renewable Energy in Finland: From Production-Centric to a Grid-Centric System'. In: P. Midford and E. Moe (eds) *Differential Success: Barriers and Solutions in Renewable Energy Development in Japan, East Asia and Northern Europe* (forthcoming).

70 Ibid.

71 Rocha, Marcia, Sferra, Fabio, Scaeffer, Michiel, Roming, Niklas, Ancygier, Andrzej, Parra, Paola, Cantzler, Jasmin, Coimbra, Alain, Hare, Bill, 'What Does the Paris Climate Agreement Mean for Finland and the European Union?' (Helsinki: Sitra 2016) https://www.sitra.fi/en/publications/what-does-paris-climate-agreement-mean-finland-and-european-union, accessed 4 February 2019.

neutral society by 2045.[72] The Government of Finland also submitted legislation to the Parliament in October 2018 to phase out the use of coal for energy generation by 2029, and pledged to halve the energy use of imported oil by 2030. Although the target set for 250,000 electric vehicles and 50,000 gas-fuelled vehicles (including biogas-fuelled) by 2030 and for increasing the share of renewable transport fuels to 40 percent do not directly flow from any obligations of EU policies, they respond to the wider global policy and the agenda of EU energy and transport policies after Paris 2015.

The new activism of Finland is not entirely unrelated to the new governance mechanism of the 2016 winter package, whereby Member States submit their national climate and energy policy plans for EU level examination. In other words, whereas previously sovereignty was highly important for Member States in energy questions, within this system they share more of it than before in order to more effectively implement common policies.

6 Conclusion

As has been noted in this chapter, energy has always undergone significant transitions. In most cases, industry and the markets have driven these transitions. They are connected with innovation and economics. Such market-driven 'real-world' transitions can be rapid and change the industry structures in a fundamental way. In these processes, the role of law and policy has been to adapt or support the transition.

Law and policy can also function as the driver for a transition. The best example of this is the ongoing transition to more sustainable energy systems. The difference between this and primary government driven transitions appears to be the pace. When policy and the reflecting laws change, the world needs to adapt. This adaptation is not obvious and is certainly not rapid. When pre-existing structures need to be altered and vested interests of market participants are in play, this moves slowly. In addition to the sustainable energy transition, there are other European examples of administratively driven changes: the introduction of competitive electricity and gas markets did not take place overnight. Instead, the change took decades of effort from the governmental side. Laws and policies had to be created, altered and adapted.[73]

Both transitions that followed changes in the markets and industry and those that followed from government policies and laws have pros and cons. Industry driven changes may be impacted by the vested interests of the industry. These and other impacting factors can lead to 'market failures'. But government driven transitions can lead to 'government failures'.[74] These failures can be traced back to inadequate understanding of markets, to inadequate policies or regulatory frameworks, or other similar factors. In both cases, there are risks involved. But despite this, transitions are a *status quo* for the energy world. Global energy adapts and evolves through these transitions. Firms succeed and fail with these transitions, but the industry as a whole moves on.

72 'Ramöverenskommelse mellan Socialdemokraterna, Moderaterna, Miljöpartiet de gröna, Centerpartiet och Kristdemokraterna' (2016), https://www.regeringen.se/49cc5b/contentassets/b88f0d28eb0e48e39eb4411de2aabe76/energioverenskommelse-20160610.pdf.

73 For this, see K. Talus, *EU Energy Law and Policy – A Critical Account* (Oxford: Oxford University Press 2013).

74 An example of this would be the miscalculation of renewable energy generation and related government subsidies in many countries, including Spain or Italy. See, for example, N. Lavranos, 'The State of Play of the Energy Charter Treaty (ECT)' OGEL 4 (2018), www.ogel.org.

33

THE FUTURE OF NUCLEAR ENERGY

Alessandro Negri della Torre

1 Introduction

On 2 December 1942, at 3:25 p.m. before a team of scientists from the Manhattan Project led by Italian physicist Enrico Fermi, the world's first nuclear reactor, the *Chicago Pile-1*, reached criticality and underwent the first controlled, self-sustaining nuclear chain reaction.[1] It was the first step towards controlled production of nuclear energy. Less than three years later, on August 6 and August 9, 1945 two explosive devices detonated over the Japanese cities of Hiroshima and Nagasaki, the first and only offensive military use of nuclear ordnance in history.[2]

Few technologies have displayed such ambivalence,[3] *i.e.* the power to light homes and power factories as well as the power to annihilate lives and infrastructure. Understandably, atomic energy – in both its destructive and peaceful applications – has inspired the most hopeful dreams and the most ominous of feelings which has led to a striking tension between the potential of nuclear technology for peaceful uses and military applications.[4] Lawmakers and sovereign powers at both the international and domestic level have long since contended with the benefits of nuclear fission technology for power generation and its drawbacks (namely radiological hazards for human health and proliferation concerns), aiming for the most delicate of balances between seemingly opposite objectives, namely regulating (and encouraging, where found appropriate) uptake and management of nuclear technology for energy production and limiting creation, transfer and use of nuclear material and technology for offensive purposes. This underlying tension inspires all modern legal frameworks and

1 'Manhattan Project: CP 1 Goes Critical, Met Lab, December 2, 1942' (osti.gov, 2019) <https://www.osti.gov/opennet/manhattan-project-history/Events/1942-1944_pu/cp-1_critical.htm> accessed 26 February 2019. The Chicago Pile-1 was very different from today's nuclear reactors as it had no shielding and appeared as an imperfect cube-like pile of fissile material and wood.

2 Michael J. Hogan, *Hiroshima in History and Memory* (Cambridge University Press, 2006).

3 Vivianne H.M. Visschers and Lasse Wallquist, 'Nuclear Power Before and After Fukushima: The Relations Between Acceptance, Ambivalence and Knowledge' (2013) 36 *Journal of Environmental Psychology* 1–2.

4 J.L. Black-Branch and D. Fleck, 'Peaceful Uses of Nuclear Energy and Its Interrelationship with Nuclear Non-Proliferation and Disarmament'. In: J. Black-Branch and D. Fleck (eds) *Nuclear Non-Proliferation in International Law – Volume III* (T.M.C. Asser Press, 2016).

has materially affected the political and social choices of States regarding nuclear energy on a global scale.[5]

In over 70 years nuclear technology has undergone significant development.[6] Progress in the understanding of physical processes, new materials and improved design and manufacturing capabilities, driven by an ever-increasing world demand for abundant, affordable and consistent energy sources has spurred significant changes in the nuclear industry towards widespread safe and secure use of nuclear energy.[7] This chapter will provide an overview of existing and developing nuclear technology with a focus on how development of nuclear technology may significantly affect existing regulatory frameworks at the international and national level. With no ambition to provide a comprehensive picture of nuclear law today and future developments, an effort will nevertheless be made to address key changes in technology and some of the most significant regulatory challenges that may follow. The final section on fusion technology will serve as a prime example of how significant developments in nuclear technology may warrant profound revision of the principles and legal architecture developed so far by nuclear jurisdictions.

2 Nuclear energy today

Fission-based nuclear energy currently provides 11 percent of the world's electricity from 450 power reactors with 60 more reactors under construction, representing 16 percent of current capacity.[8] Demand for electricity is on the rise[9] as the world population increases and so does urbanization and dependence on electricity-powered technology and infrastructure. Furthermore, several existing industrial sectors are undergoing a process of electrification, *i.e.* switching from fossil fuels to using electricity as a primary energy source. Concurrently, the pursuit of low-carbon or fully decarbonized industries and the reduction of pollution levels is at the center of countless national and international initiatives,[10] an ever-increasing concern as the human population grows, especially in rapidly-developing industrialized countries.

In this respect, nuclear energy displays several attractive properties and has garnered increasing attention as an important part of a sustainable energy mix.[11] It is among the sources

5 Intergenerational effects of use of nuclear energy (and nuclear waste) are a source of concern. See John F. Ahearne, 'Intergenerational Issues Regarding Nuclear Power, Nuclear Waste, and Nuclear Weapons' (2000) 20 *Risk Analysis*.

6 'Advanced Nuclear Power Reactors | Generation III+ Nuclear Reactors – World Nuclear Association' (world-nuclear.org, 2019) <www.world-nuclear.org/information-library/nuclear-fuel-cycle/nuclear-power-reactors/advanced-nuclear-power-reactors.aspx> accessed 26 February 2019.

7 Akos Horvath and Elisabeth Rachlew, 'Nuclear Power in the 21st Century: Challenges and Possibilities' (2015) 45 *Ambio* 38–49. John F. Kotek and James A. Lake, 'Next Generation Nuclear Power' (*Scientific American*, 2015) <https://www.scientificamerican.com/article/next-generation-nuclear/> accessed 26 February 2019.

8 'Nuclear Power Today | Nuclear Energy – World Nuclear Association' (world-nuclear.org, 2019) <www.world-nuclear.org/information-library/current-and-future-generation/nuclear-power-in-the-world-today.aspx> accessed 26 February 2019.

9 'Global Energy & CO2 Status Report: Electricity' (iea.org, 2019) <https://www.iea.org/geco/electricity/> accessed 26 February 2019.

10 Remus Prăvălie and Georgeta Bandoc, 'Nuclear Energy: Between Global Electricity Demand, Worldwide Decarbonisation Imperativeness, and Planetary Environmental Implications' (2018) 209 *Journal of Environmental Management*.

11 Barry W. Brook et al., 'Why Nuclear Energy is Sustainable and has to be Part of the Energy Mix' (2014) 1–2 *Sustainable Materials and Technologies*. See also Vladimir Knapp and Dubravko Pevec, 'Promises and Limitations of Nuclear Fission Energy in Combating Climate Change' (2018) 120 *Energy Policy*.

of energy with the lowest carbon dioxide emissions during operations,[12] it has one of the smallest carbon footprints (from construction to operations), it is among the most energy-dense sources of energy,[13] outweighing chemical reactions (such as combustion of hydrocarbons) by several orders of magnitude,[14] and energy production is not dependent on favorable weather conditions, in contrast to renewable energy sources such as solar or wind.[15] Moreover, nuclear fuel loads last several months or years, and advancements in nuclear technology have pursued the possibility of using additional fissile fuel sources,[16] increasing fuel efficiency, breeding fissile fuel,[17] and even utilizing radioactive waste inside nuclear reactors.[18] Disadvantages associated with nuclear energy include the risk of radiological release from radioactive sources or irradiated material both during production or handling of nuclear material as well as in the event of accidents at nuclear power plants or other nuclear facilities. Additionally, there is a risk of diversion of nuclear material for unlawful purposes, adding to the risk of proliferation of offensive nuclear devices. Finally, safe and effective management of spent nuclear waste is also a significant concern for regulators owing to the hazards for human health and the very long half-life of certain types of fuel waste. Despite such risks and regulatory concerns, nuclear energy has a positive track-record for safe operations. As reported by the World Nuclear Association, in over 17,000 cumulative reactor-years of commercial nuclear power operation in 33 countries, there have been only three major nuclear accidents: Three Mile Island in the USA in 1979, Chernobyl in Ukraine in 1986 and Fukushima in Japan in 2011.[19] Only the Fukushima and Chernobyl accidents resulted in a release of significant radioactivity beyond the reactor site, and only the Chernobyl accident caused human casualties as a direct result of the event. It has been suggested that among all sources of energy, nuclear energy has significantly lower fatalities.[20]

While it is undeniable that nuclear accidents are potentially a major source of harm for people and the environment, accidents at a nuclear facility are triggering events for intense, in-depth analysis of existing fleets and response and containment protocols, which, combined with the progressive phasing-out of older nuclear designs, increases the safety of existing and future nuclear technology. Recent events provide substantial evidence of the responsiveness

12 Nuclear fission itself does not emit carbon dioxide.

13 N. Touran, 'Computing the Energy Density of Nuclear Fuel' (whatisnuclear.com) <https://whatisnuclear.com/energy-density.html> accessed 26 February 2019.

14 'Fuel Comparison' (euronuclear.org, 2019) <https://www.euronuclear.org/info/encyclopedia/f/fuelcomparison.htm> accessed 26 February 2019.

15 L. Lakatos, G. Hevessy and J. Kovács, 'Advantages and Disadvantages of Solar Energy and Wind-Power Utilization' (2011) 67 *World Futures* 398–399.

16 An example is thorium, a potential nuclear fuel significantly more abundant than uranium, see 'Thorium – World Nuclear Association' (world-nuclear.org, 2017) <www.world-nuclear.org/information-library/current-and-future-generation/thorium.aspx> accessed 28 February 2019.

17 So-called breeder reactors. See Glenn T. Seaborg and Justin L. Bloom, 'Fast Breeder Reactors' (1970) 223 *Scientific American*.

18 Ehud Greenspan, *Advanced Burner Reactor with Breed-and-Burn Thorium Blankets for Improved Economics and Resource Utilization* (University of California, 2015)

19 'Safety of Nuclear Reactors – World Nuclear Association' (world-nuclear.org, 2019) <www.world-nuclear.org/information-library/safety-and-security/safety-of-plants/safety-of-nuclear-power-reactors.aspx> accessed 26 February 2019.

20 *Comparing Nuclear Accident Risks with Those from Other Energy Sources* (Nuclear Energy Agency 2010), p. 39; 'Safety of Nuclear Power Reactors – Appendix – World Nuclear Association' (world-nuclear.org, 2017) <www.world-nuclear.org/information-library/safety-and-security/safety-of-plants/appendices/safety-of-nuclear-power-reactors-appendix.aspx> accessed 28 February 2019.

of the nuclear industry. The accident at the Fukushima Daiichi Nuclear Power Plant, in fact, spurred a series of significant risk and safety assessments at reactor sites in European Union (EU) and non-EU countries.[21] Comprehensive stress tests were conducted to analyze reactor safety in the event of earthquake and flooding. Ultimately, a final stress test report was adopted by the European Commission and the European Nuclear Safety Regulators Group (ENSREG) on April 26, 2012.[22] Four main paths were identified[23] for improving nuclear plant safety, including enhanced measures to prevent and mitigate accidents resulting from extreme natural hazards. Following the report, individual States mandated active improvements (e.g., the French *Autorité de Sûreté Nucléaire* issued 32 resolutions on June 26, 2012, containing multiple additional requirements targeting power plants and nuclear facilities).[24] In the USA, the NRC also issued orders for substantial post-Fukushima enhancements to the US reactor fleet.[25]

Naturally, increased safety of nuclear power plants is of paramount importance as the demand for nuclear energy increases. Coupled with cost-reduction, better efficiency and more advanced nuclear designs, increased safety is likely to materially support uptake of nuclear technology as a response to growing energy needs on a global scale. Such aspects have been addressed in a 2018 multidisciplinary study[26] from the Massachusetts Institute of Technology (MIT) which has provided a comprehensive view of the role of nuclear energy in the pursuit of "deep decarbonization" in energy-intensive industries,[27] as mandated by both environmental concerns and international commitments in an effort to reduce global warming. The study delivers four key messages,[28] namely the central opportunity for nuclear power over the next several decades to be an effective instrument in decarbonizing the power sector, the existing challenges to widespread adoption of nuclear technology given the high cost of new nuclear capacity, the merits of reducing the cost of nuclear energy through several approaches and the role of governmental help in the form of well-designed energy and environmental policies and appropriate assistance in the early stages of new nuclear systems deployment to fully develop the potential of nuclear energy. Importantly, while construction of new nuclear power plants is planned in most mature nuclear jurisdictions, countries such as China and India (interested by significant population growth, increased industrialization and increasing pollution) have also shown firm commitment to accelerating investments in nuclear energy.[29] For example, in its

21 Id.

22 'Final Report on the Peer Review of EU Stress Tests | ENSREG' (ensreg.eu, 2019) <www.ensreg.eu/document/final-report-peer-review-eu-stress-tests> accessed 26 February 2019.

23 Id. at 48.

24 ASN's 2011 Report: 'There is a Before and an After Fukushima' (french-nuclear-safety.fr, 2019) <http://www.french-nuclear-safety.fr/Information/News-releases/ASN-s-2011-report-there-is-a-before-and-an-after-Fukushima> accessed 26 February 2019.

25 'Post-Fukushima Safety Enhancements' (2019) <https://www.nrc.gov/reactors/operating/ops-experience/post-fukushima-safety-enhancements.html> accessed 26 February 2019.

26 MIT Energy Initiative, 'The Future of Nuclear Energy in a Carbon-Constrained World' (MIT 2019) <http://energy.mit.edu/wp-content/uploads/2018/09/The-Future-of-Nuclear-Energy-in-a-Carbon-Constrained-World.pdf> accessed 26 February 2019.

27 Max Åhman, Lars J. Nilsson and Bengt Johansson, 'Global Climate Policy and Deep Decarbonization of Energy-Intensive Industries' (2016) 17 *Climate Policy*.

28 'The Future of Nuclear Energy in a Carbon-Constrained World' (n. 26) at xxiv.

29 David K. Gattie, Joshua L. Darnell and Joshua N.K. Massey, 'The Role of U.S. Nuclear Power in the 21st Century' (2018) 31 *The Electricity Journal*. Kangyin Dong et al., 'CO2 Emissions, Economic Growth, and the Environmental Kuznets Curve in China: What Roles Can Nuclear Energy and Renewable Energy Play?' (2018) 196 *Journal of Cleaner Production*.

Energy Development Strategy Action Plan (2014–2020), China has outlined a significant plan for reaching 58GWe of nuclear energy by 2020 and expanding its nuclear fleet with the additional 30GWe expected to be provided by reactors under construction by 2020,[30] including advanced AP1000 model reactors.[31] Further evidence of commitment to nuclear technology is the Chinese pursuit of nuclear fusion through the Experimental Advanced Superconducting Tokamak (EAST),[32] located in Hefei, as well as the development of the 210MWe HTR-PM reactor based on small modular reactor technology[33] and even the construction of an offshore nuclear power plant based on the domestically-developed ACPR50S SMR.[34] Against the backdrop of such firm commitments to advanced nuclear technology, the remainder of the chapter will address some of the regulatory challenges associated with nuclear technological progress.

3 Regulating nuclear energy today

Before addressing specific technological advancements and the potential effects on existing rules, it is important to note that nuclear energy (including production, transportation, storage and disposal of nuclear fuel and material) is subject to several international and regional agreements. This complex overarching international architecture is then complemented by recommendations from international bodies, as well as comprehensive primary and secondary legislation enacted by individual states. Noticeably, alongside the efforts of lawmakers and regulators in sovereign states, international organizations, such as the International Atomic Energy Agency (IAEA) and the Organisation for Economic Co-operation and Development (OECD) Nuclear Energy Agency (NEA), have played a significant role in fostering the development of an international framework both supporting the execution of treaties,[35] and entering a number of international agreements as parties in their own right. Additional guidance is provided by *soft law* which is designed to orient and direct states towards best practices and a generally harmonized approach towards management of nuclear material and nuclear installations. This highly complex and rather unique combination of international and national rules and guidance stems from the properties of nuclear energy, which is the object of detailed technical provisions at the local level (e.g., construction, licensing and operation requirements for nuclear power plants), and the risks associated with nuclear energy (e.g., harm from radioactivity and offensive uses of nuclear material), which are not inherently bound by State borders.

30 'China Nuclear Power | Chinese Nuclear Energy – World Nuclear Association' (world-nuclear.org, 2019) <www.world-nuclear.org/information-library/country-profiles/countries-a-f/china-nuclear-power.aspx> accessed 26 February 2019.

31 'Fourth Chinese AP1000 Enters Commercial Operation – World Nuclear News' (world-nuclear-news.org, 2019) <http://www.world-nuclear-news.org/Articles/Fourth-Chinese-AP1000-enters-commercial-operation> accessed 26 February 2019.

32 B. Wan (on behalf of EAST Team), 'Experimental Advanced Superconducting Tokamak' (2016) *Magnetic Fusion Energy*.

33 Wentao Guo and Michael Schorer (2018) 'Development of High Temperature Gas Cooled Reactor in China' 63(2) *Atw Internationale Zeitschrift fuer Kernenergie* 81–83.

34 'CGN to Build Floating Reactor – World Nuclear News' (world-nuclear-news.org, 2019) <www.world-nuclear-news.org/NN-CGN-to-build-floating-reactor-1301164.html> accessed 26 February 2019.

35 'Treaties | IAEA' (iaea.org, 2019) <https://www.iaea.org/resources/legal/treaties> accessed 26 February 2019.

Consequently, international agreements generally have come to address three main aspects, namely (i) nuclear safety; (ii) nuclear security; and (iii) nuclear liability.[36] The additional areas of international cooperation include technical cooperation, research and training, and specific scientific undertakings. One such example is the Agreement on the Establishment of the ITER International Fusion Energy Organization for the Joint Implementation of the ITER Project, which established the ITER organization, the purpose of which is to provide for and to promote cooperation among its members to demonstrate the scientific and technological feasibility of fusion energy.[37] Related to nuclear energy (but independent of a state's use of nuclear power plants) is the body of national and international rules including the landmark Treaty on the Non-Proliferation of Nuclear Weapons (NPT).[38] Given the specificity of non-proliferation rules, these will not be considered in this chapter.

With respect to nuclear safety, several agreements have been entered into under the auspices of the IAEA, such as the Convention on Nuclear Safety adopted in 1994, which, *inter alia*, mandates State parties to achieve and maintain a high level of nuclear safety worldwide through the enhancement of national measures and international cooperation including, where appropriate, safety-related technical cooperation; the 1986 Convention on early Notification of a Nuclear Accident,[39] which, in the aftermath of the Chernobyl accident, established a notification system for nuclear accidents that have the potential to affect States across national boundaries; and the Joint Convention on the Safety of Spent Fuel Management and on the Safety of Radioactive Waste Management adopted in 1997 with the purpose of providing an international instrument designed to address the issue of spent fuel and radioactive waste management on a global scale.[40] Nuclear security is addressed in the Convention on the Physical Protection of Nuclear Material,[41] as amended in 2005 and supplemented by the non-binding Code of Conduct for the Safety and Security of Radioactive Sources with its supplementary guidance.[42] Additional international instruments have been entered into under the auspices of the United Nations, the International Maritime Organization, and binding resolutions have been adopted by the UN Security Council pursuant to Chapter VII of the UN Charter. Currently, the principal instruments addressing nuclear

36 NEA uses a four-way classification which features "environmental protection" as a fourth topical category 'OECD/NEA – Multilateral Agreements in Nuclear Energy' (oecd-nea.org, 2019) <https://www.oecd-nea.org/law/multilateral-agreements> accessed 26 February 2019.

37 'Agreement on the Establishment of the ITER International Fusion Energy Organization for the Joint Implementation of the ITER Project | IAEA' (iaea.org, 2019) <https://www.iaea.org/publications/documents/infcircs/agreement-establishment-iter-international-fusion-energy-organization-joint-implementation-iter-project> accessed 26 February 2019.

38 'Treaty on the Non-Proliferation of Nuclear Weapons (NPT) | IAEA' (iaea.org, 2019) <https://www.iaea.org/publications/documents/treaties/npt> accessed 26 February 2019.

39 'Convention on Early Notification of a Nuclear Accident | IAEA' (iaea.org, 2019) <https://www.iaea.org/topics/nuclear-safety-conventions/convention-early-notification-nuclear-accident> accessed 26 February 2019.

40 'Joint Convention on the Safety of Spent Fuel Management and on the Safety of Radioactive Waste Management | IAEA' (iaea.org, 2019) <https://www.iaea.org/topics/nuclear-safety-conventions/joint-convention-safety-spent-fuel-management-and-safety-radioactive-waste> accessed 26 February 2019.

41 'Convention on the Physical Protection of Nuclear Material | IAEA' (iaea.org, 2019) <https://www.iaea.org/publications/documents/conventions/convention-physical-protection-nuclear-material> accessed 26 February 2019.

42 'Codes of Conduct | IAEA' (iaea.org, 2019) <https://www.iaea.org/topics/codes-of-conduct> accessed 26 February 2019.

liability are the 1963 Vienna Convention on Civil Liability for Nuclear Damage,[43] the 1997 Convention on Supplementary Compensation for Nuclear Damage, the 1960 OECD Paris Convention on Third Party Liability in the Field of Nuclear Energy and the 1988 Joint Protocol Relating to the Application of the Vienna Convention and the Paris Convention, which establishes treaty relations between the signatory parties to the Vienna Convention on Civil Liability and the Paris Convention on Third Party Liability in the field of Nuclear Energy.[44] While the current international legal framework already provides a robust system of rules, efforts to better govern nuclear energy at the international level are still very much ongoing. For example, following the accident at TEPCO's Fukushima Daiichi Nuclear Power Station in 2011, a Ministerial Conference on Nuclear Safety was convened to direct, under the leadership of the IAEA, the process of analyzing the Fukushima accident with a view to strengthening nuclear safety, emergency preparedness and radiation protection.[45] The IAEA Action Plan on Nuclear Safety, which was approved by the IAEA Board of Governors in September 2011, not only directed member states to review and strengthen national safety procedures but also to explore mechanisms to enhance effective implementation of the international instruments, join and effectively implement such instruments, and work towards establishing a global nuclear liability regime that addresses the concerns of all States that might be affected by the nuclear accident with a view to providing appropriate compensation for nuclear damage.

At a national level, international instruments are complemented by national legislation adopted to provide the necessary legal architecture to regulate production, transfer and use of nuclear material as well as licensing, operating and decommissioning of nuclear power plants, installations and facilities. As a matter of fact, as noted by the IAEA, the safe and peaceful use of nuclear energy in any given State can only be assured with the promulgation and implementation of an effective national nuclear legal infrastructure. The IAEA, as well as other international organizations, have thus undertaken considerable efforts to provide guidelines that States may follow in their efforts to equip themselves with a comprehensive body of laws and regulations addressing nuclear-related activities. According to the 2003 *Handbook on Nuclear Law*,[46] as complemented by the 2010 IAEA *Handbook on Nuclear Law: Implementing Legislation*,[47] the term "nuclear law" itself could be defined as the 'body of special legal norms created to regulate the conduct of legal or natural persons engaged in activities related to fissionable materials, ionizing radiation and exposure to natural sources of radiation'.[48] Several concepts, often expressed as fundamental principles, are considered essential in nuclear law and are often implemented by individual States. These include the safety principle, the security principle, the permission principle, the compensation principle and

43 'Vienna Convention on Civil Liability for Nuclear Damage | IAEA' (iaea.org, 2019) <https://www.iaea.org/topics/nuclear-liability-conventions/vienna-convention-on-civil-liability-for-nuclear-damage> accessed 28 February 2019.

44 'Joint Protocol Relating to the Application of the Vienna Convention and the Paris Convention | IAEA' (iaea.org, 2019) <https://www.iaea.org/topics/nuclear-liability-conventions/joint-protocol-relating-to-application-of-vienna-convention-and-paris-convention> accessed 28 February 2019.

45 'The Fukushima Daiichi Accident' (IAEA 2015), 166.

46 *Handbook on Nuclear Law* (www-pub.iaea.org, 2003) <https://www-pub.iaea.org/books/iaeabooks/6807/Handbook-on-Nuclear-Law> accessed 28 February 2019.

47 *Handbook on Nuclear Law: Implementing Legislation'* (www-pub.iaea.org, 2010) <https://www-pub.iaea.org/books/iaeabooks/8374/Handbook-on-Nuclear-Law-Implementing-Legislation> accessed 26 February 2019.

48 *Handbook on Nuclear Law* (n 6) at 4.

the international co-operation principles.[49] Furthermore, according to the schematization provided by the IAEA, domestic nuclear law should generally establish a suitable regulatory body, provide robust licensing, inspection and enforcement as key elements of an effective regulatory system, establish a legislative framework for the safe management of all sources and types of ionizing radiation, prevent unlawful or harmful uses of radiation sources as well as appropriate plans and measures for mitigating the effects of accidents, provide rules to ensure proper licensing and safe operations of nuclear facilities and effectively regulate transport and processing of radioactive material, radioactive waste and spent fuel, ensuring the highest levels of safety for human life and the environment.[50]

An analysis of the regulatory approach adopted by each State is beyond the scope of this chapter, but it is important to highlight certain key aspects that are common to the legal framework of several – if not all – jurisdictions engaged in nuclear activities. The first is that nuclear law is a highly complex and intertwined legal architecture comprised of international and national rules enriched by the unique political and legislative choices of individual states as well as the often-significant role of international organizations in providing ongoing international support and regulatory guidance. The second aspect is the assumption that, at both the international and domestic level, peaceful uses of nuclear energy must contend with the risks posed by ionizing radiations as well as the security of nuclear material. Thirdly, that nuclear energy is generated in power plants from *nuclear material*, which includes plutonium, uranium-233 or enriched uranium (fissionable material).[51] Fourth, that nuclear reactors for power generation are generally assumed to be fixed installations or, at the very least, that the process of generating power for commercial uses takes place in a stationary facility. Existing and developing nuclear technology may question such assumptions and warrant profound revisions of national and international rules. The following section will illustrate how advancements in nuclear technology may challenge such assumptions.

4 Advanced fission reactors

Nuclear reactors can be classified differently according to certain features of their designs (e.g., coolant type or moderator technology). However, given the development of nuclear technology over time, a distinction based on generations is often used to classify nuclear reactors, providing a useful chronological roadmap. That said, at present most of the world's nuclear reactors belong to the Generation II category.[52] As technology is being developed further,[53] however, Generation III, III+ and even Generation IV fission designs are set to replace older nuclear reactors as the latter approach the final stages of their life cycle and new reactor plants are commissioned. The transition from Generation II reactors to more modern designs is already underway. The first Generation III reactor was built in Japan

49 Id. 5.

50 Id. 48.

51 *Handbook on Nuclear Law: Implementing Legislation* (n. 47), 20. The definition of "nuclear material" includes plutonium, uranium and uranium enriched in the isotopes uranium-233 or uranium-235, as well as any other material the designated regulatory body determines should be classified as nuclear material. A definition based on fissionable elements would, for example, leave out material capable of generating energy by way of atomic transformation, *i.e.* fusion fuel.

52 Stephen M. Goldberg and Robert Rosner, *Nuclear Reactors: Generation to Generation* (American Academy of Arts and Sciences 2011), 4.

53 For an overview, see I. Pioro and R. Duffey, 'Current and Future Nuclear Power Reactors and Plants' (2019) *Managing Global Warming*.

in 1996 (ADBWR),[54] while the first Generation III+ design became operational in Russia in 2016 (VVER-1200/392M) at the Novovoronezh power plant.[55] Generation IV and Generation V reactors are still in the design phase and have not yet been built although Generation IV reactors are expected to make it to commercial construction between 2020 and 2030.[56] Research in next generation reactors is not limited to isolated efforts of specific nations but is also supported by a number of international organizations and international ventures. Several international initiatives are pursuing joint development of Generation III and Generation IV nuclear reactors. These include the Generation IV International Forum (GIF) initiated by the US Department of Energy in 2000 to share scientific knowledge and to pursue development of six selected Generation IV reactor technologies.[57] The Multinational Design Evaluation Programme (MDEP),[58] a joint effort of the US Nuclear Regulatory Commission (NRC) and the French Nuclear Safety Authority (ASN), is pursuing creation of a harmonized set of regulatory requirements and practices for both Generation III and future Generation IV reactors. Additionally, the European Sustainable Industrial Initiative (ESNII),[59] launched by the European Commission in 2010, will actively support Generation IV reactor technologies.

Generation III/III+ reactors display several differences compared to Generation I/II reactors, namely a more standardized design to facilitate licensing, reduced cost and construction time, simpler and easier-to-operate designs, longer operating lives, reduced risk of core accidents, better fuel efficiency, and enhanced safety features as well as load-following capabilities.[60] Additionally, some reactor designs display significant differences from the light water reactor (LWR) design and generally fall within the categories of HWR (heavy water reactors), HTGS (high-temperature gas cooled) or SCFR (sodium cooled fast reactors). The use of different coolant types and higher operating temperatures are the salient traits of such designs and raise additional technological challenges to advanced fission designs. Finally, small modular reactors (SMRs) are considered an integral part of advanced reactor research but due to their unique properties will be addressed specifically in Section 6 below.

The technological development of advanced fission designs has been acknowledged as challenging on the existing regulatory framework both in terms of the use of novel technology and the licensing process. Generation III/III+ reactors are designed to provide enhanced safety and security features while employing technology which is not found in LWR designs. Consequently, several nuclear jurisdictions have begun licensing advanced reactor designs while expressly acknowledging the regulatory challenges posed by advanced fission designs. For example, in 2005, the NRC approved certification for its first Generation III+ reactor[61] while, at

54 Id. 5.

55 'Russia Connects Novovoronezh 6 to Grid – World Nuclear News' (world-nuclear-news.org, 2019) <www.world-nuclear-news.org/NN-Russia-connects-Novovoronezh-6-to-grid-05081601.html> accessed 27 February 2019.

56 Yutaka Sagayama and Masato Ando. 'The Development Status of Generation IV Reactor Systems (1) Overview' (2018), 60(3) *Nippon Genshiryoku Gakkai-Shi (Atomos)* 162–167.

57 'GIF Portal   Home   Public' (gen 4.org, 2019) <https://www.gen 4.org/gif/jcms/c_9260/public> accessed 27 February 2019.

58 'NEA Multinational Design Evaluation Programme (MDEP)' (oecd-nea.org, 2019) <https://www.oecd-nea.org/mdep/> accessed 27 February 2019.

59 'SNETP | European Sustainable Nuclear Industrial Initiative' (snetp.eu, 2019) <www.snetp.eu/esnii/> accessed 27 February 2019.

60 'Advanced Nuclear Power Reactors' (n. 6).

61 Ian Hore-Lacy, *Nuclear Energy in the 21St Century* (Elsevier Science 2010), 65.

the same time, addressing non-LWR (advanced) reactor design licensing as part of its initiative to revise the applicable regulatory framework. The objective is to effectively address applicants' needs as advanced nuclear technology makes it to the licensing stage.[62]

Some of the most significant steps taken by the NRC in this regard were the publication in 2017 of the *Regulatory Review Roadmap for Non-Light Water Reactors*,[63] which contains design guidance for the NRC's review process for advanced reactors, and the publication of Regulatory Guide 1.232 for developing principle design criteria for non-LWRs, which is intended to provide applicants engaged in licensing applications of non-LWR designs with principal design criteria.[64] A significant development has been the recommendation by the NRC staff to the Commission on 23 May 2018 to support the creation of a new set of rules to effectively address advanced fission designs.[65] Further confirmation of the importance of developing a licensing process for advanced fission can be found in the 2018 Nuclear Energy Innovation and Modernization Act (NEIMA), which directs the NRC to modify its licensing process to support licensing of commercial advanced nuclear reactor facilities.[66] Similarly, the Office for Nuclear Regulation (ONR) in the UK has undertaken a focused review of its guidance to ensure that it is capable of adequately regulating advanced nuclear technologies (ANT),[67] which encompass a wide range of innovative nuclear reactor technologies including advanced modular reactors and small modular reactors.

As fission technology develops further and older designs are phased out of commercial operation, it is expected that regulators will review the regulatory preparedness of existing rules with increased attention. Enhanced safety, reduced staffing needs, increased reactor security as well as novel reactor designs and technologies will progressively challenge the boundaries of existing regulations. The process will probably be driven by increased demand for nuclear technology as well as industry-driven demand for faster, less onerous licensing and operating requirements from design to construction to operation. Whether the choice is to amend and complement existing provisions considering the new designs or develop entirely new licensing processes engineered to accommodate the needs of an evolving industry, additional regulatory interventions are likely to occur in the foreseeable future facilitating and accelerating development of the next generation of fission reactors.

62 'NRC: Advanced Reactors (Non-LWR Designs)' (nrc.gov, 2019) <https://www.nrc.gov/reactors/new-reactors/advanced.html> accessed 27 February 2019.

63 NRC, 'A Regulatory Review Roadmap for Non-Light Water Reactors', (2017), document no. ML17312B567 <https://www.nrc.gov/docs/ML1731/ML17312B567.pdf> drafted by the following office within the NRC 'Advanced Reactors Policy Branch Division of Safety Systems, Risk Assessment, and Advanced Reactors Office of New Reactors' in December 2017.

64 'Released: New Guidance for Developing Principal Design Criteria for Non-Light-Water Reactors' (energy.gov, 2018) <https://www.energy.gov/ne/articles/released-new-guidance-developing-principal-design-criteria-non-light-water-reactors> accessed 27 February 2019.

65 NRC, 'ML18110A187 – Achieving Modern Risk-Informed Regulation' (2018), document from the U.S. Nuclear Regulatory Commission < https://www.nrc.gov/docs/ML1811/ML18110A187.pdf > dated May 23, 2018.

66 Nuclear Energy Innovation and Modernization Act 2019.

67 'ONR – Advanced Nuclear Technologies (Ants)' (onr.org.uk, 2019) <www.onr.org.uk/advanced-nuclear-technologies/index.htm> accessed 27 February 2019.

5 Floating nuclear power plants

An historic example of regulatory concerns triggered by nuclear technological development are floating nuclear power plants (FNPP). A FNPP is generally defined as a platform equipped with one or more nuclear reactors designed to feed energy to onshore grids while power generation occurs onboard.[68] A typical use for a FNPP would be to provide heat and electricity to remote areas for, amongst other purposes, oil and gas drilling, and power provision[69] or desalination[70] for the benefit of onshore communities. In a typical use case scenario, a FNPP would either navigate (or be towed)[71] into position and generate the necessary power from beyond the coastline, providing electricity generation, heating and drinkable water through desalination of sea water. Given the growing need for affordable drinkable water and power generation, it is understandable why several coastal countries have invested in such technology, including Russia, Japan, China, Canada, Morocco,[72] and the UK. Among the coastal countries engaged in FNPP research or deployment, Russia has a distinctive track record in both nuclear manufacturing capacity and civilian use of nuclear reactors onboard naval vessels and is considered the most promising candidate for sustained deployment of FNPP designs.[73] In addition to commercial interest in FNPP, the IAEA has acknowledged that FNPPs are advantageous in that they can be manufactured and tested at ship-building sites using standardized manufacturing technologies, thus ensuring higher and more consistent quality standards. Non-proliferation concerns would be successfully addressed by exercising loading, unloading and processing of nuclear material at specific locations.[74] There are, however, strong opposing voices that highlight issues of environmental safety, nuclear security and profitability.[75]

The concept of a FNPP challenges the paradigm of a land-based nuclear installation ordinarily subject to the architecture of existing nuclear regulations at both the international and national level. Additionally, reactor technology itself is often customized to suit the needs of naval deployment. An example is the use of enriched fuel compensating for smaller reactor size, which, in turn, is a source of both safety and security concerns.[76]

As noted in scholarly contributions, the primary concern in relation to the presence or transport of FNPPs and related technology is the risk posed to human health and the environment as a result of normal operations or malfunctions. FNPPs came to the attention of the international community as early as 1974 during the United Nations Conference on the Law of the Sea in Caracas, where FNPPs were discussed with specific reference to the right of a manufacturing state to construct a FNPP without causing harm to neighboring states

68 M Dowdall and WJ F Standring, *Floating Nuclear Power Plants and Associated Technologies in the Northern Areas* (LoboMedia AS, 2008).
69 Id, 10–11.
70 Id
71 Id.
72 Id, 12–13.
73 Y.K. Panov, V.I. Polunichev and K.V. Zverev 'Nuclear Floating Power Desalination Complexes (IAEA-TECDOC--1056)' (IAEA, 1998).
74 *Economics of Nuclear Desalination: New Developments and Site Specific Studies* <www- pub.iaea.org/MTCD/publications/PDF/te_1561 _web.pdf> accessed 27 February 2019.
75 V.M. Kuznetsov et al., *Floating Nuclear Power Plants in Russia: A Threat to the Arctic, World Oceans and Non-Proliferation Treaty* (3rd ed., Agenstvo Rakurs Production, 2004).
76 Highly enriched uranium (HEU) has been used in the construction of compact naval reactors, but proliferation concerns provide a strong argument against continued use of HEU. See, *inter alia*, George M. Moore, Cervando A. Banuelos and Thomas T. Gray, *Replacing Highly Enriched Uranium in Naval Reactors* (NTI Paper, 2016).

or the marine environment, the process of taking other states' considerations into account during manufacturing and differentiating between FNPPs attached to shore and those that would provide support out to sea.[77] It has been noted that FNPP operation and transport involving maritime transport of nuclear materials intersect several frameworks and treaties in addition to nation-specific licensing and operating requirements.[78] Interestingly, some of these concerns came into existence early in the history of nuclear energy. For example, inspired by the potential of nuclear energy (and, specifically, of nuclear-powered propulsion) and the need to address liability concerns arising from vessels equipped with nuclear reactors, an attempt was made to regulate this matter at the international level with the *Brussels Convention on the Liability of Operators of Nuclear Ships* of 1962. Perhaps as a result of the controversy over international regulation of nuclear reactors onboard military vessels and the unexplored legal consequences of nuclear-powered ships docking at ports of other than licensing states, the international instrument never came into force.

Even today, multiple challenges are found to exist with international legal instruments.[79] First, certain instruments may lack the necessary specificity to address FNPP risks. Secondly, definitions contained in international treaties may be inapplicable, an example of this being the Vienna Convention on Civil Liability for Nuclear Damage, which under Article 1(j)(i) does not apply to nuclear reactors on vessels or aircraft. Thirdly, even if certain treaties are found applicable in theory, a country engaged in FNPP construction or use may not be a party to such instruments or the international instruments may lack specific enforcing rights.[80] Finally, a signatory state may still wish to engage in FNPP activities in violation of applicable international rules privileging overriding interests, and enforcement could ultimately suffer from the general limitations of legal actions against sovereign states under international law.

As demand for potable water increases and nuclear technology advances, it is reasonable to expect that FNPP may witness increased adoption,[81] and development of design variants to suit specific needs of both mature and less mature nuclear jurisdictions. Concerns regarding applicable rules, security, safety, as well as licensing and operating requirements would probably increase, spurring further legislative and regulatory efforts at both the national and international level. Technological cross-overs between FNPP and SMR designs[82] could further add to the complexity of regulating FNPPs.

6 Small modular reactors (SMRs) and micro reactors

Perhaps one of the most innovative concepts in nuclear technology currently under consideration is that of SMRs (small modular nuclear power reactors), which, given their size and theorized

77 William J.F. Standring and Mark Dowdall, *Floating Nuclear Power Plants and Associated Technologies in the Northern Areas* (LoboMedia AS, Oslo 2008), 39.

78 Id.

79 Douglas John Steding, 'Russian Floating Nuclear Reactors: Lacunae in Current International Environmental and Maritime Law and the Need for Proactive International Cooperation in the Development of Sustainable Energy Sources' (2004) 13 *Pacific Rim Law & Policy Journal Association* 721–739. Although the author expressly addresses Russian floating power plants, the legal arguments appear capable of broader application.

80 Id. at 723.

81 K-H Lee et al., 'Recent Advances in Ocean Nuclear Power Plants' (2015) 8 *Energies* 11470 <http://dx.doi.org/10.3390/en81011470> accessed 26 February 2019.

82 Wan Lei et al., 'Study on Supervision Mode of Floating Nuclear Power Plant with Small Modular Reactor' (2018) 5, 26th International Conference on Nuclear Engineering 22–26 July 2018, London.

uses display noticeable differences in comparison to the known standard of larger stationary nuclear power plants. Although there are different views as to what is the exact definition of a SMR, it is generally held that SMRs are nuclear fission reactors that are smaller than traditional reactors and capable of outputs of 300MWe or less.[83] In addition to their smaller size, SMRs display a number of significant technical properties common to most SMR designs such as: (i) factory-based production and assembly (as opposed to the *in situ* construction process for conventional power plants); (ii) enhanced safety features based on passive as well as active systems; (iii) smaller fuel loads; (iv) the ability to be physically transported after assembly; and (v) the ability to be paralleled (hence the reference to modularity) to provide grid scalability.[84] As noted by the WNA in its 2015 report,[85] the potential of SMRs resides in the fact that, by their design, SMRs could benefit from construction in controlled factory settings with increased quality control, increased construction speed, efficiency and reduced construction costs.[86] Further, their smaller size and reduced costs per unit could allow deployment in areas where larger reactors would either be too expensive, unsafe to build or inefficient.[87] The enhanced safety features, simplicity of design and reduced staffing needs could, in theory, lead to deployment of SMRs in communities less familiar with constructing, operating or even decommissioning nuclear reactors.[88] Alongside SMRs, vSMRs (very small modular reactors, up to 25 MWe) have also been considered for commercial, scientific and military uses.[89] While there are specific issues to be considered with very small or micro reactors, the fundamental regulatory concerns appear to be common to both SMR and vSMR design, and thus both technologies will be addressed together in this section. However, the reader should be mindful of the fact that as the size of nuclear reactors is reduced, the potential uses of such designs in novel settings (e.g., propulsion, power generation at remote locations) increases, further challenging the regulatory framework.

Several states have shown considerable interest in SMR designs, including those with greater experience in nuclear technology, e.g., the USA, the UK and Russia, but also countries with shorter track records of nuclear operations such as China and Korea. Several nuclear jurisdictions are currently engaged in research and the funding of SMRs with a few considering initial designs for licensing purposes. In the USA, the Nuclear Regulatory Commission (NRC) has been engaged in four application types, including the design certification of the NuScale reactor, two pre-applications and an early site permit application.[90] The Canadian Nuclear Safety Commission (NSC) is also engaged with vendors and stakeholders on the

83 'Small Nuclear Power Reactors – World Nuclear Association' (world-nuclear.org, 2019) <www.world-nuclear.org/information-library/nuclear-fuel-cycle/nuclear-power-reactors/small-nuclear-power-reactors.aspx> accessed 27 February 2019.

84 Id.

85 *Facilitating International Licensing of Small Modular Reactors* (WNA – Cooperation in Reactor Design Evaluation and Licensing (CORDEL) Working Group of the World Nuclear Association 2015).

86 Id, 3.

87 IAEA, 'Advances in Small Modular Reactor Technology Developments' (IAEA 2015), 1.

88 Mario D. Carelli and Daniel T. Ingersoll, *Handbook of Small Modular Nuclear Reactor* (Woodhead Publishing 2014), Section 20 (Section authored by D. Goodman).

89 Juan A. Vitali et al., 'Study on the Use of Mobile Nuclear Power Plants for Ground Operations' (2018) <https://apps.dtic.mil/dtic/tr/fulltext/u2/1064604.pdf> accessed 10 January 2020. The report highlights the advantages of energy-dense, long-lasting power sources in remote locations and battlefronts. The cost and logistic complexities of a steady flow of fuel to such locations is an important argument and one which appears to have application in non-military contexts.

90 'NRC: Small Modular Reactors (LWR Designs)' <https://www.nrc.gov/reactors/new-reactors/smr.html> accessed 28 February 2019.

matter of SMR deployment through a process of pre-licensing vendor design review.[91] SMR designs currently under review include the 200MWe IMSR from Terrestrial Energy, Inc., currently at the Phase 2 assessment phase, and NuScale's Integral Pressurized Water Reactor.[92]

Small modular reactors have been acknowledged as presenting unique licensing challenges.[93] The recognized advantages of SMR designs are increased safety, reduced staffing requirements and reduced hazards to human life and the environment, owing, *inter alia*, to the smaller fuel loads and enhanced safety measures. Consequently, vendors and industry stakeholders have proposed adjustments to existing regulations[94] addressing aspects such as siting criteria, emergency planning zones, insurance and liability requirements, security and safety requirements,[95] staffing levels and even multi-module licensing structures[96] to accommodate the prospective commercial applications of SMR designs. The NRC has been addressing such policy and regulatory issues[97] actively, and therefore its methodology and findings are useful to assess the challenges that several other regulators may face as uptake of SMR technology increases.

An example is emergency planning zone determination. The NRC has been actively engaged with vendors and stakeholders to determine whether the best approach to scalable emergency planning zones (EPZs) for SMR and other advanced reactor designs (also commonly referred to as other new technologies (ONTs)) which would reflect the increased safety of such designs. Existing regulations in the USA provide for a plume exposure and ingestion exposure pathway EPZ with a radius of 10 and 50 miles respectively.[98] Such current standards have been developed over time considering the features of large LWR power plants, the bulk of the US reactor fleet. Vendors and operators have questioned whether such onerous requirements are necessary with SMR designs or if smaller areas can meet the stringent safety requirements imposed by the NRC. The NRC has engaged both vendors and stakeholders, including the Nuclear Energy Institute (NEI). The process has led to the NRC proposing rules to amend regulations for emergency preparedness for SMRs and ONTs, thus creating an alternative framework characterized by a performance-based, technology-inclusive, risk-informed and consequence-oriented approach.[99]

91 Canada's commitment to SMR technology is premised on the idea that SMRs could help Canada achieve a low-carbon future. See Canadian Small Modular Reactor Roadmap Steering Committee. 'A Call to Action: A Canadian Roadmap for Small Modular Reactors'. (Ottawa, 2018).

92 'Pre-Licensing Vendor Design Review – Canadian Nuclear Safety Commission' (nuclearsafety.gc.ca) <http://nuclearsafety.gc.ca/eng/reactors/power-plants/pre-licensing-vendor-design-review/index.cfm> accessed 28 February 2019.

93 'CORDEL Facilitating International Licensing of Small Modular Reactors – World Nuclear Association' (world-nuclear.org, 2019) <www.world-nuclear.org/our-association/publications/online-reports/cordel-facilitating-international-licensing-of-sma.aspx> accessed 27 February 2019.

94 As an example of key issues, see NRC, 'ML093290268 – Potential Policy, Licensing, and Key Technical Issues for Small Modular Nuclear Reactor Designs' (NRC, 2010).

95 An example of industry-driven analysis of how SMR technology will affect source terms: Nuclear Energy Institute, 'Small Modular Reactor Source Terms' (2012).

96 NRC, 'ML110620459 – License Structure for Multi-Module Facilities Related to Small Modular Nuclear Power Reactors' (NRC, 2011).

97 See above at n. 94.

98 'NRC: Emergency Planning Zones' <https://www.nrc.gov/about-nrc/emerg-preparedness/about-emerg-preparedness/planning-zones.html> accessed 28 February 2019.

99 The official notice to the proposed issuance of rules and regulations was published in the Federal Register in Vol. 82, No. 219, on 15 November 2017. More detailed documentation is available at 'NRC: Package ML18134A086 – SECY-18-0103: Proposed Rule: 'Emergency Preparedness for Small Modular Reactors and Other New Technologies' (RIN 3150-AJ68; NRC-2015-225)' (nrc.gov, 2018) <https://www.nrc.gov/docs/ML1813/ML18134A086.html> accessed 28 February 2019.

The process of addressing this single policy issue concerning SMRs should provide evidence as to the fact that development of advanced nuclear technology will probably challenge regulatory frameworks, warranting significant revisions of current rules. Furthermore, in light of the complex relationship between national and international law on nuclear energy, it is also reasonable to believe that interventions by national lawmakers on matters such as liability or insurance requirements for SMR or advanced fission designs may reflect on those international instruments that specifically address such matters.

7 Stationary and compact nuclear fusion reactors

Fusion is the process whereby two or more atomic nuclei merge to yield different atomic nuclei and energy.[100] It is the very same nuclear process which powers our Sun, as most other stars, and is responsible for the energy output of stellar bodies.[101] Fusion differs radically from fission, which is the process where heavier atomic nuclei undergo subdivision.[102] Theorized since the 1920s,[103] fusion has long been hailed as the ultimate power source. The ample supply of lighter elements such as hydrogen and its isotopes coupled with lower radiological risks associated with fusion fuel and byproducts have made nuclear fusion an attractive and efficient[104] form of power generation.[105]

The reason why fusion is not yet a viable form of power generation for commercial uses lies primarily in the technical difficulties in achieving a stable, self-sustaining reaction. Deep in the stellar furnace, the intense heat and pressure are sufficient to overcome the natural repulsive forces between atomic nuclei and induce fusion. Successful replication of such conditions on Earth has eluded the scientific community for decades, but recent progress in the understanding of nuclear physics, materials, reactor design and construction has allowed significant progress in the quest for *ignition*. This section will provide an overview of some of the most promising approaches to nuclear fusion as well as some of the principal regulatory challenges that lawmakers and regulators will face as progress is made towards viable commercial fusion reactors.

Several different technological approaches are currently being explored to achieve controlled fusion.[106] The first is *thermonuclear fusion,* whereby fusion fuel is transformed into plasma and contained within a vessel by means of intense magnetic fields. Examples of such an approach are the ITER project currently under construction in France and set to achieve first fusion experiments in 2035,[107] the JET (Joint European Torus) located in the UK,[108] and the Wendelstein 7-X located in Germany and inaugurated in 2014.[109] A different approach is *inertial confinement fusion*, whereby fusion is achieved by heating and compressing a nuclear

100 'Nuclear Fusion: WNA – World Nuclear Association' <www.world-nuclear.org/information-library/current-and-future-generation/nuclear-fusion-power.aspx> accessed 28 February 2019.

101 Donald D. Clayton, *Principles of Stellar Evolution and Nucleosynthesis* (University of Chicago Press, 2007).

102 Stephen O. Dean, *Search for the Ultimate Energy Source* (Springer, 2013), 2.

103 Arthur Stanley Eddington, 'The Internal Constitution of the Star' (1920) XLIII *The Observatory*, 354.

104 Only a few grams of fusion fuel are used at any given time in a nuclear fusion reactor, 'Fuelling the Fusion Reaction' (ITER) <https://www.iter.org/sci/FusionFuels> accessed 28 February 2019.

105 Dean (n. 102) at 5–6.

106 Id, 8–18.

107 'What is ITER?' (ITER) <https://www.iter.org/proj/inafewlines> accessed 28 February 2019.

108 'JET– Eurofusion' (euro-fusion.org, 2019) <https://www.euro-fusion.org/devices/jet> accessed 28 February 2019.

109 'Wendelstein 7-X' (ipp.mpg.de, 2019) <https://www.ipp.mpg.de/w7x> accessed 28 February 2019.

fuel target by means of high powered lasers or ion beams. An example of such a technology is the National Ignition Facility (NIF) in the USA.[110] Finally, another approach is *inertial electrostatic confinement*, which uses powerful electric fields to accelerate ions to fusion conditions. An example of such an approach is the Polywell developed by the private company EMC2, Inc.[111] Fusion displays several fundamental differences from *fission*. In fission, fissile material must be used to cause an exothermic reaction, while fusion employs lighter elements (as light as hydrogen or helium), which are more abundant and safer than fissile elements. Furthermore, while in fission reactors damage to the control and safety mechanisms can lead to an uncontrolled, self-sustaining reaction, in fusion reactors very specific reactor conditions must be ensured for continuous operations.[112] Unless such conditions are maintained, fusion cannot occur. Furthermore, in fusion, depending on the reaction type and fusion fuel mixture, levels of radiation from fuel, fusion byproducts, operations and exposed parts of the facility are projected as being considerably less harmful than what is expected in a fission-based reactor.[113]

At this juncture, two additional key technological features must be considered. The first is that different fusion fuel mixtures can theoretically be used leading to different radiation levels, albeit at the expense of different operating conditions. For example, if a deuterium-tritium mixture is used, radiological risks are associated with both the tritium fuel, production of high energy neutrons as a byproduct of the fusion process, and the facility's irradiated materials.[114] By contrast, certain so-called aneutronic reactions,[115] such as proton-boron or deuterium-helium-3 are expected to produce lower neutron levels than even deuterium-_tritium (although x-rays are expected), with reduced risks for both life and the environment.[116] The second key feature is that fusion reactors are being conceived as both large stationary installations (such as ITER) and smaller, compact devices, small enough to potentially be fitted on vessels or aircraft.[117] Examples of such compact devices (albeit at the prototypical stage) are the compact fusion reactors announced by Lockheed Martin,[118] and the C-2W compact reactor from TAE Technologies.[119] It should be noted that stationary and compact fusion reactors have both garnered attention as potentially viable technological paths. As an example, an official recommendation to increase US funding in large and compact fusion reactors has been delivered in the 2018 *Final Report of the Committee on a Strategic*

110 'What is NIF?' (lasers.llnl.gov, 2019) <https://lasers.llnl.gov/about/what-is-nif> accessed 28 February 2019.

111 'EMC2 Fusion Development Corporation' <www.emc2fusion.org> accessed 28 February 2019.

112 'Fusion – Frequently Asked Questions | IAEA' <https://www.iaea.org/topics/energy/fusion/faqs> accessed 28 February 2019.

113 Id.

114 M. Rubel, 'Structure Materials in Fusion Reactors: Issues Related to Tritium, Radioactivity and Radiation-Induced Effects' (2010) 57(2T) *Fusion Science and Technology* 474–482 DOI: 10.13182/FST10-A9438.

115 An isolated legal reference to aneutronic fusion can be found in N.J. Legis. S. No.293 2012.

116 G.H. Miley (1982) 'Advanced Fuels and the Development of Fusion Power'. In: B. Brunelli and G.G. Leotta (eds) *Unconventional Approaches to Fusion* (Springer 1982), 397.

117 'Compact Fusion' (Lockheed Martin) <https://www.lockheedmartin.com/en-us/products/compact-fusion.html> accessed 28 February 2019.

118 Id.

119 'C2W Vessel Concept – TAE Technologies' (TAE Technologies) <https://tae.com/c2w_vessel_concept> accessed 28 February 2019.

Plan for U.S. Burning Plasma Research.[120] Both form factors (and ensuing commercial applications) should thus be considered in future regulatory processes.

The regulatory challenges of fusion are extensive and far-reaching. The first consideration is that known definitions in nuclear law such as "nuclear fuel" and "nuclear material" may be inapplicable to fusion fuel.[121] Additional safety and security requirements normally applicable to nuclear facilities (including fission power plants) could also be found to be onerous if weighed against the different radiological and risk profile of neutronic and aneutronic fusion reactors. In fact, many of the policy issues seen with SMRs and advanced non-LWR reactor designs would once again become relevant, perhaps even more so considering the inherent safety features of fusion fuel mixtures and fusion reactors. Concurrently, the use of fusion-specific technologies, such as cryogenic systems, high-powered lasers, microwave and RF emitters, and high-powered magnetic systems would trigger significant review of existing rules with respect to safety requirements,[122] security, design criteria, normal operations and waste disposal.

Compact fusion reactors pose additional challenges. While there are instances of stationary fusion licensed under existing nuclear regulations,[123] (ITER is licensed under French rules as an *Installation Nucléaire de Base*),[124] albeit most commonly under the rules laid down for experimental facilities,[125] rather than commercial power plants, the safety features and fuel types of compact fusion reactors (and, more precisely, *aneutronic* compact fusion reactors should these devices become commercially viable) could potentially unlock widespread adoption as *mobile* sources of power, like small-form fission reactors onboard nuclear vessels but capable of a multitude of additional applications. The hopeful but short-lived dreams of nuclear-powered cars and land vehicles could potentially become a reality. In this regard, the regulatory repercussions of private aircraft, vehicles and vessels being equipped with nuclear fusion devices would be significant, departing sharply from the paradigm of nuclear-fission reactors at the center of national and international regulations.

120 *Final Report of the Committee on a Strategic Plan for U.S. Burning Plasma Research* (The National Academies Press 2018).

121 It must be noted that the nuclear legislation of certain countries is inclusive of fusion fuel. For example, in the USA under NEIMA (Nuclear Energy Innovation and Modernization Act), signed into law in 2019, "advanced nuclear reactor" means a nuclear fission or fusion reactor (Sec. 3), and "advanced nuclear reactor fuel" means fuel for use in an advanced reactor or a research and test reactor, including fuel with a low uranium enrichment level of not greater than 20 percent. The link between and the content of the two definitions makes it so that "advanced nuclear fuel" may encompass fissile material other than uranium or plutonium (such as thorium) or fusion fuel such as hydrogen, deuterium or tritium. Given that fusion fuel is non fissile, it may be the case that common elements used in non-nuclear industries (e.g., hydrogen, boron or helium) could technically be classified as "advanced nuclear reactor fuel". The systemic legal effects of such a definition on the national and international level remain to be explored.

122 Y. Wu et al., 'Identification of Safety Gaps for Fusion Demonstration Reactors' (2016) 1 *Nuclear Energy*.

123 The process has yielded insight into licensing fusion reactors. See Neill Taylor and Pierre Cortes, 'Lessons Learnt from ITER Safety & Licensing for DEMO and Future Nuclear Fusion Facilities' (2014) 89 *Fusion Engineering and Design*; Lina Rodriguez-Rodrigo, Joëlle Elbez-Uzan and Carlos Alejaldre, 'ITER Licensing Process from Design and Construction to Dismantling' (2009) 59 *Fusion Science and Technology*; and G. Marbach, J. Jacquinot and N. Taylor, 'ITER at Cadarache: An Example of Licensing a Fusion Facility', (2003) 44 *Fusion Science and Technology* 251–255.

124 'ITER: une installation nucléaire de base' (ITER) <https://www.iter.org/dac> accessed 28 February 2019.

125 Taylor and Cortes (n. 23).

Fusion, with its inherent safety, would probably affect principal, well-established areas of nuclear law such as liability.[126] Yet, while fusion is likely to cause a significant change in nuclear law and in the perception of nuclear energy, some of the challenges should display some affinity with the questions and concerns raised today with respect to advanced fission (including SMRs and microreactors). In fact, the industry-driven interest in different operating and licensing requirements for advanced nuclear reactors (including SMRs and vSMRs) will probably play a role in directing regulators and lawmakers towards a more technology-inclusive, risk-based set of rules, capable of efficiently addressing new nuclear technology including fusion. For example, the determination of scalable EP zones for today's SMRs based on the lower risks associated with small modular reactors could serve as a regulatory precedent in tailoring EPZs for fusion power plants and facilities. Similarly, experience in determining staff requirements for operating safer fission reactors could also be drawn upon in determining staff requirements for fusion facilities. Finally, current efforts in devising a flexible regulatory framework to account for the fast-paced development of new fission technology in Generation III, III+ and even Generation IV (e.g., new fuel types, fuel forms, coolants and operating parameters) should serve as a stepping stone towards a legal environment capable of adequately supporting the development and uptake of commercial fusion reactors.

Perhaps the most disruptive of nuclear technologies to date, it is reasonable to expect that as progress is made on both fronts (stationary and compact reactors), profound revisions of the regulatory framework will take place to make sure nuclear fusion achieves its fullest potential.

8 Conclusions and regulatory challenges ahead

It is the author's hope that this chapter has provided the reader with an overview of some of the most promising paths towards safer, cleaner, more affordable and more sustainable nuclear energy. The regulatory challenges are considerable and are bound to increase as nuclear technology develops further and the need for abundant energy increases. Advanced fission and, even more so, nuclear fusion promise to significantly challenge the nuclear paradigm. Small, portable nuclear devices (whether fission or fusion-based) for stationary or even commercial mobile power generation or propulsion could unlock the real potential of atomic energy and usher humanity into a cleaner, safer world. If this is to happen, however, regulators and lawmakers will have to address (and overcome) some fundamental regulatory challenges – perhaps the most ambitious and demanding in the history of nuclear energy.

126 Authors have addressed liability in stationary fusion reactors, see E. W, Fork, and C.H. Peterson, 'Fusion Energy and Nuclear Liability Considerations', (2014) 1 *Nuclear Law Bulletin* 49–61.

34

THE FUTURE OF DISPUTE RESOLUTION IN THE ENERGY AND NATURAL RESOURCES SECTOR

Setting the scene and looking ahead

Gloria M. Alvarez

1 Introduction

This chapter analyses the evolution of international arbitration in the context of the energy sector by offering a dissection of the pertinent theoretical, policy and legal practice frameworks by giving evidence to uphold the contention that international arbitration will continue to gain acceptance as the most effective and suitable method to adjudicate legal disputes arising from energy transactions. It also studies the new challenges arising from energy and natural resources projects and discusses how climate change and social concerns can be resolved outside national courts at an international arbitration forum.

This chapter pins down the different ramifications of the origins of international dispute resolution in the energy sector. The chapter's main argument explains that international arbitration has been the most cost-effective and efficient legal mechanism to resolve energy disputes and that this trend will continue, including the resolution of the more complex disputes on the near horizon, ranging from regulatory changes on tax and subsidies measures, and energy transition risks, to disputes arising from climate change, and social and environmental concerns. The chapter employs different case studies on *Lex Petrolea*, low-carbon energy sources and mining to develop a business-driven justification – beyond the legal field – to claim that international arbitration is the most suitable method to resolve legal disputes in the international energy industry.

The chapter makes the proposition that international energy arbitration is a new emerging interdisciplinary field, which clusters socio-legal, business and economic concerns arising from energy as the economic sector at the epicentre of its studies. While there is legal practice orientated literature on the topic, this contribution offers a more academic justification on the symbiotic evolution between international arbitration and energy law by taking a streamlined viewpoint to cohesively explain the substantive and procedural reasons for the present and the future of the energy industry being the biggest user of international dispute resolution.

The chapter argues that particular procedural and substantive features of the international arbitration process are compatible with the specific needs of the energy industry. Given the complexity of energy projects, domestic courts can experience challenges on how to holistically adjudicate legal disputes. These challenges include issues of confidentiality, neutrality and lack of decision-making expertise. In contrast, international arbitration is a flexible process, which offers a wide range of suitable features including procedural rules and the possibility of appointing independent decision-makers with experience in the specific sector.

Furthermore, the chapter studies how substantive protections guaranteed in international instruments have been enablers of legal certainty and are attractive to foreign investors. In this respect, the possibility of bringing a claim alleging a breach of an international treaty protection has served as reassurance to energy businesses that even in the more complex type of disputes (i.e. foreign investments involving a state-entity) investments will be protected by widely recognised international law principles. Procedurally, features of the arbitration process are suitable for the resolution of disputes arising from energy matters, including those pertaining to international boundaries, social licences and investment disputes.[1] International arbitration also offers the possibility of adjudicating not only international and investment treaty disputes, but also contractually based claims, and of accommodating tailored procedural features such as different approaches on taking evidence, keeping confidentiality and appointing a decision-maker with a particular expertise and knowledge.

The chapter also employs theoretical notions and empirical evidence about the energy market as user of international arbitration. Theoretically, the rapid evolution of the energy industry requires an adjudication process oriented at ensuring due processes; a fundamental aspect of any present and future energy transaction. It is argued that due process increases the possibility of well-informed decision-making in areas such as fiscal regulations, subsidies, and legislative, judicial and policy deliberations in the deployment of energy projects. Moreover, arbitration contributes to delivering due process by means of neutral fora, while delivering biding and enforceable solutions in line with the international rule of law.[2] While it is commonly known that the energy sector is the biggest user of international arbitration, recent findings have also evidenced that energy stakeholders are confident that the industry's use of international arbitration will continue to increase in the near future (see Figure 34.1).[3]

According to the most recent International Centre for Settlement of Investment Disputes (ICSID) statistics, Figure 34.2 reveals that from 706 cases registered, 41 per cent of the disputes managed by ICSID correspond to the energy sector, including oil and gas, electric power and low carbon energy sources.[4] Empirical evidence has also revealed that arbitration institutions should continue facilitating access to databases with an arbitrator's experience in the field. Equally, evidence shows the desirability for these institutions to continue gaining knowledge in order to be well-versed in administering energy disputes.[5]

1 See, for example, Chapter 31 in this book, 'Maritime disputes and disputed seabed resources in the African Continent'.

2 Gillian Brock, *Global Justice: A Cosmopolitan Account* (Oxford University Press, 2009). See also United Nations, 'Sustainable Development Goals, Goal 16: Promote Just, Peaceful and Inclusive Society', available at https://www.un.org/sustainabledevelopment/peace-justice, accessed on 21 August 2019.

3 White & Case, 'QMUL 2018 International Arbitration Survey: The Evolution of International Arbitration', availableathttps://www.whitecase.com/sites/whitecase/files/files/download/publications/qmul-international-arbitration-survey-2018-19.pdf, accessed on 20 August 2019.

4 ICSID Secretariat, *The ICSID Caseload Statistics (Issue 19-1),* available at https://icsid.worldbank.org/en/Documents/resources/ICSID%20Web%20Stats%202019-1(English).pdf, accessed on 20 August 2019.

5 White & Case, 'Survey' (n 3).

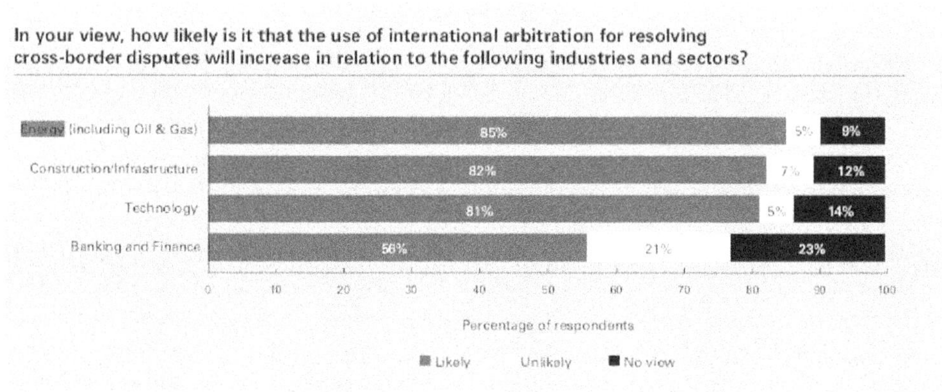

Figure 34.1 Use of international arbitration for resolving cross-border disputes

Source: 2018 White & Case and QMUL International Arbitration Survey: The Evolution of International Arbitration.

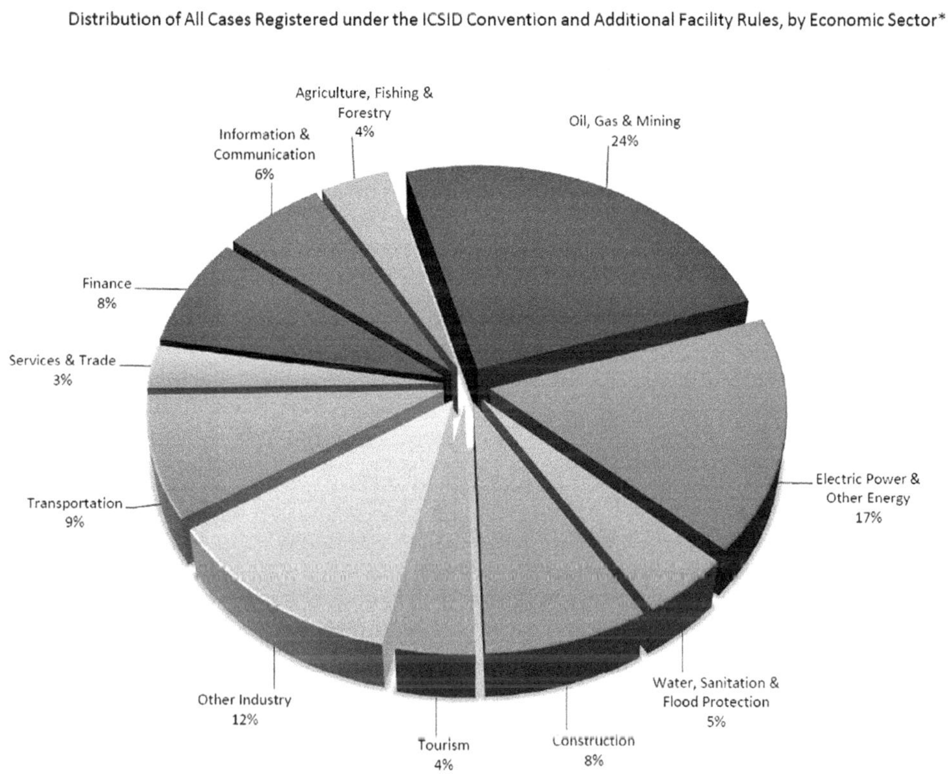

Figure 34.2 Distribution of all ICSID cases by economic sector

Source: The ICSID caseload statistics (Issue 2019–1)

2 Background

To understand international energy arbitration, it is important to contextualise how the energy industry has demanded the creation of domestic and international frameworks that regulate the way in which energy transactions and projects should be governed. The need for regulatory and legislative 'production' in the energy sector is a consequence of the twentieth century's expansion of energy transactions followed by the growth of the global economy. Energy businesses have realised that they need to become more accessible to the law (i.e. that the technical requirements of the industry are well understood by the regulator and the legislator and this is reflected in the law), while duly complying with policy and regulatory frameworks the industry is subject to. The expansion of the energy business requires the support of adequate legal frameworks, which can quickly evolve and adapt to the constant trends and challenges faced by technology, social and economic issues. To do so, legal frameworks should ensure that energy projects are carried out under legal certainty and in accordance with the applicable domestic and international standards of the rule of law.

While national economies have successfully created efficient policies and legal frameworks that have allowed them to manage energy projects at the national level, international transactions are often more complex.[6] From an international legal perspective, energy projects are often set up between different types of parties, coming from different legal cultures (i.e. a foreign investor and a government authority). Diversity in legal cultures creates the need for a level playing field where rights and obligations are mutually followed by contracting parties and in accordance with the same standards and expectations.

Moreover, energy transactions are significant for the global economy, as they are frequently driven by private and public, domestic and international interests. Therefore, private investments and public objectives are often interconnected in energy transactions, access to capital, natural resources and know-how might be placed in different jurisdictions. All of which means energy disputes are often characterised by having a high degree of technical complexity, and being capital and time intensive.

There has been a significant role of state involvement in boosting and promoting investments to expand low-carbon energy industries, including solar, wind, geothermal, biomass, hydropower, hydrogen and nuclear. To do so, governments have relied on different mechanisms to grant financial incentives to the low-carbon energy source industries. Similarly, in Colombia[7] and Spain,[8] foreign investors have relied on attractive legal incentives to undertake certain types of energy business. Legal incentives have also given rise to a series of legal disputes between investors and states, mostly due to regulatory and legislative changes considered by energy companies when deciding to invest in a particular country. Therefore, given the complexity of energy projects, it should not come as a surprise that private investors and governments have felt the need to seek expertise from decision-makers – as legal adjudicators – who understand the complexity of an energy dispute. Consequently, it is not surprising that the international energy industry is the biggest user of international arbitration and that arbitration its preferred method of resolving international energy disputes.[9]

6 See the Colombian and Mexican shale gas examples in Chapter 18 in this book, 'Shale gas regulation in Mexico and Colombia: an uncertain future' by Tina Soliman Hunter and Ignacio Herrera Anchustegui.

7 Ibid.

8 See Chapter 10 in this book, 'Dispute resolution in the European energy sector'.

9 Doak Bishop, Eldy Quintanilla Roché and Sara McBrearty, 'The Breadth and Complexity of the International Energy Industry, The Guide to Energy Arbitrations', *Global Arbitration Review* (Law Business Research, 2018) 1.

There are significant advantages for an energy business to resorting to international arbitration, including access to neutral, flexible and tailored procedural rules. In addition, resolving energy disputes through international arbitration gives the business the opportunity to avoid uncertainty associated with problems arising from national courts, including conflict of interests and corruption at the judiciary, time delays, lack of expert knowledge and a none final and binding resolution. More concretely, in terms of enforcement, an arbitration award can be enforced in other jurisdictions (i.e. countries that are signatories to the New York Convention on the Recognition and Enforcement of Foreign Arbitral Awards). As a result, parties are not concerned about national court 'protectionism' and an aversion of local courts to foreign energy investors. However, litigation of energy disputes in domestic courts has proven to be fairly successful in certain jurisdictions, particularly in Canada, the US, the UK and Australia.[10] National court proceedings in these jurisdictions have proven to be neutral, efficient and have a good record of effective enforcement of foreign judgments. In the particular context of domestic oil and gas transactions, national courts will continue to resolve legal disputes, as long as these jurisdictions offer a neutral and cost-effective judicial forum.[11]

Looking into the future, the tendency of resorting to international arbitration will continue to be the preferred choice for resolving energy disputes between international companies and governments. In investor-state arbitration, legal disputes will continue to arise from 'unexpected' regulatory measures, including indirect and (less frequently) direct expropriation, human rights and social and environmental concerns. This is particularly relevant in developing energy economies, where the new trends on the liberalisation of the energy markets will continue to require the implementation of new legislation to boost energy investment and attract private capital, while ensuring that there is sufficient state participation. For example, in Chapter 19 of this book, a study of the Mexican Energy Reform, and the potential danger that a counter-reform would represent, highlights the importance of balancing private-public interests, while respecting key legal principles such as certainty and non-retroactivity.[12] Given the ventures created by the Mexican Energy Reform, an increase in the importance given to arbitration and other alternative methods of dispute resolution is anticipated.

The synergy between energy and dispute resolution can also be illustrated by the current developments that have taken place in the European renewable energy sector. Chapter 10 highlights how developments in foreign direct investment in the renewable energy sector in Europe have been dominated by investor-state arbitration. Most of the disputes relate to challenges to regulatory measures which allegedly have affected low-carbon energy investments.[13] The analysis of these cases reveals that the fair and equitable treatment (FET) principle has played a crucial role in protecting energy investors when induced to conduct an investment project in a host-country.[14] As confirmed by most of the awards analysed by Briercliffe and Ingle, the operation of FET will continue to be the most frequently disputed substantive protection on energy arbitration under an investment agreement. The relevance of FET, and its scope and operation have been one of the most important topics of study in

10 See Chapter 16 in this book, Kristen van de Biezenbos, 'Regulation of low carbon energy sources in the U.S. and Canada'.

11 A. Timothy Martin, 'Dispute Resolution in the International Energy Sector: An Overview', 4 *Journal of World Energy Law and Business* 2011, 332–368.

12 See Chapter 19 in this book, 'Energy justice as a key driver to unlock the transition from energy reform to energy counter-reform: the rise of the immutability theory'.

13 White & Case, 'Survey' (n 3).

14 Ibid.

international economic law studies for many decades.[15] An important part of the future of energy arbitration, within the realm of foreign investment, will be the continuation of delimiting with (more) clarity the ambit of protection under FET. It is expected that policy-makers and government officials will implement the invaluable treaty practice lessons to reframe the operation of FET. Energy projects require significant financial investment and are dependent on the stability of the particular host country. Therefore, the FET standard would need to be reformulated with the objective of granting protection against unexcepted and detrimental governmental actions against energy investments. Consequently, as discussed below, the notion of FET in the Canada-EU Free Trade Agreement would not be a completely new approach. Instead, new forms of investment agreements will narrow down the FET scope by mirroring the treaty arbitration practice.

3 International energy arbitration: what is it about?

The energy industry and its recourse to international dispute resolution has been of a simultaneous growth. The first cases relating to the petroleum industry created a particular space where upstream petroleum disputes arising from political and legislative changes could be resolved by international tribunals and both parties could have more 'control' in the dispute resolution process, ensuring the sense of independence, impartiality and neutrality to settle disputes between investors and host states. Consequently, other energy industries continue using international arbitration as a process where decision-makers can offer a better understanding of the economic and political concerns surrounding energy disputes. It should not come as a surprise that transactions, even between private parties, are subject to international arbitration as the resolution forum. A good example is gas pricing arbitration, where partners in projects, outside more 'predictable' jurisdictions, often choose international arbitration to protect long-term commercial relationships, using confidentiality as well as the arbitration award to enforce international opportunities and options.[16]

3.1 Lex Petrolea

International arbitration has been a dispute resolution mechanism which has contributed to the development of the oil and gas legal practice. The *Lex Mercatoria* comprises frequent practices in the industry that have become generally accepted rules of customary law, including nationalisation, expropriation and quantification of damages. These rules have been characterised as having to constantly adapt to the specificities of the energy industry. As such, *Lex Petrolea* has become a series of customary practices, which are valid for the oil and gas industry and created in the international arbitration and other types of judicial adjudication systems.[17] In the particular context of international arbitration, it has been recognised that the oil and gas arbitration practice, to the extent that arbitration awards are not confidential, has created and developed *Lex Petrolea* over the years, even if these awards do not have binding precedents.

15 UNCTAD, 'Fair and Equitable Treatment, UNCTAD Series on Issues in International Investment Agreements II: A Sequel', available at https://unctad.org/en/docs/unctaddiaeia2011d5_en.pdf, accessed on 15 September 2019.

16 Mark Beeley and Sarah Stockley, *Upstream Oil and Gas Disputes, The Guide to Energy Arbitrations* (Global Arbitration Review, 3rd edition), available at https://globalarbitrationreview.com, accessed on 22 January 2020.

17 A. Timothy Martin, 'Lex Petrolea in International Law', in R. King (ed.), *Dispute Resolution in the Energy Sector: A Practitioner's Handbook* (Globe Law and Business, May 2012), 1–14.

The anatomy of *Lex Petrolea* is comprised of the consistent interpretation of a series of notions starting with the first generation of *Lex Petrolea,* which are the cases related to international oil and gas exploration and production from 1973 to 1998.[18] From the analysis of the first generation of *Lex Petrolea* awards, it was concluded that there was no unity of opinion as to what constituted a set of good commercial and legal practices in the petroleum industry. Customary practices shaping international arbitration can be traced back to *Aminoil v Kuwait.* The Kuwaiti Government argued that compensation for expropriation should be based on previous negotiations and agreements arising from other negotiations in the industry in the Middle East, as these previous negotiations had generated general rules for the oil industry.[19] However, the arbitral tribunal rejected these arguments on the basis that negotiations are often composed of agreements which might not have been public, where stakeholders sometimes agree to these types of negotiations under economic and political pressure and constraints.[20]

The second generation of *Lex Petrolea* (1999–2011) was characterised as a more developed set of petroleum practices, which encompassed disputes relating to regulatory fiscal measures on 'extraordinary revenues' enacted as a result of the government hosting the relevant international oil company.[21] More recently, the third (and ongoing) generation of *Lex Petrolea* refers to the wave of nationalisation of energy projects in South America, particularly in Ecuador and Venezuela. In this third generation of cases, there is a particular case which aligns with the spirit of *Lex Petrolea.* In *Burlington v Ecuador,* the tribunal acknowledged that while it is not bound by previous decisions, attention must be paid to earlier decisions made by international tribunals. A harmonious development of the law, the tribunal noted, can be achieved by adopting solutions established in a series of consistent cases.[22] In *Burlington v Ecuador,* the emphasis on the tribunal's duty to contribute to a harmonious interpretation of the law indicates that *Lex Petrolea* has developed in a way that aims to look into the petroleum industry practices as a yardstick of customary practices in trade and business. These practices have to be carried out in good faith and according to the best standards of the petroleum industry.

The concept of *Lex Petrolea* has continued to develop in the international arbitration practice and is expected to continue to be of relevance in influencing the arguments pleaded by disputing parties. While it is not certain if *Lex Petrolea* will eventually consolidate itself as a generally respected principle or provoke different reactions across schools of thought and practitioners, it will definitely be part of the future of international dispute

18 Doak Bishop, *International Arbitration of Petroleum Disputes: The Development of a* Lex Petrolea, *XXIII Yearbook Commercial Arbitration 23* (Kluwer Law International, 1998), 1131–1207.

19 Ad-Hoc-Award, *Kuwait v. The American Independent Oil Company (AMINOIL)*, 21 ILM 976.

20 John Bowman, 'Lex Petrolea: Sources and Successes of International Petroleum Law', available at https://www.lexology.com/library/detail.aspx?g=a4461c4e-4909-48fb-a908-83b6c29c0baf, accessed on 13 August 2019.

21 *City Oriente Limited v Republic of Ecuador*, ICSID Case No ARB/06/21, *Perenco Ecuador Ltd v Republic of Ecuador*, ICSID Case No ARB/08/6, *Burlington Resources Inc v Republic of Ecuador*, ICSID Case No ARB/08/5 and *Murphy Exploration and Production Company International v Republic of Ecuador*, ICSID Case No ARB/08/4. Thomas C. C. Childs, 'Update on *Lex Petrolea*: The Continuing Development of Customary Law Relating to International Oil and Gas Exploration and Production', 4 *The Journal of World Energy Law & Business* 3 (2011), 214–259.

22 *Burlington Resources Inc. v Republic of Ecuador*, ICSID Case No. ARB/08/5 (formerly *Burlington Resources Inc. and others v Republic of Ecuador and Empresa Estatal Petroleos del Ecuador (PetroEcuador)*, Decision on Jurisdiction, 2 June 2010, para 100. Professor Stern disagreed with this approach, considering it "her duty to decide each case on its own merits, independently of any apparent jurisprudential trend ...".

resolution. The current developments in Colombia and Mexico might give birth to the fourth generation of *Lex Petrolea* disputes. In contrast to the wave of nationalisation in Venezuela, the liberalisation of energy markets in Latin America is an unchartered territory for states and investors alike. Therefore, it is expected that regulatory and legislative 'teething problems' will arise in the context of pipelines and other vital infrastructure projects aiming to boost the capacity of newly liberalised energy markets.[23] It is also expected that the construction of the notion of *Lex Petrolea* will continue to be a part of petroleum disputes questioning whether tribunals should validly apply certain practices as the body of customary law.

3.2 Gas and LNG pricing arbitration

Gas supply agreements often provide for the sale and purchase of very large quantities for a long-term period, where parties would very rarely agree on fixed practices to sell/buy gas. The LNG industry generally prefers to resolve its legal disputes under international arbitration, as it would like to keep price arrangements confidential between commercial parties.[24] Unlike other circumstances where commercial arbitration disputes will be mostly based on a disputed legal issue, gas pricing arbitration requires the reframing of the pricing formula originally agreed.

The main objective of gas pricing arbitrations is to decide a final, binding, new, fairer calculation which reflects certain unexpected changes in the market affecting the profitability of the supply gas transaction.[25] In Europe, given the competition from other energy sources – which might make gas prices commercially less competitive and therefore face the need for a price readjustment – it is expected that there will be a continued increase in gas pricing arbitration in the near future. Similarly, given that Latin America possesses more than 20 per cent of the total reserves of shale gas, disputes arising from shale gas transactions are expected to arise in the near future.[26]

The projection of a steady increase in international arbitration also applies to the sale and purchase of liquified natural gas (LNG), as the decision-making process to resolve LNG pricing disputes can truly acknowledge the commercial realities particularly faced by unexpected changes in the market. More concretely, LNG arbitration requires a dual – back and forward – looking judgment; it needs to be considered what happened before the review price date and if the prices have fluctuated between the review pricing date and the hearing date. As prices continue to change across different regions, it is expected that new arbitration opportunities will be part of the future of energy gas disputes. In particular, there will be a continued growth in short-term changes in the demand and supply of LNG looking into diversions of LNG cargos to be delivered to a different destination from the one originally agreed as well as profit-sharing disputes.[27]

23 Tom Jones, 'Mexico Reaches Deal with Pipeline Operators', *Global Arbitration Review,* available at https://globalarbitrationreview.com/article/1196760/mexico-reaches-deal-with-pipeline-operators, accessed on 16 September 2019.

24 *Gas Natural Aprovisionamientos SDG, S.A. v. Atlantic LNG Co. of Trinidad and Tobago*, No. 08 Civ. 1109, 2008 WL 4344525 (SDNY 16 September 2008).

25 Steven P. Finizio, *Destination Restrictions and Diversion Provisions in LNG Sale and Purchase Agreements, The Guide to Energy Arbitration* (Global Arbitration Review), available at https://globalarbitrationreview.com, accessed on 22 January 2020.

26 See (n 6).

27 Ibid.

3.3 Stabilisation clauses and fair and equitable treatment

Economic changes do not only affect previously agreed gas pricing contracts. Generally, most energy projects are long-term commitments, which can also be subject to – unexpected – economic changes. In order to address economic changes in long-term energy projects, stabilisation clauses have been adopted to allocate and mitigate financial burdens. Stabilisation clauses are particularly designed to manage the economic effects suffered due to the implementation of new legislation or regulations made by the state hosting the energy project, the classical example being stability agreements which can limit or prohibit the possibility of tax increases.[28]

While stabilisation clauses have been used for a long time in energy contracts, their interpretation and scope continue to be the subject of study and debate.[29] The main criticism has rested on the argument that states accept stabilisation clauses favourable to the investor as a way of securing a large investment project and enticing further investment in the country.[30] The scope of the leniency of stabilisation clauses and its posterior impact in detriment on the host state laws and policies is to some extent yet to be fully exhausted by international energy treaty practice. There are a limited number of arbitration cases which have reached a final awards stage. So far it has been measured that the majority of stabilisation clauses disputes have reached settlement at an earlier stage of the dispute.[31]

The outlook of stabilisation clauses in the future of energy arbitration might significantly change its given use in international energy contracts. Diversification of the energy players due to the arrival of climate commitments has created a new type of investor, one that is particularly focused on solar and wind energy investments. International investment agreements often offer fair and equitable treatment as the treaty protection that operates to protect investors against an unexpected regulatory change which affects an investor's reasonable – and legitimate –expectations.[32]

28 *Sergei Pauschok, CISC Golden East Company, CJSC Vostokneftegaz Company v The Republic of Mongolia*, Award on Jurisdiction and Liability, 28 April 2011 (UNCITRAL), para 302.

29 Peter D. Cameron, 'Stabilisation and the Impact of Changing Patterns of Energy Investment', 10 *Journal of World Energy Law & Business* 5 (2017), 389–403. See also Constantine Partasides and Lucy Martinez, 'Of Taxes and Stabilisation', in D. Bishop and G. Kaiser (eds.), *The Guide to Energy Arbitrations* (Law Business Research, 2017) 60–76; and Sophie J. Lamb and Aimee-Jane Lee, 'The Relevance of Stabilisation Clauses in Oil & Gas Investment Treaty Arbitrations', in James M. Gaitis (ed.), *The Leading Practitioners' Guide to International Oil & Gas Arbiration* (Juris Publishing, 2015) 115–150.

30 'Stabilisation Clauses and Human Rights', a research project conducted for the International Finance Corporation (IFC) and the United Nations Special Representative of the Secretary-General on Business and Human Rights (2009) 5.

31 *AES Summit Generation Limited v Republic of Hungary*, Award, ICSID Case No ARB/07/22, 23 September 2010, at para 9.3.31: in the context of a transitional economy, "the Tribunal observes that no specific commitments were made by Hungary that could limit its sovereign right to change its law (such as a stability clause) or that could legitimately have made the investor believe that no change in the law would occur"; *Suez, Sociedad General de Aguas de Barcelona SA v Argentina*, ICSID Case No ARB/03/17, Decision on Liability, 30 July 2010, at para 214, 79: It was largely because of the country's history of instability that the Claimants required the incorporation of the specific clauses on extraordinary tariff adjustment reviews (to create stability); see also: *Alex Genin, Eastern Credit Limited, Inc and AS Baltoil v The Republic of Estonia*, ICSID Case No ARB/99/2 Award, 25 June 2001, at para 348: "the Tribunal considers it imperative to recall the particular context in which the dispute arose, namely, that of a renascent independent state coming rapidly to grips with the reality of modern financial, commercial and banking practices and the emergence of state institutions responsible for overseeing and regulating areas of activity perhaps previously unknown. This is the context in which Claimants knowingly chose to invest in an Estonian financial institution, EIB."

32 Energy Charter Treaty Secretariat, *Handbook on General Provisions Applicable to Investment Agreements in the Energy Sector*, available at https://energycharter.org/fileadmin/DocumentsMedia/Other_Publications/20171116-newHandbook.pdf, accessed on 16 September 2019.

3.4 Intra-European Union (EU) disputes and fair and equitable treatment (FET)

A handful of cases under the Energy Charter Treaty (ECT) have dealt with government actions to the detriment of investor's investments, and it is expected that FET will continue to be the most frequently invoked substantive protection in energy investment disputes, not only under the ECT or between intra-EU parties but also at a global level. While not enough emphasis can be put on the fact that arbitration tribunals are not bound to follow previous arbitration awards, there are a few takeaways relevant to the operation of FET in the energy context. In future energy disputes where FET is at stake, there is more clarity on the fact that tribunals will weight legitimate expectations against evidence that elucidates the existence of specific legal commitments between the investor and the state that supports not just a mere expectation but rather explicit and detailed commitments between that specific investor and the host state.

Moreover, although investment treaty practice will continue supporting the principle that FET is not a shield against regulatory changes, it will also weigh in the balance the legitimate state's right to regulate. Lastly, as part of the legitimate expectations evidence, tribunals might consider it pertinent to request exhaustive evidence of a due diligence process by the investor. More concretely, in order to argue for a breach of FET, it is expected that more evidence will be sought to support the argument that a proper due diligence was conducted and that no drastic regulatory changes were expected. A last point to note is that a 'legitimate' measure might have a different standard of measurement, in other words, a state measure judged as legitimate under national courts might be considered differently under international arbitration, as the arbitration tribunals are guided by international law principles.

In *Charanne v Spain,* the first intra-EU award rendered in the renewable energy industry, an investor claimed breach of FET arguing that the Kingdom of Spain's Royal Decrees have created legitimate expectations. The *Charanne* tribunal concluded that there were no specific commitments made to the investors. In contrast, international arbitration is also seen as a flexible process; a legitimate – and specific – expectation is an inherent characteristic of a stabilisation clause, as this needs to be mutually agreed between contracting parties in an investment project.[33] In *Eiser v Spain,* the tribunal concluded that even in the absence of stabilisation clauses, host-states do not have a green card to make radical legislative changes, particularly when the framework was specifically established to attract foreign investment.[34]

At first glance, it seems that having a stabilisation clause in place is more effective than seeking protection under FET. While it is true that FET protection is not a synonym for stabilisation protection, it is also true that FET is a protection against abrupt and radical legal changes made by the host-state, and which have a direct negative impact on the investment. In the same vein, the existence of a stabilisation clause serves as evidence of a specific legitimate expectation as part of the contractual commitments agreed between a particular investor and a host-state. Therefore, in terms of what is expected in the near future, in particular in the context of the diversification of energy transactions, it might be anticipated to see additional binding instruments between an investor and a host-state in order to guarantee stability and legal certainty, with the particular aim of seeking a shield against regulatory changes which might have a negative economic impact on the investment.

33 *Charanne and Construction Investments v Kingdom of Spain*, SCC Case No. V 062/2012, Award, 21 January 2016
34 *Eiser Infrastructure Limited and Energía Solar Luxembourg S.à r.l. v Kingdom of Spain,* ICSID Case No. ARB/13/36, Award, 4 May 2017.

A new way to reframe the scope of FET protection in light of changes made by a host-state is the redrafting of the FET clauses in new investment and trade agreements. For example, as discussed below more in detail, as part of the modernisation process of the ECT, it has been announced that FET is one of the treaty provisions to be updated in light of the global trend of new forms of international agreements.[35] A good example of how the scope of FET needs further redefining is the document published by the ECT Secretariat entitled 'Best Practices in Regulatory Reform'. In this document, the ECT highlights that the right to regulate investment should be balanced and developed involving all stakeholders. This balance should be clear on categorising the different types of foreign investments and investors in order to analyse the potential impact and risks from envisaged regulatory reforms.[36]

The prognosis of intra-EU disputes in the energy sector is difficult to read given the many judicial, legislative and policy developments in the EU legal order. The jurisdiction of arbitration tribunals is frequently challenged with the argument that intra-EU legal disputes are the exclusive competence of the EU judicial legal order, as it is the one that protects the autonomy of EU law. In March 2018, a judgment from the Court of Justice of the European Union concluded that the application of the dispute resolution clause in a bilateral investment treaty between two EU parties precluded the application of the EU judicial system.[37] However, at least 50 cases have been registered in relation to intra-EU cross-border energy investments and while most of them arise from transactions in the renewable energy sector, there are also a considerable number of cases arising from different regulatory actions against the EU hydrocarbons industry.

4 International dispute resolution and the energy transition

As explained earlier in this book, regional energy developments in emerging and developed markets are not isolated events, and it is expected that controversies arising from energy transactions in the short and mid-term will be consistent with the current policy and treaty negotiations taking place globally. The transformation of the energy sector from a heavily fossil-based to a lower (or zero) carbon economy will necessitate legal instruments and objectives having effective enforcement mechanisms that can hold contracting parties accountable to these commitments, including governments and private industry. Although the energy transition is underway, the future of international dispute resolution in this context will be determined by policies (i.e. the Paris Agreement) and international and national implementation.

To do so, there are relevant initiatives and new frameworks that are worthwhile analysing. As explained below, the Canada-EU Comprehensive Economic and Trade Agreement (CETA) is currently one of the flagship agreements promoting investments that can contribute to mitigate climate change. However, the uncertainty arising from the yet to be finalised multilateral investment court leaves us with some uncertainty with regard to how social, environmental and climate change related disputes are going to be properly addressed. Conversely, while the United States-Mexico-Canada Agreement (USMCA)

35 'International Energy Charter, Approved Topics for the Modernisation of the Energy Charter Treaty', available at https://energycharter.org/media/news/article/approved-topics-for-the-modernisation-of-the-energy-charter-treaty, accessed on 18 September 2019.

36 Ibid.

37 Judgment of 6 March 2018, *Slovak Republic v. Achmea BV*, Case No. C-284/16, EU: C, 2018, 158.

grants certain protections to the environment, the language is hydrocarbon-centred. In contrast to CETA, the USMCA does not explicitly refer to climate action commitments, but it does refer to the environmental scope and outreach of the agreement, which discusses obligations on the prevention and control of pollution, toxic waste and contaminants as well as mechanisms for each country to implement these commitments domestically. These agreements will be further discussed in the section below. In addition, USMCA gives more clarity on the future of international arbitration between foreign investors and Contracting Parties.

4.1 United States-Mexico-Canada Agreement (USMCA)

The new USMCA aims to replace the North America Free Trade Agreement (NAFTA). USMCA aims to steadily phase out the protections granted in NAFTA, which will remain available until 2022, in order to continue protecting those investments made between the period when NAFTA came into force and is finally terminated. While NAFTA offered investor-state arbitration between investors of one Contracting Party against another Contracting Party, USMCA does not include investor-state arbitration between Canadian investors in the US or investor-state arbitration for Mexican and US investors making investments in Canada. Investor-state arbitration will remain available under USMCA only for US investors making investments in Mexico and Mexican investors making investments in the US. If the Comprehensive and Progressive Transpacific Partnership (CPTPP) enters into force Canadian and Mexican investors would be able to have access to investor-state arbitration.

The most significant modification of NAFTA in USMCA is the substantive protections offered. Investors will be only able to bring claims on the breach of (1) national treatment; (2) most favoured nation treatment; and (3) direct expropriation. Nonetheless, in the context of energy investments, there will be additional protections of (4) fair and equitable treatment; and (5) indirect expropriation in government contracts in the oil and natural gas and power generation industries. In addition, and in line with the developments discussed previously in this book on the constitutional protectionism of the Mexican government on the ownership of hydrocarbons, USMCA contains a provision which explicitly recognises that Mexico reserves its sovereign right to reform its Constitution and domestic legislation and direct, inalienable and imprescriptible ownership of all hydrocarbons in the subsoil of the national territory, which includes the continental shelf and exclusive economic zone (USMCA, Chapter 8).[38]

4.2 Canada-EU Comprehensive Economic and Trade Agreement (CETA)

CETA is the new trade agreement between the EU and Canada and it aims to foster efficient exports of goods and services in both regions. CETA has quickly become one of the most comprehensive yardsticks in international investment law for guiding investors and states on issues relating to the environment, climate change and social concerns arising from energy

38 See (n 10).

investments.[39] Contracting Parties have agreed to use CETA as a vehicle to effectively implement the Paris Agreement.[40] CETA explicitly refers to the state's right to regulate with the objective of encouraging high levels of environmental protection (Article 24.3), and promoting transparency in the form of public awareness, availability of information and participation of the civil society (Article 24.9). CETA also makes reference to a continued cooperation on trade-related environmental issues including green and low-carbon technologies, waste management, access to water, conservation of biological diversity and public and stakeholder's participation (Article 24.13).

In terms of dispute settlement, CETA departs from the classical mechanism of investor-state arbitration and establishes a tribunal and appellate tribunal system. In the long term, the objective is that CETA's tribunal and its appellate mechanism will form part of the permanent and multilateral Investment Court System (ICS). The innovation of CETA's dispute resolution systems aims to avoid the jurisdictional and applicable law tensions experienced in the intra-EU energy disputes. In a recent decision by the CJEU, it was confirmed that CETA tribunals will not deal with EU law issues, as these will remain part of the EU judicial system. This is because CETA tribunals would not prevent the EU from acting according to its own constitutional framework.[41]

According to the CJEU, the discretionary powers of the CETA Tribunal and Appellate Tribunal do not extend to calling into question measures for the protection of public interest.[42] The CJEU clarifies that if CETA tribunals have to make findings on whether a EU measure is 'fair and equitable' this is specifically circumscribed in CETA Article 8.10.2, which gives an exhaustive list of the circumstances in which FET operates.[43] Therefore, in future energy related disputes, at least in the context of CETA, given the restricted scope of FET, there has been a significant reduction in the type of disputes that can be resolved outside the EU judicial system. How restrictive this new system will be in practice is yet to be tested. Moreover, regulatory measures often permeate more than one ambit, and hence the 'exhaustive-list' of CETA Article 8.10.2 might encounter as its first challenge the delimitation of measures arising from public order or public safety, the protection of public morals, the protection of health and life of humans and animals, the preservation of food safety, the protection of plants and the environment, welfare at work, product safety, consumer protection or, equally, fundamental rights.[44]

39 European Commission, 'EU-Canada Comprehensive Economic and Trade Agreement (CETA)', available at https://ec.europa.eu/trade/policy/in-focus/ceta/index_en.htm, accessed on 18 September 2019. Under EU law, CETA is considered to be a 'mixed agreement' which requires signature and ratification of each Member State of the EU. At the moment of writing this chapter (September 2019), this is an ongoing process.

40 European Commission, 'Recommendation 001/2018 of 26 September 2018 of the CETA Joint Committee on Trade, Climate Action and Paris Agreement', available at https://trade.ec.europa.eu/doclib/docs/2018/september/tradoc_157415.pdf, accessed on 18 September 2019.

41 Opinion 1/17 of the Court, 30 April 2019, ECLI:EU:C:2019:341, 137–161.

42 Ibid, para 156.

43 CETA Article 8.10.2 reads: "A Party breaches the obligation of fair and equitable treatment referenced in paragraph 1 if a measure or series of measures constitutes: (a) denial of justice in criminal, civil or administrative proceedings; (b) fundamental breach of due process, including a fundamental breach of transparency, in judicial and administrative proceedings; (c) manifest arbitrariness; (d) targeted discrimination on manifestly wrongful grounds, such as gender, race or religious belief; (e) abusive treatment of investors, such as coercion, duress and harassment; or (f) a breach of any further elements of the fair and equitable treatment obligation adopted by the Parties in accordance with paragraph 3 of this Article".

44 (n 37) para 160.

4.3 Energy Charter Treaty (ECT)

The landscape of energy disputes will be transformed in the near future if the modernisation of the Energy Charter Treaty succeeds. In 2015, the Energy Charter Treaty Secretariat initiated a three-phase process. First, the ECT Secretariat led an initiative to create a political declaration entitled the International Energy Charter. This has been a very ambitious and successful development as 90 countries and international organisations have signed this document.[45] The second stage consisted in developing tools for governments and the energy industry in order to streamline domestic frameworks on foreign energy investments in a more consistent manner. Most of these tools have taken the form of soft law tools. For example, the ECT Secretariat and its Legal Advisory Task Force has created a *Handbook on General Provisions Applicable to Investment Agreements in the Energy Sector*, which offers guidance to governments on how to draft and deal with complex investment agreements.[46] There is also a 'Model Instrument on Investment Dispute Management',[47] which aims to assist governments which do not have domestic legislation on the matter and a Conflict Resolution Centre aiming to assist on alternative mechanisms such as mediation and conciliation.[48]

Lastly, following the global reform on new treaty investment related provisions, the ECT Secretariat has formulated a list of aspects which have been considered suitable for modernisation.[49] This list combines all the core and crucial provisions of the ECT, including those related to procedural and substantive protections.[50] This modernisation process could deliver an amendment of the ECT itself – which, of course, requires the consent of all Contracting Parties. Consequently, this could have a significant impact on the future of energy arbitra-

45 U. Rusnák, Introduction to *The Modernisation of the Energy Charter Treaty* (Transnational Dispute Management, 2019). Energy Charter Treaty Secretariat, The International Energy Charter, available at https://energycharter.org/media/news/article/modernisation-of-the-energy-charter-treaty-discussed-during-the-celebration-of-the-20th-anniversary, accessed on 26 July 2019.

46 Energy Charter Treaty Secretariat, *Handbook on General Provisions Applicable to Investment Agreements in the Energy Sector*, available at https://energycharter.org/what-we-do/publications/handbook-on-general-provisions-applicable-to-investment-agreements-in-the-energy-sector, accessed on 26 July 20019.

47 Energy Charter Treaty Secretariat, Decision of the Energy Charter Treaty Conference, available at https://www.energycharter.org/fileadmin/DocumentsMedia/CCDECS/2018/CCDEC201826_-_INV_Adoption_by_correspondence_-_Model_Instrument_on_Management_of_Investment_Disputes, accessed on 9 January 2020.

48 Energy Charter Treaty, 'Conflict Resolution Centre', available at https://energycharter.org/what-we-do/dispute-settlement/conflict-resolution-centre, accessed on 26 July 2019. 8 Legal Advisory Taskforce and the Energy Charter Treaty Secretariat, *Handbook on General Provisions Applicable to Investment Agreements in the Energy Sector*, available at https://energycharter.org/what-we-do/publications/handbook-on-general-provisions-applicable-to-investment-agreements-in-the-energy-sector, accessed on 26 July 2019. For a detailed list of all the initiatives at phase two see Rusnák (n iii) 2.

49 Decision of the Energy Charter Conference, 28 November 2017, Document No. CCDEC 2017 23 STR, 2. See also G. Coop and I. Seif, *Modernisation of the ECT: An Institutional Perspective* (Transnational Dispute Management, 2019).

50 The themes that will be considered for modernization are: Pre-investment, Definition of "charter", Definition of "economic activity in the energy sector", Definition of investment, Definition of investor, Right to regulate, Definition of Fair and Equitable Treatment (FET), MFN Clause, Clarification of "most constant protection and security", Definition of indirect expropriation, Compensation for losses, Umbrella clause, Denial of benefits, Transfers related to investments, Frivolous claims, Transparency, Security for costs, Valuation of damages, Third party funding, Sustainable development and corporate social responsibility, Definition of "transit", Access to infrastructure (including denial of access and available capacities), Definition and principles of tariff setting, The application of treaty provisions to Regional Economic International Organisations Members, Obsolete provisions.

tion under this Treaty. It has been accepted that the ECT, in addition to its contribution to the resolution of energy disputes, has been used and observed as a document of good governance, which primarily has aided those governments lacking their own domestic laws on energy investments. Therefore, it is expected that this modernisation process will mirror the lessons and good practices of the different branches of the energy industry in order to contribute at an international policy level in guiding those countries where legal frameworks are yet to be developed. The ECT is receiving the support of its Contracting Parties in the modernisation; for example, the European Commission has adopted the European Council Proposal authorising negotiations to modernise the ECT.

The EU has highlighted its intention to contribute to the assessment and revision of some of the most frequently invoked clauses in intra-EU ECT cases, including an exhaustive list of what constitutes a breach of fair and equitable treatment and an explicit provision on the state's right to regulate.[51] In addition, as with the CETA, the European Commission has suggested including, as part of the ECT modernisation, stronger provisions related to labour standards, sustainable development, climate change and a clean energy transition. The European Commission also wishes to push for more thorough provisions on transparency and business conduct. In this respect, it should be highlighted that the ECT already addresses transparency in the context of laws, regulations, and judicial and administrative decisions affecting energy investments, which are protected under the ECT.[52] Lastly, although it is true that the ECT is energy agnostic, and it does not favour or encourage a particular type of energy source as an investment priority, it is expected that like the CETA, the ECT aims to include clearer commitment to sustainable energy investments and a balanced and steady energy transition.[53]

5 Environment, climate and social justice energy-related disputes

Two key features of the international arbitration process should be remembered: First, it usually encompasses a binominal relationship, either between two private parties, state-state or state-private company (i.e. investor). Secondly, the applicable law to resolve the relevant dispute is frequently agreed between the contracting parties. In the absence of an explicit reference to the applicable law, arbitration tribunals will often decide on the basis of a series of relevant elements applicable to the legal controversy. Often arbitrators will seek guidance from the domestic and institutional frameworks applicable to the disputing parties to make the most suitable choice on applicable law.

Having made the above clarification, it is important to pinpoint the reasons for the incremental role of climate, environmental and social concerns in international arbitration. If these types of concerns are explicitly translated into rights and obligations between the Contracting Parties – and there are clear applicable laws to the dispute regulating these concerns – then this section would be of limited relevance. However, the reality is that issues arising from climate, environment and human rights often go beyond the legal relationship

51 European Commission, 'Energy Charter Treaty Modernisation: European Commission Presents Draft Negotiating Directives', available at http://trade.ec.europa.eu/doclib/press/index.cfm?id=2017, accessed on 9 August 2018.

52 Article 20 of the Energy Charter Treaty. See also Gloria M. Alvarez, *Article 20 Transparency, Commentary on the Energy Charter Treaty* (Elgar Commentaries series, 2018).

53 See, for example, S. Maynard and A. Ason, 'Is the Energy Charter Treaty Ready to Embrace Energy Transition?' (Transnational Dispute Management, 2019).

clearly established between the disputing parties and affect a none-disputing party (i.e. local community or indigenous groups). Secondly, while it is true that climate, environmental and human rights issues are always expected to be respected in any type of investment transaction, the problem comes when there is no directly (and clear) applicable law which can guide the decision-maker on how to adjudicate these issues.

Clear rights and obligations are of utmost importance domestically and internationally, as the private sector is a crucial vehicle at the forefront of environmental protection, hence it is necessary to establish how international investment treaty law and arbitration can play a role in the protection of social and environmental concerns.[54] There have been developments in the investment treaty practice and more generally in the investment arbitration community which signpost the emergence of international arbitration as an adjudication system capable of resolving conflicts arising from social and environmental issues in foreign (energy) investments.

For example, in *Burlington v Ecuador,* Ecuador filed a counterclaim arguing that the investor's activities have caused significant environmental damage.[55] Ecuador's factual evidence was based on soil contamination, mud pits, groundwater and well site abandonment. Burlington environmental obligations were based solely in domestic law, which was not the applicable law chosen by the parties. This situation left the decision to the tribunal's discretion on finally deciding to apply either domestic or international law. The tribunal issued its decision on environmental harm, strictly based in Ecuador's liability regime for hydrocarbons enriched in the 2008 Constitution of Ecuador. Under the strict liability regime, once Ecuador proved environmental damage, Burlington could only prove that the harm was caused by a third party or *force majeure* to be excused for the repair of it. After a site visit, the tribunal determined remediation and compensation costs and rendered a decision holding the investor liable. Even though the investor's obligations were mainly found in domestic law, the tribunal granted only a partial amount of the damages requested.[56]

Environmental claims can also be made by the investor – based on domestic or international law – using the protections granted in the respective investment treaty. For example, in *Bilcon v Canada,* the investor alleged that the environmental regime applied to assess the project was arbitrary, discriminatory and unfair.[57] In the final award, the tribunal found breaches of a minimum standard of treatment (NAFTA Article 1105(1)) and national treatment (NAFTA Article 1102).

In a more complicated web of investment treaty cases, there are *Bear Creek v Peru, Alvarez y Marín v Panama* and *South American Silver v Bolivia*, all of which have highlighted the need for clarity on how an investor's social commitments on public participation should be interpreted by arbitration tribunals. In *Bear Creek v Peru,* Peru argued that one of the reasons the mining rights were revoked against Bear Creek was due to the lack of obtaining a social licence to operate from all the relevant local communities which could potentially be affected by the project. In this case, the tribunal concluded that social licences to operate

54 Sandrine Maljean-Dubois and Vanessa Richard, 'The Applicability of International Environmental Law to Private Enterprises', in Pierre-Marie Dupuy and Jorge E. Viñuales (eds.), *Harnessing Foreign Investment to Promote Environmental Protection: Incentives and Safeguards* (Cambridge University Press, 2013) 10.

55 *Burlington Resources Inc. v. Republic of Ecuador,* ICSID Case No. ARB/08/5 (formerly *Burlington Resources Inc. and others v. Republic of Ecuador and Empresa Estatal Petróleos del Ecuador (PetroEcuador)*), Decision on Ecuador's Counterclaims, 7 February 2017.

56 Ibid, para 1075 and *Burlington v Ecuador, Investment Treaty News*, available at https://www.iisd.org/itn/2018/10/18/burlington-v-ecuador, accessed on 23 September 2019.

57 *William Ralph Clayton, William Richard Clayton, Douglas Clayton, Daniel Clayton and Bilcon of Delaware Inc. v. Government of Canada, UNCITRAL*, Permanent Court of Arbitration (PCA) Case No. 2009-04.

were a concept not clearly defined in international law, which made it very difficult for the tribunal to assess the investor's obligations in light of a 'social' licence and the potential causal effects due to failure to obtain this licence.[58]

In *Alvarez y Marín v Panama,* the state's national land management authority issued a report in relation to the land acquired by the investors. The report concluded that some of the territory was under a special ownership scheme, whereby a third party may acquire the lands only when the local indigenous community decided not to make use of the land any more. As such, Panama argued that the land was acquired illegally.[59] The investor emphasised that the BIT did not impose obligations or formal requirements on how the investment should be made. While the tribunal decided that the violation of the special ownership regime made the whole investment null, this case, like that of *Bear Creek v Peru,* highlights a deeper nuance in international investment treaties. While several international agreements impose an indigenous obligation on states, investment treaties fail to develop a framework in which investment agreements make explicit reference to social commitments as part of an investment's requirements.

Lastly, another example on the lack of clarity about the source of the obligation is *South America Silver v Bolivia,* where the members of an indigenous community accused the investor of the violation of collective rights, including amongst other things polluting sacred spaces, abusing authority and threatening community members.[60] As a result, the Bolivian government reversed the ownership of the investor's mining concession in the area. In the final award, the Tribunal emphasised the importance of the social and environmental issues attached to foreign investments. Moreover, the Tribunal concluded that the investor contributed to create a 'social conflict', where the state had to take action.[61]

Also dealing with environmental and social concerns is *Copper Mesa v Ecuador,* where the investor faced difficulties in carrying out consultations with the local communities about the investment project, a planned mine development.[62] The consultative process was severely affected by the tensions between the investor and the local community, to the point that the Environmental Impact Assessment (EIA) failed to consult all the relevant communities. In response, the government rejected the EIA due the lack of consultation of all the relevant groups and terminated the investor's concessions without giving any compensation.[63] Despite the fact the Tribunal found that Ecuador had unlawfully expropriated the investor's investment and breached the FET standard, the Tribunal did not grant all the damages requested by the investor in light of the lack of engagement with the local and indigenous communities.

58 Mihaela-Maria Barnes, 'The "Social License to Operate": An Emerging Concept in the Practice of International Investment Tribunals', 10 *Journal of International Dispute Settlement* 2 (2019), 328–360.

59 *Álvarez y Marín Corporación S.A., Bartus van Noordenne, Cornelis Willem van Noordenne, Estudios Tributarios AP S.A. and Stichting Administratiekantoor Anbadi v. Republic of Panama*, ICSID Case No. ARB/15/14, *Investment Treaty News*, available at https://www.iisd.org/itn/2019/06/27/icsid-tribunal-upholds-panamas-plea-of-illegality-in-the-making-of-an-investment-in-a-tourism-project-located-in-an-indigenous-area-juan-carlos-herrera-quenguan, accessed on 23 September 2019. See also Arif H. Ali, Erica Franzetti, José Manuel García Represa and Eduardo Silva Romero, 'Mining Arbitration in Latin America: Social and Environmental Issues in Investment Arbitration Cases in *The Guide to Mining Arbitrations* (Global Arbitration Review, 2019).

60 *South American Silver Limited (Bermuda) v. the Plurinational State of Bolivia*, PCA Case No. 2013-15, Award, 22 November 2018.

61 Ibid, paras 491, 499, 656, 857.

62 *Copper Mesa Mining Corporation v. The Republic of Ecuador.* PCA Case No. 2012-2. Award, 15 March 2016, paras 6.123, 6.128–6.136 and 6.131.

63 Ibid, paras. 1.92, 1.93, 4.258, 6.55, 7.24.

These few cases illustrate the emergence of social and environmental issues being addressed by international investment tribunals. However, despite the greater emphasis, there is no clear pathway to identify the source of this type of obligation and whether international or domestic courts are more suitable to interpret and apply treaty obligations which could be better enforced. In this respect, the international arbitration community has already contributed to building a link between dispute resolution and social and environmental concerns.

Earlier discussions at the United Nations Commission on International Trade Law Working Group III have also emphasised that investment treaties should harness economic development in a way that protects the environment and is inclusive of the interests of society.[64] Therefore, the integration of social and environmental concerns in the future architecture of international dispute resolution has the potential to create a new building block in the development of a mature and rules-based system that promotes economic growth while tackling climate change.[65]

Manifestations of environmental and social principles are also embedded in the Netherlands Model Investment Agreement (Dutch BIT Model). This model includes express reference to fundamental instruments on social justice (i.e. ILO Conventions) and the Paris Agreement. The Dutch Model aims to assist energy systems on how to identify, prevent, mitigate and account for the environmental and social risks of an investment. To avoid calamities against human rights and the environment, the Dutch Model (Article 7.3) gives investors the option to incorporate different forms of investor's social commitments and public participation when pursuing an investment. The Dutch options include commissions and investment panels (before and during the investment), improved forms of impact assessments and transparency initiatives.[66]

In this regard, it is also important to take into account the current initiative lead by the International Chamber of Commerce and its Task Force on 'Arbitration of Climate Change Related Disputes'. The initiative is part of an overall institutional effort to create a new baseline in the construction of new arbitration processes tailored to resolve climate change disputes.[67] This TF main objective is to ascertain which specific features are required for dispute resolution and encompasses a set of case-by-case analysis on the potential future of climate action related disputes. The TF has developed some potential solutions to incorporate the rights of third parties including indigenous and local communities as well as environmental obligations arising from this type of transaction.[68]

6 Conclusion

Most of the writing on the importance of international dispute resolution to resolve energy disputes has been produced by legal counsels and arbitrators. The practical understanding of

64 United Nations Commission on International Trade Law, 'Working Group III: Investor-State Disputes Settlement Reform' available at https://uncitral.un.org/en/working_groups/3/investor-state, accessed on 24 September 2019.

65 United Nations, 'Sustainable Development Goals', available at https://sustainabledevelopment.un.org/sdg16, accessed on 24 September 2019.

66 Ibid, 157.

67 See, for example, Permanent Court of Arbitration, 'Optional Rules for Arbitration of Disputes Relating to Natural Resources and/or the Environment', available at https://pca-cpa.org/wp-content/uploads/sites/6/2016/01/Optional-Rules-for-Arbitration-of-Disputes-Relating-to-the-Environment-and_or-Natural-Resources.pdf, accessed on 27 September 2019.

68 At the moment of printing this chapter, the ICC TF Final Report is yet to be published. The initiative is currently a work in progress.

the emergence of the energy industry as frequent user of adjudication mechanisms outside the courts has been valuable to identify how international arbitration has extended across all the sectors of the global energy economy, from the extractive industries to the low-carbon energy technologies. This chapter advances the discussion by identifying the different sources of international energy arbitration disputes that illustrate the evolution between energy law and dispute resolution. Most importantly, this analysis identified the new trends and paths taken in the development of international energy arbitration.

The case-by-case analysis revealed that legal disputes arising from the energy industry have often faced uncertainty due to the lack of a domestic or international framework, where arbitrators have created new legal principles to identify the different stakeholders' rights and obligations. For example, early disputes on the petroleum sector incubated a type of international arbitration process in charge of creating a substantive body of principles and notions applicable to the resolution of petroleum disputes. This, however, was not an isolated event in the evolution of energy law, and similar scenarios were replicated. In Europe, in light of regulatory changes which have allegedly breached investor's expectations, international arbitration is learning to deal with the interaction between EU law and international investment law in order to give full effect to the Contracting Parties, rights as signatories of the ECT.

Similarly, tensions arising from normative frameworks have been experienced more recently in the context of natural resources and investments projects arising from the mining industry. A considerable number of cases in Latin America have highlighted the need to ascertain whether international investment frameworks contain clear social and environmental rights and obligations for Contracting Parties but also for stakeholders which can potentially be affected by these transactions. Therefore, given the current fast-track evolution of the energy sector, including the energy transition, it is pertinent that the law also takes into account the social and environmental concerns that often arise from energy transactions. This chapter determined with more precision that the energy industry will continue to invest in jurisdictions with regulatory and legal certainty as well as using forms of dispute resolution capable of taking into account economic, social and political issues surrounding complex energy transactions.

New forms of investment agreements have taken into account the permanent tension between guaranteeing investors' regulatory certainty while respecting democratic regulatory and legislative changes made by sovereign states. The future of international energy arbitration will continue to witness the attempt to balance the state's right to regulate while ensuring that investors can only be protected when genuine and legitimate legal rights were given to them and were used as the main motivation to undertake an investment project. Of course, a state's right to regulate and the scope of FET and stabilisation clauses criteria is not that straightforward, and it might have many other requirements or standards. Ultimately, treaty practice has shown that it boils down to the interpretative freedom of the arbitration tribunal as lawmaker to give a full reading to the alleged breaches, taking into account the specific facts of the dispute.

This is reinforced by empirical evidence indicating that dispute resolution mechanisms and arbitration institutions will continue to develop into a more mature field capable of responding to tensions arising from different normative frameworks (i.e. EU law) but also of adjudicating new disputes concerning climate change obligations and risks and issues relating to sustainable development including vulnerable third parties' rights. Therefore, international dispute resolution is well equipped to progress in delivering clearer investment agreements and institutions, which promote greener energy investments and sustainability, as well as enforcing investment standards on social commitments, including public participation, local content and protection of third parties' rights.

35

CONCLUDING THOUGHTS ON THE GLOBAL ENERGY TRANSITION

Penelope Crossley and Gloria M. Alvarez

The global energy sector is currently going through a once in 200-year transformation. This transformation has occurred as result of a growing global consensus that action to reduce greenhouse gas emissions is urgently required to address climate change, as well as rapid changes to the supply and delivery of energy. Indeed, the model of large unbundled utilities and companies providing unidirectional supplies of energy operating in competitive markets is now under challenge. This process is not only taking place within the power sector, but is also evident in other energy markets, with the development and exploitation of shale gas providing new sources of competition and greater flexibility being demanded in LNG contracts. At the same time, investors operating within the sector are now far more likely to avail themselves of the protections that exist under bilateral or multilateral trade agreements and are more likely to opt for adjudication mechanisms outside domestic courts. These changes, and their resulting tensions and challenges in almost every aspect of the energy sector across the world, have been highlighted throughout this book. Indeed, we believe that the overriding theme of this book is the global energy sector in transition. In this chapter, we propose to discuss how each chapter in this book highlights this theme.

1 Introduction

The introductory section of the book examines overarching themes including the recent paradigm shifts in international energy law, energy security and climate change. Soliman Hunter and Herrera Anchustegui reflect on humanity's reliance on petroleum and the great cost its consumption has had on the political, economic and – most importantly – environmental realities. The authors claim that in order to have a full understanding of the current status of energy law, it is crucial to analyse energy regulation from a geographical perspective, an objective fulfilled by this *Handbook*. Authors come from different legal backgrounds, ethnicities, ages and gender – offering their own domestic and international view of the crucial pressing points on the architecture of energy law. The authors build a bridge between the two Eras of Energy: Hydrocarbon and Electricity. The authors explain that the Age of the Hydrocarbon Man has shifted to growth of gas use. However, we are warned that in regions such as Latin America and the Arctic – two geopolitical areas with abundant natural resources – they are yet to witness the end of the Hydrocarbon Man with significant developments in the regulation of these regions. The evolution continues, however with confluence, there is more dominance by the Age of the Electricity Man. As studied in this *Handbook*, the authors explain the Electricity Man is not only reordering the energy landscape, he also represents an unprecedented business opportunity and economic growth internationally and domestically for all energy markets. Further discussed in each individual chapter, there are some conflicts that remain to be resolved by the Electricity Man, including conflicts of land use, development of smart grids, international investments and public finance.

In Chapter 2, entitled, 'From stakeholders to actors? The progressive integration of environmental, social and cultural considerations within international energy law', Ong argues that in the context of rapidly evolving social, cultural and environmental norms, the host and home state, who were traditionally the 'primary actors' within the international energy regulatory framework, no longer have absolute dominance. This is because

> [a]s humankind's search for natural resources both widens and deepens across the globe, the international finance packages for funding these projects in remote developing economies, often situated far away from the final market destinations of these resources, have become ever more intricate.[1]

This has provided previously non-legally represented 'stakeholder entities' with substantive and procedural 'actor' rights that allow them to potentially challenge unmitigated activities. It also reflects a growing recognition of foreign investors' rights under international trade and investment treaties, and their consequent growing importance within the sector.

In 'International energy law in perspective: the relationship between national and international energy law', Nordtveit focuses on how national and international law interact to jointly build a holistic energy regime. Nordveit explains the creation – and importance – of international energy law as an encompassing field regulating foreign investments and trans-border transportation of energy. The production of international energy law filters down to domestic regulations with the aim of developing legal principles modelling licensing and production contracts, trading electricity systems and transportation. In this line of argumentation, the author raises the issue of conflicting rules and values between international and domestic legal frameworks and how legal theories react in accommodating different legal relationships (i.e. monism and dualism). In response, the author explains, international law has created new forms of interaction or division of functions between national and international law where common policy objectives meet:

> International environmental law, law of the sea, human rights law, international investment law, international trade law, and international energy law are examples of new comprehensive regulatory systems aimed at coordinating regulation of important fields in different jurisdictions and to facilitate trans-border cooperation.[2]

In Chapter 4, 'Reconceptualising energy security from a legal perspective in the context of climate change', Paterson explores how the transformation of the energy sector in an attempt to address climate change has forced a reconsideration of traditional conceptualisations

1 David Ong, p. 26.
2 Ernst Nordtveit, p. 43–44.

of energy security. Paterson begins his chapter by analysing the limitations of traditional conceptualisations of energy security, identifying that '[w]hat lies ahead is not going to be straightforward and it is going to require lawyers to be ready to innovate and to embrace that which, at times, will be strange and unfamiliar'.[3] He states that a real need has arisen to create and implement innovative legal solutions in order to address emerging challenges within the energy and climate change landscape. Paterson then provides several legal strategies that could help drive legal, political and technological innovation to address energy security concerns.

The starting point of the *Handbook* warns the reader that the energy industry is at a far more complex place and therefore the legal literature in energy law needs to be written following a set of new propositions. First, law and policy are facing a diversification on the dominance of legal actors and stakeholders, as such domestic and international frameworks are currently including new legal actors that can take a legal stand to challenge unmitigated activities. Secondly, given the reformulation of legal frameworks in the energy sector, the legal field needs to identify innovative strategies and collaborate with policymakers and industry to see how best to meet and deliver on all the challenges arising from the energy transition.

2 Europe

The European Union (EU), both as a political and legal union and a region, has long been at the forefront of laws and policies to address climate change and help manage the transition of its energy sectors to address new challenges and threats. It has proactively managed the liberalisation and introduction of competition into its energy markets, taken steps to reduce its greenhouse gas emissions through the EU Emissions Trading Scheme (ETS) to address climate change, and been the first region in the world to introduce a regional approach to energy security. This has required the implementation of strict controls such as EU competition law and state aid measures, and the development of alternative pathways to resolve energy disputes under the Energy Charter Treaty.

In 'Energy market liberalisation: from monopolistic to traded markets in the European Union', Penttinen examines the process of transition within European energy markets. She begins by depicting the gradual transformation of the European energy market – from a vertically integrated national monopoly to one characterised by greater competition, privatisation and efficiency. However, she then argues that the next transition facing the European energy sector cannot be a gradual transition over 20 years due to the urgent need for change. The clean energy transition needs to accelerate the adoption of renewable energy and clean energy sources to improve energy efficiency and address climate change. It will have to be both faster and use a different approach:

> Because energy markets within the EU have traditionally evolved around the supply side where (national) monopoly energy companies produce energy from conventional energy sources (fossil fuels), energy transitions require a major shift in the whole ideology underpinning energy production and energy markets.[4]

3 John Paterson, p. 73.
4 Sira-Leena Penttinen, p. 89.

In the context of the adopted EU Clean Energy Package (CEP), the role of the EU as promoter of clean energy sources is further developed by Herrera Anchustegui and Formosa in 'Regulation of electricity markets in Europe in light of the CEP: prosumers and demand response'. By exploring how the EU's recently introduced CEP will also help facilitate the transition, the authors identified that the overarching rationale and purpose of the CEP is to incorporate the EU's climate goals into the European energy sector. However, they argue that the CEP also enables the EU to achieve significant gains in promoting energy efficiency and modernising the European electricity market during a time of technological disruption. In particular, they state that the CEP will result in a more integrated energy market, thereby enabling consumers to become 'prosumers', and actively participate and guide energy markets within the future grid. This will impose new rights and obligations on the end consumers of energy, who will increasingly become 'responsive and responsible "prosumer[s]"'.[5]

In continuing analysing EU competition frameworks, Bergqvist and Herrera Anchustegui analyse the 'Uses and abuses of EU competition law in energy', which supports the development of a single European energy market to alleviate anti-competitive conduct within the electricity and gas markets. This chapter, which adopts a chronological approach to EU competition law within the energy sector, neatly highlights how the use of Articles 101, 102 and 106 of the Treaty on the Functioning of the European Union (TFEU) has evolved within the energy sector over time. They argue that '[f]rom the pre-2003 cases, a pattern emerges where competition is applied (or not) for the purpose of supporting the single market by focusing on specific market lacunas and regulatory deficits'.[6] Bergqvist and Herrera Anchustegui believe it is the use of these powers, along with the greater use by the European Commission of their functions, that has allowed the EU's single energy market to continue to thrive.

In 'The role of state aid law in energy', Herrera Anchustegui and Bergqvist examine state aid as one of the legal mechanisms helping to support the clean energy transition. They identify that

> In practical terms, the amount of state aid designated to energy is the second largest of the approved aid in the EU and these funds are being used to transform, modernize and pursue the 'greenification' of energy markets in Europe, with renewable electricity infrastructure and energy efficiency measures at the forefront.[7]

Traditionally, state aid rules were used within the energy sector to ensure the smooth functioning of regulatory frameworks, prevent the distortion of competitive processes and provide financial assistance for remedying market failures. However, in recent years this role has evolved as growing amounts of state aid have been used to support the clean energy transition. The use of state aid for this purpose is expected to continue for the foreseeable future despite continued scrutiny of public intervention and energy aid measures by the Commission of Capacity Remuneration Mechanisms (CRM).

In 'Shale gas in Europe: a case study on EU energy and environmental law', Fleming considers the emergence of new domestic energy sources within the European market, in particular shale gas. Fleming posits that shale gas presents significant potential to alleviate

5 Ignacio Herrera Anchustegui and Andreas Formosa, p. 91.

6 Christian Bergqvist and Ignacio Herrera Anchustegui, p. 113.

7 Ignacio Herrera Anchustegui and Christian Bergqvist, p. 138.

the energy security concerns posed by the concentrated supply of gas to EU markets. Indeed, he argues that '[s]hale gas extraction is viewed as a potential 'game-changer' for the security of energy supplies in Europe'.[8] Throughout his chapter, Fleming considers whether recent technological advancements and the current primary and secondary EU legislative frameworks are sufficient to support a country seeking to develop its shale gas potential in the near future. He concludes that a number of legal and regulatory issues arise that need to be urgently addressed if Europe's shale gas potential is to be realised.

There is, however, a contradiction in the EU's role as protector of its energy market while also the promoter of a clean energy industry. This contradiction is identified by Briercliffe and Ingle in Chapter 10, 'Dispute resolution in the European energy sector'. First, this chapter notes that a growing number of cases have arisen as a result of the energy transition, particularly within the European renewable energy sector. Through its study of the awards rendered in the European renewable energy cases under the Energy Charter Treaty (ECT), this chapter critically analyses the scope of protection offered by the 'fair and equitable treatment' (FET) standard. They argue that the common approach adopted by the arbitral tribunals hearing these disputes relies on studying the disputed measures and then analysing their impact on the returns of the claimants' investments. The outcome of these cases is that investment treaties can expose states to risks arising from the disjunction between regulatory change and stability requirements.

Energy law, in the context of the EU, is well characterised by the innovative role of the EU in having strict controls on market competition, which genuinely supports an energy transition where consumers actively participate. Moreover, it is expected that the EU will work to maximise the potential of shale gas, while continuing to remove any anticompetitive conduct within the electricity and gas markets. Lastly, investment arbitration disputes in the EU renewable energy industry elucidate that while investment treaties ensure stability of the energy investments, EU laws continue to appear inconsistent with the EU's policy message regarding promotion of foreign investments in the green energy sector. The EU is facing some inconstancies in its policy message regarding promotion of greener energy sources and investment law; this is because most of the cases in international arbitration under the ECT are in relation to regulatory measures which have affected renewable energy investors. In response to this wave of cases, the European Commission has intervened in these cases and explained that these cases should be resolved at the EU judicial system and not outside it. Consequently, the jurisdictional tension between the EU and other dispute settlement mechanisms blurs and hinders the effective resolution of regulatory measures, issued by Member States, which can endanger the trust of prospective investors and deter them from making attractive low carbon investments in the region.

3 Russia

Russia is not only critical to the global energy markets as a result of its rich abundance of natural resources, holding 61 per cent of global proved oil reserves, but it also plays an important role in the geopolitics of energy. This section begins with an examination of the traditional stalwart of the Russian energy sector, that is, its oil and gas sector, which is changing. In Chapter 11, Soliman Hunter and Fodchenko simplify and systematise the complex legal framework of petroleum activities in Russia. In 'The regulation of petroleum exploration

8 Ruven Fleming, p. 141.

and production in Russia', the authors use Russia's role and example to establish regulatory and legal frameworks that delineate the principles of the state's ownership and control of its domestic energy market. More precisely, the authors use Russia's legal developments to exemplify how countries exercise their 'state's right to regulate' regardless of whose property natural and mineral resources might be, including foreign and private investments. They examine the scope of exploration and production federal laws as well as the applicable licensing legal frameworks.

Russian development of renewable energy is largely a result of its growing concern about protecting its terms of trade by maintaining its traditional fossil fuel export markets. In Chapter 12, 'Russian renewable energy: regulations and outcomes', Kozlova, Collan and Overland critically analyse Russia's renewable energy legislative framework, investment climate and the potential for renewable energy schemes in Russia. It is argued that there is an ongoing need for Russia – as one of the world's biggest energy exporters – to continue to develop and expand its renewable energy capacity, as otherwise Russia may lag behind international advances in renewable energy production, leading to undesirable consequences. However, this process appears to be fraught, with Kozlova et al. concluding that '[t]he promise of profitable investments theoretically creates a strong incentive for investors to enter the market; however, in practice, the implementation of this support is more like a steeplechase'.[9] In 'Shifting Russian energy geopolitics', Raszewski and Nowak discuss in detail the extent to which geopolitics is relevant to understanding Russia's energy security. More precisely, the authors explain Russia's attitude to global and regional (i.e. EU and Asia) shifts in the international energy market, while maintaining permanent and reliable access to energy consumers in order to maintain budget revenues.

Therefore, given the critical role of Russia's geopolitical and petroleum reserves, it is of the utmost importance to understand how they exercise their regulatory right in the aim of continuing building energy security in the most profitable scheme for the state-owned oil and gas companies. Moreover, a great deal can be learnt from Russia's sophisticated licensing schemes as well as the way it balances the new challenges which include welcoming private investments and accommodating a possible expansion of renewable energy schemes.

4 North America

Shifting to energy law in the US, in 'Shale gas development, economic impacts and regulation', Wiseman starts by offering a comprehensive analysis on the regulatory measures introduced by the federal, state and local governments in recent years. She argues that '[s]ome of the most important but overlooked regulation of shale gas development occurs at the local government level, where both municipalities (towns, townships, cities, and the like) and counties have surprisingly detailed requirements for drilling and hydraulic fracturing'. Nonetheless, Wiseman also highlights the arguments in favour of more stringent environmental regulations; overall, regulatory measures have not hindered the growth of the shale oil industry in the past.

The US has always been a pioneer and legal innovator in terms of gas regulation and pipelines. In 'Regulation of natural gas pipeline construction and operation in the United States', Talus argues that despite the existence of a sophisticated gas pipeline network in the US, there are issues pertaining to shortages in the transmission capacities and efficiency of

9 Marria Kozloca, Mikael Collan and Indra Overland, p. 216.

gas pipelines. He argues that 'pipeline companies operate a natural monopoly, which can often not reasonably be duplicated, and access to the pipeline is necessary to compete in the supply market for natural gas'.[10]

In 'Regulation of low carbon energy sources in the U.S. and Canada', van de Biezenbos compares the statutory and regulatory frameworks underpinning low carbon energy sources in the US and Canada, while also exploring prominent emerging trends relating to the use of electric vehicles, biofuels, hydropower and wind, solar, nuclear and geothermal energy generation. The chapter also argues that due to the 'politicising of energy issues', the uptake of low carbon energy sources in both countries has been relatively slow. This has made both countries highly reliant on traditional fossil fuel energy sources.

In discussing regulation of the US energy markets, it is also relevant to look into the electricity market. In the chapter 'Formula rate plans and multi-year rate plans: can they serve the public interest, and how?', the main question raised is how regulatory agencies determine their energy utility rates, specifically discussing the different approaches adopted by agencies in competitive vs. monopoly markets. Hempling critiques the inefficient practices of monopoly agencies in setting utility rates, and therefore argues for the need to establish 'appropriate expectations for public interest plans' in order to make consumers' needs central to the question of price determination. The main proposition of the author is that 'rather than accept utility proposals passively, commissions should hold generic proceedings on the positives and negatives of, and alternative designs for, FRPs [formula rate plans] and MYRPs [multi-year rate plans]'.[11] Overall, the present and the future of the North American energy market is polarised given the political position with regard to low carbon energy sources and some inefficient legal frameworks for natural monopolies and utility rates. First, it is difficult to predict the short-term development of carbon energy sources given the policy attitude in support of fossil fuel energy sources. The slow uptake of electric vehicles, hydropower, biofuels and wind, solar, nuclear and geothermal energy might also limit progress and innovation in terms of regulatory frameworks. In contrast, it is expected that the shale gas industry will continue to develop a successful path, although, more generally, consumers will continue to be more reliant on fossil fuel energy sources, despite the stricter environmental regulations. Lastly, similar to the US, Canada has a good record in addressing anticompetitive conduct in the electricity and gas markets, and in the foreseeable future it is expected to see a growth in regulation addressing access to gas pipelines.

5 Latin America

Interestingly, shale gas regulatory developments are not an isolated case in North America; similarly, in 'Shale gas regulation in Mexico and Colombia: an uncertain future', Soliman Hunter and Herrera Anchustegui address developments taking place on the American Continent. They conduct a comparative analysis of the status of unconventional hydrocarbons and shale gas in Mexico and Colombia. The chapter presents the finding that Mexico lacks certain administrative rules (relating to the exploitation of unconventional hydrocarbon), whereas Colombia's legal regulatory framework is much more mature, enabling greater flexibility overall. The authors highlight the fact that despite the (im)maturity of some legal systems, the regulatory debate regarding shale gas development is certainly not over, rather

10 Kim Talus, p. 253.
11 Scott Hempling, p. 286.

it has stepped into the legislative arena. Further developments in shale gas exploitation are necessary in the region, as these might lead to greater financial revenue, but careful and stringent laws need to be in place to manage the negative environmental consequences arising from these types of projects.

Taking a closer look into the Mexican regulatory energy framework, 'Energy justice as a key driver to unlock the transition from energy reform to energy counter-reform: the rise of the immutability theory', explores the notion of the Immutability Theory, arguing that it is crucial to ensuring and enforcing energy justice going forward. The chapter offers an analysis of Mexico's Five-Year Government Plan and the extent to which Energy Counter-Reform (ECR) impacts the current Energy Reform (ER) governance structure. Marmolejo-Cervantes claims that principles of energy justice inserted in the new Mexican energy framework will enable Mexico to promote social peace through energy.

Moving away from Mexico and Colombia, Viscidi and Graham look at the entire Latin American region to present the view that it is of the utmost importance to strengthen the regulatory framework of developing nations in order to develop energy efficiency policies. In 'Low-carbon energy in Latin America: post-Paris advances in renewable and energy efficiency policies' the authors take a comparative analysis of the development of energy related Nationally Determined Contributions (NDCs) of Latin American economies (Brazil, Mexico, Argentina, Chile and Colombia) since the Paris Climate Agreement. The authors recognise Latin America's achievements as it 'boasts extremely low per capita electricity emissions by global standards, thanks to the heavy reliance in a number of countries on hydroelectric generation'. In terms of further improvements, despite impressive investments in a 'large-scale non-conventional renewable generation', most Latin American countries have not implemented full-scale policy reforms on technologies and pricing schemes, which would actively encourage and foster the use of renewable energy sources.

Marchili and Bellera Landa recognise that the energy sector in Latin America faces significant challenges, in particular in the context of protecting ownership of natural resources while creating a reliable legal framework to attract know-how and capital from foreign investors. In 'Protecting energy investments in Latin America' the authors review some of the most relevant and well-known international arbitration cases to point out that there are valuable mitigating strategies that could be used to manage risks and build confidence in the hydrocarbons sector and the renewable energy industry. These mitigating strategies include having a clear understanding of the outreach and scope of certain notions such as what constitutes an investment and who can be an investor, protection against unexpected government treatment towards investors and neutral adjudication mechanisms outside national courts.

The debate on the state's right to regulate in light of private energy transactions is a pervasive issue when studying the energy sector in Latin America. For this reason, Montoya Pardo and Garzón Albornoz study the case of Colombia and Brazil in close detail. In 'Regulatory framework for the energy sector in Colombia and Brazil', the authors develop an explanation for the 'regulatory relationship' between energy projects and the requirements imposed on private companies. First, regulation needs to ensure energy security while diversifying the energy mix by incorporating low carbon energy sources. Secondly, regulation in Colombia and Brazil needs to continue creating legal frameworks which incentivise innovation in terms of storage, cost and reliability. Lastly, consistent with previous authors, the authors highlight the transformation of social commitment into new forms of human rights in the particular context of the extractive industries.

Overall, the Latin American landscape on the energy sector is positive given the dual commitment to hydrocarbons and renewable energy sources. However, the challenge of the disparity between the different levels of maturity of some jurisdictions remains. International frameworks offer clear rules and standards on the protection of foreign energy investments. However, domestic frameworks need to continue to create clear regulation on shale gas and the remedies against the potential negative environmental consequences of its extraction. In addition, it is also necessary to implement more reforms to implement a clear commitment to the renewable energy generation. Lastly, given the very particular geopolitical situation of Latin America, where natural resources have been a historical source and key to development, it is of great importance that national policy and law take into account how energy security is aligned with social justice commitments.

6 Asia and Australia

Raszewski argued that trade in energy, particularly coal and liquified natural gas (LNG), has been one of the defining features of the development of the Asia Pacific region. In Chapter 23, 'Asian energy markets: the impact of shifting global politics', Raszewski notes that much of this trade has been fuelled by the Australian market, as the world's largest exporter of coal, and a major exporter of LNG. This trade has presented benefits in terms of facilitating regional development and stability, which has been critical in an environment with a complex interplay of geopolitics and geo-economics. However, 'Asian energy markets are undergoing a profound change in consumption, production and transportation of energy resources'.[12] This transition will see the resetting of existing trade relationships and a new geopolitical settlement in the Asia Pacific energy sector.

In Chapter 24, 'From coal to clean energy: how the energy transition is being managed in Indian energy law and policy', Crossley examines the energy law and policy in one of the world's most populous countries. This chapter evaluates the legal and institutional structure responsible for managing the governance of the Indian energy sector, as well as considering how India is managing its transition to lower carbon energy sources:

> India is in a difficult position, its historic reliance on its plentiful coal supply means that its electricity transition will need to be more rapid and profound than many other countries. This comes with impacts on its terms of trade, as India will either have to import more foreign energy supply at great cost thereby giving up its traditional values of energy independence and self-reliance, or markedly increase its use of renewables and nuclear power … That said, such a move also presents several benefits if the renewables and nuclear option is chosen by reducing large particulate matter and air pollution, thereby lessening deaths caused by poor air quality, as well as helping India to meet their Paris commitments on climate change.[13]

Crossley argues that successfully managing this transition will require the delicate balancing of India's four key pillars of energy policy: (i) energy security, (ii) affordability and access, (iii) environmental concerns, such as air pollution and climate change, and (iv) energy efficiency. This will require difficult decisions to be made about the relative priority of each pillar.

12 Slawomir Raszewski, p. 388.
13 Penelope Crossley, p. 413.

In Chapter 25, attention shifts to the energy transition currently occurring in the world's most populous country, China. Huan in her analysis in 'Energy law and regulations in China' discusses the historical and current reliance of the Chinese economy on coal as its primary fuel source. However, Huan argues that, increasingly, international energy law and national approaches to regulating the energy sector are enabling the reorientation of the sector to become more innovative. This has made it possible for China to pursue the development of a future energy sector with a greater safety orientation which is more energy efficient and, ultimately, makes better use of low carbon energy. Effectively managing this transition is critical, with Huan concluding that '[t]he objective of having overall energy security and improving energy development strategies, policies and legislation in China is still a work in progress'.[14]

In Chapter 26, Crossley addresses how a major fossil fuel exporter, Australia, is introducing significant quantities of renewable energy into its generation mix. In her chapter, 'Renewable energy law in the context of a transforming Australian energy market', Crossley critiques the lack of a national integrated energy and climate policy and the effect that this is having on investment decisions in a new renewable generation. She argues that:

> [E]nergy policy in Australia has long been a political battleground that is ideologically driven. Because of this, there has been a lack of regulatory certainty in how the electricity sector will manage the transition to clean renewable energy sources and address climate change. This has increased the risk for those investing and operating within the energy sector and for both commercial and residential customers.[15]

In Chapter 27, Taylor examines the current supply security challenge in Australia's Eastern Gas Market, in terms of the current lack of gas availability and affordability for domestic consumers. In her chapter, 'Is gas security in the 'national interest'? An Australian Eastern Gas Market perspective', Taylor argues that this issue was precipitated by moratoria on coal seam gas exploration and production in many Australian states on the eastern seaboard, and because almost all of Australia's LNG was sold under long-term export contracts to Asian nations. She further argues that due to a lack of regulatory planning, market-based policies may be insufficient to satisfy future energy security needs, and so she proposes a 'national interest' test be applied to future LNG export projects:

> There can be no single silver bullet legislative act to exhaustively address the current Eastern Gas Market crisis. However, the introduction of a defined 'national interest' … may create a principal approach to enacting 'better' regulation to safeguard both short and long-term gas security for Australia's East Coast.[16]

The chapters in this section highlight the different impacts of the energy transition on both net energy importers such as India, China and South Korea, and on net energy exporters such as Australia. As traditional relationships of supplier and purchaser of fossil fuels shift with the growing transition to renewable energy, this is likely to significantly impact upon both the geopolitics and geo-economics of the region. It may also create a source of tension,

14 Huan Jie, p. 430.
15 Penelope Crossley, p. 444.
16 Madeline E. Taylor, p. 467.

with gas shortages being experienced in the Australian domestic market, in part due to the existence of long-term supply contracts to its Asian neighbours.

7 Africa and the Middle East

Examining the transitions of the energy sector within the African and the Middle Eastern regions is a tale of two opposites. Many countries within the African region, as the world's poorest region, are going through economic development and are experiencing rapidly growing demand for oil, gas and power, without a corresponding increase in supply. This has prompted a leap in the energy development in some countries, leapfrogging the need for large transmission and distribution networks, with growing use of decentralised energy and microgrids. In other countries, the prevalence of disputed maritime boundaries and recent oil and gas finds may create a source of conflict in the future if not amicably resolved.

This section starts with Chapter 28 authored by Oyewunmi, 'Gas commercialisation projects in West Africa: pipelines, LNG and gas-to-power'. This chapter analyses both the legal and policy frameworks, as well as the commercial and risk environments that operate in West Africa and that underlie all decisions about the exploration and exploitation of gas resources. He concludes that:

> For the developing economies in West Africa, the issues bordering on energy affordability are not merely a function of pricing, access or availability of gas upstream, but the integrity of pipeline and supply infrastructure, as well as liquidity and creditworthiness of the electricity market and electricity end-users.[17]

Ideas around affordable, reliable, sustainable and modern energy for all on the African Continent are also discussed by Obeng-Darko. Chapter 29, 'The Legal, policy and regulatory aspects of integrating electricity from renewable energy in sub-Sahara Africa: the case of Ghana, the Gambia and Nigeria', situates the energy transition within Sustainable Development Goal 7, to ask, if 'access to affordable, reliable, sustainable and modern energy for all' is a central precept within our society then how can this be achieved in sub-Saharan Africa? In particular, Obeng-Darko questions whether given the difficulty that the African region has in securing the investment needed to achieve its domestic renewable energy goals and improve its electricity generation, national law reform and policy efforts will help the 50 per cent of the population in the region without access to electricity gain access to electricity. He concludes that:

> Achieving renewable electricity integration targets across sub-Saharan Africa will be a monumental feat fraught with legal, policy and regulatory issues … these issues are all in addition to the technical, financial and technological obstacles to developing and utilising renewable energy resources for electricity production.[18]

In Chapter 31, 'Maritime disputes and disputed seabed resources in the African Continent', Khalfaoui and Yiallourides argue that there are a number of unresolved and/or disputed

17 Tade Oyewunmi, p. 488.
18 Nana Obeng-Darko, p. 506.

maritime boundaries in Africa. Disputes about maritime boundaries and seabed resources, particularly oil and gas, arise in a number of different ways, for example, through disagreements about limitations of maritime boundaries, especially when there are overlapping entitlements to maritime rights and jurisdiction. However, the existence of, or likely presence of, oil and gas often expedites the efforts to try and delimit maritime boundaries in accordance with United Nations Convention on the Law of the Sea (UNCLOS) rules. The authors argue that the use of Joint Development Agreements and the African Union Border Programme could present great benefits to countries in dispute, 'although examples of State practice have continued to accumulate there is no evidence of *opinion juris* on the part of African States on the legal necessity of establishing joint development of disputed seabed resources'.[19]

In contrast to the countries of the African Continent, many countries within the Middle Eastern region are highly dependent on fossil fuels and have, until very recently, largely ignored the transition to renewable energy. The Middle Eastern nations have played a critical role in the global supply and pricing of petroleum though their role in Organization of the Petroleum Exporting Countries (OPEC). In Chapter 30, Kelly evaluates the laws and drivers supporting the deployment of renewable energy in the Middle East and North African (MENA) region. In 'Developing renewable energy projects in the Middle East and North Africa region', Kelly states that renewable energy is now being positively viewed by MENA governments as a means of diversifying energy sources, improving their terms of trade through facilitating increased fossil fuel exports, as well as a source of capacity building and technology transfers. He argues that:

> Renewables remain a sound investment proposition to MENA economies irrespective of whether oil prices are high or low. Under high oil prices, renewables facilitate more fossil fuel exports by allowing a greater deployment of domestic generation from cheaply priced renewables; low oil prices also facilitate increased renewables deployment, with financing preferencing forms of generation with the best rates of return.[20]

8 Conclusion

A contemporary approach to energy law needs to examine how the energy transition permeates and dictates the present and the future of the structure of the energy sector. More concretely, 'Transitions are a *status quo* for the energy world. Global energy adapts and evolves through these transitions. Firms succeed and fail with these transitions, but the industry as a whole moves on'.[21] In 'Energy transitions and the law', Talus and Aalto discuss the role of law and policy in facilitating two energy transitions: the sustainable energy transition and the LNG market transition. The authors argue that the law acts as a driver for the sustainable energy transition, but merely as a facilitator for the LNG market transition. This means that the sustainable energy transition is at a greater risk of government failure whereas the LNG market transition may be impacted by vested industry interests.

Another source of energy which often produces polarised policies and literature is nuclear energy. In 'The future of nuclear energy', Negri della Torre argues that regulating nuclear energy requires lawmakers to strike a delicate balance between the opposing objectives of

19 Anna Khalfaoui and Constantinos Yiallourides, p. 545.
20 Cameron Kelly, p. 507.
21 Kim Talus and Pami Aalto, p. 560.

supporting nuclear power and attempting to limit the proliferation of nuclear weapons. He states that emerging nuclear technologies such as nuclear fusion and improvements in design, safety and the portability of nuclear power generation 'warrant profound revision of the principles and legal architecture developed so far by nuclear jurisdictions'.[22] These changes are likely to include the definitions used, safety requirements, aspects of civil liability and regulatory developments to ensure that the nuclear regime remains fit for purpose for mobile applications.

Importantly, all the legal rights and obligations generated by energy frameworks need to have their own avenues of enforcement, hence the importance of dispute resolution mechanisms adequate for the complexity of the energy industry. In 'The future of dispute resolution in the energy and natural resources sector: setting the scene and looking ahead', Alvarez argues that the energy sector has quickly evolved and become more complex and technical; where legal disputes arise they require a decision-maker with the relevant knowledge to adjudicate a dispute. Importantly, given the long-term life of energy projects and limited number of energy players in the global market, stakeholders often opt to go to legal mechanisms that are neutral, independent, impartial, confidential and comprehensive of the different legal cultures of the disputing parties. While international energy arbitration has emerged as field which successfully resolves a wide range of energy disputes, from hydrocarbons to renewable energy disputes, there are important challenges that remain unaddressed. Cases in the mining sector have indicated that international arbitrators often have difficulty in pinning down the sources of legal obligations in relation to human rights, the environment and the concerns of local and indigenous groups.

At the outset of this chapter, we stated that we were going to highlight the effect of the energy transition throughout every sub-sector of the energy sector and across every geographic region. This chapter exemplifies the profound effect that the energy transition has already had, and will continue to have over coming decades. In this new environment, we must resist the urge to continue pursuing the *status quo* by merely making piecemeal amendments to existing regulation and competitive markets; far greater change is required for the sector to continue to function effectively and efficiently.

22 Alessandro Negri della Torre, p. 562.

INDEX

Note: **Bold** page numbers refer to tables.

For Product Safety Concerns and Information please contact our EU
representative GPSR@taylorandfrancis.com
Taylor & Francis Verlag GmbH, Kaufingerstraße 24, 80331 München, Germany

www.ingramcontent.com/pod-product-compliance
Ingram Content Group UK Ltd.
Pitfield, Milton Keynes, MK11 3LW, UK
UKHW050053200926
475702UK00019B/2808
* 9 7 8 1 0 3 2 2 3 6 3 0 8 *